OMNIBUS IV

OMNIBUS IV

The Ancient World

General Editor **GENE EDWARD VEITH**
General Editor **DOUGLAS WILSON**
Managing Editor **G. TYLER FISCHER**

Veritas Press, Lancaster, Pennsylvania
www.VeritasPress.com
©2009 by Veritas Press
ISBN 978-1-932168-86-0

All rights reserved. No part of this book may be reproduced without permission from Veritas Press, except by a reviewer who may quote brief passages in a review; nor may any part of this book be reproduced, stored in a retrieval system or transmitted in any form by any means, electronic, mechanical, photocopying, recording or otherwise, without prior, written permission from Veritas Press.

Printed in the United States of America.

To my children, now all grown up, Paul, Mary, and Joanna (who is now an Omnibus teacher herself).
—GENE EDWARD VEITH

For Cinco and Pinto, with great affection.
—DOUGLAS WILSON

To my parents and to Emily's as well—George and Ann, and Glenn and Lucille. Thank you for your encouragement, kindness, patience, and love.
—G. TYLER FISCHER

TABLE OF CONTENTS

Foreword ix

Preface xi

Preface to Omnibus IV: The Ancient World xiii

Publisher's Preface xv

Introduction xvii

Using Omnibus xix

What's on the CD? xxiv

PRIMARY BOOKS FIRST SEMESTER

Essay: Philosophy 3
   Douglas Wilson

Proverbs. 13
   Essay by Peter J. Leithart
   Sessions by O. Woelke Leithart

Job 27
   Essay and Sessions by Toby J. Sumpter

Essay: Poetry 43
   Robert Siegel

The Iliad 59
   Essay by Douglas Wilson
   Sessions by Bruce Etter

Psalms. 83
   Essay by Rich Lusk
   Sessions by Jeff Moss

The Peloponnesian War 99
   Essay by Chris Schlect
   Sessions by G. Tyler Fischer

The Bacchae 117
   Essay and Sessions by William S. Dawson

The Clouds 131
   Essay and Sessions by O. Woelke Leithart

The Hippocratic Oath. 141
   Essay by Graham Dennis
   Sessions by Jennifer Harger

Essay: Politics. 157
   Frank Guliuzza

The Republic. 171
   Essay and Sessions by Graham Dennis

Nicomachean Ethics. 199
   Essay by Kevin W. Clark
   Sessions by Graham Dennis

Poetics 217
   Essay by Gene Edward Veith
   Sessions by Tim Deibler

PRIMARY BOOKS SECOND SEMESTER

Essay: Aesthetics 231
   Gene Edward Veith

Apocrypha 243
   Essay by Douglas Wilson
   Sessions by Bruce Gore

Euclid's Elements 255
   Essay by Mitch Stokes
   Sessions by Dale Siegenthaler

The War with Hannibal 267
   Essay and Sessions by Christopher Walker

On the Nature of Things 283
   Essay by Peter J. Leithart
   Sessions by Nathan Tillman

Cicero 297
   Essay and Sessions by Christopher Walker

Essay: Anthropology 309
   David Ayers

Annals of Imperial Rome 321
   Essay and Sessions by Christopher Walker

Eclogues and Georgics 339
   Essay and Sessions by Joanna Hensley

Metamorphoses 351
   Essay by Natali H. Monnette
   Sessions by Nathan Tillman

Gospel of Mark 365
   Essay and Sessions by Bruce Etter

Philippians and Colossians 377
   Essay by Peter J. Leithart
   Sessions by O. Woelke Leithart

Essay: Law 391
   John Warwick Montgomery

The Jewish War 401
Essay and Sessions by William S. Dawson

Meditations 419
Essay and Sessions by Christopher Walker

The Apostolic Fathers 431
Essay and Sessions by Stuart Bryan

SECONDARY BOOKS FIRST SEMESTER

Aesop's Fables 445
Essay by Nancy Wilson
Sessions by LaJean Burns

Death on the Nile 459
Essay and Sessions by Toby J. Sumpter

Joshua, Judges, Ruth 471
Essay by Rich Lusk
Sessions by Tom Becker

Troilus and Cressida 493
Essay by Natali H. Monnette
Sessions by Jennifer Harger

1 and 2 Chronicles 507
Essay and Sessions by Bruce Gore

Ezra, Nehemiah, Esther 523
Essay by Douglas Wilson
Sessions by Tom Becker

Augustus Caesar's World 535
Essay and Sessions by G. Tyler Fischer

Art and the Bible 551
Essay by Gene Edward Veith
Sessions by Ned Bustard

SECONDARY BOOKS SECOND SEMESTER

The Lost World 567
Essay and Sessions by Corey Piper

Knowing God 581
Essay and Sessions by O. Woelke Leithart

Antony and Cleopatra 591
Essay and Sessions by G. Tyler Fischer

Twenty Thousand Leagues Under the Seas 605
Essay by Joshua Shade
Sessions by Isaiah McPeak

Phantastes 617
Essay by Matt Vest
Sessions by Kaye Wilson

Mythology 633
Essay and Sessions by Ben House

Plutarch's Lives, vol. 2 649
Essay and Sessions by Christopher Walker

Desiring God 661
Essay and Sessions by Toby J. Sumpter

Appendix I Reading Schedule 673

Appendix II Timeline 675

Index 699

Foreword

One of the most obvious questions that Christians might ask about a curriculum like this one is, "Why study this stuff?" The question can be asked for different reasons. Perhaps a concerned parent is attracted to the rigor of a "classical and Christian approach," and yet has thumbed through a couple of the texts and is taken aback by some of the material. "It was this kind of gunk," he thinks, "that chased us out of the government school." Or perhaps the question is asked by the student himself when he "hits the wall." The rigor that is built into this course of study is significant, and about a third of the way through the year, a student might be asking all sorts of pointed questions. "Why are you making me do this?" is likely to be one of them. The student may be asking because of his workload, but if he points to the nature of the material, the question still needs a good answer. It is a good question, and everyone who is involved in teaching this course needs to have the answer mastered.

G.K. Chesterton said somewhere that if a book does not have a wicked character in it, then it is a wicked book. One of the most pernicious errors that has gotten abroad in the Christian community is the error of *sentimentalism*—the view that evil is to be evaded, rather than the more robust Christian view that evil is to be conquered. The Christian believes that evil is there to be fought, the dragon is there to be slain. The sentimentalist believes that evil is to be resented.

My wife and I did not enroll our children in a classical Christian school so that they would never come into contact with sin. Rather, we wanted them there because we wanted to unite with like-minded Christian parents who had covenanted together to deal with the (inevitable) sin in a consistent, biblical manner. We fully expected our children to encounter sin in the classroom, on the playground and in the curriculum. We also expected that when they encountered it, they would see it dealt with in the way the Bible says sin should be dealt with.

A classical Christian school or a home school following the classical Christian curriculum must never be thought of as an asylum. Rather, this is a time of basic training; it is boot camp. Students are being taught to handle their weapons, and they are being taught this under godly, patient supervision. But in order to learn this sort of response, it is important that students learn it well. That is, setting up a "straw man" paganism that is easily demolished equips no one. All that would do is impart a false sense of security to the students—until they get to a secular college campus to encounter the real thing. Or, worse yet, if they continue the path into a soft, asylum-style Christian college and then find themselves addressing the marketplace completely unprepared.

If this basic training is our goal, and it is, then we should make clear what one potential abuse of the Omnibus curriculum might be. This curriculum was written and edited with the assumption that godly oversight and protection would accompany the student through his course of work. It was written with the conviction that children need teachers, flesh and blood teachers, who will work together with them. It was also written with the assumption that many of these teachers need the help and the resources that a program like this can supply. But we also believe that, if a seventh-grader is simply given this material and told to work through it himself, the chances are good that the student will miss the benefit that is available for those who are taught.

The Scriptures do not allow us to believe that a record of sinful behavior, or of sinful corruption, is inherently corrupting. If it were, then there are many stories and accounts in the Bible itself that would have to be excluded. But if we ever begin to think our children need to be protected "from the Bible," this should bring us up short. Perhaps we have picked up false notions of holiness somewhere. In short, there is no subject that this curriculum will raise in the minds of seventh-grade students that would not *also* be raised when that student reads through his Bible, cover to cover. It is true that this curriculum has accounts of various murders, or examples of prostitution, or of tyranny from powerful and cruel kings. But we can find all the same things in the book of Judges.

So the issue is not the *presence* of sin, but of the *re-*

sponse to that sin. What we have sought to do throughout—in the introductory worldview essays, the questions and exercises, and in the teachers' materials—is provide a guideline for responding to all the various worldviews that men outside of Christ come up with. This program, we believe, will equip the student to see through pretences and lies that other Christian children, who have perhaps been too sheltered, are not able to deal with.

Of course, there is a limit to this, as we have sought to recognize. There *are* certain forms of worldliness and corruption that would overwhelm a student's ability to handle it, no matter how carefully a parent or teacher was instructing them. And while children differ in what they can handle, in our experience with many students of this age, we believe that the content of this curriculum is well within the capacity of Christian children of this age group. But again, this assumes godly oversight and instruction. The challenge here is twofold. The rigor of the curriculum can seem daunting, but we have sought to provide direction and balance with regard to the demands of the material. The second concern is the question of false worldviews, paganism and just plain old-fashioned sin, which we have addressed above.

As our students work their way through this material, and in the years of the Omnibus program that will follow, we want them to walk away with a profound sense of the *antithesis*. What we mean by this is that right after Adam and Eve fell in the Garden, God gave His first messianic promise (Gen. 3:15). But along with this promise, He also said that there would be constant antipathy between the seed of the woman and the seed of the serpent. This is what we mean by the antithesis, and we want our students to come to share in that godly antipathy. The fear of the Lord is to hate evil (Ps. 97:10; Prov. 8:13). In every generation, in all movements (whether of armies or philosophies), in all schools of literature, the men and women involved are either obeying God or disobeying Him. They are either trusting Him or they are not trusting Him. All students are learning to love God, or they are not learning to love God.

But when they love and trust Him, they must do so in the face of conflict. Jesus was the ultimate Seed of the woman, and yet when He came down and lived among us, He faced constant opposition from "broods of vipers." It is not possible to live in this world faithfully without coming into conflict with those who have no desire to live faithfully. The task of every Christian parent bringing children up to maturity in such a world is to do it in *a way that equips*. False protection, precisely because it does not equip, leaves a child defenseless when the inevitable day comes when that artificial shelter is removed. True protection equips. We do not want to build a fortress for our students to hide in; we want to give them a shield to carry—along with a sword.

Students who have faithfully worked through this course of study will not be suckers for a romanticized view of ancient paganism offered up by Hollywood. They have read Suetonius, and they have worked through a Christian response to true paganism. They are grateful that Christ came into this dark world, and they know *why* they are grateful.

—*Douglas Wilson*

PREFACE

As you are preparing to begin your work in Omnibus IV, it is at least likely that you are one of those students who began to work with us in Omnibus I. We know that we have picked up some students in the middle of this journey, but we have lined up these books in the consecutive way that we have for a reason.

Omnibus I covers the ancient world, while the second text covers the medieval period, and the third deals with the Reformation period down to the present. With Omnibus IV, we start the process over again—going back to the ancient world. Why do we do this?

There are several reasons that can be given. The first that comes to mind is related to C.S. Lewis's argument in his *Experiment in Criticism* where he maintained that the mark of a good book is that it is the kind of book you return to, in order to read through again. Classics don't wear out the way blue jeans do. In a similar way, you could argue that a period worth studying is a period worth studying *again*. We make no pretense of having covered everything that could be covered in our first pass through these eras, and we know for a fact that a return trip will be well-rewarded.

Another reason is that you, the students, are more mature now, and better able to take on more challenging work. When you return to these times, you will discover that you see more and understand more, and not just because you have gone back to a big place that you did not have time to explore fully when you were there the first time. You are going back to a big place, but you are going back to it bigger. This means that your capacities for understanding are greater, and we trust that this time through you will be gaining a great deal of wisdom— as well as enriching your earlier understanding. Aslan seemed bigger to Lucy when she came back to Narnia because *she* had grown. Return to these eras in the full expectation that much larger vistas will open up before you.

There is a third reason, related to the first one. We hope and pray that when you are done with these next three editions of the Omnibus, your attitude to the subject matter we have covered here will not be one of "There! *That's* done!" Our task goes well beyond trying to get you to learn this material—we have wanted to encourage you to love the material, and to love the study of it. We want you to be the kind of adults who return to many of the classics that you have read in the course of your education, and which you will return to for pleasure. We know that some of you will come back to the Omnibus texts for the education of your own children (which is not as far away as you might think), but apart from pragmatic considerations like that, we hope that many of you will recall many of these books with real affection. And of course those books which are stinkers—but which we had you read because of their importance—we hope you treasure your hatred of them all your days. *Mein Kampf* comes to mind.

A few years ago, I began rereading a number of C.S. Lewis's books, books that I had read many years before— some of them as a teenager. And what I found myself discovering, sometimes with a shock, was that I was encountering truths that I have been friends with my entire adult life, but was now coming back to recognize that *this* is where I must have learned that particular thing. There was a time when I didn't know that, and here was the place where this truth and I first met. Sometimes it is hard to imagine that there was a time when you didn't know your oldest friends.

And old friends are the kind of friends that you learn how to visit with repeatedly. We hope and pray in this second round of Omnibus studies that you will begin to enjoy one of the great privileges of a liberal arts education. We have certainly enjoyed the privilege of trying to provide you with that opportunity.

—Douglas Wilson

"We are all between the paws of the true Aslan."

PREFACE TO OMNIBUS IV: THE ANCIENT WORLD

Rome conquered the known world, whereupon Christianity—despite or perhaps because of intense persecution—conquered Rome. Christianity had become legal and dominant for 48 years when a new emperor named Julian took power. He grew up in a Christian home, but then rejected Christianity and embraced old-style Roman paganism. To renounce your religion is called "apostasy," so Julian became known as "Julian the Apostate." When he became emperor, he resolved to do away with Christianity and to bring the old gods back. One of his measures to undo the cultural influence of Christianity was to forbid Christians from teaching and studying the ancient pagan authors.

Julian the Apostate felt that the Christians had taken over the Greco-Roman culture. They are using the pagan writers to undermine paganism! They are using our own writers against us! That's not fair! "If they want to learn literature," his edict read, "they have Luke and Mark. Let them go back to their churches and expound on them." In other words, Christians should just read their Bibles and leave other kinds of knowledge alone. That way, he reasoned, they won't influence the civilization and will just die out.

Julian the Apostate ruled for only 19 months. He was killed in battle and was succeeded by yet another Christian. All of those ambitious plans to restore paganism—including trying to make the pagans take care of the sick and needy like the Christians did—went for nothing. Trying to stop the spiritual and cultural momentum of Christianity would be like going to the Alps and standing in front of an avalanche, ordering it to stop.

There are two major ironies here. First, some Christians today agree with the man who tried to stamp out Christianity and its influence. They think Christians should read nothing except the Bible and have nothing to do with the ancient authors who lived before the coming of Christ. Second, Julian the Apostate was right. Christianity does take over the ancient authors and the classical cultures. Christianity, with a worldview that is so much bigger than rival worldviews, really does swallow them up.

After Christianity, the classical pagan worldview lost its force. For one thing, it was evident that it could not serve as a coherent perspective that could rival Christianity. The different components of classicism contradict each other. Plato criticizes the poets, such as Homer. Aristotle criticizes Plato. Both great philosophers criticize democracy, which the Romans improved with their Republic, which, however, would be overthrown by the Empire. Cicero defends the Republic from would-be tyrants, such as Mark Anthony. Another great Roman author, Virgil, lauds the Empire of the absolute ruler Augustus Caesar.

And yet, from the vantage point of Christianity, the true greatness of all of these figures is thrown in high relief. Christianity supplies what is lacking. Plato sees that all things have an essence, an idea that gives them their form, but it's hard to imagine his realm of ideas, until Christians relate those underlying ideas to the mind of God. Aristotle reasons that the universe must have a first cause; not only that, the universe must also have a final

Julian the Apostate (331–363)

cause, an ultimate purpose, an end that fulfills all things. What these causes are remain obscure in Aristotle, but Christians see in his analysis the necessity of God. Cicero testifies to the objective reality of the moral law. And Virgil in his Fourth Eclogue written in 37 B.C. predicts that a Child will be born who will remove the wickedness of the world and usher in a Golden Age in which the lion will lie down with the lamb.

It has been observed that Christians invented fiction by rejecting the religious claims of the ancient myths while retaining them as just good stories. One of those myths was that of the Sibyl, an old woman who lived in a cave. To her was given all knowledge, which she wrote down on orderly stacks of oak leaves. The wind, though, blew the leaves away. Now, human beings must learn by finding one leaf after another, putting the isolated truths together as best they can. That's a good story. You don't have to believe in sibyls to appreciate what the story says about the nature of learning. In the *Divine Comedy*, Dante takes the story further. At the climax of the *Paradiso*, in the last canto of the comedy, Dante imagines himself in Heaven, redeemed and coming into the presence of the Trinity Himself. As he does so, Dante sees all of the scattered leaves of the Sibyl flying together, rushing into the light of God. Thus the poet expresses the biblical truth that now we know in part, but then we shall know completely (1 Cor. 13:12). This is also what it is like reading the ancients. We find one leaf of insight after another, but they all come together and make sense in light of the Triune God.

Today the latest cutting-edge ideas maintain that there is no truth and that right and wrong are just cultural constructions. Well, that is what the Sophists believed way back in the fifth century before Christ. If you know the ancients, you know that these new ideas are not only not new, but they have been thoroughly refuted by Plato. Today our scientific theorists are insisting that the only reality in the universe is material and that everything is governed by random forces. Well, that is what Lucretius said in the century before Christ. Someone familiar with the ancients can compare his ideas to those of Euclid (who saw mathematical order built into the universe) and Aristotle (who saw purpose in everything that exists).

Reading the ancients thus gives us perspective. C.S. Lewis said in his essay "On the Reading of Old Books" that each age has its mistakes, but they are usually not the same mistakes. To recognize the blind spots of our own day—and to realize that the contemporary world is not the only world there can be—we need "to keep the clean sea breeze of the centuries blowing through our minds, and this can be done only by reading old books." He adds that "books of the future would be just as good a corrective as the books of the past, but unfortunately we cannot get at them." You will, however, be able to get at the books of the past, thanks to Omnibus!

—*Gene Edward Veith*

The Cumaean Sibyl from the Sistine Chapel

PUBLISHER'S PREFACE

Have you ever stopped to think what the President of the United States in the year 2040 is doing right now? What about the next Martin Luther or John Calvin? I'll tell you what I hope they are doing. I hope they just finished reading this sentence!

There is no doubt in my mind that classical Christian education and the rigorous study of the greatest works of Western Civilization is a tool to create leaders like no other—godly leaders who understand that this is God's world, Christ inherited it, and we are to take dominion of it to His glory.

Many have begun down the path of studying this material and have not persevered—in their minds it was too hard, too salacious for Christian ears, too unrealistic, too much to grasp, the books were too old or some other "too." Be assured, like the Scriptures say in the Parable of the Sower, the work you do will *bear fruit a hundredfold* if you stick with it. In the lives of our own children we have already seen tremendous benefit and really have just barely scratched the surface.

Our goal with this text is to make the work easier for you. This text should make approaching *Omnibus,* and other material not previously encountered, come alive in a way that instills confidence, and it should convey a sense that young students (and teachers) can handle it.

We have done all we could to make this text a stand-alone guide for reading, studying and understanding these great books. One reference book in particular will prove beneficial as a resource for this year as well as the following years. *Western Civilization* by Jackson Spielvogel. If you have previously used our *Veritas Press History and Bible Curriculum,* you will want to keep the flashcards from them handy, too.

May you be blessed as you dig in and study the hand of God at work in the past and prepare for His use of you in the future.

—*Marlin Detweiler*

ADVISORY TO TEACHERS AND PARENTS

In the course of history there has been much fluctuation on what has been deemed age appropriate for young students. And for those of us alive today, there remains great variation as to what is considered age appropriate. The material we have created and the books we have assigned address numerous subjects and ideas that deal with topics (including sex, violence, religious persuasion and a whole host of other ideas) that have been the subject of much discussion of whether they are age appropriate. The judgment we applied in this text has been the same as we apply to our own children.

In the creation of this program we have assumed that it will be used by students in seventh grade and above. Furthermore, we have assumed that there is no part of the Bible deemed inappropriate to discuss with a seventh-grade student. Therefore, the material assumes that the student knows what sex is, that he understands the existence of violence, that he understands there are theological and doctrinal differences to be addressed and that he has the maturity to discern right and wrong.

The worldview we hold and from which we write is distinctly protestant and best summarized in the *Westminster Confession of Faith*. The Bible is our only ultimate and infallible rule of faith and practice.

We encourage you to become familiar with the material that your students will be covering in this program in order to avoid problems where you might differ with us on these matters.

INTRODUCTION

"At life's midpoint, I found myself lost in a dark woods," or so a certain story begins.[1] With Omnibus IV, we pass the midpoint of the project. We have been once through all of history, sampling some of the Great Books, drinking more deeply from others, hopefully finding in this reading what we so need—a connection to our fathers and to our cultural tradition. Our culture is starving for answers. The books that you have read and are reading hold many of the answers that are so desperately needed by the church and by our culture today. The path on which we tread is an old one. This has been overgrown by shrubs and thistles not because it is a bad path, but because most people have left it for easier paths that make believe that the past holds no bearing on the future, that we have no connection or obligation to our forefathers, and that the only writing worth reading is on the bestsellers list or on some blog.[2] All of this we deny! All paths that cut you off from your fathers and from the past are false, dangerous, and unsatisfying. They will eventually cut you off from your children and grandchildren and leave you all alone. Remember, it is not good for man to be alone. As we end this "halftime hiatus" in the Omnibus Project, it is good to pause, to remember and reflect. The ancient world—the world to which we return in Omnibus IV—helps us to shake free from the tethers of the Modern quest for autonomy—to be some free standing, free thinking, unencumbered being who creates reality between his ears (and then is stuck living in it all alone). The ancient world, like much of Omnibus and much of the Bible, reminds us that if we would live well we must live dependently rather than autonomously. We depend on the wisdom of our forefathers. We follow the paths they have trod. We know that outside of Christ we can do nothing. Living this way is humbling and realistic. Considering these truths puts us in our places and makes us ready to be thankful for the gifts passed on to us from the past—gifts that cost them much but which they give to us freely. Before we jump into the reading, here are a few thoughts to ponder as we begin Omnibus IV.

First and foremost, I want to thank all of you for the confidence you have placed in us by using this curriculum. I am simply staggered when I consider how many people in schools and how many home school families are reading these books. I have had the privilege of meeting many of you at conferences and speaking engagements across the country. I worried, at one point, that the creation of the Omnibus books would in a way be problematic. It would stop people from doing the hard work of creating classes from scratch or of making the mistakes (and suffering the pain) from which the first generation folks here in Lancaster have learned. What I have found, however, has been a pleasant surprise. The books, for many, have simply enabled the next level of thinking. I ran into folks at one school who put a male and female teacher in each class. The man and woman would debate different issues in front of a young class of 7th graders. They talked about how the different perspectives complemented each other. Brilliant! I discovered delightful devotion in the voice of a teacher in a home school co-op who said that after getting into the books she started having the students over to read together in the evening a couple times a weeks. I remember being introduced to a home school student whose dad introduced me as one of the editors of the Omnibus books. It was quiet for a moment and then he began to giggle. He said, "I read the footnotes." I had to smile to myself. At least one other soul shared the offbeat sense of humor laced deep into the fabric of this project and tucked away behind the guise of tiny superscripted numbers. I am so thankful that this work has been helpful to so many people. It has been a joy to see more people reading and enjoying these books. I believe that this sort of attention being paid to the thoughts of our forefathers is a necessary step if we want to survive as a culture.

While most feedback was positive, some was "constructive criticism." Perhaps this feedback has been the greatest blessing. From emails questioning the grammar of sentences to people questioning whether or not a seventh grader can write a progymnasmata in 50 minutes, I have found wisdom, truth, honest and good humor amongst the criticism. The editors have tried to listen and evolve.[3] We hope that you find this volume fitter and more able to survive.

There are a few points of advice I need to reiterate. Not listening to this advice can cause the greatest and most pernicious problems when studying Omnibus. First, you might not be able to read all of every book. Normally, at Veritas Academy, the school that I run, we skip a few books a year. You need to be careful about this, but our goal is to have enough material for almost everyone. Read according to this principle: Read as much as you can while inspiring love. Now, this does not mean that every student will love every book, but as a general rule I want to measure Omnibus by the number of students who are reading these books long after they graduate. Second, fear not! Some capture the vision for Omnibus, but also feel their own weakness ("I do not know all these books. . . . I am no expert."). I have found this: love, passion and determination mean a lot. If students can learn only from infinitely knowledgeable teachers, then we should be without hope. None of us fit the bill. If, however, God is blessing our work as we pour ourselves into the lives of our children and students, we should continue, and we should continue with good hope. I have found that my own ignorance has not been a hindrance to my teaching. My students tend to enjoy my stumbling at points. They love it when they can teach me something. The best essay I have ever graded started respectfully: "Mr. Fischer thinks that the answer to this essay is…, *but* he is wrong." Finally, remember that the first read is—for many books—only the beginning. Great books do not suffer when you go back to them. I am a big fan of *The Divine Comedy*. I read a different translation each year (I don't know Italian… yet). I tell people that when they read *The Comedy* the first time, they need to know that it is hard work. They also need to know that it is worthwhile work. The second and third and fourth reads are so much better. Think of the Scriptures. Do you read them once so that you do not have to read them again? Of course not! Do they bless you when you return to them? More and more!

There are changes that we have made in Omnibus IV. These changes follow a few principles. First, we want the students to do all the work that they can. This book can be used by all sorts of secondary students and adults.[4] Volumes IV, V and VI will be pointed more at the rhetoric age students and skills. Many of the changes that we have made simply recognize this. We have a final goal. We want students to be able to do Omnibus when they are out school—i.e., we want them to learn how to explore Great Books, ask good questions, and relish excellent conversation as thinking, Christian adults. If this goal is realized, then our work has been blessed. Second, we have stressed more rhetorical skills—more debate, more poetry (more to come in V), more aesthetic appreciation. Finally, we have been more selective about the reading. Some books are more important than others. Some parts of some books are more important than others parts.[5] We have tried to pick the most essential and most important reading. I am honestly torn on this point. If you want to read additional parts of books that we read in selection, remember that our Optional Sessions give you time to do some of this. Also, if you do not feel confident in creating your own sessions, remember that reading some sections aloud is a wonderful use of time.

Some of the largest changes to Omnibus IV are some additional session formats that we have added. Chief amongst these is the Student-Led Discussion. This follows the form of the Discussion generally, but it requires the students to write most of the questions and share their best questions with each other. They become contributors to the discussion in an even deeper and more meaningful way in the Student-Led Discussions. During this type of class, have the students read the example questions that we provide and then have them write out their own questions and answers while finishing their assigned reading. Remember that they will not produce perfect questions immediately. Encourage good effort. Also, we have added a Current Events session. This challenges

the student to take an issue from their reading and find out how it is still an issue today. We have also added a Poetry form which challenges students to try their hand at writing different forms of poetry. There will be more Poetry classes in future years. Finally, we have added a form for Aesthetics. These sessions introduce students to wonderful pieces of art and challenge them to think deeply about pieces. (These sessions might have been the most fun to edit. I believe they will be a blessing to the students in Omnibus IV.)

We have also altered a few forms. We changed the Writing sessions a lot. I have found that getting good writing from students takes a lot of editorial work. This year you will find our assignments much shorter.[6] We encourage a lot more interaction between teacher or parent and student. In many assignments the students may turn in their work product up to three times, have it graded and returned, and then they can correct it. This should give the students time to create better writing.

While we have changed some of the forms and added some new ones, we have tried to keep the core of Omnibus solid. We are committed to the same things—reading the Great Books, thinking about the great issues of the Christians West, discussing these issues and their applications today, and, finally and ultimately, learning to love our God, our forefathers[7], and our places. This love is the end of life. May you find it as you commune with the writings of the blessed (and the damned) who have gone before you, and may you find your commonality with others as you discuss these books. May that commonality be found ultimately in the source of all wisdom and knowledge—Jesus Christ—and in knowing Him, may you know true life.

—*G. Tyler Fischer*
Trinity Season, 2009

ENDNOTES

1. *The Divine Comedy*, of course.
2. This is not a condemnation of all bestsellers; some are really good. It is not a condemnation of *all* blogs—particularly the ones written by the editors of these fine volumes—just most blogs.
3. But our evolution is based on listening, faith and grace—it is a distinctively non-Darwinian form of evolution. Just think—if only the fastest, strongest and best-looking of us have a shot at surviving, most of us are… well… not going to make it.
4. Why some forward-thinking church does not start using these books for some adult training, I do not know.
5. My favorite example of this is those chapters on blubber and the whale skull in *Moby Dick*. Fascinating… maybe… but necessary?
6. This does not mean that students should not at times write longer papers. We have found that it is hard to do this in Omnibus.
7. I know some people think that the forefathers I am talking about are not their forefathers. Please do not read "forefathers" this way. I do not mean this in some ethnic sense. I am German (Austrian and Prussian), Norman and Scots. I do not think that I have any of the blood of Abraham, Aristotle or Dante. Yet I hope that in some way, some day some of them will acknowledge that in some way some part of me descends from them. I know this is true because Paul tells me that Abraham is the forefather of all who believe.

USING OMNIBUS

The second half of Omnibus—volumes IV, V, and VI—continue the journey of learning from the greatest minds of the Christian West. For those of you who have been through Omnibus I, II, and III, thank you for coming along on this journey. (I hope that you are having a good time.) For the seasoned *omnibuser*, I hope that you will enjoy the new features that we have built into volumes IV, V, and VI.

Before discussing the new aspects of these new volumes, let's walk back through the basics of Omnibus. First, know that you join an incredible group of men and women as you read through these books. These books (the Scriptures and all the Great—but lesser—Books) have nourished your forefathers. They have a lot to give as you give yourself to this study. Remember, it is important to realize that some of these books are not to be learned from uncritically—some of them we learn from by the problems they caused.

Before you get started, however, there are a few terms you need to understand. First among them is the word *omnibus*. This Latin word means "all encompassing" or "everything." So, in a very loose sense, the Omnibus curriculum is where we talk about everything. All of the important ideas are set on the table to explore and understand. In a more technical sense, however, this Omnibus focuses our attention on the ideas, arguments, and expressions of the Western Canon, which have also become known as the Great Books of Western civilization.

The *Great Books* are those books that have guided and informed thinking people in Western civilization. They are the books that have stood the test of time. They come from many sources, starting with the Hebrews and Greeks and extending to their Roman, European, and Colonial heirs. These books represent the highest theological and philosophical contemplations, the most accurate historical record, and the most brilliant literary tradition that have come down to us from our forefathers. The Great Books lead us into a discussion of the *Great Ideas,* which are the ideas that have driven discussion and argument in Western civilization throughout its illustrious history.

The Omnibus takes students on a path through the Great Books and the Great Ideas in two cycles. It follows the chronological pattern of Ancient, Medieval and Modern periods. The first cycle is *Omnibus I–III,* and focuses on sharpening the skills of logical analysis. The second is *Omnibus IV–VI,* focusing on increasing the rhetorical skills of the student.

TITLE	PERIOD	YEARS	EMPHASIS
Omnibus I	Ancient	Beginning–A.D. 70	Logic
Omnibus II	Medieval	70–1563	Logic
Omnibus III	Modern	1563–Present	Logic
Omnibus IV	Ancient	Beginning–A.D. 180	Rhetoric
Omnibus V	Medieval	180–1563	Rhetoric
Omnibus VI	Modern	1563–Present	Rhetoric

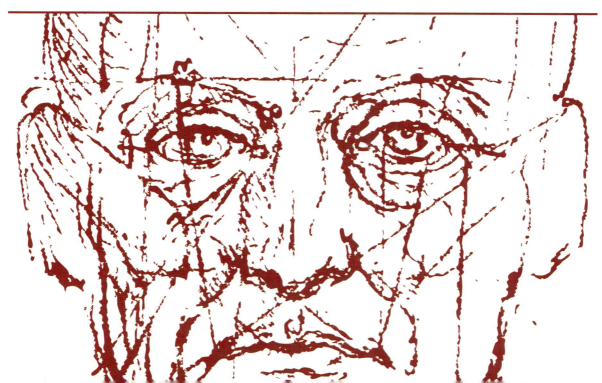

Two kinds of books are read concurrently in the Omnibus, *Primary* and *Secondary*. The list of Primary Books for each year is what might be termed the traditional "Great Books." On this list are authors like Homer, Dante and Calvin. The Secondary Books are ones that give balance to our reading (balance in the general areas of Theology, History and Literature). The secondary list contains works such as *The Chronicles of Narnia* and *The Lord of the Rings*. These books are usually easier, and less class time is devoted to them. Each year is similarly organized. There are thirty-seven weeks' worth of material. Each week is divided into eight sessions of roughly seventy minutes each, optimally. The time estimate is approximate. Home schooling situations might vary greatly from student to student. Five of these sessions are committed to the study of the Primary Books. The other three are dedicated to the Secondary Books.

In Omnibus IV, V and VI, some changes were made to encourage and challenge students to move toward greater maturity. Two of the biggest changes are the Discipline Essays and a number of new class forms.

The *Discipline Essays* aim at helping students to understand a number of important disciplines—everything from Poetry to Economics. These disciplines are areas that students might study in college. The goal, however, is not to find your college major (although, no doubt, some will find a major among these disciplines). The goal is to help students become well-rounded, mature adults who can converse with other adults on many important topics, with a basic understanding of many of the topics that move the world today. The essays are written to be both enjoyable and informative.

Omnibus IV, V and VI also employ a number of new kinds of sessions. These sessions challenge students to develop the skills necessary to wisely discuss questions in the future after they are done with their study in Omnibus and to encourage even more student involvement in class. Also, these new sessions are intended to challenge students to increase their rhetorical skills and integrate various types of knowledge.

KINDS OF SESSIONS

Prelude

Each chapter is introduced with a session called a Prelude. In each Prelude we seek to stir up the interest of the students by examining a provoking question that is or could be raised from the book. This is done in the section called A Question to Consider. When the teacher introduces this question he should seek to get the students' initial reaction to the question. These questions might range from "Can you teach virtue?" to "Are all sins equally wicked?" Usually, a student in the Logic years will love to argue his answers. Generally, it will prove helpful for a student to read the introductory essay in the student text *before* tackling A Question to Consider. Sometimes a teacher may want to introduce the question first to stir up interest. This "introductory material" will give the students both the general information on the work and a worldview essay which will unpack some of the issues that will be dealt with in the book. After reading this section, the student will be asked to answer a few questions concerning the chapter. These questions are based only on the introductory material they have just read, not on the reading of the book itself.

Discussion

The Discussion is the most frequently used class in the Omnibus. It has five parts. The Discussion seeks to explore a particular idea within a book from the perspective of the text itself, our culture and the Bible. It begins, like the Prelude, with A Question to Consider, which is the first of "four worlds" that will be explored, the world of the student. The world of the text is discovered through the Text Analysis questions. These questions unlock the answer that the book itself supplies for this question (e.g., when reading the Aeneid, we are trying to find out how the author, Virgil, would answer this question). After this, in the Cultural Analysis section, the student examines the world of the culture, how our culture would answer the same question. Many times this will be vastly different from the answer of the student or the author. The Biblical Analysis questions seek to unearth what God's Word teaches concerning this question. We can call this discovering the world of the Scriptures. So the progression of the questions is important. First, the students' own opinions and ideas are set forth. Second, the opinion of the text is considered. Next, the view of our culture is studied. Finally, the teaching of the Scriptures is brought to bear. All other opinions, beliefs and convictions must be informed and corrected by the standard of God's Word. Often, after hearing the Word of God, the material seeks to apply the discovered truth to the life of the students. Finally, the students are challenged to think through a Summa Question which synthesizes all they have learned about this "highest" idea from the session.

Recitation

The Recitation is a set of grammatical questions that helps to reveal the student's comprehension of the facts or ideas of the book. This can be done in a group setting or individually with or by students. The Recitation questions can also be answered in written form and checked against the answers, but we encourage doing the Recitation orally whenever possible. It provides great opportunity for wandering down rabbit trails of particular interest or launching into any number of discussions. Of course, we cannot predict what current events are occurring when your students study this material. Recitations can prove a great time to direct conversation that relates to the questions and material being covered in this type of class.

Analysis

This session of worldview analysis is focused on comparing a character, culture or author you are studying to some other character, culture or author. This might be done by comparing two or three characters' or authors' answers to the same questions. This type of session effectively helps students to understand the differences between cultures and characters, especially in the arena of worldview.

Activity

These classes are focused on bringing creative ideas into the mix. Activities might include debates, trials, sword fights, board games and dramatic productions. Music and art appreciation are also included in this category. These classes are harder to prepare for, but are quite important. Often, the student will remember and understand (and love) the material only if our discussions and recitations are mixed with these unforgettable activities. There are also a number of field trips that are recommended. Often, these are recommended in two categories: ones that most people can do and ones that are "outside the box" experiences that only some will be able to do. The first category might send you to the local museum or planetarium. The latter will recommend ideas like chartering a boat at Nantucket to experience what Ishmael felt on the *Pequod*. Careful pre-planning is important to be able to take advantage of these opportunities.

Review and Evaluation

Weekly testing is not recommended. Students will weary of it and will spend all of their time preparing for tests instead of learning. Choose your tests carefully. Even if a chapter has an evaluation at the end, know that you can use it as a review. The test and the review both work toward the same goal of demonstrating the knowledge of the students and cementing the material into their minds.

Evaluations are divided into three sections. The first section tests the student's grammatical knowledge of the book. Answers to these questions should be short, consisting of a sentence or two. The second section is the logic section. In this section students are asked to answer questions concerning the ideas of the book and to show that they understand how ideas connect with each other within the book. The final section is called lateral thinking. This section asks students to relate ideas in one book with the ideas that they have studied in other books. For instance, the student might be asked to compare Homer's ideal heroes (Achilleus and Odysseus) with Virgil's character Aeneas to discover how the Roman conception of the hero was different from the Greek idea. Finally, students often will be asked to compare and contrast these pagan ideas with a biblical view. So, students might be asked to contrast Homer and Virgil's teaching on what is heroic with the ultimate heroic work of Christ. In this way students demonstrate that they can set ideas in their proper biblical context, showing the relationship between the writing of one author and another. Students should be allowed to have their books and Bibles available during testing. If they have to do extensive reading during the tests, they are not going to be able to finish or do well anyway. Students should not be permitted to have notes of any kind during the test.

This sculpture of Moses, complete with horns signifying the glory of God radiating from him after Mount Sinai, is one of the statues on the tomb of Pope Julius II.

Optional Sessions and Activities

For each chapter there are also some optional classes included. These allow the teacher to be flexible and to add to, or omit classes as they think wise. Usually the number of optional classes is approximately one optional class for every week that the book is taught. There are also a number of optional activities included. These activities allow you to spend addition time on ideas that your students might find fascinating.

Midterm and final exam forms have been provided on the Omnibus Teacher's Edition CD. These tests are optional, but can be a helpful gauge of how much the student is retaining. Usually midterms are given around the ninth week of the semester, and finals are given during the last week of the semester. Midterm exams are designed to be completed in a class period. (You might want to give the students slightly more time if possible.) The finals, however, are made to be completed over two class periods (or roughly two and a half hours). Most students will finish more quickly, but some might need all of the time. If possible, give the finals when the student has no time limit. These tests, as well, are given with open books and Bibles, but no notes, and they feature the same sections as the review and evaluation (i.e., grammar, logic and lateral thinking).

Student-Led Discussions

This kind of session (new in Omnibus IV, V, and VI) fits the form of a regular Discussion, but to encourage more student involvement the students are expected to create their own questions and answers for Text Analysis, Cultural Analysis, and Biblical Analysis. The teacher is responsible for the Summa Question. The assignment appears at the end of the previous session to allow the students to work on it while doing the assigned reading. We would expect that students might need help with this the first few times they try it. These questions will quickly reveal whether or not the students have understood their reading. The teacher should collect students' questions and answers to edit and grade them. In a group setting, teachers may allow the students to ask and answer each others' questions—inserting themselves to correct or guide progress but with as gentle a hand as possible.

Current Events

This session (new in Omnibus IV, V, and VI) challenges students to see the modern relevance of the issue they are studying in Omnibus. The assignment appears at the end of the previous session, and there is no reading assignment, allowing the students to prepare their assignment for the following session. The student will find a news or magazine article and prepare a short presentation demonstrating how the article and the previous readings relate to the issue. Students will show where the issue is present in both their reading and in their articles, comparing the worldviews and critiquing both from a biblical perspective.

Poetry

This session (new in Omnibus IV, V, and VI) first introduces a kind of poetry—like a sonnet, a limerick, a quatrain, a sestina, etc. The student is expected to then write a poem related to some content or object in the book they are reading. During the Rhetoric Stage (tenth through twelfth grade) we are encouraging students to grow in their love of poetry and to begin to write poetry themselves.

Aesthetics

Aesthetics sessions (new in Omnibus IV, V, and VI) introduce students to different pieces of art, ask them to analyze the work and respond to the *content, method* and *meaning* of the work. When studying art, one or more of three general emphases should be covered:

- *Grammar of art* (e.g., why is Moses frequently depicted with horns coming out of his head?)

- *Immediate cultural connection* (e.g., colors or poses used at certain times in history). To evaluate a particular work of art, we need to place the work within its historical context: When was the work produced? And where? By whom? Man? Woman? Collaborative? What were/are the historical implications of this particular work? How does it compare to other works produced in that time and place? How does it compare to other works by this artist? And other artists of that time? And of previous periods? Do we recognize any specific artistic or cultural influences?

- *Deeper meaning* (e.g., How does the blurred focus of Impressionism relate to the worldview of the artists using the form?) All art speaks in a language of signs, symbols and semblances: It looks like some thing, sounds like some thing, feels like some thing or references some thing. In what language does the piece of art speak? Once that is determined, does it speak it well?

Trials

These sessions encourage verbal argument and debate, yielding some wonderful discussion. This kind of class appears more frequently in Omnibus IV, V, and VI than it does in the earlier years.

Writing

Writing assignments in Omnibus IV, V, and VI are shorter than in the earlier volumes. This is to encourage the teacher to edit the work more carefully and more critically. It might mean that the editorial process will take a few cycles before the work is in its final state. We hope that the writing will be shorter but much better by the end of the process.

For those getting ready to teach this curriculum, preparation should be carefully considered. The material has been designed so that it can be taught with little preparation, but this is not recommended. If you want your students to get the most out of this program, you should prepare carefully. First, make sure you are familiar with the book being studied. Also, consult the Teaching Tips on the Teacher's Edition CD before teaching. Knowing where you are going in the end will help you to effectively move through the material and interact with your students effectively.

WHAT'S ON THE CD?

Teacher's Edition of the Text

The teacher text includes teaching tips and additional pages of material, with suggested answers for all the questions, writing assignments and activities in the daily sessions.

Lesson Plans

Session-by-session lesson plans for each chapter.

Midterms and Exams

Tests with answer keys for both semesters. Three versions are provided for each test (labeled A, B and C).

Grading Tools

An explanation of our suggested grading routine, including sample and blank grading charts, as well as a grading calculator in a popular spreadsheet format.

Requirements and Use

The CD is Windows and Macintosh compatible, and requires Acrobat Reader. The installer for the latest version is right on the CD or may be downloaded for free at http://get.adobe.com/reader.

WINDOWS OS

If the main application does not appear automatically, double-click the file named "Omnibus-IV-TE".

MACINTOSH OS

Double-click the file named "Omnibus IV (Double-click)" to launch the main application. *Macintosh OS 9 and earlier—double-click the individual files you wish to view.*

PRIMARY BOOKS

First Semester

PHILOSOPHY

Philosophy can be defined simply as the study of the big questions or, looked at from another angle, the *basic* questions. What is the nature of reality? How can we define knowledge? Who or what is man? Why is there something rather than nothing at all? Why is the universe here rather than someplace else?

A Christian student might be initially puzzled by this, wondering what the difference might be between philosophy and theology. The answer is that while philosophy and theology are often covering the same "subject area" ("God," for example), theology is doing so claiming to have answers, at least in principle. Philosophy claims to have the questions, and wants on the basis of man's autonomous reason to refine the questions, and answer them in accordance with the dictates of that reason. But at its best, philosophy *does* train a student to ask and answer questions with care, and this can be training that is of great value to the Christian student.

When the questions are raised and then answered "from outside the authority of autonomous human reason," that's theology. It may be false theology or true, it may be idolatrous or in service to the true God, but at the end of the day, it is some form of theology. When the questions are raised by men, and then pursued "from within," then that is philosophy.

Philosophy as we commonly understand it began among the Greeks. The first great notable philosopher was Socrates (c. 470–399 B.C.). There were philosophers before him, known as the pre-Socratics (obviously), but these men were all eighth-graders on the JV team. Socrates taught Plato, and Plato taught Aristotle, and these three men have dominated philosophical discussion ever since. Alfred North Whitehead once commented that all of western intellectual history consists of footnotes to Plato, which is not too far off.

Now there are two ways to take this—one is to say that his philosophy was so profound that it is not possible to improve upon it, or we could say that the autonomous presuppositions inherent in philosophy mean that we are condemned to spend all our time walking in the same circles, and not very big ones either.

Socrates wrote no books, and his method of pursuing the truth was the dialectical method of asking questions that basically revealed that nobody in Athens knew what they were talking about. This was obviously not conducive to Socrates' general popularity, and he wound up being condemned to die by the city of Athens. Socrates' en-

during *ethos* is not that of a dogmatician, but rather of a questioner, a seeker after light. When the oracle at Delphi proclaimed him the wisest man in Greece, he responded to this by saying that this must be because he knew that he didn't know anything. But this *bon mot* was really part of his "aw, shucks" *persona*—there are many hidden dogmatic assumptions embedded in the questions of Socrates, rock solid assumptions about reason, truth, the nature of reality, and far more. At the same time, he *was* effective with this manner of debate. Socrates was the old timer at the pool hall, chalking his custom-made ivory cue, responding to the naïve question of the new kid in town. "No, I don't really play much . . . how about you?"

Plato (428/7–348/7 B.C.) was one of his students, and he was present when Socrates (as an old man) was forced to drink the poison hemlock as the method of his execution. We know virtually everything we know about Socrates from the pen of Plato. Plato wrote the dialogues of Socrates, and so it is not quite clear how much of what we are getting is actually from Socrates and how much was contributed by Plato. Plato taught that everything here on earth is a "shadow" of a transcendent reality in the realm of the Forms. The Forms were ethereal, rational, non-material, and perfect. So, for example, all chairs on earth are what they are because they somehow partake of the ultimate Chair. The same goes for tables and beds. All particular things on earth "answer to" some aspect of the ultimate reality. What this system seeks to do is provide some kind of integration point for all things, a way of getting all things to make sense in a unified system.

Aristotle (384 B.C.–322 B.C.) was a student of Plato's and significantly modified his theory of the Forms. For Plato, the Forms were a transcendent reality, but Aristotle brought everything down to locate the Form of each object within that object. Thus each chair had an essence of Chair within it. The *accidents* of a chair included the fact that it was made out of wood, was red, and had a cloth seat cover. All these things were not part of the *essence* of the chair. That essence or Form was within the chair, but it was not like you could actually locate it. The student should not feel bad about this—the Forms are just really weird, and *that's* why you can't find them. In addition to being a pupil of Plato's, Aristotle also became a tutor to Alexander the Great. His work had a great deal of breadth. He not only wrote on philosophical questions, but also on politics, theater, ethics, zoology, and much more.

Plotinus (c. A.D. 205–270) was the leading exponent of a system called Neoplatonism. He was writing in the context of the rising Christian faith, but does not interact with it directly. It is also important to note he was writing at the point where classical pagan philosophy was on the verge of collapse. In common with every form of Platonism, he was suspicious of the material realm, teaching that it was contemptible in comparison with the realm of ultimate reality. He taught that there was an ultimate transcendent *One,* the source of everything else. This One is infinitely simple, which is a fancy way of saying it has no parts. It also has no attributes, including the attribute of being an "existent thing." It is simply the Good, and is not a self-aware Creator God. This world is here because it is the end result of a cascading series of emanations from that One. In short, the One is an impersonal and perfect potentiality which overflows like a cascading fountain, with each level of the overflow being less perfect. The first emanations were pure like mountain streams, but by the time it gets down to us, it is like sludge from a pipe. To change the metaphor, each level is not a digital reproduction. That means each generation that is farther away from the original is increasingly corrupt.

In the history of the West, the ascendancy of the Church meant that philosophy eventually had to take a back seat for a significant period of time. Philosophical tools were certainly used by theologians, to a certain extent, and they were acquainted with the basic philosophical issues. Some, like Boethius, appeared to be doing pure philosophy without reference to Scripture, while many others honed their philosophical gifts within the confines of revealed truth. As a result, there were a number of important philosophical developments in the medieval period—the rise of nominalism in reaction to Platonic realism being one. But the theologians' central passion was theology, and so between Plotinus and Descartes, there was a significant hiatus in philosophy. If we wish to dabble in ironies, there was a thousand years of peace—the millennium spoken of by St. John perhaps?

The gap in philosophical studies that passes over some of the great Christian thinkers is really quite striking, and so the Christian philosophy student should be ready for it. He should perhaps pursue his own reading of great Christian thinkers like Augustine, Thomas Aquinas, William of

Plotinus was suspicious of the material realm, even though he was writing in the context of the rising Christian faith. His thought influenced the beliefs of major thinkers over centuries. Neoplatonic elements in the writings of Saint Augustine were no doubt acquired from Plotinus's teachings.

Ockham, or Duns Scotus. And by all means, if he sees an elective class offered in the thought of any of these gentlemen, he should by all means take it.

René Descartes (1596-1650) should be thought of as the father of philosophy reborn. In his *Discourse on Method,* he was looking for a sure point of traction, a solid footing for human thought that could not be doubted. His starting point was in his formulation of the famous *cogito ergo sum,* "I think, therefore I am." Even in moments of radical doubting, a man cannot consistently doubt that he is in fact doubting, and doubt is a form of thinking, which means that he has to *be* here in order to be thinking. Right? The methodological point to note here is that Descartes began with the solitary thinking individual, and sought to build up the whole system from that indubitable starting point. His starting point was not God. The entire Enlightenment project can really be thought of as an endeavor built up from Descartes, a Cartesian endeavor. Modern philosophy began with the rationalism of Descartes, was carried on in the empiricism of philosophers like John Locke, was driven into a tree by the skeptical doubts of David Hume, and was then supposedly *rescued* by Immanuel Kant.

John Locke (1632-1704) was an empiricist, which means that he believed that man comes to know through his sensory experience of the empirical world. While Descartes was a rationalist and began with reason, the empirical school which came later taught that knowledge was mediated to man through his senses. Locke made important contributions to political theory and social philosophy, but in philosophy proper his main contribution was in the field of epistemology. "How can we know that we actually *know?*" His *Essay Concerning Human Understanding* gave us a new approach to the self. While Descartes held that human reason contained certain innate ideas, Locke held that the mind was a *tabula rasa,* a blank slate, which was then filled by means of experience and reflection.

David Hume (1711-1776) was part of the great Scottish Enlightenment and was an important figure in the history of philosophy. His was the first modern approach to philosophy that was thoroughgoing in its naturalism, believing as Carl Sagan eventually summarized, "The Cosmos is all that is or ever was or ever will be." At the same time, the effect of his careful approach to questions resulted in a *skeptical* naturalism, as opposed to the dogmatic naturalism of later thinkers, after they had been inspired by Darwin. Hume is famous for his argument on the low probability of miracles, as well as his critique of the argument for God's existence from design. He also showed that it is not possible to derive ethical direction from a study of the way things are—in short that you cannot derive *ought*

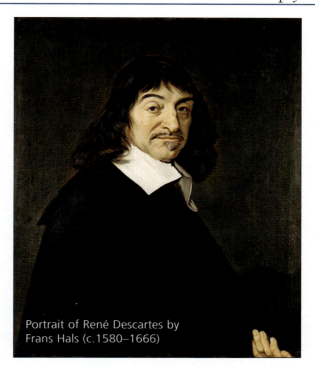

Portrait of René Descartes by Frans Hals (c.1580–1666)

from is. The cumulative effect of his philosophy was corrosive to confidence in our ability to acquire knowledge.

Immanuel Kant (1724-1804) credited Hume with waking him from his "dogmatic slumber" and sought to develop a way out of the *cul de sac* that modern philosophy had gotten itself into. The street was a one-way street, so there was no going back. It led into a *cul de sac,* and so there was no going forward. The solution that Kant offered, and which was received with great acclaim, was to float off over the houses. Kant was a crucial figure in the later Enlightenment, and he sought to give an explanation for the motto of Enlightenment—*sapere aude,* or "dare to know." Kant distinguished between the phenomenal world (which we could know after a fashion), and the noumenal realm, which he maintained we cannot know. This meant that, with regard to questions about God and the afterlife, Kant was a principled agnostic. His central contribution to the history of ideas was his transcendental idealism, which means that we have to deal with things as they appear to us, not as they actually are in themselves.

Søren Kierkegaard (1813-1855) was a fascinating Danish philosopher and theologian. In philosophy he wrote in vigorous reaction to the formalism of Hegel, and in religion and theology, he wrote in violent reaction to the dead orthodoxy of the state church of Lutheran Denmark. He is hard to pin down in many ways, but is sometimes thought of as the father of existentialism—although this is probably too facile. The Christian philosophy student

6   Omnibus IV

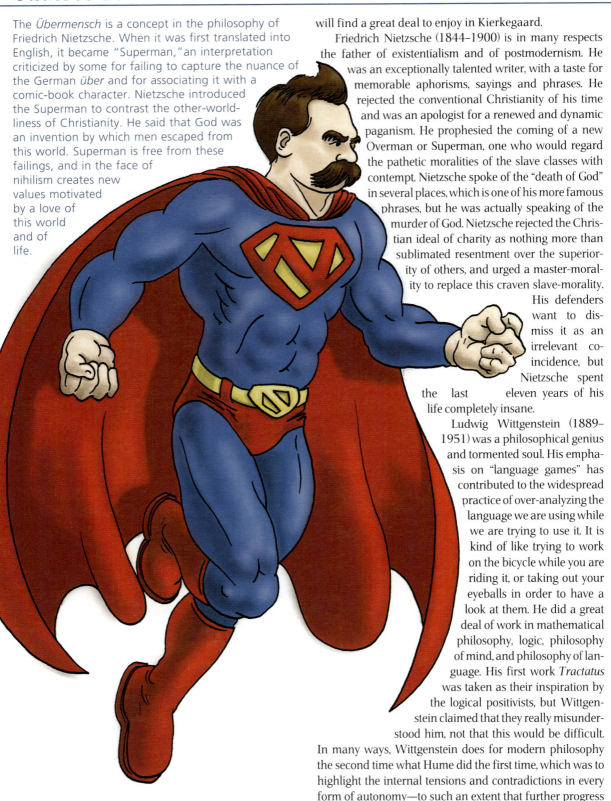

The *Übermensch* is a concept in the philosophy of Friedrich Nietzsche. When it was first translated into English, it became "Superman," an interpretation criticized by some for failing to capture the nuance of the German *über* and for associating it with a comic-book character. Nietzsche introduced the Superman to contrast the other-worldliness of Christianity. He said that God was an invention by which men escaped from this world. Superman is free from these failings, and in the face of nihilism creates new values motivated by a love of this world and of life.

will find a great deal to enjoy in Kierkegaard.

Friedrich Nietzsche (1844–1900) is in many respects the father of existentialism and of postmodernism. He was an exceptionally talented writer, with a taste for memorable aphorisms, sayings and phrases. He rejected the conventional Christianity of his time and was an apologist for a renewed and dynamic paganism. He prophesied the coming of a new Overman or Superman, one who would regard the pathetic moralities of the slave classes with contempt. Nietzsche spoke of the "death of God" in several places, which is one of his more famous phrases, but he was actually speaking of the murder of God. Nietzsche rejected the Christian ideal of charity as nothing more than sublimated resentment over the superiority of others, and urged a master-morality to replace this craven slave-morality. His defenders want to dismiss it as an irrelevant co-incidence, but Nietzsche spent the last eleven years of his life completely insane.

Ludwig Wittgenstein (1889–1951) was a philosophical genius and tormented soul. His emphasis on "language games" has contributed to the widespread practice of over-analyzing the language we are using while we are trying to use it. It is kind of like trying to work on the bicycle while you are riding it, or taking out your eyeballs in order to have a look at them. He did a great deal of work in mathematical philosophy, logic, philosophy of mind, and philosophy of language. His first work *Tractatus* was taken as their inspiration by the logical positivists, but Wittgenstein claimed that they really misunderstood him, not that this would be difficult. In many ways, Wittgenstein does for modern philosophy the second time what Hume did the first time, which was to highlight the internal tensions and contradictions in every form of autonomy—to such an extent that further progress down this road is not really possible.

Critical Issues

The problem for Christians contemplating a course of study in philosophy is that Scripture teaches us that "the fear of the Lord is the beginning of knowledge" (Prov. 1:7). We do not come to a fear of the Lord as a capstone of all our intellectual efforts, a decorative piece to crown all that we have done. Rather, the fear of the Lord is the solid foundation, upon which everything else must be built. That is where we start, not where we end. This means that Christians who are students of philosophy, or even Christians who become philosophers vocationally, cannot ever become full members of the guild. As the philosophers all get out their books, and the Christian does the same, it will soon become evident that the Christian believes he has a book with all the answers in it, which will be quickly identified as "cheating." If the Christian agrees not to use this book, then he has become a methodological philosopher, but at the cost of spiritual compromise. And as long as he uses it, as long as he is a thorough-going Christian, he will not be fully accepted as a "real" philosopher. This state of affairs is not the result of an unfortunate misunderstanding that arose just a few years ago, but rather reveals the state of affairs that has always existed between philosophy and the gospel.

At the same time, despite this tension, many Christians can be found in philosophy departments, and so over time it will be harder and harder for the secular guild to maintain their commitment to philosophical secularism. Contemporary respected philosophers like Alvin Plantinga, who are also clearly believers, have done a great deal to challenge this divide, and Christians who are committed to Christian worldview thinking and "taking every thought captive" ought to be thinking about what philosophy should look like in the future—when philosophy is again done within the context of faith as in the medieval period. There were some things that our medieval fathers did right in this regard, and there were also some blunders that we ought to be careful to avoid the second time around. But all Christian students of philosophy should be thinking in such terms—always rejecting a divided intellectual world. All of it—the whole world—belongs to Christ.

So all Christian students must understand the fundamental antithesis between autonomous philosophy and true wisdom as it is found in Christ. This does not determine whether we may study philosophy, but it absolutely must determine how we seek to do so.

The apostle Paul was acquainted with philosophy, and he took a pretty dim view of it.

As you therefore have received Christ Jesus the Lord, so walk in Him, rooted and built up in Him and established in the faith, as you have been taught, abounding in it with thanksgiving. Beware lest anyone cheat you through philosophy and empty deceit, according to the tradition of men, according to the basic principles of the world, and not according to Christ (Col. 2:6–8).

Here he contrasts the vandalism and despoliation of philosophy with the edification that is found in Christ. And he is doing this with the "golden age" of philosophy in mind. He is talking about the philosophers who show up in "great books" programs, and he is not talking about the village nihilist. He couples philosophy with vanity and deceit, and links it to the tradition of men, to the world's basic way of thinking about things. The apostle was almost certainly familiar with the content of the "wisdom of the Greeks"—he wasn't just dismissing something he knew nothing about. This meant, at a minimum, that he was warning the Christians at Colossae about the threat posed by Socrates, Plato and Aristotle. In the ancient world, the word philosophy had an understood meaning, just as the words stool, trireme, or emperor did. When he goes after the tradition of men and the rudiments of the world, he is targeting those things which carnal men believe to be virtuous. These warnings are not to be classed in the same category with your mother's warnings about pool halls, taverns, and painted ladies. Everybody knows that painted ladies represent a set of moral temptations. Almost no one knows that respected philosophers are even more dangerous.

This focus becomes even more apparent in the first two chapters of 1 Corinthians, where Paul is probably concentrating on Aristotle. But whether he is doing that or not, his central criticism of the philosophical approach is that "the world by wisdom knew not God." And if you don't come to know God as the result of what you are doing, then what good is it?

For the message of the cross is foolishness to those who are perishing, but to us who are being saved it is the power of God. For it is written:

'I will destroy the wisdom of the wise,
And bring to nothing the understanding of the prudent.'

Where is the wise? Where is the scribe? Where is the disputer of this age? Has not God made foolish the wisdom of this world? For since, in the wisdom of God, the world through wisdom did not know God, it pleased God through the foolishness of the message preached to save those who believe. For Jews request a sign, and Greeks seek after wisdom; but we preach Christ crucified, to the Jews a stumbling block and to the Greeks foolishness, but to those who are called, both Jews and Greeks, Christ the power of God and the wisdom of God. Because the foolishness of God is wiser than men, and the weakness of God is stronger than men. For you see your calling, brethren, that not many wise according to the flesh, not many mighty, not many noble, are called. But God has chosen the foolish things of the world to put to shame the wise, and God has chosen the weak things of the world to put to shame the things which are mighty; and the base things of the world and the things which are despised God has chosen, and the things which are not, to bring to nothing the things that are, that no flesh should glory in His presence (1 Cor. 1:18–29).

Paul is clear that by the "wisdom of the wise" (v. 19), or the "wisdom of this world" (v. 20), he means the wisdom of the Greeks (v. 22). As he exults in the superiority of Christ over all these intellectual systems, he acknowledges that they do have a certain impressiveness to them. He says that God has taken weak things to confound the things which are mighty (v. 27). The scribe, the scholar, the urbane debater—God has made them all foolish. In short, on the subject of intellectual and philosophical respectability, which Paul addresses directly here, he makes it perfectly plain that there is a wisdom of the world which God regards as lunacy, and the worldly wise return the favor by treating all those who begin and end with Christ in exactly the same way—as fools.

None of this means that Christians should embrace sloppy argumentation. We should not start maintaining that wet streets cause rain, or that Christianity is true because it starts with the letter C, unlike Buddhism. As mentioned earlier, Christians can learn to ask and answer questions with care, and they can learn this from their unbelieving philosophy instructor. But Paul's warnings do mean that at the center of the philosophical endeavor there is a seduction which all thoughtful Christians must be on guard against.

I was with you in weakness, in fear, and in much trembling. And my speech and my preaching were not with persuasive words of human wisdom, but in demonstration of the Spirit and of power, that your faith should not be in the wisdom of men but in the power of God. However, we speak wisdom among those who are mature, yet not the wisdom of this age, nor of the rulers of this age, who are coming to nothing. But we speak the wisdom of God in a mystery, the hidden wisdom which God ordained before the ages for our glory, which none of the rulers of this age knew; for had they known, they would not have crucified the Lord of glory. But as it is written:

'Eye has not seen, nor ear heard,
Nor have entered into the heart of man
The things which God has prepared for those who love Him.'

But God has revealed them to us through His Spirit. For the Spirit searches all things, yes, the deep things of God. For what man

Gian Lorenzo Bernini's (1598–1680) statue of Saint Paul stands in the entrance of Ponte San Angelo in Rome.

knows the things of a man except the spirit of the man which is in him? Even so no one knows the things of God except the Spirit of God. Now we have received, not the spirit of the world, but the Spirit who is from God, that we might know the things that have been freely given to us by God. These things we also speak, not in words which man's wisdom teaches but which the Holy Spirit teaches, comparing spiritual things with spiritual. But the natural man does not receive the things of the Spirit of God, for they are foolishness to him; nor can he know them, because they are spiritually discerned (1 Cor. 2:3–14).

This is more of the same. Now in verse 14, what does Paul mean by "the natural man"? An easy assumption for modern Christians to make is that this refers to a frat-boy paganism, someone who is a licentious and lustful drinker of many beers. But natural man here refers to man at his best, not man at his worst. This means that every potential student of philosophy must have his guard up, and must understand where the antithesis really is.

A Christian Response

With all this said, why would any Christian student make the choice of studying philosophy? There are actually many good reasons, but none of the good ones include a desire to "join the club." Assuming the good reasons to be sound, what are some of the basic issues that such a student should consider?

Many of these exhortations apply equally to all Christian college students, going off to study on their own for the first time. But we have to remember that philosophy is probably the only major in college you might consider that the Bible explicitly warns against. This is not the case for mechanical engineering, or forestry, or international relations. When you study philosophy, you really are endangering your soul, and so it is appropriate to take some extra precautions.

First, don't even consider a program unless it is located in a place where you can worship God every Lord's Day in a faithful, biblical church. All faithful discipleship occurs in such community, and so if you are studying secular philosophy in the midst of their community, and you have no Christian fellowship, you will be shaped by that process, however much you might have formed mental resolutions against that kind of compromise. In order to prevent that shaping, it is necessary to maintain your loyalties to God's people in a tangible, on-going way. The apostle Paul says that we are to prevent the world's attempts to drag us back, the world's attempts to make

us conform to its standards, by being transformed into something else.

I beseech you therefore, brethren, by the mercies of God, that you present your bodies a living sacrifice, holy, acceptable to God, which is your reasonable service. And do not be conformed to this world, but be transformed by the renewing of your mind, that you may prove what is that good and acceptable and perfect will of God (Rom. 12:1–2).

But note that Paul says that we are protected in our minds by what we do with our *bodies*. This seems counterintuitive to us, but it is actually testimony to the pervasive nature of certain philosophical doctrines that have gotten into the Church. The disparagement of the body's importance is a legacy of Greek thought or Hellenism, and the Church has had the devil of a time with it over the course of many centuries. The idea that what we *think* is the only "really important thing" is an idea that we have had a really hard time with—it is the philosophical gum on our shoe.

It is therefore more important for you to get your body to church (and of course your soul may go, too), even if the worship service doesn't challenge you, than it is for you to stay in your dorm room, meditating deeply on Christian themes. The reason for this is that God's people are your people, and you need to form an attachment to them as your people. And you cannot form that kind of attachment to people without spending time with them. I could not advise anybody to study philosophy if they were not plugged into a vibrant and robust Christian church.

The second caution is very similar to the first. Personal holiness is crucial, and when there has been sin, confession of that sin is even more crucial (1 John 1:9). I have a friend who, when he was a little boy, was taken down to skid row by his father to see how the bums and addicts were living. The father was not a Christian, but he wanted his son to see the end of the road, to see the final destination of a certain class of choices. I have often thought of that example when considering what the world treats as intellectual sophistication, but which an insightful Christian ought to see as an epistemological skid row full of well-groomed, sophisticated sounding ways of knowing truth that are utterly hopeless dead ends. The universities of the world are filled with intellectual refuse and *detritus*. But this is not caused because people are being stupid. Scripture teaches that folly is a moral issue, not an intellectual one.

The Scriptures teach us that men are given over to intellectual darkness and folly because they refuse to honor God as God, and refuse to give thanks to Him (Rom.

1:21). In other words, you don't protect your heart (your personal devotion) by means of intellectual exercises. Rather, you protect your ability to think in a straight line by means of personal loyalty to God, His standards, and His people. To be very specific, if an intelligent young man with a Christian upbringing goes off to college to study philosophy, the quickest way for him to start thinking that Heidegger was profound is by watching a lot of pornography or doing other activities that abandon the scriptural values of his family and community and, therefore, make the ridiculous seem profound.

We have a tendency to come up with reasons for staying away from God, and living in unconfessed sin causes such reasons to multiply like the frogs of Egypt. If a student is doing this while simultaneously engaged in a course of study designed for those who want to stay away from God, it is not hard to predict what will happen.

The third warning is this: don't accept a false head/heart distinction, thinking that you are studying difficult philosophical paganism in the course of your studies during the week, and that this requires some light devotional fluff to counterbalance it. We are called, in the greatest commandment, to love the Lord our God with all our minds—all our *brains*—and this means that your thought life is to be disciplined by Christ along with the rest of you. The points made earlier about the importance of being involved in a church and walking with God in your personal life were not meant to say that these activities counterbalance or "make up for" what is happening in your mind. It is *not* the case that the devil gets your brains, and so you have to give God your weekends and sex life in order to compensate. You are studying the way the unbelieving mind works, studying the different routes it may take, not in order to imitate it, but rather to anticipate and answer it. Another way of putting this is that every Christian studying philosophy really needs to be doing so as an intellectual evangelist or apologist. In addition, Christians who have studied philosophy do not need to worry that much about what's fashionable among unbelieving philosophers. The Christian world has its own interests that we should be addressing "in house." At a minimum, we should want to have a biblical view of knowledge, freedom, mind, language, mathematics, and so on. The Christian trained in philosophy can certainly help the Church frame her questions about these subjects carefully. This *is* an area where the Christian philosophy student can plunder gold from the Egyptians, and many doctrinal tangles and theological controversies could be sorted out if we learned how to use these philosophical tools with care.

Of course, submitting to the yoke of Christ when it comes to your intellectual life will include reading what

> "The whole problem of knowledge has constantly been that of bringing the one and the many together. When man looks about him and within him, he sees that there is a great variety of facts. The question that comes up at once is whether there is any unity in this variety, whether there is one principle in accordance with which all these many things appear and occur. All non-Christian thought, if it has utilized the idea of a supra-mundane existence at all, has used this supra-mundane existence as furnishing only the unity or the *a priori* aspect of knowledge, while it has maintained that the *a posteriori* aspect of knowledge is something that is furnished by the universe."
> — Cornelius Van Til, a Christian philosopher.

Philosophy

many Christian writers have faithfully done to answer the intellectual challenges of unbelief. Such writers should, of course, include Cornelius Van Til, C.S. Lewis, Francis Schaeffer, and G.K. Chesterton. When I was a student of philosophy, I remember that Chesterton was a lifeline of sanity to me, in a field of study where sanity did not seem to matter that much.

But at the same time, it is important to be reading other Christian writers who are in the same league with your secular studies. If all the non-believers you read are heavy-weights, and the believers are all lightweights, or you read them just to "find an answer," you will eventually get to a very bad conclusion. So even if you have a lot to read, make sure to pursue writers who are weighty and substantive, even if they are not writing in a field that addresses any of the particular questions you are working through in philosophy. Read through Calvin's *Institutes*, for example, or Augustine's *City of God*. They may not answer a particular question that came up in one of your classes, but you will be continually reminded that Christians have brains, and moreover that brains can be used in ways that are entirely constructive. As you do this, be careful to resist the temptation of trying to make Christian categories fit into the philosophical ones. It is easy to become impressed with really smart guys in theology and philosophy, and then to try to force them into the same categories, which rarely works out well.

The fourth caution is that before challenging the tenets of unbelief in the classroom—before you set yourself up to be Apologetics Man—you should strive to be the best student your philosophy instructor ever had. You should do your assignments, read everything suggested, turn your papers in on time and in a legible condition, be respectful, and above all, *do not rush to the refutation*. If the second paper you turn in to this instructor has as its thesis statement that "Kant was an idiot," what you are asking for is for that instructor to never take you seriously. Even if you had a point, which is unlikely, that point might have been made and heard had it been advanced a year or two later.

Your *ethos* as a student needs to be established first. This means that you have to take pains to make sure that you have understood what Kant is actually saying before attempting to explain to your professor how Kant became so silly. Now some might argue that sophomores have a certain divine right to be sophomoric, but Christian students should still remember that they are nineteen years old, at least for the time that they are.

As just mentioned, this is something to strive for, but sometimes things are not quite so tidy. It would be more to the point to say that Christian students should not take the offense unless they have established their credentials as hard-working, diligent students. In other words, don't carry the flag for the Christian faith, don't go over the top for Jesus, unless you have done all your homework. But where does the messiness come in? This scenario outlined above assumes that your professor is just a regular guy, trying to pay his mortgage, and he does not need an ignorant born-againer dominating all his classroom discussions.

But there are other times when the professor is actively hostile to the Christian faith, and he attacks it every chance he

gets. There are times when humble college students, who are not as well prepared as they would like to have been, have to defend the faith. But this is quite different than attacking for the faith. Both are sometimes necessary, but the former can be thrust upon you. The latter ought not to be taken up lightly.

And last, don't become a specialist—resist all temptation to become a philosophy wonk. There are two levels to this. The first is, "don't become a library rat," and the second is, "to the extent you are reading, have only about a third of it be the assigned work. This might seem like a ton of extra work, but it is actually a means of keeping your work proportioned and balanced. This exhortation is simply to make sure you have a life, and that you have one outside the realm of books, and also within the realm of books.

Outside your books, go hiking. Play flag football. Go to the movies. Attend all the church potlucks. When it comes to your reading, reserve about a third of your time to do all your reading assignments. Set aside another third for your Bible reading, and substantive Christian books. For the remainder, make sure you have a steady diet of P.G. Wodehouse, Shakespeare, Billy Collins, John Donne, J.R.R. Tolkien, and Jane Austen. Make sure you stay a reasonable human being.

—*Douglas Wilson*

For Further Reading

Plato. *The Last Days of Socrates.* Ed. Harold Tarrant. New York: Penguin, 2003.

Plato. *Parmenides.* Trans. R. E. Allen. New Haven, CT: Yale University Press, 1998.

Aristotle, *Nichomachean Ethics* in *Introduction to Aristotle.* Ed. Richard McKeon. Chicago: University of Chicago Press, 1974.

Plotinus, *Enneads.* Ed. John Dillon. New York: Penguin, 1991.

Rene Descartes, *Discourse on Method.* Trans. Desmond M. Clark. New York: Penguin, 2000.

John Locke, *Essay Concerning Human Understanding.* Ed. Paul E. Sigmund. New York: W. W. Norton. 2005.

David Hume, *An Enquiry Concerning Human Understanding.* New York: Barnes and Noble, 2004.

Immanuel Kant, *Prolegomena to Any Future Metaphysic.* Trans. Paul Carus. New York: Barnes and Noble, 2007.

Friedrich Nietzsche, *Beyond Good and Evil.* Trans. Walter Kaufmann. New York: Knopf Doubleday, 1989.

Ludwig Wittgenstein, *Philosophical Investigations.* Trans. Elizabeth Anscombe. Hoboken, NJ: John Wiley and Sons, 2008.

PROVERBS

When God created Adam, He put him in a garden, naked as a newborn. He told Adam to carry out the priestly task of "serving and guarding" the garden (Gen. 2:15). Adam was allowed to eat from the Tree of Life, but before he received the fruit of the Tree of Knowledge he had to grow up. Life is for babies; knowledge or wisdom is for adults, who have their senses trained to discern good and evil (Heb. 5:14). Eventually, Yahweh would have allowed Adam to eat the fruit of knowledge, and his eyes would have been opened to judge and rule (cf. Ps. 11:4; Heb. 4:13). Eventually, Adam would have grown up from priest to king.

Adam was just like you. For many years after your birth, your parents made all decisions for you. They decided what you would eat, what time you would go to bed, how many movies you could watch. They told you what to do and expected you to obey it. As time went on they gave you more responsibility and allowed you to make more of your own decisions. You were growing, as Adam would have done, from the Tree of Life to the Tree of Knowledge.

Adam took the fruit of the Tree of Knowledge too early, when he was still a baby. He wanted his driver's license at the age of six, and he wanted to stay out until midnight drinking and smoking with his friends when he was eight. He was impatient, and so Yahweh expelled him from the garden and didn't let him come back to eat from the Tree of Knowledge, or the Tree of Life, anymore.

Yahweh still intended for human beings to grow up from servant-priests into kings. Israel was like a new Adam, and Yahweh called His people to be servants before He gave them authority to rule. When He called Abram, He first commanded him to build altars and worship. When He brought Israel from Egypt, their first task was not to rule the land but to build the Tabernacle in the wilderness as a place of worship. After forty years of priestly service in the wilderness, Israel entered the garden-land to judge the Canaanites and become kings. Even then, Israel did not have a king for centuries.

Finally, with Saul and even more with David and Solomon, Yahweh made Israel a royal people. After many centuries, God allowed "Adam" to eat from the Tree of Knowledge and receive the wisdom needed to rule. Solomon knew he was given a privilege Adam had never received. When he asked for wisdom, he said, "[G]ive Thy servant a hearing heart to judge Thy people to discern good and evil" (1 Kings 3:9).

Israel's kings were often failures, and eventually Yahweh sent Israel and Judah into exile. Even so, He kept to His plan to train human beings to rule. Jesus is the greater Solomon, the true Wise King. His eyes are flames of fire, open to know and judge good and evil (Rev.1:14). He not only rules as the Wise King, but also teaches us wisdom so that we can rule alongside Him. He gave Himself to make us "kings and priests to God" (Rev.1:6).

Because Proverbs is a book of wisdom, it is a royal book. Solomon instructs his son, the prince, about how to rule and live well. Behind the relation of King to Prince is the relation of King Yahweh to Prince Israel, the relation of our Father to Christians. The first time Solomon uses the phrase "my son," it comes after the command to "hear" (Prov. 1:8). That reminds us of Deuteronomy 6, where Israel is told, "Hear, O Israel, Yahweh your God is one" (v. 4). Israel is Yahweh's son (cf. Ex. 4:23), and the wisdom that Solomon communicates to his prince is ultimately His Wisdom. Likewise, we are our Father's sons and daughters, and in Proverbs our Father speaks to us, training us to be His princes and princesses in His Son, the High King Jesus.

Go to the ant, you sluggard! Consider her ways and be wise, which, having no captain, overseer or ruler, provides her supplies in the summer, and gathers her food in the harvest. Proverbs 6:6–8

Omnibus IV

GENERAL INFORMATION

Author and Context

The Hebrew title of Proverbs comes from the first line of the book: "The Proverbs of Solomon" (1:1). We think of a proverb as a short, pithy saying that gives us a bit of folk wisdom. The Hebrew word (*mashal*) is broader. It can refer to a prophecy (Num. 23:7, 18; 24:3, 15, 20–23). When Israel is cursed for her sins, she becomes a "proverb," a warning, to the nations (Deut. 28:37; Ps. 44:14). Proverbs can take the form of songs (Ps. 49:4), including songs that recount historical events (Ps. 78:2). Ezekiel's parable of the eagle and the cedar tree is called a *mashal* (Ezek. 17), and when Jesus tells parables He is using a form of wisdom literature. According to the Bible, wisdom is

A depiction of wise King Solomon, one of the authors of Proverbs, from the Bible of Souvigny, produced at the end of the twelfth century at the Cluny Abbey in France.

taught by stories, sayings, songs, allegories and parables, and historical events. We can also learn wisdom from our own experience of life. In Proverbs 1:2, we're told that the Proverbs communicate "instruction." The root of the word is "chastise" and Bible scholar Bruce Waltke says that the word means "chastening lesson." Israel was supposed to take instruction from the way the Lord dealt with rebellious Egypt (Deut. 11:2), and Yahweh disciplined Israel through exile for the instruction of the surrounding nations (Ezek. 5:15). Chastening lessons also come when we act foolishly and pay for it. Receiving a spanking is a chastening lesson (Prov. 13:24; 22:15; 23:13; 29:15), and so is being fired from a job because we are lazy. We take a few steps down the road of folly, and the Lord graciously intervenes and slaps us back. He is the perfect Father, who disciples His true sons (Heb. 12:8). Chastening lessons can give wisdom only if we are open to the chastening. If we complain and murmur, or harden ourselves in anger, or hate God for chastening us, or seek to escape its lessons, or don't think about its lessons, then we are not going to gain wisdom from those chastening lessons. As Solomon says, "Fools despise wisdom and chastening." The surest way to stay a fool is to ignore the lessons God teaches us through chastening.

Solomon spoke 3,000 proverbs (1 Kings 4:32), and the Proverbs give us only a small sample. Not all of the proverbs are from Solomon, either. Proverbs 25:1 tells us that some of Solomon's proverbs were gathered together during the reign of Hezekiah, and the last chapters of the book were written by "Agur, the son of Jakeh" (chapter 30) and "King Lemuel" (chapter 31). By and large, though, the proverbs are from Solomon.

Many of them are addressed to his son, the prince. Solomon wants his son to gain wisdom, and specifically wisdom to carry out the royal tasks of providing "righteousness, justice, and equity" (1:3). Kings were supposed to meditate on the law (Deut. 17:18–20; cf. Ps. 1), and out of that meditation they were supposed to gain wisdom about judging cases that the law does not cover—like a dispute between two prostitutes over a baby (1 Kings 3).

Summary and Setting

Proverbs looks like a random collection of individual sayings arranged in several large groups.

Chapters 1–9
provide an introduction
to the whole book
Chapters 10–24
are called the "proverbs
of Solomon" (10:1)
Chapters 25–29
contain proverbs of Solomon
compiled in the reign of Hezekiah
Chapter 30
comes from Agur
Chapter 31
comes from Lemuel

Like Psalms, Proverbs is divided into five sections, which reminds us of the five books of Moses. Proverbs gives us a new Torah, five "books" of wisdom.

But there is another, more interesting arrangement in Proverbs. It is not a random collection of individual proverbs. It is arranged into a story, and it's a love story.

Genesis begins with a command to Adam to rule the earth, and ends with a new Adam, Joseph, ruling the largest empire of the world. Exodus begins with Israel in slavery and ends with God's presence descending on the Tabernacle; as James Jordan has written, the theme of the book is "From Slavery to Sabbath." The cosmic scope of the books of Chronicles is reinforced by the fact that it begins with Adam (creation) and ends with the declaration of Cyrus that the Temple would be rebuilt, an anticipation of the eschatological temple of the new creation. The book of Matthew begins with the Jewish genealogy of Jesus, depicts his escalating conflict with and rejection of the Jewish leadership and ends with Jesus commissioning His disciples to spread the gospel to the Gentile nations. Acts begins with Pentecost in Jerusalem and ends with Paul preaching unhindered in Rome.

In Proverbs, the first nine chapters are full of references to two women who compete for the prince's attention and affection. Lady Wisdom walks through the streets exhorting simpletons to abandon their simplicity and warning them of the consequences if they refuse to hear (1:20–33). Chapter 2 introduces the second woman, the adulteress, Dame Folly (cf. 9:13). Throughout the early chapters, the father alternately encourages his son, the prince, to pursue Lady Wisdom (3:13ff.; 4:1–9; 8:1–36; 9:1–6) and warns him about the dangers of following Dame Folly (5:1–23; 6:20–35; 7:6–27; 9:13–18). Wisdom brings life, riches, and honor. Folly brings poverty, shame, and ultimately death; her house is a highway to the grave (2:16–18). The Proverbs begin, then, with the son confronted by a choice of two women who are bound up with two divergent destinies.

The book of Proverbs is structurally similar to Disney's version of Hans Christian Andersen's *The Little Mermaid*, in which a prince must choose between the mermaid, who cannot speak so long as she is a normal girl, and the sea witch, who has disguised herself as a desirable young woman. The prince notices two potential brides: Which one will he choose?

We don't get the answer until the last chapter of the book, the well-known Proverbs 31. In the drama of Proverbs, the excellent wife is Lady Wisdom from the earlier chapters. Her husband, the Prince, now sits in the gates of the city. He has successfully resisted the seductions of the adulteress, Folly. He has chosen well. Together, the Prince and his bride form the royal household.

Proverbs, in other words, tells a story, a romance. In fact, it's even more of a fairy tale than that. It's a royal romance, the story of a prince finding an excellent bride who becomes his beloved princess.

Significance

Many ancient cultures passed down wisdom in short memorable statements like the ones we find in many of the proverbs, and modern writers have also used proverbs to pass on wisdom. The book of Proverbs has inspired much of the common wisdom of the West. "Spare the rod and spoil the child" is not an exact quotation from Proverbs, but it sums up a number of passages (13:24; 22:15). "A penny saved is a penny earned" comes from Benjamin Franklin, but it fits the Bible's emphasis on hard work, restraint, and foresight.

Proverbs may also be behind the medieval Catholic tradition of "cardinal virtues." The medieval church drew their cardinal "natural" virtues from Aristotle (prudence, justice, temperance, and fortitude) and added Paul's "theological" virtues (faith, hope, and love). Corresponding to these seven were seven deadly vices: pride, envy, anger, lust, sloth, greed, and gluttony. Though these lists don't derive directly from Proverbs, the notion that the Christian life involves the cultivation of godly habits of life and mind may owe something to Proverbs.

Proverbs 8 has been the most influential single chapter in the book of Proverbs. There Lady Wisdom describes herself as an assistant to Yahweh at the time of creation (vs. 22–31). Early in church history, teachers recognized that Wisdom sounded a lot like Jesus, who is called the "wisdom" of God in the New Testament (1 Cor. 1:24, 30). Arius used Proverbs 8 to support his own theology about Jesus, and the great church father Athanasius responded with long discussions of the passage.

Proverbs continued to inspire literary figures, philosophers, and even kings into the Middle Ages. An Anglo-Saxon poem known as the *Precepts* gives advice such as this: "Hold this with courage: do not carry out crime; no, never consent to it in your friend or kinsman, the less that the Measurer might accuse you, that you are a knower of sin; he will grant punishment to you as likewise he will grant to the others prosperity." Alfred the Great reputedly produced an alliterative collection of proverbs in poetic form, and centuries later the English poet George Herbert collected over a thousand "outlandish" ("foreign") proverbs like "Flies are the busiest about leane horses" and "God comes to see without a bell."

Glory of Kings

God gave us the book of Proverbs to teach us wisdom. Partly, He does that by teaching us the content of Proverbs. But he is also teaching us wisdom by the *way* He communicates wisdom. Proverbs 25:2 says, "It is the glory of God to conceal a matter, but the glory of kings to search out a matter." God hid the secrets of the universe

from us. Adam and Abraham knew nothing about atoms and nuclei, much less quarks and quasars. Until a few centuries ago, no one knew how to use electricity safely. God honors us as kings by making it tough for us to discover the truth, by forcing us to "search out a matter."

He does the same with the Bible. The Bible is a big, complicated book. It's not always easy to figure out what the Bible is teaching us. We might complain about it, but we should be honored. God doesn't treat us as children, who need to be fed from a bottle. He treats us as kings, who gain glory by investigating and studying and working hard to understand God's Word.

Proverbs in particular is a royal book, and it teaches us to be kings by making things difficult for us. Proverbs poses riddles and asks us to unravel them. Often the sayings in Proverbs seem simple and straightforward, and sometimes they are. Much of the time, though, things are deeper than we realize. Take Proverbs 24:13–14:

> My son, eat honey, for it is good,
> Yes, the honey from the comb is
> sweet to your taste;
> Know that wisdom is thus for your soul;
> If you find it, then there will be a future,
> And your hope will not be cut off.

Is Solomon giving dietary advice? Yes, but the point is less about diet than about pleasure. Honey is good because it is sweet to the taste. At the very least, we can say that Solomon wants his son to enjoy the good, very good, things that God has produced.

Honey is associated with the land throughout the Old Testament. Canaan is a land flowing with milk and honey, and when Samson kills the lion and then eats honey from it, it's a symbol of Samson's victory over the Philistines and the restoration of a honey-filled land. Enjoying the sweetness of honey means, more broadly, enjoying the goodness of the land, of the abundant inheritance God provides. Since Solomon is writing to a prince, he is also talking about royal responsibilities. A king is both a deliverer and avenger, and the chief of the festivals. Like Samson, he breaks the teeth of the oppressor, and eats honey from the lion.

But the thrust of the proverb is to speak of wisdom. The Bible frequently associates the sweetness of honey with the word and wisdom that comes from God (Ps. 19:10; 119:103; Prov. 16:24; Ezek. 3:3; Rev.10:9–10). The harlot in Proverbs 5:3 speaks honeyed words, though her words lead to bitter death; the bride's lips, however, truly are sweet as honey—not only because of the pleasure of her kisses but because of the sweetness of the words that come from her mouth (Song of Sol. 4:11). We should desire wisdom and the Word of God the way children desire candy; we should desire wisdom the way a young man desires the lips of a beautiful girl.

Now we can add this, from Proverbs 25:27:

It is not good to eat much honey,
And searching their glory [is] glory.

So, should we eat honey or not? Is it good, or is it dangerous? And if we can make sense of the comparison of honey and wisdom, what is the connection between eating honey and searching for glory?

Part of the problem with this second proverb is with the translation of the second line, which I have translated literally. The verse plays on the various meanings of the Hebrew root *kbd*, which can mean either "glory" or "heavy." Solomon is saying that to search "weighty" things lends one "weight." He means that searching into difficult or burdensome things is a glory. (Think of the honor we give to scientists who make new discoveries, after decades of long hours in the laboratory.) The verse matches the opening proverb of chapter 25: "the glory (*kabod*) of kings is to search out (*haqar*) a matter" (v. 2). Searching is glorious royal activity, but there is a particular glory in searching out things that are burdensome.

The verse is not a warning against pursuit of glory, which is the way most translations make it sound. Instead, it contrasts the dangers of over-consumption of sweet things and the delicious challenge of exploring things that require diligent and persistent effort. It is a glory to explore matters that seem to be too hard for us to figure out. Study and the search for understanding is a burden, Solomon tells us in Ecclesiastes, but it is a glorious burden.

Think of this verse next time you have to do a proof in Geometry! But think, too, of how this might apply to our entertainments. Honey is good, and so are the sweets of pop culture's movies and music. They are accessible, easy to grasp, delightful to the taste. But we can become satiated on them, and there is glory in the burden of trying to crack the code of some difficult poem or piece of music. Solomon doesn't tell us to avoid honey. We should enjoy the sweet and enjoyable things of the world. But he does tell us that the glories, and even the ultimate pleasures, of burdensome searches are superior. There's more glory and pleasure in a hard-fought game that we win with a desperate three-pointer at the buzzer than a game that ends 90–12.

We've searched a little into the matter of "honey" in Proverbs. Are you beginning to feel like a king?

Worldview

Proverbs is different from other books, so instead of the typical Worldview Essay, we will examine some of the most interesting and important themes in this book.

Wisdom

I have used the word "wisdom" a lot already, but I haven't defined it. What is wisdom? Wisdom is not the same as knowledge. Fools can know a lot of facts and figures and truth, but they are not wise. The Hebrew word for wisdom (*chokma*) means "skill" or "craftsmanship." It is the Spirit's gift of artistic skill to the men who fashioned the furnishings of the Tabernacle

Even a fool is counted wise when he holds his peace; When he shuts his lips, he is considered perceptive. Proverbs 17:28

(Ex. 28:3; 31:3; 35:31; cf. 1 Kings 7:14). When Lady Wisdom describes herself in chapter 8, she calls herself the craftsman that Yahweh used when He constructed His cosmic temple (8:30).

Wisdom is "skill" not only in art but in life. Wisdom involves skill in doing what is fitting and in producing results that are beautiful. A furniture maker displays wisdom in his craftsmanship; a musician shows his wisdom in making music; a father's wisdom becomes evident as he trains and guides his children. There is a "craft" or "art" to each of these endeavors. Proverbs is a handbook in the "art" of living. It teaches us how to live skillfully, and how to construct a life that is attractive, fitting, and beautiful. That's what kingship is all about: We want wisdom so that our lives will be filled with the royal beauty and glory of God.

We often think that art is for museums, concert halls, and artsy-craftsy people, who are usually a little effeminate. That's not the way Solomon thinks about it. Art and life are not opposed to each other. Living well means living artfully—forging a "well-crafted" life. This is why Solomon several times describes right action as action that is "fitting." Excellent speech is not fitting for a fool (17:7), neither is delight (19:10) or honor (26:1). On the other hand, the right word at the right time is fitting, and Solomon describes it as a work of art, as "apples of gold in settings of silver" (25:11). When we think about how we ought to behave, we should not only ask "Is it right?" but "Does it fit?" Not only "What are the rules?" but "What is delightful and lovely?" Solomon applies artistic standards to judge daily life.

This is one reason why Lady Wisdom's speech in chapter 8 is organized into seven speeches:

Drink water from your own cistern,
And running water from your own well.
Should your fountains be dispersed abroad,
Streams of water in the streets?
Let them be only your own,
And not for strangers with you.
Let your fountain be blessed,
And rejoice with the wife of your youth.
Proverbs 5:15–18

Proverbs 19

8:1–5 Lady Wisdom makes
public appeal to the simple
8:6–12 Lady Wisdom describes her speech
8:12–16 Lady Wisdom is the Queen
enthroned at the side of kings
8:17–21 Lady Wisdom offers
wealth and honor
8:22–26 Lady Wisdom is
begotten of Yahweh
8:27–31 Lady Wisdom was Yahweh's
foreman in creation
8:32–36 Lady Wisdom offers life

This reminds us of God's words at Creation, and Lady Wisdom claims that she was with Yahweh when He created (8:27–31). Wisdom is a creative power, the secret force behind creation. Through wisdom we discern the hidden wisdom of God and become creators ourselves. We fashion the world, and our lives, as the Master Craftsman fashioned the world.

Wisdom is about art, and it is also about life in public. Christians sometimes think that Jesus rescues us from responsibility in the world. But Lady Wisdom does not hide away in a monastery; she goes to the most public place in an ancient city—the city gates (8:3). Gates functioned as law courts, places for political campaigning and machination, centers of commerce. By taking her stand in the city gates, Wisdom is offering guidance in the practicalities of civic and economic life. Wisdom is essential if those entering the city to participate in its life are going to live in justice and peace.

Wisdom's public role is still an artistic role. Wise rulers construct and rule their kingdoms skillfully, which means beautifully. Fathers and mothers who rule wisely harmonize their families into beautiful music. A wise boss constructs a workplace that is as beautiful as a dazzling picture. A wise pastor is an architect and builder of the Lord's Temple, a glorious house (cf. 1 Cor. 3:10–15).

If wisdom is a woman, she must be wooed and won. Raping a woman is not a way to get her approval and love, nor is ignoring her. Similarly, wisdom doesn't come to those who seize wisdom, as Adam found. Nor does wisdom give herself to slackers and sluggards. Wisdom comes to those who seek her, who pursue her with the passion that a young man has for the woman of his dreams. Solomon tells his son to pursue wisdom as he would a priceless treasure. God makes the world yield its insights to people who wait, hope, and trust Him. We can also think of this more literally. A young man will gain wisdom by pursuing and choosing the right woman. Proverbs has a very high view of women. Not only does Solomon say that the *Lady* Wisdom was with

Yahweh when he created, but at the climax of the book he describes a woman of awesome energy, talent, productivity, and beauty. A young man who wants wisdom had better respect the women God places around him.

Many people think of the Proverbs as homely advice about life, the kinds of things that anyone with a bit of experience could learn. On the contrary, true wisdom, godly shrewdness or cunning, arises, Solomon says, from "fear of *Yahweh*" (1:7; 9:10; 15:33). Solomon refers to the Lord nearly a hundred times in Proverbs, and he uses the name *Yahweh*, the covenant name of the God of Israel (1:7, 29; 2:5–6; 3:5, 7, 9, 11–12; etc.). Wisdom doesn't come from following any old god, or from observing nature and history alone. Wisdom comes from the Creator.

God gives this wisdom to those who "fear" the Creator. What does it mean to fear Yahweh? Fearing God involves turning away from evil because it will displease Him (3:7; 8:13). It also means trusting His Word above our own understanding (3:5) and offering worship to God, especially with our goods (3:9). We fear God when we avoid the things that He hates (6:16) and when we remember that He sees and judges all our actions and words, and even our motives (5:21; 15:3; 16:2). We fear Yahweh when we not only "factor Him into" our plans, but when pleasing Him and avoiding His displeasure is the most important factor in all we do. When we fear God we walk obediently and uprightly (14:2). Those who fear Yahweh are humble, remembering that He abhors the proud (16:5), and the humble listen to Him. Fear seems ominous, but Solomon assures us that everything wisdom promises—life, riches, a good end, joy, creativity, insight, power, and everything else—comes to those who fear Yahweh (19:23). When we fear Yahweh, we can look on the prosperity of the wicked without envy, since we know that wickedness cannot prosper forever (23:17).

To say that Wisdom was with Yahweh "from the beginning" means that Wisdom is not some human achievement or creation, but proceeds from the depths of God. But this wisdom is communicated to us so that we can keep in step with God's own wisdom. And this wisdom which comes from God is the wisdom that creates worlds. By the wisdom that we receive from God, we establish boundaries, pass decrees, lay foundations, and rejoice in the work the Lord gives us to do.

Wisdom guides kings in their ruling, and so does Jesus, the Wisdom of God; Wisdom promises heroic valor and courage (8:14), and so does Jesus, the Wisdom of God. Wisdom promises honor and wealth and full treasuries, and so does Jesus, the Wisdom of God, who also promises persecutions (Matt. 6:33; Mark 10:29–31). Wisdom was Yahweh's agent to create the word, and through Wisdom kings establish boundaries and create worlds (cf. Eccles. 2:1–11); and Jesus is the Wisdom of God who equips us to form our worlds after the pattern of God's Word and to re-form the whole world after the pattern of His kingdom. Jesus as the Wisdom of God equips us to be kings and queens, nobles and mighty men.

Lady Wisdom has a lot to offer: skill, beauty, courage, riches, long life, success. But Lady Wisdom is not the only one trying to get the prince's attention. To woo Lady Wisdom, the prince will have to avoid other characters.

Characters

The prince is searching for the right bride. Along the way, he meets various characters. Some help him choose the right woman. Some don't. The principal help to the prince is his teacher, his father. As we saw above, Proverbs is a speech of a father to his son. The phrase "my son" occurs over twenty times in the book, and the father gives his son advice about listening to his parents (1:8; 5:1), choosing companions (1:10, 15), accepting the Lord's discipline (3:11), the sexual delights of marriage (5:20), pursuing wisdom (27:11), and diet (24:13). The father knows he doesn't know it all, so he urges his son to listen to other wise counselors as well (11:14; 15:22; 24:6). He especially urges his son to listen to his mother (1:8; 6:20; 23:22). So long as he follows the words and ways of his father and other wise men and women, things will go well, but straying from that path leads to disaster.

Other characters mislead him, but not all of them mislead in the same way. Proverbs gives several different

Pastor and poet Eugene Peterson paraphrased the section in Proverbs about the seductress as follows: *It was dusk, the evening coming on, the darkness thickening into night. Just then, a woman met him—she'd been lying in wait for him, dressed to seduce him. Brazen and brash she was, restless and roaming, never at home, walking the streets, loitering in the mall, hanging out at every corner in town. She threw her arms around him and kissed him, boldly took his arm and said, "I've got all the makings for a feast—today I made my offerings, my vows are all paid, so now I've come to find you, hoping to catch sight of your face—and here you are! I've spread fresh, clean sheets on my bed, colorful imported linens. My bed is aromatic with spices and exotic fragrances. Come, let's make love all night, spend the night in ecstatic lovemaking! My husband's not home; he's away on business, and he won't be back for a month."*

categories of bad characters. "Simpletons" are naïve and untrained, but they are not yet hardened in their ways. They lack sense (7:7) and are ignorant (9:13). They are gullible and easy to trick (14:15), and can't look ahead to see where their actions are leading them (22:3; 27:12). But there is hope for them, and Proverbs is intended partly to teach simpletons to be wise (1:4). They might turn out fine, if they, or the fools they follow, get roughed up enough to listen to wisdom (19:25; 21:11).

Lady Wisdom has to compete in the public square with Dame Folly. The two are opposites. Dame Folly sees naïve young men and preys on them (7:6–8). She goes out dressed like a prostitute to get their attention (7:9–10). The foolish woman is loud, rebellious, aggressive, and seductive (7:11–20). Solomon is writing an allegory here, but the literal sense is also important: sexual restraint, keeping distance from the loose girl or the aggressive boy, is a crucial part of growing into royal wisdom. Going to the house of Folly is disastrous. The young man who follows her is like an ox going to slaughter (7:22–23). Her guests end up being entertained in Sheol, the place of the dead (9:13–18).

People who follow Lady Folly are "fools." They are settled rebels and are not open to correction (1:7). Arrogant and self-assured, they make fun of people who try to teach them (1:22). They are very convinced of their own opinions and are more than willing to share them with you, at length (18:2). Fools talk too much (10:8, 10) and often spread damaging stories about other people (10:18). They are destructive, tearing down their own homes (14:1), often by their quick temper (14:17). Fights break out wherever they go (18:6). They make everyone around them unhappy, especially their parents (10:1; 17:21). Fools are heading for destruction, and so are the people they influence and lead (13:20). You probably have a fool in your classroom or your neighborhood. Don't get too close! A prince who wants to rule and live skillfully had better keep his distance from fools, and he certainly doesn't want to imitate them.

The "sluggard" is a particular kind of fool, someone who is so addicted to his comfort and rest that he doesn't do anything. He even has trouble getting food from his dish to his mouth (19:24). He wants things, but he won't work hard to get what he wants, so he spends his days in daydreams and disappointments (13:4). He doesn't pay attention to the time, and so plowing and harvest slip by before he gathers his food (20:4). As a result, he lives in a tumble-down shack, surrounded by weeds (24:30–34). The sluggard is a coward, making up lame excuses for not going to work (26:13). Even though he does nothing and has accomplished nothing, he thinks he knows it all (26:16). Sluggards are fools; stay away if you want to get the right girl.

The "wicked" are even worse than fools. Fools do evil, but sometimes do it almost "accidentally." Wicked people, though, delight in doing evil; their souls "delight" in evil (21:10). They might speak flatteringly, but their words hide violent intentions (10:6). They lie in wait to attack and kill (24:15), and so do their words (12:6). Even their compassion ends up being cruel (12:10), and God will spit out their sacrifices (15:8). They lead other people astray (12:26), and both they and their followers lead lives that are full of trouble and strife (12:21). They don't have a future; eventually, it's lights out (13:9; 24:20). When wicked men get into power, they take bribes and condemn innocent people (17:23). Everyone hides when the wicked rule (28:12; 29:2). Proverbs warns again and again that the wicked will not prosper, but sometimes they do well for a while. When they do, the prince is tempted to fret, but his wise father tells him not to worry about the wicked (24:19). Their prosperity won't last forever (cf. Ps. 37, 73). Instead of fretting, the prince should prepare himself for the day when he becomes king and has the privilege of clearing the wicked from his kingdom (24:25; 25:5). It won't be that hard, because the wicked get scared even when there is no danger (28:1).

By filling Proverbs with these characters, Solomon and the other writers are telling us something important about wisdom. We don't become wise by staying in our rooms gritting our teeth and trying very, very hard to be wise. We learn wisdom by listening to the right people, by making the right friends, by keeping away from fools, sluggards, and the wicked. To be wise, we need to be part of a community of the wise, and we need to have our ears open to their voices.

Ultimately, the main characters in Proverbs are Adam and Jesus. The first prince, Adam, chose to follow the wicked words of Satan and ended up, as the Proverbs say he would, in Sheol. Jesus, the Last Adam, listened intently to the Word of His Father, and died to win a spotless Bride. Now He praises His bride in the gates; she is an excellent wife. Jesus is not just the Wise Son of the Father, but is Himself the Wisdom of God (1 Cor. 1:30). Learning wisdom means, in the last analysis, following Jesus.

Speech, Work, Time

So far, we have been talking in generalities. But the Proverbs don't talk in generalities. Solomon instructs his son in many specific areas of life, too many for us to discuss here. We can take time to look at three recurring themes: speech, work, and time.

Many of the proverbs give instruction about speech, but there is no section of Proverbs that focuses exclusively on this. Solomon warns about the deceitful speech of false friends (4:24; cf. 1:8–19) and the smooth speech of Dame Folly (5:3). Sweetness makes our speech persuasive (16:21), and gracious speech gives us access to kings (22:11). The tongue of the wise is like silver (10:20), and like the leaves of the Tree of Life it brings healing (12:18). In fact, the wise tongue gives life, providing nourishing "food" for those who hear (15:4). A tongue has the power of life and death (18:21). Harsh words stir up strife, but gentle answers turn away wrath (15:1).

Solomon brings up speech when he is talking about kings and courtiers, when he is talking about wives and husbands, when he is talking about work and leisure, when he is talking about worship and taking vows. Speech is, for Solomon, woven into the fabric of life, in our families and friendship, labor and loves, at the temple and at home. All our social interactions occur through speech, and for Solomon the most important organs in our bodies are the tongue and the ear. Ears come first. Solomon's first command is to "hear" and "listen" (2:2; 4:20; 5:1). We can use our tongues rightly, wisely, only if we first hear wisdom.

What does a wise tongue do? Wisdom, we have seen, is artistic skill and cunning in rule. Wise words are words that are beautiful and words that make others and the world beautiful. Paul uses an architectural image when he says that our words should "edify" (Ephesians 4:29). "Edify" means to build, and our words should be constructing rather than destroying. Wise words are also acts of power. Like God, we are created to accomplish things by words. When a pastor or president speaks, people do what he says. He commands with his tongue. A judge decides a case by speaking "Guilty" or "Not guilty." This is what wise speech is designed to do.

Solomon also talks a good deal about work. We have already met the sluggard, the lazy fool who accomplishes nothing because he spends his life turning creakily on his bed. A diligent man, one who works hard and well, can ex-

How long will you slumber, O sluggard? When will you rise from your sleep? A little sleep, a little slumber, a little folding of the hands to sleep—so shall your poverty come on you like a prowler, and your need like an armed man. Proverbs 6:9–11

pect to have the things he needs (12:27). Hard work is the way to wealth (10:4), and also to power (12:24). Diligent people become fat (13:4), and in Scripture becoming fat is a good thing, a sign of prosperity. Wise work cannot be done haphazardly. To work wisely, we must plan ahead and then work to realize our plans (21:5).

If wise words are words that create beautiful things and rule well, wise work has the same effect. When we work diligently and carefully, the things we produce will be of the highest quality, whether those things are dining room tables, students, or an elegant dinner. When we work diligently we are exercising our godly rule over the world, and when we work wisely we will gain more and more authority.

Last, though far from least, wisdom is about having a particular attitude toward time. Have you ever known a person who says the right thing at the wrong time? Mary Bennett in *Pride and Prejudice* often says things that are true but not timely. Have you ever known anyone who can never think past the moment? Perhaps you've been that person: You step into the mall and suddenly see the best pair of shoes, and without thinking about how you're going to afford lunch or whether your mother will like the shoes, you buy them.

For Solomon, being untimely and not being able to see past the moment are both marks of folly. Fools think in the present. They see something they like, and they snap it up without thinking of the consequences. Dame Folly, in fact, encourages this kind of behavior: "Don't worry about my husband," she tells the young man she is seducing, "he's on a business trip and won't be back for days" (7:19–20). The fool never stops to ask, "Yes, but what happens when he *does* get back?"

Solomon often describes the difference between wisdom and folly in terms of two "ways" or "paths." Wise people walk along a path that leads to life, while fools stumble in the darkness along a path that will end in destruction (2:13–15; 4:14–18). But the difference can also be pictured as two different ways of walking down the same path. Here, the difference is how far ahead each one can see. Simpletons and fools cannot see where the path is leading, but wise people look ahead, anticipate danger, and change course to avoid danger. Proverbs 22:3 says, "The prudent sees the evil and hides himself, but the simple go on and are punished for it" (cf. 27:12). Solomon describes this in terms of space (the wise see further ahead on the road), but what he is really talking about is time (the wise know what is going to happen in the future). Wise people can seem like prophets. If they see a lazy person, they can foresee that he will be poor; if they see a wicked ruler, they can foresee that the righteous will hide; if they see a righteous man suffering, they can predict that the Lord will, one day, vindicate him.

Their prophetic insight doesn't depend on special revelation. It's a gift of the Spirit of Wisdom to those who pursue wisdom by hearing God's and Solomon's words.

When the wise look ahead, they are able to rule well and beautifully. Suppose you decide to have a party but don't make any plans. Everyone shows up, but there's no food and everyone stands around for two hours staring at each other. It's not beautiful because you didn't plan. You couldn't create something beautiful because you didn't look ahead to see where this path was heading.

Timeliness is also a central part of wisdom. Apt, timely answers give joy and delight (15:23). Faithful messengers refresh their masters like cooling snow in the heat of harvest (25:13). In Ecclesiastes 3, Solomon says that there is a time for "everything under heaven." God brings war and peace, times of gathering and scattering, a day of birth and a day of death. We are wise—ruling well and beautifully— if we do what each time requires, rejoicing in times of joy, mourning at death, acting decisively when the times demand it and waiting in patience at the right time.

Conclusion

Proverbs is Solomon's address to his "son," and we might speculate that the "son" Solomon addresses was Rehoboam, who succeeded him as king of Israel. If so, the first pupil of Proverbs was a failure, for Rehoboam acted foolishly and tore apart the house of Israel with his own hands (1 Kings 12). Not that Rehoboam's folly was a big surprise; Solomon himself played the fool more than once (cf. 1 Kings 11).

In the history of Israel, wise kings fail. Israel relies on her own wisdom far too often and is often seduced by idols allied with Dame Folly. We need Proverbs, of course. It is the word of God. But Proverbs also points us to the final Wisdom of God, Jesus, and in pointing us there reminds us that God's true wisdom looks like folly to the world. Proverbs reminds us that His royal rule comes through the creative craftsmanship of a cross (1 Cor. 1:25–2:16).

—Peter J. Leithart

For Further Reading

Jordan, James. *From Bread To Wine.* Niceville, Fla.: Biblical Horizons.

Leithart, Peter J. *Wise Words.* Moscow, Idaho: Canon Press, 2003.

Waltke, Bruce. *Proverbs.* Grand Rapids: Eerdmans, 2004–2005.

Session I: Prelude
Question To Consider:

Why do we need wisdom? Doesn't God just give us all the rules?

From the General Information above answer the following questions:

1. What does the Hebrew word for proverb (*mashal*) mean?
2. Who wrote the proverbs contained in the book of Proverbs?
3. How is the book of Proverbs similar to the Disney version of "Little Mermaid"?
4. Is art a manly activity according to Solomon?
5. Is Lady Wisdom concerned about public life or just private life?
6. What is the sluggard like?
7. Who are the main characters in Proverbs?

Reading Assignment:
Proverbs 1–7

Session II: Recitation
Proverbs 1–7

Comprehension Questions

Answer these questions for factual recall:

1. How does Solomon identify himself? Is this significant?
2. What does Proverbs say is the beginning of wisdom?
3. Who is Proverbs addressed to?
4. How does Solomon portray Wisdom in the first chapter?
5. Which aspects of wisdom does Solomon explain in Proverbs 3?
6. What other woman does Solomon describe in Proverbs 5?
7. To what does Solomon suggest the lazy man pay attention in Proverbs 6? Why?
8. What does Solomon say that God hates?
9. What does Solomon say about getting away with adultery?

Reading Assignment:
Proverbs 8–13

Session III: Writing
Fictional Story

Stories teach us. The Greek slave Aesop told stories with morals, some of which are still familiar today: the tortoise and the hare; the grasshopper and the ants; the boy who cried wolf. Each story illustrated some basic truth that was usually contained in a pithy statement, or proverb, at the end of the tale.

Your assignment is to write a story that illustrates one of the lessons in Proverbs 10 or 11. Choose a proverb from these chapters, and write a story that shows how this proverb is true. Remember, we are looking for quality rather than quantity. You should write no more than 750 words (if typing) or you should write about two pages if you are writing by hand.

There are two main aspects to this assignment. The first is to illustrate the proverb you have chosen, and the second is the quality of the story you tell. You should feel free to let your imaginations run, as long as you stay within the length parameter.

Some examples of this type of story are found in Peter Leithart's book *Wise Words*. Below is a short example using a verse from Proverbs 16.

Story Example

Once upon a time there were two brothers, Adam and Judah. Their father was a woodsman, but their mother had died long ago, and the brothers did not even remember her. With their father, they lived in a small house on the edge of a vast forest.

The oldest brother, Adam, had dreamed his whole life of becoming a rich and powerful king who conquered great nations and ruled many lands. Once, he had told Judah of his dream, and his brother had wondered if it was possible. The older brother lost his temper and snapped at the younger. Yet, however much the two brothers fought, Adam could never goad Judah into getting angry. Judah was always calm.

Adam knew that he could never achieve his dream while he was living in the hut of a woodsman, and so one day he told his father and brother that he was leaving. Adam knew that he wanted to win fame and fortune. So he took his sack and marched off into the forest.

Adam traveled to faraway lands. He found adventure and began to make a name for himself as a valiant warrior. He fought bravely for the king and gained his sovereign's favor. But his temper continued to plague him. He could not keep servants, and even the men assigned to his command grumbled.

One day the woodsman died, and Judah was forced to leave his home. He, too, traveled through the forest and arrived at the land that Adam had found. He found a job working for a blacksmith. Most of his time was spent shoeing horses, but the blacksmith noticed that he was a hard worker.

"Why don't you go somewhere else?" he would ask. "You could work for anyone, anywhere, and succeed."

"I am content," Judah would reply. "I will wait until it is time to move on." And so he would stay.

One day, Adam was returning from battle. He had led an army for the first time, and he had done a wonderful job. He had even conquered a city, bringing it into subjection to the king. Adam was sure that he was going to get promoted.

As his horse marched through the city, it stumbled right in front of the blacksmith's shop where Judah worked. Adam fell from his horse. Judah heard the clatter and rushed outside. His brother was on his back, and because of his armor he was unable to get up. Judah was overjoyed to see his brother and stooped to greet his brother.

"Adam, it is Judah!" he said.

"Help me up, oaf," Adam said. "I am the king's soldier."

Judah helped him to his feet. "Brother, it has been a long time."

Adam scowled at his brother. "Don't you know how important this day is to me? Leave me alone. I don't need you to help me."

Judah backed away and his brother, with the help of three or four soldiers, climbed back on his horse and continued to the castle.

At the castle, Adam discovered that he had made an error on the field. Rather than attacking one of the cities of the enemy, Adam had conquered a city belonging to the king's cousin. Adam tried to tell the king the truth, that it was not really his fault, but the king would hear none of it. Adam was thrown into a dungeon for the rest of his days.

Judah continued to work as a blacksmith until he was an old man. He eventually started his own shop and became the best blacksmith in the city. He was known for being fair and not leaping to conclusions. When he died, the king attended his funeral.

Proverbs 16:32: *He who is slow to anger is better than the mighty, and he who rules his spirit than he who takes a city.*

READING ASSIGNMENT:
Proverbs 14–22

SESSION IV: DISCUSSION
Proverbs 10–22

A Question to Consider
What does it mean to be poor?

Discuss or list short answers to the following questions:

Text Analysis
1. How does Solomon say that a man can become poor? How can one become rich?
2. What does Solomon say is the proper way to become rich?

The heart of the wise teaches his mouth, And adds learning to his lips. Pleasant words are like a honeycomb, Sweetness to the soul and health to the bones.
Proverbs 16:23–24

3. Does the fact that a man is poor mean that God is not with him?
4. How does Solomon say that wise men ought to treat the poor?
5. What does Solomon say will happen to those who ignore the poor?

Cultural Analysis

1. In our culture, what is the benefit of being rich?
2. Why does our culture believe that men become poor?
3. How does our culture believe that we should treat poor people?
4. What does our culture see as the solution to poverty?

Biblical Analysis

1. What does David say about those who care for the poor in Psalm 41?
2. What does the Bible say about those who will not work (2 Thess. 3:6–12; Eph. 4:28)?
3. How did Jesus treat the poor (Matt. 11:5; Luke 14:7–14)? What did He say about the rich (Matt. 6:24; Luke 18:24)?
4. Why does Amos condemn the people of Judah in Amos 5:11–12?

Summa

Write an essay or discuss this question, integrating what you have learned from the material above.
How should Christians treat the poor?

Reading Assignment:
Proverbs 23–31

Session V: Discussion

A Question to Consider

What makes a woman beautiful?

Discuss or list short answers to the following questions:

Text Analysis

1. What does Solomon say is worse than a continual dripping, or living outside on the corner of your roof? Why?
2. What does Solomon think a foolish woman looks like? Why?
3. What does the author prize more than charm or beauty?
4. What characteristics are shown by the righteous wife in Proverbs 31?

Cultural Analysis

1. What does our culture believe makes a woman beautiful?
2. In our culture, how do you recognize a good wife?

Biblical Analysis

1. Biblically speaking, what makes a woman beautiful?
2. Which women in the Bible made good wives?

Summa

Write an essay or discuss this question, integrating what you have learned from the material above.
What sort of woman makes a good wife?

Optional Session A: Writing Activity

Proverbs 14:4 says, "where no oxen are, the trough is clean; but much increase comes by the strength of an ox."

Explain how this verse could be applied to a fast-food business. Imagine that you own the local franchise of Burger Baron. You are a Christian, so you want to follow the biblical principles found in Proverbs. How can you understand this verse in the light of your business? Remember, you are following principles, not the literal meaning of the verse (the only oxen in Burger Baron are on the grill). Write about 500 words on the subject.

Optional Session B: Writing Activity

Proverbs 13:4 says, "the soul of a lazy man desires, and has nothing; but the soul of the diligent shall be made rich." This is one of many verses in Proverbs that seem to promise certain things to the wise. Yet if we examine the lives of God's people across the ages, we find that the diligent are not always made rich. In fact, many times the lives of the diligent get worse. John Huss, for example, worked diligently for the kingdom of God, yet he was burned at the stake.

In about a page, explain how we should understand this verse. Is this a literal promise from God that says if we work hard we will always get rich?

The Book of Job

I was almost asleep when I was attacked. It was dark under the stars, with only a piece of the moon, and it was gliding slowly down to the horizon. The man's shadow fell over me, and my stiff arm shot out, grasping for him. My fingers found his ankle, and I yanked. A moment later there was dust in my eyes, and we were tumbling. He was very strong, but I held on. My fingers and arms burned in the wild thrashing as he tried to get away. Our bodies were hot and sweaty and ground the rocks beneath us into fine sand, and on and on, out of breath in the black night, the man fought to get away.

I held his leg as he pummeled me. Finally he gasped out, "Let me go!" And between breaths I shook my head.

I have been a wrestler as long as I can remember. My mother told me I came out wrestling, which is why she gave me my name. Of course, having a twin brother gave me a natural sparring partner, but it always seemed like I was getting into some trouble, and it was all I could do to get free again. But this man was different than the others. He was stronger, swifter, and could not be tamed, so I just held on. "Let me go," he said again, and then I thought I knew who he was. My arms were burning with fire and my fingers were brittle, but I blurted out, "I will not let you go until you bless me." That seemed to only make him angrier at first. I held on for dear life. I was sure he would have me any second. Whether it was minutes or hours later, I don't recall, but he suddenly raised himself up, and I saw his mighty hand swing down and his fist rushing into my hip. The pain ricocheted through my body, and my limbs went limp, but as the world began to rush away and the stars grew fuzzy, I heard him say, "You shall be called Israel because you have wrestled with God and man and prevailed." And that's when I knew for sure that I had just seen God face to face.

This is, of course, a retelling of the story of Jacob wrestling the angel of the Lord—a striking instance of determined and resolute faith. As we consider Job, we will witness another hero of faith who wrestles with God and man and prevails.

Author and Context

We do not know who wrote the book of Job, but there have been many guesses. The descriptions of Job and his estate are reminiscent of the patriarchs (many animals and servants, like Abraham), and Job lives to be 140 years old, which was more common during that period as well. This would put Job somewhere in the first half of the second millennium before Christ, probably between 1800–1500 B.C. The dialogues that fill the middle chapters of the book are all highly poetic and match many of the themes and literary features found in the wisdom literature (Psalms, Proverbs, Ecclesiastes, etc.). Some of the themes of suffering and justice also remind us of the prophets who ministered at the end of the kingdom period and at the point of Israel's exile. It is possible that Job is the "Jobab" referred to as one of the kings of Edom, as the Septuagint suggests (Gen. 36:33–34).[1] And it is certain that Job was a great king or chieftain (1:3). But whoever Job was and however God sovereignly orchestrated the composition of Job, it comes to us in the context of the wisdom literature, and given the hand that Solomon had in so much of the wisdom literature, it may be that he played an important part in authoring this story as well.

Significance

One biblical literary scholar says that Job is "arguably the greatest achievement of all biblical poetry." Thus, from a purely literary standpoint, Job is very significant. But there are many different angles of study that make Job an intriguing part of Scripture. Job is perhaps most famous for his suffering, and in particular, from the vantage of the reader, the revelation that God is intimately involved in suggesting and allowing the suffering of Job. This makes the book of Job significant for theological and philosophical questions of *theodicy*, which seeks to justify the goodness of God in the face of evil. But the themes of justice, suffering, and mercy are wound through nearly every page of Scripture. As we look at Job more closely, the parallels between Job and many other biblical characters come into focus. We see figures like Adam and Jacob and ultimately the Lord Jesus emerging from the narrative of Job. Ezekiel is the only Old Testament book that refers to Job, and he lists him with Noah and Daniel as perhaps the most righteous men to that point in history (Ezek. 14:14, 20). James gives us an inspired commentary on Job, pointing in particular to Job's perseverance and the end of the story as proof of the Lord's compassion and mercy (James 5:11). James seems to imply that Job is an example of a prophet who spoke in the name of the Lord and endured suffering with patience (cf. James 5:10).

Main Characters

It is worth the effort to learn the main characters of Job at the outset, particularly his three friends. Job is, of course, the main character of the story, along with God Himself. Job is described as being greater than all of the "sons of the east" (1:3), which suggests that he was a Gentile, and given his wealth and greatness, he was clearly a great king (1:3, cf. 19:9, 29:25). Job's wife and children are also minor but important characters. The Accuser, literally "The Satan," is apparently an evil angelic being, probably Satan himself, who appears in the assembly of the sons of God in the opening chapter and is granted permission to test the faith of Job through inflicting him with hardship and suffering. Throughout this essay, God will be referred to as Yahweh because that is God's name in Hebrew, and one that is used in the story. Normally, English translations indicate this proper name of God by typing *LORD* in all capital letters. Similarly, Satan will be referred to as "the Accuser," since that designation was important to the author and will also prove to be significant as we consider the main themes of the book. The three friends approach Job at the end of chapter two: Eliphaz the Temanite, Bildad the Shuhite, and Zophar the Naamathite. Elihu is a latecomer to the debate. He is a young man and apparently has been listening to the discussion. Minor but significant characters also include Job's three daughters, mentioned by name at the end of the story: Jemimah, Keziah, and Keren-Happuch—the most beautiful women in all the land.

Summary and Setting

The book of Job opens describing Job, his family, and the setting of the story. A great reversal takes place in the first two chapters, which sets the stage for the substance of the narrative. The great and blameless Job loses all of his livestock, his servants, and his ten children by the hand of the Accuser, who has been granted permission by Yahweh to strike him. Finally, Yahweh allows the Accuser to afflict Job's body short of taking his life, and in these circumstances, mourning in dust and ashes, Job is joined by three friends with whom he converses and argues for most of the rest of the story. Elihu finally speaks up at the end. Yahweh ultimately answers out of the whirlwind with a couple of his own speeches. Job is justified by Yahweh in the final chapter, being declared right in what he has spoken. Job intercedes for his friends, and Yahweh restores the fortunes of Job. His relatives bring gifts of silver and gold, his livestock is restored twofold, and he is granted the same number of children again, with the beauty of his daughters particularly highlighted.

Worldview

The book of Job is a wrestling match. The famous story opens with Job, the blameless and upright king of the east, who is brought low through a series of horrific events that the reader understands to have been brought through the Accuser by the permission of Yahweh. While Job initially blesses the Lord and accepts the evil events from his hand, the majority of the book is Job's decision *not* to accept the evil events as the last word from the Lord.

Our consideration of Job should start with the structure of the book. While the opening (prologue) and the closing (epilogue) are straightforward narratives, the bulk of the book of Job is a poetic dialogue, a series of speeches, argumentation, and debate, culminating in the answer of Yahweh from the whirlwind (38:1).

Satan Smiting Job with Sore Boils by William Blake (1757–1827)

Frequently, readers find the dialogues tedious and would rather skip to the end. The response of God to Job is itself a wonderful and glorious tour of the glories of creation, closing with the exotic and terrifying leviathan, who is one of God's pets. But if we skip to the end, not only are we disregarding a sizeable portion of God-breathed Scripture, but we will also fail to really understand the conclusion. Furthermore, the writer is also taking us on a journey with Job, and our experience of reading the story of Job is meant to have a certain effect on us.

There are a number of problems that we face in the book of Job. And, as with any good story, the point of the work is to solve those problems and bring resolution by the end. First, we face some of the fundamental questions of life: How and why does God allow evil? How can God remain good and blameless if He allows evil to happen to good people? These are questions that generally go under the term *theodicy*, meaning the defense of the goodness of God in the face of sin and death and evil.

Second, we face the problem of realizing that we have a book that gives significant airplay to people who are *wrong*. If we add up the verses and figure out how much Job's three friends say, we realize that most of the book is arguing something God ultimately says is "not right" (42:7). Why has God allowed a book into the Bible that is mostly full of bad reasoning and seriously flawed theology? Furthermore, as we read about the three friends of Job, we see things that could just as easily be true and right. Much of what they say sounds like solid biblical wisdom: "He saves the needy from the sword, from the mouth of the mighty, and from their hand" (5:15) and "Behold, happy is the man whom God corrects; therefore do not despise the chastening of the Almighty. For he bruises, but he binds up; he wounds, but his hands make whole" (5:17–28).

Who could argue with these words of Eliphaz? In fact, Scripture says much the same thing in other places (e.g. Ps. 72:4,13; Prov. 3:11; Heb. 12:5). So we have not only a sizeable chunk of Scripture that is wrong, but also a sizeable chunk of Scripture that in *other* contexts would be right.

A third problem consists in the structure of the story itself. How do the prologue and epilogue relate to the main part of the book? And while there are other questions to be asked, one important one is, what about Job? Is Job right or wrong?

Job as Adam and Jacob

The book of Job opens with a number of themes that remind us of the beginning of Genesis. Job is described as "blameless," and it could just as easily be translated "perfect." Thus, Job is a "perfect man," surrounded with a world of wonderful blessings as Adam was. Of course the characters are also reminiscent: Yahweh, Satan (the Accuser), a perfect man, and even an Eve (Job's wife, who

Elohim Creating Adam by William Blake

famously counsels Job to "curse God and die" in 2:9). Job explicitly contrasts himself with Adam in one place by insisting that he has not covered his sin like Adam (31:33). Last, Job sits in the ashes after being struck with boils (2:8), and when his three friends arrive, they join him in mourning and sprinkle dust on their own heads (2:12). It was from the dust that man was formed (Gen. 2:7), and the curse pronounced for Adam's sin is that he will return to dust in death (Gen. 3:19).

The narrator opens the story emphasizing that Job was "blameless and upright" (1:1), as Yahweh reiterates this to the Accuser twice (1:8; 2:3). Jacob is also identified as "perfect" (Gen. 25:27), and like Job, Jacob finds himself persecuted by those closest to him (his brother, his father in-law); the story of his life is one of struggle and wrestling. Eventually he finds himself wrestling with God Himself (Gen. 32:24–30). God tells Jacob that his struggles have all fundamentally been with Him (Gen. 32:28). Jacob has learned wisdom through these struggles; his wrestling has made him like a king, which is why God gives him the new name Israel, which means "prince of God." Jacob is a new Adam who walks and talks with God. Likewise, as we shall see, it is Job's great desire to stand before God and speak with him—to see Him face to face, as a man with his friend, like Adam once upon a time in the garden.

Prophet, Priest, and King

James Jordan has pointed out that in Scripture, the offices of prophet, priest, and king seem to follow a progression of maturity and glory. The role of a priest is to guard and require strict adherence to the law. He must follow careful instructions regarding ceremonial and sacrificial law, and he may not deviate. The office of king follows this, where the law must be applied with wisdom. Kings must wrestle with difficult issues and questions and contemplate applications not directly addressed in the law. Solomon is a great picture of this, particularly after being granted wisdom and being required to judge between the quarreling prostitutes (1 Kings 3:16–28).

The king not only guards the law (like a priest), but he also begins to apply the law with wisdom to difficult and complex situations. He must wrestle with right and wrong, and light and darkness, and judge righteously, and eventually he will emerge as a prophet. This is the last stage in biblical maturity and glory. The prophet is one who in his most basic role is allowed access into the deliberations of God's heavenly council room. The first prophet in Scripture is Abraham, who intercedes for the afflicted and is heard (Gen. 20:7, 17). Later he speaks into the counsels of God regarding Sodom and Gomorrah (Gen. 18:16–33). The prophet is given the floor to debate

and argue his case before God and the divine assembly. This is because he has grown to maturity. He has guarded the law, and the Word of God is hidden in his heart (priest), but he has also learned wisdom and applied the Word, dividing between joints and marrow, piercing to the thoughts and intents of the heart (king). And because he has grown into this maturity, he is welcomed to the divine assembly, and his prayers and intercessions are heard. Of course, because the prophet has been involved in the divine deliberations, he is supremely qualified to announce those verdicts. This is why prophets frequently bring the Word of the Lord and foretell what He is about to do; this is because they were there when it was all decided, and they have been granted the authority to ask God what he is about to do.

This is a helpful way of looking at the entire story of Job, especially when we recognize that the bulk of Job is like a courtroom scene. Job and company may have actually been sitting outside in an ash heap, but they are arguing, reasoning, and deliberating as though they are in court. Of course, the book opens with two scenes where the "sons of God" stand before Yahweh, and the Accuser comes in among them. This famous scene reveals Yahweh suggesting that the Accuser consider Job as a worthy challenge. And after Job's family, possessions, and finally Job's body are struck by the Accuser, it is Job's wife who calls Job to action.

On the surface her suggestion seems outright blasphemous: "Do you still hold fast your integrity? Curse God and die!" The problem is that it is not clear what role she or this suggestion play in the overall story if she is merely a bitter old woman telling her husband to commit suicide or at least curse God until he strikes him dead. Job's initial response is to say that she is being foolish and insists that they ought to receive both good and evil from the hand of God (2:10). Yet what follows in the rest of the book is precisely not *that*. Job most certainly does *not* take what God has given as just and fair. What follows, after a seven-day interlude (2:13), is a plea that comes strikingly close to what his wife actually suggested. While he does not directly curse God, he begins cursing the day of his birth and the night he was conceived, wishing that time could go backward so that he might go back into darkness (see especially 3:8). Ultimately Job says he longs to be dead, that request increasingly bound up with charges that God has not been just.

The Argument

In order to follow the trajectory of the story, we need to consider the development of Job's argument. Job's initial plea is to die. He curses the day of his birth and wonders why he must go on in misery when he longs for

LEVIATHAN

O LORD, how manifold are Your works! In wisdom You have made them all. The earth is full of Your possessions—this great and wide sea, in which are innumerable teeming things, living things both small and great. There the ships sail about; there is that Leviathan which You have made to play there (Psalm 104:24–26).

The word *Leviathan* appears in five places in the Bible, with the Book of Job, chapter 41, being dedicated to describing Leviathan in detail.

In the Jewish tradition the Leviathan was created on the fifth day, both male and female, but then God killed the female leviathan to keep the species from reproducing and so destroy the world. William Blake wrote of the Leviathan: "[H]is forehead was divided into streaks of green & purple like those on a tyger's forehead: soon we saw his mouth & red gills hang just above the raging foam tinging the black deep with beams of blood . . ." But in Job, the Leviathan appears next to very ordinary creatures—like goats. So if the Leviathan was a real beast, what might it be? Some propose that it was a crocodile or a Sarcosuchus, others that it was a whale. It has also been suggested that it was a Kronosaurus—which, based on its long teeth and great length, would certainly inspire a person to associate it with Job's aquatic monster.

In the drawing below from 1515, painter and printmaker Hans Baldung (c. 1480–1545), a student of Albrecht Dürer's, created the image of a terrible creature that, if not the beast from chapter 41, certainly appears to be able to carry off the title of "Leviathan."

death (3:20–21). When confronted by Eliphaz, who suggests that Job's confidence in his own integrity has been his downfall (4:6), Job responds by insisting that he is innocent, and once again pleads for death. This time he specifically pleads with God to "crush" him, to "loose his hand and cut" him off (6:8–9). And Eliphaz's words only make him want to die more (7:13–14).

But after Bildad tries to instruct Job regarding God's dealings with the wicked, Job begins to explain that not only does he want to die because he is suffering, but his central complaint is that he cannot contend with God (9:3). This is first of all because God is not easily accessible (9:11), and furthermore, Job asks, "How can I answer Him and choose my words to reason with Him?" It is not only unlikely that he will get a hearing with God, but what would that even look like? Even if he could get a hearing and he was completely right, Job recognizes that he would still have to beg for mercy (9:15). And even if he did call upon God and He answered him, Job says that he would not even believe it was happening (9:16). How can he get a day in court with God (9:19)?

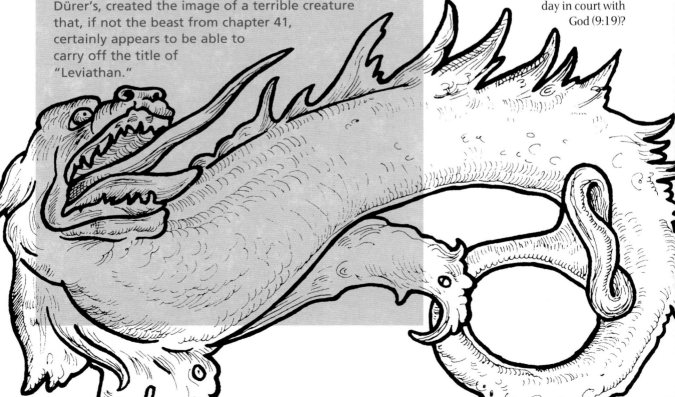

His complaint is not merely with his circumstances but with the impossibility of taking God to court. God is not a man that Job can take to court, and he sees no one who could act as a mediator between them (9:32–33). Who would act as judge between God and Job? But as Job responds to the continued criticisms of his friends, the repeated interest of Job is to speak with God and receive an answer (12:4; 13:3), and his words grow increasingly similar to the words of his wife: "Though he slay me, yet will I trust Him. Even so, I will defend my own ways before Him" (13:15).

But why all the desire for death amidst the desire to try his case? If he really wants to argue his case, why does he keep saying he wants to die? The answer begins to emerge in chapter 14 when he refers to the hope of a tree. Job says that a tree that is cut down may die in the ground, but with a little water it will spring up out of the ground again (14:7–9). Similarly, a man who dies and is buried in the ground, even a barren and dry ground, where he sleeps until the heavens are no more, will eventually be changed, and when God calls, Job knows that He will answer (14:10–15). Job's plea is to die, but to die in order that he might finally have the opportunity to stand before God—that his righteous blood may cry out for justice (16:18). What he wants is to plead with God like a man pleads with his friend (16:21).

The full force of Job's argument finally bursts forth in one of the most famous passages of Job, when he proclaims, "For I know that my Redeemer lives, and He shall stand at last on the earth. And after my skin is destroyed, this I know, that in my flesh I shall see God, whom I shall see for myself and my eyes shall behold, and not another . . . there is a judgment" (19:25–29). Job knows that there will be a final judgment, and if he cannot get his case tried in the present life, he is utterly convinced that at the resurrection he will see God face to face and finally be granted the opportunity to ask his questions and receive an answer. Again, he reiterates to his friends that what he wants is to be able to stand before God's judgment seat, to present his case before God (23:4ff).

Ultimately what Job wants is *understanding;* he wants to find out why all this evil and calamity has befallen him. He knows that the search for wisdom is a worthy cause, and one which God has called man to (28:1–11). It is the glory of God to conceal a matter, but it is the glory of kings to search out a matter (Prov. 25:2). Job is in the process of searching for wisdom, but he has come to the conclusion that it is not "found in the land of the living" (28:13) and "is hidden from the eyes of all the living . . ." (28:21). Only God has wisdom, only he has searched it out (28:27). This is why Job wants to die—so he can come face to face with God, ask his questions and receive answers, and finally

understand and know wisdom. He wants to go before the Almighty and receive an answer; he wants to approach Him like a prince (31:35–37).

This leads us to remember the story of Jacob. His struggles and wrestling ultimately culminate in wrestling with God Himself face to face. That, of course, is fundamentally what Job is pleading for. But what Job may not have realized during the course of the dialogues, readers can begin to recognize for themselves. While God remains silent until the end of the story, God is preparing Job for the very thing he is asking for. Job wants an audience with God so as to argue his case before Him, but it is the very act of arguing with his three friends that is preparing him to do that.

There are several indicators that this is the case. We see this in the fact that Job finally does speak with God when He speaks to him "out of the whirlwind" (38:1; 40:6). Job is finally granted access to Yahweh, and it is a conversation that takes place in the wind of Yahweh's presence. And allusions to that imagery have appeared throughout the rest of the book. Frequently, the words of the rhetorical combatants are referred to as "wind" (6:26; 8:2; 15:2; 16:3), which is the word *ruach*—the same word for "breath" or "spirit." That word is often used throughout the book, frequently to refer to the life-breath of man and the shortness of life, which is quickly blown away with the "wind" (21:18, 27:21). Of course, one of the disasters that befell Job was the great *ruach*—wind that struck the house his children were feasting in, killing them (1:19).

Similarly, other terms are also employed, such as the "east wind" referring to the words of Job's accusers (15:2), and the wicked are described as being stolen away in the "storm" (21:20). One way of looking at the story of Job is to picture him being drawn into the whirlwind. The narrative, the argument, and the dialogue itself is Job's transition into the whirlwind presence of Yahweh.

Taming the Accuser

Another way to look at the progression of Job is to follow the accusations. The prologue introduces the Accuser in the presence of Yahweh being granted permission to try Job's integrity, but after the Accuser leaves the stage, the accusations do not end. Job says that his counselors have turned against him (19:19), likely referring in the first instance to his three friends. They are those whom he loved who have turned against him. Job refers to the "schemes" of his friends, who seek to wrong him (21:27). In fact, Job says that they have reproached him "ten times" (19:3).

In this sense the story can be seen as a continuation of the trial that began with the Accuser in the prologue;

only after the Accuser has left the stage, three mini-accusers take his place. Far from being "friends," Eliphaz, Bildad, and Zophar are "little satans." This is suggested by the first speech of Eliphaz, who says that he had some sort of dream, and words were whispered to him and a spirit passed before his face and began to speak, asking if a "mortal can be more righteous than God?" (4:12–21) This "satan" is like the serpent of Genesis 3 who asks questions to tempt his listeners. Thus, the Accuser commissions the three men to take over for him. Job is an Adam being tempted by three crafty serpents.

It is also important to note that there is political force behind the accusations brought by the three friends. Job is a king or chieftain, meaning his disaster is not just a personal misfortune. All the people are involved, and during any economic disaster it is not long before a scapegoat must be found. This is what happened with Oedipus—when Thebes was wracked with the plague, the blame fell upon the king. Oedipus, like many good pagans, was willing to take one for the team. He did not defend himself, but if he had defended himself, the reaction he would have gotten would have been very similar to the reaction Job got. Job simply was not playing his appointed role—he needed to accept his guilt and get out of the way, as every good scapegoat knows how to do. The book of Job is striking—in all of ancient literature, there is nothing like this straight-up reply to the voices of the accusers.

Jeffrey Meyers points out that elsewhere in biblical literature, forces of evil are closely associated with the sea serpent—a dragon—and that is precisely what leviathan is (cf. Ps. 74:12–14; Isa. 51:9, Ezek. 29:3, 32:2). Of course the devil is seen in the form of a serpent in Genesis 3, and by the end of the Bible, John puts it all together: "So the great dragon was cast out, that serpent of old, called the Devil and Satan, who deceives the whole world; he was cast to the land, and his angels were cast out with him" (Rev. 12:9). This helps make sense of Yahweh's answer to Job.

It is, of course, a display of His power and sovereignty, but more than that, it is a display of all the forces of nature and even evil as Yahweh's pet. Yahweh can tame leviathan; Yahweh plays with the "king over all the children of pride" (41:34). Ultimately, the *theodicy* of Job is trust in the wisdom of the God who plays with evil and tames it. But this also suggests that Job's own struggle—wrestling with his accusers—has been the beginning of learning the same wisdom that God already possesses. Yahweh has given Job the opportunity to wrestle with the Accuser, and the conclusion is that Yahweh is pleased with Job's progress.

Notice how Yahweh calls Job "my servant" three times in 42:8. This is virtually a title that God had suggested to the Accuser in the beginning and that has now been confirmed (1:8; 2:3). Part of Eliphaz's initial accusation was that if God does not put trust in his own "servants" and even charges His angels with error, how can Job insist that he is right (4:18)? Part of Yahweh's answer, then, is that He does put His trust in Job, His "servant." This comparison with the angels is further evidence that Job has been ushered into the divine assembly. Job is now welcome when the sons of God come to present themselves before Yahweh. Job is God's son, in whom He is well pleased.

Job the Prophet

Job began as a blameless and righteous priest, but the story of Job is his king-like struggle, wrestling through difficulties, judging rightly, and emerging into the third stage of biblical maturity and glory as a prophet. In this way, the story of Job can be read as his transition from the first, through the second to the third stage of glory-maturity. In simple terms this is seen in comparing the prologue and epilogue. At the beginning, Job offers sacrifices for his children who may have sinned (priest: 1:5), and in the end, Job offers sacrifices for his three foolish accusers who have spoken wrongly concerning God, who authorizes Job to *pray* for them and promises that He will hear him (prophet: 42:8). Job has graduated from the glory of a priest, through the glory of a king, to the glory of a prophet. What Job has wanted all along—the ability to speak to God face to face, as a man to his friend—has been granted! Job has been granted access to the deliberations of Yahweh, and when Job intercedes, he will be heard. Thus, the book closes not with an Accuser in the council of Yahweh, but an Advocate. Job has become a prophet, a member of Yahweh's deliberating council.

This helps explain why the whole story is told and structured the way it is. Why is Job primarily a series of dialogues, arguments, accusations, and deliberations? Because Job must learn to speak in the assembly of the sons of God. He must patiently endure the testing of God, the accusations of his companions, and emerge clinging to his integrity in faith. When Job recognizes that he is but "dust and ashes" (30:19; 42:6), we are once again reminded of Abraham, who interceded for Sodom and Gomorrah, recognizing that he was but "dust and ashes" (Gen. 18:27).[2] Job must learn to argue his case, cling to righteousness, and "gird himself like a man." When Job speaks to Yahweh like a prophet, he is granted a prophet's mantle.

Of course, we cannot ignore the fact that in all this, Job is a picture of Jesus. If Job is faithful in the midst of suffering, Jesus is a far greater example. Just as blameless and righteous Job entrusted himself to God, Christ even more so endured suffering and death as the spotless Lamb of God for the joy set before Him. As Job saw death and resurrection as the only way to put everything right, so too, Christ fully and finally endured unjust suffering and death at the hands of many accusers and was vindicated by the Father when He was raised from the dead. As Job passes through suffering and death and emerges justified and vindicated by God, so too the justification of Christ comes in His resurrection when the verdict of God the Father was declared. Job was innocent and therefore receives everything back double. Jesus was innocent, and therefore could not stay dead and inherits the entire world. Like Job, Jesus is the ultimate servant of Yahweh (Isa. 42:1, 53:11; Matt. 12:16-18). He is the true Son of God and our great high priest and king and prophet—our Advocate with the Father, who ever intercedes for us.

Finally, if we have read carefully and followed the storyline, we ought to find that this process itself is meant to have an effect on us. If the story is about Job's graduation from the glory of a priest and king to the glory of a prophet, then one of the aims of the book is to prepare readers for the same thing. We ought to find ourselves arguing various points as we read the story ourselves. We ought to ask the same questions that Job asks. If we are reading carefully, we ought to want to talk about what is happening, we ought to want to question God, and as we imagine the possibility of God bringing some sort of calamity into our lives, it ought to make us want to wrestle with evil, to strive with God for justice and truth. It ought to drive us to prayer. In other words, not only is this story about Job being granted a prophet's mantle, but as we read it, *we* are also being asked if we are prepared to take up a prophet's mantle. We, too, have been granted access to the heavenly councils, and we, too, are invited to speak. And God promises to hear us.

—*Toby J. Sumpter*

For Further Reading

Alter, Robert. *The Art of Biblical Poetry.* New York, N.Y.: Basic Books, 1985.

Girard, Rene. *Job the Victim of His People.* Stanford, Calif.: Stanford University Press, 1987.

Meyers, Jeffrey. "Leviathan and Job" pt. 1 & 2. *Biblical Horizons,* no. 87–88, September & October, 1996.

Zuck, Roy B. *Sitting with Job: Selected Studies on the Book of Job.* Grand Rapids, Mich.: Baker Book House, 1992.

Session I: Prelude

A Question to Consider
What does it mean to be a prophet?

From the General Information above, answer the following questions:
1. How is Job like Adam?
2. How is Job like Jacob?
3. What does *theodicy* mean?
4. How do the prologue and epilogue fit with the rest of Job?
5. Who is the Accuser? Why is that significant?
6. How is Job like Jesus?

Reading Assignment:
Job 1–14

Session II: Discussion
Job 1–14

A Question to Consider
What is justice?

Discuss or list short answers to the following questions:

Text Analysis
1. What proof is given for Job's righteousness in the prologue of Job? (1:5)
2. What is Eliphaz's first speech about (Job 4–5)?
3. What is Bildad's first speech about (Job 8)?
4. What is Zophar's first speech about (Job 11)?
5. What is Job's answer to Zophar's first speech (Job 12–14)?

Cultural Analysis
1. What does our culture consider to be just and unjust?
2. What does our culture think about suffering?

Biblical Analysis
1. Recall for a moment (or quickly re-read) some of the famous judges in the book of Judges (e.g., Ehud, Deborah, Gideon, Samson). How do these judges "judge" Israel?
2. Read Leviticus 1. Job is described several times as "blameless," and the Hebrew word is *tam*. Throughout Leviticus, God requires that sacrifices be "without blemish," (*tameem*—a related word). What implications might that description have for Job given what follows?

Summa
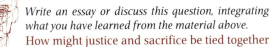
Write an essay or discuss this question, integrating what you have learned from the material above.
How might justice and sacrifice be tied together in the story of Job? How might we apply this in our lives?

Reading Assignment:
Job 15–27

Session III: Recitation
Job 15–27

Comprehension Questions
Answer the following questions for factual recall:
1. How many speeches do each of Job's three friends have in total (Job 3–27)?
2. Eliphaz asks Job if he is the "first man" to be born and whether he has heard the counsel of God (15:7,8). If he is talking about Adam, how would Adam have "heard the counsel of God"?
3. In chapter 15, what does Eliphaz say will consume the "tents of bribery"? What could he be alluding to in the events of Job?
4. What does Job call Eliphaz's words in chapter 16?
5. What does Job request of the earth in chapter 16? What does this mean?
6. According to Bildad in chapter 18, what is scattered on the dwelling of the wicked? What other biblical story does this remind us of?
7. How many times does Job say his persecutors have reproached him (Job 19)? Go back and count the speeches to this point. How do you think Job arrives at this number? What does it mean?
8. What biblical doctrine does Job refer to in 19:26?
9. How does Job describe the thoughts of his friends in chapter 21?
10. In chapter 23, how does Job describe how he will emerge from the testing of God?
11. What has God pierced with his hand according to Job in chapter 26?

Our next session will be a student-led discussion. As you are reading the following assignment, you should write down at least three questions from the text dealing with the issue listed below. These questions will be turned in to the teacher and will be used in classroom discussion. To get full credit for these Text Analysis questions you must create a question that is connected to the reading and to the issue that is the focus of our discussion; you must also answer the question correctly (and include a page or line reference at the end); and your question must be one that invites discussion and debate ("why" questions are excellent; questions that can be answered by "yes" or "no" are to be avoided).

You should also provide two Cultural Analysis and two Biblical Analysis questions. Cultural Analysis questions ask how our culture views the issue that we are discussing. Biblical Analysis questions ask what the Bible says concerning this issue. Again, to get full credit for each question, you must create questions connected to the issue we are studying, answer each question correctly and create questions that encourage and invite discussion and exploration. For an example of each type of question and answer refer to the examples provided in the next session.

If you are working alone, after creating your questions and answers, have your parent or tutor check over them. Also, if possible, share them with your family at the dinner table, helping them to understand why the issue is important, how the issue arises in your reading, how its importance is still evident in our culture, and how understanding this issue might change the way you and your family should think and live.

Issue

Friends and Envy

READING ASSIGNMENT:
Job 28–37

SESSION IV:
STUDENT-LED DISCUSSION
Job 28–37

A Question to Consider

What are some ways that jealousy and envy can affect friendships?

Students should read and consider the example questions below that are connected to the Question to Consider above. Last session's assignment was to prepare three questions and answers for the Text Analysis section and two additional questions and answers for both the Cultural and Biblical Analysis sections below.

Text Analysis

Example: What kind of "friends" are Eliphaz, Bildad, and Zophar? What about Elihu?

Answer: They really are not friends. If they were at one time, their words to Job are not helpful, and they seem to grow more and more sharp. Elihu seems more reasonable, but he is still critical. God does not say he was "wrong" in the epilogue, so the reader is left to decide whether Elihu was right or not.

Ancient of Days (God as an Architect) is a relief etching with watercolor by William Blake that appears to illustrates the query of the *Antiquus Dierum* to Job: "Where were you when I laid the foundations of the earth? Tell Me, if you have understanding. Who determined its measurements? Surely you know!"

Job Reproved by His Friends by James Barry (1741–1806)

Cultural Analysis

Example: We find that Job's "friends" are really more like little satans, mini-accusers. Frequently, envy is a root cause of mistreatment. And we can easily imagine a man of such great wealth and wisdom being envied. What does our culture think about envy and lust? What does our culture think about the Tenth Commandment?

Answer: Generally our culture says it is fine to do anything that does not directly harm others. So sins of the heart and mind are considered little or not worth worrying about. If envy and lust and covetousness stays in your own mind and heart, it's not thought by our culture to really be a problem.

Biblical Analysis

Example: How does Jesus characterize sins of the heart (Matt. 5:28)?

Answer: Jesus says that sins of the heart cannot be considered safe or harmless. Jesus says they are just as harmful as acting them out in real life.

Example: What does James imply about coveting (James 4:2)?

Answer: James implies that coveting is the root of fighting and arguing.

Other Scriptures to consider: Josh. 7:1–26, Jer. 22:17, Luke 12:15, Col. 3:5

SUMMA

Write an essay or discuss this question, integrating what you have learned from the material above.
Why is it important to fight the sin of envy?

READING ASSIGNMENT:
Job 38–42

The Book of Job

The collection of small intaglio etchings in this chapter are by artist William Blake. The series follows the story of Job but also adds elements from Blake's own imagination.

Session V: Writing
Job 38–42

Poetry

The book of Job is written in a highly stylized Hebrew verse. The arguments of Job and his companions are poems. To get an idea of what this is like, write a poem that is at least fourteen lines long in iambic pentameter that defends something or someone.

Iambic pentameter is one of the most common types of poetry in English. Poetry is made up of small groups of syllables called "feet." In iambic poetry there are two syllables per foot, and the second syllable is stressed. Pentameter means there are five feet per line. Thus, iambic pentameter is poetry with lines made of five feet, each foot having a stressed and unstressed syllable. Thus, a really uninspiring line of iambic pentameter would be:

afraid, afraid, afraid, afraid, afraid

Shakespeare has many better lines of iambic pentameter. Here is an example from Act 2 in *Macbeth*, where Lady Macbeth is speaking to Macbeth after he has murdered King Duncan (the syllables in bold receive the stress):

And **wash** this **fil**thy **wit**ness **from** your **hand**.

His poetry does not necessarily rhyme, and your poem may rhyme, but does not need to.

Example:
My son, give heed to what I say to you
Beware! Do not be led astray by cheats
Those fools who lie and beg for you to play their games
False joy is promised in their fields and courts
With rackets, balls, and pads, and hanging nets
Beware the lure of fame and false delights
Of violent striving, seeking self and gain
Of running back and forth beneath that sign
Desist to bow beneath that graven clock
That idol god whose face brings fear to hearts
O son, I beg you now to give your love
To that fair maiden, godlike sport of all
Where time does not enforce his tyrant hand
Where battle is not merely in the field
But looms in minds and faces and demands
The mind and body fully bound in love
To noble ends, to serve the common good,
To lead and to be led, to run and throw,
To hit, to dive and sacrifice yourself,
To lay your life and bunt upon the line.
There is no greater love than this on earth
As Christ our Lord has loved his bride the church
My son, of all the ways we play our lives
The sport of baseball far excels the rest.

"Curse God and die!" Job is counseled by his wife and his friends in this piece by William Blake.

The Book of Job 41

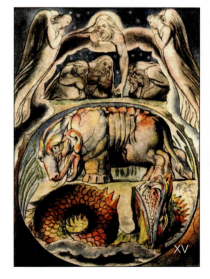

Optional Session: Aesthetics

Art Analysis

William Blake was not only a poet, he was also a great illustrator. Among his works is an illustrated commentary on the book of Job. Twenty-one drawings in his *Illustrations of the Book of Job* retell the story of Job, and wound through them are Blake's own interpretations, suggestions, and concerns. There were apparently four editions: a set of watercolors completed around 1820, a couple of others in or around 1821, and finally an edition of engravings dated March 8, 1825.

Refer to the thumbnail versions of these paintings in this chapter. For larger images to study, check out a book with these drawings or engravings from your local library or find them on the Internet.[3] Answer the following questions about Blake's illustrations.

Content Analysis

1. Compare and contrast the first and last illustrations.
2. Why does Job have a book in his hands in the first two illustrations?
3. In Illustration V, what is Job doing?
4. How is Illustration V answered in Illustration XIX?
5. What does Illustration VII suggest about Job's friends?
6. How does Blake show Elihu's youth in Illustration XII?
7. In Illustration XVII, what is God standing on? Where does this suggest they are?

8. What shape does Job take in Illustration XX? What does that imply about these sufferings, depicted behind either hand?

Endnotes

1 The Septuagint adds the following to Job 42:17: "and it is written that he will rise again with those whom the Lord raises up. This man is described in the Syriac book as living in the land of Ausis, on the borders of Idumea and Arabia: and his name before was Jobab; and having taken an Arabian wife, he begot a son whose name was Ennon. And he himself was the son of his father Zare, one of the sons of Esau, and of his mother Bosorrha, so that he was the fifth from Abraam. And these were the kings who reigned in Edom, which country he also ruled over: first, Balac, the son of Beor, and the name of his city was Dennaba: but after Balac, Jobab, who is called Job, and after him Asom, who was governor out of the country of Thaeman: and after him Adad, the son of Barad, who destroyed Madiam in the plain of Moab; and the name of his city was Gethaim. And his friends who came to him were Eliphaz, of the children of Esau, king of the Thaemanites, Baldad sovereign of the Sauchaeans, Sophar king of the Minaeans."

2 Most translations say that Job "repented in dust and ashes," but the Hebrew here is a little more ambiguous than that. At present it is not clear to me that we need to conclude that Job was wrong. It is possible that he has been reminded of God's greatness and glory, and he is merely reaffirming his humility. But Yahweh's final word seems to be that Job has spoken what is right (42:7, 8).

3 These illustrations may be found at Link 1 for this chapter at www.VeritasPress.com/OmniLinks.

POETRY

"If I feel physically as if the top of my head were taken off, I know that is poetry."

—*Emily Dickinson*

"Experience has taught me, when I am shaving of a morning, to keep watch over my thoughts, because if a line of poetry strays into my memory, my skin bristles so that the razor ceases to act."

—*A. E. Housman*

"Poetry is the spontaneous overflow of powerful feelings ... recollected in tranquility."

—*William Wordsworth*

"The poet is the sayer, the namer."

—*Ralph Waldo Emerson*

"Poets are ... the unacknowledged legislators of mankind."

—*Percy Bysshe Shelley*

Over the centuries poetry has been described or defined in numerous different ways. One of the simplest and most memorable definitions is that of Samuel Taylor Coleridge, author of *The Rime of the Ancient Mariner*. Coleridge defined it as "the best words in the best order." Simple as it is, his definition points up the truth that, in a broad sense, all artful language is poetry.

However, we ordinarily mean by the word *poetry* language written in lines, or *verse*. The rest is *prose*, writing that runs from margin to margin down the page. Unlike poetry, prose is not broken into lines by the author. The line break is the essential distinction of poetry, since prose may possess almost all the other elements of poetry.

We first encounter poetry as children in the form of nursery rhymes, skipping rhymes, advertising jingles, and in the works of writers like Dr. Seuss. We love their strong rhymes and rhythms, as in "Tom, Tom, the piper's son, / Stole a pig and away he run," though the language may be unremarkable. Here and there a line or more may rise to the level of poetry, in Coleridge's sense of "artful language," as one does in this rhyme:

> Tom, Tom, the piper's son,
> He learned to play when he was young,
> But the only tune that he could play
> Was, "Over the Hills and Far Away."

The last line evokes by its meaning, sound, and rhythm a yearning for what is romantic and far off, and the phrase

"Over the hills and far away" finds its way into many rhymes and ballads. Similarly, "Ride a Cockhorse to Banbury Cross" ends with the remarkable lines,

> Rings on her fingers and bells on her toes,
> She shall have music wherever she goes.

The lady described in the rhyme is not only impressively decked out, but the last line suggests something about her personality. She appears to be one of those magical people who carry an inner music with them. These rhymes make a strong impression on us when we're young. Recalling nursery rhymes, the Welsh poet Dylan Thomas confessed,

> I wanted to write poetry in the beginning because I had fallen in love with words. The first poems I knew were nursery rhymes, and before I could read them for myself I had come to love just the words of them, the words alone.

As we grow, we find a similar pleasure in comic or nonsense forms such as the limerick and the higgledy piggledy (or double dactyl). Here is a classic limerick:

> There was an old monk in Siberia,
> Whose life grew drearier and drearier.
> He emerged from his cell,
> With a blood-curdling yell,
> And eloped with the Mother Superior.

Similarly, we delight in the pounding rhythms and clever rhymes of a higgledy piggledy, or double dactyl, like the following:

> Higgledy piggledy,
> Ludwig von Beethoven
> Bored by requests
> For a tune they could hum,
> Finally answered with
> Oversimplicity,
> "Here's mein Fifth Symphony—
> Da da da **Dum.**"

As we read and encounter 'serious' poetry in school or elsewhere, we discover that there are many different forms of the art and that few have the rollicking rhythms and clanging rhymes of light, or comic, verse. We also learn that the purpose of poetry is "to delight and instruct," as the Renaissance courtier and poet Sir Philip Sydney wrote. Like all art, poetry must first please us or we're unlikely to stay with it, but what it finally reveals to us is much of the best that has been thought and written by humankind. Sydney says in a memorable phrase, it is like "a medicine of cherries."

As his phrase suggests, poetry appeals to us through the senses—sight, hearing, touch, taste, and smell, as well as the kinesthetic sense (the sense of the body's position or motion—as in dancing). Its musical rhythms and sounds, as well as its imagery and other components, are more concentrated and intense than those of other genres. One can say that a poem is an almost physical embodiment of thought and feeling. Mind, body, and emotions are unified in a good poem. To understand how this is achieved, it is helpful to look at the basic elements of poetry and consider how they work together to make the poem. These elements are *imagery, metaphor, sound, form*, and *content*. Although I can hardly pretend to treat these comprehensively in a short essay, looking into them—particularly from the writer's point of view—can provide a good start to understanding how poetry works.

Dickinson

How Poetry Works

Imagery

I mentioned above that a poem, both for reader and writer, can be thought of as a physical experience of thought and emotion. It should be, according to the poet Keats, "felt upon the pulses." Like all good writing, poetry is rooted in the concrete, in the experience of the five (or six) senses. Abstract words like *love, grief,* or *joy* must be incarnate in the images that make them real. Archibald MacLeish makes this clear in his poem "Ars Poetica":

> For all the history of grief
> An empty doorway and a maple leaf.

MacLeish is probably thinking here of a poem by Robert Frost. The empty doorway reminds the speaker, returning home, of the absent loved one; the single maple leaf reminds him of his loneliness and happier times in a fall now past. In the famous balcony scene in *Romeo and Juliet*, Romeo compares Juliet to the sun:

> But soft! what light through yonder
>   window breaks?
> It is the east, and Juliet is the sun!

Later Juliet expresses her love for Romeo in a similar cosmic image:

> Take him and cut him out in little stars,
> And he will make the face of
>   heaven so fine
> That all the world will be
>   in love with night.

These visual images, along with a hundred others supplied by Shakespeare, suggest the remarkable intensity of the love for which the two lovers are famous.

Visual images are the most common in poetry (as indeed they are in life), but note the other senses experienced in one line from Keats's "Ode to a Nightingale." The poet is wandering blindly among blossoming trees on a pitch-dark spring night and notes that he cannot see "what soft incense hangs upon the boughs." The senses of touch, smell, and a kinesthetic feeling of weight are all appealed to in the words *soft, incense,* and *hangs*. The speaker is alive in all his senses and alert as he listens to the nightingale's song. William Carlos Williams in his poetry repeats the dictum "No ideas but in things," and everyone beginning to read or write poetry should keep it in mind. Note the power of the images of the bones and foxes in these lines by Wallace Stevens,

> Children picking up our bones
> Will never know that these were once
> As quick as foxes on the hill,

or the effect of the Chilean poet Neruda in his "Ode to the Tomato" describing a ripe one cut in half as "a fresh,

/ deep,/ inexhaustible sun."

The popular Japanese form of the haiku works almost exclusively with images, as these two illustrate:

> Melon
> in morning dew,
> mud-fresh.

> Sudden sun upon
> the mountain path,
>   plum scent.[1]

Note that these two, like most haiku, consist of two juxtaposed natural images that complement or contrast with one another, often in very subtle ways. The following is a haiku-like poem done by a student—in two lines rather than three (it's a bit of a riddle):

> Who let the
> roaring yellow
> tigers
> out of their
> cage last
> evening?
>
> *—Janet Gummeson*

It describes a sunset. In Japan crowds of people will participate in haiku-writing contests. I urge you to try one.

Poetry, like all art, is rooted in the concrete, physical world. As Alan Watts observed, "Perhaps we need a poet occasionally to remind us that even the coffee we absent-mindedly sip comes in (as Yeats put it) 'a heavy, spillable cup.'" In my experience, poems begin in the world of the senses and stay rooted there, no matter where they end. What usually moves me to write is a desire to call things up by the power of words. A sensation, impression, or image will step out from its surroundings and demand my total attention: as the image reaches up toward the words, the words become the image, the thing itself. Thing becomes word, and word becomes thing. For one happy moment substance and meaning are fused. The terrible gap between experience and the articulation of experience is closed. The mind is one with what it perceives.

Chaucer

Metaphor

Metaphor, in the broad sense, means figurative language, and is found everywhere in poetry. Narrowly defined, it is a figure of speech in which one concrete image, thought, or feeling is put in place of another to suggest a likeness between them. Robert Frost defined it simply as "saying one thing in terms of another." When Romeo declares "Juliet is the sun," he creates a metaphor. When Juliet imagines Romeo cut "out in little stars" she creates another. If either of them had used the word "like" or "as" he/she would have made a kind of metaphor called a *simile*. Here are two similes:

> I . . . saw the ruddy moon lean over the hedge
> *Like* a red-faced farmer.
> And round about were the wistful stars
> With white faces *like* town children.
>
> —*T.E. Hulme*

Sometimes metaphors are only implied, as in this sonnet by Shakespeare:

> That time of year thou mayst in me behold
> When yellow leaves, or none, or few, do hang
> Upon those boughs which shake against
>   the cold,
> Bare ruined choirs, where late the
>   sweet birds sang.

After comparing his age to autumn, the speaker implies that his thinning hair is like the dwindling leaves of autumn and like branches abandoned by singing birds. The branches shaking against the cold also suggest other ills of advancing age (palsy, sensitivity to cold as opposed to warm-blooded youth). All of this is implicit, not spelled out; part of the pleasure of the poem is discovering it as we read the poem over several times. As in Janet Gummeson's poem, the object of the metaphor (the sunset) is only implied: "Who let the yellow roaring tigers / out of their cage last evening?"

A *symbol* is a special kind of metaphor, which says many things in terms of another. An image that is a symbol can mean many different things—even contradictory—like the ocean in Whitman's "Out of the Cradle Endlessly Rocking" that symbolizes both life and death, time and eternity, and more. Natural objects, forces, or actions often serve as symbols—the sky, mountains, birds, forests, serpents, fire, or geese flying south—but so do man-made things like the Cross, a many-faceted diamond, a sword, a veil, or an electric dynamo. In Keats's "Ode to a Nightingale" the bird becomes a symbol of many things, including immortality, mortality, art, ideal happiness, escape, and spiritual reality. In Keats's equally famous "Ode on a Grecian Urn," the urn suggests, in addition to the above, artistic perfection, human passion, frustration, truth, beauty, to name a few. Keats exclaims, "Thou, silent form, dost tease us out of thought / As doth eternity"—a good description of what a symbol will do.

There are other figures of speech, all of which can be grouped under metaphor. Aristotle, in his *Poetics* gives metaphor, or rather the maker of metaphors, a special place: "It is the one thing that cannot be learned from others; it is also a sign of genius, since a good metaphor implies an intuitive perception of the similarities in dissimilarities." Aristotle's statement might tempt you to try making a metaphor or two. One thing is almost certain, if you like metaphors, you'll love poetry.

Sound

In addition to imagery and metaphor, poetry must have the music of words. One indication of how much a person will like reading or writing poetry is how much he enjoys the sound of words. Auden said that in the case of two youths, one of whom says, "I want to be a poet," and the other, "I like fooling around with words," he would have more hope for the second. I recall as a child going by gas station signs in the car and reading them backwards for the sound. "Gulf Gas" became "Flug Sag"; and the ordinary "Standard Oil" became the mythical monster, "Dradnats Lio." Most children from infancy on play with words and other sounds; unfortunately parents and school sometimes suppress this creative oral play.

Rhyme is only the most obvious musical effect in poetry. The list includes *onomatopoeia, alliteration, assonance, consonance*, and more. Actually the sound of every word in a poem interacts with every other word. Studies show the reader is aware of these—if only subliminally—over the length of four or five lines. Every sound in language sounds either more like, or unlike, every other sound. Take the sound of the words *oil* and *critic*. They are so different one might say they clash, that they are *anti-rhymes*. The following words have much sound in common: *barn, burn, moon, moan*. So do *decrepit, creditor, medical*. Whether words clash or harmonize, the sound of all of them together is part of the music of poetry.

The sound and rhythm of the words should reinforce the poem's emotion and meaning. As Alexander Pope wrote, "The sound must seem an echo to the sense." Read the following passage aloud to hear all sound effects that it describes (*Zephyr* is the south wind, and *numbers* refers to the meter of the piece):

> The sound must seem an echo to the sense.
> Soft is the strain when Zephyr gently blows,

And the smooth stream in smoother
　　numbers flows;
But when loud surges lash the sounding shore,
The hoarse rough verse should like the
　　torrent roar.
When Ajax strives some rock's vast weight
　　to throw,
The line too labors and the words move slow;
Not so, when swift Camilla scours the plain,
Flies o'er th'unbending corn, and skims
　　along the main.

Earlier he has described an *Alexandrine* (a long six-foot line, often used to end a stanza or poem) as "a wounded

Poetry can sometimes help us "see" things even better than the visual arts. In this painting *The Adoration of the Kings and Christ on the Cross*, attributed to Benedetto Bonfigli (d. 1496), the connection is made between the Nativity and the Crucifixion. But that relationship is made quicker and stronger in a piece by Christian poet Luci Shaw (1940–) called, "Mary's Song." At the end of that poem she writes:

*. . . nailed to my poor planet, caught
that I might be free, blind in my womb
to know my darkness ended,
brought to this birth for me to be new born,
and for him to see me mended,
I must see him torn.*[2]

snake," and slows the line to a literal crawl:

> A needless Alexandrine ends the song,
> That like a wounded snake, drags its slow
>   length along.

Briefly, the sound effects of poetry include:

Onomatopoeia: words that sound somewhat like what they denote: *buzz, bang, click, snick, tintinnabulation*, and also, *skinny, slim, slender, spindly, fat, gross, huge, hog, vast*.

Alliteration: The repetition of consonant sounds. Note the m's in these lines by Tennyson as you read them aloud:

> The moan of doves in immemorial elms
> And murmuring of innumerable bees.

Assonance: The repetition and modulation of vowels. These lines by Sylvia Plath have rich vowel sounds and alliterating consonants. Again, read them aloud:

> Haunched like a faun, he hooed
> From grove of moon-glint and fen-frost
> Until all owls in the twigged forest
> Flapped black to look and brood
> On the call this man made.

Rhyme: Unlike a language like Italian, English is poor in rhymes (*true rhymes*, that is, such as *June/moon, weather/feather, bubble/trouble*). For the last century many poets have used *half-rhymes* (also called *off-* or *slant-rhymes*), expanding greatly the opportunities for rhyme. *Frost* and *forest* in the above poem are half-rhymes. Wilfred Owen, a World War I poet, provides further examples in "Arms and the Boy": *blade* and *blood, flash* and *flesh*:

> Let the boy try along this bayonet-blade
> How cold steel is and keen with hunger
>   of blood;
> Blue with all malice, like a madman's flash;
> And thinly drawn with famishing for flesh.

Finally, rhyme occurs not only at the end of lines, but within the lines, and then it is called *internal rhyme*. Here is one from Coleridge's *Rime of the Ancient Mariner*:

> The ship was *cheered*, the harbour *cleared*.
> Merrily did we drop
> Below the kirk....

In the following four lines from Gerard Manley Hopkins' "What I Do Is Me," there are twelve rhymes, eight of them internal, besides an abundance of alliteration and assonance:

> As kingfishers catch fire,
>   dragonflies draw flame;
> As tumbled over rim in roundy wells
> Stones ring; like each tucked string tells,
>   each hung bell's
> Bow swung finds tongue to fling out broad
>   its name.

Rhythm: Rhythm and meter, part of the sound, are discussed in the following section.

Form

As I noted above, the chief formal difference between poetry (or verse) and prose is the line. The line-break creates this fundamental difference between the two; all other differences follow from this one. Historically, lines have had elements added to them, such as rhyme and *meter* (a certain count of syllables or accents per line). But these features only add to, and enrich, the fundamental difference.

All English has *speech rhythms*; that is, when spoken, some syllables are stressed more than others. When one breaks speech into the lines of poetry, the line-breaks create a new, secondary rhythm modifying the primary speech rhythm. One can easily see and hear this effect in William Carlos Williams' lines about a cat:

Poem

As the cat
climbed over
the top of

the jamcloset
first the right
forefoot

carefully
then the hind
stepped down

into the pit of
the empty
flowerpot

Because of the many line- and stanza-breaks, we hear and see the slow, graceful movement of the cat. Compare these lines to the same words written out as prose:

As the cat climbed over the top of the jamcloset first the right forefoot carefully then the hind stepped down into the pit of the empty flowerpot.

In contrast to the poem, this prose sentence seems undistinguished, and perhaps a little awkward, as we speed through it.

Examining a poem's patterns of sound, rhythm, and appearance on the page reveals its *form*. There are a number of different forms of poetry. The Williams poem about the cat is written in *free verse*, that is, verse free of both rhyme and *meter* (a particular count of accents or syllables per line). In free verse pure and simple each line may be of any length the author chooses. As in the cat poem, this is the only rule. Of course, it doesn't make good free verse any easier to write, for the breaks finally must support the overall effect of the poem.

Sometimes the poet will make each free verse line a unit of *syntax*, such as a phrase, a clause, or a sentence. The end of each line corresponds to a natural pause in speech, as in these lines from "I Try to Waken and Greet the World Once Again" by James Wright:

In a pine tree,
A few yards away from my window sill,
A brilliant blue jay is springing up and down,
    up and down,
On a branch.

This *syntactical free verse* is the kind the psalmists used:

He maketh me to lie down in green pastures,
He leadeth me beside the still waters,
He restoreth my soul...

For Thou art with me,
Thy rod and thy staff, they comfort me.
Thou preparest a table before me
    in the presence of mine enemy.
Thou anointest my head with oil,
My cup runneth over.

Each line (or half-line, in the Hebrew) tends to parallel the structure of the other lines and repeat the point in a new way. This kind of free verse, with its parallel

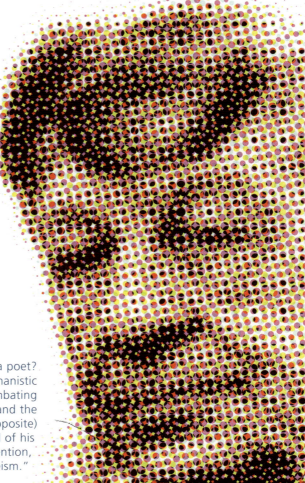

What place does Faith play in the work of a poet? W.H. Auden turned to Christianity when his own humanistic tradition failed to provide a way of explaining or combating the evil he encountered during the Spanish Civil War and the rise of Nazi Germany. In contrast, Alfred Tennyson (opposite) left the faith in which he was raised and near the end of his life said that his "religious beliefs also defied convention, leaning towards agnosticism and pandeism."

O my chief good,
How shall I measure out thy blood?
How shall I count what thee befell,
And each grief tell?

Shall I thy woes
Number according to thy foes?
Or, since one star show'd thy first breath,
Shall all thy death?

Or shall each leaf,
Which falls in Autumn, score a grief?
Or cannot leaves, but fruit be sign
Of the true vine?

Then let each hour
Of my whole life one grief devour:
That thy distress through all may run,
And be my sun.

Or rather let
My several sins their sorrows get;
That as each beast his cure doth know,
Each sin may so.

Since blood is fittest, Lord to write
Thy sorrows in, and bloody fight;
My heart hath store, write there, where in
One box doth lie both ink and sin:

That when sin spies so many foes,
Thy whips, thy nails, thy wounds, thy woes
All come to lodge there, sin may say,
'No room for me', and fly away.

Sin being gone, oh fill the place,
And keep possession with thy grace;
Lest sin take courage and return,
And all the writings blot or burn.

The poem *Good Friday* is by George Herbert, the oil painting *The Road to Calvary* is by Lorenzo Lotto (c.1480–1556).

construction, was adopted by Whitman and Ginsberg and other poets in modern times to great rhetorical effect:

> And I know that the hand of God
>   is the promise of my own,
> And I know that the spirit of God
>   is the brother of my own,
> And that all the men ever born are also my
>   brothers and the women my sisters and lovers,
> And that a kelson of the creation is love.
>
> —*Whitman*, "Song of Myself"

A third kind of free verse, uses the white space on a page to great effect, making an appeal to the eye as well as the ear. It is called *typographical* or *spatial free verse* because it depends on where the type is set on the page in relation to the white space. Here is an example from e.e. cummings' "Chanson Innocente":

> in Just-
> spring   when the world is mud-
> luscious the little
> lame balloonman

whistles   far   and wee

and eddieadbill come
running...

and from his "Portrait,"

Buffalo Bill's
defunct
                who used to
                ride a watersmooth-silver
                                stallion
and break onetwothreefourfive pigeonsjust
                        likethat....

Notice how running the words together in both these examples speeds up the way you read the words, while separating them with white space slows you down or causes you to put more emphasis on a word like *stallion*.

Typographical verse also includes *shaped verse*, where the words on the page may resemble everything from an apple to a coke bottle. I hope you'll try writing a shaped poem. (Here's a demonstration called "Urn"):

I
a m
w r i -
t i n g t h i s
v e r s e t o l o o k
l i k e a l i t -
t l e C h i -
n e s e
c e r a m i c

A popular form today, it was used by George Herbert centuries ago for his poem "Easter Wings":

Lord, who createdst man in wealth and store,
Though foolishly he lost the same.
Decaying more and more,
Till he became
Most poore:
With thee
O let me rise
As larks, harmoniously,
And sing this day thy victories;
Then shall the fall further the flight in me.

Each stanza (there are two in the poem) resembles an angel's wings when you turn the page on its side. (His example is not free verse, however, since he uses, in addition to shape, both rhyme and meter.)

Most poetry over the years has been written in *meter*, a word related to "measure." In most metrical poetry every line has the same number of *accents* (*stresses, beats*),

or *syllables*, or both. One of the simpler metrical forms is *syllabics*. In syllabic verse one counts only the number of syllables in each line. The haiku is a familiar example, often written with a syllable count of 5, 7, 5 in its three lines:

The crow twitches its   5
feathers. A few snowflakes drift   7
in the damp spring air.   5

—Trevor LeGeis

These lines from Sylvia Plath's "Dark Wood, Dark Water" each have five syllables:

This wood burns a dark
Incense. Pale moss drips
In elbow-scarves, beards
From the archaic
Bones of the great trees.
Blue mists move over
A lake thick with fish....

In contrast to syllabics is *accentual verse*, in which we count only the accents per line and ignore the number of syllables, of which there can be any number. In the opening lines to Coleridge's *Christabel* the number of stresses is four, while the number of syllables varies from four to eleven:

'Tis the middle of night by the castle clock,
And the owls have awakened the
        crowing cock;
Tu-whit!—Tu-whoo!
And hark, again! the crowing cock
How drowsily it crew.

In *scanning* the verse, that is, counting the number of stresses or feet per line, we usually mark the stressed syllables with an *ictus* (ˊ) and the unstressed syllables with a *breve* (˘). One looks like a little carrot and the other like a little hammock, as in the above verse.

The most common verse form in English is *accentual-syllabic*, where we count both the number of accents and number of syllables in a line. It has been the predominant form for hundreds of years. Robert Frost's "Stopping by Woods on Snowy Evening" is a familiar example:

Whose woods / these are / I think / I know.
His house / is in / the vil / lage though.
He will / not see / me stop / ping here
To watch / his woods / fill up / with snow.

Namesake of the Spenserian sonnet, Edmund Spenser (c. 1552–1599) composed the epic poem *The Faerie Queene* to illustrate several of the Christian virtues. The poem was written, appropriately enough, in Spenserian stanzas—that is, eight lines in iambic pentameter followed by a ninth line in iambic hexameter.

Each line has eight syllables of which four are accented, or stressed. Long ago people discovered that stressed and unstressed syllables often fall into repeated patterns within the line. These groups or clusters of syllables have been named, according to the patterns they repeat, as different kinds of *feet*. These feet have the exotic names of *iambic, trochaic, anapestic, dactylic*—names borrowed from the Greeks. (The feet in the Frost poem are separated by forward slashes.) These classifications of metrical feet are often misleading to beginning poets, as well as to readers, who mistakenly think that these patterns must be rigidly adhered to in a poem. In reality, most good accentual-syllabic verse will 'violate' metrical regularity almost as often as it fulfills it.

As Robert Frost himself said, in English we basically have two kinds of meters: a rising and a falling. The *iambic* (˘ ´) is rising, as in

Whose woods these are I think I know

and so is *anapestic* (˘ ˘ ´), as in

An old man took his dog to Detroit.

The iambic is the most common meter, while the galloping effect of anapests is useful in light verse, such as limericks. The *trochaic* is a falling meter as in

Martin married Ingrid's sister.

So is *dactylic* (´ ˘ ˘), which, like anapestic, tends to gallop—as it does quite appropriately in Tennyson's "The Charge of the Light Brigade":

Half a league, half a league,
    half a league onward
Into the mouth of Hell rode the six hundred.

The most common accentual-syllabic lines are five-foot *iambic* lines (*iambic pentameter*) and, second, four-foot iambic (*iambic tetrameter*), followed last by three-foot or *iambic trimeter*. The prefixes *penta-, tetra-, tri-* simply mean *five, four, three* respectively. All of these, plus two-foot lines, can be found in Herbert's "Easter Wings," above. Unrhymed iambic pentameter, often called *blank verse*, is the most common form of iambic pentameter and the most common verse form in English. Shakespeare wrote his plays in this form: Hamlet soliloquizes in it, "To be, or not to be, that is the question," and Romeo and Juliet declare their undying love in blank verse:

Two of the fairest stars in all the heaven,
Having some business, do entreat her eyes
To twinkle in their sphere till they return.
What if her eyes were there, they in her head?
The brightness of her cheek would
    shame those stars,
As daylight doth a lamp....

The meter sets up a pattern of stresses or beats for the accentual-syllabic poem. But there is also, playing against this, the natural rhythms of speech. The two do not always agree, in which case the speech rhythm wins and changes the meter. Note the change the rhythm of speech makes in the iambic pentameter of this line from a sonnet by John Donne: "Batter my heart, three-personed God, for you...." In the back of our minds, like the bass beat in the background of a song, we are aware of the expected iambic meter,

di DAH di DAH di DAH di DAH di DAH.

What we actually hear is quite different:

BATter my HEART, THREE-PERSoned GOD for YOU

The counterpoint, or play, of the actual speech rhythm against the anticipated pattern of the meter gives us pleasure, just as contrapuntal rhythms do in music. Now read aloud the whole sonnet by Donne, using natural speech rhythms, and you will sense that counterpoint. You'll discover that the natural rhythm of speech differs from the meter in many places:

> Batter my heart, three-person'd God; for you
> As yet but knock, breathe, shine and
>   seeke to mend;
> That I may rise and stand, o'erthrow mee,
>   and bend
> Your force to breake, blowe, burn and
>   make me new.
> I, like an usurpt towne, to another due,
> Labour to admit you, but Oh, to no end.
> Reason your viceroy in mee, mee
>   should defend,
> But is captiv'd, and proves weake or untrue.
> Yet dearely I love you, and would
>   be loved faine
> But am betroth'd unto your enemie.
> Divorce mee, untie, or breake that knot againe,
> Take mee to you, imprison mee, for I
> Except you enthrall mee, never shall be free,
> Nor ever chaste, except you ravish mee.

Notice how the pounding stresses "knock, breathe, shine" and "breake, blow, burn," sound like the battering ram of the "three-personed God" trying to enter the speaker's heart. They radically alter the iambic meter even as they "echo the sense."

I am interested in the precise observation of small twists and turns in people, including ambivalence, rather than the grandiose beauty or the terrible darkness of humanity. The poet, Scott Cairns, is a good friend of mine and this is a portrait I thought about for at least a year before asking him to pose for me. I was most interested in his conversion to Orthodoxy and the seriousness with which he attended to prayer. He had what looked like a string bracelet with beads on it around his wrist that he used to mark the repetition of The Jesus Prayer. He told me that when he first learned the prayer his priest asked him to begin by repeating it 1,000 times. The string was red and my intention was to have part of it dangle below his coat sleeve in the painting, but as I photographed him he surprised me by singing hymns, and, seeing that the prayer bracelet was not at all visible anyway, I gave up that idea and titled the painting "The Singing Poet." As time passed and I lived with the portrait in my studio, the title became more and more boring to me and had nothing of the intense feelings I had toward what I had seen in Scott; the tension between loving God and failing Him. Scott had had some whiskey at our house the night before the photo session and "I Drink Your Whiskey and Your Sorrow" came to me as a phrase that encompassed our being bound to the earth, God's care for that, and what we both do in response to it."—Catherine Prescott

OMNIBUS IV

Robert Lee Frost (1874–1963), famous American poet who received four Pulitzer Prizes for Poetry.

In the last century poets have become even more free in their use of accentual-syllabic verse. Much free verse might more accurately be called *mixed meter*, where there is a ghost of one or more metrical patterns behind the lines of a poem, though the line lengths vary so much one can't call them truly metrical. Much of T.S. Eliot's free verse, for instance, appears to be written in mixed meter. Poets will sometimes mix not only meters but the free and metrical verse. Again, Eliot gives us an example in *The Waste Land*. (This is the best-known poem world-wide written in the last century. I might add that his longest poem, *Four Quartets*, written after Eliot's conversion, is considered by many the greatest poem in English from the twentieth century.)

Poetry is an art, and therefore *prosody* (the study of form—what we've just been doing) is itself an art and not a science. There is very little that is scientifically precise about it, and much depends upon individual interpretation and point of view. Readers will often differ as to what the speech rhythm of a line or a piece is, depending on which words they think should be stressed. And some stresses receive more emphasis than others.

Content

Unlike painting or music, poetry has all the resources of language at its disposal. It can have content and meaning, therefore, in ways that music and the visual arts cannot. Poetry can tell the story of a people, put forward a philosophy, present a vision of hell and heaven, or record the growth of a poet's mind. It can in a brief lyric capture a frog plunging into a pond or the elusive moment of falling in love.

Most beginning poets tend to think a poem has to be about one of the 'big' subjects: love, grief, God, art, the meaning of life or death. It takes a while for them to realize that they're better off focusing on small things, such as a toad in the garden, a comb with broken teeth, a craving for chocolate, or a squirrel in the attic. William Carlos Williams wrote about the cat climbing over the jam jars, and an even more famous poem about a wheelbarrow:

The Red Wheelbarrow

so much depends
upon

a red wheel
barrow

glazed with rain
water

beside the white
chickens

This poem does nothing more (or less) than help us *see* the wheelbarrow and chickens and perhaps lead us to reflect on what "depends" upon them. A poem about some humble object may well wind up reflecting in a fresh way on one of the big subjects such as love, beauty or death. In a poem called "Tomes," which is ostensibly about heavy books in his library, Billy Collins weighs a history textbook on his deceased mother's food scale and finds it turns his thoughts to her,

even though it never mentions my mother,
now that I think of her again,
who only last year rolled off the edge of the earth
in her electric bed,
in her smooth pink nightgown
the bones of her fingers interlocked,
her sunken eyes staring upward
beyond all knowledge,
beyond the tiny figures of history,
some in uniform, some not,
marching onto the pages of this incredibly
heavy book.

This may be an example of how the poem that needs to be written can come along and take over the poem the poet first intended to write. Writing a poem is often a journey of discovery. At the end of the poem we learn, as perhaps Collins learned, how the tome and his mother's death fit together.

It's often helpful when looking for something to write about to get outside of yourself and the self's preoccupations. I recommend to writing students that they try to imagine themselves as someone else, either human or animal. It is helpful to imagine what it would feel like to be a tree, insect, or inanimate object and to write from that point of view. I've even suggested such alter egos as a piece of dental floss, a carpet, or coat hanger. Writing the following, I imagined myself a "Deer Tick," (the carrier of Lyme disease) addressing its victim. It begins,

No larger than a period I scramble
among the sequoia of your armhairs
unable to decide in this vast wilderness
where to drill for the life-giving well
the water of life, the warm blood.
For I am sick unto death: in my abdomen

the spirochete turns its deadly corkscrew
which I must shortly confess to the stream
pulsing from your dark red heart. . . .

Though I started by simply identifying with the insect, by the time I finished the poem I found the tick and the disease had become symbols of the general human malaise we call original sin. Here is another animal, a giant panda, often seen in zoos or nature videos:

> In the white mist of morning I find my place,
> a square of the sun where I can balance
>
> and chew the shoots, their green light
>   in my mouth.
> I sit, my footpads shiny, taking in the dim
>
> sweet music of existence. . . .

The possibilities are endless.

A word about inspiration. It's wonderful to write a poem when you feel inspired. But what seems good in the moment of inspiration may appear flat and uninspired in the cold light of the next day. On the other hand, a poem begun with a few dry facts from an encyclopedia may catch fire as one works on it. I once saw a photo of a moose crossing a bridge from Vermont into New Hampshire. That was the germ of a poem, but I had to look up facts about the moose—dry as dust—in order to write it. Only then did I feel the poem come alive. The Muse is unpredictable—and we do need to court her in a variety of ways.

A final word about content and any idea, or message, you want your poem to contain. Poems written deliberately to convey an idea or 'message' do not often succeed as poetry. It becomes too conscious a process; the Big Idea gets in the way. Save the message for an editorial , sermon, or essay. On the other hand, if you focus on writing a good poem about a moose, a heavy book, or a toothless comb, your deepest convictions will manifest themselves in it without your intending them to.

A Christian Response

Shortly after 9/11 *The New Yorker* and other magazines invited readers to send in poems (either their own or by others) to express what they felt in the face of the terrorist atrocity. Only in poetry did people find words to express adequately their grief and horror at the 'unspeakable' event.

Next to singing in the shower, poetry may be the most universally practiced art. It seems nearly everyone at some point in life tries to write a poem. Certainly most people would agree with the bumper sticker, "Poetry says it best." The fact that they are poetry is one reason the psalms are the most popular book in the Bible. The poet William Carlos Williams claimed, "It is difficult to get the news from poems, yet men die miserably every day for lack of what is found there."

Poetry captures experiences and expresses feelings and thoughts that elude our ordinary speech and our discursive prose. Among its great values is that it can help us experience vicariously the lives, thoughts, and feelings of other people in our own space and time, and of those, like Romeo and Juliet, distant in space and time. Reading and writing poetry can give us a better understanding of ourselves, of other people, of nature, and of God. Not only does it tell us in concentrated and beautiful language what we already know—"What oft was thought but ne'er so well expressed," as Pope describes it—but it provides insights into mysteries inexpressible in other forms, as does Blake's poem "The Tyger" or these lines from Wordsworth's "Tintern Abbey:"

>   And I have felt
> A presence that disturbs me with the joy
> Of elevated thoughts; a sense sublime
> Of something far more deeply interfused Whose
> dwelling is the light of setting suns,
> And the round ocean and the living air,
> And the blue sky, and in the mind of man:
> A motion and a spirit, that impels
> All thinking things, all objects of all thought,
> And rolls through all things.

Unlike philosophy, history, or the sciences, poetry does not exclude any human act, thought, feeling, belief, or intuition as not pertinent to its method; the whole spectrum is there, including the spiritual. Every conceivable human attitude, point of view, or feeling has somewhere been expressed in poetry. What is true of poetry is also true of the other genres and arts. The infinite variety of humanity is in all. Fortunately there are many poets whose works can feed us spiritually. A very short list would include Dante, John of the Cross, Spenser, Shakespeare, Milton, Donne, Herbert, Blake, Wordsworth, Coleridge, Browning, Hopkins, Thompson, Eliot, and Auden.

Even poets who do not profess faith may reflect the Christian neo-platonic tradition that has been with the Church from at least Augustine. Neoplatonism, as it has been assimilated in the theology of Augustine and others, maintains that God is the one source of the Good, the True, and the Beautiful, and that every creature radiates something of these qualities. They shine through the material world. Some might argue that this view has been with poets from the beginning. For David and other poets of the Psalms, everything in the world contains God. It is one animating Spirit or Logos in all things that the psalmist celebrates:

> Bless the Lord, O my soul!
> Who has stretched out the heavens like a tent,
> Who hast laid the beams of thy chambers
>   on the waters,
> Who makest the clouds thy chariot,

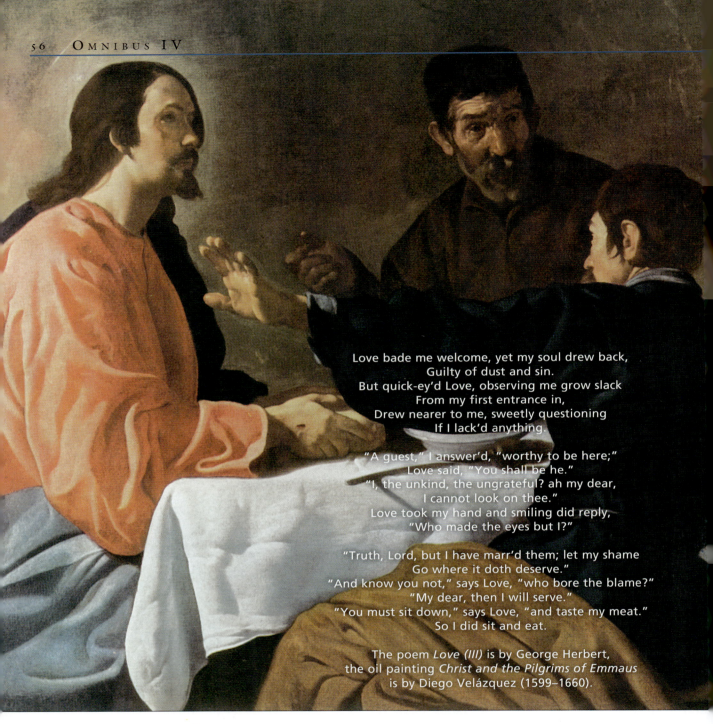

Love bade me welcome, yet my soul drew back,
  Guilty of dust and sin.
But quick-ey'd Love, observing me grow slack
  From my first entrance in,
Drew nearer to me, sweetly questioning
  If I lack'd anything.

"A guest," I answer'd, "worthy to be here;"
  Love said, "You shall be he."
"I, the unkind, the ungrateful? ah my dear,
  I cannot look on thee."
Love took my hand and smiling did reply,
  "Who made the eyes but I?"

"Truth, Lord, but I have marr'd them; let my shame
  Go where it doth deserve."
"And know you not," says Love, "who bore the blame?"
  "My dear, then I will serve."
"You must sit down," says Love, "and taste my meat."
  So I did sit and eat.

The poem *Love (III)* is by George Herbert,
the oil painting *Christ and the Pilgrims of Emmaus*
is by Diego Velázquez (1599–1660).

Who ridest on the wings of the wind,
Who makest the winds thy messengers,
  fire and flame thy ministers. (Ps. 104)

This tradition has certainly been part of poetry in English from its origins to the present. As Emerson put it, "the universe becomes transparent, and the light of higher laws than its own shines through it."

In a suggestively similar verse, the apostle James wrote, "Every good gift and every perfect gift is from above, and cometh down from the Father of Lights, with whom is no variableness, neither shadow of turning." This stunningly beautiful sentence helps remind us that poetry (and all the arts) are some of those perfect, or nearly perfect, gifts from above, from the Father of Lights. We noted earlier that poetry delights and instructs. It gives us knowledge about our world and ourselves, and stimulates us to empathize with other people and cultures. It can motivate us to good works and inspire us to seek God.

Poetry does all of these things, but one of the most important things it does is not often discussed: our imaginative response to a poem may give us an epiphany, a shining forth, a sudden intuition or realization, a communion not easy to express. As nearly perfect things, with all their parts fitting together as one, poems (and other works of art) help us to forget ourselves and experience a unity, a completeness, a wholeness, for a minute or an hour. Bruno Barnhart, a Camaldolese monk, calls this a "unitive" experience, a kind of aesthetic foretaste of the union or communion we can experience with God. In a sense, every work of art is complete, an end in itself, and invites us into its perfection. As Bruno says," It shines." As in religious experience, we forget our incomplete, divided selves, and for a moment are made one with what we are reading, looking at, or listening to. This unitive experience can lead us to see beyond the work of art itself to what shines through it—the world of meaning and spirit. Poetry may help us find such moments in the ordinary (and extraordinary) things in the world that surround us every day. Everything from a blade of grass, a stone, a certain slant of light, a human face, a song, a photo from the Hubble telescope, or a poem.

William Blake is one who understood this contemplative connection. He invites us,

To see a World in a Grain of Sand
And a Heaven in a Wild Flower
Hold infinity in the palm of your hand
And eternity in an hour.

To see a world in a grain of sand or a heaven in a wild flower, we must forget ourselves and become one with it.

Poetry and the arts are no substitute for religion, but traditionally a servant to her. The experience of beauty, or esthetic contemplation, especially the unitive experience, may lead us toward union with God. Simone Weil, a brilliant, and skeptical, young philosopher, was converted while reciting George Herbert's poem "Love III," which she had memorized for its beauty. While reciting it to herself one day, she later wrote,

Christ himself came down and took possession of me. In my arguments about the insolubility of the problem of God I had never foreseen the possibility of that, of a real contact, person to person, here below, between a human being and God."

—*Simone Weil,* Waiting for God

Her witness reminds us that the experience of beauty must finally point beyond itself or it can degenerate into mere estheticism. Like images of Paradise, it points to a Heaven beyond itself.

The English poet-priest Gerard Manley Hopkins wrote poetry filled with epiphanies in the ordinary and extraordinary. He found them even under the smoke-choked sky of nineteenth century Birmingham: "The world is charged with the grandeur of God" he wrote,

It will flame out, like shining from shook foil.
. . . .
Because the Holy Ghost over the bent
World broods with warm breast and with ah!
 bright wings.

The moment of epiphany leads Hopkins to praise God, delighting in every detail of creation in all its enormous and particular variety. Here is "Pied Beauty," where he celebrates a spotted cow, rose moles on a trout, and even a workman's ordinary tools:

Glory be to God for dappled things—
 For skies of couple-colour as a brinded cow;
  For rose-moles all in stipple upon trout
   that swim;
Fresh-firecoal chestnut-falls; finches' wings;
 Landscape plotted and pieced—fold, fallow,
  and plough;
  And all trades, their gear and tackle and trim.

All thing counter, original, spare, strange;
 Whatever is fickle, freckled (who knows how?)
  With swift, slow; sweet, sour; adazzle, dim:
He fathers-forth whose beauty is past change:
             Praise him.

The moment of epiphany leads to praise. Like the psalmists, Hopkins continually praises God for the natural world. Thoreau said that most of us spend our lives pushing our house and barn in front of us. Or we may spend our lives pushing other peoples' houses and barns, never pausing to contemplate finches wings or rose moles upon a trout. We push ahead, ignoring these promises of paradise, these foretastes of divine union. The unitive experience in poetry can lead us toward what Brother Lawrence, famous for practicing the presence of God in the kitchen among the pots and pans, called "the simple gaze: that loving sight of God everywhere present that is the most holy, the most solid, the easiest, the most efficacious manner of prayer." The exercise of the imagination through poetry can help us to discover that loving sight. The union with beauty through poetry may lead us to better experience our union with God in Christ.

When you enter college, your interest in poetry and other literature may lead you to major in English. This means that you'll read plenty of literature in other genres besides poetry: notably fiction (the short story and novel), essays, and drama. The more you read of the classics in all genres, the better your understanding of them all will be. But the student who learns to read poetry carefully will find his or her ability to read the other genres greatly enhanced. The major in English, handled rightly, can provide an excellent basis for a liberal education. It should help you to think clearly and to express yourself well in speech and writing. It is excellent preparation for law and the ministry, and even business and medicine, to mention only a few fields.

In most English departments, however, you will probably discover that most, if not all, of your professors do not share your faith. In fact, they may go out of their way to let you and the rest of their students know this. You may also discover how much time and effort literary critics spend trying to convince themselves and others that writers who clearly held a belief in the supernatural, did not. My advice is not to rashly challenge this bias when you come across it. Rather, do the reading, write good papers, and impress the instructor with your mastery of the material, so that when you do take exception to some position you will present strong, reasoned arguments that meet with her respect.

To nourish your faith, feed upon the great writers of the past, most of whom have a worldview that supports traditional Judeo-Christian values. Reading through the centuries is a great way to escape what C.S. Lewis called the narrow provincialism of our own age or century.

Definitely take a whole course—a year's course if you can—in Shakespeare. And take a course in Milton. At the end is a list of other writers you might try to read on your own, if you can't get them in class. Don't spend your valuable tuition on the light-weight courses offered in many departments today on pulp fiction, comic books, television series, or other trendy subjects. Look for those courses that take up the great writers of the past.

Take at least one creative writing course where you can write poetry. Writing it is one of the best ways to understand how to read it. Seek out literature courses from writers of poetry and fiction on the faculty. Writers love the literature itself, usually, and are less likely to spend their time on esoteric forms of French criticism or on political agendas of one sort or another. (Feminism, neo-Marxism, and neo-Freudianism, for example, are some recently fashionable critical postures.) Check with other students to find out what actually goes on in a particular class before taking it.

As an English major, you can continue to read the great works for a lifetime. Below is a selected list of poets you might want to come to know in college so that you may continue their acquaintance afterwards. Of the many contemporary poets worth reading, I've listed only an arbitrary few. For more of these, browse anthologies, libraries, bookstores, literary magazines, friends' bookshelves, and the Internet. (Most literary magazines and books can be sampled online.) Happy hunting!

—*Robert Siegel*

SO . . . WHO TO READ?

Following is a selected list of English and American poets: Chaucer, Spenser, Shakespeare, Marlowe, Jonson, Marvell, Donne, Herbert, Vaughan, Traherne, Dryden, Pope, Johnson, Blake, Wordsworth, Coleridge, Byron, Shelley, Keats, Tennyson, Browning, Hopkins, Hardy, Yeats, Auden, Dylan Thomas, Whitman, Dickinson, Frost, Stevens, Williams, Marianne Moore, Eliot, Roethke, Robert Lowell, Plath, Heaney, Heyen, Cairns, Franz Wright, Jeanne Murray Walker

. . . and a few from other languages: Homer, Virgil, Li Po, Du Fu, Dante, St. John of the Cross, Goethe, Rimbaud, Baudelaire, Lorca, Neruda, Czeslaw Milosz

For Further Reading

A History of Modern Poetry: Vols. I and II. David Perkins (Belknap Press).

The Norton Anthology of Modern & Contemporary Poetry, Ellmann, O'Clair, & Ramazani.

The Norton Anthology of Poetry, Ferguson, Salter & Stallworthy.

The Vintage Book of Contemporary American Poetry, ed. J.D. McClatchey.

Western Wind: An Introduction to Poetry, Nims and Mason, (McGraw-Hill)

Writing Poems, Robert Wallace (3rd edition or earlier, Harper Collins).

Endnotes

1   Basho, in *Love and Barley: Haiku by Basho*, trans. Lucien Stryk, Penguin.

2   Shaw, Luci. *Accompanied by Angels: Poems of the Incarnation.* Grand Rapids, Mich.: Wm. B. Eerdmans Publishing Co., 2006.

The Iliad

If there is such a thing as classical literature, and there is, then the *Iliad* has to be considered in the front rank of such literature. This was one of the foundational works for Greek civilization, and it has been a significant player in the formation of our own civilization. It is one of the most studied and praised classical works of all time.

Although it is set in an ancient world, a world largely unknown to us, the great themes of the poem have been accessible to readers ever since the poem was first composed, down to the present. The glory and tragedy of war are as much with us today as they were then, and the temptations ever present in warfare are as relevant to us as they were to Achilleus and Hektor.

The *Iliad*, set in the midst of the Trojan War, is followed by the *Odyssey*, which is Homer's account of Odysseus trying to get home to Ithaka after the war. Normally these works are read and studied in their natural chronological order, but because the *Odyssey* is less difficult and more accessible, that book was studied in *Omnibus I*. Now that we are in *Omnibus IV* and all grown up, it is time to tackle this more challenging work.

GENERAL INFORMATION

Author and Context

We know that Homer was a very great poetic genius, but we know very little else about him. He was blind, as many ancient poets were, and that is almost all we can say. At the same time, some educated speculations are possible. He was probably a Greek from the colonies in Ionia, which means that he lived (generally) where the Trojans used to live. We may remember Mark Twain's joke that we now know that the works of Homer were not by him, but rather were the work of another blind, Greek poet with the same name. Although the dating of his life is also uncertain, we may tentatively follow the dating of Herodotus and place him in the eighth century B.C. This would make him a rough contemporary of the prophet Isaiah. The Trojan War itself happened some several centuries before that.

Significance

What we have to say about the *Iliad* is very similar to what was said about the significance of the *Odyssey*. The central organizing principle of any culture is the religion of that culture. In a certain sense, following the observation of Henry Van Til, we may say that *culture is religion externalized*. But the "carrier" of religion is language, and the standardizing "carrier" of language is literature. And every body of literature has a canonical center. This is why, for example, Homer's *Iliad* had the same kind of impact on ancient Greek culture that the King James Version of the Bible had on seventeenth-century English-speaking peoples. It helped to shape the Greeks into a people, and was a very potent shaping force. Not only was this the case for the Greeks, but because of the position the Greeks had in the history of Western culture, the *Iliad* also has had a continuing effect down to the present. After all, you are studying this work now for a reason.

Main Characters

Achilleus is the main character of this story. Indeed, it would be safe to say the poem is more about the fall of Achilleus than about the fall of Troy. *Hektor* is the champion defender of the Trojans. *Agamemnon* is the commander of the Greek expedition, and one of their chief kings. *Menelaos* is Agamemnon's brother, and the cuckolded husband of Helen. *Odysseus* is one of the leading Greek warriors, a very crafty man. *Patroklos* is the warrior who dies while fighting in Achilleus's armor, fighting in his place. *Diomedes* is another leading Greek warrior. *Paris* is the Trojan prince who ran off with *Helen*, the wife of Menelaos, thus starting the hostilities.

Gods and goddesses who are important in this story are *Zeus, Hera, Ares,* and *Aphrodite*.

Summary and Setting

Some of the back story for this poem is not found in the story itself, but was clearly assumed by all who heard it. Paris was dragooned into being the judge of a beauty contest between three goddesses—Hera, Athene, and Aphrodite—which is *always* a bad idea. If you are ever asked to do this, say *no*, quite firmly. After the competition was underway, the goddesses offered Paris various inducements that would cause him to pick "the right one." Aphrodite, who clearly knew the caliber of her man, offered him the most beautiful woman in the world. That turned out to be Helen, unfortunately already married, but Paris headed back to Troy with her anyway. When Helen was being courted initially by Menelaos, her father had required all the suitors to take an oath that they would come together in an alliance if anybody tried any funny business with Helen. This is why what should have been a private quarrel between Menelaos and Paris turned into a war between the city of Troy and the various city-states of the Greeks.

Near the end of ten years of fighting at Troy, a dispute broke out among the Greeks who had been besieging Troy. Agamemnon was forced by circumstances to give up his war trophy-concubine, which he refused to do unless she was replaced by one of the concubines of the other leaders in the Greek camp. He winds up taking Briseis, the concubine of Achilleus. This infuriates Achilleus, who withdraws from the fighting, thus giving a great temporary advantage to the Trojans. Achilleus, his pride badly stung, refuses to come back into the fighting until Patroklos, fighting in his stead, falls in battle. Achilleus then comes back into the war, kills Hektor, and grossly dishonors his body. Priam, the king of Troy and father of Hektor, comes to Achilleus and begs for the return of the body, which Achilleus finally grants.

The setting of this story is near the fall of Troy, although the city does not fall in the poem. This would place it around 1100 B.C., or shortly before the time of King David, during the period of the judges in the Bible. This would make Hektor and Achilleus and Odysseus contemporaries with the prophet Samuel.

Worldview

Modern Istanbul is 726 miles from modern Jerusalem. This means that ancient Jerusalem was 726 miles from the site where Istanbul now is, which is just down the road a bit from ancient Troy. That means that the prophet Samuel, had he wanted to, could have walked that distance in about a month with his hands in his pockets. Other forms of quicker transportation were available as well, whether by sail or horseback. The point being made here is that the biblical world, so familiar to many Christian students, was a nearby part *of the same world* you will read about here in this epic poem. The gods worshipped by the pagans and the demonic forces opposed by faithful Jews were the same entities. The tactics of warfare were the same. Their methods of transport and manufacturing were the same. Their nations surrounded the same Mediterranean Sea.

It is therefore important for us to begin by reviewing briefly a few of the points made in the worldview essay for the *Odyssey*. First, the student should always remember that the basic framework of religion seen throughout the lines of the *Iliad* is the kind of religion continually opposed in the pages of the Bible. But this opposition does not consist of maintaining that the gods of the heathen were fictitious. No, in the Bible these were evil *realities*. Not every story told of the gods and goddesses was true, obviously, but the Bible does assume the basic reality of such beings, and therefore so should we. In doing this, we do not grant the background claims that the pagans made about the nature of reality, but we do assert that they were distorting some things that really were there.

Basic to the biblical position on God is that of understanding the Creator/creature distinction, with the triune God on one side and all of creation on the other. God transcends the world and is fundamentally distinct from all His creatures. The rival conception to this is necessarily that of a "great chain of being." In this chain, all beings are similar in principle and no great gap exists in the chain anywhere. Some beings are greater and some are lesser, obviously, but all inhabit the same reality. In this kind of belief system, everything runs together at some point—including the concepts of "humanity" and "deity." As I pointed out in the worldview essay on the *Odyssey*, it does not matter how high the staircase goes if each step is just eight inches higher than the previous one.

For the pagan, beings significantly higher on the chain of being were worshipped as gods or goddesses. Thus, rebellious celestials (i.e., demons) or angels were identified as deities, and the uncreated God beyond them all was ignored and forgotten. But for the biblical believer, such celestial beings would be identified as principalities, powers, thrones, demons, etc. In the Bible the existence of such beings is not denied, but the claims made on their behalf (that they are gods in the same way God is) are rejected. Their existence was real; the claims made on their behalf were not.

But still, the Bible does not reserve the use of the word *god* for God alone. God alone is the Most High God, and God alone is the Creator. But the Bible frequently uses the word *gods* to describe creatures on *our* side of the Creator/creature divide (Ps. 82:1, 6–8; Ps. 86:8; Ps. 136:2;

> "No use. Here at last the gods have summoned me deathward.... and now evil death is close to me, and no longer far away, and there is no way out. So it must long since have been pleasing to Zeus, and Zeus' son who strikes from afar, this way; though before this they defended me gladly. But now my death is upon me. Let me at least not die without a struggle, inglorious, but do some big thing first, that men to come shall know of it."—Hektor (22.297–305)

John 10: 34–36). And the gods of the various nations were closely identified with those nations. When you see this kind of thing in the *Iliad*, as you will, you are seeing nothing different from what you see in many of the battles of the Old Testament. The gods have their favorites and their loyalties, and they fight for their cities. For example, in the Bible, angelic beings stand behind the nations of Persia (Dan. 10:13) and Tyre (Ezra 28:11–16).

This is how the apostle Paul summed the whole thing up:

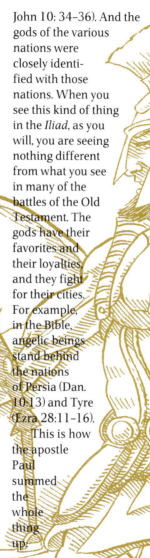

"What am I saying then? That an idol is anything, or what is offered to idols is anything? Rather, that the things which the Gentiles sacrifice they sacrifice to demons and not to God, and I do not want you to have fellowship with demons" (1 Cor. 10:19–20).

Paul is not maintaining that the Gentiles sacrificed to nonexistent beings, but rather to demons masquerading as gods. Thus, we as modern Christians have no reason to dismiss Zeus, Ares, Aphrodite, or Athena. This is very important for the student to remember in reading works like the *Iliad*. At the same time, and this is equally important, it is not this way anymore—because Christ came into this dark, pagan world in order to transform it, which He did. The New Testament speaks of this frequently (Mark 3:27; John 12:31–32; Heb. 2:5–9, 14; 6:5; 1 Cor. 2:6–7; John 16:11; Col. 2:15; Rev. 1:5–6; 11:15). So these celestials were, in some significant sense, mediators and princes. But in the Christian aeon, God has established just one Prince ... and He is one of us, a man—the Lord Jesus. We don't follow the ancient cosmology, not because we don't believe that way anymore, but rather because Christ came and changed everything.

The fact that the Trojan War occurred in the same world that many of our Old Testament stories did also helps us to understand another significant element in the stories—the important matter of giants. Remember that this is the same general time period as that occupied by Goliath from Gath, the man with a spear like a weaver's beam. It should not be surprising that Homer speaks of Hektor's strength in a similar way:

"Meanwhile Hektor snatched up a stone that stood before the gates and carried it along ... two men, the best in all a community, could not easily hoist it up from a ground to a wagon, of men such as men are now, but he alone lifted and shook it" (12.445ff).

What Homer is telling us here is that giants took to the battlefield back in the day, not like *his* day. Something to remember when reading accounts of many of these ancient battles is the likelihood that many of the heroes of old were considered such simply because they were *huge*. In modern warfare, the distinction between generals and foot soldiers is usually that of class, intelligence, experience, and education. But if you stripped them down to their skivvies, you would probably have trouble telling which one was the general and which one the corporal. But in ancient warfare, leadership was a matter of personal prowess in battle—and you would have had no trouble telling the general and the private apart at all.

Saul was chosen as the first king of Israel, and the choice seemed good to many because he was a full head taller than the rest of them. Goliath was a hero of the Philistines, and challenged Israel to produce a similar hero so they could engage in solitary combat. Samson was a judge in Israel, and you could see why at a glance. So it may be helpful, as you are imagining the battles that took place on the plains of Troy, to see the gigantic heroes fighting with one another, and the more ordinary, short little guys fighting with one another. The heroes were larger than life in our imaginations, and always have been. But they were also larger *in* life. The world of the *Iliad* was a world ruled by a warrior caste, a caste which fought for shiny objects, seized beautiful women, lived for honor, and was not really concerned with a quiet and peaceful life. The mentality is that of Achilleus, valuing a short and glorious life over against a long and boring one.

In our democratic age, a popular phrase with us is that of a "level playing field." It is hard to imagine anything in this ancient epic that even *resembles* a level playing field. The prowess and abilities of the warriors varied widely, as just mentioned. But behind the scenes, skewing things still further, in the realm where gods and goddesses intervened, various deities fought for and alongside their favorites. Only Aias fought as a great warrior without the help of any divine on-field coaching. Trying to explain the outcome of a particular battle would therefore have been like trying to predict how a punted football was going to bounce. There are reasons, but none that we have access to. And the ancients, after the fact, when they were explaining why things went as they did, would have had no trouble appealing to the intervention of Athena, or Ares, or Aphrodite. Some of the explanations might have had something to them, while many others were no doubt just convenient.

As mentioned earlier, Troy was not conquered in this poem—the story is really not about the fall of Troy at all. Actually, a more accurate name for this epic would be the *Achillead* because it is really about the tragedy of Achilleus's fall. He is a great hero, with high intelligence, but he is governed by his passion for his honor, and this noble sentiment (in the eyes of his culture) carries him away into disaster. A passion for honor was of course expected of all ancient heroes, and Achilleus was no exception. He was not faulted for that; zeal for honor was not the problem—he was expected to fight with the enemy for honor and glory. But when he was insulted by Agamemnon, his pride was stung in such a way that he was no longer able to govern himself. A hero was expected to be a sailing ship with great sails—filled with a desire for the immortality of fame. But something went seriously wrong here, and the great winds capsized his ship.

The Iliad

In the *Iliad* Briseis is shuttled between Achilleus and Agamemnon. On this pottery Briseis appears with Phoinix.

When Briseis was taken from Achilleus, according to their ancient code of honor, it was reasonable for him to be angry, and even to abandon his support of the siege of Troy. He wanted to show how much he was needed and how foolish Agamemnon was for insulting a warrior who was so badly needed by his army. But Achilleus stuck to his position long *after* his legitimate and reasonable point was made. Agamemnon saw the error of his foolish demand, returned Briseis to Achilleus with a vow that he had not touched her, and yet Achilleus was still unable to let go of his anger. "It is the anger of pride, the necessary accompaniment of the warrior's greatness that springs the tragedy of the *Iliad*. We see it in the treatment of Hektor's body and the slaughter of the captives; we see it motivate the quarrel of the first book, where the fourth word of the first line is 'anger'" (Lattimore, p. 47). Achilleus even *admits* that he is in the wrong (9.645–647), and yet he is helpless to correct himself.

And then, when the Trojans come close to the ships of the Greeks, there is no reason for Achilleus to stay out of the fight, even according to the terms he had set down in his angry pride. But he lets Patroklos fight in his place, and as a result Patroklos dies. Achilleus is furious, but he is the reason it happened. But in his anger he not only kills Hektor, he also disgraces his body afterward. But Patroklos died for two reasons—one because Hektor fought him as an enemy, and second because Achilleus had deserted him as a friend. In short, Achilleus's savage anger against Hektor is disproportionate and entirely misplaced. Through the course of the poem, he spirals downward into a number of actions far beneath where he as a noble warrior ought to have been. His behavior becomes thuggish, and the tragedy is that Achilleus was no thug.

The story ends with Priam coming to Achilleus as a suppliant, asking to ransom Hektor's body. Achilleus grants

The Judgment of Paris was a favorite subject for Lucas Cranach the Elder (1472–1553) as well as many other artists throughout history like Picasso, Burne-Jones, Raimondi, Feuerbach, Dali, and Rubens. A good friend of Martin Luther's, Cranach is also known for his religious art, including woodcuts that he made for the first German edition of the New Testament in 1522.

the request, and Priam and Achilleus weep together. Achilleus even provides Priam with a bed, and grants the Trojans a twelve-day truce so they might conduct Hektor's funeral. In this Achilleus relents, but this is not the same thing as a biblical repentance. There is a hint that he may have recovered from his runaway pride, but the audience still knows what is coming next. Achilleus is going to die—not only will he die, but he will die as a result of an ignoble arrow wound in the heel. Not only will he die of that scarcely heroic wound, but the warrior who shot that deadly arrow will turn out to be Paris, of all people. So the last book in this epic poem could be read as a hint of Achilleus recovering his senses. But it could also be read as the ominous silence before the final (offstage) tragedies. Priam will be returning to the city that will fall and be utterly destroyed. Achilleus is going to return to the battlefield where he will die at the hand of an adulterer and pretty boy. The rage of Achilleus, even though it has abated by the end of the poem, was still going on in its destructive consequences.

A secondary hero in this story is Hektor, fighting for the Trojans. His temptation is not exactly the same as that of Achilleus, but the result of his capitulation to his temptation is exactly the same. He *also* fights in a way that is far beneath him, and he does so knowing that this is what he is doing. Like Achilleus, he knows what is right, but he cannot bring himself to do it. Both Hektor and Achilleus are trapped. Hektor knew that Paris had no right to Helen, and he knew that the Trojans were completely in the wrong to have provided Paris with a refuge and to have taken up his cause as their own. This is what Hektor said to Paris about it:

> "No, but the Trojans are cowards in truth, else long before this you had worn a mantle of flying stones for the wrong you did us" (3.56–57).

Put another way, Hektor knew that the *Greek* cause was just, and that Menelaos had a legitimate grievance with Paris. He knew further that Paris had no right to the protection of Troy, and that Troy provided him with that protection anyway. Troy, and he as a leading prince of Troy, were engaged in fighting an unjust war, *and they knew it.* Even though it was a defensive war, it could have been averted or stopped at any time if Helen were simply returned to the Greeks. This they refused to do out of pride, and their tragic flaw was thus very similar to the flaw that brought Achilleus down. Achilleus would not swallow his pride, and Troy would not swallow hers.

But Hektor himself was motivated more by shame than pride. He was not afraid of battle; he was a fine warrior. But when his wife Andromache begged him not to go back into battle, his reply was revealing. He said he would feel "deep shame" if "like a coward" he shrank from the fighting (6.441–445). He was no coward in the ordinary sense, but he *was* afraid of being thought a coward. This fear of shame was deep enough to drive him to fight as an honorable prince in a very dishonorable cause.

In studying works like the *Iliad*, I never tire of reminding my students that *this is the world into which Christ came.* The astute student should come to see and understand the ancient pagan assumptions that Christ has removed forever, not in order to adopt them himself, but rather to add his own personal Amen to the rejection of them. At the same time, there is much that may be appreciated and loved. By God's common grace, the ancient pagans were able to produce literature of unbelievable beauty. That beauty can and should be appreciated. Once understood and appreciated, it may be safely appropriated and put to good use in the service of the kingdom of God. Good writers are not only good readers; they are also readers *who read good writing.* The early church fathers compared this activity to plundering gold from the Egyptians, taking what is truly valuable from Pharaoh, and putting it under the authority of Moses. But we have to be careful in ways that the early Israelites were not. God did give them favor in the sight of the Egyptians, and much gold was in fact given to them by the Egyptians (Ex. 3:22). But that same gold was later used to make a golden calf (Ex. 32:4), which means that many of the Israelites had brought a good deal more out of Egypt than just the gold. This means that the gold can be a temptation, even when it really is gold. Further, it should go without saying that the temptation is even greater when we waste valuable time watching reality television shows, which can be compared to dumpster-diving in Egypt—no gold to be found anywhere.

Just a quick note on some of the features of the poetry: the *Iliad* is epic poetry, which is formulaic poetry. Because it is a very long poem, and has the settled meter of dactylic hexameter, the recurrence of certain phrases should not really be a surprise. These phrases recur for the sake of the meter— brilliant Achilleus, crafty Odysseus, white-armed Hera, and so on. Dactylic hexameter is the basic *heroic line* for the epic in the original Greek. This is very difficult to make work in English, although some have tried from time to time. Here is an approximation of that meter in English: *strawberry strawberry strawberry strawberry strawberry jam pot.*

In sum, considering this poem as a whole, the Christian student should seek to appreciate and enjoy the beauty of the poetry, appreciating what is noble and good about it. But he should not be fooled. C.S. Lewis said somewhere that the genius of Homer took the granite of despair, and shined it up to look like marble.

—*Douglas Wilson*

For Further Reading

Leithart, Peter. *Heroes of the City of Man.* Moscow, Idaho: Canon Press, 1999. 53–84.

Spielvogel, Jackson J. *Western Civilization.* Seventh Edition. Belmont, Calif.: Thomson Wadsworth, 2009. 57–60.

Veritas Press History Cards: *New Testament, Greece and Rome.* Lancaster, Pa.: Veritas Press. 3, 6.

Session I: Prelude

A Question to Consider

Is it really fear to be afraid of being thought afraid by others?

From the General Information above, answer the following questions:
1. What is this poem not about?
2. What is the basic theme of this poem?
3. When is the poem set? Who are some biblical contemporaries?
4. Why does Achilleus withdraw from battle?
5. Is his anger reasonable?
6. When did Homer live?
7. Was the cause of Troy just?
8. Why does Hektor continue to fight, even though his heart is not in it?
9. Was the contest of heroes conducted on a level playing field?

Optional Activity

Memorize the first ten lines of the *Iliad*.

 **Reading Assignment:**
Book 1

Session II: Discussion
Book 1

A Question to Consider

Think about one of your heroes. How would you like to become like that person? Do we become like those whom we admire? How? Do we become like the god(s) we worship?

Discuss or list short answers to the following questions:

Text Analysis

1. Read aloud the first 105 lines of Book I. Count the number of times a form of the word "anger" is used. To whom does it refer?
2. Why is Apollo angry? What is he doing as a result of his anger?
3. Why is Agamemnon angry?
4. What is the stated theme of the *Iliad*?
5. Why is Achilleus so angry?

The Iliad

Judgement of Paris was created by the artist Peter Paul Rubens and was commissioned for the Spanish court. The oil-on-canvas painting was completed in 1638–39 and now hangs in the Museo del Prado in Madrid. Aphrodite is in the center and is supposedly a likeness of the artist's wife. Peter Paul Rubens was quite a prolific Flemish painter of the seventeenth century. His paintings, often of mythological themes, tended to emphasize color and sensuality.

Cultural Analysis

1. What were the Greek gods like?
2. If you can remember back to the good old days of *Omnibus I*, in what ways were the Greeks just like their gods?
3. What are the gods of our culture?
4. How has our culture become like those gods?

Biblical Analysis

1. In Psalm 115:1–7, what does the writer say about idols?
2. What does Psalm 115:8 teach about the relationship between these idols and those who worship them?
3. What does 2 Corinthians 3:18 teach about the relationship between God and believers?
4. What does 1 Corinthians 10:18–22 teach about the nature of false gods?
5. What is the clear implication of these passages?

SUMMA

Write an essay or discuss this question, integrating what you have learned from the material above.
What is the connection between the anger of Apollo and the anger of Achilleus? Do we become like the god(s) we worship? How might this apply to both individuals and entire cultures?

OPTIONAL ACTIVITY

A Bee In The Mouth

What would it be like to have a bee in your mouth? In the past, Christians have preached and practiced virtues like self-control and restraint. Today, many seem to think that expressing rage is, if not a constitutional right, at least the healthiest choice. We are told to let our anger out. Peter Wood recently has written a book called *A Bee in the Mouth: Anger in America Now*. It is a fine read for mature readers in a culture where rage is all the rage.

READING ASSIGNMENT:
Book 2

SESSION III: AESTHETICS

The Judgement of Paris by Rubens

In this session, you will get to know a particular piece or type of art related to our reading. It is our job as believers to be able to praise, love, and protect what is beautiful and to condemn, hate, and oppose all that is truly ugly. This task is often harder than we think. We have to discipline ourselves to first examine and understand the piece reflectively. After we understand the content of a piece, we can examine the author's intention concerning the piece and attempt to figure out what the piece of art is communicating. Sometimes this will be easy; other times it will be difficult or impossible. Finally, we need to make a judgment about what this work of art communicates. Sometimes we will be able to clearly condemn a work of art as untrue, badly done or wicked. Sometimes we will be able to praise a work as glorious, majestic, and true. Oftentimes, however, we will find ourselves affirming some parts of a work and condemning others. Remember, maturity is harder than immaturity—but also more rewarding. Also, remember that our praise or condemnation means more when we have disciplined ourselves to first reflect on the content and meaning of a work.

Questions on the content and meaning of the work:
1. What is most striking about the artist's abilities?
2. What is happening here? (Review Summary and Setting of the essays.)
3. Do you notice someone in the sky pointing toward the right? Any thoughts as to who this might be?
4. Is this work life-like?
5. Compare the Cranach rendition of the *Judgement of Paris* to Rubens'. How do the artists' depictions of costume in these paintings affect the way we relate to them?

Writing and Debate

We use the Latin term *in medias res* to describe the way Homer writes. It means "into the middle of things." You may remember this from reading the *Odyssey* in *Omnibus I*. No background, no history—the story begins with Odysseus stranded, lonely and weeping on an island with the goddess Kalypso. You do not find out until later how he got there and why he is so sad. Homer is doing the same thing here in the *Iliad*. The story begins with an argument between two Greek leaders, Agamemnon and Achilleus, who are far from home fighting in a war. You find out later all about Helen and Paris and why they are there.

We have discussed the painting, the beauty contest, and Paris. But why exactly were they having this beauty contest? What prompted it? Do some research and find out why it all began and write a "Once upon a time" version of the whole story from beginning to end. Once we have put all the pieces together, we will attempt to answer the question, "Who was the real cause of the Trojan War?" You can do this research using one of the books you will be reading later in the year, *Mythology* by Edith Hamilton (Book IV, chap. I).

Our next session will be a student-led discussion.

As you are reading the following assignment, you should write down at least three questions from the text dealing with the issue listed below. These questions will be turned in to the teacher and will be used in classroom discussion. To get full credit for these Text Analysis questions you must create a question that is connected to the reading and to the issue that is the focus of our discussion; you must also answer the question correctly (and include a page or line reference at the end); and your question must be one that invites discussion and debate ("why" questions are excellent; questions that can be answered by "yes" or "no" are to be avoided).

You should also provide two Cultural Analysis and two Biblical Analysis questions. Cultural Analysis questions ask how our culture views the issue that we are discussing. Biblical Analysis questions ask what the Bible says concerning this issue. Again, to get full credit for each question, you must create questions connected to the issue we are studying, answer each question correctly and create questions that encourage and invite discussion and exploration. For an example of each type of question and answer refer to the examples provided in the next session.

If you are working alone, after creating your questions and answers, have your parent or tutor check over them. Also, if possible, share them with your family at the dinner table, helping them to understand why the issue is important, how the issue arises in your reading, how its importance is still evident in our culture, and how understanding this issue might change the way you and your family should think and live.

Issue

What separates the men from the boys?

READING ASSIGNMENT:
Book 3

SESSION IV: STUDENT-LED DISCUSSION
Book 3

A Question to Consider

What separates the men from the boys?

Students should read and consider the example questions below that are connected to the Question to Consider above. Last session's assignment was to prepare three questions and answers for the Text Analysis section and two additional questions and answers for both the Cultural and Biblical Analysis sections below.

Text Analysis

Example: What proposal does Paris make to end the war?

Answer: He challenges any Greek who will take him on in single combat. When Menelaos steps forward to take him up on his offer, he has second thoughts (2.1–75).

Cultural Analysis

Example: Based on the advertising that bombards you, what is the most prevalent image of a manly man?

Answer: The manly man in our culture is either drinking beer and hanging out with beautiful women, or he is busy showing his brawn by beating up on someone.

Other cultural issues to consider: Other images of a true man. What are his goals? Aspirations? What does the culture view as a wimpy man?

Biblical Analysis

Example: Consider David in 1 Samuel 16 and 17. What qualities make him a truly manly man?

Answer: Even though he was not the tallest of the brothers, he was fearless and tough. He was in the habit of killing large animals when he tended sheep. He bravely took on Goliath and brought down the man that our very culture would hail as the manly man. At the same time, he was a man after God's own heart. He was no wimp, and he loved God with great passion.

Other Scriptures to consider: In pondering the biblical teaching on what constitutes a manly man, there are two avenues to explore: a. examples of godly men like Abraham, Moses, Joshua, and Paul. b. passages that describe a manly man like 1 Timothy 3:1–7 and Titus 1–2.

SUMMA

Write an essay or discuss this question, integrating what you have learned from the material above.
What separates the men from the boys?

READING ASSIGNMENT:
Book 4

SESSION V: RECITATION
Books 1–3

Comprehensive Questions

Answer these questions for factual recall.
1. What is the stated theme of the *Iliad*?
2. What argument is going on at the beginning of the book? What role does Apollo play?
3. To whom does Achilleus appeal? What is his request?
4. What dream does Zeus send to Agamemnon? What happens the next day?

5. When the troops decide to go back to Greece, who calls them back? What reminder does he give them?
6. Once the leaders are convinced of victory and make the final decision to stay and fight, what does the Poet request of the Muses?
7. What brilliant idea does Paris propose to end the war?
8. What is Helen doing before the fight between Paris and Menelaos?
9. How does the single combat end?
10. What is Helen's response to Paris?

Reading Assignment:
Book 5

Session VI: Debate

The story of the Trojan War is told by several writers of the ancient world, and the details are not always the same. Remember Herodotus from *Omnibus I*? He claims that Paris never made it back to Troy with Helen. Rather, their ship was blown off course and landed in Egypt. When the Greeks arrived at Troy and demanded the return of Helen, the Trojans were actually telling the truth when they said she was not there. The Greeks, thinking the Trojans were mocking them, attacked, burned the city and only then discovered that Helen was not there. Menelaos then went to Egypt, recovered his bride, and returned to Sparta (*Histories*, 2.113–120).

Euripides throws a fascinating twist to the story in his play, *Helen*, claiming that because Hera was so upset at not being chosen the "fairest of all," she gave Paris a ghost-like image of Helen, an "airy delusion" that fooled him enough into carrying her (it) back to Troy. Hermes carried off the real Helen to Egypt to remain pure until her husband could arrive and rescue her. After sacking the city of Troy, Menelaos was blown off course and landed in—yes, you guessed it—Egypt (a common theme in the ancient world was getting blown off course and landing in Egypt). When he realized that the real Helen was there, he quickly "broke up" with the ghost version and made away with his bride back to Sparta.

So, what really happened? We are going to have a debate over which is the most believable version of the story. Since we do not know for sure what actually transpired, we are debating which makes the most sense.

If you are working alone, choose either Homer or Herodotus. Write down your arguments and share your conclusions with your parents. Before you share your arguments, make sure to explain the issue of the debate to your family. Be ready to answer questions concerning the strong points for the other side of the argument.

Divide the class into two groups: Homer vs. Herodotus. Structure the debate in the following manner:

Opening Statement: Homer
Herodotus questions Homer
Opening Statement: Herodotus
Homer questions Herodotus
Allow for rebuttals when necessary.
Closing Statement: Homer
Closing Statement: Herodotus

Reading Assignment:
Books 6 and 7

Optional Activity

Creative Writing

Write your own alternate version of the story that you believe explains all the facts.

Session VII: Activity
Books 1–7

Current Events

We are going to do a bit of a twist on the typical current events session. Instead of dealing with current events in our day, we are going to focus on current events of the time in which the Trojan War was fought.

If you could have been in Troy to read the *Trojan Times*, what would it have said? Well, let's find out. We are going to actually create the *Trojan Times*, complete with front page, editorials, international news and, of course, the best part of any newspaper, the comic strips!

Divide the class into groups and assign the various categories you wish to create and include in the newspaper. Some suggestions are listed above. Consider adding the following: religious news, sports, financial news and obituaries. The teacher may need to give each group more than one category depending on the number of students involved. A student working alone can pick a few of the options and put the paper together. Once all the parts are done compile them into a completed *Trojan Times*.

Focus on the following specifically:

International news: Refer back to the Worldview Essay for contemporary events recorded in the Old Testament.

Headlines: Draw from Books 4–7 in the *Iliad* for the front-page headlines.

Editorials: express opinions about world events.

Religious News: Articles that focus specifically on the actions of the gods

Obituaries: Quite a few characters die in Books 4–7. Do a write-up on several of them in the form of obituaries.

Comic Strips: Have some fun with this one. Make up some comic strips that might have proved comic relief for both the Greeks and the Trojans. Go ahead and throw one in from the Egyptians!

Once you have completed all the parts of the *Trojan Times,* compile it all into a newspaper form. Make use of desktop publishing software, if available.

If working alone, do an abbreviated version with a front page and a couple of articles. If you are part of a group of homeschoolers doing *Omnibus IV,* assign the various parts in the same manner and put it all together.

READING ASSIGNMENT:
Books 8–9

SESSION VIII: RECITATION
Books 4–9

Comprehensive Questions

Answer these questions for factual recall.
1. What does Zeus send Athene to do? How does she do it?
2. What does Diomedes do as a result of being wounded?
3. What man/god combination drives the Greeks back into retreat?
4. What two men on opposing sides meet and have a chat on the battlefield? What do they discuss? How does the conversation end?
5. With whom does Hektor converse? What is the content of these conversations?
6. Who agrees to a duel with Hektor? How does it end?
7. What Trojan offers a proposal that will end the war? What is his proposal? How is it received?
8. When the gods meet in council, what command does Zeus give the gods?
9. Which two goddesses disobey Zeus's command? What is the result?
10. What does Agamemnon decide to do after the speeches of Diomedes and Nestor?
11. How does Achilleus respond?

READING ASSIGNMENT:
Book 10

SESSION IX: DISCUSSION
Books 9–10

A Question to Consider

What's the biggest decision you have ever made? Did you seek counsel? If not, should you have sought the advice of someone in making this decision?

Discuss or list short answers to the following questions:

Text Analysis
1. What three men among the Greeks go to Achilleus to advise him?
2. What are they advising Achilleus to do?
3. What reasons does Odysseus offer? How does Achilleus respond?
4. What is Phoinix's counsel to Achilleus? How does Achilleus respond?
5. Finally, what does Aias say to Achilleus? How does Achilleus respond?

Cultural Analysis
1. What are the biggest decisions that are common to most people? How do you think most people make those big decisions?
2. Do most people focus on the long-term ramifications of big choices? Why or why not?
3. Why do you think some people find it difficult to seek counsel of others?

Biblical Analysis
1. In 1 Kings 12, Rehoboam has to make a great decision. Whose counsel does he seek? Whose counsel does he accept and follow? What is the result?
2. Seeking counsel is a significant theme in the book of Proverbs. Read the following passages and relate what they teach about this issue: Proverbs 1:5; 11:14; 12:15; 13:10; 15:22; 19:20; 24:6.
3. Based on the Proverbs passages above as well as Psalm 37:4 and Philippians 4:6-7, lay out a plan for making a big decision like where to go to college, whom to marry or changing careers.

Summa

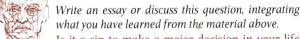

Write an essay or discuss this question, integrating what you have learned from the material above.

Is it a sin to make a major decision in your life without seeking counsel? If so, what are the consequences? From what you know of the rest of the *Iliad*, discuss the ripple effects of Achilleus's decision to reject wise counsel.

Reading Assignment:
Books 11–12

Session X: Writing
Dear Aphrodite . . .

Throughout the *Iliad* we see that gods and goddesses are influencing men to do and say things. In the reading you just completed, Zeus sends Iris to influence Hektor's decisions (Book 11) and also inspires Sarpedon in Book 12. In Book 2 Zeus sends Agamemnon a dream in an attempt to encourage him to attack, and in Book 3 Aphrodite saves Paris from certain death at the hands of Menelaos.

But who is it that is actually influencing humans when "false gods" are doing this? Paul discusses the true nature of false gods in 1 Corinthians 10, calling them demons. So, when false gods communicate with men, it is really demons communicating with men. We know that demons do not have man's best interests at heart.

C.S. Lewis provides striking insight into the communications and plans of demons in his book *The Screwtape Letters*. In this book an elder demon, Screwtape, writes letters advising his nephew Wormwood as to how to manipulate his "patient." You may remember this book from *Omnibus I*.

We are going to write a letter from one demon (let's call him Zeus) to another, advising him on how to manipulate humans to bring about their desired ends. Choose an incident in Books 1–12 in which a god or goddess has intervened in the affairs of man. Remember, this is a "behind the curtain" view of what's *really* going on. What we read is Homer's perspective, and he certainly did not have our insight that these "gods" were actually demonic forces. In your letter be sure you include the advice coming from the higher demon and also the true "why" of the action, not the reason given in the story. You also might want to include a section in which the elder demon is advising as to how the action should come across to the poets as they write their epics.

Reading Assignment:
Book 13

Session XI: Writing
Homeric Similes

One of the fascinating aspects to Homer's work is his unique use of the simile. When we use similes we typically use the words "like" or "as," and we end it with one phrase; for example, *He shouted like a crazed beast after sacking the quarterback.* Not Homer! As you may have noticed, Homer's similes often go on and on and on and on.

Read these examples from the Iliad *and then answer the questions that follow.*

A description of the army moving out and preparing for battle:

> So he spoke and led the way departing from
>   the council,
> and the rest rose to their feet, the sceptred kings,
>   obeying
> the shepherd of the people, and the army
>   thronged behind them.
> Like the swarms of clustering bees that
>   issue forever
> in fresh bursts from the hollow in the stone,
>   and hang like
> bunched grapes as they hover beneath the
>   flowers in springtime
> fluttering in swarms together this way and
>   that way,
> so the many nations of men from the ships
>   and the shelters
> along the front of the deep sea beach marched
>   in order
> by companies to the assembly . . . (2.84–93)

Paris confronting Menelaos:

> But Alexandros the godlike when he saw
>   Menelaos
> showing among the champions, the heart
>   was shaken within him;
> to avoid death he shrank into the host of his
>   own companions.
> As a man who has come on a snake in the
>   mountain valley
> suddenly steps back, and the shivers come
>   over his body,
> and he draws back and away, cheeks seized
>   with a green pallor;

so in terror of Atreus' son
    godlike Alexandros
lost himself again in the host
    of the haughty Trojans.
(3.30–37)

Other examples are found in 2.459–543 and 5.159–178.

1. What are Homer's similes about?
2. For many of his similes Homer uses images from nature that would have been familiar to his readers. Why do you think he does this?
3. What effect do Homer's similes have on the story?
4. Why do you think some of them are so long?

Writing Your Own Homeric Similes
1. Choose a section in the book we have already read and fill in the text with a Homeric simile.
2. Write a few of your own Homeric similes using themes that would appeal more to a twenty-first century audience. Your topic can be either a scene from the *Iliad* (preferably from more recent reading) or one you create.

The next session will be a student-led discussion. Students will be creating their own questions concerning the issue of the session. Students should create three Text Analysis Questions, two Cultural Analysis questions, and two Biblical Analysis questions. For more detailed instructions, please see Session III.

Issue:

Do the soldiers in the *Iliad* have free will?

A detail from *The Loves of Paris and Helen* by Neoclassical French painter Jacques-Louis David (1748–1825). In the full painting, a statue of Aphrodite is included as well as two wreaths of myrtle—an emblem of conjugal fidelity. In a preliminary drawing for the painting Cupid flew near the lovers to further underscore the theme of love in the artwork.

Reading Assignment:
Book 14

Session XII: Student-Led Discussion
Books 1–14

A Question to Consider

Do the soldiers in the *Iliad* have free will? What exactly does it mean to have free will?

Students should read and consider the example questions below that are connected to the Question to Consider above. Last session's assignment was to prepare three questions and answers for the Text Analysis section and two additional questions and answers for both the Cultural and Biblical Analysis sections below.

Text Analysis

Example: What involvement does Poseidon have in the action in Book 14?

Answer: Hera seduces Zeus to take him out of the action, and thus Poseidon is freed up to lead the Greeks in battle (14.159–387).

Cultural Analysis

Example: What is the common view of fate in our culture?

Answer: Even people who do not believe in God seem to have an understanding that something greater than they are controls their lives. They may call it "fate" or "the Force."

Other cultural issues to consider: How do people behave if they have resigned to "fate"? What do they believe is behind fate? Do they believe it is personal or impersonal? Do most people believe in any form of "fate working along with individual responsibility"?

We often hear of someone committing a terrible crime and blaming their dysfunctional family and upbringing. We also hear of someone who commits adultery and lives as though this is the will of God: "I love her. How could it be wrong? How could God possibly not be in this? It feels so right!"

Biblical Analysis

Example: Consider Romans 9–11. Is God in control of all things? If so, does this mean we have no responsibility for our actions?

Answer: Yes, God is indeed in control of all things, but the Bible clearly teaches that we are responsible for what we do.

Other Scriptures to consider: Proverbs 16:1, 9, 33; Romans 8:28; Ephesians 1:11.

In these passages be sure to address a common objection made to the sovereignty of God—namely, that if God is in control of all things, then we must surely be puppets, and He is the puppeteer moving our strings and making us do whatever He wants. Is that a true view of things?

Summa

Write an essay or discuss this question, integrating what you have learned from the material above.
How are our lives like or not like the soldiers in the *Iliad*?

Reading Assignment:
Books 15 and 16

Session XIII: Activity
Books 15 and 16

Debate

Using the rules below, debate the following question: *Whose fault is the death of Patroklos, Achilleus or Patroklos himself?*

Split into two teams of roughly equal size. Amend the following rules for the debate as suits your needs.

Rules

For a school setting:

Turn the students' chairs so that each team is facing the other.

Each side will speak for no more than two minutes before letting the other side speak.

The teacher will make sure that during the course of the debate everyone speaks, which may involve calling on quieter students.

The teacher will give one point for every helpful comment given; two points will be given if what the student says is particularly insightful or if the student points out a logical fallacy the other team has committed.

One point will be taken away if any student speaks out of turn. Though the students must remain quiet, they will be permitted to communicate through written notes to help them consult during the debate.

Remember that reasons are required. A statement without a reason is an opinion and does not contribute to your side.

If you intend to have a formal debate (with opening statements, closing statements, rebuttals, etc.), then the

The Iliad 75

students will need to determine who will speak when. After each side is prepared, determine who will go first. Then proceed with the debate.

For a homeschool setting:
If more than one student is doing this reading, follow the rules above, but move back and forth between the students representing the different points of view. If there is only one student, you could:

Meet with someone in your area to have your own debate.

Have Mom or Dad represent the opposite side of the debate.

Have the student represent both sides of the debate, but give them a short time for looking over their notes between presentations (you would also allow longer times than two minutes in this option because there is no need to back and forth).

The student may write out what he would say as a "position paper" for the debate.

READING ASSIGNMENT: Book 17

SESSION XIV: RECITATION
Books 10–17

Comprehensive Questions

Answer these questions for factual recall.
1. Who agrees to spy on the Trojans? What is the result of their expedition?
2. As Hektor is killing Greeks and Odysseus and Diomedes are killing Trojans, who takes Diomedes out of action?
3. What god is helping the Greeks?
4. What plot does Hera hatch to assist the Greeks?
5. What results from Hera's assistance of the Greeks?

"So much stronger am I than the gods, and stronger than mortals."
—Zeus (8.27)

6. Who is Patroklos? Why is he weeping? What request does he make of Achilleus?
7. How does Achilleus respond to his request? What warning does he give?
8. Does Patroklos heed the warning? How does it all end?
9. What are Patroklos's last words?
10. What happens to Patroklos's body?

The next session will be a student-led discussion. Students will be creating their own questions concerning the issue of the session. Students should create three Text Analysis Questions, two Cultural Analysis questions, and two Biblical Analysis questions. For more detailed instructions, please see Session III.

Issue

How are others affected when we slack off?

READING ASSIGNMENT:
Books 18 and 19

Session XV:
Student-Led Discussion
Book 16

A Question to Consider

How are others affected when we slack off?

Students should read and consider the example questions below that are connected to the Question to Consider above. Last session's assignment was to prepare three questions and answers for the Text Analysis section and two additional questions and answers for both the Cultural and Biblical Analysis sections below.

Text Analysis

Example: Why is Achilleus not fighting? What is the mood of Patroklos when he comes to him at the beginning of Book 16 and why?

Answer: Achilleus is not fighting because he remains stubborn in his resolve that he has been wronged by Agamemnon over the concubine incident. When Patroklos comes to Achilleus, he is weeping. He is in great anguish because the Greeks are losing the war (16.1–48).

Cultural Analysis

Example: Do you think most people think they are affecting others when they sin?

Answer: No. It is common for people to believe their sin is a private matter and not the business of anyone else and that they are not hurting anyone else with their actions.

Other cultural issues to consider: How is this issue dealt with in the workplace? In sports? How about a woman who makes certain health choices when pregnant? For example, what happens when a woman smokes or drinks alcohol during a pregnancy? What about a woman who simply does not eat well during a pregnancy?

Biblical Analysis

Example: Consider Achan in Joshua 6–7. What happened to others as a result of Achan's sin?

Answer: Because of Achan's disobedience, men died in battle and his family was stoned along with him (Joshua 7:1–16).

Other Scriptures to consider: Adam in Genesis 3; David in 2 Samuel 11–13; and Solomon in 1 Kings.

SUMMA

Write an essay or discuss this question, integrating what you have learned from the material above.
What are the affects of our sin on others?

The next session will be a student-led discussion. Students will be creating their own questions concerning the issue of the session. Students should create three Text Analysis Questions, two Cultural Analysis questions, and two Biblical Analysis questions. For more detailed instructions, please see Session III.

Issue

What does it take to reconcile a severely broken and damaged friendship?

READING ASSIGNMENT:
Book 20

Session XVI: Student-Led Discussion
Book 19

A Question to Consider

What does it take to repair and reconcile a friendship that has been severely damaged?

Text Analysis

Example: Who encourages Achilleus to reconcile with Agamemnon? What does she tell him?

Answer: Achilleus's mother, Thetis, encourages him to make things right with Agamemnon, telling him to "unsay his anger against him" and then to "arm at once for the fighting" (19.28–36).

Other themes to pursue in the text: Are they seeking to mend the relationship for the right reasons? Do you think a true reconciliation occurs on both ends? Are all the necessary elements present to truly rectify past wrongs and heal the broken friendship? Who admits fault? Is there genuine forgiveness?

Cultural Analysis

Example: What do you think is most often left out of the process of healing a broken friendship?

Answer: Too often we want to brush things under the rug in an attempt to get it over and move on. The problem with this approach is that lingering bitterness can resurface later and true healing has not occurred.

Other cultural issues to consider: What elements in our culture cause us to lean toward this "quick fix" solution mentality? What does our culture encourage us to do when we've been hurt by someone else?

Biblical Analysis

Example: Read Luke 6:37–42. What principles do you see here for healing broken friendships?

Answer: This passage reminds us of the importance of forgiveness and doing away with a judgmental attitude. We are also reminded of the need to look at ourselves to see that we all are vile offenders in the eyes of God.

Sterbender Achilles ("Dying Achilles,"), by German sculptor Ernst Herter (1846–1917), greets visitors to the Achillion Palace on the Greek Island of Corfu. The palace was built for Empress Elizabeth of Austria in 1890–91.

Other Scriptures to consider: Leviticus 19:17, 18; Proverbs 17:17; 18:24; 27:14, 17; Matthew 5:21–26; 18:15–20.

SUMMA

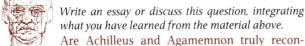

Write an essay or discuss this question, integrating what you have learned from the material above.

Are Achilleus and Agamemnon truly reconciled? What is the most important element of healing a broken friendship?

READING ASSIGNMENT:
Books 21 and 22

SESSION XVII: WRITING

Writing a Eulogy

Many good men have fallen. As the Greeks continue to mourn the loss of Patroklos, the Trojans grieve the death of Hektor and watch in horror as Achilleus drags his dead body over the battlefield in humiliation. The last few books focus on the retrieval of Hektor's body so that he can receive a proper burial. Write a eulogy that might be delivered at Hektor's funeral. Think of the things that make him a great man. Give the eulogy from the perspective of someone close to him. If time permits, read some of them in class.

READING ASSIGNMENT:
Books 23 and 24

SESSION XVIII: RECITATION
Books 18–24

Comprehensive Questions

Answer these questions for factual recall.
1. What does Thetis do for Achilleus?
2. What action does Achilleus take concerning Agamemnon? How does Agamemnon respond?
3. What conversation takes place between Achilleus and his horse?
4. What happens when Achilleus and Aeneas meet?
5. Why is the River god upset with Achilleus?
6. What comes of the confrontation between Hektor and Achilleus? What is Hektor's last request?
7. Who witnesses his death?
8. Who appears to Achilleus in a dream? What is his request?
9. Who comes to negotiate for Hektor's body?
10. What three women lament the loss of Hektor?

Chart 1: **COMPARISON OF ETHICS AS SEEN IN THE *ILIAD***

ACTION IN THE *ILIAD*	GREEK HEROIC ETHIC	BIBLICAL VIEW
Achilleus chooses a short life and glory over a long life with no glory.	Above all, the Greeks prized glory. The true hero had no concern about how long he lived, but rather put a total premium on glory in battle.	Personal glory is not the end of the Christian life. Rather, the glory of God is the highest and greatest end (WCF Q1).
Achilleus refrains from battle as a result of having his concubine taken away by Agamemnon.		
At first, Achilleus refuses to accept Agamemnon's apology.		
Odysseus and Diomedes lie to Dolon, the Trojan spy, saying they would not kill him if he would divulge information to them.		

Session XIX: Analysis

Comparison

Many actions of individuals in the *Iliad* may be difficult for us to understand because we are 3,000 years removed from the times in which it was written. The Greeks operated on what is commonly called the Greek Heroic Ethic, a code of living that may be foreign to us.

Fill in Chart 1 with the Greek Heroic Ethic and the Biblical View corresponding to the Action in the Iliad.

Session XX: Evaluation

All tests and quizzes are to be given with an open book and a Bible available.

Grammar

Answer each of the following questions in complete sentences. Some answers may be longer than others. (2 points per answer)

1. What do we know about Homer? When did he live? What is the time period for the setting of his great work?
2. What is this book not about?
3. What argument is going on at the beginning of the book? What role does Apollo play?
4. What brilliant idea does Paris propose to end the war? How does it end?
5. Who agrees to a duel with Hektor? How does it end?
6. What does Agamemnon decide to do after the speeches of Diomedes and Nestor? How does Achilleus respond?
7. Who agrees to spy on the Trojans? What is the result of their expedition?
8. What plot does Hera hatch to assist the Greeks? What is the result?
9. Who is Patroklos? Why is he weeping? What request does he make of Achilleus?
10. How does Achilleus respond to his request? What warning does he give? How does it all end?
11. What happens to Patroklos's body?
12. What does Thetis do for Achilleus?
13. What action does Achilleus take concerning Agamemnon? How does Agamemnon respond?
14. What comes of the confrontation between Hektor and Achilleus? What is Hektor's last request?
15. Who comes to negotiate for Hektor's body?

Logic

Demonstrate your understanding of the Roman worldview as set forth in the Iliad. Answer the following question in complete sentences; your answer should be a paragraph or so. Answer two of the four questions. (10 points per answer)

1. What is the connection between the anger of Apollo and the anger of Achilleus? Do we become like the god(s) we worship? How might this apply to both individuals and entire cultures?
2. On the issue of free will, compare the truth in Scripture with what we see in the *Iliad*.
3. Whose fault was the death of Patroklos, Achilleus or Patroklos himself?
4. Are Achilleus and Agamemnon truly reconciled? What is the most important element of healing a broken friendship?

Lateral Thinking

Answer one of the following questions. These questions will require more substantial answers. (15 points per answer)

1. Compare the biblical view of a true hero with the ideal Greek hero as seen throughout the *Iliad*.
2. Was the Trojan War a just war? Explain why or why not. Here are the *jus ad bellum* (Just War) principles:
   1. A competent authority must declare war.
   2. The war must have a just cause.
   3. The force used must be proportionate to the cause.
   4. All peaceful means of settling the dispute should be exhausted.
   5. And finally, the goal of the war must be a just and equitable peace.

Optional Session A: Aesthetics

Hektor Berlioz: *Les Troyens*

Bearing the same name as the Trojan hero, Berlioz was a French composer in the nineteenth century. While he composed many great works, his opera *Les Troyens* (*The Trojans*) is recognized by many as his greatest. The story follows the Trojan Aeneas as he flees with his father from the burning city of Troy. As Virgil tells the story in the *Aeneid,* he goes on to found a "New Troy": Rome.

At the beginning of the opera the people are rejoicing because after ten years of siege the Greeks have left a giant wooden horse and are apparently gone. Listen to the opening chorus and answer the following questions.

(If you do not already own a recording of this opera, you may download just the opening chorus from your favorite online music service (like iTunes, Rhapsody, or Amazon MP3). The track is entitled "Act I, No. 1, Ha, Ha! Après dix ans.") Here is the translation:

> After ten years passed within our walls,
> Ah! what happiness to breathe
> The pure air of the fields, which the battle cry
> Will no longer tear asunder.

(young men and children running and carrying debris in their hands)

> Naught but debris—a spearhead!
> I found a helmet!—And I, two javelins!
> Look at this vast shield!
> It would carry a man over the waves.
> What cowards, these Greeks!

1. What is the general mood of the music? Use as many adjectives as you can to describe the mood of the people.
2. What particular instruments heighten this mood?
3. Does the music match the lyrics? Explain.

Do some research on the opera and answer the following questions. A book that would be helpful is The New Kobbé's Complete Opera Book, *edited and revised by the Earl of Harewood, Putnam. You might also explore the information found on the web at http://www.musicwithease.com/berlioz-les-troyens.html and http://en.wikipedia.org/wiki/Les_Troyens.*

1. When did Hektor Berlioz live?
2. When was this opera first performed and where?
3. What other operas did he compose?

The next session will be a student-led discussion. Students will be creating their own questions concerning the issue of the session. Students should create three Text Analysis Questions, two Cultural Analysis questions, and two Biblical Analysis questions. For more detailed instructions, please see Session III.

Issue

Was the Trojan War a just war?

OPTIONAL SESSION B: STUDENT-LED DISCUSSION

A Question to Consider

Was the Trojan War a just war?

Students should read and consider the example questions below that are connected to the Question to Consider above. Last session's assignment was to prepare three questions and answers for the Text Analysis section and two additional questions and answers for both the Cultural and Biblical Analysis sections below.

Text Analysis

Example: What started the war? Who attacked whom?

Answer: Well, Paris actually started the war when he stole Helen. The Greeks, however, initiate military action.
Walk through the Just War principles for each side of the conflict.

Cultural Analysis

Example: How do we judge if a war is just in our culture?

Answer: War is rarely popular these days. It seems as though it is quite trendy to be anti-war. It does not matter what the issues are.
Other cultural issues to consider: What do the media have to do with public opinion of war?

Biblical Analysis

Example: What do we see in Deuteronomy 20:19?

Answer: We see some specific instructions as to how wars should and should not be waged. This and other passages reveal that the Bible is not silent on the matter.
Other Scriptures to consider: Psalm 2; Psalm 109; Deuteronomy 20:10–12.

SUMMA

Write an essay or discuss this question, integrating what you have learned from the material above.
Was the Trojan War a just war?

The Iliad

The next session will be a student-led discussion. Students will be creating their own questions concerning the issue of the session. Students should create three Text Analysis Questions, two Cultural Analysis questions, and two Biblical Analysis questions. For more detailed instructions, please see Session III.

Issue

Given the choice, would you choose a short life with glory, or a long life with no glory?

OPTIONAL SESSION C: STUDENT-LED DISCUSSION

A Question to Consider

Given the choice, would you choose a short life with glory, or a long life with no glory?

Students should read and consider the example questions below that are connected to the Question to Consider above. Last session's assignment was to prepare three questions and answers for the Text Analysis section and two additional questions and answers for both the Cultural and Biblical Analysis sections below.

Text Analysis

Example: What does Achilleus do with this choice? Why? What is his motivation? How does his life end?

Answer: Achilleus, of course, true to Greek ideals, chooses the short life with glory. He wants to be remembered for his exploits. He is driven by his pride and anger.

Other themes to pursue in the text: What do some of the other Greek heroes choose? Odysseus? Nestor? Agamemnon? Are they just as heroic as Achilleus?

Cultural Analysis

Example: If you were to take a random survey, what do you think would be the percentage of people who would choose the short life and glory?

Answer: Hard to say, but we do know that everybody seems to want their "15 minutes of fame," and many are willing to make great sacrifices to get it.

Other cultural issues to consider: Does our culture

This is the Trojan War, right? So where is the Trojan Horse? The famous faux filly is mentioned briefly in Books 4 and 8 of the *Iliad's* "sequel"—the *Odyssey* and is also described in detail in Book 2 of Virgil's *Aeneid*.

value longevity in any way? Why or why not? What is behind the common desire for "15 minutes of fame?"

Biblical Analysis

Example: Consider Solomon's insightful words in Ecclesiastes 12:1–8. After pursuing all sorts of pleasure and glory in his youth, what does Solomon conclude?

Answer: His final assessment is that the object of our pursuits should be the Creator rather than all the pleasures and glory he sought. He explains that if we indulge in pleasure and glory in our youth, they will be unknown to us in our later years. We will also not know our Creator in our later years. The point, says Solomon, is to look to the future years of maturity. We can be so much more productive for the kingdom if we have grown into the mature years of wisdom.

Other Scriptures to consider: Proverbs 15:25,33; 16:18, 19; 22:4; Philippians 2:1–4.

SUMMA

Write an essay or discuss this question, integrating what you have learned from the material above.

Is it noble to choose a short life with glory over a long life with no glory?

The Psalms

Can music change the world? In the 1960s, rock stars thought so, and styled themselves as cultural prophets. Their songs were going to transform society, end war, and bring in an age of love and peace. In 1971, Jann Wenner, co-founder and publisher of *Rolling Stone,* explained the philosophy behind his magazine and the music it covered:

> Rolling Stone was founded and continues to operate in the belief that rock 'n roll music is the energy center for all sorts of changes revolving rapidly around us: social, political, cultural, however you want to describe them. The fact is for many of us who've grown up since World War II, rock 'n roll provided the first revolutionary insight into who we are and where we are at in this country.[1]

There can be no doubt that rock is a high-energy cultural form that has pervaded our society (though it has been giving way to other popular music forms for some time now). As Wenner suggests, rock music had political and cultural goals from the start of the genre. Some might say that the musicians eventually sold out, giving up politics to focus on sex, drugs, and money. Or maybe sex, drugs, and money *were* the political agenda from the beginning. Whatever the case, there is no doubt rock music played a role in bringing the counterculture of the 1960s into the mainstream culture within a generation. But the quest of rock artists to usher in a new age of love and peace quite obviously never materialized. Nevertheless, the mission of changing the world through music is still very much with us.

Those who looked for revolution to take place through rock had the right idea, but the wrong music. Music really *can* change the world. Indeed, God has given his people a collection of songs aimed at doing just that. Right in the center of our Bibles is God's very own hymnbook, known as the book of Psalms. The Psalms were written as poetic prayers, designed to be sung in corporate worship. They were inspired by God's Spirit to change us, as his covenant people, and ultimately to change the world. Using the Psalter in prayer and song is one of the most powerful tools the church has to bring about the transformation of culture. Of course, the Psalms will not bring in the kind of revolution the 1960s rockers were trying to ignite; it will be a different kind of revolution, one based on the love and justice of God, as defined by his Word.

General Information

Author and Context

The main author of the book of Psalms is David. Moses, Solomon, Asaph, and a handful of other figures also made contributions, as the titles in the Psalter indicate. It is important to understand that while many Psalms may have originated in a private context, these songs have been brought together into a book intended for public, corporate use. We should not think of the Psalms as David's private prayer journal, but as Israel's (and now the church's) foundational hymnbook. The experiences of the psalmists should be considered personal, but not private. The Psalms give us a paradigm for understanding, exploring, and expressing the life of faith, including its pains and struggles, in the context of the covenant community.

One of the church fathers, Diodore, wrote,

> When our souls find in the psalms the most ready formulation of the concerns they wish to bring before God, they recognize them as a wonderfully appropriate remedy. For the Holy Spirit anticipated all kinds of human situations, setting forth through the most blessed David the proper words for our sufferings through which the afflicted may find healing.[2]

Martin Luther called the Psalter "the Bible in miniature" in which "you have before you a fine, bright, spotless mirror that will show you the kind of thing Christianity is."[3] John Calvin spoke in glowing terms about the Psalter, saying, "I have been accustomed to call this book, I think not inappropriately, the anatomy of all the parts of the soul,"[4] meaning it covers the whole breadth and range of human experience from a sanctified perspective.

The fact that the Psalms were written largely by David—a great man, but also one who stumbled many times, as we do—comforts us. We can truly use the Psalms as a textbook of our own souls, for the psalmists share in our weaknesses and trials. There is a Psalm for every legitimate human emotion and every situation we face.

For many men today, poetry seems effeminate, and church music in

The Psalms have been called the war songs of the Prince of Peace. By praying them, we learn to trust in Christ as our King and Savior, as well as imitate His life of faithfulness. Here King David, the main author of the Psalms, plays the harp (from the Westminster Psalter, c. 1250).

general seems wimpy. David would beg to differ. He was both a warrior and a poet. His songs are full of passion and fire. Singing the Psalms will form our character in unique ways—certainly very few uninspired hymns cover the same territory as the Psalter (e.g., Ps. 139:19–22). Singing the Psalms can make us tough enough to face the kinds of battles David faced, such as when he killed a wild bear and took down Goliath. In a narcissistic, therapeutic culture like our own, the Psalms get us out of our own little private, self-centered worlds and help us focus our energies on God's warfare against evil and oppression in the world. The Psalms are distinctively militant, calling on God to bring judgment against those who oppose his kingdom and stand in the way of his grace.

But if the Psalms can make us tough, they can also make us tender. There are psalms that, if sung faithfully, will tenderize our hearts and minds to God's grace and the needs of others. In the Psalms we learn how to confess our sin, we learn true humility, we learn our smallness before the overwhelming majesty of God, and we learn the importance of showing mercy to others in need even as the Lord has shown us mercy. The Psalms teach us about the importance of community with other believers and our obligation to pursue the lost with the good news of God's gracious reign. The Psalms fill us with a desire to worship the living God and give us a heart for the global mission of God's kingdom.

Of course, the most important function of the Psalms is to point us to Christ, who fulfills them all. Christ is the King the psalmists prayed for; more than that (as we will see), Christ prayed *through* the psalmists as his forerunners. In this book, we not only have prayers *about* Christ but prayers *of* Christ. The Psalms have rightly been called the war songs of the Prince of Peace.[5] By praying them, we learn to trust in Christ as our King and Savior, as well as imitate His life of faithfulness. The Psalter celebrates Christ's gifts of forgiveness and renewal, as well as His ultimate victory over His enemies.

Significance

The Psalter came to hold a unique and central place in the life of Old Covenant Israel. It's been rightly said that ancient Israel enjoyed life as a whole through the medium of music. Psalm singing was central to their corporate life and culture. They not only sang psalms in temple and synagogue worship, but also made liberal use of the Psalter in the midst of daily activities. They were a musical people, and the Psalms served as the soundtrack of their lives.

David, the chief author of the Psalter, was also responsible for organizing Israel's priesthood to include trained musicians, orchestras, and choirs. The record of David's kingship in 1 and 2 Chronicles pay special attention to his musical reforms, which must stand among his life's greatest achievements. If Moses was responsible for organizing Israel's worship through the sacrifice of animals, David was responsible for organizing their worship through the sacrifice of musical praise. He glorified the national liturgy by giving sacred song a new place of prominence.

From the earliest days of the church, the Psalms have formed the basic prayer book and hymnal for Christians. Clement of Alexandria gives a little snapshot of how psalm singing fit into the joyous, thankful life of the Christian:

> Holding festival, then, in our whole life, persuaded that God is altogether on every side present, we cultivate our fields, praising; we sail the sea hymning. . . . And his whole life is a holy festival. His sacrifices are prayers, and praises, and readings in Scripture before meals, and psalms and hymns during meals and before bed, and prayers also again during the night. By these he unites himself to the divine choir.[6]

For Clement, Christians sang psalms not only to shape noble character but also to express thanks and praise to God. This was considered the highest function of music.

Other church fathers, like Basil, also extolled the importance of the Psalter in the life of the church:

> A psalm drives away demons, summons the help of angels, furnishes arms against nightly terrors, and gives respite from daily toil; to little children it is safety, to men in their prime adornment, to the old a solace, to women their most fitting ornament. It peoples solitudes, it brings agreement to market places. To novices it is a beginning; to those who are advancing, an increase; to those who are concluding, a confirmation. A psalm is the voice of the church. It gladdens fast days, it creates grief which is in accord with God's will, for a psalm brings a tear even to a heart of stone.[7]

Likewise, Jerome wrote to Demetrias that she should "always [pray and sing psalms] at the third, sixth, and ninth hours, at evening, in the middle of the night and at dawn." In another case, he advised a young Christian woman to "learn the Psalter by heart."[8] One of the reasons for the spread of early Christianity though the Roman Empire was the beauty and attractiveness of its psalmody and hymnody.

At the Reformation, the book of Psalms played a vital role in theological and liturgical reforms. Calvin commissioned musicians to put the Psalms to singable melodies, which became known as "Genevan jigs" for their lively style. According to Calvin, the Psalms give us the gospel:

In one word, not only will we here find general commendations of the goodness of God, which may teach men to repose themselves in him alone, and to seek all their happiness solely in him; and which are intended to teach true believers with their whole hearts confidently to look to him for help in all their necessities; but we will also find that the free remission of sins, which alone reconciles God towards us, and procures for us settled peace with him, is so set forth and magnified, as that here there is nothing wanting which relates to the knowledge of eternal salvation.[9]

The Reformation was, among other things, a revival of congregational psalm singing, the likes of which had not been seen since the early days of the church.

Historian James Hastings Nichols explains the centrality of the Psalter in Reformational church life and piety, focusing especially on the French Reformers, known as Huguenots:
As the staple of private and family worship as well as of the services of the church, the psalms became known to many by heart. No other book of the Old Testament, at least, could rival the psalms in the affections and knowledge of Reformed laymen. Ministers frequently preached from the psalms also; the Psalter was the only Old Testament book on which Calvin preached on Sundays. For every occasion, it seems an appropriate verse would leap to the tongue of a Huguenot.

When the Huguenots were facing persecution, they turned to the Psalter for strength and encouragement. Again, Nichols:
And all over France, wherever Huguenots of the first generation were confined, often sometimes by the score, guards and jailers became familiar with the psalms, even to the prisons on Santo Domingo and Martinique. The colporteurs who carried the psalters, with Bibles and catechisms, all over France, were frequently caught and burned. Many martyrs died with the words of the Apostles' Creed, but it is surprising to what a range of the psalter was drawn on by others. The courage and joy of these martyrs who, like the ancient Christians, could have had release for a word, won converts among the onlookers. The authorities tried gags, but the cord would burn and from the smoke the psalm would again begin. The bishops then ordered that the tongues of the Huguenots should be cut out before they were burned. This became the general practice. . . .

"A psalm drives away demons, summons the help of angels, furnishes arms against nightly terrors, and gives respite from daily toil. . . ." It is easy to imagine what would be on St. Basil's iPod if he were alive today —the Psalms!

When the fifty-seven Protestants of Meaux were led off to the dungeons they lamented [using Psalm 79]. . . . [T]he fourteen of them who were later led out to execution sang from the same psalm until their tongues were cut out. . . . When armed resistance began, Ps. 68 became the Huguenot [war chant]. . . . At the Battle of Coutras, the Reformed soldiers knelt and prayed and sang. Roman Catholic courtiers, observing, cried out that they were afraid and were confessing, but a more experienced officer said it was not so. They were singing [Psalm 118].[10]

It's hard to imagine any other songs sustaining these saints as they faced such suffering and grueling tests of faith. Of course, the Huguenots are hardly alone in their love for psalm singing. Throughout church history, the Psalms have played a vital role in Christian faith and practice.

These stories echo through the churches of the Reformation in Scotland, in the Netherlands, in Puritan England and in America. Wherever Protestants went, they loved and sang and lived by the Psalter.

Summary and Setting

Historically, it is obvious that the Psalter had to undergo a process of development, as individual psalms were written, collected, and canonized. The bulk of the Psalms were written at the time of David (about 1000 B.C.), but some came before (e.g., Ps. 90) and some came after (e.g., Ps. 72). We do not know exactly when the Psalms were put into their final canonical form. Most likely, inspired editors during the post-exilic era of Ezra and Nehemiah shaped the Psalter into the form in which we have it today.

It is important to note that the Psalms are not thrown together haphazardly or randomly. There is an order and logic to the 150 songs that compose the book. In fact, the book of Psalms is actually organized into five books, each of which has a narrative flow and concludes with a doxology (or series of doxologies).[11] Each book within the Psalter has its own distinctive characteristics and themes. For example, most of Book I was written by David and generally uses the name YHWH for God, the Psalms in Book 2 are by David (or the sons of Korah), and the name Elohim is normally used for God, and so forth. While the inner logic may not always be immediately clear to us, the arrangement and organization of the Psalter is deliberate.

The five books are divided this way:

Book I	Psalms 1–41
Book II	Psalms 42–72
Book III	Psalms 73–89
Book IV	Psalms 90–106
Book V	Psalms 107–150

Psalm 1 introduces the entire Psalter, as well as Book I in Psalms. It serves as a transitional bridge from the era of Moses (focused on the law) to the era of David (focused on the kingdom). If Psalm 1 is a gateway to the Psalter as a whole, then Psalms 146–150, a block of praise songs, serve as resounding conclusion not only to Book V, but to the book of Psalms in its entirety. The trajectory of the Psalter is from law (Ps. 1) to praise (Pss. 146–150). In other words, the piety of the Psalter is not only focused on giving God obedience but ultimately giving Him delighted and vigorous worship. This joyous, exuberant praise described in the final group of Psalms is the goal of all creation and history. The overall structure of the Psalter shows us that a life of meditation on God's law and walking in God's ways has its proper outcome in victorious worship and celebration.

As mentioned, each of the five books within the Psalter tells a story. To give one example of how narrative flow works within the Psalter, consider Book V. This book, from beginning to end, tells the story of exodus, exile, and new exodus.

In Psalm 107, we find God rescuing and gathering His people just as He delivered them out of Egyptian slavery. Psalms 108–110 describe God's victory over His enemies, again reminding us of the defeat of Pharaoh in the first exodus. Psalms 111–118 praise God for His mighty deliverance, much as the Israelites celebrated the Red Sea crossing with the Song of Moses (Ex. 15). Not surprisingly, we find next a meditation on the law given at Sinai (Ps. 119). Psalms 120–136 are known as "Psalms of Ascent" and continue the story by focusing on worship. After God gave the law to Moses, the Israelites built the tabernacle as a center for worship, so naturally, worship Psalms come next in the sequence of Book V. Psalm 137 then stands on its own, asking a critical question: How can Israel sing Zion's songs in a foreign land? This might correspond to the time of wilderness wandering or to the period of exile in Israel's history.

The answer to the question forced upon Israel by exile is answered in Psalms 138–145. These are royal psalms describing the kind of righteous king Israel needs. The answer to exile will ultimately be found in the coming of a new and greater David, a messianic king. What will happen when the king comes? God's people, and indeed all of creation, will burst with praise. In Psalms 146–150, we find an explosion of joyous worship, a final crescendo of honor and adoration given to Israel's covenant Lord, as the whole creation fulfills its purpose of glorifying God.

This is at best a bird's-eye view, and there is no space here to fill in the details. But it should be clear how the themes and progression of Book V track with the story of Israel from exodus, to exile, to the coming of the kingdom, to the kingdom's consummation. It is a stylized narrative summary of redemptive history.

Artistic Structure

David and the other psalmists were brilliant composers, and these songs display their consummate wisdom and skill. The Psalms are musical poetry at its finest. As poetry, the Psalms make use of a number of literary forms. Literary analysis of these songs usually pays rich dividends. We cannot explore all these literary features, but a few major ones should be mentioned. The Psalter is full of metaphors, symbolism, and lively imagery. But we will focus more on the literary structures the authors built into their texts.

The poetry we are familiar with in the modern West tends to use rhyme or meter as a structuring device. For the Hebrews, parallelism was the basic poetic form.[12] One cannot understand the Psalms without understanding the role and function of parallelism. For example, consider these lines from Psalm 2:

Why do the nations rage,
And the people plot a vain thing?

Or these lines from Psalm 139:

Where can I go from Your Spirit?
Or where can I flee from Your presence?

In each case, the second line repeats, but elaborates on the first. Traditionally, when the Psalms would be used in a liturgical setting, the first line would be called out by the leader; the people would then echo back with the second line. In other words, the Psalms are designed for congregational participation.[13]

There are a wide variety of parallelisms, including synonymous, in which the two lines reverberate with the same basic meaning (e.g., Ps. 1:1); antithetic, in which the two lines form a sharp contrast (e.g., Ps. 44:3); and climactic, in which the meaning intensifies (Ps. 29:3–9).

Chiasm is another literary form deeply pervasive in the Psalter. A chiastic structure follows the kind of pattern seen in Psalm 70:

A. Appeal to God: "Deliver me O God; hasten to help me" (70:1)
   B. Malediction toward enemies (70:2–3)
   B.' Benediction toward those who seek God (70:4)
A.' Appeal to God: "Hasten O God; You are my help" (70:5)[14]

There are chiasms of various sizes in the Psalter, from just a few lines to entire, lengthy psalms. The matching sections are generally mutually interpretive, so the first A and B sections above help us understand the later B' and A' sections because they balance each other.

Some psalms use an acrostic (or partial acrostic) device. In these psalms, each line (or section) begins with each successive letter of the Hebrew alphabet. (Obviously, this cannot be captured in translation.) Examples include Psalms 9, 10, 25, 34, 119 (a celebration of the law of God "from A to Z"—each section of this longest chapter in the Bible begins with a different letter of the Hebrew alphabet), and 145.

Finally, some Psalms use refrains (e.g., Ps. 136). These repeating lines are by no means the "vain repetition" Jesus condemned (Matt. 6:7). Instead, they are ways of powerfully driving the truth into the minds and hearts of those who sing and pray them. Like water flowing over a rock, slowly softening its edges, repeated phrases and lines in the Psalter mold and shape us with regular usage.

Worldview

"Tell me what you sing, and I'll tell you who you are." "I don't care who makes the laws as long as I get to the write the songs people sing." These proverbial sayings capture the power of music to shape culture and form personal identity. Music is never neutral; it has an effect on us that reaches into the very depths of our being.

Music and the Christian Life

The Bible is not given to us first and foremost as a theology textbook but as a storybook and a songbook. God is a musician (Zeph. 3:17); in fact, the church fathers described God the Father as Singer, God the Son as Word/Lyric, and God the Spirit as Melody.[15] Because we are made in the image of the music-making God, music is foundational to human life. Martin Luther grasped this, and expounded frequently on the importance of music:

I have always loved music. He who knows this art is in the right frame, and fitted for every good pursuit. We can not do without music in our schools. A schoolmaster must know how to sing, or I would not allow him to teach. Nor ought we to ordain young theologians to the sacred office, unless they have first been well-tried and practiced in the art in the school.

For whether you wish to comfort the sad, to terrify the happy, to encourage the despairing, to humble the proud, to calm the passionate, or to appease those full of hate . . . what more effective means than music could you find?….[Music] is a mistress and governess of those human emotions.

Next to the Word of God, the noble art of music is the greatest treasure in the world. . . .

Music is a fair and lovely gift of God which

has often wakened and moved me to the joy of preaching.... Music drives away the Devil and makes people gay.... Next after theology I give to music the highest place and the greatest honor. I would not change what little I know of music for something great.

Experience proves that next to the Word of God only music deserves to be extolled as the mistress and governess of the feelings of the human heart.

We know that to the devils music is distasteful and insufferable. My heart bubbles up and overflows in response to music, which has so often refreshed me and delivered me from dire plagues.[16]

Given the importance of music, it is not surprising that the longest book in the Bible is a hymnbook. The Psalms are at the heart of biblical worship and theology. Because the Psalms are songs, we must remember they were written not merely to be studied, or to be read, or even to be spoken, but primarily to be sung. Thus, we should ask: How does the Psalter (and the rest of the Bible) help us develop a biblical theology of music? How should we make practical use of the Psalter in the church? And how can the Psalms train us in righteousness?

Obviously, God has given us inspired texts to sing, but not inspired melodies. We do not know exactly how the Psalms were sung in ancient Israel, and scholarly attempts to reconstruct their musical forms have met with mixed success.[17] There is no doubt the Psalms can be matched with a variety of musical styles, and have been in the past. For example, the medieval church chanted the Psalms (as some churches—Protestant and Catholic—continue to do today), while Calvin and the Puritans set them to meter. The key is for composers to provide melodies that mesh well with the content of the texts and the corporate usage for which the Psalter was intended. It would not be fitting to put Psalm 51 to a lively dance tune, or Psalm 150 to a slow, somber dirge. It is essential that the church have singable melodies for the Psalms so as to employ them in public worship.

The Psalter calls attention to the importance of instrumentation. Again and again, the psalmist instructs us to praise God using a variety of instruments (e.g., Ps. 150). We also find that these instruments are to be played skillfully (Ps. 33:3, 149:3), so there is also a concern for the aesthetic quality of our musical praise.

The references to instrumental accompaniment point us to the fact that the Psalms are really war songs. For example, trumpets are prominent in the Psalter (e.g., Ps. 98:6; 150:3), but trumpets throughout Scripture are primarily used for mustering troops and/or worshippers (e.g., Num. 7:7–10; Neh. 4:20; Ezek 33:2–6). In Psalm 144:1, David asks God to train his fingers for war, but we find a few verses later that he's really talking

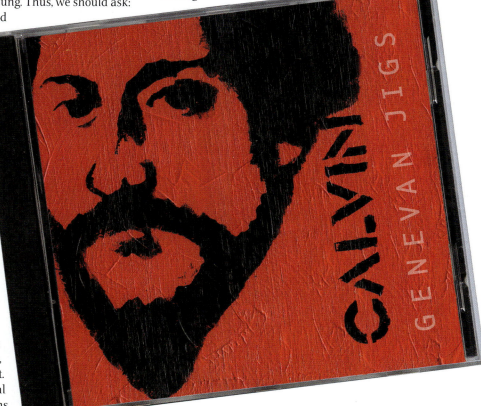

"As to public prayers, there are two kinds: the one consists of words alone; the other includes music. And this is no recent invention. For since the very beginning of the church it has been this way, as we may learn from history books. Nor does St. Paul himself speak only of prayer by word of mouth, but also of singing."—John Calvin

about learning to play the harp (144:9)! God calls His people to fight their spiritual battles first and foremost through worship (e.g., 2 Chron. 20:1–30), and the Psalter belongs on the front lines in this "holy warfare" (note that according to 2 Chronicles 20:21, Jehoshaphat's army/choir sang Psalm 106:1 as they marched into battle).

In the book of Psalms, we learn that worship is holistic, involving not just the heart but the body. The heart religion of the Psalter is evident from beginning to end. But we also find bodily actions accompanying the music and singing. In the Bible, worship is not purely a mental or attitudinal matter. We also find bodily gestures such as clapping, shouting, kneeling, and processing playing a vital role. In fact the word for worship in both the Old and New Testaments basically means "to bow down," obviously a bodily action. As C.S. Lewis pointed out, the Psalms show us that true worship is full of "gusto"; it is not just contemplative, but loud, vibrant, and energetic.[18]

Biblically, the purposes of music go beyond mere enjoyment and include the formation of character. The church fathers and Reformers recognized this reality. Thus, Clement of Alexandria wrote, "Music then is to be handled for the sake of embellishment [to glorify words] and for the composure of manners [to shape character]."[19] Music shapes our attitudes and habits over time. It has the power to mold people, for better or worse. Music can stimulate and even manipulate our emotions, which is why some (like the ancient philosopher Plato and the sixteenth-century Reformer Ulrich Zwingli) have been suspicious of it. But throughout Scripture, we find God's Spirit using music to stir up holy desires (2 Chron. 29:20–30; Eph. 5:18–20), as it did for Augustine:

> How I wept during your hymns and songs! I was deeply moved by the music of the sweet chants of your church. The sounds flowed into my ears and the truth was distilled into my heart. This caused the feeling of devotion to overflow. Tears ran, and it was good for me to have that experience.[20]

Augustine obviously loved music and gave it a central place in Christian experience. He also recognized that music is a form of rhetoric. That is, it is designed to persuade us, to move us to action, to train our senses in the recognition and appreciation of beauty, and to shape us holistically. John Calvin believed the same. Noting the power of music, he said songs could be used by God "to

The Psalms are not simply songs *about* Christ; they are actually spoken *by* Christ. They are His prayers, His songs, inspired by His Spirit and written down by His forerunners. Jesus prays in Gethsemane in this painting entitled *Christ in the Garden of Olives* (oil on wood, c. 1460).

recreate man and give him pleasure." The influence of music makes it all the more important to consider carefully the songs that fill our ears and mouths: "Wherefore, we must be the more diligent in ruling it in such a manner that it may be useful to us and in no way pernicious."[21]

The Psalter shows us that ultimately all of creation exists to praise God. In fact, the church fathers talked about creation singing a "cosmic hymn" and medieval Christians spoke of the "music of the spheres"; more recent theologians have spoken of the universe existing in "musical harmony" and performing a "cosmic dance according to God's tune." The Psalter affirms that all of creation in some way sings to God's glory (e.g., Ps. 98:4–9, 150:6; cf. Isa. 44:23; Rev. 4–5); man's role is to join in this song and articulate creation's song as a royal priesthood before God's throne. God has given us the songs of the Psalter that we might "get in tune" with this cosmic hymn and sing our part in the cosmic choir. In the words of Origen,

> So we sing to God and his only begotten as do the sun, the moon, the stars and the entire heavenly host. For all these form a sacred chorus and sing hymns to the God of all and his only begotten along with those among men who are just.[22]

At the end of the Bible, when Babylon is destroyed, the wicked city is told that "the sound of harpists, musicians, flutists, and trumpeters shall not be heard in you anymore" (Rev. 18:22). In hell, there will no singing, only the sounds of weeping and wailing and the gnashing of teeth. But the joyous songs of the righteous go on forever and ever.

The Prayers of Christ

The question is sometimes asked, "Which Psalms are messianic? That is, which Psalms specifically point us to Christ as the Greater David, the promised King?" The right answer is "All 150 Psalms are messianic!"

In Luke 24:44, we find that Jesus viewed the entire Old Testament, including the Law of Moses, the Prophets, and the Psalms, as prophetic of His person and work, His sufferings, and His glory. But the Psalms are not simply songs *about* Christ; they are actually spoken *by* Christ. They are His prayers, His songs, inspired by His Spirit and written down by His forerunners.

In Hebrews 2:12, we find the words of Psalm 22:22 put in the mouth of Jesus. The words of the psalmist are treated as the words of Jesus. He is the choirmaster, leading God's people in song when they gather for worship. But what's interesting is this: We have no record in the Gospels that Jesus actually quoted these words (though He did cite Psalm 22:1 on the Cross), but they are treated as His own speech nevertheless.

Hebrews 10:5–7 does the same thing with Psalm 40.

We have no record of Jesus quoting Psalm 40 or making these words His own. The original human author was probably not thinking of the incarnation of the Son in human flesh when he wrote them. And yet these verses in Hebrews are treated as Jesus' own prayer, sung when He entered the world.

If we combine these examples with the numerous psalms Jesus speaks directly with his own voice in the Gospel records (e.g., Psalm 22:1 in Matthew 27:46; Psalm 6:3–4 in John 12:27; Psalm 69:4 in John 15:25; Psalm 69:21 in John 19:28; Psalm 31:5 in Luke 23:46; Psalm 6:8 in Matthew 7:23; etc.), as well as those applied to Him indirectly (e.g., Psalm 78:2 in Matthew 13:35; Psalm 69:9 in John 2:16–17), we must conclude that *the book of Psalms is ultimately the prayer book of Jesus.* Just as Jesus is portrayed as a new David, so He is the true Psalmist.

Augustine wrote, "The voice of Christ and His Church was well-nigh the only voice to be heard in the Psalms . . . we ought to recognize his voice in all the Psalms."[23] Dietrich Bonhoeffer explains more elaborately:

> According to the witness of the Bible, David is, as the anointed king of the chosen people of God, a prototype of Jesus Christ. What happens to him happens to him for the sake of the one who is in him and who is said to proceed from him, namely Jesus Christ. . . . David was a witness to Christ in his office, in his life, and in his words. The New Testament says even more. In the psalms of David the promised Christ himself speaks. . . . These same words which David spoke, therefore, the future Messiah spoke through him. The prayers of David were prayed also by Christ. Or better, Christ himself prayed them through his forerunner David.[24]

Reading the Psalms as the prayers of Christ also brings a new dimension to our understanding of Jesus' humanness. When we see that the weakness of the psalmist is really the weakness of the Son of God in human form, we see His humility and sufferings on our behalf in a deeper way. We have a Lord and Savior who fully understands human suffering and temptation (cf. Heb. 4:15; 5:7–8). The God-man knows what it is like to endure betrayal by a friend (Ps. 38:11), loneliness (Ps. 25:19–20), doubt (Ps. 22:1–2), and the ultimate forms of pain and torment (Ps. 22:1, 14–16). Because He has been through the most difficult aspects of human experience, He can strengthen us. Indeed, because He has faced all these trials while keeping "clean hands and a pure heart" (Ps. 24:4), He can help us live faithfully in any circumstance.

Reading the Psalms as the prayers of Christ also reveal to us something of the inter-Trinitarian relationship between Father and Son. In the book of Psalms, we find the Father and Son serving one another in bonds of perfect love (e.g., Ps. 18). The Son calls upon the Father, and the Father answers. The Son trusts and obeys the will of the Father, fulfilling his assigned mission; therefore the Father vindicates Him against His enemies, exalts Him to the highest position, and promises Him the nations as His inheritance (see Ps. 2, Ps. 110; cf. Phil. 2:5–11). The Son proclaims His loyalty to the Father (Ps. 7), while the Father expresses His delight in the Son (Ps. 2:7–9; 18:19).

The Trinitarian structure of the Psalter has huge implications for Christian worship, as Charles Drew suggests:

> At the most profound theological level, worship is a spectator sport. We gather to watch the Father vindicate his Son in the preaching of the gospel and to watch the Son give praise to the Father in the praises of our lips. For the Spirit of Christ indwells us, and that Spirit lives to extol the Father and Son.... When next you gather for public worship, why not ask the Lord to catch you up into the praises of the Godhead? Ask him to give you in abundance the Spirit of Christ so that your songs might be the songs of the One who loved his Father to the end, and your joy might be the joy of the Son who was lifted from the tomb by the Father's embrace.[25]

If we see the Psalms as the prayers of Christ, several apparent problems with these songs get sorted out. For example, there are several imprecatory Psalms; that is, prayers in which the psalmist asks God to execute the wicked (e.g., Pss. 69, 109, 137, 139, etc.). It would seem difficult to reconcile such prayers of cursing with other biblical admonitions to love our enemies, pray for those who persecute us, and bless rather than curse. But if we understand these psalms as the prayers of Christ, the problem resolves itself. Christ came to establish God's merciful reign and to show grace to sinners. But Christ also calls on His Father to execute vengeance on those who simply will not repent, instead choosing to persist in their rebellious and idolatrous ways. For us to ask judgment on our enemies would be an act of self-righteousness, but for us to pray in union with Christ that God would judge His enemies is entirely appropriate.[26]

It might be asked: How can the Psalms be the prayers of Jesus, if the Psalter contains prayers of confession, and Jesus never sinned (e.g., Ps. 32, 51)? Further, how can *we* pray the parts of the Psalter that claim righteousness when we still sin in many ways (e.g., Ps. 7:8)? These theological conundrums are most clearly answered in the Pauline epistles, because Paul most fully develops the doctrine of the church's union with Christ.

In becoming incarnate as man and in His baptism, the Son of God united Himself to us; thus, He is made a sin offering, representing us (2 Cor. 5:21), and we are made participants in His death, resurrection, and reign (Rom. 6:1–14; Eph. 2:6; etc.).

The Son became one of us in order to take what was ours and make it His own; thus, all our wrongdoings were charged to Him at the Cross, where He died a sinner's death. In a very real sense, Jesus not only died *for* us, but He also died *as* us. Thus, because of His union with us, all the psalms in which the speaker confesses his guilt and iniquity become Christ's own prayers on our behalf. If what happened at Calvary has any saving significance for us, it is only because Jesus claimed our sins as His own; He can truly say, "O God, you know my foolishness and my sins are not hidden from you" (Ps. 69:5) because He has made Himself one with us, His weak and sinful people.

Even as Christ takes what is ours, He gives us what is His. He takes our poverty so we can share in His riches (2 Cor. 8:9). Christ is perfectly righteous; in union with Him we come to share in that righteous status and character. We can pray, "Judge me, O Lord according to my righteousness, and according to my integrity within me" (Ps. 7:8) because we are one with Christ, legally and experientially. Again, He took what was ours (sin and condemnation) in order to give us what is His (righteousness and life).

The "I" of the Psalter is both Christ *and* His people together (or *totus Christus*, the whole Christ, head and body, in the words of Augustine). Christ is the key to the book of Psalms even as He is the key to the whole of the Bible. The Psalms, with the rest of Scripture, find fulfillment in our loving, gracious, and holy Savior. We must pray and sing the Psalms in union with Him.

—*Rich Lusk*

For Further Reading

Adams, James E. *War Psalms of the Prince of Peace: Lessons from the Imprecatory Psalms.* Phillipsburg, N.J.: Presbyterian and Reformed Publishing, 1991.

Jones, Paul S. *Singing and Making Music: Issues in Church Music Today.* Phillipsburg, N.J.: Presbyterian and Reformed Publishing, 2006.

Mays, James Luther. *Psalms.* Louisville, Ky.: John Knox Press, 1994.

Peterson, Eugene H. *Answering God: The Psalms as Tools for Prayer.* San Francisco: Harper Collins, 1989.

Veritas Press Bible Cards: *Judges through Kings.* Lancaster, Pa.: Veritas Press. 53.

Session I: Prelude

A Question to Consider

Music and worship style are among the most controversial topics in the church today. What role should the Psalms play in current debates? How could a recovery of the Psalter help the church resolve at least some of these disputes? What do the Psalms teach us, explicitly and implicitly, about worship and worship and music?

From the General Information above answer the following questions:

1. Rock star Bono said the following about the Psalms:

   Words and music did for me what solid, even rigorous, religious argument could never do—they introduced me to God, not belief in God, more an experiential sense of GOD.... As a result, the Book of Psalms always felt open to me and led me to the poetry of Ecclesiastes, the Song of Solomon, the book of John.... My religion could not be fiction, but it had to transcend facts. It could be mystical, but not mythical.[27]

   How has God used music, especially the Psalms, in church history? How has God used the Psalms (and other music) to open your life to the gospel?

2. The Psalms put a great deal of stress on public worship. The Psalter as a whole was written for congregational use (though it can obviously be used by Christians in other contexts as a vehicle of praise). Eugene Peterson writes the following:

   God gives us various means to grow: prayer and Scripture silence and solitude, suffering and service. But the huge foundational means is public worship. Spiritual growth cannot take place in isolation. It is not a private thing between the Christian and God. In worship, we come before God who loves us in the presence of others whom he loves. In worship, more than at any other times, we set ourselves in deliberate openness to the action of God and the need of neighbor, both of which require us to grow up to the fullness of the stature of Christ, who is both God and man for us. Regular, faithful worship is as essential to the growing Christian as food and shelter to the growing child. Worship is the light and air in which spiritual growth takes place.[28]

   Is Peterson right to focus the primacy of corporate worship in the way? Do the Psalms support this view?

3. What is the relationship between worship and "holy war" in the Bible?
4. How does music shape character? Can you see examples of music shaping people in positive and negative ways in our culture?
5. What does the literary artistry of the Psalter teach us about the way the church is to use the Psalms?
6. If you had to summarize the overarching theme of the Psalter, how would you do it? How does the New Testament's use of the Psalter help you grasp its overall meaning?
7. How can the Psalms teach us how to pray?

Optional Activity

Imagine you are shipwrecked on a desert island together with a large group of other people. Most of the people stranded together are Christians, but they come from different churches and denominations. You all decide to form a church together. You have no songbooks, but you have

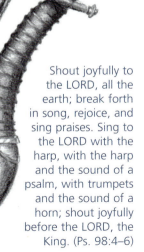

Shout joyfully to the LORD, all the earth; break forth in song, rejoice, and sing praises. Sing to the LORD with the harp, with the harp and the sound of a psalm, with trumpets and the sound of a horn; shout joyfully before the LORD, the King. (Ps. 98:4–6)

Bibles, so you agree to write new songs based on the Psalms. All the Christians on the island are going to meet to talk about how to compose songs for the new church. You will be one of the speakers at this meeting.

Write a speech that presents your thoughts about how the Psalms should be set to music. Should all available musical styles be used—classical, jazz, Gregorian chant, rock, hip-hop, etc.? Should only some of these styles be used, or only one? Should different musical styles be used for different psalms? Give biblical and logical arguments for your position.

READING ASSIGNMENT:
Psalms 1 and 120–150

SESSION II: DISCUSSION
Psalms 1 and 120–150

A Question to Consider

What difference could it make for a church if they sang the Psalms in their worship services, and not just songs composed in modern times? You may focus on Psalms 120–134 (the "Songs of Ascents") as your formulate your answer.

Discuss or list short answers to the following questions:

Text Analysis

1. In Psalm 1, what sort of man is described as blessed? What is the difference between his future and the future of the wicked?
2. Look at the first verse of each of the following psalms of ascents: 120, 121, 123, 130. What theme do they all have in common, and why is this theme important to the book of Psalms?
3. What are the psalmist's attitudes toward "enemies"? In your answer, consider several of the following psalms: 120, 124, 129, 136, 139, 140, 143, 149.
4. Based on the information given about "the gods" in Psalm 135:5; 136:2; and 138:1, who are these beings and what do we know about them? See also Psalm 82; 86:8; 96:4–5; and 97:7–9.
5. In Psalms 148 and 150, each section of each psalm talks about a different aspect of praising the Lord. How many different sections are there in each of these psalms, and what is the theme of each one? Example: Psalm 148:1–4 calls the heavenly beings to praise Him.

Cultural Analysis

1. Many Bible scholars believe that Psalm 136 was meant to be sung antiphonally—that is, a leader or trained choir would sing the first half of each verse, and then another choir or the whole congregation would sing the refrain ("For His mercy endures forever"). On the other hand, most modern church music involves either the whole congregation singing together, or a soloist or choir singing separately. What are some advantages and disadvantages of antiphonal singing as opposed to these other two methods?
2. Psalm 137 ends with a blessing on anyone who would smash Babylonian children against rocks. Is this statement relevant to our culture today?
3. Describe an event in modern, secular Western culture where people gather together in large numbers to praise someone or something. (Hint: These events often take place in the areas of entertainment and sports.) How is this event like the corporate praising of God described in the Psalms? In what ways is it different?

Biblical Analysis

1. What are the themes of the first and last psalms (1 and 150)? How do they help to connect the book of Psalms to the rest of the Bible?
2. What do we learn about David elsewhere in the Bible? Consider both Old and New Testament references. Since David is the primary author of the Psalms, what light does his personal and family history shed on this book?

SUMMA

Write an essay or discuss this question, integrating what you have learned from the material above.

If a nation had a widespread practice of singing from the book of Psalms, how would it transform that nation's culture?

READING ASSIGNMENT:
Psalms 2–40

SESSION III: RECITATION
Psalms 1–40, 120–150

Comprehension Questions

Answer the following questions for factual recall:

1. Who is named as the author of the first 24 psalms? Are there any of these psalms where he is not men-

tioned as the author?
2. Summarize what happens in Psalm 2.
3. For what time of day is Psalm 5 written?
4. What does Psalm 8 say about man's role in creation?
5. What is the difference between the people who are the focus of Psalm 14, and the people described in Psalm 15?
6. What was the situation in which Psalm 18 was written?
7. What does Psalm 19 say about God's voice in creation? About His voice in His law?
8. What experiences does the Psalmist describe in Psalm 22?
9. Describe the two figures who are making ceremonial entrances in

PSALM FORTY

I waited patiently for the LORD;
   And He inclined to me,
   And heard my cry.
He also brought me up out of a horrible pit,
   Out of the miry clay,
   And set my feet upon a rock,
   And established my steps.
He has put a new song in my mouth—
   Praise to our God;
   Many will see it and fear . . .

King David originally wrote these lyrics for the chief musician. Then in the 1980s "Saint" Paul David Hewson of Dublin (Bono) borrowed them for the last song of U2's album, *War*. The band had less than two hours left of studio time and were one song short. So Steve Lillywhite, the album's producer, sliced up a song that had been recorded and abandoned earlier in the sessions in an attempt to pull together another song. In the book *U2 by U2*, The Edge describes the final process: *So then we had this slightly unusual piece of music and we said, 'OK, what are we going to do with it? Bono said, 'Let's do a psalm.' Opened up the bible and found Psalm 40. 'This is it. Let's do it.' And within forty minutes we had worked out the last few elements for the tune, Bono had sung it, and we mixed it.*

"40" has become the closing song at U2's shows, and now hundreds of thousands of people all over the world have sung the Psalm together, along with the song's chorus, taken from Psalm 6:3.

Psalm 24. Who are they, and what are the places that they are entering?

READING ASSIGNMENT:
Psalms 41–88

SESSION IV: WRITING

A Musical Experience

This session is a writing assignment. Remember, quality counts more than quantity. You should write no more than 1,000 words, either typing or writing legibly on one side of a sheet of paper. You will lose points for writing more than this. You will be allowed to turn in your writing three times. The first and second times you turn it in, your teacher will grade it by editing your work. This is done by marking problem areas and making suggestions for improvement. You should take these suggestions into consideration as you revise your assignment. Only the grade on your final submission will be recorded. Your grade will be based on the following criteria: 25 points for grammar, 25 points for content accuracy—historical, theological, etc.; 25 points for logic—does this make sense and is it structured well?; 25 points for rhetoric—is it a joy to read?

Write about a memorable experience you have had with music. Your description should include answers to the following questions: How were you involved with the music? What kind of music was it? What was the setting? Who else was present, and what was their relation to the music being played? How did the music affect you? If the music had words that went with it, how did the effects of the words mix with the effects of hearing or playing the music itself?

READING ASSIGNMENT:
Psalms 89–119

Chart 1: WORLDVIEW ANALYSIS

	GOD	MAN	EXPECTATIONS FOR THE FUTURE	RESPONSES TO SUFFERING	SOURCES OF JOY AND PLEASURE
Psalms	Worthy of praise		The ends of the earth will turn to the Lord (Ps. 22:27)		
Oedipus the King	The gods are not to be trusted. They trick men and destroy them.	Men are pawns of the gods. Even as they try to find justice and to avoid wrong, they offend the capricious deities and suffer the terrible consequences, like killing your father and marrying your mother by accident.	There can be no set expectations for the future. The gods are treacherous and will do whatever they desire to men. They destroy Oedipus and give him no answers.	The response to suffering must be humility built on the foundation of despair. Oedipus sees his life and family destroyed and learns humility through this, but has no abiding hope.	There are no set sources of joy and pleasure. Oedipus can find no joy in his great exploits and quest for justice. Through these, the terrible secret of his identity is revealed to him and to all.
Other work you choose					

SESSION V: WORLDVIEW ANALYSIS

Pop Culture vs. the Psalms

Choose a work of art or a work of popular culture that you know very well (e.g., a song, movie, or novel). Compare and contrast the worldview expressed in this work with the worldview presented in the book of Psalms, by filling out Chart 1 as thoroughly as possible. A few sample answers for the book of Psalms have been provided for you as well as an example from Sophocles' *Oedipus the King* from Omnibus I.

OPTIONAL SESSION: WRITING

Writing a Psalm

This session is a writing assignment. Remember, quality counts more than quantity. You should write no more than 1,000 words, either typing or writing legibly on one side of a sheet of paper. You will lose points for writing more than this. You will be allowed to turn in your writing three times. The first and second times you turn it in, your teacher will grade it by editing your work. This is done by marking problem areas and making suggestions for improvement. You should take these suggestions into consideration as you revise your assignment. Only the grade on your final submission will be recorded. Your grade will be based on the following criteria: 25 points for grammar, 25 points for content accuracy— historical, theological, etc.; 25 points for logic—does this make sense and is it structured well?; 25 points for rhetoric—is it a joy to read?

Write a short hymn in the style of one of the following types of Psalms: praise (cf. Ps. 111; 116), lament (cf. Ps. 6; 13), or historical doxology (cf. Ps. 78; 126; see also 136). Be careful to speak to and about God with the same mixture of reverence and directness you see in the biblical psalms. In your "psalm," you must also use at least one of the literary structuring devices discussed in the Artistic Structure section above: parallelism, chiasm, acrostic, and/or refrain. Write in poetic lines, just as the Psalms are written, noting that each "verse" of a biblical psalm is generally two or three poetic lines in length.

ENDNOTES

1 Quoted in Ken Meyers, *All God's Children and Blue Suede Shoes.* Grand Rapids: Eerdmans (1989), 138. There are numerous examples of the kind of rock-driven revolution Wenner is talking about. Perhaps the most famous rock song of all, Led Zeppelin's "Stairway to Heaven," explicitly describes the new age that will

dawn if we will only follow the music:

And it's whispered that soon
If we all call the tune
Then the piper will lead us to reason
And a new day will dawn
For those who stand long
And the forests will echo with laughter.

The "piper" is probably the pagan god Pan, who was known to play the flute.

2 Quoted in Christopher Hall, *Reading Scripture with the Church Fathers.* Downers Grove, Ill.: InterVarsity Press (1998), 158–9.

3 Quoted in Roderick Campbell, *Israel and the New Covenant.* Philadelphia: Presbyterian and Reformed (1954), 56.

4 John Calvin, *Commentary on the Book of Psalms,* translated by James Anderson. Grand Rapids, Mich.: Baker (1993 reprint), xxxvi-xxxvii.

5 Jay E. Adams' book on imprecatory Psalms goes by this title.

6 Quoted in Calvin R. Stapert, *A New Song for an Old World: Musical Thought in the Early Church.* Grand Rapids, Mich.: Eerdmans (2007), 58.

7. Quoted in Stapert, 151.

8 Quoted in Stapert, 163.

9 Calvin, *Commentary of the Book of Psalms,* xxxix.

10 James Hastings Nichols, *Corporate Worship in the Reformed Tradition.* Philadelphia: Westminster Press (1968), 38ff.

11 Some scholars believe that when a psalm was sung in ancient Israel, at the end, the singers would conclude with the doxology drawn from the end of that book in the Psalter. So, for example, if they sang Psalm 3, they would conclude it with the last verses of Psalm 41. If this is indeed the case, there are several interesting implications. For example, Psalm 88 is a psalm of lament from beginning to end. It is perhaps the only psalm of lamentation that never "turns" to praise and thanks at the end. It seems to conclude in despondency and despair. But if the doxology from Psalm 89 would have always been tacked onto it, it puts the entire psalm in a new light. Also, this may be where early Christians got the notion of singing a doxology or Gloria Patri at the end of their hymns, which was a standard practice for several centuries, until it was finally reduced to a mere "Amen."

12 C.S. Lewis pointed out that parallelism is the only poetic form in the world that can be translated from one language to the next without loss. The Psalms were seemingly designed by God to ultimately function as the basic hymnbook of an international, multilingual church. Other literary forms in the Psalter do not carry over to other languages, but they are not nearly as foundational to the structure and usage of the Psalms as parallelism.

13 When Psalm lines are sung alternately, it is known as "antiphon."

14 See David Dorsey, *Literary Structures of the Old Testament.* Grand Rapids, Mich.: Baker (1999), 177.

15 This is why J.R.R. Tolkien and C.S. Lewis present the divine figure singing his creation into existence in their creation myths (in the *Silmarillion* and the *The Magician's Nephew,* respectively).

16 These quotations are from various places in Luther's works. For an overview of Luther's theology of music, see Roland Bainton, *Here I Stand,* Nashville: Abingdon (1978), 266ff, and Paul S. Jones *Singing and Making Music: Issues in Church Music Today.* Phillipsburg, N.J. (2006), 3ff, 171ff.

17 See, for example, Susan Haik-Ventoura, *The Music of the Bible Revealed,* San Francisco: Bibal Press (1991).

18 See C.S. Lewis, *Reflections on the Psalms,* San Diego: Harcourt Brace (1958).

19 Quoted in Stapert, 196. By "manners," Clement means one's

98   OMNIBUS IV

whole course of life and conduct in the world.

20 Quoted in Stapert, 181. Sometimes Augustine sounds quite suspicious of music because of its power over the emotions. While music can be dangerous, it can also be used to encourage the right kind of feelings. See, for example, 2 Chronicles 29:30, where we find that the Israelites sang until there was gladness. In this case (as in Augustine's testimony), music is used not just to express devotion but to stimulate it.

21 Quoted in Stapert, 195.

22 Quoted in Stapert, 38.

23 Quoted in Adams, 32.

24 Quoted in Adams, 26-7.

25 Charles Drew, *The Ancient Love Song: Finding Christ in the Old Testament,* Phillipsburg, N.J.: Presbyterian and Reformed (1996), 100.

26 There are other dimensions to the imprecatory Psalms. The judgments prayed for could include a petition that the wicked be converted. For example, in Psalm 139, David prays God would slay the wicked. But such slaying could include asking God to kill the "old man" so that the sinner is remade a "new man" (cf. Paul's description of conversion as death of the old self and a rising to life of the new self in Romans 6-7, Gal. 2:19-20, etc.). Likewise, when Psalm 137 speaks of dashing Babylon babies against the rock, it could be stretched to mean bringing children to Christ, who is the Rock. But these interpretations hardly solve the problems posed by the imprecations. John N. Day, in *Crying for Justice* (Grand Rapids, Mich.: Kregel [2005]), sees these imprecatory prayers as cries for justice and covenant vengeance, in accord with Genesis 12:3, Deuteronomy 28–32, 1 Corinthians 16:22, Revelation 6:9–11 and other texts that describe or pronounce curses for the wicked. Day argues that believers live within a tension, simultaneously loving and hating the wicked, both blessing and cursing them. This is true, of course, but Day wrongly disconnects these prayers from the church's union with Christ, which is the essence of the covenant relationship.

27 From the article "Psalm Like It Hot," available through www.VeritasPress.com/OmniLinks, Link 1 for this chapter.

28 Eugene Peterson, *Living the Message,* San Francisco: HarperCollins (2003), 284.

The Peloponnesian War

Aristotle was the first to attempt a careful explanation of how historical writing differs from other types of writing. In his day, this meant distinguishing historical writing from epic poetry, which was the only other type of writing about the past known to him.

The distinction between historian and poet is not in the one writing prose and the other verse—you might put the work of Herodotus into verse, and it would still be a species of history; it consists really in this, that the one describes the thing that has been, and the other a kind of thing that might be. Hence poetry is something more philosophic and of graver import than history, since its statements are of the nature rather of universals, whereas those of history are singulars (Aristotle, *Poetics* 9).

Thucydides does not neatly fit Aristotle's notion of history. He saw the singulars of history as a window to universals. Thucydides believed that the specific events of the Peloponnesian War manifested the general way humans will act in similar circumstances. The human impulses that animated Athens and Sparta in the fifth century B.C. are the same impulses that guided human behavior in the Punic Wars, the Thirty Years War, the Napoleonic Wars, the Second World War, and America's war in Iraq at the dawn of the twenty-first century.

GENERAL INFORMATION

Author and Context

What little we know of Thucydides comes from autobiographical traces we find in his work. He was Athenian, son of a man named Olorus. Thucydides operated gold mines in Thrace which gave him wealth and influence (1.1.1, 4.104.3). He began recording the events of the war immediately from the time it first began in 431 B.C. (1.1.1) and pointed out that at that time he was "of age to comprehend events" (5.26.5). These remarks suggest that he was in his early adulthood at the outbreak of the war, which would mean that he was born sometime in the 450s. When plague hit Athens in the summer of 430, the disease afflicted Thucydides, but he survived (2.48.3). We find him commanding Athenian forces in Thrace in 424 and 423 B.C. During his command the city of Amphipolis, an Athenian ally in Thrace, defected to the Spartans. Thucydides claims he reacted to the crisis as soon as possible, and thanks to his quickness he prevented nearby Eion from defecting to Sparta as well (4.106.3–4). Nonetheless, the people of Athens held Thucydides responsible for losing Amphipolis and imposed a 20-year exile upon him.

Thucydides reports that his exile proved advantageous for the writing of his history because it gave him access to the Peloponnesian view of events, which was unusual for an Athenian (5.26.5). Indeed, Thucydides was aware that his judgment could be clouded by the fact that he was a participant in the war. "I did not even trust my own impressions," he said (1.22.2). The Roman Lucian praised Thucydides' relentless pursuit of objectivity:

> There stands my model, then: fearless, incorruptible, independent, a believer in frankness and veracity; one that will call a spade a spade, make no concession to likes and dislikes, nor spare any man for pity or respect or propriety; an impartial judge, kind to all, but too kind to none; a literary cosmopolite with neither suzerain nor king, never heeding what this or that man may think, but setting down the thing that befell.[1]

Thucydides' attitude toward truth and objectivity exem-

plifies an intellectual movement that moved among some elites at the time. Proponents of this movement were highly skeptical of supernatural claims and sought truth through the careful observation of nature. A good illustration is Thucydides' highly clinical description of the plague that swept through Athens in 430 B.C. (2.48–54). Among Thucydides' contemporaries who also adhered to this secular and rationalistic view of knowledge and reality were the physician Hippocrates, the philosopher Anaxagoras, and Pericles the Athenian statesman.[2] Thucydides' earlier contemporary, Herodotus, did not share these ideas.

Significance

Secretary of State George C. Marshall was the architect of U.S. foreign policy immediately following World War II when the U.S. entered into a tense Cold War with the Soviet Union. He also read Thucydides. In 1947 he contemplated a new global situation that placed the United States as a global superpower. He said, "I doubt seriously whether a man can think with full wisdom and with deep conviction regarding certain of the basic international issues today who has not at least reviewed in his mind the period of the Peloponnesian War and the fall of Athens."[3]

Thucydides' analysis of the Peloponnesian War has shaped intellectuals and statesmen alike throughout modern times. His outlook deeply influenced early modern political theorists such as Niccolò Machiavelli and Thomas Hobbes. It also guided many nineteenth-century heads of state in Europe, most notably Otto von Bismarck. Twentieth-century advocates of Thucydides' outlook include Hans Morgenthau and Edward Carr. Among American statesmen, we see his influence in the policies of Secretary of State George Marshall, ambassador to the U.S.S.R. George F. Kennan, and Secretary of State Henry Kissinger. Thucydidean ideas have also been proposed as a guide for U.S. policy for the post-Cold War era by Dennis Ross, who held influential diplomatic posts in the administrations of George H.W. Bush, Bill Clinton, George W. Bush and Barack Obama.[4] Whether you agree or disagree with Thucydides' perspective, it is a perspective that has shaped many statesmen and is one that we must take into account.

Main Characters

The second half of the fifth century B.C. is often called the "age of Pericles," so named after Athens' leading man of the era. We first encounter Pericles in history when he sponsored the playwright Aeschylus in around 472. Ten years later he came to prominence in Athenian politics when he opposed a faction that wanted Athens to befriend Sparta. Beginning in 460 and for 29 years thereafter, the Athenians annually elected Pericles to the office of military archon, or *strategos* (often translated into English as *general*). His policies led to a string of skirmishes against Sparta that are collectively known as "The First Peloponnesian War" of 461–446, which concluded in the "Thirty Years Peace." Pericles also oversaw a massive public building campaign that included the construction of the Parthenon. He died in a plague that swept through Athens in 429.

Thucydides had great respect for Pericles, but little respect for Athenian leaders who came after him. Among them was Cleon, who figures prominently in books 3 and 4. Thucydides uses Cleon as a foil to set up Diodotus's brilliant speech in book 3, and also blames him (and the Athenians who supported him) for refusing a generous offer of peace from Sparta, a peace that Pericles would surely have accepted (4.17–22, 41.4).

While Cleon is leading Athens in some bad decisions, Brasidas, an effective Spartan leader, enters the narrative. Brasidas was important because he seems to be the only Spartan who understood how to defeat Athens: not by a direct invasion of their territory, but by supporting rebellions among Athens' subject states. Athens' allies were the source of Athenian strength (cf. 2.13.2, 65.7). Thucydides recognizes Brasidas's valor in a few places (e.g., 2.35.2, 3.79.3, 4.11.4) and shows that his leadership was especially effective in a campaign through Thrace (book 4).

Other significant characters include Nicias and Alcibiades, who are discussed below.

Summary and Setting

Our name for this conflict, the "Peloponnesian War," was coined a few centuries ago. It reflects the western affinity for classical Athens that pervaded early modern Europe. (What Americans refer to as "the Korean War" is surely not what Koreans call it!) Interestingly, though Thucydides was Athenian, he called the conflict by a less partisan name than we give it: "the war between the Peloponnesians and the Athenians" (1.1.1). This great war lasted from 431 to 404 B.C.

Some people today mistakenly think of the Peloponnesian War as a civil war because it was a war in which Greeks fought Greeks. But this overlooks the fact that Greek cities in this era were separate political entities, distinct from one another. Thus the Peloponnesian War was an international conflict that convulsed the entire Greek-speaking world. Even Persia, the great near-eastern empire of that age, became

Thucydides thought highly of Pericles, the Athenian leader who consistently opposed Sparta. Among other notable acts, he sponsored the playwright Aeschylus and oversaw the construction of the Parthenon.

deeply involved. From the Greek perspective, this was literally a world war.

In book 1, Thucydides outlines his approach and then addresses the causes of the war. This book is divided into five sections. The first is a brief introduction in which Thucydides asserts that the war between the Peloponnesians and the Athenians was the "greatest movement" in history up to his time (1.1.2). Then follows the second section, called the *Archaeology,* in which Thucydides defends his "greatest movement" claim while at the same time he explains methods of fact-finding (1.2–23). Here he reviews the most important Greek wars of the past, the Trojan War and the Persian Wars, in order to minimize their greatness in comparison to the war he is writing about. At the end of this section (1.23.5–6), Thucydides distinguishes two causes of the Peloponnesian War, which form the structure of the remainder of book 1. The first cause is the pretext for war, or the grievances each side had against the other. It boils down to a quarrel over who broke a treaty to which they had agreed back in 446 B.C. Then Thucydides mentions the "real cause," kept hidden, that actually motivated Athens and Sparta to fight one another. In the third part of book 1 Thucydides recounts the first kind of cause, or the pretext for war, which features Corcyra and Potidaea (24–88). In the fourth part, Thucydides narrates background to what he deems to be the war's real cause, which is the growth of Athens and the fear it aroused in Sparta (89–117). Finally, in the remaining fifth part of book 1, he returns to the pretext for war, describing negotiations prior to the outbreak of war (118–146).

Thucydides turns to the war itself beginning in book 2. The first phase of the war is called the *Archidamian War* after the Spartan king Archidamus. The Archidamian war lasted from 431–421 B.C. and spans books 2 through 5.24 in Thucydides' account. This first phase concluded when Athens and Sparta reached an agreement called the *Peace of Nicias,* named for the Athenian leader who represented Athens in the negotiations. Tensions continued under the Peace, which Thucydides describes in the rest of book 5. Books 6–7 recount Athens' magnificent but ill-fated expedition to Sicily. Many have said that Thucydides' account of the Sicilian expedition is the greatest narrative in all western literature. Toward the end of the expedition, Athens and Sparta came to blows once again, shattering the Peace of Nicias. This brought the war into its final phase from 413–404 B.C. This phase is called the *Decelean War,* so named because an important strategic feature of this phase was the Spartan occupation of Decelea, a small city dangerously close to Athens. The final book of Thucydides, book 8, opens with events in 413 B.C. and continues to an abrupt end in the middle of 411 B.C. Leaving his work unfinished, Thucydides does not record the final seven years of the war. The Greek historian Xenophon, not Thucydides, is our most important source for the end of the Peloponnesian War and the fall of Athens.[5]

Worldview

Historians inevitably infuse their own understanding of human nature and society into their narratives of the past. This is certainly true of Thucydides. He believed that political ties are more important to one's identity than ties of kinship, friendship, religion or business. He saw the office of *citizen* as more important than the office of *mother* or *husband.* Not surprisingly, his history focuses on politics to the exclusion of other dimensions of society and culture. In this way he differed sharply from Herodotus, who wrote a good deal about religion, diet, marriage and child rearing, clothing, and other aspects of culture. Thucydides' approach to history resembled that of many modern historians from the enlightenment era through the nineteenth century. A good representative is Edward Gibbon, who wrote in his famous *Decline and Fall of the Roman Empire* that "wars, and the administration of public affairs, are the principal subjects of history" (ch. IX). Like many who came after him, Thucydides saw this as the most rational or scientific way to look at human society. We find almost nothing in his work about private life, religion or kinship. As an observer of politics, however, Thucydides has much to offer.

Thucydides sometimes refers to himself in the third person, as though he as a writer stands with Olympian detachment from the events he describes (1.1.1, 4.104–106). He cleanly separates Thucydides the historical actor from Thucydides the writer of history. Indeed, Thucydides believes that history is made up of an objective body of facts about the past, and that these facts can be accessed and understood by any observer who employs the proper method to get at them. Any intelligent observer should see the same facts the same way. Thus, in the age-old debate over whether history should be grouped among the sciences or the humanities, Thucydides is a science man.

A key assumption underlying any scientific pursuit is that the thing being studied behaves in a law-like manner—it acts consistently, predictably. This is how chemists and physicists think about the natural world, or at least the parts of it they study. Some disciplines treat humans in a similar way. Sociology and modern economics are good examples. Practitioners of these *social* sciences treat human actions as data points, compile and organize them, analyze them with statistical tools, and use the results to form theories about human behavior in general. Social sciences arose a little over a century ago. Around the turn of the nineteenth century, intellectuals began viewing humans as part of nature rather than above, distinct from, or different from nature. If humans function within the ordinary operations of nature, then they can be studied using the same methods we use to study nature—that is, with scientific methods. Out of this intellectual transformation came many new developments in the nineteenth century, including an evolutionary view of human origins, advances in modern medicine, and the rise of the social sciences. Thucydides would probably have been comfortable with these changes. While he seldom used numbers, averages or statistics (though one place where he does is 1.10.4–5), he certainly analyzed the past in a systematic way in order to theorize about human behavior in general. For Thucydides, social and political laws are like natural laws. This is why, for more

Thucydides believed that no city-state answered to any law higher than itself. This means that the realm of international relations is a free-for-all. Put simply, the world is in a perpetual state of international anarchy.

than a century now, scholars have described Thucydides' approach to history as "modern."

Thucydides believed that anyone who understands the general rules or common habits of human action will be able to predict how people (or nations) are likely to behave in certain situations. He measured the value of his work by how well it fostered this skill: "... if it be judged useful by those inquirers who desire an exact knowledge of the past as an aid to the understanding of the future, which in the course of human things must resemble it if it does not reflect it, I shall be content." Thucydides' project was far more ambitious than merely setting forth a reliable account of the Peloponnesian War. He treated the war as a lens through which to study the general workings of human society, which can be applied to any age. "I have written my work," he says, "not as an essay which is to win the applause of the moment, but as a possession for all time" (1.22.4).

Political science is the social science that captured Thucydides' attention. His political philosophy can be summarized in five basic principles. The first principle is the most important. Thucydides held that nations act according to three basic motives: *fear, honor,* and *interest*. When Peloponnesian cities complained about Athenian supremacy, Athenian representatives explained that their city's actions were grounded in these three motives. When the Greek cities invited Athens to lead them in their campaigns against Persia, Athens accepted the invitation—as any city would have—because it suited her interest to do so. Later, when their leadership became irksome to the various Greek allies, Athens tightened her grip on these allies because she feared what could happen if they lost control of cities that despised her leadership. These disgruntled allies would surely look for help from Athens' rival, Sparta, thereby causing Athens to lose face (honor), not to mention the tribute she received from these allies (interest). "It follows," they explained,

> that it was not a very remarkable action, or contrary to the common practice of mankind, if we did accept an empire that was offered to us, and refused to give it up under the pressure of the three strongest motives, fear, honor, and interest. And it was not we who set the example, for it has always been the law that the weaker should be subject to the stronger (1.76).

Notice that Athens' policy toward her allies accorded with "the common practice of mankind" and reflected an unchanging "law." This is a law of national behavior that the Spartans themselves followed, just as any nation would (1.75–76).

In Thucydides' outlook, the motives *fear, honor,* and

interest sometimes converge, but at a given moment one may be more prominent than the other two. *Interest* is the motive that seeks national gain, whether it is a gain in wealth, strategic advantage, or honor. *Fear* is the motive that seeks to prevent the loss of any of these qualities. *Honor* is a motive that seeks prestige, eminence or "face." It has more to do with a nation's standing relative to others than with being known as a virtuous nation. Of the three, *honor* is the most confusing to us because our western notion of honor is laden with Christian underpinnings. Remember that Thucydides lived in Greece five centuries before the arrival of Christianity. In Thucydides, Pericles' speeches illustrate the motive of honor nicely. He urged Athens not to yield to a trifling Spartan demand, saying, ". . . make them clearly understand that they must treat you as equals" (1.140.5). He praised Athens in his famous funeral oration by saying, "Our constitution does not copy the laws of neighboring states; we are rather a pattern to others than imitators ourselves" (2.37.1). This same sense of honor figures prominently in Homer's *Iliad*. Achilles quarrels with Agamemnon and leaves the battle because Agamemnon slighted his honor.

Second, Thucydides believed that nations (or in his Greek context, city-states) are truly sovereign. No nation answers to a law above itself. Thus, when two nations come into conflict, there is no higher court of appeal that can rightly claim jurisdiction over both. No legitimate authority exists that can preside over and adjudicate the dispute. This means that the realm of international relations is a free-for-all. Put simply, the world is in a perpetual state of international anarchy.

Third, in the absence of an enforcer to which all the nations are beholden, nations work out their differences by appealing to power or force. This does not mean that nations will always fight all the time, as many mistakenly assume. Fighting is often disadvantageous to one or both sides in a dispute. Nonetheless, weaker nations tend to make concessions to stronger nations, and stronger nations tend to place demands upon weaker nations. Thucydides filled his work with examples of such complex power relationships among the Greek cities.

Thucydides acknowledged that nations justify their policies by appealing to justice and morality. Every nation will *claim* that it is always "doing right." This is certainly true of nations in a dispute with one another. Thucydides believed that, in the end, neither justice nor righteousness can settle the dispute. But power can, and always will, settle such disputes. The cleanest summary statement of this principle appears in an Athenian speech to the ignorant leaders of the puny island of Melos: ". . . you know as well as we do that right, as the world goes, is only in question between equals in power, while the strong do what they can and the weak suffer what they must" (5.89). Thucydides believed that morality has a place in political events, but only a subordinate place. Power sits in the driver's seat.

Fourth, Thucydides believed that hegemony brings order and peace among the nations. Hegemony is a condition in which one nation is preeminent and exercises control or influence over the others. The presence of a hegemonic power diminishes the chaos of international rivalry due to several factors. Less powerful nations will either ally with or oppose the hegemonic power. Allying with the powerful nation brings trade and military protection to a smaller nation. The small nations who dislike the hegemonic power are unlikely to take up arms against it for fear of being crushed. The hegemonic power, in turn, shapes its own policies to preserve its superiority. Because war tends to disrupt the *status quo*, a hegemonic power is unlikely to instigate war. If war does break out, the strongest nation will step in to contain it and bring it to a speedy end.

Thucydides credits hegemonic power with the highest attainments of Greek antiquity. For example, in the Minoan era, King Minos of Crete wielded hegemonic power over the Aegean islands. He expelled the Carians (who were pirates that disrupted trade) and through his power he ushered in a heyday of trade and communication among various Greek peoples (1.4, 7–8). Thucydides had a similar view of Mycenean power under Agamemnon's leadership during the Trojan War. According to legend that survives in Homeric epic, leaders of the Achaean armada assembled against Troy to fulfill an oath. But Thucydides attributes the fleet to Agamemnon's "superiority in strength;" those who followed his command did so out of fear (1.9). During the half-century interval between the Persian Wars and the Peloponnesian War, Athens became the greatest hegemonic power in Greek history (1.10.3; cf. 1.118.2, 3.10–12, *passim*), an assessment that figured into Thucydides' claim that the Peloponnesian War was the greatest disturbance yet known.

The fifth principle has to do with the political order within a nation rather than between nations. Thucydides believed that it is advantageous to align the personal ambition of a capable leader (or leaders) with the national interests of his city. In Thucydides, this principle plays out in the careers of Pericles and Alcibiades.

Thucydides admired Pericles for exercising independent control over the Athenian people, going so far as to say that during his tenure Athens was a democracy in name only (2.65.9). Pericles urged Athens not to give in to Sparta's ultimatum, thereby bringing on the war (1.139–146). He also orchestrated Athenian strategy in the early years of the war (2.13.2, 65.7), a strategy

Thucydides believed would have brought success. After Pericles succumbed to the plague in 429 B.C., various factions fought to fill the void of leadership he left behind. It was the petty squabbling of these factions that caused Athens' downfall (2.65). Thucydides believed that petty factions are the bane of democracy.

To illustrate the ills of faction in a democracy, Thucydides uses prominent Athenians who came into leadership after Pericles. None of these successors possessed Pericles' ability to exercise independent control over the Athenian people. Among them was Cleon, whom Thucydides describes as "a popular leader of the time and very powerful with the multitude"—which are negative attributes in Thucydides' outlook (4.21.3; cf. 3.36.6). Another leader was the incompetent Nicias, whom the Athenians placed in leadership because he was nice and pious, in contrast to the highly capable Alcibiades. Alcibiades came under fire because his ostentatious personal habits offended the Athenian people. When Nicias attacked Alcibiades' character on this point, Alcibiades admitted to being ambitious. But he was quick to add that the fame he sought for himself brought fame to Athens as well, and this benefited all Athenians (6.12.2, 4.16). This reasoning reflects Thucydides' own outlook. But Athens did not embrace this principle, to her own destruction. Once the Sicilian expedition got underway, a faction of Alcibiades' opponents implicated Alcibiades in a scandal. Because they loathed Alcibiades' personal habits, the simpleminded Athenian people were duped. They recalled Alcibiades from the expedition, though he was an outstanding military leader, and they kept the incapable but virtuous Nicias in command. By preferring Nicias over Alcibiades, the naïve Athenians sided with morality over competence. In Thucydides' assessment, the factional squabbling caused the Sicilian expedition to end in disaster for Athens (cf. 2.65.11 and 6.15.4).

In Federalist #10, the most famous of the Federalist Papers, James Madison took a page from Thucydides when he criticized democracies for their inability to control the violence of faction. Madison, of course, preferred a republic. Thucydides did not mind republican rule so long as a voice in government was given to only those who had a direct personal or financial investment in the nation. Rulers who directly benefit from their position have a personal stake in the well-being of the state. Thus they have personal incentive for the state to succeed (cf. 8.97).[6] Many of America's early founders agreed, and applied this principle by extending voting privileges only to those who owned land. This principle fell into disfavor during the Jacksonian era.

These five principles about nations (they are motivated by fear, honor and interest; they are sovereign over their own affairs; they will appeal to force if not forced to peace by a greater power; the hegemony of one nation over many others brings order and peace; and that wise states align the personal interests of ambitious and able

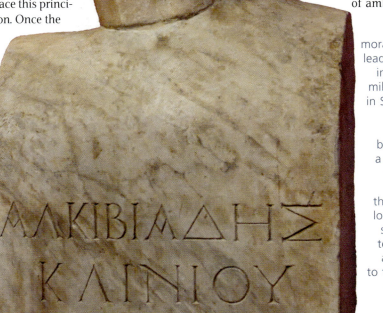

Does personal morality matter in a leader? While leading the Athenian military expedition in Sicily, Alcibiades was recalled to Athens after being charged in a scandal. Rather than returning, he defected to the Spartans. The loss of his leadership was a blow to the Athenians and contributed to their calamitous defeat in Sicily.

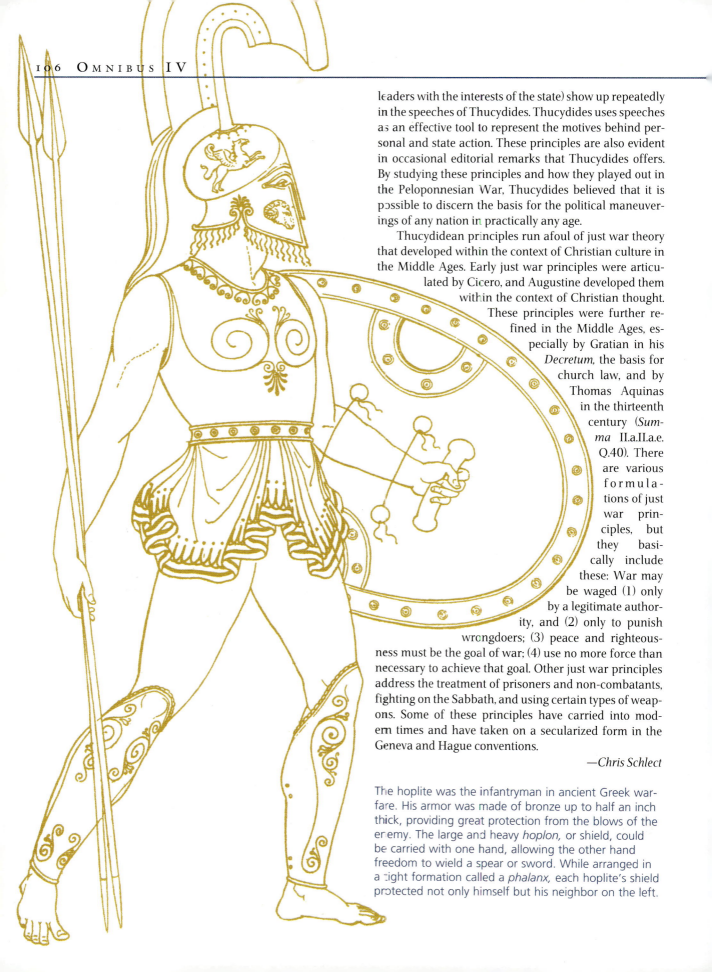

leaders with the interests of the state) show up repeatedly in the speeches of Thucydides. Thucydides uses speeches as an effective tool to represent the motives behind personal and state action. These principles are also evident in occasional editorial remarks that Thucydides offers. By studying these principles and how they played out in the Peloponnesian War, Thucydides believed that it is possible to discern the basis for the political maneuverings of any nation in practically any age.

Thucydidean principles run afoul of just war theory that developed within the context of Christian culture in the Middle Ages. Early just war principles were articulated by Cicero, and Augustine developed them within the context of Christian thought. These principles were further refined in the Middle Ages, especially by Gratian in his *Decretum*, the basis for church law, and by Thomas Aquinas in the thirteenth century (*Summa* II.a.II.a.e. Q.40). There are various formulations of just war principles, but they basically include these: War may be waged (1) only by a legitimate authority, and (2) only to punish wrongdoers; (3) peace and righteousness must be the goal of war; (4) use no more force than necessary to achieve that goal. Other just war principles address the treatment of prisoners and non-combatants, fighting on the Sabbath, and using certain types of weapons. Some of these principles have carried into modern times and have taken on a secularized form in the Geneva and Hague conventions.

—Chris Schlect

The hoplite was the infantryman in ancient Greek warfare. His armor was made of bronze up to half an inch thick, providing great protection from the blows of the enemy. The large and heavy *hoplon*, or shield, could be carried with one hand, allowing the other hand freedom to wield a spear or sword. While arranged in a tight formation called a *phalanx*, each hoplite's shield protected not only himself but his neighbor on the left.

For Further Reading

Connor, W. Robert. *Thucydides.* Princeton, N.J.: Princeton University Press, 1984.

Crane, Gregory. *The Blinded Eye: Thucydides and the New Written Word.* London: Rowman and Littlefield Publishers, Inc., 1996.

Crane, Gregory. *Thucydides and the Ancient Simplicity: The Limits of Political Realism.* Berkeley, Calif.: University of California Press, 1998.

Dewald, Carolyn. *Thucydides' War Narrative: A Structural Study.* Berkeley, Calif.: University of California Press, 2006.

Forde, Steven. *The Ambition to Rule: Alcibiades and the Politics of Imperialism in Thucydides.* Ithaca, N.Y.: Cornell University Press, 1989.

Hornblower, Simon. *A Commentary on Thucydides; Vol. I: Books I–III,* and *Vol. II: Books IV–V.24.* New York: Oxford University Press, 1991 and 1996.

Hornblower, Simon. *Thucydides.* Baltimore, Md.: The Johns Hopkins University Press, 1987.

Kagan, Donald. *The Peloponnesian War.* New York: Viking, 2003.

Orwin, Clifford. *The Humanity of Thucydides.* Princeton, N.J.: Princeton University Press, 1994.

Rood, Timothy. *Thucydides: Narrative and Explanation.* New York: Oxford University Press, 1998.

Spielvogel, Jackson J. *Western Civilization.* Seventh Edition. Belmont, Calif.: Thomson Wadsworth, 2009. 73–78.

Veritas Press History Cards: New Testament, Greece and Rome. Lancaster, Pa.: Veritas Press. 14.

Session I: Prelude

A Question to Consider

How would you think Thucydides would react to this statement by Theodore Roosevelt? Roosevelt wrote, "War, like peace, is properly a means to an end—righteousness. Neither war nor peace is in itself righteous, and neither should be treated as of itself the end to be aimed at. Righteousness is the end."[7]

From the General Information above, answer the following questions:

1. What did Aristotle mean when he said that the statements of history are "singulars"? Explain how it is that this attribute does not describe Thucydides' approach to the past.
2. Though Thucydides was Athenian, why did he believe he could faithfully represent both sides of the war in his account?
3. How did Athens function as a democracy during the height of Pericles' rule? How did it not?
4. Explain how Thucydides reasoned that democracy contributed to the failure of Athens' expedition to Sicily.
5. Though World War II began in 1938 or '39, the United States did not enter the war until December of 1941 following the Japanese attack on Pearl Harbor. Briefly explain the United States' motives for entering World War II in terms of the Thucydidean motives of *fear, honor* and *interest.*

Reading Assignment:
The Peloponnesian War, Book 1.1–46

Session II: Discussion
The Peloponnesian War, Book 1.1–46

A Question to Consider

In book 1 Thucydides traces some of the events that led up to the Peloponnesian War. At points, participants in these events seem to take the coming of the war as something almost predestined. In some of the *Star Trek* movies, there is an inevitable conflict scenario—the famous Kobayashi Maru Flight Simulator Test. In this test there is no possibility of victory. War and defeat are inevitable—or so everyone seems to think.[8] Are events inevitable?

Discuss or list short answers to the following questions:

Text Analysis

1. What caused the conflict between Corcyra and Corinth to erupt?
2. Why did the Epidamnians seek help from the Corinthians?
3. Why did the Corcyraean and Corinthian envoys end up in Athens?
4. What arguments did the Corcyraeans make to attempt to win Athenian support?
5. What arguments did the Corinthians make to encourage Athens to refuse support to Corcyra?
6. What decision did the Athenians make? Why did they make this decision?

Cultural Analysis

1. Where do you see examples in our culture of conflicts that are deemed inevitable?
2. How does our culture view genetics as an inevitable cause of actions?

Biblical Analysis

1. What was the string of events that led Cain to kill Abel? Do these events exonerate Cain (Gen. 3)? and 4
2. Do pagans have an excuse for the sins that they commit? Why not, if they have never heard someone preach the gospel (Rom. 1:18–22, Acts 17:30)?
3. Was the crucifixion an inevitable event? Does God's hand in the event exonerate those who crucified Him (Acts 2:22–23)?

SUMMA

Write an essay or discuss this question, integrating what you have learned from the material above.
Does understanding that God is sovereign over all events make them easier to bear?

The next session will be a student-led discussion. Students will be creating their own questions concerning the issue of the session. Students should create three Text Analysis Questions, two Cultural Analysis questions, and two Biblical Analysis questions. For more detailed instructions, please see the chapter on the *Iliad*, Session III.

Issue

Acting in one's own best interest

READING ASSIGNMENT:
The Peloponnesian War, Book 1.47–117

Thucydides believed naval power was a key factor in Athenian dominance in the Aegean Sea. He himself had commanded a squadron of triremes. These light but strong ships were used for ramming enemy ships with their reinforced prows. Their name (*trieres*, "three-fitted") comes from the three levels of rowers who powered and maneuvered the ship.

SESSION III: STUDENT-LED DISCUSSION
The Peloponnesian War, Book 1.47–117

A Question to Consider

Is it ever wrong for a person or a country to act in its own best interest?

Students should read and consider the example questions below that are connected to the Question to Consider above. Last session's assignment was to prepare three questions and answers for the Text Analysis section and two additional questions and answers for both the Cultural and Biblical Analysis sections below.

Text Analysis

Example: How did the Athenians justify the accumulation of power and the creation of their empire?

Answer: They did not apologize for it. On the contrary, they claimed they were simply acting in their own interest. They reminded the Spartans that everyone would hate them too if they had had the good fortune to have built an empire. They argued that they had been more gentle and considerate of others than they had had to be. In summary, they claimed it is only natural to act in one's own best interest and that is all they have done (1.72–78).

Cultural Analysis

Example: Where do we see people acting in their own interest in our society today? Is this often wrong? When is it wrong?

Answer: We see this everywhere. We can note that it occurs in business—one businessman tries to sell more widgets than his competitor by selling for less. Customers shop ceaselessly for widgets, plasma screen TVs, and candy bars, trying to find the best deal, because keeping their money is in their own best interest. We see this in politics where speakers carefully measure their words to try to communicate their message without offending any voters, because they wish to be re-elected. Often acting in one's own interest is fine so long as it is done within the confines of God's commandments. If we look at the world as He does and see our best interest in light of His perspective, we can see that our best interest and righteousness will always coincide. Seeing this, however, is often difficult. One large problem that has prevailed since the Enlightenment is that we tend to see the world (and reckon our interests) individually rather than covenantally.

Other cultural issues to consider: Capitalism v. socialism, supply and demand, pre-nuptial agreements (which are not in one's best interest) and focus groups.

Biblical Analysis

Example: In Proverbs 22:7, it says that the "borrower is slave of the lender." If we want to be humble and avoid "acting selfishly in our own interest," should we then become the borrower?

Answer: This is not what the Scripture is trying to convey. It recognizes that debt can turn the borrower into a slave. While the Scriptures recognize that sometimes we can not avoid debt and slavery, it recommends that we avoid debt-slavery and commends savings, hard work, and frugality. The Bible expects us to act shrewdly with the resources that we are given. It commends reasonable risk so that we can make a profit and use that profit to further serve God. Remember, all that we have belongs to the Lord—not just the tithe. He gives to us that we might give to others.

Other Scriptures to consider: Genesis 12:1–3; Proverbs 14:1; Hebrews 12:2.

SUMMA

Write an essay or discuss this question, integrating what you have learned from the material above.
With so many people shouting so many ideas today, how can we determine our best interest?

READING ASSIGNMENT:
The Peloponnesian War, Book 1.118–146

SESSION IV: RECITATION
The Peloponnesian War, Book 1.1–146

Comprehension Questions
Answer the following questions for factual recall:
1. What caused the Greeks to colonize?
2. Who was the first city-state to develop the trireme?
3. What was the cause of the Peloponnesian War according to Thucydides?
4. What started the strife between Corcyra and Corinth?
5. Which side—the Athenians/Corcyraeans or the Corinthians—erected trophies and celebrated victory at Leukimme?
6. What did Athens tell the Potidaeans they must do?
7. What arguments did the Corinthian envoys use to convince the Spartans to defend Potidaea?
8. What did King Archidamus of Sparta wonder concerning the conflict with Athens?
9. Why did Themistocles go to Sparta to discuss the Spartan demand that Athens not rebuild their city wall?
10. When the Helots revolted against their Spartan masters, what did the Athenians do? What became of this?
11. What are "The Long Walls?"
12. Whom did the exiled Themistocles end up serving?
13. What did Pericles recommend concerning the Spartan pressure on Athens to rescind the Megarian Decree?

READING ASSIGNMENT:
The Peloponnesian War, Book 2.34–65, 71–85 and Book 3.1–21

SESSION V: WRITING

Speech for the Nation
The Peloponnesian War, Book 2.34–65

This session is a writing assignment. Remember, quality counts more than quantity. You should write no more than 1,000 words, either typing or writing legibly on one side of a sheet of paper. You will lose points for writing more than this. You will be allowed to turn in your writing three times. The first and second times you turn it in, your teacher will grade it by editing your work. This is done by marking problem areas and making suggestions for improvement. You should take these suggestions into consideration as you revise your assignment. Only the grade on your final submission will be recorded. Your

Birthplace of Artemis and Apollo according to mythology, the "heaven-built isle" of Delos served as the treasury for the Athenians. The Terrace of the Lions featured snarling marble lions guarding the Sacred Way.

grade will be based on the following criteria: 25 points for grammar, 25 points for content accuracy—historical, theological, etc.; 25 points for logic—does this make sense and is it structured well?; 25 points for rhetoric—is it a joy to read?

Your objective is to imagine yourself as the leader of your country or the speech writer for the President. Imagine that your country is at war and that you are speaking at the memorial service for a number of fallen soldiers. Write a speech imitating Pericles' Funeral Oration.

Optional Activity

Watch another interesting example of a speech inspired by Pericles' Funeral Oration in the movie *City Hall* starring Al Pacino. Pacino plays the mayor, and he is eulogizing a child killed by gang violence. Note, however, the similarities and differences between what Pericles and Pacino say in their speeches. Both are talking about the state and virtues and problems of their cities. You can watch the speech online.[9]

Reading Assignment:
The Peloponnesian War, Book 3.22–85

Session VI: Discussion

A Question to Consider

When is revolution (the overthrow of an established government) justified?

Discuss or list short answers to the following questions:

Text Analysis

1. After the Athenians put down the revolution in Mytilene, Cleon and Diodotus argued for very different treatment of the rebels. For what did they each argue?
2. What did the Athenians decide concerning Mytilene?
3. When the Plataeans surrendered to the Spartan siege, what did they hope to receive from Sparta? What did the Thebans want for the Plataeans?
4. What did the Spartans decide concerning Plataea?
5. What did the Corcyraean oligarchs do in the summer of 427 B.C.?
6. How did the Peloponnesians and the Athenians again become involved in Corcyra's politics?
7. In book 3.82–85, how does Thucydides describe the results of revolution? Particularly, how does revolution affect the meaning of words, the perception of masculinity, promises and oaths, and nobility?
8. What motive drives the destructive forces of revolution?

Cultural Analysis

1. Where do you see a lust for power in our political culture?
2. Where do you see greed at work in our culture—particularly in people using force to take property from their enemies?

Biblical Analysis

1. Does Adam's rebellion against God count as a revolution (Gen. 3)?
2. Why did the people rebel against God's leadership and demand a king "like the other nations" (1 Sam. 8)?

Summa

Write an essay or discuss this question, integrating what you have learned from the material above.
How can we oppose the forces of revolution in our days? When should we become the forces of revolution?

The next session will be a student-led discussion. Students will be creating their own questions concerning the issue of the session. Students should create three Text Analysis Questions, two Cultural Analysis questions, and two Biblical Analysis questions. For more detailed instructions, please see the chapter on the *Iliad,* Session III.

Issue

How the strong should treat the weak

Reading Assignment:
The Peloponnesian War, Book 4.1–41 and Book 5.84–116

Session VII: Student-Led Discussion

A Question to Consider

How should strong groups of people treat weak groups of people?

Students should read and consider the example questions below that are connected to the Question to Consider above. Last session's assignment was to prepare three questions and answers for the Text Analysis section and two additional questions and answers for both the Cultural and Biblical Analysis sections below.

Text Analysis

Example: What does Thucydides think of the fact that Athenians treated the Melians based on the principle that the strong do what they can and the weak suffer what they must?

Answer: Thucydides thinks this is simply the way the world works. His observations have a lot of history behind them. Strong nations tend to do what they want to do and then figure out ways to justify their actions after they have accomplished their objectives (5.89).

Cultural Analysis

Example: In our culture where do we see the weak suffering at the hands of the powerful?

Answer: We see this in many places. It is typical of what happens when political divisions occur within a society. It also occurs often in wars. When stronger forces meet weaker ones, they typically have their way with them—even if the results are atrocious. We also see this sort of oppression financially when people are trapped in debt.

Other cultural issues to consider: Abortion and euthanasia, families trapped by gang violence, war.

Biblical Analysis

Example: In 1 Samuel 11, Nahash the Ammonite besieged God's people at Jabesh Gilead. What were Nahash's terms for a treaty? Why did the people consider complying? How were they spared?

Answer: His terms were that he would only make a treaty with them and break the siege if he were allowed to put out the right eye—the eye used by the archers of Israel—of all the men in Jabesh Gilead. This would both neutralize the men of Jabesh Gilead as a fighting force and "bring disgrace on all Israel." The men of Jabesh Gilead considered taking these terms because otherwise he might kill all of them simply by keeping up the siege and starving them to death. They, like Thucydides, realized the weak often have to suffer terrible injustice. God, however, sent Saul to break the siege and rescue Jabesh Gilead.

Other Scriptures to consider: Exodus 1, Exodus 20:8–11, Matt. 23:14, James 1:27, Romans 5:8, Romans 14, Proverbs 13:23.

SUMMA

Write an essay or discuss this question, integrating what you have learned from the material above.
How should we as believers treat those weaker than us? How should we act when we are weaker and others are stronger?

READING ASSIGNMENT:
The Peloponnesian War, Book 6.1–72

SESSION VIII: RECITATION
The Peloponnesian War, Book 2.34–6.72

Comprehension Questions
Answer the following questions for factual recall:
1. In the Funeral Oration what did Pericles say that Athens was for Helles and what it was worthy to do?
2. In the Funeral Oration what did Pericles say should be done by widows, and what did he say would be done for the children of the dead soldiers?
3. Each year an army from the Peloponnesus invaded Athenian territory, burning crops and homes. What did Pericles say about this?
4. When the Peloponnesians attacked Plataea, what did the Athenians ask the Plataeans to do?
5. Why did the Mytilenians join with the Athenians—and what did they say was not the reason they joined them?
6. What happened when the Spartan, Salaethus, armed the common people of Mytilene?
7. On what point of debate did Cleon and Diodotus disagree?
8. What did the Spartans and Thebans do to Plataea when they surrendered?
9. When the Athenians had the upper hand at Pylos, Spartan envoys offered terms of peace to Athens. How did the Athenians react to these terms?
10. What tactic did Demosthenes use to defeat the Spartan forces on Sphacteria? What was he trying to avoid?
11. What was the outcome of the Athenian siege of Melos?
12. Why was Alcibiades recalled from Sicily and condemned to death in absentia by Athens?

Tomorrow's session will be a Current Events session. Your assignment will be to find a story online, in a magazine, or in the newspaper that relates to the issue that you discussed today. Your task is to locate the article, give a copy of the article to your teacher or parent and provide some of your own worldview analysis to the article. Your analysis should demonstrate that you understand the issue, that you can clearly connect the story you found to the issue that you discussed today, and that you can provide a biblical critique of this issue in today's context. Look at the next session to see the three-part format that you should follow.

Issue
Personal life affecting national politics

READING ASSIGNMENT:
The Peloponnesian War, Book 6.73–Book 7.19

SESSION IX: CURRENT EVENTS

In *The Peloponnesian War,* we meet a number of leaders. Some of them are good leaders, others are failures. One leader, Alcibiades, stands out because he works for both the Athenian and Spartan side. He is young, brash, excessive, and proud. He is also able, but his flamboyant lifestyle earns him many enemies who believe that he wants to overthrow democracy and introduce oligarchy or tyranny to Athens. He recognizes this fact, but simply claims that his arrogant attitude comes from his own excellence. Basically, he says, his pride is part of the package. This, of course, alienates and aggravates many Athenians, who hatch a plan to humiliate the proud Alcibiades. They use a case of vandalism to trump up charges of blasphemy against him. They delay the trial and stir up public sentiment against him before he returns to Athens, leaving the Sicilian Expedition in the hands of Nicias, who has few enemies but is not the caliber of general that Alcibiades is. Eventually, Alcibiades flees to the Spartan side and helps them understand how to defeat Athens by making them fight wars on two fronts, Syracuse and Attica. Thucydides recognizes Alcibiades' abilities and sees the ruin of Athens in Alcibiades' excesses, saying, "... and although in his public life his conduct of the war was as good as could be desired, in his private life his habits gave offense to everyone, and caused them to commit affairs to other hands, and thus before long to ruin the city." All too often today, leaders want to divorce private and public life. This, however, can not be done. Our private lives affect the trust that people have in us.

Issue

Personal life affecting national politics

Current events sessions are meant to challenge you to connect what you are learning in Omnibus class to what is happening in the world around you today. After the last session, your assignment was to find a story online or in a magazine or newspaper relating to the issue above. Today you will share your article and your analysis with your teacher and classmates or parents and family. Your analysis should follow the format below:

Brief Introductory Paragraph

In this paragraph you will tell your classmates about the article that you found. Be sure to include where you found your article, who the author of your article is, and what your article is about. This brief paragraph of your presentation should begin like this:

> Hello, I am (name), and my current events article is (name of the article) which I found in (name of the web or published source)...

Connection Paragraph

In this paragraph you must demonstrate how your article is connected to the issue that you are studying. This paragraph should be short, and it should focus on clearly showing the connection between the book that you are reading and the current events article that you have found. This paragraph should begin with a sentence like

> I knew that my article was linked to our issue because...

Christian Worldview Analysis

In this section, you need to tell us how we should respond as believers to this issue today. This response should focus both on our thinking and on practical actions that we should take in light of this issue. As you list these steps, you should also tell us why we should think and act in the ways you recommend. This paragraph should begin with a sentence like

> As believers, we should think and act in the following ways in light of this issue and this article.

Reading Assignment:
The Peloponnesian War, Book 7.20–87

Session X: Discussion
The Peloponnesian War, Book 6.1–7.87

A Question to Consider

How does a person or a country turn a defeat into a ruinous calamity like the Sicilian Expedition?

Discuss or list short answers to the following questions:

Text Analysis

1. How did Nicias try to convince the Athenians to reconsider their decision concerning the invasion of Sicily? What did his argument do?
2. Who was chosen to lead the expedition? Why was one of them recalled? Why?
3. How did Nicias display his indecisiveness after Gylippus' arrival?
4. Why did the Spartans fortify Decelea? What effect did this have on the Athenians?
5. What was the structural advantage of the new Corinthian triremes?
6. On what strategic steps did Demosthenes and Nicias disagree? What sorts of things were convincing Nicias that he was correct?
7. How did the different sides seek to motivate their fighters before the final battle?
8. What was the outcome of the Sicilian Expedition?

Cultural Analysis

1. Where do you see short-sighted or wrong-headed actions being taken by governments today?
2. Where do you see leaders avoiding hard decisions in order to curry the favor of the people?
3. Where do you see pride at work in the leadership of our culture?

Biblical Analysis

1. How did Rabshakeh's arrogance lead to a disaster for the Assyrians? How did Hezekiah's humility save his people (2 Kings 18:9–19:37)?
2. How did Hezekiah's pride lead to disaster (2 Kings 20:12–19)?

Summa

Write an essay or discuss this question, integrating what you have learned from the material above.

How can we help our nation avoid disasters like the Sicilian Expedition?

Optional Session A: Activity

The Democracy Game

Athenian democracy was a model for future republics like America. We might have warm feelings in our hearts when we hear words like "democracy." Many philosophers down through the ages, however, have been terrified of it. Democracy in Athens was a dangerous game for some who used the state for their own personal gain. (Of course, this could not happen in America, right? Seriously, democracies can be swayed by demagogues. Constitutional republics, like America, have protections—like hopefully having wise representatives—but we could and sadly do see the American Republic being swayed by demagogues in our day.) Often, politicians had a deep personal stake in the decisions that the government was making. Alcibiades longed for fame and fortune, thereby burning through the trust of many.

Today, we are going to do an experiment that will help us understand the dangers of democracy when people use the state for their own personal gain; to make it fun and to sharpen our persuasive abilities, we are going to play for some rewards.

Choose at least two, but preferably three, people as speakers. Each speaker will be given a Position and Reward Slip—see Rule #1 below. (These slips can be found in the Teacher's Edition. Print out the page containing them, cut out each slip, and distribute one to each speaker randomly.) If you are playing this game at home, you may limit the speakers to two. Parents and siblings are welcome to play. There should be at least one person in the audience. The audience will decide which position they will support after hearing the speeches. One person must be designated as the G.O.C. (Guardian of the Candy) and must, in fact, actually guard it until the game is over. This should be a teacher or parent if at all possible. The winning proposition will be the one with the most votes in the election. To begin this activity the G.O.C. is given a candy bar for each participant and one dollar is given to each participant. (If you have time and resources, play more than once with different speakers).

Rules

1. Each of the speakers has received a Position and Reward Slip. It tells them the position they must persuade the audience to support and what reward they (and possibly the audience) are to receive if they successfully get the most votes for their position.
2. All participants have been given one dollar. At the end of the game you might be allowed to keep it, or make a purchase with it, depending on the outcome of the vote and the reward on the winning speaker's slip.
3. Each speaker will have two chances to speak.
4. The speakers will present their speeches in turn. During the second round of speeches they will speak in reverse order.
5. Each speech will be limited to two minutes.
6. After all the speeches are completed there will be a short time for questions and answers.
7. Speakers should vote, but they may not vote for their own proposal.
8. Speakers may not reveal what the reward is or anything about the reward promised on their slip.
9. After the speeches hold the election to determine the winning speaker. If there is a tie, hold a run-off election between those speakers only.
10. When the game is over, each speaker reads the reward on his slip. Follow the instructions for the winner's reward.

A bust of Thucydides

THE QUESTION
Should participants in this game receive a candy bar?

Consider the following questions after the game is over:
1. What types of arguments were persuasive? (Did people argue emotionally or rationally? Did they twist people's arms to try to get their votes?)
2. Did personal interest corrupt the process?
3. Was the interest of the entire group served by the final decision or not?

OPTIONAL SESSION B: STUDENT-LED DISCUSSION
The Peloponnesian War

A Question to Consider

In *The Peloponnesian War*, we see a battle between the Athenian empire and the forces led by Sparta. Athens was a democracy, but she ruled her empire as though it were made up of slaves. Sparta was an oligarchy, but for many Greek city-states Spartan victory meant freedom from Athenian oppression. Which then is better: an empire (if you can have it) or a confederacy where one party does not have to submit to the other?

Students should read and consider the example questions below that are connected to the Question to Consider above. Last session's assignment was to prepare three questions and answers for the Text Analysis section and two additional questions and answers for both the Cultural and Biblical Analysis sections below.

Text Analysis

Example: In 1.23 Thucydides says that the cause of the Peloponnesian War was Sparta's fear of growing Athenian power. Should the Spartans have feared the growth of Athenian power?

Answer: Yes, they should have. The Athenians consistently proved that they wielded power unapologetically in their own interest. This interest might mean the total destruction of another city. When a group of people say that "the strong will do what they can and the weak will suffer what they must," it makes those who are seeking to keep their own freedom nervous. The Athenians continued to act arrogantly throughout the war. They wiped out Melos. They started a new war in Syracuse. They rejected generous peace terms on the part of Sparta.

Cultural Analysis

Example: Where are the forces of empire loose in our world today?

Answer: Since the end of World War II—and especially since the end of the Cold War—America has held a sort of hegemony over the nations of Europe and over the rest of the world. Our temptation is to act increasingly like an empire—rather than being a republic. Today, we are tempted to insert ourselves into many conflicts across the globe. Our interests are broad. America must carefully consider its place in the world and whether we should continue on the path of empire or look more to be the republic that our Founders envisioned.

Other cultural issues to consider: U.S. aid for foreign countries, peacekeeping, international treaties, internationalism, American Empire.

Biblical Analysis

Example: What form of government did ancient Israel have? Does this tell us anything about God's perspective on empires (singular or narrow freedom) or confederacies (freedom being spread more broadly)?

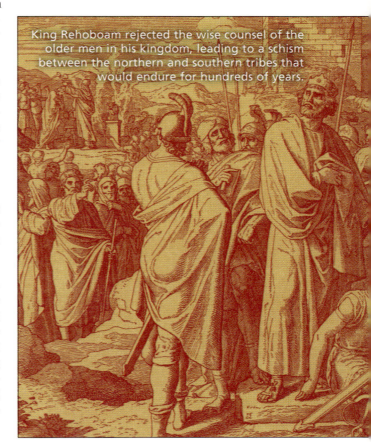
King Rehoboam rejected the wise counsel of the older men in his kingdom, leading to a schism between the northern and southern tribes that would endure for hundreds of years.

Answer: Israel was much more confederacy than empire. For most of the history of the nation, the leadership of each tribe was critical to the functioning of the state. Elders, since the time of Moses, were the functional local government of Israel. During the reign of Solomon, Israel became more centralized. After Solomon, however, Rehoboam was asked to decrease the control of the central government. Sadly, he rejected the wise counsel of the older men and tried to increase the centralized control (and worked the people like slaves). This rejection of wise advice led to the schism between the northern tribes, Israel, and the southern tribes, Judah. God, however, makes it clear that His people can thrive under the rule of many different kinds of governments. Still, governments, if they wish to please God, need to be servants of their people, protecting their freedom and liberty to serve Him and do what is righteous.

Other Scriptures to consider: Deuteronomy 17:14ff, 1 Samuel 8, Jeremiah 29:7, Isaiah 9:6–7, Revelation 11:15.

Summa

Write an essay or discuss this question, integrating what you have learned from the material above.

As we have influence over our government, what type of government should we desire, hope for, and work to have?

Endnotes

1. Lucian, "The Way to Write History" 42, in *The Works of Lucian*, trans. H.W. Fowler and F.G. Fowler, four volumes (Oxford University Press, 1905), vol. 2, 129.
2. Plutarch, Life of Pericles VI.
3. "Feb. 27, 1947," *Time* (10 March 1947).
4. See Alexander Kemos, "The Influence of Thucydides in the Modern World," *Point of Reference: A Journal of Hellenic Thought and Culture* (Harvard University, Fall 1994), available at http://www.hri.org/por/thucydides.html; also Dennis Ross, Statecraft: *And How to Restore America's Standing in the World* (Union Square West, NY: Ferrar, Straus and Giroux, 2007). Ross does not mention Thucydides, but his outlook is laden with Thucydidean practicality.
5. See Xenophon's *Hellenica* I–III.
6. Thucydides praised the rule of the 5,000 that Athens instituted in 411 B.C. (8.97.2). Aristotle informs us that an important feature of this government was that members of the 5,000 needed to have a personal or financial stake in Athens. "The whole of the rest of the administration was to be committed, for the period of the war, to those Athenians who were most capable of serving the state personally or financially, to the number of not less than five thousand" (*Athenian Constitution*, 30).
7. Theodore Roosevelt, *Fear God and Take Your Own Part*. (New York: George H. Doran Co., 1916), 66.
8. Film clips concerning the infamous the Kobayashi Maru Flight Simulator Test (the test where victory was impossible) from various *Star Trek* movies both old and new can be found through Links 1 and 2 for this chapter at www.VeritasPress.com/OmniLinks.
9. Watching the scene online is best because the movie was not memorable and has some vulgar language and violence. A video of this speech is available through Link 3 for this chapter at www.VeritasPress.com/OmniLinks.

The Bacchae

It is one of those moments when C.S. Lewis catches you off guard. It can't be . . . but it is. Then you think, "What is *he* doing here?" Certainly it must be an invasion—new forces of destruction have been imported from ancient Greece to wreak some new havoc in Narnia. It seems the pagan god Bacchus or Dionysus has risen. He and his maenads are dancing around bringing who knows what sort of mischief to the forest. *"Watch out Lucy! Watch out Susan!"* you think. *Where is Father Christmas when you need him?*

But wait . . . Bacchus . . . has come with someone. He is with Aslan! *Didn't see that coming!* Lewis, however, the master storyteller has a point. He has imported this rascal and put him in the service of the Lion to show us how misguided our views of the faith often are. Sadly, modern Christians mistake the faith for something that would remove all joy from the world. They think Christ came to bring a sanitized, tightly controlled world where everyone would walk in lines and no one would play jazz. In *that version of* a Christian world sanctification would be evident by the length of one's dour countenance. No one would climb trees. No one would pitch on the inside part of the plate. No one would spit or bleed or feast. Not so fast, says Lewis. The point of his use of Bacchus in service to Aslan is that a pharisaical world of mint, dill and cumin counting is *not* the world that God intended. Christianity replaces dour tasteless food with feasting. It replaces water with wine. It replaces minimalist silence and clashing cacophony with a symphony. It means to fill the world with laughter and joy. It will not stop until all of have been banished or joined the dance.

Notice, however, that Lewis's Bacchus brings freedom, but he is not free. His joy and laughter comes in the service of Aslan. Wine, finally, finds its place not as the purveyor of drunkenness, but as in the chalice of the Lord's Supper.

Euripides, however, is not a believer—not even close—and his Bacchus is not bound to Aslan. He is free, and with that freedom, he brings madness.

GENERAL INFORMATION

Author and Context

Euripides (485–406 B.C.) was the youngest of the three great classical Greek tragedians. Roughly speaking, Aeschylus represents the conquering generation, Sophocles the conserving generation, and Euripides the collapsing generation of classical Athens. Born of "good family" he lived nearly his entire life in Salamis on a family estate, not far from Athens, until he was self-exiled to Macedonia in his last years. This may partially explain why he apparently was considered something of a loner for a public writer. It was said he wrote most of his plays in a cave by the sea. He was obviously familiar with the leading intellectual lights of his day, including Protagoras and Socrates, and acted as a lay priest in the sanctioned cult of Zeus. Euripides seems to have been an "edgier" writer, less "politically correct" than Aeschylus and Sophocles, and he was criticized during his lifetime for his innovations in tragic drama and his inclusion of "common people" in his plays. This may have been one reason why Euripides won only five first prizes (including one for *The Bacchae*) in the annual Athenian theatrical competitions, compared to twenty first-place awards for Sophocles and a dozen for Aeschylus.

Apparently disturbed at the disintegration of classical Athens in his lifetime, he exiled himself to Macedonia where he lived the last few years of his life and wrote his final plays, including *The Bacchae*. Euripides intuitively sensed that the classical Greek city-state, based as it was on a formal Apollonian law and order, could not sustain peace and harmonious community any more than the old tribal societies, because the city-state failed to adequately address the need for Dionysian joy and freedom within their formal legal order. The setting of the play is the Greek city-state of Thebes in mythical times. The Dionysian takeover of Thebes was one of five famous mythological cycles of stories related to Thebes, which had the predominant mythological history of all city-states in ancient Greece. Euripides wrote the play near the end of the famous Peloponnesian War (431–404 B.C.), an ancient Greek military conflict, fought by the Greek city-state of Athens and its empire against the Peloponnesian League, which included Thebes and was led by the Greek city-state of Sparta. This is the time of Ezra and Nehemiah, when the Israelites first returned to Jerusalem to rebuild the temple after their exile in Babylon, then Persia. This would make Ezra and Nehemiah contemporaries of Euripides.

Significance

Euripides' *Bacchae* is significant not merely because it is the last play written by Euripides and the classical Greek tragedians. The play itself questions the very worldview of the classical Greeks, and their attempt to control what they perceived to be fickle and inscrutable gods by rational organization and law. Euripides intuitively understood that the Greeks could not save themselves through the political device and organization known as the city-state. *The Bacchae* makes it clear that an imposed formal order based on the reason of man—whether of the individual through stoic self-control or of society through formal systems of government—cannot suppress sin, control our "irrational" impulses, or bring peace to a society. Such a solution will fail largely because it misunderstands the depths of humanity's real problem. As a result, the rational imposition of law and order ironically creates the very same violence, chaos, and disorder it seeks to avoid by the suppression of nature, freedom, and change.

The Bacchae unintentionally witnesses to the truth of Scripture's view of mankind and society—man, individually or collectively—cannot save himself or keep himself "pure" by imposing rational law, because such systems merely cover over the real problem—man's sin and his failure to love his Creator. Similar in some ways to the Pharisees' strategy in New Testament Israel, the Greeks' attempts to prevent sin and disorder amounted to "whitewashed tombs, which outwardly appear beautiful, but within are full of dead people's bones and all uncleanness." Inevitably, as Euripides understood, the impurity and dead bones of the classical Greek

The Greek god of wine, Dionysus, appears on this pottery, which is an example of red-figure vase painting. This technique was developed in Athens in the sixth century B.C., and its greater flexibility in rendering detail soon supplanted the black-figure painting style which had dominated previously.

city-states such as Athens were exposed by history. Euripides could not solve this vexing problem of humanity, but by pointing to the failure of the Greek solution he also unknowingly pointed to the truth of the gospel.

Main Characters

Dionysus and Pentheus are the main characters in *The Bacchae*. Dionysus is the Greek god of wine and ecstasy, as well as a fertility god. He is son of Zeus and the human Semele. In the play Dionysus has two roles: the traditional god on high, and his disguised role as the "Stranger" who comes to Thebes to punish the Greek city for slandering his mother.

Pentheus is the King of Thebes, son of Agaue, grandson of Cadmus and first cousin of Dionysus. Opposite in personality to his cousin, he is a law-and-order type, determined to keep control of Thebes by force if necessary. Despite his domineering, puritanical personality he is also a curious voyeur, secretly attracted to the Dionysian cult.

Semele, mother of Dionysus and daughter of Cadmus, is already dead when the play begins. Cadmus is the legendary founder of Thebes. He is the grandfather of Pentheus and Dionysus, and the only male public worshipper of Dionysus in his family. His friend and famous Theban seer (prophet) is Teiresias, who persuades Cadmus to worship Dionysus.

Agaue is the daughter of Cadmus and mother of Pentheus. At the beginning of the play she is already one of the *maenads* (from the Greek *mainad*, "to be mad"), the secret cult worshippers of Dionysus, but her major role is near the end of the play. The Chorus represents female *bacchants* (followers of the secret Dionysian rites) from nearby Lydia, who are led by Dionysus in his disguised human form as the Stranger.

Summary and Setting

Dionysus' mother Semele was a princess in the royal Theban house of Cadmus. She has an affair with Zeus, becoming pregnant with Dionysus. Zeus's jealous wife Hera tricks Semele into requesting Zeus to appear in divine form. Zeus's appearance as a lightening bolt unfortunately burns Semele to a crisp. Zeus manages to rescue the unborn Dionysus stitching him into his "thigh" from which he is later born. (More appropriate chuckling!) Semele's family maligns her name, does not believe her child was from Zeus, and rejects the young god Dionysus.

As the action of the play begins, Dionysus returns to Thebes disguised as a human stranger, in order to vindicate his mother and punish the insolent city for refusing to acknowledge his divinity. In the meantime Cadmus's proud and arrogant grandson Pentheus has become King of the city, and promptly forbids the worship of Dionysus. Upon his arrival Dionysus first drives Semele's sisters mad, and they promptly flee to the mountains to worship Dionysus.

Though threatened by the Dionysian rites, Pentheus refuses to believe the women's madness is divine and assumes they are purposely violating the orderly customs of Thebes. He orders his soldiers to arrest the stranger (Dionysus disguised) and his maenads. Dionysus permits himself to be arrested and taken back to Pentheus.

Pentheus attempts to bind and torture the boyishly handsome stranger, without success. Attempting to tie up Dionysus, Pentheus finds he has only tied up a bull. Attempting to plunge a knife into Dionysus, he finds only the blade passing through the stranger like a shadow. Suddenly, an earthquake shakes the palace foundations starting a fire, and Pentheus is left dazed and confused.

As Dionysus attempts unsuccessfully to persuade Pentheus that his path of resistance is destructive, a cowherd is brought before the King. The cowherd has witnessed a blissful scene of the maddened Theban women (including Pentheus's mother) in the forest, alternately resting peacefully and feasting, singing and dancing, playing music and suckling wild animals. When, however, the women see the cowherd, they suddenly fly into a murderous rage and chase him within inches of his life. He barely escapes, and his poor cows are torn apart by the crazed women with their bare hands.

Frightened but intrigued by the cowherd's story, Pentheus is about to order another military expedition to arrest the Bacchants, when Dionysus the stranger offers Pentheus a chance to see the maenads in person, but undercover. Unable to resist, Pentheus accepts the offer. Dressing himself in a wig and long skirts, Pentheus becomes an effeminate cross dresser—a vain, arrogant and lecherous parody of a man of authority. When Pentheus at first cannot get a clear view of the women, Dionysus miraculously places him in a treetop. Instantly the maenads spy Pentheus atop the tree, and Dionysus signals them to attack. Friends, I must here hide from your eyes the horror of what follows. Let us just say it involves lots of violence, a lion, a beheading, and lots of tears.

Worldview

You may have heard about the Sixties and an American phenomenon called the "Hippie" movement. The Hippie generation believed in "peace and love," and a more "back to nature" lifestyle, reacting against "the establishment" and what it perceived to be the lifeless materialism, dead religion, corporate conventionalism, and militarism of modern American society. At the end of the 1960s, a host of confusing and frightening things were happening. The Vietnam War was escalating and dividing the country, while the nuclear arms race between the United States and Soviet Union accelerated, the civil rights movement was in its prime with much racial tension, NASA was sending the first men to the moon, the radical student movement was at its zenith on many college campuses, demanding changes in education and government, and rock concerts

The Who, Janis Joplin, Grateful Dead, Creedence Clearwater Revival, Blood, Sweat & Tears, Santana, and Jimi Hendrix were among the performers at the infamous "3 Days of Peace & Music."

and festivals became a staple of the youth scene.

The most famous rock festival in history was held over three days in August 1969 on a large farm near rural Woodstock, New York. Over half a million young people showed up (originally expecting 50,000, the promoters planned for 150,000); the facilities were not adequate to handle this many people. There were copious amounts of drugs consumed, the New York Thruway was shut down due to traffic jams, and it rained off and on during the festival. Yet miraculously there were no riots, murders or serious criminal incidents. A book extolling "Woodstock Nation" lauded the event, and it seemed the Hippie spirit of Woodstock might live up to its "peace and love" claims. More big rock festivals promoting peace and love were planned, and on December 6, 1969, just four months after Woodstock, the Altamont Free Concert was held at a raceway in central California and approximately 300,000 people attended. Unfortunately, the spirit of peace and love turned to a spirit of anger and violence. Numerous riots broke out, one of the big name bands refused to go on stage for fear of the violence, another performer was knocked unconscious following a fight on stage, one man was murdered by a Hell's Angel gang member, and three others were killed by a hit and run driver. As soon as their set was over, the members of the headlining band, the Rolling Stones, ran off the stage and into their limousines, and police had to be called to restore order. The whole sordid concert scene was filmed, including the murder. It was the effective end of "Woodstock Nation," and the innocence of the Hippie movement. The famous classic rock song by Don McLean entitled "American Pie" includes these lyrics reportedly written about the Altamont affair:

> Oh, and as I watched him on the stage
> my hands were clenched in fists of rage.
> No angel born in hell
> could break that Satan's spell.

The maenads in a frenzy attack Pentheus in this wall painting from the Casa dei Vettii in Pompeii, excavated in the 1890s.

And as the flames climbed high into the night,
to light the sacrificial rite
I saw Satan laughing with delight
the day the music died.

Like the young concertgoers in the Hippie era, the Bacchants, worshippers of Dionysus, can suddenly change from peaceful nurturers of young animals to murderers who tear their sacrificial victims apart in ecstasy. At one level, *The Bacchae* is a story about not enough of and then too much of a good thing. Ultimately, at a much deeper level, it is a story that, however dimly, perceives a flaw in man's nature so fundamental that no formal government structure, organization or set of laws can successfully suppress it.

Dionysus's mother Semele is slain by the grandeur of his father Zeus in this painting by Gustave Moreau (1826–1898).

Although *The Bacchae* reflects the unbiblical classical Greek worldview, Euripides was able to perceive, however imperfectly, this fundamental flaw of man's nature because of the times he experienced. Placing *The Bacchae* in its historical and literary context will better help us see this. You may remember from your last trip to the ancient world (Omnibus I) reading some wild and wacky plays called *Oresteia* (by Aeschylus) and *The Theban Trilogy* (by Sophocles). *Oresteia*, written at the height of Athens classical glory was all about the transition of Athens from a society based on the *oikos* (Greek for "household"), governed by household gods and the laws of blood vengeance, to a society based on the *polis* (Greek for "city-state"), governed by the Olympic gods (Zeus and company) and a republican rule of law. In the *oikos*-based society, the most sacred bond of community had been "blood" (family or tribal relations) but because of constant family feuds the newer *polis*-based society was organized around a sacred "contract" between citizens and elected rulers. *Oresteia* was a celebration of the triumph of the city-state over tribal organizations, a change that initially seemed to bring so much peace, prosperity, and greatness to classical Athens.

The Theban Trilogy, written a generation later, as the dark clouds of the Peloponnesian War gathered over Athens, is set in Thebes, where the city-state's peace and prosperity are threatened by a devastating plague. It turns out that the Theban king violated the sacred contract of the city-state by engaging in unintended but forbidden sexual relations with his mother. The only way to end the plague and save the city-state is to make a scapegoat of the king, exiling him outside the city-state forever. Although there was still hope that the city-state concept would be successful and bring lasting peace, Sophocles' play implies that maintaining the purity of the city-state, which was necessary to avert disasters, would not be easy.

Euripides' *Bacchae* was written as the Peloponnesian War was drawing to its destructive end and Athens was about to lose its classical glory forever. As the translator of the play notes:

> For three generations, ever since the repulse of Persian power, many Greek states had tried in varying degrees to order their public life according to reason; autocracy had given place to [limited] assembly, debate and the vote. This change had been followed by a generation of war; it had led to a degree of organization which had taken from life much of its liberty and beauty and joy and given anxiety in return. The life of reason was proving a heavy strain. Dionysiac worship offered an escape from reason back to the simple

joys of a mind and body surrendered to unity with nature.

Euripides witnessed the impact of more draconian laws and the conflicts they engendered in Athenian society as the war dragged on. He also noticed that fear of violence from excessive Dionysian freedoms often led ironically to violent means to repress those very Dionysian freedoms.

The Bacchae highlights a universal situation of man's condition—the fractured nature of both individuals and communities, and the resulting contradictions in our nature. We are disordered and fearful creatures, as well as guilty and lost creatures, but we react in different ways to our situation based on our personalities, our culture and our experiences. Additionally, we tend to swing between extremes in responding to our plight. Looking about for a solution to our dilemma, we often choose to favor one part of our nature as superior to another part based on the false assumption that one aspect of our nature, or one aspect of creation, is more righteous or pure than another. In a futile attempt to save (and justify) ourselves, we then repress, by force of law or violence, the aspect of our nature we deem impure or unrighteous.

The Greeks recognized this to some extent in their mythological gods, which were of course simply projections of their own human nature and culture. Hence Apollo and Dionysus represented two divergent tendencies of man's nature—his desire for order and control of his environment through reason on one hand, and his desire to be one with nature and experience authentic joy and freedom on the other. Both gods, that is both tendencies, manifest themselves at different times in the same person or society. Because we are broken and fractured creatures, Apollo and Dionysus battle for control within each of us, as well as in society. Each "side" of our nature tends to fear and despise the other side.

The main point of Euripides' play is that societies and people who tend toward the law and order of Apollo ignore at their own peril the demand of the human spirit for Dionysian experience. Those who in the name of law and order suppress that demand in themselves or others, as Pentheus attempts to suppress his own desires as well as those of Thebes, become unwitting agents of the very disintegration and destruction they sought to avoid by rejecting the Dionysian spirit in the first place. Pentheus had decided to protect the Apollonian civilization of Thebes from the excesses and chaos of Dionysus by banning him completely from the city. He refused to acknowledge or worship the god and prohibited all Thebans from doing the same. His measures were in fact a mirror image of Dionysian excess, using excessive force

under the guise of law and order to keep out what he feared most.

Dionysus is not just the god of wine and revelry, but also of fertility. In the play the stranger turns into a bull—the ancient symbol of fertility—when Pentheus tries to tie him up. This is an apt image given that the futility of controlling Dionysus can be compared to the futility of riding a bull—the best bull riders in the world can only control the bull for a matter of seconds. As Euripides makes clear, the Dionysian bull is in fact impossible to control.

Yet this is precisely what the Greeks were attempting to do in their fifth century B.C. city-state organizations. They considered their city-states as islands of law and order in a sea of chaotic nature. Thus, when Pentheus is forced to deal with Dionysus the stranger, who has led the maenads out to the wild mountain, he brings him inside the city of Thebes, hoping thereby to tame him through the civilization devices of the city. The Dionysian-inspired earthquake destroying Pentheus's palace soon reveals that this strategy is hopeless and foreshadows the eventual takeover of the city by Dionysus himself. Pentheus' refusal to acknowledge the divinity of Dionysus (that is the reality of the Dionysian side of the human spirit) is the height of folly because it is the denial of an undeniable fact. Pentheus had been warned: after reprimanding the old men, Cadmus and blind Teiresias, for participating in Bacchic rites, the blind prophet responds to Pentheus: "Power and eloquence in a headstrong man spell folly; such a man is a peril to the state . . . pay heed to my words. You rely on force; but it is not force that governs human affairs."

After Teiresias implores Pentheus to acknowledge the divinity of Dionysus, the Chorus chimes in, noting that worshipping Dionysus "shows no disrespect to Apollo." Euripides thus implies that the Apollonian and Dionysian sides of man's nature are not mutually exclusive, not an "either-or" proposition. Both sides of man's nature need to be heeded. Yet other than implying this need, Euripides gives us no clue as to how the multiple aspects of man's nature can come together. His is only a negative warning about the need to somehow have them come together.

Christians also sometimes mistakenly assume that either the Apollonian or Dionysian side of our nature is "more Christian" than the other side. In so doing they fall into the trap of favoring certain aspects of nature and creation over others. Self-styled "conservative" Christians are especially prone to make the mistake of Pentheus, preferring an Apollonian law-and-order approach to life while trying to shut out other, Dionysian aspects of creation, such as creativity, wine, music, dance and theater. Because

Bacchus is the Latin name of Dionysus. In his piece entitled *Bacchus*, Jusepe de Ribera (1591–1652) imparts a somber tone to the revelries with his flat color palette and deep shadows

they easily perceive the sinful perversions in Dionysian life, but fail to perceive the sinful perversions in their own Apollonian life, the Dionysian things are deemed too dangerous and are therefore banned. There are two tragic consequences of this unbiblical "Pentheus strategy." First, the Christian life is stunted by the suppression of valid aspects of our nature and creation. As a result unbelievers end up controlling the Dionysian aspects of life in society by default. Second, as with Pentheus, walling ourselves off from aspects of creation is ultimately counter productive, and Christians who take such a strategy risk becoming, along with their children, victims of the very perversions they sought to suppress. At bottom, this "Christian" Pentheus strategy is a form of escapism and an unbiblical attempt at purification based on works rather than the imputed righteousness of Christ.

The Bacchae also demonstrates the destructive nature of both Apollonian and Dionysian extremes in several contexts.[2] For instance, Pentheus and Dionysus have conflicting and distorted definitions of wisdom and justice. Pentheus sees the rites and festivals of Dionysian worship as unwise, the very height of folly. By contrast, Dionysus considers Pentheus a fool for his refusal to acknowledge the Bacchus, the source of true wisdom. Similarly, Pentheus thinks that justice is established by maintaining order through the use of force. Dionysus, on the other hand, uses the term to describe the vindication of his mother through revenge against his enemies.

Neither Pentheus nor Dionysus represent a biblical understanding of wisdom and justice. Biblical wisdom and justice are not possible without the redeeming of our minds through the power of Christ, in whom reside all the riches and treasures of wisdom. True wisdom does not consist in worshipping any aspect of man's nature, Apollonian or Dionysian. Nor does true justice involve authoritarian force or savage human revenge.

Euripides also gives us a glimpse of the conflicted nature of man in the double sidedness of Bacchic madness. The Bacchants are first described in peaceful harmony with nature, joyful in song and dance, making sweet music and nurturing young animals. Yet later they fly into a rage, savagely attack and tear apart the very same animals, dancing like whirling dervishes and destroying anything in their path.

Although Euripides has insights into the contradictions and conflicts within human nature, he has no ability to point us to a resolution of those conflicts because of his unbiblical view of God and man's relationship with God. He is a man of his place and time, and cannot see beyond the classical Greek worldview. He lives in a world controlled by inscrutable fate, where in fact nobody is in control, not even the gods. The gods seek to be acknowledged as superior to man and as an integral part of the universe, but are otherwise not interested in real relationships with man. The gods do not communicate any coherent revelation about reality to man, and are every bit as fickle, unpredictable, and unreliable as man is. As a result, man is at the mercy of the gods and cannot in any meaningful way be responsible for his problems. Yes, Pentheus failed to acknowledge Dionysus, yet in Euripides' view his blindness is not so much moral (for the gods are amoral) as it is a defect ordained by the gods or fate. As a result Euripides cannot point us to a positive solution to the problem caused by the conflict of our Apollonian and Dionysian natures. The Greeks' only recourse, implies *The Bacchae*, is to add more Dionysian festivals to the city-state, as an outlet for the Dionysian passions, and hope that excesses are kept to a minimum. This is at best a patchwork approach to a much deeper problem. It is also eerily similar to the modern American approach of working hard during the week (Apollonian style), then "doing-your-own-thing" on the weekend (Dionysian style) to counterbalance the grind of the week. It is sort of a balancing approach to our nature which, given the unpredictability of the gods and fate, gives little confidence or comfort, although our American "balance" consists of falling into the Apollonian ditch of excess for five days so that we can fall into the Dionysian ditch on the weekend—which is, of course, not getting a balance of anything.

The biblical solution to the problem raised by Euripides goes to the root of the matter, and therefore is ultimately much more comforting to man. The world is not subject to the whims of fate but is under the direct control of the Triune God who loves us and ordains everything ultimately for our own good. No matter how messy the world may appear to us because of our sin and lack of comprehensive knowledge, we can trust in the Lord Jesus Christ precisely because of His sovereignty and character. He has communicated to us a coherent revelation of reality in His word and has given us His Spirit to guide us. In His word, He has revealed to us that it is neither anything in the creation nor any aspects or characteristics of our nature, whether Apollonian, Dionysian or otherwise, that are bad in themselves, but rather the sin that so easily besets us in all aspects of our character. Sin is our refusal to submit to our loving Creator in all areas of life. The only solution to sin is faith in the One who died for our sins and is in the process of redeeming us and the whole world. Submitting to Christ in society will heal the conflicts between Apollo and Dionysus, both within us and in our communities, thereby permitting all aspects of our nature (law and spirit, nature and civilization, freedom and responsibility, Apollo and Dionysus) to be redeemed and act harmoniously together, as God intends. Christians who really seek to be a part of God's redeeming history must focus their efforts on transforming and bringing together the Apollonian and Dionysian aspects of life for the sake of the world and the glory of our Lord and Savior.

—*William S. Dawson*

For Further Reading

Girard, Rene and Yvonee Freccero. *The Scapegoat*. Baltimore: Johns Hopkins University Press, 1989.

Kitto, H.D.F. *Greek Tragedy*. New York: Routledge, 2002.

Leithart, Peter J. *Heroes of the City of Man*. Moscow, Idaho: Canon Press, 1999.

Spielvogel, Jackson J. *Western Civilization*. Seventh Edition. Belmont, Calif.: Thomson Wadsworth, 2009. 78.

Session I: Prelude

Question To Consider:

Why do you think people sometimes feel like running away from home or school or work? Why do you think people sometimes feel trapped by "civilization" and just want to escape? Are these inclinations wrong?

From the General Information above answer the following questions:

1. In what time period and where did Euripides live? Who were the two other great Greek Tragedy playwrights?
2. The Bacchae unintentionally witnesses to what fundamental truth of Scripture?
3. What is the main point of Euripides' play?
4. What were the classical Greeks attempting to do by organizing city-states in 5th century B.C.?
5. What trap do Christians fall into when they assume that either the Apollonian or Dionysian side of our nature is "more Christian" than the other side?
6. Why can't Euripides offer any real solution to the Bacchanalian dilemma raised in *The Bacchae*?

Reading Assignment:
The Bacchae, lines 1–493

Session II: Discussion
The Bacchae, lines 1–493

A Question to Consider

What does it mean to be natural? Is it a good or bad thing to be natural?

Discuss or list short answers to the following questions:

Text Analysis

1. In the opening of the play how does the Bacchant chorus describe the "mystic" power of Dionysus and what are the attributes that the Chorus warns Thebes to reverence?
2. According to the Bacchant Chorus who is the "blest man" and what "spirit" is Dionysus said to embody?
3. What are some of the Bacchic rites that are encouraged by the Chorus for reverencing Dionysus in the mountains?
4. What does The Bacchae story imply about the Greek's understanding of nature (represented by Dionysus in the play) and civilization (represented by Pentheus and Apollo in the play)?

Cultural Analysis

1. How does modern Western culture deal with the Apollonian and Dionysian aspects of life in its social structures and customs?
2. Why can't modern Western culture adequately integrate these two aspects of life?

Biblical Analysis

1. How does the Bible portray the Apollonian and Dionysian aspects of life? (Ex. 7-12; 32; Eccles.)
2. What is the biblical solution to the Greek dilemma regarding Apollo and Dionysus?

Summa

Write an essay or discuss this question, integrating what you have learned from the material above.

Is it more important to be civilized or to be natural?

Reading Assignment:
The Bacchae, lines 494–841

Session III: Worldview Analysis
The Bacchae, lines 1–841

Fill in the following Chart 1 for Apollo, Dionysus and the Bible's view of each of the subjects or questions in the right-hand column.

Reading Assignment:
The Bacchae, lines 842–1392

Chart 1:. **WORLDVIEW OF APOLLO AND DIONYSUS COMPARED WITH THE BIBLE**

	APOLLO	DIONYSUS	BIBLE
God and the gods	The gods are superior beings who guide humans who do what the gods want and punish those who don't. The gods are in competition for the worship of men and societies, looking for their proper due.		
Man's Problem		He is too artificial and repressed by his reason and fear of disorder to live well.	
Salvation			Worship and love your Creator and Savior Jesus the Christ with all your heart, soul, and mind, and love your neighbor as yourself.
Fate or Predestination		Fate is inscrutable and even impacts the gods, therefore we can never be sure of anything but only hope for the best—chance is always a threat.	
How can you stay out of trouble?	Set up a very ordered, hierarchical system of self and societal government and avoid any change or emotional responses that may disrupt the order.		
Which is better: civilization or nature?		Nature—it lets you be who you really are, and creates an authentic rather than an artificial, hypocritical society.	
What are justice and mercy?			Ultimate justice and mercy come together in the incarnation of Christ who delivered mercy to man while keeping the justice of the Father.

Session IV: Recitation
The Bacchae

1. Why did Dionysus turn Semele's sisters mad?
2. Why do the maenads "catch wild snakes, nurse them and twine them round their hair"?
3. According to the prophet Teiresias, why are Cadmus and Teiresias the only Thebans who will dance to Dionysus early on?
4. When Pentheus first hears of "this astounding scandal" (the Bacchanalian activities) in his city, what does he claim he is going to do to the Bacchants and to the foreigner (Dionysus in disguise)?
5. What does the prophet Teiresias tell Pentheus about his plans to stop the Dionysian worship by force?
6. When Pentheus first puts the foreigner Dionysus in prison how does Dionysus respond?
7. What happened when the Bacchants, including Pentheus's mother, saw the cowherd on the mountainside watching them?
8. What does Dionysus suggest and Pentheus agree to do so that he can spy on the female Bacchants?
9. Why did Pentheus's mother not recognize him when he implored her to recognize him, as the women were about to tear him apart?
10. When Agaue returned to Thebes with the head of her son Pentheus, what did she think she was carrying?
11. Who brought Agaue to realize what she had done after killing her son?
12. Why has all this calamity happened, according to Cadmus?

Session V: Discussion
The Bacchae

A Question To Consider
What is a "scapegoat"? Have you or anyone you know ever experienced being or been made into a scapegoat?

Discuss or list short answers to the following questions:

Text Analysis
1. Who controls Thebes when Dionysus first comes to town?
2. Who is responsible for leading the women of Thebes to worship Dionysus?
3. How does Pentheus end up being a "sacrifice" to Dionysus?
4. Who are the scapegoats in Thebes at the end of the play?

Cultural Analysis
1. Do we have scapegoats in our society? If so, give some examples.
2. Rarely are our culture's scapegoats physically exiled or killed. How are they made scapegoats in our culture?

Biblical Analysis
1. What does the Bible say about the origins of the scapegoat in ancient Israel? (Lev. 16:8–26)
2. What is the relationship of Jesus Christ to the scapegoat? (Isa. 43:4; John 1:29; Heb. 9–10)

Summa

Write an essay or discuss this question, integrating what you have learned from the material above.

Why is Pentheus an ineffective scapegoat, and why is Christ the only effective scapegoat in history?

Optional Session: Current Events

Assignment

Instead of a reading assignment you have a research assignment. Tomorrow's session will be a Current Events session. Your assignment will be to find a story online, in a magazine, or in the newspaper that relates to the issue that you discussed today. Your task is to locate the article, give a copy of the article to your teacher or parent and provide some of your own worldview analysis to the article. Your analysis should demonstrate that you understand the issue, that you can clearly connect the story you found to the issue that you discussed today, and that you can provide a biblical critique of this issue in today's context.

Issue

Identify Apollonian—or Dionysian—Worship in our culture today.

Current events sessions are meant to challenge you to connect what you are learning in Omnibus class to what is happening in the world around you today. After the

The Triumph of Bacchus by Cornelis de Vos (1585–1651).

last session, your assignment was to find a story online or in a magazine or newspaper relating to the issue above. Today you will share your article and your analysis with your teacher and classmates or parents and family. Your analysis should follow the format below:

BRIEF INTRODUCTORY PARAGRAPH

In this paragraph you will tell your classmates about the article that you found. Be sure to include where you found your article, who the author of your article is, and what your article is about. This brief paragraph of your presentation should begin like this:

> Hello, I am (name), and my current events article is (name of the article) which I found in (name of the web or published source)...

CONNECTION PARAGRAPH

In this paragraph you must demonstrate how your article is connected to the issue that you are studying. This paragraph should be short, and it should focus on clearly showing the connection between the book that you are reading and the current events article that you have found. This paragraph should begin with a sentence like

> I knew that my article was linked to our issue because...

CHRISTIAN WORLDVIEW ANALYSIS

In this section, you need to tell us how we should respond as believers to this issue today. This response should focus both on our thinking and on practical actions that we should take in light of this issue. As you list these steps, you should also tell us why we should think and act in the ways you recommend. This paragraph should begin with a sentence like

> As believers, we should think and act in the following ways in light of this issue and this article.

CLOUDS

Have you ever beaten your parents with a stick? Let's assume the answer is no—I hope it is. But if you did do this, how would you defend your actions? Could you defend your actions?

You certainly couldn't defend your actions from the Bible. The Bible is clear that parents need to be respected and obeyed. It doesn't say anything about beating parents. In fact, the Old Testament law explains that one punishment option for a rebellious son is execution (though this was for extreme cases).

But let's say you aren't using the Bible as a standard for behavior. Could you defend beating your parents? Perhaps you could. You could argue that they have punished you with a stick before, perhaps as discipline. What goes around comes around, right? Perhaps you could argue that you've seen someone else do it. You could even turn to the animal world, where the dominant male of a herd is routinely defeated by his younger, stronger offspring.

This is exactly where reasoning and argument outside of Scripture can lead us. When you leave out the moral standard of the Bible, you can defend almost any action, even one as horrible as beating your parents. In the play *The Clouds* there is no scriptural standard. And by the end of the play, the lack of moral standards has led to precisely this place.

Have you ever beaten your father with a stick? Pheidippides has.

GENERAL INFORMATION

Author and Context

Aristophanes was a playwright who lived in Athens in the fifth century B.C. He lived in Athens during the Peloponnesian War, which you may have read about in the works of Thucydides. Though he didn't know it, he lived at about the same time as Ezra and Nehemiah.

Aristophanes wrote at least forty plays, though only eleven remain today. History indicates that he was the dominant comic playwright of his generation. He satirized the establishment in Athens, mocking what he saw as the silliness of fashion, sophistry, and tradition. From what we can tell in his plays, he spared no one, and Aristophanes was occasionally sued for slander (most notably by a prominent Athenian politician named Cleon).

The tension between Athens and the rest of Greece,

particularly Sparta, dominated most of Aristophanes' life. Even after the conclusion of the war, Athens and Sparta still had little love for one another.

Significance

The comedy of the Athenian stage went through several periods, and Aristophanes' plays are the only surviving example of the Old Comedy. Comedies were performed at festivals, particularly the festival of Dionysus. They were bawdy and coarse and often satirized aspects of Athenian life. In fact, there are many similarities with modern American comedies in that way (though the Greek ones were better written).

When *The Clouds* was first performed, it was a failure. Athenian audiences rejected it, and although Aristophanes revised it for a second performance, there is no evidence that this version was actually performed. In the middle of the play, the chorus refers to this revision (lines 518–525).

Part of the significance of *The Clouds* lies in the treatment given to Socrates. It lampoons him as a foolish thinker, out of touch with reality, and willing to argue anything. Several decades after *The Clouds* was first performed, Socrates was actually put on trial and executed for corrupting the youth of the city, which is very similar to what occurs in the play. It is unknown how much of an impact the play may have had on damaging Socrates' reputation, but it certainly fits with the picture painted of him at his trial. In one of his works, Plato blames part of the ill will towards Socrates on this play.

Main Characters

Strepsiades is an old farmer who is badly in debt, largely due to his son. He is willing to try anything to get out of his debts.

Pheidippides is Strepsiades' son. At the beginning of the play, Pheidippides is lazy and only interested in horse racing. Strepsiades wants to enroll him in the Thinkery, but he refuses.

Socrates is the head of the Thinkery. He teaches his students how to be philosophers. He also engages in debate himself. In western culture, although there are pre-Socratic philosophers, Socrates is still widely thought of as the founder of philosophy. His famous pupil, Plato, recorded his ideas in several different works, some of which you may have read.

As you may be aware, Greek plays involved the use of a chorus. In this play, the chorus is a group of clouds. Rather than just commenting on the action, this chorus occasionally interacts with the characters. Socrates says that these clouds are "the only real divinities" (line 365).

Right and Wrong are two possible arguments that an orator can use. At one point in *The Clouds*, they are personified and engage in a debate with one another.

Summary and Setting

The play opens with Strepsiades tossing and turning on his bed, unable to sleep because he is worried about his debts. Pheidippides has wasted most of his money on the races.

Strepsiades decides he will enroll his son in the school of philosophy run by Socrates, the Thinkery. Once his son learns how to be an orator, he will be able to argue his father out of all of his debts. Pheidippides, however, is less than enthusiastic about this plan, and so Strepsiades enrolls in the school himself.

While at the school, Strepsiades proves himself a very poor pupil. He is more interested in cracking crass jokes than he is in learning how to argue. Socrates quickly gets exasperated with his new pupil, and Strepsiades leaves the Thinkery.

After he leaves, Strepsiades is able to convince his son to join the school, where he quickly excels. Strepsiades is very excited as the due date for his bills grows close. He knows that his son can now argue his way out of anything, and he hopes this will be beneficial for his finances. His hopes are realized when the creditors are shooed away.

But this is not a happy ending for Strepsiades. Pheidippides has also figured out how to argue against his father. Pheidippides beats his father, and then uses his new-found sophistry to argue that this beating is justified. Strepsiades tries to argue with his son, but it is no use.

Strepsiades is angry and disappointed. Feeling betrayed by Socrates and his school, he goes to the Thinkery and burns it down.

Worldview

What is the purpose of humor? God created man with a sense of humor. He made us so that we laugh at various things in the world around us. In fact, God Himself has a sense of humor. One only has to go to the zoo and watch the monkeys for a few minutes to realize this. And it's not just monkeys who are funny-looking. We've also got the platypus, the puffer fish, and the dodo bird (okay, maybe we don't have that last one anymore). Our God loves to create funny-looking things.

Why did God do this? He did this in part because humor makes us laugh, and laughing is good for us (Prov. 17:22). God wants us to be joyful and filled with laughter (Ps. 126). Laughter and happiness are part of the rich Christian life to which we are called. When we go to live with the Lord in heaven, it will be a place of joyful laughter, not tears of sorrow.

But that's not the only reason God gave us humor. Humor is also one way we can be taught. If we see that something is joyfully hilarious, we might try to replicate it in our own lives. On the other hand, when we see that something is funny and ridiculous, we can see that we ought to avoid it. We can learn about the world through humor.

One of the ways humor can teach us is through satire, the use of humor or mockery to criticize. You may have already seen examples of this in other parts of *Omnibus*, such as *Gulliver's Travels*, which satirized the British culture of its time. An excellent modern example of satire is a political cartoon in a newspaper. In these cartoons, artists use exaggerated characteristics and animals, such as elephants and donkeys, to get their points across. Usually they make fun of a silly aspect of a recent political event, but each cartoon still makes a point.

Aristophanes' play *The Clouds* is a satire. He is making fun of Athenian society. His goal is not to provide an historically accurate description of what Athens was like in the fifth century B.C. He is not attempting to accurately portray Socrates or his school. Aristophanes is teaching his audience, making the point that the philosophy of the sophists is self-important and flawed, and he does this through humor.

Although *The Clouds* is a comedy, there are significant tragic elements. For example, we would expect a comedy to end well for the characters involved. In *The Clouds*, however, none of the central characters end well: Strepsiades has been beaten and has lost his son's favor, Pheidippides is a full-blown sophist, and Socrates' Thinkery (the satirical name for the real Socrates' Academy) is on fire. This is an odd ending for a comedy.

The reason for this is the satire. Aristophanes uses elements of comedy, but he is trying to show that sophists will reach a tragic end. Since the main characters fall victim to the sophistry the play is mocking, they must end badly.

The Clouds 133

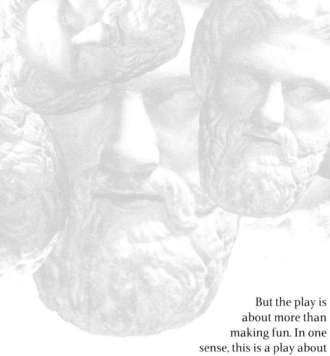

The forecast calls for slightly Aristophanes all day with a chance of guffaws in the morning, followed by giggles in the afternoon, turning to chuckles in the evening.

But the play is about more than making fun. In one sense, this is a play about education. Strepsiades is concerned about educating either himself or his son, and so he goes to the best educator in town. The motivation for this education varies depending on the characters: Socrates wants education for education's sake, while Strepsiades has financial motivations for learning from the philosophers. The method is the same, but the goal is different. Not all the characters have this goal, of course. At the beginning of the play, Pheidippides is happy just gambling on the races—he does not want any sort of education at all.

None of these attitudes is biblical. As Christians, we should not seek education for its own sake, nor should our primary goal be to make lots of money. We are called by God to glorify God and to enjoy Him, as the Westminster Shorter Catechism famously begins. When we learn, our goal is to learn more about our God and His creation. Everything we do should be done in the light of this calling. We educate ourselves because we have a calling from God, and we want to do that well. Parents are called to begin this process in their children (Eph. 6:4), and that process continues throughout life (Prov. 22:6). By contrast, the motivations for education in *The Clouds* are flawed and empty.

Another key theme of the play is the kind of education that the student receives. When we examine the work of Plato around this time period, it becomes clear that there was some tension between two groups of educators in Athens: the philosophers and the sophists. As Plato portrays it, the philosophers focused on trying to understand the world. They took no money for their teaching since their primary focus was supposed to be on knowledge itself. This group included Plato himself and Socrates. The sophists, by contrast, offered their teaching services for sale. They were willing to teach anyone who could pay them, and they would teach them how to argue and win. The philosophers looked down on the sophists, feeling they had "sold out" their knowledge.

We can see this tension in Plato's work Gorgias. In that dialogue, Socrates discusses rhetoric with Gorgias. Gorgias is willing even to admit that his use of rhetoric requires no real knowledge of the subject matter, since all one has to do is argue well. A rhetorician can be an expert in anything without studying, since he knows how to argue. This goes against what the philosophers believed, since they believed in gaining knowledge for its own sake.

Like Plato, Aristophanes portrays sophistry as empty and meaningless. Oddly, however, he portrays the leader of the sophists as Socrates himself. The philosophers from Socrates' Thinkery can prove anything they like through oration. This is part of the attraction for Strepsiades: he wants to be able to win all his arguments. These sorts of victories are hollow. They can win arguments, as Pheidippides does multiple times in the closing scenes of the play, but that does not make them right. In particular, Aristophanes shows that this sort of empty sophistry leads to the collapse of morality.

If Socrates opposed sophistry, then why did Aristophanes put him in charge of the sophist Thinkery? There are a couple of possibilities. Maybe Plato is misleading us, and Socrates really was a sophist. Perhaps Aristophanes was right after all. A more likely explanation is that Aristophanes is simply using the most prominent Athenian philosopher of his day to satirize philosophy in general. Either way, Plato apparently didn't have bad feelings toward Aristophanes, since he featured him uncritically in one of his later dialogues.

We need to recognize that Aristophanes' view of Socrates is complicated. It is alternatively unjust and also beneficial. To make a full assessment of this play, we must understand these three facets of Aristophanes' view of Socrates.

Aristophanes is, in fact, quite unjust to Socrates. Socrates most specifically did not argue so as "to make the worse argument appear better." He explicitly argued against that position. He is the great enemy of the sophists who bragged that they could prove anything. The sophists were the first relativists, anticipating many of the ideas of today's postmodernists. They believed that truth was just a language game, that different cultures had different moralities—nothing was set or absolutely true. Socrates was the one who argued for absolute truth, and for that we owe him a debt of gratitude.

And yet Aristophanes is right to satirize certain tendencies of Socrates, Platonism, and the rest of us intellectualoids—including classically-educated students. We sometimes do, to allude to the title of the comedy, "have our heads in *The Clouds*." Aristophanes is satirizing the danger of being overly-abstract and theoretical, ignoring the concrete reality in front of our faces. Sometimes we do use our intellects to rationalize bad behavior, to justify ourselves, to create excuses. Abstract theoretical ideologies, however well-constructed, have consigned many tangible human beings during the past hundred years to concentration camps and gulags. We can talk ourselves into all kinds of things, even beating our parents and neglecting our bills. We have to beware of thinking up in the "clouds." Christians too must remember that our faith is not just abstract theology, which also can become a pretext for misusing people; rather our faith lies in the very clear and real words of Scripture, in the tangible Person of the Word made flesh, Jesus Christ, and in His historical work on the Cross. (We sometimes even turn God into an abstract idea, a being up in the "clouds," rather than a very real, objective Person who went so far as to become Incarnate.)

In *The Clouds* Socrates is in charge of more than just a school of speaking. The Thinkery is not just about oration. It is also about discovering knowledge. This, however, is just as empty as the speaking, at least as it's portrayed in the play. Aristophanes shows that the scholars' way of seeking knowledge is just as frivolous as their speaking. For example, when Strepsiades meets one of Socrates' students, the young man describes how Socrates is trying to figure out how far a flea can leap by fitting it with little, wax boots. He tells Strepsiades that Socrates studies the moon by examining the ceiling (lines 171–174).

One aspect of the description of a scholarly university holds true, however. Like most institutions that place knowledge on a pedestal, the Thinkery is atheistic. Socrates denies the existence of the Greek gods and their accomplishments and, of course, knows nothing of the true God. The "atheism" of the real Socrates, however, was not quite like Aristophanes' portrayal. Christians have respected Socrates because he saw through the obvious inconsistencies in the pagan deities. We should

The Clouds makes the point that Zeus is infamous for having no self-control when it comes to women. The god of the sky and thunder also seems to have problems when it comes to men, as illustrated by *The Rape of Ganymede* by Correggio (1489–1534). In that myth, the god swoops down to earth in the form of an eagle to carry off a shepherd boy. Another event in the history of Zeus's notoriously "fowl" behavior is his seduction of Leda in the form of a swan. From this union Leda bore Helen of Troy. Shown on the next page is a preliminary drawing for *Leda and the Swan* by Leonardo da Vinci (1452–1519). The actual painting has been lost.

commend the way Socrates rejected the Greek gods and the humanistic idolatry that underlay them. Socrates had inklings that there must be only one transcendent Creator, though, tragically, he did not know Him or His Son, not knowing God's Word. While Aristophanes is making fun of Socrates, he misses this important point.

So what is the place of the Greek gods in this play? On the one hand, Aristophanes uses his characters to lampoon their behavior and question their very existence. Socrates explains to his new pupil, Strepsiades, that they are not real (line 365). During the argument between Right and Wrong, Wrong points out that Zeus has no self-control when it comes to women, so why should anyone else (lines 1079–1083)? Aristophanes seems to be saying that the gods are too silly to be considered real.

But is this really what the play is teaching? By the end of the play, Strepsiades has returned to the gods and apologized for his lack of faith. He knows that Socrates does not support the gods, and this is part of the reason that he burns the Thinkery down—it is an atheistic institution. *The Clouds* themselves, whom Socrates says are the only real divinities (lines 250–253), call upon the gods (lines 564–565). At the very least, the relationship of the play with the Greek gods is more complex than simply denying or affirming.

It is also noteworthy, as Alan Sommerstein points out in his Introduction to the Penguin Classics edition[1], that Aristophanes holds back from satirizing any religious activities. He mocks the gods, but his mocking is relatively gentle compared to his treatment of the sophists. All religious festivals are left alone, perhaps because this would have been out of place—his plays themselves were performed at a religious festival—but it may also be due to the fact that Aristophanes did not really want his audience to abandon the Greek religion. He simply wanted to point out a few, silly inconsistencies among the Greek pantheon.

This is not too far different from our culture today, which is willing to have its gods gently mocked but not removed. For example, you could include Abraham Lincoln as a ridiculous character in a comedic movie (or have him racing other presidents at Washington Nationals baseball games), but you cannot suggest that Lincoln was a terrible president, or that his "temple" on the National Mall is a little much for a mere mortal. We may gently mock, but we may not seriously criticize. In a similar vein, Aristophanes realizes that the gods are silly, but he does not have anything better to offer in their place. And so he mocks them, but does not expect his audience to abandon their worship.

The play touches on other important subjects with the same satiric tone. In the opening scene, Strepsiades complains about his marriage. He was a poor farmer from the country, and he married a rich girl from the city. He and his wife had very different ideas about their son. His wife wanted to name Pheidippides one name, he another. His wife dreamed of their son becoming a successful Athenian, while Strepsiades hoped his son would one day drive goats (lines 68–73). Strepsiades bemoans the marriage that forces him into such compromise.

This complaint reveals Aristophanes' thoughts about the institution of marriage, and they're not far different from his thoughts on the gods. He recognizes that it leads to strife, and so he mocks that aspect of it. His audience, many of them married themselves, would probably have laughed right along.

Aristophanes also thinks very little of lending institutions. The entire plot of the play is structured around Strepsiades trying to avoid having to pay Pheidippides' debts, and when the creditors finally show up near the end, he gets rid of them quickly. The first creditor bemoans the fact that he lent out anything at all. "Better to face the embarrassment of having to say no at the outset rather than have all this trouble afterwards," he says (lines 1215–1216). When the second creditor arrives, Strepsiades beats him to make him go away. Being a creditor is a poor life, and the people seem to be constantly scheming how to avoid repayment of their loans.

Through all of this, you will notice that Aristophanes does what comics throughout history have done. He mocks the institutions without offering anything substantive in return. As a result, his satire is not as harsh as it could be. He wants his audience to see the flaws in their thinking, he wants to help them see where they need to improve, but he does not have anything serious to offer in return.

As you read this play, you will also notice that Aristophanes is very clever with words. Some of the puns he makes are clear to us in English, while others are invisible (and this is where the notes come in handy). Words have multiple meanings, and sometimes the name of a character is important. For example, Strepsiades means "twister," and this is shown as he twists and turns in his bed at night. He twists from idea to idea. Pheidippides' name is the subject of a joke about the relationship between Strepsiades and his wife. The double meanings in so much of what is written remind us that we ought not to necessarily take what the characters say at face value.

Another aspect of Aristophanes that you will, no doubt, notice is that he is crass. This was a common feature of Greek plays at this time period, and it is somewhat reminiscent of modern American comedy. This is the sort of thing that garners big box-office receipts at the local multiplex, and apparently it won prizes at the festival of

Dionysus in ancient Greece. Bawdy humor worked, then and now.

What is the place for this sort of humor for a Christian? Christians are called by God to have pure lips and hearts, and this includes our jokes. Paul tells the Ephesians to avoid "obscenity, foolish talk or coarse jesting, which are out of place" (Eph. 5:4). If we are going to get laughs, we need to do it without scatological humor.

So should we even read this stuff? Obviously, we think that you ought to, since we have placed this play in the *Omnibus* curriculum. There are several reasons for this. The play has literary merits that are important for you to study, such as its themes and witty banter. Aristophanes is also important because of his influence on later writers. Another reason to read this play is to understand the other side. Like a football team before the big game, we want to see what the other side is up to in order to beat them. Ultimately, Christians must reach a maturity where they can examine sin without being seduced by it. God does not call Christians to cloister themselves from sin, but to confront and defeat it.

Christians are also called to reject the sophistry that Aristophanes presents. We must reject any philosophy which teaches that any side can be correct, depending on how it is argued. God does not tell us in His Word that whatever we argue can be correct. Christians believe in absolute standards of morality that are based on the Bible.

For example, Pheidippides argues that he is allowed to beat his father. His reasoning is based on the idea that his father disciplined him as a child, so why shouldn't he return the favor (lines 1411–1419)? After all, old age is called

The Thinkery is a cult in which young men pay to learn the latest scientific lore and rhetorical skills in order to achieve fame, power and wealth.

a "second childhood." Pheidippides also argues from the treatment of roosters, who fight their fathers (line 1427). From a Christian perspective, both of these arguments are deeply flawed. The central problems are the equation of children with parents, and the equation of people with chickens. Christians understand that God created the world with separation between man and beast, and between father and son. The rules for one do not necessarily apply equally to the other, and we can go to Scripture to show this.

From a pagan perspective, however, Pheidippides' argument is fair. Apart from the Word of God, there is no reason to believe that human beings are any better than animals. Within the worldview that Aristophanes and his audience inhabit, there is no valid reason not to agree with Pheidippides—no reason except tradition.

Ultimately, Aristophanes falls back on this. Like so many comics, Aristophanes is not really offering anything in return. He is wise enough to know that sophistry is flawed, and he shows it well. Yet he does not offer up an alternative knowledge in response. The best that Strepsiades can do in response to the moral relativism of his son is to appeal to tradition. But tradition changes. The avant-garde of one period is the tradition of the next.

To find out what a story means, we have to look at the ending. Is it a righteous story or a wicked story? That all depends on who wins in the end. Think of the story of a thief who wants to rob a bank. If he succeeds and evades capture at the end of the story, then it is a wicked story, since it teaches that one can get away with theft. If he is caught and reaps what he sowed, then it is a righteous story. In the latter example, what happens is what was supposed to happen. The resolution of the plot shows us what the story means.

The Clouds ends with the burning of the Thinkery. Sophistry is shown to be morally empty, since it leads to men behaving like roosters (lines 1427–1428). Yet at the same time, the argument between Right and Wrong shows that belief in the gods is also flawed, since the gods are inconsistent. Strepsiades follows the atheistic thinking of Socrates, and it leads to his ruin. He has even become a sophist—he said early on that he was willing to be beaten if it meant that he could learn how to argue his way out of his son's debts (line 440), but this is clearly not the case.

Strepsiades, however, did not do this by himself. *The Clouds* themselves are part of the fall of Strepsiades. They wanted him to fear the gods, and they also felt that he was too "in love with wickedness." They tell Strepsiades that when they see such a person they will "cast him into

misery" (lines 1458–1462). In spite of the fact that he gets some revenge on the Thinkery at the end, Strepsiades ends up in misery, with a ruined family and no prospect for evading future debt.

How can such a play show us Jesus? The Bible teaches us that everything shows us Christ (Col. 1:17). Something can either show us Christ directly, as the Bible does when it speaks about Him, or it can show us how much someone needs Christ. *The Clouds* demonstrates the utter emptiness of a world without Christ.

Christ is the answer to Socrates' problems. Socrates cannot truly solve any problems, because he founds his thinking on sophistry. His Thinkery does not train anyone for moral behavior—in fact, just the opposite. But Christ shows us the way to true knowledge, knowledge based on observation of creation and the Word of God.

Christ is the answer to Strepsiades' problems. Through Christ and the Bible, we see the biblical way to deal with debt: if we are the debtor, we return the money that we owe. If we are the lender, we may forgive the debt (Matt. 18:21–35), and we should not charge exorbitant interest to our brothers (Neh. 5:10–11). The Bible also shows us how children are to behave toward their parents, and vice versa.

Christ is the answer to Aristophanes' problems. Satire is not an end in itself. There are times when the Bible uses satire to make its point, just as Aristophanes did. But God does not stop there. God knows that it is not enough simply to expose the foolishness of man. Christ also shows us how we ought to treat our parents by His example of love, respect, and obedience.

Just as Christ is the solution to the problems posed in this play, so He is also the solution to ours. When we follow the Word of God, we can avoid being tricked by *The Clouds*, and we can avoid the problems of sophistry. Through Christ, we can truly be set free.

—*Woelke Leithart*

For Further Reading

Leithart, Peter J. *Heroes of the City of Man*. Moscow, Idaho: Canon Press, 1999.

Sommerstein, Alan H., trans. *Lysistrata and Other Plays, Revised Edition*. London: Penguin Books, 2002. Introduction.

Spielvogel, Jackson J. *Western Civilization*. Seventh Edition. Belmont, Calif.: Thomson Wadsworth, 2009. 78.

SESSION I: PRELUDE

A Question to Consider

What is the purpose of humor?

From the General Information above answer the following questions:

1. What war took place during Aristophanes' life?
2. What period of Athenian comedy was Aristophanes a part of?
3. Which politician sued Aristophanes for slander after he appeared in one of his plays as a character?
4. Whom did Aristophanes satirize in *The Clouds*? What happened to this person afterwards?
5. Who plays the chorus in the play?
6. What sort of trouble has Pheidippides made for his father?
7. Who is the leader of the school in Athens? What is the school called?
8. What does Strepsiades do to the school at the end?

READING ASSIGNMENT:
The Clouds, lines 1–220

SESSION II: DISCUSSION
The Clouds, Lines 1–220

A Question to Consider

How should Christians handle debt?

Discuss or list short answers to the following questions:

Text Analysis

1. Why is Strepsiades currently in debt? Does he believe that this is good?
2. How did Strepsiades' marriage contribute to his money worries?
3. How does Strepsiades plan to get out of debt?
4. What does Strepsiades think about money?

Cultural Analysis

1. Why does our culture believe we should get into debt?
2. Does our culture encourage getting out of debt?
3. What does our culture believe is the place of money?

Biblical Analysis

1. What does the Bible teach us about paying back a debt (Ps. 37:21, Prov. 22:7)?
2. What is the result of charging exorbitant interest (Prov. 28:8)?
3. What does Jesus teach us about money in the Sermon on the Mount (Matt. 6:24)?
4. Does the Bible really teach that money is the root of all evil (1 Tim. 6:10)?

SUMMA

Write an essay or discuss this question, integrating what you have learned from the material above.
How should Christians behave with money?

READING ASSIGNMENT:
The Clouds, lines 221–627

SESSION III: RECITATION
The Clouds, lines 1–627

Comprehension Questions

Answer the following questions for factual recall:

1. How does Socrates enter the stage?
2. Why has Socrates been in the air?
3. Why has Strepsiades come to the Thinkery?
4. Whom does Socrates summon? Why does he do this?
5. What form do *The Clouds* take? Why?
6. How does Socrates convince Strepsiades that Zeus does not send rain?
7. What is Socrates' explanation for thunder?
8. Does Strepsiades have a good memory?
9. About what does the leader of the chorus complain to the audience?
10. Why is the Moon displeased with Athens?

READING ASSIGNMENT:
The Clouds, lines 628–889

Session IV: Writing
The Clouds, lines 1–889

Poetry

Writing poetry can be a real challenge, so we are going to provide forms for you. Remember, poetry is hard, but rewarding work.

An epigram is a short poem that is often used as a pithy, brief expression of satirical wit. It is often used in politics to expose flawed thinking or actions on the part of a political opponent. Today, we are going to work on writing epigrams that are couplets. So your epigram should have:

1. Two lines
2. These two lines should rhyme
3. These two lines should have the same meter (meter is the rhythm of your line—so the lines in your epigram should have the same number of syllables and should have emphasis on the same syllables in each line).

Epigram

Imagine what poetry Socrates would write to Strepsiades.

Example:

> You, the debtor, sent the son to learn,
> While you, the father, came to school to burn.

Optional Activity

If time allows, write other epigrams from Strepsiades to Socrates, Strepsiades to Pheidippides, and Pheidippides to Strepsiades.

Reading Assignment:
The Clouds, lines 890–1510

Session V: Debate
The Clouds, lines 1–1510

Question to Debate

Is it right to argue a position you don't believe?

Directions

Split into two sides of roughly equal size. If you are assigned a position you don't hold, then you have first-hand experience in the question at hand, and you might want to bring that up in the debate. You should first determine what the rules for the debate will be, such as how long each person will speak, or whether or not you will allow cross examination. If you are going to have a formal debate (with opening statements, closing statements, rebuttals, etc.), then you will need to determine who will speak when, and for how long. After each side is prepared, determine which side goes first. Then proceed!

Rules for a homeschool setting:

If more than one student is doing this reading, follow the rules above, but move back and forth between the students representing the different points of view.

If there is only one student, you could:
- Meet with someone in your area to have your own debate.
- Have Mom or Dad represent the opposite side of the debate.

> *"The rich rules over the poor,*
> *And the borrower is servant to the lender."*
> — Proverbs 22:7

- Have the student represent both sides of the debate, but give them a short time for looking over their notes between presentations (you would also allow longer times than two minutes in this option because there is no need for back and forth).

The student may write out what he would say as a "position paper" for the debate.

OPTIONAL SESSION A: DISCUSSION
The Clouds, lines 1214–1510

A Question To Consider
How should we treat our fathers?

Discuss or list short answers to the following questions:

Text Analysis
1. What does Pheidippides do to his father? Why?
2. How does Strepsiades object to this treatment?
3. How does Pheidippides defend himself?
4. Does *The Clouds* support Pheidippides' actions?

Cultural Analysis
1. What does our culture believe is the place of fathers?
2. How does our culture believe that parents should treat children?
3. How does our culture believe that children should treat parents?

Biblical Analysis
1. How are children commanded to treat their parents?
2. How does the law command us to treat our elders (Lev. 19:32)?
3. How did Absalom treat his father? How do we know that this was wicked?
4. How did Isaac honor his father Abraham (Gen. 22)? How is this like Christ Himself?

SUMMA

Write an essay or discuss this question, integrating what you have learned from the material above.
What sort of relationship should children have with their parents?

OPTIONAL SESSION B: ACTIVITY

Drama
Get together and perform a section from The Clouds. *Since the entire play may be too long to perform, choose some sections that illustrate the key theme of fathers and sons (or another theme of your choice). Or perform an abridged version of* The Clouds.

GUIDELINES:
1. Try to isolate the necessary sections of the play. Remember your theme. Which sections of the play best illustrate that theme?

   Here are the sections to emphasize if the theme of "fathers and sons" is chosen:
   a. The opening scene between Strepsiades and Pheidippides, from when Strepsiades wakes up until he enters the Thinkery (lines 1–130).
   b. The scene when Strepsiades returns to Pheidippides and forces him to enter the Thinkery (lines 815–885).
   c. The scene when Pheidippides returns from the Thinkery (lines 1165–1213).
   d. The final scene, from when Pheidippides beats his father until the end of the play (1323–end).

2. Delete any bawdy jokes that might offend your audience. Remember, we are Christians, and we are not performing for the festival of Dionysus.

ENDNOTES
1 Sommerstein, Alan H., trans. *Lysistrata and Other Plays*, Revised Edition. London: Penguin Books, 2002.

THE HIPPOCRATIC OATH

"A voice was heard in Ramah,
Lamentation and bitter weeping,
Rachel weeping for her children,
Refusing to be comforted for her children,
Because they are no more."
— Jeremiah 31:15

This passage from Jeremiah is directly quoted in the Gospel of Matthew. Both passages "resurrect" Rachel to weep over her children. The passages echo a very particular kind of sadness, that of great loss and the fear that comes from being terrorized by a bloodthirsty tyrant. Jeremiah's context is the Babylonian invasion of the southern kingdom. Matthew's context is the fulfillment of Herod's decree—the murder of all the boys two years old and younger in Bethlehem and its surrounding villages (Matt. 2:16). But why does Matthew's Gospel quote Jeremiah's passage of lament regarding Nebuchadnezzar's bloody siege of Jerusalem? And why does Jeremiah refer to Rachel?

There is one very interesting answer to these questions, an answer that does justice to the larger purpose of both authors. This answer is hope: just as Moses escaped Pharaoh's bloody decree, and a remnant of exiles survived the annihilating forces of the Babylonians, so too Jesus escaped the murderous decree of Herod.

God's covenant purposes are fulfilled in spite of the wickedness of men. But why Rachel? Why does Jeremiah refer to Rachel weeping over her children? Rachel was often viewed by Jewish rabbis as the mother of Israel. Thus "Rachel's children" are the children of the covenant promises. Throughout the history of Israel, the children of Israel were often subject to great suffering and the terrible pain of exile. In this condition of exile they waited—for the coming fulfillment of the covenant. As they waited, they wept, often bitterly.

As Rachel was dying, she named the son she had borne Ben-Oni ("son of my sorrow"). Rachel was buried on the way to Ephrathah, in Bethlehem. In Matthew's Gospel, the obvious link is both to Bethlehem, the sight of weeping and bitter lamentation for the children of Rachel who "are no more," and to Rachel's son Ben-Oni, "son of my sorrow" (the son whose name is changed by his father, Jacob, to Ben-Jamin, "son of the right hand"). Rachel's sorrow, however, is interrupted by the great joy of the birth of the Messiah—the Messiah who will be the end of all sorrows. By God's providence, Jesus escaped Herod's decree so that one day He would end Rachel's weeping. In the biblical narrative of salvation history, great sorrow is often punctuated by even greater joy.

Central to the events that both Jeremiah and Matthew record is the tyrant. The tyrant is the corrupt and godless ruler who wantonly destroys life and has no concern for the innocent. The tyrant wields the sword in the name of unchecked power. Nebuchadnezzar's imperial commander, Nebuzaradan, had wielded the sword cruelly and rapaciously in the name of such power. He also wielded the sword as he gathered the remaining exiles at Ramah to take them into captivity in Babylon. The children of Israel ("Rachel's children") wept as they saw their once great nation in ruins—their women and children cruelly and rapaciously massacred by a bloodthirsty tyrant. The children of Israel also wept as another tyrant, Herod, massacred the baby boys in and around the city of Bethlehem.

In the hands of tyrants (and those who do their bidding), the sword is an instrument of unchecked power, wanton devastation, and ultimately genocide. Have we made progress since then? The record of our most recent century suggests that humanists have not learned their lesson. The twentieth century, which began with unbridled humanistic optimism, tragically experienced the result of such optimism. The humanist, godless ideologies of the twentieth century spawned men like Hitler, Stalin, Mussolini, Pol Pot, and Idi Amin, state-sponsored genocidal machines such as the German National Socialist Party (Nazis), the Soviet Union, and the Khmer Rouge, and massive and mindless bloodletting events such as the death camps at Auschwitz, the Rape of Nanking, and the killing fields at Choeung Ek. Clearly, humanism is a form of regression, not progress.

Whereas in the hands of a tyrant the sword is death, devastation, and unchecked power, another art has been practiced for the opposite purpose: the preservation and protection of life. This is what the guild of doctors in the ancient world referred to as the "healing art." However, the doctor and the tyrant are potentially not so different. Both wield power over life and death. Patients, not unlike the subjects ruled by tyrants, are quite vulnerable. Although the tyrant wishes to wield unchecked power, what of the doctor? Is there some means whereby the power that the doctor has over life and death might be restrained by a moral code?

For thousands of years, those practicing the "healing art" have taken an oath to place a restraint on the great power they wield. This oath is the Hippocratic Oath. Simply put, the Hippocratic Oath provides a very clear picture of the way that doctors should practice their craft. According to the central principle of the oath, doctors shall preserve and not destroy life when it is most fragile and vulnerable. Thus, the Hippocratic Oath explicitly set out to protect life where it is most vulnerable—the unborn, sick, infirm, and elderly. Therefore, the Hippocratic Oath explicitly forbids doctors either to abort babies or to euthanize patients. As the Hippocratic Oath is increasingly ignored in our society, and as doctors are murdering unborn babies and euthanizing the elderly, a question arises for us: has our medical profession become tyrannical?

GENERAL INFORMATION

Author and Context

It is difficult to identify a single author of the oath. It is quite possible that the oath was originally penned by Hippocrates (460–380 B.C.), a contemporary of Socrates. It is important, if we are to understand the context of the oath, to understand the central theme of the oath. The central theme of the oath is a simple distinction: healers versus killers. The oath determines, by its basic orientation, to make this distinction clear and undeniable.

The followers of the Greek god Asclepius (the god of healing) were referred to as Asclepiads. They were part of a guild of practitioners of the medical art. The history of Asclepius in mythology may be an interesting clue to the central purpose of the guild. According to one myth, Asclepius was the son of Apollo. His mother died during childbirth. As she was about to be consumed by flames on the funeral pyre, Apollo rescued his unborn son. He was cut out of his dead mother's womb and hence given the name Asclepius ("to cut out"). Being instructed in the art of medicine (by the centaur Chiron), Asclepius gained great power and the ability to restore patients to health. His art, therefore, was considered "the healing art." Followers of the Asclepiad guild, therefore, were practitioners of the healing art.

Significance

The Hippocratic Oath was a central feature of the guild of healers from the fourth century B.C. to Galen (129–200 A.D.), the last of a great tradition of Asclepiad Greco-Roman philosopher-physicians. It has formed the foundation for the contemporary practice of doctors taking oaths as an essential element in the practice of medicine. Its significance is found in the way it helped to establish a "school" of physicians with a standardized moral vision. We take it for granted that a doctor is a medically and scientifically trained expert at his craft. But that was not always the case.

For the most part, those practicing the medical arts were nothing more than *shamans*, that is, witch-doctors performing ritualistic, occult activities. Divinization, crying, reading runes, sacrifice, controlling spirits—these were all activities considered to be "medicinal" in nature. Little to no attempt was made to study the body scientifically or to understand the relationship between anatomy, biology and healing. This is what set the Hippocratic, Asclepiad tradition apart. The members of the guild passed knowledge down from generation to generation. And according to some ancient scholars, by the time of Galen the science of medicine had become quite sophisticated. Possibly the greatest ancient inheritor of the Hippocratic tradition, Galen was truly a philosopher and scientist. He had developed the art of anatomy and possessed a quite advanced understanding of such complex systems as the nervous and circulatory systems.

Perhaps the greatest significance of the Hippocratic tradition, however, is the way the oath defined the *telos*, or purpose, of the doctor. The most basic principle of the oath is defined in this simple Latin phrase: *primum non nocere* ("first do no harm"). In succinct form, the oath clearly articulates the basic goals and aims of medicine. This section of the oath helps us understand how clearly the oath articulates the moral purpose and function of the doctor's art:

> Whenever I go into a house, I will go to help the sick and never with the intention of doing harm or injury. I will not abuse my position to indulge in sexual contacts with the bodies of women or of men, whether they be freemen or slaves.

The oath, therefore, clearly recognizes the possibility of doctors having tyrannical power over their patients. Not only did the Hippocratic tradition encourage doctors to be scientists and not shamans or witch doctors, but it also encouraged them to practice their art with great moral self-restraint and with the highest respect for the sacredness of life and of the doctor/patient relationship.

For some time now, medical students have taken some version of the Hippocratic Oath, as almost every medical school administers some form of the oath as an essential part of its tradition. It is important to note, however, that most medical schools have removed key elements of the oath. Most notably, references to abortion and euthanasia have been removed from many of the modernized versions of the oaths administered at medical schools.

For thousands of years, those practicing the "healing art" have taken an oath to place a restraint on the great power they wield. Hippocrates is the namesake of this oath.

Setting

As with any oath that has value, the context for this oath is religious. Since a man can swear by nothing higher than God (or the gods, for the Greeks and Romans—Christian doctors, of course, could not take an oath to a false deity[1]), the oath begins with the following: "I swear by Apollo the physician, and Asclepius, and Hygieia, and Panacea and all the gods and goddesses as my witnesses, that, according to my ability and judgment, I will keep this Oath and this contract."

Hygieia was the offspring of Asclepius and was the goddess of good health (the word *hygiene* is derived from her name). Her sister Panacea's name means "all-cure." As was traditional in Greco-Roman religion, practitioners of certain arts dedicated their activities to the gods who were considered to be the divine benefactors or patrons of their craft. In devoting their activities to the gods, the Asclepiads (the guild of doctors) were recognizing the sacred responsibilities and moral boundaries of their craft. Another important element in the opening declaration is the recognition of the legally binding quality of the oath. Many translations give the following version of the binding nature of the oath: "... to keep according to my ability the following oath and promise." Some will put in place of "promise" the word "agreement." This is closer to the appropriate translation. Better is the translation given previously: "contract." The Greek word being translated is *syngraphe*. It refers to a written (legally binding) agreement, not merely a verbal agreement. So the best translation would not be "promise" or "agreement," but something like the following: "... to keep according to my ability the following oath and *legal agreement*."

The oath has seven main elements, with a final, capstone promise (to keep everything contained in the oath). They can be broken up into the following abbreviations:

- **A** Responsibility to fellow practitioners of the art
- **B** Prohibition against doing harm and promise to do good
- **C** Prohibition against euthanasia and abortion
- **D** Promise to preserve purity of life and practice
- **E** Recognition of the need for specialists to provide specialized services (like certain specialized surgical activities)
- **F** Prohibition against abusing power to seduce patients
- **G** Prohibition against teaching the secrets of the craft to those untrained or who have not taken the oath

Worldview

During World War II, Nazi doctors practiced medicine in a horrific manner. What was their stated purpose? Their purpose was to pursue the "common good" of the state as a whole. Who suffers when this objective operates unchecked? Given the history of Nazi Germany, it is clearly the weak and vulnerable, the unwanted or "useless," who suffer the most. Many of the Nazi experiments were employed with the justification that they served the greater common good.

For instance, Nazi doctors conducted hypothermia (freezing) experiments on human subjects to simulate the conditions Nazi soldiers might face in extreme cold conditions. The experiments attempted to determine how quickly someone would typically freeze to death and, if possible, how best to resuscitate the body. They used two basic methods to bring patients to a point of freezing: putting them in tanks filled with ice water, and putting victims outside, naked, in freezing temperatures. In the concentration camp at Auschwitz, the extreme cold conditions in the winter made it the perfect place to perform cold-weather "exposure" experiments. The "warming" experiments (used to bring the person back from a state of extreme hypothermia) were no less cruel than the

Asclepius, the Greek god of medicine, is depicted practicing his art on a patient.

"cooling" experiments. One of the worst warming techniques was one in which the unconscious victim had boiling hot water forced into such internal organs as the stomach and intestines. This was done to see how quickly the body temperature would return to normal (and to see if the patient could be revived).

The stated justification for such horrific experimentation was to promote the common good of the Nazi army (and, by implication, the German state). What kind of ethic does this presume? The ethic it presumes is utilitarian. On this ethical theory, the "greater good" (the end) justifies the morally questionable means employed to achieve such a "good."

On this reasoning, the value of an action (or a thing—even a person) is determined by its utility or use-value in relationship to the end or goal that is pursued. Use-value is often based upon the following principle: an action has utility (use-value) insofar as it best promotes the greatest good of the largest number. Nazi freezing; bone, muscle and nerve regeneration; bone transplantation; mustard gas; sulfanilamide, and seawater experiments, were all justified according to this principle.[2]

Unlike a *deontological* ethical system (in which the moral worth of actions is not determined with respect to outcomes or consequences), utilitarian ethics are *consequentialist*. This means the value of an action is not only based upon its utility, but also upon the desirability of the outcome. The desirability of the outcome becomes the overriding moral principle that justifies the means used to achieve the outcome.

Nazi medical ethics were explicitly utilitarian and consequentialist in form. They determined that achieving the greatest good for the greatest number in the German state demanded the sacrifice of some (the weak, infirm, Jews, captured enemy soldiers, etc.). Often, this principle was justified on the basis of utilitarian social Darwinism: the herd as a whole (the German state) is strengthened when the weaker members of the herd (the weak, elderly, infirm, ethnically inferior, genetically inferior, etc.) are killed.

Out of this terrible and horrific moment in the history of medicine emerged a very important document. It was influenced by the important work of Dr. Leo Alexander (expert medical adviser to the U.S. Chief of Counsel for War Crimes, and important participant in the Nuremberg war crimes trials). The document is called the "Nuremberg Code."[3] The purpose of the document is to provide a moral framework for experimentation on human subjects. In it the principle of "informed consent" is established as preeminent. In it we can also see the influence of the Hippocratic Oath. The goal of the Nuremberg Code is the same as that of the Hippocratic Oath: to define the moral objectives (and limits) of medical practitioners. Nazi Germany provides an important reminder—those practicing medicine need to be limited by a binding moral code. From this we can see that the 2,400-year-old lesson Hippocrates sought to teach us is no less relevant today than it was in 400 B.C.

Nazi Germany provides such an explicit and historically memorable example of heartless inhuman injustices, we are tempted to see it as an anomaly—something that happened *once* in history but will never happen again. However, the biblical picture of man suggests that he is always tempted to act according to naked self-interest and according to a "way" whose end is death: "There is a way that seems right to a man, but its end is the way of death" (Prov. 14:12). In our pride we may believe we have learned the lessons we needed to learn from the medical horrors of the Holocaust. And yet the evidence suggests the opposite.

Contemporary medicine has strayed quite far from the basic principles of the Hippocratic Oath. There are two obvious instances of this: abortion and euthanasia/physician-assisted suicide. For some time the Netherlands has been the most supportive of euthanasia and

THE HIPPOCRATIC OATH (Original Version)

I SWEAR by Apollo the physician, Aesculapius, and Health, and All-heal, and all the gods and goddesses, that, according to my ability and judgement, I will keep this Oath and this stipulation.

TO RECKON him who taught me this Art equally dear to me as my parents, to share my substance with him, and relieve his necessities if required; to look up his offspring in the same footing as my own brothers, and to teach them this art, if they shall wish to learn it, without fee or stipulation; and that by precept, lecture, and every other mode of instruction, I will impart a knowledge of the Art to my own sons, and those of my teachers, and to disciples bound by a stipulation and oath according to the law of medicine, but to none others.

I WILL FOLLOW that system of regimen which, according to my ability and judgment, I consider for the benefit of my patients, and abstain from whatever is deleterious and mischievous. I will give no deadly medicine to any one if asked, nor suggest any such counsel; and in like manner I will not give a woman a pessary to produce abortion.

WITH PURITY AND WITH HOLINESS I will pass my life and practice my Art. I will not cut persons laboring under the stone, but will leave this to be done by men who are practitioners of this work. Into whatever houses I enter, I will go into them for the benefit of the sick, and will abstain from every voluntary act of mischief and corruption; and, further from the seduction of females or males, of freemen and slaves.

WHATEVER, IN CONNECTION with my professional practice or not, in connection with it, I see or hear, in the life of men, which ought not to be spoken of abroad, I will not divulge, as reckoning that all such should be kept secret.

WHILE I CONTINUE to keep this Oath unviolated, may it be granted to me to enjoy life and the practice of the art, respected by all men, in all times! But should I trespass and violate this Oath, may the reverse be my lot!

Oregon were the first U.S. citizens to be recipients of a legally supported physician-assisted suicide. These patients were killed under the terms of the 1994 Death with Dignity Act.

Christians are also painfully aware of how the legalization of abortion in the infamous *Roe v. Wade* Supreme Court decision has profoundly changed the landscape of American medicine. Since the 1973 *Roe v. Wade* decision, there have been over fifty million abortions. If we use the round number of five million Jews killed in the Holocaust, we have had the equivalent of ten Holocausts in the United States since 1973. Also, we have heard arguments from the floor of Congress, from presidents, and from medical experts justifying selective (eugenic) abortion, abortion as population control, and embryonic research. These arguments are philosophically utilitarian and consequentialist in nature. So are we really that far from the ethic used to justify the Nazi approach to life issues? In removing explicit references to euthanasia and abortion from the modernized versions of the Hippocratic Oath, are our doctors in danger of becoming indistinguishable from tyrants?

Another sign that America is in danger of being unable to avoid the temptations of a utilitarian ethic is the career of Peter Singer. Peter Singer is an open and self-avowed proponent of infanticide—killing a baby after he has been born. Not only is Peter Singer pro-abortion, but he also believes that infanticide is morally justifiable by the principles outlined in his utilitarian ethics.[4] That an ethicist would hold this view is not especially remarkable in our time. That such an ethicist would be the Ira W. DeCamp professor of bioethics at Princeton University *is* remarkable.

Operating with a strange form of strict and cold consistency, Singer is both a proponent of abortion on demand and infanticide and yet an avid supporter of

physician-assisted suicide. In 2002 euthanasia and physician-assisted suicide were officially legalized in the Netherlands (although for over twenty years doctors had not been prosecuted if they had euthanized patients or assisted in suicide). In 1998 two terminally ill patients in

animal rights. Singer claims to have been a vegetarian since 1971, and his famous *Animal Liberation* has become a sort of bible for animal rights activists. That Singer could be promoted to such a prestigious position at a top Ivy League school suggests that the outrage we experience in relationship to the Holocaust, which is visceral, natural and immediate, doesn't exist when it comes to an exactly equivalent moral issue (infanticide) that should be just as visceral, natural, and immediate.

Singer and his ilk promote a utilitarian bioethics. Utilitarian bioethics uses a quality-of-life argument to determine how to make basic ethical decisions. Yet this is exactly the kind of reasoning used to justify human experimentation and the euthanization of infants, the sick, and the elderly in Nazi Germany. To determine how little we've learned from World War II Germany, we will take a look at a chilling passage from Dr. Leo Alexander's now famous article from the July 1949 *New England Journal of Medicine*, titled "Medical Science Under Dictatorship."

Whatever proportions these crimes finally assumed, it became evident to all who investigated them that they had started from small beginnings. The beginnings at first were merely a subtle shift in emphasis in the basic attitude of the physicians. It started with the acceptance of the attitude, basic in the euthanasia movement, that there is such a thing as life not worthy to be lived. This attitude in its early stages concerned itself merely with the severely and chronically sick. Gradually the sphere of those to be included in this category was enlarged to encompass the socially unproductive, the ideologically unwanted, the racially unwanted and finally all non-Germans. But it is important to realize that the infinitely small wedged-in lever from which this entire trend of mind received its impetus was the attitude toward the non-rehabilitable sick.[5]

THE HIPPOCRATIC OATH (A Modern Version)
Written by Louis Lasagna in 1964

I swear to fulfill, to the best of my ability and judgment, this covenant:

I will respect the hard-won scientific gains of those physicians in whose steps I walk, and gladly share such knowledge as is mine with those who are to follow.

I will apply, for the benefit of the sick, all measures which are required, avoiding those twin traps of overtreatment and therapeutic nihilism.

I will remember that there is art to medicine as well as science, and that warmth, sympathy, and understanding may outweigh the surgeon's knife or the chemist's drug.

I will not be ashamed to say "I know not," nor will I fail to call in my colleagues when the skills of another are needed for a patient's recovery.

I will respect the privacy of my patients, for their problems are not disclosed to me that the world may know. Most especially must I tread with care in matters of life and death. If it is given me to save a life, all thanks. But it may also be within my power to take a life; this awesome responsibility must be faced with great humbleness and awareness of my own frailty. Above all, I must not play at God.

I will remember that I do not treat a fever chart, a cancerous growth, but a sick human being, whose illness may affect the person's family and economic stability. My responsibility includes these related problems, if I am to care adequately for the sick.

I will prevent disease whenever I can, for prevention is preferable to cure.

I will remember that I remain a member of society, with special obligations to all my fellow human beings, those sound of mind and body as well as the infirm.

If I do not violate this oath, may I enjoy life and art, respected while I live and remembered with affection thereafter. May I always act so as to preserve the finest traditions of my calling and may I long experience the joy of healing those who seek my help.

For all of Dr. Alexander's chilling warnings, we clearly haven't learned our lesson. Alexander warns against approaches to bioethics based upon quality-of-life reasoning and utilitarian ethical principles. The slippery slope to Nazi medical ethics began with a shift away from a deontological, rule-based ethics to a utilitarian ethic based upon quality-of-life judgments. As a nation, we continue to use quality-of-life reasoning and utilitarian ethical principles.

For instance, aborting babies with disabilities has become a common practice. Some estimates have the abortion rates for babies identified with Down syndrome as high as 80 to 90 percent. Furthermore, we are constantly hearing that abortion reduces the number of "unwanted pregnancies" and "unwanted children" and therefore increases the percentage of "happy children." In short, abortion increases the overall quality of life of American children. The rationale given for selective (eugenic) abortion and abortion to control population or reduce "unwanted pregnancies" is exactly the same as what Dr. Alexander warns us against; it is the "small beginning" that led to the terrible and horrific consequences of the Holocaust. It assumes that we can, by playing God, calculate the status of a life "not worthy to be lived."

So how has our "enlightened" and "progressive" world become so deluded as to have failed to learn the important (and obvious) lessons from the Holocaust? As Christians, we cannot be reminded enough of one of the most basic aspects of sin: "suppressing the truth in wickedness." Romans 1:18 tells us that sinners *actively* and *intentionally* suppress the truth in wickedness. The Greek verb for "suppress" means "to actively hold back" or "restrain" or "hold down."

This is precisely what we as a society are doing as we ignore (intentionally) the most basic elements of the Hippocratic Oath. If the majority of medical colleges throughout the country have removed references to abortion and euthanasia from their modernized, updated versions of the Hippocratic Oath, we can be certain they are "suppressing the truth in wickedness." What is frightening is that this active suppression of the truth is done in the name of justice and liberation.

So how might we respond to this trend in our culture? We must return to the most basic elements of the doctrine of creation and the anthropology that emerges from it. One of the most basic responsibilities that Christians have is to be "fruitful and multiply" and to "fill the earth and subdue it." In order to do this, however, we must have an ethic, theology, and anthropology that explicitly and unwaveringly protects the mystery and "gift quality" of life. The mystery of life is an essential component of our situation as finite and limited human beings. We do not see the future, and we are not called to attempt to manipulate the future through some kind of alchemical calculus that reduces (and even destroys) the mystery of the gift of life. There are many instances in Scripture in which disastrous consequences come from people attempting to control life through some kind of alchemy or technique.

Synonymous with the mysterious quality of life is its gift character. According to Exodus 3:14, God *is life*. We, on the other hand, merely *have life*. For this reason, life is a sacred gift given to us from the fountain of all life. It is never something that we *own*, nor is it ever something that is an ungifted "right." This understanding is in danger of being lost when we articulate life as a "right." Although it is true that human beings have a "right" not to have life unjustly taken away from them by another human being, it does not follow that we have a "right to life" *per se*.

For creatures who are created and whose essence is not to exist—only God has essential existence—life always retains its gift quality. Even the universe does not uphold itself, but is actively upheld by the power of Christ (Col. 1:17; Heb. 1:3). As St. Augustine reminds us in *Confessions*, if God withdrew His sustaining power, the universe would fall back into the nonexistence out of which it came (this is a logical extension of the doctrine that God created the universe *ex nihilo*).

What does this mean for ethics? It means we must promote an ethic that recognizes the mystery, sanctity, and gift quality of life and our role as Christians to protect it. It is hard to do this without an explicitly theological approach to ethics. It is interesting to note that the Hippocratic Oath invokes the gods at the beginning. Although these gods are obviously false, it is no less true that the Hippocratic Oath begins with recognition of the sacred nature of the doctor's vocation. This understanding translates into an ethic that asks doctors to avoid the temptation to abuse their vocation as autonomous tyrants. They have a sacred vocation to protect and preserve the sanctity of life. To do this they must respect the gift quality of life. Therefore, we Christians have a great responsibility to take the insights at the heart of the Hippocratic Oath and support (and develop) the tradition it represents.

So how do we protect doctors from becoming tyrants? We do so by reminding them of the sacred mystery and gift quality of life, and asking them to hold themselves to a rule-based standard that promotes respect for these things. Supporting an appropriate ethic in the context of life issues is an essential part of the cultural mandate that God has given the church. The church has a powerful responsibility: to take what is most noble and true in the Hippocratic tradition of medicine and support that tradition, enlightening it with the clearer and more certain truths revealed in sacred Scripture and the luminous dogmas forged in the nearly 2,000 years of church history.

—*Graham Dennis*

The Hippocratic Oath 149

For Further Reading

Cameron, Nigel M. de S. *The New Medicine: Life and Death After Hippocrates.* Chicago: The Bioethics Press, 2001. 23-34, 49-91, 171-177.

Colson, Charles (ed.). *Human Dignity in the Biotech Century.* Downers Grove, Ill.: InterVarsity Press, 2004. 21-39, 60-74.

Guinan, Patrick. *Hippocratic and Judeo-Christian Medical Ethics.* Bloomington, Ind.: AuthorHouse, 2007. 3-8, 13-18, 77-82, 93-116.

Session I: Prelude

A Question to Consider

Is it ever right for a doctor to intentionally kill a patient?

From the General Information above answer the following questions:

1. Who is Asclepius, and what is his role in the history (or mythology) surrounding medicine?
2. How did the Hippocratic Oath define the *telos* of the medical profession?
3. What horrifying experiments did Nazi doctors practice, justifying

Jack Kevorkian (1928–), nicknamed "Dr. Death," is a former pathologist and promoter of euthanasia who claims to have assisted more than 130 terminally ill patients in committing suicide. He is infamous for inventing a "death machine" that allowed patients to self-administer lethal drugs to end their lives.

their horrendous actions by claiming they were for the "common good"?
4. What are utilitarian ethics, and what does this ethic lead to in medical practice?
5. What are some changes that medical colleges have made to the Hippocratic Oath recently?
6. Do human beings have a "right" to life?

Reading Assignment:
The Hippocratic Oath (original and modern versions)

The Hippocratic Oath explicitly set out to protect life where it is most vulnerable—the unborn, sick, infirm, and elderly.

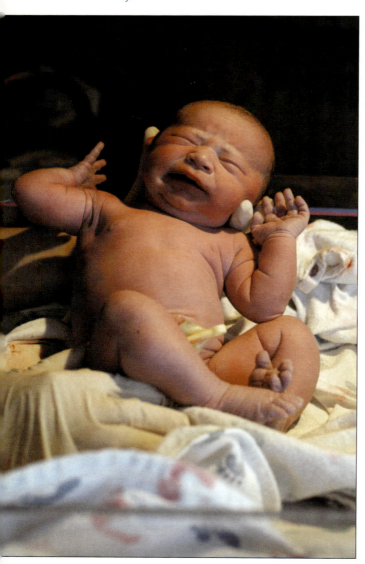

Session II: Discussion

A Question to Consider
What are the responsibilities of a physician to his patient, and what relevance does that answer have to anyone who is not in the medical profession?

Discuss or list short answers to the following questions:

Text Analysis
1. What are the five major elements of the original Hippocratic Oath? What central principle unifies these tenets?
2. What is meant in the original oath by the promise not to cut "persons laboring under the stone"? (Think of stones you might have in your body—or your parents might have in theirs.)
3. What are the significant differences between the ancient and modern versions of the oath? What do these differences tell us about how culture has changed since Hippocrates' time?
4. In the third paragraph of the original oath, what specific examples of respecting life does this oath promise to uphold? How are these examples possibly surprising in light of current medical practice in America today?

Cultural Analysis
1. Hippocrates was instrumental in forming the basis for medicine in the West. Medicine in ancient Greece was originally practiced by temple priests, and characterized by superstition, charms, and religious ritual. Hippocrates and others like him rejected the idea that diseases were arbitrary punishments by the gods; they sought natural causes and rational treatments through observation and experimentation. Many people today believe that the conflict between religion and reason in Hippocrates' day is a permanent conflict, and that religious faith (considered superstitious and irrational) impedes scientific advancement. How should the Christian respond to such an attitude when he encounters it?
2. How does our culture today view the principles of the original Hippocratic Oath?
3. How does our culture justify practices that violate the principles of respect for life set forth in the oath?
4. Christians ought to be vigilant against compromising biblical truth and practice. Yet not all change is compromise, any more than all change is positive progress. As the field of medicine changes rapidly with advances in technology, what standard can we use to

determine the difference between true improvement and ethical compromise?

Biblical Analysis

1. What is the biblical teaching on protecting and respecting life (Gen. 1:26–28, Deut. 30:15–20, John 1:4, 10:10, 14:6)?
2. What is the biblical teaching on ethics, especially as applied to medicine (Matt. 22:34–40, Rom. 13:8–10, 1 John 4:7–13)?
3. What is the importance of healing imagery in the Scriptures (Gen. 3:22–24, Matt. 9:12–13, Rev. 22:2)?

Summa

Write an essay or discuss this question, integrating what you have learned from the material above.

What are the responsibilities of a physician to his patient, and what bearing does that answer have on your own Christian life and witness?

Instead of a reading assignment you have a research assignment. Tomorrow's session will be a Current Events session. Your assignment will be to find a story online, in a magazine, or in the newspaper that relates to the issue that you discussed today. Your task is to locate the article, give a copy of the article to your teacher or parent and provide some of your own worldview analysis to the article. Your analysis should demonstrate that you understand the issue, that you can clearly connect the story you found to the issue that you discussed today, and that you can provide a biblical critique of this issue in today's context. Look at the next session to see the three-part format that you should follow.

Issue

Medical Ethics and the Dignity of Human Life

Session III: Current Events

Issue

Medical ethics and the dignity of human life

Current events sessions are meant to challenge you to connect what you are learning in Omnibus class to what is happening in the world around you today. After the last session, your assignment was to find a story online or in a magazine or newspaper relating to the issue above. Today you will share your article and your analysis with your teacher and classmates or parents and family. Your analysis should follow the format below:

Brief Introductory Paragraph

In this paragraph you will tell your classmates about the article that you found. Be sure to include where you found your article, who the author of your article is, and what your article is about. This brief paragraph of your presentation should begin like this:

> Hello, I am (name), and my current events article is (name of the article) which I found in (name of the web or published source)…

Connection Paragraph

In this paragraph you must demonstrate how your article is connected to the issue you are studying. This paragraph should be short, and it should focus on clearly showing the connection between the book you are reading and the current events article you have found. This paragraph should begin with a sentence like:

> I knew that my article was linked to our issue because…

Christian Worldview Analysis

In this section, you need to tell us how we should respond as believers to this issue today. This response should focus both on our thinking and on practical actions that we should take in light of this issue. As you list these steps, you should also tell us why we should think and act in the ways you recommend. This paragraph should begin with a sentence like

> As believers, we should think and act in the following ways in light of this issue and this article.

Reading Assignment: None

Session IV: Worldview Analysis

Medical Ethics Comparison

Choose a current medical topic. Research the ethical questions surrounding it, as well as our culture's—and the medical community's—common position on that topic.

152 OMNIBUS IV

Then, compare and contrast the worldviews expressed in the oaths, current medical practice, and Christianity by completing Chart 1. In the last column write in your selected topic—then identify the position of each of these three on that issue. In your answers, you must explain why each entity takes that position (or why you believe it would), based on its worldview.

Suggested topics to research and evaluate: abortion, forms of birth control that can result in the loss of a fertilized embryo, euthanasia, in vitro fertilization, the use of human embryos in stem cell research, and human cloning.

"Above all, I must not play at God." Although human cloning is not (yet) a reality, proponents believe it could bring mankind a host of medical blessings. It also raises a host of ethical issues. Simply by engaging in human cloning experiments scientists are certain to destroy human lives "in the name of science." Is it up to our healers to decide who must die that others might live?

SESSION V: ACTIVITIES

Medical "Examination"

1. Interview someone in the medical profession to learn their perspective on how modern medicine upholds the ethical values stated in the Hippocratic Oath. Some questions you might want to ask are:
    - Did you choose to take the oath (or another one), and if so, why?
    - If you did, how do you interpret and specifically apply the principles of the oath in your daily practice?
    - How do those in the medical field who support violations of the oath justify those violations?
    - What long-term effects do you predict for the practice of medicine and for our culture due to the increased acceptance of practices that do not protect and preserve life? (You will learn more if you ask

Chart 1: **MEDICAL ETHICS COMPARISON**

	DUTY TOWARD GOD	**DUTY TOWARD FELLOW MAN**
Hippocratic Oath	The original oath calls on the witness of the healing gods of its polytheistic pantheon. The modern version omits all reference to God except to call on doctors to avoid playing God. The language in the original oath implies a responsibility toward the divinities to honor with reverence and dignity the arts they practice, and it presumes that these gods have the power to punish as well as heal.	The original oath recognizes that man has gifts and abilities and the choice to exercise them for good or ill. While not explicitly acknowledging the *imago Dei,* this oath reflects an ancient understanding of the nobility of man, in both himself (the physician) and others (the patient). This understanding results in an obligation not to harm one's neighbor, nor use him for selfish benefit. The concept of treating others with dignity and respect was understood and honored, even if not always practiced (as is still the case today).
Current Cultural Values	In a postmodern culture, there is little consensus on the nature—much less the very existence—of God. These beliefs will, of course, depend upon the individual physicians and patients. Still, the medical profession and society as a whole tend to look mostly toward materialistic explanations for diseases and their treatments and cures. In many cases, today's society tends to view religious faith as a private matter, and thereby focuses more on one's duty to fellow man than to God. This can result in the presumption of ignoring God's law and creating a standard for ethics apart from Him; sometimes those ethics still hit upon the law of God written on our hearts—as the Hippocratic Oath did in a pre-Christian, pagan society—but sometimes it does not.	Today's cultural understanding of the nature of man is informed by Christianity, but does not always explicitly follow it. There is often a tension between recognizing the *imago Dei,* with its attendant responsibility to protect and respect life—yet at the same time "rating" human life on a utilitarian scale instead of seeing intrinsic value. Thus, our society can at the same time believe that individual patient rights must be respected, and require informed consent before a medical procedure—but at the same time believe that some lives are more valuable than others. So, for example, many consider abortion acceptable because the concerns and "rights" of the mother outweigh those of the baby; similarly, some see embryonic stem-cell harvesting as acceptable because the babies' lives are not as valuable as those already born who are suffering from diseases that might be cured by research done with those stem cells. This utilitarian view of human life is dangerous and unbiblical.

Chart 1: **MEDICAL ETHICS COMPARISON** *continued*

	DUTY TOWARD GOD	**DUTY TOWARD FELLOW MAN**
Christianity	Christianity starts with the foundational understanding that God created the cosmos, and all of it is by and for Him: "The earth is the Lord's and the fullness thereof, the world and those who dwell therein" (Ps. 24:1). Because we belong to Him, we owe all obedience and reverence to Him. Jesus tells us that our first duty—the greatest commandment—is to love the Lord our God with all our heart, soul, and mind (Matt. 22:36–38). He also tells us that loving Him means obeying His commandments (John 14:15). Thus our duty to God is to love and obey Him, and a great part of this duty to God is to love our fellow man, whom He has also created in His image (Matt. 22:36–40).	Our duty to our fellow man is inextricably linked with our duty to God. If the greatest commandment is to love God, the second—to love our neighbor—is "like unto it" (Matt. 22:39) and completes the central message of the Scriptures. Man is made in the image of God; we, especially believers, are called to honor others above ourselves, and in so doing we honor God.

POSITION ON CURRENT MEDICAL TOPIC:

Hippocratic Oath		
Current Cultural Values		
Christianity		

open-ended questions, and avoid those that can be easily answered with a *yes* or *no*.)

2. Expand upon the topic you chose for the Current Events or Worldview Analysis Sessions. Conduct further research on that topic and write a paper or give an oral presentation on it. Your paper or presentation should be both informative and persuasive; educate your audience on the topic and its surrounding ethical issues, and evaluate it biblically, offering a Christian response.

3. Research various systems of health care (such as managed care or socialized medicine). Examine how each system affects the physician's ability to uphold the ethical guidelines, established in the Hippocratic Oath, to make his patient's health his first priority.

OPTIONAL SESSION

Writing Your Representative

Biblical medical ethics are vitally important to the cultural health of our society, as well as its physical health. Our attitudes toward the weak, the sick, the elderly, and the unborn—and how we practically care for them—reflect the foundations of our culture's character and indicate the direction it will take in the future. Therefore, we all have a stake in the medical ethics and practices of our society. Because many people today base their practice on what is legal, rather than what is right, it is important to be aware of—and involved in—legislative decisions surrounding medical ethics and practice.

Choose a medical-ethics issue currently being considered in a legislative context. (This could be on a national, state, or local level—or perhaps more than one of these.) Identify your appropriate representatives and write them about this issue, urging them to uphold principles of wisdom, justice, and respect for life in their decisions. Do not merely ask them to vote a certain way; your letter should use solid information, sound logic, and persuasive rhetoric to show them why you request such a vote. Clearly state the issue in question and the position you request they take, then argue an effective case using the facts you have learned, citing sources where applicable. Be sure that your communication is clear and gracious.

ENDNOTES

1 Christian physicians actually altered the oath, removing references to the pagan deities and replacing them with references to Christ. Here is a version of the revised Creed used by Christian physicians in the Middle Ages:

From the Oath According to Hippocrates in so far as a Christian May Swear It (*Urbinus 64 mss*)

Blessed be God the Father of our Lord Jesus Christ, who is blessed for ever and ever; I lie not.

I will bring no stain upon the learning of the medical art. Neither will I give poison to anybody though asked to do so, nor will I suggest such a plan. Similarly I will not give treatment to women to cause abortion, treatment neither from above nor from below. But I will teach this art, to those who require to learn it, without grudging and without an indenture. I will use treatment to help the sick according to my ability and judgment. And in purity and in holiness I will guard my art. Into whatsoever houses I enter, I will do so to help the sick, keeping myself free from all wrong-doing, intentional or unintentional, tending to death or to injury, and from fornication with bond or free, man or woman. Whatsoever in the course of practice I see or hear (or outside my practice in social intercourse) that ought not to be published abroad, I will not divulge, but consider such things to be holy secrets. Now if I keep this oath and break it not, may God be my helper in my life and art, and may I be honoured among all men for all time. If I keep faith, well; but if I forswear myself may the opposite befall me.

2 For an exhaustive treatment of these experiments, and of the Nuremberg trials in general, see *Doctors From Hell: The Horrific Account of Nazi Experiments on Humans* (Vivien Spitz, First Sentient Publications, 2005).

3 Text for the Nuremberg Code can be found through Link 1 for this chapter at www.VeritasPress.com/OmniLinks.

4 See Peter Singer's chapter in *Practical Ethics* entitled "Taking Life: Humans." (Cambridge University Press, 1993.)

5 This article can be found through Link 2 for this chapter at www.VeritasPress.com/OmniLinks.

POLITICS

I was the oldest child of an American serviceman—a military brat. Economically, we were at the tail end of that spectrum identified as the middle class. In reality, we were probably among the more affluent of American's lower class. Neither of my parents had attended college. To my knowledge, no one on either side of our family had gone to college. We certainly did not enjoy wealth, privilege, or social standing. Nevertheless, my parents gave me a gift that was priceless—the ability to dream. They were raised in the cautious optimism that characterized post-World War II America. Therefore, while I was growing up they enabled me to believe that I could accomplish anything.

The standard line that optimistic members of the lower/middle-class told their children was, "You can grow up to be anything you want. You might even become president of the United States." That sounded good to me. I might as well aim for what everybody thought to be the top job. So, even as a young child, my ambition was to fulfill that objective. When other kids were asked what they might like "to be" when they grew up, the standard answers included fireman, policeman,

"If you join government, calmly make your contribution and move on. Don't go along to get along; do your best and when you have to—and you will—leave, and be something else."—Peggy Noonan, columnist, author, and former speech writer to President Ronald Reagan.

teacher, or nurse. I told my kindergarten teacher, with some degree of confidence, that I would someday become president of the United States.

And I meant it. When I reached the advanced age of seven, armed with a round, fat pencil and that paper we all used when we started elementary school—with the wide spacing and the dotted lines—I decided I need to get about the business of preparing for my future career. Therefore, I wrote a letter to President Johnson. Shortly thereafter, I received a packet of information from the White House that included a signed letter from the President. I cannot recall what words of wisdom I included in my missive, but now that I was in direct and personal communication with the leader of the free world, I was certain that I would someday occupy the space that Lyndon Johnson called home.

As I grew up, I supplemented my political ambition with some other interests. I was all too obsessed with sports—watching them and playing them. I also started to compete in interscholastic and, later, intercollegiate speech and debate. Instead of making "connections" with a political party or running for student council president, I was "cutting cards" and traveling extensively as a scholarship debater for my university. All the while, however, I still harbored that dream of running for the presidency.

A New and Different Calling

At the end of my senior year in college, I had one more rather dramatic interruption to my political pathway (a pathway that would lead to the White House). I gave my life to Jesus Christ. I became a Christian. Suddenly, my life moved in a very different direction. Initially, I did not anticipate much of a change in my career plans. I entered a master's degree program in political science determined to enroll in law school shortly thereafter. Despite my new-found faith in Christ, I saw no reason why my career in law and eventually politics would not unfold much as I had planned.

Boy, was I wrong. Within a year of my conver-sion, I felt a calling into the ministry. The debate days were over. The preoccupation with sports diminished to a hobby. Instead of law school, I went off to a theological seminary in Kentucky. And, even as a seminary student, I started to minister in small churches throughout southwestern Michigan.

Although my political aspirations might appear to have been self-centered, I was certainly motivated by more than personal ambition. I love America very much. Hence, I wanted to enter politics, in part, because I felt it to be the best way to serve my country.

After I came to Christ, I started to question that conclusion. As a minister of the gospel, I would have specific responsibilities under the direction and power of the Holy Spirit: First, I would be required to help lead a congregation in worshipping "our Father which art in heaven" and His Son Jesus Christ. Second, I would disciple brothers-and-sisters in Christ by doing the same things that Jesus did—to preach, teach, and minister to those who were hurting. Third, I would do the work of an evangelist—I must share the good news of Christ to those who had yet to receive Him as Savior and Lord. Finally, I would help to lead a congregation in those things that Jesus taught us to do: to put food in the mouths of those hungry, to put water in the cups of those who are thirsty, to put clothes on the back of those who are naked, to minister to those in jails, nursing homes, mental institutions, hospitals, and the like.

In fact, when I entered the doctoral program in Government at the University of Notre Dame, it was not to enhance a political career. After seminary, we were supposed to receive some denominational support for our little church in Michigan. That support fell through. I entered Notre Dame to acquire the credentials and preparation necessary to teach at the college level. I wanted to have a tent-making ministry like the apostle Paul so that I could be as free to minister as possible—and free to minister as the Lord might lead since we wouldn't be receiving the bulk of our livelihood from a

Politics

particular church or ministry.

I reached the conclusion that service to the Lord was not only my obligation as a minister, but it was also the best way for me to serve my country. I was convinced that I could change America for the better by changing individual lives. And I believed I could best change individual lives by helping to lead people to Christ and by ministering in His name. I still was interested in politics and government. After all, I am an American citizen, and I do enjoy the give-and-take of political debate. But I assumed that I would never seek elected office.

An Unexpected Return

A few years after I started teaching in Utah, things began to change. At the urging of one of my students, I attended a caucus meeting in the Republican Party and was elected a delegate to the state convention. Five years later, a couple of elected officials drafted me to run for Chair of the Republican Party in our county. They prepared the campaign. I gave a speech at the convention. To my surprise, I was elected. Suddenly, I was the Chair of a political party in a county with between 80–100,000 registered voters—most of whom were Republicans. I was responsible for about 150 voting precincts, fielding candidates for six districts to the Utah House of Representatives and two to the Utah Senate, and to raise money and govern the party on a day-to-day basis.

It was during my term as Weber County GOP Chair that I began to consider something much more dramatic: a candidacy for the United States Senate against the popular incumbent senator, Orrin Hatch. There are a variety of reasons why I considered the run. The most important was my concern that the Senator had been in Washington so long that his real constituency had become folks in and around the District of Columbia rather than the people of Utah. I felt like he had reached the point where he believed that he owed Utahans his inspiration and perspiration, but that he no longer owed them an explanation for his activity in the Senate. He was much like Colonel Nathanson in the film *A Few Good Men*. The Colonel told the young attorney in court that they should be thankful for the protection that he provided without asking questions. Hatch essentially told Utahans that we should be thankful for the representation he provided in the Senate without asking questions.

Note that this campaign was not an attempt to jumpstart my childhood dream. I wasn't planning to use my election to the Senate as a launching pad for a long-term career in politics culminating with a presidential run. In fact, I was pretty certain that I would not be elected. I did believe that my campaign would give me the opportunity to say some important things and, perhaps, prompt the Senator to see himself as more accountable to the people in Utah.

I presented a paper shortly after the 2000 election cycle which describes the experiences in the campaign in much greater detail. A campaign against Senator Hatch within the Utah Republican Party certainly was akin to smacking the nose of a big dog in his own back yard. In the paper, I describe the highs and lows, the experience of traveling across the state to speak at county conventions, and what it feels like to speak to 7,000 people at the state convention in the arena where they later held the hockey tournament at the 2002 Winter Olympic Games in Salt Lake City.

"Don't fall in love with politicians, they're all a disappointment. They can't help it, they just are."—Peggy Noonan

The inauguration of President Barack Obama, January 20, 2009 in Washington D.C.

Ministering through Citizenship?

As a boy I had dreamed of a career in politics. As a young Christian, called into ministry, I decided that the best way for me to serve both God and country was to become an excellent pastor rather than a politician. A few years later, opportunities surfaced that provided an opportunity to return to the political arena. I embraced those opportunities, although at times maybe a bit more like one who approaches the water by sticking in a big toe rather than fully plunging in.

What prompted the change of heart? I still consider myself, first and foremost, a minister of the gospel. I preach and teach whenever I have the opportunity and would maintain that America would be a better place if more of us were transformed through a relationship with Jesus Christ. I simply learned over the years that it is possible to minister in and through the political arena. Too often Christians, called to be salt and light to our government and culture, fail miserably if we cede the political arena to those outside of the body of Christ. We fail both as citizens of heaven and as American citizens.

In the body of Christ there has been a concern that if one is enmeshed in the affairs of government and, much worse, politics, then one is of little value to God. Although one might identify several periods in post-New Testament history where this concern served to compel individuals to separate from the political realm, one obvious and fairly recent case study would be the reaction to politics within a large portion of the body of Christ in America from the 1920s through most of the 1970s.

During this fifty year period, many Christians extricated themselves from the political arena in order to emphasize evangelism. "We haven't the time to be concerned with the goings on of this world," they might have observed. "Our obligation to the Lord is to prepare souls for the next one." Thus, while one might exercise many of the responsibilities of citizenship, political engagement pulled one away from one's primary obligation to God. Consequently, the participation in politics was likely an utter waste of time.

There is a whole cottage industry devoted to the re-emergence of Christians back into the political arena (as critics of culture, as would-be "kings," and, increasingly, as would-be kingmakers). Several scholarly books chronicle the importance of evangelical Christians as an important player in electoral politics. There are also a large number of popular and scholarly books that are very shrill in their opposition to Christian involvement in politics.

Rank-and-file Christians in America are reaching a point where they will make an important decision: Do we as believers challenge those aspects of our society that are the most ungodly, or do we retreat back from the political arena in favor of evangelism? This question becomes particularly prescient when many believers think that their brothers and sisters in Christ who are most shrill in the political arena are actually hurting the ultimate work of the Church.

I hope I've made it clear that for Christians to retreat from dialogic politics, the world of political ideas and discussions, would be a big mistake. Yes, I did make a clear decision that I could better serve God as a minister rather than as a public servant and believed that God was calling me in that direction. I always understood that the Bible teaches us that there is a clear connection between one's faith and the responsibilities of citizenship that call us all into politics at least at some level.

It certainly is safe to say that the political battle that Christians have fought since the late 1970s has not been without consequences. Christians are taking casualties from an enemy that is powerful, accomplished, educated, and determined not only to separate church from state but also religion from politics.

I have noted elsewhere that with regard to Christians and culture, it seems like we have only a limited number of choices:

1. We can withdraw from the secular-political world and concentrate on preparing souls for the next one as so many have suggested. This option would badly impoverish the nation.
2. We can resist by taking up arms in an attempt to purge and remake the state in God's image—a terrifying option that all but the most fervent extremists have opted to reject.
3. We might resist passively and nonviolently. Like Ghandi or King, the Church could speak out against the evils of the state and suffer—even welcome—arrest, torture, and death.
4. We can resist, from within the political arena, what we find to be immoral and unjust (whether practiced within the public or private sectors). The Constitution guarantees that, as citizens, we have a right to engage in combat in the political arena: To concede that "if we can't join them—and we can't join them—we can beat them."

If we embrace the latter, and as I suggested, I am not certain that evangelical Christians will continue to do so indefinitely into the future, then we need young believers who will run for office, run for political party leadership, speak out and write editorials, teach in colleges and universities, even start colleges and universities, start professional schools, and sponsor think tanks. While this kind of Christian activities scares the pants off of some in and out of the

"Beware the politically obsessed. They are often bright and interesting, but they have something missing in their natures; there is a hole, an empty place, and they use politics to fill it up. It leaves them somehow misshapen."
—Peggy Noonan

Church, it seems to me to be quintessentially American. And fortunately America provides Christian citizens a way to impact the culture positively without stepping outside of our obligation to honor the government.

An Unlikely Political "Arena"?

Serious students of God's Word will recognize that there is an intersection between politics and governing and our responsibility as believers. It is not a connection invented by the so-called Christian Right in the late twentieth century.

The Old Testament describes man's original relationship with God, man's fall from God's favor and fellowship, and the impact of God's wrath upon the apex of His creation, mankind (Gen. 1–3). As a consequence of the Fall, man inherited a nature inclined toward sin (Rom. 5:12–21). Thus, man was in serious need of governing and law. In the Pentateuch, God governed directly and/or articulated His law through His prophets. But increasingly throughout the Old Testament, the prophets assumed a tremendous amount of authority to govern and to interpret the law.

By the time the New Testament was written, the Jewish people had participated in many of history's most important empires: Egypt, Assyria, Babylon, Persia, and Greece. The New Testament provides a glimpse, through the lenses of these Jewish authors, of the powerful Roman Empire. When we read the Gospels, and Luke's book of Acts, we are privileged to watch the decisions of many secular and religious leaders—and there is serious question which tyranny was worse. We also get to see the importance of the law in the Roman Empire (and note that the Romans had a fairly well-developed judicial system of trial courts and even appellate "courts" available to Roman citizens). The on-going disputes between the Pharisees and Sadducees offers an example of party politics and at least a partial justification for separating church and state.

But the New Testament provides more than a glimpse into what life was like for the Jews and Gentiles under an ancient empire. It tells us how God would have us live today. Through the authors of the New Testament we learn that:

1. He commands us to love—indicating that love fulfills all of the Old Testament's laws and rules (John 3:23–24, Rom. 13:8);
2. He requires us to pray for those in authority so that we might lead quiet and peaceful lives (1 Tim. 2:1–2);
3. He provides legitimacy to existing governments—and even legitimizes the authority of government to punish with the sword (Rom. 13:1–7);
4. He says that, generally, it is our duty to obey those in authority (Rom. 13:1–7, Matt. 22:21);
5. He also provides us with examples of those who legitimately disobeyed authority when rules would have them run afoul of God's commandments (Acts 4:16–20—and of course they are buttressed by the Old Testament examples of Shadrach, Meshach, Abednego, and Daniel in Daniel 3 and 6).

The New Testament provides a sweeping presentation of our duty to secular and ecclesiastical leadership and, perhaps even ironically, illustrates why we have a greater duty to obey those secular leaders in authority rather than those in the Church who might wish to compel us to taste not, touch not, drink not, etc., without a sound biblical basis (Col. 2:16–23).

Even though God's Word is principally intended to describe our relationship with Him through our Savior, Jesus, it instructs us substantially as to how He would have us operate in this world (as citizens of Heaven while here on Earth) In fact, to be a serious student of God's Word requires us to be a student of politics at least at a cursory level. If it is true that God ordained three institutions for the benefit of man; the Family, the Church, and Government, then it is important, if not imperative, that in every generation there are some smart and educated Christians who are experts in the field of government and politics. Just as Christians have an increasingly significant voice in philosophy, there should be committed Christian believers in the scholarly study of politics.

Hence, there is one additional way for Christians to be effective citizens without ever once filing to be included on a ballot: *as teachers and scholars in the field of politics.*

Can Any Good Come from Politics?

A major portion of this essay is supposed to be about the academic study of politics for students who are considering which direction they might go when entering college. I would like to do so by placing it within the context of calling and citizenship.

As I have suggested above, I think that everyone in the body of Christ has an obligation to be effective citizens as a part of our reasonable service to Him. Some undoubtedly will act on that responsibility by paying attention to our government and seeking God's wisdom when it comes time to vote. They will raise their children, pay their taxes, and do their best to obey good laws and change bad ones.

Others will engage the political arena a bit more directly. Some will play the role of the Old Testament prophets—

> # We have one country, one Constitution, and one future that binds us.
>
> **—George W. Bush**

serving as public critics of those in power, hoping to hold them accountable to God's standards. Some will seek to be "kings"—a general way of saying that they hope to hold elected office (whether Dog Catcher or President). Increasingly, some Christians will operate as "kingmakers"— they will not run for office, but will do their best to elect people of like mind.

One might argue that there is at least one more way in which Christians might be called into service—as scholars who formally study political science for a living, and who use their expertise to teach politics/government to students. What does it mean to study and teach political science?

What is Politics?

I recall a conversation I had with a fellow graduate student at the University of Notre Dame more than two decades ago. He was a student in contemporary political theory; I was focusing upon constitutional theory and law. As such, we were both less than charitable toward the name of our discipline, *Political Science,* primarily because we did not believe that it best characterized the wide range of study that fell under the discipline's vast umbrella.

I suggested that the field of study might be better labeled as *Government.* He countered with an even better suggestion. He noted that the more accurate label for the broader field of study would be *Politics.* I agree.

If one looks at a variety of political dictionaries, a political encyclopedia, the ever-popular internet sites, or an introductory political science textbook, one is likely to find a whole range of definitions for the discipline of political science.[1] A composite of the many definitions might lead one to conclude that political science is the study of several things:

- The state and how it is governed;
- The various institutions of government;
- The effectiveness of government;
- How power is transferred legitimately in particular governmental structures;
- Democracy (direct or representative; its origins and effectiveness and what factors enhance or restrict participation by "the people;"
- Who governs in the absence of democracy (e.g., tyrants, elites, interest groups)?
- How do people behave politically (What factors stimulate particular kinds of political behavior? Are people rational actors who strive to bring about their desired outcomes?
- From where do the ideas that those involved in politics come?

The distinction I identified above, between the study of politics and the formal discipline of political science, is an important if one hopes to trace out the origins of the discipline. If one is talking about the former, then ours is a very old discipline indeed. If one is asking about the latter, then political science is a relatively new addition to the modern social sciences.

For instance, in the Western tradition, one can certainly trace the study of politics back to the ancient

Greeks—and even well before the famous studies authored by Plato and Aristotle. Plato and Aristotle did much to contribute to our understanding of politics.

Plato, in a variety of dialogues, used his mentor Socrates to articulate many of his most important political ideas, e.g., one's duty to the *polis* (state or government). He presupposes that one's duty to the *polis* transcends one's claim to rights that might be asserted against the *polis*. Further, he provides an evaluative hierarchy for the various types of government in existence during his lifetime. While he offers a critique of the argument that those with the greater military or economic clout should hold power (or at least challenges the notion that might makes right), he also offers an equally devastating critique of democracy. Still, Plato's treatment of politics is largely from a philosophical framework. One might argue that his greatest work of politics, *The Republic*, is not a political treatise at all—it is hardly a blueprint for government. Rather, it is an illustration to help Plato define justice.

Aristotle, Plato's prize student, did provide a much more systematic and direct discussion of politics. In his work by that name, *The Politics*, Aristotle describes his study of the world's constitutions of government. He finds that they all might be placed into three categories: governments of the "one," governments of the "few," and governments of the "many." Further, he notes that within each of these types of government, there are those who are selfish and those who seek the common good. Thus, he argues that governments of the one can be identified either as tyrannies or monarchies depending upon whether the leader in charge was selfish or commons regarding (i.e., one that looked out for the interests of the people). Similarly, governments ruled by the few are either oligarchies or aristocracies. And, of course, the same thing holds true when a state is governed by the many. Aristotle holds when the state is governed by a selfish people, it is a democracy. Alternatively, when it is governed by a commons regarding people, it is a polity.

Hence, it is obvious that the study of politics emerged from philosophy. It is the important study of "political philosophy" or "political theory." Consequently, some of the seminal work in analyzing politics is offered by philosophers.

St. Augustine's work offers a seminal argument addressing the ways in which religion and politics should be separate—and the ways in which they intersect or overlap. Niccolò Machiavelli's *The Prince* discussed eco-

Many Christians became engaged in politics after hearing the teaching of Francis Schaeffer but often made the mistake of thinking that a political party, Democrat or Republican, was *the* party for Christians.

nomic, social, and military policy and their impact upon government. British social contract thinkers Thomas Hobbes and John Locke provided very different critiques of classical republican thought in favor of what has been described as classical liberalism as a remedy for the consequences of a hypothetical "state of nature." Georg W.F. Hegel provided a comprehensive evaluation of politics in his work, *The Philosophy of Right*, and Karl Marx's economic philosophy, perhaps unintentionally, gave birth to a form of communism that would prove devastating to millions around the world. And in eighteenth century America a group of politically active thinkers like John Adams, Alexander Hamilton, James Madison, and Thomas Jefferson borrowed heavily from their theoretical predecessors to put together a political theory articulated in the form of a statement of separation from Great Britain, "The Declaration of Independence." The theory was built upon seven basic principles:

- That there are self-evident truths;
- That all men are created equal;
- That they are endowed by their Creator with unalienable rights;
- That among these are life, liberty, and the pursuit of happiness;
- That it is the duty of government to affirmatively protect these rights;
- That governments derive their legitimacy from the consent of the governed; and, finally,
- When government fails to accomplish these ends, it is the right of the people to alter or abolish it.

Several years later, in defense of the proposed United States Constitution,

Many try to bank on Uncle Sam, but he makes a poor god and will never really be mistaken for Jehovah Jirah.

Hamilton, Madison, and Jay authored a series of papers defending constitutional republican government in America, *The Federalist Papers*.

Thus, it is evident that the study of politics emerged from ancient philosophy and that throughout history the world was blessed with important political thinkers. The study of politics is very old indeed. In the nineteenth and twentieth centuries, however, there was a movement afoot suggesting that politics should be studied like a science—that there might be an objective way to look at constitutions and governments, so that politics was not simply the analysis of particular political personalities or the presentation of comprehensive political theories.

One might argue that the modern discipline of political science was born in the mid-to-late 1800s. During the latter half of the nineteenth century several events occurred to create this new discipline. For example, Francis Lieber was named Professor of Political Science at Columbia College in 1858. In 1876, the Johns Hopkins University created the study of History and Politics. Columbia University, under the direction of John Burgess, formed the School of Political Science in 1880. Between 1880 and early twentieth century, a number of universities founded political science journals. Too, a small number of colleges and universities created separate political science departments, and American universities began to offer the doctorate in the field.

From this genesis in the late nineteenth century, a full-fledged academic discipline emerged. A national organization, the American Political Science Association (APSA), emerged in 1903. The APSA served to promote the organization by hosting an annual national convention, and by providing opportunities for political scientists—professional teachers of politics—to have a conversation about the discipline. It also developed a committee structure to offer some rudimentary governance to the organization and, therefore, indirectly to the discipline.

Shortly thereafter, the APSA sponsored an academic journal, the *American Political Science Review* (APSR). The *APSR* serves as the flagship journal in political science ready to showcase the best scholarship in the field that might emerge through the peer-review process.

For the next several decades, the discipline of political science continued to grow across the colleges and universities in the United States. More institutions offered programs in political scientist. Consequently, they hired a larger number of jobs to political scientists. More universities offered advanced degrees in the field therefore increasing the number of Ph.D.s.

Although the discipline continued to grow, it was not free from disputation. For example, there were some political scientists who maintained that the purpose of the discipline was to prepare political activists or train college students, generally, in public affairs and citizenship (what might be similar to the call to prepare students for "civic engagement" that is so popular today). Others insisted that, primarily, political scientists were scholars who should do cutting edge work within the broader study of politics.

Moreover, even within the camp of those who urged political scientists to prepare scholarship, there were significant methodological disputes and debates about how to subdivide the burgeoning field of study. For instance, the discipline largely emerged as an extended study of "comparative politics" looking largely at the differences between politics in the United States and Europe. Increasingly, political scientists began to focus on "American politics" and the vast array of research questions available for study in the United States. Further, a considerable number of those in the discipline emphasized the study of political theory/philosophy with an aim toward understanding and explaining the great books in the study of politics (e.g., the list of political philosophers identified above).

Many in the field used the case study as their principle methodological tool. Other political scientists rejected the great books and case study methods in favor of what they believed to be the more sophisticated scientific methodological approaches used in other social sciences like psychology (e.g., Behaviorists) and economics (rational choice theorists). Accordingly, they tried to use an extensive literature review to form a testable hypothesis; they tried to draw from an increasingly larger number of methodological strategies to find the appropriate way to test the hypothesis; and, finally, they made an effort to write up the findings so that future political scientists might replicate and build upon the results.

Today, political science has become an increasingly specialized discipline. Since it emerged as an addition to the modern social sciences in the late nineteenth century, political science divided into several of the standard subfields one might find at many colleges and universities. As I mentioned above, American Politics became a large subfield distinguishable from Comparative Politics (although the latter remains as a standard within the discipline). International Politics is an important component of the discipline particularly as political scientists started to study countries outside of the United States and Europe. And, of course, Political Theory remains the cornerstone of the discipline, though sometimes to the chagrin of those who might emphasize the "science" in political science.

The movement toward specialization has pushed beyond the boundaries of the standard subfields of American Politics, Comparative Politics, International Politics, and Political Theory. At many of our outstanding universities graduate students in political science are trained in Political Economics or Political Psychology. They study Public Administration and Public Law. In American Politics they might focus upon Political Ethics or the Politics of Women. And, while quite a number of political theorists still study the classic thinkers, others engage the modern political theorists of the twentieth century like Strauss, Arendt, Habermas, Pocock, Marcuse, Rawls, Nozick, and the like.

Political science is indeed a discipline of contrasts. In many respects its roots are in ancient philosophy. Alternatively, it is a relatively modern social science. And while many institutions of higher education might teach some very basic courses in the discipline, clustering around the larger subfields identified above, many universities will offer a vast array of courses that reflect the increased specialization in the field.

As I suggested above, it is more accurate to think of the discipline as the study of politics. Hence, like so many other fields of study, it is almost impossible for any one political scientist to fully master the discipline—anymore than any one person could master the study of politics itself.

Critical Issues

Political science is not like some academic disciplines where Christians might be automatically wary about participating therein. For example, some believers might be suspicious about the study of biology–particularly if taught exclusively through the lenses of an evolutionary framework (specifically when "evolution" becomes a philosophy/theology and scientists take on the role of advocates for that philosophy). Others might misconstrue the second chapter of Colossians to be a warning by Paul to steer clear of philosophy. Despite the fact that many mothers warned their children that the two things we should not discuss in polite company are religion and politics, there is nothing, per se, that should deter Christians from political science.

One concern might be the fear of indoctrination by professors in many of the outstanding political science departments across the United States. Again, this problem might be more acute in other fields. When I took philosophy as an undergraduate, my professor told the class that the ancient question about whether individuals have souls that are independent from the mind had been fully answered. He stated, without equivocation, that anything that one might consider to be a "soul" is simply the result of physical activity within the brain. Hence, he noted, sci-

ence has demonstrated that there really is no soul. I was not a Christian at the time, but even I was dubious of this very arrogant conclusion. There are also now a number of articles, books, and films that identify the stranglehold that evolutionary theory has over all of the sciences—and the consequences that students and even faculty face when they challenge the dominant paradigm. Evidence of this sort tends to support the concern held by some parents that their children will face indoctrination when they go to college.

Such is also the case in the social sciences (disciplines like political science, anthropology, sociology, and history). Several years ago, survey data of professors from a number of major political science departments revealed that 90-plus percent were registered Democrats and self-identified liberals/progressives. It is not just that the professors hold positions associated with those on the Left, it is also the intensity with which they hold them—and their willingness to proclaim them boldly to their students.

I have been to many a meeting with political scientists, pre-law advisors, or those working in law schools who nearly always fall on the same side of a given political issue. Furthermore, they discuss the issue with a certainty that assumes there is no other competing point of view. Thus, the concern that young Christians might be indoctrinated or otherwise face some sort of retaliation for challenging the professor's point of view is presumptively one that cannot be dismissed out-of-hand.

And, of course, there is another concern that Christian students share with everyone who might consider majoring in political science: Can someone who majors in political science get a job? For years I attended an annual "Major Fair" at my previous institution. During this festival, all of the academic departments would set up booths in the Union Ballroom. Some of the disciplines would set up elaborate displays to make their programs appear more attractive to prospective students. To entice students to come, the university held drawings for prizes during the event. We provided food and beverages. We invited juniors and seniors from the local high schools to come so that they might start to consider their future majors.

I would sit at my more modest booth advertising programs in political science, philosophy, and information about pre-law advising. I had brochures on the university's nationally-ranked mock trial team and moot court team. I was prepared to share much of the information that I presented above about our major.

Invariably, however, the first question I was asked was, "So, what can I do with a degree in political science?" Although it was frustrating to answer the same question over and over, and I suspect that the folks in the next booth had memorized my answer and could recite it as well I as might have, in an age when it seems that the primary purpose of attending a college or university is to prepare for a job, it is probably a fair question. I am guessing that you might be asking the same question, and wonder why I have taken so long to at least raise the subject (one I will address further below).

One final concern is the "scientific" component in political science. As I indicated above, over the last century nearly every serious political science department requires its students to be familiar with how to construct a research design—to move beyond descriptive papers (or those that simply construct an argument) to papers where the writer uses his or her knowledge of the existing literature to develop hypotheses or testable questions. Even some political theory professors will ask students to present their analysis of a thinker through the structure of a research design. Further, graduates from most of these departments will know at least some of the basic methodologies necessary to test these hypotheses and analyze data.

This requirement often comes as a serious shock to even the brightest students, who are used to writing papers where they identify an issue that they wish to discuss (e.g., the death penalty); then they take a position on the issue (e.g., capital punishment is wrong); finally, they go out and find authorities that support their point of view. Such students often think that rigorous research is discussing authors from both sides of the issue (the standard descriptive paper). Preparing a research design is often difficult for even the smartest students to do because it is so much different from what they have typically been asked to do in a history or civics class.

A Christian Response

While there might be a number of reasons for a Christian student to be concerned about a concentration in political science/government/politics, there are more than enough reasons to do so. These would include the very solid biblical reasons identified above as well as some important secular considerations (ah, the "Can I get a job?" answer).

Previously, I noted that although political science is a relatively new academic discipline within the social sciences, the study of politics is very old. I briefly mentioned a few of the famous western political thinkers, beginning with Plato.

Political science also offers one of the best liberal arts educations one might find in a university setting. One will have an opportunity to study everything from Plato and Aristotle to sophisticated quantitative methods. One can concentrate on any of the many general and specialized subfields that I discussed in the first section.

Increasingly there is the dilemma in higher education over the need to provide our students with a general or liberal arts education at the same time most departments are asking for a greater number of hours to provide quality major programs of study. Both sides are right.

There is so much information that we think our students need to know so that they might be generally educated. Most universities expect their students to demonstrate competencies in writing, mathematics, and government/history. They want their students exposed to art, literature, philosophy, science, and social sciences. Some now expect students to take courses in ethics, leadership, diversity, and perform some form of service learning. It is tougher and tougher to do that within the boundaries of the 30 to 40 hours many schools require for general education.

Likewise, many departments are requiring an increasing number of hours to complete their majors. They insist that the knowledge one needs to "major" in a given field has exploded over the previous decades. It is true. Even non-technological fields like history simply have much more ground to cover. I use a book in Constitutional Law that is several thousand pages (actually two volumes of the same soft-cover book; there is no way we read it all in the semester, but I need the entire book to cover all of the cases). I kid students about what a constitutional law book must have looked like prior to 1945 (skinny!).

Thus, one of the problems in contemporary higher education is how to provide an excellent broad-based education and not shortchange the major courses of study. Political science provides a way to accomplish both goals. To enjoy a full and rich major in the discipline actually *enhances* one's general education.

Ah, but what about the $64,000 question? What can I do with a degree in political science? How will a degree in political science help me get a job when I leave school? Here is what I told folks at the aforementioned Major Fests. If you are looking for a major that will prepare you for a specific job, e.g., to program computers, to work in respiratory therapy, to serve as a corrections officer or a nurse, then political science will not prepare you. But it is my experience that most employers want students who can think, speak, and write. If they can find a smart employee, they will teach him or her all the particulars of a specific job. A good political science program will enhance your ability to think, speak, and write.

As a result, I have watched our graduates step into a variety of jobs. Some go on to graduate school and study to become political scientists. Some go to graduate programs in a form of practical politics so that they might have the training necessary to manage political campaigns and work for political parties. Some enter graduate programs in public policy or public administration. I have former students who, for all intents and purposes, run cities and towns. Others enter into other forms of public life working in a wide variety of government jobs at the local, state, or national level. Still others find jobs in the private sector: they work in corporations, they own their own businesses, they are officers in the military, they are in sales, they work as journalists (print, radio, and television), they are ministers, and the like. And, of course, many go on to law school. As Chair of the Pre-Law Advisors' National Council, I have a particular passion for this career field and could likely write another essay on why political science is simply an unbeatable "pre-law" major (an argument I raise often with law school admissions representatives).

Hopefully, in this brief presentation I was able to do justice to an important academic discipline. It will be almost impossible for you to avoid "poly sci" when you go to school. Fortunately, that is because so many universities are recognizing the importance of educated people knowing something about government and politics.

It All Comes Back to Citizenship

It is also important to study politics for another reason. Even though political science is an academic discipline with serious expectations of it scholars, it has never fully gotten away from its purpose to help prepare citizens and, further, those who would be active in the political process (just as historians, economists, and others shoulder some of that obligation).

In case any of you are confused, I was not elected to

the United States Senate. Senator Hatch is now in his sixth term, and I am still teaching politics to college students.

I did have one more entry into the political arena. Based upon my performance during the 2000 Senate campaign, a group of citizens asked me to run as a candidate for Vice Chair of the Utah Republican Party. That meant another full-scale statewide campaign to more than 3,000 delegates. After I prayed about it, I agreed to run. This time, however, I was not entering the race to call attention to an issue or to otherwise make a point. I wanted to win. I ran in a tandem with a former candidate for governor. We put together a coalition of grass roots supporters from across the state. We prepared for a showdown against the heavy favorites for Chair and Vice Chair.

All of this work paid dividends. At the state convention, featuring the keynote speaker, Vice President Dick Cheney, we campaigned and presented our speeches. When the ballots were counted, we lost the bid for Chair, but I was elected Vice Chair (meaning that two different "factions" within the Party each captured one of the top-two prizes). To recount the range of experiences that I enjoyed in this party office would require another essay, but once again, I had the chance to marry the theoretical—the things I would teach in class—with the practical ("okay, that's what the book says, but here's how it really works").

I did have one experience in party leadership that made me appreciate the role of the scholar-teacher in helping to foment civic engagement. I would often be asked to attend large fund raising events as Vice Chair. At one particular event, I was at a large round dinner table with about eight to ten party activists and "fat cats." One started to share how much he always disliked politics until he took a freshman-level American Politics class at his university from a particular professor. It turns out that several of the others also were apathetic about politics or actively disliked the subject until they, too, took a course from the same professor.

It served as a good wake-up call for me as to the importance of those of us who teach these basic, required introductory courses. They might serve as the light bulb moment for so many students who previously had no interest in politics or government. I hope that you might have the chance to take a class from a dedicated, passionate, excellent political scientist. It might serve as a source of inspiration for you—a call to the importance of citizenship.

For those of you who already love the subject, I hope that you might view the study of politics as a calling—as a way to serve the LORD. If so, it can become your contribution to the kingdom of God—and you will be as excited about your work as any other area of ministry.

—Frank Guliuzza III

For Further Reading

Almond, Gabriel A. *A Discipline Divided: Schools and Sects in Political Science.* Newbury Park, Calif.: Sage Publications, 1990.

Collini, Stefan, Donald Winch, and John Burrow. *That Noble Science of Politics: A Study in Nineteenth-Century Intellectual History.* Cambridge, U.K.: Cambridge University Press, 1983.

Crick, Bernard. *The American Science of Politics: Its Origins and Conditions.* Berkeley: University of California Press, 1959.

Crotty, William, ed. *Political Science: Looking to the Future.* 4 vols. Evanston, Ill.: Northwestern University Press, 1991.

Farr, James, and Raymond Seidelman, eds. *Discipline and History: Political Science in the United States.* Ann Arbor: University of Michigan Press, 1993.

Finifter, Ada W. *Political Science: The State of the Discipline.* Washington, D.C.: American Political Science Association, 1983.

Finifter, Ada W. *Political Science: The State of the Discipline II.* Washington, D.C.: American Political Science Association, 1993.

Guliuzza, Frank. *Over the Wall: Protecting Religious Expression in the Public Square.* Albany, NY: SUNY Press. 2000.

Guliuzza, Frank. "Smacking the Nose of the Great Big Dog in His Own Backyard: A Brief Glimpse at the Quixotic Political Campaign of One Christian Political Scientist." Presented at the Third National Conference for Christians in Political Science, San Diego, Calif., June 7–10, 2001.

Pye, Lucian W., ed. *Political Science and Area Studies: Rivals or Partners?* Bloomington: Indiana University Press, 1975.

Seidelman, Raymond, and Edward J. Harpham. *Disenchanted Realists: Political Science and the American Crisis, 1884–1984.* Albany: State University of New York Press, 1985.

Somit, Albert, and Joseph Tanenhaus. *The Development of American Political Science: From Burgess to Behavioralism.* Enlarged ed. New York: Irvington Publishers, 1982.

Endnotes

1 To put together the background information on political science, I borrowed from some of the works cited in the brief bibliography at the end of the essay and other materials produced by the American Political Science Association. I also looked at some of the sources that a student might use should he or she wish to find out about the discipline.

The Republic

The sound of the gavel rang sharply throughout the courtroom. The decision had been made. The reverberating shockwave of angry wood on wood immediately gave way to silence. But far from a peaceful, sleeping silence, this was a brutal and waking silence. The convicted man was stoic in appearance. He appeared unfazed by the shocking result: guilty on all charges. Unlike so many before him, the terrible judgment did not buckle his knees. No cry of anguish escaped from the bowels of his soul.

I, on the other hand, was not so brave. The silence choked me. My knees grew weak. The world suddenly seemed irrational and wild. My master, the great conscience of our once noble city, had been unjustly condemned to die. Instead of dying with a laurel crown to grace his noble head, he would die a criminal's death, surrounded on all sides by the ridicule of petty men. A dark doubt entered into my mind for the first time in my life: does the justice that rules the stars above also rule the affairs of men?

It is likely that Socrates' trial and death at the hands of his fellow Athenian citizens caused Plato to ponder the following questions:

1. Is there a divine Justice beyond the human injustice with which men are all too familiar?
2. Assuming such perfect Justice exists, is it possible for a city ruled by such Justice to be realized in this imperfect world?

But are these questions simply too abstract to pursue? Would it even do us any good to pursue questions like this? Inspired by the poet Aristophanes and his famous portrayal of Socrates in the *The Clouds*, many have concluded that philosophers are simply too heavenly minded to be of any earthly good. In some instances, these detractors are correct. However, this kind of approach can also serve as an illegitimate excuse not to engage the most difficult (and pressing) ideas. It is very easy to paint a silly portrait of a complex man, thereby making it unnecessary to confront his ideas. This illegitimate shortcut in reasoning is called an *ad hominem* fallacy. As we approach Plato's *Republic*, we need to resist such reasoning.

Plato's desire to understand the true nature of justice likely came not from an unhealthy fascination with otherworldly trifles, but from a very concrete, heartrending, real experience in *this* world. That experience was a painful face-to-face encounter with human injustice; that experience was the trial and death of his beloved master at the hands of self-proclaimed Athenian "patriots."

The reader who takes this journey with Plato must keep in mind that the elements drawn from Plato's own city-state are not intended to distract us from our own particular communities but to *reflect upon them in a new way*. Eight hundred years later a great Christian thinker would ask us to do the same thing. This thinker would ask us to think about the insufficiency of our own earthly cities by comparing them to the "heavenly city" (the New Jerusalem, the "City of God"). With the aid of God's divine revelation in Holy Scripture, St. Augustine's *City of God* compares the "city of man" to the divine city founded by Christ, the "city of God." Plato had to rely upon reason alone to arrive at his celestial city; St. Augustine's reason was enlightened by Scripture.

GENERAL INFORMATION

Author and Context

Plato was born in 427 B.C. to an established and wealthy aristocratic Athenian family. He was born during a time that scholars refer to as the golden age of Athens. Although Plato was born during that era, his adolescent years and young adulthood were marked by its tragic decline. Plato's awareness that the greatness of Athens was a very mortal and flawed greatness provided a powerful reason for writing a book like *The Republic*. Plato's *Republic* is a book seeking True Justice, a Justice beyond the imperfect human justice Plato found in his own Athens.

Two events would have been prominent in the minds and hearts of Plato's fellow Athenians:

1. The defeat of the Persians and the subsequent rise of the "golden age" of Athens
2. The more recent war with Sparta (the Peloponnesian War), its disastrous outcome, and the political chaos that ensued

One was a cause of great pride; the other, great shame. Stories and songs about the heroic deeds performed by the Athenians in their stunning victory over the Persians would have been a source of great pride for the city. On the other hand, the Athenians would also have been painfully and shamefully aware of the disastrous outcome of the more recent war with Sparta. Prior to the war with Sparta, the Athenians were the most powerful Greek city-state. After the war they were destitute, having lost all of the wealth they had so painstakingly amassed in the years after their victory over the Persians. Athens was, to put it bluntly, a real life Greek tragedy—a great city experiencing a swift and heroic rise to fame followed by an equally swift and tragic fall.

In 415 B.C., when Plato was twelve years old, the Athenians began a fateful military campaign—the "Sicilian expedition" (see Thucydides, *Peloponnesian War* VI–VII). Just two years later (413 B.C.), when Plato was fourteen, Athens received quite unbelievable news. The Sicilian expedition had been an awful failure: the great Athenian navy had been utterly decimated and the

A statue of Plato stands before the modern Academy of Athens. The site of Plato's original Academy had been a sacred grove and then a gymnasium for athletics. Its name was derived from a local Attic hero named Hekademos.

The Republic 173

army undertaking the Sicilian expedition had been completely routed. By 404 B.C. (the twenty–third year of Plato's life) Sparta had thoroughly routed the Athenians and occupied the city. The Peloponnesian war had mortally wounded Athenian pride. Thus, some of the most formative years of Plato's life were marked by key events in the tragic decline of Athens.

In order to understand Plato's Athens, we need to understand how the Greeks viewed themselves. Surprisingly, the Greeks didn't really view themselves as, well, "Greeks." The Greeks viewed themselves as Spartans, Corinthians, Athenians, etc. The imperial despotism of the great Empires to the east—like the Persians—was considered to be inferior to the sophisticated and superior life of the *polis*. "Polis" is the Greek word for "city" or "city-state." This was the central cultural and political feature of Plato's world. Although the Greeks were very proud of their city-states, each Greek was especially proud of *his own city-state*. In Thucydides, for instance, we see the great diversity of character and culture of some of the Greek city-states. Athens is depicted as a bold, proud, even brash city full of rhetorically gifted speech-makers and brilliant engineers; Sparta is a slow-moving, cautious and laboriously tactical city-state not as given to rhetorical flourish.

The centrality of the city-state gave the Greeks a unique form of patriotism.[1] In the Greek world of Plato's time, to be patriotic meant not to love Greece (*hellas*), but to love one's own city-state. We might try to understand this by comparing Athenians and Spartans to New Yorkers or Bostonians. We can easily imagine a New Yorker taking great pride in being from New York City or a Bostonian taking great pride in being from the city of Boston. Anyone who has been to a Yankees/Red Sox game knows this first hand. There is, however, a very important difference. One who is from the city of New York or Boston is also from the State of New York or Massachusetts. And, moreover, these city-dwellers are also citizens of the United States of America. Athenians and Spartans, on the other hand, were citizens not of Greece but of Athens and Sparta. Thus, whereas New Yorkers and Bostonians both pledge allegiance to the same flag, Athenians and Spartans had no such national allegiance to bind them together. At best, the Greeks had shaky alliances; at worst these alliances were simply convenient ways for the stronger city-states to manipulate the weaker ones.

As a well-born Athenian, Plato was undoubtedly very aware of the fierce patriotism that his fellow Athenians felt towards their own city-state. But Plato was also painfully aware that such loyalties made criticizing one's own city a very dangerous activity. In the political chaos and embarrassing disorder that had ensued after the Athenians lost the Peloponnesian War, the patriots within the city desperately needed a scapegoat. Socrates was to become the needed scapegoat. In 399 B.C., when Plato was twenty-eight years old, his great master was put to death. The death of Socrates is the tremor that reverberates throughout Plato's dialogues. It is the biographical detail that gave Plato a longing, an almost desperate longing, for a Truth that could rise above the fickle and shifting opinions of men and a Justice not subject to the injustice of men.

Significance

Plato's *Republic* is important for many reasons. Alfred North Whitehead (a twentieth- century philosopher) famously said that all philosophy is "a series of footnotes to Plato." Whitehead was suggesting that Plato's thought provided the groundwork for all subsequent philosophical discussion. Or, to put it more simply, Plato's thought is important because he is good at identifying the basic problems that philosophy must deal with. Does this mean that in his works Plato says everything that can possibly be said? Certainly not. Does this mean that Plato is correct about everything he says? As Christians, we can also be certain that this is not the case. Therefore, we might say that his value lies not so much in his answers but in the quality and perceptiveness of his questions.

For Christians, Plato is also important because his thought was transformed by subsequent followers into a comprehensive worldview. This worldview grew into a "thinking man's religion" that would become a genuine rival to Christianity in the late ancient and early medieval world. Many Christian thinkers were either influenced by Platonic doctrines (for better or worse), or made it their life's work to establish the philosophical superiority of Christianity over them. In his *Confessions*, St. Augustine tells us that he owed much to the Platonists. They helped him to overcome certain errors in Manichean theology. One of the errors St. Augustine couldn't overcome was his "too corporeal thinking." In other words, St. Augustine couldn't imagine anything unless it was corporeal (i.e., a body). He tells us that he viewed God as nothing but a giant body—the "biggest body" of all. This problem is not unlike the central problem of Greek religion (and, incidentally, all man-made religion). The Greeks had a tendency to view their gods as nothing more than exaggerated men and women—men and women who are distinguishable as gods not because they are *better* than mortals, but simply because they have more *power* than ordinary mortals. In other words, the Greeks tended to view their gods as men writ large. In the *Republic*, Plato will make this very complaint: the great poets of the Greeks gave their people gods that are not suitable models for virtue. What is needed, according to Plato, is a new kind of poetry/religion.

Plato will argue in the *Republic* that the Greeks need gods who can be models of virtue, not models of vice. In this, we can see a rough outline of St. Augustine's critique of pagan Roman religion in *The City of God*.

Although St. Augustine tells us in *Confessions* that the Platonists helped him overcome his "too corporeal thinking," he also tells us that there were certain things that he could not have learned without revelation (the Bible), and without the teachings of great Christian men like St. Ambrose. St. Augustine makes it very clear that there are many things that the Platonists *could not tell him*. Ultimately, then, St. Augustine needed to bid farewell to the Platonists when he found greater men—men whose minds had been transformed by God's Word. For thinkers like St. Augustine, the fact that Christ is the *Logos* means that he is the definitive Word who is the ground and support of all reality and all truth. For Christians, then, Plato is a transitional figure: his critique of Greek religion is at one and the same time the beginning of the end of the classical age and the rise of the new Christian era.

Main Characters

In a Platonic dialogue, the characters are quite often essential to the argument. For this reason, it is important to pay special attention to who they are. In this dialogue, we need to familiarize ourselves with the following characters: Socrates, Cephalus, Polemarchus, Thrasymachus, Glaucon and Adeimantus. Socrates is, of course, the main character in the dialogue. He will keep the conversation moving along by asking his dialogue partners questions and, somewhat uncharacteristically, making long speeches. In the worldview section, we'll take a closer look at Socrates.

In one way, Cephalus is what we might call the "benefactor" or "patron" of the conversation. The dialogue takes place in the home of Cephalus (and his son Polemarchus). From hints in the dialogue, we can presume that Cephalus is a very wealthy man. It is important, however, to point out that Cephalus is not an Athenian citizen. Cephalus is a "metic." This means that he is a foreigner who is allowed to live in Athens—and who must, therefore, pay Athenian taxes—but who doesn't enjoy all of the privileges of Athenian citizenship. Why might this be important? We should keep in mind that Socrates was murdered by his fellow Athenian citizens. Ancestral loyalty can be a nasty thing, and it's possible that an outsider (like Cephalus) would be less suspicious of a man like Socrates than a fiercely loyal Athenian citizen. Cephalus's home provides a safe environment for a discussion that will touch upon (and criticize) all of the things that are most dear to the Athenians: politics, literature and religion.

Polemarchus is the son of Cephalus, but whereas Cephalus is a wealthy businessman—and is therefore too concerned about practical affairs to be engaged in a long philosophical conversation—Polemarchus is slightly more philosophically inclined than his father. He is one step removed from the tyranny of the practical. And yet, Polemarchus does not seem to be sufficiently philosophical to move the dialogue along very far. He will make a showing at the beginning but fade into the background as the dialogue proceeds.

Thrasymachus is the character that really gets the dialogue moving. Like Cephalus and his son Polemarchus, Thrasymachus is a non-Athenian. Unlike them, however, his trade is in words. Thrasymachus is a wandering wordsmith-for-hire who teaches the art of rhetoric for a fee. These men, often referred to as "sophists," were hired by wealthy Greek citizens. These masters of the art of rhetoric were hired to teach aspiring young Greeks the art of public speaking. This art would have been necessary to master if a well-born Athenian wanted to become a respected member of the assembly. Rhetoric was considered to be absolutely essential to the art of politics. Although not a philosopher, Thrasymachus introduces the greatest challenge to philosophy. The rest of the dialogue will be devoted to a refutation of the challenge presented by Thrasymachus.

The final two characters that we encounter in the dialogue are brothers: Glaucon and Adeimantus (they are also brothers of Plato). These men are very important, and they occupy the great majority of the dialogue. They are the only characters in the dialogue capable of becoming Athenian statesmen. This makes them very interesting to Socrates. As brothers of Plato, we know that they would not only have been nobly born, but also would have been expected to pursue political careers. If Socrates' philosophic movement is to get off the ground, these are precisely the kind of men that need to be persuaded to become "friends" of philosophy.

Summary and Setting

The *Republic* is a book about the nature of Justice. That, however, is not the only theme of the book. Plato's *Republic* is essentially a book about the relationship between the human soul and the city-state (or, more generally, the real communities within which human souls find themselves). Like Aristotle after him, Plato believes that man is inherently a social and political animal. This means that human beings are, by nature, meant to live together in communities. But the moment we see the political sphere emerge we immediately encounter a terrible problem: human beings have different abilities, interests, and ideas about the "good life," and this makes getting along quite difficult. Getting human beings to coexist in a manner that promotes the "common good"—that contributes to the happiness and fulfillment of each member of society as far as possible—is the central problem of politics.

The occasion to reflect upon justice provides the opportunity to reflect upon the ideal city. Throughout the dialogue, the interlocutors, with the help of Socrates, will create a "city in speech." They create such a city because Plato believes that one cannot simply think about justice *in the abstract*. We cannot, in other words, think about justice without thinking about it in the context of a human community—a community in which people with different ends and interests are bound together. Justice is an inherently *political* concept. However, the city in speech that the dialogue partners will create is not any real, existing, concrete city but a city that will be constructed from the ideas about justice developed during the dialogue. In a way, this makes the setting of the dialogue *anywhere*, and the time of the dialogue *anytime*.

Although the *ideal* city is not some particular, existing city, it is important to point out that many of the elements of the city are drawn from things that were part of Plato's Greek world, the concrete world that the participants in the dialogue inhabit. In this way, the ideal city that is created is, nevertheless, quite Greek. For this reason, Plato's *Republic* gives us great insight into the Greek mind of one of her most famous individuals living in one of the world's most famous and historically significant cities.

Worldview

Plato's student Aristotle referred to politics as "the master science." What did he mean by that? In order for us to understand what Aristotle *did* mean, it may help us to reflect upon what he *didn't* mean. For the Greeks the word 'politics' didn't carry the narrower meaning it does for us. When we think of politics we immediately think about elections, government, corruption, backstabbing, selfishness, and dishonesty. For the Greeks, on the other hand, the word *politics* was tied to the word "polis" (city-state). The word *polis* carried with it many important meanings, and many that help stretch the word politics far beyond the narrow connotations it has for us. Rather than simply referring to political activity (as we conceive it), politics for the Greeks was a word that primarily referred to the art and science of being civilized. In this way, politics was viewed as an essential component of the ultimate goal of human existence. The Greeks viewed that ultimate goal, the *summum bonum* or "greatest good," in the following way: to rise up out of the animal-like existence

of the barbarian and become civilized, cultured, and educated human beings capable of reaching their ultimate potential. An Athenian like Socrates would have viewed the city-state as the place in which this might happen. After the death of Socrates, student Plato was profoundly aware that even in a "civilized" city-state like Athens men can quickly descend back into barbarism. Beneath the veneer of civilization lies a potentially uncivilized, even irrational, monster.

The Greeks were proud of their city-states. And the Athenians living during the "golden age" of Athens were especially proud of the way that their city-state enabled human beings to be civilized. Therefore, when Aristotle suggests that politics is the "master science" he means that it is the discipline that deals with the ultimate human problem: human beings living together in a community in a way that enables them to achieve *arete*, that is, human excellence.[2] Thus, politics for the Greeks was *both* the activity of writing constitutions, making speeches, and constructing public policy, *and* the science of reflecting upon how it is that human beings might achieve their ultimate potential in the context of communities (like a city-state). Political philosophy is the latter of these two activities.[3]

Just as for us, the Greeks knew that there were many ways of being human. Any city-state would certainly be full of people with different interests, abilities and ideas of happiness. In this dialogue the characters themselves form a city-state in speech. Anyone who has ever formed a little miniature world—e.g., playing cowboys and Indians or war—consisting of good guys and bad guys, with laws and rules that govern that existence, has engaged in a little political philosophy.

In many ways, Plato is the father of a new genre of literature. He uses all of the tools made possible by allegory and imagination to critique some existing political arrangement. In all likelihood, Plato did not want us to take his "city in speech" literally (there are many hints throughout the dialogue that this is the case), but instead used it as an elaborate mechanism to critique his own beloved Athens. This new form of literature—allegorical political philosophy—would inspire many great thinkers after him. Men like Cicero, St. Augustine, Dante and Spencer would (with some stylistic amendments) use a similar device to engage in political philosophy.

In order to understand this dialogue, it is important for us to have a working understanding of the method of Plato's beloved master, Socrates. Socrates practiced a method of questioning that is called *elenchus*. The point of this method is not to argue for the sake of winning, but to engage in a dialogue for the sake of coming to the truth. Most of the professional debaters and rhetoricians of Socrates' time argued for the sake of point-scoring, fame, and pay. The better they were at winning arguments, the better their pay! The Greek word for this kind of argumentation—argumentation for the sake of point-scoring—is *eristic*. Anyone who has ever had a conversation with someone who just wanted to win and wasn't interested in learning knows what *eristic* is. It can be a terribly frustrating experience. In fact, it really isn't possible to have a *conversation*. Thrasymachus, whom you will meet in Book I, is the sort of person with whom it is not possible to have a conversation. He is a practitioner of the art of *eristic*. In fact, Book I of *The Republic* is a miniature "war" between the method of Socrates (*elenchus*) and the method of Thrasymachus (*eristic*). The point of Book I is to silence Thrasymachus. Without this silencing of Thrasymachus, the dialogue cannot possibly take place.

In another dialogue, Plato gives us a very interesting simile to help us understand the method of Socrates. According to Plato, Socrates viewed himself as a midwife who does what he does as a service to the gods. The famous midwife analogy (which we can find in Plato's dialogue *Theaetetus*) suggests the following. Socrates, by his method, helps his dialogue partners *give birth* to noble ideas. In other words, Socrates is a midwife of ideas. The simile is an interesting one. It entails the following things:

1. Giving birth to ideas is a *laborious* process (pun intended!)
2. It is helpful to have a "midwife" facilitate the birth of ideas
3. The potential to "give birth" to ideas is inside Socrates' dialogue partners, but his method helps them to actualize that potential

We should pause for a moment on the analogy and see how Socrates' method would differ from that of Thrasymachus. A typical Socratic dialogue involves a process of questioning in which the dialogue partners of Socrates try out a variety of ideas. Socrates' method helps them to "give birth" to ideas that will, subsequently, be tested. Continuing the midwife analogy, Socrates tells us that many ideas are "still-born." In other words, they are not "living" ideas, but "dead" ones. This means that they are not viable and that we should not view them as such. It is Socrates' method which helps men to give birth to ideas and then to test their merits.

Thrasymachus, on the other hand, immediately engages in a war between ideas. In a war, the two sides are trying to kill one another. Socrates, however, prefers verbal dialogue over verbal warfare. Thrasymachus wants to win and views an argument as a public spectacle, a contest, and even an opportunity to make money. Built into the word *eristic* is the Greek word for "strife," *eris*.[4]

As a Sophist, Thrasymachus views the process of coming to the truth as a sport and, therefore, a public spectacle in which the stronger man—the more rhetorically gifted man—wins. Socrates and Plato were concerned that this kind of attitude towards "truth" would destroy the most genuine motivation for truth, the desire to know. The desire to win and the desire to know are not often compatible.

Plato shares much with the biblical position at this point. The importance of humility in the process of searching for the truth is mirrored quite clearly in the book of Proverbs. The following passages are strikingly similar:

> "He who does not fly from correction will be sure to take more heed of his afterlife"
> (Plato, *Laches* 188b).

> "Do not rebuke a mocker or he will hate you; rebuke a wise man and he will love you" (Prov. 9:8).

> "When pride comes, then comes disgrace, but with
> humility comes wisdom"
> (Prov. 11:2).

Thrasymachus is clearly a "mocker" who must be silenced. It is never clear that Thrasymachus is thankful for being rebuked. Rather, he is simply silenced. But he must be silenced because he does not have sufficient intellectual humility to engage in a dialogue. Those who practice *eristic* do not search for the truth. Rather, they are simply attempting to display their own power.

A reading of the entire Platonic canon reveals that Socrates is not only a "midwife" but is also presented as a "savior." He is a savior, sent by the gods, to help to release human beings from the chains of ignorance. We can see this most clearly in both *The Apology* and *The Republic*. The controlling image in the dialogue that you are about to read is that Socrates is like Orpheus—a man who descends into Hades to free prisoners from chains.[5] The chains that Socrates is to free men from are the chains of false opinion. The *Republic* opens with a "descent": "I went down…" (327a). This descent of Socrates prefigures

The Republic 177

the famous descent of the philosopher into the "cave" to free prisoners from the chains of ignorance and false opinion (Book VII). This famous allegory implies something quite obvious: the Athens of Plato's day (the cave) is dominated by false opinion. The philosopher (Socrates) descends into the city to free the prisoners from the chains placed upon them by men like Thrasymachus—men who are masters of false opinion. From this imagery, we can conclude that Socrates is not only a midwife, he is also a savior of men who, like Orpheus, descends into "Hades" to free prisoners from chains. It is at this point

Texas artist Mary McCleary has been described as "the Seurat of collage." Her artwork is made by carefully combining beads, string, kewpie doll eyes, costume jewels, foil, glitter, and many other ordinary and neglected materials to create shimmering images of wonder. In the past her mixed media collages were based directly on Bible stories. In recent years her work has become more allegorical, drawing from sources of literature, history and popular culture. In *Plato's Cave* McCleary shows the moment when the prisoner has broken free of the shadowlands and has come out into the sun.

Although a fairly obscure figure in Greek thought, Orpheus figured prominently in the Orphic mystery religion, and many scholars believe that this religion had a great influence upon Plato. It gave Greeks a totally different conception of the afterlife than Homeric thought had, presenting a doctrine of the immortality of the soul. According to the story of Orpheus, he was torn to death by Thracian Maenads, his lyre was placed among the stars, and the Muses gathered up the fragments of his body. Sculptor Edward Berge (1867–1924) regarded *Muse Finding the Head of Orpheus* as one of his most important works.

that Christians might begin to become a little uncomfortable. Is Socrates being presented as a Christ-figure? The comparison to Orpheus is very important if we are to answer this question.

If Orpheus is not a character in the dialogue, why are we concerning ourselves with him? And who is he anyhow? In a way, Orpheus *is* a character in the dialogue. He is, however, only insofar as Plato borrows an image from the Thracian religion of the Orphics (followers of Orpheus) to create a great allegory for Socrates' work. The Thracian followers of Orpheus viewed him as something like a divine pied-piper. As a great musician and patron of the musical arts, Orpheus had the ability to draw the human soul above the mortal, bodily sphere of human existence.[6] For the Greeks, this meant that he was like Apollo. And just as Apollo came to represent reason and all that is orderly, Orpheus was the benefactor of a certain kind of music and a certain kind of poetry—music and poetry that reflects order and harmony.[7] The religious experience promoted by the music and poetry of Orpheus and Apollo could be contrasted to the wild and irrational experiences that were associated with the followers of the god Dionysus. Plato's Socrates is a messenger of the rational religion of Orpheus and Apollo, not the irrational and wild religion often associated with Dionysus. By comparing Socrates to Orpheus, the following connection emerges: like Orpheus, Plato's Socrates is a sort of savior, a pied-piper leading men not by the art of the lyre but by the philosophic art. Through his art (*elenchus*), Socrates is drawing men above the irrational chaos of the opinions of men.

Another important use of Orpheus, for Plato, is to be found in the connection between Orpheus,

Apollo, and the sun. In Plato's famous allegory of the cave, the sun is pictured as a source of light by which we can see everything *truly*. It is compared to the man-made light of the cave by which men only see "shadows." The connection between Orpheus, Apollo, and the sun provides an important context for what Socrates is doing. Through this elaborate image, Plato is telling us what Socrates' art attempts to do. Socrates is drawing men *from* the imperfect light of the cave of human opinions *to* the true light by which men might see things truly. Just as Orpheus descended into Hades to free prisoners, so too Socrates is going to descend into the bowels of his own city to free prisoners from the chains of the false opinions of men.

As Christians, there are certainly themes in this book that overlap with concerns that we find in Scripture. Here are some obvious instances in which Plato's *Republic* and scriptural concerns overlap:

1. The need to establish the difference between imperfect human justice and divine Justice
2. The need to establish the difference between imperfect human truth and divine Truth
3. The need for someone not enslaved to imperfect justice and imperfect truth to save human beings from their enslavement to these things
4. The longing for a perfect city

It is in reading this dialogue, however, that the difference emerges between the Christian and the Platonic solutions to these problems. For this reason, the *Republic* is a very important piece of literature. It helps us to see human beings doing their best to solve human problems *without the aid of divine revelation*. Plato's Socrates is, therefore, like Dante's Virgil. But there is one very important difference. Plato wasn't aware that something better had come. Dante's Virgil knows that Christian truth is superior to the best that the classical world had to offer, just as Dante knows that Christ is infinitely superior to Virgil himself. Sadly, Virgil has to spend all eternity in Limbo lamenting that for all his wisdom and virtue he will "see through a glass darkly," never experiencing the refulgent light of the beatific vision.

We should also ask if Plato's Socrates is a rival of Christ. Isn't Christ the divine Word who descends into the "cave" of human opinion to reveal God's divine Truth? One important distinction obviously emerges. Whereas Socrates claims to *point men to the truth*, Jesus *is the truth*: "I am the way, the truth, and the life" (John 14:6). In the comparison between Socrates and Jesus we are immediately drawn to the Apostle Paul's distinction between the "wisdom of the world" and the "wisdom of God." Christians would obviously be very uncomfortable with the Platonic claim that Socrates is a quasi-divine savior who by his method does

exactly what Christ himself would ultimately do—make it possible for men to know the truth. The radical insufficiency of philosophy in the face of divine revelation is made explicitly clear in Paul's first letter to the church in Corinth: "Where is the wise? Where is the scribe? Where is the disputer [philosopher] of this age? Has not God made foolish the wisdom of this world?" (1 Cor. 1:20)

If this is the case, why should we read Plato? Can we learn anything of great significance from Plato? Moreover, if Christ is indeed the Logos (the Word of God), why should we read *any* pagan literature? Should we follow Tertullian's advice and despise that which comes from "Athens" on the supposition that it has nothing to do with "Jerusalem?"[8] The question is a good one. What value *does* lie in pagan literature if Christian revelation (and the teaching which derives from it) makes "foolish the wisdom of the world?"

One possible way of answering this question would be as follows. It is often the case that in comparing the false to the true the great virtue of the truth emerges. The Bible uses this method all of the time. Quite often the "false view" is given a hearing only to be shattered by the truth. Two instances come to mind: Job and the Psalms. In Job, a variety of opinions about Job's condition are heard—and explored quite exhaustively—before the truth is revealed. In the Psalms, it is quite often the case that the Psalmist introduces a problematic view that is subsequently replaced by a triumphant perspective. Psalm 22 (a very famous Messianic Psalm) presents such a structure. The Psalm begins with the following words:

My God, My God, why have You forsaken Me?
Why are You so far from helping Me,
And from the words of My groaning?
O My God, I cry in the daytime,
But You do not hear (Ps. 22:1–2a)

God appears to be aloof, unconcerned, and distant. And yet, the Psalmist concludes (as does Christ[9]) that God has not left him, and that God does hear.

For He has not despised nor abhorred the
affliction of the afflicted;
Nor has He hidden His face from Him;
But when He cried to Him, He heard. (Ps. 22:24)

Our curriculum as a whole intends to follow such a structure. The problems of men are presented in the books that we read. In those books we see our humanity *nakedly* displayed—warts and all. We see our flaws and faults. We see our insufficient solutions and incomplete answers to the problems encountered in these books. So many books in our curriculum present problems that are greater than their solutions. Plato's *Republic*, like so many of these books, does the same.

What is the human problem with which Plato's *Republic* is concerned? The problem that Plato presents to us in *Republic* can be simply stated as follows: every existing human community is flawed and imperfect. However, if we are to judge these communities as *flawed* and *imperfect* we must, in principle, be able to compare them to a perfect model. Once one has experienced injustice *as injustice*, a desire to know True Justice often emerges. We can imagine Jews suffering in the concentration camps at Auschwitz and slaves suffering at the hands of cruel masters longing for human injustice to be replaced by divine Justice. And yet, longing for justice does not necessarily entail an adequate understanding of it. A small child has many longings that he can't articulate and doesn't understand. The pagan person is likely in quite the same situation.

If it is indeed true that no human regime is perfectly just, a terribly difficult problem immediately arises: How can we possibly know what justice is? Plato's answer is interesting. He argues that we must rise above every imperfect regime and gaze at "Justice-itself" if we are to distinguish between justice and injustice in the imperfect cities in which we dwell. But what is "Justice-itself"? Plato's answer is, in a way, quite simple. Just as we can arrive at an unarguable and certain definition of a triangle, it is likewise possible that we can (in principle) arrive at a definition of perfect Justice. Like the Pythagoreans (yes, the very same Pythagoreans of the "Pythagorean theorem"), Plato thought that our capacity to do mathematics provides us with a model for how we might imagine something like perfect justice. Those who have gotten far enough in mathematics know that for every triangle the sum of its interior angles is 180 degrees. Does one have to inspect every triangle (the possibilities are endless, mind you) to know that this is true? No. We can know that this is true because we can identify the necessary properties which are true for every triangle we will ever encounter. In the same way, Plato is telling us that we must first imagine and define perfect justice if we are to attempt to create a city-state patterned after it or if we are to critique our own political structures.

We can be very thankful for Plato at this point. Plato is pointing out something that we should not take for granted. Plato is suggesting that every regime founded by man (including the beautiful and "golden" Athenian regime under which he lived) is flawed. This insight does, in a way, prepare the Greek world for the Christian solution. A deeper understanding of Plato's conclusion reveals that Socrates *was* indeed guilty of impiety. The logical conclusion of the position presented by Socrates and Plato (if we read between the lines) is that Athens is not only flawed, but tragically *human*. Ancient people (the Greeks included) tended to view their cities as not only founded by the gods, but also as legitimate objects of worship. Patriotism and religion were much more closely tied together for the Greeks (and ancient people in general) than they are for us. Plato's criticism of the poets in *Republic*—and the view of the gods that the poets offer—could be nothing less than blasphemy for a Greek of his time. This is why it is prudent for a conversation that will criticize Athenian religion and politics to take place in the house of Cephalus, a non-Athenian.

The astute reader will have recognized a flaw in the triangle analogy that was offered above. A tenacious thinker—someone Socrates would want to hang around with—wouldn't let the analogy go without sufficient criticism. So let's criticize the idea. We might suggest, in Socratic fashion, that thinking about the qualities of triangles is different than trying to understand the nature of perfect justice. Why is that? In order to understand justice, we must first understand the human soul. As created in the image of God, the human soul is infinitely more complex than triangles (this is why the soul can understand a triangle, but a triangle can't understand the soul). Moreover, in order to understand justice we not only need to understand the soul, but also the relationships between the human beings who possess these souls (boy, things get really complicated at this point!). As we've already mentioned, human beings have different abilities and interests and these different abilities and interests lead people to arrive at different conceptions of what it means to be happy. This is why it's fairly easy to get people to agree on the nature of triangles, but it's notoriously difficult to get people to agree on definitions of happiness and "the good life." The pre-Socratic philosopher Heraclitus gives us a clue as to why this is so. He claims that the soul has a "logos" that is too deep to measure: "You could not find out the boundaries of soul, even by traveling along every path: so deep a measure [logos] does it have."[10] It is precisely the complexity of the human person—and the corresponding complexity of persons as they exist together in society—that makes it so difficult to arrive at a conception of perfect justice.

However, what is difficult is not necessarily impossible. If it were impossible, Socrates would not even begin to engage in this quest for a definition of perfect justice. This alone tells us that Socrates is not a skeptic. And yet, Socrates' quest to arrive at the perfect city fails. This interpreter is quite confident that Plato knows this, and that he certainly doesn't expect us to take seriously the "city in speech" created by the interlocutors. The secret teaching of the *Republic* seems to be this: achieving justice in the individual soul (which like a state is complex, not simple)

Christ has led prisoners out of the cave of sin and is Himself the bright light by which truth can be seen. *The Last Supper (La Ultima Cena)* was painted by "the Spanish Raphael," Juan de Juanes (c. 1510–1579).

is more possible than achieving justice on the larger level of the state. The picture of the ideal society in *Republic* is terribly flawed. But Plato would take some more cracks at it. Plato's *Timaeus* was likely far more influential on the medieval mind than *Republic* (possibly because *The Republic* was lost for most of the medieval period). Unlike *The Republic*, the *Timaeus* uses the universe as a model for justice and the soul. Obviously, this suggests that the city is an imperfect model.[11]

It is precisely at this point that Christianity becomes so relevant. In order to have a conception of perfect justice it is necessary to see things from a divine perspective. St. Augustine's *City of God* acknowledges this flaw in Plato and introduces a solution to the problem—divine revelation. An individual, like Socrates, suffers from the very same problem that every concrete human city suffers. Human beings, like earthly cities, are imperfect.

Therefore, they cannot conceive of perfect justice *on their own*. Instead, it must be revealed to them. We should at this point compare the Platonic (philosophic) solution to the Christian solution. The philosophic solution is to begin from our humanity and rise up to a trans-human perspective. This is why Aristotle says in *Metaphysics* that "it is the philosophers task to be able to view things in a total way" (1004a, 35). The philosopher is trying to see things "from above," from a divine perspective. But the Greek philosophers were too optimistic about the powers of human reason to rise above its limitations (especially the limitation of sin). Not only did they tend to overestimate the powers of human reason, but they tragically underestimated the power of human sin. According to Romans 1, men are not sinful because they are ignorant, but they are ignorant (fools) because they are sinful. Throughout the Platonic dialogues we see Socrates claiming that people commit injustice because they are ignorant. In other words, ignorance produces injustice. The solution, then, is to cure people of their ignorance. Socrates is a philosophic savior sent to cure men of their ignorance.

The New Testament presents a quite different analysis of the problem. Rather than obscuring the truth by their ignorance, Paul says that men become fools by "suppressing the truth in wickedness." It is this problem of "truth-suppression" which makes it necessary for God to descend into our world and reveal the truth to us. The problem, then, is twofold: we are indeed ignorant, but we are ignorant because we are sinful. Any solution which attempts to deal with the ignorance without dealing with the sin is not only insufficient, it is dangerously naïve. Paul's own personal story is quite relevant in this regard. Even as a Hebrew (a "Hebrew of Hebrews"), Paul—at that point he was still 'Saul'—couldn't see the truth. Why was that? It was not until the scales of sin were removed by Christ that Paul could "see" the truth. From the standpoint of the Scriptures, we cannot "see" the truth until the problem of sin is dealt with. Clearly, Plato has no solution for the problem of sin. Therefore, the philosophic solution is terribly naïve and radically incomplete.

What then of the quest for a "perfect city?" Plato's quest brings an end to the classical world, preparing it for the Christian answer. This is the conclusion that one of the greatest Christian philosophers, St. Augustine, would argue for in *The City of God*. Pagan man's longing for a perfect city can only be fulfilled by the city that is created, founded, and ruled by God. Is it an accident, then, that our Scriptures end with the consummation of this longing in the revelation of the "city of God?"

> Then I, John, saw the holy city, New Jerusalem, coming down out of heaven from God, prepared as a bride adorned for her husband. And I heard a loud voice from heaven saying, "Behold, the tabernacle of God *is* with men, and He will dwell with them, and they shall be His people. God Himself will be with them *and be* their God. And God will wipe away every tear from their eyes; there shall be no more death, nor sorrow, nor crying. There shall be no more pain, for the former things have passed away." (Rev. 21:2–4)

We must therefore conclude that a very real and deep longing that began in the heart of an Athenian citizen (one of her greatest citizens) can only be fulfilled by the heavenly city, the New Jerusalem. What does Athens have to do with Jerusalem? The Scriptures tell us that the longings of the Athenian or Spartan, the New Yorker or Bostonian, can only find fulfillment in that city founded by the God-man, the city of God. Philosophy must give way to theology, Greek thought must give way to Christianity, and Socrates must give way to Christ.

—Graham Dennis

For Further Reading

Bloom, Allen (trans.). *The Republic of Plato*. Second Edition. Basic Books, 1991. Interpretive Essay, 307–436.

Copleston, Frederick. *A History of Philosophy*, Vol. I: Greece and Rome. New York, NY: Image Books, 1993. 225–233.

Kraut, Richard (ed.), *The Cambridge Companion to Plato*. New York, NY: Cambridge University Press, 1995. 311–337.

Spielvogel, Jackson J. *Western Civilization*. Seventh Edition. Belmont, Calif.: Thomson Wadsworth, 2009. 57–60.

Veritas Press History Cards: New Testament, Greece and Rome. Lancaster, Pa: Veritas Press. 15.

Session I: Prelude

A Question to Consider

Why is it important for human beings to have a working definition of justice?

From the General Information above answer the following questions:

1. What two events would have been prominent in the hearts and minds of Plato's fellow Athenians?
2. What was the central political structure in the Greek world of Plato's time?
3. What is the "biographical detail" that made Plato so concerned about the nature of justice?
4. Why do the dialogue partners, with the help of Socrates, create a "city in speech"?
5. What does Aristotle mean when he says that politics is the "master science"?
6. What is the difference between *elenchus* and *eristic*?
7. Why is Socrates a "savior" figure for Plato?
8. Why is revelation a necessary solution to the problem Plato so astutely recognizes?

Reading Assignment:
Book I (327a–354c)[12]

Session II: Discussion
Book I (327a–354c)

A Question to Consider

What is justice?

Discuss or list short answers to the following questions:

Text Analysis

1. At the very beginning of the dialogue, Socrates runs into Polemarchus. What are the two options presented (one by Polemarchus the other by Socrates) regarding Polemarchus's request that Socrates stay instead of returning to town?
2. According to Cephalus, what is the greatest use of money? How does this relate to his conception of justice?
3. Polemarchus provides one of the oldest definitions of justice, and the one that probably comes most naturally to men. It is the next definition after they explore justice as "giving to each man what is owed" (331e). What is the dialogue's second definition of justice, as articulated by Polemarchus?
4. How is Thrasymachus's entrance into the dialogue described?
5. What is Thrasymachus's first definition of justice?
6. What weakness does Socrates find in Thrasymachus's first definition of justice?
7. What is the restatement of Thrasymachus's definition of justice? What has changed from the first definition to the second?

Cultural Analysis

1. Does our culture still engage in vigorous and intelligent public debate over great and important political matters?
2. What role does popular culture play in defining conceptions of justice and injustice?

Biblical Analysis

1. What aspect of justice is emphasized in Exodus 23:2–6?
2. According to 2 Chronicles 19:7 human judges are to reflect God's character as the True Judge. What three things are never aspects of God's office as judge, and what does this tell us about Divine Justice?

Summa

Write an essay or discuss this question, integrating into your essay what you have learned about justice from the material above.

What is justice and how can we know it?

The next session will be a student-led discussion. Students will be creating their own questions concerning the issue of the session. Students should create three Text Analysis Questions, two Cultural Analysis questions, and two Biblical Analysis questions. For more detailed instructions, please see the chapter on the *Iliad,* Session III.

Issue

Is justice always more profitable than injustice?

Reading Assignment:
Book II (357a–383c)

Session III: Discussion
Book II (357a–383c)

A Question to Consider

Is justice *always* more profitable than injustice? If so, why is it? If not, why not?

Students should read and consider the example questions below that are connected to the Question to Consider above. Last session's assignment was to prepare three questions and answers for the Text Analysis section and two additional questions and answers for both the Cultural and Biblical Analysis sections below.

Text Analysis

Example: Why is the "ring of Gyges" introduced into the argument?

Answer: The ring of Gyges is introduced into the argument to demonstrate that people only act "justly" because they are afraid of the consequences. Remove the fear of being "unjust" (i.e., remove the consequences of committing an injustice) and men will behave in an "unjust" manner—they will do whatever they want (359b–360d).

Cultural Analysis

Example: What are some examples of people in our culture getting ahead because they've committed an injustice?

Answer: There are many instances of professional athletes setting records and significantly altering their performance by using illegal performance-enhancing drugs. Some of these athletes have been caught and have suffered the consequences for committing an injustice. However, many of them have not. It is also the case that many investment bankers, CEOs of corporations, financial advisors, and others working with money have managed to accumulate great wealth by committing injustices. Some have been caught, but many have managed to evade the justice system. However, St. Augustine tells us that an unjust soul is its own punishment. And Christ says in Matt. 16:26, "For what profit is it to a man if he gains the whole world, and loses his own soul? Or what will a man give in exchange for his soul?" (NKJV)

"Unless communities have philosophers as kings
. . . or the people who are currently called kings and rulers practice philosophy with enough integrity
. . . there can be no end to political troubles . . ."
(*Republic*, 473d)

Other cultural issues to consider: Praising deception, that which is dishonorable, falsehood, and that which is unholy.

Biblical Analysis

Example: What do the Psalms tell us about following the law of God and pursuing justice rather than pursuing injustice? Look at the following Psalms: Ps. 1; Ps. 19:7–11; Ps. 112.

Answer: In these Psalms we learn that following God's law makes us firmly rooted, so that we will not be blown and tossed by trials. Unjust men, therefore, cannot "uproot" us from being firmly rooted in God's grace. God watches over those who fear Him and desire to keep His law. Also, the commandments of God are a source of wisdom, joy and divine blessing. Finally, the man who fears the Lord and His commands can have no fear of bad news. His heart is made steadfast because his security is found in God, who is the source of all riches and who alone can give us triumph over the strongest and most deadly foes. Thus, even though a man might suffer injustice for do-

ing what is right, justice is more powerful than injustice because justice is rooted in God.

Other Scriptures to consider: Ps. 119; Prov. 14:12; Phil. 4:8–9

Summa

Write an essay or discuss this question, integrating into your essay what you have learned about justice from the material above.

In light of all that we've learned, why doesn't it profit a man to act unjustly?

Instead of a reading assignment you have a research assignment. Tomorrow's session will be a Current Events session. Your assignment will be to find a story online, in a magazine, or in the newspaper that relates to the issue that you discussed today. Your task is to locate the article, give a copy of the article to your teacher or parent and provide some of your own worldview analysis to the article. Your analysis should demonstrate that you understand the issue, that you can clearly connect the story you found to the issue that you discussed today, and that you can provide a biblical critique of this issue in today's context. Look at the next session to see the three-part format that you should follow.

Issue

Ill-gotten gain.

Reading Assignment:
None

Session IV: Current Events
Book II (357a–383c)

Issue

Ill-gotten gain.

Current events sessions are meant to challenge you to connect what you are learning in Omnibus class to what is happening in the world around you today. After the last session, your assignment was to find a story online or in a magazine or newspaper relating to the issue above. Today you will share your article and your analysis with your teacher and classmates or parents and family. Your analysis should follow the format below:

Brief Introductory Paragraph

In this paragraph you will tell your classmates about the article that you found. Be sure to include where you found your article, who the author of your article is, and what your article is about. This brief paragraph of your presentation should begin like this:

> Hello, I am (name), and my current events article is (name of the article) which I found in (name of the web or published source)...

Connection Paragraph

In this paragraph you must demonstrate how your article is connected to the issue that you are studying. This paragraph should be short, and it should focus on clearly showing the connection between the book that you are reading and the current events article that you have found. This paragraph should begin with a sentence like

> I knew that my article was linked to our issue because...

Christian Worldview Analysis

In this section, you need to tell us how we should respond as believers to this issue today. This response should focus both on our thinking and on practical actions that we should take in light of this issue. As you list these steps, you should also tell us why we should think and act in the ways you recommend. This paragraph should begin with a sentence like

> As believers, we should think and act in the following ways in light of this issue and this article.

Reading Assignment:
Book III (386a–417b)

Session V: Recitation
Books I–III (327a–417b)

Comprehension Questions

Answer these questions for factual recall.

1. Who is the person who orders Socrates to stay with him, introducing a tone of mock and playful violence to the dialogue?
2. Why does Cephalus hand the argument over to his son Polemarchus?
3. How is Thrasymachus's entrance into the conversation depicted?
4. What is Thrasymachus's first definition of justice?
5. How does Socrates demonstrate that there is a problem with Thrasymachus's definition?
6. What is the basis of Socrates' criticism of the poets in Book II?
7. With what kind of god does Socrates replace the imperfect gods of the poets? What are the chief characteristics of this god?
8. When Socrates is discussing the opinions that poets and prose writers have of men (Book III), what does he suggest is wrong with the way that these writers characterize human life?
9. According to Socrates, being overly attentive to the body while neglecting the soul has terrible consequences. What kind of man does this produce?
10. What is the "noble lie" that Socrates tells Glaucon must be told to the citizens?

Reading Assignment:
Book IV (419a–445e)

Session VI: Writing
Books II–IV (357a–445e)

This session is a writing assignment. Remember, quality counts more than quantity. You should write no more than 1,000 words, either typing or writing legibly on one side of a sheet of paper. You will lose points for writing more than this. You will be allowed to turn in your writing three times. The first and second times you turn it in, your teacher will grade it by editing your work. This is done by marking problem areas and making suggestions for improvement. You should take these suggestions into consideration as you revise your assignment. Only the grade on your final submission will be recorded. Your grade will be based on the following criteria: 25 points for grammar, 25 points for content accuracy—historical, theological, etc.; 25 points for logic—does this make sense and is it structured well?; 25 points for rhetoric—is it a joy to read?

Description

Your assignment is to write a description following the direction provided below. This may be more difficult than it sounds! Make sure your description guides a reader into an experience of the object. Use language that stirs the senses (what does it look, sound, feel, smell, or taste like?). Make judgments about the object as you describe it. Remember the great rule of description—Show us; don't tell us. Do not tell us that something is good or beautiful or likable. Describe it in a way that shows your reader the object's beauty or ugliness, its goodness, or wickedness.

Describe a noble and heroic action by a hero—one that Socrates would suggest is sufficient for the education of the guardians. Your hero should display one of the following virtues: courage, faithfulness to a duty, sacrificing oneself for a noble cause, or love for one's county.

Your challenge is to *reform* Greek poetry. Thus, you should take a character like Achilles, Agamemnon, or Creon and have him do something profoundly noble (you pick one that you've encountered, one that needs reforming; if you can't think of one ask your teacher, or make one up).

Here is an example written from Achilles' perspective.

> How I've raged in my heart against Agamemnon! Does he not understand how proud and noble is the heart that beats beneath this battle-worn armor? Will such a heart allow itself to be disgraced and defamed—openly mocked? And yet, our cause is greater than the petty squabbles of

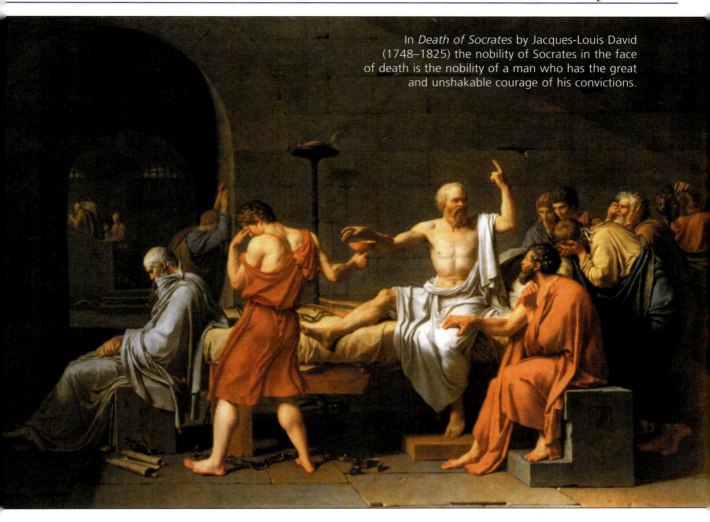

In *Death of Socrates* by Jacques-Louis David (1748–1825) the nobility of Socrates in the face of death is the nobility of a man who has the great and unshakable courage of his convictions.

men. If I be truly noble, a man of virtue and not just valor, I cannot allow a small disgrace to torture my soul. I must be the better man.

Two beasts tear at a piece of flesh. Their jaws are set like immovable iron. They will not relinquish their grip. They tear and rage. Foam escapes from each contender's angry maw as guttural growls gurgle. Are we like they? Are we not men? The gods have given men souls with which to reason, and virtue so that we may not be beasts. Am I a beast or a man?

The heat in my tent is unbearable. Steam-like tributaries of sweat pour down my brow. It is difficult to think. I know what I must do, but the doing is not as easy as the knowing. If our cause is to be victorious, if we Achaeans are to restore our honor, I must sacrifice my pride for greater glory. Let this great agitation, this sweat-filled scuffle in my soul, be my path to virtue. Let the sweat on my brow signify my hard-won path to virtue. It is decided, I rise to meet Agamemnon.

READING ASSIGNMENT:
None

SESSION VII: AESTHETICS

In this session, you will get to know a particular piece of art related to our reading. It is our job as believers to be able praise, love and protect what is beautiful and to condemn, hate and oppose all that is truly ugly. This task is often harder than you think. We have to discipline ourselves to, first, examine and understand the piece reflectively. After we understand the content of a piece, we can examine the author's intention concerning the piece and attempt to figure out what the piece of art is communicating. Sometimes this will be easy; other times it will be difficult or impossible. Finally, we need to make judgment about what this work of art communicates. Sometimes we will be able to clearly condemn a work of art as untrue, badly done or wicked. Sometimes we will be able to praise a work as glorious, majestic and true. Oftentimes, however, we will find ourselves affirming some parts of a work and condemning others. Remember, maturity is harder than immaturity—but also more rewarding. Also, remember that our praise or condemnation means more when we have disciplined ourselves to first reflect on the content and meaning of a work.

David's *Death of Socrates*

This famous work was created by Jacques-Louis David (an artist whose work you will also encounter in the sessions on *Antony and Cleopatra*). The work was first exhibited in 1787. Revolution, of course, was in the air. The American colonists had already successfully claimed their independence from King George, and it was the eve of the French Revolution. For Jacques-Louis David, Socrates represented a great philosophical hero challenging political corruption. The nobility of Socrates in the face of death is the nobility of a man who has the great and unshakable courage of his convictions. The painting has a trinity of characters: the stoic master himself (Socrates); the self-possessed yet grief-ridden disciple (Plato, Crito); the weak man overcome by emotion (the jailer and Socrates' other disciples). Socrates is a picture of absolute calm in the face of the greatest horror—death. The martyr for ideas is ultimately so certain of the truth of his cause that he is undeterred by death. Plato and Crito (Plato is at the foot of the bed, Crito is the man with his hand on Socrates' thigh) are the only disciples who are self-controlled, in spite of their obvious grief. The other disciples are clearly incapable of controlling their emotions, and therefore, likely incapable of martyrdom. It is interesting to note that Thomas Jefferson was present when the painting was unveiled. Anecdotal evidence suggests that he was a great admirer of the painting, especially the appropriateness of the sentiment it conveyed on the eve of the French Revolution. At the time of the painting many of David's fellow Frenchmen were either in prison or had been exiled for opposing the king. The painting is neo-classical in style, and was greatly praised for the quality of its execution of the style.

Jacques-Louis David was an artist and advocate for the French Revolution. He often painted scenes from Greek and Roman History as well as scenes from the French Revolution. His primary goal as an artist was to inspire people to pursue noble ideals in the face of injustice and oppression.

Technical Analysis

1. Does this work demonstrate the artist's ability and expertise?
2. Describe the scene. What is happening?
3. Does this have balance and symmetry? What is the central or most important element of this work? (To what are your eyes most attracted?)
4. Is this work realistic and proportional or not?
5. How is light used in this work?
6. What colors are used in this work?

Subject Analysis

1. Who do you think the woman is in the background (through the arched passageway)?
2. Is there any significance to the fact that Plato and Crito are both sitting beneath Socrates, while the others are standing?
3. What is the significance of Socrates pointing up with his left hand, while grasping at the hemlock with his right?
4. Plato has clearly laid down his parchment and inkpot. His duty—chronicling Socrates argument—is finished. Why do you think his back is turned to Socrates?

Content Analysis

1. What is the message of this work?
2. What is worthy of praise in this piece of art? What is worthy of condemnation?

The next session will be a student-led discussion. Students will be creating their own questions concerning the issue of the session. Students should create three Text Analysis Questions, two Cultural Analysis questions, and two Biblical Analysis questions. For more detailed instructions, please see the chapter on the *Iliad*, Session III.

Issue

What is a philosopher? (What virtues must one have in order to pursue the truth vigorously and consistently?)

READING ASSIGNMENT:
Book V (449a–480a)

SESSION VIII: DISCUSSION
Book V (449a–480a)

A Question to Consider

What virtues must one have in order to pursue the truth vigorously and consistently?

Students should read and consider the example questions below that are connected to the Question to Consider above. Last session's assignment was to prepare three questions and answers for the Text Analysis section and two additional questions and answers for both the Cultural and Biblical Analysis sections below.

Text Analysis

Example: In Book V, 475a and following the philosopher is introduced. What is it that the philosopher pursues that the "lover of sights" (the unphilosophical man) doesn't pursue?

Answer: The "lovers of sights" pursue the many instances of beauty, not beauty itself. The philosopher, however, will not be satisfied until he moves from the many particular instances of beauty to beauty itself—the ground of the imperfect beauty that is expressed in the many beautiful things that the "lovers of sights" pursue.

Cultural Analysis

Example: Plato is convinced that knowledge and reality are connected. This assumes that we have souls that are *built* to understand reality—if they are properly attuned. He believes that opinion, however, is less real than knowledge because it is not grounded in reality. Clearly, Plato believes that there are truths which are non-negotiable, what we might call "objective truths." Does our culture believe in "objective truth?" If it does, what kinds of truths qualify as "objective truths?"

Answer: Our culture tends to suggest that there are some truths that we can know with a great degree of certainty. However, there are many people in our culture who suggest that the most important truths cannot be known with any degree of certainty. The kinds of truths that we cannot know with any degree of certainty are the ones having to do with religion, and therefore, with things like our eternal destiny, the true nature of beauty, how to worship a holy God, and the essence of moral goodness. We are often told something like the following: whereas we can know that the square root of 5,929 is 77 or that water freezes at 32 degrees Fahrenheit, or that the chemical formula for trifluoroacetic acid is CF_3CO_2H, we cannot know (with any degree of certainty) that Jesus is the Son of God or that God hates sin or that marriage is a divinely established institution and is to be between a man and a woman. You may have noticed that this means that we can be certain about things which don't concern our eternal destiny, but we're left in the dark about the most important questions. This soft or partial relativism suggests that objective truth is relevant when we are discussing the sciences or mathematics but not when we are discussing religion or morality. There is another obvious consequence: whereas it makes sense to try to demonstrate the truth of one's propositions in science and mathematics, it doesn't make much sense to do so in religion and morality.

Biblical Analysis

Example: According to 1 Peter 3:15, how are Christians to approach questions which might be asked regarding the truthfulness and content of their beliefs? What does Acts 17:2–3 tell us about the role of reasoning and argumentation in the Apostle's Paul's presentation of the gospel?

Answer: First Peter 3:15 tells us that we are to set apart Christ as Lord in our hearts, and we are to be prepared. What kind of preparation is this passage suggesting we need to have? We need to be prepared to "give an account." The Greek word that is used for "give an account" is *apologia*. It means, literally, "to give a reasoned defense" or "to provide an orderly and persuasive account." Socrates made his famous "apology," which was an orderly and reasoned defense of his activities in Athens. When unbelievers see that we are different (because we have set apart Christ as Lord in our hearts) and, as in the age of the martyrs, they become interested in that difference, we are to be prepared to articulate to them why we have the hope that we have—why we have a living faith in a living God.

Acts 17:2–3 tells us that the Apostle Paul reasoned in the Synagogues, presenting an apologia, a reasoned defense, that Christ is the Messiah. We are told that he did the following things: he reasoned with them from the Scriptures; he explained that Christ is the Messiah; and he demonstrated that his reasoning was sound. The two passages together suggest that Christians must love God with their entire person. They must set apart Christ as Lord in their hearts, and they must likewise prepare their minds to express the Lordship of Christ in their hearts. Their lips must also be willing to express their thoughts by proclaiming the gospel—Jesus is Lord.

Other Scriptures to consider: Acts 18:4–11; Acts 18:18–23

SUMMA

Write an essay or discuss this question, integrating into your essay what you have learned about justice from the material above.

How can we know the difference between knowledge and opinion?

Reading Assignment:
None

Session IX: Activity

Short Essay

Socrates has made a strong argument that cultural decline begins with the arts. He takes his argument one step further: he argues that in order to stop such decline, censorship is necessary. This strikes right at the heart of democracy. Socrates seems to have been a critic of the Athenian democracy. One of his greatest concerns was that everything reduced to the art of persuasion—politics and the arts become arenas for unscrupulous men to control the weak-minded. In this short essay you are to explore the question of censorship. Here are some important items to consider as you write your essay:

1. Is the potential good created by a governmental body censuring harmful images and ideals expressed in literature, theater and music overshadowed by a greater evil? If so, what is that greater evil?
2. What role does censorship have in the life of a Christian? Examine 2 Cor. 10:4–5. What does this Scripture passage tell us about censorship?
3. If Christians do practice censorship in their own lives, should we also pursue government censorship?
4. Do we have censorship in our own democratic society? If so, provide some examples. If you found examples, what principles motivate such censorship?
5. Do you think that Plato is correct about the role that the arts play in corrupting the young? Also, do you think that this is Plato's defense of Socrates in the face of the criticism that Socrates had "corrupted the youth" (*Apology*)?

Your essay should be between 800–1,000 words.

Reading Assignment:
Book VI (484a–511e)

Session X: Recitation
Books IV–V (419a–480a)

Comprehension Questions

Answer these questions for factual recall.

1. According to Socrates, changes in what always lead to the greatest political changes?
2. According to Socrates, what attitude should the founder of the city have towards ancestral religion (especially the Temple of Apollo at Delphi)?
3. According to Socrates, the class which is the wisest will also be what?
4. Which is the virtue that is, according to Socrates, the common virtue that stretches throughout all of the classes in the city?
5. In the new "city in speech," an entirely new definition of justice emerges. This definition clearly reflects an important characteristic of the soul (remember, the city is the "soul writ large"). What is the new definition of justice that emerges in Book IV?
6. At 435e, Socrates compares the soul and the city. How are the three parts of the soul described by Socrates in that passage?
7. At 439d and following, Socrates attempts to demonstrate that the soul has "parts" (i.e., that it is complex). Briefly explain how his demonstration works.
8. According to Socrates, the city's justice is most perverted when one part of the city overpowers another part of the city. Briefly explain this.
9. A second notion of justice (really a restatement of the one mentioned earlier) emerges at 443d–e. It is based upon the analogy of the soul and the city. What is this second comparison of the city and the soul like?
10. According to the quite shocking argument of Socrates (at least for his time), men and women do not have different souls. The differences are matters of degree, not essence. Describe how Socrates suggests that men and women share in the same nature.
11. In order to preserve the purity of the higher classes, what abomination (for Christians) must be practiced?
12. Why is the communism (i.e., "common" or "public ownership") of women and children necessary?
13. What indications do we have that this city is too fanciful to come into existence? (Hints: 466d; 471c; 471e; 472d; 473a–b; especially 592b)
14. According to 478e–480a, the philosopher is not the lover of opinion, but the lover of something else. What is this something else, and how is it described?

Session XI: Activity
Book VI (484a–511e)

Plato's Divided Line

Many of Plato's most important ideas come to us in images. At the end of Book VI is one of Plato's most important images. In a very important way, it also anticipates another important image—Plato's most famous—the allegory of the cave. Using information from the text, create a model of Plato's famous "divided line." The "divided line" is described from 509d–511e. In this exercise you will create a drawing that makes the divided line as clear as possible. Be careful to read the text with care, and make every effort to create a chart that is as accurate as possible.

Reading Assignment:
Book VII (514a–541b)

Session XII: Activity
Book VII (514a–541b)

Cave Drawings

As with the previous lesson, it is extremely important to figure out the allegory of the Cave by imagining it and mapping it out. It is an allegory, so we need to know what an allegory is in order to proceed. There are some famous allegories, and the one that you have read in Book VII is certainly one of the most famous. However, in order to understand what an allegory is we'll look at a much simpler Platonic allegory. In the dialogue *Phaedrus*, Plato gives us the following allegory (*Phaedrus* 246a–254e). The soul, according to the allegory, is like a chariot being pulled by two horses and driven by a charioteer. The horses pulling the chariot are white and black. The white horse is a very well-bred and well-trained horse. It runs smoothly and obediently—and it does so without having to be whipped and beaten. The black horse, however, is not well-bred. It is also untrained and constantly in need of correction. The challenge is to get the horses to cooperate so that the chariot can go in the direction that the charioteer wishes it to. Following the Platonic tripartite soul, we can see the way that the allegory represents the human soul:

SYMBOLIC IMAGE	WHAT IT REPRESENTS
The whole chariot: chariot, driver, horses	The soul
Charioteer	Reason
White Horse	Moral passions
Black Horse	Immoral, irrational passions

The way that the allegory works is pretty simple. If the charioteer keeps the black horse under control, then it is possible for the chariot to go where the charioteer pleases. However, if the charioteer does not control the black horse, it will not work in harmony with the white horse and the chariot will be thrown into chaos, unable to follow the course it is supposed to follow.

The allegory of the cave is best understood if it is drawn out and then labeled. It is quite an elaborate allegory, so it is helpful to draw out the symbolic images and then to label them, determining what each symbolic element of the allegory represents. In this assignment, you should carefully read Plato's allegory of the cave (Book VII, 514a–521c). Then, you should sketch out the parts of the allegory, and attempt to label them. Finally, you should consider how the allegory of the cave and the "divided line," as you sketched it out in the last assignment, might work together. Below are some important questions to consider:

1. What issue is this allegory trying to address?
2. What is the significance of the two different sources of light?
3. What happens when a prisoner is made to turn around?
4. What kind of person is it who descends into the cave?
5. What can happen to this person who descends into the cave? How might this be related to events in Plato's own life?
6. Who are the shadow-casters?
7. What is the cave?
8. What role does nature play in the allegory?
9. Is it significant that one fire is man-made and the other is natural?
10. How might the Prometheus story figure into this allegory?

Read through the passage (514a–521c). Make a basic sketch of the allegory of the cave. Label each of the parts on your sketch (making your best judgment as to what each symbolic element refers to). Then make an attempt to determine what relationship might exist when compared to the sketch that you drew for the "divided line." Finally, write a brief paragraph explaining what the allegory of the cave tells us about the condition of human nature with respect to education (knowledge of the true, good and beautiful).

READING ASSIGNMENT:
Book VIII (543a–569c)

Chart 1: **WORLDVIEW ANALYSIS**

	VIRTUE	POWER
Thrasymachus	According to Thrasymachus, there are two kinds of virtue. There is the "virtue" of the weak man and there is the "virtue" of the strong man. The "virtue" of the weak man is to be moral and law-abiding. The virtue of the strong man is to do what nature intended him to do—to rule. The weak secretly wish that they were strong, but lacking the ability, they call that shameful which they would do if they had the strength.	
Socrates		Socrates presents a notion of "power" that is exactly the opposite of Thrasymachus's notion. True power is not simply doing what one wants, but doing what is actually best for the soul. Because the soul is complex, it can be divided between its wants. The wise man chooses between options based upon a judgment regarding what is best for the soul. True power, therefore, is having the capacity to (a) make a proper judgment about what is best and (b) having the capacity to do what one judges to be the best course of action.
Christianity		

SESSION XIII: DISCUSSION
Book VIII (543a–569c)

A Question to Consider

Why is it that political structures created by man seem to suffer from the phenomenon of rising and falling?

Discuss or list short answers to the following questions:

Text Analysis

1. Why do all regimes tend to fall apart, according to the insight Socrates presents at 546a?
2. How does the democratic regime come into existence? (Hint: 556d–557a).
3. What is the dominant feature of the democratic regime?
4. Describe the decline of the democratic regime.

HAPPINESS

VICE (DOING EVIL)

For the Christian, to be happy is to be blessed by God. In the famous "beatitudes" passage (Matt. 5:3–11), Jesus again gives us a paradoxical formula. Those who are blessed are, strangely, those whom the world would view as cursed: the poor in spirit, those who mourn, the meek, and the persecuted. It is interesting to note that this list is the opposite of that presented by Thrasymachus. The logic of this position is simple: those who are dependent are blessed. All of those listed are precisely those who are dependent. And of course, they are those who are dependent upon God. This is why Jesus says that we must be like little children.

5. To what kind of regime does democracy lead after it dissolves?
6. What is it that most enslaves those living in a democratic regime?

Cultural Analysis

1. Plato's account of democracy suggests that freedom actually enslaves. Do we see this in our own culture? If so, where do we see it?
2. At 560c–d, Socrates talks about the tendency in a democracy not only to elevate license to a virtue (license means "doing what one wants"), but to view morality as something old-fashioned and quaint. In our culture, this seems to have happened especially in the arts—and most especially in Hollywood. Can you think of examples in our culture that represent this tendency to praise license and blame morality, as though it were for the simple?

Biblical Analysis

1. What do the following passages suggest is the purpose of the freedom that we have in Christ: Jude 1:4; 1 Corinthians 10:23; 1 Peter 2:16; 2 Peter 2:19?
2. Do a careful reading of Genesis 11. What was the basic impetus behind building the Tower of Babel? And what is so problematic about the way that they went about it?

Summa

Write an essay or discuss this question, integrating into your essay what you have learned about justice from the material above.

Read through Romans chapter 1. See if you find signs that our culture is beginning to follow the pattern of degeneration outlined in the chapter. Using Romans chapter 1 as your guide, try to determine if we likewise are in danger of falling under the "wrath of God revealed from heaven against all ungodliness and unrighteousness of men, who suppress the truth in unrighteousness" (Rom. 1:18). If we are in such danger, what role does the Church have in such a culture?

Reading Assignment:
Book IX (571a–592b)

Session XIV:
Worldview Analysis
Books I–IX (327a–592b)

What Would Socrates Do?

Fill out Chart 1. Do your best from your knowledge of the text and your knowledge of Scripture. If you are not certain of an answer, try to infer from your knowledge of the positions of each character how they might view each particular category. For each character, we have provided you with one of the answers.

Reading Assignment:
Book X (595a–621d)

Session XV: Evaluation

All tests and quizzes are to be given with an open book and a Bible available.

Grammar

Answer each of the following questions in complete sentences. Some answers may be longer than others. (2 points per answer)

1. According to Cephalus, what is the greatest use of money? How does this relate to his conception of justice?
2. How is Thrasymachus's entrance into the dialogue described?
3. What is Thrasymachus's first definition of justice?
4. What is the basis of Socrates' criticism of the poets in book II?
5. With what kind of god does Socrates replace the imperfect gods of the poets? What are the chief characteristics of this god?
6. What is the "noble lie" that Socrates tells Glaucon must be told to the citizens?
7. Socrates attempts to demonstrate that the soul has "parts" (i.e., that it is complex). Briefly explain how he demonstrates this.
8. According to Socrates, the city's justice is most perverted when one part of the city overpowers another part of the city. What does this "overpowering" look like?
9. To what kind of regime does democracy lead after it dissolves?
10. What is it that most enslaves those living in a democratic regime?

Logic

Demonstrate your understanding of Plato's Republic. Answer two of the four following questions in complete sentences; your answer should be a paragraph or so. (10 points per answer)

1. Explain the Socratic/Platonic tripartite soul. What are its basic parts, and what are each part's basic characteristics?
2. What is the purpose of the "ring of Gyges" in relation to Thrasymachus's view of human nature?
3. What is the plot of the myth of Er? Explain what the central point of the myth is.
4. What is the weakness that Socrates finds in Thrasymachus's notion of "justice" (his first definition)?

Lateral Thinking

Answer one of the following questions. These questions will require more substantial answers. (20 points per answer)

1. Plato suggests that it is important for human beings to arrive at a model or standard so that we can distinguish between the standard and a counterfeit, flawed or deviant example. Explain the difference between the Christian means for arriving at standards and the method that Plato's philosophical solution presents. Use quotations from the book and from Scripture to justify your answer.
2. What similarities do you see between the Platonic notion of the soul and the Christian? What differences do you see?

OPTIONAL SESSION A: ACTIVITY

Listening to a Symphonic Portrayal of Socrates

Socrate is a piece of music composed by Erik Satie. Erik Satie is a French composer of classical music whose work dates from the late nineteenth century through the early twentieth. He is most famous for his *Gymnopédies*. Satie's *Socrate* was described by the composer himself as "a symphonic drama in three parts." The style is interesting. It has been considered anything from a secular oratorio to an operatic symphony. The piece is divided into three parts:

Part I: Portrait of Socrates
Part II: On the Banks of the Ilissus
Part III: Death of Socrates

The vocal parts are all taken from works of Plato. The first section is taken from Plato's *Symposium*. The second is taken from Plato's *Phaedrus*. And the third section is taken from Plato's *Phaedo*.

Listen to Satie's *Socrate* (you may obtain this piece in a store, online or, maybe, at your local library—especially if there is a university or college library nearby). The piece is part of a genre of classical music that will likely be very new to you. It is not liked by all. It has been seen as the beginning of minimalist music—even some of the forms of absurd art that we find in figures like John Cage (who did his own arrangement of this piece). As you listen to the piece consider the following:

1. Does the piece of music convey the honor and nobility that Plato would want us to see in Socrates? If so, how does it do this? If not, why do you think that it doesn't?
2. After listening to the Death of Socrates section (the last movement), does it convey the sadness that his friends certainly felt? From what perspective do you think that the piece presents his death? Is it triumphant? Heroic? Tragic?
3. In many films the music helps us to feel what is being depicted on screen. Does this music move you in any way? If so, how? If not, why not?

OPTIONAL SESSION B: ACTIVITY

Writing

Aldous Huxley's *Brave New World* presents a picture of a society much like the society that Socrates and Glaucon create—replete with philosopher kings, eugenics, thought police, and "noble lies." If you've not read this novel, search online for a brief synopsis.[13]

In this assignment, you will be asked to think about the "utopia." From the standpoint of Aldous Huxley, the "city in speech" created by Socrates would actually be a "dystopia." A "dystopia" is a parody of a utopia. In other words, a dystopia is an ironic treatment of utopian literature. During Huxley's lifetime, many thinkers were taking seriously the idea of creating a technologically-based utopian society. These thinkers believed that science and education were rapidly advancing to the point that human beings would, in the not-too-distant future, create perfect societies. H.G. Wells' utopian literature, for instance, is thought to be an inspiration for Huxley's *Brave New World*.[14] Wells was extremely optimistic about the possibilities of education and technology to create a greater future society. He believed that in order to do so, however, the English would have to get over their puritan sensibilities—namely, their Christian belief that man's sinfulness renders the creation of such a utopia impossible (at least without God's divine intervention). Huxley's dystopian *Brave New World* attempts to show us the dangers of such utopian dreaming.

In this essay consider the following questions:

1. What would Huxley have thought about Plato's "ideal city"?
2. *Brave New World* pokes fun at the dreamy-eyed idealism found in utopian literature. Should we, as Christians, accept Huxley's critique of utopias?
3. What do Christians think about the concept of a utopia? Is the "New Jerusalem" a utopia? If so, is the Bible utopian? Be sure to read Revelation chapter 21 before writing your paper.
4. Do you think that Plato intended us to take his "city in speech" seriously? Or, did he have some other purpose?
5. Is our democratic form of government, with its system of checks and balances, inherently dystopian in nature?

The essay should be roughly 1,000–1,200 words.

Aristotle Contemplating a Bust of Homer was painted in 1653 by Rembrandt van Rijn.

OPTIONAL SESSION C: AESTHETICS

Rembrandt's *Aristotle Contemplating a Bust of Homer*

Study this famous work of art and think through the impressions it makes upon you and the questions it raises. Be encouraged to notice details and write your own questions.

This work was produced in 1653 when Rembrandt was quite poor. Unlike Aristotle, who had Alexander the Great as a patron, Rembrandt identifies with Homer because both men were penniless artists. Rembrandt, however, was a man who lived beyond his means. He loved to collect art and rare antiquities and artifacts. So we might wonder at his identification with Homer, especially since Aristotle is almost certainly a self-portrait (Rembrandt often inserted himself into paintings). In a way, Rembrandt may have identified with the wealth and worldliness of Aristotle, but admired (and sympathized with) the simplicity and poverty of Homer.

Aristotle (384–322 B.C.) was a Greek philosopher who had studied under Plato. He was also the personal teacher to Alexander the Great. Aristotle was especially appreciated in the ancient world for his ability to systematize thought. He separated subjects of study into distinct categories (many of which we still use today). He also was one of the first philosophers to create a formal logical system. Much of Aristotle's thought influenced medieval Muslims, Jews and Christians (influencing both the Eastern Orthodox Church and the later medieval scholastics). Homer's dates are uncertain. Herodotus suggests that Homer was writing 400 years before his own works. If true, that would make Homer's dates roughly 880–800 B.C. Homer is often referred to as the "blind poet." He is especially known for his mastery of the epic poetic style. Both thinkers have greatly influenced western culture and literature.

We would like you to do something a little bit different for this session. After reading through the sample questions (with provided answers), you will write your own questions. In order to do this, you will really need to analyze the painting. This involves not simply looking, but looking well. Rarely do we, as busy modern people, have the opportunity to spend a long time to listen attentively to a great piece of music or to take some time to gaze at a painting until its hidden secrets are revealed. Great works of art have secrets that are only discovered through attentiveness and keen observation. We would like you to begin practicing these skills. In order to do this, you will be asked to do the following:

a)   Come up with three questions that can be presented to the class.
b)   Answer those questions.

You will present the questions to the class (or your parents if working alone), and they will have an opportunity to respond. Then, when they are finished you should provide the answers that you've prepared. Below is a sample question with an answer provided.

Example: Does Aristotle seem to be looking down on the poet (from a higher perch of philosophical genius), or is he contemplating the great poet as a humble admirer?

Answer: Aristotle's face does seem to have a look of reverence upon it. However, it is hard not to think that Aristotle feels somehow superior to the humble "blind bard."

Example: Does Aristotle believe that his great wealth somehow vindicates his own enterprise (as philosopher)? Or, is Aristotle genuinely impressed by the simplicity and humility of Homer?

Answer: Many interpreters have suggested that Aristotle is contemplating the value of worldly success as compared to spiritual depth. Homer represents spiritual depth, and Aristotle (the tutor of Alexander) represents worldly success.

Time yourself. Give yourself five minutes to stare at the painting. Notice as much as you can. As you are studying the painting, write down some thoughts that come to mind. After you are finished, compose three questions with answers. Have fun!

OPTIONAL SESSION D: ACTIVITY
Book X (595a–621d)

Literary Analysis

In Book X we see Socrates creating a new genre of poetry—a genre that meets the demands that he has for properly didactic poetic discourse. Socrates is, in Book X, a philosophic poet. In this exercise you will analyze the basic elements of the "myth of Er." At 605b–c, Socrates says that poets tend to make a bad regime in the soul. The most important part of his argument is that poets cause things to water and grow in the soul which ought to be dried up. In short, the poets "water wickedness."

This is, in part, because they are committed to entertaining people, and what is most entertaining is not always what's best for the soul. Clearly, the philosophic myth is intended to reverse this error. But in order to understand how it might reverse this error, we need to understand the central components of the myth, and what it is intended to convey.

We have a very important hint as to what the true art of the poet ought to be at 618b–c. The chief art is that which enables a man to distinguish between the good and the bad. If the poetic art tends to make this impossible (because it "waters wickedness"), it seems to follow that that tendency needs to be corrected. Consider this as you do your literary analysis of the "myth of Er." The myth of Er begins at 614b–620d.

BASIC PLOT
Briefly write a condensed version of the plot of the myth.

BASIC POINT
Briefly describe what the "moral" or "point" of the myth is.

IMPORTANT QUESTIONS TO ASK
In attempting to understand a story it is important to ask the right questions. Below, write down four questions that when answered would help a reader to gain better insight into the story. Here is an example question:

Question 1: What role do the fates play in the story?

Note: Tomorrow's class will be an Evaluation. To prepare for this test you should review your earlier answers to the questions in previous lessons.

ENDNOTES
1   By the way, if you've read Dante's *Inferno* you've already encountered a quite similar form of patriotism. The city-state was a dominant feature of Dante's Italian world. In fact, Dante's Florence (itself a city-state) is probably the city closest to Athens. Both cities are quite famous for producing a remarkably large number of the world's most famous men.
2   "Arete" is a Greek word often translated as "virtue."
3   Plato's Republic, Aristotle's Politics, and other works like Machiavelli's Prince and Rousseau's Social Contract are instances of political philosophy.
4   Eris was the Greek goddess of discord or strife. The opposite of

this goddess was Harmonia—the goddess of peaceful coexistence and concord.

5   Although Orpheus doesn't appear in Homer or Hesiod, he had become quite popular by the time that Plato was writing. Amongst other things, he was a son of one of the Muses and, most importantly, one of the rare mythological figures who had descended and returned from Hades. He was also connected to music (and especially to Apollo), and the patron god of a religious cult that began to teach the doctrine of the immortality of the soul.

6   According to the legend as it had developed in Plato's time, Orpheus' music retained their great power to draw and woo even in Hades. Socrates, therefore, is like Orpheus in that his art (philosophy) draws men up from the Hades of ignorance and false opinion into the "heaven" of truth, goodness and beauty.

7   An important hint that Orpheus (and Orphic religion) is somehow involved in the text comes at the very beginning of the dialogue. Socrates and Glaucon go to the Piraeus to observe religious festivals. It is not only a religious festival put on by Athenians, but Thracians were also involved. Orpheus was often presented as a Thracian god.

8   Tertullian (c. 160–220 AD) is one of the early Fathers of the Church. He was one of the first Fathers of the Church to write in Latin, not Greek. He famously asked the following: "What has Athens to do with Jerusalem, or the Academy [Plato's school of philosophy] with the Church?" By this he meant to highlight the difference between "natural theology" (the attempt to speak about the soul and God without revelation) and Christian truth (which depends upon divine revelation). He thought that the attempt to do theology without revelation was demonic and led, inevitably, to heresy.

9   Psalm 22 is a Messianic Psalm. Jesus directly quotes this Psalm from the Cross (Matt. 27:46; Mk. 15:34).

10 Herakleitos, Fragment 45, Diogenes Laertius ix, 7.

11 The Timaeus is one of the few Platonic dialogues to which medieval people had access. As such, it was also one of the greatest inspirations for the medieval model of the universe and was a great source of inspiration for men like Boethius and Dante.

12 The traditional ten books are often referenced using the following numbering system:
Book I: 327a–354c
Book II: 357a–383c
Book III: 386a–417b
Book IV: 419a–445e
Book V: 449a–480a
Book VI: 484a–511e
Book VII: 514a–541b
Book VIII: 543a–569c
Book IX: 571a–592b
Book X: 595a–621d

13 A good summary can be found at Link1 for this chapter at www.VeritasPress.com/OmniLinks.

14 Many scholars believe that Wells' *Men Like Gods* was the inspiration for Huxley's dystopian response, *Brave New World*.

Nicomachean Ethics

What is the *chief end of man*?

As you quite possibly know, this is the first question of the Westminster Shorter Catechism. You might even be able to rehearse the answer: "To glorify God and enjoy Him forever." And this is certainly the right answer. What you might not be aware of, however, is that it is a really profound question—one that has occupied the minds not only of theologians but also of philosophers down through the ages.

Take a look at your own life and the lives of those around you. It is pretty obvious that we all do the things we do for a reason. Take brushing your teeth, for instance: Why do you do it? Because your parents told you to? To make sure you have fresh breath? To prevent tooth decay? Any or all of these may be the right answer for you, and there are probably many others I did not list. The point is this: whenever you perform any action, you are doing it for some reason—it is just part of being human.

Now brushing one's teeth is not the sort of thing philosophers examine. They do not simply try to discern our reason for doing some particular action; rather they try and discover why we do *everything* we do. That is, they want to know what we are seeking in life, what we are aiming at. To use Westminster's language, they want to know what our chief end is. It is to people who want to answer this question that Aristotle addresses his *Nicomachean Ethics*.

General Information

Author and Context

Aristotle, Plato's most brilliant disciple and founder of the Lyceum, is a man who perhaps needs no great introduction. Known simply as "the Philosopher" throughout the Middle Ages, he is one of the most influential thinkers in the Western intellectual tradition. In addition to his skill as a philosopher, however, Aristotle was something of a polymath. He was interested in all sorts of things. This intellectual curiosity led him to coin both the names for such academic disciplines as logic, rhetoric, physics, and meteorology, and also the terms employed in these fields of study. It is a special testament to his genius that the study of "formal logic" meant the study of Aristotle's logical writings for some 2,000 years after his death.

Aristotle was born at Stageira, Thrace, in 384/3 B.C. His father, Nichomachus, was a physician and friend of the Macedonian king

Amyntas II. This connection with Macedonian royalty would prove to be both a great opportunity and a great liability in Aristotle's life. In 368/7 he moved to Athens, where he would study with Plato at the Academy for the next 20 years. When Plato died, Aristotle spent a brief time as the director of the branch of the Academy in Assos before moving to Macedonia to become the tutor of then-thirteen-year-old Alexander the Great. He would keep this position for seven years. When Alexander ascended his father's throne in 336/5, Aristotle returned to Athens to found his own school, the Lyceum.

Aristotle spent the rest of his working career at the Lyceum in Athens. It is during this twelve-year period that he composed his most important works, including the *Nicomachean Ethics*. After Alexander the Great's unexpected death in 323, anti-Macedonian sentiments were on the rise in Athens, and Aristotle was suspect due to his and his family's Macedonian connections. In order to escape almost certain death, Aristotle left Athens. He spent the year 322, which was his last, living in exile on his mother's estate in Euboea.

Significance

We have all probably heard Socrates' famous maxim: "The unexamined life is not worth living." They are wise words, indeed, and one would do well to remember them. But according to Mortimer Adler, in his great little book *Aristotle for Everybody*, Aristotle himself took it back one step further—for him, the *unplanned* life is not worth examining. To examine your life without knowing what it is you are aiming at is kind of like Alice asking the Cheshire Cat what the right way is when she doesn't know where she is going. There is just no real way of making a decision without a goal.

The *Nicomachean Ethics* is significant because it focuses our attention on the vitally important issue of the purpose of human life. Furthermore, after focusing our attention, it then helps us to discover the surest course to achieve that purpose. Although Aristotle was not a Christian—he lived three centuries before Christ—his exhortation here to live circumspectly is clearly in line with the teaching of the Scriptures.

Moreover, the *Nicomachean Ethics* has further significance for people in our own day. Aristotle notes that some people in his day had argued that the purpose of life is to have as much pleasure as possible, while others argued for wealth, power, or honor instead. Still others argued that the attainment of virtue is the real goal of life. In short, there were in his day any number of conflicting opinions about the purpose of life. The thoughtful person will see that we find ourselves in a similar situation today. The *Nicomachean Ethics* is a useful tool not only in learning to ask the right questions and think about important matters, but they also help us to make sense of our own world in our own time.

Aristotle assumes that all human actions are directed toward an end, and the end they are striving for, ultimately, is happiness, or "the good life."

Summary and Setting

The *Nicomachean Ethics* is best described in the following three ways. It is *teleological*, for Aristotle assumes that all human actions are directed toward a *telos* (Greek for "end" or "goal"). He understands this goal to be what he calls in Greek *eudaimonia*, which means felicity, happiness, or the "good life." Hence Aristotle's work here is often called *eudaimonistic* by philosophers. Finally, it is practical; Aristotle argues that the good life is not achieved merely by *thinking* about what constitutes a good life, but by putting those ideas into *practice*.

A brief outline of the text goes as follows. In Book One Aristotle notes that all human actions are teleological and that the *telos* they are striving for, ultimately, is *eudaimonia*, or happiness. He then sets limits on his work, saying that the conclusions he will reach in his argument will be *probable* rather than *certain*. That is due to the fact that ethical reasoning is largely based upon *inductive* arguments (those that attempt to arrive at general principles by studying particular instances) rather than *deductive* arguments (those that attempt to understand the particular things in light of general principles).

In Books Two through Five, Aristotle defines moral virtue, considers how it is acquired, and discusses the individual moral virtues at length. Key to this part of the text is Aristotle's famous *Doctrine of the Mean*, by which he shows that the virtues are performed by avoiding extremes either of deficiency or excess in any action. In Book Six he discusses the intellectual virtues, while in Book Seven he considers pleasure. Books Eight and Nine contain Aristotle's famous philosophy concerning friendship, while the whole work is drawn to a close with a consideration of happiness in Book Ten.

Worldview

Written in the mid-fourth century B.C., the *Nicomachean Ethics* is one of the most frequently studied works of one of the most important philosophers in Western history. It was read widely in Aristotle's day and has continued to captivate the minds of the greatest philosophers ever since, especially since its reintroduction to Europe in the high Middle Ages 750 years ago.

When reading an ancient book, it is hard to imagine that it was once a novelty, but this is precisely what the *Nicomachean Ethics* was in many ways. For Aristotle's was the first work ever to be written on the subject of ethics, the branch of philosophy concerned with evaluating human actions. Now it is true that Plato's *Dialogues* display an intense concern for ethical truth; this is especially the case in his *Republic*, where he focuses upon justice

and the ordering of the ideal society. But Plato, seeing man's good to be identical with the good of the state, fails to address man as man. He simply describes the ordering of the good state and assumes that it will be good for the man as well. It was Aristotle, however, who first took a serious look at human nature and action in order to explain what the good of man was and how it could be achieved.

The influence the *Nicomachean Ethics* has had in Western civilization is great, both inside and outside the Church. In the Greco-Roman world, Aristotle's teachings were embraced by the Peripatetics (the name given to Aristotle's followers because they walked around while he taught them), while a good number of his ethical ideas were also embodied in various other philosophical schools such as the Stoics and Epicureans. Christian thought about ethics has also been greatly influenced by Aristotle. To give two notable examples, the great medieval theologian St. Thomas Aquinas produced what many scholars think to be the most profound commentary on the *Nicomachean Ethics*, and the influential sixteenth-century protestant reformer Peter Martyr Vermigli is noted for his fine commentary as well.

Potential Difficulties

The fact that the *Nicomachean Ethics* is an influential work notwithstanding, the Christian reader is often unsure of the value or even the legitimacy of studying ethics from someone who was, frankly, a pagan. For writing 350 years before the coming of Christ, and ignorant of the Lord's revelation of Himself to Israel, Aristotle never even conceives of the Triune God, much less addresses Him in his work. Although this fact should not surprise us, it does necessarily raise a difficult question about the value of reading Aristotle for the thoughtful Christian.

Christians have disagreed over this issue, but for those who value the study of Aristotle's *Ethics*, the following three principles are most important. First, as Christians we affirm that although all men are sinners in Adam, we are nevertheless made in God's image and after His likeness. This truth applies even to pre-Christian pagans like Aristotle. As a bearer of God's image, we should expect him to express important truths about many areas of human life and experience, sometimes even very profound ones. As a fallen sinner, however, we should not be surprised to find great errors as well.

Second, we believe with Psalm 19 that the "heavens declare the glory of God; and the firmament proclaims his handiwork. Day to day pours forth speech, and night after night declares knowledge. There is no speech, nor are there words; their voice is not heard; yet their voice goes out through all the earth, and their words to the end of the world." Simply put, there is truth to be found by giving attention to the world that God has made. Aristotle was deeply concerned with observing the world around him and attempting to make sense of it as best he could. In his *Ethics* he is concerned with studying that peculiar part of the world we call *man*. Insofar as human beings are part of God's creation, we ought to expect that studying human nature and human actions will likewise yield knowledge.

Behold, I send you out as sheep in the midst of wolves. Therefore be wise as serpents and harmless as doves.—Matt. 10:16

Finally, we believe the apostle Paul's teaching in Romans 2 that all men, in some sense, have the law of God "written in their hearts" (v. 15). Now exploring the full implications of this doctrine would be a great undertaking, but Paul seems to make it clear that even without biblical revelation, Gentiles (literally "Greeks") can know the law of God to an extent (v. 14). This is because their consciences bear witness to the law God has written in their hearts (v. 15).

The Christian reader, therefore, should be confident that there is value in reading the *Nicomachean Ethics*—and indeed any work of human learning—since it is the product of a man made in God's image, who lives in God's creation, and who has God's law written in his heart. As we have seen, however, this does not mean Aristotle is without error, for he is a fallen image living in a fallen world, with a conscience that does not infallibly interpret God's law. We should proceed carefully, then, testing all things by the standard of God's Word. And yet we should proceed as so many of our forebears in the Christian faith have: as wisely as serpents and as innocently as doves, studying the Scriptures, but willing to accept truth wherever it might be found.

In addition to this potential theological difficulty, there is also a potential practical difficulty in reading the *Nicomachean Ethics*. In his masterful book on ethics, *After Virtue*, the philosopher Alasdair MacIntyre refers to the *Nicomachean Ethics* as "the most brilliant lecture notes ever written." These are great accolades for Aristotle, but they also reveal something important for the reader to keep in mind as he approaches this text. The *Nicomachean Ethics* is essentially an edition of lecture notes Aristotle delivered to his students at the Lyceum.

As lecture notes, the *Nicomachean Ethics* present at least two difficulties for the reader. First, they are terse and profound: Aristotle will make the most thought-provoking comment and move right along to the next idea without any further explanation. In the actual lectures—oh, to have been there!—the master teacher would have taken time to explain these things to his students. We who have only the notes are often left to ourselves to fill in the missing commentary and explanation.

Another difficulty in interpreting this work, and one which seems to be the opposite of the first, is that Aristotle feels free to digress frequently in the course of his exposition. That is to say, he discusses material that at times seems ancillary, if not tangential, to his argument. But if the reader keeps in mind that this is the text of a *lecture*, he will not be surprised by this. How many times in a class has a teacher thought of an example, formed a connection, or made an allusion to something that might seem unimportant to an outsider, but was quite appropriate in the context of the class? We can all probably think of any number of these occasions. This is doubtless the case with Aristotle's teaching. Keeping this in mind, the reader might find that he is delighted rather than distracted by Aristotle's digressions.

About Worldview

Anyone familiar with thinking about worldview issues is accustomed to asking three important questions of any work he reads: What is the author claiming/assuming about the nature of reality? What does he or she assume about whether and how I can know it? What does the author think I should do? There are whole branches of philosophy dedicated to dealing with each one of these questions—in fact, the study of philosophy is customarily divided into three main branches corresponding to these three questions.

The first question covers the discipline that philosophers, following Aristotle's coinage, call metaphysics.[1] This branch of philosophy studies existence and the natures of God, man and the world. The second question covers the discipline we call epistemology, the branch of philosophy that tries to discern such things as whether anything can be known, what knowledge is, and how a person arrives at knowledge. The final question covers the discipline we call ethics, and it is concerned with what a person ought to do and how he or she ought to do it.

So there are three traditional branches of philosophy and three "worldview questions" associated with them. For the remainder of this essay, we will interact with the worldview Aristotle has given expression to in his *Nico-machean Ethics*, discussing it in terms of his metaphysics, epistemology, and ethics. As we do so, however, it is important to keep in mind that we will be distinguishing things that in reality are never separate. Our understanding of reality (metaphysics), for example, is always affecting both our view of knowledge (epistemology) and of what we ought to do (ethics). The same is true of the effect our ethics have on our metaphysics and epistemology, and so forth. All three are always present together and, as it were, interpenetrate one another.

Ontology: What Is Reality?

What does Aristotle assume about the natures of God, the world, and man? When we seek to discern Aristotle's *theology* (what he assumes about the nature of God), it comes perhaps as a surprise that he doesn't seem to be concerned with deity at all in his discussion. It is commonplace for Christians to associate ethics, the study of human actions, with theology—God is, after all, very concerned with human actions, how we live our lives, and the choices we make. This is due to the fact that although we are distinct from God by our very essence as created beings, we are nevertheless made in God's image, after His likeness. Furthermore, He has assumed our human nature in the Incarnation, and He is also the source of all goodness, truth, and beauty in the universe. For the Christian thinker, then, the study of ethics *must* be connected with theology, because God is goodness Himself.

Not so for Aristotle. Although it was not uncommon in ancient Greek culture to view the gods as being concerned with human actions—think of Homer's *Iliad* and *Odyssey*—the Greeks did not seem to think there was any *necessary* relationship between them. That is to say, for the Greeks, man is not made in some god's image, the gods are not themselves the standard of right and wrong, and it is not to the gods that a man must give account of his life after death. Not to mention the fact that there was no authoritative revelation from the gods upon which to base any certain knowledge.

In Greek thought, the gods were concerned with human actions only insofar as those actions affected them. Consider an example from the opening of Homer's *Iliad*. Apollo was very angered by the fact that Achilles abducted Briseis, the daughter of Chryses, but not because of the immorality of taking a girl captive. Apollo was angry with Achilles' actions simply because Chryses was Apollo's priest; Apollo was merely taking Chryses' side. Whether Achilles' actions were right or wrong just did not come up.

As Christians we find Aristotle's theology quite foreign, though we can, perhaps, understand the lack of emphasis he places on the gods. Greek mythology is, after all, at best the result of the corrupt speculation of men, and at worst the result of demonic deception. It is no surprise, then, that a man striving to understand the good—even in the form that a fallen mind can perceive it—would have to leave this mythology behind. It simply can not bear the weight of the truth.

When we consider Aristotle's cosmology (what he thinks about the nature of the world), however, we find something with which we are much more familiar. For Aristotle, ours is a real world, a rational world, and a moral world. Plato, you might recall, thought that the world of our experience—the world we touch with our hands, see with our eyes, hear with our ears, and so forth—is largely an illusion. It is an unsubstantial copy or image of ideal reality. Such a world is not, and could not be, the proper object of knowledge. Aristotle, however, thought that this world we experience with our senses is in fact a substantial reality. If anything is "real," then the world is certainly real, and so are we.

Because our world is real, it is also rational—i.e., it makes sense and can be known. We do not think of it very often, but the fact that studying the particular events in our experience allows us to come to a general knowledge of things is really staggering. It is truly astounding that by studying this particular tree, this horse, or this rock, we come to learn things about trees, horses, and rocks in general. As we will see more clearly when we study his epistemology, Aristotle assumes all along this know-ability of the world.

Our world, finally, is a moral one, and this fact has two important consequences. First of all, the practice of virtue, which for Aristotle means living "according to reason," will really lead to the "good life," and folly will really bring failure. Second, morality can be derived from nature. That is to say, what ought to be the case (ethics/morality) is derived from what is the case (metaphysics/being). Aristotle will tell us, for example, that we ought to devote our leisure to the use of reason and the acquisition of wisdom. Why? Because man by nature is a rational animal. We share all our other characteristics with other creatures, save our reason. Thus, argues Aristotle, reason is understood as the perfection of the other qualities of man and should be developed. In short, for Aristotle, abilities imply obligations.

Epistemology: What Is Truth?

Aristotle's epistemology is widely known, and is captured famously in Raphael's masterpiece, *The School of Athens*. This painting, the reader will recall, depicts many of the famous philosophers of ancient Greece gathered variously in a large ambulatory. There are a good number of sages present, but the painting clearly draws our attention to the center, where Plato and Aristotle are walking, books in hand, engaged in philosophical dialogue.

There are a number of fascinating things about this painting, but two are of particular significance for us here. First, our two philosophers are carrying the books for which they were most noted during the Renaissance. Plato carries his dialogue *Timaeus*, while Aristotle holds the *Nicomachean Ethics*. Second, and more importantly, Plato and Aristotle are depicted in curious though significant postures. Plato stands looking to Aristotle with his index finger extended upward to the heavens. Aristotle,

returning the gaze, stands open-handed with fingers extended toward the ground.

With these images, Raphael brilliantly captures the profound distinction between Plato's and Aristotle's worldviews. Plato, believing this multifaceted and ever-changing world to be but a copy of the ideal realm, directs our attention toward the heavens to contemplate this unchanging and unified truth. Aristotle, on the other hand, understands this world, though given to multiplicity and change, to be the proper object of man's knowledge. He thus directs our gaze earthward towards the things around us.

Aristotle, in fact, is often called the philosopher of this world. He does not doubt that human beings have minds and souls, and that truth is eternal and unchanging. Yet he understands that we are irreducible complexes of body *and* soul, mind *and* matter, and that our theory of knowledge must take this into account. When we do, two things become clear immediately: all our knowledge is derived from, or somehow dependent upon, our senses; and we learn best by doing or making things ourselves. Philosophers often call the former type of knowledge *empirical* knowledge, while the latter is called *poetic* knowledge, from the Greek word *poesis* ("doing" or "making").

These two facts are the foci around which Aristotle's epistemology revolves. As such, his ethics are *inductive*—that is, his arguments seek to arrive at ethical principles by reasoning from observation, experience and tradition. This contrasts with the *deductive* reasoning of a discipline like geometry, which proceeds from general principles to understand *this* circle or *this* triangle.

Moreover, his ethics are based in poetic knowledge. The most important principles for ethics are "learned" by living virtuously. He claims at the beginning of his work, for example, that "the man who has been well brought up has or can easily get starting points" for ethical reasoning (Book I, chap. 4). In fact, for Aristotle, almost all of the starting points for the particular disciplines—he calls them first principles—are derived neither from deductive nor inductive reasoning, but from *intuition* (the name Aristotle gives to the process whereby we arrive at poetic knowledge). The discipline this applies to *par excellence* is ethics.

One final item we must discuss here is Aristotle's notion about the limits of certainty. He assumes in the *Nicomachean Ethics* that goodness itself is objective: good is simply good and bad is simply bad. He notes, however, that the knowledge we gain about it through reasoning is only *probable*—it is only true *for the most part*, or *to a point*. By reasoning about it, we cannot have complete certainty whether an action is good or bad.

Why not? Aristotle explains that there are two ba-

Nicomachean Ethics

In *The School of Athens* Italian painter Raphael (1483–1520) brilliantly captures the profound distinction between Plato's and Aristotle's worldviews. Plato points heavenward to the realm of the ideals while Aristotle, holding a copy of his *Nicomachean Ethics,* directs our gaze toward the earth and the things around us.

sic ways of reasoning through an argument: *deduction,* reasoning *from* first principles; and *induction,* reasoning *to* first principles. The former kind of reasoning, which is the domain of mathematics and geometry, results in certain conclusions. The latter kind of reasoning, which is that of the rhetorician, does not arrive at certainty, but results only in more or less probable conclusions.

Now our first reaction may be to identify Aristotle as some kind of proto-relativist who thinks there are no absolute standards of right and wrong. But this would miss his point entirely. Keep in mind that Aristotle is not working from the standpoint of the revealed Word of God. He does not have any *certain* principles from which to base his argument, no sure guide in all matters of faith and practice. For Aristotle, moral and ethical principles are neither revealed (like the *Decalogue*) nor rationally self-evident (like the fact that the whole is greater than the parts) but passed down from one generation to the next and contained in the wisdom of the sages and poets. This tradition is a real mixed bag, so he acknowledges at the outset of his argument the limitations any of his conclusions will have.

Interestingly, this is also the context for his discussion of poetic knowledge. He notes that it is only the person who develops good moral habits and lives righteously who will be able to recognize ethical truth when he encounters it. Hence Aristotle encourages a life lived in humility and respect for tradition and the wisdom of previous generations.

Aristotle concludes that "it is the mark of an educated man to look for precision in each class of things just so far as the nature of the subject admits" (Book I, chap. 3). His entire work, therefore, will proceed carefully by considering the wisdom of older generations, the sayings of other philosophers, and the customs of Athens. He will consider these sources of ethical wisdom like a scientist: analyzing the data, testing hypotheses, and attempting to arrive at general conclusions.

Ethics: How Should We Live?

Aristotle speaks of man as being a political animal by nature. Humans are relational, and in a profound sense are not fully human unless they are living in community with other people. As Greeks living prior to the revelation of Jesus Christ, philosophers like Plato and Aristotle have no higher aspirations than to live well within the Greek *polis,* or city-state. Aristotle's ethics are the first part of his politics—he says as much in the first book of the *Nicomachean*

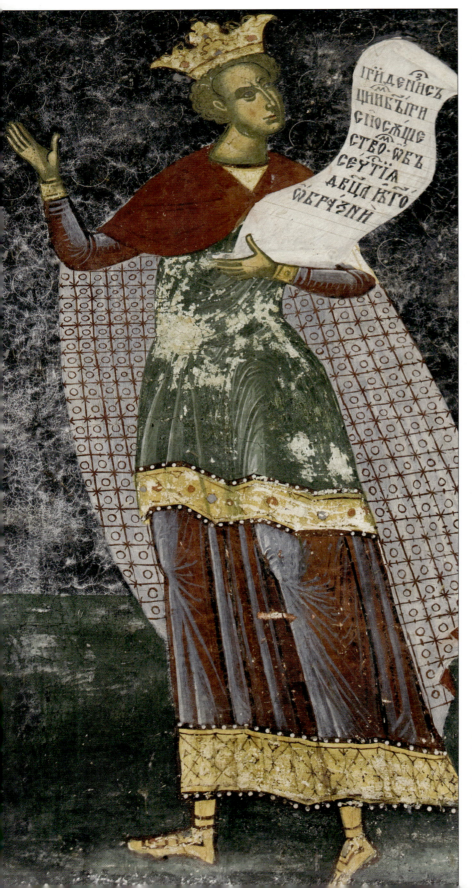

Ethics—and Plato's celebrated *Republic* presents the well-ordered society as the goal of philosophy. Ethics, then, is the goal of personal formation and one of man's most important studies.

It may strike the Christian reader that Aristotle saw man's highest goal as living the good life within the *polis*, for we know rightly that man was created for fellowship with God the Father and Son, and with each other, through the power of the Holy Spirit. It is a great shame that Aristotle and Plato, to use St. Paul's words from Acts 17, were left to grope in the darkness after the truth of God. We should, however, note the profound truth that Aristotle understood concerning man.

Although Aristotle completely lacks the concept of creation, and the particular emphasis of man's being created in God's image, he does nevertheless perceive the inherent dignity of man. Man, for him, is an animal endowed with reason, and as such his actions have both purpose and gravity. Among living beings, man is unique in the fact that his actions have a moral quality, and render him liable to praise or blame.

Now thoughtful Christians disagree as to the virtue of Aristotle's view of man. Many have argued that he thought of man as an autonomous being, and was actually at fault for attempting to build his philosophy on the basis of reason apart from his religion. But this is to fail to understand Aristotle's context. The ancient Greek religion was, as we noted above, an inconsistently compiled set of what is at best corrupt human tradition, and at worst demonic ritual. In the most profound sense, then, the turn to reason and

Christian thought about ethics has been greatly influenced by Aristotle. This painting of "the Philosopher" from the Middle Ages can be found in the Sucevita monastery church in Romania.

philosophy from pagan mythology as a means to living justly was actually an affirmation of the dignity of man made in God's image.

We do not know how Aristotle would have responded to the Word of God proclaimed by the apostles and prophets if he could have heard it. What we do know, however, is that many who sought the truth in philosophy rather than pagan Greek mythology received the word of the apostles and evangelists gladly when in the fullness of time they did hear the gospel preached.

Furthermore, Aristotle did not have the concept of faith and righteousness we have as Christians. He did, however, think that man's happiness lay in living virtuously and acting justly. In fact, he contends in chapter 8 of Book One that man's happiness is contingent both on *performing* just actions and in *taking pleasure* in performing just actions. That is, he thought both man's outward acts and his inward disposition to be significant in moral actions. This is quite in line with the biblical teaching about the law.

Taken as a standard of life, Aristotle is certainly wanting. He fails to comprehend the most fundamental truths of man's origin and his destiny in Christ. He does, however, express profound truths and remarkable insights about human nature. We will close our discussion of his worldview by examining a few of his most significant ideas.

First, Aristotle perceived that man acts *teleologically*; that is, all of man's actions are directed towards attaining some end. This comes as no surprise; a rational creature would, after all, think about what he was going to do before he did it. But Aristotle takes it further. He says that simple reflection shows us that most of these "goals" are themselves mere means to another end. Unless we are going to retract our first premise and say that all our actions are merely an endless chain of getting to the next purposeless cog, we have to admit there is some *telos*, or goal, toward which we *ultimately* direct all our actions. This goal Aristotle terms the "good of man" and identifies it as *eudaimonia,* a Greek word that has been translated variously as "happiness," "the good life," and "flourishing."

In any case, man is moving toward a goal, and this goal is his own good, the perfection of his natural inclinations. This brings us to the second point: Aristotle's ethics are grounded in nature. Man has a concrete nature—he is a rational animal—and according to that nature he is proceeding to the ultimate goal (*telos*) of the good life (*eudaimonia*). There is, therefore, a right way and a wrong way to achieve this goal, and this will be determined, argues Aristotle, by reflection upon man's nature.

Man is a rational animal, and thus his happiness must address man as both an animal and a rational being. As we read his argument we will see that man must

have a certain degree of health, companionship, possessions, and wealth in order to be happy. Who could be happy, he asks, if he were starving? And yet man's purpose is not located merely in material or bodily goods. His goal is to live according to reason, and this means living virtuously.

But how are we to live reasonably? Virtuously? How are we to discern between right and wrong? Aristotle answers these questions, all the while maintaining the antithesis between right and wrong, and still allowing for the use of reason and discernment by his famous *Doctrine of the Mean*. In Book Two, chapters 6–9, he formulates a standard for judging between virtue and vice, but he does so not by proposing a set of timeless, absolute laws. Rather, he argues that virtuous living takes wisdom and prudence—the ability to discern the proper action with respect to the circumstance and the motivation.

Right actions, he maintains, are those that stand as an intermediate point between two extremes: an extreme of *excess* and an extreme of *deficiency*. With respect to the giving and taking of money, for example, Aristotle notes that both miserliness (hoarding money) and prodigality (careless indulgence) are vices. Miserliness is a vice of deficiency with respect both to the acquisition and the use of money, whereas prodigality is a vice of excess in the same category. The virtuous use of money—what Aristotle calls *liberality*—is the reasonable mean between these extremes. For the man possessed of liberality neither hoards nor carelessly spends, for he knows by the prudence gained from experience when to save and when to spend.

—*Kevin W. Clark*

For Further Reading

Adler, Mortimer J. *Aristotle for Everybody.* New York: Macmillan Publishing, 1978

Copleston, F.C., "Aristotle's Ethics," in chapter xxxi of *History of Philosophy*, volume 1, New York: Doubleday, 1993. 332–350.

Hutchinson, D.S., "Ethics," in *The Cambridge Companion to Aristotle.* New York: Cambridge University Press, 1995. 195–232.

MacIntyre, Alasdair, *A Short History of Ethics.* Second Edition. South Bend, Ind.: University of Notre Dame Press, 1998.

Spielvogel, Jackson J. *Western Civilization.* Seventh Edition. Belmont, Calif.: Thomson Wadsworth, 2009. 80–82.

Veritas Press History Cards: New Testament, Greece and Rome. Lancaster, Pa: Veritas Press. 15.

Session I: Prelude

A Question to Consider

What is the "good life"?

From the General Information above, answer the following questions:
1. What does the term *teleological* mean?
2. Toward what goal does Aristotle think all of man's thoughts and actions are directed?
3. What is the good toward which all men are striving?
4. What are the main things people identify with happiness?
5. What does Aristotle identify as true happiness; that is, what does he think is the good life?
6. In what ways is the Doctrine of the Mean similar to biblical teaching about ethics, and in what ways is it different?

 **Reading Assignment:** *Nicomachean Ethics*, Book I

Session II: Discussion
Nicomachean Ethics, Book I

A Question to Consider

What is happiness?

Discuss or list short answers to the following questions:

Text Analysis
1. What is Aristotle's initial (basic) definition of the "good"?
2. What is more noble than securing the good for a single man?
3. Why is a young man not equipped to be a student of politics?
4. What is the "common" or "vulgar" definition of the good?
5. In Book One, chapter 7, Aristotle arrives at a definition of the "ultimate" or "final" good. What is it?
6. In Book One, chapter 7, Aristotle defines the "proper function of man." What is his definition of the proper function of man?

Cultural Analysis
1. What relationship does our culture believe exists between virtue and happiness? Does our culture tend to think that virtue is essential to happiness?
2. Aristotle's conception of "politics" is entirely and radically different than ours. Aristotle views politics as a "master science." For him, it is a reflection on the totality of human relationships—a view of human activity from "above." This means that in order to do "politics," one must also have a complete account of the nature of man. Modern politics certainly doesn't operate this way. How is our conception of politics different than Aristotle's?

Biblical Analysis
1. What does Ecclesiastes 12:13-14 say about the "chief end" of man?
2. Proverbs 4:18-19 seems to suggest the opposite of the "subjectivist" view of happiness. Why can't the "wicked" be truly happy according to these verses?

Summa

Write an essay or discuss this question, integrating what you have learned from the material above.
Why must happiness be more than a feeling if we are to arrive at a notion of happiness that makes happiness relevant to virtue?

The next session will be a student-led discussion. Students will be creating their own questions concerning the issue of the session. Students should create three Text Analysis Questions, two Cultural Analysis questions, and two Biblical Analysis questions. For more detailed instructions, please see the chapter on the *Iliad*, Session III.

Issue

The role of habituation—continually repeating right acts—in the acquisition of virtue.

 **Reading Assignment:** *Nicomachean Ethics*, Book. II

Session III: Student-Led Discussion
Nicomachean Ethics, Book. II

A Question to Consider

What role do good habits play in the acquisition of virtue?

Students should read and consider the example questions

below that are connected to the Question to Consider above. Last session's assignment was to prepare three questions and answers for the Text Analysis section and two additional questions and answers for both the Cultural Analysis and Biblical Analysis sections below.

Text Analysis

Example: Aristotle divides virtue into two basic categories. What are they?

Answer: Aristotle divides virtue into intellectual and moral (character) virtue (I.13).

Cultural Analysis

Example: What are some of the virtues that our culture considers most important if we are to be "good" or "moral" human beings?

Answer: Our culture has gone through a profound change recently. Whereas biblical, Judeo-Christian virtues once formed the basis for our view of moral human action, today more secular attitudes have pushed for value-neutral virtues (civic virtues) that might replace the explicitly moral ones provided by the Judeo-Christian tradition. Fairness, tolerance, conservation, and empathy are examples of virtues considered to be sufficiently value-neutral (they don't seem to depend upon any religious tradition and are therefore suitable to teach in public schools and to espouse in the context of the promotion of secular values). Interestingly, our culture has also abandoned classical virtues because they—although they are not biblical—rely on a truth outside of the subjective.

Biblical Analysis

Example: In chapter 4 of Book Two, Aristotle talks about the importance of self-control to a life of virtue. What do the following passages suggest about the importance of self-control to a life devoted to holiness and virtue: 1 Thessalonians 5:6–8; Titus 2:12; 1 Peter 1:13, 4:7, 5:8?

Answer: Self-control helps us be alert and live "in the daylight." Those who do not possess self-control are not vigilant (as the sleeping metaphor suggests), and therefore they are not actively thinking about how to please Christ (see 2 Corinthians 10:4–5). Those who are self-controlled, however, can be vigilant and are capable of reflecting on their actions and testing them to see if they conform to the pattern of virtue laid out in the New Testament.

READING ASSIGNMENT:
Nicomachean Ethics, Book III

The incontinent man, according to Aristotle, is one whom passion masters so that he cannot act rightly. He is able to reflect on his actions and thus is better than the self-indulgent man, who stubbornly sticks to his vices.

Session IV: Recitation
Nicomachean Ethics, Books I–III

Comprehension Questions
Answer the following questions for factual recall:
1. What is the definition of the good with which Aristotle opens his *Nicomachean Ethics*?
2. According to Aristotle, what is the "master science of the good"?
3. What is the "common" or "vulgar" notion of happiness?
4. According to Aristotle's definition of happiness, happiness is an activity of the soul in conformity with what?
5. Aristotle divides virtue into two basic categories. What are they?
6. Aristotle suggests that virtue is a mean between what two things?
7. According to Aristotle, we should treat what in the same way that the elders of the Trojans treated Helen?
8. What is Aristotle's definition of choice?
9. According to Aristotle, if we leave the appetites unchecked, they will ultimately push what aside?

Reading Assignment:
Nicomachean Ethics, Book IV

Session V: Aesthetics
Art Analysis

In this session, you will get to know a particular piece of art related to our reading. It is our job as believers to be able praise, love, and protect what is true, beautiful, and good and to condemn, hate, and oppose all that is false, ugly, and evil. This task is often harder than one might think. We must discipline ourselves first to examine and understand artwork reflectively. After we understand the content of a piece, we can examine the author's intention concerning the piece and attempt to figure out what it is communicating. Sometimes this will be easy; other times it will be difficult or nearly impossible. Finally, we need to make judgments about what this work of art communicates.

Sometimes we will be able to clearly condemn a work of art as untrue, badly done, or wicked.

Sometimes we will be able to praise a work as glorious, majestic, and true. Oftentimes, however, we will find ourselves affirming some parts of a work and condemning others. Remember, maturity is harder than immaturity—but also more rewarding. Also, remember that our praise or condemnation means more when we have disciplined ourselves first to reflect on the content and meaning of a work.

Washington Crossing the Delaware

This is an oil painting (on canvas) completed in 1851. The painting commemorates a now-famous event in American lore: Washington's crossing of the Delaware River on Christmas Day, 1776. Like many nineteenth-century paintings, the artist wanted the painting to convey a political message through the depiction of an important moment in history. Leutze hoped to encourage liberal reforms in Europe (the proposed reforms following the revolutions of 1848) through the influence of the painting. This is clear from the aesthetic license he took. The real crossing took place in the dead of night during a driving snowstorm. Leutze, however, uses light to convey a message about Washington's role in bringing about a new dawn of hope and freedom. In the original painting, the morning star is just barely visible above Washington. This would obviously suggest a Christmas theme. Those following Washington are like the wise men following the morning star to find the Christ child. This makes Washington a Christ-like figure—a figure through whom a radical transformation of the world takes place. This "soft messianism" is common in many of the political paintings in the nineteenth century. The painting is of interest to us as we study Aristotle because it nicely depicts Washington as a man of courage clearly motivated not by rashness and violent warmongering but by reflective prudence and self-control.

Emanuel Gottlieb Leutze was born May 24, 1816, in Germany. His parents moved to the United States when he was a child, but Leutze would later return to Germany as an adult. After studying painting in Germany and living in Dusseldorf for fourteen years, Leutze would return to the United States where he lived until his death in Washington, D.C. in 1868.

Technical Analysis
1. Does the work demonstrate the artist's ability and expertise? Explain.
2. Does the work have balance and symmetry? What is the central or most important element of this work (to what are your eyes most attracted)?
3. How do you think the author is using light to convey a message?

Subject Analysis
1. If you look closely, it is possible to pick out different kinds of characters (wearing quite diverse kinds of clothing). What do you think Leutze is trying to communicate through this device?

Content Analysis
1. Describe the scene. What is happening?

Washington Crossing the Delaware by Emanuel Gottlieb Leutze (1816–1868) commemorates the opening move of Washington's famous surprise attack against Hessian troops in Trenton, New Jersey.

2. Aristotle goes to great pains to distinguish between true courage and what often passes as courage but is merely rashness. The key element is prudence or practical wisdom. Does the painting strike you (especially Washington as the key figure in the painting) as reflecting an Aristotelian picture of courage?

The next session will be a student-led discussion. Students will create their own questions concerning the issue of the session. Students should create three Text Analysis Questions, two Cultural Analysis questions, and two Biblical Analysis questions. For more detailed instructions, please see the chapter on the *Iliad,* Session III.

Issue

How does the concept of justice relate to individuals and communities?

Reading Assignment:
Nicomachean Ethics, Book V

Session VI:
Student-Led Discussion
Nicomachean Ethics, Book V

A Question to Consider

Is justice an inherently social concept—in other words, does justice refer primarily to individuals or primarily to relationships between individuals in the context of a concrete community?

Text Analysis

Example: In Book Five, chapter 5, Aristotle treats the question of reciprocity. He suggests that reciprocity (proportionate return) is what "holds the city together." What has been introduced, according to Aristotle, to make reciprocal (proportionate) exchange possible in the city-state?

Answer: Aristotle argues that money has been introduced in order to provide a reciprocal relationship between

For seven years as a teenager Alexander the Great received a direct education from Aristotle, who was his tutor in science and politics.

goods so that exchange is proportionate to the value of the good. For example, the number of shoes exchanged in payment for the building of a house should be proportionate to the value of the shoes in relation to the value of a house (V.5).

Cultural Analysis

Example: As with Plato in the dialogue *Gorgias*, Aristotle argues that it is far better to suffer injustice than to commit injustice. What would our culture say about this? Also, consider the following scenario: what if one commits an injustice to avoid suffering an injustice?

Answer: Our culture thinks it is worse to suffer an injustice than to commit an injustice. This is why we would forgive one for committing an injustice in order to avoid suffering one. This is because we have placed the value of the temporal higher than the value of the eternal. Consider someone cheating on a college entrance exam because the college had traditionally practiced racial discrimination when it came to selection. This might seem justified, but why? Clearly the soul is not considered. If the soul is harmed more by committing injustice than by suffering it, then it would follow that we would consider the eternal state (the corruption of the soul) against the temporal benefit gained from cheating on the exam (getting into the college). The important thing is that one cannot exchange the soul for anything (Matt. 16:26).

Biblical Analysis

Example: In Book Five, chapter 7, Aristotle says that some people believe that all forms of justice are merely a form of convention. In other words, there is nothing that is "just by nature," but only what is "just by convention." This would mean that justice is relative—it would be relative to the laws of the state. In other words, justice would simply be whatever each society (and possibly what each person) says is just. There would be no standard against which to compare what justice is. What does Proverbs 29:26 say about the nature of justice?

Answer: According to Proverbs 29:26, justice does not flow from men but from God. He is the author of justice. This would mean there is a divine standard of justice beyond the merely human standards of rulers. There is what Aristotle would have referred to as a "natural" justice that is beyond human convention. Of course, the biblical view is not that it is "natural" (having its origins in the structure of nature), but that it exists as an extension of God's nature (having its origins in the structure of God's nature). This is the personal dimension of justice that distinguishes a Christian view of natural law from pagan conceptions. Even Christian natural law traditions suggest that the structure of nature reflects the structure of God, the author of nature.

Reading Assignment:
Nicomachean Ethics, Book VI

Session VII: Writing

Progymnasmata: Chreia

This session is a writing assignment. Remember, quality counts more than quantity. You should write no more than 1,000 words, either typing or writing legibly on one side of a sheet of paper. You will lose points for writing more than this. You will be allowed to turn in your writing three times. The first and second times you turn it in, your teacher will grade it by editing your work. This is done by marking problem areas and making suggestions for improvement. You should take these suggestions into consideration as you revise your assignment. Only the grade on your final submission will be recorded. Your grade will be based on the following criteria: 25 points for grammar, 25 points for content accuracy—historical, theological, etc.; 25 points for logic—does this make sense and is it structured well?; 25 points for rhetoric—is it a joy to read?

What is a *chreia*? A chreia is an ancient rhetorical form used to examine and unfold a wise saying or deed. It is an excellent way to explore the depths of riches in a pithy quotation. The French have a phrase, *les juste mots,* which means "exactly the right word or expression." Sometimes great sayings are very compact and use just the right words. But the saying might be profound enough that it cannot be appreciated without exploring it in greater detail. The chreia is an excellent vehicle for exploring a profound saying.

A typical chreia is composed of the following eight parts:
1. Panegyric: Praise of the speaker.
2. Paraphrastic: Retelling the saying in your own words.
3. From the cause: Explaining what caused the person to say what he did.
4. From the contrary: Explaining what would happen if the opposite of the saying or action would occur.
5. Analogy: Likening the saying or action to something else, usually something more concrete and easier for people to understand (e.g., "Education is like a farmer planting his crops in hope of the harvest"). It has to be general and not pointed at one specific person.
6. Example: Likening the saying or action to a saying or action of another person.
7. Testimony of the ancients: Quoting a sage person from the past who testifies to this same truth.
8. Epilogue: Summing up the chreia.

In this writing assignment you will do the following parts: 1, 2, 4, 5, 7, 8 (omit 3 and 6). If you desire, you may do all eight. A typical chreia is not long-winded. Each of the sections is very brief and to the point.

Assignment

Write your own chreia using the six parts listed above. Remember to keep it concise. When you are finished, read it out loud to your class (or your parents and siblings). A good chreia will do two things: (a) it will help the audience to understand the quotation, and (b) it will make the audience want to read more from the author you've quoted. Use the following quotation from Book VI of the *Nicomachean Ethics* as the starting point for your chreia. Have fun!

Quotation: "It follows that in the general sense also the man who is capable of deliberating has practical wisdom." —Aristotle, *Nicomachean Ethics* VI.5

Reading Assignment:
Nicomachean Ethics, Book VII

Session VIII: Discussion
Nicomachean Ethics, Book VII

A Question to Consider
What is "moral strength"?

Discuss or list short answers to the following questions:

Text Analysis
1. According to Aristotle, what was Socrates' position on "incontinence," or moral weakness?
2. Why is an incontinent man curable, but a self-indulgent man incurable?
3. Why can a man not have both practical wisdom and incontinence at the same time and in relation to the same action?
4. What are the three basic views of pleasure to which Aristotle is responding?
5. Why does Aristotle think that "simplicity" and "goodness" are synonymous?

Cultural Analysis
1. What attitude does our culture have toward pleasure?
2. Does our culture conflate passion and incontinence? Or do we correctly distinguish between them?

Biblical Analysis
1. What does the following passage suggest happens to the incontinent—"Whoever has no rule over his own spirit is like a city broken down, without walls" (Prov. 25:28)?
2. Reading the following verses together and reflecting upon them, what conclusion should a Christian come to regarding the importance of self-control (continence) if one is to pursue righteousness (1 Thess. 5:6–8; 1 Pet. 1:13; 5:8)?

Summa

Write an essay or discuss this question, integrating what you have learned from the material above.
How could someone in your setting pursue "moral strength"?

Reading Assignment:
Nicomachean Ethics, Books VIII–IX

Session IX: Recitation
Nicomachean Ethics, Books IV–VII

Comprehension Questions
Answer the following questions for factual recall:
1. With respect to wealth or money, what are the two excesses and deficiencies? What is the mean?
2. In Book Four, chapter 3 Aristotle says that something is the "crown of the virtues." What does he suggest seems to be the crown of the virtues?
3. Which of all the virtues is thought to be "another's good"?
4. In Book Five, chapter 5 Aristotle suggests that some aspect of justice "holds the city together." What aspect of justice holds the city together?
5. In Book Five, chapter 7 Aristotle divides justice into two basic forms. Explain the two forms and the difference between them.
6. In Book Six, chapter 1 Aristotle distinguishes between two basic kinds of virtues. What are the two basic categories of virtues?
7. Why, according to Aristotle, is practical wisdom not a "science" or an "art"?
8. In Book Six, chapter 12 Aristotle talks about the relationship between (moral) virtue and practical wisdom. Explain that relationship.
9. According to Aristotle, a self-indulgent man is different than an incontinent man. What is the chief difference (VII.8)?
10. What are the three views of the relationship of pleasure to the good (or virtue) to which Aristotle is going to respond (VII.11)?

Reading Assignment:
Nicomachean Ethics, Book X

Session X: Evaluation
All tests and quizzes are to be given with an open book and a Bible available.

Grammar
Answer each of the following questions in complete sentences. Some answers may be longer than others. (3 points per answer)
1. According to Aristotle, why is a young man not equipped to be a student of "politics"?
2. According to Aristotle, virtue is a mean. It is a mean between what two things?

3. What is the "common" or "vulgar" definition of the good?
4. Why is an incontinent man curable but a self-indulgent man incurable?
5. Identify the two basic forms of justice and the chief difference that distinguishes them.

Logic

Demonstrate your understanding of Aristotle's Nicomachean Ethics. Answer the following question in complete sentences; your answer should be a paragraph or so. Answer three of the four questions. (10 points per answer)

1. Briefly explain why it is better to suffer injustice than to commit it. Do you agree with Aristotle's conclusion?
2. Explain why all forms of justice cannot be merely "conventional." In other words, why must there be a justice based on absolute truth rather than the traditions of particular cultures which is "just by nature" or is objectively just?
3. Aristotle suggests that human beings have a "proper function" in relation to which their happiness will be determined. If they fulfill their "proper function," they can achieve happiness. If not, they cannot. Briefly describe Aristotle's notion of the "proper function of man."
4. Why, according to Aristotle, is practical wisdom not a science or art?

Lateral Thinking

Answer one of the following questions. These questions will require more substantial answers. (40 points per answer)

1. In Book Four, chapter 3 Aristotle discusses the mean of high-mindedness or pride and the deficiency of slavish flattery and the excess of haughtiness or vanity. The Greek word for this virtue is *megalapsuchia* and the Latin is *magnanimity.* They both can be translated as "greatness of soul." This is often referred to as "proper pride." On Aristotle's aristocratic account of virtue, "proper pride" is an essential quality of the great and virtuous man. However, this virtue seems to be at odds with the virtue that St. Augustine argues makes men like angels. St. Augustine argues that humility is the virtue that Christians must have in order to become Christ-like. St. Chrysostom agrees with St. Augustine on this matter. He says the following: "Humility is the root, mother, nurse, foundation and bond of all virtue." These great church fathers are only echoing Scripture (see Proverbs 11:2; 15:33; Philippians 2:3; Titus 3:2; 1 Peter 5:5; Matthew 18:4, 23:12). Do you think that "proper pride" (as Aristotle describes it) is compatible with the Christian emphasis upon humility as the "bond" and "foundation" of the virtues?

2. In Book Ten, chapters 7–8 Aristotle suggests that the highest happiness for men must correspond to an activity in accord with what is highest in men. On Aristotle's account of the soul, the highest in man is the fully rational element of the soul. For this reason, contemplation is the highest form of happiness, and this would mean that a life lived in contemplation (as far as possible) would be the happiest kind of life. This kind of activity is, according to Aristotle, "divine activity." It is a "divine life." However, human beings cannot attain to a "divine life" because they are not completely rational. Thus, the closest that men can come to complete happiness is to live a life that closely resembles a divine life. This account of happiness necessarily would make it impossible for most of humanity to live a life we would call "happy" or "blessed." This aristocratic view of happiness depends heavily upon an excellent education and a life not overly cluttered by practical affairs. In short, this is a life of leisure. Is this view compatible with a Christian notion of happiness? Are their points at which we might recognize divergences between the two?

OPTIONAL SESSION A: WRITING

Aristotle's Fables

Create a fable to illustrate a theme from *Nicomachean Ethics.* A fable is an imaginary story used to teach a moral. Fables use animals to represent a variety of characteristics. There is a correspondence between the animal and a particular virtue or vice. For instance, a rooster might be used to represent a sort of strutting, self-satisfied pride, and a fox might be used to represent self-confident cunning. Using your imagination, create a beast-fable in order to represent some moral that Aristotle highlights in his *Nicomachean Ethics.* You will need to start with a proverbial statement of some form. Here is an example from *Aesop's Fables:*

TITLE
The Ass, the Rooster, and the Lion

PROVERB/MORAL
False confidence often leads into danger.

An Ass and a Rooster were in a straw-yard together when a Lion, desperate from hunger, approached the spot. He was about to spring upon the Ass, when the Rooster (to the sound of whose voice the Lion, it is said, has a singular aversion) crowed loudly, and the Lion fled away as fast as he could. The Ass, observing his trepidation at the mere crowing of a Rooster, summoned courage to attack him, and galloped after him for that purpose. He had run no long distance, when the Lion, turning about, seized him and tore him to pieces.

A good fable is often short and sweet. It also is very important that it is very clear. The relationship between the parts of the story, the characters and the proverb or moral should be very clear and obvious. It shouldn't take a lot of reflection to see the connection between the story and the proverb or moral. If you can't create a proverb from elements in *Nicomachean Ethics*, try using a proverb from the Book of Proverbs. However, be sure to use a proverb that confirms a point that Aristotle makes in *Nicomachean Ethics*.

OPTIONAL SESSION B: ACTIVITY

Historical Research

Do some research on your own, then write a 1,000-word essay on Aristotle's relationship to Alexander the Great. Include the following elements in your essay:

1. A hand-drawn map of Aristotle's world including the following: Athens, Sparta, Thebes, Macedonia, Persia.
2. Information on Philip II of Macedon and his relationship with Aristotle and Alexander.
3. The Lyceum. Use at least two resources to complete your work. Here are some suggestions:
    a) The Internet Encyclopedia of Philosophy can be found at Link 1 for this chapter at www.VeritasPress.com/OmniLinks.
    b) Volume I of Frederick Copelston's famous *History of Philosophy*.
    c) The General Introduction to your copy of *Introduction to Aristotle*.

ENDNOTES

1   I use the term *metaphysics* here because it is the one Aristotle used. The reader should be aware that some later philosophers use the term *ontology* to refer to the subjects we will study. There is good reason for this. Since we are addressing Aristotle specifically, however, I thought it best to retain Aristotle's own term for the subject.

2   *This note appears only in the teacher's edition.*

Poetics

Some years ago, our family gathered together in our living room to watch a comedy entitled *Throw Momma from the Train*. Our son Paul was 14, our daughter Joanna was 10, and our daughter Mary was seven. You might be wondering why a parent would let young children watch something entitled *Throw Momma from the Train*. I honestly cannot remember nor otherwise account for this lapse in parental judgment.

The movie is a comical take-off on Alfred Hitchcock's *Strangers on a Train*, in which two men agree to murder each other's nemesis. In this version, the character played by Danny DeVito throws the ex-wife of the Billy Crystal character off a cruise ship. In return, Billy Crystal will deal with Danny DeVito's mother—played by Anne Ramsey as the most overbearing, obnoxious, hateful, non-maternal mother of all time—by throwing her off of a train.

As this plot unfolded, the young daughters were getting rather disturbed. They had already witnessed one murder. And the storyline was building up to the climax promised in the title. Noticing their agitation, I said, "Don't worry. Nobody is going to die in this movie. Momma isn't going to get thrown off the train, and the lady that was thrown off the cruise ship is going to turn out not to be dead."

"How do you know?" they asked.

"Because Aristotle said that in a comedy no one is slain."

Sure enough, at the end of the movie, we learn that the woman we thought had been murdered had only fallen overboard and was living it up in a Polynesian island paradise. Far from throwing Momma off the train, Danny DeVito and Billy Crystal actually *prevent* her from falling off the train. The act of saving her life turns her into a loving mother. No one was hurt after all. And everyone lives happily ever after—especially me, having been proven right and having my parental authority restored.

Later, Joanna asked me, "How did Aristotle know that?"

What a good question. Aristotle had not seen *Throw Momma from the Train*, having been born some 2,400 years too soon. Even if he was somehow able to get hold of a copy, and even if he somehow had a television monitor, and if he had acquired an even more primitive playback device than the already primitive VHS tape player that we were using, there would have been no place in ancient Athens to plug it all in. And yet, Aristotle knew how this movie would end. Not only that, he knew what would happen in *all* comedies. How did he know?

I told her that Aristotle was talking about the nature of comedy. Comedy needs to be light-hearted enough to make us laugh. If someone were to be slain in a comedy, that would spoil the comic mood. Death is not funny. Death is tragic, which means that it belongs to the nature of tragedies. In comedies, the characters often *think* that bad things are happening, but they never are, really. Tragedies have sad endings, but comedies have happy endings.

Actually, there are some modern day comedies that violate Aristotle's principles. For example, *Weekend at Bernie's* is about two characters that carry around a dead body, a movie I watched but our children did not. That is an example of a "black comedy." Today, many people no longer believe in either Christianity or the ordered universe that Aristotle analyzes. They think that life has no meaning. So they think comedy is a way to show the absurdity of life. So people get killed in them.

The Greeks also believed that comedies should ridicule vice; but many comedies today instead ridicule virtue. This is because many people today no longer have a basis for morality and ignore the difference between right and wrong.

These modern comedies might make you laugh while they are going on, but they end up depressing us. I could tell that *Throw Momma from the Train*, despite the title, was a light-hearted comedy that was making fun of bad behavior. That made it more of a classical comedy. So I assumed that it would also follow Aristotle's rule about no one dying in a comedy.

I like to think that our conversation played a role in making Joanna the classicist she is today. She survived my parenting and grew up to become a classics major who today teaches Latin and the online Omnibus courses. She is even a contributor to this volume.

General Information

Author and Context

Aristotle was born in 384 B.C. in the city of Stagira. This was in Macedonia, about 30 miles from Thessalonica, to whom, much later, the apostle Paul would write his letters to the Thessalonians. When he was 17 or so, Aristotle went to Athens to study under Plato at his famed Academy. When Plato died 20 years later, Aristotle traveled in Asia (Minor) for a few years until his career took a new turn. King Philip of Macedon was looking for a teacher for his precocious but rather violent 13-year-old son. He wanted the best for his boy, so he hired Aristotle. Yes, Aristotle homeschooled Alexander the Great.

Alexander proved a worthy pupil. Later he would send his old teacher specimens of the exotic new animals and plants that he was discovering in the course of conquering the world. It is said that the two had a falling out toward the end of Alexander's life due to Aristotle's harsh scolding of his former student when he started claiming to be a god. You can expect your Omnibus teachers to do the same if you ever claim to be a god.

When Alexander became king in 336 B.C., Aristotle considered that a graduation and left for Athens. Here he founded a new school to rival Plato's Academy. He called it the Lyceum, after a nearby shrine to Apollo Lykeios—literally, Apollo the Wolf. It was located just outside the walls of Athens in a grove of trees. Aristotle's school included a temple to the Muses and a building with lecture rooms and a library. Classes, though, would be conducted outdoors, as the teacher would lecture and have dialectical conversations with his students as they walked around amidst the trees. For this reason, the students at the Lyceum were called *peripatetics*, from the Greek word for walking around.

There was a reason why Aristotle was not given leadership of the Academy after Plato's death and had to start his own school. Though Plato evidently followed and even extended the precepts of his teacher, Socrates, Aristotle found himself disagreeing with his teacher Plato. Plato was more interested in the realm of ideas. Aristotle was more interested in the realm of things.

Plato dismissed poetry—including myth, epic, tragedy, and comedy, which was known to skewer Socrates as in *The Clouds* by Aristophanes—as being untrue. For Plato, art was a mere imitation of an imitation, one step further away from the universal reality that resided in the purely abstract realm of the ideals. Aristotle, though, who believed that the universals inhere in particular examples, saw great value in poetry and in aesthetics.

He was writing at a time when Athenian drama had reached heights exceeded only in England at the time of Shakespeare. Aristotle knew the work of the great tragedians Aeschylus, Sophocles, and Euripides, all of whom had lived a century earlier. Each year the city continued to award vigorously-contested prizes for the best tragedies and comedies.

Aristotle wanted to think through how poetry worked and why stories, plays, and specifically tragedy can move us so deeply. He wrote the *Poetics* in 335 B.C., which would have been the first year of his Lyceum. If you find its style to be somewhat meandering, just remember that it was probably composed—or was possibly transcribed by his students—as he was walking among the trees.

When Alexander died in 323 B.C., Athenians found it safe to react against him and his supporters, including his old teacher. Aristotle found himself about to be legally accused of not sufficiently believing in the mythological gods. Though Socrates, faced with the same charge, stayed in Athens, accepted the verdict of his trial and drank the hemlock, Aristotle disagreed once more with Plato, who celebrated the submission of Socrates. Saying that he did not want the Athenians "to sin twice against philosophy," Aristotle fled the city. He died the next year, 322 B.C., at the age of 62.

Significance

According to the myth, Athena, the goddess of wisdom, was born when she sprang out of the head of her father Zeus, already fully grown and fully armed.

Western literature is that way, springing fully grown and fully armed out of the head of Homer. Evolutionists believe that complex organisms— including, presumably, literature— developed gradually out of simpler forms. And yet, the very first literary author that we have, writing the very first sustained, long, fictional poetic narratives, is still among our very greatest authors, and in the *Iliad* and the *Odyssey*, we see literary art already fully formed and at a level of quality few later works can measure up to.

Philosophy is that way too, only with two fully-armed intellectual warriors springing up as if from nowhere. Plato and Aristotle are still the two greatest philosophers, mighty adversaries yet kindred spirits like Achilles and Hector, with all other philosophers to come merely their minions or their feeble challengers.

And in the *Poetics* we have literary criticism springing fully grown and fully armed out of the head of Aristotle. This is the first essay on literary art, and it is still one of the best. It will give you tools—and a language—to help you understand the other Greek plays that you will read in Omnibus.

These plays and Aristotle's principles continued to shape European drama. An important strain of English drama—the academic plays of the Renaissance, the neoclassicism of Ben Jonson, the plays of the Restoration and the Enlightenment—continued this tradition. Much of the drama of the other European countries, especially France with its great playwrights such as Racine and Moliere, never strayed from the classical style. The only reason English-speakers have had more options is because

This bronze statue shows Athena with her shield. The owl on the shield denotes her wisdom.

of Shakespeare, who combined the multiple plotlines and narrative freedom of medieval drama—such as the biblical mystery plays—with the depth of character required by Aristotle.

Though Aristotle concentrates here on plays, what he has to say about plot and character applies also to other kinds of literature, including much later literary forms such as the novel. Aristotle was analyzing existing plays, but in doing so, he established principles that later playwrights and other authors would follow. The *Poetics* is also a model for later literary criticism. From scholars who analyze literature to film critics who review movies, they all owe a debt to Aristotle's *Poetics*.

Summary and Setting

Aristotle's method is usually to break down everything he considers into categories which themselves often get subdivided; he then analyzes each possibility in exhaustive detail. At one point in the *Poetics*, in a discussion of poetic diction, he breaks down language into its nouns and verbs, and then breaks those down into syllables and then letters—to not much effect, as far as we readers can tell! And yet, even while he seems lost in the woods, he tosses off observations about metaphorical language and how to create a poetic style that are incisive and priceless.

So you will get lost as you walk with Aristotle through the groves of Lyceum. Do not be discouraged. He is referring to a multitude of plays, most of which have been lost. If only the barbarians had not burned the library at Alexandria! Do not get bogged down with what you do not understand. Watch for what you do understand.

Keep in mind that when Aristotle refers to "poetry," he has in mind not so much lyric poetry, which expresses an emotion, but narrative poetry, which tells a story. Specifically, he is thinking of epics and the two kinds of plays that were performed in Athens, tragedy and comedy, both of which were written in verse. Thus, Aristotle comments on the various kinds of poetic meter. Remember too that Greek plays incorporated music and dance, especially with the chorus that sang and danced its parts. Thus, Aristotle comments on melody and rhythm.

Eventually, Aristotle gets around to his main topic: tragedy. He considers tragedy to be the highest form of literary art.

According to Aristotle, tragedy is better than epic because a play can be taken in at one sitting; as a result, the audience can better experience its *unity*, a major value in classical aesthetics. Longer works, such as epics or the later-to-be-invented novel, take many sessions to read. How long did it take you to read the *Odyssey*? That breaks up the work, taking away from the intensity of its effect. We can experience an entire play, television program, or movie, though, in a couple of hours. We can read the whole thing at one time, which is good to do when you read the Omnibus plays; as a result, we get the whole impact at once. Actually, the authors of longer works made up for this problem with unity by breaking up their stories into separate "books," as Homer did, and "chapters," as novelists did, each of which usually has a unity of its own and can be read in one sitting.

Tragedy is more serious and more noble—and thus "higher"—than comedy. In addition to saying that in comedy no one is slain at the end, Aristotle says that the characters of comedy are "worse than average." We are supposed to look down on the characters of classical comedy. Classical comedy ridicules vice. This distances the audience from their bad behavior. We shouldn't want to be like the Three Stooges or the Simpsons. We laugh at them, and our laughter is a kind of moral judgment. The characters of a tragedy, though, are better than average. We look up to them. We also care about them. That means they affect us more deeply.

Aristotle's typical mode of analysis is to zero in on the purpose of whatever he is examining. The purpose of tragedy, he says, is to create a "catharsis" of pity and fear. In other words, a story with a sad ending evokes in the members of its audience certain powerful emotions. And somehow, these emotions are cathartic, that is to say, cleansing.

Not being a fan of either roller coasters or horror movies, I have often asked people who are why they pay good money to get scared. It isn't pleasant to be afraid. Isn't fear a negative emotion, something we try to avoid? Perhaps a person is so courageous that it doesn't bother him to go hurtling along a winding track high in the air at great speed, sometimes even looping upside down. But I know that is not the case. When I go to amusement parks and watch the people who ride the roller coaster, I can hear them scream. And then, after they survive and the ride is over, I can hear the screamers say, "I want to do it again!" Evidently, fear, in this context, is enjoyable.

When roller coaster fans such as my wife try to explain the appeal, they talk about the "rush" of emotion and adrenaline that they find to be exhilarating. When the ride is over, they feel drained but elevated. It is cathartic.

A jump-out-of-your-seat horror movie can have that same effect. So can a tragedy. But Aristotle speaks of another kind of emotion that tragedy evokes: pity. When we see someone suffering, it is natural to feel pity for that person, to feel compassion. The more we know the person—a friend who has a death in the family; a family member who is hurt in an accident—the more compassion we feel.

Compassion is a "good feeling;" it is morally good. Strangely enough, compassion also feels good, even though it takes something bad—someone suffering—to bring it on. Compassion can also be cathartic, making us feel cleansed. Pity or compassion is a species of love. Jesus extends the claims of compassion. He says that we should have compassion not only for our friends but also for our enemies. More than that—since we at least know our enemies and have a strong emotional tie to them—Jesus wants us to have compassion on people we do not know but whom God brings into our lives, like the Samaritan did for the "neighbor" bleeding on the side of the road (Luke 10:25–37).

A successful tragedy makes us feel compassion for the characters who suffer. It is proof of our fallen nature that we sometimes find it easier to feel sorry for fictional characters—to get all teary-eyed over the fate of Bambi's mother or Old Yeller or the misunderstood musician who finally finds true love just as he dies of cancer—while being utterly callous about the actual suffering of the real human beings we encounter: the handicapped child that other kids make fun of; the World War II veteran in the nursing home; a member of your family who is hurting. Still, a work of fiction can help us cultivate positive emotions, training us to be more sensitive and compassionate, and thus play an important part in our moral formation.

So Aristotle determines that the purpose of tragedy is to give us a cleansing rush of pity and fear: pity for the hero, and fear for ourselves. We feel close to the hero and so sympathize with him in his suffering. We feel pity. But then we consider that his fate might be our own. That makes us afraid. Those emotions—one pulling us outside ourselves and the other forcing us to look inward—come together at once in a powerful and healthy emotional impact.

Having established that "end," that purpose, Aristotle then reasons backwards. What kind of hero does a tragedy need in order to make the audience feel such pity and fear at the point of the catastrophe? The hero cannot be purely evil, Aristotle reasons. When the bad guy in a movie gets killed, we don't feel pity or fear. We are glad. But the hero cannot be purely good, either. Here, Aristotle and the classical tradition start to differ from our modern sensibility. When the good guy in a movie gets killed, we may feel pity and fear, but we also feel frustrated and angry. When Teen Angel rushes back to the car to recover her boyfriend's high school ring only to get run over by a train, we feel cheated. It's not fair! Things like that shouldn't happen! Aristotle believed that a good tragedy needs to be satisfying. We need to think, "Yes, it's sad, but that's how it has to be."

Aristotle concludes that, to fulfill the purpose of tragedy to create in the audience a catharsis of pity and fear, the hero needs to be noble—having certain qualities that we admire and look up to—whose fall comes about because of some *hamartia*. This was traditionally rendered in English as a "tragic flaw." More modern translations have "mistake" or "error." But those of you who have studied New Testament Greek should recognize the word. In translations of the Bible, *hamartia* is the word for "sin."

Here the theologians and the literary critics should get together and learn from each other. "Sin" is not just a bad thing we do. "Sin" is our tragic flaw. It inheres in our fallen nature so that we keep hurting people we care about, spoiling things we touch, bringing disaster upon ourselves through our own fault. Conversely, the "tragic flaw" is more than just the hero's error or mistake. It is the hero's sin. The hero is not evil, as such; indeed, he usually has many virtues. The audience is on his side. But the hero has a sin. His character is flawed. His *hamartia* is what brings on the catastrophe, the tragic ending. Thus, he brings his downfall upon himself. He is responsible for what happens, as horrible as it is. This is what makes it so tragic.

Again, this classical perspective is different from the modern view of tragedy. We speak of "tragic accidents," as when an innocent person dies in a car wreck. Aristotle would say that such an event is unbearably sad, but it is not "tragic." If someone dies in a car wreck because he was drinking and driving, so that he was responsible for what happened, that would be tragic.

Many of today's sad stories and tear-jerking songs—including some that I have used as examples—are not really tragedies by Aristotle's standards. Bambi's mother dies because she is a deer, not because she has done anything wrong; the Teen Angel who runs back into the car when the train is coming is just being stupid. This is because our contemporary culture does not believe much in personal responsibility. All suffering is presented as accidental

A successful tragedy makes us feel compassion for the characters who suffer. It is proof of our fallen nature that we sometimes find it easier to feel sorry for fictional characters while being utterly callous about the actual suffering of the real human beings we encounter: the handicapped child that other kids make fun of; the World War II veteran in the nursing home; a member of your family who is hurting. A work of fiction can help us cultivate positive emotions and thus can play an important part in our moral formation.

Because Oedipus solves the Sphinx's riddle, the Thebans make him their king. This is one more link in the seemingly irresistible fate that leads to his ruin.

true. Such plays are dizzying in their irony, but watch for the hero's *harmartia*.

Notice too that classical tragedy uses "hero" somewhat differently than what we moderns do. We tend to think of "hero" as the good guy, who is opposed by the "villain," the bad guy. Heroes are handsome and wear white hats; villains are ugly and wear black hats. We do not necessarily know what the heroes do that is so good, nor why the villains are so evil. The conflicts are all external and symbolic. The characters tend to be simple and one-dimensional.

But when we go beyond Saturday morning cartoons or Hollywood blockbusters to truly great literature, the characters tend to be complex. There may well be an external conflict of good vs. evil, but the good guy may have some bad qualities that he has to overcome; the villain may have some good qualities. Or, perhaps more often, the conflict between good and evil takes place within the hearts of the characters.

In the classical literature of ancient Greece, to speak of a "hero" usually means the character who is flawed. This applies not only to tragedy but to epic as well. Achilles is the hero of the *Iliad*, but his wrath and injured pride are his flaws. He is the protagonist and Hector is his antagonist, but Hector is not evil. Rather, Hector is a complex character himself, nobly trying to protect his family while being too tolerant of his adulterous brother.

Aristotle says much more: about how plots must not just be one episode after another, but have a purposeful beginning, middle, and end; about how plots often turn upon some discovery; about how "spectacle" is the least artistic part of a drama. We can thus imagine what Aristotle would think about today's movies that have hardly any plot and superficial characters but lots of special effects.

Worldview

Aristotle lived several centuries before Christ, and he apparently knew nothing of the Jews. He did, however, believe in an orderly, meaningful universe. As such, he has often been treated as an ally of Christianity. For example, in the Middle Ages, the Roman Catholic scholar Thomas Aquinas made Aristotle's philosophical system the founda-

because life is absurd and we are all passive victims of our environment. Thus, even stories that could be tragic because the hero brings the downfall on himself because of a sin—say, a drama about someone dying of AIDS contracted because of immoral behavior—are presented as meaningless accidents happening to an innocent victim.

The principle that the tragic hero is responsible for his downfall holds true even for classical dramas in which the events seem determined by an irresistible fate. Oedipus is trying to escape the oracle's prophecies, but it is his own hot temper and his pride that make the prophecies come

tion of his whole theology. For Aquinas, Aristotle accounts for what can be known by reason. This is complementary to what can be known only by revelation.

Aquinas used Aristotelian arguments for his proofs of the existence of God. Aristotle argued that the universe had to have a "first cause." He also argued that the universe had to have a "final cause," that is, a purpose, a design, and thus a designer. Aristotle had no conception of a personal God, but for Aquinas, that knowledge is supplied by the revelation of Scripture. Aristotle's analysis of morality became the foundation for what would be described as "natural law," the rational proofs for the moral law. The purpose of sex in its biological design is the engendering of new life. Therefore, sex outside of marriage and potential parenthood is wrong. Aquinas's theology with his Aristotelian methods became, more or less, the official position of the Roman Catholic Church and is called Thomism.

The Reformers took issue with the way the medieval church exalted Aristotle as an authority, in effect, on a par with Scripture. For example, Aristotle's distinction between "substance" and "accidents" became the basis for the Roman Catholic teaching about transubstantiation in the Lord's Supper, the belief that the bread and wine on the altar is changed into the physical body and blood of Jesus Christ. More importantly, Aristotle's confidence in the human will and human virtues downplayed sin and supported a works-righteousness that undermined the gospel of Christ.

In general, the Reformers considered that the medieval church's reliance on Aristotle was a manifestation of rationalism, that impulse that is not unknown among Protestants too, to think that we must understand everything perfectly with our limited minds, as opposed to trusting God's Word in faith. The Reformers believed not only in Scripture but in *sola Scriptura*, that the Bible *alone* is the only ultimate and infallible authority for doctrine and life. Luther called Aristotle a "many-headed serpent" whose influence must be purged from theology. Nevertheless, after excoriating Aristotle's writings on metaphysics, the soul, and ethics in his "Open Letter to the Christian Nobility," Luther writes, "I should be glad to see Aristotle's books on Logic, Rhetoric and Poetics retained."

And yet, it is evident that the *Poetics*, for all of its value, is not the work of a Christian. When Aristotle talks about the catharsis of pity and fear, he says that the value is in "purging" those emotions—that is, to get rid of them. We can see how it is helpful to purge ourselves of fear. Feeling vicarious fear can be a way to help us conquer that fear so as to become more courageous. But for many of the ancients, pity was also a feeling to overcome. You will not find much compassion in Homer—think of Odysseus mowing down the suitors—or in other Greek authors.

The pagan Greeks and Romans spoke of the four cardinal virtues: justice, self-control, courage, and prudence. You will find those everywhere in the literature, philosophy, and history of this great civilization. But, as Dante noted, they lacked the theological virtues: faith, hope, and love. They had no faith, being ignorant of Christ. They had no hope, assuming that all the dead descended into Hades, so that life itself ended in misery. With their tragic sense of life, no wonder they were so good at writing tragedies. And they had no love in the Christian sense. Yes, they would love their spouses and children and country. But they had little sense of *agape*, the love of the undeserving, the love of forgiveness and grace with which God loves us and which He expects us to extend to our neighbors.

Instead, their writings—whether epics or tragedies or philosophical discourses—often praise revenge and retaliation, and, while often lifting up hospitality, loyalty, and friendship, tend to be weak when it comes to compassion.

Pity was one of the few things Alexander the Great—leveler of cities, destroyer of kingdoms—never learned from Aristotle. But he could probably tell a very good story. And in his greatness and in his flaws, he made a very good tragic hero.

—*Gene Edward Veith*

> Martin Luther called Aristotle a "many-headed serpent" whose influence must be purged from theology. Nevertheless, he appreciated his books on Logic, Rhetoric, and Poetics.

For Further Reading

Adler, Mortimer. *Aristotle for Everybody*. New York: Touchstone, 1978.

Kaplan, Justin D., ed. *The Pocket Aristotle*. New York: Washington Square Books, 1958.

Rorty, A.O., ed. *Essays on Aristotle's Poetics*. Princeton, N.J.: Princeton University Press, 1992.

Spielvogel, Jackson J. *Western Civilization*. Seventh Edition. Belmont, Calif.: Thomson Wadsworth, 2009. 80–82.

Veritas Press History Cards: Old Testament, Ancient Egypt. Lancaster, Pa.: Veritas Press. 31.

Veritas Press History Cards: New Testament, Greece and Rome. Lancaster, Pa.: Veritas Press. 15, 17.

Session I: Prelude

A Question to Consider

How were dramas in Aristotle's time, both tragedies and comedies, similar to and different from dramas today? How might this affect our understanding of Aristotle's *Poetics*?

From the General Information above, answer the following questions:

1. Who was Aristotle's famous teacher?
2. Who was Aristotle's famous pupil?
3. What was the name of the school Aristotle founded, and how did he conduct his classes there?
4. Why is this work of Aristotle's called *Poetics* when it deals mostly with drama?
5. Briefly compare and contrast the overall philosophical approaches of Plato and Aristotle. How do their approaches affect their respective views of art, poetry, and drama?

Reading Assignment:
Poetics, chapters 1–7

Session II: Discussion
Poetics, chapters 1–7

A Question to Consider

What is your favorite movie or play? Why?

Discuss or list short answers to the following questions:

Text Analysis

1. Is Aristotle giving a descriptive (by examining different poems) or prescriptive (using language like "ought" and "should") account of poetry? How do you know which? How does this relate to his overall philosophical approach?
2. How does Aristotle compare and contrast tragedy or comedy? Which does Aristotle think is the superior form of drama, and why? Do you agree or disagree? Why?
3. How does epic poetry differ from tragedy? Why does Aristotle think that tragedy is superior to epic poetry?
4. How does Aristotle define tragedy?
5. What constitutes a well-formed plot, according to Aristotle?

Cultural Analysis

1. What do people today think makes a good movie or play?
2. Does everybody have the same standards for judging this question, or are they different? How do you know?

Biblical Analysis

1. The Bible contains beautiful poetry in the book of Psalms, e.g., Psalm 1 and 136. What are the major features of this Hebrew poetry, and is it in any way similar to any of the poetry Aristotle analyzes?
2. Does Hebrew poetry appeal to the heart or to the mind?
3. Are there any examples of drama, either comedy or tragedy, in the Bible? If so, what role does each one play (Ezek. 4)?

Summa

Write an essay or discuss this question, integrating what you have learned from the material above.

You might know a person who always says of the last play or movie that he or she watched, "This is the greatest movie ever!" What should we be looking for if we are to judge a work of art as great?

Reading Assignment:
Poetics, chapters 8–14

Session III: Discussion

Poetics, chapters 1–14

A Question to Consider

In *Poetics* chapter 10, Aristotle maintains that a simple plot or "story" is just a series of events, one following another, with no necessity attaching from previous events to subsequent events, and which contains no reversal of situation or recognition. A complex plot, on the other hand, does have this sort of necessity attaching to subsequent events (so he says), and does contain reversal and recognition. The key issue is whether subsequent events follow previous events in a merely *post hoc* ("after this") sort of way or a *propter hoc* ("because of this") sort of way. Can you think of any simple plots or "stories," as Aristotle describes them? What about any "complex plots?"

Discuss or list short answers to the following questions:

Text Analysis

1. According to Aristotle, how does poetry imitate life?
2. For Aristotle, must a piece of writing use verse in order for it to be considered poetry? Why or why not?
3. Tragedy is sometimes said to incorporate three "unities:" unity of action, unity of time, and unity of place. Does Aristotle "require" a tragedy to have all three? Which one or ones does he require?
4. Aristotle claims that human beings are by nature imitative creatures that delight in imitation. Why does he say this?
5. How does Aristotle distinguish between poetry and history?
6. What are the various parts of the performance of a Greek tragedy?
7. What are the four elements in a really good tragic plot, according to Aristotle?
8. Aristotle claims that pity and fear are the "pleasures" of tragedy. He says that this fear and pity arise in

Aristotle taught that comedy needs to be light-hearted enough to make us laugh. The Greeks believed that comedies should ridicule vice, but many comedies today instead ridicule virtue. This is because many people today no longer have a basis for morality and ignore the difference between right and wrong.

the audience during a good tragedy and should ideally result from the plot itself rather than from "spectacle"—i.e., the costume, the music, the scenery, etc. Why does he say this?

Cultural Analysis

1. How do contemporary tragedies compare to ancient Greek tragedies?
2. Does modern American culture seem bent toward tragedy or comedy?

Biblical Analysis

1. How does the worldview instantiated within ancient Greek tragedy differ from the Christian worldview?

Summa

Write an essay or discuss this question, integrating what you have learned from the material above.
Why were the Greek drama festivals so popular in ancient Greece?

Reading Assignment:
Poetics, chapters 15–21

Session IV: Discussion
Poetics, chapters 11–21

A Question to Consider

A good tragic plot is often compared to the tying and untying of a knot. Why or how is this a good metaphor for the plot in a good tragedy?

Discuss or list short answers to the following questions:

Text Analysis

1. What does Aristotle say about the role of choral songs in tragedy? Why?
2. What role do pity and fear play in the plot, according to Aristotle? Why?
3. How does Aristotle describe the tragic hero?
4. What are the six different kinds of Discovery that Aristotle points out?
5. Chapter 20 comprises a fairly rigorous analysis of language and its various parts. Why do you think Aristotle includes this here?

Cultural Analysis

1. Where do we see examples of catharsis in the movies and in plays today?
2. Do audiences today still look for the same qualities that Aristotle claimed should characterize the tragic hero?

Biblical Analysis

1. Identify two or three tragic figures in Scripture. Do they meet the requirements that Aristotle sets forth for a tragic hero? Why or why not?
2. According to the Scriptures is life tragic or comedic? How is this different for ancient pagans?

Summa

Write an essay or discuss this question, integrating what you have learned from the material above.
Can Aristotle help believers build excellent tragedies?

Reading Assignment:
Poetics, chapters 22–26

Session V: Activity
Create Your Own Tragedy

Today we will sketch out and outline our own tragedy. Remember the requirements that Aristotle has for tragedy. The goal is for our audience to reach a catharsis and be purged of their own feelings of fear and pity. Answer the questions below and create an outline of your own tragedy.

Create your hero with his tragic flaw
He needs to be a character with a good character with correspondingly good moral purpose. His good qualities should be appropriate for him, not for someone else. He must be realistic. He must act consistently, if only in his inconsistency. Hero goes from fortune to misfortune. The misfortune must be caused by *hamartia*, an error or character flaw. The hero's character must never be worse than that of the average person. So, what will your tragic hero be like?

Create a plot that focuses on one issue

Poetics 227

HOW WILL THE DISCOVERY OR RECOGNITION OCCUR?
Remember, there are basically six ways that this happens.
1. By means of signs or marks
2. That is contrived by the author
3. That is prompted by memory
4. Through deductive reasoning
5. Through faulty reasoning or speech on the part of a disguised character
6. That follows naturally and logically from the sequence of events in the play

HOW WILL THIS REVERSAL HAPPEN WITH YOUR TRAGIC HERO?

CREATE A CLIMAX
All plays have a point where the main issue of the play is resolved. How will this occur in your tragedy?

Optional Activity

FROM TRAGEDY TO COMEDY
What would be needed to change your tragedy into a Christian comedy?

Optional Activity

DEVELOP YOUR TRAGEDY FURTHER
Write out a short version of your tragedy using the outline you created in Session V. Then perform the play for your classmates, church group, or family.

A jump-out-of-your-seat horror movie is cathartic. Roller coaster fans describe the same kind of appeal, the "rush" of emotion and adrenaline that they find to be exhilarating. When the ride is over, they feel drained but elevated.

OPTIONAL SESSION: WRITING

Film Review

This session is a writing assignment. Remember, quality counts more than quantity. You should write no more than 1,000 words, either typing or writing legibly on one side of a sheet of paper. You will lose points for writing more than this. You will be allowed to turn in your writing three times. The first and second times you turn it in, your teacher will grade it by editing your work. This is done by marking problem areas and making suggestions for improvement. You should take these suggestions into consideration as you revise your assignment. Only the grade on your final submission will be recorded. Your grade will be based on the following criteria: 25 points for grammar, 25 points for content accuracy—historical, theological, etc.; 25 points for logic—does this make sense and is it structured well?; 25 points for rhetoric—is it a joy to read?

Your assignment is to write a review of a movie or play that is connected in some way to the book that you have been reading—in this case you will be using Aristotle's standards to judge the worth of a play or movie. Your review should be persuasive—fitting, of course, for the rhetoric years. You should tell your reader if this movie is worth watching and why. Your teacher may ask you to write a positive review or a negative review, or leave it up to you. You should be encouraged to praise or condemn the content, the worldview and the style of the movie. Also, remember that you are responsible for representing a Christian worldview, so you need to critique the movie for language, any glorification of violence, and any sensuality. Remember that you need to learn to both condemn and praise, and that both skills must be more than a simple affirmation or denial of "liking" it.

PRIMARY BOOKS
Second Semester

AESTHETICS

A detail from Vermeer's work *The Art of Painting* (also known as *The Allegory of Painting* or *Painter in his Studio*). In this piece, the woman crowned with a laurel wreath and carrying a book by Herodotus or Thucydides represents Clio, the Muse of History.

Postmodernists believe "there are no absolutes." Christians, on the other hand, do believe in absolutes. They sometimes, however, do not raise the obvious question: What are absolutes? Classical thinkers, both ancient and Christian, spoke of three kinds of absolutes: the true, the good, and the beautiful. Most Christians have no problem believing that truth and goodness are absolute—that they are objective, transcendent reality grounded ultimately in God. And yet, when it comes to beauty, Christians are often as subjective and relativistic as postmodernists.

What is Aesthetics?

Aesthetics, put simply, is the study of beauty in its different varieties and in its different manifestations in nature and in the arts. Aesthetics is indeed about pleasure, which often makes people assume that it is merely about subjective feelings. But, properly understood, aesthetic pleasure is a perception of objective quality that also points, ultimately, to God.

Say you are walking outside on a fall day and across the road you see a gigantic maple tree, its leaves turned a bright red and its branches trembling in the breeze. It takes your breath away. Why?

Or say you are watching *American Idol*, the popular television talent show. One singer croaks and yells and has an attitude. Another sings in such a way that you are utterly captivated. What is the difference? What makes one singer bad and the other one good?

Plato would say that aesthetic experience is a glimpse of perfection. That tree across the road gave us a momentary manifestation of the ideal tree that exists in the mind of God. The skilled singer is approaching perfection of sound and expression.

An Aristotelian approach to aesthetics would look at the tree and the *American Idol* performance in terms of their purpose and how the parts—the leaves and branches, the words and the music—cohere into a whole.

Other aesthetic analysis might attend to matters of form. How the color of the leaves harmonize against the blue sky; how the branches trace intricate patterns; how the singer's techniques of phrasing, breathing, and improvisation contribute to an excellent, effective performance.

Christian thinkers, ranging from the medieval scholastic Thomas Aquinas to the American Puritan Jonathan Edwards, said that the feeling we get when we experience beauty is a kind of love. You love that maple tree. You love that song and feel a love-like connection to the artist who sings it. For Aquinas and Edwards, something is beautiful when it provokes love. They went on to connect beauty to Christian ethics and to the love of God, whose own love for His creation is expressed in the beauty that He lavishes everywhere.

For Edwards the beauty of the natural world is a testimony to the God who created it. Christian artists such as Thomas Cole, founder of America's first distinct ar-

tistic movement, the Hudson River School, saw nature as God's art. Like an artist creating a painting, a song, or a novel—only much, much more so—God created the entire universe in all of its variety, intricacy, and detail. And He made it beautiful. Human artists, in turn, who are themselves God's self-expression as having been created in His image, can imitate, however faintly, God's creativity by creating works of beauty and meaning themselves.

The British critic John Ruskin said that God alone is the source of our highest pleasures. Therefore, he reasoned, the standards of aesthetic excellence please us because they reflect the attributes of God.

For example, one aesthetic criterion is the principle of unity and complexity. Some works of art, such as the black canvas in a modernist art gallery, have unity. Others,

Thomas Moran (1837–1926), a painter from the Hudson River School, evokes a sense of infinity through this detail from *Grand Canyon of the Colorado River*.

such as Jackson Pollack's random paint drippings, have complexity. But the best works—a Rembrandt portrait, a Thomas Cole landscape—have both unity and complexity at the same time. The paintings have a plethora of intricate details, but somehow they all harmonize together into a whole. In a Bach concerto every instrument may be doing something completely different from all of the others; and yet all of the sounds harmonize to form a wondrous whole. In a Shakespeare play each character has his own story, plots and subplots interweave with each other, and multiple themes emerge in the complex, multi-leveled language. And yet, everything in the play comes together into a unity.

Why do we respond so positively to the synthesis of both unity and complexity? Ruskin says it's because the Triune God is both unified and complex—a perfect unity of Father, Son, and Holy Spirit. Ruskin tells us that even unbelievers cannot help responding in love at the faintest glimpse of God's attributes.

Ruskin explains other aesthetic criteria along the same lines. Anything that evokes a sense of infinity, he says, gives us aesthetic pleasure—the can't-take-it-all-in vastness of the Grand Canyon; the Crab Nebula; the mind-boggling sublimities of Milton's *Paradise Lost;* a Hudson River School landscape of waterfalls and mountain ranges. Intimations of infinity give us pleasure because God is infinite.

According to Ruskin's aesthetic theory, symmetry, the way parts are in balance, is a sign of God's justice. Light is a sign of God's energy. Moderation is a sign of God's law, which is fulfilled in "self-restrained liberty." Craftsmanship, technical skill, and attention to detail call to mind the artistry of God.

Another dimension to the field of aesthetics concerns the different kinds of aesthetic experience. Both Longinus, a Greek in the Roman empire, and Edmund Burke, the eighteenth-century father of conservatism, explored the category of the "sublime," that is, creations in nature and in the arts that create a sense of awe. Again, think of the Grand Canyon. If beauty evokes a feeling of love, said Burke, sublimity evokes a feeling of fear. And yet that fear, that sense of being overwhelmed, is a positive and particularly powerful aesthetic experience. Other categories include the "picturesque"—the quaint and unusual—and the "homey," creating feelings of comfort and the warmth of ordinary life, as in the Hobbiton scenes in *The Lord of the Rings*.

Notice that beauty in its various guises is not the same as "pretty." The horror of tragedy can create in us a feeling of compassion, which is a kind of love and thus a perception of beauty. A portrait by Rembrandt, arguably the greatest Protestant painter, shows ordinary human beings through whom traces of God's image shine. The lined faces of his old women stirs more love than a stereotyped, made-up, shallow expression of a fashion model, and thus shows a greater beauty.

Aesthetics is not an exact science. Different styles and different movements have their own aesthetic quirks.

The Garden of Eden, painted in 1828, was Thomas Cole's first painting to explore spiritual themes. "A number of critics have seen the Hudson River School landscapes evocations of the American Eden, an unspoiled paradise to be inhabited by the new American Adam. Certainly, Bible-saturated Protestants of the time could hardly view an example of natural beauty without thinking of the biblical paradise, but it should be noted that such associations would have been understood to be only analogies, not literal identifications."
—Painters of Faith: The Spiritual Landscape in Nineteenth-Century America

The Past and *The Present* by Thomas Cole

Just how much aesthetic judgments can be rationalized is a matter of debate. But people debate about truth and goodness also. Controversy and elusiveness do not keep beauty from being an absolute.

Aesthetics as a subject in itself is a branch of philosophy. Just as epistemology is the philosophy of how we know, and metaphysics is the philosophy of the nature of existence, aesthetics is the philosophy of beauty. The field of aesthetics explores questions such as: What is art? How does art work? How can we say that one piece of art is better than another?

All branches of philosophy have their controversies and contending schools of thought, and aesthetics is no exception. Is a work of art something that has no purpose other than itself? Or does art always have to communicate something? Is the meaning of a work of art determined by the artist's intention? Or is the meaning determined by its audience? Or is the meaning independent of both the artist and the audience? Is art self-expression or a representation of objective truth? Does art appeal to emotion or to the mind? Is the beauty of a work of art simply a matter of form? Or intensity? Or technique and craftsmanship?

Such questions are not easily answered. Like other philosophical issues, they resist resolution, cropping up in different guises throughout the history of philosophy.

But aesthetics is not simply an academic philosophical exercise. Like ethics, another branch of philosophy, it manifests itself more clearly where it is applied.

Thus, aesthetics is an intrinsic part of many other fields. Whether you pursue singing or photography or writing or filmmaking or industrial design, you must operate in the realm of aesthetics.

Keep in mind that "art" refers not only to painting and sculpture, but also to music, literature, drama, movies, and similar human creations. Even "practical" creations—such as architecture, clothing, and manufactured products—have their "design" and thus have aesthetic qualities.

Aesthetics is for both artists and critics, the ones who make the work and the ones who receive it. The latter include professional scholars who try to understand and to help other people understand significant works of art.

At college you can learn to be a critic. Art criticism, literary criticism, music criticism are all valuable enterprises. This does not mean "criticizing" or "being critical" in the sense of always being negative and tearing down other people's creations. (That *can*, of course, be part of a critic's calling when dealing with bad work that deserves that kind of treatment.)

A critic is someone who analyzes and evaluates a work of art. To do so requires knowledge of the art form—its genre, techniques, and history—as well as the cultural knowledge to put it into context. To explicate a painting or a novel or a movie, a critic needs, among other things, to be a historian, a philosopher, and (ideally) a theologian. That is, a critic needs a strong classical liberal arts education.

If you study the arts in college—whether the visual arts, music, literature, or film—you can learn how to *do* the art. You draw, perform music, write poetry, make movies. You can also learn how to *understand* the art. You can analyze paintings, appreciate music, interpret poetry, and evaluate movies.

These two dimensions are related. Performance classes involve the professor and your peers critiquing your presentations. And if you are going to become good at your art, you also need to learn how to critique yourself.

But it is also possible to specialize on the critical side. Most English majors focus on literary criticism. In fact, critical theory is currently dominating the field, to the point of sometimes overshadowing the great authors. A promising subfield for would-be critics is the history of the art form. You will learn much about aesthetics from courses in literary history, music history, and art history.

You do not, however, have to be a professional artist or a professional scholar or journalistic review-writer to be involved with aesthetics.

Cooking a good meal, painting and decorating the house, making yourself presentable when you get dressed are all manifestations of artistry in everyday life. These ordinary activities call for the exercise of aesthetic taste.

Going to a movie, listening to your iTunes, reading for pleasure, watching TV are all examples of receiving works of art. You can consume artistic dreck that contaminates your intellect and your morals. Or you can take in art that enriches your life.

In our entertainment-saturated culture, understanding aesthetics and cultivating high aesthetic standards have become survival skills.

Critical Issues

I have sometimes overheard some of my students talking about what they did last weekend, and one of them will make an innocent remark, "That was a really good movie."

Whereupon I jump into the conversation. "What was good about it?"

"Uh, I don't know."

"Was the movie good because it conveyed a profound insight into moral behavior?" I will say, as the student looks around for an escape.

"Not really."

"Was the movie good because of the excellent construction of its plot?"

"No. It really didn't have much of a plot."

"Was the movie good because it had good acting? Good camera work? Was it well edited?"

"I really didn't notice."

"So what was so good about the movie?"

"Well, I really liked when they had the big car chase, and they had some really cool explosions, and at the end when the bad guy was killed his guts all came out. It was an awesome movie!"

Aesthetics

At that point, saving for another day a discussion about the sublime, I say, "Oh, I get it. You liked the movie. You didn't mean that the movie was good. You just meant that you liked it."

I then go on to help the fledgling critic see the difference between saying something is "good" and saying, "I like it." The former tells us something about the work. The latter tells me something about him.

We can "like" things that are not "good." In fact, such is our fallen nature that we have a proclivity for liking things that are bad.

To take an innocent example, we take pleasure in food that is, as we say, "bad for us." We gorge ourselves with sugar and fat in all its various guises, even though a steady diet of such fare makes us fat, decays our teeth, and destroys our health. Still, we "like it." For some people, that is all that matters. Or, to take a guilty example, we take pleasure in sin, in activities that are morally "bad."

This is what many movies and other popular entertainment forms exploit. It is possible to make a movie that is aesthetically good—one that is technically excellent, that conveys a valuable meaning, a work of art whose form effectively conveys its theme, a movie with actors and directors and cinematographers and writers who display a high level of skill and craft. But a movie like that is hard to make.

It is far easier to get people to "like" a movie by bringing in a beautiful actress and having her take off her clothes, or by appealing to viewers' latent sadism with a ramped up torture scene. Viewers also "like" the feeling of rebellion that can come from admiring an immoral hero or from mocking good institutions, such as the family or the church.

Aesthetics does have to do with taking pleasure in something. It does have a subjective element, the enjoyment of a work of art or a natural phenomenon. But aesthetics also has an objective element, having to do with the perception of qualities in a work of art, as well as the ability to make evaluative judgments based on objective standards.

I am not saying that aesthetic criteria are the only pleasure we can take from a work of art. Some pleasures are innocent. There is nothing wrong with eating junk food occasionally, as long as it doesn't dominate our diet. There is nothing wrong with enjoying a movie for its car chases, even though the rest of it is incredibly stupid and ineptly put together. We can even enjoy movies that are so bad they are unintentionally hilarious, as in *Plan 9 from Outer Space*.

Some people, though, eat so much junk food that they "like" nothing else, destroying their taste for good, healthful, wholesome food. And some people "like" nothing but entertainment that gives them cheap thrills and so cut themselves off from works of beauty and meaning.

This is the condition of many people today. They are culturally obese, out-of-shape, and malnourished. They require constant stimulation; otherwise, they succumb to that chronic spiritual ailment of our times: boredom.

According to the classical Christian writers, chronic boredom can be part of the sin of sloth, a spiritual laziness that can grow into a paralyzing apathy. Those who are chronically bored often treat their condition by pursuing ever greater sensations, including the overtly sinful kinds.

In contrast, the Bible teaches us to cultivate high standards: "Finally, brothers, whatever is true, whatever is honorable, whatever is just, whatever is pure, whatever is lovely, whatever is commendable, if there is any excellence, if there is anything worthy of praise, think about these things" (Phil. 4:8).

Often called the "worst movie ever made," the 1959 sci-fi film *Plan 9 from Outer Space* is about aliens who, in hopes of stopping mankind from developing a doomsday weapon, create zombies to get the planet's attention.

There is a "whatever" of contemporary boredom. Here, though, we have "whatevers" that open us up to the best of what life has to offer. This is a list of what is good, including not only the moral ("whatever is honorable . . . just . . . pure") and the intellectual ("whatever is true") but also the aesthetic ("whatever is lovely . . . commendable . . . any excellence . . . anything worthy of praise").

A Christian Response

Learning to "like" (subjectively) what is "good" (objectively) is what we mean by developing good taste.

Christians should develop good taste. Not because there is any spiritual or even moral merit in good taste, in itself. But beauty is better than ugliness; and good art is something of an antidote to bad art. Christians should equip themselves to tell the difference and to prefer the good to the bad.

In our current pop culture we are immersed in entertainment that is decadent, immoral, and mind-dissolving. It generally conveys a worldview that is utterly hostile to that of the Bible. Since God is the source of true beauty, art that is truly beautiful will tend to conform to His will.

Usually what is beautiful accords with what is true and what is good. The moral flaws in a work often turn out to be aesthetic flaws also, such as when a complex and involving plot is interrupted for a sex scene, causing the audience to respond with a different kind of pleasure and thus breaking the aesthetic spell.

This is not always the case, however. Some well-written literature advances a false worldview. Sometimes the form of a work is beautiful or sublime, while the content it communicates is false. Awareness of aesthetics, though, enables you to make that kind of distinction. This frees you to appreciate the form while refusing to let it manipulate you into accepting the content.

Conversely, sometimes the content is true and good—indeed, Christian—though the form is aesthetically bad. Thus the plethora of embarrassing Christian music, romance novels, movies, and knickknacks that fill up the shelves of so many Christian bookstores. Now a Christian might agree with the message of a Christian romance novel and might even "like it." But a poorly-written novel, whatever its message, will generally have little lasting impact—on Christians, much less non-Christians—and it will have zero influence on the culture as a whole.

As I hope you are noticing in the *Omnibus* series, Christians have an aesthetic legacy that is unparalleled by any other worldview. The heirs of Rembrandt and Bach, T.S. Eliot and Tolkien, Hopkins, Donne, Herbert, Milton, Shakespeare . . . and the list could be extended indefinitely, should aspire to create and to enjoy work that

is simultaneously true and good and beautiful, thereby glorifying God and edifying man.

But the Christian appreciation for aesthetics must go beyond the important but separate question of whether or not the artist was a Christian. Christians are empowered to appreciate beauty wherever they find it and to turn it into an occasion for glorifying God.

Ruskin observed that when we experience beauty, we are also filled with a sensation of thanksgiving and praise. We are grateful for what we see or hear, and we praise whoever made it possible. When we see a beautiful tree, we are thankful for that tree, and we praise the One who made it. When we hear a beautiful song, we are thankful and full of praise—to whom?

Some people see no further than the artist who created the art, with their thanksgiving and praise going entirely to him, turning themselves into often-pathetic, star-worshipping fans. Christians can appreciate the artist, but they can also see through him to Someone looming behind the artist's talents. God Himself is the source of every good and perfect gift (James 1:17). Christians, in faith, can recognize the greater Artist behind the artist, the One who bestowed the artist's gifts and who creates beauty through the artist's vocation. When Christians perceive the beauty, whether of nature or of art, it becomes an occasion to glorify God.

So how can Christians learn to notice the aesthetic dimension and grow in their tastes? That is, how can we learn to take pleasure in what is good?

Let me recreate another conversation that I have had with students. A group of them will be talking about music. Someone will say something like this: "Hymns are boring! Contemporary Christian music is a lot better!"

"Better?" say I. "In what way?"

"Well, the old hymns have a lot of words I don't know. And, the old hymns are like, old. But the praise songs are more modern, and I can relate to them better."

"OK," I say, with considerable self-restraint. "You don't understand the hymns. Does that make them bad?"

"No, not really."

"Which has more to say, a six-stanza hymn, or a praise stanza that you sing over and over? Which has more words? Which has more notes?"

"Well, I guess the hymn."

"Which tells us more about Christ, the Bible, the will of God, and the Christian life?"

"OK. The hymn."

"Which has not only one melodic line but different voices all coming together into a harmony?"

"The hymn."

"So how can you say that a contemporary praise song is better than a hymn?"

"I don't know!" my interlocutor concludes, "I just like it better!"

"Ah!," I say. "You don't mean to say that the praise song is objectively good. You just mean that *you like it better.*" Whereupon I move to the other discussion described in the previous section.

I have come to the point where I can prove to the satisfaction even of the person I am debating that, for example, the music of Mozart is objectively better than the music of the pop star currently at the top of the charts.

I hesitate to name the pop star, since by the time this essay gets into print, that singer, defended then with such ardour, will have fallen far out of fashion. That is one measure of the difference between great art and commercially-churned-out popular art. The latter wears out its welcome; people get tired of it, even sick of it. It has to give way to the next fashion. Whereas the best art never ages. I have read Shakespeare's *Hamlet* probably hundreds of times, and I still see new facets of the play every time I read it. Whereas I can hardly sit through reruns even of TV shows that I originally enjoyed. I never tire of listening to Bach's *Brandenburg Concertos.* The first time I heard "Don't Worry, Be Happy," I found it catchy. But it wasn't long before whenever it came on, I wanted to shoot my radio.

Nevertheless, my students who preferred contemporary Christian music and pop songs do illustrate some important principles of aesthetics. The best art demands understanding. Poorer art is simple and accessible. It makes few demands. It's easy. Great art, though, is demanding. It demands attention. It demands knowledge.

Consider sports. Actually, many aesthetic theorists consider sports to be equivalent to art. An athlete, like an artist, performs his exploits for their own sake, seeking to attain standards of excellence.

To enjoy a game of football, you need to understand the game. And the more you understand it—if you pick up on the different plays, the blocking patterns, and techniques of the various position players—the more you will enjoy the game.

To enjoy the best music, you need to know about music. The more you know about literature, painting, architecture, movies—or baseball, woodworking, or cars—the more you will enjoy them. And also, the more you will be able to make judgments about them.

My daughter, currently an *Omnibus* teacher, was in the Milwaukee youth orchestra when she was a kid. Playing the violin in a youth orchestra is a competitive sport, with everyone trying to beat out their friends and rise through the ranks from the easy ensembles all the way up to the higher-ranked orchestras. The program also offered a music theory course, teaching the concepts behind the music.

That was the time when heavy-metal, head-banging music was all the vogue. Many Christian parents we knew had all kinds of conflicts with their teenagers over the salacious content and purposefully rebellious attitude cultivated in this music. But we never had any problems like that. Our daughter dismissed her friends' music not because of its immorality but because she knew about music. "That stuff just has three chords!" she told me. There just wasn't enough to that kind of music to interest her. Another time, when their conductor made them play some atonal modernist abstract music, she and her friends whined and complained until they could play music they could really enjoy— specifically, Mozart.

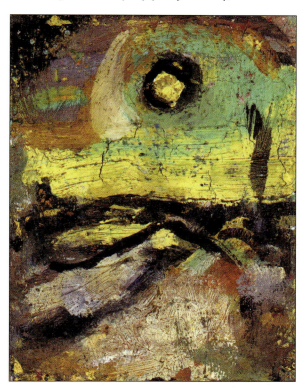

Landscape by Georges Rouault (1871–1958). About art, Rouault once wrote, "Adore everything which lives beneath the sky. The light is so beautiful, the dusk and even the shadows."

You need to understand the art form before you can enjoy it at its highest level. This is why you take music lessons, go out for sports, and study *Omnibus.*

I really couldn't expect those students I was tormenting to know any better, though as their professor I was trying to teach them to open their sensibilities to higher things. It also wasn't completely fair to compare rock groups to Mozart.

Different genres of art have their own standards. Within a genre, it is also possible to perceive different levels of merit. Some pop stars are better singers than others, which makes *American Idol* possible. Some rock musicians thrash their guitars to make noise. Then there is Eric Clapton, a guitar virtuoso.

In the genre of country music, Hank Williams, Patsy Cline, and Merle Haggard are objectively *better* than the latest hot act on country radio. By the standards of creativity, musicianship, and originality, these artists are far better than those of lesser talent who simply follow conventions and trade on their good looks.

We can apply aesthetic standards on nearly every level. The principle of complexity and unity? That describes an Eric Clapton guitar solo, a riff by Aretha Franklin, and a Johnny Cash ballad.

Some genres have such complexity and unity built in. We have discussed how in a Bach concerto all of the instruments are playing different music, which nevertheless coheres into a whole. That is also a good description of jazz.

Whereas classical music has been composed so that the musicians are following a score, jazz depends on improvisation. Each musician makes it up as the music goes along, though the whole ensemble is following a strict chord progression and must listen carefully to every other member in the group so that they play off of each other so as to avoid cacophony. Jazz, arguably, grows out of a different worldview—one that values individualism and existential self-invention—as opposed to Bach's objective, God-centered ordering. But jazz requires the very highest musicianship.

Bluegrass is similar to jazz. It too demands musicians that are creative enough to improvise. Taking traditional tunes as a jumping off point, bluegrass musicians trade off solos at blinding speeds.

One might say that the highest form of American popular music is jazz, and that the highest form of American country music is bluegrass. There is just more going on in jazz and bluegrass than in a three-chord rock song or honky-tonk ballad. A still higher form of music is classical orchestral music, which is capable of even more musical complexity.

This is not to say that songs in the simpler genres cannot be complex and unified in their own terms. We should look for quality and appreciate excellence of every kind. You should develop aesthetic taste. But don't become an aesthetic snob.

Another concept that will help you cultivate your taste is the distinction between the levels of culture. As the Christian culture critic Kenneth Myers explains in his book *All God's Children and Blue Suede Shoes,* works of art exist in the folk culture, the high culture, and the pop culture.

Folk culture is the product of a historical community. It is traditional, conservative, and communal. When it comes to works of art, no one person wrote the fairy tale *Cinderella,* or composed the ballad "Barbara Allen," or patented the recipe for barbecued ribs. All of these were passed down from generation to generation, with different families creating their own variations. We have regional folk cultures—that of the deep South, New England, the wild West, the different neighborhoods of Chicago—and we have ethnic cultures with roots in Africa, Italy, Scotland, and wherever.

High culture is the product of talented individuals who create contributions that everyone else can then draw on. High culture grows out of education and genius. Great statesmen such as George Washington and Thomas Jefferson, inventors like Thomas Edison and Bill Gates have contributed immeasurably to our American culture. The great poets, painters, and thinkers that you read and learn about in *Omnibus* have given us our high culture.

Pop culture, according to Myers, has to do with the commercial realm. It is entertaining, technologically-driven, and instantaneously gratifying. Pop culture goes in and out of fashion. Pop culture turns art into a commodity to buy and sell. Achieving popularity and thus making money is its only purpose.

What determines whether or not a television show stays on the air is not its valuable moral lessons (the concern of folk culture) or its aesthetics merits (the concern of high culture), but its ratings. Networks will put on anything that will draw an audience. Music executives give out recording contracts not so much to the most talented musician but to performers whose music, for one reason or another, will sell. The entertainment industry does depend on the talent of the high culture—musicians, actors, photographers, technicians—but the artists often end up frustrated by the commercial demands of the marketplace, which sometimes distorts or degrades the artistic impulse.

Food in the folk culture is your grandmother's home cooking; food in the high culture is a gourmet meal created by a chef in a fine restaurant; food in the pop culture is a hamburger wrapped in paper shoved at you from a drive-through window. There is nothing wrong with eating a fast-food hamburger. But if that is all you eat, you will not only develop malnutrition, you will miss out on the love and good company of a family meal and the heights of deliciousness of a fine meal.

Similarly, I am not against all pop culture. Again, even within pop culture, there are gradations of excellence, and it is possible to develop a taste for the best TV shows, the best rock music, and the best fast food. But if your only artistic diet is pop culture, you will be aesthetically malnourished and you will miss out on some of the deepest and most edifying pleasures.

Pop culture traffics in what we "like," rather than what is "good." Though it sometimes attracts us with cheap tricks such as sex and sadistic violence, pop culture can be innocent. The problem with pop culture is that it drives out the other kinds of culture. As Neil Postman has shown in his book *Amusing Ourselves to Death*, the entertainment mentality is now taking over every other cultural realm, from education (where high culture is supposed to be cultivated) to the church (whose hymns and customs reach deep into the folk culture and whose theology and scholarship exemplifies the high culture).

The antidote to the pop culture diet is to make a point of enjoying also the folk culture and the high culture. I myself love the blues, an art form that emerged from the folk culture of poverty-stricken black Southerners. I also love traditional country music, an art form that emerged from the folk culture of poverty-stricken white Southerners. Later, these strains would be fused together by artists such as Elvis Presley, and rock 'n' roll was invented. Even after this new art form was co-opted by the pop culture, in its best examples you can still pick out the blues styl-

In *Angle of a Dream* painter Joel Sheesley uses reflective surfaces to pose an interesting riddle for one of the 20th century's major concerns about painting: its persistent valorization of "flatness." Two dimensional reflective surfaces simultaneously embody three dimensional space. Sheesley is interested in the dynamic tension between abstraction and representation; between the virtues of analytic reduction and metaphorical expansion.

ings in a particularly fine guitar solo and the country heritage in a particularly plaintive lyric.

So grow your musical sensibility by listening to the music of the folk culture: to blues and bluegrass; Irish dirges and Appalachian folk songs. Also listen to music of the high culture: to Bach and Mozart; jazz artists like Duke Ellington and Charlie Parker; great singers like Luciano Pavarati, Mahalia Jackson, and (I would say) Patsy

Cline. Similarly, don't just watch TV for your entertaining stories. Delve into the fairy tales, myths, and legends of the world's folk cultures. Read Shakespeare, Milton, Dickens, Tolkien, and other masters of the high culture. All of this will give you a richer aesthetic experience. You will learn to take pleasure in what is good. You will develop good taste.

There is one other thing you need to realize as a Christian going deeply into aesthetics. When you go into the upper reaches of the art world or of the academic establishment, you will find that you, as a Christian, have a profound advantage.

Just as postmodernists reject the true and the good, they also reject the beautiful. In their relativistic minds, standards of beauty—like intellectual truth and moral principles—are nothing more than oppressive constructions by those in power. Since Beauty expresses ideals and perfections, it needs to be subverted. Thus, many contemporary artists create work that is, as they say, "subversive" and "transgressive." They make art that is purposefully ugly. Instead of trying to make their art give aesthetic pleasure to their audience, they try to outrage and shock their audience (thus the art made of excrement and bodily fluids, the blasphemies and desecrations, the pornographic images and gross-out carnage). Ironically, the biggest enemies of art today happen to be artists.

This should not surprise us. Those who have no basis for truth and goodness have no basis for beauty. Christians, though, do have a basis for them all.

As the secularists create a world that is uglier and uglier, increasingly void of order and meaning, and as they become capable of no pleasures other than sensuality and vulgar entertainment, Christians can resist by recovering beauty. The aesthetic treasure that the unbelievers have thrown away Christians can take up for themselves. And when Christians go back to creating compelling works of art like they used to, they will once again shape Western civilization.

—*Gene Edward Veith*

For Further Reading

M.C. Beardsley. *Aesthetics.* Second Edition. Indianapolis: Hackett Publishing Company, 1981.

Steven M. Cahn and Aaron Meskin, ed. *Aesthetics: A Comprehensive Anthology.* Malden, Mass.: Blackwell Publishing, 2008.

Nicholas Wolterstorff. *Art in Action: Toward a Christian Aesthetic.* Grand Rapids, MI: Wm. B. Eerdmans Publishing Company, 1980.

Ned Bustard, ed. *It Was Good: Making Art to the Glory of God.* Baltimore, Maryland: Square Halo Books, 2006.

John Ruskin. Ed. David Barrie. *Modern Painters.* New York: Alfred A. Knopf, 1987.

Gene Veith. *Painters of Faith: The Spiritual Landscape in Nineteenth-Century America.* Washington, D.C.: Regnery Publishing, 2001.

Calvin Seerveld. *Rainbows for the Fallen World: Aesthetic Life and Artistic Task.* Toronto: Tuppence Press, 1980.

Gene Veith. *State of the Arts: From Bezalel to Mapplethorpe.* Wheaton, Ill.: Crossway Books, 1991.

APOCRYPHA

Suppose your great-grandfather left you several boxes of books in his will. After he passed away, the boxes were delivered to your house, and you had a terrible time figuring out what the two boxes were supposed to mean. One of the boxes was straightforward and easy—on the outside of the box, in black marker, he had scrawled "66 books I would want to have with me on a desert island." You would rightly infer from this that these were his favorite books, or books he believed to be very significant and important. But the other box was unmarked, and contained some very fine literature, almost in a class with the books in the first box, along with a couple of romance novels and a western, and some Garfield cartoon books. "What is all this?" you would wonder. "Why did he want me to have *this*?" To make things more complicated, the second box was smaller and had been transported to your house on top of the books in the first box. "Would grandfather really have taken these books with him to a desert island?"

In *Judith Slaying Holofernes* blood and violence takes center stage with delicate details like the bracelet on Judith's arm making the scene even more disturbing. Artemisia Gentileschi (1593–1653) was one of the best painters in her day, even becoming the first female painter to become a member of the Accademia di Arte del Disegno.

Throughout our history, the Christian church has puzzled over the Apocrypha in much the same way, and different parts of the church have settled the problem in different ways. Some parts of the church have included the second box as part of the first. Other parts of the church have made a sharp distinction between them, keeping them in separate places entirely. But virtually all portions of the church have recognized that there is something different about that deutero-box, or box of secondary books, that is beneficial but not part of the Bible.

GENERAL INFORMATION

Author and Context

We don't know who the authors of these books were, but we do know the general period in which they wrote. The books of the Apocrypha were largely written in the inter-testamental period, the time between Malachi and Matthew. Some of the histories are about events during that time, while other stories from the Apocrypha are set in a time period a little earlier, during the time of Israel's exile. And some of the books are wisdom literature and so have more of a "timeless" feel to them. This period in Israel's history was a time when there was great pressure for God's people to accommodate themselves to the surrounding assumptions of Hellenistic culture. Israel's rejection of that pressure (and in some cases, accommodation to it) is recorded for us in the Apocrypha.

Significance

Nations are shaped in large part by their literature. The ancient Greeks were shaped by the Homeric literature. The nation of Germany was made possible by Luther's translation of the Bible. There is a similar effect in differing Christian communions—not to mention heretical sects. For example, the fact that Mormons believe that *The Book of Mormon* is divinely inspired affects more than just the content of what they believe; it has helped to shape their corporate identity. With the various Christian communions, our differences over the exact boundaries of sacred Scripture have a more profound effect than simply restricting (or expanding) the number of available proof texts for us. The Protestant churches have been shaped by their rejection of the Apocrypha as Scripture. The Roman Catholic churches have accepted the Apocrypha, although usually while granting it secondary status, and this has helped shape Roman Catholic culture. Eastern Orthodox churches have accepted more of these books as

canonical than even Rome has, and this in turn has had its effect. Some of these distinctive emphases should become more obvious as we proceed through our discussion.

Summary and Setting

Alexander the Great did not conquer the entire world, but he conquered enough of it to make people notice what he was doing. His family was from Macedonia (northern Greece), and when the southern cities of Greece (Achaia) had exhausted themselves by fighting one another in the Peloponnesian Wars, Alexander's father Philip defeated them and established the supremacy of Macedonia. Alexander wanted much more than that, and so when he assumed the throne he began a pattern of unbelievable conquest. He marched to the east, overthrowing the Persians, conquering Egypt, and still keeping on, subduing nations as far out as the borders of India. Alexander wanted to keep right on going, but his troops decided that enough was enough and that they had no real interest in seeing Japan. Alexander died on the way home, in Babylon, in 323 B.C.

The empire that he established was then divided up between his generals (eerily prophesied in the book of Daniel), but all the pieces of Alexander's conquest remained Hellenistic—shaped by Greek culture and language. This is why the New Testament was written in Greek, even though the Latin-speaking Romans were in control at the time. But before the rise of Rome, the tiny nation of Israel happened to be right in between two of these fragments of Alexander's legacy—the Seleucid dynasty (in Syria) and the Ptolemaic dynasty (in Egypt).

The general outlook found within the Apocrypha is the outlook of believers greatly outnumbered by the pagans, and living in a position where they have to deal with those pagans constantly. The pressure to submit to the "spirit of the times" was enormous. When the Old Testament closed, the Persians were in control. When the New Testament opened, the Romans were in control. In the four hundred years in between, some very great changes had occurred—and it was not a straight transition from Persia to Rome. The intervening force was Alexander, and all he brought in with him. We don't have very much inspired history of that period, but we do have some very good information—much of it from the Apocrypha.

Worldview

This series of Omnibus textbooks is written from the classical Protestant worldview, and so it is not surprising that our study of the Apocrypha here is a study that will not treat these books as part of sacred Scripture. At the same time, it might be surprising to some misguided but ardent Protestants that we are giving any time at all to these books—isn't this like giving credence to *The Book of Mormon*? Well, no, it is not like that at all. It is our position that these books ought not to be studied as though they were inspired by the Holy Spirit, but that they may be read seriously and even devotionally. So let us begin with that question: What is the basis for rejecting the Apocrypha as Scripture? And if that question is successfully answered, what could be the reason for giving these writings the time of day?

In the ancient world, the Old Testament came in three basic versions—Hebrew and Greek, and Latin a little bit later. The Hebrew version of the Old Testament, the version maintained by the Jews in Palestine, *did not* contain the Apocrypha. But you should also recall that this was a time when many Jews were living outside Palestine in colonies throughout the Greek-speaking world. The Septuagint was a translation of the Hebrew Scriptures into the Greek for use out in that Greek-speaking world. The word *Septuagint* comes from the tradition that this translation was accomplished by seventy Jewish scholars—it was the work of the "Seventy." The Hellenized Jews outside Palestine were not as conservative as those within, so they felt at liberty to include these books in their translation. Their view of the boundaries of Scripture was a bit looser. Then a few centuries later, when Jerome was asked to translate the Bible into Latin, he worked from the Greek, and wound up including these books as well. But he knew something was fishy about them, and remarked on that in prefatory notes that he included. Over time, however, those prefatory notes were dropped, and a large part

The story of Susanna and the Elders is an apocryphal addition to the book of Daniel that has been a popular subject for painters from about 1500. Sir Anthony van Dyck (1599–1641) takes a similar approach to Rembrandt and Gentileschi's paintings of Susanna, showing a virtuous young wife who is vulnerable, frightened, and repulsed by the demands of the lecherous men.

"Then Tobias asked the angel, and said to him: I beseech thee, brother Azarias, tell me what remedies are these things good for, which thou hast bid me keep of the fish? And the angel, answering, said to him: If thou put a little piece of its heart upon coals, the smoke thereof driveth away all kind of devils, either from man or from woman, so that they come no more to them. And the gall is good for anointing the eyes, in which there is a white speck, and they shall be cured." —Tobit 6:7–9

of the Western church just considered these books "part of the Bible" because, *practically* speaking, they were.

With the arrival of the Reformation, one of the great rallying cries was *ad fontes*—"back to the sources" or "back to the headwaters." The Reformers were very interested in checking current abuses against the originals. This included the study of the early church fathers—the Reformers included in their midst the best patristic scholars in Europe—as well as the originals of Scripture. This meant abandoning the Latin Vulgate and going back to the Greek New Testament and the Hebrew Old Testament. The Reformation was very much tied in with the "new learning," which brought with it a great zeal for original research of ancient languages and sources. For example, a number of the early Reformers studied Hebrew with the Jewish rabbis and became some of the foremost experts in Hebrew. But as soon as the Reformers went back to the study of the Hebrew Old Testament, they found themselves studying a Bible without an Apocrypha. A Greek-speaking Jew who grew up in Ephesus would have had occasion to use the Septuagint and would have read the Apocrypha. But someone who grew up in Jerusalem and studied there would have had a Bible without an Apocrypha. And in an argument that was quite compelling for Protestants, this meant that the Bible Jesus used, along with all the apostles, was a Bible without an Apocrypha. It would seem to follow from this that if the Lord didn't have an Apocrypha, then we don't need to have one either.

As a result of this pressure from the Protestants, the Roman Catholic church finally determined at the Council of Trent that the Apocrypha was to be included. But it is noteworthy that this "ecumenical" decision to include the Apocrypha did not occur until a millennium and a half after the time of Christ. The inclusion of the Apocrypha up to this point had been informal. And the Protestants responded confessionally as well. For example, the Westminster Confession in the seventeenth century begins in its first chapter by itemizing the books of the Bible that are to be received as canonical. Because the Protestants placed so much emphasis on *sola Scriptura*, it is not surprising that they were keenly interested in defining the boundaries of those Scriptures. And what did they say about the Apocrypha?

> The Books commonly called Apocrypha, not being of divine inspiration, are no part of the canon of the scripture; and therefore are of no authority in the Church of God, nor to be any otherwise approved, or made use of, than other human writings (WCF 1.3).

Related to this was the fact that the New Testament nowhere quotes the Apocrypha directly, and as an obvious consequence nowhere uses it to settle any point of doctrine. This is all the more striking because one of the most obvious features of the New Testament is the constant citation of Old Testament passages. But with all these citations, there is not one direct quotation from the Apocrypha. And all it would have taken to settle the matter would have been for the apostle Paul to have said, "As the Spirit says in Scripture, 'From a woman sin had its beginning, and because of her we all die" (Sirach 25:24), which somehow we cannot imagine Paul saying. But if he *had* said it, and called it Scripture, then there would have been apostolic warrant for treating the Apocrypha as Scripture. We don't have anything like that.

The apostle Paul tells us in several places that the Jews were entrusted with the oracles of God. They were responsible for the transmission and preservation of the Old Testament Scriptures. "What profit is there in being a Jew?" he asked. Well, *chiefly* he says, "unto them were committed the oracles of God" (Rom. 3:2; cf. 9:4). If the Jews were entrusted with the Old Testament Scriptures, as the Apostle says, and the Bible that Jesus and the apostles used in Israel was an edition without an Apocrypha, then the church (entrusted with the New Testament) ought not to mess around with the boundaries of the Old Testament. Whether or not Tobit is in the Bible is not in the church's department—that was one of the chief responsibilities of the Jews. When we fairly consider how they exercised that responsibility, and how the Lord interacted with what they did, it seems plain that we ought not to receive the Apocrypha as inspired.

But at the same time, we can see that the biblical writers were aware of the Apocrypha, and they did not keep their distance. If they considered it to be at least *instructive*, then so may we. For example, many of the citations of the Old Testament in the New are in Greek and are from the Septuagint, which contained the Apocrypha. In other words, the mere presence of the Apocrypha in the scroll did not keep them from quoting other portions of that same scroll. In a similar way, the first editions of the King James Version, used commonly by Protestants, included the Apocrypha while at the same time recognizing its non-canonical status. Believing it to be uninspired is not the same thing as believing it to have had cooties. The Swiss Reformer John Oecolampadius said in 1530 that the Reformed did "not despise" these books. At the same time, he said, "we do not allow them divine authority with the others." The issue for Protestants was whether it was inspired or not, and not whether we approved of it or not.

While there are no quotations, there are apparent allusions to the Apocrypha in the New Testament. Consider these passages from the Wisdom of Solomon and from Romans:

> "For from the greatness and beauty of created things comes a corresponding perception of their Creator . . . yet again, not even they are to be excused" (Wisdom 13:5, 8).

> "For the invisible things of him from the creation of the world are clearly seen, being understood by the things that are made, even his eternal power and Godhead; so that they are without excuse" (Rom. 1:20).

> "For who will say, 'What have you done? Or will resist your judgment'" (Wisdom 12:12).

> "Thou wilt say then unto me, Why doth he yet find fault? For who hath resisted his will? (Rom. 9:19).

And in the book of Hebrews, there is a plain allusion to a story out of Maccabees: "Women received their dead raised to life again: and others were tortured, not accepting deliverance; that they might obtain a better resurrection" (Heb. 11:35). This is a pretty clear reference to a story you will read shortly—see if you can identify someone enduring through torture in the hope of a better resurrection.

For these and other reasons, the Apocrypha can be quite an edifying read. There is great wisdom here, and there are many passages that are fully in accord with Scripture. As we consider a few selections from the Apocrypha, please review the chart on page four of your edition. The Protestants don't receive any of the Apocrypha as inspired. The Roman communion does not receive 1–2

Esdras and 4 Maccabees, for example, while the Greek Orthodox communion receives 1 Esdras, but not 2 Esdras, and the Russian Orthodox receive 2 Esdras but not 4 Maccabees. But *all* the communions that receive the Apocrypha do receive Tobit, Judith, the Esther outtakes, Wisdom of Solomon, Ecclesiasticus (not to be confused with Ecclesiastes), Baruch, the Daniel outtakes, and 1–2 Maccabees. It is also worth noting, in passing, that even for the communions that agree on the need for an acceptance of the Apocrypha, the exact boundaries of that Apocrypha remain a little fuzzy for them.

Tobit is a rollicking good story, but we can be grateful it is not in the canon. Any story that includes a demon-suitor killing seven grooms on their respective wedding nights with the same woman is a story that belongs in the folk-tale genre and not in Scripture. The book of Judith is also a great story, resembling Esther in some respects, but it is told at an exaggerated pitch. The story is about a gorgeous Jewish widow who beguiles the head of the Assyrian army, assassinates him, and gets clean away. The book also contains some historical inaccuracies that might be classified as howlers, so we are grateful we are not left to defend it as the inspired Word of God. But the student should sit back and enjoy the story anyway. The additions to Esther should be read as pious attempts to improve on something that didn't need improving.

The Wisdom of Solomon falls into a different category. It really is wisdom literature, and is full of helpful insights:

> "Love righteousness, you rulers of the earth . . ." (Wisdom 1:1).

> "Because the hope of the ungodly is like thistle-down carried by the wind . . ." (Wisdom 5:14).

> "A potter kneads the soft earth and laboriously molds each vessel for our service, fashioning out of the same clay both the vessels that serve clean uses and those for contrary uses, making all alike; but which shall be the use of each of them the worker in clay decides" (Wisdom 15:7).

Ecclesiasticus is similar and has many wise observations—although periodically you will want to say, "No, *that* can't be right:"

> "Do not glorify yourself by dishonoring your father" (Ecclesiasticus 3:10).

The seige of Jerusalem by Antiochus IV imagined through the lens of a medieval artist. This picture is from the *Chronique Universelle* (1480–1482).

Apocrypha

"When you gain friends, gain them through testing, and do not trust them hastily" (Ecclesiasticus 6:7).

But sometimes there appears to be a little bit of works-righteousness:

"For kindness to a father will not be forgotten, and will be credited to you against your sins" (Ecclesiasticus 3:14).

"As water extinguishes a blazing fire, so almsgiving atones for sin" (Ecclesiasticus 3:30).

And sometimes there are head-scratchers, like this one from Baruch:

"The giants were born there, who were famous of old, great in stature, expert in war. God did not choose them, or give them the way to knowledge; so they perished because they had no wisdom, they perished through their folly" (Baruch 3:26–28).

The prayer of the three friends, and the story of Daniel, Bel, and the snake, and the story of Susanna are all additions to the book of Daniel. Susanna is, like Judith, another heroic story of a "Jewess-babe."

In 1–2 Maccabees we find important historical information. First Maccabees is written in a straightforward historical style and is a reliable source of information about that period. For the Christian who wants to know more about the history between the close of the Old Testament and the opening of the New, this is an important book to read. Second Maccabees is written more vividly, in more of a partisan way, and records numerous speeches for the instruction of the reader.

Throughout our discussion, we have been talking about "inspiration." But what does this mean? We have been assuming that Galatians has it and that Judith doesn't, but what is it exactly? When you go out on a very cold morning, as you fill your lungs and exhale, you can see a cloud of your breath in front of you. The apostle Paul teaches us that Scripture is to God what that cloud is to you:

"All Scripture is given by inspiration of God, and is profitable for doctrine, for reproof, for correction, for instruction in righteousness: that the man of God may be perfect, thoroughly furnished unto all good works" (2 Tim. 3:16–17).

The New International Version renders the word *inspiration* literally, translating it as "God-breathed." The English Standard Version says, "All Scripture is breathed out by God." The clear implication is that the Scriptures, like the God who exhaled them, are perfect. It is popular in these days of unbelief to dispute or question the perfection of Scripture, but if we want to be faithful to God and His Word, we can't go this route.

Now this is why the question is a very important one. If the Apocrypha is included in this, then as we study it, we will be forced to recognize that we need to "downgrade" our definition of perfection. This is what unbelievers are trying to force us to do with regard to the 66 books of the Bible, which *are* perfect. If the Apocrypha is thrown in, and we are trying to accommodate the historical errors of Judith, for example, then we will be forced into the position of saying that perfection isn't what it used to be.

This will lead to various devices and arguments that might win us a little time, but which are very ill-advised in the long run. To say that the Scriptures are perfect when it comes "to spiritual things," but that they can be mistaken on matters of science or history, is to open the door wide to every form of unbelief. We don't really have a basis for dividing one kind of truth from another, and so it is best to do what evangelical believers have always done—accept the absolute infallibility of the Word of God, holding that it is without error in all that it affirms.

—Douglas Wilson

For Further Reading

Bruce, F.F. *The Canon of Scripture*. Downers Grove, Ill.: Intervarsity Press, 1988.

Carson, D.A. and Douglas Moo. *An Introduction to the New Testament*. Grand Rapids, Mich.: Zondervan, 2003.

Metzger, Bruce. *An Introduction to the Apocrypha*. New York: Oxford University Press USA, 1977.

Williamson, G.I. *The Westminster Confession of Faith*. Philipsburg, NJ: Presbyterian and Reformed Publishing, 2003.

Session I: Prelude

A Question to Consider

Why should the exact boundaries of Scripture be important to us?

From the General Information above, answer the following questions:

1. In your Bible reading, have you ever read a book or a passage that made you wonder why it was included in the canon of Scripture?
2. In your reading of other ancient literature, have you ever wondered why something was not included in the Bible?
3. Which book of the Apocrypha might Paul have been alluding to in Romans 1 and 9?
4. Which book of the Apocrypha is similar to an exaggerated version of Esther?
5. Which historical book of the Apocrypha informs us concerning the Jewish rebellion and cleansing of the Temple, which is celebrated in Hanukkah?
6. What is the basic argument that Protestants would present for the non-inspiration of the Apocrypha?
7. What are secondary arguments against the Apocrypha's inspiration?
8. What book in the Bible is most like the literature of the Apocrypha?

In reading the Apocrypha, we are not reading the Bible itself, but literature from the biblical world. This can be a great help in coming to understand the context of the writings we do consider to be Scripture.

Optional Activities

Memorize five memorable aphorisms from Wisdom of Solomon and Ecclesiasticus.

The next session will be a student-led discussion. Students will be creating their own questions concerning the issue of the session. Students should create three Text Analysis Questions, two Cultural Analysis questions, and two Biblical Analysis questions. For more detailed instructions, please see the chapter on the *Iliad*, Session III.

Issue

What qualities is the story of Judith intended to inspire in the reader?

Reading Assignment:
Judith

Session II: Student-Led Discussion
Judith

A Question to Consider

What qualities is the story of Judith intended to inspire in the reader?

Students should read and consider the example questions below that are connected to the Question to Consider above. Last session's assignment was to prepare three questions and answers for the Text Analysis section and two additional questions and answers for both the Cultural and Biblical Analysis sections below.

Text Analysis

Example: What are some examples of apparent historical errors and anachronisms that show up in the story of Judith?

Answer: The story of Judith refers to Nebuchadnezzar as the king of Assyria who reigned in Nineveh. In fact, Nebuchadnezzar was king of Babylon, and Nineveh had been destroyed in 612 B.C., some seven years before Nebuchadnezzar had taken the throne. The city of Bethulia, and the narrow pass it occupies, appears to be fictional. Although Nebuchadnezzar actually destroyed Jerusalem and its temple in 586, the narrative of Judith has him foiled in the effort.

Cultural Analysis

Example: Although Judith represents a genre of loose historical fiction, what lessons can be learned from this narrative that are applicable to God's people at all times in history?

Answer: At times when the move of culture continues to shift away from the foundations of biblical principle in public and private policies, there may be individuals who, in the spirit of Judith, are called to infiltrate the "camp" of the enemy, using strategies of subterfuge to bring down strongholds of evil. Although Judith used controversial tactics that some might find questionable, she is celebrated as a heroine of Jewish history for her courage and resourcefulness.

Other cultural issues to consider: In the so-called contemporary "culture war," Christians can use the methods of infiltration to reach goals. This can be done successfully or it can cause Christians to lose their saltiness through compromise. Look at topics like the religious right, religious conservatives, and the founding of Westminster Seminary and J. Gresham Machen. As you study these topics, consider what strategies were employed and whether these strategies led to faithfulness and fruitfulness.

Biblical Analysis

Example: What are some examples of personalities in the Bible that adopt a strategy like that of Judith, using deceitful tactics to achieve righteous purposes?

Answer: Probably the best-known example is Rahab, who lied to the officials of Jericho to conceal the presence of Israelite spies, thus contributing to the defeat of Jericho and the preservation of her own family. David also engaged in deceit in his dealings with the Philistine king Achish (1 Sam. 27).

Other scriptures to consider: Jeremiah 38:14–28

Summa

Write an essay or discuss this question, integrating what you have learned from the material above.

How can a Christian ascertain the limits to which deceitful tactics may be used to accomplish godly purposes? Is the example of Judith applicable to Christian people seeking to be "salt" and "light" in a dark world? When does a Christian go too far in adopting such tactics?

Optional Activity

While it would be impious to try to write Scripture or to try to pass off as Scripture something you had written yourself, it can still be instructive to try to mimic the cadences of different kinds of writing. In this exercise, write a "verse" and try to mimic the timbre of different books you have read:

ROMANS

1 SAMUEL

WISDOM OF SOLOMON

2 MACCABEES

READING ASSIGNMENT:
Tobit

Session III: Recitation
Tobit

Comprehension Questions

Answer the following questions for factual recall:

1. What is the general time frame purported in the book of Tobit with respect to Old Testament events?
2. What concern occupies the life of Tobit, and what happens to him as a result?
3. What are the circumstances of Tobit's return to Nineveh after his exile?
4. Who is Sarah, and what is her situation?
5. Who is Raphael, and how is he introduced into the story?
6. What adventures befall Tobias as he makes his journey to Media?
7. How do the stories of Tobias and Sarah intersect?
8. What is the response of Sarah's father when he learns that Tobias has survived his wedding night with his new bride?
9. How does the story conclude?
10. Re-read chapter 4 of Tobit. What virtues are especially praised in this section of the book?
11. From your reading of Tobit, are there doctrinal matters suggested by its content?

READING ASSIGNMENT:
1 Maccabees

Session IV: Writing
1 Maccabees

First Hand Account

This session is a writing assignment. Remember, quality counts more than quantity. You should write no more than 1,000 words, either typing or writing legibly on one side of a sheet of paper. You will lose points for writing more than this. You will be allowed to turn in your writing three times. The first and second times you turn it in, your teacher will grade it by editing your work. This is done by marking problem areas and making suggestions for improvement. You should take these suggestions into consideration as you revise your assignment. Only the grade on your final submission will be recorded. Your grade will be based on the following criteria: 25 points for grammar, 25 points for content accuracy— historical, theological, etc.; 25 points for logic—does this make sense and is it structured well?; 25 points for rhetoric—is it a joy to read?

Description

Your assignment is to write a description following the direction provided below. This may be more difficult than it sounds! Make sure your description guides a reader into an experience of the object. Use language that stirs the senses (what does it look, sound, feel, smell, or taste like?). Make judgments about the object as you describe it. Remember the great rule of description—Show us; don't tell us. Do not tell us that something is good or beautiful

The Martyrdom of the Seven Brethren and their Mother by Julius Schnorr von Carolsfeld (1794–1872) depicting an event from the Second Book of the Maccabees.

or likable. Describe it in a way that shows your reader the object's beauty or ugliness, its goodness, or wickedness.

Objective

Give a firsthand (first person) description of the experience of Mattathias when he confronted the Seleucid soldiers who came to Modin and demanded that he and the other citizens of the town participate in pagan ritual.

Reading Assignment:
Wisdom of Solomon

Session V: Poetry
Wisdom of Solomon

Writing like Solomon

In this session you will be challenged to write in the poetic literary genre found in The Wisdom of Solomon. The style, similar to that found in the wisdom literature of the Old Testament (e.g., Ecclesiastes, Song of Solomon), seeks to communicate in a kind of "didactic exhortation"—that is, in a manner that teaches precepts while at the same time encouraging obedience to them.

Writing in this style can present some challenges, especially for those less familiar with the rather concrete and pictorial style of ancient Middle Eastern languages. This type of literature, however, is common in the Old Testament and can express in very beautiful ways the call to a life of virtue and wisdom. Consider the following well-known text from Ecclesiastes:

> Rejoice, O young man, in your youth,
> And let your heart cheer you in the days
>   of your youth;
> Walk in the ways of your heart,
> And in the sight of your eyes;
>
> But know that for all these
> God will bring you into judgment.
> Therefore remove sorrow from your heart,
> And put away evil from your flesh,
> For childhood and youth are vanity.
>
> Remember now your Creator in the days
>   of your youth,
> Before the difficult days come,
> And the years draw near when you say,
> "I have no pleasure in them":
>
> While the sun and the light,
> The moon and the stars,
> Are not darkened,
> And the clouds do not return after the rain;
>
> In the day when the keepers of the house tremble,
> And the strong men bow down;
> When the grinders cease because they are few,
> And those that look through the windows grow dim;
>
> When the doors are shut in the streets,
> And the sound of grinding is low;
> When one rises up at the sound of a bird,
> And all the daughters of music are brought low.

As you read the Wisdom, focus especially on chapters 7–10, which celebrate the figure of the divine Sophia (wisdom). Notice how the author extols this virtue, and at the same time encourages his readers to follow in the path illuminated by her guidance.

Now think of another virtue—perhaps temperance, courage, integrity, or fidelity—and write some lines that provide a comparable example of instruction.

Optional Session: Recitation
1 and 2 Maccabees

Comprehension Questions

This session is on 1 and 2 Maccabees. Please read 2 Maccabees then answer the following questions for factual recall:

1. How would you compare the style and content of 1 Maccabees with 2 Maccabees?
2. What is the object of the discussion of Jeremiah in the letter to the Jewish people in Egypt found in 2 Maccabees 2, and what significance might that have with respect to popular speculation about the identity of Jesus (cf. Matt. 16:14)?
3. Who was Heliodorus, and what significance did he have in connection with the temple?
4. Who was Jason, and what role did he play in connection with the religious life in Jerusalem?
5. What lessons does the writer hope to teach by his recital of the accounts of martyrdoms found in chapters 6–8 of 2 Maccabees?
6. How would you compare the view of a hope of resur-

rection and afterlife found in 2 Maccabees 7 with that contemplated by the apostle Paul in 1 Corinthians 15?

7. What were the circumstances of the death of Antiochus IV, and how is his death interpreted by the writer of 2 Maccabees?

8. What did Judas Maccabeus do after he recovered control of the Temple following its desecration at the hands of the Syrians?

9. What were the subsequent experiences of the Jewish people under the reigns of Antiochus V and Demetrius I?

10. Judas Maccabeus appears to authorize prayers for the dead in 2 Maccabees 12. How does the practice implied in this text compare with what you otherwise know from biblical teaching?

11. What lesson does the author of 2 Maccabees hope his readers will learn from his accounts of the deaths of Andronicus (4:30–38), Menelaus (13:1–8), and Nicanor (15:1–28)?

12. If you had to summarize the overall theological theme of 2 Maccabees, how would you do so?

Euclid's Elements

"Credo ut intelligam." [*"I believe in order that I may understand."*] —St. Anselm of Canterbury

How do you know that you weren't adopted? No, really—think about it. What *conclusive* evidence do you have? (If you actually *were* adopted, you'll have to use your imagination for a moment.) Is your evidence that your parents have always said that you weren't adopted? Well, you can't simply *assume* they're trustworthy here. It's always possible that they've hidden the truth from you—maybe for a very good reason. All the pictures of your mom in the hospital, the birth certificate, everything, could have been staged. It seems you really have no *absolutely* conclusive evidence to go on. Apparently, then, you *don't* know that your mom really gave birth to you.

But hold on. You'd be *crazy* not to believe your parents. They've shown themselves trustworthy in countless ways. Sure, it's always *possible* they've constructed an elaborate conspiracy to fool you, but it's highly unlikely. You have every right to trust them. And this is the real issue here: trust. To know at least some things, you have to take people at their word. But can we ever be *certain* about things we believe, without merely trusting what we're told? Western thinkers have asked this ever since they started thinking about thinking. And they've usually answered *yes* because there has been one shining example of absolutely certain knowledge: Euclid's *Elements*.

General Information
Author and Context

Euclid is an intriguing figure. On the one hand, his work has proven to be wildly important in establishing Western culture's overall personality, for better or worse. His fingerprints show up in the most unexpected places. On the other hand, we know hardly anything about him. And the little we *do* know about him is from authors who lived centuries after he died. Of course, this situation isn't uncommon in historical research. Scholars argue, for example, whether there even *was* a Shakespeare. So we shouldn't be surprised in the case of Euclid. But it still evokes a sense of mystery—in Shakespeare's case as well as in Euclid's.

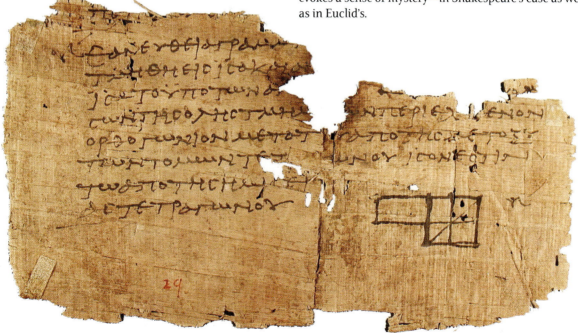

Believed to be from the first century A.D., this papyrus fragment was discovered at the important archaeological site at Oxyrhynchus in Egypt. The diagram is from Euclid's *Elements*, Book II, Proposition 5.

Here are some of the things about Euclid we can piece together from the clues. Euclid was, not surprisingly, a mathematician. He lived and taught in Alexandria, Egypt, around 300 B.C. There is some evidence, however, that he learned mathematics in Athens: the only people who could have taught him such advanced mathematics were from Plato's Academy. Moreover, he was apparently familiar with the teachings of Aristotle, who had his own school in Athens, called the Lyceum. Euclid's main work (though not his *only* work) was his *Elements* (*of Geometry*). The *Elements* is a summary of classical Greek mathematics.

Significance

Euclid's place in history would be difficult to overstate. The *Elements* was so influential that all previous mathematical books became obsolete, and the *Elements* became the primary mathematics textbook for more than two thousand years. Even in the late 1800s every schoolboy learned mathematics by going through many of the *Elements*' proofs. Even today, the geometry we learn in school is called *Euclidean geometry*.

But these facts alone aren't the most important reasons for including Euclid in the Omnibus, as important as these facts are. Rather, the most important reason is that Euclid's *method* (called the "axiomatic method") is the ideal way at getting at the truth for *any* discipline, whether philosophy, theology, science, etc. If you want to be *absolutely certain* about something (so it's claimed), then follow Euclid's method. So, then, studying Euclid's *Elements* allows us to understand why people would think this. Moreover, by learning how the *Elements* influenced Western intellectual history, we see why one of our culture's strongest "personality traits" is the desire for absolute certainty.

In fact, we can tell the story of Western culture's intellectual history through the story of Euclid's influence. Throughout Western history's search for knowledge, mathematics has always been there, guiding the way. And this hasn't always been a good thing.

This statue of Euclid stands in the Oxford University Museum of Natural History.

Historical Setting

Euclid wrote the *Elements* at a critical time of transition in Greek history. Historians usually divide ancient Greek history into two periods, before and after Alexander the Great's death in 323 B.C. The period before 323 is called the *classical* or *Hellenic* period. The period after 323 is called the *Hellenistic* period. As you probably recall, Alexander conquered most of the "known world" at the time. Of course, gaining power was a great motivator for him, but he also wanted to spread Greek culture to the "barbarian" lands, to enlighten them.

Before he traveled eastward to conquer the Middle East and India, Alexander chose a site in Northern Egypt as the center of his expanding empire. He named the city, naturally enough, after himself. Actually, he liked himself so much that he named a few other cities the same thing. His new city was strategically located on the Mediterranean and very near the juncture of three continents: Europe, Asia, and Africa. (To understand how strategic this location was, remember that this was very near the location God had chosen for Israel, a choice that helped spread the knowledge of God far beyond that little country.)

Unfortunately (at least for Alexander), he died before Alexandria was fully established as a cultural center. Upon his death, his great empire collapsed into three smaller realms. Ptolemy I, one of Alexander's closest generals, took over the Egyptian portion of the empire. He then founded Alexandria's famous library and museum (the House of the Muses). The library and museum formed what some consider the first genuine university: people from all over the empire came together to learn and discuss ideas, attempting to unify the learning of various cultures. Much of the knowledge of the ancient past comes to us through Alexandria. The Alexandrian university gave birth to a world that, in turn, produced modern culture. And Euclid was one of its most famous faculty members.

Worldview

Doubt, Trust, and Mathematics: Descartes' Doubt

It might seem strange, but we're going to begin with René Descartes, the seventeenth-century philosopher and mathematician. The reason for this should become clear shortly. Descartes, you'll probably recall, lived during a time when controversies and turmoil racked Europe. People constantly bickered over politics, religion, science, and philosophy—bickering that often resulted in people getting killed.

Whenever there's a disagreement, it helps to appeal to some authority to decide which side is right. When you're playing Scrabble, for example, and your brother or sister comes up with a dubious word like *qaxezer*, you naturally object: "That's not a word!" Yet your sibling isn't giving up that easily: "Is too!" You respond with your own subtle bit of reasoning: "Is not!" Of course, the easy solution (other than "I'm telling!") is to appeal to the dictionary, the Scrabble-sanctioned authority: "See, I *told you* it's not a word!"

Notice that one of the reasons this is an easy solution is that both of you agree that the dictionary gives the final (ahem) word in this situation. Furthermore, it's easy to tell exactly what the dictionary *says*. There's no troublesome issue of interpretation; *qaxezer* is either in there or it isn't. Case closed.

So when there's a disagreement or doubt about something, it's nice to have a clear, agreed-upon authority that can tell us what the right answer is, that can tell us what to believe. When we don't have this kind of authority, or we don't think we do, we can become confused, frustrated, and even violent, as Descartes knew.

Before Descartes' time, during the Middle Ages, there *were* agreed-upon authorities: the Church and Aristotle (sometimes these two were mixed and hard to tell apart). But during Descartes' time, people didn't always see these authorities *as* authoritative; people doubted their trustworthiness. They saw that, for centuries, the authorities continually debated the same theological and philosophical issues.

Moreover, traditional views of the physical universe were being questioned, views that the Church and Aristotle had endorsed. For example, the Church and Aristotle had been wrong about Earth's location in the universe, further diminishing their credibility. The reason you've heard the phrase "Seeing is believing" is that it's a good rule of thumb; we can usually trust our senses. And what's more obvious to our senses than that the earth is stationary? All our ordinary evidence suggests—no, *screams*—that the earth doesn't move: we don't *feel* it move, our hair doesn't blow as we (supposedly) travel really fast through space, and objects don't fly off in all directions as the earth spins. Clearly, our senses can be very wrong, and such mistakes can go unnoticed for a long time.

Descartes had tired of the uncertainty. He was particularly frustrated with the scholasticism of Europe's universities (simply put, scholasticism is a mixture of Aristotelianism with Christianity). Here's what he says about the traditional education he received:

> From my childhood I enjoyed the benefits of a literary education; and because I was persuaded that by this means one could acquire a clear and certain knowledge of all that is useful in life, I was extremely eager to learn. But as soon as I had completed the course of study at the end of which one is normally admitted to the ranks of the learned, I completely changed my opinion. For I found myself beset by so many doubts and errors that I came to think I had gained nothing from my attempts to become educated but increasing recognition of my ignorance. And yet I was at one of the most famous schools in Europe, where I thought there must be learned men if they existed anywhere on earth.

Adelard of Bath (c. 1080–c. 1152) reintroduced the *Elements* to Western Europe with his Latin translation from an Arabic edition in 1120. In the frontispiece to that work Lady Geometry uses a compass and square to teach a group of students.

Descartes had reached an intellectual crisis: he no longer trusted what the intellectual authorities had told him. He needed a solution; he needed intellectual therapy.

Look where he finds the solution:

> Those long chains composed of very simple and easy reasonings, which geometers customarily use to arrive at their most difficult demonstrations, had given me occasion to suppose that all the things which come within the scope of human knowledge are interconnected in the same way.

He finds inspiration in the method of "geometers." He's referring here to Euclid's way of proving mathematical statements. Descartes' idea is this: if we follow Euclid's lead, we can be certain of anything—or at least anything that we're *able* to know. (Notice, then, that there's a difference between knowing something and knowing it *with certainty*.)

Why would Descartes copy Euclid? Because he believed that mathematics is our best example of certainty. Look what reason can do for us! We can, says Descartes, appeal to reason when we are uncertain; reason is the authority we can go to when we need to decide what to believe. In fact, Descartes believes we *must* go to reason if we want certainty. That's the only way; every other method—scientific observation, for example—can go very wrong. The closer we can approximate mathematical methods, the closer we can approach certainty.

And he's not alone in thinking this. Many others have believed that the way to certainty is to follow the *Elements*: Thomas Hobbes, Galileo, Spinoza, Leibniz, and Sir Isaac Newton all applied Euclid's methods outside mathematics to philosophy and science. And these men, along with Descartes, were the ones who set the modern world in motion, the world in which reason is exalted above all other sources of knowledge. In fact, Descartes is often called the Father of Modern Philosophy. Although there's some truth to this, it's a bit misleading. Descartes was carrying on the Greek tradition of putting reason in charge of our beliefs, a tradition he and others learned from Euclid's *Elements*.

To understand the logical structure, we're going to imagine that Euclid's system of statements is a brick building. Think of each brick as a mathematical statement. The building, or *superstructure*, is supported by a strong *foundation*, which is also made out of bricks (that is, it too is made out of mathematical statements—but *special* statements). In Figure 1 there are ten "bricks" in the *Elements*' foundation and over four hundred in its superstructure. Imagine now that mortar holds the bricks together; this "mortar" is logic, the rules of correct reasoning.

Now let's look more closely at the foundation. As we said, the ten bricks in the foundation are special: they are extremely "strong" in the sense that we are absolutely sure they're true, so sure that we don't need to prove them. To put it another way, it's not enough that the foundational statements *be* true, they must be *obviously* true. One of Euclid's foundational statements is *the whole is greater than the part*. If someone asks you *why* this is true, slowly step away without making eye contact. Today we call these unique foundational statements *axioms*, although Euclid divides them into two groups called *postulates* and *common notions*.

The axioms must be completely certain because Euclid will *prove* the rest of the statements from them. The proven statements are called *theorems* or *propositions*; these make up the superstructure. A proof is simply a logical argument—it begins with premises and ends in a conclusion. The axioms, then, are Euclid's very first premises, his logical starting points—his *assumptions*. If we didn't allow Euclid any assumptions, he could never begin any proof (do you see why?). And proofs are only as good as their starting points, so the axioms had better be very good.

The axioms, however, are the only statements Euclid can simply assume. He has to *work* for his theorems; he has to prove them. A theorem, then, is just a proof's conclusion. Every proof must have premises. Although the ten axioms will get Euclid started, he will eventually need more premises. Here's how he can get them: once Euclid proves a theorem, its strength is upgraded, and it can now be used as an assumption in subsequent proofs. The rule is this: any premise that Euclid uses in a proof must be either (a) one of the ten axioms, or (b) a *previously proved* theorem.

For example, in Book I, in the very first proof—the proof of Proposition 1 (or I.1 for short)—Euclid is

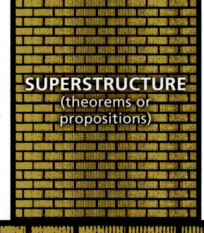

Figure 1. The ten axioms support the "superstructure" of over four hundred propositions.

allowed only the axioms as premises, since there aren't yet any previously proved propositions. In the proof of I.2, however, he can assume the axioms *as well as* I.1. After he proves I.2, he can, if he wants, use I.2 in the proof for I.3 (and in any other proof after).

So Euclid constructs the entire building from the axioms up. Starting with only the axioms, he derives the first proposition. From there he derives the *next* proposition, and so on, continuing until he derives all four hundred or so propositions.

We now call this the *axiomatic method,* and by it Euclid achieved certainty in mathematics. Descartes and many others naturally thought if they just followed this method (but in political theory, ethics, philosophy, and science, rather than in mathematics), then they, too, could have certainty.

Modernism and Mathematics

To copy Euclid's method, Descartes first needed a foundation for his philosophy; he needed beliefs he couldn't possibly doubt. Unfortunately, he didn't find many that could meet this standard. There was one, however: he found he couldn't doubt the statement, *I think.* To doubt is to think, since doubting is simply a form of thinking. This sentence, then—*I think*—became an axiom in his system, the only one, really. Not much of a beginning, but at least it was certain. He then reasoned—using logic, of course—that if he is thinking then he must exist. (You might say to yourself, "Well, duh." But remember that Descartes had set the highest possible standards for his beliefs. He wanted *super* certainty.) *I exist,* then was his first theorem. This little bit of reasoning is Descartes' famous "cogito": *cogito, ergo sum* or *I think, therefore I am.* From "I exist," he attempted to build up an entire system of undeniable beliefs.

So Descartes seemed to have solved his problem of doubt, and he did it by appealing to *reason's* authority. After all, to follow the axiomatic method is simply to follow logic, the rules of right reasoning. (As an aside, when Aristotle—a few decades before Euclid—"invented" the discipline of logic, he really took it from mathematics. But that is another story.) According to Descartes' way of thinking—a silly way of thinking, as we'll see—you can be certain of something only if you can deduce it from undeniable as-

The thirteen books climax with a discussion of the Platonic solids and a proof that these five polyhedra are the only regular polyhedra that can exist. The Greeks placed great philosophical significance on these geometric shapes.

sumptions or axioms. If, for example, you can derive "God exists" from your axioms, from things you can't possibly doubt, then—*and only then*—you can be certain that God exists. We must have reason's permission to believe something before we can be certain of it. Reason has become the ultimate authority over our beliefs.

The view that we should exalt reason above all other authorities is often called *modernism*, but we see that this view goes back to Euclid and the Greeks. Since Euclid's time, the apparent success of mathematics encouraged people to place their ultimate trust in reason; after all, they believed, the mathematicians' method was the best way to gain knowledge, and mathematicians used reason alone. Descartes took this view very seriously and put it into practice, beginning the modern age.

After Descartes, the West became even more confident in the reliability of mathematics (and therefore in the reliability of human reason). In fact, optimism in mathematics began the eighteenth-century Enlightenment. Sir Isaac Newton developed calculus as the language of his new physics, and Europe hailed his physics as the highest achievement of human reason. Mathematics, and therefore reason, is the key to understanding the universe. The motto of the Enlightenment, according to the famous philosopher Immanuel Kant, was "Have courage to use your own understanding!" Turn to reason, think for yourself, break the shackles of traditional authorities like the Church, and overthrow The Man. *Viva la revolution!*

A Closer Look at Arguments

If reason is the only way to real knowledge, it looks like faith is merely a second-rate path to belief. But when we look more closely at Euclid's method—at *logic's* method—we find something surprising.

Remember that the propositions in Euclid's system can be only as certain as the axioms. If the foundation is weak, so is the building. But where did the axioms come from? How exactly are we certain of *those*?

Of course, we can't ask for a *reason* to believe the axioms, because to ask for a reason is to ask for an argument. And axioms—by definition—aren't argued for, they're simply *assumed*. But what makes us believe the axioms? Take one of Euclid's axioms: *The whole is greater than the part*. We just "see" that it's true; there's nothing more to say, really. We simply have to trust our own judgment (perhaps this is another job that reason performs, in addition to producing arguments). Another way of saying this is that we have to *have faith* in our ability to "see" that some truths are obvious. The process of reasoning actu-

Archimedes, the master of ancient mathematicians, plans the defense of Syracuse in this engraving from 1740.

ally begins with a type of faith.

One of the sad facts, however, is that obviousness is often only in the eyes of the beholder. The human race has found itself mistaken about many things it took for granted. Think back to the belief that the earth doesn't move. We had every reason to believe that it was at a dead standstill. But our evidence was dead wrong, of course. Truth and obviousness sometimes come apart. That was the whole problem to begin with: Descartes realized that we can be wrong about things we *think* we know; that's why he struggled with doubt. Did he really solve the problem, then?

Postmodernism and Mathematics

Speaking of being wrong about the obvious, here's where Euclid's story gets really interesting—and really weird. In the 1800s, mathematicians made a "terrible" discovery: Euclid's system of geometry wasn't the only "right" geometry. There were systems that contradicted Euclid's. These systems represented alternative geometrical worlds where, for example, the sum of the interior angles of a triangle *isn't* 180 degrees and a "straight line"— still the shortest distance between two points—can curve back on itself.

To construct these new systems, these new "buildings," mathematicians took one of Euclid's axioms out of the foundation and replaced it with its *opposite*. The opposite of a Euclidean axiom *should* make for a very weak brick, a brick so weak that it jeopardizes the entire building. Yet with this brick, mathematicians still built a perfectly sound building, a consistent system with no contradictions. This would be like replacing 2+2=4 with 2+2=5 in arithmetic and still getting a consistent system of arithmetic! For these mathematicians, imagining a legitimate geometry that was different from Euclid's would have been like imagining a square circle.

And to make matters worse, scientists discovered that one of these "non-Euclidean" geometries actually describes the space we live in. In the early 1900s, Albert Einstein used non-Euclidean geometry to formulate his General Theory of Relativity. If Einstein's theory is right, then the system of the *Elements* contains false statements. This is because one of Euclid's axioms—which, remember, seemed obviously true—turned out to be false. And this falseness spread to other parts of Euclid's system. (By the way, the axiom that some modern mathematicians think is false is Euclid's fifth postulate.)

Although Western thinkers copied Euclid's method because it could turn doubt into certainty, non-Euclidean geometry showed them that this method isn't as trustworthy as they once believed. We can't really be sure that our axioms are true. People even began to doubt mathematics: if we could be surprised like this after two millennia of trusting Euclid, then what's to prevent us from being surprised again? It was like learning that your mom, after all these years, had been lying to you. If you can't trust your mom, who can you trust? Similarly, they thought, if you can't trust Euclid, who can you trust? And because Euclid's *Elements* was reason's ideal, reason itself came into doubt.

To make things worse, it's now quite agreed that Descartes' project of certainty is a big loser. We simply can't derive very many beliefs from "I think" using logic alone. We can't, it turns out, have the kind of certainty Descartes wanted.

Euclid's "failure" showed us that we can't trust reason as much as we thought. Absolute faith in reason is misplaced. But some people took this line of reasoning very far indeed, becoming overly pessimistic about reason. We often call such folks *postmodernists.* They have supposedly moved beyond the modernists' overzealous exaltation of reason. (But, of course, to conclude that we can't trust reason, postmodernists had to *use* reason. To doubt reason is to trust it. Ironically, modernists and postmodernists both put their ultimate trust in reason— the postmodernists just didn't realize it.)

Euclid is largely responsible for these two attitudes toward human reason: the extreme optimism of modernism and the extreme pessimism of postmodernism. Both attitudes are widespread today. Modernists haven't gone away; today they live right alongside postmodernists. But both extremes are misguided. The story of Euclid's influence ends in a twisted view of reason.

So what *is* the right view?

Reason and Say-So

I've suggested that postmodernists have to *use* reason to doubt it. This, however, makes it look like reason really *is* the ultimate judge of truth, the inescapable foundation of thought, our ultimate authority when it comes to what we believe. But is it really?

Think back to the *Elements'* axioms. According to the axiomatic method, we aren't allowed to give an *argument* for axioms. But what if we didn't want to merely trust our judgment of what is obvious? What if we *wanted* to give a reason for believing an axiom? Could we? Let's see. Remember the axiom, "The whole is greater than the parts"? Once we understand what the sentence means, it seems there's nothing more to say. But maybe it only *seems* this way. Maybe we could use our experience, our sense perception, to show ourselves that the whole is greater than the parts: "Take a look at this whole pie and its slices ..."

Even if we could, however, we'd have a new problem: we could always ask, "Is our *sense perception* reliable? Why do we think it delivers true beliefs?" And notice that we couldn't use sense perception to show that sense perception is reliable, because our senses are in question here. To appeal to our senses would be circular: "our senses are reliable because our senses are reliable." Not a very convincing argument (although it's valid and probably even sound!).

Could we use *reason* to justify our sense perception, to show that our sense-perception beliefs are true? You can probably see the problem with that: we could then ask, "Why think reason is reliable" Why believe what reason tells us?" It looks like we can always ask, "Why believe that?" What can stop this series of "why questions" so we can finally believe something, for Pete's sake?

Trust is the only way to stop it. In order to use either our senses or reason, we must first trust them. We have to assume that they're reliable; we have to first believe that what they *tell us* is true. To put it yet another way, we have to take them at their word, on the basis of their say-so or *testimony.* We must have faith in reason and our senses.

It seems that *faith*—believing what we're told—is at the root of all our beliefs. So even though reason and sense perception are important sources of beliefs, they don't come first in terms of importance. We have to trust their testimony first; we have to have faith in them. Faith comes before knowledge. This gets close to what Anselm meant when he said, "*Credo ut intelligam*" or, "I believe in order that I may understand."

In fact, much of what you know is based on testimony and so is ultimately based on faith: believing the say-so of parents, teachers, books, television, movies, and radio. Some of these are more trustworthy than others. But none of them are perfect. None of them has the *ultimate* say-so. Only *God's* testimony does. What He tells us is absolutely trustworthy—His say-so is the final authority on *everything*. That's why Scripture is so important for Christians. Many people—especially since the Enlightenment—have believed that faith is a substandard source of knowledge and understanding. Little did they know, however, that in order to have any knowledge at all, we must have faith and must first believe testimony.

Worshiping Yourself

The real question, then, is which testimony is most reliable? When the answer is *reason's testimony*, we fall into either modernism or postmodernism. Both attitudes resulted from putting reason on the throne, though it's easier to see in the case of modernism than in postmodernism. Notice, however, that postmodernists were disillusioned when they discovered that reason could make big mistakes. Something they unreservedly *trusted* let them down. Hero worship eventually results in disappointment. Or to put it more blatantly: idolatry is always a letdown. And the ultimate problem here is idolatry.

We've been talking as if reason is some *thing* or *object* independent of us. But really it's just another way to refer to *us*. Reason isn't a *thing* at all. Rather, *we* are the "things" that perform the action of reasoning. Therefore, to make reason the *final* judge of what to believe is to actually make yourself the final judge. Worshiping reason is worshiping yourself.

We can also see that we're trying to be God when we desire absolutely certain knowledge. No one except God has *that* sort of knowledge. To ask for it is like asking to be God.

Learning from Euclid

Euclid taught the West to put reason, and therefore the self, on the throne of knowledge. Our culture learned this lesson all too well. But almost nobody knows that *Euclid* taught us this. This is why understanding the *Elements* and its cultural significance is so important.

In other words, we can learn a different lesson from Euclid's story. By following the influence of the *Elements*, we see that reason is often very reliable but is not infallible. Reason is a gift from God that helps us navigate our lives, but it's not a perfect guide. Only Scripture is *that*.

—Mitch Stokes

Session I: Prelude

A Question to Consider

List four sources of information that you trust the most. Why do you trust them? Have they ever been wrong? Are any sources of information perfectly reliable?

From the General Information above, answer the following questions:

1. What is the most important reason for studying the *Elements*?
2. What is trust? What is faith? What does the Worldview Essay say they are? What does the dictionary say? What does the Bible say that faith is?
3. Open your copy of Euclid's *Elements* to Book I. What does Euclid present before his axioms (also called *postulates* and *common notions*)? Why does he do this?
4. Look at Euclid's ten axioms. Can you see any important difference between postulates and common notions?
5. Can you see a way to doubt any of the axioms? If so, which ones, and how would you convince someone that they might possibly be wrong? Look particularly at the fifth postulate. Is there anything "strange" or "different" about it?
6. What is postmodernism? What is modernism? How do both *exalt* reason?
7. Why must we begin any reasoning or argumentation by first assuming something?

 Reading Assignment:
Book I: Definitions, Postulates, Common Notions, and Propositions I.1–I.6. (Try to follow I.1 with your own straight edge and compass).

Note: The reading assignments from the Elements are unlike others you will encounter this year. They are very short and require very careful attention to each statement in the development of the proof. Read slowly, redraw your own diagrams as you follow the argument, and refer back to the axioms and propositions as they are referred to in the text.

Session II: Discussion
Definitions, Axioms and Early Propositions

A Question to Consider

No doubt you believe in God. Why do you believe this? What assumptions enable you to believe in God?

Discuss or list short answers to the following questions:

Text Analysis

1. What is the difference between a definition and an axiom?
2. Why does Euclid begin with the construction of an equilateral triangle in his first proposition?
3. The two tools Euclid allows in his proofs are an unmarked straight edge and a *collapsible* compass. The function of these tools is described in the first three postulates. However, the compass you are using in your construction is almost certainly a *non-collapsible* compass. In other words, it holds the same distance between its two end points when you pick it up from your paper. In propositions I.2 and I.3, Euclid proves that even with a compass whose end points fall back together, the instant you lift it from your paper, it is still possible to transfer or "cut off" line segments with equal length. Why does Euclid *prove* this very basic function of a compass rather than *assume* it?
4. You may recognize the statement of proposition 4 from a course in geometry. It is commonly referred

to as the SAS "side-angle-side" congruence theorem. What earlier propositions does the proof of proposition 4 depend on?
5. Proposition 5 is often referred to as the *pons asinorum* ("bridge of asses"). In the history of Euclid's *Elements* being used as a teaching tool, a student who was able to grasp this proof was ready to "cross the bridge" into more difficult propositions. What makes this proposition more challenging than the ones before it?
6. Propositions 5 and 6 are very closely related. What is the difference between these two propositions? Do you recall the name for this relationship from any previous study of logic?

Cultural Analysis

1. In what ways do we use the logical framework Euclid established in daily life or other areas of study? When do we begin by carefully defining language and presenting our assumptions?
2. Compare and contrast what you have read so far in Euclid's *Elements* with your previous experience studying mathematics. How is Euclid different than most of our experience learning math?

Biblical Analysis

1. Some verses in the Bible could be called definitions or axioms. Sort the following verses into two categories, definitions or axioms: Hebrews 11:1; Genesis 1:1; 1 Corinthians 13:4–8; John 1:1, 2; and Proverbs 14:16–17.

SUMMA

Write an essay or discuss this question, integrating what you have learned from the material above.
How did Euclid's *Elements* impact Western civilization? Did it affect other subjects outside mathematics?

READING ASSIGNMENT: Propositions I.7–I.15

SESSION III: ACTIVITY
Propositions I.1–I.15

Deduction Flow Chart

Science is inductive. The scientific process begins by looking at the world around you, making a hypothesis about what you observe, and testing this hypothesis through experimentation until, after repeated success, the hypothesis becomes theory or, after failure, the hypothesis is modified and retested. Truth moves from specific observations to general theories.

Mathematics is different. Unlike scientists, mathematicians begin by making very general assumptions and, once established, move to the more specific logical implications of these assumptions. Once a proposition is validated by a proof (using only definitions, axioms, and previously proven propositions), it is then added to the arsenal of established truth that can be used to prove later propositions. Truth moves from general assumptions to specific implications. This process is called deduction and will be the focus of this activity.

In a deductive system, propositions can be arranged into a logical flow chart allowing us to see their relationships and interdependence. See Figure 2 for an example.

Figure 2. Structure of Propositions 1 to 5

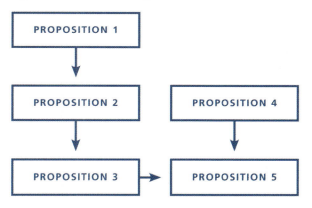

In the last session, we observed that proposition 4 does not rely on any previously proven propositions, whereas proposition 5 relies on them all. This can clearly be seen in a flow chart. Using a flow chart, it is possible to analyze how a deductive system would change as a result of changing axioms. For example, if we assumed that postulate 3 was not true, then proposition 4 would still stand valid, but the rest of the first five would crumble. When mathematicians in the 1800s replaced Euclid's fifth postulate with its opposite, they used this kind of analysis to determine what parts of Euclidean geometry were still valid.

Create your own flow chart of the first 15 propositions of Euclid's *Elements*. Make note of which postulates and common notions are used in each proof. In our translation of Euclid there is bracketed notation in the text of the proof indicating when an axiom or proposition is used. A preliminary rough draft will almost certainly be necessary to create a final, neat flow chart.

After you have drawn your chart, discuss or list short answers to the following questions:
1. Which proposition is used to support the first 15 propositions most often?
2. Which propositions are not used at all in the first 15 propositions?
3. In order for proposition 11 to be valid, which of Euclid's 5 postulates must be true?
4. What postulates are not used at all in the first 15 propositions?

Reading Assignment:
Propositions I.16, I.20, I.29, I.32, I.46–48

Session IV: Discussion
Later Propositions

A Question to Consider

Euclid has been studied by countless students over the past two millennia, not the least of whom was the sixteenth president of the United States. As James Mellon writes in *The Face of Lincoln,*

> "At last I said, Lincoln, you never can make a lawyer if you do not understand what demonstrate means; and I left my situation in Springfield, went home to my father's house, and stayed there till I could give any proposition in the six books of Euclid at sight. I then found out what demonstrate means, and went back to my law studies."[1]

Carl Sandburg mentions in his biography of Lincoln that, as a young lawyer trying to sharpen his reasoning skills, Abraham Lincoln

> "bought the Elements of Euclid, a book twenty-three centuries old. It went into his carpetbag as he went out on the circuit. At night he read Euclid by the light of a candle after others had dropped off to sleep."

Why would reading Euclid's *Elements* help Abraham Lincoln be a better lawyer? How does your study of mathematics help you in other areas of life?

Text Analysis

1. Euclid had a goal he was trying to reach. The thirteen books climax with a discussion of the Platonic solids and a proof that these five polyhedra are the only regular polyhedra that can exist. This proof would have been very important to the Greeks, who placed great philosophical significance on these geometric shapes. Taken one book at a time, Euclid usually has one particular proposition he is trying to reach that guides and organizes the preceding propositions. In Book I, this goal is perhaps the most famous theorem Euclid ever proved, proposition 47, also known as the Pythagorean theorem. Euclid's proof of this theorem is so famous that a mathematician's statement "I.47" must be a reference to Euclid in the same way that John 3:16 must be a reference to the Bible. It is this proposition and a survey of those leading up to it that are the topic of this session. What is another name for proposition I.16?[2]
2. Proposition I.20 is usually called the Triangle Inequality and states that the sum of two sides of any triangle is greater than the third. When stated another way, "The shortest distance between two points is a straight line," this seems obvious. Even a farm animal knows that the shortest distance to its food is to walk in a straight line. Why would Euclid choose to prove this theorem rather that make it a postulate?
3. Proposition I.29 is the first time in the *Elements* that Euclid uses the fifth postulate in his proof. Why would he wait so long before making use of this assumption?
4. In proposition I.32, Euclid proves that the three interior angles of a triangle are equal to two right angles. How does this language differ from the way we as modern students of mathematics talk about the angles of a triangle?
5. Look at the diagram for proposition I.47. Of what does it remind you? Why do you think Euclid demonstrated how to construct a square in proposition I.46?
6. We often hear the Pythagorean Theorem stated, "In any right triangle *a* squared plus *b* squared equals *c* squared" or shown mathematically,

$$a^2 + b^2 = c^2$$

Euclid's statement is mathematically identical. Take time to carefully read through the proof of this important proposition. There are some useful interactive resources on the Internet to help understand Euclid's proof of the Pythagorean Theorem. Why do you think this proposition has amazed scholars for millennia?

Cultural Analysis

1. How would our culture benefit from being more familiar with Euclid's *Elements?*
2. Euclid has received a fair amount of criticism in

recent centuries from mathematicians who do not think Euclid meets the modern standard of rigorous mathematics. There have been many attempts to "patch up the holes" in Euclid or begin with a different set of axioms. How valid is this criticism? Is there still value in studying Euclid?

3. The fifth postulate was eventually replaced with several different postulates, each leading to a different system of geometry. These geometries are called "non-Euclidean" geometries. They help modern scientists understand the geometry of the planet we live on and even outer space. One of these alternate postulates essentially says that lines we consider parallel (i.e., perpendicular to the same line) would eventually intersect. Can you think of one example of these lines (think of maps and globes)?

Biblical Analysis

1. As Christians, there are many truths we believe that do not have a simple scriptural proof text. Important parts of our theology come from combining many different beliefs and truths from Scripture with previous conclusions from our study of the Bible. Give an example of something you believe that is supported by Scripture but also depends on several other beliefs in order to be true.

SUMMA

Write an essay or discuss this question, integrating what you have learned from the material above.

Think of something you believe to be true. How do you know it is true? On what other beliefs does this truth depend? Can you identify the underlying assumptions of this belief? Begin with these assumptions and see if you can arrange a logical demonstration of your original belief.

SESSION V: RECITATION

Elements, Book I

Comprehension Questions

Answer the following questions for factual recall:

1. What does Euclid present before he begins proving propositions?
2. How does Euclid define a point?
3. How does Euclid define a line?
4. Which postulate was the most controversial in the history of mathematics? What was it about?
5. Explain the goal of Euclid's *Elements*.

6. What does Euclid prove in his very first proposition?
7. Explain the difference between induction and deduction.
8. Why did Abraham Lincoln study Euclid's *Elements*?
9. What proposition was Euclid working toward as the goal of Book I? What is another name for this proposition?

OPTIONAL SESSION: AESTHETICS

Art Analysis

"Don't disturb my circles." These are the apocryphal last words of Archimedes, the undisputed master of all ancient mathematicians. The events surrounding his death are the subject of this session. See the mosaic in this chapter.

The year was 214 B.C. in the middle of the Second Punic War between Carthage and Rome. The setting was Syracuse on the island of Sicily. In order to prevent an alliance between Syracuse and Carthage, General Marcus Claudius Marcellus, "The Sword of Rome," was sent to besiege the city. Syracuse was a coastal city and heavily fortified. In addition, Archimedes had invented great weapons of war that held the Roman forces at bay until 212 B.C. The Syracusans had grown confident in their ability to hold off the attack of the Romans and lowered their defenses to celebrate a religious festival to the goddess Artemis. A small group of Roman soldiers scaled the walls of Syracuse and opened the gates to the waiting Roman army. Marcellus is said to have wept at the sight of the beautiful city, knowing the devastation his army was about to unleash.

Marcellus ordered that Archimedes be captured unharmed. He had grown to respect and fear this man who had engineered devices that had foiled him for so long. Undoubtedly, he wanted Archimedes to design this same weaponry for the Romans.

Here is Plutarch's account of what happened next:

. . . Archimedes, who was then, as fate would have it, intent upon working out some problem by a diagram, and having fixed his mind alike and his eyes upon the subject of his speculation, . . . never noticed the incursion of the Romans, nor that the city was taken. In this transport of study and contemplation, a soldier, unexpectedly coming up to him, commanded him to follow to Marcellus; which he declining to do before he had worked out his problem to a demonstra-

"Don't disturb my circles." In this mosaic, the great mathematician Archimedes is interrupted in his work as the city of Syracuse is overrun by the Romans and a soldier attempts to take him prisoner.

tion, the soldier, enraged, drew his sword and ran him through. Others write that a Roman soldier, running upon him with a drawn sword, offered to kill him; and that Archimedes, looking back, earnestly besought him to hold his hand a little while, that he might not leave what he was then at work upon inconclusive and imperfect; but the soldier, nothing moved by his entreaty, instantly killed him ... Certain it is that his death was very afflicting to Marcellus; and that Marcellus ever after regarded him that killed him as a murderer; and that he sought for his kindred and honoured them with signal favours.[3]

Technical Analysis

1. Describe what is happening in this scene.
2. What points of interest are our eyes drawn to in this mosaic?

Subject Analysis

1. Who is the man seated at the table? What is his occupation?
2. Describe Archimedes' attitude toward the attacking soldier.
3. What do you think will happen next?

Content Analysis

1. What is the message of this work?
2. How does this painting compare and contrast the Greek and Roman civilizations? In what ways is our culture similar to one of these two?

Endnotes

1. James Mellon, ed. *The Face of Lincoln*. New York: Viking, 1979. 67.
2. Students who have taken Geometry should know this answer. If a student has not taken Geometry, try searching online using the key words *Euclid* and *Exterior Angles*.
3. Arthur Hugh Clough, ed. "Marcellus," *Plutarch's Lives* vol. 1. New York: Random House, 2001. 421–422.

The War with Hannibal

The season comes down to this game. If your team wins, they have a chance to become world champions. If they lose, they go home, and their season ends with failure rather than success. But even more is at stake in this game, because with so much on the line, your team is playing their most bitter rivals. A loss not only means failure, it also means humiliation over another defeat to your most hated opponents.

Despite the emotional hype and the fans packing the stadium, your team not only loses, they get pummeled. In the stands a nine-year-old boy cries over the loss, overcome by disappointment in the face of such high expectations. There in the stands he vows to dedicate his life to the game, so that when he grows up, he can play for his home team and help them avenge this humiliating loss.

Imagine if the stakes in this game were not a world championship, or team pride, or a win over a bitter rival, but death, exile, and the subjugation of your country. Imagine if that nine-year-old boy wasn't vowing to dedicate his life to baseball or football, but to military strategy; not to avenge a loss in a sporting event, but to avenge a defeat on the battlefield. Imagine that the result is not a more intense hatred of, say, the New York Yankees or the Pittsburgh Steelers, but an all-encompassing dedication to wreak military destruction on another nation. These scenarios are exactly those of Hannibal in Livy's history of the second Punic War. At nine years old, the Carthaginian general Hamilcar places his son's hand on the altar and watches Hannibal swear to dedicate his life to fighting Rome in order to reclaim his country's honor and empire. Livy's history is the account of Hannibal's fierce and passionate efforts to fulfill this promise.

General Information

Author and Context

Titus Livius (Livy) was born in Patavium (Padua), Italy in 59 B.C. During the first half of his life, Livy witnessed a world torn apart by civil war. He was fifteen years old when Julius Caesar was stabbed on his way to the Senate, and he was twenty-eight when Octavian defeated Mark Antony at Actium, bringing peace to a shattered nation by consolidating power and becoming the first emperor of the Roman world.

About the time Octavian (Augustus) became emperor, Livy moved to Rome and began writing his history of the city. This history of Rome was unlike any writing assignment you or I will ever attempt. It was no mere class writing assignment or even doctoral dissertation—it was a project that took Livy 40 years to complete, consisting of 142 books (chapters) when all was said and done! Of this massive history, the largest section remaining today is the account of Rome's struggle against Hannibal in the second Punic War.

We know very little about Livy's life apart from his dedication to writing, perhaps because his historical magnum opus dominated his career. He was not actively involved in politics, though he seems to have found favor with many political figures because of his work. Unlike many Roman authors, Livy was recognized as a great writer in his own day. Tacitus tells us that Augustus himself appreciated Livy's writing, while Pliny the Younger famously relates that he was too engrossed in Livy's history to go watch the eruption of Vesuvius! Livy died in A.D. 17, shortly after the death of Augustus. As far as we know, he was still working diligently on his history when he died.

After losing Sicily and Sardinia to the Romans, the Carthaginian general Hamilcar prepared to move his armies into Spain. His young son Hannibal begged to go along. Hamilcar prompted Hannibal to swear an oath at a sacrificial altar that he would forever be an enemy of Rome.

Significance

Livy's work is a masterful example of rhetorical skill. He is no mere historian engaged in collecting facts and putting them in order; he is a rhetorician and an artist as well. Although his Latin is difficult, his speeches and battle descriptions have inflamed hearts and minds throughout western civilization. His accounts of speeches were used in Roman schools of rhetoric starting in the first century A.D., his story of the gold rings at Cannae found its way into Dante's *Divine Comedy*, and his rhetoric, along with that of Cicero and Plutarch, was used to inspire supporters of the French Revolution in the eighteenth century.

But of all the events in his 750-year history of Rome, Livy himself finds no period more important than the second Punic War. As he himself writes in the opening paragraph, "Most historians have prefaced their work by stressing the importance of the period they propose to deal with; and I may well, at this point, follow their example and declare that I am now about to tell the story of the most memorable war in history."

From our vantage point two thousand years later, this war between Rome and Carthage has not diminished, but has perhaps grown in significance. It is surely a harsh irony for Hannibal that as a result of his life-long efforts against Rome he *did* change the entire course of western civilization . . . by losing.

For some of you as students, the most tangible significance of this war may be that you now learn Latin rather than some African language. But Livy summarizes the importance of the war for Rome when he writes of the decisive battle at Zama, "Before the next night they would know whether Rome or Carthage was destined to give laws to the nations, for the prize of victory would be not Italy or Africa, but the whole world." The course of Western history set by the Roman empire, including the influence of such men as Caesar Augustus, Nero, Vespasian, and others; the political and social environment into which God sent His Son Jesus; and the legal and philosophical heritage we have today as members of western civilization are all what they are because Rome, rather than Carthage, won at Zama, becoming the undisputed master of the Mediterranean world.

Main Characters

A number of significant characters march across the stage of this seventeen-year war. However, the one figure dominating Livy's history from the first page to the last is not a Roman hero, but Rome's fiercest enemy. Hannibal is indisputably the central character in this section of Livy's history. One commentator argues that Livy seems fascinated by the personal qualities of Rome's arch-enemy which demanded admiration, even as he describes Hannibal's faults, which distinguish him from the virtue of the best Roman generals.

Other notable Carthaginians include Hamilcar, Hannibal's father and the general who was defeated in the first Punic War; Hanno, the senator who opposes the war against Rome; and Hasdrubal, the brother of Hannibal and one of his most trusted generals. However, keeping track of Carthaginians in the story can be very confusing since many different characters have the same name. In fact, there are no fewer than seven *different* men named Hamilcar mentioned in Livy's history, along with six Hannos and five Hasdrubals!

On the Roman side there is not one figure who dominates the story throughout. Because the Roman system of government required that praetors and consuls (who serve as the army commanders) be elected each year, the men leading the Roman forces constantly changed. However, the most significant character is clearly Publius Cornelius Scipio. He first enters the story as a mere boy who rescues his wounded father from the battlefield shortly after the war begins, but he emerges as the savior of Rome more than a decade later when he defeats Hannibal at Zama and forces Carthage to surrender.

Summary and Setting

Livy's *War with Hannibal* describes the events of the second Punic War, the second of three wars fought between Rome and Carthage for mastery of the Mediterranean world in the second and third centuries B.C. This war lasted for seventeen years, beginning in 218 B.C. when Hannibal crossed the Ebro River in Spain (the boundary between Roman and Carthaginian territory established by treaty) and ending with a new treaty restricting the territory and resources of Carthage in 201 B.C.

However, the war was not a long string of Roman victories. In fact, as Livy notes, "The final issue hung so much in doubt that the eventual victors came nearer to destruction than their adversaries." Hannibal began by leading his army through Spain, defeating Roman armies and their allies, and then accomplishing one of the most famous marches in military history by taking his army, elephants and all, through the Alps and down into northern Italy. He then proceeded to decimate Roman armies at Trebia, Trasimene, and Cannae. Livy argues that the panic and despair in Rome were greater at this point in the war than when the Gauls had actually sacked Rome a century earlier.

But Hannibal paused after his victory at Cannae, both to allow his troops to rest and to woo Roman allies over to his side. Unfortunately for Hannibal, his delay allowed

Rome to recoup some of its losses, and in one of the most significant marks of loyalty in history, nearly all of Rome's allies in central Italy refused to join Hannibal despite his crushing military mastery up to that point. This delay led to a decade-long stale-mate which swung dramatically to Rome's advantage when Scipio transferred the war to Africa, swept aside every army Carthage and its allies put in the field, and finally defeated Hannibal himself at the decisive battle of Zama in 202 B.C.

Worldview

The Gods

My wife is currently enrolled in a statistics course at a local college. She decided to take the course by distance so that she would not have to go to the campus each week for classes, but she has run into a frustrating problem. The professor offers inadequate instructions for solving the required problems and consistently fails to email full explanations in response to questions. As a result of this poor communication, my wife has the challenge not only of doing the problems themselves, but also of trying to guess how exactly such problems are solved and in what format the professor wants them completed. Far from seeking to correct the problem, however, the professor actually boasts about the high percentage of students who fail his course. In the end, his class seems more designed to fail as many students as possible rather than to help them understand statistics!

But what if instead of inadequately explaining his subject matter, a professor actually changed the right answers from time to time. What if the correct answer to $2 + 2$ suddenly became 5 without warning? Such a situation would not merely be frustrating, it would turn school work into a constant guessing game as each student tried to figure out what the teacher wanted on that particular day.

Such seems to have been the way of life for a Roman citizen when it came to their religion. Livy describes the horror that omens and portents inspired in the people of Rome and the struggles they endured as appointed Romans tried to figure out how to appease the wrath of the gods. In these descriptions we catch a glimpse of what it was like to believe in the Roman gods and to live life trying to please them.

In one example, Livy recounts the anxiety and fear sweeping over the people as numerous strange portents filtered into Rome: a javelin burst into flames, a hen turned into a cock, shields sweat blood, the sun and the moon appeared to war against each other, and red-hot stones rained down on Praeneste. The senate immediately met to discuss how to respond to these portents. They offered sacrifices of purification, they performed every ceremony ordered by the divine writings, and they set aside a period of prayer for divine favor. The result of the Romans' religious efforts at appeasing the gods was ... one of the greatest military disasters in Roman history at Lake Traisimene!

After this defeat, the Senate appointed Quintus Fabius Maximus dictator, and he immediately ordered new investigations into how Rome might satisfy the gods' displeasure. A new set of books was consulted, hundreds more oxen were sacrificed, games were dedicated to Jupiter, a shrine was built to Venus, and additional religious ceremonies were performed. And when the results of their redoubled religious efforts were in ... *two* Roman armies had been destroyed by Hannibal at Cannae! We are left with the picture of an entire nation scrambling to find a solution to a divine problem. Rome tried every possible method of appeasing the wrath of the gods, only to meet with new disasters after each new religious ceremony.

Of course, Rome did eventually win the war, so perhaps they finally found the magic festival or sacrifice. But even on the eve of victory the gods did not prove themselves trustworthy, for the weeks leading up to Rome's victory were full of more disastrous portents. In the final year of the war, Rome witnessed crows eating gold off the Capitol, a foal born with five legs, and fire and meteors blazing across the sky. This time, however, the bad omens did not end in utter defeat, but in final victory. In other words, the Roman people swayed between hope and fear based upon divine portents that had no bearing on the events that would actually take place, they trusted in sacred writings that did *not* adequately explain how men might be reconciled with them, and their priests were forced to spend their days guessing at how best to serve these gods. What a depressing religion to dedicate oneself to!

In many ways, Livy's description brings to mind another story in which men desperately try to figure out how to serve their false god. In 1 Kings 18, four hundred servants of Baal pray to their god, leap about his altar, prophesy for hours on end, and even carve themselves up with lances, all in an effort to get a response out of Baal. But the silence of this god justifies the mocking of Elijah rather than the passionate dedication of these four hundred prophets. Elijah's jibes that perhaps Baal is sleeping, busy, or on a journey make all too clear that even if Baal were a real god, he can not be compared with the One True God who answers Elijah's prayer with divine fire.

What a contrast the God of Scripture offers to these faithless divinities who offer so little to a Roman people suffering through one of the worst crises in their history! Rather than send portents which frighten and forebode disaster regardless of the eventual outcome, the God of the Bible sends prophets who truly and accurately prophesy what the sovereign Lord of the universe will bring to pass; and rather than fill a book with religious ceremonies which may or may not satisfy divine wrath on a particular day, God tells His people how to worship Him and faithfully responds if they keep His word.

But the greatest differences between the Roman divinities and the God of the Bible are expressed by the incarnation of Jesus Christ. The first great difference relates to what theologians refer to as God's *immanence*. God is not only an incomparably majestic being who is greater than anything we can contemplate, He is also a God who has chosen to come down and interact with His people. He has not remained aloof, a mystery for each of us to solve as best he can. Rather, God has chosen a particular people and revealed to them His power, His law, and His mercy in the story of the Old Testament. In the New Testament, God further reveals Himself by making known the mystery which had previously been hidden (Col. 1:27). Of course, this revelation comes in the person of Jesus Christ. While the Romans must try and try again to figure out exactly what their gods want and how in the world they might please them, the One True God reveals Himself through creation, gives specific messages to His people through prophets, and, ultimately, comes to dwell with His people on earth. In each of these instances, God makes known to us who He is and how we ought to serve Him, rather than remain high above us and force us into a frustrating cycle of divine trial and error.

The second great difference between the gods of Rome and the God of Scripture is the result of the final, perfect sacrifice Jesus accomplished on the cross. Livy paints a picture of a never-ending struggle to atone the lat-

The Romans offer a fifty pound golden thunderbolt to their god Jupiter as they deal with horrific omens and defeat in war. When that offering apparently fails to appease his anger, they dedicate games and offer him 300 oxen. Will it ever be enough? For Christians, this repetitive pattern of displeasure, sacrifice, and satisfaction ends on the Cross.

est divine wrath with bigger and better sacrifices and festivals. When a fifty pound golden thunderbolt doesn't quite satisfy Jupiter, gifts of silver don't appease Juno, or three days of public prayer aren't enough pleading to win the gods' favor, then the stakes increase. Next time, the Romans offer Great Games and three hundred oxen to Jupiter, they dedicate a series of shrines to a host of gods and goddesses, and another period of public prayer takes place. But even if the golden thunderbolt had been enough to satisfy Jupiter, his wrath would only be averted for a short time. A few months, or weeks, or days later, the priests would again be discussing how to win back the gods' favor.

For Christians, this repetitive pattern of displeasure, sacrifice, and satisfaction ends on the Cross. As the author of Hebrews emphasizes repeatedly, Christ shows Himself better than any previous sacrifice by offering Himself *once*, and by that one sacrifice bringing about *eternal salvation*. Because of Christ we do not need to wear a beaten path to and from the altar, constantly seeking forgiveness, satisfaction, and divine approval. Rather, our faith in His one sacrifice unites us with Him in a relationship that never lacks divine favor. As Jesus explains to His disciples, they are united to Him, and therefore God the Father loves them even as He loves His own Son. Livy's description of the hopeless repetition of religious ceremony only highlights the glorious truth that our religious ceremonies are repeated because we constantly rejoice in a great promise of salvation, rather than because we need to find new and better ways to appease divine wrath.

Virtue

Have you ever watched the Academy Awards or some reality TV talent contest and found yourself yelling at the TV screen because you can't imagine how in the world the judges chose *that* actor or singer? Or perhaps you've perused the awards for Best of Show at a local county fair and there is no way the dog that won was really better than the cute collie you preferred. We've probably all experienced this feeling that we're sure is righteous indignation on behalf of the slighted party, but why do these decisions happen? Why isn't the best performance obvious to everyone? Of course, the reason is that we make our choices based on a different set of standards than the judges. Perhaps our checklist ends with the awesome battle scene from the movie we wanted to win Best Picture, or the cute face of the dog we were rooting for, while the judges have a different set of categories they use to make their selections.

In the same way, the moral standards we operate under determine what we consider virtuous or depraved. Part of Livy's purpose for writing his history is to offer moral examples for future generations. In light of this, he comments throughout the story on the virtue or vice of various characters. But he makes his moral judgments based on a specific standard of virtue which he refers to as Roman character and tradition.

There are a number of specific actions that appeal to Livy's moral tastes based on this standard of virtue. For instance, Livy praises the courage and determination of the Roman people in the face of their repeated defeats at the hands of Hannibal. Livy points out that despite losing one army after another and watching Hannibal clear a path to Rome itself, the people never breathed a word about peace, but always talked about how they could renew their efforts to defend Rome from its enemy. At another point, Livy extols the loyalty of Rome's allies, who watched Hannibal ravish their land and conquer the Roman armies whose duty it was to protect them, yet remained faithful to Rome and withheld support from Hannibal. Scipio is lauded for not taking revenge on the Carthaginians after they treacherously violate an armistice. According to Livy, the reason for Scipio's actions was his refusal to go against the tradition of the Roman people and his sense of what was right.

Livy also recounts the actions of men who fail to live up to his standard of virtue. Despite his admiration for Hannibal's skill and courage as a military leader, Livy condemns Hannibal for disregarding truth, honor, religion, and oaths; Masinissa received a lecture from Scipio on the importance of self-control after he sacrificed honor to personal lust; and Varro's pride and arrogance are displayed as an example of what happens when a man puts his own greatness ahead of the interests of the country.

From a biblical standpoint, Livy is right to praise self-control and condemn lust, to commend loyalty and oppose treachery, to applaud

The War with Hannibal 273

courage and criticize cowardice. Further, Livy's moral code as a whole seems to be driven by the virtue of self-sacrifice, which Jesus and his apostles also commend. On account of this similarity, it may seem that Livy's moral standards basically agree with the standards established by God for His people.

In reality, however, a vast chasm separates Livy's moral code from the morality of the Bible. While the particulars may appear similar at times, the underlying motivation for virtue is quite different. For Livy, self-sacrifice is oriented around Rome. A man passes the test of life and accomplishes his purpose as a Roman citizen by living honorably for his country and by sacrificing his own interests and desires for his city. It is *patria*, the fatherland, which motivates selfless virtue and inspires courage and honor. Thus, lust and self-indulgence, cruelty and treachery, cowardice and disregard for the gods deserve condemnation because they are not worthy of the honor and tradition of Rome, not because they violate the example of a holy, righteous God. But just as we would condemn a man who carefully controlled his desires in order to improve his own honor and reputation, and just as we condemn politicians whose motivation for acting honorably is to earn votes in an election, so we should condemn a standard of morality driven by nothing other than the tradition of a city or country.

Self-sacrifice is not admirable because a city or government deserves our first love; self-sacrifice is worthy of praise because God sacrifices Himself for His people. As God's people, we are to be holy, just as He is holy; we are to love each other because He first loved us; and we are called to deny ourselves and pick up our crosses because He first denied Himself and picked up His cross on Calvary. While some may complain that this is a circular argument which demands some other justification for commending selfless virtue, this is the only standard of virtue that will last. Contrary to the arguments of Socrates in the *Euthyphro*, God *does* determine what is holy and righteous. There is no standard higher than the perfect, loving moral code decreed by the eternal, self-existent Creator of the universe, with the decree arising out of His eternal nature and character. His word and His example are the rock upon which we are to build our moral houses.

In the end, Livy's foundation of morality must fail, for

Livy's moral code seems to be driven by the virtue of self-sacrifice, but for him, self-sacrifice is oriented around the city of Rome. In Christ Carrying the Cross *by Hieronymus Bosch (1453–1516) we see that self-sacrifice is not admirable because a city deserves our first love; rather, it is worthy of praise and imitation because God sacrifices Himself for His people.*

Snow Storm: Hannibal and His Army Crossing the Alps was completed in 1812 by the British painter Joseph Mallord William Turner. The painting brings together two of Turner's own experiences, including a snowstorm he witnessed in Yorkshire, England and his travels in northern Italy. Turner tries to capture the chaos and fear that grip Hannibal's troops as they watch an impending snowstorm descend upon them during their march across the Alps in 218 B.C.

Rome is neither eternal nor immutable. Just as a house collapses when the foundation shifts, so Livy's standard of morality collapses when Rome crumbles or when its citizens find ulterior motives for action. In contrast to this temporal and changeable foundation, the eternal God offers an immutable standard of virtue, and He Himself gives us the strength to live according to it.

The Sovereign Lord of History

As a final comment, it is worth pausing and considering how a Roman historian interested in lauding his country's virtue and tradition still demonstrates God's sovereign rule over history. It may seem like analyzing Livy in light of a biblical worldview is like trying to stuff the square block into the circle opening of a toddler toy. After all, Hannibal's march on Rome happens thousands of miles from God's people in Palestine and hundreds of years before Jesus and His apostles enter the narrative. Livy's history is meant to recount the history of Rome and to inspire Rome's citizens to live lives worthy of their country's tradition, not to argue for or against the God of the Bible. Why shouldn't we just admire Livy's work for its compelling style and content, enjoy a good story, and leave it at that?

Of course, we ought to admire the excellence of Livy's work and enjoy the story he has to tell. His rhetorical skill draws readers into a storyline already full of drama and suspense. The daring marches of Hannibal, the deliberations of German and Latin leaders who must decide which power to join and which to fight, the politics of the Roman world and the personalities of their consular commanders, and the personal interests which drive Syphax and Masinissa to battle each other in Africa all contribute to one of the most fascinating historical narratives in ancient history. In addition, Livy brings this narrative alive with the passionate speeches he puts in the mouths of generals and senators and by developing the personalities of his characters with compelling reality.

But once we have enjoyed Livy's narrative, we must step back and consider where this story fits in the overall context of history. When we take this step, God's sovereignty stares us full in the face. The second Punic War is part of His plan to prepare the Mediterranean world for the incarnation of Jesus Christ. If Rome had not defeated Carthage, the western Mediterranean would not have fallen under the control of one nation. If Rome and Carthage had continued to co-exist, it is doubtful that Rome would have had the military strength to extend its empire east, through Greece and into Palestine. In other words, as Livy argues, the stakes in the battle at Zama in 202 B.C. were not Italy or Spain, but the whole world. This victory, then, was part of God's sovereign plan to bring His Son into a world under the rule of one empire, which spoke one language, and which ensured peace throughout the Mediterranean world. Such a situation allowed for the introduction and spread of the gospel, fulfilling God's promise of a kingdom comprised of all people and all nations. Thus, even in the gripping narrative of Hannibal's elephants and the struggle between two of the greatest military leaders in history, God's hand is at work, fulfilling His purposes and preparing the world for salvation in His Son, Jesus Christ.

—Christopher Walker

For Further Reading

Spielvogel, Jackson J.. *Western Civilization*. Seventh Edition. Belmont, Calif.: Wadsworth/Thomson Learning, 2009. 122-124, 135.

Veritas Press History Cards: New Testament, Greece and Rome. Lancaster, Pa: Veritas Press. 19.

SESSION I: PRELUDE

A Question to Consider

How should we respond to failure?

From the General Information above answer the following questions:

1. What was the historical context for Livy's early life?
2. How is Livy different from many of his fellow Roman authors?
3. How have Livy's writings impacted men and women throughout Western history?
4. What was the significance of Rome's victory in the second Punic War?
5. What makes keeping track of Carthaginian characters so difficult?
6. What changed the course of the second Punic War, bringing Hannibal's momentum to a halt and eventually allowing Rome to conquer?

READING ASSIGNMENT:
The War with Hannibal, XXI.1–XXI.24

SESSION II: DISCUSSION
The War with Hannibal, XXI.1–XXI.24

A Question to Consider

How do our desires and goals affect our character as well as reflect it?

Text Analysis

1. What life purpose drove Hannibal's actions? When did this become his goal?
2. After Hamilcar died, what debate took place in the senate regarding how Hannibal should be raised?
3. What good qualities result from Hannibal's time with the army?
4. How was Hannibal's character negatively influenced by his desires and his upbringing?

Cultural Analysis

1. What goals does our culture encourage us to pursue in life?
2. Is it possible to have good character and also pursue our culture's goals?

Biblical Analysis

1. What does Matthew 6:21 have to say about the relationship between our desires and our character?
2. What fundamental contrast is introduced in 1 John 2:15–17? What does this contrast tell us about the possibility of pleasing God and setting up goals motivated by earthly desires?

SUMMA

Write an essay or discuss this question, integrating what you have learned from the material above. How can we establish goals for our life that will yield good character?

READING ASSIGNMENT:
The War with Hannibal, XXI.25–XXI.46

Session III: Aesthetics
The War with Hannibal, XXI.25–XXI.46

Art Analysis

Joseph Mallord William Turner (1775–1851), a British Romantic artist, was perhaps the most successful landscape artist of the nineteenth century. The Royal Academy of the Arts first displayed one of his paintings when he was 15 years old! As a Romantic, he believed that art should display the *sublime*. Edmund Burke described the *sublime* as that which produces the strongest possible emotion upon the human mind. While beauty or joy may be sublime, Burke believed that terror produced the strongest possible emotion. Turner used nature and the world around him, in addition to poignant moments from ancient history, to produce such strong emotions in his work. Unfortunately, Turner's own life ended in emotional turmoil. He became radically eccentric, isolated himself from all his acquaintances, refused to sell any of his paintings, and finally disappeared for months before being found in hiding, ill and on the verge of death.

Technical Analysis

1. Does this work demonstrate the artist's ability and expertise?
2. Describe the scene Turner paints for us.
3. Is this work realistic and proportional or not?
4. Are the details of the men and animals significant to the central appeal of the painting, or are they strictly in the background?
5. How is light used in this work?
6. What colors are used in this work?
7. What are the men doing in the painting?

Subject Analysis

1. Why might Turner want the snowstorm to dominate this painting?
2. Why might Turner limit himself to painting scattered groups of regular soldiers instead of Hannibal himself, or a large portion of the army?
3. How does the impressionistic, or non-realistic, painting of the snowstorm produce greater terror than a realistic painting of swirling snow could do?

Content Analysis

1. What is the message of this work?
2. What is worthy of praise in this piece of art? What is worthy of condemnation?

READING ASSIGNMENT:
The War with Hannibal, XXI.47–XXI.63

Session IV: Recitation
The War with Hannibal, XXI.1–XXI.63

Comprehension Questions

Answer these questions for factual recall.

1. What command did Hannibal act as if he had received since his first day as commander?
2. How did the war between Rome and Carthage begin?
3. Whose aid did Rome seek against Hannibal, and what was their response?
4. What dream encouraged Hannibal on his quest to conquer Italy?
5. According to Livy, how did the first cavalry skirmish of the war foreshadow the final outcome?
6. What did the Carthaginian troops fear more than Roman soldiers?
7. Why did Hannibal and Scipio feel mutual respect for each other prior to the first battle in Italy?
8. Why did Scipio hastily retreat after the first battle with Carthage?
9. What was the significance of the Roman army gathered at the Trebia?
10. What was Hannibal's strategy in the Battle at Trebia?

11. What was the result of the battle?
12. What controversy surrounded the new consul Flaminius when he took office?

READING ASSIGNMENT:
The War with Hannibal, XXII.1–XXII.21

The next session will be a student-led discussion. Students will be creating their own questions concerning the issue of the session. Students should create three Text Analysis Questions, two Cultural Analysis questions, and two Biblical Analysis questions. For more detailed instructions, please see the chapter on the *Iliad,* Session III.

Issue

To whom do we owe loyalty? Why is loyalty admirable?

SESSION V: STUDENT-LED DISCUSSION
The War with Hannibal, XXII.1–XXII.21

A Question to Consider

To whom do we owe loyalty? Why is loyalty admirable?

Students should read and consider the example questions below that are connected to the Question to Consider above. Last session's assignment was to prepare three questions and answers for the Text Analysis section and two additional questions and answers for both the Cultural and Biblical Analysis sections below.

Text Analysis

Example: What policies did Hannibal employ in trying to win the support of Rome's allies?

Answer: Hannibal went back and forth between attempting to frighten the allies of Rome into joining him by devastating their lands and trying to win their favor by showing mercy and compassion. However, in the end, very few Roman allies deserted to Hannibal's side. The majority remained loyal to Rome, which Livy attributes to their "just and mild" rule.

Cultural Analysis

Example: What motivates loyalty in our culture today?

Answer: As with many virtues, loyalty is still recognized as a good thing by our culture at times, but this admiration has little foundation. Our culture does not see any reason to sacrifice its own interests for the interests of others, so loyalty, as with so many other virtues, becomes an empty action performed merely because it is admired or in order to gain trust or respect. In other words, the only motivation for loyalty in our culture is actually a selfish desire for greater admiration or respect.

Other cultural issues to consider: To what extent is loyalty still admired in marriage relationships? In friendship? In family relationships? What will happen to a society which no longer respects or values loyalty in relationships?

Biblical Analysis

Example: What does the story of Jonathan and David in 1 Samuel 20 teach us about loyalty?

Answer: The fear of the Lord leads to wisdom. Instead of being driven to compromise our standards in the face of fear, the fear of the Lord reinforces our moral standards. God is both just and almighty. We ought to fear the consequences of displeasing our heavenly Father. But this fear drives us back to God and His will, rather than away from it.

Other Scriptures to consider: Prov. 18:24, Prov. 17:17, Ruth 1:16, Mark 6:1–6.

SUMMA

Write an essay or discuss this question, integrating what you have learned from the material above.

What distinguishes the loyalty urged in Scripture and the loyalty demonstrated in *The War with Hannibal*?

READING ASSIGNMENT:
The War with Hannibal, XXII.22–XXII.42

Session VI: Writing
The War with Hannibal, XXII.22–XXII.42

Historical Fiction

In this session, you are going to complete a short writing assignment. Remember, we are looking for quality rather than quantity. You should write no more than 1,000 words (if typing) or you should write on one side of a piece of paper legibly if you are writing by hand. You will lose points for writing more than this. You will be allowed to turn in your writing three times. The first and second time you turn work in your teacher will grade it by editing your work. This is done by marking what is wrong and by making suggestions for improving your writing. Your job is to take these suggestions and rewrite your assignment. Your final submission's grade will be recorded. It will be graded in the following manner: 25 points for English grammar; 25 points for content accuracy— historical, theological, etc.; 25 points for logic— does this make sense and is it structured well?; 25 points for rhetoric—is it a joy to read?

Your assignment is to write an imaginative story based on the following historical setting. Your goal is to create a story that is factually and grammatically accurate, that makes sense and that people will enjoy reading.

Historical Setting: Imagine that you are a soldier in Hannibal's army just days before the battle of Cannae. Livy describes the situation as desperate—Hannibal was out of provisions and his Spanish troops were ready to desert. Write a letter or a journal entry describing the atmosphere in the camp.

Here is an example for your inspiration:

Journal Entry

I have given up trying to discover what an army must do to enjoy the fruits of victory. We demolished the Romans under Sempronius at Trebia, we crushed a second Roman army under Flaminius at Lake Trasimene, we have yet to suffer a single defeat, and yet we stand on the brink of starvation, desertion, and retreat. The thrill of success that drove us through the hardships of mountains, floods, cold, and forced marches only makes the sting of failure all the sharper. The joy of victory only leaves us more discouraged in the face of defeat.

This morning I wandered aimlessly around camp striking up conversations with the off-duty sentries in an effort to ignore the noises coming from my empty stomach. The food shortage has grown daily, and in little more than a week there will be no food left for any of us. With such a prospect, our daily rations have been cut to a bare minimum. Despite our continued successes on the battlefield, the surrounding towns universally gathered their grain and flocks within the walls of their towns as soon as we entered the district. I suppose it wouldn't be wise to attempt a siege with a consular army hemming us in, but I sure wish our battle plans were aimed more directly at conquering hunger than just another proud Roman consul! Just as the sight of the enemy retreating inspires new strength, so the sound of an empty stomach grinding against its own walls makes every muscle feel limp. Even if we lay siege to a town, I'm sure I wouldn't have the strength to breach the walls without increasing the size of my breakfast and adding lunch back on the menu.

I had hoped that conversation would drive out the ever present feeling of discouragement and despair, but the impending disaster apparently dominates the thoughts of all the other soldiers as well. During one conversation with a sentry named Mago, I learned that some Spanish troops had secretly met to discuss deserting to the Romans. The irony struck me immediately: how many times in history had a group of soldiers considered deserting *from* a repeatedly victorious general *to* an army whose general had changed with each new defeat and whose troops were fresh recruits due to the loss of an entire army the year before? Victorious against any sword or spear, Hannibal is losing to the dinner plate. I continued my aimless wandering through the camp, my gloom growing heavier rather than lighter with each conversation.

This afternoon, new rumors spread about that even Hannibal has begun to despair. One soldier went so far as to accuse him of considering a dash to the safety of Gaul with his cavalry while leaving those of us serving in the infantry to the mercy of Varro and the Romans. Even if I refuse to grant any truth to this rumor, it still demonstrates the hopelessness and terror hanging over all the soldiers. And what if they are right? What if Hannibal does desert us? We certainly won't find any friends in Rome. But I don't believe it. Even a cruel general such as Hannibal won't leave the soldiers he's marched with since he was a boy to be butchered or enslaved by a new, proud Roman consul.

Meanwhile, sounds of celebration and a tremor of brash courage float to our ears from the Roman camp. As great an irony as a despairing Hannibal seems to me, a confident Roman camp seems even more incongruous! Here their commander finds himself in the same position as two others who met death and destruction at the hands of Hannibal, and with untested recruits this new consul Varro thinks he can crush Hannibal and the Carthaginians like a millwheel grinding grain. I can't decide which position I'd rather fill, that of a hopeless victor or that of a confident, but defeated soldier.

Our one hope is that this unfounded confidence will lead yet another Roman general into a trap. Hannibal has proved the superiority of his battle strategies time and time again. Personally, I don't think Varro knows what he's up against. Not every general could lead an army, elephants and all, over the Alps through the storms of winter. Not every general could out-maneuver three Roman armies. This is the general we have leading us. But Hannibal will have to hurry. He doesn't have the luxury of patience this time. I'd like to say, "time will tell the end of the story," but my stomach doesn't have the patience for time to tell.

Perhaps tomorrow these pages will bear more hopeful thoughts. For now, since ambling about camp and chatting with other disgruntled infantrymen has only made my limbs feel weaker and heavier and has only filled my mind with more thoughts that I'd rather not think, I am off to try sleep.

READING ASSIGNMENT:
The War with Hannibal, XXII.43–XXII.61

Hannibal's feat of leading his army over the Alps inspired the respect of even his opponent Scipio, the Roman general.

SESSION VII: DEBATE
The War with Hannibal, XXII.43–XXII.61

A Question to Debate

Should the Roman soldiers captured at the battle at Cannae be ransomed?

Note to homeschoolers: This activity will prove meaningful enough to make special efforts to include others. Try to enlist the participation of other homeschool children near the same age or the entire family.

DIRECTIONS

Today we are going to serve as judge and jury as we consider the case for and against ransoming the captured Roman soldiers after the battle of Cannae. To do this, follow these steps:

• Elect a judge, two defense attorneys (to set forth the soldiers' case) and two prosecutors (who are against ransoming the soldiers).

• Others will be members of the Roman Senate. After reviewing the speeches made in favor and in opposition to the proposed ransom in XXII.59-60, list reasons why the soldiers should or should not be ransomed. The judge should write out the charges on the blackboard for all to see. The prosecuting and defense attorney should write the charges on notebook paper.

• The prosecution will then set forth its case. Then the defense will present its case. (Limit the time of each side.)

• The Senate should then decide whether the soldiers should be ransomed, or whether their character and actions or the situation of the Roman state preclude their being ransomed.

READING ASSIGNMENT:
The War with Hannibal, XXX.1–XXX.15

Session VIII: Recitation
The War with Hannibal, XXII.1–XXII.61

Comprehension Questions

Answer these questions for factual recall.
1. Why did the Romans argue that they had only one legitimate consul despite electing two?
2. What two bad omens terrified the Roman troops before the battle of Lake Trasimene?
3. Describe Hannibal's strategy at the battle of Lake Trasimene.
4. After the defeat at Lake Trasimene, what significant step did Rome take for its protection during the time of crisis?
5. What tactic did the dictator, Quintus Fabius Maximus, take against Hannibal? How did his Master of Horse respond to this tactic?
6. What caused the Spanish tribes to contemplate breaking with Carthage and supporting Rome?
7. What plan did Hannibal employ to turn popular opinion against Fabius?
8. Describe Varro's attitude as he left Rome for the battlefield.
9. What was Hannibal's situation in the weeks leading up to the battle of Cannae?
10. What was generally considered to be Rome's salvation in the face of its defeat at Cannae?
11. What steps did the Senate take to curb the confusion that reigned in the city as a result of its fear, sorrow, and despair?
12. What facts does Livy cite to demonstrate the courage and heart of the Roman people in the face of repeated defeats?

Reading Assignment:
The War with Hannibal, XXX.16–XXX.30

The next session will be a student-led discussion. Students will be creating their own questions concerning the issue of the session. Students should create three Text Analysis Questions, two Cultural Analysis questions, and two Biblical Analysis questions. For more detailed instructions, please see the chapter on the *Iliad*, Session III.

Issue

Are we more ready to complain about trials than to give thanks for blessings?

Session IX: Student-Led Discussion
The War with Hannibal, XXX.16–XXX.30

A Question to Consider

Are we quicker to complain about trials than to give thanks for blessings? Why or why not?

Students should read and consider the example questions below that are connected to the Question to Consider above. Last session's assignment was to prepare three questions and answers for the Text Analysis section and two additional questions and answers for both the Cultural and Biblical Analysis sections below.

Text Analysis

Example: What inspired the Roman people to offer public thanks to the gods for their deliverance from the threat of Hannibal's army?

Answer: Several older senators reminded the people of the fear and panic that spread throughout the city when Hannibal was knocking at the gates and the desperate prayers offered to the gods at that time. But these senators also rebuked the people, for now the gods had answered their prayers, but no motion to give public praise and thanksgiving had been put forward.

Cultural Analysis

Example: To what extent is thankfulness admired in our culture?

Answer: There are places where "old-fashioned thankfulness" is still respected, but there is little reason to place a high value on thanksgiving. Taking time to show your appreciation, either through a thank you note or a phone call, or even an email, is practiced less and less. In many cases, this is because there is a sense of entitlement. Many people feel they deserve to be treated well, so just as a parent doesn't reward a child for doing what is expected, thankfulness seems a bit superfluous. In other cases it is because the focus is so bent inwards on the self, that the person assumes everything is fine and normal when people are doing things for him, but he must make his complaints known as soon as anything crosses his will.

Other cultural issues to consider: How does our culture view grumbling and complaining? What reasons might our culture have for continuing to show thanks and appreciation? Does our culture still have any place for giving thanks to God?

Biblical Analysis

Example: How does Jesus' response to the thankful leper in Luke 17:11–17 highlight our sinfulness as well as the proper response to God's goodness?

Answer: Jesus marvels that even in the face of a miracle ninety percent of the men still neglected to give glory to God. At the heart of our rebellion is a refusal to give God the glory and honor He deserves. The one who returns, however, becomes an example of proper, God-glorifying thankfulness.

Other Scriptures to consider: Col. 3:15, 1 Thess. 5:18, Jude 16, Numbers 11.

Summa

Write an essay or discuss this question, integrating what you have learned from the material above.
Why should we cultivate a habit of thankfulness?

Reading Assignment:
The War with Hannibal, XXX.31–XXX.45

Session X: Activity

The War with Hannibal, XXX.31–XXX.45

Poetry Analysis

Read the following poem by the Roman author Juvenal and answer the following questions:

> Put Hannibal in the scales:
>   how many pounds
>   will that peerless
> General mark up today?
> This is the man
> for whom Africa
> Was too small a continent, though it stretched
>   from the surf-beaten
> Ocean shores of Morocco east to the
>   steamy Nile,
> To tribal Ethiopia, and new elephants' habitats.
> Now Spain swells his empire, now he surmounts
> The Pyrenees. Nature sets in his path
> High Alpine passes, blizzards of snow:
>   but he splits
> The very rocks asunder, moves mountains
>   with vinegar.
> Now Italy is his, yet still he forces on:
> 'We have accomplished nothing,' he cries,
>   'till we have stormed
> The gates of Rome, till our Carthaginian
>   standard
> Is set in the City's heart.' A fine sight it must
>   have been,
> Fit subject for caricature—the one-eyed
>   commander
> Perched on his monstrous beast! Alas, alas
>   for glory,
> What an end was here: the defeat, the
>   ignominious
> Headlong flight into exile,

We last read of Hannibal in Livy's account as he is about to flee to the Seleucid king of Syria, Antiochus III. Several years later, as admiral of the naval forces of the king of Bithynia in Asia Minor, he again found himself up against the power of Rome and poisoned himself rather than surrender to Roman authority.

282   OMNIBUS IV

everyone gawping at
The once-mighty Hannibal turned humble
    hanger-on,
Sitting outside the door of a petty Eastern despot
Till His Majesty deign to wake. No sword,
    no spear,
No battle-flung stone was to snuff the fiery spirit
That once had wrecked a world: those
    crushing defeats,
Those rivers of spilt blood were all wiped out
    by a
Ring, a poisoned ring. On, on, you madman, drive
Over your savage Alps, to thrill young
    schoolboys
And supply a theme for speech-day recitations!

Juvenal, *Satire X*, lines 147–167
Translated by Peter Green

1. How does Juvenal express Hannibal's ambition in the poem? How does Juvenal's summary of Hannibal's ambition compare with Livy's account of Hannibal's motivation for war with Rome?
2. Juvenal begins the poem by portraying Hannibal as an unstoppable force. What images does Juvenal use to create this impression?
3. What does Juvenal mean by "moves mountains with vinegar"?
4. How does Juvenal demonstrate the extent of Hannibal's fall and express the contrast from his former glory?
5. To what does Juvenal attribute the change of Hannibal's fortunes? (See XXIII.12 for the specific image.)
6. According to the final lines, what did Hannibal ultimately accomplish for all his ambition and initial success?

OPTIONAL SESSION A: ACTIVITY

Speech Craftsman

Livy was more than a historian; he was a craftsman of words. The speeches he composed for his characters provide excellent examples of good rhetoric for readers who desire to understand the art of speaking well.

Choose one of the speeches made by a senator, Hannibal, or Scipio, and analyze it in light of the following questions:
1. How does the speaker establish his *ethos* (his trustworthiness and authority to speak in this matter)?
2. How does the speaker use images and examples to stir the emotions of his audience (referred to as *pathos*)?
3. What logical arguments does the speaker use to convince his audience of his position (the *logos* of the speech)?
4. Is the speech structured effectively (i.e., Does have it have an introduction that grabs attention? Does it flow logically? Does it conclude in a manner that ties the speech together? Does it use evidence effectively to prove its claims)?
5. Is the speech enjoyable to read? Why or why not?

OPTIONAL SESSION B: REVIEW

Comprehension Questions

Discuss or list short answers to the following questions:
1. How did Hannibal draw Rome into war with Carthage?
2. Summarize the three disastrous defeats suffered by Rome in Northern Italy after Hannibal descended from the Alps.
3. What events led the Carthaginian senate to recall Hannibal from Italy?
4. How and why did Carthage treacherously break the armistice after they had sued for peace?
5. Summarize Hannibal's speech to Scipio asking for peace before the battle of Zama.
6. What convinced Scipio to grant Carthage terms of peace rather than attacking the city itself?

ON THE NATURE OF THINGS

Ancient philosophy is sometimes very hard to follow, detached as it is from everyday life. No one has ever seen one of Plato's forms, the eternal "intellectual" objects that Plato believed were more real than the "sensible" objects that we bump into every day. Aristotle said that every thing is a combination of two realities, form and matter. Matter by itself has no shape, color, no properties of any kind, and "form" is even more elusive. Since what we actually see, taste, touch, and hear is always something that is "formed matter," why even make the distinction between form and matter? What difference does it make?

In fact, ancient philosophers were all after one main thing: they wanted to know how to live well. As the historian Pierre Hadot noted, ancient philosophy was not a collection of ideas but a choice of a way of life. All the difficult words and high-falutin' concepts are ways of explaining and defending the way of life that the philosopher chooses to follow. Modern philosophy students often think of Plato and Aristotle and all the rest as people who taught certain ideas, but for the philosophers themselves philosophy was more like a religion, a pathway leading to wisdom.

Epicurus, the philosopher who inspired the work of Lucretius, certainly saw things that way. He did have elaborate "scientific" beliefs about the world, but the point of those beliefs was to explain how we are to live. "The study of nature," he wrote, aims to produce "men who are strong and self-sufficient, and who take pride in their own personal qualities and not in those that depend on external circumstances."[1] Epicurus and Lucretius both developed theories about the world, but the goal was to form a certain kind of human being.

Ancient philosophers were wrong about many things, but they did get this one thing right: Our beliefs about the world shape the life we lead. For the Christian, the world

is, above all, a surprising, overwhelmingly good gift, a gift that we have done nothing to earn or deserve. The very fact that you and I are alive at all is a gift. God gave us the gift of life when we didn't even exist to receive that gift. Every thought, every new dawn, every sight and sound, every other person, every book we read and every meal we eat—it is all gift from top to bottom.

If this is what the world is, then the only proper way of life is the way of gratitude. And if Jesus has risen from the dead, then we will live, and die, in the light of that triumph.

On the other hand, if we think, as Epicurus and Lucretius did, that the gods take little notice of human beings, we will take little notice of them. If we think that our souls die with our bodies, then we are going to live, and die, in a particular way. *On the Nature of Things* is all about that way of death, and life.

General Information

Author and Context

The world into which Titus Lucretius Carus was born around 99 B.C. was a chaotic one. The Roman Republic was in shambles, and there was not yet a Julius Caesar or an Octavian to take the reins of power and bring the bolting horse to rest. Roman virtues—patriotism, justice, loyalty, self-control—were collapsing as well. Soldiers no longer felt loyalty to Rome, but swore allegiance to the strongman of their choice. The Senate sent one Verres to govern a province, but he plundered it instead. A nobleman, Clodius, persuaded a plebian family to adopt him so he could qualify to run for office as a Tribune, a position he used to carry out a plot against the republic. Cicero and Sallust charged Cataline with gathering reckless former soldiers to burn Rome and frighten creditors into canceling debts. As historian William Leonard put it, it was "an age of desperate and bloody self-seeking on the part of the few; while the populace in the city cried now for one leader and now for another, knowing only that it was hungry; and while the yeoman in the Italian fields was run down by disbanded soldiery or bewildered by ever-diminishing returns from his plowing and sowing a depleted soil which he had neither science nor means to restore."[2]

In such a world, it is no wonder that a philosopher such as Lucretius would be attracted to the promise of the teachings of the Greek philosopher Epicurus. In the summary of Epicureanism found in the "Principal Doctrines," Epicurus wrote that "a blessed and indestructible being has no trouble himself," and therefore is "free from anger and partiality."[3] Epicurus urged his disciples to withdraw from the public world of competition and conflict into small communities of calm pleasure and languid friendship. Human nature, Lucretius said, "yelps after" only one thing: "that the body / Be free of pain, the mind enjoy the sense / Of pleasure, far removed from care or fear!" (2.17–29).[4] His ideal is

> when friends in the soft grass lie at ease,
> In the shade of a tall tree by the riverside,
> Their bodies refreshed and gladdened,

> at no great cost,
> Most pleasantly when the weather smiles and the season
> Sprinkles the grassy meadow with new flowers. (2.29–33)

The connection between Lucretius's tumultuous world and his dreams of peaceful country picnics give us some hint about the man himself. Beyond that, we know almost nothing about him. He died young, at the age of 44. By the time he died, he was an admired poet. Cicero wrote his brother, "The poems of Lucretius are as you write: they exhibit many flashes of genius, and yet show great mastership," and Virgil alludes to the poetry of Lucretius in the second book of his *Georgics*. One ancient writer informs us that Virgil identified with the older poet because he received his *toga virilis*, token of his entry into manhood, on the very day that Lucretius died.

The church father Jerome provides us with more colorful biographical information: "Titus Lucretius the poet is born. Later he was driven mad by a love potion, and when, during the intervals of his insanity, he had written a number of books, which were later emended by Cicero, he killed himself by his own hand in the 44th year of his life." Many centuries later, Alfred Lord Tennyson dramatized Lucretius's madness and death in his poem "Lucretius." Finding her husband "cold," disappointed when he greets her kisses with "small notice" and austerity, Lucilla, Lucretius's wife, hires a witch to brew a potion that she slips into his drink. The "wicked broth / Confused the chemic labor of the blood, / and ticking the brute brain within the man's / Made havoc among those tender cells, and check'd / His power to shape." Driven mad by the potion, he gives up his legendary calm and raves about a thunderstorm, about Venus and the gods, about all that his philosophy was designed to protect him against, until

> he drove the knife into his side.
> She heard him raging, heard him fall, ran in,
> Beat breast, tore hair, cried out upon herself
> As having fail'd in duty to him, shriek'd
> That she but meant to win him back, fell on him
> Clasp'd, kiss'd him, wail'd.

Titus Lucretius Carus

Lucretius recovers himself enough to warn his wife not to sorrow over death: "Care not thou! / Thy duty? What is duty? Fare thee well!"

Unfortunately, this dramatic story is probably not true. We have no more idea about how Lucretius died than we do about how he lived.

Significance

Tennyson was not the only Victorian to take note of Lucretius. Of *On the Nature of Things*, Thomas Babington Macaulay commented that the "philosophy is for the most part utterly worthless; but in energy, perspicuity, variety of illustration, knowledge of life and manners, talent for description, sense of the beauty of the external world, and elevation and dignity of moral feeling, he had hardly ever an equal." Lucretius was interesting to Victorians partly because he seemed so contemporary. Matthew Arnold noted that "Depression and *ennui*" (boredom), the "characteristics stamped on how many of the representative works of modern times," were also "the characteristics stamped on the poem of Lucretius." Nineteenth-century scientists were intrigued by Lucretius's scientific theories, which seemed to anticipate their own. As we shall see, he developed an early form of atom-theory, and his description of the origin of the universe sounded familiar to readers of Darwin's *Origin of Species*.[5] In the twentieth century, the Spanish philosopher George Santayana ranked Lucretius with Dante and Goethe as great "philosophical poets."

Lucretius was also influential in earlier centuries. In his treatise about the origin of the state, *Leviathan*, Thomas Hobbes famously described man's life in the state of nature as "solitary, poor, nasty, brutish, and short." He could have been quoting Lucretius:

For many revolutions of the sun
They [early humans] led the life of the pack,
    like beasts that roam.
There was no ruddy farmer to steady the plow;
Unknown were iron tools to till the fields,
How to plant out new shoots, or from tall trees
Prune away the old branches with the hook....
They had no foundry skills, no use for fire;
They didn't know how to clothe themselves
    with skins
But lived in the wild woods and the mountain caves,
Stowing their dirt-rough limbs among the bushes
When driven to flee the wind's lash and the
    downpour. (5.928–954)

There was no society to speak of: "They could not recognize the common good; / They knew no binding customs, used no laws." They were motivated by a need for survival, and by primitive desires for sex and food. They slept naked in "a thatch of leaves and branches," "fearing the night" (5.955–974). Their life, like their diet, was hard, but "ample, for wretches born to die" (5.941). Hobbes's treatise provided a rationale for absolutist states, and to that Lucretius made his unintended contribution.

The greatest of Lucretius's "disciples" was Virgil himself. Anthony Esolen, a recent translator of *On the Nature of Things*, suggests that "the most important intellectual and poetic influence upon Virgil was neither Homer nor Homer's Roman admirer Ennius but Lucretius." Virgil was "steeped in Lucretius," but he resisted Lucretius's influence. Esolen writes,

Lucretius excited and disturbed Vergil, as I think he did most of the poets of the early Empire and, much later, the poets of the Renaissance. By Vergil's day it had become impossible for a sophisticated person to believe all of the myths of the Greek and Roman gods.... But Vergil longed for some divinity in things, some plan or fate that men had to obey and that would justify Rome's dominance in the world. Lucretius posed a serious problem for him. On the one hand, he understood both Lucretius's love of nature and his desire to reveal how the universe works.... On the other hand, there were strains in Lucretius which stirred Vergil to intellectual struggle: the emphasis on chance, the retreat from the political, the utter disdain for war, the meaninglessness of history.[6]

Summary and Setting

Lucretius's goal is to explain how the world works. He starts by describing the basic building-blocks of the world—atoms and empty space; then describes human nature, knowledge, and sensation; and ends with an overview of the origins of the universe, development of the human race, and wonders in heaven (like thunder and lightening) and on earth (earthquakes, volcanoes, and magnetism among them). The six books of Lucretius's poem can be divided into three sets of two books. Books I–II start on the microscopic scale, with atoms; Books III–IV move up the scale to human nature; and the final two books deal with the world in its totality.

At the same time, the poem can be divided in half. Book I begins with a song to Venus, Lucretius's name for "Nature" that brings all things to life, causes the winds and storms to move across the sky, and makes plants spring from the ground and the ocean waves surge (1.1–9), and the first half of the poem ends with a reminder that life leads inevitably to death: "This much is sure: the end of life awaits us, / The summons must be answered; we must die.... And long life won't allow us to pluck out / One moment from our span beyond the grave / That we might spend a shorter time in death." In short, "eternal death awaits" (3.1075-1089).

The second half of the poem moves through the same cycle. With the help of the Muses, Lucretius claims to be "singing" to bring "dark matters into the light" (4.7) so that his readers can "grasp the entire / Nature of things" (4.25). He is the singer of life. But if you thought the end of Book III was grim, it is nothing compared to the end of the poem as a whole, a long and painful description of a plague in Athens:

> all was chaos, fear, and every man
> Had his own buried as his means allowed.
> The suddenness and poverty incited
> Horrors. On funeral pyres heaped up for others
> People would lay their own kin down, and wail,
> And set their torches underneath, and sometimes
> Brawl and shed blood, rather than leave their dead.
> (6.1279-1285)

A number of the individual books in the poem have the same shape. Book II, for instance, begins with a famous passage in which Lucretius reflects on the sweetness of watching from a distant shore as a ship struggles against the waves. "Your freedom from those troubles is what's sweet," he remarks (2.1-4). But the sweetness is no longer there at the end, as he portrays an "old plowman" who sees that "all of his hard work has come to nothing" and complains that the world has gotten worse since the days of his fathers but "doesn't / Grasp that, slowly, wasting away, all things / Go to the tomb, worn out by the long years" (2.1163-1173). Each book begins in life and ends in death; each acknowledges Venus the "creatoress," and Venus the destroyer. The exception is Book V, which celebrates the achievement of human beings throughout.

Macaulay believed the poem was unfinished, and

On the Nature of Things is a philosophical poem. Unlike Homer, whose poetry catches the imagination with swords and sirens and the gory blinding of the Cyclops, Lucretius chose to write philosophy in poetic form to sweeten the hard truth that he wanted to teach.

many others have agreed. But the overall pattern matches the pattern of each book, which makes it likely that the poem ends exactly where Lucretius meant it to end, with a disturbing reminder of the grave. In this too, Lucretius may have influenced Virgil, who ends the *Aeneid* not with a celebration of the grandeur of Rome but with the shade of Turnus howling toward hell.

Worldview

Many students are put off by poetry. Even more are put off by philosophy. Homer's poetry is redeemed by the story and the gore—swords crashing through brain pans, seductive sirens, a heated olive-wood pole sizzling in the eye-juice of a Cyclops. Lucretius has something to annoy both types of students: *On the Nature of Things* is a philosophical poem. It may seem the worst of all worlds.

That's not the way Lucretius saw it. He chose to write philosophy in poetic form because he thought the poetry would sweeten the hard philosophical truth that he wanted to teach. He is a physician of souls, and just as "doctors try to coax children to take / Foul wormwood" by brushing "the rim of the cups / All around with the sweet and golden juice of honey" so Lucretius reveals the "harsh" teaching of Epicurus in "sweet-throated song, / Touching it with the honey of the Muses" (4.11–22).

Philosophy might sound rather boring, and all his talk of death might even be a little frightening. But Lucretius spices up his philosophy with delightful observations on nature, satire on human follies, accounts of wars and illness. Lucretius loves the world, and the things of the world, and he helps us see things that we would often ignore. Unlike some other philosophers, who are so obsessed with unseen realities that they miss what they do see, Lucretius keeps taking us back to ordinary life. As Esolen says, "there are the boys spinning around and making themselves so dizzy they think the roofs are about to tumble on them; snakeskins dangling from the briars; the yelp of a dog when she licks her puppies, and the different yelp when she slinks away from a beating; the 'applause' of a rooster's wings; the shimmering blue and coral plumage that rings the throat of a dove."[7]

Homer is the master of mayhem, but the pacifist Lucretius can be nearly as good: "Fighters fall where they are stricken, the blood spurts/ In the direction from which we suffer the hit; / In hand-to-hand combat the red gush strafes the enemy" (4.1040–1042). Men have tried nearly everything to gain advantage in battle, sometimes unleashing lions on their enemies, which go "lunging for the attacker's face / Or ripping the unsuspecting from behind, / Clamping them, mortally wounded, to the ground, / And fixing them fast with healthy bites and

claws" (5.1316–1319). Sometimes his descriptions of war are metaphorical. Elsewhere he describes the frenzied movement of atoms as a microscopic battle.

Few satirists in history have captured better than Lucretius the pathetic puppyism of a lover who transforms his beloved's every blemish into a thing of rare beauty:

> Men laugh at a fellow who's stuck with
>   an ugly girlfriend,
> "You better go keep your Venus happy!" Fool!
> Their own troubles are worse, and they
>   can't see them.
> She's black as soot? "Honey-tan."
> She never washes? "Casual!"
> Cat-eyed? "Like Pallas!"
> She's knobby and wiry? "A gazelle."
> A dwarf's "ma petite," "my little charmer,"
> A big bruiser's "One who'll take your breath away";
> The stammerer "lisps," the stock-still,
>   she's just "bashful,"
> While the spiteful little spitfire's "A real sparkler"
> It's "svelte" for a woman too withered to keep alive,
> And the half-dead hacker's got a "delicate frame."
> (4.1148–1158)

"I could go on forever with such stuff," Lucretius says, and he probably could, but he is more interested in reminding the infatuated, "Hey, there are others!" (4.1164).

On the Nature of Things is philosophy, and it talks about hidden things. Unlike Plato's, though, it is philosophy that starts from the world as we know it, and keeps returning us to that world.

Lucretius's main aim is ethical. He wants to teach people how to live well, and in his mind living well means being liberated from care, anxiety, and fear. As he looks around him, and reviews history, he sees two main things that cause fear: religion and death. We are overly serious and anxious about life because we fear that the gods will punish us if we slip up. Fear of death stirs us to care in many ways—because we recoil from the empty blankness of death, because the shortness of life makes us fear that we will never accomplish all we want to accomplish, because our limited time and limited resources prick us to competition for fame and far more money than we can ever use. If we can be liberated from religion and the fear of death, we can live without fear, and if we can live without fear, we can be truly happy. The contemporary atheist Christopher Hitchens is updating an argument from Lucretius when he claims that "religion poisons *everything*."

Lucretius takes a roundabout way to make his point. Instead of simply exhorting his readers "Fear not," he gives an account of the nature of things that makes fear

According to Lucretius, the gods live in an eternal state of bliss and couldn't care less about our world. The immortal beings make merry in Jacopo Tintoretto's (1518–1594) *The Concert of the Muses*.

and care seem absurd. All his discussions of science, of the nature of reality, of knowledge are designed to show two things. First, he wants to show that reason can explain the world without having to call in the gods to fill the gaps. If he can explain thunder as an effect of atoms bumping into each other, then thunder is no longer the voice of Jupiter; if he can explain earthquakes as natural phenomena, then he relieves us of the fear that an earthquake is punishment from the gods. Gods exist, Lucretius believes, but they live in an eternal state of bliss and couldn't care less about our world. Best to return the favor and ignore them. Second, he aims to show that death is the natural course of all things. It is no more to be feared than a flower petal, or spring, or a butterfly dipping his proboscis into a flower. It is just as natural as an avalanche or a tsunami. We ought no more grieve at death than we grieve over sunsets.

According to Lucretius, the world consists of essentially two realities. On the one hand, there are atoms. Atoms are the smallest bits of matter, so small that they are invisible in themselves. Esolen sometimes translates the word "atom" as "first-beginning," since the atoms that make up a thing are like seeds that make the thing grow into a particular kind of thing. Atoms have only a few properties of their own: they come in a variety of sizes and a variety of shapes, and they move at different speeds. They have no "accidental" qualities like color or taste. These properties emerge only when atoms assemble into things like iron and sea water and stars. There are an infinite number of atoms, but a finite number of different types of atoms. Everything that we experience in the world is a conglomeration of atoms of different sizes and shapes.

Atoms are hard and simple; there is no space within an atom. Beside atoms, and surrounding them, is empty space, what Lucretius calls the "void." Unless there is void, the atoms would have no place to move, and everything would be at a complete standstill, like a late afternoon traffic jam. Even apparently solid objects are combinations of atoms and void. As Lucretius summarizes his point, "The universe is made up of two things / Which exist in themselves: atoms, and void" and there is no "third thing" that helps "compose the world" (1.419–420, 431). No wonder modern writers have been intrigued by Lucretius. He seems to have hit upon the scientific view that the world consists of nothing but matter in motion.

Lucretius attempts to explain virtually everything in terms of these two fundamental realities. Why are some objects heavier and more solid than others? Because the atoms are packed together more tightly: Iron has less "void" than water. Why are some objects smooth and others rough? Because they have atoms of different shapes. Why are liquids so liquidy? Because they have smooth, round atoms. Why does air move faster than lava? Because its atoms are smaller, lighter, and faster. Why is my shovel handle narrower at the place where I grip it? Because it's losing atoms. Why do trees grow? Because they're gaining them.

He explains our experience of the world through the senses in the same way. Why are some liquids bitter? Because they contain sharp-edged atoms, while more pleasant liquids are made of round atoms that slip down the gullet without getting caught. Why do sounds travel through doors when sights cannot? Because the atoms of sound are smaller and can fit through the gaps in the door, while vision atoms are larger and get stuck. Given his ignorance of chemistry (shared by everyone in the ancient world), Lucretius's atomic theory is childishly physical; but it is no less ingenious for that.

Though Lucretius says that the universe consists of atoms and void, he finds that he cannot do without a few other forces. The world is not random, but why not? What keeps atoms from combining in any old way, constantly generating dogheads and centaurs, liquid flowers and trees with eyes and eyebrows? And what makes atoms stick together in the first place? How can Lucretius explain the reality of kinds? When a lion mates with his lady, why do the atoms form into another lion instead of a pomegranate?

Lucretius gives several answers to these questions. At times, he attributes the regularity of the world to "nature" or "Creating Nature" (1.628), sometimes personified as "Venus":

> She forces the atoms
> To be bounded by void, and to bound
>   the void in turn;
> By alternating these she gives the world
> Endlessness. If they did not bound each other
> One of them in pure form would stretch forever.
> (1.1005–1010)

To answer the question about "kinds," he speaks of "laws" in the universe. "Don't suppose atoms link in every way," for if they did we "would meet freaks and monsters" on every street corner. Things grow into kinds because "they must; a fixed law makes it so." He explains,

> For the atoms proper to each—

> from the right food—
> Stream into the limbs and, linking, bring about
> Suitable motion. By contrast, we see Nature
> Shed to earth the foreign stuff, and much
> The body will expel with unseen blows,
> Atoms that can't link up or replicate
> The inner motions and the bonds of life.
> (2.700–717)

So, there are atoms, there is void, and there is some force or power that keeps things together and guides the atoms to combine in a finite number of ways.

Like his teacher, the godlike Epicurus, Lucretius believes that we can trust our senses. When I see an iguana, there is actually an iguana there. Lucretius attempts to explain the reliability of sense in terms of his atomic theory. Very thin sheets of very, very tiny atoms are constantly peeling off and floating away from things, floating, mind you, in the exact shape of the thing and in every direction at once. These wraith-like "semblances" or "films" enter our eyes and "strike / Our minds when we're awake" and give us the sensation of "seeing" (4.26–44). For Lucretius, all senses are a form of touch—the film of atoms banging into the atoms of our eyes.

Lucretius runs into a problem here. He does not think our senses ever deceive us. Rather, deception arises from misinterpretation of what our senses receive from these shimmering drapes of atoms that come from things. As Esolen points out, this does not solve the problem, since for Lucretius thought itself is a kind of sight: "we see films thick enough for the eye, but we 'think' films so thin that only the soul can notice them." But then can the eye of the soul be deceived? If so, why can't the physical eye? Lucretius wants to say that all our thought comes from information provided by the senses, but he gets tangled up in contradictions. Besides, Esolen says, Lucretius leaves the mind passive, but when we think it "feels active, willed, creative." Lucretius has no account of memory, or logic, or imagination.[8]

The problems that Lucretius runs into with knowledge and the mind are evident also in his attempt to explain the soul within his atomist theory. The soul is, like everything else, a body composed of atoms, though soul-atoms are, of course, an extremely fine silky kind of atom: "the soul is super-subtle, / Composed of tiniest particles" (3.179–180). They are so fine and small, in fact, that their presence cannot be detected. Bodies don't get lighter when the soul and mind leave (3.212–214). This is a central part of Lucretius's argument. If he can prove that the soul simply passes out of existence along with the body at death, then he can relieve fears of hell or the uncertainties of a life beyond death.

But he
can't quite stay
true to his atomism here.
A thoroughly atomistic theory—in which atoms and void
were absolutely the only things about—could not explain
our experience of free will, our experience of mental resistance to outside forces. As many moderns have concluded, if we are nothing more than atoms randomly
assembled, then the idea that we can will, desire, think,
plan, remember, reason is nonsense. What we think we
experience as "will" is only the random jostling of atoms,
genes, and whatnot. When we think that we are resisting
the influence of the world outside, we are actually just
doing what our atoms and genes and chemical reactions
make us do. Lucretius does not have the courage of his
atomism because he knows that his heart has a power of
its own that cannot be reduced to atoms and void. When
someone physically coerces us,

How patently clear that all our body's atoms
Are then dragged, kidnapped, going in spite of us,
Till through the limbs the will bridles them in.
So you see that although an outside force can push
Many men forward against their will, and drag them
Or pitch them headlong, still in our hearts there is
Something which can stand up to block it, fight it,
At whose decision to multitude of atoms
Are meanwhile spurred, in the joints
        and the limbs, to turn
And be reigned in from the gallop and stand still.
(2.275–284)

Lucretius can explain this only by changing his theory. Atoms have some unexplained power "beyond collision and weight," a power of motion that gives our hearts
an "inborn power" to resist. This is one implication of the
Epicurean doctrine of the "swerve," a random variation,
a tilt, in the motion of an atom. On the slender thread of
atomic "swerve" rests all the interior life of the soul that is
so much a part of being human.

This is not the only difficulty in Lucretius's theory.
He attempts to explain the nature of things by rational
explanation, without appeal to divine forces. Yet, to make
it work, the atoms have to have remarkable attributes.
They are eternal, indestructible, simple, *just like God*. As
the Dutch theologian Herman Bavinck observed a century ago, at the atomic level matter suddenly takes on very
non-material qualities, for none of the material things we

"Then God said, 'Let there be
light'; and there was light. And
God saw the light, that it was
good; and God divided the light
from the darkness" (Gen. 1:3–4).
Detail from the Sistine Chapel
ceiling, painted by Michelangelo
between 1508 and 1512.

know are eternal, indestructible, or simple. The smaller the bit of matter, it seems, the closer it resembles spirit. Further, Esolen points out that Lucretius shoots himself in the foot by trying to urge moderation without religion: "the traditional moderator has been religion itself, which in Lucretius's own words clamps its bit in our mouths and reigns us in. But if religion does not bridle us, what will?"[9]

Conclusion

For all its flaws, *On the Nature of Things* isolates a key problem in human life, namely, the fear of death. The New Testament is in agreement with Lucretius at this point: Fear of death enslaves and inhibits the fullness of human life (Heb. 2:15). Instead of the Epicurean resignation to death, however, the New Testament announces Jesus' triumph over death through His resurrection, a triumph that transforms death itself into a way to life. As much as Lucretius, the New Testament teaches us to overcome fear, but it dispels fear of death by inculcating another fear, the fear of Yahweh that is the beginning of wisdom.

—Peter J. Leithart

For Further Reading

Epicurus, "Principal Doctrines" and "Vatican Sayings," available at http://www.epicurus.net/index.html.

Esolen, Anthony, trans. and ed. *On the Nature of Things*. Baltimore: Johns Hopkins University Press, 1995. "Introduction" and "Notes."

Minadeo, Richard. *The Lyre of Science: Form and Meaning in Lucretius' De Rerum Natura*. Detroit: Wayne State University Press, 1969.

Session I: Prelude

A Question to Consider

What practical differences do our beliefs about the "nature of things" make? Why does it matter whether we are Epicurean atomists or Aristotelians or Platonists? Does the Bible provide an explanation of the "nature of things" different from Lucretius?

From the General Information above answer the following questions:

1. Why was Lucretius interested in "science"?
2. Describe the world of Lucretius and how it influenced his thought.
3. How did Lucretius influence Virgil?
4. According to Lucretius, what are the two main components of reality?
5. What is wrong with religion, according to Lucretius?
6. According to Lucretius, how can we see and hear things?
7. How does Lucretius explain free will?

Reading Assignment:
On the Nature of Things, Books I–II

Session II: Discussion
On the Nature of Things, Books I–II

A Question to Consider

Lucretius's strategy is to make the bitterness of Epicureanism sweet by using poetry. Do you think his strategy works successfully or not?

Discuss or write answers to the following questions:

Text Analysis

1. According to Lucretius, of what two elements is the universe composed? Lucretius rejects any third element—what is he implicitly rejecting?
2. Lucretius notes and rejects the theories of three philosophers concerning which elements the universe is composed of. Who are these philosophers? State their positions and explain Lucretius's objections.
3. According to Lucretius's expression of Epicureanism, what are the only two things that a person needs in life? Why does Lucretius say this?
4. What conclusion does Lucretius draw from seeing dust floating in sunbeams?
5. Which qualities do atoms have, and which do they not have?
6. Why does wine flow through a sieve more freely than oil, according to Lucretius?
7. How does Lucretius explain bad and good tastes, smells, and sounds?

Cultural Analysis

1. Review your answer question 3 in the Text Analysis above. Compare the Epicurean view of life expressed in this section with what modern secular society says about the purpose of life.

2. Where does a modern scientific understanding agree with Lucretius about atoms, the size of the universe, and the idea of other inhabited worlds?

Biblical Analysis

1. Lucretius posits an infinity of worlds which are too big for the gods to rule. What are the qualities of God that enable Him to rule the universe? (Gen. 1 and 2, Job 38 and 39)
2. In question 1 of the Cultural Analysis above, we asked you to consider the purpose of life according to Epicureanism and modern secular society. What does a Christian view say about the purpose of life (l Cor. 10:31; Ps. 16:5-11; Isa. 12:2; Luke 2:10)?
3. Consider Lucretius's descriptions of men striving for fame and success in 2.1-61. Compare this to Ecclesiastes chapters one and 12. Locate at least two points of agreement between Epicureanism and Christianity in these passages.

SUMMA

Write an essay or discuss this question, integrating what you have learned from the material above.

Following his conversion to Christianity in A.D. 386, St. Augustine became suspicious of rhetoric—of using elegant speech to persuade others to your point of view—because it seemed to be more concerned with elegant packaging rather than with the truth (or lie) that packaging contained. At the beginning of this session you discussed Lucretius's rhetorical strategy: he wanted to coat the bitter message of Epicureanism (the gods do not care about you, and there is no afterlife) with the honey of poetic language. As you encounter people and ideas in life, both Christian and non-Christian, how can you distinguish between "packaging" and content in order to decide what is true and what is false?

Like Lucretius, Carl Sagan believed, in his own famous words, that the "Cosmos is all that is or ever was or ever will be." Sagan produced beautiful television shows and interesting novels based on this flawed premise. Lucretius—an ancient materialist—bested Sagan by writing beautiful poetry about a meaningless universe.

READING ASSIGNMENT:
On the Nature of Things, Books III–IV

SESSION III: RECITATION
On the Nature of Things, Books III–IV

Comprehension Questions

Answer the following questions for factual recall:

1. Where does Lucretius believe the mind is located?
2. Where does Lucretius believe the soul is located?
3. What are the four elements that make up the mind?
4. Name one argument that Lucretius offers for the mortality of the soul.
5. List two reasons why Lucretius says we should not fear death.
6. How is an object visible to the eye?
7. Why can sound pass through things that visual images cannot?
8. When speaking about bodily organs like eyes and ears, which comes first: existence or use? Why is this important?
9. How can lust cause a person to neglect responsibilities?

READING ASSIGNMENT:
On the Nature of Things, Books V–VI

Venus is Lucretius's name for Nature, that which brings all things to life. Detail from "The Birth of Venus" by Italian painter Sandro Botticelli (1445–1510).

Session IV: Discussion
On the Nature of Things, Books V–VI

A Question to Consider

Look up the word teleology in the dictionary. Lucretius is very concerned with arguing against the idea of teleology in the formation of the universe—he is anti-teleological. Christians believe in a teleology of the formation of the universe: God created it for His own glory and called it good. However, according to Lucretius, there was no purpose in how the universe was formed; it would be just as well (or better) if he had never been born and if the world had never been created. Would it be better if you hadn't been born? Why or why not?

Discuss or write answers to the following questions:

Text Analysis

1. According to Lucretius, how was the world formed?
2. In what ways did human life during the savage period resemble that of the animals? How did they transition to becoming civilized and different from the animals?
3. What role did technology play in the development of human civilization? According to Lucretius, was technology good or bad for humans?
4. What causes thunder and lightning?
5. Why do oceans neither diminish nor overflow?
6. What causes diseases?
7. Given that Lucretius is trying to persuade his readers that they should not fear the gods or death, why do you think Lucretius chose to end his epic with the plague at Athens?

Cultural Analysis

1. What do you make of Lucretius's claim that people used to follow leaders who were beautiful or strong, but after the discovery of gold they began to follow the rich? Whom do we follow today and why?
2. Lucretius believes that the first humans were physically larger and stronger than humans are today, and he seems to suggest that the earliest societies were better because there was no war, greed, or selfish-

Chart 1: THREE VIEWS OF CREATION

	GENESIS	LUCRETIUS	DARWINIAN
Creation of the cosmos	God creates it for His glory by speaking it into existence 294 (Gen. 1).	Floating atoms clump together at random and form planets and stars (5.416–768).	In the Big Bang, matter explodes out into space and clumps together at random to form everything in the universe.
Creation of the earth, seas, and sky			
Creation of plant life			
Creation of animals			
Creation of humans			
Creation of tools/ weapons			
Creation of clothing			
Creation of language			
Creation of cities and kingdoms			

ness. Contrast the way in which Lucretius views the world as getting worse with the modern Darwinian view of human progress.

Biblical Analysis

1. Compare the Genesis account of Adam naming the animals (Gen. 2:19–20) with Lucretius's theory of how things first got their names. Why is it important how things were named?
2. According to Lucretius, humans falsely attributed the control of nature and morality to the gods. What does Lucretius think the gods do with their time? How would Jeremiah 29:10–14, Exodus 20, and Matthew 5–7 comment on Lucretius's position?
3. Contrast your answers for number 2 in Cultural Analysis above with a Christian view: Are the world and

the human race getting better, worse, or neither? Does Ecclesiastes 1:9 complicate your answer? Is Darwin or Lucretius more similar to Christianity on this issue?

SUMMA

Write an essay or discuss this question, integrating what you have learned from the material above.

Do you remember what you found out about teleology at the beginning of this session? Remember that Lucretius's view was anti-teleological: he did not believe there was a purpose in the forming of the universe. There is no goal that human society is heading for. With this in mind, re-evaluate your answers about how Lucretius viewed the savage period of human society. In what ways do his descriptions of this period look like a "Golden Age" or idealized past, and in what ways do they seem worse than the present?

Session V: Worldview Analysis

Lucretius and Creation

Fill out Chart 1 comparing what Lucretius and Genesis 1–11 say about the formation of the universe and the development of civilization. Then, if you have time, use what you know about the Darwinian/secular scientific theory of evolution to fill in the third column.

Optional Session: Activity

Poetic Creed

As you have seen in *On the Nature of Things*, Lucretius uses poetry to describe his Epicurean philosophy and to convince others to follow that philosophy. Whether you are aware of it or not, you have your own philosophy of life, which has been shaped by your experiences. Have a think: what is the purpose of life? Why are you here? How was the world created, and for what purpose? How does God relate to humans? What is the story of civilization? How is the universe made up physically, and what physical laws govern it?

Lucretius wrote in dactylic hexameter, which was a very flexible meter for Greek and Latin. In English, however, unrhymed iambic pentameter or blank verse serves a similar role.

Write a poem of at least ten lines in blank verse describing one or more parts of your philosophy of life (faith, family, education, the construction of molecules, et cetera).

Endnotes

1. Epicurus, "Vatican Sayings," #45.
2. William Ellery Leonard and Standley Barney Smith, eds. *T. Lucreti Cari De Rerum Natura Libri Sex* (Madison: University of Wisconsin Press, 1942), 6.
3. Epicurus, "Principal Doctrines," #1.
4. I am using the translation of Anthony Esolen (Baltimore: Johns Hopkins University Press, 1995). Line citations are taken from this translation.
5. All the quotations here were taken from Frank M. Turner, "Lucretius Among the Victorians," Victorian Studies 16:3 (1973), 329–348.
6. Esolen, "Introduction," 15–16.
7. Esolen, "Introduction," 4.
8. Esolen, "Notes," 263.
9. Esolen, "Introduction," 12.

Just as we entice children to take their medicine by sweetening it, so Lucretius sweetens the bitter teachings of Epicurus in "sweet-throated song, / touching it with the honey of the Muses" (4.11–22).

Cicero

Have you ever looked closely at your tongue? Probably not. Ok, go right now to a mirror and take a look at your tongue.

Not very attractive, is it? Now, find a classmate, brother, sister or parent and ask them if you can examine their tongue—especially the bottom.

Yuck! The tongue is possibly the ugliest, nastiest part of the body—covered with bumps and taste buds on top, filled with blood vessels and skin flaps on the bottom, slimy and wet—sometimes covered with color from your last Powerade. Yuck and double yuck. Also, it is long. It goes way back down your throat.

The tongue is gross, but many would agree that it is the most powerful organ in the body. With it the thoughts of the heart can be verbalized and spoken to others. These spoken words can move hearts, change minds, overthrow conspiracies and rail against tyranny.

This chapter is a story of a tongue—one of the most powerful tongues in the history of the world, for that matter. It did all of the things listed in the previous paragraph. Because of its power, it was sought out often as a friend, it was feared as an enemy, it was hunted down, and its owner was murdered, and, finally, it was cut out and nailed to the rostrum in Rome. The wife of its greatest political enemy even mutilated it to make sure that it would no longer raise opposition to her husband's schemes. It fought tyranny, trying desperately to save the Roman Republic. It failed, but it was glorious in both success and failure. This tongue belonged to Cicero, one of the greatest orators, statesmen, philosophers, lawyers, conspiracy theorists, and ardent republican patriots in history.

General Information

Author and Context

The most famous Roman orator lived through one of the most tumultuous periods in Rome's history. Born in 106 B.C., Cicero spent his youth studying and training in oratory. He survived the harsh civil war between Marius and Sulla in 83 B.C. and navigated a political scene full of civil strife and confusion for the next forty years. Cicero first gained his reputation as a lawyer by defending Roscius, a man no other orator dared defend because he had lost his property based on Sulla's condemnation. But Cicero's boldness and his stunning speaking ability won the case and secured his place in the public forum.

Although Cicero was not born to a family in the governing class, he rose through the ranks, serving as quaestor

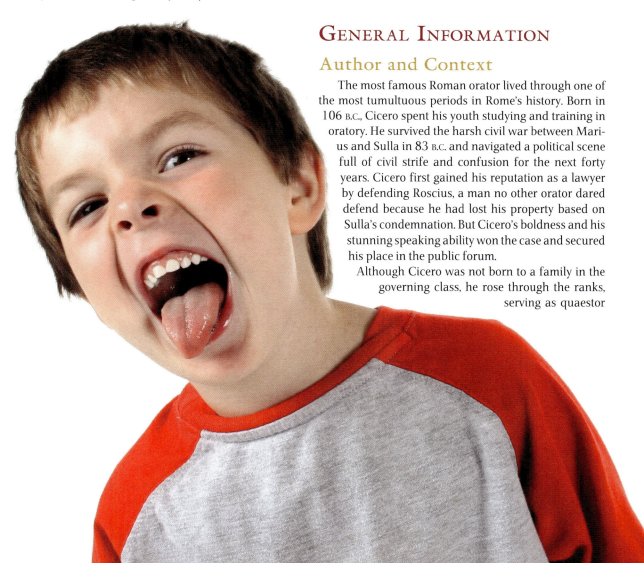

(a sort of local governor) over Sicily and provincial governor over south-east Asia before being elected consul in 63 B.C.. Cicero's most significant accomplishment as consul was his discovery of Cataline's plot to overthrow the Roman government. His efforts in defeating the conspirators led Rome to hail him as father of his country and savior of the state.

Perhaps because of his success in rising to national prominence, Cicero was fiercely attached to the Roman Republic. Unfortunately, he lived to see the Republic collapse upon itself. The First Triumvirate (Pompey, Caesar, and Crassus) demonstrated the senate's impotence, while Pompey and his troops had to forcibly bring order to the anarchy in Rome. Civil war broke out with renewed vigor when Caesar marched on Rome to oppose Pompey's growing influence. Cicero, ever an opponent of tyranny, opposed Julius Caesar and rejoiced at his assassination. His joy was short lived, however, as Mark Antony began to increase his authority in Caesar's footsteps. As a result of his harsh condemnation of Antony, Cicero ended up on the proscription list—the list of those who were to be put to death and whose property was to be confiscated. He was murdered by Antony's men in 43 B.C.

> According to Plutarch, Marcus Tullius Cicero's "natural talent shone out clear, and he won name and fame among the boys, so that their fathers used to visit the schools in order to see Cicero with their own eyes and observe the quickness and intelligence in his studies for which he was extolled."

Significance

Cicero's reputation as one of the most powerful and effective orators in ancient history probably overshadows the significance of his ideas. However, the combination of Cicero's *Second Philippic* and his *On Duties* aptly summarizes the influence Cicero's ideas have had on Western civilization. On the one hand, Cicero has been remembered as a fierce defender of freedom and a model for opposing tyranny and government oppression in favor of rights and liberties. As Camille Desmoulins notes, "Republicans [of the French Revolution] were mostly young people who, brought up on the readings of Cicero at school, were fired by them with the passion for freedom."[1] The American colonists were also familiar with Cicero, whose explanation of natural law was important for establishing a higher authority of right and wrong that justified their break with Britain and whose oratory helped shape the style and habits of early American politics. Even his style of writing was highly influential for rhetoricians. He is known particularly for his lofty tone, his elegant use of language, and his use of tripartite sentences, which have been employed by many great Western speakers (e.g., *we shall battle on the land, we shall fight in the air, we shall win on the seas*). Also, Cicero is known for his use of periodic sentences—sentences whose meaning does not become clear until the final word.

On the other hand, Cicero was a Stoic philosopher concerned with morality and right living. In this capacity, Cicero exercised strong influence over many church leaders (although Pope Gregory the Great wanted to burn his works for distracting men from the Scriptures). Lactantius thought Cicero's philosophy was helpful for the church, and Ambrose included Cicero's ideas and style in his own writings. The Medieval church included Cicero's philosophy in its curriculum, while the Reformers continued to appreciate his work. Luther reportedly regarded Cicero's work more highly than Aristotle's, and Melancthon called *On Duties* a work of perfection.[2]

Summary and Setting

Cicero's *Second Philippic* opens a window into Roman imperial politics. Through this window the reader finds himself witnessing a verbal whip-lashing, a long series of personal abuses that would surely land Cicero in court for libel today. Cicero does not even attempt to mask the personal interest at play in this speech, noting from the beginning that this is an opportunity to defend himself against Antony's attacks. But the bulk of the speech addresses the base excesses and criminal actions of Antony's career. Cicero makes his case from direct evidence and clear examples as well as offering the reader a number of not-so-subtle implications, which purposely do not define the limits of Antony's corruption. Cicero's accusations basically fall into three categories. First, he paints Antony's character as one of utter debauchery and gluttony. Cicero claims that Antony is constantly throwing wine-doused feasts. Bribery, gambling, sexual perversion, and dishonesty round out Cicero's description of Antony's life. Second, Cicero charges Antony with undermining the Roman Republic. According to Cicero, Antony played a key role in sparking civil war, in supporting tyranny, and in stealing the rights and freedoms of Rome's citizens. (We know a lot about Antony's character from his portrayal in *Julius Caesar, Antony and Cleopatra* and other works about that tumultuous time in Rome as the republic became the empire. Here was an exceptional soldier, but a moral failure.) And finally, Cicero carefully examines Antony's words and actions, making him appear ignorant, inconsistent, and a model of stupidity. Cicero's attack on Antony's character may or may not be perfectly accurate, but it does offer an excellent example of Cicero's oratorical style.

Cicero's comments in *On Duties* are quite different from his *Second Philippic* in both character and style. In this treatise Cicero wrestles with questions of morality, examining situations in which what is right seems to conflict with what would be most beneficial. For instance, if a man could earn a small fortune and keep a good reputation by fudging some numbers, should he do it? Cicero calls this a false dilemma, however, because something can be beneficial only if it is morally right. Cicero concludes, therefore, that every decision must be made exclusively based on what is right; financial, social, or political advantage never excuses an evil or immoral action.

Worldview
Harsh Words

Imagine a playground full of third graders at recess. Billy and Jimmy dash out of the building headed for their favorite swing—the one that goes just a little higher than the others. At the same instant they both grab the swing. With one side of the swing locked in his arms, Billy pulls with all his might, screaming at his friend (or former friend) Jimmy who is hanging on the other side.

> Billy: "I got here first!"
> Jimmy: "No, you didn't."
> Billy: "Yes, I did!"
> Jimmy: "It doesn't matter anyway, I get the swing."
> Billy: "Why!?"
> Jimmy: "Because you're a stupid idiot!"

(Ah, the joys of third grade fallacies. The *ad hominem* will never be as fulfilling as it was in third grade.) This is hardly the pinnacle of logical argumentation. In fact, hurling insults most often serves to escalate controversy rather than solve it. Unfortunately, the discourse between many of our politicians and media members barely rises above the elementary school playground. A conservative commentator on FOX News recently summarized his case against a liberal by calling him "an angry, bitter guy"; his opponent, however, outdid him by calling him a typical, sexually repressed Republican, full of hatred, vile, and bile. Ouch!

So what exactly is wrong with this exchange of insults? The problem is not that these two men aren't playing nicely with each other; the problem is that they have left out any logical or substantive arguments in favor of personal attacks. In other words, these commentators have committed the classic *ad hominem* logical fallacy, in which a speaker assumes that a well-aimed personal attack sufficiently rebuts his opponents' beliefs. This does not mean, however, that any attack on a person's character is illegitimate. After all, the Old Testament prophets had some harsh things to say about the people of Israel (Hosea, for instance, called the people robbers, murderers, villains, and whores), while Jesus was at no pains to hide his opposition toward the Pharisees. Take a look at Luke 11:39–52, for instance. You can imagine the Pharisees' reaction to that judgment!

In his attack on Mark Antony, Cicero is actually employing a particular kind of speech known as a *philippic.* The Greek orator Demosthenes first employed the form in his attacks against the Macedonian king, Phillip. The purpose of a *philippic* was to denounce a person's moral and political failures through harsh invective.

So what separates a legitimate attack on a person's character from an *ad hominem* attack? The difference between an *ad hominem* fallacy and a legitimate attack on a person's character is whether or not the attack is made as an insult which distracts from the debate, or whether the attack is part of the debate itself. In other words, if two men are arguing over taxes, calling each other names will not solve the problem. But if the debate is whether a candidate is fit for public office, or whether we should follow a certain leader, points of personal character are essential to the debate! Accusing a politician of failing to show self-control is not an *ad hominem* attack; it is a legitimate reason not to allow him to continue as a government leader. For Cicero, Antony's moral failures are a perfect reason for rejecting his leadership and for the necessity of a republican government to check the power of such corrupt leaders.

As Christians, we are called to a high standard when it comes to using our words. Proverbs argues that our words can either pierce like a sword or heal like medicine (Prov. 12:18), while Paul commands us to use speech that is gracious, so that we may know how to answer everyone (Col. 4:6). Clearly, even if a person does deserve a verbal whiplashing, we need to be careful how we speak! Paul offers some direction for the use of harsh words in 1 Corinthians 5:9–13. Here, he argues that Christians should not judge those who are of the world; after all, we should not expect moral behavior from those who don't know Christ! But the Christian is right to judge the unrepentant believer, whose evil must be purged from the community of saints. This is the same standard Jesus used in the Gospels. His harsh invectives were reserved for the religious leaders who should have known better and who refused to repent. The common standard that both Paul and Jesus employed was that harsh words were reserved for those within the community of believers who refused to repent of their evil. In both cases harsh words were a condemnation of sin before a holy God, used not to shame, embarrass, or humiliate, but to keep sin away from God's people and to bring about repentance.

Duties and Natural Law

In his *On Duties,* Cicero's goal is to find a key for determining right from wrong. As he puts it, he wants to "master the rules for leading a good and consistent life"[3] through the philosophy of moral obligations. Cicero's first step toward developing a test for right and wrong is to prove that doing what is morally right is always the most advantageous action. Even if resetting the mileage on a used car, hedging facts on a resume, or "not mentioning" the rotting foundation of a house might lead to greater material benefits, Cicero argues that the crime of dishonesty cancels out any advantage this person would have gained. In order to prove his point, Cicero carefully defines his standards for morality then demonstrates how moral goodness trumps material advantage. In the process of establishing this standard, Cicero sets down one of the clearest arguments in ancient literature for what philosophers refer to as "natural law."

Natural law refers to an authoritative standard of right and wrong inherent in the way the world works. The Stoics believed that if a man used his reason to examine the world, humanity, and his own soul, he would be able to chart a moral course in life. They described this as "living according to Nature." Cicero certainly agrees with the Stoics that a man should live according to nature, but he gives a more detailed explanation of natural law. For Cicero, the law that governs humanity and defines morality is a set of rational principles based on the way the world works. For instance, to take something away from someone else is contrary to natural law because it destroys the foundation of society. Murder, causing pain, or seizing property all undermine human fellowship and so lead to the collapse of human community. These actions are "contrary to nature" and therefore immoral. On the other hand, justice, courtesy, and generosity comply with the law of nature since they promote community and the good of humanity. As Cicero summarizes it, "Everyone ought to have the same purpose: to identify the interest of each with the interest of all . . . just precisely because they are all human beings . . . [and] having identical interests means that we are all subject to one and the same law of nature: and, that being so, the very least that such a law enjoins is that we must not wrong one another."[4]

The founding fathers of the United States of America also strongly believed in a natural law. They argued that the laws inherent in nature governed all men and clearly indicated that each man has rights to life, liberty, and property. This became the basis for their revolution against Britain. Although the king of Britain was their legitimate ruler, when he took away their liberty or property, he was violating the higher "natural law" and therefore forfeited his authority.

In Romans, Paul discusses God's creation in a way that lends some support to the natural law. Paul writes that, "For since the creation of the world His invisible attributes are clearly seen, being understood by the things that are made, even His eternal power and Godhead, so that they are without excuse."[5] In other words, Paul says that God's creation offers a powerful testimony to who He is and what He requires of men. C.S. Lewis further develops this argument in his book *The Abolition of Man*, noting there are certain moral laws that all nations in all times have followed. Despite many different practices and customs, no society has ever argued that killing your mother is a *good* thing, nor praised a man for stealing from his neighbor. Some societies may believe in capturing their enemies while others believe in eating them, but all reject betraying friends into such a fate. In other words, because God has created all men in His image and placed them in a world He created, there are certain things that all men have known intuitively as right and wrong. God has written His law on our hearts and testified to it in His creation.

But as Paul also says in Romans 1, sin deceived men so that they exchanged the truth they knew from nature for the lies of their sinful passions. In a world separated from God, the idea of the natural law as a universal standard for right and wrong quickly breaks down into dissension and disagreement. Even among men legitimately trying to follow the natural law, disagreements will occur. What happens when two "universal laws" seem to come into conflict? Cicero argues that although most men are imperfect, reason will solve many difficulties. In addition, Cicero believes that the soul is the most godlike part of man, so a man should follow the dictates of his soul, not violating his conscience. The problem is that both of these standards are individual; neither offers an authority above the individual for determining truth or morality. In the end, each person's priorities will determine his own ultimate moral standards. Thus, if Cicero's own priorities tell him that it is fine to lambast his opponents (hardly conducive to nature, community, and humanity) even while pursuing virtue and morality, then fire away!

So what are Cicero's priorities? How does he determine his moral standards? Cicero consistently reveals that liberty in the Roman Republic is his highest priority. In his *Second Philippic* he calls on Antony to think of his country, he speaks of the glory of killing a tyrant, he claims that every action and decision he has made has been for his country, and he closes his attack with a prayer that every man's fortune in life will correspond to his services to his country. In other words, he defends himself and accuses Antony based on their service to a free Roman state. In *On Duties*, as Cicero contemplates situations in which moral decisions are unclear or natural laws seem to come into conflict, he makes his commitment to liberty and country even more clear.

"For since the creation of the world His invisible attributes are clearly seen, being understood by the things that are made, even His eternal power and Godhead, so that they are without excuse" —Romans 1:20. In medieval art goldleaf was often used in the sky to indicate Heaven. In this illustration the glory of Heaven is all around the figure, and yet he refuses to see it, just like the stubborn dwarves refuse to see the beauty of Aslan's country in C.S. Lewis's *The Last Battle*.

Cicero notes that the natural law condemns killing a man, particularly a close friend. However, what if that close friend happens to be a tyrant or an oppressive ruler? One might think that the murder would be worse than suffering some oppression; Paul, in Romans 13, certainly argues that God requires submission to authority regardless of their political stance. But Cicero contends that saving one's country from a tyrant so outweighs the evil of murder that killing an oppressive ruler is the noblest deed a Roman can perform. If your friend turns tyrant, Cicero seems to argue that you should kill him as quickly as possible so that someone else doesn't get the privilege and glory of performing the deed!

Cicero then poses the question of whether a wise but starving man should steal from someone rich but useless. Cicero responds that theft contradicts the natural law, even if the victim is a useless man ... *unless* the wise man could render "great services to your country." If done for that reason, argues Cicero, the theft becomes legitimate. In the end, Cicero has made the assumption, because of his experiences and desires, that the best thing for humanity is a thriving state, free from oppression or tyranny. While this may be a pleasant state to live in, it is not inherent in the natural law Cicero has established. It is possible to have a happy, thriving community with a king on the throne. In fact, using Cicero's logic, one might just as well argue that his own success and wealth will most greatly benefit his city, since he will buy its products, generously give to charity, and host parties in his mansion. Therefore, his attempts to get richer trump the immorality of any theft or dishonesty that leads to his wealth.

In the end, Cicero runs up against a wall because he tries to establish the authority of natural law without recognizing the authority of the God who created nature's laws. Natural law only has authority and can only be applied consistently when a person also submits to the revealed will of the one, true God. C.S Lewis can use natural law in his argument because God is his source and his goal. Paul can appeal to natural law because the Spirit of God lives in him and reveals God's truth to him. Natural law works as a guide to God who created nature, but it cannot authoritatively solve the dissensions that arise between men driven by sinful passions and personal commitments.

Of course, I have focused on the weaknesses in Cicero's moral code. His desire for truth, justice, and self-control along with his promotion of courage and generosity reflect his honest attempt to obey the laws of nature, which do reveal God's truth. But his commitment to his country, rather than a commitment to God, dominated his attempt to live a consistent, moral life.

Stoicism in Cicero

Cicero identified himself as a follower of Stoicism, but his beliefs represent a unique strain of Stoic philosophy worth examining. As a refresher, Stoics believed that God was pantheistic, that is, God fills, or is, everything in the natural world. This means that trees, flowers, clouds, and even the ant crawling across your kitchen floor are actually divine. The Stoic God is a force which guides and directs all things, much like a man's reason ought to guide and direct his life. Cicero certainly agreed with this description of God, but he adds a bit more information. When Cicero discusses the responsibility of a judge to render justice in the law court, he argues that the judge should remember that God is his witness. However, Cicero immediately adds that in his opinion, God and a man's own soul have the same force and authority, since a man's soul is the most god-like part of humanity. In other words, the Stoic God, who exists in and through the natural world, grants semi-divine authority to a man's soul. But just as Cicero's commitment to reason lowers the standard of morality to each individual, so granting divine authority to each man's soul leaves humanity in hopeless confusion. If every soul has the quality and authority of God, no higher standard, no external authority exists for clarifying, asserting, and demonstrating truth, beauty, and goodness! In other words, while Cicero *correctly* recognizes that man is made in God's image, he *incorrectly* concludes that the mind and soul of man have divine ability to guide us to truth and virtue. Only when the Creator remains distinct from the creature, and only when God defines and determines the standard for right and wrong apart from the general operation of a man's reason and conscience can man hope to have a clear picture of truth, beauty, and goodness.

In his discussion of oaths, Cicero further clarifies his understanding of God. He declares that a man should not fear divine retribution for breaking an oath because divine anger *does not exist*. An oath breaker violates "good faith" but not a promise before God. The most significant consequence of Cicero's theology here is that God is no longer the focus of religion. Cicero declares that an oath has the "whole force of religion" behind it, but this "whole force of religion" has nothing to do with fearing God or God's faithfulness to punish those who sin, because divine anger does not exist! Violating religious beliefs, according to Cicero, becomes a matter of undermining honesty and "good faith," which turns out to be sacred *not* because a man swears before a holy God, but because society cannot function unless men uphold honesty and good faith.

But as Peter reminds us in Scripture, our duty to pursue holiness does not come from general human necessity, but from God's own holy character (1 Pet. 1:16).

Despite identifying human reason as divine, Stoics readily admitted the existence of sin. But rather than viewing sin as a deadly consequence of the fall that corrupts the whole person, Stoics relegated sin to the influences of bodily passions and emotions. Thus, for Stoics, reason

Gene Roddenberry, creator of the *Star Trek* television and movie franchise, conceived of the many alien races in the show to correspond with various nationalities and groups on Earth. Among them are the Vulcans, the most famous of which is Mr. Spock.

The rigorously logical Vulcans correspond with ancient Greeks because of their love of philosophy in general and logic in particular. The Romulans are, as their name implies, Romans, who maintain a vast galactic empire ruled by a military class (their home planet is Romulus, in reference to Romulus and Remus). In the warlike Klingons we are to see Asians or Soviets of the Vietnam era. More broadly, we see logic and philosophy as leading to peace versus a preoccupation with the military that leads only to imperialism and endless war.

would guide a man to godliness; passion and emotion, however, drive a man to sin and suffering. Again, Cicero adds a twist to this Stoic doctrine. For Cicero, the central conflict between right and wrong is more practical than the general opposition of reason and emotion. He argues that the good man seeks what is right, while the corrupt man seeks what is most advantageous. In other words, Cicero's definition of morality depends on a man's goals, regardless of the degree to which reason or emotion is involved. Anyone who places his own advantage above doing what is right will fall into sin and corruption, whereas a commitment to virtue leads to a man of wisdom and moral goodness. The Bible, however, makes it clear that a decision to seek one thing or another does not solve the problem of sin. A pagan who commits himself to virtue and moral goodness rather than his own success may be less of a scourge to society, but he will still fail to achieve the perfect requirements of a holy God.

This distinction introduces the most profound difference between Christianity and the host of very moral pagan philosophies. Comparing Cicero's ideal of moral goodness to Christian virtue, there are far more similarities than differences. Thanks to God's general revelation (natural law), many pagans understand and admire the wisdom of living a virtuous life. But for Cicero and his fellow philosophers, the virtuous life was the end goal. There was no need for salvation, no desire to live well now in preparation for the future, no passion for pleasing and glorifying God. These philosophers were dedicated to virtue because they believed it yielded the most happiness in this life. As Christians, virtue is *not our end goal*. Glorifying God is our chief goal in life. Of course,

Looted for building materials in the centuries after the fall of Rome, the Forum is hardly recognizable today as the crucial center of the empire it once was, serving as the seat of government and the main business district and marketplace.

due to the fall and the omnipresence of sin in humanity, glorifying God is only possible once God has renewed our lives by His Spirit through faith in Christ. Such a renewal in the Spirit also yields fruit, which, according to Galatians 5:22–23, looks quite a bit like the fruit virtuous pagans sought to produce. But despite the similar desire for moral goodness, Christians break radically with the ancient philosophers by finding their identity in Christ, not in their virtue.

—Christopher Walker

For Further Reading

Everitt, Anthony. *Cicero: The Life and Times of Rome's Greatest Politician.* New York: Random House, 2003.

Hamilton, Edith. *The Roman Way.* New York: W.W. Norton, 1993.

Spielvogel, Jackson J. *Western Civilization.* Seventh Edition. Belmont, Calif.: Thomson Wadsworth, 2009. 137–142.

Veritas Press History Cards: New Testament, Greece and Rome. Lancaster, Pa.: Veritas Press. 12, 19.

Session I: Prelude

A Question to Consider

How might the concept of natural law be helpful to Christians? In what ways might natural law be unhelpful to Christians?

From the General Information above, answer the following questions:
1. How did Cicero first gain his reputation as an able lawyer and orator?
2. What was the highlight of Cicero's consulship?
3. Why was Cicero proscribed by the Second Triumvirate?
4. In what two ways has Cicero influenced Western thought?
5. What central question does Cicero address in *On Duties*?
6. What is natural law?
7. What is Cicero's core commitment in life?

The next session will be a student-led discussion. Students will be creating their own questions concerning the issue of the session. Students should create three Text Analysis Questions, two Cultural Analysis questions, and two Biblical Analysis questions. For more detailed instructions, please see the chapter on the *Iliad*, Session III.

Issue

Does anger or personal attack have a place in persuasion? What is the most effective way to persuade an audience to follow you rather than your opponent?

Reading Assignment:
Second Philippic, I.1–XXXI.78 (pp. 101–135[6])

Session II: Student-Led Discussion

Second Philippic, I.1–XXI.53 (pp. 101–126)

A Question to Consider

Does anger or slander have a place in persuasion? What is the most effective way to persuade an audience to follow you rather than your opponent?

Text Analysis

Example: What are two examples where Cicero's bitterness influences his rhetoric against Antony?

Answer: Just in the first few pages of his philippic there are several examples. He discusses laws which Antony passed and his actions as a consul but then immediately begins attacking Antony as a "drink-sodden, sex-ridden wreck," whose "ill-reputed house" can't pass a day without repulsive orgies. Later he lashes out against Antony, saying, "just see how unbelievably stupid he is!" These are not logical arguments; they are results of Cicero's passionate anger towards and dislike of Antony.

Cultural Analysis

Example: How is anger expressed in our culture's public forum?

Answer: In many ways, little has changed. While political campaigns can stay positive for a time, nearly every campaign cycle degenerates into mud-slinging attack ads. Political parties often support their position, but their dislike of men and women "on the other side of the aisle" comes across in both logical disagreement and passionate dislike.

Other cultural issues to consider: How is anger expressed privately and among friends and acquaintances? Does our culture find expressions of anger persuasive? What sorts of things would be persuasive to men and women in our culture?

Biblical Analysis

Example: How does Proverbs 15:1 explain anger in political disagreement as well as offer a solution?

Answer: The author of Proverbs here explains that harsh words (Cicero's use of terms such as "drink-sodden" and "unbelievably stupid" are certainly harsh) stir up anger. In other words, once ad hominem attacks (attacks against a person himself rather than his position) and harsh jabs start, it is very difficult to stop. On the other hand, a soft answer, one which responds reasonably and meekly, actually turns away wrath.

Other Scriptures to consider: Mark 3:5 and 11:15–19 (How does Jesus' anger apply to this discussion?); 1 Peter 3:15 (note the context of godly persuasion); Ephesians 4:26–31; Psalm 103:8–10.

SUMMA

Write an essay or discuss this question, integrating what you have learned from the material above.
How should a believer respond to anger and bitterness?

Instead of a reading assignment you have a research assignment. Tomorrow's session will be a Current Events session. Your assignment will be to find a story online, in a magazine, or in the newspaper that relates to the issue that you discussed today. Your task is to locate the article, give a copy of the article to your teacher or parent and provide some of your own worldview analysis to the article. Your analysis should demonstrate that you understand the issue, that you can clearly connect the story you found to the issue that you discussed today, and that you can provide a biblical critique of this issue in today's context. Look at the next session to see the three-part format that you should follow.

Issue

Ad Hominem Attacks against Political Opponents

READING ASSIGNMENT:
None

SESSION III: CURRENT EVENTS

Issue

Ad Hominem Attacks against Political Opponents

Current events sessions are meant to challenge you to connect what you are learning in Omnibus class to what is happening in the world around you today. After the last session, your assignment was to find a story online or in a magazine or newspaper relating to the issue above. Today you will share your article and your

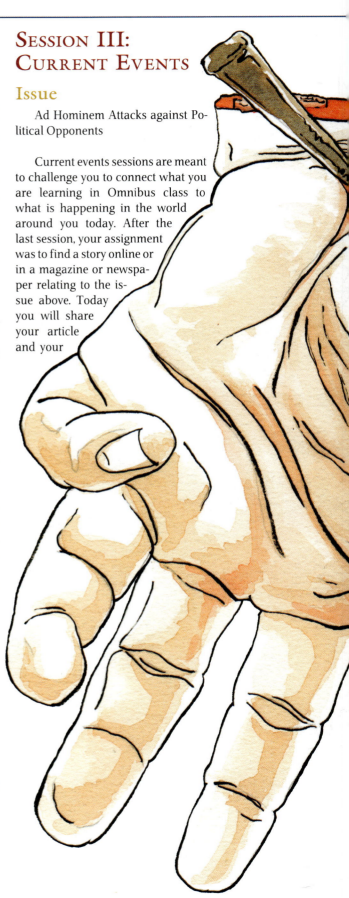

After having Cicero killed, Mark Antony ordered that his head and hands be hung above the rostra, where the orators spoke. Never again would Cicero write another Philippic against Antony.

analysis with your teacher and classmates or parents and family. Your analysis should follow the format below:

BRIEF INTRODUCTORY PARAGRAPH

In this paragraph you will tell your classmates about the article that you found. Be sure to include where you found your article, who the author of your article is, and what your article is about. This brief paragraph of your presentation should begin like this:

Hello, I am (name), and my current events article is (name of the article) which I found in (name of the web or published source)...

CONNECTION PARAGRAPH

In this paragraph you must demonstrate how your article is connected to the issue that you are studying. This paragraph should be short, and it should focus on clearly showing the connection between the book that you are reading and the current events article that you have found. This paragraph should begin with a sentence like

I knew that my article was linked to our issue because...

CHRISTIAN WORLDVIEW ANALYSIS

In this section, you need to tell us how we should respond as believers to this issue today. This response should focus both on our thinking and on practical actions that we should take in light of this issue. As you list these steps, you should also tell us why we should think and act in the ways you recommend. This paragraph should begin with a sentence like

As believers, we should think and act in the following ways in light of this issue and this article.

READING ASSIGNMENT:

Second Philippic, XXXII.79–XLVI.118 (pp. 135–153) and *On Duties* III, X.1–VI.32 (pp. 157–170)

SESSION IV: ACTIVITY
Second Philippic

Cicero's Rhetorical Devices and Fallacies

Despite the fact that Cicero is considered one of the greatest orators in western history, his rhetoric is not always sound. Although many times his logic and his appeal to emotions are entirely appropriate, he also employs many arguments that fall under the category of rhetorical fallacies. In this activity, you will analyze Cicero's rhetoric, looking for both positive and negative examples of rhetoric and argumentation.

In classical rhetorical theory, a good persuasive speech was characterized by logos, pathos, and ethos. Logos referred to the logical soundness of the argument, pathos referred to the emotional appeal of the speech, and ethos referred to the author's attempt to appear credible and gain his audience's trust. Rhetorical fallacies also fall into these three general categories—fallacies of logic, emotional appeal, and efforts to gain credibility.

Review Cicero's Second Philippic *and answer the following questions:*

1. Find an example of logos, or good logical argumentation.
2. Find an example of pathos, or appropriate appeal to the audience's emotions.
3. Find an example of Cicero's attempt to establish his ethos.

Define the following rhetorical fallacies (feel free to use a dictionary or Internet resources to find the definitions of any of these fallacies) and find an example of each of them in Cicero's speech.

1. Hasty Generalization
2. Non Sequitur
3. Post hoc ergo propter hoc (or Faulty Causality)
4. Scare Tactics
5. Slippery Slope
6. Guilt by Association
7. Ad hominem
8. Straw man

OPTIONAL ACTIVITY

Analyze Rhetoric

The above session could be profitably repeated by reviewing modern political speeches or articles. You could examine the rhetoric of a speech that is famous for its good rhetoric (Martin Luther King, Jr.'s *I Have a Dream* speech, for example), or you could choose an article written by a politician or media member notorious for rhetorical fallacies (Ann Coulter, Rush Limbaugh, Sean Hannity, Dennis Miller, James Carville, and Bill Maher are popular examples at this writing).

Reading Assignment:
On Duties III, VII.33–XXXIII.121 (pp. 170–209)

Session V: Discussion
On Duties III

Question to Consider

Can something that is to our advantage ever conflict with what is right? Would we be sufficiently performing what is right if we serve our interests without harming anyone else in the process?

Discuss or list short answers to the following questions:

Text Analysis

1. Why does Cicero believe we should pursue what is right?
2. Besides actually preferring advantage to right, what else does Cicero say would be sin?
3. Why does Cicero believe that doing wrong against another person for your own profit is always wrong and never advantageous?
4. According to Cicero, what characterizes the greatest heroes and men in history?
5. What analogy does Cicero offer to explain why it is acceptable to serve our own interests, as long as we don't harm another?

Cultural Analysis

1. Would our culture agree that it is always advantageous to do what is right?
2. Would our culture agree with Cicero that we should strive to serve our own interests as long as we don't harm anyone else?

Biblical Analysis

1. According to 1 John 3:16–17, what example has Jesus laid down for our lives?
2. What does Philippians 2:3–4 have to say about our priorities in life? How does this contrast to Cicero's analogy of the runner in a race?

Summa

Write an essay or discuss this question, integrating what you have learned from the material above.

How should we balance enjoying God's gifts and providing for ourselves while living a self-sacrificial life?

Optional Session: Recitation

Comprehension Questions

Answer the following questions for factual recall:

1. In his *Second Philippic* what does Cicero claim about all enemies of Rome for the previous 20 years? What does this imply about Cicero?
2. According to Cicero, what contradiction has Antony committed regarding the murder of Caesar?
3. Why does Cicero call Antony "our Helen of Troy?"
4. What "present" did Antony give Cicero at Brundisium?
5. How does Cicero use Antony's purchase of Pompey's estate to criticize Antony's character?
6. How did Antony use Caesar's death to his own advantage?
7. What two things does Cicero pray for at the end of his *Second Philippic*?
8. According to Cicero, what is the most "fertile field" of philosophy?
9. What three questions does the philosophy of moral obligations seek to answer?
10. According to Cicero, what is the relationship between what is right and what is advantageous?
11. What purpose ought every man to have in life? What are the consequences of not living life according to this purpose?
12. What are the Four Cardinal Virtues Cicero discusses?

Endnotes

1. *Cicero, Selected Works*, Michael Grant, trans. (London: Penguin Books, 1960), 101.
2. Ibid., 29.
3. Ibid., 160.
4. Ibid., 168.
5. Rom. 1:20.
6. All page citations are from *Cicero, Selected Works*, Michael Grant, trans. (London: Penguin Books, 1960).

Cultural Anthropology

What is Cultural Anthropology?

Unfortunately, it is not possible to discuss an academic discipline of this nature without using some of its jargon. Please bear with me. There is also a brief glossary at the end of this essay in case you need to refresh your understanding of a particular term or field.

Cultural anthropology is part of the "anthropology" family of academic disciplines. *Anthropos* (Greek) refers to "human beings" and *logy* (also rooted in Greek) is commonly used to designate something as a "science, theory, or doctrine" (as in physiology, theology, or biology). Thus, anthropology can be concisely defined as the "scientific study of mankind" (or in the current politically correct style, "humankind").

The term *cultural anthropology* can refer broadly to all those subfields of anthropology that are not specifically part of *physical anthropology*, the latter having to do with "the study of human biological characteristics and variation across time, place and condition." In this more general designation, cultural anthropology includes archaeology (the study of the material remains of past human populations in order to describe and understand their cultures), linguistics (the systematic study of language), and ethnology (which involves analyzing and explaining different cultures, generally in comparison to one another, or to themselves over time). The "ethnography," a detailed and comprehensive written description of a culture resting mostly on sustained, direct

Beautifully displaying her culture by what she wears, this girl from Longsheng, China, wears a traditional costume of the Dong minority group.

interaction with it ("participant observation" or "fieldwork"), is the most important source of information for doing ethnology.[1]

More narrowly, the term *cultural anthropology* is often used to refer to the field that includes ethnology as well as ethnographic study of individual cultures. Scholars who do this tend to treat archaeology and linguistics as separate anthropological subfields, despite the fact that both certainly involve analyzing cultures or cultural phenomena. Regardless, it is generally recognized by cultural anthropologists that their work often requires incorporating material from, and being conversant in, all anthropological subfields to at least some extent. The current essay treats cultural anthropology in this more restrictive sense.

Cultural anthropology as a discipline or field of study did not formally emerge until the mid- to latter part of the nineteenth century. Certainly, before this time there had been people interested in studying cultures other than their own, both deep description of particular groups and some types of comparative studies.

What student of classical education is not aware of the ancient Greek historian Herodotus (484–425 B.C.), who in his time traveled throughout, and wrote extensively about, the known world around the Mediterranean and places as far-flung as India? There was Julius Caesar, who wrote of the customs of the Gallic and Germanic peoples in his *Commentaries*, even describing things like marital rules and dowry in detail. In *Germania*, the Roman historian and senator Tacitus (A.D. 56–117) essentially provided a study of the German ethnic groups, and he tackled other tribes in some sections of his *Agricola*.

Actually, the detailed study and description of other cultures and their habits (essentially early "ethnography") held an honored position among the ancient Greeks and Romans. There are the writings of later traders and explorers, such as the famous thirteenth-century work, *The Travels of Marco Polo*. And a more immediate precursor to cultural anthropology, French aristocrat and Enlightenment thinker Baron Montesquieu (1689–1755), did what amounted to early ethnology in his *Spirit of the Laws*, searching for general laws behind social variation and development across different cultures through systematic comparison. In fact, his "general spirit" (roughly, the ways of thinking, feeling and seeing common to a people) anticipated later notions about "worldview" and "culture." He also explored the effect that different physical ecologies may have upon the content of cultures, a major concern for many cultural anthropologists today.

However, these early analyses and descriptions of various people groups differed from what was to become cultural anthropology in some pretty important ways. Two appear to be especially important.

First, cultural anthropologists consciously sought to be more "scientific" in studying cultures, utilizing practices such as direct observation, cross-checking, verification, and standardizing methods. Later on, some quantification was even introduced. They tried to get away from "armchair anthropology"—that is, just reading about the experiences of others such as missionaries, traders, explorers, soldiers, and colonial government workers.[2]

Second, in something that especially reached fruition in the twentieth century, cultural anthropologists worked hard to be more objective in looking at other cultures, trying to understand them on their own terms, and not assuming the superiority of their own civilization's way of life. They were also more likely to use ethnographic work to question their own cultural practices, values, and beliefs.

Edward Burnett Tylor

Two of the earliest major thinkers in what was to become cultural anthropology were Edward Burnett (E.B.) Tylor (1832–1917) and Lewis Henry Morgan (1818–1881). The latter's work *Iroquois* (1851) is a real ethnography based on extensive firsthand interaction with the group. In Tylor's *Primitive Culture* (1871) and Morgan's *Ancient Society* (1877) both men advanced the idea of "unilineal evolution." That is, despite differences in their theories with regards to the exact nature of the stages and processes involved, they both believed that all cultures progress over time, from lower to higher, through the same stages in the same order. This idea is now widely discredited.

In a more important and lasting contribution, in the former book E.B. Tylor sought to define the very idea of "culture" as something possessed by all people groups. Formerly, normal usage was that "culture" was something only possessed by certain folk, particularly elites or more advanced peoples, or at least some people had more culture (or "civilization") than others. Culture, Tylor said, was a "complex whole" that included any habits or capacities that were acquired by people through their involvement in societies.

The idea of culture has developed in the field a great deal since then, but owes a lot to Tylor's pioneering efforts. Certain features are pretty consistently held to across the (probably) hundreds of definitions of "culture" advanced by cultural anthropologists over the years.

Cultures are learned through social interaction and not inborn, therefore they are transmitted from one generation to another; they are generally held in common by members of the society that generated them; they tend to be integrated (that is, they are internally coherent, with different elements of cultures supporting rather than undermining other elements of the same cultures); and they include things like knowledge, beliefs, behavior, values, norms, and even emotions.

Most of all, cultures are, at the core, symbolic. That is, they involve representations—visible things that stand for ideas and thus convey meanings that must be interpreted in culturally appropriate ways. The most obvious example of the symbolic nature of culture is language in all its elements, but things such as rituals, ceremonies, art, literature and stories, traditions, images, and even repetitive practices of everyday life also convey and sustain meaning symbolically.

The real foundation of American cultural anthropology was laid by Franz Boas (1858–1942), a German Jew who emigrated to the United States in 1887, eventually becoming a professor at Columbia University in New York City. He taught and shaped the approach of many who went on to become influential cultural anthropologists, including Alfred Kroeber (1876–1960), Robert Lowie (1883–1957), Edward Sapir (1884–1939), Ruth Benedict (1887–1948), and his most famous disciple, Margaret Mead (1901–1978).

Boas was a talented ethnographer, known especially for his work among the Inuit of the Baffin Islands, and the Kwakiutl of a coastal region in British Columbia. He decisively rejected the theory of unilineal evolution and sought to make anthropology even more empirical and rigorous methodologically by basing it even more on observation rather than conjecture, promoting fieldwork done by scholars who master the native language of their subjects, living with them over a fairly lengthy period of time. Although Boas did not use the term, he advanced the idea of "cultural relativism." Embracing this became a virtual requirement for doing cultural anthropology. He also promoted the doctrine of "cultural determinism."

His program was substantially laid out in his *The Mind of Primitive Man* (1911), and each of the latter three elements, especially the first two, became central features of American anthropology.

Cultural relativism basically states that the beliefs and actions of people can only be evaluated within the context of their own cultures. This means that a culture's morals, too, can only be understood in light of the values of that culture. The doctrine also clearly asserts that no culture is inherently superior or inferior to any other culture.

Understanding other cultures in light of any supposed universal truths or absolutes, or from the standpoint of one's own culture, is not only flawed epistemologically, Boas believed, but undermines good methodology; objectivity in studying other cultures requires that one embrace cultural relativism. Ethnocentrism, the belief in the superiority of the ways of one's own culture and evaluation of others by its standards, is also seen as bad for humans generally. Cultural anthropologists believe that one of the most valuable consequences of their work is to combat excessive ethnocentrism in their own cultures, and to help people become more critical of their own cultures and their basic assumptions. A quote from Ruth Benedict's *Patterns of Culture* (1934) illustrates this doctrine: "... taboos on killing oneself and others relate to no absolute standards."

The doctrine of cultural determinism states that people, and variation among individuals and cultures, are not shaped by biology much, if at all. Humans are quite "plastic," easily able to adapt to the vastly different cultures in which they might be raised. An almost infinite variety of cultural practices will "work" for people, so long as they are enculturated (raised within and taught the culture) to it. As Benedict said in the above, "Man is not committed in detail by his biological constitution to any particular form of behavior." Every culture is a kind of "personality," which imprints itself on its members (an idea that became especially associated with Benedict and Mead). At the cultural level, cultures are ultimately responsible for their own nature and content; culture begets culture. They are influenced, may be limited, but are not determined, by various forces both cultural and non-cultural.

This idea is somewhat associated with those eventually leading to the approach of Boas and his disciples being labeled "historical particularism." That approach emphasized the uniqueness of each culture and the forces that shape it, such that even cultures that arise at the same point (say, embracing monotheism) often do so by very different means and for disparate reasons. Boas' view makes universal theories about culture difficult if not impossible. Put another way, he resisted ethnology while emphasizing ethnography.

At the same time, in Britain and elsewhere in Europe a different approach to cultural anthropology was being developed, known as "functionalism." This approach stressed the functional nature of cultures; that is, as wholes and in their particulars they are ultimately designed to promote the survival and well-being of the societies that generate them. Cultural practices that are not functional are either abandoned, or they harm and perhaps even destroy their society.

The version of functionalism advanced by the Polish-born Bronislaw Malinowski (1884–1942), working mostly at the London School of Economics, focused on the ways that cultures are designed to directly and indirectly meet the individual biological, psychological, and social needs of their members. In the process they necessarily develop means for emotionally attaching people to their societies. These ideas were set forth especially in two posthumous volumes, *The Scientific Theory of Culture* (1944), and *The Dynamics of Cultural Change* (1945). Malinowski was also known for his ethnographic work among the Trobriand Islanders (just northeast of Papua New Guinea), published in the classic *Argonauts of the South Pacific* (1922).

Alfred Reginald (A.R.) Radcliffe–Brown (1881–1955) developed an approach known as "structural functionalism." This considered more the functions that cultural beliefs and practices had for the society as a whole. The key thing he sought to explain was social stability, or order. The culture provides means for maintaining or restoring equilibrium, or balance, to cope with inevitable disruptions and strains that arise within society. People within a culture are united by common interests and views.

Radcliffe–Brown also promoted an "organismic" view of culture and society. That is, these are like living organisms, in that the various parts are mutually dependent upon and affect one another. Changes in one area of culture (say, birth preferences) lead to changes elsewhere (for example, the military, business markets, or education), often in ways that are hard to predict or trace. For the whole to be healthy, each part must function properly. Much of his theoretical system is laid out in *Structure and Function in Primitive Society* (1952). He was also active in doing field research, especially in the Andaman Islands (in the Bay of Bengal southeast of India) and in Australia.

A slightly later development is the school of thought known as neo-evolutionism, which, like the nineteenth-century work of Tylor and Morgan, sought to explain cultural evolution over time. This approach stresses the extent to which cultures are shaped by, and thus deeply reflect, the ways that people have adapted to, and survived within, given physical ecologies. It rose to a great extent in opposition to Boas' approach, stressing things like cultural progress, the development of general theories about culture rather than just deep description of particulars, and the clear notions that cultures were strongly determined by external factors.

One major proponent of this was Leslie White (1900–1975). He argued that technology is key to human survival, enabling people to get energy from their natural environment (as in getting energy from food) and turn it to human use. Advances in technology that enable people to do this better propel their cultures forward (as in the shift from hunting and gathering to agriculture, or oil to nuclear energy).

Note that for White, unlike among the followers of Boas, some cultures were more advanced. Such technological shifts lead to changes in every other area of cultures such as the economic, marital, military, religious, and political. Thus, his position is sometimes called "technological determinism." His most important theoretical works were *The Science of Culture* (1949) and *The Evolution of Culture* (1959).

Another key thinker in this school was Julian Steward (1902–1972). He stressed the idea that how people acquire what they need within specific ecologies shapes every other aspect of their cultures. Thus, for example, we would expect the cultures of people living in Arctic tundra to be different from those of folk in the Sahara Desert. His position, set out in books such as *Theory of Cultural Change* (1955), gave rise to the study of "cultural ecology," namely, the relationship of cultures to their immediate physical environments.

Later still is an approach called "cultural materialism," championed especially by the provocative Marvin Harris (1927–2001). A kind of "cultural ecology on steroids," Harris argues that cultural contents are completely determined (not just influenced) by the interaction between people and their immediate physical ecology, with all its assets as well as limitations. Change is often forced by the inevitable pressures of population growth upon societies' ability to survive within particular environments. Unlike Steward and White, he also emphasized the fact that cultures can and do also shape their physical environments. The basic elements of his theory are captured in *The Rise of Anthropological Theory* (1968).

Today, cultural anthropology can be said to be divided between followers of the more "natural science"-modeled tradition and a more "humanistic" approach. The former, characterized by Steward, White, and Harris, seeks as much as possible to use the techniques and approaches of the "hard sciences" in the study of culture, and to develop theoretical generalizations about it. The latter, rooted in the work of Boas and his followers, sees the field as more historical and descriptive, argues for the uniqueness of each culture, and is more interested in describing and understanding individual cultures than in explaining them.

The modern humanistic approach, which could be described as "Boas on steroids," includes "interpretative anthropology," which treats cultures almost as if they were texts to be interpreted (and thus with a heavy emphasis upon the symbolic dimensions of culture), and seeks to acquire and convey an "insider's view" of that culture. The leader in developing this approach was Clifford Geertz (1926–2006), with his key work in this regard being *The Interpretation of Cultures* (1973). He did extensive field research in Southeast Asia and North Africa.

"Postmodernism" is even sharper in its critique of the scientific approach. To postmodernists, science is inescapably bound to its own culture, and thus "scientific" statements about other cultures reflect more the anthropologist's own culture than the one he is analyzing. Cultural materialists reflect their own materialist cultures, technological determinists are shaped by the technological obsession in their own societies, and so forth. And to postmodernists, beliefs of those in positions of power are designed to perpetuate the same. Thus, "scientific" cultural anthropology, like all science, becomes a kind of tool of domination.

Critical Issues

There are many problem areas for thoughtful, serious Christians in cultural anthropology, not only within particular schools of thought but across the field as a whole. For one thing, practitioners overwhelmingly accept Darwinian evolution at least as an explanation for the emergence of man and other species.

With some exceptions, cultural anthropologists tend to be very hostile to endeavors such as Christian missions, or indeed even to many attempts at cultural reform based on broadly Western values and knowledge. In fact, the typical cultural anthropologist wants to see indigenous cultures preserved, not changed. This is true even for cultures that accept high levels of violence and crimes such as rape; hold views of health and disease that increase sickness and death; embrace destructive, magical ideas about the spiritual world; ritually use powerful hallucinogenic drugs; practice extensive body mutilation; and so forth.

Where both anthropologists and missionaries are at work in the field, they are often "at war" as a result of this animosity of the former to the basic work of the latter. Organizations such as Wycliffe Bible Translators must often devote significant time and resources to dealing with such conflicts.

Cultural anthropologists are usually left-wing personally and politically. Despite the "toleration" they extend to the cultures they study, they are not usually accepting of biblically orthodox Christians, or indeed any conservatives who value and embrace the Western tradition. This is not only irritating, but is also a fundamental contradiction of their stated values, such as being non-judgmental and culturally relative.

Those who are cultural determinists are not only guilty of circular reasoning ("culture causes culture;" "they are different because they are different"), but rule out by fiat a host of relevant external factors that influence cultural variation. On the other hand, those who posit some kind of material factors to explain cultural beliefs and practices tend to view those as deterministic, as if the people had no choice but to adopt them and are thus (where relevant) absolved of any moral blame.

But the most important and systematic challenge facing any Christian working or taking courses in cultural anthropology is its widespread acceptance of the doctrine of cultural relativism. Therefore, that will be the focus of this section, beginning with an extended examination of cultural relativism's central claim that all human standards are relative to the cultures in which they are found and cannot be judged by any external moral norms.

By necessarily rejecting the idea of absolutes, or at least that any can be known with certainty, this position is in direct opposition to what is revealed to us propositionally in Scripture, not only in the areas of morals but also in the claims God makes about Himself, His world, mankind, and any other areas the Bible addresses. The fact is that the Bible is also full of records of God "judging" entire cultures in terms of His absolutes, regardless of what (indeed, typically *because* of) the "cultural values, beliefs, and practices" they embrace. Consider the litany of judgments against entire civilizations in places like Isaiah chapters 14–23.

And lest we think this is just an Old Testament reality, consider the negative judgment of the Cretans in Titus 1:12, or the first two chapters of Romans, in which Paul points out with regards to a litany of practices that are accepted in various cultures that "those who practice such things are deserving of death" (1:32).

The fact is that God is sovereign over every nation; He sets them up and He tears them down (see for example Daniel 2:21; 5:34, 35). His truth proclamations are not subject to or bound by any human culture. So while it is certainly true that our own cultures are imperfect, and affect and often even distort how we understand and apply Scripture, by grace we know that absolutes are in the Bible and that many are at least made clear *enough* to us. For example, things like murder, adultery, theft, pride, oppression, false religion, envy, homosexuality and fornication are wrong everywhere and for all people. Christians

must insist upon people repenting of such things, and turning to the one and only true God, in all cultures.

Besides, the positive statement "there are no absolutes" is in itself an absolute, and so is logically self-refuting. If true, it is not true. Cultural relativists will sometimes dodge this by claiming that there *may* be absolutes, but either (a) no one knows for sure what they are, as there is widespread disagreement about them among cultures, or (b) scholars have to generate or discover absolutes. The latter can only be done after much careful, ethnographic study of the world and seeing what "universals" there are. For example, all human cultures have moral norms, and a statement like "all cultures need moral rules" is an absolute.

Besides rejecting God's propositional revelation in the Bible, view (a) above understates the degree of similarity that exists among cultures. For example, in terms of moral systems, in *The Abolition of Man* (1943) C.S. Lewis's excellent discussion of "the Tao" underscores the extent to which various moral ideas, such as "the Golden Rule," are embraced across a wide range of civilizations and religions.

Moreover, disagreement doesn't prove that no one is right or another wrong about what is or is not an absolute. View (b) at best confuses "something universally done among cultures" with "absolutes." If something is the former, it is certainly an absolute of some kind. But to be an absolute, something certainly need not be accepted in all cultures. Peter's bold statement, "Nor is there salvation in any other, for there is no other name under heaven given among men by which we must be saved," (Acts 4:12) is not commonly accepted in all cultures (sadly, including the modern West), but it is absolutely and everywhere true.

It is also not an illegitimate "slippery slope" argument to point out that cultural relativism leads logically to epistemological (that is, relativism about what we can know) and moral relativism, both of which have destructive impact. If all truth claims are culturally contingent, at some levels both forms of relativism are the logical consequence. Certainly, many cultural anthropologists, especially older ones, have resisted this slide, especially in the moral area, but have simply lacked theological and philosophical means to do so once they embraced cultural relativism.

For example, some anthropologists have pointed out that just because something is morally acceptable in one culture does not make it so in another. For a Tibetan woman to be married to several brothers (fraternal polyandry) at the same time does not give a New Yorker a "free pass" to do the same, as the conditions that justified this in Tibet do not apply in New York. But what if the relevant conditions in New York become similar to those in Tibet? Or what if a polyandrous Tibetan family moves to New York?

Christians throughout history have championed various social and cultural reforms, and this is an important part of the cultural mandate. Cultural relativism logically undermines the fundamental rationale for such efforts, namely, that some existing cultural practices are objectively wrong and need to be changed.

Cultural anthropologists often deny the latter charge. One way they do this is by distinguishing between their duties as scholars, and those they have as private citizens who can and should make value judgments. But this is a bit like believing in Jesus on Sunday and in Buddha the rest of the week. If cultural relativism is true, it is as true for the private citizen considering outlawing widow burning in India or female circumcision in the Sudan as it is for the anthropologist studying the same things.

Another way around this for some cultural anthropologists is to claim they will use values within a culture to challenge obnoxious practices within those same cultures. But what if these other necessary values are not present? And by what standards do we identify which objectionable practices to assault in the first place, if that culture has accepted them? Nothing is more contorting and mind-twisting than to study the debates among cultural anthropologists whenever they try to figure out if they should oppose some practice of any non-Western culture.

Second, briefly consider the idea that no culture, as a whole, is superior to any other. This kind of claim, with its surface humility, appeals to many Christians, but we must reject it. Christianity is true, and it is transformative. We ought to expect that cultures in which the gospel is being embraced by increasing numbers of people, in thought and deed, will experience real advancement of civilization. We cannot throw that away. This is not an occasion for pride in such cultures, but thankfulness, as it is all about grace from beginning to end.

It is certainly true that in all cultures, including Christianized ones, many problems will remain, and there will be many steps backward along the path of cultural progression. Further, every culture that is permeated by the gospel won't end up the same, but there will continue to be some uniqueness among cultures, as when we see "nations" in the plural in the New Jerusalem (Rev. 21:24–26). But the gospel does bring cultural advances, and if it does so in ours, we should not be ashamed to export these blessings to others.

It must also be remembered that one of the most fundamental facts is that the natural state of all men, at all levels, but for the intervention of God, is rebellion against Him. All non-Christian cultures or cultural elements involve the rejection of God and indeed the attempt to hide from, suppress, and replace Him (Rom. 1:18–23).

So what of the claim that objective study of other cultures is not possible unless one embraces cultural relativism? There are Christian alternatives to this. Overall, simply being dedicated to understanding and relaying truth, as much as possible, in the study of other cultures will go a long way toward overcoming the real dangers of illegitimate types of ethnocentrism.

First, Christians can certainly, through careful study, learn about the substance of different cultural beliefs and practices, even those they know to be wrong, including the culture's rationales for them, and the forces and conditions that promote them. They should also be able to convey these findings in truthful, non-judgmental (in the best sense of the term) ways. For example, we can explain that Aztec cannibalism was partly a result of a large population trying to meet its needs for animal protein without claiming that it was acceptable for them to do this under the conditions, as if Aztecs had no alternative means of meeting these physical needs.

Second, believers should look at the flaws in their own cultures as they look at others, to help clarify their thinking and to be able to relate to members of these cultures in winsome ways. In considering Muslim po-

lygyny, remember the high rates of divorce and sex outside marriage in the West. In examining cultures that practice human sacrifice, consider the United States, which has enough abortions to depopulate an entire large city, or even one or two states, every year. In a twist on a familiar parable, we end up realizing that we must remove the speck from our eye before we try to take the plank out of theirs (Matt. 7:3).

Third, believers should be self-critically aware of the degree to which we *do* possess "cultural blinders." We tend to take many things from our cultures for granted, and judge other cultures based on them, that are not in Scripture or that go beyond it. For example, do we have to treat all arranged marriage practices as wrong? Provided it is done in a good spirit, should we condemn wives eating separately from and after their husbands? There may be answers to these types of questions, but they won't be arrived at easily, and addressing them properly means distinguishing our cultural assumptions and training from what Scripture teaches.

Paul Gauguin painted *Nafea Faa ipoipo? (When will you marry?)* in 1892. Gauguin had abandoned his wife and children about a decade earlier to devote himself to his painting. In 1891 he sailed to the South Seas to escape European civilization (that is, he was in serious debt). An aesthetic cultural anthropologist of sorts, Gauguin's depictions of Polynesian culture led the way for Primitivism, an art movement characterized by exaggerated body proportions, colorful contrasts, and geometric designs.

A Christian Response

Is cultural anthropology a legitimate field for a Christian to enter? Well, certainly there is nothing inherently sinful about wanting to study other cultures in a systematic, even scientific way (with all the qualifications we need in applying that latter term to studying humans). There are many valuable insights and facts about the human race throughout anthropological literature, much of which is inherently fascinating. Any endeavor that requires cross-cultural, international work can benefit from being familiar with the relevant ethnographies or doing anthropological studies of one's own. This includes much work in business, politics, the military, and of course, missions. Consider the global missions and Bible translation work of an organization such as Wycliffe Bible Translators, which keeps an extensive collection of ethnographic materials and works with cultural anthropologists quite a bit.

Moreover, throughout the Scriptures, acquiring wisdom includes the careful observation of human beings and their ways. The wisdom book of Proverbs contains scores of insights about human beings, given by God, of course, but obviously acquired through careful observation.

Our understanding of the Bible has been enhanced greatly by the insights of students of the ancient world back to at least Ur at the time of Abraham. This has included archaeology used to reconstruct, among other things, the cultural ways of people involved in the biblical records.

Moreover, much of what is in the Bible is much more understandable if one has a better grasp of cultural anthropological terms, concepts and facts. In the Bible we find polygyny and concubinage and its consequences; beliefs in oracles and other magic; men like Jacob having to per-

GLOSSARY

Anthropology: the scientific study of mankind.

Archaeology: the study of the material remains of cultures.

Cultural anthropology: in its broadest use, those parts of anthropology that involve the study of human cultures, including archaeology and linguistics, as well as ethnology and ethnography (see below for definitions of these last three terms). Sometimes, the term is used more narrowly, applying only to ethnology and ethnography, which is how it is generally used in this essay.

Cultural determinism: at the level of individuals, the idea that people are easily shaped by their cultures, which are far more important than biology in affecting their personalities, and that many types of practices will work so long as people are taught by their cultures to do and accept them. At the level of cultures, the idea that cultures are ultimately responsible for shaping themselves ("culture begets culture").

Cultural ecology: the study of the relationship of cultures to their immediate ecological (material) environments, with the belief that the latter strongly shape every aspect of the former.

Cultural materialism: cultural ecology (see definition above) "on steroids"; the idea that material, ecological constraints, typically aggravated by various population pressures, determine every aspect of any culture.

Cultural relativism: the idea that beliefs (including morals) and actions of people can only be evaluated within the context of their own cultural context and not in light of any absolutes, and that no culture is inherently superior or inferior to any other culture.

Culture: something that is produced by societies, learned through social interaction, transmitted from one generation to another; generally held in common by members of the society that generated it, which tend to be integrated (that is, internally coherent with different elements of cultures supporting rather than undermining each other), and which include things like knowledge, beliefs, behavior, values, norms, and even emotions. Any culture is essentially symbolic (see definition below).

Enculturation: the process of being raised within, taught, and personally absorbing a culture.

Ethnography: a detailed and comprehensive written description of a culture.

Ethnology: analysis, explanation and comparison of cultures.

continued on the next page

GLOSSARY continued

Fieldwork: the study of a culture through sustained, direct observation of, and participation within it. (See also "Participant observation" below.)

Functionalism: the idea that different aspects of cultures exist because they support the survival of individuals and whole cultures.

Historical particularism: an approach within cultural anthropology that emphasizes the uniqueness of each culture, and denigrates the idea of general theories about culture.

Linguistics: the systematic study of language.

Neo-evolutionism: a modernization of some of the major ideas of unilineal evolution (see below) that emphasize the progress of societies, and the importance of advancing general theories to explain cultural development.

Participant observation: the study of people by observing and interacting with them while being directly involved in their life and activities. (See also "Fieldwork" above.)

Postmodernism: in cultural anthropology, a viewpoint that sharply rejects the very idea of a science of culture. Postmodernists see science as a Western tool of domination and oppression that is bound to Western culture and believe that scientific claims by anthropologists tell us more about the anthropologists' own biases and cultural blinders than about any of the cultural realities they claim to be analyzing.

Symbolic: involving representations; that is, visible things that stand for ideas and thus convey meaning.

Unilineal evolution: the idea that over time all cultures develop, from lower to higher, through the same stages, in the same order.

form bride service before they could marry other men's daughters; patrilineal systems (tracing ancestry through the male line) carefully maintained; the levirate, kinship-based property systems; tribal governments; incest and menstrual taboos; and much else that is the basic stuff of ethnographies. A book like Victor Matthew's *Manners and Customs in the Bible* (2006) is just one of many valuable resources that use such information to shed light on Scripture.

For example, learning about how men with multiple wives in contention with each other handle the problems that arise in polygamous cultures around the world, illuminates much of what we read in Genesis concerning Jacob, his two wives, and his two concubines. The beautiful story of Ruth can only be understood in terms of the levirate (where a man is encouraged to marry the wife of his dead brother, a responsibility that then can fall on other male relatives by some rule should this not be possible or desirable). Boaz was Ruth's "kinsman-redeemer," and Jesus Christ is ours. Or consider the refusal of Naboth to sell his vineyard to Ahab in 1 Kings 21, saying, "The Lord forbid that I should give the inheritance of my fathers to you" (v. 3). This is understandable to anyone in a patrilineal system in which land belongs to the larger kinship group and not to individuals in the strict sense of the word, as was true in ancient Israel.

However, the obstacles that one is likely to encounter in cultural anthropology, especially in terms of the prejudice and discrimination from professors and fellow students, are considerable for the serious Christian. Doing cultural anthropology really means getting a master's and probably a doctoral degree in the field. In today's politically correct academy, it would be very tough for the orthodox, believing Christian to get through this process intact, without being either rejected or co-opted. To get something like an academic post, and then tenure afterward, would be challenging as well, except perhaps in a Christian college. However, the latter don't typically hire many cultural anthropologists, and those within these settings have often ended up pretty compromised themselves. All this would require a great deal of discretion, including a lot of very careful picking of battles.

Attending a Christian college could help, if one can find one with a sound program in cultural anthropology. This means carefully talking to the college's professors in the major field about many of the problematic ideas described in this essay and finding out where they stand on them. The history of compromised "evangelical" colleges and professors is pretty dismal, and any social science especially (of which cultural anthropology is one) must be approached with caution. Some Roman Catholic colleges may also be very good choices if they are still

Brahma bulls are considered holy to Hindus and are seen freely walking the streets of India. This one was photographed sitting leisurely outside a typical street vendor's market in Chennai.

seriously Catholic and offer a cultural anthropology major, since they may enforce respect for basic, orthodox Christian beliefs. Another option is to study a different but supportive field (such as history or sociology) and then tackle cultural anthropology at the graduate level. Getting into a good cultural anthropology program does not require an undergraduate degree in the field.

But whatever precedes it, if he is to move on in the field, the Christian student will almost certainly find that he needs to do graduate work in a secular setting, unless (once again) he chooses a strongly Roman Catholic university. Given the close relationships between professors and students that are normal in good graduate programs, the differences in values and beliefs that the Christian student will encounter, and the prejudice of these academicians towards biblical Christianity, are likely to lead to real problems. But recalling that fine Christians regularly successfully navigate programs where most practitioners hold key beliefs that are hostile to scriptural approaches—such as sociology, biology, psychology—it is certainly possible to do so.

One good piece of advice at the graduate level is to look for programs that are more rooted in the "objective science" side of the field, and to at least avoid like the plague those that are heavily "postmodern." The former will generally respect good logic and hard evidence, and will tend to subscribe to academic norms that judge students on the quality of their work more than on their private religious beliefs, even when the professors are personally liberal in outlook. It is also possible to find conservative cultural anthropologists. Normally, on the objective science side of anthropology, they will usually treat Christian students with respect.

A good organization for any academician to join, especially one in a heavily politically correct field like cultural anthropology, is the National Association of Scholars. The NAS is committed to resisting political correctness, defending the study of Western civilization, and promoting sound, objective scholarship. It includes academicians of many religions and political stripes, and sections organized around academic disciplines. The encouragement and networking at NAS meetings both local and national can be invaluable, particularly for the student looking for good graduate programs and professors to work with.

However, nothing can replace the quality of the personal preparation and wise Christian walk of the student himself. Someone contemplating, or engaged in, the study of cultural anthropology should be thoroughly familiar with the Scriptures, with a particular focus on what the Scriptures teach us about human beings. The Bible has a wonderful, rich anthropology that, unlike the secular variety, is completely true. This should be the starting point, and the check and balance, on all of our inquiries into the field. But understanding the Scriptures, including so many of the difficult passages and problems that arise when studying humans in the Bible, means also learning to read good books, including commentaries on the Bible.

For example, consider the Onan incident in Genesis 38, where the latter is killed by God after refusing to complete the sex act with his dead brother's wife (a levirate incident). How can we understand this? What place did the levirate have in God's economy here, and is the violation of the levirate the source of God's anger with Onan? Does this record suggest that birth control is obnoxious to God? Would God demand something that, in many practical instances, required that men engage in polygyny? These are tough but important issues, and a good student will want to know what scholars like John Calvin, Martin Luther, Matthew Henry, and many others had to say about this difficult passage.

Students in this field should also devour scholarly works that critique cultural anthropology, or social science generally, from a Christian viewpoint. For example, C.S. Lewis's *The Abolition of Man*, mentioned earlier, is among other things a cogent commentary on the error and consequences of relativism, including the cultural variety. His fine "Space Trilogy" (*Out of the Silent Planet, Perelandra,* and *That Hideous Strength,* 1945) also has embedded, in literary form, some excellent critique of the social sciences, as well as some fine Christian anthropology. Another excellent choice is Leslie Stevenson and David Haberman's *Ten Theories of Human Nature* (2008).

Some books that set forth a Christian vision for the social sciences (at least partly) are Abraham Kuyper's *Lectures on Calvinism* (1898) and Herman Dooyeweerd's *A New Critique of Theoretical Thought* (four volumes, 1953–58). Although too long out of print, Alan Storkey's *A Christian Social Perspective* (1979) is also a fine book, inspired by Dooyeweerd. Herbert Schlossberg's *Idols of Destruction* (1983) is a masterpiece. David Hegeman's *Plowing in Hope* (1999) has some excellent insights on establishing a truly biblical theology of culture.

With this, Christian students in all fields should be familiar with the best work on integrating biblical faith with scholarship. Some suggestions in this vein are: *A Francis Schaeffer Trilogy* (1990), which comprises Schaeffer's three most essential books (*The God Who is There, Escape from Reason,* and *He Is There and He Is Not Silent*); George Marsden's *The Outrageous Idea of Christian Scholarship* (1998); Mark Noll's *The Scandal of the Evangelical Mind* (1994); Gary North's (Ed.) *Foundations of Christian Scholarship* (selected essays, 1976); and the demanding but essential *The Defense of the Faith* (1967) by Cornelius Van Til.

Finally, while this has certainly been mentioned elsewhere in this volume, meaningful, sustained involvement with and commitment to fellow Christians, especially in a local church, is vital. This needs to include interaction with wise believers able to understand and respond intelligently to problems and issues encountered in the study of cultural anthropology. They need not be anthropologists of course, but can easily include those schooled in disciplines such as theology, philosophy, sociology, communication, psychology, and history, all of which regularly tackle challenges similar to those confronted in cultural anthropology.

—*David Ayers*

For Further Reading

Ruth Benedict. *Patterns of Culture*. New York: Houghton Mifflin Harcourt, 2006.

Franz Boas. *The Mind of Primitive Man*. Whitefish, Mont.: Kessinger Publishing Company, 2007.

Jared Diamond. *Gun, Germs and Steel*. New York: W.W. Norton, 1999.

Mary Douglas. *Purity and Danger*. Oxford, UK: Taylor and Francis, 2002.

Derek Freeman. *Margaret Mead and Samoa*. Jackson, Tenn.: Perseus Publishing, 1999.

Clifford Geertz. *The Interpretation of Cultures*. New York: Basic Books, 1977.

Marvin Harris. *Cannibals and Kings*. New York: Knopf Publishing Group, 1991.

Bronislaw Malinowski. *Argonauts of the South Pacific*. Long Grove, Ill.: Waveland Press, 1984.

Margaret Mead. *Coming of Age in Samoa*. New York: HarperCollins, 2001.

Lewis Henry Morgan. *Ancient Society*. Tucson, Ariz.: University of Arizona Press, 1985.

Julian Steward. *Theory of Cultural Change*. Champaign, Ill.: University of Illinois Press, 1972.

ENDNOTES

1   Although the author is drawing on a number of sources and general knowledge for these definitions, he is especially grateful to Jean-Luc Chodkiewicz ("What is Anthropology All About?," pages 1–5, in Chodkiewicz (Ed.), Peoples of the Past and Present. Toronto: Harcourt Brace. 1995) for his concise definitions of these subfield terms.

2   Though certainly figures such as Herodotus, Caesar, and Marco Polo were not stuck in their armchairs!

Annals of Imperial Rome

Have you ever noticed anything funny about ordering coffee at a fast food drive-through window? "Yes, I'd like one large hot coffee, please," you say. "Here you are, sir," comes the reply. "Please be careful; the coffee is hot."

Why does the restaurant employee think it is necessary to *warn* you that they are giving you exactly what you ordered? You ordered *hot* coffee and then are told to watch out! The reason, of course, is that in 1994 McDonald's was sued by a woman who burned herself with the hot coffee she had ordered.

Similarly, doctors today must be extremely careful when performing surgeries, because even in their attempt to help save a person's life or replace a bad knee, one wrong step and they could be sued for millions of dollars. The "industry" of lawsuits for such mistakes has played a large role in the escalating cost of health care in recent years. But doesn't it seem a bit strange that a person or business can be ruined financially for an accident made while trying to serve someone?

In his *Annals of Imperial Rome*, Tacitus describes the slow but steady corruption of Roman politics under the emperors of the first century A.D. Tacitus describes a situation in which not just a person's money, but his life and the lives of his whole family, could be lost because of one wrong word spoken in the wrong company. Of course, many of those killed or exiled were guilty and corrupt. But for Tacitus, the corruption of Roman politics is most evident when innocent citizens, doing their best to serve Rome, are punished on account of vague rumors, or even just an emperor's displeasure. Tacitus hopes that his history of four emperors in the first century will make clear the decisions and actions that led to this atmosphere of fear and violence.

Portrait of Emperor Nero recarved as Claudius (c. A.D. 54–68, recarved c. A.D. 70). This head shows signs of re-carving in antiquity on its cheeks and jaw, and the area around the mouth has been reworked. The deep grooves recall portraits of the emperor Claudius, an elderly man when he came to power. It is likely that after Nero's unpopular rule, the portrait was re-carved to resemble his well-liked predecessor, Claudius.

No one knows exactly when or where Tacitus was born, only one contemporary of his wrote about his existence, and even his first name is up for debate! Even this "portrait" of Tacitus is only conjecture as to his appearance.

General Information

Author and Context

Imagine that you are given the assignment of writing a report about an author named "C. Smith." As you begin your research, you encounter several major obstacles. No one knows when or where this "C. Smith" was born, only one contemporary seems aware of his existence, and even his first name is up for debate! Such is the case with Publius (or Gaius) Cornelius Tacitus. He was probably born around A.D. 55, perhaps in northern Italy or southern Gaul (France), and he died sometime around A.D. 117.

From his own writings, several letters from a friend, and a single inscription in Turkey, we can piece together a few highlights of Tacitus's career. He attributes his rise in the political world to the emperors Vespasian, Titus, and Domitian. While the reigns of Vespasian and Titus would have offered a generally stable political environment in Rome, the proud and ever-suspicious Domitian conducted a fifteen-year reign of terror from A.D. 81–96. Tacitus would have needed tact and care to survive a reign that ended the lives and careers of hundreds of Roman politicians. After Domitian's death, Tacitus served as consul under the emperor Nerva in A.D. 97, and fifteen years later, under the emperor Trajan, he became governor of western Anatolia (Turkey).

The *Annals* are the first half of Tacitus's history of Roman emperors from the death of Augustus through the rule of Domitian. The *Annals* cover the reigns of Tiberius, Gaius (Caligula), Claudius, and Nero. The *Histories* pick up the narrative with the death of Nero and continue through Domitian's reign. Unfortunately, a significant portion of both texts is missing from the manuscripts available to us. Books VII–X and the end of Book XVI are missing from the *Annals*, and about two thirds of the *Histories* are missing.

Stylistically, Tacitus is a master of implication. He loves to give his readers an innocent explanation for the death of a popular figure, only to contradict that explanation with a vague yet ominous hint that some more sinister cause may lie behind the death he just described. Tacitus's love for implication also shapes how he describes imperial corruption. Rather than let his readers into the gory details of crime and debauchery as Suetonius might have done, Tacitus prefers to leave things up to the imagination of the reader. He leaves no doubt as to what happened, but rarely does he actually describe crimes or debauchery in detail.

Significance

Tacitus is generally considered by modern historians to be one of the most reliable sources for the events and actions surrounding the early Roman emperors. However, as with Plutarch and many other ancient writers, Tacitus's writings were not appreciated in his own day. In fact, we have little evidence of his works being read or appreciated at all until the Renaissance. Today, Tacitus's work is significant not only for historians interested in the events of imperial Rome, but also for those who are interested in the beliefs, practices, and culture of the Roman Empire in the first century A.D.

As Christians, we find particular significance in Tacitus's account. In addition to his general description of Roman culture, which aids our understanding of the environment in which the Church began and grew, Tacitus offers a brief history of Christianity itself when he describes Nero's attempt to blame the great fire of Rome on the Christians. In the process, he provides the only non-biblical reference to Pontius Pilate and confirms the biblical account of Christ's death as an historical event. Although we believe that the Bible is historically accurate because it is inspired by God Himself, this confirmation of biblical history helps to confirm our faith and is excellent evidence for apologetic situations.

In spite of Tacitus's help historically, his description of Christianity is extremely negative. He refers to it as a "deadly superstition" deserving "ruthless punishment," noting that Christians are "notoriously depraved" (*Annals*, XV.44). Even this negative perspective is helpful for us, however. This verdict from a Roman historian helps us understand the general attitude toward Christians in the first century, and helps to explain the persecution under Nero that many believe led to the deaths of Peter, Paul, and countless other believers.

Main Characters

Tacitus's brilliance as an author is especially evident in the development of his characters. One commentator argues that "in the delineation of character, Tacitus is unrivalled among historians and has very few superiors among dramatists and novelists."[1] Tacitus's characters come alive, their motives are explored, and their actions are natural in the context of Tacitus's descriptions. In fact, in many ways, the *Annals* are not driven by plot so much as by character development, as Tacitus gives us one lesson after another in virtue and depravity.

Tacitus has chosen four emperors as the main characters of the *Annals*: Tiberius, Gaius, Claudius, and Nero (although his entire account of Gaius is part of the text that has been lost). These four men dominate his account, though several other characters are important to the story. Tacitus attributes the decline of Tiberius's reign to the influence of his commander of the guard, Lucius Aelius Sejanus. Sejanus draws Tiberius into a long line of murders and seductions until he, along with anyone associated with him, is murdered because of the emperor's suspicions. Agrippina, mother of Nero, holds immense authority at the end of Claudius's reign and the beginning of Nero's. She commits a host of crimes, first to ensure Nero's rise to the throne, and then to protect her own power. However, her violence is surpassed by that of Nero, who has his own mother killed because she was "intolerable." Seneca is Nero's tutor and counselor through his youth and throughout much of his reign as emperor. Seneca continually seeks to steer Nero away from disastrous decisions, but finds himself forced to commit suicide when Nero turns his hatred toward innocent friends.

Tacitus's history is not limited to a few notable characters, however. Into the story come countless men and women, many of whom are just names that cross the pages as they fall victim to the plots and suspicions of the emperors. In fact, one of the difficulties of reading Tacitus can be keeping track of which names appear once and are gone, and which names he expects his readers to remember from an earlier episode.

Summary and Setting

Tacitus is very open about the reason for his history and what he hopes to accomplish in the process. He argues that during their reigns, these four emperors were described in false and flattering terms, whereas immediately after their reigns they were wrongly slandered out of spite and anger. Tacitus hopes to write a fair and accurate account, noting that neither of these incentives has influenced his writing.

His purpose in writing is not just to give an accurate account of imperial history, however. Rather, it is "to let no worthy action be uncommemorated, and to hold out the reprobation of posterity as a terror to evil words and deeds" (*Annals*, III.65). His purpose is distinctly moral. He argues that it is often difficult to know what is right and wrong, but he hopes a history of the consequences of particular decisions made by men and women in the past will help future generations know what is right. However, while his purpose is to demonstrate right and wrong choices, Tacitus focuses almost exclusively on the corruption and evil choices made by his characters.

Tacitus's account is clearly oriented around this goal. He never loses an opportunity to explain how corruption came to pass, or what motivated a character to make a bad decision. Particularly, Tacitus is interested in showing how great power and personal *hubris* lead to corruption and violence in the leader, as well as how the desire for success over virtue leads to corruption among the rest of the people. For each of the emperors, a similar storyline unfolds. Their reigns begin modestly as they seek to gain the goodwill of the people and establish their reign. However, as time goes on, increasing fear and suspicion along with the desire to be loved and admired drives each of the emperors to greater and greater acts of violence.

Worldview

While at my grandparents' house for Christmas one year, a storm covered northern Mississippi with a thick sheet of ice. Because of the weight of the ice, branches continuously snapped and fell from trees. It sounded like we had been transported into a war zone as branch after branch crashed onto the roof, rolled off, and landed among the bushes out front. During the night, a large branch hanging high above the roof of my grandparents' bedroom snapped and came hurtling down toward the house. Unlike the other branches that had fallen, this one was pointed straight down like a spear. It pierced straight through the roof, continued through the attic, and smashed through the ceiling into one of the bedrooms, stopping about five feet above the bed. My aunt slept downstairs for the rest of the night.

If such an occurrence had taken place in Tacitus's day, the potential victim would have undoubtedly taken this frightening surprise as much more than a narrow escape. It may have been considered a supernatural warning, or perhaps an omen of disaster to come. Tacitus describes a world quick to find meaning and guidance in unusual or dramatic events. Today, we might think of this tendency to find divine revelation in storms, deformed births, withering trees or other natural anomalies as ridiculous superstition.

But the Roman world was not irrational. Paul argues that "since the creation of the world, [God's] invisible attributes are clearly seen, being understood by the things that are made" (Rom. 1:20), while David writes that "the heavens declare the glory of God" (Ps. 19:1). In other words, the instinct to look for revelation from God or about God from the created world is, in itself, not misguided. God has, in fact, revealed Himself in the natural world. Violent thunderstorms and soaring eagles do have something to tell us about God. The problem for the Roman world was that their understanding was flawed on account of sin and was incomplete without God's divine explanation found in Scripture. Paul also writes in Romans 1 that men knew God was revealing Himself in creation, but they rejected Him. Because of their sin, Paul says that they "became futile in their thoughts . . . professing to be wise, they became fools."

Roman society was thus stuck with a broken pair of glasses that clouded its vision of reality. It was attempting to build an understanding of its world without the necessary tools. Instead of seeing thunderstorms and eagles as evidence of God's power and majesty, or reminders that He is present with us and sovereign over every event in our lives, the Romans tried to twist them to fit their needs in a broken, directionless world.

Agrippina the Younger had numerous imperial family ties. She was the great-granddaughter of Augustus, the sister of Caligula, the niece (and wife) of Claudius, and, as proved unfortunate for her, the mother of Nero.

Sin and Salvation

In the midst of this blindness, however, Tacitus was not unaware of the problems facing his culture. Despite his inability to understand God's revelation in nature, he was equipped with a mind and soul fashioned after the image of God. It should not surprise us, therefore, that Tacitus, pagan though he was, was keenly aware of the moral failure of his world. In fact, the Greek and Roman philosophers and historians as a whole were very good at identifying problems with the beliefs and practices of their cultures. Unfortunately, without the light of Christ, their solutions are less profitable than their indictments.

The problem, as Tacitus sees it, is a growing moral laxity in Roman society. From personal flattery, political sycophancy (flattering influential people for personal gain), greed, and suspicion to adultery, murder, and debauchery, Tacitus cries out against the downward spiral of sin in his culture. Tacitus continually deplores the moral depravity that has buried Roman politics in lying,

criminal efforts to succeed—or just to stay alive. In fact, the whole purpose of Tacitus's writing is to expose the deadly consequences of sinful actions. History, for Tacitus, has a distinctly moral purpose. He tells us that it is from the study of histories such as his that "men learn to distinguish right and wrong" (*Annals*, IV.32).

Tacitus reminds us that the most basic tenets of morality have been written upon our hearts by the finger of our Creator. His critique of Roman culture often sounds very much like Paul's criticism of the sinful nature Christians are to put off. Tacitus would readily agree with Paul's indictment of "adultery, fornication, uncleanness, lewdness, idolatry, sorcery, hatred, contentions, jealousies, outbursts of wrath, selfish ambitions, dissensions, heresies, envy, murders, drunkenness, revelries, and the like" (Gal. 5:19–21). Tacitus is not a Christian, but he understands that something is deeply wrong with the world around him. He is watching sin wreak havoc upon lost humanity, and he knows there is a problem.

Of course, one might say that an emperor who roves the city streets beating up strangers, a judge who perverts justice, or a son who kills his own mother are rather obvious indications that something is wrong. But that misses the point. As Tacitus points out, many people in his day used these examples as encouragement to vice, rather than as evidence of corruption.

Tacitus not only understands what actions are wrong, he also seems to have a deep understanding of the effects of sin on the human soul. In deploring Tiberius's wickedness, Tacitus cries out, "How truly the wisest of men used to assert that the souls of despots, if revealed, would show wounds and mutilations—weals left on the spirit, like lash-marks on a body, by cruelty, lust, and malevolence. Neither Tiberius's autocracy nor isolation could save him from confessing the internal torments which were his retribution" (*Annals*, VI.5) What a description of the sufferings of a lost sinner! Tacitus is no advocate for unrestrained pleasure and debauchery. He has a crystal-clear vision of the pain and suffering that result when sinners serve their own passions.

But despite the clarity of Tacitus's vision for the problem with humanity, he lacked understanding in two very important areas. First, Tacitus did not know the root cause of humanity's sin and suffering, and because he didn't know the cause, he did not have an adequate solution.

How did the world get to the point of moral depravity that existed under these four emperors? For Tacitus, the slide into corruption must be explained historically. His answer is that the increase in power belonging to the position of emperor increased the risks and rewards of Roman politics. In the first century A.D., the stakes were raised as the emperor came to hold more and more sway over Roman life. There was suddenly more to gain and more to lose by being in favor with the emperor. Men gave up striving for virtue because success, admiration, and even life itself depended upon the political favor of one man.

The first pages of Tacitus's *Annals* describe the decline of the Republic and the rise of the Empire, with special attention placed on the violence, favoritism, and bribery that attended the change. Tacitus makes it very clear that he sees a link between the system of government and the character of Roman citizens. With the loss of political equality, everyone became focused on one man. This increased focus on pleasing one man eroded the old Roman virtue that relied on valuing the community and its interests over your own. And so, argues Tacitus, with the loss of republican government came the loss of "the old Roman character."

For Tacitus, not only does the concentration of power in an emperor naturally undermine virtue, but the rise of each emperor individually demonstrates a similar pattern. The reign of Tiberius went from eight years of stability and prosperity to a growing bloodbath of internal conflict, suspicion, and crime because of the "unbounded lust for power" sparked by Sejanus, Tiberius's commander of the guard. Once Sejanus got the ball rolling, the cycle of violence caused by each man's bid for the emperor's goodwill, along with the emperor's increased fear of losing his power, never ceased. Similarly, Nero's reign started well. He increased the senate's power and reversed unpopular and tyrannical trends from Claudius's reign. But once again, the "greater attraction of forbidden pleasures" and increasing fear for his own position of power led Nero into the most bloody and corrupt reign Tacitus has yet described.

Since Tacitus's explanation for the collapse of virtue lies in a change in Rome's political structure, it is not surprising that his solution to the problem lies in the same direction. Tacitus looks back on the Republic as a golden era, not only in terms of prosperity or peace, but also in terms of virtue and good character. The Republic and the virtue that accompanied it become Tacitus's standard for judging right and wrong. In other words, much of Tacitus's condemnation agrees with Paul's indictment of sin in Scripture. But rather than God's standard of truth, beauty, and goodness, Tacitus makes his judgment based on the character of the old Romans during the time of the Republic.

This shift in standard eventually leads Tacitus astray.

Nero's persecutions did not take place in the Colosseum because it had not yet been built. This famous building is nevertheless connected to the history of Tacitus because of its name and its location. After the fire of Rome in A.D. 64 Nero seized for himself a large plot of land that had been devastated in the fire and built a grandiose villa with gardens, a lake and numerous outbuildings on the site. At the entrance to the elaborate villa an immense bronze colossus (statue) of Nero was erected. It was at this location that Vespasian began the construction of the *Amphitheatrum Flavium*, which came to be called the Colosseum after the bronze colossus that still stood there.

For instance, it is largely because Tacitus's judgment is based on a political system that he refers to Christianity as a "dangerous superstition." The Christian religion undermines Roman citizens' sense of primary responsibility to the state. A religion that changed a citizen's allegiance from Rome to a Jewish criminal could not help but further destabilize society.

But more fundamentally, Tacitus's hope in a system of government is bound for failure. Humanity's moral dilemma cannot be fixed by a system of government, because any such system will be created by and run by sinners. The cycle of violence, oppression, and suffering will continue so long as men are left in their sin. Only a divine act of redemption that changes the very core of humanity can solve the problem Tacitus sees destroying his own culture.

So while Tacitus is able to recognize moral depravity, he knows nothing of the biblical doctrine of sin that explains the problem. As Christians, we know that the root cause of evil and suffering has nothing to do with a political system. Rather, evil and suffering result from disobedience to God, starting in the Garden of Eden and continuing throughout history in every human being. Further, this rejection of God not only brought sin into the world, but it also trapped all mankind in slavery under sin and death. This slavery is such that men are incapable of pleasing God (Rom. 8:7). Their lives are naturally defined by pride of life, lust of the flesh, and lust of the eyes (1 John 2:16). For this reason, Christians should not be surprised at an empire mired in political corruption. We know that since all mankind fell in Adam, sin has motivated every thought and desire, leaving no option but moral depravity.

But into this picture comes the good news that Tacitus wasn't aware of—the only viable solution to the problem of sin. The same God whom humanity rejected has provided a solution to the problem of sin. He has come down into our enslaved world and has lived among our corrupted political systems, in fact in the very empire Tacitus was writing about. In the person of Jesus Christ, God died and rose again, conquering the enslaving power of sin and providing a way of escape from the cycle of violence and corruption. Through faith in His Son, Jesus Christ, the core of humanity can be changed, and the problem Tacitus felt all around him can be solved. This is the glorious news of the gospel!

Stoicism

Tacitus belonged to a school of philosophy known as Stoicism. Stoicism began in Greece about three hundred years before Christ, and the philosophy encouraged its adherents to transcend their fickle emotions that resulted from the changing circumstances of life. The Stoics believed that there was a divine providence, a sort of impersonal guiding force, that got the world started and now keeps things running in an orderly fashion. However, under the guidance of this providence, an individual and the circumstances of his life are of little importance compared to the overall order of the universe. Thus, the sooner one realized that the details of his own life were not important to the overall good of the universe, and the sooner he freed himself from the emotional responses that came along with these details, the happier he would be.

Now, Stoicism was not the philosophical embodiment of the soldier keeping a straight face and saying, "Yes, sir, may I have another?" while his drill sergeant ran him until the pain was too great to continue. Stoics were not supposed to grimace, bear life, and be happy. Rather, they believed that their knowledge about how the universe worked and their ability to free themselves from emotion would enable them to be truly happy.

In the first centuries B.C. and A.D., a number of prominent Romans adopted this philosophy, but they added to it the more practical element of virtue. Roman Stoics, of which Tacitus was one, agreed about the impersonal divine force guiding the universe, and they agreed that one should rise above the changing circumstances of life. But for the Roman Stoics, the means for accomplishing this goal was not limited to knowledge and emotional detachment, but also included living a virtuous life. The virtuous man could be happy regardless of what circumstances he met as he went through life because virtue was not dependent on chance. It depended only an individual's choice. If an individual consistently made the choice to be virtuous, his happiness would be freed from the fickle events of life.

Seneca was one of the most well-known Roman Stoics. Tacitus goes into great detail describing the sentence and death of Seneca in the *Annals*. Here we get a picture of Stoicism in real life. Seneca, who has spent his life tutoring and counseling Nero, is commanded to commit suicide by his emperor-student. In the face of such a decree, Seneca calmly hugs his wife, discourses briefly on virtue and happiness in the face of trials, and slits his wrists.

The result of this philosophy was a group of men and women whose standards of right and wrong, as well as their belief that the world was governed by sovereign providence, were in many ways similar to the standards and beliefs of Christianity. Both emphasized the need to live a moral life, many of the actions each considered moral were the same, and both trusted that everything was in control thanks to a sovereign divinity. Of course, these similarities also masked some important differences.

I am a perpetual competitor, and I remember challenging a friend to a race—through our college cafeteria, which was full of tables, chairs, and students carrying trays of food. I took a straight path through the obstacles, while my friend took a route longer, but less congested. My decision to take the obstacles straight on was a mistake. I came up short in the race thanks to chairs that frequently tripped me up while my friend made a clean run through the course. Perhaps our race provides a picture for comparing Christianity and Stoicism. Both come to some similar (though *not* the same) conclusions, but get there in very different ways, and the path of Stoicism lacks the truth of the gospel, meaning it will come up short in the final analysis.

The central division between Christianity and Stoicism is that the "god" of Stoicism, the impersonal providence that got the world started and keeps it in line, is very different from the God of Scripture. God did indeed create the world, and He has sovereignly guided all that has happened since Creation. But our God is no impersonal force. He is a personal God who has entered into a covenant with a particular people and come down into His creation to save that people after they broke His covenant. He is a God who has spoken to us, loved us, and given Himself for us in the person of Jesus Christ. He is no mere force; He is a personal, Triune being who calls us to live in communion with Him forever.

This fundamental difference also reveals the distinction between the two systems of ethics. Stoic ethics is based on the premise that virtue is the one aspect of our lives that changing circumstances cannot take away since each individual always has a choice to be virtuous. Thus, we can be happy, even in the face of evil and suffering, because our happiness is based upon our virtue, which is untouched by chance. Christian ethics is based on the more fundamental premise that since God

SENECA THE YOUNGER

Lucius Annaeus Seneca (Seneca the Younger) wrote numerous works, ranging from philosophical essays to tragic plays to dialogues. It is thought that his tragedies influenced later playwrights, including Shakespeare fourteen centuries later.

A tutor to young Nero and then one of his advisors after he became emperor, Seneca was a proponent of stoic philosophy. Considering the self-disciplined behavior promoted by the Stoics, the licentious lifestyle of Seneca's charge gives rise to the idea that he may not have been a very effective teacher. Nero's final act against his teacher was to order his execution after his name was implicated in a conspiracy. Tacitus relates that after Seneca was commanded to commit suicide, he responded, "Surely nobody was unaware that Nero was cruel! After murdering his mother and brother, it only remained for him to kill his teacher and tutor."

When the bleeding from slitting his veins proved ineffective, Seneca drank poison, just like Socrates with the hemlock. But unlike Socrates, the poison seemed to be ineffective, and he died finally after suffocating in the vapors of a hot bath.

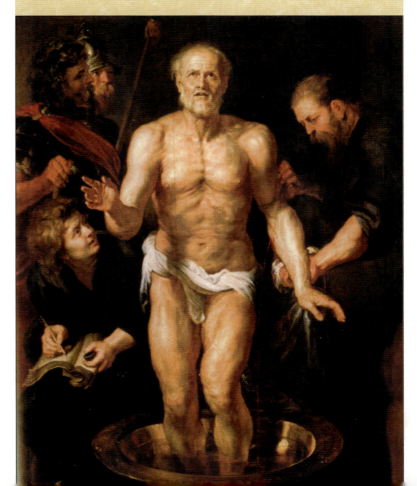

has created us in His image, joy will be the natural result of a life lived in conformity to His perfect will. The God who created us also revealed a set of standards consistent with His own goodness. Our joy reaches its greatest heights when we do the will of Him who created us; that is, when we live the way our Creator intended us to when He made us.

In the end, Stoic happiness is based upon the decision to find joy in one's own virtue. If a decision wavers, so does happiness. Christian happiness, on the other hand, is according to our nature as God created it. Our joy as Christians springs from fulfilling the purpose for which God created us and saved us. As Jesus said to His disciples, by keeping His Father's commandments and abiding in His love, "my joy [will] remain in you, and your joy [will] be full" (John 15:11).

In the *Annals*, Tacitus's main goal is to demonstrate what is right and wrong. He places the lives of virtuous men such as Seneca next to emperors, such as Nero, whose lives are living chronicles of the consequences of evil choices. But no amount of moral examples can save humanity from the problem of a sinful heart. Little did Tacitus dream that the criminal executed during Tiberius's reign by Pontius Pilate, the originator of the "notoriously depraved Christians," had the only viable solution for men who were wicked to their core. This "Christus," after all, was the Creator and Savior of the world, in whom alone we find forgiveness of sins, the will to act virtuously, and fullness of joy forevermore.

—Christopher Walker

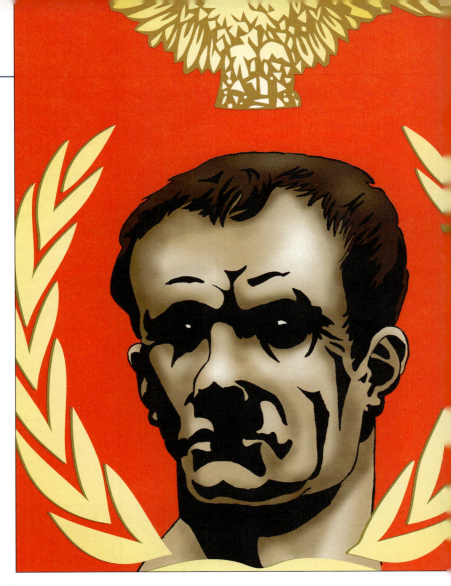

Sejanus was the evil henchman of Emperor Tiberius. Tacitus considers Sejanus, the commander of the Praetorian Guard, to have been a corrupting influence on Tiberius and a major cause of the decline of his reign.

For Further Reading

Spielvogel, Jackson J. *Western Civilization*. Seventh Edition. Belmont, Calif.: Thomson Wadsworth, 2009. 147–162.

Veritas Press History Cards: New Testament, Greece and Rome. Lancaster, Pa.: Veritas Press. 21, 25, 26.

Session I: Prelude

A Question to Consider

To what extent should a person be allowed to disagree with his government or rulers? When does criticism become treason?

From the General Information above, answer the following questions:

1. What obstacles stand in the way of learning about Tacitus's life?
2. How does Tacitus's description of the moral degradation in Roman politics differ from that of Suetonius and other Roman historians?
3. How does Tacitus's account of the persecution of Christians in Rome support the historicity of the Bible?

4. Who are the main characters in Tacitus's *Annals*?
5. What is Tacitus's main purpose for writing history?
6. Tacitus and other ancient authors were very good at identifying problems in society but are repeatedly short on solutions for those problems. Why?

READING ASSIGNMENT:
Annals of Imperial Rome, I.1–15 and IV.1–25

SESSION II: DISCUSSION
Annals of Imperial Rome, I.1–15 and IV.1–25

A Question to Consider

Should we seek friends with bad character in order to try to influence them for good?

Discuss or list short answers to the following questions:

Text Analysis
1. To what does Tacitus attribute the turn of Tiberius's reign from prosperous and stable to tyrannical and corrupt?
2. What was Tiberius willing to do with Sejanus that he seemed unwilling to do with anyone else?
3. How does Tacitus describe Sejanus's character?
4. Did Sejanus have Tiberius's best interest at heart?

Cultural Analysis
1. What does our culture think of evaluating another person based on character?
2. What sorts of people does our culture encourage us to spend time with?

Biblical Analysis
1. What does Proverbs 13:20 say about the impact our closest associates have over us? See also 1 Corinthians 15:33.
2. What does the Bible say about the purpose of friendship, particularly in the context of the church? Consider Hebrews 10:24–25, 1 Thessalonians 5:11, Proverbs 17:17, and John 15:13–15.

SUMMA

Write an essay or discuss this question, integrating what you have learned from the material above.
How should we balance a desire to influence ungodly people while not being corrupted ourselves?

READING ASSIGNMENT:
Annals of Imperial Rome, IV.26–V.5

SESSION III: ACTIVITY
Annals of Imperial Rome, IV.26–V.5

Sejanus's Informers

As a class or with your family, play the game Sejanus's Informers. The rules for the game are as follows:

Setup

The narrator (the teacher) should prepare the right number of playing cards to set up the game. Select two aces (the Informers), two kings (the Plebian Police), and several number cards (so that the total number of cards equals the number of players in the game). Therefore, if there are 12 people playing, there will be two aces, two kings, and eight number cards. The narrator shuffles these cards, and each player randomly selects a card without revealing his or her identity to the others. The person assumes the role for the round.

Roles

Aces are **Informers**. Their goal is to keep secret that they are Informers and blend in with the Townspeople. For them to win the game, they want to eliminate the Townspeople one by one each round but not to get eliminated themselves.

Kings are members of the **Plebian Police**. The Police try to figure out who is guilty of being an Informer and who is innocent. Thus, their goal is to help the Townspeople vote correctly in who to eliminate. They generally want to keep their identity secret so that the Informers cannot eliminate them, but they are not required to do so.

All other cards (number cards) are **Townspeople**. Their goal is to figure out who the Informers are and to eliminate them from the town.

How to Play

The players should sit in a circle. Each "day" of the game, the narrator takes the entire town through the following commands in this order:

1. Nighttime

    "It is nighttime, so everyone please go to sleep." (Everyone puts their head down and closes their eyes.)

    "Informers, please wake up." (Only the Informers open their eyes. They quietly and unanimously choose a person to eliminate by pointing to someone in the group. The narrator takes note of the person chosen.)

    "Informers, please go to sleep." (The Informers close their eyes and put their heads down again.)

"Plebian Police, please wake up." (The Police open their eyes and quietly point to one person who they suspect is an Informer. The narrator quietly nods or shakes his or her head to indicate whether that person is indeed an Informer).

"Police, please go to sleep." (The Police close their eyes and place their heads down.)

"It's morning. Everyone please wake up."

2. Daytime Update

The narrator announces the person who was eliminated. The person who was eliminated must leave the circle. This person may not speak to anyone for the remainder of the entire game, but he may now keep his eyes open to watch everything.

3. Daytime Discussion/Voting

The Townspeople (along with the Informers and Plebian Police who may pretend to be Townspeople) then nominate and vote on people who they suspect are Informers. Each person nominated should make a defense and plead his case. The person receiving the most votes after all accusations and defenses are heard is eliminated. After someone is eliminated, the day is over. The day may also end without any eliminations if the entire group decides to do so. The day ends, and the pattern starts again (Nighttime, Daytime Update, Daytime Discussion/Voting).

How to Win

The Plebian Police or Townspeople win if they successfully eliminate all Sejanus's Informers. Sejanus's Informers win if they successfully eliminate all the townspeople.

After the game is finished discuss the following questions based on your reading in Tacitus and your experience in the game. Also reference the following quotation from Tacitus: "Some, however, reappeared and showed themselves again—alarmed because they had displayed alarm. For it seemed that no day would be free of convictions when, at a season in which custom forbade even an ominous word, sacrifices and prayers were attended by manacles and nooses" (IV.70).

1. Based on your experience in the game, what does Tacitus mean by "alarmed because they displayed alarm"? Did you try to defend your innocence with one tactic, only to have another player accuse you as guilty based on your very tactic of innocence?
2. What sorts of ominous words helped convict players in the game? What sorts of ominous words do you think served as a fast track to exile or execution under Tiberius?
3. What would it be like to live in an environment in which every word you spoke to anyone, including friends and family, could lead to your accusation and conviction?

The next session will be a student-led discussion. Students will be creating their own questions concerning the issue of the session. Students should create three Text Analysis Questions, two Cultural Analysis questions, and two Biblical Analysis questions. For more detailed instructions, please see the chapter on the *Iliad*, Session III.

Issue

Are suicide or physician-assisted deaths ever appropriate?

Reading Assignment:
Annals of Imperial Rome, V.6–VI.51

Session IV: Student-Led Discussion
Annals of Imperial Rome, V.6–VI.51

A Question to Consider

Are suicide or physician assisted deaths ever appropriate?

Students should read and consider the example questions below that are connected to the Question to Consider above. Last session's assignment was to prepare three questions and answers for the Text Analysis section and two additional questions and answers for both the Cultural and Biblical Analysis sections below.

Text Analysis

Example: What decision did Marcus Cocceius Nerva make, against the wishes of the emperor?

Answer: Nerva decided to commit suicide through starvation. All of the emperor's pleadings were insufficient to deter Nerva from his resolve. His friends asserted that Nerva was both indignant and afraid of the corruption and misfortune spreading throughout Rome, so that death seemed the only honorable way to die.

Cultural Analysis

Example: Does our culture offer any moral reasons against committing suicide?

Answer: Our culture's primary standard of morality seems to be whether or not everyone involved is willing. As long as all parties are willing, all bets are off. Working within this standard, there is no reason we should not commit suicide if life ceases to offer positive reasons for living. The victim is the only one involved, and if he is willing, there is no moral argument against it (there may be pragmatic arguments against the suicide, but nothing moral).

Other cultural issues to consider: The lack of any eternal punishment after death, the view that life is a waste if you can't enjoy it now, and the willingness to end any life that doesn't seem to be enjoyable or fulfilling.

Biblical Analysis

Example: Why would suicide be considered a breach of God's law based on Genesis 9:5-6?

Answer: This passage discusses the consequences of shedding blood. The central distinction here is the shedding of an animal's blood as opposed to shedding human blood. God shall require judgment of anyone who sheds human blood because man is made in the image of God. Notice that the litmus test for guilt is not whether the person is willing, or who the victim is, but rather the fact that a man kills a person made in God's image. Just as vandalizing a statue is an affront to the one represented, so killing a man, even if that man is himself, is an affront to God, in whose image we were created.

Other Scriptures to consider: Jonah 4:3-11, Matthew 27:3-10, and Exodus 21:12-14 (focus on the issue of premeditation).

SUMMA

Write an essay or discuss this question, integrating what you have learned from the material above.
Why should a man not consider suicide if his life is full of pain, grief, and suffering

READING ASSIGNMENT:
Annals of Imperial Rome, XIII.1-XIII.33

ROMAN EMPERORS	
27 BC–AD 14	Augustus
14–37	Tiberius
37–41	Caligula
41–54	Claudius
54–68	Nero
68–69	Galba
69	Otho
69	Vitellius
69–79	Vespasian
79–81	Titus
81–96	Domitian
96–98	Nerva
98–117	Trajan
117–138	Hadrian
138–161	Antoninus Pius
161–180	Marcus Aurelius
161–169	Lucius Verus
177–192	Commodus

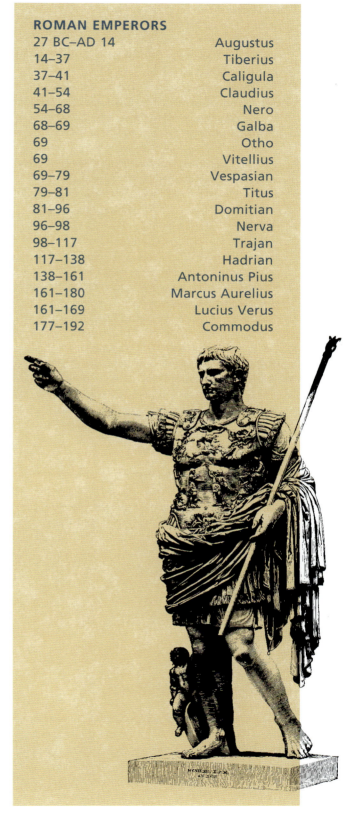

SESSION V: RECITATION
Annals of Imperial Rome, I.1-15, IV.1-VI.51

Comprehension Questions

Answer the following questions for factual recall:
1. How did Octavian gain the goodwill of the people while consolidating various political powers in himself?

2. What was the first crime of Tiberius's reign as emperor, and how did he attempt to explain it?
3. What and who does Tacitus credit with turning Tiberius's reign from one of stability and prosperity to one of crime and corruption?
4. Why did Sejanus grow bolder in his criminal acts?
5. What intensified the Thracians' troubles and ensured a Roman victory over the Thracian tribes?
6. What caused the Frisian tribes to rebel against Rome?
7. Why did Tiberius's reign, already full of corruption and crime, turn to one of absolute and crushing tyranny?
8. To what does Tacitus compare the acts of evil debauchery performed by Tiberius around Rome?
9. What two unheard-of features marked this "reign of terror"?
10. Women could not be accused of aiming at supreme power, but of what could they be accused?
11. How did Tiberius gain some goodwill from the people after the fire in Rome?
12. What was the death of Tiberius like?

The next session will be a student-led discussion. Students will be creating their own questions concerning the issue of the session. Students should create three Text Analysis Questions, two Cultural Analysis questions, and two Biblical Analysis questions. For more detailed instructions, please see the chapter on the *Iliad*, Session III.

Issue

How should we respond to fear?

Reading Assignment:
Annals of Imperial Rome, XIII.34–XIV.13

Session VI: Student-Led Discussion
Annals of Imperial Rome, XIII.34–XIV.13

A Question to Consider

How should we respond to fear?

Students should read and consider the example questions below that are connected to the Question to Consider above. Last session's assignment was to prepare three questions and answers for the Text Analysis section and two additional questions and answers for both the Cultural and Biblical Analysis sections below.

Text Analysis

Example: When the collapsing-boat trick failed, what caused Nero to openly order Agrippina's assassination?

Answer: Nero was driven by fear for his power. He had been told that Agrippina desired power, and now he was afraid she might come with armed slaves or go to the senate and accuse him, either of which could have jeopardizes his position as emperor.

Cultural Analysis

Example: What do people in our culture fear, and how does it drive them to bad decisions?

Answer: People usually fear losing things that are important to them. Therefore, it is no surprise that our culture is often driven by a fear of not having enough money to lead a comfortable life, of not feeling secure with the positions they hold, or of being made fun of in a way that undermines their social status. These fears drive many in our culture to unethical decisions that they might not make were it not for their fears.

Other cultural issues to consider: how fear motivates decisions in various contexts, including politics, business, and a classroom; peer pressure as an example of fear driving decisions; the lack of moral standards as a reason why a person's fears hold such a great sway over individual decisions; and how fear motivates decisions.

Biblical Analysis

Example: What sort of fear leads to wisdom rather than sin according to Proverbs 1:7? Why?

Answer: The fear of the Lord leads to wisdom. Instead of being driven to compromise our standards in the face of fear, the fear of the Lord reinforces our moral standards. God is both just and almighty. We ought to fear the consequences of displeasing our heavenly Father. But this fear drives us back to God and His will, rather than away from it.

Other Scriptures to consider: Matthew 10:28, Exodus 18:21 and 20:18–21, and Job 28:28.

Summa

Write an essay or discuss this question, integrating what you have learned from the material above.
How should a person overcome his fears?

Instead of a reading assignment you have a research assignment. Tomorrow's session will be a Current Events session. Your assignment will be to find a story online, in a magazine, or in the newspaper that relates to the issue that you discussed today. Your task is to locate the article, give a copy of the article to your teacher or parent and provide some of your own worldview analysis to the article. Your analysis should demonstrate that you understand the issue, that you can clearly connect the story you found to the issue that you discussed today, and that you can provide a biblical critique of this issue in today's context. Look at the next session to see the three-part format that you should follow.

Find a story in a current magazine, in a newspaper, or online relating to the issue stated in the next session. Prepare an analysis of your article to share with the class.

Issue

Selfishness (or, one could say, making decisions based on achieving personal security or success rather than following moral principle)

 READING ASSIGNMENT:
None

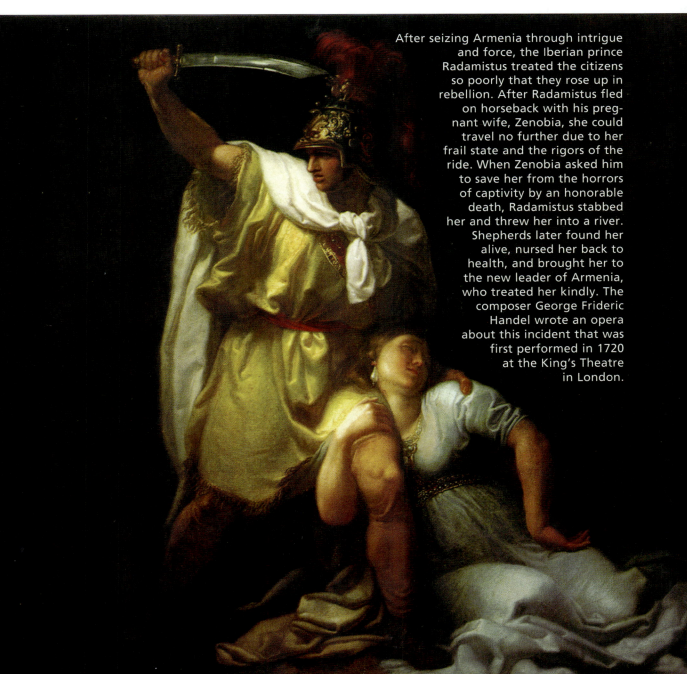

After seizing Armenia through intrigue and force, the Iberian prince Radamistus treated the citizens so poorly that they rose up in rebellion. After Radamistus fled on horseback with his pregnant wife, Zenobia, she could travel no further due to her frail state and the rigors of the ride. When Zenobia asked him to save her from the horrors of captivity by an honorable death, Radamistus stabbed her and threw her into a river. Shepherds later found her alive, nursed her back to health, and brought her to the new leader of Armenia, who treated her kindly. The composer George Frideric Handel wrote an opera about this incident that was first performed in 1720 at the King's Theatre in London.

Session VII: Current Events

Annals of Imperial Rome, I.1–15, XIII.34–XIV.13

Issue

Selfishness (or, one could say, making decisions based on achieving personal security or success rather than following moral principle)

Current events sessions are meant to challenge you to connect what you are learning in Omnibus class to what is happening in the world around you today. After the last session, your assignment was to find a story online or in a magazine or newspaper relating to the issue above. Today you will share your article and your analysis with your teacher and classmates or parents and family. Your analysis should follow the format below:

Brief Introductory Paragraph

In this paragraph you will tell your classmates about the article that you found. Be sure to include where you found your article, who the author of your article is, and what your article is about. This brief paragraph of your presentation should begin like this:

> Hello, I am (name), and my current events article is (name of the article) which I found in (name of the web or published source)...

Connection Paragraph

In this paragraph you must demonstrate how your article is connected to the issue that you are studying. This paragraph should be short, and it should focus on clearly showing the connection between the book that you are reading and the current events article that you have found. This paragraph should begin with a sentence like

> I knew that my article was linked to our issue because...

Christian Worldview Analysis

In this section, you need to tell us how we should respond as believers to this issue today. This response should focus both on our thinking and on practical actions that we should take in light of this issue. As you list these steps, you should also tell us why

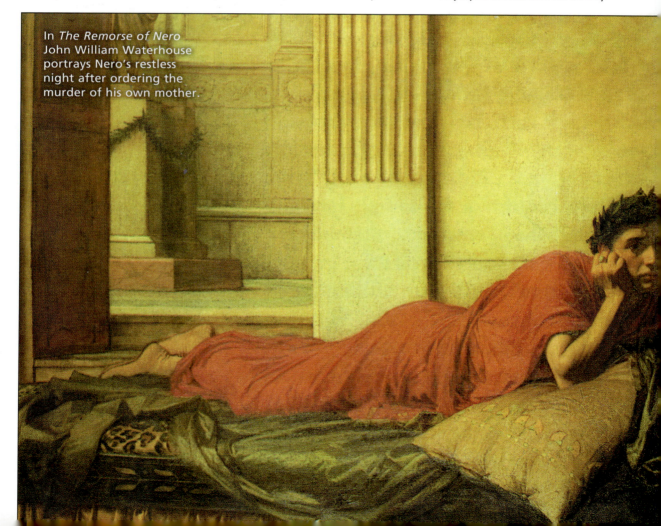

In *The Remorse of Nero* John William Waterhouse portrays Nero's restless night after ordering the murder of his own mother.

we should think and act in the ways you recommend. This paragraph should begin with a sentence like

> As believers, we should think and act in the following ways in light of this issue and this article.

Reading Assignment:
Annals of Imperial Rome, XIV.14–65

Session VIII: Aesthetics
Annals of Imperial Rome, XIV.14–65

Art Analysis

In this session, you will get to know a particular piece or type of art related to our reading. It is our job as believers to be able to praise, love, and protect what is beautiful and to condemn, hate and oppose all that is truly ugly. This task is often harder than you think. We have to discipline ourselves to examine and understand the piece reflectively.

After we understand the content of a piece, we can examine the artist's intention concerning it and attempt to figure out what it is communicating. Sometimes this will be easy; other times it will be difficult or impossible. Finally, we need to make judgments about what this work communicates. Sometimes we will be able to clearly condemn a work of art as untrue, badly done, or wicked. Sometimes we will be able to praise a work as glorious, majestic, and true. Oftentimes, however, we will find ourselves affirming some parts of a work and condemning others. Remember, maturity is harder than immaturity—but also more rewarding. Also, remember that our praise or condemnation means more when we have disciplined ourselves to first reflect on the content and meaning of a work.

The Remorse of Nero

The Remorse of Nero was completed in 1878 by the British painter John William Waterhouse. It seeks to capture the emotion that overcame Nero after he ordered the assassination of his mother, Agrippina. Tacitus describes Nero's emotional state after the murder in the following terms: "For the rest of the night, witless and speechless, he alternately lay paralyzed and leapt to his feet in terror—waiting for the dawn which he thought would be his last" (XIV.10). Waterhouse communicates his understanding of Nero's emotional state in this painting. Waterhouse also seeks to capture the tensions between luxury and cruelty and wealth and corruption that characterized Nero's reign.

John William Waterhouse was a British artist who painted during the late nineteenth century. He witnessed the decline of British imperialism. Many of his contemporaries sought to emphasize the glory of the British Empire by comparing it to the Roman Empire. Waterhouse, however, was interested in reminding his culture that an empire is not all about glory but also includes a temptation towards corruption and cruelty.

Technical Analysis

1. Does this work demonstrate the artist's ability and expertise?
2. Describe the scene Waterhouse paints for us.
3. Is this work realistic and proportional or not?
4. Make a list of the details in the picture.
5. Are these details significant to the central appeal of the painting, or are they strictly in the background?
6. How is light used in this work?
7. What colors are used in this work?

Subject Analysis

1. What might be the significance of Waterhouse choosing the color red for Nero's toga?
2. Why would Waterhouse emphasize the luxury of Nero's bedroom in this scene?
3. How does the contrast between light and shadow on Nero's face illustrate his emotional state?
4. Why might Waterhouse have included the laurel wreath—a prize for poetic or musical performance—on Nero's head?

Content Analysis

1. What is the message of this work?
2. What is worthy of praise in this piece of art? What is worthy of condemnation?

READING ASSIGNMENT:
Annals of Imperial Rome, XV.1–47

Session IX: Recitation
Annals of Imperial Rome, XIII.1–XV.47

Comprehension Questions

Answer the following questions for factual recall:

1. What did Nero say that made the audience laugh at Claudius's funeral?
2. When Nero exempted Lucius Antistius Vetus from swearing allegiance to him, why did the senate praise him so highly?
3. What did Nero do that inspired increasing violence by gangs roaming the streets of Rome?
4. What role does Poppaea play in Nero's matricide?
5. Describe Nero's plot to murder his mother secretly. Is it successful?
6. Whom did Nero appoint to replace his counselor Burrus and why?
7. What did Nero do to his wife, Octavia?
8. What rivalry developed on the Eastern frontier?
9. What did Nero do in an attempt to inspire confidence in the citizens of Rome with regard to the food supply?
10. Why did Nero's efforts to help those hurt by the fire fail to earn him the people's goodwill?
11. Why did the people pity Christian martyrs despite their general dislike of Christianity?

READING ASSIGNMENT:
Annals of Imperial Rome, XV.48–XVI.35

Session X: Writing
Annals of Imperial Rome, XV.48–XVI.35

Educating Nero

This session is a writing assignment. Remember, quality counts more than quantity. You should write no more than 1,000 words, either typing or writing legibly on one side of a sheet of paper. You will lose points for writing more than this. You will be allowed to turn in your writing three times. The first and second times you turn it in, your teacher will grade it by editing your work. This is done by marking problem areas and making suggestions for improvement. You should take these suggestions into consideration as you revise your assignment. Only the grade on your final submission will be recorded. Your grade will be based on the following criteria: 25 points for grammar, 25 points for content accuracy—historical, theological, etc.; 25 points for logic—does this make sense and is it structured well?; 25 points for rhetoric—is it a joy to read?

Fictional Story

Your assignment is to write an imaginative story based on the following historical setting. Your goal is to create a story that is factually and grammatically accurate, that makes sense and that people will enjoy reading.

Historical Setting

Imagine you are a servant of Nero with the privilege of attending him during a tutoring session from Seneca. Show the flaws in Nero's character as Seneca seeks to counsel the young royal.

Optional Session A: Worldview Analysis

Tacitus vs. Nero

Compare and contrast the worldviews of Tacitus (a pagan interested in virtue) and Nero (a licentious pagan) with Christianity by completing Chart 1. For our purposes here, we are exploring four categories: God, man, sin, and commitments. There could be other areas in which to compare their views.

Chart 1: **WORLDVIEWS OF TACITUS AND NERO**

	GOD	MAN	SIN	COMMITMENTS
Tacitus		Although birth and destiny play a role in a man's life, he is ultimately defined by his choices. Man is a rational being who will either choose to live honorably according to the "Old Roman character" or he will engage in flattery, corruption, and debauchery to stay alive and to succeed by any means possible.		
Nero			It is hard to imagine any standard of virtue or morality that Nero fails to violate in his personal life. However, the central sin he opposes is disloyalty to the emperor. Any threat to his rule is dealt with harshly.	
Christianity	Specifically in response to the Annals, God is personal as well as sovereign. He is a guiding force, but also lovingly interacts with His creation to save His people from the suffering of sin and give them eternal hope.			

OPTIONAL SESSION B: REVIEW

Comprehension Questions

Discuss or list short answers to the following questions:

1. In what way did Tiberius suffer from the same harsh injustice at his death that he practiced on others in his life?

2. How did Tacitus summarize the progression of Tiberius's life from one above reproach to one of complete perversion?

3. What was it that angered Agrippina most during Nero's affairs with Acte and Poppaea?

4. How was Piso's conspiracy finally discovered?

5. How did Seneca's death demonstrate the integrity of his life as a philosopher?

6. What lie did Nero believe that led him to waste money and to look like a fool?

ENDNOTES

1   See the Introduction in *Complete Works of Tacitus*, Moses Hadas, ed., p. XIV.

Eclogues and Georgics

Have you ever seen that classic 1960s television show *Green Acres*? Here's the gist: A successful New York City banker named Oliver Wendell Douglas longs, literally, for greener pastures. Weary of the hustle and bustle of big-city life and frustrated with the Big Apple, Mr. Douglas sings in the opening theme song:

> *Green acres is the place to be*
> *Farm living is the life for me*
> *Land spreading out,*
> *So far and wide*
> *Keep Manhattan,*
> *Just give me that countryside.*

Mr. Douglas follows his dream, buys a dilapidated farm, packs up his socialite wife and moves to Hooterville, U.S.A., where he and Mrs. Douglas have six television seasons' worth of zany adventures with their farmhand Eb and a pig named Arnold Ziffel, who seems to understand English as well as the rest of the Hootervillians.

Mr. Douglas's frustration with urban life and his longing for the countryside are as old as antiquity. Although most viewers watch the ridiculous antics on the Douglas farm with mild amusement, *Green Acres* actually illustrates a profound truth: Wherever there is a city, be it present-day New York City or ancient Rome, there are people who long to escape it, return to a simpler life, and enjoy a breath of fresh air. This seemingly universal desire to escape to the countryside is at the heart of Virgil's pastoral poetry.

In this mosaic from the third century, Virgil is accompanied by the muses of history and of tragedy.

General Information

Author and Context

Publius Vergilius Maro (known today as Virgil or Vergil) lived from October 15, 70 B.C. to September 21, 19 B.C. Virgil spent his boyhood growing up on a farm near Mantua, Italy, where, according to Macrobius, he was "brought up amongst the woods and shrubs" (*Saturnalia*, Book V). Virgil moved to Rome as an adult, where he became quite popular for his collections of poems called the *Eclogues* (originally called the *Bucolica,* or *Cowherd Songs*, published around 39 B.C.) and the *Georgics* (published around 29 B.C.). These pastoral poems, called such because the Latin word *pastor* means "shepherd," celebrate the rustic life of the countryside, a fashionable subject among urbanite Romans feeling the pinch of city life and wishing to get back to nature.

The successful poet had friends in high places—even Emperor Caesar Augustus himself. Virgil lived during a time of great transition in Rome, and with the assassination of Julius Caesar in 44 B.C. (*Beware the Ides of March!*), he watched the Roman Republic as it was transformed into the Roman Empire.

Virgil is best known for his epic poem the *Aeneid*, which traces the founding of Rome from the ashes of Troy to the shores of Italy, illustrating the inevitable greatness of Rome and her destiny to become a powerful empire. Virgil died before he was able to finish the *Aeneid*, and according to tradition, he left orders to have the manuscript destroyed upon his death. Ignoring his friend's dying wish, Augustus preserved the poem and published it, providing the people of Rome with an epic on par with that of Homer. Virgil's self-composed epitaph summarizes well his literary accomplishments: "*Cecini pascua rura duces:* I sang of pastures, fields and kings."

Significance

Virgil was the first Roman poet to write pastoral poetry in Latin. Before him, pastoral poetry was a genre belonging to Greek poets such as Theocritus and Hesiod. It was common for Romans to borrow elements of Greek culture, whether religious, political, philosophical or artistic, which they then developed into uniquely Roman concepts. The same is true of Virgil's treatment of pastoral poetry. As tribute to the Greek pastoral tradition, he uses Greek names for the characters in his poems, such as Meliboeus and Menalcas, and makes references to Greek mythology and religion. And yet, his political references and descriptions of the countryside—from the names of rivers to flowers and plants—are local to Italy and distinctly Roman.

The influence of Virgil's pastoral poetry spans centuries. Read the Duke's speech in Shakespeare's *As You Like It* or the King's soliloquy in *Henry the Sixth*. Spenser's *The Shepheardes Calendar*, Marlowe's *Passionate Shepherd*, Milton's *Lycidas*, Keats' *Ode to a Nightingale*, and Frost's *Build Soil* prove translator David Ferry's point: "The *Eclogues* are everywhere."[1] Why would a few Latin poems about shepherds hold such sway? Man cannot escape that timeless tendency: Wherever there is a city, there are people who want to leave it, to find "the other side" where the grass really *is* greener, to return, once and for all, to the Garden, to the natural and spiritual perfection man lost in Eden.

Main Characters

The big stars in Virgil's pastoral poems are humble shepherds. This is a dramatic shift from the epic heroes

Eclogues and Georgics 341

in Virgil's *Aeneid* who are princes, warriors, and noble founding fathers driven by destiny and descended from the gods. Yet, these shepherds are not without dignity. Indeed, they enjoy what the Roman nobility can only dream of. Consider Tityrus in Eclogue I, who rests "'neath a broad beech-canopy / Reclining on the slender oat . . . careless in the shade . . . play[ing] on the shepherd's pipe what songs [he] will." What Roman, or even what Omnibus student, isn't envious of such a life?

Consider Menalcas and Damoetas, who, in Eclogue III, challenge each other to a singing contest while they tend their flocks when "Now is burgeoning both field and tree / Now is the forest green, and now the year / At fairest." Not a bad way to pass the time in spring.

The shepherds may live and work in an idyllic environment, but that doesn't mean they are always happy. Consider Damon in Eclogue VIII, who sang his "pastoral ditties" about true love scorned. Damon is driven to suicide because the fair Nysa, the girl he first met while "[p]lucking the dewy apples," the girl he had loved since he was twelve years old, the girl who loathed his "shepherd's pipe, [his] goats, [his] shaggy brow / And untrimmed beard," has married another—Mopsus, of all men! Being thwarted in love is just as romantic as being successful in love, at least when it is happening to someone else, and so Damon's sorrows, as far as the city-living reader is concerned, seem to add even more romance to the countryside.

Consider, too, the boy child, found in Eclogue IV, who is said to bring peace to the earth and usher in a new Golden Age. More will be said about this character later in this essay, but any discussion of the main characters in Virgil's *Eclogues* would be incomplete without mentioning this figure, which attracted the attention of Augustine and the early Christian church.

Chart 1: **A GUIDE TO VIRGIL'S *ECLOGUES***

Eclogue I	Meliboeus, having recently lost his land, runs into Tityrus, who comforts him with apples, cheese, and song.
Eclogue II	Corydon is hopelessly in love with the boy Alexis. He admits his madness and sings sometimes of his love and sometimes of his own unworthiness.
Eclogue III	Menalcas and Damoetas challenge each other to a singing contest while they tend their flocks. Palaemon determines it a tie.
Eclogue IV	In this Messianic Eclogue, Virgil announces the arrival of a Golden Age, when a boy will usher in a time of peace for man and beast.
Eclogue V	Mopsus and Menalcas take turns singing about Daphnis, who has died. They mourn him, and they bless him with offerings.
Eclogue VI	Two boys and a naiad come upon a drunken satyr, Silenus, who is sleeping in a cave. They tie him up with garlands and paint his face with mulberry juice for a joke. Silenus then sings stories for them about the origins of the earth, Prometheus the fire-stealer, and Scylla the deadly whirlpool.
Eclogue VII	Daphnis and Meliboeus take a break from their labor to hear a singing contest between Thyrsis and Corydon. Corydon wins the day.
Eclogue VIII	The heartbroken Damon sings of the faithless Nysa and threatens to fall from a cliff to his doom. In reply, Alphesiboeus sings the song of a woman who looks to spells and enchantment to secure the fidelity of the man she loves.
Eclogue IX	Moeris tells Lycidas while they walk into town together that his land has been taken from him. Lycidas attempts to comfort him with song as they pass a friend's tomb on the roadside.
Eclogue X	In the final poem in the collection, Gallus ends his song with the lament, "Love conquers all." His farewell to the woods and the Hamadryads is echoed by Virgil himself who ends his Eclogues: "Now homeward, having fed your fill / Eve's star is rising—go, my she-goats, go."

Summary and Setting

The *Eclogues* is a collection of ten poems about shepherds, encompassing three basic themes: the beauty of the Italian countryside, the pleasure of music, and the joys and sorrows of love.[2] Refer to Chart 1 as a summary guide.

The *Georgics* is less about individual characters and more about the nobility of agrarian pursuits. Book I deals with crops and the calendar, what to plant, and when to plant it. Book II is about the trees and man's transformation of nature. Book III discusses livestock and the effects of love on both man and beast. Book IV describes that ideal working community: the beehive. Do not think, though, that the *Georgics* is an ancient-day *Farmer's Almanac*. It is far too poetic to offer practical farming advice, but what it lacks in practicality it gains with beauty.

Worldview

Thinking back to Mr. Douglas's life on *Green Acres*, do you think he was ever truly happy, either as a New York banker or as a farmer in Hooterville? Do you think saying goodbye to city life actually satisfied the inner yearning in his heart? The problem with escapism, or the attempt to avoid the reality of the daily grind by running away from it, is that it never works. The distant views of nature look so appealing from the desk of a skyscraper's corner office, or from atop the seven hills of Rome, but the comforts offered are shallow and short-lived.

Eclogues

Even the best nap under the shade of "a broad beech-canopy" is nothing compared to resting under the shadow of God's wings (Ps. 17:8). Plowing the fields, even in the most idyllic setting, is aimless without Christ, who promises: "My yoke is easy and My burden is light" (Matt. 11:30). There is no peace in this world without the Prince of Peace (Isa. 9:6). In his own, limited way, Virgil recognizes the shortcomings of his own pastoral scenes. Virgil makes it clear that sorrow can exist even in the most beautiful places on earth.

Take, for example, the splendor of the countryside. The shepherds live, work, and sing of the Italian landscape, as in Eclogue IX:

Here glows the Spring, here earth
Beside the streams pours forth a thousand flowers;
Here the white poplar bends above the cave,
And the lithe vine weaves shadowy covert . . .

What beauty! What magnificence! And yet, the joy in the land quickly dissolves when in the same poem, the unfortunate Moeris confides to his friend that a stranger has taken ownership of his farmland and his flock:

O Lycidas,
We have lived to see, what never yet we feared,
An interloper own our little farm,
And say, "Be off, you former husbandmen!
These fields are mine." Now, cowed and out of heart,
Since Fortune turns the whole world upside down,
We are taking him—ill luck go with the same!—
These kids you see.

Consider, too, the shepherds' experiences with love, a central theme in many a pastoral song. In Eclogue VIII, Damon's constant but unrequited love for Nysa drives him to consider suicide: "I from the tall peak / Of yon aerial rock will headlong plunge / Into the billows. . . ." In Eclogue X, the love-sick Gallus, upon hearing that his love has abandoned him, accuses *Amor* of never having enough of tears:

Love wrecks not aught of it: his heart no more
With tears is sated than with streams the grass
Bees with the cytisus, or goats with leaves.

Fewer than ten lines from the end of the final poem, Virgil writes, "*Omnia vincit Amor*: Love conquers all." Far from today's romantic idea of love overcoming all obstacles so that happiness might prevail, this phrase leads the reader to understand that love leaves its victims conquered, defeated, and subdued.

So, is there any hope for these shepherds? Is there any hope for the world today? If man cannot escape a life of frustration and chaos by becoming a shepherd, retreating to the country or by falling in love, is there any message of comfort in Virgil's *Eclogues*?

Virgil shifts gears abruptly in the middle of his *Eclogues*. He silences the shepherds' singing and invokes the Muses for "a somewhat loftier task." This is Eclogue IV, that famous and mysterious *Messianic Eclogue*, in which Virgil announces the coming of a new Golden Age. A Virgin[3] returns and with her a baby boy under whose guidance:

Whatso tracks remain
Of our old wickedness, once done away,
Shall free the earth from never-ceasing fear.
He shall receive the life of gods, and see
Heroes with gods commingling, and himself
Be seen of them, and with his father's worth
Reign o'er a world at peace.

In this new Golden Age, the earth will bring forth fruits freely, without the toil of agriculture, and even the animals will be at peace with each other:

Untended, will the she-goats then bring home

Their udders swollen with milk, while flocks afield
Shall of the monstrous lion have no fear...
The serpent too shall die...

Thanks to this new Golden Age, Virgil is able to describe the truly idyllic landscape without the pains and sorrows we see in the other *Eclogues*. Sin still remains ("Yet shall there lurk within of ancient wrong / Some traces") and "New wars too shall arise," but when that boy reaches the maturity of manhood:

> The glebe no more
> Shall feel the harrow's grip, nor vine the hook;
> The sturdy ploughman shall loose yoke
> from steer...

Virgil then gives this fantastic description of multi-colored sheep's wool, which even the Fates find delightful for their spinning:

Nor wool with varying colors learn to lie;
But in the meadows shall the ram himself,
Now with soft flush of purple, now with tint
Of yellow saffron, teach his fleece to shine.
While clothed in natural scarlet graze the lambs.

Does any of this imagery sound familiar to you? Compare Eclogue IV with Isaiah 9:6–7:

> For unto us a Child is born,
> Unto us a Son is given;
> And the government will be upon His shoulder.
> And His name will be called
> Wonderful, Counselor, Mighty God,
> Everlasting Father, Prince of Peace.
> Of the increase of His government and peace
> There will be no end,
> Upon the throne of David and over His kingdom,

A fourth-century depiction of Christ as the Good Shepherd (Museum for Epigraphy, Terme di Diocleziano, Rome).

To order it and establish it with judgment and justice
From that time forward, even forever.
The zeal of the Lord of hosts will perform this.

A boy is born, one who is sent by the high god, who himself is called god because he takes after his father. This boy brings peace and increase to the world and establishes justice. See why this poem is known as the *Messianic Eclogue*? Now compare Eclogue IV with Isaiah 11:6–8:

The wolf also shall dwell with the lamb,
The leopard shall lie down with the young goat,
The calf and the young lion and the fatling together;
And a little child shall lead them.
The cow and the bear shall graze;
Their young ones shall lie down together;
And the lion shall eat straw like the ox.
The nursing child shall play by the cobra's hole,
    And the weaned child shall put
    his hand in the viper's den.

The boy has not merely brought political advancement, but see how he has also restored peace to nature. In language that is itself pastoral, Isaiah describes a time when flocks are safe from lions and wolves, when, because of the shepherd boy—the Good Shepherd Himself—even the serpent is no threat to babes at play.

Modernist scholars are quick to link Virgil's new Golden Age with the consulship of Pollio in 40 B.C., and they claim that Virgil's boy savior is the anticipated child of Mark Antony and Augustus's sister Octavia. If they are right, Virgil's hopeful prophecy doesn't amount to much. Pollio's consulship wasn't *that* great in reality, and the fighting triumvirs in 40 B.C. hardly brought peace to the government or to nature. Mark Antony's affair with the Egyptian queen, Cleopatra, kept him from raising a savior boy with Octavia, so that hope didn't pan out either.

A merely political understanding of this new Golden Age makes little sense in the context of the poem itself. Why would Mark Antony's baby want to do away with the world's *wickedness*? Why would their offspring do away with *war*? That seems so un-Roman! Why would he bring peace to *nature*? Why would

Pieter Aersten (1508–1575), who was an important figure in the development of still-life painting, produced this work entitled *The Adoration of the Shepherds.*

anyone—even a supreme flatterer—think of associating the birth of a child with such things? And even if Virgil was thinking that the child would be Antony's, wasn't he still predicting a Messiah? Nevertheless, views that Eclogue IV has anything to do with the prophecies of the Old Testament, whether directly or indirectly, are considered by most secular scholars to be old-fashioned and superstitious. Their skepticism leaves no room for hope for Virgil's shepherds or for the world today.

Contrast this modern attitude with that of the early Christian church. Saint Augustine found great hope in Eclogue IV, and he writes in Book XXVII of *The City of God* that Virgil is prophesying Jesus' birth. Emperor Constantine also understood Eclogue IV as a reference to the coming of Christ and used this as part of his justification for legalizing Christianity. The Italian poet Dante certainly agreed (see *Purgatorio*: Canto XXII), which is a major reason why Dante imagined Virgil as his guide. This is why early Christian monks worked so diligently to preserve the writings of Virgil after the fall of Rome and throughout the Middle Ages. This is also why Virgil has been so respected in the centuries-old heritage of classical Christian education.

Now, before we get too far ahead of ourselves, we must ask the question: Can a pagan ever be a prophet? Eclogue IV might be very much like sections of Isaiah, but it is decidedly *not* Isaiah. Virgil's *Eclogues* is not a book of the Bible, nor does Scripture suggest that God has chosen Virgil to bring His Word to the nations. If we were to travel back in time to 40 B.C. and ask Virgil if he meant to talk about Jesus in Eclogue IV, he would no doubt give us a strange look and mumble something about Pollio and Augustus before running away. It is dangerous for Christians to believe in extra-biblical prophecy in the strict sense. What if the similarities are just coincidence? What if Virgil somehow acquired a copy of the Septuagint, copied some of Isaiah's imagery, but didn't understand what he was referring to? Or what if God was providentially preparing a culture for Christianity through great literature?

Like Jill and Eustace, we need Puddleglum to help us sort through these issues. If you have your copy of C.S. Lewis's *The Silver Chair* handy from the days of Omnibus I, open it to chapter 10. At this point in the story, Jill, Eustace, and Puddleglum have made their way to the Deep Lands, and they are explaining to the still-enchanted Knight that they were told to follow the words "UNDER ME" carved in the stone of the City Ruinous. The Knight laughs at them:

"You were the more deceived," he said. "Those words meant nothing to your purpose. Had you but asked my Lady she could have given you bet-

ter counsel. For those words are all that is left of a longer script, which in ancient times, as she well remembers, expressed this verse: *Though under earth and throneless now I be / Yet, while I lived, all Earth was under me.*"

Eustace and Jill are devastated to learn that what they thought was a sign from Aslan turned out to be yet another mistake. They fear they've muffed another sign, been duped into believing in an accident, and this was like cold water down their backs. Thankfully, the wise marshwiggle has an answer:

"Don't you mind him," said Puddleglum. "There *are* no accidents. Our guide is Aslan; and he was there when the giant King caused the letters to be cut, and he knew already all things that would come of them; including *this*."

What, then, would Puddleglum say about Eclogue IV? He would say that there are no accidents when God is guiding His people. So what if secular scholars think the early church's interpretation of Eclogue IV is old-fashioned? So what if Virgil is a pagan and would never purposefully write anything about the coming Messiah? God was there when Virgil caused the letters of this poem to be cut, and He knew already all things that would come of them. God was providentially using great literature to prepare the culture for the spread of Christianity in Rome, then throughout the Empire and throughout the world.

The yearning in Virgil for the shepherd life, for the countryside, for the Garden is a sign of human beings' universal pining for that time before the Fall. The yearning in Virgil that a child would be born who would usher in a new age of salvation is a sign of God's perfect solution to the Fall. Because of the Good Shepherd, the lion really will lie down with the lamb, and God's children will live forever in the New Jerusalem (Rev. 21), that idyllic city they will never want to escape, where God, who is Love, conquers all.

Georgics

If *omnia vincit Amor* in the *Eclogues, Labor omnia vicit* in the *Georgics*. Work is a central theme in this poem. Virgil makes no more mention of a new Golden Age, as he did a decade before in Eclogue IV, when the earth would bring forth crops on its own without anyone having to do any work. Instead, Virgil sees the necessity of agriculture, writing about farming tips, seasonal weather, and honeybees.

This work is constant and difficult. As soon as Ceres "first / Set mortals on with tools to turn the sod," farmers discover that they must pursue weeds ceaselessly, shout to scare away the birds, and pray to bring on the rains. Anyone who has planted a veggie patch can certainly relate to that! Just as in the *Eclogues*, life in the beautiful Italian countryside is far from ideal. Even when a farmer reaps a successful crop, the seasons change and bring with them new possibilities for failure and degeneration. Again and again, the earth must be tamed.

Love adds to the conflict between man and nature. Read in Book III how *Amor* drives animals to battle each other "horn to horn." The lioness prowls, heedless of her whelps. The bears deal "wide-spread havoc-doom" through the forests. Virgil continues the *omnia vincit Amor* theme found in the *Eclogues* when he writes: "Every race on earth of men, and beasts / And ocean-folk, and flocks, and painted birds / Rush to the raging fire: love sways them all."

What is a farmer to do when farming leads to thistles and love to havoc-doom? Georgics IV offers one solution: live life like a bee. (By the way, if you ever have free time and wish to write a paper on some aspect of antiquity, write your paper on bees. These sweet little honey-makers create quite a buzz in classical literature—pun intended.) Bees live in a "settled, sure abode," which, while surrounded by thyme, savory and violets, is safe from wind, cold, and scale-clad lizards. Bees take great care of their "cozy subterranean home" by filling any crevices with pollen to protect their honey and their community.

Community is most important to bees. If ever there is a conflict, the bees unite as one mob in loyalty to their king. Bees "house / Together in one city, and beneath / The shelter of majestic laws they live." According to Virgil, they raise their offspring as a community, and even though bees may have different jobs within the hive, they are united in their commitment to the community and their common love of flowers.

In some ways that is an attractive lifestyle. It is picturesque to be sure, and it does recognize the moral value of hard work and cooperation. Missing, though, is any consideration for the individual. There are no arts in the beehive, and no room for individual creativity. Love does not reach beyond loyalty, and there is no place for unique families within the community, especially since baby bees were described as coming forth from an ox carcass. There is no answer for sin, either, which abounds when men live in community. Human beings cannot, by nature, live like the bees. So, again, what is a farmer to do when farming leads to thistles and love to havoc-doom?

See how Scripture gives a better answer. Ecclesiastes 1:2–3 acknowledges that farming with thistles is wearisome: "'Meaningless! Meaningless!' says the Teacher. 'Utterly meaningless! Everything is meaningless.' What does man gain from all his labor at which he toils under the sun?" The Hebrew word *hebel*, which is here translated as *meaningless* but is sometimes construed as *vanity*, literally means a "puff of smoke" or a "breath," like the wisp of vapor you see when you breathe out on a cold day. As brief as man's time of labor is, God wants us to enjoy our work as a gift. See Ecclesiastes 3:12–14: "I know that there is nothing better for men than to be happy and do good while they live. That everyone may eat and drink, and find satisfaction in all his toil—this is the gift of God. I know that everything God does will endure forever."

So everything God does endures forever. Though our labors are but a breath, when God is working through our labors, suddenly these wearisome, meaningless tasks take on profound—even eternal—significance. When we Christians pray for our daily bread, for example, God uses the thistle-fighting farmers to give it to us. Not only the farmers, but also the grain-grinders, the bread-makers, the grocery stores, the checkout girls, and our own parents are all instruments God is using to give us our daily bread. When you help wash the dinner dishes, though it seems like a wearisome and meaningless chore, God is using you to bring blessing to others. The Reformers called this understanding of work *vocation*, and it became a major doctrine of the Reformation.

Unlike the bees, who elevated the community above the individual, God uses individuals to serve other individuals within a community. People are free to be creative, free to love, and free to live in families, since God uses all of these things to bless His people. We do not perform works to benefit God, as if He needed us, nor to earn our own salvation, as if we were good enough; rather, we perform works, as commanded by our Father, to benefit our neighbors through our vocations. Thinking about work in this way, the farmer can see many fruits of his labors even while he toils under the sun, for when God is at work, everything He does endures forever.

—*Joanna Hensley*

For Further Reading

Ferry, David. *The Eclogues of Virgil.* Bilingual Edition. New York: Farrar, Straus and Giroux, 1999.

Groton, Anne H. and James M. May. *38 Latin Stories.* Fifth Edition. Wauconda, Ill.: Bolchazy-Carducci, 2004. 38–39.

Spielvogel, Jackson J. *Western Civilization.* Seventh Edition. Belmont, Calif.: Thomson Wadsworth, 2009. 137–138, 294.

Veritas Press History Cards: New Testament, Greece and Rome. Lancaster, Pa.: Veritas Press. 21, 22.

Session I: Prelude

A Question to Consider

Have you ever wished you could escape it all and become a shepherd? What makes people accustomed to city life long for the countryside?

From the General Information above, answer the following questions:
1. How did Virgil's boyhood make him ideally suited to write pastoral poetry?
2. Compare Virgil's pastoral poetry with his other literary achievements.
3. Were Virgil's shepherds happy?
4. Why is Eclogue IV called the *Messianic Eclogue*?
5. Why is it dangerous to look outside of Scripture for prophecy?
6. How does Puddleglum's understanding of Providence help us understand Eclogue IV?
7. Define *escapism*. What is the problem with escapism?

Reading Assignment:
Eclogues I–X

Session II: Discussion
Eclogues I–X

A Question to Consider

What do you like to do when you are out in nature? Why?

Discuss or list short answers to the following questions:

Text Analysis
1. What do the Shepherds do for fun in the *Eclogues*?
2. Do the Shepherds ever work?
3. Describe the nature enjoyed by the Shepherds.
4. What role do the gods play in the *Eclogues*?

Cultural Analysis
1. How does the culture at large view the relationship between man and nature?
2. Does the culture recognize anything divine in nature?

Biblical Analysis
1. How does the Bible present the relationship between man and nature? (Gen. 1:26–29, 3:17–19; Jer. 12:4; Rom. 8:19–22)?

In Eclogue VI the satyr Silenus tells the story of Scylla, the monster which, along with Charybdis on the other side of the narrow channel, was so dangerous to ancient shipping. The phrase "being between Scylla and Charybdis" describes an almost hopeless situation where you must tread carefully, since by retreating from one danger, you will be threatened by another danger just as bad.

2. Does the Bible recognize anything divine in nature? How does Scripture address the problem of nature worship (Ps. 19:1; Isa. 44; Deut. 4–28; Jer. 2:27)?

SUMMA

Write an essay or discuss this question, integrating what you have learned from the material above.
How should recognizing God as the Creator affect the way we enjoy and use nature?

READING ASSIGNMENT:
Reread Eclogue IV

SESSION III: DISCUSSION
Eclogue IV

A Question to Consider
Do Christians benefit from the writings of pagans?

Discuss or list short answers to the following questions:

Text Analysis
1. Make a list of references or images in Eclogue IV that are reminiscent of the Old Testament prophecy about the Messiah.
2. Describe the Golden Age.
3. Is this Golden Age political or spiritual?
4. How is Eclogue IV different from the rest of the *Eclogues*?

Cultural Analysis
1. Why is it so important for modernist scholars to call a Messianic interpretation of Eclogue IV old-fashioned and superstitious?
2. How does our culture rely upon political saviors rather than the true Savior?

Biblical Analysis
1. Read Isaiah 9:6–7 and Isaiah 11:6–8. Some scholars insist that Virgil must have been familiar with these passages and that they influenced him when he was writing Eclogue IV. What specifically connects Eclogue IV with these passages in Isaiah? What does this insistence tell us about the worldview of these scholars?
2. Read 2 Peter 1:21, 2 Timothy 3:16, and 2 Samuel 23:2. What do these verses teach about the nature of prophecy?

After stealing the sacred fire and giving it to men, Prometheus was punished by being chained to a rock, where every day an eagle would eat his liver. He is prepared for his sentence in *Prometheus Being Chained by Vulcan* by Dirck van Baburen (1595–1624).

3. Virgil is not considered one of God's prophets, and so we would not elevate Eclogue IV to the level of Scripture. What, then, is the value of such a poem? Read Psalm 89:11, Job 42:2, Acts 1:8 and Acts 17:22–34.

SUMMA

Write an essay or discuss this question, integrating what you have learned from the material above.
Is the *Messianic Eclogue* really about Jesus Christ?

READING ASSIGNMENT:
Georgics I and II

SESSION IV: ACTIVITY

Compose a Pastoral Poem
Now that you have studied Virgil's poetic style, try writing a pastoral poem of your own. Be sure to stay true to the pastoral themes of the beauty of the countryside, the pleasure of music, and the joys and sorrows of love.

Set your poem to music and challenge a classmate to a sing-off worthy of Menalcas and Damoetas. If the weather is nice, be sure to perform outside, preferably in a violet-studded meadow or 'neath the shade of a flowering tree.

Optional Activity

Translate your poem into Latin. If you do not know Latin well enough to translate the poem entirely, do as much as you can, beginning by finding the appropriate vocabulary words in your dictionary. Swap poems with your classmates and see if you can translate each other's work.

READING ASSIGNMENT:
Georgics III and IV

SESSION V: DISCUSSION

A Question to Consider

What are your vocations?

Text Analysis

1. What makes bees such good workers?
2. In the beehive, is creativity important?
3. What are the benefits of living in a hive? What are the drawbacks?
4. In what ways does work conquer all in the *Georgics*?

Cultural Analysis

1. Work is often seen as a problem in our culture. Why?
2. In what ways is work abused in our culture?
3. Does the culture praise or scorn people who work purely for the benefit of others?

Biblical Analysis

1. Why is it impossible for men to live and work like the bees (Isa. 53:6; Rom. 3:23)?
2. How does the Bible discuss work (Gen. 3:17–19; Eccles. 1:2–4, 2:4–11)?
3. What is the Bible's solution to the "problem" of work (Eccles. 3:9–15; 1 Cor. 7:21, 10:31; Eph. 6:5–6; Col. 3:22)?

SUMMA

Write an essay or discuss this question, integrating what you have learned from the material above.
How do your vocations show God's hand at work?

OPTIONAL SESSION: POETRY STUDY

Spenser, Marlowe & Co.

Read one of the following pastoral poems or another one suggested by your teacher: Spenser's *The Shepheardes Calender,* Marlowe's *The Passionate Shepherd to His Love,* Milton's *Lycidas,* Keats' *Ode to a Nightingale,* or Frost's *Build Soil.*

Discuss or write answers to the following questions:[4]
1. In what way is this poem pastoral?
2. How has this poet been influenced by Virgil?
3. How does this poem differ from the *Eclogues* or the *Georgics*?
4. What, if any, are the political references made in this poem?

ENDNOTES
1. David Ferry, The Eclogues of Virgil, A Bilingual Translation (New York: Farrar, Straus and Giroux, 2000) xv.
2. Robert Coleman, Eclogues (London: Cambridge University Press, 1977) 9.
3. James Rhoades translates this as "Justice returns" in the Dover edition, but the Latin clearly reads: *Iam redit et Virgo.*
4. These pastoral poems may be found online by clicking Links 1 to 5 for this chapter at www.VeritasPress.com/OmniLinks.

Metamorphoses

No doubt one of your elderly female relatives, looking upon you after an intervening absence, has sighed and said, "My, my, you are getting so grown up! Last visit you were only this high . . ." or words to that effect. As you patiently endured these and similar comments, and then left the room as soon as politely possible, she more likely than not turned to your mother and said, "They do grow up so fast. Do you ever wish things didn't change?" And your mother no doubt made a sensible answer. However, great-aunts are not the only ones who remark on the changes around them. For students, the freedoms of summer inevitably yield to autumnal scholastic pursuits; the excitement of the first snowfall wanes after Christmas, and winter is always finally conquered by the new life of spring. Change in our own lives is also unavoidable. Perhaps you remember the day when imagining things lost its charm, or how your best friend in first grade gradually grew away from you, and, now, you don't even really talk to one another. We all have mourned the loss of a favorite pair of jeans to a growth spurt or just wear and tear.

The Roman poet Ovid capitalized on the idea of change in his poem the *Metamorphoses*. He drew from mythology and history to weave together a tapestry of stories about creation, gain, loss, destruction, and above all, shape-changing. For that is what *metamorphoses* means in Greek—changes or transformations of shape.

Proserpina, the daughter of Jupiter and Ceres, was abducted by Dis, who made her his queen. She was not permitted to go home because she had eaten seven pomegranate seeds from the underworld. *Proserpine*, painted by Dante Gabriel Rossetti (1828–1882), resides at the Tate Gallery in London.

GENERAL INFORMATION

Author and Context

Publius Ovidius Naso (yes, his last name means "nose") lived from 43 B.C. to A.D. 17, during the age of Augustus. He was a younger contemporary of Virgil (70–19 B.C.), and the son of an *eques,* (a "knight," basically the upper-middle class of the empire, socially one rank below a senator). His father sent him to be educated in Rome (finished by a Grand Tour through Greece) so that he could pursue a career in government or law. Ovid distinguished himself in his rhetoric classes and went on to hold some inconsequential judicial posts, but he soon abandoned his practical career for a poetic one. He gained almost immediate success as a writer of *elegy* (first-person love poems generally written in self-contained couplets) and was regarded as Rome's most prominent poet by A.D. 8.[1] Among his more famous early elegiac works were the *Amores* ("Loves"), erotic poems relating the woes and joys of a poet in love, and the *Ars Amatoria* ("The Art of Love"), a how-to guide on courtship and seduction.

Also in A.D. 8, just after Ovid completed the *Metamorphoses*, the emperor Augustus abruptly banished him to the remote and chilly town of Tomis on the Black Sea. Ovid writes of two reasons for his exile: his *carmen*, or "songs" (the *Ars Amatoria*, which apparently Augustus deemed corrosive to good old traditional Roman morals) and his *error*, or "indiscretion" (there is much speculation about this indiscretion, presumably Ovid stumbled upon some court intrigue or scandal). Aggrieved by the barbaric and harsh surroundings, Ovid nonetheless continued to write elegies such as the *Tristia* ("Sorrows"). He died in exile in A.D. 17.

Significance

Ovid boldly concludes the *Metamorphoses* with the prediction that after his death "in spirit I will be borne up to soar beyond the distant stars, immortal in the name I leave behind; wherever Roman governance extends over the subject nations of the world, my words will be upon the people's lips, and if there is truth in poets' prophesies, then in my fame forever I will live" (XV.1105–1112). Thus far Ovid's prophecy has proved true. After his immediate success and fame as an imperial poet, Ovid's works were used as a school text in the Middle Ages (just as Virgil's were). The themes, content, and style of both his elegiac and epic poetry influenced literature throughout the medieval period as well, and his *Art of Love* was especially well-suited to the courtly love tradition. When medieval authors turned to allegory and moralizing, Ovid was metamorphosed into scriptural and abstract truths. Succeeding great authors such as Dante, Chaucer, Boccaccio, Petrarch, Spencer, and Milton all paid tribute in some fashion to this Roman poet.[2]

In the *Metamorphoses* specifically, Ovid preserved some myths for us that otherwise would have gone extinct and retold other well-known tales in his own distinctive style. His influence on Western civilization is profound and difficult to measure. You can go see Bernini's incredible Apollo and Daphne sculpture in Rome and relive Ovid's description of Daphne's transformation. You can open up Shakespeare and find Ovid's story of Pyramus and Thisbe recast seriously as *Romeo and Juliet*, or related humorously by Bottom and his Mechanicals in *A Midsummer Night's Dream*. Perhaps you have seen George Bernard Shaw's play *Pygmalion*, or its movie version *My Fair Lady*. Even a basic knowledge of Ovid's repertoire is necessary for true Western cultural literacy.

Publius Ovidius Naso as imagined in the *Nuremburg Chronicle*, 1493

Main Characters

Ovid relates well over 200 transformations in his *Metamorphoses*, which makes it difficult to pin down who the main characters are. Obviously the Olympians figure prominently in many of the stories, as the gods fall in love, conceal affairs, or become enraged by the hubris of mortals. On several occasions, Ovid seems to be drawing a parallel between Jove and the emperor Augustus, in particular, when Jove calls together a council of the gods to determine what to do about the wicked race of men (I.222ff). Some scholars take this comparison as a superficial compliment but at the same time a subversive jab at the emperor.[3]

In addition to tales about the gods, Ovid also writes of shape-changing associated with the great heroes of Greek and Roman legend: Cadmus, Perseus, Jason, Theseus, and Hercules. Ovid writes about some of the interactions between the characters of the *Iliad* and *Odyssey*, and he selectively retells Aeneas's adventures as well. Ovid's last transformation of the book is Julius Caesar's deification, which Virgil also wrote about (perhaps more seriously than Ovid) in the *Aeneid*.

However, many of Ovid's stories relate the adventures, escapades, and mishaps of mortals and lesser deities (such as nymphs and river gods) who may not be familiar to the modern reader. Conveniently, the translator of your book (Charles Martin) has included a glossary of names in the back for your reference.

Summary and Setting

Unlike his other poems (written in elegiac couplets), Ovid composed the *Metamorphoses* in the epic meter of dactylic hexameter. With an epic poem, we might expect tales of wars or foundings of kingdoms (as in the second half of the *Aeneid* or in the *Iliad*), or perhaps a hero's journey, complete with a trip to the Underworld (as in the first half of the *Aeneid* or the *Odyssey*). Ovid, however, informs the reader what his epic's purpose is in the opening lines (which, incidentally, is good epic procedure): "My mind leads me to speak now of forms changed into new bodies. O gods above, inspire this undertaking (which you've changed as well) and guide my poem in its epic sweep from the world's beginning to the present day" (I.1–5). Despite his claim to unfolding stories of transformation chronologically, after he tells of the creation of the world, the first four ages, and the flood, Ovid's stories don't

Having intuited his wife's approach, Jove had already metamorphosed Io into a gleaming heifer—a beauty still, even as a cow.
(*Metamorphoses* I.846–849)

really seem to have that—or any—principle of organization. In fact, each is usually connected to the previous one, and sometimes a story will begin, spin off into a couple of tangents about metamorphoses, and then conclude. Many of the fifteen books are connected one to another, ending on a "to be continued…" note as the story is resumed in the next book. Thus, the very feel of the work is one of flux and change, which handily reinforces Ovid's purposes.

Despite the fluid structure of the work, it does begin and end in a parallel way. Initially, the world is brought forth from chaos and then renewed after the Flood. The last book contains the significant speech by Pythagoras on the changing nature of the world and then brings Roman history up to the present time with Julius Caesar's deification and a nod to Augustus. Thus, although it may have meandered a bit in the intervening thirteen books, Ovid does bring his epic to a chronological and thematic close.

Worldview

You are already familiar with the religious systems of Greece and Rome from reading other works in the Omnibus series. Ovid vividly paints for us numerous interactions of the gods among themselves and with mere mortals. It is a polytheistic world, with Jove as the king of the gods. Yet even above Jove rules Fate (and perhaps the Nature that Pythagoras discusses in Book XV). It is also important to keep in mind while reading the *Metamorphoses* that Ovid's theme is change: the only thing that doesn't change is that things change; change is inevitable (whether for the individual's good or ill) and even necessary. The second striking theme of the *Metamorphoses*, which Ovid does not declare explicitly but stares up from every page, is the moral tension between the realms of gods and mortals.

Book I begins with the creation of the world, and for Ovid, creation begins with Chaos. In the *Metamorphoses*, something new must always come from something already existing, and thus we see the unnamed god (or "kindlier nature") shaping and separating the chaotic substance into an orderly heaven and earth (or rather, I should say air, earth, fire, and water). This manner of the creation sets the stage for all the subsequent transformations. We see gods in pursuit of nymphs or maidens who pray to be transformed before the worst could happen; these women often become trees. The gods will often take on disguises to aid them in their lustful pursuits. Other victims of the gods' attentions are transformed in an after-the-fact punishment by a jealous wife (usually Juno) or lover. Sometimes Ovid is merely relating an etiological myth, that is, a story of some physical phenomenon's origin—such as how the mulberry's once white fruit became

dark (Pyramus and Thisbe, IV.87–227). In other tales, human arrogance against the gods is punished by a transformation into an animal, monster, or stone. We also see women transformed into men, a man and nymph melded into one bisexual being known as Hermaphroditus, and animals or stones becoming humans. Yet not all the changes are physical. Rapid and violent swings of emotion are also all too common in these stories—indifference is enflamed by passion; love becomes consumed by jealousy and revenge; unrequited or disappointed love is swallowed up by inconsolable grief.

All of these varied transformations culminate in the doctrine of change expressed in the lengthy speech by Pythagoras in XV.89–546. The discourse begins and ends with a vivid appeal to stop eating animals and become vegetarian. This might seem odd to us until we remember the preceding fourteen books' worth of stories: that steak you are about to bite into might have once been a poor girl like Io, who was impregnated by Jove and then punished by Juno to wander as a cow (I.784–1037). Pythagoras even accuses the gods of delighting in the slaughter of poor innocent beasts. The middle and longest portion of his speech is devoted to the topic of change. He begins asking the people why they fear death:

Here is what happens after you die: your body, whether consumed on the pyre or slowly decaying, suffers no evil; souls cannot perish, and always, on leaving their prior abodes, they come to new ones, living on, dwelling again in receptive bodies.…

Everything changes and nothing can die, for the spirit wanders wherever it wishes to, now here and now there, living with whatever body it chooses, and passing from feral to human then back from human to feral, and at no time does it ever cease its existence; and just as soft wax easily takes on a new shape, unable to stay as it was or keep the same form, and yet is still wax, I preach that the spirit is always the same even though it migrates to various bodies. (XV.199–217)

Pythagoras then proceeds to lecture on changes in nature—the sea and waters, night and day, the four seasons, changes in man, the entropy that befalls the human body when young and strong or beautiful flesh becomes wrinkled and saggy, and changes in kingdoms—how the empire of Rome evolved out of the fallen ruins of Troy. He concludes with another appeal not to eat flesh of any kind.[4]

Christian doctrine emphasizes the resurrection of the body rather than some inherent immortality of the soul. The Latin of the Apostles' Creed is very explicit: we believe in *carnis resurrectionem*, the "resurrection of the flesh." Our bodies will be changed and reunited with our souls for eternity. When Christ first appeared to His disciples after He rose from the dead, they knew Him as Jesus (even though they thought He was a ghost). This tells us that Jesus' resurrected body was similar in some recognizable way to His previous body. He also reassured them in several ways that He was flesh: look at Me, touch Me, give Me something to eat (Luke 24:36–43). In his great chapter on the resurrection, Paul also teaches us about the renewal of our flesh:

> But someone will say, "How are the dead raised up? And with what body do they come?" Foolish one, what you sow is not made alive unless it dies. And what you sow, you do not sow that body that shall be, but mere grain—perhaps wheat or some other grain. But God gives it a body as He pleases, and to each seed its own body.
>
> All flesh is not the same flesh, but there is one kind of flesh of men, another flesh of animals, another of fish, and another of birds. There are also celestial bodies and terrestrial bodies; but the glory of the celestial is one and the glory of the terrestrial is another. There is one glory of the sun, another glory of the moon, and another glory of the stars; for one star differs from another star in glory.
>
> So also is the resurrection of the dead. The body is sown in corruption, it is raised in incorruption. It is sown in dishonor, it is raised in glory. It is sown in weakness, it is raised in power. It is sown a natural body, it is raised a spiritual body. There is a natural body, and there is a spiritual body.
>
> And so it is written, "The first man Adam

Pythagoras warns against eating the flesh of animals in Book XV of the *Metamorphoses*, since an animal might have once been a human. Christians emphasize the resurrection of the body, rather than some inherent immortality of the soul that migrates from body to body. In *Noli Me Tangere* (1511–12) by Titian, Jesus tells Mary Magdalen after his resurrection, "Touch me not."

became a living being." The last Adam became a life-giving spirit. . . . And as we have borne the image of the man of dust, we shall also bear the image of the heavenly Man.

Now this I say, brethren, that flesh and blood cannot inherit the kingdom of God; nor does corruption inherit incorruption. Behold, I tell you a mystery: We shall not all sleep, but we shall all be changed—in a moment, in the twinkling of an eye, at the last trumpet. For the trumpet shall sound, and the dead will be raised incorruptible, and we shall all be changed. For this corruptible must put on incorruption, and this mortal must put on immortality. So when this corruptible has put on incorruption, and this mortal has put on immortality, then shall be brought to pass the saying that is written: "Death is swallowed up in victory." (1 Cor. 15:35–54)

Arachne dared to challenge the goddess Minerva in a weaving contest. She still spins thread, but now she does it as a spider.

This passage is critical to understanding the Christian notion of change as opposed to the pagan one expressed by Pythagoras. First, we learn that God has made distinct types of flesh: man, animals, birds, fish, even celestial versus terrestrial beings—these are all different. Pythagoras preaches that really all flesh and matter are the same and are in flux (they all originated in the same Chaos, after all, so what's to prevent them from dissolving back into that chaotic state and reshaping into something else?). However, when God created the formless earth and shaped that chaos into heaven and earth, He declared that separation and distinction "good." When He formed man from the dust of the earth, He distinguished him forever from earth by stamping him with His image and breathing His spirit into him. God also created man male and female, another distinction that is blurred in some of Ovid's transformations.

We also learn from Solomon that animals have some type of spirit that is different from man's: "Who knows the spirit of the sons of men, which goes upward, and the spirit of the animal, which goes down to the earth?" (Eccles. 3:21). In Pythagoras's view, there is only spirit versus matter (does this sound familiar, like, say, Gnosticism?). Spirit can inhabit different types of matter. In the Bible, however, different types of spirit have been "assigned" to different types of matter. When the Christian's corruptible body dies, his soul is not at liberty to find a new type of flesh to inhabit; rather, his body will be raised incorruptible. Paul teaches us elsewhere that we long for our incorruptible (human) bodies: "For we who are in this tent groan, being burdened, not because we want to be unclothed, but further clothed, that mortality may be swallowed up by life" (2 Cor. 5:4).

As much as we would disagree with Pythagoras on his doctrine of reincarnation, we can still grant that yes, the world is constantly changing around us. This is the subject of the book of Ecclesiastes: vanity of vanities, all is vanity. However, the world we see in the *Metamorphoses* remains at that level: everything is always changing into something else, world without end. There seems to be no end goal or purpose to all of this change, unless it be "try not to anger any gods in your next life, would ya?" There is no conclusion of the matter such as that given in Ecclesiastes: "Fear God and keep His commandments, for this is man's all. For God will bring every work into judgment, including every secret thing, whether good or evil" (12:13–14). The Christian story is not an endless cycling of repetitive change unto infinity. Our story has a beginning, conflict, redemption, and grand conclusion. God created the world *ex nihilo* and divided the chaos into a perfect order. Man marred Eden with sin, and corruption brought its deathly change to the world. God did not simply wipe out mankind and start over, but the most miraculous metamorphosis occurred: God became flesh and dwelt among us. The Immortal God died on a cross, His body was laid in a tomb for three days, and He rose again and ascended into heaven. His followers are also reborn: first God gives them a new heart of flesh to replace their old heart of stone, and in the final resurrection He will clothe these souls with new incorruptible bodies. The Bible tells of creation, fall, and re-creation; Ovid relates tales simply of shaping and reshaping.

Another striking feature of the *Metamorphoses* that unifies this collection of tales is the ethical system displayed both by gods and men. The first story about man's transgression is that of Lycaon, who violates sacred laws of hospitality by serving Jove a stew made from a slave (to test Jove's deity). This is the last straw for the gods, and Jove sends the flood on the earth. However, immediately after the earth regenerates itself following the flood, we read of Apollo's thwarted rape of Daphne. How is Apollo any less wicked than Lycaon? This type of troubling question comes up repeatedly throughout this work. Jupiter's adulterous rapes and seductions alone take up quite a number of stories. Mars and Venus are caught in the act of adultery by her husband Vulcan. The gods have enough jealousies and rivalries among them to furnish sufficient material for any teenage reality show. Cupid is employed multiple times to inflict love or rejection upon gods and mortals. Gods get offended by the pride or indifference or jealousy of mortals and change them into a spider (Arachne), a childless stone (Niobe), or a monster (Scylla). Yet the mortals are really no better. You will not be reading some of the more gruesome stories, but they are there—a sister who burns with passion for her brother (Byblis and Caunus), a girl who grows up disguised as a boy to prevent her father's wrath and falls in love with her fiancée (Iphis and Isis—happily she is turned into a man right before the wedding—a close call), a king who rapes his wife's sister and cuts her tongue out so that she cannot reveal his sin (Tereus, Procne, and Philomela), and a girl who commits incest with her own father (Myrrha).

Given the behavior of the gods, we should be asking the question "Why are the mortals 'wrong' for doing these things as well?" Even Byblis, the girl who is in love with her own brother, tries to justify herself by saying, "The gods took their own sisters, to be sure!" But then she concludes, "The gods, though, are a law unto themselves!—Why should I try to use them as my models when their behavior is so unlike ours?" (IX.726–732). Ovid even introduces this story by saying, "This Byblis serves to illustrate a moral: that girls should not desire what's forbidden; she did not love her

brother as a brother, or as a sister should" (664–667). Somehow, although the gods behave exactly in the same ways as the mortals do, they are above the law. We get the impression that "their behavior is so unlike ours" only because the gods are bigger and more powerful than mortals, and thus they can do what they want. They can turn mortals into beasts at a snap of the fingers if they so desire.

The folly of this pagan system is obvious. Psalm 115:3–8 says,

> But our God is in heaven; He does whatever He pleases. Their idols are silver and gold, the work of men's hands. They have mouths, but they do not speak; eyes they have, but they do not see; they have ears, but they do not hear; noses they have, but they do not smell; they have hands, but they do not handle; feet they have, but they do not walk; nor do they mutter through their throat. Those who make them are like them; so is everyone who trusts in them.

In the *Metamorphoses* we can clearly see how the worshippers are like the gods they worship. The gods burn with passion for men or women they ought not to love; the mortals also pursue illicit relationships. When a god sees a nymph or girl he wants, he takes her; mortal men also rape the helpless.

In her jealousy Juno changes the nymph Callisto into a bear. Before Callisto's son can unwittingly thrust his spear at her, Jupiter casts them both into the sky as two new constellations, Ursas Major and Minor.

The gods lose their tempers and lash out at men; men and women also are consumed by anger and destroy one another. But, inconsistently, mortals are held to some standard of morality that is not even found in the Olympian heaven they look to for guidance.

The Christian and Triune God is not simply a bigger version of us. His ways are not our ways, nor His thoughts our thoughts (Isa. 55:8). He is completely and utterly good, holy, righteous, merciful, and just. Our Creator so far transcends us, that apart from our Mediator, His Son Jesus Christ, we would be utterly lost and condemned in our sins. The poor mortals struggling along in the *Metamorphoses* have no such redemption or hope of salvation. They must cling to the very tenuous hope that if they are pious and serve the gods, they might escape their notice or please them somehow (e.g., Baucis and Philemon). However, even if a maiden is piously following the virgin goddess Diana, she still has to be on the lookout for the lustful king of the gods himself (e.g., the story of Jove and Callisto). Our God, however, is not at odds with Himself; Father, Son, and Spirit are in complete harmony and do not require contradictory things of us. Lust, unrighteous anger, rape, and incest are all wrong because they are contrary to God's nature as revealed in His law to us.

If Ovid so vividly portrayed the follies and moral defects of the gods, did he himself even believe in the deities and myths he portrayed in the *Metamorphoses*? It is difficult to answer this question from the *Metamorphoses* itself, since as the storyteller Ovid manages to keep himself removed from much of the work. However, we see a few comments of reservation or skepticism. For example, when Orpheus is pleading for his wife Eurydice before the King and Queen of the Underworld, he adds "unless that tale of long-ago rape was invented" (X.39). In his other works, Ovid comes across as some sort of agnostic who holds to the old religion for the sake of tradition or "just in case": "It is useful that there be gods, so let us believe in them as it is useful, let us offer incense and wine on the old altars. And they do not keep aloof in quiet unconcern, as if slumbering. Live

without doing harm, and divine power will be with you. Return to the owner whatever he entrusted to you; abide loyally by your mutual ties; abstain from deceit, and let your hands be clean from murder."[5]

Yet the overall tone of the *Metamorphoses* is far from that of a systematic theology. We do not get the impression that Ovid is laying out the intricacies of Roman religion for its devotees. Rather, his swift and vivid storytelling sends the reader rushing from heaven to earth to river to woodland, witnessing the transforming effects of sincere love and impure passion. While we should not simply withhold judgment as we read these myths, we should also appreciate them as they are set out: stories for entertainment and edification.

—*Natali H. Monnette*

Medusa with her snaky hair was decapitated by Perseus.

For Further Reading

Hardie, Peter. *The Cambridge Companion to Ovid.* Cambridge: Cambridge University Press, 2002.

Lee, A., ed. *Ovid: Metamorphoses Book I.* Mundelein, Ill.: Bolchazy-Carducci Publishers, Inc., 1988.

Leithart, Peter. *Heroes of the City of Man.* Moscow, Idaho: Canon Press, 1999.

Perkins, Caroline and Davis-Henry, Denise. *Ovid: A Legamus Transitional Reader.* Mundelein, Ill.: Bolchazy-Carducci Publishers, Inc., 2008.

Taylor, A.B., ed. *Shakespeare's Ovid: The Metamorphoses in the Plays and Poems.* Cambridge: Cambridge University Press, 2006.

Session I: Prelude

A Question to Consider

Is change good or bad?

From the General Information above answer the following questions:
1. How was Ovid's poetry received by the Romans of his day?
2. What is the difference between an elegy and an epic? Into which category does the *Metamorphoses* fall?
3. In what ways has Ovid's poetry influenced Western civilization?
4. What is the basic structure of the *Metamorphoses*?
5. What kinds of changes occur in the *Metamorphoses*?
6. How does the Christian view of flesh and spirit differ from that of Pythagoras?

Reading Assignment:
Metamorphoses, Books I–II

Session II: Discussion
Metamorphoses, Books I–II

A Question to Consider

Think about any superhero movies you might have seen recently. In most of these movies, the main character experiences a physical transformation. Often an evil character also undergoes a transformation. Choose a movie about a superhero. How does the main character's physical transformation accompany a mental, moral, or spiritual transformation? In other words, how does the physical transformation change how the character sees his or her mission in life?

Discuss or write answers to the following questions:

Text Analysis

1. How does the creator god (whichever one it was) transform the primordial Chaos into the created universe?
2. Describe the transformations of the four ages of the world—gold, silver, bronze, and iron. How does Ovid explain the seasons? How does he explain human evil?
3. Why does Jove finally decide to flood the earth? Why do the gods initially worry about killing the entire human race?
4. When he takes the reins of Phoebus's sun chariot, Phaethon seems to be trying to transform himself into

A victim of Fate, Actaeon wanders inadvertently upon Diana bathing in a pool. She splashes him with water, beginning his transformation into a stag. His own hounds and his friends, not realizing it is he, hunt him down and kill him.

a god like his father. Does he succeed or not? Why?
5. List the transformations that occur in the story of Jove, Callisto, and Arcas and explain why they happen.

Cultural Analysis

1. Our God is a God of order. He created the universe and

gave it form. One of the primary effects of the Fall was the un-shaping of what God had made—our bodies no longer function the way they were made to, human societies do not exist in harmony, and the earth is blighted by diseases, droughts, and natural disasters. Evil has a clear cause in the biblical narrative, and good and evil are clearly distinguished from Eden onward. In the *Metamorphoses* we have encountered another perspective: the gods are neither clearly good nor evil. They demand a kind of moral behavior of humans, but they do not practice this behavior themselves. Moreover, righteous living does not necessarily ensure favor with the gods. How do secular Americans today view good and evil? What is their origin? Are they clearly distinguished? Choose one or two examples from popular culture and discuss.

2. You have now encountered a number of stories in which Jupiter rapes a female character; Juno his wife is understandably outraged whenever this happens. But note whom Juno blames and punishes each time–not Jupiter, but the female victim. What cultural assumption might the Romans have possessed to explain this blame? Most Americans today would probably disagree with the Romans on this point. Whom would we tend to blame in such situations? What do you think accounts for the change in cultural perspective?

Biblical Analysis

1. Ovid's creation account bears some striking similarities to the biblical version. What are some of these similarities? What are some major differences?
2. The Greeks and Romans were not the only ancient peoples to tell tales of immortal beings fathering children by mortal women. Read Genesis 6:1–4. While there is much dispute over the meaning of these verses, one reading would seem to suggest a situation similar to those mentioned by Ovid. Compare and contrast the biblical version with those in the *Metamorphoses*.

Summa

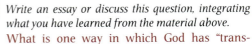

Write an essay or discuss this question, integrating what you have learned from the material above.

What is one way in which God has "transformed" you into a better person? How did that transformation affect how you saw yourself as a person? Your relationship with God and others? Your purpose on earth?

Reading Assignment:
Metamorphoses, Books III–V

Session III: Recitation
Metamorphoses, Books II–V

Comprehension Questions

Answer the following questions for factual recall:

1. In the story of Jove and Europa, into what does Jupiter transform himself and why?
2. In the story of Cadmus's founding of Thebes, how does Athena instruct him to replenish his people? What happens?
3. For what deed did Diana transform Actaeon into a stag? What happens to him in the end?
4. In what way does the story of Narcissus and Echo reverse the usual trope, the pattern of the story or figure of speech, of a male deity accosting a mortal female?
5. In the story of Pyramus and Thisbe, what was the original color of the mulberry tree's fruit? What color is it now, and why?
6. In what condition does Perseus find Andromeda? Why has this happened to her? What does Perseus demand from her parents in return for saving her?
7. Who instructs Cupid to make Pluto fall in love with Proserpina, and why?

Medea mixes a potion to restore youth to her father-in-law. She was married to Jason, leader of the Argonauts.

8. Following Ceres' plea for her daughter's return, Jupiter tells her that he will give Proserpina back to her mother under what condition? Does Proserpina meet this condition? Why or why not?

READING ASSIGNMENT:
Metamorphoses, Books VI–IX

SESSION IV: DISCUSSION
Metamorphoses, Books VI–IX

A Question to Consider

What qualities make a person admirable?

Discuss or write answers to the following questions:

Text Analysis

1. What is the primary fault of both Arachne and Niobe?
2. In the three stories you read about Medea, what are some of the qualities that she exhibits that make her an evil character?
3. What quality or virtue does Daedalus urge Icarus to use as he flies away from Crete?
4. What positive characteristics do Baucis and Philemon demonstrate to Jupiter and Mercury? How do the gods reward them?
5. Which qualities make Hercules heroic? Which qualities don't seem heroic? Give examples of at least three.

Cultural Analysis

1. What are two primary sources for what qualities Americans value in a person? Give examples of each.

Andromeda, chained to a rock in punishment for her mother's trust in her own beauty, is saved by Perseus, who conquers the sea serpent.

2. Considering Daedalus, what would our culture admire or criticize about him? Why?

Biblical Analysis

1. Compare the story of Baucis and Philemon with that of Sodom and Gomorrah.
2. What are some of the qualities that the Bible values? What are some that it rejects?

Summa

Write an essay or discuss this question, integrating what you have learned from the material above. How can we inspire our culture to practice and value humility?

Reading Assignment:
Metamorphoses, Books X–XII

Session V: Aesthetics
Metamorphoses, Books X–XII

Retelling Mythology on Canvas

One of the most remarkable aspects of mythology is how adaptable the myth is as a vehicle for meaning. Ovid's *Metamorphoses* has proved to be fruitful material for visual artists throughout the centuries. The following questions ask you to locate historic works of art and to consider how the artist has adapted the Ovidian myth to suit the purposes of his/her work. Discuss the following questions aloud in a small group or, if you are working alone, write out answers to the questions.

1. Re-read the Deadalus and Icarus selection from Book VIII and compare it to Pieter Bruegel the Elder's painting *Landscape with the Fall of Icarus* (1558). (You can find an online version of this piece by clicking on Link 1 for this chapter at www.VeritasPress.com/OmniLinks.)

When Apollo pursues Daphne, her father Peneus hears her pleas for help and turns her into a laurel tree. Apollo declares that even though he cannot have her as a woman, the laurel would forever be his tree. Laurel would henceforth grace the brow of Greek champions and Roman generals and emperors. *Apollo and Daphne* by Gian Lorenzo Bernini (1598–1680) shows the moment when Daphne is changing into the tree.

Metamorphoses 363

Locate Icarus in the painting. Why do you think Bruegel chose to re-tell the myth in this way? How does this make you think about Ovid's story differently? What message does this adaptation of the story convey that the Ovidian version did not?
2. Re-read the selection on Venus and Adonis from Book X and compare it to John William Waterhouse's painting *The Awakening of Adonis* (1900). (You can find an online version of this painting by clicking on Link 2 for this chapter at www.VeritasPress.com/OmniLinks.)

Why do you think Waterhouse chose this moment in the story to paint? Who does Waterhouse focus on, Venus or Adonis, and why might this be?

READING ASSIGNMENT:
Metamorphoses, Books XIII–XV

SESSION VI: ACTIVITY
Metamorphoses, Books XIII–XV

Ovid in Poetry

In this session you will examine how myths have been adapted to send differing messages in the arts. You will question how these same Ovidian myths have inspired poets to refashion them in vastly different ways and to convey different meanings depending on which details the authors select or omit.

Read the poems aloud and discuss the following questions in a small group. Read each of the following poems and answer the questions below:
1. Read Percy Bysshe Shelley's "Adonais." (You can find an online version of this poem by clicking on Link 3 for this chapter at www.VeritasPress.com/OmniLinks.) It is a pastoral elegy written on the death of his friend John Keats (1821). Why is the story of Adonis fitting for this occasion?
2. Another English poet who was inspired by Ovid centuries after his death was John Gower, whose most famous work is the *Confessio Amantis* (c. 1390). Here is a quick synopsis of the poem. Divided into a prologue and eight books, the poem is a frame narrative, like the *Canterbury Tales* of Geoffrey Chaucer, a contemporary of Gower. The frame story of the *Confessio* details the Lover making a confession structured around the seven deadly sins (lust, gluttony, greed, sloth, wrath, envy, and pride) to Genius, the priest of Venus. For each of the sins there are a number of tales, many from Ovid's *Metamorphoses* and Greek mythology, which (more or less) demonstrate either the dangers of that sin or the benefits of avoiding it. In his section on sloth in Book 4, Gower recounts the story of Pygmalion, emphasizing the role of diligent love in how Pygmalion creates the statue and desires it to become a real woman.

Read lines 371–450 of the *Confessio Amantis*. (You can find an online version by clicking on Link 4 for this chapter at www.VeritasPress.com/OmniLinks. It is in the original Middle English. You should be able to decipher most of it. Try it!) Why do you think Gower chose to tell this story in the section on sloth? How is this different from the moral of Ovid's story?

OPTIONAL SESSION
Graphic Novel

In the *Silmarillion,* his book outlining the early mythology of Middle-earth, J.R.R. Tolkien includes the story of Beren and Luthien. Some readers may be familiar with the version of their story sung by Aragorn in *The Fellowship of the Ring*. The story presents an interesting variation on the Ovidian formula of a male god pursuing and violating a mortal woman.

In Tolkien's narrative, Beren is a mortal man who, fleeing a devastating battle against Morgoth, wanders into the elvish realm of Doriath. On an evening deep in the woods of Neldoreth Beren spies the beautiful elvish princess Luthien dancing and singing, and he falls in love with her. He advances toward her, but she runs from him. Throughout the winter and into the spring Beren pursues her, until one day Beren cries out to her and gives her a new name, Tinuviel. The sound of his voice and of the new name causes Luthien to fall in love with Beren, and she brings him to her elvish father to ask permission to marry him. In the end, Luthien becomes a mortal to marry Beren.

Note how Tolkien reworks the Ovidian myth: instead of an immortal male dominating and abusing a mortal female, in Tolkien's story it is the female who is immortal, and she chooses whether to permit the mortal man's love or not. The man wins the Elf not by physical force but by crying out in desperation the only name he knew for her.

Illustrate two brief graphic novellas (comic strips) for the story of Beren and Luthien and for a comparable story from the *Metamorphoses*. Be sure to highlight both similarities and differences between the stories.

Endnotes

1. Stephen E. Hinds, "Ovid." *The Oxford Classical Dictionary*. Ed. Simon Hornblower and Anthony Spawforth (Oxford: Oxford University Press, 2003). Oxford Reference Online (Oxford University Press. Regent University. 22 January 2009).
2. For a detailed treatment of Ovid's presence throughout the centuries and in these authors, see Edward Rand, *Ovid and His Influence* (New York: Cooper Square Publishers, Inc. 1963).
3. See the translator's introduction to your book, 5–6. Charles Martin, trans. *Ovid: Metamorphoses* (New York: W.W. Norton & Company, 2005).
4. I do not intend to address the question of vegetarianism in this essay. Regardless of a Christian's views on the subject, we can all agree that Pythagoras's reasons against eating meat are rooted in shallow soil indeed.
5. *Ars Amatoria* I.637ff, quoted by Hermann Fränkel in his discussion of Ovid's religious views in chapter 11 of *Ovid: A Poet Between Two Worlds* (Berkeley: University of California Press, 1969), 90–93. See also Rand, 72–76.

Mark

Which would you prefer, a short, action-packed movie, or a long, drawn out chick flick? Well, we all have our preferences, but I know I would go for the former any day! Nothing wrong, mind you, with a long, drawn out serious movie, but I prefer a little action: a few explosions, a high-speed chase. Throw in a car flying across a huge canyon, and I'm happy.

The Gospel of Mark is kind of like that. Mark gets right to the point. It is a fast-moving narrative and a unique look at the action-packed ministry of Jesus Christ. He does not mention the birth of Jesus at all. By the end of the first chapter, John the Baptist has already announced His coming and has baptized Jesus, Jesus has been tempted in the wilderness by Satan and begun His ministry, four men have been called to follow Him, and Jesus has cast out several demons and healed Peter's mother and a leper. (And it's not even a long chapter!) Luke, by comparison, takes five chapters to get to the same point in the life and ministry of Jesus. It was Luke's purpose, of course, to give a more detailed, historical narrative of the birth, life, and death of Jesus.

Mark uses a particular word throughout his account which highlights his style, the Greek word ευθυς (euthus). The word is often translated as *immediately*. Skim over the first chapter alone and count the number of times it occurs. In the narrative material of the New Testament (Matthew through Acts), ευθυς occurs 51 times. Of these, 41 instances are in Mark! Matthew has 5, Luke and Acts have 1 each, and John has 3 instances of ευθυς.

Mark also commonly uses the present tense for a past action. He uses this "historical present" no less than 150 times when other writers would have simply used the past tense. You get the feeling that you are right there in the middle of the action. His unusually frequent use of ευθυς and his abundant use of the present tense give his relatively brief sixteen-chapter Gospel a powerful sense of movement and urgency.

In the context of critical times Mark communicates a compelling message of who Jesus is and the radical truth of what it means to follow Him.

GENERAL INFORMATION

Author and Context

Like the other three Gospels, Mark is anonymous. The title "According to Mark" was added later to distinguish it from the other three. So how do we know who wrote it? The early church fathers attributed the second Gospel to Mark, and the most important testimony comes from Papias, a man who was serving as bishop of Hierapolis in Phrygia of Asia sometime before A.D. 130. His words are recorded by Eusebius (remember his *Church History* from Omnibus II?). Eusebius, writing in A.D. 325, quotes Papias as saying that Mark wrote this Gospel and that he obtained most of his information from Peter (*The Church History*, 3.39.15).

He is sometimes referred to as John Mark, and Luke first mentions him in Acts 12:12. His mother Mary is holding a prayer service at her house. Peter had been imprisoned, and the church is praying for his release. In the middle of their prayer they hear a knock at the door and, lo and behold, there's Peter. Talk about a quick answer to prayer! Mark certainly would have been strongly moved by this miracle, and he later decides to join his cousin, Barnabas (Col. 4:10), and Paul on their first missionary journey. For some reason, however, Mark left them after they arrived in Pamphylia, in Asia Minor. It is possible that early on Mark had sympathies with the circumcision party within the church—he left immediately after the gospel was presented to the first Gentile who had no connection to Judaism. But while scholars have speculated, no one knows the exact reason for this seemingly abrupt departure from the mission. We do know that Paul was not happy about it and refused to take Mark along on the second journey. Barnabas and Paul agreed to disagree and went their separate ways as a result. Paul chose another partner, Silas, and Barnabas and Mark set sail for Cyprus (Acts 15:36–40). It seems, however, that the friendships were later healed, as Paul speaks highly of Barnabas (1 Cor. 9:6) and Mark (Col. 4:10). Paul even mentions that Mark was with him during his imprisonment, and he describes him as "useful to me for ministry" (2 Tim. 4:11).

Peter mentions that Mark was with him as he wrote 1 Peter from Rome, and Peter refers to him as his "son" (1 Pet. 5:13), implying that perhaps Mark had been converted through his ministry. It seems that Mark was not only converted through Peter's ministry, but that he became a faithful companion of Peter and gleaned much of the information for his Gospel from Peter as well.

And finally, there is at least a possibility that Mark was the famous rich, young ruler who went away from Jesus saddened by the requirement that he give up everything.

The Book of Kells was produced around 800 A.D. and is one of the most beautifully illuminated manuscripts in the world. It contains the four Gospels written in insular majuscule script accompanied by magnificent pages of decoration. This detail from one of those pages shows a winged lion—the symbol of Saint Mark. The lion comes from Mark's description of John the Baptist as a "voice of one crying out in the desert" (Mark 1:3), whom artists compared to a roaring lion. The lion's wings are derived from the application of Ezekiel's vision of the four winged creatures to the four Gospel writers.

From the house and servant (Acts 12:12), we know that Mark was from a wealthy family. And Mark's Gospel is the only one that includes the detail that Jesus looked on the rich, young ruler and loved him (Mark 10:21).

Significance

Matthew, Mark, and Luke are called the "Synoptic Gospels" (literally, "seeing together"). They are set apart from John because these three bear striking similarities. Not only do they relate the same events, in several places the wording is exactly the same. And while they contain a great deal of material that is the same, John contains a great deal of material that is not found in any of the three synoptics.

The natural question, of course, is "How do we explain the overlap that is identical?" It seems likely that one of the writers wrote his Gospel first and the other two used it as a source when they wrote theirs. Since Matthew and Luke have significant variation in content and order of events, and the basic content of Mark is reproduced almost entirely in the other two, a common theory is that Mark was written first and the other two used his document independently as a source. This explanation works until we realize that there is material common to Matthew and Luke, but not found in Mark. Scholars have proposed the idea of a second source for Matthew and Luke, "Q" (for the German word *quelle*, which means "source"). This theory has some credibility, but it should be noted that no one has ever found this "Q" document.

If indeed Mark was the first Gospel, it deserves special consideration, for it shaped what the other Gospels would look like. It provided the model of the genre that we know and call today "Gospel." Matthew and Luke take on the form they do because of Mark.

Summary and Setting

Mark's Gospel is the shortest, and he spends almost half of the book on the last week of Jesus' life. The miracles and sermons are clearly important, but it is in the suffering, death, and resurrection that Mark finds the essence of Jesus' mission. He is writing to encourage

his audience to believe that Jesus is the Son of God, that He suffered for us, and that being a true believer means *following* Him. Following Him means denying self, taking up the cross, and following Jesus (8:34).

Several issues make it likely that Mark was written from Rome and was intended to encourage the body of believers there. First, there are an unusual number of Latin technical terms (called "latinisms"). Some examples: *legion, praetorium, centurion, speculator, flagellare, denarius, quadrans.* (The quadrans, the monetary amount of two copper coins, was not in circulation in the east.) Second, Mark translates Aramaic expressions and makes a point of explaining Jewish customs, which suggests an audience far removed from the world of Judaism. This would, of course, be consistent with an origin of Rome. Third, Mark mentions a man named Rufus, an individual whom Paul addresses when greeting the Roman church (Rom. 16:13). Finally, the many allusions to suffering make it consistent with the persecution of believers in Rome.

Coming up with an exact date for the writing of Mark is difficult. It is likely, however, that Mark was written before A.D. 62. Remember our discussions of the writing of Luke in Omnibus I? Since Luke was written around that time, and Mark was likely a source Luke used, we have to place the writing of Mark either in the late fifties or early sixties. As the eye witnesses to the life and ministry of Jesus (like Peter) were dying, it became necessary to have a record of their account, so Mark fills this need by giving us a Gospel based on Peter's observations.

Worldview

Once upon a time in ancient Rome, there was a man described as being of average height, with light blond hair, and a "squat" neck. His body is described as being "pustular" (covered with pimples), and he is said to have had "pretty" (not handsome) features. He apparently had a "protuberant" (bulging) belly and "spindling" (long and skinny) legs. Wow, what a specimen. So, who is this guy? Hang on . . . a little more suspense, please. He grew up poor, but was

Lucius Domitius Ahenobarbus

years! He was born Lucius Domitius Ahenobarbus, but most people refer to him as Nero. (All the information in this paragraph comes from Suetonius's *The Twelve Caesars*.)

Rome began as a monarchy (753 B.C.) but transitioned to a republic after the rape of the noble Lucretia by the son of the king around 510 B.C. (*recall Livy's Early History of Rome from Omnibus I*). The Romans vowed they would never revert to a monarchy again until, riddled with civil war and chaos, a man named Octavian rose to power. With the help of Virgil, Octavian, later called Augustus, was welcomed to the throne as a messianic figure. Upon his death, Augustus was elevated by the Senate to the status of god and was worshiped by the Romans. He had adopted Tiberius and appointed him as heir to his estate. Tiberius, therefore, was the "son of god." Tiberius ruled Rome after the death of Augustus in A.D. 14 until his own death in A.D. 37. After Tiberius, Caligula ruled, then Claudius. It was common for the standing emperor to adopt the next emperor, so Claudius adopted Nero, and Nero ruled Rome from A.D. 54–68. Since Claudius was elevated to godhood upon his death, Nero was the "son of god."

So, how do you think it would have sounded to residents of Rome (including Nero himself, Rome's emperor at the time Mark was written) when they first read Mark's Gospel stating the following:

"Then a voice came from heaven, 'You are My beloved Son, in whom I am well pleased'" (1:11).

"And the unclean spirits, whenever they saw Him, fell down before Him and cried out, saying 'You are the Son of God'" (3:11).

"When he (a demon-possessed man) saw Jesus from afar, he ran and worshiped him. And he cried out with a loud voice and said, 'What have I to do with You, Jesus, Son of the Most High God?'" (5:6–7a).

"And a cloud came and overshadowed them; and a voice came out of the cloud, saying, 'This is My beloved Son. Hear Him!'" (9:7).

"But He kept silent and answered nothing. Again the high priest asked Him, saying to Him, 'Are you the Christ, the Son of the Blessed?' Jesus said, 'I am. And you will see the Son of Man

adopted by a rich man and tutored by one of the most prestigious teachers of his day. He grew up to be one of the most deranged and twisted men ever to live. He committed several murders, including involvement in his own father's death and multiple attempts on his mother's life. He is said to have driven his teacher to commit suicide. He engaged in every kind of unthinkable and unspeakable sexual aberration. Believe it or not, this man was actually the most powerful man in the world for seventeen

sitting at the right hand of the Power, and coming with the clouds of heaven'" (14:61–62).

"So when the centurion, who stood opposite Him, saw that He cried out like this and breathed His last, he said, 'Truly this Man was the Son of God!'" (15:39).

It was common for the deified emperor to have a temple built in his honor after his death and be worshiped there. The Imperial Cult was central to Roman religion and the key to maintenance of loyalty among the Roman subjects. They believed they had achieved their power and ability to conquer the world from the favor of the gods. Continuing to remain in good standing with the gods was vital. Understood in this light, the Gospel of Mark is a direct assault upon the very heart and soul of the Roman Empire. In the midst of this religious environment, Mark, most likely living in the capital of Rome itself, takes aim at this pagan system and cries out that Nero is not the son of God. How powerful is the passage in chapter fifteen in which the Roman centurion, a government employee, exclaims that Jesus (*not* Nero) is the Son of God!

Mark's message is loud and clear. Neither Nero's father Claudius nor any other emperor is to be worshiped. Temples should *not* be built to honor these men because they are not gods, nor are they sons of gods. Jesus Christ is the only Son of God, and He alone is worthy of our adoration. Jesus as the Son of God is one of Mark's primary themes, and it is an even more powerful message when understood in its historical context.

Claiming that the emperor was not God was not the only issue that caught the attention of the authorities. At least four charges were leveled at Christians in the first century. The first of these was cannibalism. Cannibalism? Christians? Well, imagine you are a curious Roman citizen, and you decide to peek in on one of those Christian meetings, and you hear the following, "'Take, eat; this is My body.' Then He took the cup, and when He had given thanks He gave *it* to them, and they all drank from it. And He said to them, 'This is My blood of the new covenant, which is shed for many'" (Mark 14:22b–23). What is this? People eating one another!

The second charge leveled against Christians was that of incest. Christians engaged in "love feasts" during which they were encouraged to "love their brothers and sisters." Again, we can imagine how the Romans might have interpreted these innocent events.

The third charge was that of atheism. As mentioned above, Christians refused to acknowledge the emperor as God. If someone is not going to recognize the most important god, then he might as well be an atheist.

In contrast to Emperor Nero, this mosaic, *Christ in Majesty*, depicts the *true* Son of God. The mosaic is from the ceiling of the Basilica di Sant'Apollinare Nuovo in Ravenna, Italy.

And finally, Christians were charged with laziness. By honoring the Fourth Commandment to "Remember the Sabbath Day to keep it holy" and refraining from work, Christians were viewed as making an excuse to lie around and not work.

Because they were viewed in this way, Mark, along with his message that Jesus is God, stressed the nature of true discipleship. How were believers to respond to these accusations? How were they to endure the attacks? What did it mean to follow Jesus in this setting?

Roman citizens could worship as many gods as they liked, as long as one of them was the state (in the form of emperor worship). But if the emperor is not God, he is not to be worshiped. What does this mean for someone who has embraced the truth of the gospel of Jesus Christ and is living in first-century Rome? Surely there is some compromise for those who grew up in the context of the imperial cult, right? First-generation Christians must be allowed some concessions, right? Well, you be the judge. Here are the words of Mark:

> When He had called the people to Himself, with His disciples also, He said to them, "Whoever desires to come after Me, let him deny himself, and take up his cross, and follow Me. For whoever desires to save his life will lose it, but whoever loses his life for My sake and the gospel's will save it. For what will it profit a man if he gains the whole world, and loses his own soul? Or what will a man give in exchange for his soul? For whoever is ashamed of Me and My words in this adulterous and sinful generation, of him the Son of Man also will be ashamed when He comes in the glory of His Father with the holy angels" (8:34–38).

Mark does not mince words. If someone is going to be a disciple of Jesus he must be willing to defy the emperor, which could lead to his death. Disciples of Jesus are called to imitate Him in His sufferings. Jesus willingly endured the disdain of the people and great suffering at the hands of Roman authorities. There is nothing the Christian could endure at the hands of Nero that Jesus has not already suffered. Remember, almost half of this Gospel focuses squarely on the last week of Jesus' life, His road to the cross, His brutal crucifixion and resurrection. By refusing to worship and follow anyone but Jesus, Christians are making themselves targets for the same kind of suffering Jesus endured. To those who might question the sanity of becoming a Christian in this Roman world, Mark makes sure his readers are counting the cost.

> But watch out for yourselves, for they will deliver you up to councils, and you will be beaten in the synagogues. You will be brought before rulers and kings for My sake, for a testimony to them. And the gospel must first be preached to all the nations. But when they arrest you and deliver you up, do not worry beforehand, or premeditate what you will speak. But whatever is given you in that hour, speak that; for it is not you who speak but the Holy Spirit. Now brother will betray brother to death, and a father his child; and children will rise up against parents and cause them to be put to death. And you will be hated by all for My name's sake. But he who endures to the end shall be saved (Mark 13:9–13).

He records the words of Jesus, "Follow Me," several times (1:17; 8:34; 10:21), but for those doing the "cost / benefit analysis," he also records the following:

So Jesus answered and said, "Assuredly, I say to you, there is no one who has left house or brothers or sisters or father or mother or wife or children or lands, for My sake and the gospel's, who shall not receive a hundredfold now in this time—houses and brothers and sisters and mothers and children and lands, with persecutions—and in the age to come, eternal life. But many who are first will be last, and the last first" (Mark 10:29–31).

Indeed, many received Mark's challenge and welcomed death as a result. The Roman historian Suetonius, referring to Christians as a "sect professing a new and mischievous religious belief," says that Nero "inflicted punishments" upon them. Tacitus is more specific. Here is a quote from his *Annals of Imperial Rome* as he discusses a great fire that destroyed much of the capital city in A.D. 64.

> Yet no human effort, no princely largess nor offerings to the gods could make that infamous rumor disappear that Nero had somehow ordered the fire. Therefore, in order to abolish that rumor, Nero falsely accused and executed with the most exquisite punishments those people called Christians, who were infamous for their abominations. The originator of the name, Christ, was executed as a criminal by the procurator Pontius Pilate during the reign of Tiberius; and though repressed, this destructive superstition erupted again, not only through Judea, which was the origin of this evil, but also through the city of Rome, to which all that is horrible and shameful floods together and is celebrated.

> Therefore, first those were seized who admitted their faith, and then, using the information they provided, a vast multitude were convicted, not so much for the crime of burning the city, but

for hatred of the human race. And perishing they were additionally made into sports: they were killed by dogs by having the hides of beasts attached to them, or they were nailed to crosses or set aflame, and, when the daylight passed away, they were used as nighttime lamps. Nero gave his own gardens for this spectacle and performed a Circus game, in the habit of a charioteer mixing with the plebs or driving about the race-course. Even though they were clearly guilty and merited being made the most recent example of the consequences of crime, people began to pity these sufferers, because they were consumed not for the public good but on account of the fierceness of one man (*The Annals of Imperial Rome*, xv.32–47).

Writing in the midst of this persecution, Mark issues both a challenge to endure the suffering and also an encouragement to those who are currently being persecuted in some way. And by spending so much time on the end of Jesus' life, Mark reveals that Christians are both imitators of the Son of God in His sufferings and

Mark's Gospel gives us the longest account of the story of Herodias's daughter and the beheading of John the Baptist. This painting by Rogier van der Weyden is a detail from the right panel of the *St. John Altarpiece*. Completed around 1460, this work shows the beheading of John, the presentation of the head to Salome and her offering of the head to her mother all in one painting. Notice that van der Weyden clothes all the characters in the styles of his day, a practice often used by artists over the years to help the viewer identify with the biblical event.

that they are vindicated by His glorious resurrection in the end. The Romans killed Him … but they were *not* able to keep Him down. In the end, Jesus wins! Roman believers can take heart in the truth that while they may face brutal and undeserved persecution, in the end they win. Around the same time Mark was ministering to Christians in Rome, Paul wrote a letter to this same group of believers and said the following, "For I consider that the sufferings of this present time are not worthy *to be compared* with the glory which shall be revealed in us" (Rom. 8:18). Is it worth it to suffer for Jesus? Is it worth it to go so far as dying for the faith? Both Mark and Paul respond with a resounding yes! And Paul would write another letter that eventually made its way to Rome in which he explains that because Jesus rose from the dead, we also will rise with new and improved bodies and live a glorious existence in the presence of God for eternity (1 Cor. 15).

To summarize, then, two of the main emphases in Mark are: 1) Jesus as the Son of God, and 2) the nature of true discipleship. A third key theme is the power of the gospel. Mark reveals the power of God in the gospel in at least three areas: healing of disease, victory over evil, and forgiveness of the sinner.

Mark pictures a Jesus who is moving from one miracle to another: Peter's mother-in-law, cleansing the leper, healing the paralytic, etc. In these healings and exorcisms Jesus shows Himself as the Son of God, and as such, He is almighty (see Mark 1:27). At the same time Mark records a significant amount of teaching and preaching, and in the message of Jesus the power of the gospel is revealed. His miracles serve to authenticate the power of His message (Mark 1:38–39).

The ultimate power of the gospel, however, is revealed in the forgiveness of the sinner. By the time the believers in Rome were reading Mark (probably in secret in the catacombs), Peter had already established himself as a significant leader of the church in that part of the world. Remember, it is likely that Mark gleaned most of his material for his Gospel from Peter. Peter would have been highly respected in these circles. Yet Mark records a dark hour in the life of this saint. In Mark 14:66–72 he tells the story of Peter denying Jesus three

The Parable of the Growing Seed (Mark 4:26–29) is found only in Mark's Gospel.

times. The very thing Mark has been challenging his readers to do, namely, stand firm in the face of persecution, be willing to accept the consequences of following Jesus, Peter himself had failed to do. This incredible saint denied the Lord, yet, as the Roman Christians also knew, he was forgiven and restored. For those who had caved in the face of Nero's punishing of the Christians, there is forgiveness; there is restoration.

Finally, another fascinating theme that runs throughout Mark is what scholars call the "messianic secret." On several occasions Jesus demands silence about who He is and what He has done. In chapter one He heals a leper and then demands that he not tell anyone about it (1:44). After preaching to the multitudes, Jesus encounters "unclean spirits" who proclaim that He is the Son of God (how ironic that these demonic beings, many of whom had taken on names like Jupiter, Juno, Minerva, and Neptune, were calling Him God). He then warns them "not to make Him known" (3:12). Jesus brings a twelve-year old girl back to life and "commands them strictly that no one should know it" (5:43). Later, Jesus heals a deaf and mute man, and even though the people disobey Him He commands them to "tell no one" (7:36). He does the same with a blind man (8:26). Afterwards He is speaking with His disciples about His identity and what the people think about it. Upon Peter's confession that He is the Christ, Jesus once again warns them not to let the secret out (8:30). Finally, after the Transfiguration Jesus reminds them not to tell anyone until after the resurrection (9:9).

So why would the Son of God, who came to "seek and save the lost" and "give His life as a ransom for many" and "proclaim the acceptable year of the Lord" (Luke 4:19–20), want to hide His identity? Scholars do not agree, but there are some common ideas. Some say that Jesus commanded demons not to reveal who He was in an effort to disassociate with them. He did not want them proclaiming the truth. Others say that Jesus did this in some healing contexts because He did not want to get bogged down in this aspect of His ministry. Rather, He wanted to devote ample time to preaching and teaching. Finally, some scholars say that Jesus, realizing that His disciples did not fully grasp the gospel, wanted them to wait until they were "ready" to go out and preach. They needed more time to understand the true nature of the gospel before they could be cut loose.

It seems more likely that since the crowds would have desired to exalt Him as King and usher Him to a throne, Jesus commanded silence because He knew that God's perfect and sovereign plan needed time to work out. His earthly ministry was to be three years, no more, no less. Jesus tells His own mother that His "hour has not yet come" at the wedding in Cana (John 2:4). Jesus knew that He was to proceed in stages and according to the timetable of His Father so as not to be overrun by the excesses of the masses. Jesus was declared with power to be the Son of God by His resurrection (Rom. 1:4). It was appropriate that our declarations wait for the Father's declaration. But now that He has been raised, we are told to preach the gospel to every creature.

Mark presents us with an action-packed, fast-moving picture of the life and death of Jesus Christ, the Son of God. He boldly challenges us to faithfully follow the suffering Servant even to death, if necessary. When we read Mark today, how do we apply his Gospel to our lives? First, we must believe that Jesus is the Son of God. All groups who deny this basic tenet of the Christian faith are heretical and should be exposed and condemned. Further, are we willing to embrace and publically ascribe to doctrines that open us to ridicule and persecution? Are we willing to stand up in the face of our modern culture and deny the deity of the gods of our times? Are we willing to preach the truth about pluralism and tolerance, the official gods of our day? Are we willing to proclaim that Jesus is *the* only way to salvation? Most of us will not face a Neronian persecution like the original recipients of Mark's Gospel. However, the message of Mark is the same: stand firm in the midst of persecution, proclaim the truth about Jesus, follow Him in whatever context you find yourself, know that He forgives and restores the sinner and finally, remember, in the end . . . we win.

—*Bruce Etter*

For Further Reading

Carson, D.A., Moo, Douglas, Morris, Leon. *An Introduction to the New Testament.* Grand Rapids: Zondervan, 1992, 89–109.

Elwell, Walter A., Yarbrough, Robert W. *Encountering the New Testament.* Grand Rapids: Baker, 1998, Second Edition, 87–96.

Lane, William L. *The Gospel According to Mark, The New International Commentary on the New Testament,* F.F. Bruce, General Editor. Grand Rapids: Eerdman's, reprint, 1993.

Suetonius. *The Twelve Caesars.* Trans. Robert Graves. New York: Penguin Publishers, 2003, chap. 6.

Tacitus. *The Annals of Imperial Rome.* Trans. Michael Grant. New York: Penguin Publishers, 1996, xv.32–47.

Tenny, Merrill C. *New Testament Survey Revised.* Grand Rapids: Eerdmans, reprint, 1989, 160–172.

Session I: Prelude

A Question to Consider

Have you ever been persecuted for something you believed? How did you respond? How did your persecutor respond? If not, have you ever witnessed someone being persecuted?

From the General Information above answer the following questions:

1. What two literary features make the Gospel of Mark move along at a brisk pace and give the sense of being right there in the action?
2. Name some things we know about the writer of this Gospel.
3. What does the word synoptic mean? What is the "Synoptic Problem?"
4. From whom do scholars think Mark got much of the material he used to write his Gospel account? Where was Mark when he wrote the book, and whom is he addressing?
5. Who was the Roman emperor when Mark wrote his Gospel? Why is this significant?
6. What were some of the charges leveled at Christians in the first century?
7. According to the Roman historian Tacitus, what did Nero do to Christians?
8. What is the "messianic secret?"
9. What are the two most important themes of the Gospel of Mark?

Reading Assignment:
Mark 1–8

Section II: Discussion
Mark 1–8

A Question to Consider

What does it mean to be a true follower of Jesus Christ?

Discuss or list short answers to the following questions:

Text Analysis

1. What accompanies Jesus' command to follow Him in Mark 1:17? Why do you think Mark includes this detail?
2. What is Levi doing when Jesus approaches him and commands him to follow Him (Mark 2:13–14)? Why do you think Mark mentions this fact?

3. Read Mark 8:34–38. Jesus lists two specific commands before the command to follow Him. What are they? What do you think these commands mean?
4. What do you think Jesus means by "gains the whole world" (Mark 8:36)? Can you think of any examples of individuals in Scripture who "gained the world" but "lost their souls"?
5. According to Mark 8:38, what is also involved in following Jesus? What do you think this has to do with being a true follower of Christ?

Cultural Analysis

1. Who are the people that have the greatest "following" in our culture? Why?
2. What religious leaders have the greatest following in our culture? Why?
3. What is our culture's view of the individual who follows Christ and Him alone? What is behind this thinking?

Biblical Analysis

1. Read Romans 12. After eleven chapters of sublime theology, Paul begins a discussion of what it means practically to be a follower of Jesus Christ. What are some commands in this chapter that point to the heart and soul of being a follower of Jesus?
2. How does Jesus summarize the Christian life in Mark 12:28–31? What are the "Two Tables of the Law?" How do the Ten Commandments relate to what it means to be a true follower of Jesus Christ?

Summa

Write an essay or discuss this question, integrating what you have learned from the material above.

What does it mean to be a true follower of Jesus Christ?

Reading Assignment:
None

Session III: Recitation
Mark 1–8

Comprehension Questions

Answer the following questions for factual recall:

1. What is the first event Mark records?
2. Where does Jesus go after His baptism? What happens there?

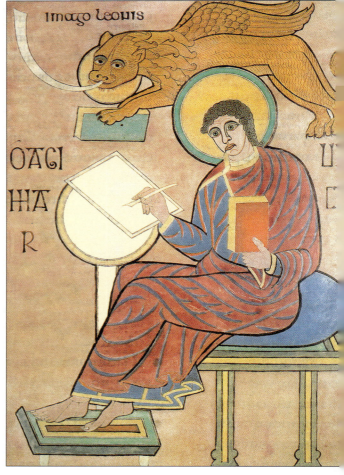

Sitting beneath the winged lion that symbolizes him, Mark the Evangelist writes his Gospel.

3. Name some of the miracles Jesus works early in His ministry.
4. On what day of the week does Jesus make a point of doing some of His healings?
5. What does Jesus say He is trying to communicate by doing so?
6. What does Jesus say is the "unpardonable sin?"
7. What does Jesus say is the reason He tells parables?
8. What does the demon call Jesus while being cast out of the man in the country of the Gadarenes?
9. Who are the only three individuals Jesus permitted to accompany Him as He healed the daughter of the ruler of the synagogue?
10. What happens to John the Baptist?
11. What does Jesus predict in Mark 8:31–33? Jesus predicts His own death.

The next session will be a student-led discussion. Students will be creating their own questions concerning the issue of the session. Students should create three Text Analysis Questions, two Cultural Analysis questions, and two Biblical Analysis questions. For more detailed instructions, please see the chapter on the *Iliad,* Session III.

Issue

Think of famous Christians from the past. Which ones do you think are the "greatest"? Why? Think of well-known Christians in our day. Which ones do you think are the greatest? Why? What about ordinary people you know? Which believers are the greatest and why?

READING ASSIGNMENT:
Mark 9–16

SESSION IV: STUDENT-LED DISCUSSION
Mark 9–16

A Question to Consider

Think of famous Christians from the past. Which ones do you think are the "greatest"? Why? Think of well-known Christians in our day. Which ones do you think are the greatest? Why? What about ordinary people you know? Which believers are the greatest and why?

Students should read and consider the example questions below that are connected to the Question to Consider above. Last session's assignment was to prepare three questions and answers for the Text Analysis section and two additional questions and answers for both the Cultural and Biblical Analysis sections below.

Text Analysis

Example: Jesus perceives that His disciples had been debating a certain issue as they traveled to Capernaum. What was the debate topic that day, and what did Jesus have to say about it? See Mark 9.

Answer: His disciples were actually embarrassed by the fact that they had been debating who was the "greatest." He responds and explains true greatness to them (Mark 9).

Cultural Analysis

Example: What generally makes someone "great" in our culture? Why?

Answer: Clearly, our culture sees greatness as a successful career in sports or in some field in which you have money, power, and prestige. It is usually measured in monetary gain.

Other cultural issues to consider: Think of people who are featured in magazines and those who receive special awards. Why do we think they are great? What accomplishments make them great?

Biblical Analysis

Example: What individuals in Scripture are considered to be truly great? What about them does God praise as great?

Answer: True greatness in Scripture is not, contrary to what some may think, the person who sins the least. David was considered great, but it was because he was humble and quick to confess his sins when confronted with them. The truly great person in Scripture is the one who is a humble servant (Joshua, Ruth, Samuel, and Josiah are a few examples).

Other Scriptures to consider: 1 Samuel 16; Ruth; John 13.

SUMMA

Write an essay or discuss this question, integrating what you have learned from the material above.
What constitutes true greatness?

SESSION V: RESEARCH ACTIVITY
Mark 16:9–20

Canonicity

Open up any version of the Bible except the King James Version or the New King James Version and read Mark 16. Then read the same chapter in the King James or New King James. What do you notice? If you did not notice a tremendous difference in the reading of these two different versions you might want to read it again.

Do some research. Why is there such a radical difference in the two translations of Mark 16? What do scholars think about this issue? What do you think? Here are some sources you can consult:

Carson, D.A., Moo, Douglas, Morris, Leon. *An Introduction to the New Testament.* Grand Rapids: Zondervan, 1992, 102–104.

Links 1 and 2 for this chapter at www.VeritasPress.com/Omnilinks.

Scholars do not agree as to whether or not Mark 16:9–20 was a part of the original. Some earlier manuscripts do not contain these verses, but the majority of manuscripts do contain them. The debate is over whether the earlier manuscripts should be trusted because they are earlier (closer to the actual time of writing) or if the fact that the majority of manuscripts contain the verses, this should lead us to include them (because, as they say, majority rules!). The earlier manuscripts were compiled into a single manuscript and became the basis for one particular Greek New Testament. The majority texts, however, came together into a single Greek text that has become the basis for the King James Version. It is an ongoing debate and not likely to be settled any time soon.

The question that arises is whether or not there are any significant issues here that would change our theology in any way. The answer to that questions is "no." The only issues that generally come up in the discussion are those which arise from verses 17–19. After the Great Commission Jesus says, "And these signs will follow those who believe: In My name they will cast out demons; they will speak with new tongues; they will take up serpents; and if they drink anything deadly, it will by no means hurt them; they will lay hands on the sick, and they will recover." While some have used these verses as proof that Christians should still be doing these things today, it is clear that God actually empowered individuals to do these things in New Testament times.

A twelfth-century fresco of Christ, the Son of God, seated as King over all.

OPTIONAL SESSION: RECITATION
Mark 9–16

Comprehension Questions

Answer the following questions for factual recall:

1. Who was with Jesus as He was transfigured?
2. Who came to Jesus testing Him concerning His views on marriage and divorce?
3. What did Jesus tell the Rich Young Ruler to do?
4. In chapter 10 Jesus predicts what event for the third time?
5. After entering Jerusalem upon a colt, what does Jesus do in the Temple?
6. What religious group questioned Jesus about the doctrine of the resurrection?
7. Jesus predicts the destruction of what great edifice?
8. How is Jesus anointed for burial before He dies? How did the people around Him respond?
9. What were the disciples doing as Jesus was praying in the Garden of Gethsemane?
10. What did Peter do once he realized the prophecy that he would deny Jesus came true?
11. Who brought spices to Jesus' tomb?

Philippians and Colossians

"Be perfect, as your Father in heaven is perfect," Jesus tells His disciples in Matthew 5:48. When we hear that, we usually cringe, thinking that Jesus is being totally unreasonable. How can we be perfect? Don't we still sin? Jesus' demands are too hard for us, and we might decide that Jesus doesn't really mean what He says.

Jesus does mean what He says, but we often misunderstand it. In the Bible, the word "perfect" doesn't usually mean "without sin." Instead, it means "mature." Jacob was a "perfect" man (Gen. 27:25), and so was Job (Job 1:8). Neither one was sinless, but they were both "complete." They were both "grown-ups."

That is what the Bible is all about—showing us how to be "perfect," to be "grown-ups." Adam was a baby in the Garden of Eden, as naked as a newborn. God planned for him to grow up and put on a crown and a royal robe of glory. But Adam acted just like a baby, grabbing the food he wasn't supposed to have, and so God put him out of the Garden. When Jesus came, though, He came to bring us to maturity. Jesus came make us "perfect"—all grown up.

"And seeing the multitudes, He went up on a mountain, and when He was seated His disciples came to Him. Then He opened His mouth and taught them . . ." Notice the clever way Judas Iscariot is identified in this fresco of *The Sermon on the Mount* by Fra Angelico (c.1400–1455).

378 OMNIBUS IV

Children are often eager to grow up. "I can't wait until I can boss people around," says my five-year-old daughter. But being an adult is hard. Adults have responsibilities and challenges that children don't have. Because of this, many adults would prefer to be children. Many adults, in fact, act like children—using their money to buy very expensive toys, following their whims and desires, and competing with others for attention and approval.

Paul had to deal with Christians who wanted to become children again. That's what the letter to the Galatians is all about. In Galatians 4:1–11, he says that the Jews in the Old Testament were really God's sons, the heirs of everything. But while they were young, God treated them like slaves. He gave them rigid laws and put them under babysitters ("guardians and managers") until they were grown up enough to receive their inheritance. That happens in the "fullness of time," when God sends His Son Jesus and His Holy Spirit, so that Jews and Gentiles can become full-grown sons.

But the whole letter is about how the Galatians want to go back to the old covenant, back to childhood. Paul barely controls his anger and surprise at the foolish Galatians, who seem "bewitched" (Gal. 3:1–5). How could any adult want to go back to wearing diapers and eating baby food? But that's what the Galatians want.

The Philippians and Colossians are tempted by the same things, and Paul writes to both churches to urge them to grow up, to become "perfect." Paul is confident that God will complete and perfect His work in the Philippians (Phil. 1:6), and he actually describes the Philippians as "perfect" (3:15). Similarly, Paul hopes that the Colossians will be able to stand "perfect and fully assured in the will of God" (Col. 4:12).

Just like Jesus, Paul wants the churches to be perfect as the Father in heaven is perfect. But what does perfection look like? What does it mean to be grown up? That's what Paul's letters show us.

GENERAL INFORMATION

Author and Context

Paul came through Philippi on one of his missionary journeys and, as usual, got into trouble.

Founded by Philip of Macedon, Philippi became world-famous as the site of the battle in which Antony and Octavian triumphed over Brutus and Cassius. When Octavian later defeated Antony at Actium in 31 B.C., he rebuilt Philippi, established a military base, moved in Roman soldiers, and made it a colony. Philippi was brought under the *jus Italicum,* a legal status equal to the legal status of cities in Italy. It was the highest standing a city in the Roman provinces could get.

When he was in the city, Paul got a glimpse of the Philippians' pride in their standing as a Roman colony. Paul and Silas exorcized a girl who was being used as a fortune-teller, and as a result her owners became enraged and brought Paul before the magistrates. Their charges are revealing: Paul and Silas, they said, were "throwing our city into confusion" by encouraging "customs (*ethe*) which it is not lawful for us to accept or to observe, being Romans" (Acts 16:20–21). Paul and Silas's teaching was seen as a threat to Philippi's Roman identity and way of life, and he promptly got plopped into a Philippian jail, which, again as usual, couldn't hold him (Acts 16:23–40). As in Thessalonica (Acts 17:1–9), the apostles were seen as subversives, both of the city and the empire.

By the time Paul wrote the letter to the Philippians, there were serious conflicts inside the church. After a long introduction, his first exhortation is to "conduct yourselves in a manner worthy of the gospel," which means working "with one mind" (Phil. 1:27) with "one purpose" (2:20). The most famous passage of Philippians, Paul's "song" about the humility of Jesus, follows immediately from this: the church becomes united in mind and purpose by following the example of Jesus' humility (2:3–11). Paul emphasizes unity because the church is not unified. All this is vague until chapter 4, when Paul names two women, Euodia and Syntyche, and urges them to "live in harmony in the Lord" (4:2). Perhaps others were bickering too, but it doesn't take a mob to fill a church with turmoil. Two angry women, or men, are plenty.

What was causing these divisions? Most likely, the Philippians were fighting among themselves because they were under attack from outsiders. The Philippians are "partners" in the gospel with him (1:5, 7) because they have sent gifts to help him (4:10–16). But they also share in the gospel by sharing in the persecution that Paul suffers. The ones attacking them are the unbelieving Jews. In chapter 3, Paul spends a lot of time reminding the Philippians of his own background as a Jew (3:4–11). He does this as part of a warning to "beware of the dogs, beware of the evil doers, beware of the false circumcision" (3:2). With each of these words, Paul turns a Jewish insult against the unbelieving Jews. Jews regarded Gentiles as "dogs" (see Matthew 7:6; 15:26–27); Paul calls them dogs. Jews claimed to be the circumcised sons of Abraham, but Paul describes their circumcision as a form of mutilation. Jews dismissed others as workers of evil, but Paul says that these Jews do evil. The Philippians Christians, on the other hand, are the "true circumcision," not workers of evil but people who "worship in the Spirit of God and glory in Christ Jesus" (3:3).

Philippians and Colossians 379

The situation in Philippi is the same as it is in many of the early churches: Jews, and later Gentile Romans, attack the church, putting pressure on the members of the church, some of whom want to escape persecution by compromising or turning away from Jesus. This creates conflict within the church. Paul warns the Philippians that some are "enemies of the cross of Christ" (3:18). This doesn't just mean that they reject the gospel of Jesus. It means they turn from Jesus because it's too hard to take up a cross and follow Him.

From this, we get a hint about what Paul means by "maturity." To be mature is to share in the work of the gospel, and to bear the cross that comes with that work. To be mature is to unite with one mind and purpose in proclaiming and serving Jesus.

While Paul was familiar with the Philippians, and knew them by name, he never visited the small town of Colossae, of which we know very little. The Colossians received the gospel from one of Paul's "fellow slaves," Epaphras (Col. 1:7). Still, Paul knew something about the struggles and problems of the church in Colossae. He warned them not to be captured by "philosophy and empty deception" (2:8) and reminded them that "self-abasement and worship of angels" only looked impressive, but are merely "self-made religion" (2:18, 23).

While it is obvious that Paul is dealing with some heresy or false teaching in Colossians, it is not so obvious what this false teaching was. Some have seen it as a form of gnosticism. Gnostics deny that creation comes from God and that it is good. Material reality is gross, and no self-respecting God is going to get Himself mucked up by making a world of dust and mud or human beings made of meat and blood. According to gnostics, the true God got somebody else to do His dirty work for him. Paul says that the false teachers

The Conversion of Paul by Girolamo Francesco Maria Mazzola (1503–1540), also known as Parmigianino

are imposing commands such as "Do not handle, do not taste, do not touch" (2:21), and that could be a sign that they hated matter.

More likely, though, Paul is dealing with false teachers who are urging the Colossians to adopt a Jewish way of life. Such teachers, known as "Judaizers" (see Galatians 2:14, which uses the Greek word *joudaizein*), claimed that Gentile Christians had to be circumcised, keep the Jewish Sabbath, follow the dietary laws of the Old Testament, and avoid contact with uncleanness if they wanted to be fully Christian. For reasons we will explore below, Paul sharply disagreed, but the Judaizers remained a recurrent headache for the apostle, seducing not only the Galatians, but also some Christians in Rome and elsewhere. The Colossians were also seduced. The false teachers were urging them to keep festivals and Sabbaths (2:16), pay reverence to the angels who delivered the law (2:18; see Acts 7:53; Galatians 3:19; Hebrews 2:1–4), and keep the Old Testament regulations about touching unclean things and tasting unclean food (2:21).

Two words that Paul uses support this. In 2:8, he warns the Colossians to resist being taken captive by these "philosophers," and he uses a rare verb, *sylagogein*. N.T. Wright has said that the word makes a "pun with the word *synagogue*." Paul's warning is not just about those who would take captive, but also about the temptation to lapse back into an Old Covenant way of life. He has earlier described the Colossians' conversion as a "new exodus" (1:13–14), and he urges them not to return to "Egypt"—that is, the Egypt that Judaism had become. The other word is translated as "elementary principles" (stoicheia in 2:8, 20). Elsewhere, Paul uses this word to describe the regulations of the Old Covenant (Gal. 4:1–11), and in Colossians he uses it when talking about the Mosaic law's rules about tasting and touching unclean foods and objects (2:20–21).

Paul writes both Philippians and Colossians from prison (Phil. 1:7; Col. 4:18). Paul was in and out of prison many times, and we can't be sure which prison he was in when he wrote these letters. Most likely, though, he wrote during the series of imprisonments described in the last chapters of Acts, when he is arrested in Jerusalem, appeals to Caesar, and is transported to Rome. Whatever prison he writes from, it's important to see that Paul's sufferings as an apostle are not random accidents. They are part of his calling; his sufferings don't disqualify him from being an apostle, but are instead his apostolic

credentials (see 2 Corinthians 11:16–33). In Colossians 1:24, he makes the strange claim that his sufferings for the sake of the Colossians "fill up what is lacking in Christ's affliction." He doesn't mean that Jesus' death was inadequate, or that his own work saves anyone (see 1 Corinthians 1:13). He means that when he suffers, he suffers in union with Jesus, and therefore his sufferings both display the gospel he preaches and also bring that gospel more fully into effect. As he tells the Philippians, his imprisonment emboldens other believers (Phil. 1:14). When people hear Paul, they hear him talking about the cross of Jesus, and when they see Paul suffering, they see that Paul has taken up his cross to follow his Lord.

Like the Philippians, the Colossians need to grow up, or better, to recognize that in Christ they are already grown up. They don't need circumcision, or laws about food and purity, to be mature. They have all they need in Christ, and Paul's main fear is that, now that they have come to maturity, they will be tempted to start playing with toys again.

Significance

As we will see below, both Philippians and Colossians include passages that describe Jesus—His nature and His work. These passages were crucial in the early centuries of the church, as faithful Christians struggled against heretics. Along with the opening chapters of John's Gospel, Philippians 2:2–6 and Colossians 1:15–22 and 2:9–10 revealed to the early Christians that the crucified and risen Jesus was God in human flesh.

After Constantine's conversion, Colossians quickly became one of the key biblical books to defend the Christian empire. From Colossians, the church historian Eusebius drew the insight that Jesus is the ruler of all things, and he added that the emperor, Constantine, was the earthly image of the heavenly King. Jesus overcomes principalities and powers (Col. 1:16, 20; 2:15), and so did Constantine. Jesus governs a people that includes Jews, Greeks, barbarians, Scythians, slaves, and freemen (Col. 3:11), and so did Constantine. Jesus is the great "peacemaker" (Col. 1:20), and the very same Greek term was used to describe the *pax Romana*, the Roman peace that Augustus established and Constantine renewed.

In modern times, Philippians 2:7 has been particularly important in the development of the theory of *kenosis*. Paul uses the verb form of *kenosis* to describe Jesus' "emptying," and some modern theologians have argued that

"Christ Jesus, who, being in the form of God, did not consider it robbery to be equal with God, but made Himself of no reputation, taking the form of a bondservant, and coming in the likeness of men. And being found in appearance as a man, He humbled Himself and became obedient to the point of death, even the death of the cross. Therefore God also has highly exalted Him and given Him the name which is above every name . . ." —Philippians 2:6–9

Philippians and Colossians 381

this means that the Son "emptied" Himself of His divine attributes when He took on flesh—being all-powerful before He became man and afterward not, and present everywhere before the Incarnation and afterward not. This is not what Paul was talking about, and the kenotic idea of the Incarnation is a heresy. As the church fathers said, the Son "added" humanity to His divine nature, but did not cease to be divine.

Another passage of Philippians has been widely used in Christian discussions of art, literature, and culture. Toward the end of the letter, Paul urges the Philippians to think on things that are true, honorable, right, pure, lovely, and excellent (4:8). This certainly includes "Christian" things like the Bible, theology, heroes of the faith, the Lord's Supper, and so on. But Paul says that we should devote ourselves to "whatever" has these qualities. If a painting is lovely, Paul encourages us to muse on it, even if it is not about a Christian theme. Playing a sport with "excellence" is something Paul encourages. If a novel or a history book is "true," we should love it, because it will somehow reveal Jesus, who is the Truth behind every truth.

Finally, Philippians is notable for its emphasis on joy. Paul, remember, is writing from prison, a situation that most of us would find deeply depressing. But from the first verses to the end, he can't stop expressing his joy. He offers his prayers "with joy" (1:4), and he is convinced that he will continue to encourage joy in the Philippians (1:25). Even when people preach the gospel for bad reasons, he rejoices that the gospel is preached (1:18). As the letter closes, he tells the Philippians to "Rejoice in the Lord always," and in case they didn't get the point, he repeats it: "Again I say, rejoice" (4:4). By rejoicing, they share in Paul's own joy (4:10), a joy that he has whether he is full or empty, hungry or satisfied, imprisoned or free (4:11–12).

Artistic Design

Paul begins Philippians with a long personal introduction. He rejoices in the Philippians' share in the gospel and describes his prayers for them (1:3–18), and then he tells them about his own situation and plans (1:18–26). Only then does he launch into the main point of the letter. Philippians 1:27–30 raises a number of concerns that run through to the end of chapter 3. Paul repeats some of the same words at the end of chapter 3 and the beginning of chapter 4 that he uses at the end of chapter 1. The Greek verb translated as "conduct yourself" (1:27) is *politeuo,* and the word for "commonwealth" in 3:20 is *politeuma.* Both words come from the Greek word for "city," *polis.* In 1:27, he tells the Philippians to "stand firm" and repeats that exhortation in 4:1. "Striving together" appears in both 1:27 and 4:3. In between these two sections, Paul develops his themes of unity, humility, and harmony. As he often does in his letters, Paul summarizes his main themes (1:27–30), develops them (2:1–3:16), and then summarizes them again (3:17–4:3).

In Colossians, Paul does something similar. As in Philippians, the key exhortation is about the way Christians are to "walk" (2:6), and Paul then develops that theme by reminding the Colossians that they share in Christ's death (2:12) and exaltation (3:1–4). Because of the Cross, they are dead to the "elementary principles of the world" (2:8, 20); because of the Resurrection, they are "hid with Christ in God" (3:4) and therefore must "set your mind on things above" (3:2). As in Ephesians, Paul gives specific exhortations to wives, husband, children, masters, and slaves, all of which are to walk according to the gospel. Finally, he returns to the original theme in 4:5: "Walk with wisdom toward outsiders, making the most of the opportunity."

Philippians is also organized in a chiastic order:

CHIASTIC ORDER OF PHILIPPIANS
A. Greetings & grace (1:1–2)
  B. Thanksgiving for their partnership (1:3–8)
    C. Prayer for love to abound in discernment (1:9–11): "approve what is valuable"
      D. Paul's situation: advance in spite of ill-will (1:12–18a): rejoice.
        E. Paul's expectation & plans (1:18b–26)
          F. Conduct: unity (1:27–30)
            G. Having the "in Christ Jesus" thinking (2:1–11)
          F'. Conduct: unity (2:12–18)
        E'. Paul's plans: send Timothy & Epaphroditus (2:19–30)
      D'. Enemies of the gospel (3:1–4:4): "rejoice in the Lord."
    C'. Prayer & discernment (4:5–9): "think on these things"
  B'. Their partnership (4:10–20)
A'. Greetings and grace (4:21–23)[1]

Worldview
Fullness of the Times

What does Paul write about in general? Obviously, he writes about Jesus. But what does he say about Jesus? To grasp the shape of Paul's gospel in general, we need to grasp the meaning of some basic concepts. One is "eschatology," and another is "covenant."

Let's start with covenant. Paul does not use the word very often, but it is a basic part of his belief and preaching. The Hebrew Bible Paul studied as a Pharisee began with Creation. Yahweh created the heavens and the earth and made a good and glorious world. He created man to rule the world under Him as His prince and to turn the glorious creation into something even more glorious. Almost immediately, the creation was spoiled by the sin of Adam, then by Cain's murder of Abel, then by the sins of the sons of God. Even after the Lord destroyed and remade the world in the Flood, sin continued to spread and dominate God's good creation. At Babel, the nations banded together in rebellion against their Maker, and Yahweh scattered them. Instead of glorifying creation, sinful human beings ruined it.

Yet Yahweh never gave up on creation or on humanity. Immediately after He scattered the nations at Babel, He called Abram and made him a promise: In him all the nations of the earth would be blessed, and the damage done at Babel would be

"But when the fullness of the time had come, God sent forth His Son, born of a woman, born under the law, to redeem those who were under the law, that we might receive the adoption as sons" (Gal. 4:4–5). Raphael's (1483–1520) *The Small Cowper Madonna* is one of the seventeen images of the Virgin and Child that survive from the years Raphael was in Florence.

reversed. And Yahweh backed up His promise by taking an oath. This is the covenant that shaped the hopes of Israel for centuries: Yahweh, the Creator God, was not going to leave His creation to rot; He was going to fix it through Abram's descendants.

From the time he met Jesus on the road to Damascus, Paul's message was that this promise to Abram has been fulfilled. The Seed of Abram has come, and His name is Jesus. Jesus is the one who is putting the world back together again, and He's doing it through His death and resurrection. This is what *eschatology* means. *Eschatology* comes from a Greek word meaning "end," and it is about the end of things. According to Paul's gospel, what Israel had always hoped for, the *end* that they awaited from the moment Yahweh spoke to Abram in Haran, has already come, in the middle of time, through Jesus. Jesus is the Last Adam, making a new humanity out of the old; He is the true Israel, forming a new people of God where the old distinctions of Jew and Gentile no longer matter; He is the "firstborn of creation" who is recreating all things. All things are being made new, now, in fulfillment of the covenant Yahweh made with Abram. Through Jesus, God has started fixing the creation. God is not just fixing what's broken—He's also raising His people to full maturity. Through Jesus, the first adult in human history, he is "perfecting" His people.

That is Paul's message in all his letters, including Philippians and Colossians. In Philippians, it focuses on the fact that Jesus has been proclaimed Lord. According to Paul, Jesus is not like the first Adam. The first Adam seized what was not his, because he wanted to become God. He thought "equality with God a thing to be grasped" (Phil. 2:6). Jesus doesn't. Instead, Jesus willingly took a lower position, willingly became obedient, and willingly gave Himself to death on a cross (2:6–8). Because of His obedient humility, Jesus is exalted in a way that Adam never was. He is raised up and exalted and given the title "Lord" (2:8–10). "Lord" here does not mean "God." To say that Jesus is "Lord" is to say that He has authority; He is the King of all, the master of creation.

And that's good news—very, very good news. One of the great problems from the beginning of creation was that the most brutal men often had the most authority and power. Lamech boasted of his cruelty and vengefulness (Gen. 4:23–24), and down through the centuries there have been Lamechs in every nation under heaven. Israel was little better. Alongside the Davids and the Hezekiahs and the Josiahs were the Ahabs and the Manassehs who filled the land with innocent blood. Paul announces, though, that this has all changed. Tyrants are still around, but they are now running scared. There is another King, another Lord, and His name is Jesus. By exalting Jesus to His right hand, the Father has begun to remake the world, to renovate the human race.

Colossians makes many of the same points in different terms. According to Paul, Jesus is the creator of everything in heaven and earth, including "thrones or dominions or rulers or authorities" (Col. 1:16). These are angelic powers that stood behind the human rulers of the ancient world (see Deuteronomy 32:8; Daniel 10:13, 20). All these were from and for Jesus (1:16), but they did not all submit to Him. Through His death and resurrection, Jesus has reconciled all things in heaven and on earth to Himself, including the thrones and dominions and rulers (1:20). Alluding to the Roman practice of parading defeated kings through the streets of Rome, Paul says that Jesus has "disarmed the rulers and authorities and made a public display of them, having triumphed over them" (2:15). By defeating the powers, Jesus has been made Lord.

Earlier in Colossians, Paul expressed a similar point in a somewhat different way. He begins the letter with a prayer of thanksgiving, and this comes to a climax with thanks to the Father for giving us an inheritance with the saints (1:12). How do we come into that inheritance? Paul says that we have been translated from one kingdom to another. We have been delivered from the domain of darkness and brought into the kingdom of the Son, where God forgives our sins (1:13–14). This means that being saved, for Paul, means coming into the realm of the Lord Jesus, coming under His rule. This is true life, and the people who have been translated from darkness to light make up the new human race, the new creation.

Jesus

Covenant and eschatology provide the framework of Paul's gospel. God made a covenant with Abram, promising to put creation right in the end; God has fulfilled that promise. But this framework makes sense only because of what's at the center of it all. The center is Jesus.

We've already seen that Paul teaches in Philippians 2 that Jesus is Lord. But that is not all he says about Jesus. According to verse 6, Jesus "existed in the form of God." Through the centuries, most Bible students have thought that Paul is talking about the eternal Son. "Form" here doesn't mean simply a shape or an outline. In the sense in which Paul uses the word, the Son was everything the Father was. In Plato's thought, the "form" of the good is not just an outline of the good; it is the fullness of all that is good. Jesus is the "form of God" in that sense. On this reading, being in the "form of God" is the same as being "equal to God" (v. 6).

Most likely, this is not the focus of Paul's exhortation. The whole section is about the mindset of Christ Jesus (v. 5), the incarnate Son of the Father. The passage assumes the incarnation of the Son in human flesh, and is describing how *Jesus* obeyed His Father and became obedient to death on the cross. When Paul says that Jesus is in the "form of God," he is saying that Jesus is the new Adam, who was made in the image of God. Unlike Adam, however, He did not grasp for equality with God, but emptied Himself out in death (see Isaiah 53:12: "he poured out his soul in death"). Paul is not saying, "Imitate the Son who humbled Himself when He became human." He is saying, "Imitate the incarnate Son who humbled Himself on the cross."

Even on this reading, though, Paul tells us that Jesus is eternal God and Lord. But that revelation comes at the end of the story, not at the beginning. Paul begins with the incarnate Son, but then describes the incarnate Son, and in doing so quotes from Isaiah 45:22–23:

> Turn to Me and be saved, all the ends of the earth; for I am God, and there is no other. I have sworn by Myself, the word has gone forth from My mouth in righteousness and will not turn back, that to Me every knee will bow, every tongue will swear allegiance.

Yahweh here says that He alone is God, and that He alone has glory and authority. Yet Paul quotes the last part of this passage and applies it to Jesus. Paul is doing one of two things: Either he is committing blasphemy by making a mere man equal to God, or he is confessing that Jesus is Himself Yahweh in the form of a servant, giving Himself for His people on the cross.

N.T. Wright explains the meaning of the exaltation of the Son (Phil. 2):

> It is the affirmation, by God the Father, that the incarnation and death of Jesus really was the revelation of the divine love in action. In giving to Jesus the title *kurios* [Lord] and in granting him a share in that glory which, according to Isaiah, no one other than Israel's God is allowed to share, God the Father is as it were endorsing that interpretation of divine equality which, according to v. 6, the Son adopted. Christ's exaltation and divine honor are the public recognition that what was accomplished in his obedience and death was the outworking of the very character of God, the revelation of divine love.[2]

Jesus shows us what it means to be a completely mature man. Through Jesus, Christians become mature when they share in Jesus' exaltation, becoming new Adams, lords of the creation.

One other point is worth making before turning to what Paul says about Jesus in Colossians. According to most translations, Paul introduces his song to Jesus by saying "although he existed in the form of God . . . He humbled Himself" (vs. 6, 8). This implies that Jesus humbles Himself *in spite of the fact that* ("although") He is in the form of God. Humility appears to be a *contradiction* of God's nature. The Greek is not nearly so definite. It says, "existing in the form of God . . . He humbled Himself." The word "although" is not in the Greek, and the Greek is better translated "*because* He existed in the form of God . . . He humbled Himself." Humility is not a contradiction of God's character—it *is* God's character. In His humble service for His people, Jesus reveals that God is not a pompous lecher like Baal, Zeus, or Jupiter. He is not a splendidly isolated power like Allah. He is not the demanding, testy, proud God that many Christians, in spite of the Bible, believe in. Jesus shows the face of the Father; if you have seen Jesus, you've seen God. And Jesus is meek, humble, gentle, kind, good, generous, merciful, and compassionate. That is our God, the God who humbles Himself for us.

Our God humbles Himself for us because He is a God who exists in *eternal* humility. The Son eternally bows before the Father, glorifying Him in the Spirit; the Father eternally shines the light of His pleasure upon His Son, glorifying Him in the same Spirit. The Father doesn't compete with the Son to see who can get the greatest honor, nor the Son with the Father. Each exalts the other, each serves the other, each humbles himself to lift up the other. As Paul says, "let this mind be in you, which was also in Christ Jesus."

This, too, is a mark of true maturity, even though it looks like the opposite. Adults sometimes think that being humble, preferring others ahead of ourselves, is foolish and childish. Paul thinks differently. He looks at Jesus, the image of the invisible God, and he sees what it means to be perfect, as the Father is perfect. He recognizes that being humble as a child is part of true adulthood.

Paul's Christological "poem" in Colossians 1:15–20 makes some of the same points as Philippians 2. The passage has a chiastic order:

A. Firstborn of creation; creator of heaven and earth, vs. 15–16
  B. Who is before all things, v. 17
  B'. Who is head of the church, v. 18a
A'. Firstborn from the dead; reconciler of heaven and earth, vs. 18b–20

The poem begins with Jesus as firstborn of creation, and ends with Him as firstborn from the dead; it begins with saying that He has created everything in heaven and earth, and ends with saying that He has reconciled everything in heaven and on earth. At the center, we learn that this Jesus, who was Creator and has died and risen, is the preeminent one in "all things" and is the head of the church. The structure by itself shows that Jesus is both Creator and re-Creator. He is the one who made all things and the one for whom all things were made. Everything exists from the Father for His benefit.

Paul says that Jesus is the image of the invisible God (v. 15). In context, Paul is talking about the eternal nature of the Son, not about the Son as the incarnate God-man, Jesus. Eternally, the Son is the image of the Father, just as a human son has all the qualities of his father. Clearly, Paul is also using language the Bible uses to describe the character of human nature. Human beings are made in the image of God, but above and beyond the human image, the Father has an eternal image in the Son. Because the Son is eternally the "image" of the Father, it is appropriate that He becomes the Last Adam to renew the image of God in man.

Twice here Paul calls Jesus the "firstborn." What does that mean? It seems strange that Paul would use this language, since it seems to imply that Jesus was produced by the Father—born of Him. The second use, "firstborn from the dead," does have the connotation of being given birth. Jesus was in the grave and emerged from it, as a child emerges from the womb. And the first also hints at this. In John's Gospel, Jesus is the "only-begotten" Word of the Father, and here Jesus is the firstborn of all creation, the firstborn before all creation, the One who is begotten of the Father before all worlds, light of light, very God of very God, begotten not made.

In Scripture, the word "firstborn" includes the idea of birth, but includes other connotations as well. The first use of the phrase in the Bible refers to Abel's righteous offering (Gen. 4:4). While Cain brings fruits and vegetables to the altar, Abel brings a righteous offering of "firstborn and their fat."

Elsewhere in the Old Testament, too, the "firstborn" is the substitutionary sacrifice. The Passover lamb in Egypt dies in the place of the "firstborn" of Israel, the firstborn of every animal and woman in Israel belonged to Yahweh as a result, and the Levites then substituted for the firstborn. Jesus is the firstborn in the sense that He is sent to be the Passover, to initiate the new exodus—from darkness to light, from the old creation to the new. Yahweh claims the firstborn. They are his (Ex. 34:19–20; Num. 3:13; Deut. 15:19). Yahweh says that everyone that opens the womb belongs to Him. Jesus is the firstborn of creation, and so belongs wholly to the Father; He is the firstborn from the dead, opening the womb of the grave, and so also belongs to the Father.

This has heightened significance because the firstborn of Israel stands in the place of Israel herself. When Yahweh comes to Pharaoh to tell him to release Israel, he identifies Israel as his "son," his "firstborn" (Ex. 4:23). Passover is a matter of multiple substitutions: Yahweh kills Pharaoh's firstborn, the firstborn of Egypt, in retribution for Pharaoh's slaughter of Israel's sons; Yahweh instructs Israel to slaughter lambs and spread blood to save their own firstborn; and in saving the firstborn of Israel, Yahweh is also

N.T. Wright is the Bishop of Durham in the Church of England. His supporters say that he is one of the world's foremost New Testament scholars and an expert in the times and beliefs of first century Palestine. His teaching is steeped with biblical history and orthodoxy in a time of rampant apostasy; and he has taken firm stands against theological liberalism, abortion, euthanasia, and the sanctioning of homosexual practice. However, his opponents charge him with abandoning crucial doctrines and equivocating in his use of theological terms in an attempt to appear to endorse these doctrines while actually refuting them.

saving Israel. Jesus as the firstborn is also the true Israel.

The firstborn in Scripture is also the chief heir and represents the future of the family. According to the inheritance laws of Deuteronomy, the firstborn son received an inheritance double that of his siblings (21:17). The firstborn son was responsible for carrying on the family, caring for parents in old age. He was the one who kept the family going through generations. Jesus is the firstborn also in this sense, as the chief heir of his Father's fortune, who is preeminent in all things. And so it's as the firstborn, as the only begotten of the Father, as the new Israel, as the heir, as the Passover sacrifice, that Jesus goes to the cross. And the cross, Paul says, has the effect of "reconciling" and "making peace."

Much of Paul's terminology is borrowed from the propaganda of the Roman Empire. According to Roman imperial ideology, the emperor is the preeminent "peacemaker," and this actually became a title of the emperor. In some Roman texts, the peace that the Roman emperor brought to earth is an image of heavenly peace, so there is a cosmic dimension even to Rome. Paul says there is another peacemaker, another who reconciles all things. He is the one in whom, as Paul says later, all things are renovated, a renovation that extends to Greek and Jew, circumcised and uncircumcised, barbarian and Scythian, slave and free (3:10–11).

Jews and Gentiles

What we have said about covenant, eschatology, and Jesus helps us understand why Judaizers are among Paul's most important opponents. Paul preaches a gospel that implies that the system of the Law established at Sinai was temporary (Gal. 3–4). Yahweh called Abram to form a people, but the purpose of that people, that seed, was always to bring blessing to the Gentiles, not merely to Jews. God always intended to put the nations, and even the whole creation, back together again, through Israel. Now that the end has come in Jesus, now that a new creation is beginning, now that a new Lord is on the throne, the restrictions and divisions of the Old Covenant no longer matter. Circumcision means nothing, and neither does uncircumcision. In Jesus, there is no difference between slave and free, man and woman, Jew and Gentile.

This is a message that gets unbelieving Jews riled up. Jews considered themselves God's special people, and Paul tells them that they aren't special anymore. Paul knows that the Jews are angry at his gospel, but it doesn't make him back off. He describes his Jewish opponents as dogs, evil workers, and "false circumcision" (Phil. 3:2). As we have seen, in chapter 2, he urges the Philippians to follow the example of Jesus in humility, self-emptying, and restraint. He urges the Philippians to renounce privileges, becoming obedient and trusting the Father to exalt them, just as Jesus did. In the following chapter, Paul tells the Philippians that he himself has followed Jesus' example. Like Jesus, Paul has privileges, the privileges of his Hebrew background and training (3:1–6). He was a Jew himself. Yet, all this he willingly gives up for the sake of the gospel (v. 7–8). He does not think that Judaism is something to be held tightly. He gives up his great heritage for the sake of the gospel.

But how are the predominately Gentile Philippians supposed to follow this example? Beginning in chapter 3, Paul has basically equated Judaism and paganism (as he frequently did). In 3:2, he urged the Philippians to beware of the *katatome*, translated as "false circumcision" in the New American Standard Bible but actually meaning "mutilation." Verse 3 makes clear that Paul was talking about Jews: The contrast is between the *katatome* that the Philippians are supposed to avoid and the *peritome* ("circumcision") that belongs to those who "worship in the Spirit of God and glory in Christ Jesus and put no confidence in the flesh" (or in the lack thereof). Though he is talking about Jews, however, Paul described them in a shocking and utterly pagan manner. Since the new age had come, Jews who continued to cut the flesh of the foreskin were no better than the *castrati* who served pagan temples.

Further, as Wright explains, Paul was mounting a polemic against the imperial ideology, affirming that Jesus, not Caesar, is "Lord" and "Savior," both prominent terms in imperial propaganda. Paul's claim that Christians are citizens of a heavenly *politeuma* further indicates that the Philippian Christians are to consider themselves a colony of heaven more than as a colony of Rome. Paul imitated Christ by giving up his privileges as a Hebrew of the Hebrews, exhorting the Philippians to follow his example by treating their Roman citizenship and attachment to the Roman emperor as "rubbish" for the sake of Christ and His heavenly *politeuma*.

In short, throughout Philippians, which some identify as one of the least political of Paul's letters, Paul was treating the church as an alternative to the politico-religious organization of the city and of the empire.

The political dimensions of Paul's gospel come to more explicit expression in Philippians 1:27–30, where Paul employed a cluster of friendship terms and phrases: "come and see you or remain absent," "one spirit," "one mind," and "striving together." Verses 27–30 are a single sentence in Greek, and the main verb is *politeuo*, which means "to live as a citizen." All these "friendship" terms expound on what it means to "live as a citizen in a manner worthy of the gospel." Philippians 1:27–30 anticipates the language of Philippians 3:20, where Paul declared that the Philippian Christians were citizens of a "heavenly commonwealth (*politeuma*)." The Philippians, so proud of being Roman citizens and so protective of Roman custom, needed to learn to live as citizens of a different commonwealth that placed new demands on its citizens.

Colossians, as we have seen above, is more explicitly concerned with the issues of Judaism and Christianity. The heretics of Colossae are Judaizers, who want the Gentile Christians to conform to Jewish regulations before embracing them as brothers. Paul views this with horror. He wants the Colossians to grow up to maturity or "perfection" (1:24; 4:12; see Philippians 3:15), and turning back to Judaism is turning back to childhood. They are in danger of going back to the ABCs of the world ("elementary principles, Colossians 2:8, 20) instead of pressing on to maturity. Jesus has taken away the law, with its regulations and its curses; all of that was nailed to the cross along with Jesus (2:13–14). Submitting to these regulations again is turning the clock back, acting as if Jesus never died in the first place.

Paul is again teaching about the character of true perfection. Jews in the first century considered themselves the most mature, the perfect race. Paul says, on the contrary, that Jewish regulations are childish. Don't touch this, don't eat that, don't put that in your mouth—these are rules for children. But in Jesus, the Colossians, and we, have grown up, and we are no longer under the "elementary principles" of the world.

Conclusion

When we put Philippians and Colossians together, we get at least the outline of mature human life. Being mature means cultivating the humility of Jesus, living in unity with other believers, resisting the temptation to fall back into childish bickering, giving up privileges so that we can serve others, and rejoicing in all circumstances. In a word, being mature means following in the way of Jesus, the Last Adam, the first and last fully human human.

—Peter J. Leithart

For Further Reading

Thielman, Frank. *Philippians*. NIV Application Commentary. Grand Rapids: Zondervan, 1995.

Wright, N.T. *Colossians and Philemon*. Tyndale New Testament Commentaries. Grand Rapids: Eerdmans, 1986.

Wright, N.T. *Climax of the Covenant: Paul and the Law in Pauline Theology*. Minneapolis: Fortress, 1993.

Veritas Press Bible Cards: Acts through Revelations. Lancaster, Pa.: Veritas Press. 146, 149.

This statue of the author of Philippians and Colossians stands in front of the Basilica di San Paolo fuori le Mura (Basilica of Saint Paul Outside the Walls) in Rome. The basilica was founded by Constantine over the traditional burial place of the Apostle.

Session I: Prelude

A Question to Consider

Jesus tells us to be perfect. What does He mean? How do we become perfect?

From the General Information above answer the following questions:
1. What does gnosticism teach concerning creation?
2. How is Jesus' lordship part of remaking the world?
4. Is it a contradiction to say that God is humble? How do we see this answer in Philippians?
5. What does it mean for Paul to call Jesus the "firstborn"?
6. How is Christ the "firstborn" who represents the future of the family?
7. Why was it important that Paul calls Jesus "Lord" and "Savior"?

Reading Assignment:
Philippians 1–2

4. Does everyone preach the gospel with good motives? What does Paul think about this?
5. Why is Paul unconcerned about death?
6. What sort of mind does Paul want the Philippians to have?
7. How does Paul illustrate the humility he wants the Philippians to have?
8. According to Philippians 2, what is the result of Jesus' coming to earth?

Reading Assignment:
Philippians 3–4

Session III: Writing

Poetry

In this session, you will be challenged to write poetry in a certain form about a particular object, person, event, or idea. The challenge for the poet is to lay bare the heart of the truth in language that is beautiful and that inspires its reader to love what is pure and righteous or to hate what is wicked and evil. The best poetry marries true philosophy and beautiful rhetoric.

Writing poetry is a real challenge, so we are going to provide forms for you. Remember, poetry is hard but rewarding work.

This mosaic, designed by Florentine artist Coppo di Marcovaldo (c. 1225–1274), is found in the Florence Baptistery.

Session II: Recitation
Philippians 1–2

Comprehension Questions

Answer the following questions for factual recall:
1. Who wrote Philippians?
2. Where does Paul say he is? How long does he expect to be there?
3. Why does Paul tell the Philippians not to worry about the terrible things that have happened to him?

Hymn in Long Meter

Most hymns are written with a set meter and rhyme, with the ending of each line rhyming with another line in the hymn. The rhymes will usually alternate. In long meter, there are four lines per verse, all of which are iambic tetrameter (four emphasized syllables). The Doxology ("Praise God from Whom All Blessings Flow") is an example of a hymn written in long meter.

Your assignment is to write a hymn celebrating the work of Christ. Use things you have learned from Philippians 2 about Christ's humiliation and exaltation. Feel free to paraphrase biblical passages, but try to use your own wording as much as possible. Your hymn should be at least six verses long; use half to speak of Christ's humiliation and half to speak of His exaltation. You can test whether or not it is in long meter by singing your hymn to the tune of "When I Survey the Wondrous Cross," or the Old Hundredth (in most hymnals this is the Doxology).

READING ASSIGNMENT:
Colossians 1–2

SESSION IV: ACTIVITY

Jehovah's Witnesses

Since Jesus Christ's ascension into heaven, many people claiming the title of "Christian" have denied that He was truly and eternally the Son of God. These beliefs have been held by groups ranging from the fourth-century heretic Arius to the modern-day Jehovah's Witnesses. Rather than deny Christ's deity outright, as a secular atheist would, such Arians instead deny that the Son is equal to the Father. They argue that He was created (or "begotten") at some point before the creation of the world. The Son of God is thus the first creation of the Father, before the world was created, merely "a god," rather than fully God. All of this was officially designated heresy by the church over 1,500 years ago at the Council of Nicea (A.D. 325).

You may have experienced Jehovah's Witnesses preaching this heresy in your neighborhood. How would you answer someone who came to your door and taught these things? How can you show from Scripture that these beliefs are false?

1. List and describe some of the things in Colossians 1 that demonstrate that this view of Jesus Christ is inconsistent with Scripture.
2. What other passages do you know of in the New Testament that would demonstrate that Jesus is not just "a god"?
3. For further research: How does the New World Translation, used by the Jehovah's Witnesses, differ from the New King James Version (NKJV) in its translation of Colossians 1:15–20? See Chart 1.

READING ASSIGNMENT:
Colossians 3–4

Chart 1: **COLOSSIANS 1:15–20**

NEW KING JAMES VERSION	NEW WORLD TRANSLATION
He is the image of the invisible God, the firstborn over all creation. For by Him all things were created that are in heaven and that are on earth, visible and invisible, whether thrones or dominions or principalities or powers. All things were created through Him and for Him. And He is before all things, and in Him all things consist. And He is the head of the body, the church, who is the beginning, the firstborn from the dead, that in all things He may have the preeminence. For it pleased *the Father that* in Him all the fullness should dwell, and by Him to reconcile all things to Himself, by Him, whether things on earth or things in heaven, having made peace through the blood of His cross.	He is the image of the invisible God, the firstborn of all creation; because by means of him all [other] things were created in the heavens and upon the earth, the things visible and the things invisible, no matter whether they are thrones or lordships or governments or authorities. All [other] things have been created through him and for him. Also, he is before all [other] things and by means of him all [other] things were made to exist, and he is the head of the body, the congregation. He is the beginning, the firstborn from the dead, that he might become the one who is first in all things; because [God] saw good for all fullness to dwell in him, and through him to reconcile again to himself all [other] things by making peace through the blood [he shed] on the torture stake, no matter whether they are the things upon the earth or the things in the heavens.

SESSION V: DISCUSSION

A Quetion to Consider
How should Christians treat others?

Discuss or list short answers to the following questions:

Text Analysis
1. What does Paul say that the Colossians ought not to do to one another?
2. How are families supposed to behave toward each other?
3. How should masters behave toward their bondservants (i.e., slaves)?

Cultural Analysis
1. How does our culture believe that people ought to treat one another? Why?
2. How does our culture believe that husbands and wives ought to treat each other?
3. What does our culture believe about community?

Biblical Analysis
1. How does Abraham behave towards Lot after their herdsmen dispute over pasture (Gen. 13)?
2. How does Jesus treat His community of disciples (John 13)?
3. What does John tell us is the mark of a true Christian (1 John 1:7; 2:9–11)?

SUMMA

Write an essay or discuss this question, integrating what you have learned from the material above.
What does it mean to live in Christian community?

OPTIONAL SESSION: DISCUSSION

A Question to Consider
Is it good to suffer?

Discuss or list short answers to the following questions:

Text Analysis
1. What benefit does Paul explain has come from his persecution? Why does he rejoice if he suffers?
2. Why does Paul boast about his accomplishments?
3. How does Paul say that he has made it through his trials?

Cultural Analysis
1. For our culture, what is the most important goal? (For what two things are many people living?)
2. Does our culture see suffering as a benefit or a detriment? Explain.

Biblical Analysis
1. Why is Stephen willing to suffer (Acts 6–7)?
2. What does Jesus tell us about what we should hold to be most important (Matt. 16:24–27)? How does this relate to suffering?
3. What does James tell us is the purpose of suffering (James 1:2–3)?

SUMMA

Write an essay or discuss this question, integrating what you have learned from the material above.
What benefits can Christians see in suffering for their faith?

ENDNOTES
1. I owe this outline to John Barach and use it here with his permission.
2. Wright, N.T. *Climax of the Covenant: Christ and the Law in Pauline Theology.* Minneapolis: Fortress Press, 1993. 86.

Law

What is "law"? You have certainly heard of the law of gravity and are acquainted with the law the policeman enforces when he stops the motorist (you?) for speeding. How do these different kinds of law connect with each other? And is there a deeper meaning to the notion of law in general?

All law—whether physical law or societal law—involves two elements: *order* and *compulsion*. We can see this if we consider the major varieties of law: scientific law, custom, moral law, and juridical law.

Scientific law involves finding regularities in nature. We observe the world, see patterns, and then attempt to describe them in general terms. Our first attempts are often called "hypotheses." We then test those hypotheses by examining more and perhaps better data; this results, perhaps, in a rejection of our initial explanation, or, if we are on the right track, in a refining of our hypothesis. Such refinements raise our hypotheses to the level of a "theory." Finally, if our theory holds up under even more and better investigations of the physical world, and there appears to be no evidence contradicting it, we may be able to present the result as a scientific law.

Scientific laws describe regularities in the physical universe. They also—and inevitably—entail *sanctions*, that is to say, negative consequences if we disregard or violate them. The law of gravity, for example, tells us that on this planet all physical objects fall toward the center of the earth and that they do this in

This 300-year-old statue of Lady Justice oversees the "Well of Justice" at Frankfurt's Roemer Square in Germany.

accord with a strict mathematical formula. If you try to defy the law of gravity—by attempting to fly from the roof of your house without benefit of aircraft, for example—the *sanction* is that you will break a leg (if not worse).

Customs are part of every society. They are regular, widely accepted social patterns, and disregarding them can result in ostracism. For example, if you insist on wearing a swimsuit to a wedding, you will not be invited to other weddings—and maybe people will hesitate to invite you out at all!

Moral law is often confused with custom (Latin, *mores*). But moral law cuts much deeper. To treat shabbily a person weaker than oneself or to take advantage of someone who cannot protect himself or herself will be considered far more serious than not wearing the right clothes at a social occasion. The treatment of Jews by the Nazis during the Second World War is regarded almost universally today as heinous—as deserving ethical condemnation and the severest of societal punishments. When immoral acts are committed and someone "gets away with it," people often say, "There ought to be a law!" But often there are no laws to cover such acts, and many immoral actions (such as lying, unkindness, selfish use of family property, hurtful treatment of friends) cannot be effectively treated by the state. One comes to see that moral law has a *transcendent* dimension—that is, it touches matters so fundamental that without a Last Judgment to punish the disregard of it, the universe would be inherently immoral and irrational.

Finally, we come to the law of the land—*juridical law*. This is the law that is enforced not by social ostracism (as is custom) or by moral opprobrium such as being publicly disgraced (as is the moral law), but by state sanctions. Most modern nations have legal systems that distinguish civil law and criminal law. Civil law attaches penalties (generally money payments or injunctions forcing people to do what they should) to acts which cause quantifiable or objectively provable harm to others. Criminal law deals with those far more serious acts which are inherently harmful to the society as a whole (homicide, physical attacks, stealing, corruption, etc.), and attaches much more serious penalties to their commission (incarceration and sometimes even the death penalty).

Juridical law comes about through the passing of general laws and regulations by legislatures, reinforced by the decisions of judges in particular cases. Constitutions set forth fundamental law, thereby restraining legislators from passing laws which would go against the general will of the people.

Like the moral law, juridical law has a *transcendent* dimension. This is reflected in the building of courthouses (often, as in the case of the Royal Courts of Justice in London, England, they are styled like cathedrals), in the robes worn by judges, and in the formal, often majestic style of courtroom proceedings. When the death penalty was still imposed in England, the judge would don a black cap in pronouncing the fateful sentence. Again, one inevitably thinks in terms of Last Judgment. People often say that a murderer who has not been found guilty—who has "gotten off" because of a legal technicality—won't get away with it when he stands before the bar of God's justice on the Last Day.

If we focus our attention on juridical law, what are the major issues we should consider? Three very important problem areas are *the connection between law and morality, legal reasoning, and how law can be justified.*

First, how does morality relate to juridical law? As we have seen, they are certainly not the same thing. There are laws having a very minor moral element—for example, the rule that one must drive on the right-hand side of the road (in the British Isles and former British colonies, one drives on the left-hand side of the road). There are also many immoral acts that cannot effectively be punished by the juridical law—especially subjective immoralities such as envy and covetousness, but also instances where a greater evil would be produced by legal action, such as allowing forced confessions or tainted evidence to be used against the accused.

But clearly law and morality are interrelated. One of the major purposes of the law is to make sure that a decent society is maintained. This immediately raises the issue for the Christian believer of the extent to which Christians should "enforce morality" through legislation. This was the subject of an important controversy in England some years ago—the so-called Hart-Devlin debate. H.L.A. Hart, an eminent philosopher of law at Oxford, argued that one should not attempt to enforce morals, whilst Lord Devlin maintained that doing so is quite legitimate, indeed, inevitable. The concrete issue in that debate was homosexuality—should it be criminalized?

Here is a suggested approach; think about it and come to your own conclusion. The moral laws of the Bible are absolute, since they come from the God of the universe who has created mankind. But we live in a fallen world, where everyone desperately needs to receive the gospel of Jesus Christ for eternal salvation. Therefore, we should do all that we can to promote biblical morality through the law—*as long as* by doing so we don't misrepresent Christ and so alienate the unbeliever that he or she will no longer listen to the gospel. In practice, this will mean that we will not create "Christian coalitions" to force Sunday closing laws on the community where this would drive the non-Christian to the view that we are trying to ram our Christian beliefs down the throats of those who are not themselves believers.

Exceptions to this approach come only at the point of mission critical issues like the right-to-life. We would not want to hold the unborn hostage to the possibility of successfully evangelizing the pro-choicer—any more than during the Third Reich Christians would have been right not to oppose the death camps on the ground that to do so might have been to offend Nazis and reduce the effectiveness of evangelism to them! But short of right-to-life, evangelism should trump efforts at moral improvement. After all, our Lord's "Great Commission" to the church, was "Go and preach the gospel to every creature"—not "Be sure to raise the moral tone of society"!

Second, how do lawyers and judges reason? Answer: just like scientists or historians—or anyone else who uses one's head. That is to say, the lawyer or judge collects facts (the facts bearing on the case and the record of similar and relevant past cases), creates the best theory or argument to account for those facts and their legal implications, and then sets forth a reasoned conclusion. Analytical philosophers Ludwig Wittgenstein and Karl Popper employed a very effective analogy for this process: the shoe and the foot. The "foot" is the factual situation; what we try to do in science, history, law, or ordinary life is to develop an explanation which, like a good shoe, will exactly "fit" that situation. We don't want explanations that so pinch the facts that they distort them; nor do we want explanations so general and vague that they would fit *any* facts.

To be sure, the law has special reasoning techniques appropriate to the nature of legal procedure. Thus, evidence will be excluded if it is so prejudicial that it would inflame the jury and keep them from coming to a balanced, reasonable conclusion. Precise "standards of proof" are set forth—a "preponderance" of evidence (51%) to win in a civil case, but "proof to a moral certainty, beyond reasonable doubt" to convict in a criminal case, where the consequences are so much more severe.

Fascinatingly, these high standards of legal evidence have been employed by legally trained Christian apologists to show the soundness of the case for reliability of the gospel records and the facticity of the resurrection of Jesus Christ; we shall have more to say about this below.

Ludwig Wittgenstein

Finally, how can law—legal rules—be justified? The problem here is that if laws are merely *relative*—like customs—then why should one obey them if one can get away with not doing so? To be effective and enforceable, laws must have an authority beyond the changing mores of society. And where constitutional principles are involved, we must somehow reach the level of what the Declaration of Independence termed *"inalienable rights"*—legal standards so immutable that no one has the right to change them.

Secular philosophers of law have tried very hard to find and justify such standards. Probably the most influential attempts have been the *natural law* and the *neo-Kantian* approaches. Let's look at both of these very briefly.

Natural law thinkers have argued that everyone has built-in moral standards—therefore we naturally *know* what should be legally accepted and what should be rejected. In consequence, we are told that law can appeal to undeniable universal standards.

Modern secular philosophy of law has been deeply influenced by the ethical thought of eighteenth-century rationalist philosopher Immanuel Kant. Kant did not believe that one could prove God's existence, but he did believe an absolute ethical principle could be set forth. He called it the "categorical imperative": so act that your action can become a universal rule. In the twentieth century, a major political philosopher (John Rawls) and a major philosopher of law (Alan Gewirth) have used this Kantian approach to try to justify law.

Rawls suggests that if, hypothetically, people were placed under a "veil of ignorance"—so that they did not know anything about their particular advantages over against other people—they would logically and inevitably arrive at a society built upon two "principles of justice" entailing civil liberties and an economic and social life which would benefit the least advantaged. Gewirth claims that since every human being is a "purposive agent," each of us must make "freedom and well-being" available to others, not just to oneself. We must not base our personal freedom (civil liberties) and well-being (social and economic rights) on any special characteristic we may possess—our race, our wealth, our social position, our family background—but only on the humanity we share with everyone else, i.e., our common characteristic of being "purposive agents." For Rawls and Gewirth, then, fundamental civil and social rights can be justified on a purely secular, humanistic basis.

Let us analyze these philosophies in our next section.

Critical Issues

What is the problem with secular attempts to provide a basis for law? The fundamental difficulty is illustrated by the two positions we have just been describing.

Secular Natural Law

Natural law thinking may seem like a viewpoint consistent with biblical revelation. After all, does not the Apostle Paul say in Romans 1 that God's law is "written on our hearts"? Yes, he does, but he follows this with the condemnation of the entire human race—Jew and Gentile alike—for having consistently violated that law: "All have sinned and come short of the glory of God" (Romans 3:23).

The problem with secular natural law theory in a fallen world is threefold: (1) It assumes that everyone will agree on moral and legal standards, but, obviously, people don't: there are great differences in moral standards and legal rules across the globe. (2) Even if everyone agreed, that would not necessarily mean that what was agreed upon was right. *Consensus gentium*—the agreement of the peoples—is not a sufficient test of truth (and, indeed constitutes a logical fallacy when so used—"Fifty million Frenchmen can be wrong"). (3) To arrive at any kind of commonality of standards, the natural law rules have to be stated in so general a way that they can mean almost anything and are capable of being applied in almost any direction—including frightening ones. Example: the great principle of classical natural law (in the *Digest* of the sixth-century *Justinian's Code*) that "each person should get what he deserves" was placed in German translation (*Jedem das seine*) by the Nazis on the gate leading into the Buchenwald death camp.

The great Christian legal thinkers, such as Sir William Blackstone, have stressed that a special revelation (Holy Scripture) is absolutely essential to show a sinful and fallen humanity which "writing on the human heart" comes from God and which from self-interest. Jiminy Cricket's philosophy of "let your conscience be your guide" is naïve at best, highly dangerous at worst.

Neo-Kantian Approaches

Kant's categorical imperative sounds a bit like the Golden Rule. But Jesus never used it as a rationalistic principle—as an argument to explain societal action. Rather, Jesus employs the principle of "doing unto others as you would have them do unto you" to show us how far our actions deviate from God's standard as to the way we should be treating others. (Like everything in the Sermon on the Mount—summed up in the command, "Be ye therefore perfect, even as your heavenly Father is perfect"—the object is to show us how desperately we need Jesus' sacrifice on the cross for our sins.)

Rawls and Gewirth hypothesize a situation in which people act rationally without any regard for their own advantages. This, however, is hopelessly unrealistic. In fact, people *always* take into account their own strengths—and the weaknesses of others—in their actions. Rawls and Gewirth, like their mentor Kant, have no serious awareness of *sin*—of the radical self-centeredness of a fallen race.

Suppose we were to try to convince, let us say, Ghengis Khan, to institute a proper legal system—one involving civil liberties and socio-economic equality. We might say to Ghengis: "Ghengis, have you been out raping and pillaging again?" Reply: "Well, yes. Frankly, I enjoy raping and pillaging." "But Ghengis, you should be acting

Immanuel Kant

so that your action could become a universal rule! You should be thinking in terms of just legality—civil and social rights—for everyone, not just your own interests. How would *you* like it if others treated you as you are treating them? You should be thinking in terms of a universal rule of law!" Ghengis: "GRRRHH! Listen up! I happen to be bigger and stronger than they are. There is no chance that *they* could get away with raping or pillaging *me.*"

The point here is that in a fallen world, even if people will admit a rational principle (such as the categorical imperative), this in no way ensures that they will follow it. Fallen creatures are perfectly happy with a rule of law for their *own* protection; but they invariably balk when attempts are made to apply legal standards to their personal *disadvantage*. Think of the popular legal area of human rights: everyone favors them—including the worst dictators—but human rights are invariably interpreted to protect the political interest group or dictator, and disregarded when to do so is to the advantage of that state or individual.

The problem with all secular efforts to justify law is that, arising from human sources—and sinful, self-centered sources at that—they cannot possibly arrive at the absolute ethical principles needed to ground legal systems.

Water doesn't rise above its own level. Remember Archimedes? Said he, "Give me a lever long enough and a fulcrum outside the world, and I shall move it." This is sound physics—and an equally sound ethical and legal principle. The necessary condition for moving the world is that the fulcrum lie outside it; otherwise, one is trying to pull oneself up by one's own bootstraps—and a painful fall is inevitable! To arrive at the needed absolute principles to ground a legal system, one needs a source outside the world—a source uncontaminated by the sinful and finite human condition.

Two thinkers have seen this clearly, though they were not themselves believers. Jean-Jacques Rousseau, in his *Social Contract,* wrote: "It would take gods to make men laws." And Ludwig Wittgenstein asserted: "The sense of the world must lie outside the world. . . . Ethics is transcendental"—explaining this by saying, "I can only describe my feeling by the metaphor, that, if a man could write a book on Ethics which really was a book on Ethics, this book would, with an explosion, destroy all the other books in the world."

That book, of course, is the Holy Scriptures. In the inerrant word of God, one finds the absolute principles capable of providing a sound foundation for human legal systems. These principles are absolute—inalienable—because they have been revealed by a God who is the only source of the absolute and the inalienable. Moreover, the Bible gives a fallen race *not only* the legal principles it so desperately needs as the criterion for identifying the proper content of the law written on the heart, *but also* the solution to fallen mankind's self-centeredness: the cross of Christ as the way of redemption and a new life in which one will indeed "love one's neighbor as oneself" and seek to establish and implement legal systems reflecting God's standards.

One might, of course, raise the question as to the

Taizu, better known as Genghis Khan. This portrait of paint and ink on silk is a detail from an album now located in the National Palace Museum in Taipei depicting several Yuan emperors.

effectiveness and the application of such biblical standards in our modern secular, pluralistic world. We have already noted that morality (including biblical standards) must not be forced on a non-Christian society in a way that reduces the effectiveness of evangelism to that society. But in our culture, impregnated as it has been with the western Christian tradition, the unbeliever is "living off the inherited capital" of biblical morality. He or she can then be appealed to on the basis of that morality and legal perspective. "Surely," we can argue, "you want your children not to be impacted by internet porn—or suffer the psychological miseries of abortion—or lose the opportunity for a decent marriage as a result of a redefinition of it to include homosexual unions?" Common ground arguments of this kind can persuade the unbeliever to move in the direction of biblical morality and biblically based legislation without imperiling evangelism.

A Christian Response

How can one personally respond to the issues in this vital area of legal thinking? Let us consider a number of possibilities.

The Biblical Aspect

We have argued that only Holy Scripture can serve as a proper foundation for law, since only the Bible is a transcendent book capable of providing absolute principles—principles uncontaminated by the sinful and limited human perspective.

Fine. But this will hardly work if you yourself do not know the Scriptures. Are you well enough acquainted with the actual content of biblical revelation to know what its fundamental principles *are*? This, of course, is a lifetime task. But why not start now? Plan to read the Bible through, say, every three years. Take good courses on particular books of the Bible. Consider the possibility of going to a Bible school for a year after high school—especially if you are planning to attend a secular university.

And there is the problem of "rightly dividing" the word of God, that is to say, properly interpreting it. In the history of the church, even those who have been convinced of the total truth of the Bible have sometimes interpreted it in a manner that has badly hurt its message and impact.

For example, there is the viewpoint that all proper law is given in Scripture and that we should not be allowed to do anything that is not expressly commanded in the Bible. On this basis, during the Commonwealth period in England (seventeenth century), people were fined for celebrating Christmas—since nowhere in the Bible is it commanded to keep that holiday! To be sure, the proper approach to law is that we are allowed by God to do whatever is *not condemned in Scripture*. The Bible is not an "encyclopedia Britannica," giving specific rules for all particular actions. We are expected to use the heads God has placed on our shoulders to handle particular issues. Just as the Bible does not provide rules for television repair, so it does not set out statutes for promissory notes or traffic safety. We are to employ sanctified common sense, through the guidance of the Holy Spirit, in drafting our laws and choosing our actions in a manner that will maximally glorify the Christ who has died for us.

Moreover, one must face the question of the relationship between the Old Testament and the New. There are Christians who have thought that the entire Old Testa-

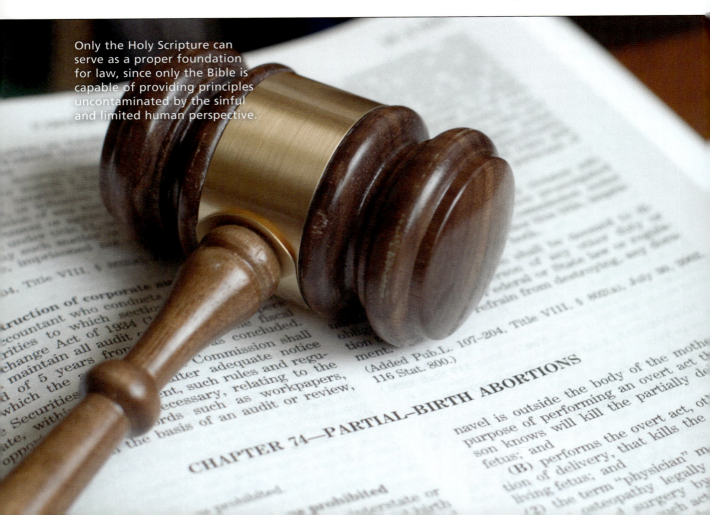

Only the Holy Scripture can serve as a proper foundation for law, since only the Bible is capable of providing principles uncontaminated by the sinful and limited human perspective.

ment law is (or should be) applied today. These folk have wanted to legislate the levitical law—much as orthodox Jews try to do. One of them has actually said that it would be desirable today to stone prostitutes and kill children who will not obey their parents. You need to understand that whilst the *moral* law of the Old Testament is permanently applicable, the *civil* and *ceremonial* law of ancient Israel definitely is *not*. That law, unique to the preservation of the nation Israel as the cradle for Messiah's coming, was abrogated by its fulfillment in our Lord's advent, as is plain from the apostles' refusal in the New Testament to require circumcision of gentile converts. Occasionally it may be difficult to draw the line between Old Testament moral law on the one hand and the civil and ceremonial law on the other, but the critical importance of the distinction remains nonetheless.

Going further, one needs to understand what Martin Luther termed "the proper distinction between law and gospel." He declared that "the true doctor of theology is the person who can properly distinguish law from gospel." What did he mean? Luther was referring to the two great doctrinal themes that run through the entire Bible. He was not suggesting, as some have thought, that one can divide the Bible into law, equivalent to the Old Testament, and gospel, equivalent to the New Testament! In point of fact, law and gospel are inherent to both Testaments. Law, in the theological sense, refers to *what we do in response to God's commands;* gospel, on the other hand, describes *what God does for us to save us.* Grave problems arise whenever law and gospel are confused. When gospel is turned into law, people try to save themselves by their own moral and law-abiding efforts. (Haven't you heard a non-Christian say, "I don't need salvation—I've led a good moral life—never been in jail"?) When law is turned into gospel, people and societies become unaware of their sin and think that God is a Santa Claus who saves them—maybe everybody—without there being any moral or legal standards at all. Theologian Dietrich Bonhoeffer called this the notion of "cheap grace."

The Reformers distinguished three main "uses" of the law—meaning the functions of the revealed law in the Bible as well as the functions of human legislation. The first use of all law is *political*—the law which structures sinful society and keeps us from eating each other! The second use is the *pedagogical* use—the "law as a schoolmaster [Greek, *paidagogos*] to bring us to Christ" (Galatians 3:24). This is—for Luther—the most important of the three uses, for it points up the fact that *all* law, biblical and juridical, if taken seriously, demonstrates that our fallen race does not conform to God's standards—or even to the human ideals it sets for itself—and therefore needs the salvation provided by Christ alone. (Incidentally, in classical times the *paidagogos* was not the teacher, but the mere slave who brought the child *to* the teacher! This is what the law properly does: it drives us to the cross by showing us how far short we fall from divine standards.) Christ interiorized the Old Testament law, making it even more stringent—leaving no one without excuse: "Has it been said of old time, thou shalt not kill? I say unto you, he who hates his brother has already committed murder in his heart;" etc., etc. The third use of the law—unlike the first two—applies only to believers: it is the *sanctifying* use. Only the believer can come to "love God's law" as the expression of His character and will. The unbeliever will always and ever see God's law as a threat—and rightly so—since, as the Reformers put it, *lex semper accusat* ("the law always accuses"). Only at the cross is the law seen as reflecting God's own loving nature, since He was willing to take the hideous violations of it by a fallen race on Himself, expiating our sin by the blood of His cross.

These kinds of theological and biblical understandings are essential if one wishes to apply law in the fullest sense to one's personal situation and to the society of which one is a part.

The Political Aspect

More than a few evangelical Christians have beliefs which reduce the effectiveness of their witness in the political and legal world of our time. You need to engage in self-examination to make sure that you are not unknowingly hurting the cause in this way.

There are evangelicals who hopelessly confuse biblical religion with conservative politics. They may not believe that no Democrats go to heaven, but they would be surprised if the number was very great! As for socialists, WELL *they* are surely in outer darkness with gnashing of teeth . . .

Now, I have almost always voted Republican, and I certainly believe that "the best government is the government that governs least" (I'm for less government, rather than more). But this is a far cry from being an anarchist (no government at all) or a libertarian (who may not even want the state to license doctors or lawyers). The facts are that Holy Scripture does not mandate any single form of government and, since original sin is universal, there is no assurance that either Democrats or Republicans will always be right! In some situations, government should stay out of things; in others, government intervention and an increase in legislation can be badly needed. The point is that each policy and each piece of proposed legislation and each legal case needs to be evaluated *as such*—by biblical standards. Sometimes the "conservatives" will be right; sometimes the political "liberals" will be right. We must not become doctrinaire, lock-step rightists who refuse to "test the spirits" on an issue-by-issue, case-by-case basis.

The same point needs to be made in regard to "Americanism." There are Bible believers among us who give the impression that the American constitutional documents are a kind of infallible extension of Holy Scripture, and that the founding fathers of our country were all saints. Theologically and historically, this is simply not correct. We are blessed with a constitutional and legal system deeply impregnated with biblical ideals, but this is not to say that ours is in fact a Christian nation. *No country is.* The kingdoms of this world will all pass away one day and will be replaced by "the kingdom of our God and of his Christ." Just as in the case of conservative vs. liberal, so in our beliefs concerning our own nation, we need to place everything under the authority of the Holy Scriptures—meaning that we need to judge our country's actions (not just the actions of other nations) by God's eternal standards as set forth in his holy word. Often our nation will show itself a beacon light in a dark world; at other times we may need to speak prophetically to its leaders, its legislators, and its judges.

This brings us to the matter of international law. Some evangelicals seem to think that there is something inherently demonic about things international. Is international law always bad—always worse than our national law? True, there is often less direct accountability to legislatures in the case of international law. But here's a sobering example: The American Convention (= Treaty) on Human Rights, ratified by most of the North and South American countries—but not by the United States—protects the right to life "from the moment of conception." Why has the U.S. Senate not ratified this treaty? Because, were it to do so, the U.S. would immediately be brought before the Inter-American Court of Human Rights for violating the treaty owing to our federal law (*Roe v Wade*), which allows abortion on demand during the first trimester of pregnancy. Here, again, the issue is not whether something is national (supposedly always good) or international (supposedly always bad). National law *as well as* international law needs to be evaluated by biblical criteria, and there is no guarantee that the one will always be right or the other always wrong. Only God's word "lasts forever."

The Professional Aspect

Do you really want to move your country and your world in a more biblical direction? Here are some suggestions.

First, analyze why things are a mess (or, at least, why they aren't better than they are). The reason will *not* be because your favorite candidate didn't get elected or your fa-

vorite law did not get enacted—or because someone on the U.S. Supreme Court didn't get a fatal heart attack.

The fundamental problem will turn out to be much more profound than that, involving such considerations as the perspective of the citizenry (in the 2008 national election, economics was more important—right across the country—than right-to-life). How could such a perspective be changed for the better?

Answer: *by influencing the climate of opinion.* And how is this done? Let's begin by noting how it *won't* be done. It will not be accomplished by the typical evangelical style of separating oneself from the society. We have tended to take the approach, "if we can't beat 'em, we'll separate from 'em." We go to isolated churches; we build our Bible schools and Christian colleges in the middle of nowhere (so that we won't be contaminated by secular society); we avoid the social atmosphere and recreational activities of "the world," etc. Result: though we have the eternal gospel in our hearts (and, hopefully, also in our heads), the non-Christian never hears it—for we are simply not on his or her planet. We need to be like our Lord and like his apostles: "in the world, but not of it."

The apostles, it is seldom noted, focused their evangelism *in the cities*—at the centers of political and cultural influence in their day. They expected, quite rightly, that the gospel would spread from there into the hinterlands. We, however, often do the very opposite: we go out into the bush, as far as possible from the "pagan" centers of our society, and hope that the gospel will somehow trickle to the points of power. Sadly, it seldom works that way. One might think that we are more concerned with our own spiritual health—our personal sanctification—rather than the needs of a dying world.

Practically speaking, why not think of going to a Christian college having the goal of impacting the political and legal climate for Christ? These schools are rarer than the proverbial hen's teeth, but they exist. Or why not go to a fine secular university—one with a strong Christian student work on campus so that you can maintain solid Christian fellowship whilst presenting the eternal gospel of salvation to those who might never hear it otherwise?

Of course, to do the latter, you need to know how to defend the faith—how to present the powerful evidence in its behalf and show the fallacies of the views that contradict it. This means doing what the Apostle Paul clearly did: learning the views of the non-Christian so as to be able to speak intelligently to them. (In Athens, Paul quoted the Stoic poet-philosophers to move the Stoics away from their "unknown god" to Jesus Christ; Paul hadn't studied Stoicism in his rabbinic education—he'd gone to the trouble of learning it because he wanted to reach the Stoics for Christ.) Start, therefore, studying apologetics now. In a secular society, wherever you go to college, you'll need to follow the Apostle Peter's instruction to "be ready always to give an answer [Greek, *apologia*] for the hope within you."

Fascinatingly, as we alluded to earlier, many great lawyers have examined the case for Christianity using the rigorous standards of legal evidence—and have ended up as Christian believers. Here are but three examples: Theophilus Parsons, nineteenth-century chief justice of the Massachusetts Supreme Court, who declared: "I examined the proofs and weighed the objections to Christianity many years ago, with the accuracy of a lawyer; and the result was so entire a conviction of its truth, that I have only to regret that my belief has not more completely influenced my conduct." Professor Simon Greenleaf of Harvard, the greatest nineteenth-century authority on the law of evidence, and author of *The Testimony of the Evangelists*, who showed that the four Gospels would be accepted in any common law court as solid evidence for the life and divine claims of Jesus Christ. Sir Norman Anderson, late head of the School of Advanced Legal Studies at the University of London, and the greatest non-Muslim specialist of his generation on Muslim law—who wrote several books defending Christian truth, including a treatise entitled, *The Evidence for the Resurrection.*

Here apologetics and law come together—and this is highly significant, since the law deals with the most serious evidential issues in society, those on which life and death depend. The "ancient documents rule" will allow the New Testament books to be admitted into evidence.

Moses carries the Ten Commandments in this stained glass detail from a window at the Scottish Rite Cathedral in Indianapolis, Indiana.

Examining the witnesses to Jesus Christ in those sound historical documents will show them to be reliable. Thus, if one subjects them to "internal" and "external" juridical examination, one can say that the witnesses had no reason to present anything other than the truth about Jesus' life and ministry; and if one looks, again "internally" and "externally," at what they wrote, one finds the four Gospels to present what one would expect of four witnesses to the same event describing it from their own personal angles—in harmony but not collusively; and the archeological confirmations of the New Testament during the last century and a half have supported again and again the veracity of the documentary material. And it is well worth emphasizing that if the disciples had tried to introduce a false or skewed picture of Jesus' ministry, or of the Old Testament prophecies He fulfilled, they could hardly have gotten away with it: the Jewish religious leaders had "the means, the motive, and the opportunity" (as lawyers put it) to refute any such false claims, since the events of Jesus' life took place in full public view. The great New Testament scholar F.F. Bruce has observed that the presence of these hostile witnesses is the functional equivalent of cross-examination in a court of law.

As for the central attestation of the truth of Jesus' claims, his resurrection from the dead, we have the powerful legal argument of Frank Morison in his book, *Who Moved the Stone?*, that if one doesn't accept the miraculous resurrection, one has to explain the missing body—and the Romans and the Jewish religious leaders would hardly have stolen it (it was, to use the technical legal term, "against their interest") and the disciples would certainly not have stolen it and then died for what they knew to be untrue. As the juridical phrase has it, *res ipsa loquitur* ("the thing speaks for itself"). And when unbelievers claim that one can't prove a unique event like the resurrection, we have the devastating rebuttal of Thomas Sherlock, master (chief pastor) of the barristers' Temple Church in London, who noted that a resurrection is simply a person dead at point A and alive again at point B; granted that in our experience, people are alive at point A and dead at point B—but the evidential problem is identical in both instances: we certainly know the difference between a dead man and a live one (eating fish, for example, means the person is alive—as Jesus was when, after Easter morning, He ate fish with His disciples on the road to Emmaus).

So the answer is to learn to present and defend the gospel effectively. This is not just an option; it is a spiritual duty in the secular world in which we live. Legal skills can offer much assistance in this regard. And getting our own legal philosophy straightened out is equally vital. After all, when we witness to unbelievers, we must be able to point them to the proper distinction between law and gospel—which will occur only if we have reached the point of making that vital distinction ourselves!

Luther noted that the way to change society is to "become a little Christ to your neighbor." What we really need is more Christians per cubic inch. Can you imagine the effect of just one more solid Christian believer teaching a critical course at Harvard? Serving in the Senate? Having the role of American ambassador to the United Nations? Sitting as a U.S. Supreme Court justice—or acting in the capacity of judge or lawyer in your community?

Why not aim high? Maybe the way you can impact the law is by making a career of it. Law school isn't easy, but there is no reason why you can't handle it. And if the Lord is leading you in some other direction, aim high there too. Scripture tells us that "He who is within you is more powerful than he who is against you." If you believe that, act on it.

—*John Warwick Montgomery*

For Further Reading

Carl Joachim Friedrich. *The Philosophy of Law in Historical Perspective*. Chicago: University of Chicago Press, 1963.

Irwin H. Linton. *A Lawyer Examines the Bible*. Grand Rapids: Baker Book House, 1977.

John Warwick Montgomery. *The Law Above the Law*. Minneapolis: Bethany, 1975. Contains Simon Greenleaf's Testimony of the Evangelists.

John Warwick Montgomery. *Human Rights and Human Dignity*. Calgary, Alberta, Canada: Canadian Institute for Law, Theology and Public Policy, 1989

John Warwick Montgomery. *The Shaping of America*. Minneapolis: Bethany, 1976.

C. F. W. Walther. *God's No and God's Yes: The Proper Distinction between Law and Gospel*. Saint Louis: Concordia Publishing House, 2005.

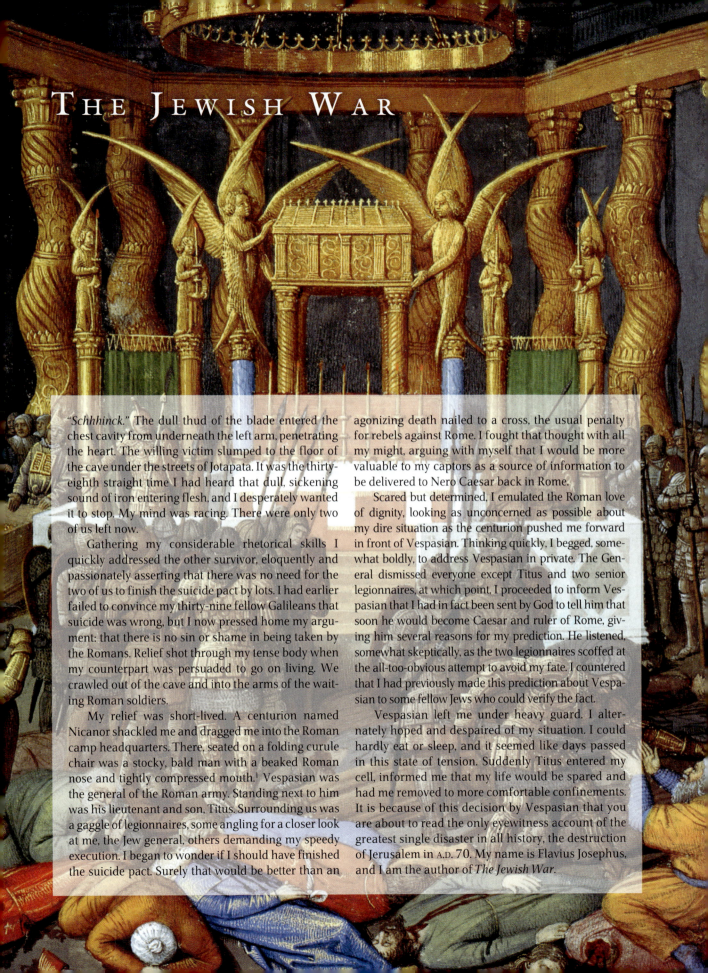

The Jewish War

"*Schhhinck.*" The dull thud of the blade entered the chest cavity from underneath the left arm, penetrating the heart. The willing victim slumped to the floor of the cave under the streets of Jotapata. It was the thirty-eighth straight time I had heard that dull, sickening sound of iron entering flesh, and I desperately wanted it to stop. My mind was racing. There were only two of us left now.

Gathering my considerable rhetorical skills I quickly addressed the other survivor, eloquently and passionately asserting that there was no need for the two of us to finish the suicide pact by lots. I had earlier failed to convince my thirty-nine fellow Galileans that suicide was wrong, but I now pressed home my argument: that there is no sin or shame in being taken by the Romans. Relief shot through my tense body when my counterpart was persuaded to go on living. We crawled out of the cave and into the arms of the waiting Roman soldiers.

My relief was short-lived. A centurion named Nicanor shackled me and dragged me into the Roman camp headquarters. There, seated on a folding curule chair was a stocky, bald man with a beaked Roman nose and tightly compressed mouth.[1] Vespasian was the general of the Roman army. Standing next to him was his lieutenant and son, Titus. Surrounding us was a gaggle of legionnaires, some angling for a closer look at me, the Jew general, others demanding my speedy execution. I began to wonder if I should have finished the suicide pact. Surely that would be better than an agonizing death nailed to a cross, the usual penalty for rebels against Rome. I fought that thought with all my might, arguing with myself that I would be more valuable to my captors as a source of information to be delivered to Nero Caesar back in Rome.

Scared but determined, I emulated the Roman love of dignity, looking as unconcerned as possible about my dire situation as the centurion pushed me forward in front of Vespasian. Thinking quickly, I begged, somewhat boldly, to address Vespasian in private. The General dismissed everyone except Titus and two senior legionnaires, at which point, I proceeded to inform Vespasian that I had in fact been sent by God to tell him that soon he would become Caesar and ruler of Rome, giving him several reasons for my prediction. He listened, somewhat skeptically, as the two legionnaires scoffed at the all-too-obvious attempt to avoid my fate. I countered that I had previously made this prediction about Vespasian to some fellow Jews who could verify the fact.

Vespasian left me under heavy guard. I alternately hoped and despaired of my situation. I could hardly eat or sleep, and it seemed like days passed in this state of tension. Suddenly Titus entered my cell, informed me that my life would be spared and had me removed to more comfortable confinements. It is because of this decision by Vespasian that you are about to read the only eyewitness account of the greatest single disaster in all history, the destruction of Jerusalem in A.D. 70. My name is Flavius Josephus, and I am the author of *The Jewish War*.

General Information

Author and Context

Born in Jerusalem in A.D. 37 (shortly after the crucifixion of Jesus) Josephus's original Aramaic name was Yosef bar Mattathyahu. A Jewish aristocrat from two lines of priestly families, he was a negotiator, general, and historian. Josephus led a truly unique and unusual life, ending up a participant and eyewitness to world changing events. Educated in the Temple, the bright Josephus grew up exploring the many different first- century Jewish sects, including the Pharisees, Sadducees, Essenes, and Zealots. Interestingly, there is no evidence that he investigated the new Christian movement. Although attracted to the austere Essene sect, Josephus ended up something of a lukewarm Pharisee.

In A.D. 64 Josephus traveled to Rome on a mission to obtain the release of some Jewish priests imprisoned by Roman Governor Felix. Impressed with the power and grandeur of Rome, Josephus returned as a peace advocate. However, when the Jewish revolt broke out in A.D. 66, Josephus became the commander of Jewish forces in Galilee, where he was captured by the Romans in the first major campaign of the war. Subsequently, he accompanied Titus to the siege of Jerusalem in A.D. 70, acting as a mediator and interpreter between the opposing camps. Unsurprisingly, he was well rewarded by the Romans and hated as a traitor by the Jews. After the destruction of Jerusalem he returned to Rome with Titus, where he was given a pension to live on and proceeded to write his famous histories. Josephus died shortly after A.D. 100.

Like other Jewish aristocrats, Josephus had a conflict of interest, for it was the Romans who sanctioned the local power of Jewish aristocrats in exchange for keeping the Jewish population under control. As the century wore on, the greed and corruption of the aristocracy, combined with accelerated lower-class crime, created a deep hostility between the classes in Judea.[2] Josephus reflected these hostilities in his own life. Clearly too impressed with himself, he was a snob who inaccurately puts all the blame for the war against the Romans on the Jewish lower classes. He held the common ancient viewpoint that people of material wealth were simply better people than those without material wealth. Although his personal evaluations of the leaders and groups involved in the war cannot be completely trusted because of his biases *toward* the Jewish aristocrats and *against* the Zealots and lower class Jews, all scholars agree that his overall narration of events is very reliable. Readers should also be aware that Vespasian and Titus were his patrons (meaning that they gave him a lot of money to write his books) and some of the Jewish rebel leaders were his personal enemies.

Yosef bar Mattathyahu

Josephus was a prodigious writer. He wrote *The Jewish War* in A.D. 77, as well as *Jewish Antiquities* (his version of Jewish history), the *Vita* (about his own life), and *Against Apion* (a defense of the antiquity of the Jews).

We need to go back in history to understand the context of *The Jewish War*. Although the Jews first rebuilt the Temple in 516 B.C. (during the time of Ezra and Nehemiah), by the time of the last Old Testament prophet, Malachi, Jerusalem and the land of Israel were not in good spiritual shape. Haggai, Zechariah and Malachi all spoke of the coming restoration of Israel, its full return from exile, and the coming of the Messiah. However, the hearts of the people were cold and full of unbelief, and their leaders were corrupt. Malachi's last word is one of judgment unless God's people repent and return to the Lord.

During the time of God's silence (approximately 300 to 400 years between Malachi and John the Baptist), the Jews were still ruled mostly by foreign powers. After the Persians came the Greeks under Alexander the Great, followed by his successors the Ptolemies and the Seleucids. In 175 B.C. the Seleucid King Antiochus IV Epiphanes, fearing the growing power of Rome, tried to unify his empire by making everybody, including the Jews, adopt Greek culture and religion. In 167 B.C. he terrorized the Jews and desecrated the Temple by sacrificing pigs to a statue of Zeus. Jews were outraged by this "abomination of desolation" foretold in the book of Daniel. The incident sparked the famous revolt led by Judas Maccabeus, who defeated the Seleucid army and took control of Jerusalem in 164 B.C. (The Jewish feast of Hanukkah still celebrates this event, and it is the subject of 1 & 2 Maccabees in the Apocrypha.)

By 142 B.C. Judea was independent and ruled by the Hasmonean dynasty, led by descendents of Judas Maccabeas. Surprisingly, however, the Hasmonean leaders progressively adopted Greek cultural ways, loosely obeying or ignoring biblical laws regarding the priesthood. Different Jewish factions like the Essenes and Pharisees opposed the Hasmoneans, while the aristocratic Sadducees supported the regime. Torn by internal strife, the Hasmoneans were defeated by Roman General Pompey in 63 B.C. The Romans installed the half-Jewish Idumean King Herod the Great (famous for trying to kill the baby Jesus and for the spectacular rebuilding of the Temple) to rule the Jews.

When Herod died (shortly after the birth of Jesus), Judas the Galilean led an unsuccessful revolt against the Romans in A.D. 6. From then on a succession of Roman governors (including Pontius Pilate) ruled Judea until the great destruction of Jerusalem in A.D. 70. From the time of Jesus to the destruction, there was intermittent but constant agitation between the Romans and Jews, as well as in-fighting among the many Jewish factions who claimed to represent the truth of God. Tragically, every one of these factions rejected the truth of God Himself, the true Messiah, at the time of His visitation. Only the minority of Jews in the small Christian community of Jerusalem recognized that Jesus the Messiah was the true King and Savior of Israel. They represented the first fruits of the true restoration of God's people and escaped the judgment of God on Jerusalem reported so graphically by Josephus and foretold by Jesus.

Significance

It is difficult to overstate the significance of Josephus's *The Jewish War.* Quite simply it is the only eyewitness account of the greatest catastrophe in history. That it has survived almost completely intact is somewhat of a miracle in itself, given that the vast majority of written works from that age have long since disappeared. As Josephus himself testifies, the fact that he even *lived* to write about this crucial event is due solely to God's surprising providence. He experienced several miraculous escapes from death, including surviving a shipwreck on his way to Rome in A.D. 64 (reminiscent of the apostle Paul's similar experience), avoiding final participation in the suicide pact, and escaping execution on a cross by the Romans.

It is not too difficult to envision why God decreed this role in history for Josephus. An intelligent, capable writer who had personal or "inside" knowledge of both the key Jewish and Roman characters and movements of the time, Josephus was able to unintentionally, independently, and without any direct ties to Christians or Christianity corroborate and confirm in detail the historic event that Jesus himself predicted would occur within a generation of His death and which confirmed for all time

the permanent transition from the Old Covenant to the New Covenant.

Of additional significance is the fact that the writings of Josephus, including *The Jewish War,* are *the* primary sources for our knowledge of both the time between the close of the Old Testament and the beginning of the New, and the times immediately following the end of the New Testament. Josephus's works also corroborate much biblical information, as well as substantially add to our knowledge about biblical times.

Main Characters

The main characters of our story, in order of importance, are:

GOD

The triune God of Scripture is the main character of *The Jewish War,* in a way that Josephus himself does not even understand. Despite declaring several times in his work that the catastrophe he describes is due to God's displeasure with the behavior of the Jews, Josephus appears oblivious to the larger context within which his story unfolds. Josephus believes the Jews have brought God's punishments upon themselves because of immoral or unrighteous behavior and rebellion. He is unaware of the fact that these behaviors are merely symptoms of a much greater issue: the rejection of their Messiah, Jesus of Nazareth, by the very people of God. This is the all-pervasive, unstated context within which the story unfolds, and, without which, the story cannot be properly understood or accounted for.

ROME AND JERUSALEM

Josephus's story is also the culmination of the clash between two great ancient civilizations. "Rome and Jerusalem have existed for centuries in the Western imagination as opposite ideals of grandeur and sanctity." Rome, the Eternal City, is seen as the "epitome of magnificent power imposed through military might," while Jerusalem represents "a holy place of revelations, miracles, and spiritual intensity."[3] The worldviews of Rome and Jerusalem were irreconcilable. Ironically it was the Jews' failure to follow their spiritual legacy (by embracing the true Messiah), and instead adopting Rome's legacy of power by the sword, that led to the destruction of Jerusalem.

VESPASIAN AND TITUS

The father/son Roman generals in the story. Vespasian initiates the response to the Jewish rebellion, conquering Galilee, and taking Josephus prisoner. Then in A.D. 69, Vespasian is called to Rome to become the next emperor after a series of civil wars in Rome. Titus is sent to finish the Jewish War by sacking Jerusalem. From Josephus's perspective both Vespasian and Titus are treated as heroes in the story, even though they are responsible for destroying Jerusalem.

JOHN OF GISCHALA AND SIMON BAR GIORA

The leading Jewish Zealots (or rebels) who fight each other for control of Jerusalem even as they fight off the Romans during the siege of the city. Josephus paints these characters in a very negative light, both because they were personal enemies of his and because he blames the Zealots for the catastrophe. In his book Josephus almost always refers to the Zealots and other rebels as tyrants, brigands, thieves, or criminals.

ARISTOCRATS AND ZEALOTS

Josephus generally paints the Zealots and other rebels as bad guys and the nobles or aristocrats as good guys. However, it is clear from the narrative that there were aristocrats who were Zealots or rebels and were often as treacherous.

JOSEPHUS

Being a participant and eyewitness in the events of his story, the author of *The Jewish War* is also a main character. The story is told from his perspective, even as he plays the different roles of peacemaker, rebel general, and ultimately prisoner and aide to Titus in the siege of Jerusalem.

Summary and Setting

The Roman governor of Judea was Gessius Florus, an extremely corrupt governor, even by Roman standards. To cover up his criminal activities he sought to provoke the Jews to rebellion. In A.D. 66 Florus orchestrated robberies for his own gain that were so outrageous that Jewish authorities decided to stop making the customary offerings at the Temple on behalf of the emperor and Rome. According to Josephus this act laid the foundation for the war with Rome. Factional fighting among the Jews intensified. Since many wealthy and powerful Jews obtained their status in Judea through deals with the Romans, they became targets of the rebels, and their houses were often plundered. The High Priest Ananias was murdered for this reason. When the small Roman garrison in Jerusalem tried to protect the wealthy Jews, they were defeated by the Jewish rebels. After surrendering with a promise of free passage out of the city, the Romans were summarily slaughtered by the rebels.

The Roman Governor of nearby Syria, Cestius Gallus, now marched on Jerusalem with a sizable force. The rebels refused an offer pardoning their misdeeds if they would disarm and return their allegiance to Rome. Cestius proceeded to march his troops through the city gates and began a siege of the inner city and Temple areas. Roman success was all but assured when Cestius inexplicably called off the siege, apparently figuring his show of strength and the rebels losses to this point were sufficient to quell the rebellion. (Josephus alleges that Cestius was bribed by Florus to retreat because Florus was not interested in a quick ending to the conflict.) This decision proved disastrous to the Romans, who subsequently lost over five thousand men and all their artillery to rebel guerilla assaults as they marched back through the Judean hills to Caesarea. The rebels were encouraged and emboldened by this unanticipated victory.

When news of this debacle reached Rome, Emperor Nero instructed Vespasian to take several Roman legions and re-conquer Israel. In early spring of A.D. 67, Vespasian launched his operation against Galilee, where he captured Josephus. For the next two years Vespasian methodically gained control of the areas surrounding Jerusalem, and laid waste to the countryside. By June A.D. 68 the Romans were in control of all the important areas outside Jerusalem, when the unexpected happened—Nero committed suicide.

Vespasian put his operations on hold as events in Rome spun completely out of control. For the first time in over a century there was no clear successor to the throne in Rome. Civil Wars broke out as generals backed by various Roman legions struggled for control of the empire. In the "year of four emperors," A.D.69, the empire teetered on the brink of collapse as four emperors—Galba, Otho, Vitellius, and Vespasian—served in one tumultuous year. Two emperors died violent deaths in the early months of the year. Subsequently, forces backing Vespasian triumphed over a third emperor and installed Vespasian as Caesar. In order to solidify his leadership, Vespasian sent his son Titus (accompanied by Josephus) back to Judea to re-conquer Jerusalem.

This delay allowed the Jews to solidify their defenses in Jerusalem. However, the factional fighting among the Jews increased. Three radical groups, led by Eleazar ben Simon, John of Gischala, and Simon bar Giora fought for control of the city. None was successful. During this time frame the Christians of Jerusalem, remembering Christ's prophecies concerning the destruction of Jerusalem, abandoned the city before the final return of the Romans, probably taking refuge in Pella on the eastern side of the river Jordan.

Suddenly in the spring of A.D. 70, Titus took the Jews by surprise, arriving with a large army to lay siege to Jerusalem, shortly after many Jews from the surrounding country and villages had gone up to Jerusalem to celebrate Passover. They were trapped inside the city with the natives. During the siege, Titus surrounded the city with a continuous wall, protected by armed guards, in order to cut off all supplies into the city and prevent anyone escaping. Ultimately deciding not to wait for the population to starve, but to destroy the entire city, Titus prosecuted the siege with vigor despite the imposing defenses of the fortress-like city and Temple. By August the deed was done, with incredible destruction of life and property. Over one million Jews were dead, the city was leveled, and the Temple destroyed, never to be built again.

Worldview

Jesus turned resolutely from his brief exchange with the inquisitorial lawyers and chief priests back to the people. Standing in the shade under the roof of the Portico of Solomon in the Temple courts he decided to tell them a simple story about a landowner who had rented his vineyard to some tenants.

"Once there were some tenants who would work a vineyard and then split the share of the profits with the landowner, who lived overseas," he explained. "When the landowner sent back an employee to collect his share of the profits, the tenants beat him up and sent him away empty handed. The landowner sent a second employee, and the tenants promptly beat him up as well. He sent yet a third employee who also was ill-treated and kicked out by the tenants. Finally the owner decided to send his only son. Surely the misbehaving tenants would listen to the owner's son. But it was not to be. Thinking they could gain control of the vineyard for good by killing the heir to the property, the tenants murdered the son." Jesus looked intently at the people. "What do you think the owner of the vineyard will do?" he asked rhetorically. "Of course, he'll come back and kill the tenants and give the vineyard to others." The people, disturbed by the story, responded, "No, this shouldn't happen." Jesus approached closer to the people, looking directly at them, and inquired, "Then what is the meaning of the Psalm which states 'The stone the builders rejected has become the cornerstone'?" Jesus concluded,

Christ Driving the Merchants from the Temple by Jacob Jordaens (1593–1678)

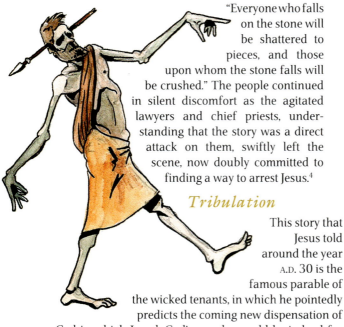

"Everyone who falls on the stone will be shattered to pieces, and those upon whom the stone falls will be crushed." The people continued in silent discomfort as the agitated lawyers and chief priests, understanding that the story was a direct attack on them, swiftly left the scene, now doubly committed to finding a way to arrest Jesus.[4]

Tribulation

This story that Jesus told around the year A.D. 30 is the famous parable of the wicked tenants, in which he pointedly predicts the coming new dispensation of God in which Israel, God's people, would be judged for rejecting the Messiah, and the Church would become the new Israel, the new people of God. The destruction of Jerusalem and the Temple approximately forty years later would be the final event establishing this new dispensation. As Passover celebration began, and Jesus approached Jerusalem in a royal manner with much fanfare, palms, and hosannas from the people, some of His excited but bewildered disciples had heard him cry out in anguish about the great city.

> If you had known, even you, especially in this your day, the things that make for your peace! But now they are hidden from your eyes. For days will come upon you when your enemies will build an embankment around you, surround you and close you in on every side, and level you, and your children within you, to the ground; and they will not leave in you one stone upon another, because you did not know the time of [God's] visitation.[5]

Shockingly, not long after all this kingly adulation, Jesus proceeded to the Temple, the most sacred symbol of the Jews' religion, and ransacked it, driving the money changers out in anger. Jesus' action was *not* a moral temper tantrum, but a symbolic act in conjunction with his warnings of judgment. Later, while walking by the Temple, some of His disciples were remarking proudly about its impressive size and beauty when Jesus responded with more astonishing and confusing words. He casually informed them that within a generation the entire Temple would be demolished, with no stone left standing. Confused, the disciples asked when this would happen. Jesus responded that the time would be near, after the disciples had experienced much first-hand persecution, many false prophets, warfare around the empire, and various fearful events and great signs. "But when you see Jerusalem surrounded by armies, then know that its desolation is near. Then let those who are in Judea flee to the mountains, let those who are in the midst of her depart, and let not those who are in the country enter her. For these are the days of vengeance, that all things which are written may be fulfilled."[6]

Like zombies in a video game, the Jews kept rebelling against the Romans. Jerusalem in early A.D. 70 was literally, not just metaphorically, the land of the "living dead," surviving only on hearts fueled by hatred and revenge. The truly shocking thing about this state of affairs was that the "zombies" involved were the people of God.

Jesus the prophet, in word and deed, continued to hammer home this theme of the judgment of God against the Jewish nation that rejected His visitation, as part of His ministry's overarching theme—the advent of the Kingdom of God and the vindication of the Son of God as the rightful King, not only of Israel but of the whole world. Those who repented and embraced Jesus would be saved. Unfortunately, the leaders of Israel and many of the Jewish people rejected His Kingship and cosmic view of redemption in favor of their own narrower, worldly expectations of redemption. As a consequence, there would be judgment and destruction, and God would now see fit to make His Church the new people of God. It is Jesus' life and message, and the Jews' tragic rejection of the Son of the very God who had created and chosen them for a special role in history that make the destruction of Jerusalem narrated by Josephus more than just a spectacular national disaster, but rather a tribulation "such as has not been since the beginning of the world until this time, no, nor ever shall be."[7]

The Land of the Living Dead

Have you ever played one of those video games where you're trying to reach some goal or conquer some territory but zombies with hatchets or chainsaws keep attacking you and getting in your way? And they just keep coming: for every zombie you mow down, three more attack, and, after awhile, the bodies are lying all over the place? You keep thinking, "come on, when are these guys going to give it up!" Finally, exhausted, you reach your goal. If you never see another zombie again it will be too soon! This is probably how the Roman soldiers felt after their terrible destruction of Jerusalem. If they never saw another Jewish rebel again it would be too soon. But this was no video game, and it wasn't virtual slaughter. This carnage really happened.

When you read the gory details in Josephus it is hard not to shake your head in disbelief and ask, "How could they? Why did they act like that?" The ultimate reason was the judgment of God predicted by Jesus. (Even Josephus and some of the Romans understood it was God's judgment, though for the wrong reasons.) But Jesus also gave us a glimpse of the "how and why" of what was to come at Jerusalem. While explaining to the disciples privately about the timing and signs of the destruction, he tells them that "many will be offended [by the faith], will betray one another, and will hate one another," false prophets will "deceive many," "lawlessness will abound," and the "love of many will grow cold."[8]

The increasing hatred and violence, not only between the Romans and Jews, but especially among the Jews themselves is palpable throughout the story, brother betraying brother, class betraying class in endless rounds of revenge and violence. Even the hardened Roman soldiers were amazed at the ferocity of the Jews' implacable hatred. It is difficult, if not impossible to find any human character in *The Jewish War* who is faithful and who does not betray somebody (including Josephus himself). Near the end of the story, for most people involved, the only thing that fueled their life was hatred and a ravenous thirst for violence and destruction. They would rather die fighting each other than compromise or try to understand, let alone love their enemies. Like the Somalis in the movie *Black Hawk Down*, they had completely lost any concept of the dignity of human beings, having degenerated to the level of ravenous animals. Jerusalem in early A.D. 70 was literally, not just metaphorically, the land of the "living dead," surviving only on hearts fueled by hatred and revenge. Soon most of them would be the "dead dead." The truly shocking thing about this state of affairs was that the "zombies" involved were the people of God. This was happening to God's chosen people! How could this be?

Worldviews in Conflict

One way to get a better handle on this unique and ghastly situation is to look at the worldviews (the way people see and explain their world) of the key participants. Worldviews, of course, are fairly complex things, but there are some key questions that all worldviews address in some form: Who are we? Where are we (in history)? What's the problem? and What's the solution?

The Jews and Jewish Rebels

Who are we? Virtually all Jews of the time believed that Israel was the chosen nation of the one creator God of the Universe.

Where are we? Most Jews thought they were in the holy land, with the Temple being the focus of their national life, but that their return from the Babylonian exile had gone wrong somehow, so they were still in exile, waiting for God's deliverance.

What's the problem? Most Jews thought that they had the wrong rulers: pagan Romans, corrupt priests who ruled under the thumb of the Romans, and half-breeds (such as Herod and his family). They believed the present situation cried out for deliverance from God.

What's the solution? Again most Jews believed that God needed to act again in history to provide a true priesthood and king. Many Jews believed this would only happen if Jews were faithful in following the covenant laws and in resisting the corruptions of the pagan Romans and their Jewish lackeys.

Because there were many Jewish factions, there were several different perspectives on these answers. Remember, the vast majority of Jews did not become followers of Jesus, and thus had rejected Jesus as the answer to their national dilemma. The Sadducees, mostly priests and aristocrats with ties to the Romans (a small but rich and powerful minority), did not believe there was a major problem with leadership or that a change in rulers was the solution to Jewish problems or that the Jews were in any sense in exile still. The Pharisees generally emphasized the need for more purity and faithfulness of Jews to the laws of God as the Pharisees understood them, so that God would be willing to act on the Jews' behalf. The Essenes, separatists living out in the wilderness, believed that the priests and leaders were so corrupt that God had called the Essenes to be the first fruits of the new kingdom of God, wholly set apart from the corrupt Jews, and that God would act soon to vindicate them.

Most importantly from the standpoint of Josephus, the Jewish Zealots and radicals (whom Josephus usually calls brigands, thieves or tyrants) agreed with the majority of Jews that they were still in exile as the people of God, and that the main problem was the corrupt Roman and Jewish leadership. They believed that if they took the initiative in courageously defending, by violence, the purity of the Temple against the abominations of the pagan Romans, that God would, in essence, be forced to give them the victory and protect His dwelling place. Surely God would not let anything happen to the Temple, His dwelling place. Josephus records amazing evidence of this mentality when rebel leader John of Gischala refused to stop his suicidal defense because in his view of things God would never let His Temple be captured by pagans.

As the tensions between the Jews and Romans increased, the radical Jews were able to persuade many other Jews that God was going to act through the rebellion to save Israel from the Romans. These Jews were further encouraged by the surprising victory of the rebels against the Roman legions under Cestius in A.D. 66. Those Jews who were not persuaded by the words of the radicals often were terrorized into supporting the rebellion.

The Romans

Who are we? The Romans believed they were the rulers of the world, fated for that role by the gods.

Where are we? The Romans believed they were in the god-forsaken land of the Jews, doing their duty to the world by keeping order in the empire and shoring up de-

Roman soldiers carry the plundered contents of the Temple in this detail from the Arch of Titus in Rome.

fenses against eastern barbarians such as the Parthians. The Romans believed, in essence, that they were the policemen of the world, bringing order and justice to inferior peoples such as the Jews.

What's the problem? To the Romans the answer was simple. The stiff-necked Jews are the problem. They refused to meld into the Roman society and behave as they should. The Jews were extremely fussy about their religious laws and their exclusive God, and the Jewish radicals had become too troublesome and too powerful.

What's the solution? The Romans believed that force and violence were the solution to the Jewish rebellion, which must be put down as a lesson to other inferior peoples who might think about rebelling against the rulers of the world.

The Romans had no way of comprehending the Jews' religious zeal and focus. Roman religion was classic pagan polytheism (many gods), and there was no central focus to the religion. Religion played a supporting role in Roman life, rather than being at the center of life. This contrast can be seen in the physical layout of the two great ancient cities of Rome and Jerusalem. The Temple was at the center of and dominated life in Jerusalem. The imposing physical presence of the Temple overshadowed all other structures in the city. All other aspects of life in Jerusalem, including business and politics, revolved around Temple activities and personnel. By contrast, there were several temples to pagan gods in Rome, but none of them dominated the landscape or presented a central focus for the city. Neither were they the main focus of business or politics in the capital of the empire.

Additionally, the Romans were always open to "acquiring" more and better gods, wherever they found them. For example, several of the most important gods in the empire were originally Egyptian gods. The more the merrier so to speak. This, of course, was in direct contrast to the Jews: their God had specifically prohibited the worship of any other gods. Neither could the Romans fathom a god without an image. How could the Jews worship their God when they were not even permitted to have any images of Him? Thus there was a profound cultural disconnect between the first century Romans and Jews which may be hard for us to appreciate today. Their religious worldviews could hardly be further apart.

The one thing the two cultures did share was a belief, in some form, of prophecies and signs. It is for this reason that Josephus could successfully save his life by predicting that Vespasian would become emperor. It is also why both parties during the war could assert, in effect, that God (or the gods) was on their side.

Josephus's Worldview

So where did Josephus stand amidst these various worldviews? Given his unique experiences and position, it is not surprising that Josephus's worldview at the time of his writing did not conform exactly to the Jewish or Roman worldviews. Josephus agreed with all other Jews that they were the chosen people of the creator God. He also believed that the Jews, in some sense, had not been fully restored since exile and that their current leaders (both Romans and Jews) were at least part of the problem. To some extent he agreed with the Pharisees that the Jews' problem was their own lack of faithfulness and purity. But unlike most Jews of his day, by the time of the destruction and subsequent writing of *The Jewish War*, he believed that the Romans *were the answer rather than the cause* of the Jews' problems and that the Jews needed to reform their behavior and accept the fact that God had put the Romans in charge of them. Josephus even believed that the circulating prophecies about a new world leader arising out of Judea ultimately referred to the Roman Emperor Vespasian who was crowned emperor by his troops while still in Israel. The relevant fundamental belief of Josephus is that the destruction of Jerusalem was the judgment of God on the Jews, and more particularly the radicals, for their horrible moral behavior and rebellion against the Romans.

Josephus tells us that shortly after the daily sacrifice in the Temple was stopped (for lack of men and lambs) he went to the Temple wall to encourage the rebel leader John of Gischala and his men to "come out of the temple and fight somewhere outside" so they would stop polluting the Temple and save it instead. When "the tyrant John" cursed Josephus, saying he did not fear capture because the city was God's, Josephus responded that everybody knew about the Old Testament prophets forecasting the destruction of "this miserable city." Josephus concluded, "It is God Himself who is using the Romans to purge the temple with fire and exterminate a city so choked with pollution."[9] This was certainly true, although Josephus was unaware of the ultimate reason for this judgment.

Biblical Analysis

How does the Bible view the events laid out by Josephus in *The Jewish War*? In summary form the biblical view answers the questions as follows:

Who are we? The Jews were the Old Covenant people of the creator God of the Universe. The pagan Romans had been given power by God to build their empire for God's purposes, including the coming of His Son and the

After Jerusalem fell, other Jewish rebels withstood a Roman siege in the fortress of Masada. When in A.D. 73 the Romans built a rampart and finally breached the wall, they found its 960 defenders had committed suicide rather than surrender.

propagation of the gospel. (The Romans, of course did not acknowledge the true God or give Him thanks, and used their God-given power for their own, usually wrongful, purposes.)

Where are we? Crucially this generation was the time of God's judgment on his rebellious people, the Jews, and the end of the Old Covenant. God used the Romans to execute that judgment, although the Roman Empire itself will be judged and dismantled 300 years later.

What's the problem? The problem was the rejection of God's Son by His own people, as dramatized in the parable of the wicked tenants. This rejection led to all sorts of other schemes by the Jews to fix what they consider to be the problem—the rule of Rome.

What's the solution? The only solution is God's judgment of the Jews and the saving of all the New Covenant followers of Jesus to participate in the New Israel, the Church.

The biblical perspective on this crucial time is far more comprehensive than the narrow worldviews of the Jews, the Romans, or Josephus. The destruction of Jerusalem and the Temple is an integral part of God's big story, confirming to the first generation Christians (as well as all subsequent generations) the prophecies of Jesus and his status as Ruler of the world sitting at the right hand of the Father. It marked the permanent end of the Old Covenant (the last sacrifices of the rebels under John were the final sacrifices ever made in the Temple in history). The Jews who survived in the world but rejected Jesus, having no Temple, had no choice but to create an essentially new religion called rabbinic Judaism. Whatever doubts the Christians had about their upstart faith were now erased, even as the Jews now had to come to terms with the loss of their spiritual center and place of sacrifice. The New Covenant of the blood of Christ was affirmed and established for all time, as was the status of the Church as the new Israel, the new people of God. This was the main point of the events of A.D. 70.

Josephus thought of himself as a prophet. In some minor ways God used him in this role. Josephus's details were accurate in his explanations regarding the Jewish War. Yet despite all of his experience and learning, because he did not acknowledge Jesus as the Messiah, he missed entirely the main point of the incredible event known as the destruction of Jerusalem.

—William S. Dawson

For Further Reading

Goodman, Martin. *Rome and Jerusalem.* London: Allen Lane, 2007.

Holford, George, *The Destruction of Jerusalem.* Nagadoches, Tex.: Covenant Media Press, 2001

Mason, Steve. *Josephus and the New Testament.* Peabody, Mass.: Hendrickson, 1992.

Seward, Desmond. *Jerusalem's Traitor: Josephus, Masada, and the Fall of Judea.* Cambridge, Mass.: Da Capo Press, 2009.

Spielvogel, Jackson J. *Western Civilization.* Seventh Edition. Belmont, Calif.: Thomson Wadsworth, 2009. 173.

Veritas Press History Cards: New Testament, Greece and Rome. Lancaster, Pa.: Veritas Press. 27.

Session I: Prelude

Question To Consider

You might recall the gospel passage where Jesus effectively warns God's people not to fear those who have the power to destroy the physical body only, but fear Him who has the power to destroy body and soul (Luke 12:4–5). How do you think this warning might be connected with the destruction of Jerusalem?

From the General Information above answer the following questions:

1. How did Josephus escape execution after being captured by the Romans in Jotapata?
2. Why can't Josephus be totally trusted in his evaluation of the Jewish lower classes and the Jewish rebel leaders?
3. What famous parable did Jesus tell the people predicting the destruction of the Jews and confirming the Church as the new people of God?
4. Why were the Jews in Jerusalem in A.D. 70 like zombies, and what was so shocking about this situation?
5. According to the worldview of the Jewish rebels, what were the problem and solution regarding their situation?
6. According to the worldview of the Romans, what were the problem and solution regarding their situation?
7. According to the biblical view of the world, what were the problem and solution regarding their situation?

Reading Assignment:
The Jewish War, W II:280–W III:399

Session II: Discussion
The Jewish War, W II:280–W III:399

Question to Consider
What is a prophet?

Discuss or list short answers to the following questions:

Text Analysis

1. Why did Josephus consider himself in some sense having the gift of prophecy?
2. Why did the Romans even consider that Josephus could possibly be prophetic even though he was a Jewish general who did not believe in the Roman religion?
3. After Vespasian questioned the other Jewish soldiers about Josephus's "prophecy," what happened?
4. Later in the text you will read that rebel leader John of Gischala asserted to Josephus that he did not fear capture by the Romans because Jerusalem was God's city. Josephus responded, "It is God Himself who is using the Romans to purge His temple with fire and exterminate a city so choked with pollution!" Was this "prophecy" of Josephus true?

Cultural Analysis

1. What is the current Western view of "prophecy"?
2. How are some modern Western views of "prophecy" similar to ancient pagan views?

Biblical Analysis

1. What is the biblical view of prophecy?
2. Moses pointed to and spoke of a prophet to come who would be greater than himself in Deuteronomy 18:15–22, through whom the ultimate rest and salvation of the people would come. Who was Moses speaking about even though Moses never knew him or his name?
3. How do you know a true prophet according to the Bible (Read Deut. 13:2; 18:20; Jer. 23:14; Isa. 8:19; Heb. 11)?

Summa

Write an essay or discuss this question, integrating what you have learned from the material above.
Was Josephus a "true" prophet?

"Eleazar, however, did not intend to flee, nor would he allow anyone else to do so. When he saw the wall in flames, he thought it would be nobler for all to die than fall into Roman hands . . . ." (Jewish War, VII:320)

Session III: Discussion
The Jewish War, W II:280–W III:399

Question to Consider
What are "factions," and are they good or bad?

Discuss or list short answers to the following questions:

Text Analysis
1. Name three factions of Jews in the first century who had different worldviews and are referenced in Josephus and the Bible.
2. Who were the three main rebel leaders who organized different factions of rebels according to Josephus?
3. According to Josephus, how did the "leading men" and "people who favored peace" respond to the takeover of the Temple by the Zealots and radicals?
4. From your reading of the Worldview Essay, what factions developed that nearly destroyed the Roman Empire itself in A.D. 69?

Cultural Analysis
1. Can you think of factions in the modern world who are or have fought each other literally or figuratively within the recent past?
2. What has happened to the Church's witness in the modern world as a result of the Protestant factions regularly splitting?

Biblical Analysis
1. What does the book of James tell us about our conflicts and fighting? (James 4:1–3)
2. What did Jesus make clear about the results of disunity in a body or household? (Mark 3:25; Matt. 12:25)
3. What does the Apostle Paul tell the Corinthians about divisions within the Church? (1 Cor. 1:10–13)
4. What did Paul tell the Christians of his generation, the generation of the destruction of Jerusalem, regarding complaints, disputes and arguments? (Phil. 2:14–16)

Summa

Write an essay or discuss this question, integrating what you have learned from the material above.
Why is it important that Christians today avoid falling into contentious factions?

Reading Assignment:
The Jewish War, W III:409–W IV:84

SESSION IV: RECITATION
The Jewish War, W III:409–W IV:84

Comprehension Questions
Answer the following questions for factual recall:
1. When Vespasian marched his troops to Caesarea after capturing Jotapata, who did the Caesareans loudly demand be punished and why?
2. When the people of Jerusalem heard that Josephus had surrendered to the Romans how did they react?
3. What was the name of the Jewish rebel leader based in Tarichaeae?
4. How did Titus surprise and overtake Tarichaeae after he learned that the rebels and townspeople were fighting and arguing among themselves?
5. To where did the Jewish fugitives of the initial Tarichaeae action run? What did the Romans do as a result?
6. After taking control of Tarichaeae, how did Vespasian brutally trick the surviving rebels?
7. When Vespasian advanced on the town of Gamala, who tried to persuade the people of the city to surrender, and what happened when he did?
8. How did the Roman officer Placidus trick the rebels on Mount Tabor?
9. What cowardly order did John of Gischala give his rebels as they left Gischala under cover of darkness to escape to Jerusalem?
10. How did Titus react in the morning when he found out about John's escape the night before?

READING ASSIGNMENT:
The Jewish War, W V:1–98

SESSION V: ACTIVITY
The Jewish War, W V:1–98

Biblical Research
If you pay attention in your reading of the Gospels, you will see that most of the teaching of Jesus, as he closes his ministry approaching and then entering Jerusalem, dwells on the theme of coming judgment. It is remarkable how much of his teachings from this time are focused not directly on His approaching death but on the impending catastrophe of Jerusalem and judgment of the Jews. Read Matthew 21–25 and Luke 19–21. Identify as many parables and actions of Jesus as you can that are about the destruction of Jerusalem or judgment of the Jews. Both identify the parable and give a brief explanation of why it applies to the time of the destruction of Jerusalem:

READING ASSIGNMENT:
The Jewish War, W V:136–348

SESSION VI: DISCUSSION
The Jewish War, W V:136–348

Question to Consider
How do you think redemption and judgment are related?

Discuss or list short answers to the following questions:

Text Analysis
1. From your reading of the Worldview Essay, who is being judged in the story of *The Jewish War*?
2. Who is redeemed in the limited sense of vindication (rather than salvation by God) in the way that Josephus tells the story?
3. Who is redeemed and vindicated with respect to true salvation in this story, even though Josephus is largely unaware of this fact?
4. What does Josephus show us about the collective nature of judgment in this story?

Cultural Analysis
1. How does the modern Western world view the concepts of redemption and judgment?
2. Why do modern Westerners have trouble with the concept of God's judgment?

Biblical Analysis
1. How do we know that the ideas of redemption and judgment are directly linked (Matt. 25)?
2. How is God's revelation, both in creation and through His word, related to redemption and judgment (Isa. 55:10–12)?

SUMMA

Write an essay or discuss this question, integrating what you have learned from the material above.
How is Josephus's story of the Jewish War the perfect example of the power of God's Word to redeem and to damn?

READING ASSIGNMENT:
The Jewish War, W V:424–W VI:157

Session VII: Recitation
The Jewish War, W V:424–W VI:157

Comprehension Questions

Answer the following questions for factual recall:
1. As the famine raged in the city of Jerusalem because of the Roman siege, what did the rebels do?
2. What is Josephus's fearful summary about the sufferings of the people and the crime of the rebels in Jerusalem during the siege?
3. What did Titus do to those Jews captured for venturing out of the city to look for food?
4. What were rebel leaders John and Simon able to do to the first Roman earthworks around the Antonia Fortress?
5. After the Romans rebuilt the earthworks and finally broke through the Antonia wall, what were they surprised and dismayed to see?
6. What did Titus urge his troops to do when they saw this second wall?
7. How did the Romans finally take the Antonia Fortress?
8. When the Romans tried to press on and take the Temple after the Jews fled inside it, what happened?
9. According to Josephus, Titus sent Josephus to tell rebel leader John that Titus would permit the Jews to fight outside the Temple in order to keep from desecrating the holy structure. How did John respond to Josephus's offer?
10. How did Josephus respond to John?

Reading Assignment:
The Jewish War, W VI:177–271

"But when you see Jerusalem surrounded by armies, then know that its desolation is near. Then let those who are in Judea flee to the mountains, let those who are in the midst of her depart, and let not those who are in the country enter her. For these are the days of vengeance, that all things which are written may be fulfilled."—Luke 21:20–22

Chart 1: WORLDVIEW ANALYSIS

ISSUE	JEWISH REBEL WORLDVIEW	ROMAN WORLDVIEW	JOSEPHUS WORLDVIEW	BIBLICAL WORLDVIEW
Nature of God	Yahweh is the only God, He dwells in the Temple in Jerusalem which is the center of the world, and He will not let His Temple be destroyed	Many gods who are jealous and not in complete control of events—superior to men and immortal but like men subject to fate	Yahweh is the one true God, He dwells in the Temple, but will leave if His people are not faithful and obedient to His laws	
God has sent the Romans to . . .				
Salvation will be attained by . . .				
The fate of Jerusalem and the Temple are . . .				
The future will bring . . .				

Session VIII: Activity
The Jewish War, W VI:177–271

Warnings of the End

Jesus was not the only person to warn the first generation Christians about the destruction of Jerusalem and the end of the world as they knew it—the Old Covenant dispensation—and the beginning of a new world—the New Covenant kingdom of God. The apostles also regularly alerted the first Christians to this cosmic change in reality—the judgment of the Jews and the vindication of the New Israel, the new people of God. Find the warnings for the nearness of the end of the Old Covenant dispensation confirmed by the destruction of Jerusalem. Search in your Bible or Bible dictionary or commentary for the multiple passages by the apostles alerting the faithful to the nearness of the time of this momentous change in the world. In the books of Romans, 1 Corinthians, Philippians, James, 1 Peter, 1 John, and Revelation there are at least 14 references to the nearness of time for these momentous changes and the need of the first century Christians to be aware.

1. Review the following scriptures and write a short summary of what each one says about the coming end of the Old Covenant:
   1 Corinthians 7:31
   1 Corinthians 10:11
   1 Peter 4:7
   1 John 2:18
   Revelation 1:1
   Revelation 22:6–7
2. What other passages in the New Testament point to this same truth?
3. What conclusion should believers in the early church have been able to draw from these passages?

Reading Assignment:
The Jewish War, W VI:281–420

Session IX: Recitation
The Jewish War, W VI:177–420

Comprehension Questions
Answer the following questions for factual recall:
1. How did a certain Roman soldier Artorius save himself from the flames along the Temple's western portico set by the Jews?
2. During the excruciating famine caused by the siege, what was the incredible horror of Mary of Bethezuba described by Josephus?
3. What did Mary say and how did the rebels react when they arrived, curious about the "unholy smell" coming from her house?
4. According to Josephus, how did the Roman generals decide to deal with the Temple?
5. According to Josephus, the Temple was doomed on what important date?
6. How did the fire that eventually helped destroy the Temple get started?
7. How did the Roman troops respond to Titus' command to stop the burning of the Temple?
8. While the Temple was in flames how did the Romans act toward Jewish people and property?
9. Josephus tells us that before the siege of Jerusalem "portents had appeared, foretelling the impending devastation, but the Jews had disregarded these warnings of God." Describe at least three such portents.
10. According to Josephus what "ambiguous oracle" most incited the Jews to war?
11. How did Josephus say the Jews misinterpreted this prophecy, and how did Josephus interpret it?
12. When the rebels had fled from the Temple into the lower city, what did the Romans do?
13. When Titus saw up close the strength of the city towers and walls abandoned by the rebels, what did he say according to Josephus?
14. According to Josephus what was the total number of prisoners taken by the Romans, and how many died in the siege?

Reading Assignment:
The Jewish War, W VII:1–454

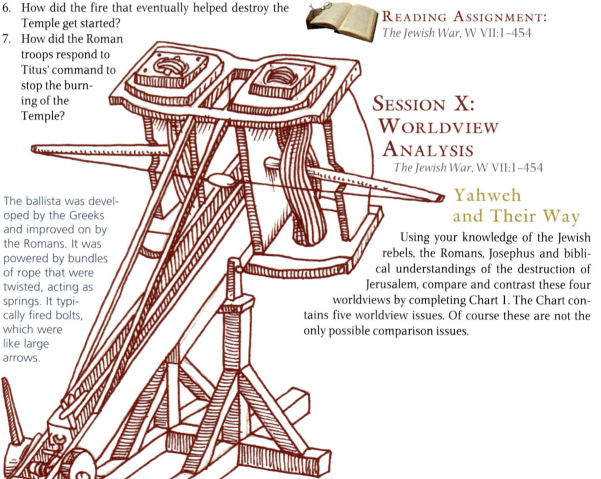

The ballista was developed by the Greeks and improved on by the Romans. It was powered by bundles of rope that were twisted, acting as springs. It typically fired bolts, which were like large arrows.

Session X: Worldview Analysis
The Jewish War, W VII:1–454

Yahweh and Their Way

Using your knowledge of the Jewish rebels, the Romans, Josephus and biblical understandings of the destruction of Jerusalem, compare and contrast these four worldviews by completing Chart 1. The Chart contains five worldview issues. Of course these are not the only possible comparison issues.

OPTIONAL SESSION A: ACTIVITY

Siege Weapons Research

Do some research in the library or online on Roman siege equipment and weapons and write a paragraph or two describing the equipment listed below and how it was used by the Romans.[10]
1. The Ram
2. The Onager
3. The Ballista
4. The Carro-ballista

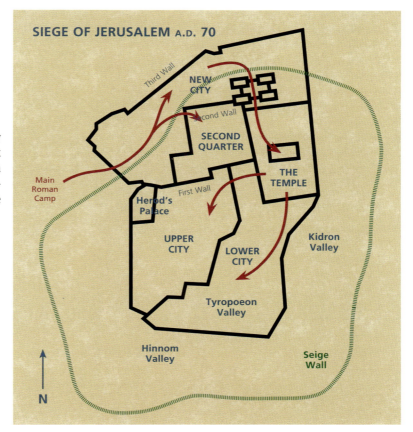

OPTIONAL SESSION B: ACTIVITY

Map Study

Using the map of the Roman siege of Jerusalem, answer the following questions:
1. From what direction did Titus approach Jerusalem and break through the third (outer) wall?
2. In what direction was the main

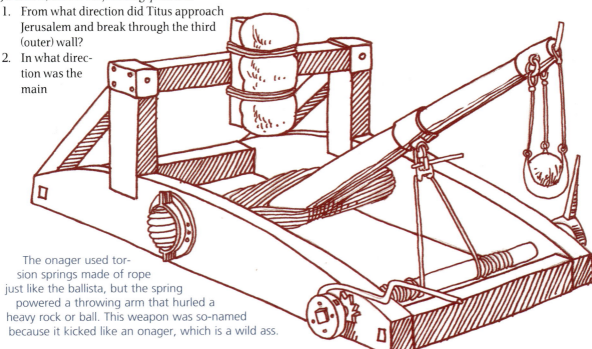

The onager used torsion springs made of rope just like the ballista, but the spring powered a throwing arm that hurled a heavy rock or ball. This weapon was so-named because it kicked like an onager, which is a wild ass.

Roman camp from the city?

3. Once the Romans captured and destroyed the Antonia fortress, what did they capture next?

4. Which side of the city contained the Temple?

5. On which side of the city was Herod's Palace?

6. In what section of the city is the Tyropoeon Valley?

ENDNOTES

1 Description of Vespasian taken from Seward, Desmond, *Jerusalem's Traitor*, p. 99.

2 The Judean aristocracy had emerged only during the past century, under the Herods or still more recently. In a country where the harvest was dependent on an uncertain rainfall, their wealth had been acquired by lending money to peasants in bad years and seizing their holdings when they defaulted. In addition, just as the prophet Amos had written long ago, they manipulated the price of wheat so that "we may buy the poor for silver, and the needy for a pair of shoes" (Amos 8:6). Understandably, they were unloved by the tenants they gained in this way and hated by even the peacefully minded among the poor because of their greed, corruption, and ostentation. Throughout Judea there was deep hostility between the classes. From Seard, Desmond, *Jerusalem's Traitor*, p. 11.

3 Goodman, Martin, Rome and Jerusalem, p. 29.

4 See Luke 20:9–19.

5 Luke 19:42–44

6 See Luke 21:5–22

7 Matthew 24:21

8 See Matthew 24:10–12.

9 *The Jewish War* (W VI:93).

10 Information on Roman siege equipment can be found by following the links for this chapter at www.VeritasPress.com/OmniLinks.

MEDITATIONS

once you had explained the Internet, what would Benjamin Franklin write on his blog?

Reading Marcus Aurelius's *Meditations*, I often imagine his thoughts in the context of modern technology. I can picture his reflections appearing in an online journal, or perhaps filling space on his personal home page. "Meditations" could be the title of a pastor's or college professor's blog. But thinking of the second century Roman emperor in the context of modern technology only highlights the difference between him and the millions of bloggers typing away on their laptops. Today, those in the blogging world watch their hit count, hoping to see evidence that someone else in the world stopped to read their (usually poorly written and unimportant) thoughts. But what are the chances of a student reading anything posted on one of our blogs 2,000 years from now? Marcus Aurelius, on the other hand, has been read by millions of men and women for nearly two millennia, and he didn't intend for a single person to read his thoughts!

Have you ever wondered how the founding fathers of our country would respond if they saw the United States today? What would it be like to give Benjamin Franklin a tour of Philadelphia in 2009? I can imagine the conversation. "Mr. Franklin, would you like to visit New York, Baltimore, or Washington, D.C. this afternoon?" "This afternoon?! Even if you drove the carriage until the horses collapsed we wouldn't get to Washington until late tonight!" How would he respond if you offered to take him to Paris in a day, if only he would hop inside a giant flying machine? How would you explain the Internet? And

GENERAL INFORMATION

Author and Context

Marcus Annius Verus was born on April 26, A.D. 121, during the reign of Hadrian. His father died while he was still young, so his grandfather raised him and directed his education. Marcus was introduced to Stoicism, a belief that people should strictly restrain their emotions in order to attain happiness and wisdom, during these early years of his education, and this philosophy guided him the rest of his life. But Marcus's life changed dramatically in A.D. 138. Upon the death of Hadrian, Rome chose

420 OMNIBUS IV

Aurelius Antoninus, Marcus's uncle, as the next Roman emperor. Having no son of his own, Antoninus adopted Marcus as his future successor and changed his name to Marcus Aurelius Antoninus. From this point on, Marcus spent his days learning to run a government and preparing to lead the empire.

Marcus Aurelius became emperor himself in A.D. 161. The empire was still technically enjoying the *Pax Romana,* the period of peace and prosperity that had begun under Caesar Augustus over a century before. But during Marcus's reign, an outbreak of the plague, a series of natural disasters, and threats of war from Germans in the north and barbarians in the east threatened the *Pax Romana.* The emperor spent much of his reign personally directing the efforts to defend the borders, and it was during these years of war, holding back the rising tide of barbarians on the edge of the empire, that Marcus Aurelius wrote his *Meditations.*

Marcus Aurelius died from a disease that swept through his camp in A.D. 180. His son, Commodus, took the throne after him, but he did not follow his father's example of virtue and dedication. He is generally considered one of the more useless emperors in Rome's history.

Significance

The desire to be famous, to make a difference, to leave a significant mark on society seems to be built into mankind. Dying men leave money for buildings that will perpetuate their name, and young boys and girls dream of being the president, a famous baseball player, an

Marcus Aurelius reigned as emperor in Rome from 161 to 180. The first eight years he was co-emperor with his adoptive brother Lucius Verus until Lucius's death in 169.

actor, or a well-known singer. Of course, most of us won't be remembered by anyone beyond our own grandchildren. Marcus Aurelius, on the other hand, didn't have any pretensions to greatness. His *Meditations* were meant for his own personal use, yet he didn't think even he would re-read his journal. He wasn't trying to impact the ages with his great philosophical thought; he was merely attempting to live a virtuous life.

But unlike most of us, Marcus Aurelius has made a significant contribution to Western thought. The most important contribution of the *Meditations* is the picture it gives us of the worldview of a Roman Stoic. Stoicism was the predominate worldview throughout the first two centuries of the Roman Empire, and although we have other examples and writings of professed Stoics, it is the *Meditations* that offers the most complete guide to Stoic philosophy. In the process, it also gives us a glimpse into the life of virtue a disciple of Stoicism would seek to live.

The book is especially important for us to understand as Christians. As you read through this book, you will notice that many of Marcus Aurelius's thoughts sound similar to Jesus' commands from the Sermon on the Mount. In fact, philosophers and commentators often point to Marcus Aurelius's *Meditations* as evidence that Christianity stole many ideas from Stoicism, and that Stoicism offers almost the same moral standards found in Christianity. We will better understand our own faith if we can thoughtfully read Marcus Aurelius and see how his attempts at peace, happiness, and virtue fall short of the power and good news of the gospel.

Summary

It is difficult to summarize Marcus Aurelius's *Meditations* because this work is not a story; it lacks any one theme or overarching narrative and has no characters other than Marcus himself, the author and recipient of the book. What we have in the *Meditations* is really Marcus's journal; his collection of thoughts, advice, and maxims on life, virtue, and the world. Many of these are his own exhortations, but he also includes principles he learned from family members and companions. Quotes from other philosophers that Marcus considers worth remembering, especially Plato, also find their way into his *Meditations*.

Unlike many ancient works, we are not missing any sections from the *Meditations*. It consists of twelve books in all, and each contains a fairly random collection of thoughts. While there is some coherence to the first book in that it lists what Marcus has learned from various figures in his life, there is no theme, pattern, or division to the content of remaining eleven books. In fact, the material often seems a bit repetitive, since Marcus reminds himself over and over of many of the same principles of virtue, arguing that he has not attained the level of virtue or philosophy that he is striving for. Perhaps the best way to bring together all the material in the *Meditations* is to think of it as a personal exhortation to live a virtuous life based on Stoic beliefs.

Worldview

Have you ever experienced the disappointment of thinking you have found a spectacular deal, the opportunity of a lifetime, only to discover a devastating "catch" that sends your dreams spiraling into the dust? I remember grabbing the mail one day and pulling out an envelope from a flower and garden store announcing that I was a specially chosen finalist for a grand-prize sweepstakes of $25,000. All I needed to do was mail back the enclosed form with a single dime attached, and I was on my way to winning hundreds of prizes. I had a mental spreadsheet of what I was going to buy with the $25,000 before I even had the return envelope stamped. Sadly, after sending in my dime, I received another lengthy letter and survey that made me "almost a winner," followed by a request for a purchase of $25 or more, after which I was again "about to win" the stated prizes. By this point, I realized that the promised $25,000 was not going to appear in my mailbox as I had initially dreamed.

My dashed sweepstakes hopes taught me to look closely at glowing mail offers. But far more important than catchy slogans telling us to "click here to claim your prize," many ideas, beliefs, and philosophies appear true, good, and helpful, only to reveal devastating falsehood upon closer examination. This is why it is important for us to be able to think clearly and logically, and to "test the spirits to see whether they are from God."

Marcus Aurelius gives us a long list of such ideas, beliefs, and philosophies. As you read through his *Meditations*, many of his thoughts may strike you as being very similar to biblical principles. He encourages us to be humble, truthful, selfless, generous, kind, patient, and self-controlled. He calls us to honor others as our brothers, urges his readers to consider whether their lives line up with divine standards, and talks about the importance of life after death. All of this sounds very similar to Christian doctrine. However, underneath many true statements, Marcus has built on a flawed foundation that inevitably brings his system of morality crashing to the ground.

Marcus Aurelius and Stoicism

Marcus Aurelius dedicated his life to the philosophy of Stoicism from a young age. Because of the *Meditations,* he is probably the most famous Roman Stoic in history. Stoicism was a comprehensive worldview that sought to answer questions about God, the world, and life after death, as well as offer a path to a happy and virtuous life.

Stoicism is essentially pantheistic. *Pantheism* comes from two Greek words: $\pi\alpha\nu$, meaning "all," and $\theta\epsilon o\varsigma$, meaning "god." Pantheists believe that deity dwells in all things, or, more to the point, that it is to be identified with all things. Of course, as Christians, we believe that God is everywhere and that He dwells in us if we have placed our trust in Christ. But we mean that God's presence is in all places and that we have fellowship with Him, not that our skin and bones, or the rocks and trees, are actually part of God. That, however, is exactly what pantheism holds. When the pantheist says that God dwells in all things, he means that every material thing is actually part of God. According to the Stoics, pantheism is something like a fiery energy existing in all things. It is also a sovereign, guiding force that determines all that comes to pass.

Stoics would have been very comfortable saying that men were created in god's image, because they believed that every man consisted of a body ruled by a rational soul, just as the world was a mass of material things governed by god. This led the Stoics to posit that the best life was a life lived "according to Nature." A life lived "according to Nature" meant that just as god ruled the material world, so a man's reason would rule his body, along with its passions and emotions. Reason was also responsible for guiding a person toward a virtuous and happy life, just as the Stoic god sovereignly guided the affairs of the world.

Marcus Aurelius consistently comes back to these beliefs. Happiness through virtue is his main goal, and

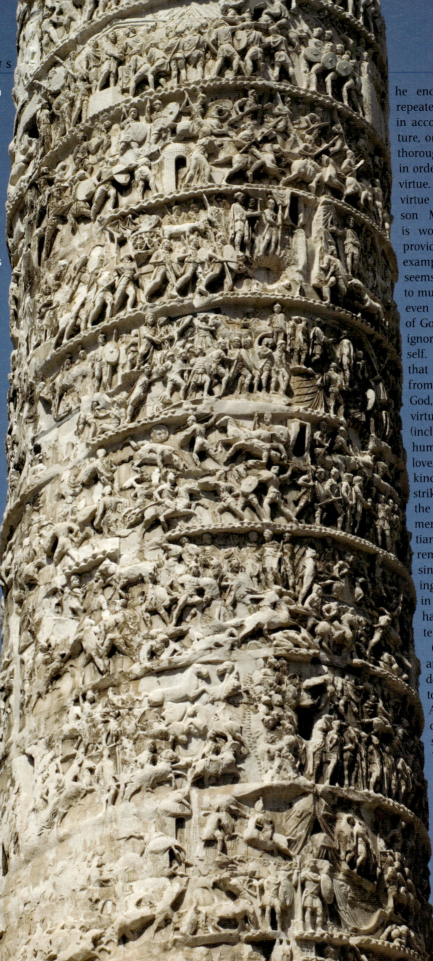

422 OMNIBUS

The Column of Marcus Aurelius was built in the late second century in honor of the late emperor. It is formed of 28 blocks of marble and stands 100 feet tall in the Piazza Colonna in Rome. The spiral relief celebrates two of Aurelius's military expeditions.

he encourages himself repeatedly to live more in accordance with Nature, or to submit more thoroughly to his reason in order to maintain his virtue. His emphasis on virtue is part of the reason Marcus Aurelius is worth reading. He provides an excellent example of a man who seems to live according to much of God's truth even though outside of God's covenant and ignorant of God Himself. Aurelius argues that happiness results from obedience to God, while the specific virtues he strives for (including integrity, humility, self-control, love, patience, and kindness) sound strikingly similar to the fruit of the Spirit mentioned in Galatians 5:22. All this reminds us that even sinful human beings are still made in God's image and have His truth written on their hearts.

Of course, humans are still sinful, and despite his desire to promote virtue, Aurelius fell short of biblical truth in several key areas. The foundation for Stoic virtue rests on two key principles: submission to whatever fate Nature brings into his life and ordering life according to one's own reason. On both accounts, Aurelius built his house upon the sand rather than on the rock of scriptural truth.

Upon first glance, submitting to the sovereignty of the Stoic god may seem right in line with what Scripture teaches. After all, we ought to be content with whatever God puts in our lives. But the problem isn't so much the idea of a sovereign, guiding force in the universe, but with who (or what) that guiding force is. For the Stoic, this god is an impersonal force that makes sure the world doesn't collapse. It's something similar to a supercomputer that keeps everything in order as the world moves along. This sort of sovereign force may assure you that the universe won't explode in the next few minutes, and it may be able to ensure that things generally will work out for the common good, but it offers no comfort or hope in the face of life's challenges, or during times of suffering and persecution.

As Christians, it is not just the fact that God is *sovereign* that is so comforting, but that *God* is sovereign. As you make your way through the clouds, thirty-five thousand feet above the earth, it is not the fact that a person is flying your plane that gives you a sense of security (the planes used on September 11, 2001, were flown by people), but the fact that your pilot has the ability and intention to carry you safely to your destination. We delight in the fact that the God of the Bible has planned everything that has and will occur, but only because of the character of the God in whom we trust. He is a good God, who has sacrificed His own Son in order to save us from sin and death, who provides for our needs and cares for us as His children, who is just, and who will not allow the wicked to prosper beyond their time. This hope and assurance springs from who God is. In the end, an impersonal, fiery force that happens to keep things running looks a lot different from the personal, loving, just God of the Bible.

The second pillar of Stoicism is the ability of reason to guide a person into all truth and virtue. Reason acts as the connection between the human and the divine, and it provides both the standard and the source of all good in humanity. This doctrine, however, diverges from Scriptural truth is several important ways.

To begin, in order to elevate reason to this lofty role, Stoicism must have a different understanding of the nature and source of evil. If all men are rational, and reason provides a path to virtue, the question remains why men so often are *not* virtuous. A Stoic would quickly agree that men are sinful...as long as we are referring to men's bodies, passions, or emotions. But for the Stoic, reason, or the capacity to think, is the work of god in man. Man is most like god when he exercises his reason. Thus, to suggest that reason is fallen, corrupt, or sinful would be an attack on the divine itself.

So, if reason will never lead a man to a sinful or corrupt conclusion, why are crimes committed, and why does suffering consume humanity? If reason leads to virtue, vice must be the result of . . . not thinking! And that is just what the Stoics believed. They held that evil and suffering were the result of ignorance or stupidity, rather than active or intentional evil. A man does something evil because he just isn't *thinking,* or because he doesn't know better. If he would exercise his reason, he would realize that what he is doing is wrong. Marcus Aurelius notes that "men are not intentional evildoers," and that the ill will and selfishness he encounters is "due to the offender's ignorance of what is good or evil." In fact, he even goes so far as to say that rational beings should be *incapable* of indiscretion!

Unfortunately, the Stoics were neither the first nor the last to hold such a position about humanity's ability to think or to reason to righteousness. Much of modern education is based on the premise that if children are educated, they will turn out to be moral, upstanding citizens. While a well-educated person may be more apt to weigh the consequences of his actions, education does nothing to change the heart or make a person moral. Sociologists and educators constantly argue that viewing children as naturally sinful damages their self-esteem and impedes our ability to love them and help them appropriately. If we look at people's natural goodness, then we'll be able to see their potential to improve themselves.

But it seems to me that anyone who has ever had a brother, a sister, or a child should realize fairly quickly that humans are not naturally good people. We seem to delight in teasing, mocking, and annoying far more naturally than we learn to obey or to love. As G.K. Chesterton has put it, sin is the one Christian doctrine that is scientifically provable: all we need to do is look around us!

Scripture tells a very different story about the nature and source of evil. Sin does not result from ignorance; rather, we know from Scripture that mankind is fallen in every capacity, including his reason. While it is certainly true that men who do not think will be fools, Scripture makes it clear that those who *do* think are also fools and sinners. Genesis 6:5 states that humanity's wickedness extends to its thoughts and intents, while Paul argues that the world's wisdom has actually impeded it from coming to the true source of virtue in Christ (1 Cor. 1:18–25). As Paul summarizes in Ephesians 2:3, by nature we are children of wrath who fulfill the desires of both the flesh *and* the mind. In the end, men do not have moral minds struggling to control sinful bodies; our minds are fallen along with our passions and emotions.

Now, the logical corollary of the idea that sin is just a result of ignorance is that the only thing a man needs to lead a virtuous life is his own reason. In other words, for the Stoic, the source of virtue is found within man himself. Aurelius repeatedly appeals to the divinity within him and constantly encourages himself to remember, to focus, to think, to act, or to obey. He finds both the motivation and the source of his virtue within himself. In fact, the very idea of a collection of his own thoughts to guide him along the path of virtue emphasizes his focus on his own ability to achieve the virtuous life.

Once again, however, Stoicism finds itself running against biblical truth. Scripture makes it abundantly clear that mankind in utterly incapable of living a virtuous life. Paul emphasizes that all men are dead in their sins (Eph. 2:3) and are actually incapable of pleasing God (Rom. 8:7–8). In other words, men are no more capable of living virtuous lives than a corpse is capable of shooting a free throw or kayaking down a river.

The only way anyone can live according to God's moral standard is through the power of the Holy Spirit given him through faith in Christ. When a person dedicates his life to Christ, God changes his nature and enables him to obey God. But this is not natural. In fact, the Bible uses the language of resurrection to describe mankind's renewed ability to obey God. In other words, the change that God needs to work in a person before he can live a virtuous life is equivalent to raising a dead body to life! Thus, Scripture emphasizes that Marcus Aurelius's efforts to be truthful, kind, self-controlled, and humble the majority of the time will not make him a virtuous person; only the forgiveness of God can cover our failures, and only the resurrecting, life-changing power of God can provide the strength to live according to His moral standards.

The Ends Define the Means

The differences between Stoicism and Christianity become even more evident when we consider the question of salvation. For a Stoic, the use of the term "salvation" is rather odd, since he really isn't looking to be rescued from anything. Stoicism does not have the same idea of eternal destiny that Christianity has. While at times Marcus Aurelius seems to wrestle with the idea of an afterlife, he also reflects the general Stoic belief that after death, the body decomposes materially while the soul "decomposes" spiritually, becoming part of the fiery force that constitutes god. Thus, living a virtuous life is not oriented toward a future destiny, but toward happiness on earth now. Stoicism's goal, the end it strives after, is happiness in this life. Salvation, then, is a bit of an odd idea. The Stoic doesn't need salvation so much as a guidebook on how to live a life that brings happiness. The guidebook given by the Stoic instructs one to live a virtuous life guided by reason—no outside help needed and no future destiny to be rescued.

How different from the end the Bible urges Christians to yearn for! Christians are less concerned with happiness in this life (though joy in this life is a result of trusting and obeying God!) than with life and fellowship with God in the next life. This eternal destiny must be rescued because all men are fallen in Adam and are hopelessly at odds with God. Salvation is necessary because nothing in our power can restore the fellowship with God necessary to dwell with Him forever. Thus, for the Stoic, virtue through reason brings the final goal of happiness in this life, while for the Christian, virtue is only a result or a manifestation of a restored relationship with God that will culminate in life and joy forever.

Conclusion

There may be some who are still impressed by Marcus Aurelius's attempts to live a life so concerned with treating others justly and generously or with guiding his own life by truth, humility, and self-control. One might assume that at the very least Marcus Aurelius would have viewed Christians favorably since they sought to live by many of the same virtues he himself was striving to adopt.

However, nothing could be further from the truth. The emperor who sought to be tolerant of his fellow men, who desired to treat others with justice and humility, and who rejected the passions of earlier emperors for a life of quiet virtue, also attacked the church with a vigor unknown under any previous Roman emperor. Under Marcus Aurelius, the policy established by the emperor Trajan, which was roughly equivalent to our "don't ask, don't tell" policy, was repealed in favor of more active persecution intended to halt the growth of the Christian "superstition." Why would a man so dedicated to humanity and virtue (and a virtue that at times appears so similar to Christian virtue) try to stamp out the church?

The answer lies in the different core commitments of Marcus Aurelius and God's church. To begin with, Aurelius was dedicated to virtue and honor. While the church does strive to live virtuous lives, virtue does not set the church apart from the world. Every religion under the sun promotes virtue. Rather, it is the solution to man's inability to live a virtuous life that sets Christianity apart from other religions.

In addition, Aurelius believed that part of the way in which he could honor "the god within him" was by doing all things with humanity and justice as "a statesman, a Roman, and a ruler." Aurelius's standards of virtue were defined by his position as Roman emperor. It is important to remember that especially at this point in Roman history, religion played a huge role in unifying a large and diverse empire. By religion, I don't mean living a moral life or seeking salvation—for the Romans that was the realm of philosophy. When it came to religion, the Romans expected all citizens to participate in the sacrifices, festivals, and worship of the state gods. For Christians, their core commitment to worship their Creator and Savior exclusively meant they were not willing to participate in Roman religion.

Aurelius couldn't care less about Christianity's understanding of salvation or virtue, but a group of men and women who refused to participate in state religious practices was tearing apart the social fabric of the empire. Thus, for Marcus Aurelius, virtue as a Roman and a ruler demanded that he oppose Christianity.

In the end, Marcus Aurelius missed the central point. While the Romans Stoics sought happiness by living a virtuous life "according to Nature," they missed the fact that Nature is the creation of the one true God. Virtue is impossible without this God at its core, and once Stoicism rejected the God of Scripture for a divine "fireforce," it lost its ability to achieve either the virtue or the happiness it sought.

—Christopher Walker

Everything exists for some end, a horse, a vine. Why dost thou wonder? Even the sun will say, I am for some purpose, and the rest of the gods will say the same. For what purpose then art thou? To enjoy pleasure? See if common sense allows this.
—Meditations 8.19

For Further Reading

Eusebius. *The Church History.* Paul Maier, ed.. Grand Rapids, Mich: Kregel, 1999. 144–246.

Gonzalez, Justo. *The Story of the Church.* San Francisco: HarperCollins, 1984. 45–48.

Needham, N.R. *2000 Years of Christ's Power.* London: Grace Publications Trust, 1997. 77–87.

Spielvogel, Jackson J. *Western Civilization.* Seventh Edition. Belmont, Calif.: Thomson Wadsworth, 2009. 168–169.

Session I: Prelude

A Question to Consider

What does it mean to be made in the image of God? In what ways are we like God, and in what ways are we not?

From the General Information above, answer the following questions:

1. How did Marcus Aurelius's life change in A.D. 138?
2. What was the condition of the Roman Empire during Marcus Aurelius's reign?
3. Why is Marcus Aurelius's *Meditations* so significant for our understanding of the Roman world?
4. What are some of the main categories of information Aurelius includes in his *Meditations*?
5. What are the two key Stoic principles for living a virtuous life?

Reading Assignment:
Meditations, Books 1 and 2

Session II: Discussion
Meditations, Books 1 and 2

A Question to Consider

How is God's sovereignty similar to and different from the sovereignty of the Stoic god?

Text Analysis

1. What guides all things that come to pass according to Marcus Aurelius?
2. How does Marcus Aurelius argue we should live, given the sovereign role of Providence?
3. What is Marcus Aurelius's moral judgment of Nature's sovereign guidance?

Cultural Analysis

1. What does our culture think about living in a world ruled by a sovereign God?
2. Who would men and women in our culture trust to guide their lives?

Biblical Analysis

1. How does Matthew 6:25–33 summarize the extent of God's sovereignty and our proper response to His sovereignty?
2. How does Philippians 2:12–13 summarize our responsibility to do what is right even though God has perfectly planned out all that comes to pass?
3. How does Romans 8:28 assess God's sovereignty morally?

Summa

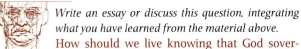

Write an essay or discuss this question, integrating what you have learned from the material above.
How should we live knowing that God sovereignly guides whatever comes to pass?

Reading Assignment:
Meditations, Books 3 and 4

Session III: Activity
Meditations, Books 3 and 4

Writing Your Own *Meditation*

In this activity, you will be writing your own journal, or, in Marcus Aurelius's language, your own *Meditations.* You should take time now in class to write down your core convictions, the most important principles you seek to live by, and your greatest weaknesses you attempt to overcome. In addition, you should make an entry each evening this week, writing down principles to live by, quotations worth remembering that you ran across during the day, or helpful advice given to you by a teacher, family member, or friend. Compile your thoughts in a notebook. You may think that not even you yourself will ever read these thoughts again . . . but Marcus Aurelius thought the same thing!

Marcus Aurelius is often found in very good company. We should be as careful of the books we read as the company we keep. The dead very often have more power than the living. *He who walks with wise men will be wise, but the companion of fools will be destroyed.*
—Proverbs 13:20

Below are a few sample entries for your inspiration:

SUNDAY, MAY 17

This morning's sermon recalled my mind to the subject of God's calling in my life. There are many things God commands us to do in Scripture. Obedience in many areas is a mark of being filled with the Spirit. However, there are other choices God has not mandated universally, but in which He calls each Christian differently. The job I seek, the choice of whether or not to marry, and the hobbies I enjoy in my free time are not mandated scripturally, but are still part of God's calling for my life specifically. This encourages me to seek God's will in my life in all things, and to honor Him in all that I do, even if that thing is not specifically required in the Bible.

MONDAY, MAY 18

In order to live a life of wisdom, I must avoid speech that insults, mocks, or belittles another person. I must resolve through the strength of the Spirit to let only what builds others up come from my mouth.

I must also avoid a life driven by pride and self-esteem. How often I have made decisions on whether or not I will be admired, rather than on the scriptural truth or goodness of the thing at hand!

Daily seek strength for obedience, forgiveness for error, and grace for increased faith. All these the Spirit of God offers.

TUESDAY, MAY 19

"The mighty Casey had struck out." I heard this line quoted in class today, and it brought to mind the comforting truth that just as the best baseball players strike out, so even the godliest man lacks perfection. Christ has not laid on us the burden of perfect obedience but a renewed desire to obey and an offer of forgiveness for a humble man who seeks grace from Him.

READING ASSIGNMENT:
Meditations, Books 5 and 6

Our next session will be a student-led discussion. As The next session will be a student-led discussion. Students will be creating their own questions concerning the issue of the session. Students should create three Text Analysis Questions, two Cultural Analysis questions, and two Biblical Analysis questions. For more detailed instructions, please see the chapter on the *Iliad,* Session III.

Issue

Should reason be your guide in life? What is good about reason? What are reason's limits?

Session IV: Student-Led Discussion

Meditations, Books 5 and 6

A Question to Consider

Should reason be your guide? What are the limits of reason?

Students should read and consider the example questions below that are connected to the Question to Consider above. Last session's assignment was to prepare three questions and answers for the Text Analysis section and two additional questions and answers for both the Cultural and Biblical Analysis sections below.

Text Analysis

Example: In 5.27, how does Marcus Aurelius describe our minds and our reason?

Answer: He describes our mind and reason as an "inward divinity," given by Zeus as our ruler and guide. In other words, reason is not only reliable, it is actually divine!

Cultural Analysis

Example: In what ways might our culture agree or disagree that reason is an "inward divinity?"

Answer: Our culture is apt to agree with this statement because it suggests that we and our own minds have the right and authority to direct our lives. There is no being outside ourselves that can tell us what to do if reason is an inward divinity. However, our culture would probably reject this statement for two reasons. First, our culture would deny that any part of us actually reflects a divine being, whether Christian, Stoic, or any other. Second, our culture often relies on emotions, feelings, and expression. More and more people in our culture seem to care little for reason or rationality as long as they can express their feelings!

Other cultural issues to consider: How and why does our postmodern culture reject reason? What role does reason play in science? Does reason have any place in an entertainment-driven culture?

Biblical Analysis

Example: What does 1 Corinthians 1:18–30 have to say about the use of reason?

Answer: Paul argues here that the wisdom of the world has become foolish before God. He says that the philosophy and rationality of the Greeks has become the very stumbling block to their salvation, because a resurrected divine/human just doesn't make sense! In the end, Christ is our wisdom, for only when we submit to the Creator of our minds can we truly be rational.

Other Scriptures to consider: John 1:1 (note that *word* is from the Greek λογος, which is the root of our word *logic*), Matt. 11:25, Isa. 29:14, Dan. 1:17–21, Prov. 1:1–7.

Summa

Write an essay or discuss this question, integrating what you have learned from the material above.
Where does Aurelius go wrong in thinking about reason?

Reading Assignment:
Meditations, Book 7

Session V: Recitation
Meditations, Books 1–7

Comprehension Questions
Answer the following questions for factual recall:
1. For what things does Marcus Aurelius say is he indebted to the gods?
2. In Book Two, how does Aurelius believe we ought to respond to those who do us wrong, and why?
3. In Book Two, how does Aurelius define a philosopher?
4. From Book Three, what question ought a man always be ready to answer without hesitation in order to ensure he is focused on the proper things?
5. In Book Three, what does Aurelius identify as the marks of a good man?

Chart 1: **COMPARING WORLDVIEWS OF MARCUS AURELIUS AND PAUL**

	GOD	REASON	SIN	SALVATION
Marcus Aurelius	God is a Mind-Fire; a force that is the source of all things; the end of all things; the sovereign ruler of all things past, present, and future. This god works all things for a common good, but is not individual or personal.			
Paul			Sin is enmity with God; it is active rebellion against our Creator. At its core, it is an inheritance from Adam *that* each individual actively joins through his disobedience. There is no one who does not sin, and nothing in man, who is fallen in all his capacities, can save him (Rom. 3:10–11; 5:12; 8:7–8).	

6. In Book Four, what does Aurelius claim is the quietest and most untroubled retreat for man?
7. In Book Five, how does Aurelius believe we should respond to our failure to live up to our principles?
8. In Book Six, how does Aurelius describe the appropriate response to life if there is a god, and if there is not a god ordering the universe?
9. In Book Seven, what does Aurelius say we can learn by looking back over the past?
10. In Book Seven, what three features ought man's constitution demonstrate?

OPTIONAL SESSION: WORLDVIEW ANALYSIS

Comparing Aurelius and Paul

Compare and contrast the worldviews of Marcus Aurelius's Roman stoicism and Paul's Christianity by completing Chart 1.

The Apostolic Fathers

"What is the meaning of this?" demanded the general, blue eyes ablaze, voice choked. "What is the meaning of this?" he repeated.

"You know," the man replies, cringing, "that—that the attack was contrary to my advice and opinion."

A touch of scorn flashed in the general's eyes, his voice calm, "You should not have undertaken the command unless you meant to carry it through."

And then he was off. The British were charging, and the American lines were in disarray. But at the sight of their general the Americans began to reform their line, commanders securing the flanks. As the general rode to and fro, organizing the men who had been anticipating defeat, volley after volley was fired their way by the British. But the British regulars were ineffective, their troops so compressed in the narrow valley between the hills that the men in rear had to fire high for fear of hitting their companions in front.

The general gave order, and the American lines opened fire, the flanks pouring artillery into the massed infantrymen. The British fled and rallied, then fled again in defeat, many dying from musket balls and others from the sweltering heat. The Battle of Monmouth was an American victory snatched from the jaws of defeat.

The general was George Washington; the subordinate General Charles Lee. It seems that Lee disagreed with Washington's plan of attack that day. Though given the option to refrain from fighting, Lee demanded one of the most critical spots in the line. Once in command, with Washington at a safe distance (or so he thought!), he refused to engage the enemy. American disgust with Lee's behavior was intense. After the battle, Lee was court-martialed and suspended from the military for a year. Within that time he was convicted of receiving bribes from the enemy and dishonorably discharged from the army.

The Battle of Monmouth highlights for us some important principles of war. In order to achieve victory, an army must have a united front combined with skillful leaders who will direct the troops effectively. Victory is the goal—but victory will not be achieved without unity.

In the early history of Christianity, the contest between Christianity and its opponents—paganism and Judaism—was much more clearly conceived as a type of battle. The early Christians understood that a war was raging, that they had enemies, and that they needed to remain unified if they were to succeed. The men whom the

America needed a united front and strong leaders in the War for Independence. The men the apostles appointed to lead the Church in her early days knew the absolute necessity for skillful leadership and unity as they battled the opponents of Christianity.

apostles appointed to lead the Church knew the absolute necessity of unity and skillful leadership for the honor of God's name and for victory. Consequently, the letters and books they wrote frequently return to these twin themes.

General Information

Author and Context

The authors that you will be reading are collectively called the *apostolic fathers*. This is not because they were apostles, nor even because they had children (though many of them did). Rather, it is because these men were the first generation of teachers following the apostles: many of them were taught by the apostles themselves.

The custom of calling revered teachers "fathers" is witnessed in the New Testament and became common in later church history. Paul calls himself the "father" of the Corinthian congregation (1 Cor. 4:15; cf. Gal. 4:19) and calls Timothy his "true son" in the faith (1 Tim. 1:2). Hence, we mustn't take Jesus' words out of context when he urges us to call no one on earth our father (Matt. 23: 9). Provided that we are distinguishing between the voice of God and the voices of these men, it is fitting to call them our fathers in the faith.

Their writings span the period from shortly after the destruction of Jerusalem (A.D. 70) to about the middle of the second century (c. A.D. 150). These are the first great theologians of the church. Their writings form the theological foundation on which even greater theologians like Augustine would later build. Of course their words are not directly inspired by the Holy Spirit as the canon of Scripture is! Yet their devotion to Christ as well as their passion for the purity and unity of the Church is evident and cannot fail to elicit our love and respect.

Significance

The apostolic fathers present us with a taste of early Christianity. We often wonder what happened to the Church after the apostles died. The apostolic fathers give us a glimpse—albeit a partial and unsatisfactory one—of the post-apostolic church.

The remarkable thing is that we have so few writings from the apostolic fathers. While in the New Testament we possess the writings of several apostles, we possess very few writings from those taught by the apostles. Why is this? One reason is that, as important as the apostolic fathers were, their significance pales in comparison with the apostles themselves.

The church father, Augustine, whose book *The Confessions* was read in *Omnibus II*, remarked on the difference between the canonical writings—that is, the Old and New Testaments—and the writings of others like the apostolic fathers. The canonical writings, he insists, are to be received as an authority in and of themselves, speaking with the very voice of God. The apostolic fathers, on the other hand, "however excellent in purity of doctrine, I do not therefore take a thing to be true because they thought so; but because they can persuade me, either through those canonical authors, or probable reason, that it does not differ from the truth." Augustine considered the apostolic fathers an authority *under* Scripture not *alongside* Scripture; we should think the same.

Setting

We actually know very little about the state of the Church during the period of the apostolic fathers. So little information remains at our disposal that it is difficult to reconstruct the history. After Luke wrote his account of the apostolic period, The Acts of the Apostles, no one took the time to write another history until Eusebius picked up his pen in the time of Constantine—hundreds of years after the apostolic fathers lived and ministered.

What we glean from the apostolic fathers themselves is that during this time the Church was a collection of growing and fledgling communities of believers spread throughout the Roman world. Sometimes they faced severe persecution from their unbelieving countrymen as is witnessed in the martyrdom of Polycarp and in the letters of Ignatius. More often they faced the threat of disunity and false teaching from within.

Consequently, the apostolic fathers felt compelled to fulfill their calling as leaders in the church by shepherding the Church of God which had been entrusted to them. They insisted on the need to study the Word of God, to preserve the faith once for all delivered to the saints, to protect the peace of the churches, and to honor the various officers appointed in the churches.

Worldview

Imagine that you've been assigned the task of summarizing the military tactics of the leaders of the War for Independence. A lover of military history, you take up the task with verve and enthusiasm. You research and study, learning the names of many famous commanders in the war—George Washington, Commander of the Continental Army; Nathaniel Greene, Washington's right-hand man; Francis Marion, the Swamp Fox of the Revolution; etc. But as you study, you quickly become distraught. "How can I possibly summarize their tactics," you ask yourself, "when they're all so different?"

A similar problem arises with the apostolic fathers. While they were all engaged in the same battle, they're all so different. They wrote at different times to different people on different occasions for different purposes in different styles. Consider:

The Apostolic Fathers   433

Clement of Rome's *Letter to the Corinthians* (c. A.D. 95)[1] was written as a result of divisions that were emerging in the Corinthian church. His style is closest to many of the Pauline letters and he exhorts the Corinthians to faithfulness, harmony, and unity in Christ.

The *Homily by an Unknown Author* (c. A.D. 120 to 140), sometimes called Clement's *Second Epistle to the Corinthians*, seems timeless and unconnected with any specific problem in a local church. It is called a "homily" because it reads like a sermon. It is an earnest exhortation to faith in Christ and to a righteous life.

The *Epistles of Ignatius* (c. A.D. 105) were written as their author, Ignatius, the Bishop of Antioch, was on his way to Rome to be executed for his faith in Christ. He writes intensely personal letters, encouraging the churches to remain faithful to their charge, preserve the unity of the faith, and submit lovingly to their leaders. He even writes a letter to the church at Rome, begging them to facilitate rather than oppose his coming martyrdom.

The correspondence surrounding Polycarp, the Bishop of Smyrna, resembles closely the letters of Ignatius. Polycarp's *Epistle to the Philippians* (c. A.D. 107) urges them to faithfulness and purity in light of Ignatius's recent passage through their city. Some time later the church at Smyrna writes (c. A.D. 155 to 156) to other believers to recount Polycarp's own faithfulness unto death.

The author of the *Didache* (c. A.D. 100) is unknown. It is the earliest extant manual of church discipline. After contrasting the two ways of life and death, it urges its readers to pursue life and the things attached to it. It regulates such things as baptism, fasting, the Lord's Supper, thanksgivings, teaching in the churches, support for ministers, and the Lord's Day.

The *Epistle of Barnabas* (c. A.D. 70 to 79) is an extended critique of Judaism written by an unknown author. Its purpose is to demonstrate that Jesus is the fulfillment of everything that the Old Testament anticipated. Unfortunately its argumentation is at times fanciful and speculative rather than textual and historical, laying a foundation for later generations of allegorical interpretation.

The *Shepherd of Hermas* (c. A.D. 140 to 155) is by far

Foxe's Book of Martyrs recounts Polycarp's answer to the Roman soldier who demands that he renounce Christ: "Eighty and six years have I served him, and he never once wronged me; how then shall I blaspheme my King, Who hath saved me?" Polycarp died during what Foxe names the Fourth Persecution, under Marcus Aurelius.

Clement was an early bishop of Rome in the late first century and wrote the *Letter to the Corinthians*. The Roman Catholic Church claims him as the fourth pope.

the longest of the writings. Written in the middle of the second century for the benefit of the Roman church, it is full of visions, commandments, and allegorical revelations. The reader sometimes feels that it would be profitable to be an artist and draw Hermas's visions, so difficult is it to keep track of the numerous details.

Finally, *The Epistle to Diognetus* (c. A.D. 150), author unknown, contrasts Christianity with both paganism and Judaism. Though incomplete in its present form, it highlights the superiority of the Christian revelation and is one of the most winsome of these early writings.

So how can we possibly summarize such disparate writings? The task seems daunting at first glance. Fortunately, however, despite their differences, the apostolic fathers do have a remarkable number of similar objectives. Lurking beneath the surface differences is a collection of common concerns—and these concerns bring us back to our opening story of George Washington and Charles Lee. The three major concerns that unite the apostolic fathers are (1) that the church hold true to apostolic teaching, (2) that the churches maintain peace, unity, and harmony by submitting to their leaders, and (3) that the witness of Christians to their Lord be unstained by cowardice or corruption. Let us examine each of these in turn.

Unity of Belief

The first thing that characterizes the writings of the apostolic fathers is a concern for unity of belief. What was Christianity after all? It was not an ethnic religious movement connected with only one people group. On the contrary, Christianity made universal claims—claims upon all men from every nation under heaven. What was the nature of these claims? What was it that drew Christians together and united them as one? That gave them a reason to stand against both paganism and Judaism?

It is questions of this sort that lead the apostolic fathers again and again to return to the importance of apostolic doctrine. That which unites Christians is their faith. The apostolic fathers understand that their task as leaders is to preserve and pass on to succeeding generations the teaching that was delivered to them. They are not concerned to be novel, to be innovators. They are trying to preserve what was given, "to contend earnestly for the faith which was once for all delivered to the saints" (Jude 3).

Their attitude reflects well the commission that was given them by the apostles. Paul envisioned and articulated this very process in his letter to Timothy. "You therefore, my son, be strong in the grace that is in Christ Jesus. And the things that you have heard from me among many witnesses, *commit these to faithful men who will be able to teach others also*" (2 Tim. 2:1–2). Timothy's task was to hand on the faith to the next generation of leaders so that they could pass it on to the next. The apostolic fathers are that next generation.

The concern of the apostolic fathers for apostolic doctrine is evident both in their descriptions of true doctrine and in their warnings against false doctrine (heresy). Repeatedly they urge their readers to cling to Christ, to follow the way of righteousness, and to shun unbelief. But the unbelief against which they warn is at times subtle. Not only do they contend with the unbelief of paganism and Judaism from the outside (witness *The Epistle to Diognetus*), they also contend with false teaching from within the Church. Ignatius exhorts the Philippians, "As children therefore of the truth, shun divisions and wrong doctrine" (5:2).

In the time of the apostolic fathers, two major errors circulated the church which later historians have identified with the names *Docetism* and *Ebionism*. Docetism (from the Greek *dokew*—"to seem") was a false teaching that grew out of the Greek hatred for the body. For the Greeks "salvation," if it meant anything, meant to be released from our bodies. Docetists were those who professed to believe in Christ but who thought it impossible that the one sent to save us would have a body—yuck!

How can he rescue us from our body if he himself has one? And so these folks insisted that Jesus only "seemed" to have a body, only "seemed" to suffer on the cross. In actual fact, they maintained, he did not come in the flesh. Hints of the early church's battle with Docetism are found in the New Testament (cf. 1 John 4:1–3; 2 John 7) and frequently in the apostolic fathers.

In contrast to Docetism, the apostolic fathers insist on the goodness of creation. The first principle of the gospel is "to love the God that made thee" (*Didache*, 1). The same God who made you is the One who sent His Son Jesus Christ *in the flesh* to suffer and die for the forgiveness of His people. Jesus didn't just *appear* to be human and to suffer. He *actually* was human and suffered on our behalf. Not only this but He was raised from the dead by the power of God and thereby secured the resurrection of all men from the grave. The apostolic fathers insist that Christianity is enmeshed with the created order. Listen to Ignatius:

> Be ye deaf therefore, when any man speaketh to you apart from Jesus Christ, who was of the race of David, who was the Son of Mary, who was truly born and ate and drank, was truly persecuted under Pontius Pilate, was truly crucified and died in the sight of those in heaven and those on earth and those under the earth; who moreover was truly raised from the dead, His Father having raised Him, who in the like fashion will so raise us also who believe on Him—His Father, I say, will raise us—in Christ Jesus, apart from whom we have not true life. (Trallians, 3:9)

The second major error which the apostolic fathers denounce is Ebionism. The Ebionites were (largely) Jewish Christians who said that Jesus was not divine but only a great teacher like Moses and who insisted on the continuing obligation of many distinctive Jewish ceremonial regulations. They rejected the authority of Paul's letters and used only the Gospel of Matthew. Apparently, there were many Christians who were tempted to revert to some form of Judaism like Ebionism.

The apostolic fathers, particularly the *Epistle of Barnabas* and the *Epistles of Ignatius,* repeatedly warn against this temptation. Now that Christ has come, the sacrifices and ceremonial regulations of the Old Testament are superfluous and, in the case of the sacrifices, offensive to God. This does not mean that the Old Testament itself is inferior or irrelevant. On the contrary, the Old Testament is Scripture, and the apostolic fathers frequently use it to establish the truth of Christianity. Christians, they insist, are the true heirs of the Old Testament. As Paul had taught, "We are the [true] circumcision, who worship God in the Spirit, rejoice in Christ Jesus, and have

no confidence in the flesh" (Phil. 3:3). The Old Testament pointed to Christ and, now that He has come, many of its regulations are like the scaffolding erected around a construction site. The scaffolding is not bad; indeed, it is absolutely essential for the construction of the building. But when the building is finished, only a fool grows so accustomed to the scaffolding that he refuses to take it down and admire the building.

Both in their instruction to the churches and in their warnings against false teaching, therefore, the apostolic fathers are passionately concerned about preserving the faith which was delivered to them by the apostles.

Harmony in the Church

Alongside this unity of doctrine, the apostolic fathers emphasize the necessity of peace and harmony in the churches themselves. Not only should the churches be teaching the same thing, they should be loving and serving one another in a way that honors their Lord. As Ignatius declares, "If any man followeth one that maketh a schism, he doth not inherit the kingdom of God. If any man walketh in strange doctrine, he hath no fellowship with the passion." Jesus, after all, had prayed for the unity of the Church (cf. John 17:20-23) and the apostolic fathers want to see this lived out in the Church in their own day.

The main threats to harmony in the Church are false teachers on the one hand and sin on the other. The false teachers are those who subvert apostolic doctrine and refuse to submit to the authority of the men who were appointed to lead the local congregations. Even as a false general like Charles Lee can cause great havoc in the midst of battle, so false teachers can cause great havoc in the Church. Consequently, the apostolic fathers are vigilant to warn the congregations not to harbor them.

It is in opposition to these false teachers that the role of the officers in the congregations becomes so critical. Again and again the apostolic fathers urge believers to submit to the lawful authorities in the churches. The key for God's people is to know who their lawful leaders are and then to follow them. Clement writes to the Corinthians, "It is shameful, dearly beloved, yes, utterly shameful and unworthy of your conduct in Christ, that it should be reported that the very stedfast and ancient Church of the Corinthians, for the sake of one or two persons, maketh sedition against its presbyters" (*1 Clement to the Corinthians,* 47). Likewise, Ignatius declares time after time "be ye united with the bishop and with them that preside over you as an ensample and a lesson of incorruptibility" (*Magnesians,* 2:6).

This concern to honor the officers in the churches continues a New Testament theme. The book of Hebrews commands, "Obey those who rule over you, and be submissive, for they watch out for your souls, as those who must give account" (13:17a). The apostles, of course, were the earliest leaders of the Church, appointed by Christ himself to be the foundation of the Church (cf. Eph. 2:20). The apostles selected gifted men to serve after them either as presbyters/elders (sometimes called overseers/bishops in the New Testament—cf. Acts 20:17, 28; Titus 1:5, 7) or as deacons (cf. 1 Tim. 3:1–15; Titus 1:5–9). The primary responsibility of the presbyters was to preach, teach, and shepherd the people (cf. 1 Pet. 5:1–5) and to protect the church from false teachers (cf. Acts 20:28–30; Titus 1:9). The deacons were responsible to serve the poor and needy (prefigured in Acts 6).

As time passed, early church leaders separated existing offices and/or added new ones to respond to new difficulties. We witness some of this transformation in the writings of the apostolic fathers. While some of them seem to speak of only two offices—the presbyters (elders) and deacons—others speak of three—the bishop, the presbyters, and the deacons. In these latter writings the term "bishop" seems to be used as the functional equivalent of our word "pastor"—the one man among the elders who was in vocational ministry. (Note that some theological traditions see even more in this early threefold division of offices believing that bishops were overseers over a number of congregations.)

While assessments of the value of this change vary considerably among Christians, the apostolic fathers spend very little time discussing the merits of the changing terminology. They simply use it to enforce on the minds of their hearers the importance of honoring those whom God placed over them in the Church. The presbyters, bishops, and deacons were the leaders of God's people, their generals as it were. The layman's task was to follow them and give heed to what they had to say.

None of this, of course, means that the officers are free from the danger of sin and error themselves. After all, Paul warned the elders at Ephesus that "savage wolves will come in among you, not sparing the flock. Also *from among yourselves* men will rise up, speaking perverse things, to draw away the disciples after themselves" (Acts 20:29–30). We see that this warning was not frivolous in the remarks which Polycarp makes about a former presbyter named Valens who had fallen into grave sin and endangered the Church of the Philippians (*Polycarp to the Philippians*, 11).

Not only is the peace and harmony of the Church threatened by false teachers, it is also threatened by sin. Consequently, the writings of the apostolic fathers are full of admonitions and warnings against sin. A common way of contrasting Christianity and unbelief is found in the *Didache* which contrasts "two ways"—in other words,

two paths or roads. There is the way of life found in Christ and the way of death found in the world. The call upon God's people is to walk in the way of life and practice those virtues which are consistent with this walk.

While numerous exhortations to righteousness are given by the apostolic fathers, some are particularly interesting in light of modern controversies and problems. The fathers are very clear on the issue of abortion and infanticide—both are grievous sins to be shunned by those walking in the way of life (e.g., *Didache* 2, *Barnabas* 19). In addition, there are frequent admonishments to fathers to instruct their children in the ways of the Lord—a very relevant topic for many readers of this essay (e.g., *Didache* 4). Indeed, the primary sin for which Hermas is rebuked is his failure to shepherd his wife and children (cf. *Hermas* Visions 1.3, 2.2).

Glory of God

The apostolic fathers, therefore, are concerned for the unity of the church doctrinally and the unity of the church personally under the direction of the officers appointed to lead her. But what was the overarching purpose of this unity? Why submit to the leaders? When Washington rallied the troops at Monmouth and defeated the British, he wasn't doing it just for the sake of fighting. The fighting had a greater end in view. So too the labors of the apostolic fathers. Their writings have a greater end in view. Why is it important for their readers to give heed to the things they say? Why is it important to record the sufferings of the martyrs? To defend the faith from its detractors? To strive to convert unbelievers to the fold? The purpose of unity (both doctrinal and personal) as well as sound leaders is that something even greater may be accomplished. Unity is not an end in and of itself, and good leaders must be leading folks *somewhere*. What is this overarching purpose or goal for which the apostolic fathers yearn? The glory of God manifest in the victory of the gospel.

There is a reason the apostolic fathers frequently evoke the language of two roads to describe the contrast between Christianity and unbelief. One truly is the pathway to life and the other the pathway to death. Christians love and have compassion upon all men, longing for all to enter into the way of life, to experience the favor of God in this life and the blessing of salvation at the time of judgment. The apostolic fathers want to see others repent and enter into life and so glorify the Maker and Creator of all.

This overarching goal helps explain the passion and expectation with which the apostolic fathers write. Consider, for example, the words of Ignatius on his way to Rome to suffer death. He writes to the Romans, "Come fire and cross and grapplings with wild beasts, cuttings and manglings, wrenching of bones, hacking of limbs, crushings of my whole body, come cruel tortures of the devil to assail me. Only be it mine to attain unto Jesus Christ" (4:5). Astounding! Christianity, the apostolic fathers remind us, is the way of life and so "we are more than conquerors through Him that loved us" (Rom. 8:37). And the end, the goal, of the conquest is the glory of God.

> Finally may the All-seeing God and Master of spirits and Lord of all flesh, who chose the Lord Jesus Christ, and us through Him for a peculiar people, grant unto every soul that is called after His excellent and holy Name faith, fear, peace, patience, long-suffering, temperance, chastity and soberness, that they may be well-pleasing unto His Name through our High-priest and Guardian Jesus Christ, through whom unto Him be glory and majesty, might and honour, both now and forever and ever. Amen. (*I Clement*, 64)
>
> —*Stuart Bryan*

For Further Reading

Gonzalez, Justo. *The Story of Christianity*. San Francisco: HarperCollins, 1984. Vol. 1. Part 1 The Early Church.

Kerr, Hugh. Ed. *Readings in Christian Thought*. Nashville, Tenn.: Abingdon Press, 1966.

Spielvogel, Jackson J. *Western Civilization*. Seventh Edition. Belmont, Calif.: Thomson Wadsworth, 2009. 170–175.

Walker, Williston. *The History of the Christian Church*. New York: Scribners, 1985. Periods 1 and 2.

Session I: Prelude

A Question to Consider

How important is unity in the local church? In the universal Church?

From the General Information above answer the following questions:
1. Who were the Apostolic Fathers?
2. How did Augustine think we should treat the writings of the apostolic fathers in comparison with Scripture?
3. Why is summarizing the work of the apostolic fathers so challenging?

Modern Christians may have trouble identifying this figure as Jesus, since he is shown without a beard or the obligatory red sash over a white robe. But for viewers in the past, the cross within the halo would have been enough to show them that the figure is meant to be Jesus.

The purpose of unity and sound leadership is that something even greater may be accomplished. Unity is not an end in and of itself, and good leaders must be leading folks *somewhere*. What was this overarching purpose or goal for which the apostolic fathers yearned? The glory of God manifest in the victory of the gospel.

4. What were the two major doctrinal errors the apostolic fathers warned against? Explain.
5. How did the appointment of leaders in the churches serve to preserve the unity of the Church?
6. What change is taking place in the number of officers in the Church during the days of the apostolic fathers?
7. What is the overarching goal for which the apostolic fathers are striving?

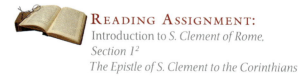

Reading Assignment:
Introduction to *S. Clement of Rome, Section 1*[2]
The Epistle of S. Clement to the Corinthians

Session II: Discussion
The Epistle of St. Clement to the Corinthians

A Question to Consider

What is the authority and purpose of officers in the Church?

Text Analysis

1. What serious problem in the Corinthian congregation prompted Clement to write his letter to them?
2. What observation does Clement make about the nature of the military, of political order, and of the body? How does this observation relate to the position of leaders in the Church?
3. What should we prefer to disturbing the harmony of the Church and the authority of duly appointed presbyters?
4. What exhortation does Clement deliver to those who are causing the sedition in the Corinth?

Cultural Analysis

1. List authorities that are commonly recognized in our culture.
2. Is the authority of officers in the Church highly respected? What proofs can you give for your contention?

Biblical Analysis

1. What officers does Paul instruct Timothy to ordain in the church at Ephesus (1 Tim. 3:1ff)? Titus in Crete (cf. Titus 1:5ff)?
2. What are the relative duties of presbyters (elders) and church members in the following passages (Acts 20:28-30; Heb. 13:7, 17, 24; 1 Pet. 5:1-7)?
3. Why have Church officers been entrusted with their authority (cf. Mark 10:35-45; Eph. 4:11-16)?
4. Is it possible for Church officers to exceed or misuse their authority? What does this say about the nature of their authority (cf. Acts 20:28-30; Gal. 2:11-13)?

SUMMA

Write an essay or discuss this question, integrating what you have learned from the material above.

What should be our attitude toward officers in the Church?

The next session will be a student-led discussion. Students will be creating their own questions concerning the issue of the session. Students should create three Text Analysis Questions, two Cultural Analysis questions, and two Biblical Analysis questions. For more detailed instructions, please see the chapter on the *Iliad*, Session III.

Issue

How important is the unity of the church?

READING ASSIGNMENT:
Introduction to the Epistles of S. Ignatius, Section 13
The Epistles of S. Ignatius

Giovanni Battista Tiepol painted *Pope St. Clement Adoring the Trinity* in 1737–1738. Tiepol was a Venetian painter and printmaker and was widely esteemed throughout Europe for his frescoes.

Session III: Student-Led Discussion
The Epistles of S. Ignatius

A Question to Consider
How important is the unity of the church?

Students should read and consider the example questions below that are connected to the Question to Consider above. Last session's assignment was to prepare three questions and answers for the Text Analysis section and two additional questions and answers for both the Cultural and Biblical Analysis sections below.

Text Analysis
Example: What does Ignatius say we should value over our own peace and safety?

Answer: Ignatius insists that more important than our own peace and safety is the unity and harmony of the body of Christ. Better our own troubles increase than create troubles for the Church of God.

Cultural Analysis
Example: What is the approach of organizations like the World Council of Churches (WCC) to this question?

Answer: The WCC and similar organizations make unity a higher principle than truth. Consequently, they endeavor to unify Christians of various traditions on a least common denominator principle: what are the minimums necessary for us to cooperate with one another? The danger of this is that it can obscure Paul's insistence on the absolute necessity of believing and preaching the true gospel (in Galatians Paul says that even if an apostle or an angel comes and preaches a different gospel to the Galatians then they are to not only split from the false preacher but to consider them accursed or damned).

Biblical Analysis
Example: How should Jesus' prayer in John 17 shape our opinion of the importance of church unity?

Answer: Jesus prays that his disciples "may be one as You, Father, and I are one." In other words, Jesus prays that the unity and diversity within the Trinity may be manifest in the life of His people—that despite our diversity we would be joined together by the bonds of love and affection. Given that Jesus prayed earnestly for this unity, it should be a high priority for us as the people of God.

Summa

Write an essay or discuss this question, integrating what you have learned from the material above.
How important is the unity of the Church?

Reading Assignment:
Introduction to the Epistle of S. Polycarp, Section 14
The Epistle of S. Polycarp to the Philippians
Introduction to the Martyrdom of Polycarp[5]
The Letter of the Smyrnaeans (The Martyrdom of Polycarp)
Introduction to the Didache, Section 1[6]
The Didache (The Teaching of the Twelve Apostles)

Session IV: Activity
The Epistle of S. Polycarp to the Philippians; The Letter of the Smyrnaeans (The Martyrdom of Polycarp); The Didache (The Teaching of the Twelve Apostles)

Debate
Resolution: Feasts honoring the Christian dead are inherently idolatrous.

If working in a class of students, divide up into two groups. One group will take the affirmative (they will be in favor of the resolution); the other will take the negative. Give equal time to each group to make its case. After each side presents its case, let each team question the other. After this round of questions, let the teacher or audience ask questions to each group. Finally, let one member of each group make his or her final appeal to the teacher or audience. After that, the teacher will choose a winner and give his reasons for his choice. The losing team might then serve snacks to the winners.

If you are working at home, make a brief summary of both sides to your parents and siblings and then present an argument for one side. They will then ask you questions and you have to give the answers. Afterwards, let them vote on whether your case was convincing. If you convince a majority, you might get extra dessert.

The Letter of the Smyrnaeans offers a brief explanation of why they celebrate the memory of Polycarp. The challenge today is to determine if you agree with their reasoning or find it inadequate.

READING ASSIGNMENT:
Introduction to the Epistle to Diognetus, Sections 1–2[7]
The Epistle to Diognetus

READING ASSIGNMENT:
Introduction to the Shepherd of Hermas, Sections 1–3[8]
The Shepherd of Hermas, Visions 1–4 (This reading is only for those students doing Optional Session.)

Session V: Writing
The Epistle to Diognetus

Book Review

This session is a writing assignment. Remember, quality counts more than quantity. You should write no more than 1,000 words, either typing or writing legibly on one side of a sheet of paper. You will lose points for writing more than this. You will be allowed to turn in your writing three times. The first and second times you turn it in, your teacher will grade it by editing your work. This is done by marking problem areas and making suggestions for improvement. You should take these suggestions into consideration as you revise your assignment. Only the grade on your final submission will be recorded. Your grade will be based on the followi sng criteria: 25 points for grammar, 25 points for content accuracy—historical, theological, etc.; 25 points for logic—does this make sense and is it structured well?; 25 points for rhetoric—is it a joy to read?

Your assignment is to write a review of the book that you have just completed, *The Epistle to Diognetus*. Your review should be persuasive (fitting, of course, for the rhetoric years). You should tell your reader if this is a good book or a bad book and why. Your teacher may ask you to write a positive review or a negative review, or leave it up to you. You should be encouraged to praise or condemn the writing style, the content or the worldview of a book or author. (Also, remember that you are responsible for representing a Christian worldview, so you need to critique the book for language, the glorification of violence, and any sensuality.) Remember that you need to learn to both condemn and praise and that both skills must be more than a simple affirmation or denial of "liking" it.

Optional Session: Recitation
Introduction to the Shepherd of Hermas, Sections 1–3[9];
The Shepherd of Hermas, Visions 1–4

Comprehension Questions

After reading the Introduction to the Shepherd of Hermas and Visions 1–4, answer the following questions for factual recall:

1. Who is Rhoda? In the introduction, to which figure in Dante's *Inferno* does Lightfoot compare her?
2. For what sins does Rhoda rebuke Hermas in the opening vision?
3. Who is the aged woman that appears to Hermas after Rhoda's departure? What happens to her appearance in subsequent visions? Why?
4. For what sins does the aged woman rebuke Hermas?
5. What is the vision which the woman shows to Hermas? How detailed is the explanation of each type of stone?
6. Who are the seven women round about the Church? Explain.

Endnotes

1. All dates are taken from Lightfoot, J.B. and J.R. Harmer, eds., The Apostolic Fathers, Berkeley, Calif.: Apocryphile Press, 2004.
2. This introduction is found in Lightfoot and Harmer, p. 3.
3. This introduction is found in Lightfoot and Harmer, pp. 97–99.
4. This introduction is found in Lightfoot and Harmer, pp. 165–166.
5. This introduction is found in Lightfoot and Harmer, pp. 185–187.
6. This introduction is found in Lightfoot and Harmer, pp. 215–216.
7. This introduction is found in Lightfoot and Harmer, pp. 487–488.
8. This introduction is found in Lightfoot and Harmer, pp. 291–292.
9. This introduction is found in Lightfoot and Harmer, pp. 291–294.

SECONDARY BOOKS
First Semester

Aesop's Fables

Sometimes when you have dealt with certain things forever, you don't know they are even there. Explaining water to a fish would be difficult, and it might be hard for you to understand just how strange the word *Wednesday* is. Wed-*nez*-day? We see through certain things so often that it is sometimes very difficult to look *at* them. Some of the stories found in the fables of Aesop are very much in this category.

Even if you have never read through *Aesop's Fables*, you are no doubt acquainted with many of them. Who has not heard of the boy who cried wolf? And everyone knows who won the famous race between the hare and the tortoise. These fables have made their way into many children's books and animated films, and they have had whole stories develop around them. They have been passed down and around in many forms for literally ages and ages. These simple short tales have inspired artists and authors alike. An original 1912 edition translated by V.S. Vernon Jones (with an introduction by G.K. Chesterton and illustrated by Arthur Rackham) sells now for hundreds of dollars. But you can find a facsimile edition for much less and still enjoy Rackham's fabulous illustrations, and in addition to the text used for this course, you can read the fables in many different and easily available versions.

So perhaps we should begin by discussing the genre of fable. What *is* a fable? Technically speaking, *The Harper Handbook to Literature* defines a fable as "a short, allegorical story in verse or prose, frequently of animals, told to illustrate a moral." The word *fable* comes from the Latin *fabula* and simply means "little story." A fable's purpose is didactic, though many are quite entertaining as well. But the purpose of the fable is to teach a little lesson, to give a little advice, to comment on the ways of the world, or to satirize man and his foibles. This is why *Aesop's Fables* have become such popular material for children's books—it contains just the sort of life lessons that children need.

One of the most popular fables used in children's books is "The Hare and the Tortoise." Disney made a memorable cartoon of this story as well.

General Information

Author and Context

Though the fables themselves predate the man known for them, Aesop became credited for passing them on, though he never wrote them down. G.K. Chesterton says, "... his fame is all the more deserved because he never deserved it. The firm foundations of common sense, the shrewd shots at uncommon sense, that characterize all the Fables, belong not to him but to humanity." In other words, these morals resonate with everyone at all times in history.

Nothing too certain is known about Aesop himself, but the legendary tradition surrounding him is that he was a slave and a storyteller who lived in ancient Greece six centuries before Christ (from 620–560 B.C.). According to Herodotus, he was thrown off a cliff in Delphi by the citizens there, though the reason for this is unknown. Some have speculated that he was troubling the populace with his wisdom. Plato mentions that Socrates spent some of his time in prison putting Aesop's fables into verse. The first known written collection of his fables appeared around 300 B.C., and a few centuries later a Thracian slave named Phaedrus (15 B.C.–A.D. 50) translated them from Greek prose into Latin verse. In 1484 William Caxton printed the first English edition, and in 1692 the first English version specifically written for children appeared. Over the ages collections have been translated and retranslated into many languages, some with additional fables from other sources. Now there are many volumes of *Aesop's Fables* available worldwide, where they continue to endure as a well-loved form of folk literature.

Herodotus asserts that Aesop was a slave (*Histories*, II.134) and that he met his death by being cast from a cliff at the hands of the citizens of Delphi. A medieval legend that he was deformed and ugly is not corroborated by more ancient sources, but despite this the myth persists, and this bust from the Villa Albani in Rome is said to depict a deformed Aesop.

Significance

G.K. Chesterton observes that in a fable, "The wolf will be always wolfish; the fox will be always foxy. . . . by using animals in this austere and arbitrary style . . . men have really succeeded in handing down those tremendous truths that are called truisms." Whenever men are in the story, they are capable of a change of heart, but when you use animals, you can expect the nature of the animal to be fixed. Thus we have the industrious ants showing no mercy to the hungry, idle grasshopper, or the sneaky fox stealing the proud crow's cheese by flattery. To quote Chesterton again: ". . . all these are deep truths deeply graven on the rocks wherever men have passed. It matters nothing how old they are, or how new: they are the alphabet of humanity. . . ." The fables illustrate simple truths about life, taught in memorable ways through exchanges with talking beasts and the occasional man or woman. Whether an individual man or woman repents or not, the way things *are* stays the same.

Main Characters

The main characters in the fables are animals, objects like pots or even a pail of milk and a honey jar, the gods (Venus, Mercury, Jupiter, or Hercules), and nature itself, as in "The Wind and the Sun" or "The Farmer and the Sea." Many of the fables have unnamed human characters, like a boy, a blacksmith, a shepherd, a farmer, a fisherman, a maid, a goatherd, a widow, or a woodcutter.

Summary and Setting

Each fable is driving to a point, and the point is a maxim or pithy saying. Consider this small sampling: *The value of an object is in the eye of the beholder. Uninvited guests are most welcome when they leave. Only fools try to take the credit due to others. The more you want, the more you stand to lose. Grasp at the shadow, and you will lose the substance.* So the plot in each fable is merely a vehicle to carry the point home. Some of the fables are as short as three or four sentences. Some, like "The Country Mouse and the Town Mouse," can run a page and a half. Characterization depends largely on what we might expect from the animal in the story. No one has to tell us to expect the lion to think highly of his own status, the wolf to be cunning, or the ass to play the fool. The fables are timeless because they portray episodes in life that we can readily imagine at any time or any place in history. So they continue to have wide appeal. Common sense never goes out of style.

Worldview

Though people of any religion and background can identify with the stories in the fables, it would be superficial to identify them as representing any particular religion. Though some may sound similar to biblical proverbs (who could disagree with "honesty is the best policy"?), they deal mostly with hard luck and hard consequences, very much like the world of the blues. This is a very strict reap-what-you-sow world. We do not see the biblical virtues of mercy and forgiveness in the fables, but rather common sense that comes from living in a dog-eat-dog world. The wolf dressed like a sheep is caught and killed; the hungry grasshopper begging for food is left to starve. So the moral always presents us with an incomplete picture, though true as far as it goes. The Bible does teach that a man reaps what he sows—but that is not all it teaches. Aesop is strong on law, while in Scripture we find both law and grace. In one sense, these fables demonstrate life in the raw: the strongest wins; the weakest loses. It pays to be shrewd sometimes, and sometimes it doesn't.

For the Christian student, reading the fables can and should be delightful. Not only are they enjoyable in themselves, but it is always enlightening to read literature that has survived millennia and been honored throughout that time for good reason. Such endurance certainly lends a respectability that should continue to be honored.

The common sense found in the fables that comes from practical experience in the world, though admirable, is not the same thing as the complete wisdom that comes from above. Paul says in 1 Corinthians 3:18–19, "Let no one deceive himself. If anyone among you seems to be wise in this age, let him become a fool that he may become wise. For the wisdom of this world is foolishness with God." And James says, "But the wisdom that is from above is first pure, then peaceable, gentle, willing to yield, full of mercy and good fruits, without partiality and without hypocrisy" (James 3:17). The fables do not attain to this level of wisdom, although they certainly teach the value of common sense. God bestows His common grace on the world, and mankind loves to teach one another these precepts as far as they go. These fables were most likely stories passed down from fathers to their children, teaching them the ways of the world. So the Christian reader can appreciate the fables and the limited picture they portray.

The fables are more about law than grace, which is always easier for fallen man to relate to. We gravitate to law-making, and we look to the rule, moral, or lesson being taught. Man was born to learn and born to teach. Man has a harder time understanding pure grace because it goes against our nature. It is much easier to understand the law: work hard, do not listen to liars, always be wary of flatterers. Much common sense is like this and falls in the category of good advice. Man will always devise moralistic, cautionary tales to instruct others on how to get on in this life. The Christian is no exception when it comes to devising rules and looking for the law. Yet the Christian must look for grace beyond this, and view life as a means of bringing God glory, not as an opportunity to get by with the least trouble and the most success.

Though our text includes over two hundred fables, we will consider just a sampling of them, looking at a number of the more well-known fables. We'll begin with "The Fox and the Grapes" where we get the expression "sour grapes." The hungry fox spies some delicious-looking grapes, but try as he might, he cannot reach them for all his jumping. So rather than being disappointed with his loss, he decides that the grapes were probably too sour to eat anyway. This is the behavior of the poor loser, and it is self-deception as well. He knows full well that the grapes were delicious, but he would rather tell himself a lie than admit his own defeat. So we have a prideful and lying fox, which is consistent with what we expect from the crafty nature of the fox. The tale does not condemn the fox; neither does it commend him. Rather, it is simply illustrating for us the typical, fleshly response to defeat.

"The Ants and the Grasshopper" has as its moral "Idleness brings want." It readily reminds us of Proverbs 6:6–11: "Go to the ant, you sluggard! Consider her ways and be wise, which, having no captain, overseer or ruler, provides her supplies in the summer, and gathers her food in the harvest. How long will you slumber, O sluggard? When will you rise from your sleep? A little sleep, a little slumber, a little folding of the hands to sleep—So shall your poverty come on you like a prowler, and your need like an armed man." In this fable the lazy, half-dead grasshopper appeals to the industrious little ants for a handout, but he meets with no pity. Again, this illustrates all law and no grace. They told him that since he had spent his summertime singing, perhaps he could dance all winter. Not only do they shut him out, they laugh as they do so. No mercy here. In contrast consider Proverbs 14:20–21: "The poor man is hated even by his own neighbor, but the rich has many friends. He who despises his neighbor sins; but he who has mercy on the poor, happy is he." God blesses the merciful because He is the father of all mercies Himself (2 Cor. 1:3). In this fable the law slams down on the grasshopper, and the ants are exonerated. In Scripture, the same principle is operative—laziness does lead to poverty—but another principle is operative as well: mercy triumphs over judgment.

One of the fables that Disney has used for a cartoon is "The Country Mouse and the Town Mouse," though Disney named it *The Country Cousin*. This is one of the longest fables in the collection, and it also evokes a teaching found in Proverbs: "Better is a dry morsel with quietness, than a house full of feasting with strife" (17:1). The country mouse concludes the fable with, "But I'd rather have a crust in peace and safety than all your fine things in the midst of such alarm and terror." This is basic to understanding contentment and also illustrates the dangers and temptations associated with living in wealth and luxury. The town mouse is captured by his worldly friend's fine talk, and he was quite pleased with the new arrangement, thinking contemptuously of his previous situation, until the revelers and the dogs burst in. It was then that the country mouse came back to his senses, seeing that his lowly life had some things money could not buy. The self-respecting country mouse had gleaned from the fields (barley, nuts, etc.), and the conceited city mouse was eating leftovers off the tables of the rich.

"The Hare and the Tortoise" must be the most popular fable for children's books, and Disney made a memorable cartoon of this story as well. *Slow and steady wins the race* is a maxim with plenty of applications. This is reminiscent of *Poor Richard's Almanac*, or Proverbs again: "Pride goes before destruction, and a haughty spirit before a fall" (16:18). The hare is full of himself, boastful and ridiculing the tortoise. But the tortoise is game for the contest and exhibits the good quality of follow-through. He does not flake out like the hare. Another biblical quotation illustrating the same principle comes to mind: "Let not the one who puts on his armor boast like the one who takes it off" (1 Kings 20:11).

"The Shepherd Boy and the Wolf" is a cautionary tale that many parents have told their children to illustrate the dangers of lying. "Even when liars tell the truth, they are never believed" is true as far as it goes. As we know, Satan is the father of all lies (John 8:44). But we also know that lies can be forgiven, that God can apply His grace to the liar's heart and wash away the sinfulness of it all. In this fable, the sheep were left to the mercy of the wolf, which is to say they received no mercy at all. They were ravaged by the wolf because of the careless shepherd boy's foolishness. Sin always has consequences, and sometimes they fall on the innocent bystanders. A liar always leaves destruction in his wake. The townspeople had lost patience with the shepherd boy, and again we see law, not grace, and we don't even know if the shepherd boy learned his lesson. This story is good incentive for truth-telling because of the consequences that befall the liar. But the Christian loves the truth because Jesus proclaimed Himself to be the way, the truth, and the life. It is not *just* about consequences.

"The Wind and the Sun" is an unusual fable whose characters are neither animals nor humans, but elements of nature. In this fable, the wind and the sun have a contest to see who can get a traveler to take off his coat. Never mind that the wind was at a serious disadvantage to start with because windy weather seldom causes one to take off a coat, but nevertheless, he blew up quite a gale, so the traveler kept his coat on tightly. Then the sun shone, the traveler got warm, and off came the coat. The moral of the story is "Sunshine of a kind and gentle manner will sooner open a poor man's heart than all the threats and force of blustering authority." Of course, sometimes that may in fact be true, but it is not a universal truth. Sometimes a poor man's heart won't open without God's intervention. Consider the apostle Paul, for instance. He had to be knocked off his horse and blinded!

In "The Wolf in Sheep's Clothing" we see what happens to those who seek to deceive others: they are found out and quickly dealt with. At least in this fable that's what happens. "Be sure your sin will find you out" (Num. 32:23) is the principle that comes to mind. The wolf dressed up like a sheep, hoping to eat a sheep for his supper, but the shepherd mistook him and killed him for his supper instead! Proverbs 26:27 says that "Whoever digs a pit will fall into it, and he who rolls a stone will have it roll back on him." It is hard not to think of the shepherd here as quite similar to the wolf: both of them just want their supper.

"The Fox and the Crow" has a very clever moral: "Whoever listens to the music of flatterers must expect to pay the piper." In this fable we have the crow stealing some cheese and the fox stealing the stolen cheese from the crow by means of flattery. Though the fox is the winner, he is in no way the "good guy" in this exchange. The fox covets the cheese that is not his, lies to the crow, and then insults the crow after winning the cheese. But the crow's foolishness is remarked on in the fable, not the fox's dishonesty or thievery. It is easy to imagine a follow-up fable where the fox gets his just reward from the crow.

We will read these and a number of other fables.

Having considered all this, it is important to note that Christians can often mistake Jesus' parables for fables. A parable (as Jesus told them), though similar in some ways to a fable, has additional subtleties and a very different point. *The Harper Handbook to Literature* defines a parable in a way that is too similar to their definition of fable—a "short tale encapsulating a moral or religious

How often have we nursed our disappointment by convincing ourselves that what was not obtained was probably not worth having anyway? The fox maintains his self-esteem by speculating that the grapes were no doubt sour.

lesson." *The New Geneva Study Bible* note on Matthew 13:3 has this to say about Jesus' parables: "Most of Jesus' parables are clear, but they also contain a depth of meaning that only one with a right relationship to Jesus can comprehend. It is only to the disciples that Jesus gives the

Dr. Seuss was a modern fabulist. Born Theodor Seuss Geisel in 1904, he published more than 60 children's books, including *The Cat in the Hat*, *Green Eggs and Ham*, *If I Ran the Zoo*, and *Horton Hears a Who*. As both storyteller and illustrator, he filled his stories with catchy rhymes, easily understood moral lessons, and whimsical creatures. Geisel died in 1991.

arrive shortly before the end of the day, but they are all paid the same amount for their labor. If we are just looking for a simple moral, we might say, "Be content with your pay" or "Don't compare yourselves to others" or "An employer can overpay his workers if he wants." These are all good lessons, and so the story could work as a didactic lesson. But Jesus was speaking about Israel and the Gentiles. The Jews had been "working in the vineyard" for many centuries, serving God, obeying His law, and worshiping Him as He commanded. Then along came Jesus preaching the Good News, with the intent to include even the Gentiles and other sinners within Israel. And the Jews were grumbling. How could God give the kingdom to the latecomers, those who had not been working all day? This is a good example of how we can mistake the message of God's abundant grace and just get some good moral instruction from the parable instead.

A modern fabulist would be someone like Dr. Seuss. If you have read stories such as *The Sneetches* or *Horton Hears a Who*, you know he is using funny animals to teach moral lessons to children about how to treat one another, about the foolishness of competition and peer pressure, and the importance of standing up for the little guy. These are fables, not parables, but because he lived thousands of years after the Incarnation, Dr. Seuss understands something of grace. He sees the goodness of the self-sacrificing Horton who is persecuted by his community. Perhaps the difference between Seuss and Aesop is that *Aesop's Fables* originated in the darkness of ancient Greece before the advent of the gospel, while Dr. Seuss was writing in the light of the Christian era.

By bringing Scripture to bear on these fables, I am not trying to undermine their purpose of teaching or their ability to delight us. We ought to take them as they are intended and enjoy them. But this enjoyment should only be as far as they go. So, if you have the opportunity, look at some children's editions of the stories and check out a couple of the cartoon versions.

—*Nancy Wilson*

interpretation of the parable of the sower and the parable of the tares. The ungodly miss this deeper meaning because their lack of a proper relationship with God has darkened their thoughts and hearts." In addition to this, Christ's parables were more context-dependent. Aesop's fables bring their own context with them; they are universally accessible. Christ's parables often function well at the same level (treated as a fable), but if we stop there, we will miss a great deal.

Jesus' parables were not just giving little morals like a fable, but were actually prophetic pronouncements against Israel. Consider, for example, the parable of the Laborers in the Vineyard in Matthew 20:1–16. In this parable some workers come early in the morning and others

For Further Reading

Frye, Northrop, et al. *The Harper Handbook to Literature.* New York: Harper and Row, 1985.[1]

The New Geneva Study Bible, Thomas Nelson Publishers, 1995.

Vernon Jones, V.S., trans. *Aesop's Fables: A Facsimile of the 1912 Edition*, with introduction by G.K. Chesterton. New York: Avenel Books, 1975.

Zipes, Jack, ed. *Aesop's Fables.* New York: Signet Classics, 1992.

Session I: Prelude

A Question to Consider

If fables are not factually possible (animals do not speak —the serpent in the Garden and Balaam's ass excepted), why should we read them?

From the General Information above, answer the following questions:
1. Why do the fables have such a universal appeal?
2. What is the relationship of law and grace for Christians?
3. What is the relationship of law and grace in Aesop?
4. Does this reliance on law mean that Christians cannot enjoy Aesop?
5. What common mistake do we make with regard to the parables of Christ?
6. What is significant about the use of animals in Aesop?

Reading Assignment:
"The Fox and the Grapes," "The Ants and the Grasshopper," "The Hawk and the Pigeons," "The Eagle and the Fox," "The Cock and the Jewel," and "The Fox and the Lion"

Session II: Discussion
"The Fox and the Grapes," "The Ants and the Grasshopper"

A Question to Consider

When we hear a "poor loser" make up excuses for why he lost or didn't get his way, why does it bother us so much? What is a typical fleshly response to defeat?

Discuss or list short answers to the following questions:

Text Analysis
1. In "The Fox and the Grapes," what condition is the fox in at the beginning of the fable? Might this condition affect his attitude to some degree? If so, how?
2. In "The Fox and the Grapes," how does the fox respond to defeat?
3. In "The Ants and the Grasshopper," how do the ants first respond to the half-dead grasshopper's request for "a morsel to save his life"?
4. In "The Ants and the Grasshopper," at any point in the fable do the ants show compassion or have mercy on the grasshopper?
5. In "The Ants and the Grasshopper," the moral of the fable is "Idleness brings want," which applies to the grasshopper's situation. What might the moral be if it were to apply to the ants?

Cultural Analysis
1. Where do we see "sour grapes" attitudes in our culture?
2. How does our culture react to people claiming "sour grapes"?
3. Where do we see sluggardly behavior in our culture?
4. How does our culture react to sluggardly behavior?

Biblical Analysis
1. How does the fox's response compare with Proverbs 21:23–24?
2. What does Luke 6:44–46 say about this sort of response?
3. What connection do we see between the fox's heart and mouth (Matt. 12:34)?
4. The Scriptures paint a very clear picture of how the sluggard is to look to the ant and learn from her ways. How is the grasshopper an excellent illustration of Proverbs 6:6–11?
5. In this passage, how does the ant fall short of a Christian response to poverty?

Summa

Write an essay or discuss this question, integrating what you have learned from the material above.
What is a Christian reaction to "sour grapes" and sluggardly behavior?

Optional Activity

Narrative Mime

Let's bring this fable to life with a narrative mime! While the teacher reads the following adaptation of "The Fox and the Grapes," the students act out the role of the fox without speaking. Be sure not to read too quickly. The students need time to mime all of the actions. There are no "physical" props... everything is mimed. Have fun!

Our next session will be a student-led discussion. As you are reading the following assignment, you should write down at least three questions from the text dealing with the issue listed below. These questions will be turned in to the teacher and will be used in classroom discussion. To get full credit for these Text Analysis questions, you must create a question that is connected to the reading and to the issue that is the focus of our discussion; you must also answer the question correctly (and include a page or line reference at the end); and your question must be one that invites discussion and debate ("why" questions are excellent; questions that can be answered by "yes" or "no" are to be avoided).

You should also provide two Cultural Analysis and two Biblical Analysis questions. Cultural Analysis questions ask how our culture views the issue that we are discussing. Biblical Analysis questions ask what the Bible says concerning this issue. Again, to get full credit for each question, you must create questions connected to the issue we are studying, answer each question correctly, and create questions that encourage and invite discussion and exploration. For an example of each type of question and answer, refer to the examples provided in the next session.

If you are working alone, after creating your questions and answers, have your parent or tutor check over them. Also, if possible, share them with your family at the dinner table, helping them to understand why the issue is important, how the issue arises in your reading, how its importance is still evident in our culture, and how understanding this issue might change the way you and your family should think and live.

Issue

Wolves almost always appear in fables as villains. Is this consistent portrayal of wolves good or is this just a prejudice?

Reading Assignment:

"The Wolf in Sheep's Clothing," "The Wolf and the Crane," "The Wolf and the Goat," "The Wolf and the Horse," "The Wolf and the Lamb," "The Wolf and the Lion," "The Wolf and the Sheep," and "The Wolf and the Shepherd"

Go to the ant, you sluggard! Consider her ways and be wise, which, having no captain, overseer or ruler, provides her supplies in the summer, and gathers her food in the harvest. How long will you slumber, O sluggard? When will you rise from your sleep?
—Proverbs 6:6–9

Session III: Student-Led Discussion

"The Wolf in Sheep's Clothing," "The Wolf and the Crane," "The Wolf and the Goat," "The Wolf and the Horse," "The Wolf and the Lamb," "The Wolf and the Lion," "The Wolf and the Sheep," and "The Wolf and the Shepherd"

A Question to Consider

Wolves almost always appear in fables as villains. Is this consistent portrayal of wolves good, or is this just a prejudice?

Students should read and consider the example questions below that are connected to the Question to Consider above. Last session's assignment was to prepare three questions and answers for the Text Analysis section and two additional questions and answers for both the Cultural and Biblical Analysis sections below.

Text Analysis

Example: Do wolves have a fixed nature in *Aesop's Fables* or are there all sorts of different wolves?

Answer: We see a clear pattern as to the wolf's fixed nature. There is not a single fable that paints the wolf as being an honorable, merciful character. We see this in the world as well. Since the wolves are known for being cunning, liars, thieves, deceivers, bullies, and tyrants, we also know that the wolf will not choose a respectable way to "earn a living." We need to keep in mind that this fable illustrates a simple truth about life as far as it goes. It's simply showing that a liar lies, a thief steals, a deceiver deceives, and so on. It doesn't go the extra step in showing that God can change hearts and forgive those who repent.

Cultural Analysis

Example: Where do we see the twisting of symbolic language in our culture today?

Answer: We often see it in children's books and cartoons. Dragons and snakes and ghouls are often portrayed as kind, nice, heroic and all-around good (or at least vastly misunderstood).

Other cultural issues to consider: *Dragontales, Super Why, Beetlejuice*

Biblical Analysis

Example: Are dragons and snakes ever good in the Bible?

Answer: They are mainly bad, but not always. Remember that when the Israelites are attacked by "fiery serpents," Moses raised up a bronze serpent on a pole. Those that looked at the serpent and trusted in God's provision were saved. This serpent represented Christ. Throughout the Scriptures, however, serpents and dragons are generally wicked.

Other Scriptures to consider: Genesis 3, Psalm 58, Psalm 140, Matthew 23:33; Revelation 12:9, but also cf. Exodus 7 and Numbers 21.

Summa

Write an essay or discuss this question, integrating what you have learned from the material above.

Should we seek to preserve the symbolic meaning of certain animals like wolves when we write children's stories?

Reading Assignment:

"The Country Mouse and the Town Mouse," "The Fox and the Crow," "The Fighting Cocks and the Eagles," "The Mouse and the Frog," "The Peach, the Apple and the Blackberry," "The Lion and the Mouse," and "The Lion, the Ass and the Fox Who Went Hunting"

Session IV: Activity

Drama

Let's bring this fable to life with a little acting! Act out the fable "The Country Mouse and the Town Mouse." In addition to being a lot of fun, acting is a great way to reinforce material being taught.

Divide up the parts between the students or family members. Casting is very flexible. One person can play numerous parts. Read through the entire script. Once you are familiar with the script, set up a "stage" and run the show. Work together to create the blocking and imaginative sound effects. Have fun!

Here is a short synopsis of some of the issues concerning the "The Country Mouse and the Town Mouse." Read through this and consider how these issues should affect your play.

Have you ever heard, "The grass is always greener on the other side (of the fence)?" For a brief period of time, the simple country mouse was definitely won over by the greener grass! Compared to his meager, quiet home, the town mouse's home is luxurious, and every meal is a feast. Is there anything wrong with being wealthy and having nice things? No, not at all. However, there are dangers and temptations associated with living in wealth and luxury. We need to remember that nice things in and of themselves are not bad. We know from the Scriptures that the Lord blessed Job, Abraham, Isaac, David, and Solomon (and the list goes on) with great wealth. Let's look closely at what Hebrews 13:5 has to say about money: "Keep your lives free from the love of money and be content with what you have because God has said, "Never will I leave you; never will I forsake you." Note here that he does not say, "Keep your lives free from money," but rather "from the *love* of money." Money in and of itself is not bad—it's the way in which we use it, think about it, and value it. Clothes, money, gadgets, and food can all become idols, but in and of themselves they are all just *stuff.* Let's take a look at how the country mouse is affected by *stuff.*

Let's look at the after-dinner chat between the town mouse and country mouse. The town mouse says, "How is it, my good friend, that you can endure this boring and crude life? You live like a toad in a hole. You can't really prefer these solitary rocks and woods to streets teeming with carriages and people. Upon my word of honor, you're wasting your time in such a miserable existence. You must make the most of your life while it lasts. As you know, a mouse does not live forever. So, come with me this very night, and I'll show you all around the town and what life's about." Several things can be gleaned from this conversation:

The town mouse is the country mouse's good friend. Because of this relationship, the country mouse values the opinion of his friend. He trusts him.

How is it, my good friend . . .

The town mouse persuasively and convincingly tells the country mouse that he truly cannot prefer his country way of life over that of town.

You live like a toad in a hole. You can't really prefer these solitary rocks and woods . . .

The town mouse very confidently and unapologetically gives the country mouse counsel as to how he needs to change his country way of life for his own good.

Upon my word of honor, you're wasting your time in such a miserable existence.

The town mouse uses the "sense of urgency" to convince the country mouse that he needs to make a life change.

You must make the most of your life while it lasts. . . . [A] mouse does not live forever. Come with me this very night . . .

The town mouse portrays himself as being an expert in knowing what life is all about.

. . . I'll show you all around the town and what life's about (the essence of the entire discourse).

Though the town mouse believes that what he is saying is true, his words are tempting, deceptive and false and will lead his friend astray.

List of Characters

Narrators: One or more
Birds, Cows, Trees
Country Mouse
Town Mouse
Revelers
Dogs

Set/Props

For Country Mouse's home use one chair to represent rocking chair. Two chairs and a small table can be used to represent the kitchen. For Town Mouse's home two chairs and a table can be used to represent the dining room.

Sound-Effects

Use the voice to create birds tweeting, trees blowing and whistling, a telephone ringing, cows mooing, a roaring car engine, and traffic noises. Use bells for a telephone ringing, along with a triangle for the elevator going up and down, stopping at each floor.

Staging

Use one half of the stage/room for the country mouse's house, and the other half for the town mouse's house. As the mice travel from one home to the other, they could drive their car around the edge of the stage/classroom.

Reading Assignment:

"The Hare and the Tortoise," "The Hares and the Frogs," "The Farmer and the Stork," "The Man and the Lion," "The Bundle of Sticks," "Jupiter and the Bee," "Mercury and the Woodcutter," and "The Goose with the Golden Eggs"

Benjamin Franklin once said, "A wolf eats sheep but now and then, ten thousands are devoured by men." In fables wolves are almost always depicted as villains.

SESSION V: WRITING
"The Hare and the Tortoise"

Extending the Story

This session is a writing assignment. Remember, quality counts more than quantity. You should write no more than 1,000 words, either typing or writing legibly on one side of a sheet of paper. You will lose points for writing more than this. You will be allowed to turn in your writing three times. The first and second times you turn it in, your teacher will grade it by editing your work. This is done by marking problem areas and making suggestions for improvement. You should take these suggestions into consideration as you revise your assignment. Only the grade on your final submission will be recorded. Your grade will be based on the following criteria: 25 points for grammar, 25 points for content accuracy—historical, theological, etc.; 25 points for logic—does this make sense and is it structured well?; 25 points for rhetoric—is it a joy to read?

Fictional Story

Your assignment is to extend or lengthen the story of "The Tortoise and the Hare" by imagining what would happen after the race is over. "The Tortoise and the Hare" is one of Aesop's most popular fables. We tend to think of it as being a fable for children since it is so often adapted for children's books and movies. It points out how the proud and boastful hare loses in a race against a slow but steady tortoise. Though the hare has the ability to win the race, he makes an arrogant decision to stop and rest, which enables the tortoise to pass him by and win. The tortoise is an excellent example of one who perseveres until the end. Thus, we have the moral "Slow and steady wins the race." Have you ever wondered what happened

after the race? Was the hare a "bad loser" or did he learn his lesson? Was there ever a rematch? Wonder no more. A new, extended version of this fable answers all your questions.

"The Tortoise and the Hare . . . Extended Edition"
Author Unknown

Once upon a time a tortoise and a hare had an argument about who was faster. They decided to settle the argument with a race. The tortoise and hare both agreed on a route and started off the race. The hare shot ahead and ran briskly for some time. Then seeing that he was far ahead of the tortoise, he thought he'd sit under a tree for some time and relax before continuing the race. He sat under the tree and soon fell asleep. The tortoise, plodding on, overtook him and soon finished the race, emerging as the undisputed champ. The hare woke up and realized that he'd lost the race.

The moral of the story is that slow and steady wins the race. This is the version of the story that we've all grown up with.

But the story doesn't end there . . .

Here is an example of what the rest of the "Extended Edition" might look like. (This version is written to affirm certain business principles. It is used by professionals as a tool to teach teamwork throughout the English-speaking world and beyond. In addition to the United States and Canada, this version is popular in the United Kingdom, Australia, New Zealand, Philippines, Taiwan, Vietnam, Thailand, Malaysia, Indonesia, China, Hong Kong, India, Korea, Japan, Jamaica, Saudi Arabia, Croatia, and the list goes on. Some or all of the morals are focused on the business world.)

The hare was disappointed at losing the race and he did some soul-searching. He realized that he'd lost the race only because he had been overconfident, careless, and lax. If he had not taken things for granted, there's no way the tortoise could have beaten him. So he challenged the tortoise to another race. The tortoise agreed. This time, the hare went all out and ran without stopping from start to finish. He won by several miles.

The moral of the story? Fast and consistent will always beat the slow and steady. If you have two people in your organization, one slow, methodical and reliable, and the other fast and still reliable at what he does, the fast and reliable chap will consistently climb the organizational ladder faster than the slow, methodical chap.

It's good to be slow and steady; but it's better to be fast and reliable.

But the story doesn't end there . . .

The tortoise did some thinking this time, and realized that there's no way he can beat the hare in a race the way it was currently formatted. He thought for a while, and then challenged the hare to another race, but on a slightly different route. The hare agreed. The tortoise and hare started off. In keeping with his self-made commitment to be consistently fast, the hare took off and ran at top speed until he came to a broad river. The finishing line was a couple of kilometers on the other side of the river. The hare sat there wondering what to do. In the meantime the tortoise trundled along, got into the river, swam to the opposite bank, continued walking and finished the race.

The moral of the story? First identify your core competency and then change the playing field to suit your core competency.

In an organization, if you are a good speaker, make sure you create opportunities to give presentations that enable the senior management to notice you. If your strength is analysis, make sure you do some sort of research, make a report and send it upstairs. Working to your strengths will not only get you noticed, but will also create opportunities for growth and advancement.

The story still hasn't ended.

The tortoise and hare, by this time, had become pretty good friends, and they did some thinking together. Both realized that the last race could have been run much better. So the tortoise and hare decided to do the last race again, but to run as a team this time. They started off, and this time the hare carried the tortoise till the riverbank. There, the tortoise took over and swam across with the hare on his back. On the opposite bank, the hare again carried the tortoise, and they reached the finishing line together. Both the tortoise and hare felt a greater sense of satisfaction than they'd felt earlier.

The moral of the story? It's good to be individually brilliant and to have strong core competencies, but unless you're able to work in a team and harness each other's core competencies, you'll always perform below par because there will always be situations at which you'll do poorly and someone else does well.

Teamwork is mainly about situational leadership, letting the person with the relevant core competency for a situation take leadership.

There are more lessons to be learned from this inspirational teamwork story.

Note that neither the tortoise nor hare gave up after failures. The hare decided to work harder and put in more effort after his failure. The tortoise changed his strategy because he was already working as hard as he could. In life, when faced with failure, sometimes it is appropriate to work harder and put in more effort. Sometimes it is appropriate to change strategy and try something different. And sometimes it is appropriate to do both.

The tortoise and hare also learned another vital lesson in teamwork. When we stop competing against a rival and instead start competing against the situation, we perform far better.

For example, when Roberto Goizueta took over as chief executive officer of Coca-Cola in the 1980s, he was faced with intense competition from Pepsi that was eating into Coke's growth. His executives were Pepsi-focused and intent on increasing market share 0.1 percent. Goizueta decided to stop competing against Pepsi and instead compete against the situation of 0.1 percent growth.

He asked his executives what was the average fluid intake of an American per day. The answer was 14 ounces. What was Coke's share of that? Two ounces. Goizueta said Coke needed a larger share of that market. The competition wasn't Pepsi. It was the water, tea, coffee, milk, and fruit juices that went into the remaining 12 ounces. To this end, Coke put up vending machines at every street corner. Sales took a quantum jump, and Pepsi has never quite caught up since.

To sum up, the story of the hare and tortoise teaches us many things. Chief among them are that fast and consistent will always beat slow and steady; work to your competencies; pooling resources and working as a team will always beat individual performers; never give up when faced with failure; and finally, compete against the situation, not against a rival.

Reading Assignment:
""The Wind and the Sun," "The Fox and the Crow," "The Maid and the Pail of Milk," "The Mice in Council," "The Ass and His Master," "The Mice and the Weasels," "The Eagle and the Crow," and "The Lion and the Three Bulls"

Session VI: Activity

Creating an Oral Fable

In the true spirit of Aesop, we are going to create an oral fable. In addition to being a great learning experience, this exercise is a lot of fun! An important factor to making this a success is to do a thorough job creating the storyline. The more information you have, the better the oral fable will be!

Copy the headings from Chart 1 onto a large sheet of paper or the board. Fill in the information. Remember, the moral drives the storyline. The storyline is simply the tool used to drive the point home.

Sit in a large circle. (If you are working at home, do this activity with family members. If you are working alone, write the fable and present it to your family at dinner.) Pass around a "talking stick" (any simple item, such as an eraser, ruler or ball). The person holding the "talk-ing stick" adds a line or two to the oral fable being created. The last one holding the "talking stick" tells the moral of the story. Encourage the students to include creative dialogue! (Each student may contribute to the story one or several times depending upon the size of the class.)

Here is an example of what you might produce:

Chart 1: **CREATING AN ORAL FABLE**

CREATING THE STORYLINE	EXAMPLES
Moral	"Whoever harms his neighbor will bring a curse upon himself."
	"Little friends may prove great friends."
	"Never underestimate the help of the small."
General plot	Characters "A" and "B" are walking down the road. "B" falls into a pit. "A" runs away, leaving "B" in the pit. "C" comes upon "B" in the pit and rescues him. "C" invites "B" to his home for dinner and lodging. The next day "B" and "C" come upon "A" captured in a drop-net trap. "B" and "C" do not rescue "A."
Select characters whose characteristics are appropriate for the plot.	Character "A": a fox; Character "B": an old hound; Character "C": a mouse
Additional storyline details: Setting, Relationships, Motives, Outcome (can be completed in any order)	Setting: Summertime on a forest path just as the sun is setting. Shadows are covering the ground. It is the middle of the night when the mouse helps the old hound. It is mid-morning when the old hound and mouse come upon the fox.
	Relationships: The fox and the old hound with poor eyesight meet earlier that day on the road. They realize they are both traveling in the same direction and decide to travel together. The forest dwelling mouse doesn't know either the fox or the old hound.
	Motives: The fox knows the old hound has poor eyesight and that a pit lies on their path. The fox wants the old hound's travel pack which contains food and money. The mouse has no ulterior motive. He shows kindness to the old hound. The old hound and mouse do not rescue the fox because he showed no mercy to the old hound.
	Outcome: The old hound retrieves his travel pack and continues his journey accompanied by the mouse. The fox is captured by hunters.

458 OMNIBUS IV

Once upon a time there was a possum and a field mouse. The possum thought little of the field mouse because he was so tiny, but the field mouse desperately wanted to be friends with the possum. "What can a field mouse do?" asked the possum sarcastically as he strode away from the friendless mouse into the deep dark woods. That night some hunters were in the woods and saw the possum. He scurried away. But just when he thought he was safe, he stumbled into a patch of vines and was trapped. Soon the hunters would find him, kill him, and have him for dinner. Along came the listless field mouse, who saw the possum trapped and heard the hunters coming. He quickly ran to where the possum was trapped and began to gnaw at the vines that held him fast. The last vine snapped seconds before the hunters arrived, and the possum and the field mouse darted into a hollow tree for safety. The possum looked at his tiny friend with gratitude. "Little friends may prove great friends," he said.

Optional Activity

A great way to practice rhetoric skills while applying what the students have learned about Aesop is to host an *Aesop's Fables* production! Invite parents, siblings, and younger students.

Aesop was a master storyteller. He was known for his quick wit and his ability to captivate and entertain large audiences. Captivate your audience! In honor of Aesop, be energetic, witty, and creative. Leave a lasting impression on your audience. Have fun!

Below is a sample 30-minute performance schedule. If time permits, add more to the schedule. For example:

- Add a reading of the original "The Shepherd Boy and the Wolf" as well as a rewrite.

- Read an Aesop's fable but don't include the moral. Call on audience members to share what they think a fitting moral might be. End with reading the real moral.

- If the audience is composed of older students and parents, include a reading of "The Tortoise and the Hare … Extended Edition."

SAMPLE PERFORMANCE SCHEDULE

- Present a brief background of Aesop.

- Do a brief introduction of "The Wind and the Sun." Perform the play (make it like the one you did for "The Country Mouse and the City Mouse."

    Following the performance, expand upon the moral by adding that in some instances we need more than a kind word to open a poor man's

heart. We need God's intervention.

- Read the original version of "The Ants and the Grasshopper."

    Explain how this fable shows all law and no mercy.

    Read one rewrite of "The Ants and the Grasshopper" and explain how it demonstrates mercy.

- Do a brief introduction of "The Country Mouse and the Town Mouse." Perform the play.

- End with the actors and audience members participating in a mime of "The Fox and the Grapes." (See the Optional Activity for Session II.)

OPTIONAL SESSION: RECITATION

Comprehension Questions

Answer the following questions for factual recall:

1. Looking at the fable "The Country Mouse and the City Mouse," at what point do you notice that the country mouse is finding the town mouse's living situation more agreeable than his own? What is the country mouse's initial attitude toward this "positive" change in his living situation?
2. In "The Country Mouse and the City Mouse," after spending some time in the "lap of luxury," the country mouse goes through a transformation. What seed has sprouted and is growing in the country mouse's heart, which affects his attitude and thoughts?
3. What actions occurred that brought the country mouse back to his senses?
4. In "The Wolf in Sheep's Clothing," why did the wolf dress up like a sheep in the first place?
5. In "The Wolf in Sheep's Clothing," are the wolf and shepherd really so different?
6. In "The Fox and the Crow," is the crow a more honorable creature than the fox in this fable?
7. In "The Fox and the Crow," can you think of an instance in your life where you listened to smooth talking and ended up "paying the piper"?
8. In "The Wind and the Sun," we see that the sunshine of a kind and gentle manner will sooner open a poor man's heart than all the threats and force of blustering authority. Do you agree or disagree with the moral? Why?

ENDNOTE

1 There are a number of online sources for Aesop. For starters try Link 1 for this chapter at www.VeritasPress.com/OmniLinks.

DEATH ON THE NILE

What motivates a murderer? Is it greed? Is it lust? Power? Revenge? The question of murder always goes back to the early chapters of Genesis, when the first murder occurred. Every murderer is a Cain and under the curse of God. Every murder victim is an Abel whose blood cries out to God for justice.

Cain was the first son of Adam. The promise of God had been that a Seed would come from Eve and crush the head of the serpent, but instead of her firstborn seed crushing the serpent, he embraced the serpent. Instead of ruling over evil, Cain invited the evil in, and he was cursed like the dragon before him and driven from the land of the living.

The name Adam literally means "man," and frequently in the Old Testament, a "son of Adam" is translated "son of man." To label someone a son of Adam, a son of man, is to label him as Cain, a son of the Fall, a murderous brother.

There was another Son of Man who was also born of a woman, but this Cain ruled over the sin that crouched at His door. This Cain did not allow the dragon in; this Cain fought the dragon and won. But this Cain became an Abel, and was slain for all the sons of Adam. And when this Cain died, He took all evil and sin into Himself,

and He took it into Himself not so that it could find a home but so that it might finally be destroyed. For when this Son of Man died, sin died with Him.

Death on the Nile is in many ways a traditional detective mystery novel. We know that someone is going to be murdered. But every good murder mystery is always a faint reflection of the story of history. It's always a story of the murderer being revealed, justice being done, and the wisdom and wit of the hero leading us to the truth.

GENERAL INFORMATION

Author and Context

Agatha Mary Clarissa Miller was born on September 15, 1890, the third child of a fairly affluent family. While she would not have been old enough at the time to appreciate them, her family's dinner parties included such esteemed literary giants as Henry James and Rudyard Kipling. Her father died when she was eleven, leaving the family in a hard spot, and eventually she and her mother moved to Egypt and rented out their home in England. She married Archibald Christie in 1914. While she would eventually be known formally as Lady Mallowan (taking her second husband's last name), she has always been known popularly around the world as Agatha Christie and playfully as the Duchess of Death. She also authored romances under the pseudonym Mary Westmacott. Christie's first novel was *The Mysterious Affair at Styles,* published in 1920, which introduced and started the career of her fictional Belgian detective hero Hercule Poirot (pronounced "Airkewl Pwa-ro") who would go on to star in 33 novels and 54 short stories. By the end of the 1930s she would begin to grow tired of Poirot, but she is said to have been concerned to please the public who so enjoyed the character. As the final episode in the Poirot series, she wrote *Curtain* during World War II, but it was sealed in a bank vault for over thirty years until 1975.

Poirot, however, is not Christie's only great detective.

She was the writer of many great mysteries and so created many great characters. Her other great detective is Miss Jane Marple, an elderly lady in a small English village, who most people ignore as a doddering senior citizen but who always finds the killer.

Much of Agatha Christie's life and experiences are seen in the settings and characters of her novels. She traveled extensively, and even some of the more difficult experiences of her life can be found as echoes in her novels. Christie lived through both World Wars and witnessed the many challenges and transitions of those periods. She served as a nurse during World War I and found it very rewarding. Some years after the war her first husband was unfaithful and divorced her. She married Max Mallowan, an archaeologist, in 1930. Knowledge of medicine, wounds, history, not to mention personal experience with love and betrayal, are significant themes in a number of Christie novels, *Death on the Nile* no less than others.

Christie was wildly popular and successful during her own lifetime, and is still known for the eighty mystery novels she wrote and a number of highly successful stage plays. Her stage play *Mousetrap* is the longest running play ever, still running as of this writing. Christie received a number of awards during her life: a Commander of the Order of the British Empire in 1956, President of the Detection Club in 1957, a Dame Commander of the Order of the British Empire in 1971. Agatha Christie died on January 12, 1976.

Agatha Christie

Significance

Agatha Christie deserves recognition for the broad popularity and appeal she had throughout so much of the twentieth century. *Guinness Book of World Records* ranks her with William Shakespeare as having sold more books than any other author. It lists only the Bible as having more sales. John Dickson Carr, a celebrated detective novelist, judged *Death on the Nile* to be among the ten greatest mystery novels of all time.

Christie herself noted *Death on the Nile* as holding a

special place in her own mind: "I think, myself, that the book is one of the best of my 'foreign travels' ones. I think the central situation is intriguing and has dramatic possibilities, and the three characters, Simon, Linnet, and Jacqueline, seem to me to be real and alive."[1] *Death on the Nile* not only enjoys favorite status by Christie, but it is also the favorite of many fans and critics alike. Today there are Death on the Nile Cruises which offer the opportunity for vacationers to not only enjoy a cruise on the Nile, but also the intrigue and fun of a murder mystery aboard the ship. Actors and actresses play their parts aboard the cruisers, and vacationers are called on to act as detectives to solve the crime.

Main Characters

As might be expected, Hercule Poirot, the careful and brilliant detective, is the most important character in the novel. In the opening chapter we are introduced to Linnet Ridgeway (later Linnet Doyle) by two townsfolk discussing her wealth and her beauty. Her best friend, Jacqueline de Bellefort, has fallen on hard times in the aftermath of the great stock market crash, and she appears early in the story looking for employment for her fiancé, Simon Doyle. Part 1 ends with the news spreading that the rich and lovely Linnet Ridgeway has married Simon Doyle and is honeymooning in Egypt. In fact, as Part 2 opens, we find the Doyles aboard the S.S. *Karnak* along with a number of other passengers: Mrs. Allerton and her son, Tim; Linnet's maid, Louise Bourget; Miss Van Schuyler and her niece, Cornelia Robson; Miss Schuyler's nurse, Miss Bowers; Salome Otterbourne and her daughter, Rosalie; Linnet's American lawyer and trustee, Andrew Pennington; a mysterious man named Mr. Ferguson; the archaeologist Signor Richetti; the silent man James Fanthorp; the Austrian Dr. Bessner; and Jacqueline De Bellefort. We meet Joanna Southwood in the first couple of chapters, and we know that she has a somewhat mysterious relationship with Tim Allerton. Colonel Race, a government agent, is also aboard the *Karnak* tracking an anonymous terrorist of sorts. He becomes the assistant of Poirot as the mystery unfolds.

Summary and Setting

As has already been noted, the rich and beautiful Linnet Ridgeway steals the fiancé of her best friend, Jacqueline de Bellefort. The Doyles are on their honeymoon in Egypt, taking a cruise on the Nile, and to their great dismay they are being stalked by Jacqueline. And the rest of the colorful cast aboard the *Karnak* brings a host of their own tangles with them. After Jacqueline finally does seem to crack, pulling out a gun and shooting Simon in the leg, she is taken back to her room and kept under observation. The next morning Linnet Doyle is found dead in her cabin, shot in the head.

Not to be confused with the hero of our story, Hercules displays amazing feats of strength on this red-figure vase painting. Hercule Poirot, on the other hand, amazes us with intellectual feats using his "little grey cells."

While the setting does not appear to play an absolutely essential role in the story, it is nevertheless notable. One aspect of this includes the fact that the Aswan Dam was built on the Nile around the turn of the century. This dam caused the river banks to rise considerably, a fact that is noted in the novel: "There was a savage aspect about the sheet of water in front of them, the masses of rock without vegetation that came down to the water's edge—here and there a trace of houses abandoned and ruined as a result of the damming up of the waters. The whole scene had a melancholy, almost sinister charm" (Pt. 2, chap. 6). Many villages and archaeological sites were buried beneath the reservoir created by the dam (known as Lake Nasser); only some survived, and that with great effort. The temple of Ramses II at Abu Simbel was perhaps the greatest site along the Nile, and it was preserved by cutting it into some 950 pieces, hoisting them up the banks to a new sight safely away from the edge of the river, and reassembling them. There is something haunting, something sinister in the waters covering those houses and ruins. And one wonders if there are parallels underlying *Death on the Nile*.

Worldview

G.K. Chesterton once wrote that the "first essential value of the detective story lies in this, that it is the earliest and only form of popular literature in which is expressed some sense of the poetry of modern life."[2] So detective stories reveal the poetry of modern life. They do this by hiding the truth and then proceeding to slowly and methodically uncover it.

W.H. Auden defined the plot of a detective novel as "a murder occurs, many are suspected; all but one suspect, who is the murderer, are eliminated; the murderer is arrested or dies."[3] Another commentator says that a detective story may be defined as "a tale in which the primary interest lies in the methodical discovery, by rational means, of the exact circumstances of a mysterious event or series of events."[4] In other words, the primary point of a detective mystery novel is the *dénouement*. This is a French word which means "to untie," from Old French and Latin roots associated with untying knots. The dénouement is the outcome or resolution of the central plot in literature or drama. And that is precisely what a detec-

"O'er Egypt's land of memory
   floods are level,
And they are thine, O Nile!
   and well thou knowest
The soul-sustaining airs
   and blasts of evil,
And fruits, and poisons spring
   where'er thou flowest."
—Percy Bysshe Shelley

Still a popular destination for holiday cruisers, the Nile exudes an aura of exotic mystery.

tive novel is all about. Detective novels are frequently almost entirely all dénouement, all untying, all unraveling. Everyone knows that someone will die fairly early on and by the end the brilliant detective will have uncovered the truth, but the story is all about the unearthing of the truth. While all stories usually have some sort of dénouement, some sort of resolution, many other genres spend more time leading up to a climax through rising action and the resolution comes at the end, pulling the loose ends all together. And while the detective novel also follows this pattern in some ways, in another sense, for the detective novel, the plot *is* the resolution. The rising action is the slow uncovering of information leading up to the final revelation of "whodunit."

Poirot describes this very process of dénouement with archaeological imagery toward the end of the novel. His friend and assistant, Colonel Race, is growing frustrated with the case (and with Poirot) because all of the most likely suspects, for all their faults and other crimes, have not yet been pegged with the murder of Linnet. "Why all this beating about the bush?" Race asks, and Poirot responds,

> You think that I am just amusing myself with side issues? And it annoys you? But it is not that. Once I went professionally to an archaeological expedition—and I learnt something there. In the course of an excavation, when something comes up out of the ground, everything is cleared away very carefully all around it. You take away the loose earth, and you scrape here and there with a knife until finally your object is there, all alone, ready to be drawn and photographed with no extraneous matter confusing it. That is what I have been seeking to do—clear away the extraneous matter so that we can see the truth—the naked shining truth (Pt. 2, chap. 27).

A detective story is a riddle, and the fun of the riddle is found in the fact that certain rules must ordinarily be observed. The riddle must be solved through erudition, logic, and meticulously observing the tendencies of people. Mary Wagoner points out that in *Death on the Nile* there is particular attention paid to a number of relationships that revolve around tensions with power and authority. Of the sixteen people on board the *Karnak,* most of them are struggling with wielding authority, enduring unjust authority, or preparing to rebel against it. Linnet Ridgeway is the most powerful of all the characters. She is powerful in riches, in beauty, and in intelligence. And she bends all of these gifts to serve her purposes. Jacqueline has power in her will, in her determination and relentlessness to achieve her goals. Poirot himself is looked up to by all. He is as famous as Linnet Ridgeway, an intellectual celebrity, but his authority ultimately rests in the truth, in his ability to unearth the original players and actions. In addition to Poirot, there are mothers who are authoritarian or meddlesome and their children, who struggle in various ways beneath them; Mr. Pennington, Linnet's guardian; Mr. Fanthorp, the representative of Linnet's English solicitor; there is Mr. Ferguson, a socialist revolutionary; and an old, wealthy woman who constantly complains and manipulates the people under her.

Part of the challenge of *Death on the Nile*, like many murder mystery tales, is all the suspects. *Death on the Nile* is packed with people, too many people, too many stories colliding. And of course that is part of the fun. There's a crowded room, a crime is committed, and you have a front row seat to the investigation. As Poirot unravels the facts, we find that it is not so simple as one bad guy, lots of innocent bystanders, and an innocent victim or two. While this is not always the case in Christie novels, *Death on the Nile* explores the complications of crime and sin when everyone is a sinner, when there are several criminals, and even when the victim is not at all very innocent. And this becomes both a challenge for readers and part of the poetry of the story. There isn't really any character who seems altogether sympathetic. Everyone has flaws; everyone has weaknesses. Even the hero, Hercule Poirot, is not particularly winsome. He's brilliant and smart, but he does not appear to be a great man. He seems odd, a little picky and irritable in places, and in the end he even seems a little ambivalent to justice and overly pessimistic.

The name Hercule Poirot is not unrelated to his character. The first name "Hercule" conjures up Hercules, the Greek adventurer and warrior, while a *poirot* is something of a buffoon. And thus we have the juxtaposition of the fierce and valiant son of the gods with a "funny little man" with a black mustache who puts all his ability in his "little grey cells" and occasionally borders on being annoying with his overly fastidious nature. One commentator goes so far as to suggest that Poirot has something of the feminine in his style and methods. Throughout the novels, Poirot frequently notices details that we would ordinarily credit a woman with noticing. In *Death on the Nile*, this

The jackal-headed Anubis, Egyptian god of the dead, was guardian of the underworld and associated with the mummification process.

manifests itself in the curious notice of a fingernail polish. Would an ordinary man be bothered by the presence of two bottles of nail polish and notice a slight difference in color? Poirot was, and that is how he came to examine the bottles and find a telling clue.

All of these elements in *Death on the Nile* actually blend together quite nicely. Let's see: a story full of flawed characters, where power struggles, resistance, and manipulation figure prominently, and by the time it's all over, several corpses are being carried ashore. It sounds a lot like the world we live in, the story of history. Of course, the story of the world is a mystery. God is the genius story teller, and he knows all the answers to all the riddles, all the mysteries. And yet God also loves the story, loves the mystery, and has written Himself into the story. Like Hercule Poirot, the story of history is God the Spirit, digging away at a treasure, a fossil, brushing away the dirt, clearing away debris, unearthing His glory in the world through the intrigue and fallible stories of His people.

While there are a number of important scenes and conversations in the first part of the book, one occurs when the reader is introduced to Hercule Poirot in the restaurant Chez Ma Tante. While the detective is there taking in the crowd, he notices one couple dancing who end up sitting at a table near him. While Poirot does not yet know who the couple are, readers quickly realize that this is Jackie, Linnet's best friend and her fiancé, of whom she has already spoken to Linnet about, Simon Doyle. Even as Poirot watches them, he notes to himself, "She cares too much, that little one," and he adds, "It is not safe. No it is not safe." Poirot is suspicious of Jacqueline's love for Simon here, and by the end of the story he concludes, "That is why most great love stories are tragedies."

There are several references to the Bible throughout the novel. There is an explicit reference to the David and Bathsheba story and to Nathan's confrontation of David in particular (2 Sam. 11–12), as well as the incident with Ahab and Naboth's vineyard (1 Kings 21). In both episodes there is murder, of course, but both also highlight the misuse of power in taking advantage of the weak.

A less explicit reference to Scripture is in Poirot's warning to Jacqueline, when he urges her not to seek her revenge against Simon and Linnet. "Do not open your heart to evil," he urges Jackie, "Because—if you do—evil will come... Yes, very surely evil will come... It will enter in and make its home within you, and after a little while it will no longer be possible to drive it out." This is very close to God's own warning to Cain in Genesis 4: "If you do well, will you not be accepted? And if you do not do well, sin lies at the door. And its desire is for you, but you should rule over it" (Gen. 4:7). Like Poirot's warning, God urges Cain not to allow evil through the door, to make its home within him. For if sin and evil are allowed in, they will rule over him. The wording here is exactly parallel to one of the curses in Genesis 3 where God says that sin will create a particular kind of adversity between a husband and a wife, where a woman's desire will be for her husband, and he shall rule over her (Gen. 3:16).

Poirot appears to be overly pessimistic. It may be true that many great love stories have had tragic elements, but we know that the story of the world is the greatest love story, the story of God's love for the world and the giving of His Son for us. And that story is not a tragedy but a comedy, a story that ends in a wedding and in joy. Yet Poirot's suspicions with regard to misplaced love seem consistent with Scripture. Recognizing that love is Jackie's problem, he warns her, "Love is not everything, Mademoiselle . . . It is only when we are young that we think it is." This is why the greatest commandment is to love God with all that we are. Anything less than wholehearted devotion to God is dangerous. It is not safe.

But our love for God is of course all the result of His love for us. He has sought us out in Jesus; we love Him because He loved us first. And this love is to die for. He came to be a righteous Cain, to rule evil and put it to death in His death. In order for Jesus to rule over evil, He had to be a wise king. Like a greater Solomon, Jesus was anointed with the Spirit of Wisdom and knew that to destroy all sin and death and evil, He had to take these things into Himself and die. He had to die like a murderer, for all murder to be destroyed. And the glory of it all is that in the death of Christ, true power was revealed. When Jesus was lifted up on the cross, He was revealed to be the Messiah, the true King of Israel.

And it is this enthronement on the cross, the wisdom of God revealed in the death of Jesus, that answers the curse of sin on the woman. In the death Christ, He took a bride to Himself, the Christian Church (Eph. 5:2, 25). And that Bride is being revealed *as* the wisdom of God; the church united to Christ is where the treasures of wisdom and knowledge are found. She is where God's glory is being revealed from glory to glory. By the power of the Spirit her desire is for her Husband, but He rules her in wisdom and has exalted her and seated her with Him in the heavenly places to reign with Him until every enemy has been put down.

Death on the Nile is not high art. Christie was not producing great literature in her mystery novels, but the mass production and hugely popular following of fans certainly reveals something "classic" about them. People are attracted to the universal themes of love and greed, loyalty and betrayal, and the multiplicity of ways humans have to take perfectly wonderful things and turn them into horrific tales of sadness and misery. There is also something fundamentally true about a mystery. It's the glory of God to conceal a matter, but it is the glory of kings to search it out (Prov. 25:2). There is something built into humans created in the image of God, a certain nobility, that loves a good challenge, a good mystery. And perhaps that is something of the poetry of a detective story, something of the glory in a mystery. Kings are called to wisdom, and wisdom must be searched out, untied, and unearthed. In Christ, we have all been made kings and called into that great treasure hunt, the adventure of life, the mystery of the universe which ultimately finds all dénouement, all resolution, and every solution in the Father, Son, and Holy Spirit. And *that* is the naked shining truth.

—*Toby J. Sumpter*

For Further Reading

Most, Glen W., and Stowe, William W. *The Poetics of Murder*. New York: Harcourt Brace Jovanovich Publishers, 1983.

Murch, A.E. *The Development of the Detective Novel*. London: Peter Owen Limited, 1968.

Osborne, Charles. *The Life and Crimes of Agatha Christie*. New York: St. Martin's Press, 2001.

Session I: Prelude

Question to Consider
What is power?

From the General Information above answer the following questions:
1. How did Agatha Christie's life inform her writing?
2. What is dénouement in literature and drama?
3. How is a detective novel in one sense almost entirely dénouement?
4. What biblical allusions appear in *Death on the Nile*? How are they significant?
5. How might Poirot be accused of being somewhat feminine? How does that fit with the idea of wisdom?
6. What is the glory of God and the glory of kings (Prov. 25:2)? How does that fit with wisdom?

Reading Assignment:
Death on the Nile, Part 1– Part 2, chapter 3

Session II: Discussion
Part 1 – Part 2 chapter 3

A Question to Consider
When is it the hardest to do what is right?

Discuss or list short answers to the following questions:

Text Analysis
1. What does Joanna Southwood tell Linnet she would do if Linnet lost all her money?
2. What does Linnet notice that Jacqueline does which she remembers as being "characteristic of her?"
3. What does Poirot overhear Jacqueline and Simon talking about at the Chez Ma Tante restaurant?
4. What makes Mr. Andrew Pennington angry? And what does he decide to do?
5. Why is Jim Fanthorp sent to Egypt?
6. What reason does Poirot say is causing Linnet to feel guilty? What does Poirot agree to do for Linnet?

Cultural Analysis
1. Linnet says that an engagement is not really binding, and therefore it was actually heroic and right for Simon to break it off with Jacqueline since he had discovered that he really loved Linnet. Would our culture agree with Linnet?

2. Poirot says that Linnet is upset because she feels guilty. What is our culture's view of guilt?

Biblical Analysis
1. Read Psalm 51. The note at the beginning of the Psalm says that this was the prayer of David after Nathan the prophet confronted David about his sin with Bathsheba and his murder of Uriah. What does David's prayer of confession teach us about guilt with regard to sins committed against other people?
2. Read Josh. 7 and Acts 5:1–11. What are some of the similarities between the two stories? What do both of these stories teach regarding hiding sin?

Summa

Write an essay or discuss this question, integrating what you have learned from the material above.
What's the difference between obeying out of guilt and obeying out of gratitude?

Reading Assignment:
Death on the Nile, Part 2, chapters 4–10

Session III: Recitation
Death on the Nile, Part 2, chapters 4–10

Comprehension Questions
Answer the following questions for factual recall:
1. According to Jacqueline, why did Simon Doyle leave her for Linnet Ridgeway?
2. When Poirot asks Simon Doyle if there's any of the "old feeling left" for Jacqueline, how does Doyle respond? Why is Poirot startled by his answer?
3. What does Simon Doyle plan to do in order to give the slip to Jacqueline?
4. In chapter 7, what does Poirot hear as he is drifting off to sleep?
5. While Linnet is signing papers with Mr. Andrew Pennington, what does Mr. Fanthorp say and do that seems to annoy Mr. Pennington?
6. While out touring the great temple of the Ramses, what near-miss occurs?
7. What old acquaintance shows up aboard the *Karnak*? Why is he aboard?

Reading Assignment:
Death on the Nile, Part 2, chapters 11–16

Death on the Nile 467

Chart 1: **CHARACTER ANALYSIS**

CHARACTER	PERSONALITY	POSSIBLE MOTIVE	ALIBI	QUESTIONS/ SUSPICIONS
Jackie De Bellefort	Hot, fiery, jealous	Jealousy	She tried to shoot Simon, missed, and has been under surveillance since.	She's been talking about getting revenge and killing the Doyles.
Andrew Pennington			He has no clear alibi, although he says he was writing in his room when the murder occurred.	
Mr. Ferguson			He has no clear alibi.	
Signor Richetti			He has no clear alibi.	
James Fanthorp				Why did he rush down to be on the cruise after hearing that Mr. Pennington was also along?
Simon Doyle				Is he really so cruel to have betrayed Jackie for Linnet?
Marie (Former Maid)			Not on board the *Karnak* (although her former fiancé was)	
Joanna Southwood			Not on board the *Karnak*	
Dr. Bessner		No clear motive		

SESSION IV: ACTIVITY

Planning a Detective Novel

Imagine that you are preparing to write a detective/ mystery novel like *Death on the Nile*. On one page, sketch out the basic plot of the story, all of the main characters, and the resolution. Give enough detail to show how the various characters will make the real perpetrator difficult to identify.

Or find a murder mystery game to play as a class or with your family. Try to use as many names and situations from *Death on the Nile* as possible. Discuss factors such as motives, opportunity, methods, and various circumstances that make suspects more or less likely to have committed the crime.

Reading Assignment:
Death on the Nile, Part 2, chapters 17–23

Session V: Character Analysis

Deduction

Fill in Chart 1 to help you remember and identify the various characters. After completing the chart take a thoughtful guess as to who murdered Linnet Ridgeway.

Our next session will be a student-led discussion. As you are reading the following assignment, you should write down at least three questions from the text dealing with the issue listed below. These questions will be turned in to the teacher and will be used in classroom discussion. To get full credit for these Text Analysis questions you must create a question that is connected to the reading and to the issue that is the focus of our discussion; you must also answer the question correctly (and include a page or line reference at the end); and your question must be one that invites discussion and debate ("why" questions are excellent; questions that can be answered by "yes" or "no" are to be avoided).

You should also provide two Cultural Analysis and two Biblical Analysis questions. Cultural Analysis questions ask how our culture views the issue that we are discussing. Biblical Analysis questions ask what the Bible says concerning this issue. Again, to get full credit for each question, you must create questions connected to the issue we are studying, answer each question correctly and create questions that encourage and invite discussion and exploration. For an example of each type of question and answer refer to the examples provided in the next session.

If you are working alone, after creating your questions and answers, have your parent or tutor check over them. Also, if possible, share them with your family at the dinner table, helping them to understand why the issue is important, how the issue arises in your reading, how its importance is still evident in our culture, and how understanding this issue might change the way you and your family should think and live.

Issue

Justice and Punishment

Reading Assignment:
Death on the Nile, Part 2, chapters 24–30

To control flooding on the Nile River, the British built the Aswan Low Dam in 1902. Over the years this proved inadequate, so a second dam was completed farther upstream in 1970. To prevent the temples of Ramses II at Abu Simbel from being covered by the lake that resulted, they were moved and reassembled further from the water's edge on higher ground.

Session VI: Student-Led Discussion
Death on the Nile, Part 2, chapters 24–30

A Question to Consider
In order to achieve justice, must punishment occur?

Students should read and consider the example questions below that are connected to the Question to Consider above. Last session's assignment was to prepare three questions and answers for the Text Analysis section and two additional questions and answers for both the Cultural and Biblical Analysis sections below.

Text Analysis
Example: How is Mr. Allerton a criminal? Is he punished for his crime?

Answer: Mr. Allerton is a thief, and he has stolen a pearl necklace from the deceased Linnet Doyle. He is not punished for his crime. He flings the fake string of pearls into the river, and Poirot lets him off the hook since he was not Linnet's murderer.

Cultural Analysis
Example: What does our culture think about punishment and justice?

Answer: Our culture puts a lot more emphasis on rehabilitation than on punishment. Retributive justice has been replaced by protection and re-education.

Biblical Analysis
Example: How can Christians not worry about punishing personal offenses (Rom. 12:17–21)?

Answer: Paul says that we should do good to those who do us wrong since we know that God is the God of vengeance. He will repay.

Other Scriptures to consider: Romans 13:4

Summa

Write an essay or discuss this question, integrating what you have learned from the material above.
Does the coming of Jesus change how we should view crime, justice and punishment?

Optional Session A: Recitation
Death on the Nile, Part 2, chapters 24–30

Comprehension Questions
Answer the following questions for factual recall:
1. What does Mr. Ferguson think about the three murders?
2. Who was "practically ruined" by Linnet's father?
3. Why is Mr. Fanthorp on board the *Karnak*? How did Poirot come to suspect his involvement?
4. What is Mr. Tim Allerton's relationship with Joanna Southwood?
5. Who killed Linnet Doyle? How?
6. Who killed Louise Bourget and Madame Otterbourne? Why?
7. How do Jackie and Simon end up at the end of the book?

Endnotes
1. Cited in Osborne, Charles. *The Life and Crimes of Agatha Christie*. New York: St. Martin's Press, 2001. 147.
2. "In Defence of the Detective Story," *The Defendant*, London: Dent, 1901. Cited in Murch, A.E. *The Development of the Detective Novel*. London: Peter Owen Limited, 1968. 10.
3. Wagoner, Mary. *Agatha Christie*. Boston: Twayne Publishers, 1986. 33.
4. Murch, A.E., 11.

JOSHUA, JUDGES, AND RUTH

Do you ever find anything in the Bible that offends your moral sensibilities? Anything that embarrasses you? For many people today, the Old Testament is a rock of offense and a stone of stumbling. Probably the most scandalous section of the Hebrew Scriptures is the conquest of Canaan recorded in the book of Joshua. It looks like God is commanding full-scale genocide, more diabolical than anything the Hitlers, Maos, and Pol Pots of our era have cooked up.

Celebrity atheist Richard Dawkins puts his distaste for the Old Testament in rather colorful terms:

> The God of the Old Testament is arguably the most unpleasant character in all fiction: jealous and proud of it; a petty, unjust, unforgiving control freak; a vindictive, blood-thirsty ethnic cleanser; a misogynistic, homophobic, racist, infanticidal, genocidal, filicidal, pestilential, megalomaniacal, sadomasochistic, capriciously malevolent bully.

Dawkins' charges against the Christian God can, of course, be refuted. But even inside the Church it's not uncommon to find people who pit the harsh, angry, blood-thirsty God (or god?) of the Old Testament against the sweet, loving, tenderhearted deity revealed in Jesus.

As we will see, the conquest of the land of Canaan was not genocidal. It was not an "ethnic cleansing" at all. It was actually a revelation of God's perfect justice. And more than that, it was an important chapter in the unfolding narrative of God's plan to bring His saving grace to all peoples.

How do Joshua, Judges, and Ruth fit together? These three books form an interlocking story in the midst of a crucial, transitional period of Israel's history. Joshua records Israel's entrance into the new Eden of the Promised Land. God gives a holy land to His holy people. Judges records Israel's Adam-like fall in the new Eden. The Israelites forget God is their king: instead each Israelite believes the Satanic lie and makes himself a king in his own eyes. Finally, Ruth gives us a glimpse of Eden restored, reminding Israel of God's gracious promise by showing the nation what the true Redeemer-King will look like. In the midst of Israel's misery, she should long for a servant-ruler like Boaz. The fact that Boaz takes a Gentile bride is obviously a significant indicator of God's ultimate intention to bless all the nations of the earth through Israel's coming King.

"Then Joshua, and all Israel with him, took Achan the son of Zerah, the silver, the garment, the wedge of gold, his sons, his daughters, his oxen, his donkeys, his sheep, his tent, and all that he had, and they brought them to the Valley of Achor. And Joshua said, "Why have you troubled us? The LORD will trouble you this day." So all Israel stoned him with stones; and they burned them with fire after they had stoned them with stones. Then they raised over him a great heap of stones, still there to this day. So the LORD turned from the fierceness of His anger. Therefore the name of that place has been called the Valley of Achor to this day."—Joshua 7:24–26

472 Omnibus IV

"By faith the walls of Jericho fell down after they were encircled for seven days."
—Hebrews 11:30

General Information

Author, Context, and Setting

Joshua, Judges, and Ruth are an important threesome in the unfolding story told by the Hebrew Scriptures. God had promised to the patriarchs a seed and a land, an abundant posterity and a country of prosperity (Gen. 12:1–3, 7; 15:5–7, 13–21). The first of these promises came to initial fulfillment while the Israelites were still in Egypt (Ex. 1:7). The second of these promises comes to initial fulfillment after the exodus, as the Israelites conquered the land of promise under Joshua (Josh. 23–24). Joshua was chosen to be Moses' successor, and the conquest should be viewed as the completion of the exodus. Unfortunately for Israel, once they settled into the land, things became rocky. Israel triumphed over the Canaanites militarily, and yet spiritually never quite eradicated the influences of Canaanite culture. This failure would come back to haunt them, as the period of the judges plainly reveals. Israel was chosen by God to model His righteousness in the sight of the nations (Deut. 4:6–7), but during much of this period, Israel looks just like the other nations. By the end of Judges, the tribes of Dan and Benjamin have nearly completely apostatized (they were Canaanite-ized).

The book of Joshua emphasizes God's side of the covenant. God has been faithful in fulfilling His promise to give the land to Israel. In Joshua, God trains His people to fight, an important stepping stone in their maturation. Because God has given them success, they are able to rest in the land. Joshua 11:23 gives a thematic summary: "So Joshua took the whole land, according to all that the Lord had spoken to Moses; and

Joshua gave it for an inheritance to Israel according to their tribal allotments. And the land had rest from war."

The book of Judges emphasizes Israel's failure to finish the conquest. Throughout the days of the judges, Israel wrestles to break free from pagan influence so she can live as God's holy people in His holy land. But her faith falters, and she never quite finishes the job Joshua began. Like a skipping compact disk, we find Israel going in repeated cycles, rising in righteousness only to fall back into idolatry, again and again. Instead of doing what is right in her own eyes, Israel must learn to acknowledge that the Lord is her king; rather than crowning her own king like the nations, she must trust and obey the Lord alone as her king (Judg. 21:25). When the time is right for her to have a human representative of the Lord's kingship (and that time would come, according to Deuteronomy 17), she should look for a righteous and mighty man like Boaz, the redeemer of Naomi and husband of Ruth.

In Joshua, men led by the Lord do all the fighting. In Judges, women play important roles in battles (Judg. 4–5; 9:53–54). As in Genesis 1–2, the woman comes after the man and serves as his helper. The book of Judges shows faithful women acting as classic female archetypes. We find mothers (e.g., Judg. 5:7; 13:2), daughters (e.g., Judg. 11:34), and brides (e.g., Judg. 1:12) in prominent positions—twelve women in all, matching the twelve judges. We also find women playing immoral roles (Judg. 16).

Literarily, Judges is full of irony, intrigue, and humor. We should not read the Bible so seriously that we miss the hilarity of stories like Ehud overcoming Eglon by deceptively thrusting a sword into his fat belly, or the comedic wisdom in Samson's riddles and military tactics.

Ruth is a beautiful narrative in which content and form perfectly merge. Ruth is the Bible's very own romantic comedy. But it is also a gospel-shaped story, a death-and-resurrection story, prefiguring the redemption of the nations in Christ. God works behind the scenes through Boaz to bring Naomi (a Jew) and Ruth (a Gentile) from desolation to fullness, from sadness to joy, from curse to blessing. The book of Ruth is a ray of light shining into a dark period in Israel's history.

From where did these books come? Who wrote them and when? We cannot say for sure; the books themselves do not tell us, so their origins are shrouded in mystery. But we can use circumstantial evidence to piece together some of the basic facts, and on that basis we can make some educated guesses.

Joshua seems to be the primary author of the book that bears his name (Josh. 24:26; cf. 18:1–10), but he could not have been the one to put it into its final form (cf. Josh. 24:29–33). It was probably completed later by an inspired prophet, though there are some clues indicating

Samuel had been dedicated to the Lord's service as a child by his mother Hannah. Besides being the last judge of Israel and anointing King Saul and then King David, Samuel may have written the books of Judges and Ruth.

it could not have been much later. For example, Joshua 6:25 was written while Rahab was still alive, and Joshua 9:27 was written before the Gibeonites were nearly slaughtered by Saul (1 Sam. 21:1–2). If the conquest began approximately in 1406 B.C., and lasted seven years, we may place the primary composition of Joshua shortly thereafter.

Samuel is a very likely candidate for the authorship of Judges. Samuel himself was the last judge. Because the people demanded a king prematurely, Samuel crowned a Benjamite named Saul for them (1 Sam. 8–10). But Saul fell into sin and forfeited his claim on the throne (1 Sam. 13–15). Following God's lead, Samuel anointed David, a man of Judah and a descendant of Boaz, to take his place (1 Sam. 16). By the way in which the book of Judges treats the tribes of Judah (David's tribe) and Benjamin (Saul's tribe), it provides a strong apologetic for David's claim to the throne at a time when the Israelites were having to decide with which royal house to side (cf. Judg. 1 and Judg. 20).

Finally, Samuel probably also authored Ruth. The story takes place during the days of the judges (Ruth 1:1); the retrospective language suggests the monarchy has been set up by the time of writing. The genealogy at the end of Ruth concludes with David, which means it was likely written while David was still on the throne. Like Judges, Ruth provides a strong apologetic for Davidic kingship, especially with its closing genealogy (Ruth 4:13–22). We can date the writing of Judges and Ruth to roughly 1000 B.C., sometime after the beginning of David's reign.

Significance

The books of Joshua, Judges, and Ruth are significant because they serve both as a testimony of God's ongoing care of His people and His faithfulness to His covenant promises. They also serve as a bridge between Moses and the giving of the law, and David and the establishment of the kingdom. These books of the Bible play a very significant role in setting out Israel's purpose. They show us God's faithfulness in fulfilling His promise to Abraham and completing what He began in the exodus under Moses. But these books also show us Israel's failure and her need for a Redeemer greater than Joshua or any of the judges.

These books also contain some of the most discussed and controversial issues in the entire Bible. First among them is the Israelite conquest of Canaan and the extermination of the Canaanites. This "holy war" is presented as proof-positive that God either is or was a capricious dictator who sanctions the slaughter of the innocent and the guilty and plays racial favorites with His special peo-

ple Israel. There is plenty of evidence to the contrary, but unbelievers often point to these very books as evidence of God's injustice and the barbarism of religion in general.

These books do have application for us as well, but Christians have struggled to figure out how to apply them, especially Joshua. In the book of Joshua, the Israelites wage a "holy war" against the inhabitants of the land of Canaan. We know that God does not want us to fight this kind of violent, bloody battle today. Paul said our warfare is not against flesh and blood (Eph. 6:10–20) and our weapons are not carnal (2 Cor. 10:4–6). We will inherit the nations, but not through bloodshed (Rev. 2:26–27). What, then, do we do with the holy war theme found in the Old Testament? Specifically, how do we reconcile the conquest with God's love and the Church's mission? If we look at the Bible's story from beginning to end, we can arrive at satisfactory answers.

Worldview

The book of Joshua begins with a transition. Moses has preached his farewell sermon and passed from the scene. Joshua has been appointed his successor. Can the people follow Joshua the way they did Moses? Will God give them the victory under Joshua's leadership? Is there life after Moses?

The book shows us that Joshua is a new Moses. Here are several clues:

- Moses led the people through the Red Sea on dry ground; Joshua will lead them through the Jordan River on dry ground.
- Moses sent spies into the land; Joshua sends spies as well.
- The people saw the miracles of Moses and trusted; in the same way, Joshua was exalted before the people, and they feared him because of what God did through him.
- Moses met with the Lord at the burning bush and took off his shoes because he was on holy ground; Joshua met the commander of the Lord's army and took off his shoes as well.
- Moses is called the "servant of the Lord;" Joshua is as well.

The point is clear: Moses may have died, but a new Moses has taken over. Under Joshua's Moses-like leadership, the people will be able to conquer the Canaanites just as they overcame the Egyptians.

The New Testament Scriptures show us how we should apply the conquest of Canaan in our own day. First, warfare imagery is used to describe the Christian's

Joshua, Judges, and Ruth 475

battle against sin (Gal. 5:17). We are called to "conquer our personal Canaanites," as it's been put. The same kind of *herem* warfare Israel was supposed to wage on the inhabitants of the land is now to be waged on sin that dwells in our own hearts (Matt. 5:29–30; 1 Pet. 2:12). Just as God enabled Israel to drive out the Canaanites "little by little" (Ex. 23:29–30; Deut. 7:22), so our growth in grace and obedience is often a slow and grueling process.

But more importantly the New Testament shows us that the conquest serves as a blueprint for the Church's mission. Joshua's "little commission" points to Jesus' Great Commission. Luke constructed the early chapters of the book of Acts so that they track with the early chapters of Joshua. In other words, the Church's fulfillment of her mission (Matt. 28:16–20; Luke 24:46–49) witnessing to the nations is the New Covenant counterpart to Joshua's conquest of Canaan. Joshua and Acts show a number of striking parallels:

- In each case the leader of God's people has just left the scene (Moses in death, Jesus in His ascension).
- In the book of Joshua, Joshua is called to be Moses' successor and carry forward God's purposes in the conquest; in Acts, the Holy Spirit comes to be Jesus' successor and carry forward the Church's mission.
- The Lord commands Joshua to be strong and courageous at the beginning of the book; at the beginning of Acts, the Lord promises that power will come upon the disciples to make them strong and courageous (as seen in the sudden transformation of Peter from coward to preacher).
- In Joshua Israel is commanded to conquer the land; in Acts the Church is commanded to bear witness to the ends of the earth.
- In Joshua the people are led through a clear sequence of events: they cross over the Jordan in a kind of baptism (cf. 1 Cor. 10:2), they are circumcised, and they celebrate Passover. In Acts the sequence is similar: the Spirit baptizes the Church, 3,000 are baptized with water (the New Covenant equivalent of circumcision per Colossians 2:11–12), and they break the bread of the Lord's Supper together (cf. Acts 2:42–46; the Lord's Supper is the New Covenant fulfillment of the Passover according to 1 Corinthians 5:7–8).
- In both books the first move of God's people is to invade a key city; Jericho falls by shouting and trumpeting, while Jerusalem is invaded by means of prayer and preaching.
- Almost immediately in both books we find the people of God hindered by sin in the camp: in Joshua, Achan steals booty that belongs to the Lord, and is put to death on the spot (Josh. 7). Likewise, in Acts 5, Ananias and Sapphira steal from the Lord by lying about selling some property, and they are executed on the spot. The word for stealing in Acts 5:2 is a rare term, but it is also used in the Greek (Septuagint) translation of Joshua 7:1. Further, in Acts 20:33, Paul explicitly repudiated having committed the sin of Achan (Josh. 7:21), showing he understood his mission work as a successful "holy war" campaign.
- In both books fear enters the enemies of God's people, allowing the covenant community to score significant victories (Josh. 2:9–13; 5:1–2; Acts 2:2:43, 5:5, 11; 9:31; 19:17).
- In both books we see Gentiles brought in, though with significant controversy (Josh. 9; Acts 15) and attack (Joshua 10; Acts 6–7).

Judges 3:12–30 recounts the story of Ehud, an agent from God licensed to kill. A corpulent despot must be stopped, so Ehud straps a secret gadget to his right thigh and enters the headquarters of the evil Eglon with a "secret message." Once inside the lair of the Moabitish king, the left-handed Benjamite kills the villain. After deftly making his escape, he rallies the soldiers of God's chosen people, and they strike down ten thousand of the enemy. Scripture doesn't record whether Ehud preferred his martinis shaken or stirred.

Acts is about New Covenant holy war, as the Church "invades" Jerusalem, Judea, Samaria, and the ends of the earth. But the nature of her warfare has been transformed. There is a shift from killing to converting. Unlike Joshua, in the book of Acts Peter and Paul do not inflict suffering, but bear suffering. Unlike Joshua, Peter and Paul advance the kingdom through service rather than force.

Thus, God's people no longer fight with a literal sword and fire; instead they use the sword of the Spirit (the Word of God; Heb. 4:12) and witness in the fiery presence of God's Spirit (Acts 2:3). The weapons of holy war have morphed. The Church can learn a great deal about her mission from the book of Joshua, but to do so she must apply Joshua's use of sword and flame in a metaphorical way, guided by Acts and the rest of the New Testament.

Further, the battleground and promised territory is no longer a strip of land in Palestine, but the entire earth. The New Testament is very clear that the land promises God made to Abraham have been expanded to include the entire globe (although it is also clear from the Old Testament this was God's intention all along; cf. Gen. 12:3 and Rom. 4:12). The New Testament ascribes no special importance to any geographic area; what was called the "holy land" in the Old Covenant is now theologically irrelevant. All the blessings associated with the land in the Old Testament (such as inheritance, rest, and holiness) are now found in Christ and the Church. Christ and His people fulfill the Old Covenant priesthood, Temple, sacrifices, and kingdom (1 Pet. 2:4–10). In the Old Covenant, Gentiles were called "aliens" and "strangers" to the covenant because they had no home in the land of promise. But now they are full members of Israel, totally apart from living in a certain geographic region (Eph. 2:11–22). Thus, Paul can change the wording of the promise in the fifth commandment from "land" to "earth" (Eph. 6:3), and Jesus can do the same with Psalm 37:11 in the beatitudes (Matt. 5:3). Hebrews 3:12–4:11 assures us that, in Christ, we have the true rest that Joshua's conquest could attain only in a provisional, shadowy way (Josh. 1:13, 23:1). In sum, the privileges and responsibilities of God's covenant people are no longer defined by living in Palestine but by living in union with Christ. Or, as Christopher Wright has put it, being "in Christ" has taken over the meaning of being "in the land" (cf. 2 Cor. 1:20).[1]

Finally, note the importance of worship. Earlier, Abraham and Jacob had journeyed through the land, setting up altars (Gen. 12:7, 8; 28:18–22; 35:1, 16–22). The worship of the patriarchs had already marked out the land as God's chosen dwelling place, serving as a kind of liturgical "proto-conquest."

Worship continues to be important when Israel finally invades the land. In Joshua worship and warfare go hand-in-hand. Israel's battles start off looking more like worship services than military conflicts. In the battle of Jericho, Israel's army seems to be more like a priesthood and choir than a traditional regiment of soldiers. The seven day circling of the city puts the climactic act of warfare on the seventh day, a Sabbath, which is associated with worship. The ram's horn (Lev. 25:9) and Ark (Ex. 25:10–22) are obviously liturgical objects, rather than ordinary weapons. In short, Joshua did *not* fight the battle of Jericho; rather the Lord fought for His people when they worshipped Him.

We see this same theme unfold repeatedly throughout the book of Joshua. In fact, the goal of the conquest may be viewed as replacing Canaanite altars with the worship of the true God. Israel cannot rest in the land until God's house, the Tabernacle, is set up in Shiloh as a centralized place of worship (Josh. 18:1).

There is an instructive lesson here for the Church. We will not "conquer" any area with the gospel using "normal," worldly means. We cannot rely on political activism, improved education, or the latest technology. That's not to say these tools and methods are bad or should be totally shunned. They just aren't powerful enough to win the battle. We will transform the culture around us only if we turn to God in praise and prayer. We must preach and sing our way to victory. We can win unbelieving cities for the gospel only if we worship God faithfully as Joshua and the Israelites did in Joshua 6. As Peter Leithart puts it, "When Israel worships God, He brings the walls down."[2] Liturgical warfare is the key to the Church's success in her mission to the nations.

Politics Human and Divine

In Joshua the conquest advances because God fights for Israel. By the end of the seven-year period recorded in Joshua, Israel has established herself in the land, and God's land promises have been definitively fulfilled. However, Israel still has to drive out remaining Canaanites, lest they prove to be a temptation and a trap to the covenant people.

As the book of Judges opens, the tribe of Judah has success in claiming her promised inheritance. But the other tribes fail in taking full possession of their allotted land (Judg. 1:21–36). In Joshua Israel's success was related to faithful worship; in Judges the nation's failure is linked to her unwillingness to tear down the altars of the Canaanites (Judg. 2:1–3). In fact, before long, we find Israel worshipping at Canaanite altars (Judg. 2:11–23)!

Israel moves several times through an easily identifiable spiritual cycle in the book of Judges. Again and again

Joshua, Judges, and Ruth 477

Israel falls into idolatry, and so the nation is subjugated by a pagan oppressor. It's as if God says, "If you want to worship pagan gods, let me show you what life is like under pagan rule!" The Lord "sells" (Judg. 1:14) Israel back into slavery, reversing the exodus and conquest. When Israel finally comes to her spiritual senses and repents, God sends the nation a deliverer. Each judge is a new Moses and a new Joshua who acts to free the people from bondage and re-establish rest in the land. But the peace never lasts. Israel can't stand prosperity. And so the cycle repeats itself. However, as we move toward the end of the book, we see that not only is Israel seriously flawed as a people, but even the judges themselves begin to show serious blemishes. The early judges are presented as having very minor defects, at most. But the later judges, like Gideon, Jephthah, and Samson have very significant problems, to say the least.

Towards the conclusion of Judges, we find an emerging refrain that serves as one of the interpretive keys to the whole era (albeit an ironic one): "In those days there was no king in Israel; everyone did what was right in his own eyes" (Judg. 17:6; 21:25; cf. 18:1; 19:1). Of course, Israel *did* have a king in those days: the Lord was her king (cf. Judg. 8:23)! But because the nation refused to submit to the Lord's rule, her kinglessness became her undoing.

Having a human monarch, per se, would not have solved Israel's problem. We know this from lat-

er history. Many of Israel's kings would actually lead the nation further into idolatry, rather than saving her from such rebellion. But even within the book of Judges we see that human kingship cannot be the answer because Israel actually had a king during the era of the judges, at least briefly.

Gideon started out well, serving God faithfully and delivering Israel from the Midianites (Judg. 6:1–8:21). He even refused the offer of kingly office, pointing the people to the Lord as king (Judg. 8:23). But toward the end of his life, he decided to seize kingly privileges and prerogatives that did not belong to him. He collected gold, multiplied wives, and led Israel into idolatry (Judg. 8:24–35). He even named one of his sons Abimelech, meaning, "my father is king." This is the turning point of the entire book of Judges.

The seed of rebellion planted by Gideon becomes a full-grown thorn bush in the next generation. Abimelech one-ups his father's sin by explicitly trying to create a monarchy in Israel, with himself on the throne. He kills his 70 brothers (minus one) to eliminate possible rivals (Judg. 9:5). The entire episode turns into a disaster (Judg. 9:22–57), until Abimelech's head is finally crushed by a woman with a millstone, and he dies in shame (Judg. 9:53–54; note the allusion to Genesis 3:15).

While we should give the twelve judges their due as men of faith (cf. Heb. 11:32–40), we should also examine why Israel was not able to sustain multi-generational faithfulness in this period. The repeated declaration that Israel has no king (Judg. 17:6; 21:25) is not a statement about Israel's governmental structure so much as it is a commentary on their spiritual condition. Israel's problems cannot be solved merely by a new political arrangement. A king is not going to help, especially if that king is like the kings of the surrounding pagan nations.

The concluding chapters of Judges identify the problem beneath the problem, as it were. We find that, ultimately, Israel is failing to submit to the Lord not because she lacks a human king but because her priests (remember these men not only performed sacrifices, they also served as Israel's pastors) fail to guide her according to the law. The priests are not teaching the people the ways of the Lord; instead, they

"Then Judah went up, and the LORD delivered the Canaanites and the Perizzites into their hand; and they killed ten thousand men at Bezek. And they found Adoni-Bezek in Bezek, and fought against him; and they defeated the Canaanites and the Perizzites. Then Adoni-Bezek fled, and they pursued him and caught him and cut off his thumbs and big toes." —Judges 1:4–6

"So she gleaned in the field until evening, and beat out what she had gleaned, and it was about an ephah of barley. Then she took it up and went into the city, and her mother-in-law saw what she had gleaned. So she brought out and gave to her what she had kept back after she had been satisfied." —Ruth 2:17–18

conquering them?

Again, there is a lesson here for the Church, and it echoes the lesson of Joshua. The nation of Israel falls apart when her spiritual leaders are unfaithful. The deepest problems of any culture cannot be solved through political means. The faithfulness of the Church in teaching and worship is always the key to cultural strength and transformation. Only when the Church faithfully proclaims the kingship of the Lord, and worships Him as true king, will the nation as a whole follow suit and mature in righteousness. If we want the Lord visibly enthroned in our society, we must enthrone Him upon our praises. In the New Covenant we are now a nation of priests (1 Pet. 2:4–10), and so it is our job to inspire people through our teaching, service, and example to submit to the Lord as their true King.

Gospel Typology

Following Jesus' lead (Luke 24:25–27, 44–45; John 5:39), the Church has traditionally read the Scriptures in a typological fashion, looking for ways in which the Old Covenant prefigured the new, and the new fulfills the old. We do not need to turn the Old Testament Scriptures into Christian literature, because the whole Old Testament is *already* all about Christ. We just have to learn how to see Him there. The New Testament writers build their theology out of various Old Covenant typologies. For example, we find Jesus presented as the new Adam (Rom. 5:21–21), the true tabernacle/temple (John 1:14; 2:19–21), the Passover lamb (John 1:28), the Greater Solomon (Matt. 12:42), and so on. Likewise, the Church is portrayed as the new Israel and new priesthood (1 Pet. 2:4–10); baptism fulfills sea and river crossings (1 Cor. 10:2) as well as the Flood (1 Pet. 3:18–22); the Lord's Supper fulfills the Passover meal (1 Cor. 5:7–8); and our worship, mercy, and obedience are New Covenant counterparts to the animal sacrifices (Rom. 12:1–2; Phil. 4:18; Heb.

are falling into idolatry themselves, creating a counterfeit temple and system of worship (Judg. 17–18). In Judges 17–18, a Levite hires himself for money to lead worship at Micah's idolatrous image. With Levites like this, is it any wonder Israel is imitating the Canaanites rather than

13:15–16). Of course, the typologies explicitly developed in the New Testament are not comprehensive; rather, the New Testament gives us selected interpretive models, showing us how we should read the rest of the Old Testament Scriptures as a whole. We should not treat types as isolated "snapshots" of Christ and/or His people; rather, typology flows out of the biblical story taken as a whole, as God's plan progresses from promise to fulfillment, and His people move from childhood to maturity.

As expected, then, the narratives of Joshua, Judges, and Ruth abound in typological structures that point us to Jesus and the Church. Ruth, in particular, is a masterpiece of typological literature, a tragic-comedy that points us to Christ in profound ways. However, to understand the story, we have to do more than recognize the story's archetypes and the way they come to fulfillment in the New Covenant. We have to understand a couple of key Old Testament institutions on which the whole narrative turns, namely the levirate and the kinsman-redeemer.

The levirate marriage is described in Deuteronomy 25:1–10. When an Israelite man died without a son, his surviving brother (or, by extension, another close male relative) was to marry his widow, so as to continue his brother's family line, name, and inheritance. The first-born son of a levirate marriage belonged to the deceased man and, essentially, took his place. The tribe of Judah was implicated for failure to practice this custom in Genesis 38, resulting in judgment falling on Judah and illegitimate children being brought into the tribal line. The levirate institution is what stands behind the otherwise cryptic language in Ruth 1:11–13 and 4:10, 12, 17. The book of Ruth shows us a man of the tribe of Judah who did what Judah himself failed to do, namely, act as a faithful *levir* (Latin, meaning "husband's brother") on behalf of a helpless widow, Ruth, who is a new Tamar.

The kinsman-redeemer institution is outlined in Leviticus 25:25, 28, 48, 49. The obligations of the kinsman-redeemer fell on the nearest male blood relative and included redeeming a lost inheritance and/or buying the person out of slavery. The kinsman-redeemer could also act as an avenger of blood in cases of murder (Num. 35:21). The pattern for the kinsman-redeemer is ultimately God himself, who frequently goes by the name "Redeemer" (Ex. 6:6; Isa. 43:1; 41:14; 44:6, 22; 48:20; Ps. 103:4; Job 19:25).

In the story of Ruth, Boaz plays the role of both levirate husband and kinsman-redeemer. There is some ambiguity about this because he is not Elimelech's brother, and not even Naomi seemed to know exactly how close a relative he was (cf. Ruth 2:20, 3:1–4). Nevertheless, these two institutions explain Ruth's action on the threshing floor in chapter 3 and the transaction between Boaz and the nameless relative in chapter 4. In Ruth 3, Ruth decks herself out as a bride and approaches Boaz, essentially proposing marriage to him. But nothing immoral happened on the threshing floor that night (and so the passage reverses, rather than recapitulates, the events of Numbers 25 and Genesis 19:30–38). Ruth is simply calling on Boaz to play his role as a close relative, a potential levir and kinsman-redeemer. Boaz graciously agrees to do so (Ruth 3:10–13) and then follows through in a timely and lawful manner (Ruth 4:1–12).

What, then, is the story of Ruth about? The story abounds in exquisite and ironic detail. Elimelech's name means "My God is king"—but this is a period in Israel's history in which the Israelites, by and large, refuse to acknowledge the kingship of the Lord over them (cf. Judg. 21:25). Elimelech and his family live in Bethlehem, which means "house of bread." But there is no bread in the breadbasket! The land that was supposed to produce abundant food has been hit with famine (cf. the curses in Leviticus 26 and Deuteronomy 28). And so, like Adam and Eve, Elimelech goes into self-imposed exile from the place where God dwells. Elimelech's family goes eastward to Moab (an odd choice to find refuge in light of Numbers 21–22; cf. Deut. 23:4), but there the curse only intensifies. Elimelech's sons marry Moabite women, but soon all the men in the family are dead. Naomi, Ruth and Orpah are left as powerless widows. Naomi pleads with both of her daughters-in-law to turn back to their families, but Ruth, like Abraham, insists on leaving her homeland and journeying with Naomi to a land she does not know. In an account that resonates with exodus themes, the lonely pair returns to Bethlehem.

Naomi and Ruth are widows mired in poverty when they arrive in Bethlehem. Resourceful, hard-working Ruth goes out to glean (Lev. 19:9–10; 23:22; Deut. 14:28–29) and "chances" upon a field belonging to Boaz (note the touch of irony in 2:3). What a wonderful providence this turns out to be, since Boaz is a relative of Naomi's and therefore a potential kinsman-redeemer (Ruth 2:20)! Boaz, as a merciful, kind-hearted man, takes good care of Ruth, ensuring that her gleaning is successful. When Naomi finds out that Ruth has connected with her relative Boaz, she concocts a plan to bring the two together and, as the saying goes, the rest is history!

What's the meaning of the story? The narrative begins "when the judges ruled." But the last word is the name of Israel's most famous king, David. At one level, this historical account is a parable of Israel's plight. Naomi (and her sidekick Ruth) represents Israel, with no food, no husband, and no sons. When God shows her mercy and restores her, it is a picture of what God has promised to do for Israel. By the end of the narrative, Naomi and

Ruth have been given abundant food (Ruth 1:6; 2:14, 17–19; 3:15, 17), Ruth is married (Ruth 4:13), and a child has been born to take the place of Naomi's fallen husband and sons (Ruth 4:13–22). This is a true rags-to-redemption story.

The writer makes critical connections apparent by means of some very clever word plays and symbolism. For example, the same word used for Elimelech's sons in chapter 1 (best translated "lads") is used of Obed in chapter 4. Obed is the replacement son (though in light of Ruth 4:15, we must note that Ruth is too, since she's even better to Naomi than seven sons!). In Ruth 1:21, Naomi says she has come home *empty-handed* (apparently ignoring the fact that Ruth is with her!). In Ruth 3:17, Boaz gives Ruth six ephahs of barley so that she will not return to Naomi *empty-handed*. The fact that Boaz provides *six* ephahs is a crucial piece of symbolism, one that does not escape Naomi's notice since she says the man will not *rest* until he has settled the matter. That is to say, the six ephahs serve as a pledge of a seventh, a Sabbath, to come when Boaz has secured Ruth's future. In Ruth 3:1, Naomi spoke of rest as the goal of approaching Boaz; at the end of the chapter, Ruth can rest because Boaz has made it clear he will not rest until he has provided her permanent rest.

In Ruth 2:12, Boaz commends Ruth for her faithfulness in gleaning and caring for her mother-in-law. Boaz blesses her, saying, "A full reward be given you by the Lord God of Israel, under whose wings you have come for refuge." In Ruth 3:9, Ruth gives Boaz an opportunity to fulfill this blessing, when she asks him to "[t]ake your maidservant under your wing." The "wing" language in these texts is covenantal and marital (cf. Ezek. 16:8). In Ruth 3:9, it refers to a garment that a husband and wife share when they become one flesh.

The twist in the plot is the threshing-floor revelation of a rival kinsman-redeemer, a relative closer to Naomi than Boaz (Ruth 3:12). The narrator has led us to pull hard for a Boaz-Ruth marriage, but now that outcome is in doubt. The next day will be decisive. Boaz has men from the city assemble at the gate to serve as witnesses (Ruth 4:1–2). He summarizes the situation for the closer relative to digest so he can make his decision. The closer kinsman says he will redeem Naomi's land; after all, Naomi is old and won't be having any more children to take Elimelech's place, so this is a relatively painless way for the man to expand his own estate in the end (Ruth 4:3–4). The plot thickens and suspense builds. Boaz then plays his trump card: he tells the closer kinsman that actually he will have to marry Ruth, and in so doing, raise up a seed to take Elimelech's place and reclaim his land (Ruth 4:5). Suddenly the situation has changed: the nameless kinsman will have to buy back Elimelech's property, but he won't get to keep it. When the son he has with Ruth gets old enough, he will claim that land as his own. The closer relative does a quick recalculation and decides to pass the redeemer duties off to Boaz (Ruth 4:6).

Not everything about Boaz' strategy is clear, but we can discern that he acted in righteousness and in wisdom, with the result that he was able to both obey the law and get what he desired. Ironically, the closer kinsman passed up his redeemer duties because he was so concerned about preserving his own name—and yet the text leaves him nameless! He refused to perpetuate the name of the dead, and yet it's his name that has not been perpetuated in history! He

In this detail from *The Crucifixion*, a painting by Anthony van Dyke (1599–1641), Mary takes Ruth's place at the feet of their Redeemer.

missed his chance to make his name great in Israel because he would not make a sacrifice for a fellow covenant member in need. Boaz, on the other hand, demonstrated his true worth as a self-giving, merciful leader in Israel. He married Ruth and the Lord gave the happy couple a son (Ruth 4:9–15) to perpetuate the name of the dead (Ruth 4:16–17).

Of course, as Christians, we cannot help but see the Christ/Church relationship in the marriage that takes place at the end of the book. This book is the gospel in miniature; it is "the littlest gospel" as it's been called. It is a microcosmic retelling of all of redemptive history. Elimelech and his sons represent the first Adam. They are associated with curse, famine, and death. Boaz represents Jesus as the second Adam. He becomes what Elimelech and his sons should have been. Through him, the Lord shows His covenant love. Today, we put our hope in the greater Boaz, the greater David, a mighty man of valor, who has shown us mercy and provided for our every need. The fact that Boaz marries a Gentile, but in so doing also cares for a Jewish woman, is a beautiful foreshadowing of the New Covenant, which weaves Jew and Gentile together into the redeemed bride of Christ.

Jesus is the Greater Boaz, acting as both the Church's levirate husband and kinsman-redeemer (Rom. 7:1–6; Heb. 2:14–18). The first Adam had widowed us by his rebellion, leaving us in exile, under the reign of death and the curse. Jesus is the second Adam who marries us, restores our inheritance, and buys us out of slavery. Naomi's story is the Church's story: we have moved from emptiness to fullness, from barrenness to fruitfulness, from cursed to blessed, through the work of the True Boaz.

—Rich Lusk

For Further Reading

Davis, Dale Ralph. *Such a Great Salvation*. Ross-shire, Scotland: Christian Focus Publications, 2003.

Harstad, Adolph. *Concordia Commentary: Joshua*. St. Louis, Mo.: Concordia Publishing House, 2004.

Hubbard, Jr., Robert L. *The Book of Ruth*. Grand Rapids, Mich.: William B. Eerdmans Publishing, 1988.

Jordan, James B. *Judges: God's War Against Humanism*. Tyler, Tex.: Geneva Ministries, 1985.

Veritas Press Bible Cards: *Genesis through Joshua*. Lancaster, Pa.: Veritas Press. 28–32.

Veritas Press Bible Cards: *Judges through Kings*. Lancaster, Pa.: Veritas Press. 33–39.

SESSION I: PRELUDE

A Question to Consider

One of America's more famous politicians once said, "Change in America begins in the ballot box." In light of your study of Joshua and Judges, what do you think about that statement? Can we really change our culture through politics or should we rely on prayer?

From the General Information above, answer the following questions:

1. How would you answer Richard Dawkins' claims that the God of the Old Testament is "blood-thirsty" and "genocidal?" Is the conquest really an act of genocide?
2. What is typology? Explain how one or two characters in Joshua, Judges, or Ruth serve as a type of Christ.
3. One of the pillars in Solomon's temple was named after Boaz (1 Kings 7:21). What does this tell you about Boaz's character?
4. Assuming that Judges and Ruth were first composed during the early days of the monarchy, explain how the books address the pressing questions of the day for Israel? Specifically, how do these books compare Judah and Benjamin, the tribes of David and Saul, respectively?
5. If holy war has been transformed into worship and evangelism in the New Covenant, does that mean all Christians should be pacifists? Is *all* warfare now immoral?

 **READING ASSIGNMENT:** Joshua 1–6

SESSION II: WRITING
Joshua 1–6

Progymnasmata

This session is a writing assignment. Remember, quality counts more than quantity. You should write no more than 1,000 words, either typing or writing legibly on one side of a sheet of paper. You will lose points for writing more than this. Note, since this is a slightly longer assignment you will only be able to turn this assignment in twice. When you turn it in, your teacher will grade it by editing your work. This is done by marking problem areas and making suggestions for improvement. You should take these suggestions into consideration as you revise your assignment. Only the grade on your final submission will be recorded. Your grade will be based on the following criteria: 25 points for grammar, 25 points for content accuracy—historical, theological, etc.; 25 points for logic—does this make sense and is it structured well?; 25 points for rhetoric—is it a joy to read?

In this assignment you will be writing a *chreia*. A chreia is one of the ancient *progymnasmata*. These were rhetorical exercises meant to hone the skills of young rhetoricians like you. The chreia is an exposition of some memorable saying or deed, generally for good counsel. It means "saying exercise." Some chreia are of words, others of deeds, still others of both. It must be concise.

Sanitized Sunday school classes can make it easy to forget that the mother of Boaz, and therefore an ancestor of Jesus Christ, was a prostitute. Rahab hid the spies, then deceived the king's men to keep them safe. Turning away from her old life, Rahab, along with her parents and her brothers, were blessed by being rescued from the city when it fell. Hebrews 11:31 says that it was "by faith" that she did not perish.

A chreia has eight paragraphs. The first is the *Panegyric* which is a paragraph in which you praise the person who uttered the wise saying. The second is called the *Paraphrastic*. In this short paragraph you put the saying into your own words. This paragraph often begins with something like: "When Saint Augustine said that evil was the deprivation of good, he meant that . . ." In the third paragraph, called *From the Cause*, you explain the motivation of the person. The fourth paragraph is called *From the Contrary*, and in it you explain what would have happened if the opposite of the saying or action had occurred. For example, "If Diogenes had not struck the inept teacher, bad education would have continued." In the fifth paragraph, called the *Analogy*, you liken the saying or action to something else, usually something more concrete and easier to understand.

The sixth paragraph is similar to the fifth. It is called *Example*, and in it you show the wisdom of the saying or deed by pointing your reader to a specific instance in which this wisdom was demonstrated. The *Analogy* is different from the *Example* in that it is about a general practice (e.g., "Education is like a harvest: you work hard and reap great reward.") whereas the *Example* is about a specific person, place or thing (e.g., "Erasmus studied many things and became a learned man."). The seventh paragraph is called the *Testimony of the Ancients*. Here you quote a sage person from the past who testifies to the truth of the saying. Finally, in the eighth paragraph called the *Epilogue*, you sum up the chreia.

Here's the context for your writing assignment: Starting in Joshua 5:1 we read that the kings of the Amorites (on the west side of Jordan) and of the Canaanites (by the sea) were frightened by the report that Yahweh had "dried up the waters of the Jordan from before the children of Israel." Having walked through the river on dry ground, the Jews camped at Gilgal. They made a memorial from 12 stones of the river Jordan, just as Yahweh had instructed Joshua to do (4:15–18). While at Gilgal, Yahweh instructed Joshua to circumcise all the males. These were the young men who would replace the fighting-aged men who died, wandering in the wilderness. So this is how Gilgal got its name: On that day Yahweh "rolled away" (literally, "rolling") the reproach of Egypt from Israel. The children of Israel celebrated the Passover and the next day ate the fruit of their promised land. Manna ceased falling from heaven; a new era had begun. Then something very strange happened to Joshua. Sometime later, he saw a man "opposite him" near Jericho. This man would turn out to be the Lord Himself, a pre-incarnate Christ, if you will. We suppose that's the case because it is at this point that the Lord gives Joshua instructions and encouragement for sacking the city of Jericho (6:1–5). At first meeting this messenger, Joshua, acting as captain of Israel's army in Moses' place, asks him a critical question: "Are you for us or for our adversaries?" His perfectly honest question was answered in a perfectly mysterious way.

Write a chreia on the statement made by the commander of the Lord's army to Joshua in chapter 5, verse 14: "No, but as Commander of the army of the Lord, I have now come."

I. Panegyric
   - Praise the person who uttered the saying.
II. Paraphrastic
   - Put the saying in your own words
III. From the Cause
   - Explain the motivation of the speaker
IV. From the Contrary
   - Explain the consequences if the opposite of the saying or action had occurred
V. Analogy
   - Liken the saying or action to something else.
VI. Example
   - Point the reader to a specific instance in which the wisdom of the saying was demonstrated
VII. Testimony of the Ancients
   - Quote a sage person from the past who testifies to the truth of this saying
VIII. Epilogue
   - Sum up your previous paragraphs

READING ASSIGNMENT:
Joshua 7–12

Session III: Recitation
Joshua 1–12

Comprehension Questions

Answer the following questions for factual recall:

1. What is the gist of Yahweh's commission to Joshua in 1:1–9?
2. How can you tell that the author treats events in the book as truly historical?
3. Does the author consider their crossing of the Jordan a miracle? How can you tell from the text?
4. Who went first into the Jordan, and why? How far ahead were they?
5. What was Yahweh's stated purpose for that special day?
6. In 6:17–18 Joshua calls the inhabitants and belongings of Jericho "devoted to the Lord for destruction." Why should they be destroyed? What *is not* to be destroyed, and why?
7. Later, other towns are taken over by the Israelites. Why, then, is Jericho singled out as completely given over to destruction?
8. What would happen if the Israelites spared some of the devoted things or spared some of the women to make them their wives?
9. Why did Joshua's spies stay at a prostitute's house on the wall of Jericho?
10. What was the "deal" the spies struck with Rahab? Who was to do what?
11. Describe the Israelites' loss at Ai. Why did they lose the battle?
12. What happened to Achan?

READING ASSIGNMENT:
Joshua 13–18

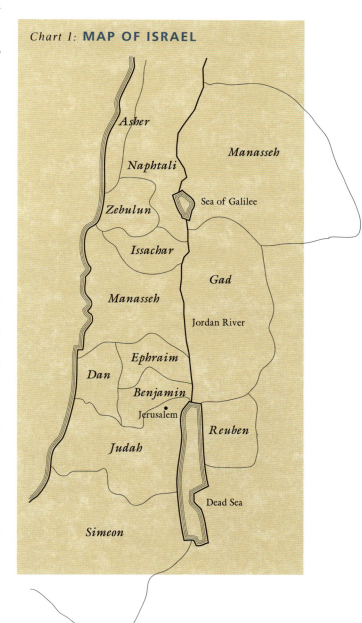

Chart 1: **MAP OF ISRAEL**

Session IV: Discussion
Joshua 13–18

A Question to Consider

If you own a piece of land in the United States, do you *really* own it? Do you have a right to do with it as you please? What does it mean to "own land?"

Discuss or list short answers to the following questions:

Text Analysis

1. After the conquest, which tribes were given land on the east side of the Jordan? Why?
2. Refer to the map in Chart 1 showing the boundaries of the tribes of Israel. Do the allotments appear well-distributed?
3. Caleb was of the tribe of Judah. What special request did he make of Joshua in chapters 14 and 15?
4. Why didn't the Levites have an allotment of land?

Cultural Analysis

1. How was America's War for Independence centered on land?
2. Who should enforce the right use of land in our country? Federal, state, or local governments? Industry? Families? Churches?

Biblical Analysis

1. By the New Testament era, were the tribes of Israel still in a settled state throughout Canaan? Why is their location significant for the growth of the Church?
2. How did Jesus' Great Commission in Matthew 28:18–20 change how God's people should view the Promised Land?

Summa

Write an essay or discuss this question, integrating what you have learned from the material above.

If you own a piece of land in the United States, do you *really* own it? Do you have a right to do with it as you please? What does it mean to "own land?"

Reading Assignment:
Joshua 19–24

The Maciejowski Bible is an illuminated manuscript produced in the mid-thirteenth century. It was commissioned by King Louis IX of France. This scene depicts Deborah leading the Israelites against the Canaanites.

Session V: Activity
Memorializing a Witness to God

In this activity, your class will imitate the Israelites and Joshua by erecting two kinds of memorials that future generations of students will see. Your class may choose to work in small groups of five or so. If you are working alone, choose one of the two memorials and erect it for your family, perhaps in a garden or flower bed.

The first memorial centers on collecting 12 large rocks to be placed in a pile. These rocks represent the 12 tribes of Israel in their safe deliverance across the flooded Jordan (Josh. 4:20). By erecting this memorial, your class will identify with Israel in that future generations of students will ask the question, "What are these stones doing here?" Your memorial will be a reminder of God's gracious hand at your school in years past.

The second memorial is reminiscent of Joshua's memorial stone that he set up "under the oak that was by the sanctuary of the Lord" (Josh. 24:26). His memorial, as acting messiah of God's people, pre-figures the covenant Jesus initiated with His body and blood. When future groups of students observe this monument, they will be directed to meditate on the work of Christ in keeping Israel's covenant demands for the sake of sinners, both Jew and Gentile.

For the first project, you will need rocks large enough to be seen from a distance yet small enough to be carried by individual students in your class. For the second memorial, each group should have access to a large, exposed rock or wall somewhere on the school property (Be sure you have permission to turn an exposed rock into a memorial!). In the absence of a permanent rock, you may also use a large, portable rock to be placed in a garden.

To customize the memorials and ensure their "permanence," the rocks should be inscribed or chiseled with words from Scripture or small phrases your class makes up. It will be critical to devise a simple and safe way to do this. We suggest that your inscriptions be simple, able to be etched in one or two class periods.

Before you start hunting, collecting, inscribing and placing memorials stones, be sure to read carefully Joshua 4 and 24.

Further optional memorial activities

- Once your rocks are completed, you may wish to read selections from these passages in a ceremony.
- For a twist you might want to make your memorial apostolic. Your 12 rock memorial could be called "The Church Memorial." Inscribe the names or historical symbols of the Twelve Apostles on the rocks.
- To commemorate the work of Jesus Christ as the "second Joshua" who delivered His people, call your second memorial "The Christ Rock." Inscribe it with one of many historical logos the Church has used for Christ, e.g., the Ichthus (fish), INRI (Jesus of Nazareth, King of the Jews), a shepherd, a loaf of bread, a chalice, a cross, a lamb.
- Post a framed description of your memorials and your ceremony on an inside wall of your school, pointing people to the memorial. Sign your names as "a witness" to future generations that God had been gracious to your class. Include a photo.

Reading Assignment:
Judges 1–5

Session VI: Writing
Judges 1–5

Poetry

In this session you will be witness to the power of poetry in the Bible. You will also be challenged to interpret an exciting historical event poetically.

Conveniently, Judges 4 and 5 showcase for us two literary genres back to back: narrative and poetry. Think of Francis Scott Key, beholding the tattered colonial flag creeping up its pole over Baltimore harbor amid the "rockets red glare." How did he respond? By writing a poem, "The Star Spangled Banner" which became the American national anthem. Consider also how our nation responded to the 9/11 attacks on our soil. Poets were enlisted to aid our grief, to memorialize in vivid language our national tragedy and to solidify our resolve to fight for freedom. The same thing happens in redemptive history in the Bible. For believers, at times it seems that only poetry is capable of conveying our deepest longings, immense gratitude, and honest worship of God.

Read aloud about Deborah's victory over Jabin, king of Cannan, and his army commander Sisera in chapter 4. A student should read this aloud for the whole class, or if working alone, read it to your family. Notice that the language is historical and straightforward.

Next, ask a student with a flare for the dramatic to read Judges 5. This passage recounts the song of Deborah and Barak after their victory. Note especially the use of vaulted language, repetition, and imagery.

Discuss these questions:
1. How do chapters 4 and 5 compare? Make a list on

Joshua leads the children of Israel across the Jordan. The priests who carried the Ark of the Covenant stood in the middle of the riverbed until all the people had passed by.

the board of similarities and differences in word usage, structure, emotional impact, etc.
2. Do both chapters say the same thing? If not, what's the difference? If so, why, then are there two chapters devoted to the same event?
3. Why is the mixture of genres significant?

Reading Assignment:
Judges 6–16

Session VII: Discussion
Judges 1–16

A Question to Consider

Is the Christian God really the same God Richard Dawkins describes in this quotation?

> The God of the Old Testament is arguably the most unpleasant character in all fiction: jealous and proud of it; a petty, unjust, unforgiving control freak; a vindictive, blood-thirsty ethnic cleanser;

a misogynistic, homophobic, racist, infanticidal, genocidal, filicidal, pestilential, megalomaniacal, sadomasochistic, capriciously malevolent bully.

Discuss or list short answers to the following questions:

Text Analysis

1. In Judges 1, which tribes did not fully drive out the inhabitants of the land?
2. What effect did this partial conquest have on Israel?
3. A cycle of deliverance is the prevailing theme in Judges, and it's found in 2:13–22. What were the main elements of this cycle?
4. How many judges were there, and where did they come from?
5. Why is Deborah's victory over Jabin and Sisera bittersweet for Israel?

Cultural Analysis

1. Why do many people pray when they are in dire straights?
2. Should Christians put stock in their political leaders to save them?

Biblical Analysis

1. Is there a New Testament corollary to the cycle we see in the life of Israel in Judges?
2. Read 1 Samuel 7:15–8:22. After the Book of Judges, we learn that Samuel rules Israel faithfully as judge, prophet and priest, foreshadowing the three main offices of Jesus Christ. Clearly, Yahweh was their king. Why then did God give Israel a king?

SUMMA

Write an essay or discuss this question, integrating what you have learned from the material above.
Is the Christian God really the same God Richard Dawkins rails against?

Reading Assignment:
Judges 17–21

This oil painting, *Samson Bound at the Mill* by Tanja Butler, is one of a twelve-piece series exploring parallels between the life and ministry of Samson and that of Christ. The similarities are striking. Both births were announced by angels, both men were called to free their people from oppression, and both suffered and died in fulfilling their ministries. "Samson Bound" can be seen as a metaphor for the brutal bondage and blindness in which sin has imprisoned humanity.

Session VIII: Activity
Judges 1–21

Note to homeschoolers: This activity will prove meaningful enough to make special efforts to include others. Seek out other homeschool children near the same age or involve your family members.

Judges on Trial

In the letter to the Hebrews, the author urges the early Christians (most of them Jewish in his audience) to press on knowing and serving Jesus Christ. As examples of faith, he holds up a list of Old Testament "witnesses." Curiously, he holds up some characters that were . . . let's just say, characters.

In Hebrews 11:32, the following four men are said to be examples of true, saving faith in the Lord: Gideon, Barak, Samson, and Jephthah. With a quick reading, a student might not stop to contemplate the irony. Clearly, each of these men was a sinner and did not follow God perfectly.

That begs the question: If these men in fact had true, saving faith, how was their faith evidenced? Why in the world are they in the list of biblical heroes?

In our nation, a person on trial is presumed innocent until proven guilty. The job of the prosecution is to "prove beyond a reasonable doubt" that the party is guilty. The defense's job is to create doubt in the judge's or jury's minds so that their party's innocence of the crime is maintained. In the case of our trial, we are not determining the defendants' guilt or innocence. Rather, we are looking for evidences of true, saving faith. To use courtroom language, we might say we are seeking to determine beyond a shadow of doubt if

each man had faith (despite his good or bad deeds).

To be true to God's Word, we must not let the students feel that they are putting God's Word on trial. Each of these four men clearly demonstrated saving faith, even though in critical ways, they failed to act in faith. This trial should demonstrate that saving faith is not about acting perfectly, but acting in tune with God's promises. As the Puritan saying goes, "God uses crooked sticks to draw straight lines." And that same God has a way of making saints out of sinners over a lifetime. Our faith should be directed toward Christ who fulfilled all righteousness, even as these heroes of the faith believed and trusted in Yahweh in the midst of their brokenness.

To examine this question, your class will hold a trial of each of these men.

- Elect a judge.
- Elect four defense and four prosecuting attorneys to accuse or represent each man.
- To prepare for either defending or accusing the saints in question, each attorney should carefully read these pertinent passages:

    Gideon: Judges 6:11–9:35
    Barak: Judges 4:1–24
    Samson: Judges 13–16
    Jephthah: Judges 11, 12

- The rest of the class will act as witnesses and the jury (with Bibles at hand).
- One prosecutor sets forth his case. Then the defender does the same. Go through each man this way.
- The judge should list charges made against each man that point to his acting in unbelief as well as list, in his defense, examples of each man's deeds extending from faith. Also, any statements the men make about their faith or about God should be taken into consideration.
- The jury should be taking notes as well.
- When the cases have all been heard, allow for a time of questioning of the attorneys by the jury.
- The judge should then call for a recess so that the jury can determine the presence of true, saving faith in each defendant's life.
- The judge will ask four different members of the jury to read their verdicts.

The next session will be a student-led discussion. Students will be creating their own questions concerning the issue of the session. Students should create three Text Analysis Questions, two Cultural Analysis questions, and two Biblical Analysis questions. For more detailed instructions, please see the chapter on *Death on the Nile*, Session V.

Issue

How should the grace of God shape a believer's life?

READING ASSIGNMENT:
Ruth

SESSION IX: STUDENT-LED DISCUSSION
Ruth

A Question to Consider

How should the grace of God shape a believer's life?

Students should read and consider the example questions below that are connected to the Question to Consider above. Last session's assignment was to prepare three questions and answers for the Text Analysis section and two additional questions and answers for both the Cultural and Biblical Analysis sections below.

Text Analysis

Example: What nationality are Naomi and her husband Elimelech? Why do they move to Moab, and how does this affect their lives?

Answer: Naomi and Elimelech are Israelites from Bethlehem. They move out of the Promised Land because of a famine. Things don't go very well in Moab. Though their sons find Moabite wives, those sons and Elimelech all die.

Other important parts of Ruth that might be explored:
- The levirate marriage and kinsman redeemer provisions in Ruth 1:11–13, 4:10–17, as well as in Leviticus 25:25–55, and Deuteronomy 25: 5, 6
- Naomi's perception of God's providence from bitterness (1:20) to fullness (4:13–17)
- The godliness of Boaz demonstrated in how he treats Ruth and Naomi generously and righteously. He serves as a wonderful picture of Yahweh "under whose wings [Naomi and Ruth] have come for refuge" (2:12).
- The importance of family, name and inheritance in Israel.
- The blood line leading up to King David (and eventually to Jesus of Nazareth)

Cultural Analysis

Example: To what degree does our culture value the input of extended families into such personal matters as money, marriage, and inheritance?

Answer: Our culture today is still operating, for the most part, off the fumes of Christendom. At least formally, a young man still tends to ask for a young woman's hand in marriage by talking to her father. Ceremonies of marriage tend to be traditional as well. However, Romanticism has influenced much of what we do in marriage. We tend to ignore bigger issues surrounding marriage, like our parents' wishes, our family name, our family businesses and hometowns. Where faith in Christ is lacking, young people simply marry the person they "fall in love with," regardless of their relationship to Christ. The Hebrew law reminded Jews that God owned everything: the land and all money. Believers were expected to steward their possessions and run their families in ways that were in the best interest of the community and for God's glory. Breaking God's law only brought misery and disruption to their peace. As we see in Boaz's treatment of Ruth, redemption and blessing are possible if believers keep covenant with their God in light of His amazing grace.

Other cultural issues to consider: Redemption and its modern equivalents, the "romance" of Ruth's story, and the imperfect constituents in the lineage of the perfect Christ as being a boasting point and not something of which to be ashamed.

Biblical Analysis

Example: Why is it significant that the story of Ruth takes place "when the judges ruled"?

Answer: The significance of the historical context is this: The era of the judges was tumultuous. God would discipline Israel for their disobedience by sending them oppression from their enemies. He would raise up a judge to deliver them, but they always fell back into idolatry. We can surmise that the famine in Ebimelech's time was deserved. The land, being under God's curse, was no place to live a decent life. Still, Ebimelech could have remained in Bethlehem (ironically, the name means "House of Bread"!); instead he fled to Moab. His sons take pagan wives. The author is trying to show us that the further we go from God's presence, the worse life gets. Naomi loses everything but Ruth and heads back to Bethlehem because she hears that Yahweh has favored them again. The real "romance" of this story is that a pagan woman and her

Ruth and Boaz Meet by Russian-Jewish artist Marc Chagall (1887–1985).

Hebrew mother-in-law find refuge in the Lord and His people.

Other Scriptures to consider: 1 Samuel 3:21-25, 2 Samuel 11 (especially v. 1), 1 Corinthians 7:32-33.

Summa

Write an essay or discuss this question, integrating what you have learned from the material above.
How should the grace of God shape a believer's life?

Optional Session A: Activity

Constructing a Family Tree of the Messiah

In this activity you will work with two or three others to create a family tree for Jesus of Nazareth. You have probably worked on a similar schematic for your own family. The point of this assignment is not only to help you track the physical line of Christ from ancient times; it is also designed to showcase how God, in His plan of redemption, included many sinful people. Some of these ancestors in Jesus' line will surprise you!

Before you begin, it will be necessary to familiarize yourself with Jesus' earthly family. Begin with the genealogy in Ruth 4:18-21. Remember, Ruth the Moabitess married into the tribe of Judah by being redeemed by Boaz. She was to become the great-grandmother of King David.

Next, to find Boaz's ancestry all the way back to Adam, see Luke 3:32-38. See Matthew 1:6-16 for the genealogy from David to Christ. (Note: If you stray from these exact verses, you may soon notice that these two genealogies trace two different lines after David. Matthew follows Solomon, listing Jesus' ancestors on his earthly father Joseph's side of the family, while Luke traces His ancestors through Mary's side to Nathan, a different son of David. Researching why this is so could provide another good optional activity for another day.)

With this information you will be able to create a family tree. Which direction should your tree run? You may start with Jesus as one of the fruits, or start with him at the root. Either way, Ruth and Boaz will show up somewhere in the middle.

Here are some more suggestions:

In the book of Ruth, Boaz provides for a destitute Ruth and Naomi by leaving extra grain in his fields for them to glean and also by giving six measures of barley directly to Ruth. Her gleaning of grain from the fields is strongly reminiscent of the Israelites collecting the manna that God provided for them in their wanderings. The association of manna with the bread in communion and the even stronger association of grain with bread make this scene in Ruth a foreshadowing of Jesus giving bread and wine to his Church in the form of the elements in communion.

- Since Jesus' family tree could become huge, emphasize his direct line only, as the genealogies do. You will end up with a line running up or down the whole tree. Fill in as many "side" relatives as you wish. For example, the 11 brothers of Judah are worth noting (Gen. 48:8–21; remember that Manasseh and Ephraim are the sons of Judah's brother Joseph).

- Be creative! It's a tree, so "go green." Using a poster board for your final product, employ colors, real leaves or other kinds of relief. If you're really daring, you could construct your family tree in three dimensions using a small Christmas tree.

- Split up the various ancestors among your group. Do research in the Bible to uncover one memorable aspect of their character. For example, Rahab was a prostitute who found refuge in the Lord by exercising her faith in hiding Israelite spies. Or an interesting note about Joseph is found in Luke: Jesus … "being (it was supposed) the son of Joseph" (3:23). This is a significant detail because in reality, Christ is the Son of God.

- Create the family tree online using one of many services that organize your genealogical information. Your teacher will be able to find some free platforms or may currently own access to a more polished version.

- Include mothers. Typically the genealogies follow the fathers. An exception is where Matthew mentions Bathsheba, but not by name (1:6). To find wives, you'll need to locate their stories in the Old Testament history books.

- Once you create the family tree, give an oral presentation for five minutes to the rest of your class.

OPTIONAL SESSION B: EVALUATION

Grammar

Answer each question in one or two sentences for factual recall. (2 points per answer)

1. What is the gist of Yahweh's commission to Joshua in 1:1–9?
2. Who went first into the Jordan, and why? How far ahead were they?
3. In Joshua 6:17–18 Joshua calls the inhabitants and belongings of Jericho "devoted to the Lord for destruction." What is *not* to be destroyed, and why?
4. What would happen if the Israelites spared some of the devoted things or spared some of the women to make them their wives?
5. Describe the Israelites' loss at Ai. Why did they lose the battle?
6. After the conquest, which tribes were given land on the east side of the Jordan? Why?
7. Why didn't the Levites have an allotment of land?
8. Who were the major judges?
9. What nationality are Naomi and her husband Elimelech? Why do they move to Moab, and how does this affect their lives?
10. Where did the levirate marriage and kinsman redeemer provisions in Ruth 1:11–13, 4:10–17 originate?

Logic

Answer the following questions in complete sentences; your answer should be a paragraph or so. Answer two of the four questions. (10 points per answer)

1. Why is the location of the tribes of Israel significant for the growth of the Church?
2. How did Jesus' Great Commission in Matthew 28:18–20 change how God's people should view the Promised Land?
3. How do chapters 4 and 5 of Judges compare? Why is the mixture of genres significant?
4. In what ways does Boaz demonstrate godliness in how he treats Ruth and Naomi?

Lateral Thinking

Answer one of the following questions. These questions will require more substantial answers. (15 points per answer)

1. A cycle of deliverance is the prevailing theme in Judges, and it's found in Judges 2:13–22. What are the main elements of this cycle? Does God treat his New Covenant people in the same way?
2. Should we consider Deborah a model of godly femininity?
3. How should the grace of God shape a believer's life?

ENDNOTES

1 Wright, Christopher J. H. *The God I Don't Understand*, Grand Rapids, Mich.: Zondervan, 2008. 168. A good deal of this discussion about Joshua, holy war, and the land is drawn from Wright's work.
2 Leithart, Peter J, *A House for My Name*, Moscow, Idaho: Canon Press, 2000. 111.

Troilus and Cressida

Have you ever broken a promise? Maybe it was as insignificant as telling a friend you'd meet him for lunch somewhere, and then you forgot all about it. Maybe it was more deliberate, such as telling your dad you would clean the garage on Saturday as he asked, but then you decided to go play soccer instead. Many of our minor broken promises don't seem to have any real consequences; in the first example, your friend no doubt forgave you because "you forgot," and you rescheduled your lunch; your dad hopefully instituted certain consequences for your failure to clean the garage. However, other promises and vows have devastating, long-term consequences if they are violated—a broken marriage vow, for instance, or perhaps a messy lawsuit arising from some broken business contract. Promises get more complicated when love, honor, and duty are involved. A marriage vow does not only involve love, but responsibility and reputation as well. When a man enlists in the military, he has pledged his service and cannot get out of it unless he receives his discharge, whether honorable or dishonorable.

William Shakespeare's play *Troilus and Cressida*, although a very difficult and ambiguous play in many ways, addresses these issues of vows, promises, loyalty, fidelity, duty, and honor. By juxtaposing the two main plots of the lovers (Troilus and Cressida) and the warriors (Achilles and those he affects with his actions), Shakespeare raises the issue of keeping promises in the midst of love and war.

Award-winning artist Barry Moser crafted this relief engraving from photographs of the Bard's death mask, rendering an accurate likeness of Shakespeare's visage. Moser has illustrated hundreds of books including *Moby-Dick*, *The Divine Comedy*, *Alice's Adventures in Wonderland*, and his monumental work, the *Pennyroyal Caxton Bible*.

General Information

Author and Context

See this section in the chapter on Antony and Cleopatra.

Significance

As one of Shakespeare's "problem plays," *Troilus and Cressida* is important to study because of its content and its performance history. It has been described as "a demanding play, Shakespeare's third longest, highly philosophical in tone and with an exceptionally learned vocabulary."[1] The obvious themes of honor, duty, and fidelity in love and war are on the surface of a much more complex script. Part of the difficulty in understanding the play simply is due to the nature of theater—we don't know how Shakespeare would have directed this when it was performed, or how he would have portrayed each of the characters. The play has also been categorized variously as a tragedy, comedy, and history play—so which is it? Perhaps because of the play's ambiguous and often bawdy content, it has not really known popularity until the twentieth century. John Dryden cleaned it up, rewrote the end to make it an official tragedy, and put it on in 1689, but the play did not really come into its own, because it was not often performed until about 200 years later.[2] This was due in part to all of the wars that rocked Europe and the rest of the world in the twentieth century which were accompanied by growing disillusionment with the glory of war. The content of *Troilus and Cressida* was also no longer taboo, as the English-speaking world moved away from the Victorian Era toward the sexual revolution of the 1960s. Thus, many scholars believe that Shakespeare was far ahead of his time in the way he addressed war, disorder, and flawed characters. The play continues to appeal to our fragmented postmodern society.

Main Characters

Readers familiar with Trojan War stories will recognize most of the characters in this play. The two title characters are new additions to the myth, however, since the Troilus-and-Cressida love story developed in medieval retellings of the Trojan War, crystallizing in Boccaccio's *Il Filostrato* (c. 1338) and refined in the lengthy poem *Troilus and Criseyde* (1385–1387) by Geoffrey Chaucer.[3] Troilus is one of King Priam's sons and therefore a prince and warrior of Troy. Cressida is a Trojan lady, the daughter of Calchas (a priest who has gone over to the Greek side—again, a medieval twist to the Homeric story) and the niece of Pandarus, a Trojan courtier whose object in life seems to be to get Troilus and Cressida together. Other Trojan princes also appear—Paris with his abducted lover Helen, Hector and his wife Andromache, and Aeneas. Cassandra also makes a few frenzied prophecies, as is her wont.

In the Greek camp, the familiar commanders are present (but of course Shakespeare changes their Homeric characterizations for his own purposes): Menelaus, the husband of Helen; his brother Agamemnon; the clever Ulysses; aged Nestor; hot-tempered Achilles and his friend Patroclus; and the warrior Ajax (portrayed here as a swaggering buffoon rather than a great fighter). Finally there is Thersites, who plays a minor role in Homer as an ugly deformed man who is beaten by Odysseus for reviling Agamemnon (see Book 2 of the *Iliad*) but in this play is a sort of court jester who makes acid and often ribald commentary on the action.

Summary and Setting

Act I opens during the seventh year of the Trojan War in Troy, where Pandarus is busily trying to bring Troilus and Cressida together. Troilus openly loves her; she secretly loves him. The act concludes in the Greek camp, where the leaders bemoan their disordered state due to Achilles, who has withdrawn from the fighting along with Patroclus. A challenge arrives from Hector to the Greeks; Ulysses and Nestor plot to have Ajax meet Hector in the duel to shame Achilles into fighting again.

In Act II, Ajax seeks to find out more about Hector's challenge. Nestor, meanwhile, has sent another demand to Troy to let Helen go, and the Trojan courtiers debate about whether or not she is worth it (they decide she is). Agamemnon comes to Achilles' tent to ask him to rejoin the fighting; Achilles still refuses. The Greek leaders continue to butter up Ajax so that he will take on Hector's challenge.

Pandarus finally brings a reluctant Cressida to Troilus in Act III; she eventually yields, and Pandarus sends them off to bed to consummate their love. In the Greek camp, Cressida's father Calchas asks the leaders to make a prisoner exchange—the Trojan captive Antenor for his daughter Cressida. They agree to this and send Diomedes to accomplish the exchange. Ulysses manages to speak with Achilles and continues to manipulate him (using the Ajax-Hector duel) to get him to fight, but only Patroclus is convinced to rejoin the battle.

Act IV focuses on the forced separation of Cressida from Troilus. After their one night together, Cressida must depart to the Greeks. The lovers weep and promise faithfulness to one another, exchanging tokens of their loyalty. Diomedes then escorts her to the Greek camp. The act concludes with the duel between Ajax and Hector, which is halted because Ajax is half-Trojan and thus they do not want to harm each other. Achilles finally agrees to meet Hector in battle the next day. Troilus, who had also come to the Greek camp, asks Ulysses to take him to Calchas (and Cressida).

Ulysses and Troilus make their way to this tent in Act V (followed by Thersites, who watches and comments on the following scene). They witness Diomedes make advances to Cressida, who hesitates but finally accepts his overtures. Troilus, of course, is angered against Diomedes, but he must return to Troy before taking any action. In Troy, Hector prepares to go out to battle, despite the pleadings of his wife Andromache and others. As Troilus is also heading out to battle, Pandarus brings him a letter from Cressida, which he reads and promptly rips to pieces. The rest of the act is a series of skirmishes, and Achilles finally joins the action after Hector kills Patroclus. Achilles has his Myrmidons slaughter the unarmed Hector and then takes credit for it. Troilus returns with the evil news to Troy, vowing his revenge. Pandarus concludes the play with a rather depressing monologue.

Worldview Essay

One week my friend and I decided to watch a number of different movie versions of the Cinderella story to see how its retelling differed through the decades and at the hands of various directors. It was actually quite fascinating that a simple plot line could be portrayed in so many ways, often with radically different agendas. The Trojan War story is similar. From Homer down to the present, this basic collection of myths and characters has taken on different roles in storytelling. Achilles is portrayed quite differently in Homer, Chaucer, Shakespeare, and even in our day (in the rather unfortunate 2004 movie *Troy*, for instance). Even Shakespeare's version of *Troilus and Cressida* has been interpreted in radically different ways by directors over the last century or so (as mentioned above). Thus, as we read this play we should consider not only what is happening, and how the characters are interacting, but also what changes Shakespeare has made in his retelling of this portion of the Trojan War. The way the characters handle loyalty in love and war, as well as how they view their own responsibility, is quite different in Shakespeare's play when contrasted to earlier versions of the story.

The two basic plots of this play—the lovers Troilus and Cressida, and the Achilles story—highlight conflicts in

Troilus and Cressida, Act V, Scene II by Angelica Kauffmann. In Kauffmann's own words: "[Troilus] sees his wife in loving discourse with Diomedes and he wants to rush into the tent to catch them by surprise, but Ulysses and the other keep him back by force."

love and loyalty, honor and duty. The play takes place in the context of the Trojan War, which of course was begun by broken vows. Every audience knows that Helen broke her marriage vow with Menelaus by running off with Paris, and Paris also broke basic rules of hospitality by taking his host's wife. We should not be too surprised therefore when another woman in this play simply follows Helen's example by also forsaking her first love. When Helen left Menelaus for another man, she also left her own country for a new one. Cressida is in a slightly different position, because she is forced to abandon her country when she is traded over to the Greeks, but note how quickly she gets over her loyalty to Troy and Troilus once she is amongst the Greeks. We see this more clearly in Chaucer's version of the story, when Diomedes uses every available means of persuasion to woo her and basically argues: "Look. Troy is a lost cause anyway; we all know the prophecies, and we know that it will fall. You might as well get used to being a Greek and forget about your Trojan lover for a new Greek one, namely, me" (V.123ff).

Loyalty to one's nation is also important among the warriors. Paris is known from Homer on as being a bit of a wimpy warrior—sure, he can go out and fight, but he prefers to stay in Troy polishing his armor or making love to Helen. His brothers, Hector and Troilus, however, are fiercely loyal to Troy.

Hector especially is willing to sacrifice personal and familial happiness to preserve his city. In a tender scene in Homer, and a rather curt scene in Shakespeare, he brushes off his wife Andromache's concerns as he insists upon going to battle for the sake of his city and his own honor. On the Greek side, disorder is caused by those who care more for their personal honor than loyalty to their cause. Achilles is, of course, the prime example of this. In Homer we learn that the cause of his withdrawal from battle is that Agamemnon took away his concubine Briseis (because Agamemnon had been compelled to give up his own), and Achilles felt so disgraced that he wanted to teach the Greeks a lesson by not fighting so that they would lose and really miss him. In Shakespeare, we see a more juvenile and immature Achilles, who with Patroclus mocks all the Greek leaders with imitations of their foibles. His bad example influences Ajax to pull out of the fighting as well. In Homer, the Greeks begin to lose without Achilles' involvement because he also has the backing of Zeus. However, in Shakespeare, although there are references to the gods, we see a more medieval view of the world at work, where the planets influence people and events, and where order and harmony are prized above all.[4] Ulysses has a lengthy and significant speech to the other Greek leaders in I.3, where he talks about the planets and orderliness: "O when degree is shaked, / Which is the ladder to all high designs, / The enterprise is sick. . . . / Take but degree away, untune that string, / and hark what discord follows. . . . / Troy in our weakness lives, not in her strength" (101–103, 109–110, 137). His point goes beyond the Homeric argument that without Achilles, the Greeks won't be able to win. He is arguing that as long as they are disunified in their own camp, they will be unable to defeat the Trojans. Winning Achilles back therefore is much more than simply winning a battle; it will restore cosmic order.

Shakespeare also chooses to portray war and war heroes in a much different light than Homer did. The *Iliad* is an epic poem, and Homer treats his heroes in true epic fashion. One of Achilles' common descriptors is "god-like;" these men are superhuman fighters who seek honor and everlasting glory. True, they behave in a rather petty fashion from time to time, but so do the gods. Shakespeare takes most of these great warriors and deflates this epic feel. In *Troilus*, we feel more as if we are watching a crisis in a high school boys' basketball team, where the best player is mad about something and refuses to play. The coaches then scramble to sooth and eventually deceive the player into rejoining the team. Achilles, Patroclus, and Ajax are not the great leaders and warriors of

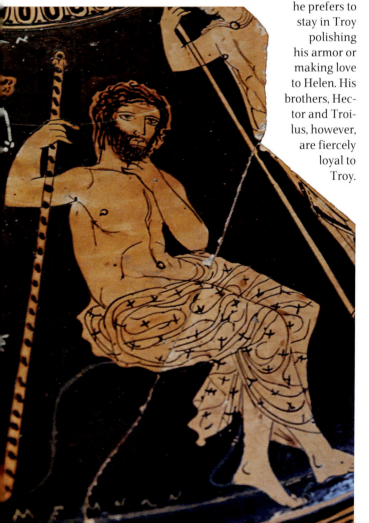

This red-figure representation of Agamemnon is thought to have been produced by the Meidias Painter, 410–400 B.C. The works of the Meidias Painter are identified by his distinctively ornate style.

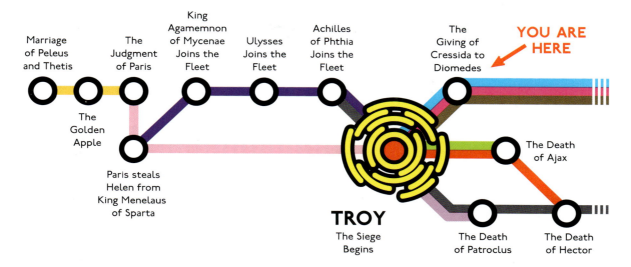

It can be a difficult task to keep track of events in the Trojan War, especially because the epic storyline unfolds over numerous poems, books and plays. This map may help readers sort out where they are in the epic.

Homer anymore; they are jocks and oafs. The whole Trojan War feels pointless and not worthwhile. Diomedes is an excellent spokesman for this attitude of disillusionment in Act IV, when he comes to fetch Cressida from Troy. Paris asks Diomedes to decide whether Paris or Menelaus deserves Helen. Diomedes, instead of rising to the defense of his fellow Greek, bitterly attacks Helen (to the face of the man who stole her away and started the whole war): "Hear me, Paris. / For every false drop in her bawdy veins / A Grecian's life hath sunk; for every scruple of her contaminated carrion weight / A Trojan hath been slain. Since she could speak / She hath not given so many good words breath / As, for her, Greeks and Trojans suffered death" (IV.1.70–76). There seems to be no glory or honor in this contest in the eyes of Diomedes.

The general feel of the two stories told by Chaucer and Shakespeare is also quite different. Chaucer's tale drips with chivalry and courtly love; the battles and war fade in comparison to the trauma of the two lovers. Shakespeare's knights are hardly chivalrous. Even Troilus, who approaches Cressida as on a pedestal, does not die or duel for her honor. He simply accepts the decision that she must be taken from him. Achilles violates the very basic warrior honor code by watching Hector disarm, and then jumping out at him with his Myrmidons—so not only does he attack a defenseless man, but he also pits numerous of his own warriors against the one man. This is a very different portrayal than in Homer, where Achilles slays Hector in battle, man-to-man, and only after that does he reject social decency by defiling Hector's body.

So which characters are to blame in this story for these various conflicts and disappointments? Again, reading Homer, Chaucer, and Shakespeare's versions, we see different spins on that question. They all in some way address the age-old question of personal responsibility versus divine foreordination. In Homer, as with the other ancient Greek and Roman authors you have studied, you have seen how Fate and the gods are at work, and how individuals cannot escape their fate. Yet at the same time, individuals are held accountable. In *Oedipus Rex*, for example, even though Oedipus is merely fulfilling prophecy and fate by murdering his father and marrying his mother, he is still held responsible for his actions—and blinds himself as punishment. So also in Homer, we know from prophecies that Troy will fall after 10 years and that Achilles will die young with eternal glory or else live long and in anonymity.

Chaucer, although he does refer to the gods since he's retelling a classical myth, more often than not discusses Fortune and her famous wheel. Throughout the war, the alternate successes of the Greeks or the Trojans are explained because "Fortune hath uncertain courses, / And now her wheel goes up, and now goes down, / And now she wears a smile and now a frown" (I.20).[5] Interestingly, the reason that Troilus first falls in love with Cressida is because he mocks love, and the god of love (in a very Ovidian fashion) is angered and shoots him with arrows of love for Cressida (I.27–37). Pandarus encourages Troilus in love because it seems that Fortune's wheel is turned to grant him luck (I.122), and for a time he seems to be right: "Too short a fleeting time, alas the while, / Great joy

Hector and Ajax duel.

endures, and Fortune wills it so, / Who truest seems when most she will beguile, / And most allures when she will strike a blow, / And from her wheel some hapless victim throw; / For when some wretch slips down and disappears, / She laughs at him and comforts him with jeers" (IV.1). When he learns that the Trojans have decided to send Cressida away, he prays to and then reproaches Fortune (IV.38ff., 56). A little later, however, he embarks on a long discourse trying to reconcile predestination and free choice, beginning, "I must believe and cannot other choose, / That Providence, in its divine foresight, / Hath known that Cressida I once must lose, / Since God sees everything from heaven's height / And plans things as he thinks both best and right, / According to their merits in rotation, / As was arranged for by predestination" (IV.138; his entire speech takes up IV.137–155). Chaucer concludes his version of Troilus and Cressida by stepping out of his narrative and explaining that he is portraying the folly of pagan beliefs and the loyalty of Christ, who will never betray those who love Him:

And love ye him who on the cross did buy
Our souls from timeless death to live for aye,
Who died and rose and reigns in heaven high!
Your deepest love his love will ne'er betray,
Your faith on him I bid you safely lay;
And since his love is best beyond compare,
Love of the world deny with all its care.

Here, lo, the vanity of pagan rites!
Lo, here, how little all their shrines avail!
Lo, here, the end of worldly appetites!
Lo here, how all the Gods at last shall fail,
Apollo, Jove and Mars and all the tale!
Lo, here the song that time hath held in fee,
Rescued from crumbling, grey
antiquity! (V.264–265).

Shakespeare has no such overt, tidy explanation of his purpose. Although like Chaucer he incorporates the ancient Greek and Roman gods with the medieval and Elizabethan notion of Fortune, he perhaps takes advantage of the nature of a play and forces the audience to interpret the characters' motives without the assistance of a narrator. When the reader finishes Troilus and Cressida, he could interpret Shakespeare's portrayal in a number of ways. In the realm of the warriors, blame seems to fall squarely on Achilles; he's the one acting childishly and bringing disharmony to the Greeks, isn't he? Ulysses appears to be his opposite—he is the one who restores order. However, the play is not so simple. Notice how Ulysses brings harmony back to camp—by driving a wedge between two of the great warriors, Ajax and Achilles. He uses more disorder to achieve his goal of unity. The Trojans also, although seeming to have more order in their ranks than the Greeks, are also on shaky foundations. They agree that they are right in keeping Helen and quickly agree to hand over Cressida to the Greeks. But is that unity necessarily good? They are self-consciously supporting an adulterous relationship (Paris and Helen), and they willingly hand over a defenseless woman to get a good warrior back. The audience also knows (even if the Trojans try to ignore Cassandra's prophecies among others) that Troy is doomed.

So how does the audience view the two lovers, and how do Troilus and Cressida view themselves? It is easy to condemn Cressida—she seems to be the one who promises fidelity and then quickly gives it up. Chaucer tends to be a bit more sympathetic to Cressida's plight than Shakespeare does, pointing out that it took her quite a long time to yield to Diomedes. Even though she is guilty of breaking her vow to Troilus, she is repentant and proves loyal to Diomedes (V.150–157). In Shakespeare, Cressida comes across as a somewhat contradictory character. She seems like a flirt from the very beginning, who interacts with men chiefly by sparring wittily with them (in fact, she only speaks to men during the play)—from Act I in her banter with her servant Alexander and then her uncle Pandarus (scene 2), to her reluctance to yield to Troilus in Act III, to her open flirting with the Greek leaders when she is brought to their camp in IV.6. When she finally yields to Diomedes, she simply says: "Troilus, farewell. One eye yet looks on thee, / But with my heart the other eye doth see. / Ah, poor our sex! This fault in us I find: / The error of our eye directs our mind. / What error leads must err. O then conclude: / Minds swayed by eyes are full of turpitude" (V.2.109–114). So is she simply an insecure flirt, or is she a calculating woman who is trying to protect herself in the only way she can in a time of war?

Troilus at first seems to be the blameless and faithful lover of the pair. He is the one who swears faithfulness, and loves her to the end. However, Shakespeare changes the story from Chaucer slightly to leave some doubt in the audience's mind about the actual depth of Troilus's love. In Chaucer's version, when the news comes from the Trojan council that Cressida must leave, Troilus thinks through a number of different plans to get around this decree—he and Cressida could run away, for instance. However, he also knows that his city is at war because of that very thing, and he does not want to be disloyal to Troy by suggesting that his father change the deal (IV.79–80). Shakespeare's Troilus, however, moans a bit but acquiesces so quickly that it makes us wonder if he was really sincere in all of his oaths of eternal love and fidelity. Incidentally, Pandarus too does not question the council's decision (at least in Chaucer's version he tried to work with Troilus to figure out a way around it).

Tales of love, war, and broken loyalties are standard in great myths and stories throughout the ages. However, each age has approached these issues and the people involved with different sets of worldviews and attitudes. As we follow the versions of the Trojan War story through time, we can perhaps learn more about the storytellers than the story itself. As you read Troilus and Cressida, think not only about *what* Shakespeare is telling, but how he is telling it. What conclusions can we draw about war, love, or promises? Perhaps Cassandra (the ever-misunderstood prophetess) is right when she says, "It is the purpose that makes strong the vow, but vows to every purpose must not hold" (V.3.23–24).

—Natali H. Monnette

For Further Reading

Chaucer, Geoffrey. *Troilus and Criseyde in Chaucer,* Vol. 22 in *Great Books of the Western World.* Chicago: Encyclopedia Britannica, Inc., 1952.

Girard, Rene. *A Theater of Envy.* South Bend, Ind.: St. Augustine's Press, 2004, 135ff.

Homer. Translated by George Chapman. *Chapman's Homer: The Iliad and the Odyssey.* Wordsworth Editions, Ltd., 2005.

Lewis, C.S. *The Discarded Image.* Cambridge: Cambridge University Press, 1998.

Veritas Press History Cards: New Testament, Greece, and Rome. Lancaster, Pa.: Veritas Press, 3.

SESSION I: PRELUDE

A Question to Consider

Is it ever right to break a promise?

From the General Information above answer the following questions:

1. Is *Troilus and Cressida* a comedy, tragedy, or history play?
2. What were some of Shakespeare's sources and influences for this play?
3. What are the two basic plots in Troilus and Cressida?
4. How is Achilles portrayed in Homer versus Shakespeare?
5. Are Troilus and Cressida sympathetic characters?
6. Why might Shakespeare's play Troilus and Cressida be more complex and difficult to understand than Chaucer's poem?

The next session will be a student-led discussion. Students will be creating their own questions concerning the issue of the session. Students should create three Text Analysis Questions, two Cultural Analysis questions, and two Biblical Analysis questions. For more detailed instructions, please see the chapter on *Death on the Nile,* Session V.

Issue

The word *true* has implications for both honesty (telling the truth) and fidelity (being true to someone). How are these two-fold responsibilities of truth necessary for the preservation of order in both personal and in public arenas?

READING ASSIGNMENT:
Troilus and Cressida, Act I

SESSION II: STUDENT-LED DISCUSSION
Troilus and Cressida, Act I

A Question to Consider

The word *true* has implications for both honesty (telling the truth) and fidelity (being true to someone). How are these two-fold responsibilities of truth necessary for the preservation of order in both personal and in public arenas?

To be "true" means to be both honest and faithful. This play explores the consequences of failure in both areas, and its effects in love and in war, in private lives and in public community—and insists that all these strands are linked. Most people understand that dishonesty, unfaithfulness, neglect, and betrayal are destructive in personal relationships; yet it is important to note the effect of such sins on the community as well. Part of the problem in this play is that characters want freedom and privacy to make poor choices and renege on their duties. (Troilus, for example, is obsessively in love with Cressida—but he will not let anyone in his family know, and his choice to keep their relationship secret leads to disastrous consequences later.) But as John Donne notes, "No man is an island, entire of itself; every man is a piece of the continent, a part of the main" (Meditation XVII). We are all connected in community, and our virtues and vices have effect beyond our own lives. Helen's flight with Paris has staggering implications for two great nations; Achilles' choice to lounge in his tent with Patroclus, instead of fighting for his general, infects the entire Greek army with listlessness and disorder; and Troilus and Cressida's failures toward each other have implications for societal stability as well.

In this messy play, characters consistently fail to follow the behaviors and values appropriate to their respective roles (lover, warrior, leader, etc.) and Shakespeare shows us that the resulting disorder in their personal lives has public ramifications for the community as well. These warriors are not heroes, and these lovers are not faithful. When people are not true to their duties, but instead follow their individual appetites, then honor, love, and heroism are undermined. These values depend upon self-sacrifice and obedience to a higher standard than appetite or personal desire. Ulysses' speech about order and degree (I.3.75–137) emphasizes the patterns that ought to be followed for an ordered society. Take careful note of this speech, as it is key to understanding the rest of the play.

Text Analysis

Example: Already in Act I, several characters are discovered failing to be "true" in their roles—whether this means dishonesty, deception, or neglect of their duties. This failure manifests itself in various degrees, ranging from the seemingly innocuous (secrecy and coyness in love, for example) to outright deception and manipulation. Choose one of these characters and identify his or her failure to be true.

Answer: When Hector issues a challenge to the Greek army for a single combat, Ulysses hatches a plan with Nestor to falsely rig a "lottery" to choose the opponent. Everyone in the Greek army knows that Achilles is the best choice, but because he refuses to fulfill his responsibilities as a warrior and hero, the Greek leaders wish to punish—and goad—him by choosing the lesser Ajax instead. This manipulation and deception sows seeds of discord among the Greeks, who admittedly are not in great unity to begin with (I.3.310–390).

Culture Analysis

Example: How does our culture view obligations of duty in regard to a person's place in the community?

Answer: On the one hand, privacy and individual "rights" are defining values for most of American popular culture today. This is seen in a variety of issues from abortion (commonly considered to be a woman's choice regarding her own body), to questions of romance (where morality and duties to others are often thrown out in the pursuit of "love" and happiness), to consumer culture (where advertisements frequently urge us to indulge in luxuries, telling individuals they "deserve" whatever product is being sold). Yet areas still remain where individual actions are recognized to have effect on the community, and the culture does press individuals to conform where it perceives a duty to "community" values—in areas such as environmental practices like "going green," for example. Our culture rightly recognizes that individuals are not isolated from their community, and that individual actions do affect others. The question is not whether our culture believes in duties of individuals to their communities, but rather, which issues it believes ought to be private matters and which public, and also how those matters affecting "community" ought to be enforced (by means of individual conscience, social pressure, or by law). In these questions, unfortunately, our culture often uses different criteria for its decisions than the Scriptures (such as the abortion issue previously mentioned).

Biblical Analysis

Example: What does the Bible teach about a person's responsibility to be "true" in his duties toward others, individually and in community?

Answer: The Scriptures show that man's actions have always affected others in relationship with him. From the narrative passages of Scripture, we see beginning with Adam that one man's actions affect many (Rom. 5:12–19). We see that the sin of Achan affected the entire nation of Israel (Josh. 7), and that on the other hand righteous living can bring blessing to one's children and descen-

Achilles and his faithful friend Patroclus appear on this red-figure pottery.

dants (Ex. 20:1–6). Scripture also teaches that after loving God, man's next highest duty is to love his neighbor (Lev. 19:18; Matt. 22:37–39). Jesus instructs us to do unto others what we would have them do unto us (Matt. 22:35–40), and Paul urges us to esteem others more highly than ourselves (Phil. 2:3–4). All these commandments indicate our duty to respect others and be mindful of our place in community. As we practice this individual love, the watching world will observe our works (John 13:34–35), and this individual obedience will have lasting effects for the Kingdom of God.

SUMMA

Write an essay or discuss this question, integrating what you have learned from the material above.

Why is it so important for believers to be "true," in honesty and in faithfulness, to the people and principles important in their lives?

Instead of a reading assignment you have a research assignment. Tomorrow's session will be a Current Events session. Your assignment will be to find a story online, in a magazine, or in the newspaper that relates to the issue that you discussed today. Your task is to locate the article, give a copy of the article to your teacher or parent and provide some of your own worldview analysis to the article. Your analysis should demonstrate that you understand the issue, that you can clearly connect the story you found to the issue that you discussed today, and that you can provide a biblical critique of this issue in today's context. Look at the next session to see the three-part format that you should follow.

Find a story in a current magazine, in a newspaper, or online relating to the issue stated in the next session. Prepare an analysis of your article to share with the class.

Issue

Faithfulness and honor

OPTIONAL ACTIVITY: DISCUSSION

Taming the Wolf

One of the most powerful and memorable speeches in *Troilus and Cressida* is the famous "Universal Wolf" speech in Act I, scene 3, lines 119–124. Here it is:

Then everything includes itself in power,
Power into will, will into appetite;

And appetite (an universal wolf,
So doubly seconded with will and power)
Must make perforce an universal prey,
And last, eat up himself.

This speech gives us through the lips of Ulysses Shakespeare's biblical diagnosis of the political problems in the Greek army. The application, however, is much broader.

Reread Ulysses' speech in lines 75–137 and answer these questions:
1. What does Ulysses diagnose as the reason for all of this strife?
2. According to the "Universal Wolf" speech, what are the results of letting everything become a mad grab for power?
3. Where do you see tracks of the "Universal Wolf" in our world today?
4. Where do you see these tracks in your own life at school and home?
5. How should you respond to the wolf tracks in your life?

Like in *Aesop's Fables,* where the wolf appears as a villain, *Canis lupus* is used in this play as a metaphor for the ravenous appetite for power.

SESSION III: CURRENT EVENTS

Issue

Faithfulness and honor

Current events sessions are meant to challenge you to connect what you are learning in Omnibus class to what is happening in the world around you today. After the last session, your assignment was to find a story online or in a magazine or newspaper relating to the issue above. Today you will share your article and your analysis with your teacher and classmates or parents and family. Your analysis should follow the format below:

BRIEF INTRODUCTORY PARAGRAPH

In this paragraph you will tell your classmates about the article that you found. Be sure to include where you found your article, who the author of your article is, and what your article is about. This brief paragraph of your presentation should begin like this:

Hello, I am (name and my current events article is (name of article) which I found in (name of the web or published source)…

CONNECTION PARAGRAPH

In this paragraph you must demonstrate how your article is connected to the issue that you are studying. This paragraph should be short, and it should focus on clearly showing the connection between the book that you are reading and the current events article that you have found. This paragraph should begin with a sentence like

I knew that my article was linked to our issue because…

CHRISTIAN WORLDVIEW ANALYSIS

In this section, you need to tell us how we should respond as believers to this issue today. This response should focus both on our thinking and on practical actions that we should take in light of this issue. As you list these steps, you should also tell us why we should think and act in the ways you recommend. This paragraph should begin with a sentence like

> As believers, we should think and act in the following ways in light of this issue and article.

READING ASSIGNMENT:
Troilus and Cressida, Acts II and III

SESSION IV: RECITATION
Troilus and Cressida, Acts II and III

Comprehension Questions

Answer the following questions for factual recall:
1. When the Trojan Council meets to determine whether to return Helen, Hector and Troilus offer opposing arguments. Identify each man's position and his explanation for it.
2. How do the Trojans respond to Cassandra's wild prophecies warning that Troy will burn if they do not let Helen go?
3. In the context of the rest of the scene, what does Ajax's servant, Thersites, mean when he says that "all the argument (cause of contention) is a whore and a cuckold" (II.3.71)? How does this contrast with the attitude of the Trojan council in the previous scene?
4. How does Achilles demonstrate disrespect for the rest of the Greek commanders in II.3, acting out the behavior that Ulysses condemned as "out of degree" in his earlier speech from Act I?
5. What does Pandarus want from Paris and Helen when he approaches them in III.1? Why is this request necessary?
6. Why isn't Paris fighting at the time of this scene, like most of the other Trojan men (except Troilus)? What is he doing instead? How does this decision relate to the play's theme of being true to one's duty?
7. When Pandarus brings the lovers together to pledge their love and fidelity to one another, what fear does Cressida suddenly express amid their declarations and kisses?
8. What is unusual about the conclusion these three come to after discussing the possibilities of future infidelity?
9. Who is Calchas, and what is his plan to free the captured Antenor?

READING ASSIGNMENT:
Troilus and Cressida, Acts IV and V

SESSION V: WRITING
Movie Treatment

This session is a writing assignment. Remember, quality counts more than quantity. You should write no more than 1,000 words, either typing or writing legibly on one side of a sheet of paper. You will lose points for writing more than this. You will be allowed to turn in your writing three times. The first and second times you turn it in, your teacher will grade it by editing your work. This is done by marking problem areas and making suggestions for improvement. You should take these suggestions into consideration as you revise your assignment. Only the grade on your final submission will be recorded. Your grade will be based on the following criteria: 25 points for grammar, 25 points for content accuracy—historical, theological, etc.; 25 points for logic—does this make sense and is it structured well?; 25 points for rhetoric—is it a joy to read?

Your Assignment: Because Shakespeare's plays were always meant to be performed, rather than merely read or studied, he rarely describes his characters and settings in vivid sensory detail. Instead, he primarily provided the extraordinary dialogue and left the portrayals to the actors and directors.

In this session, imagine yourself as the director of a stage or movie production of *Troilus and Cressida.* You will envision the characters and the setting as you would bring it to life (with unlimited budget and technical capabilities, of course—dream big!). Your paper will be your artistic vision for this production and must address three important elements: 1) the cast you will choose to portray the major characters, 2) the setting—including both time and place—that will best serve as a foil for the themes that this play addresses, and 3) your thoughtful reasons for all of these choices.

As the director you have free imaginative reign in selecting the actors for your cast. You may choose a glamorous film icon from the 1930s to co-star with the lead from a recent summer blockbuster. However, this is a serious writing assignment: choose actors according to their onscreen charisma and presence, and how well they match the character they will play, and not based on popularity. The characters for whom you must choose actors are: Troilus, Cressida, Pandarus, Ulysses, Achilles, and Hector.

As for the setting, directors have always been creative in re-telling Shakespeare's stories. One famous example is *West Side Story,* a musical which re-set the story of *Romeo and Juliet* in 1950s New York City, in which the two feuding families become rival gangs with ethnic tensions. You may choose a setting other than the Trojan War, such as a different historical war, or in another kind of conflict (such as warring Mafia clans, for example). The important thing is that if you choose a different setting, you will need to explain why—that is, how elements of that different setting match and reflect elements or themes of this play. This would be done by describing your new setting first, and then explaining its similarities to the original. In either case, whether or not you choose to change the setting, you will need to give a basic but vivid visual description: how does the landscape look? How would the camp scenes be portrayed? What kinds of uniforms or costumes will the characters wear?

Your paper does not need to follow a particular paragraph form. Rather, the emphasis is on creative thinking and using good rhetorical skills to present your ideas well—with vivid, specific details—and to persuade the reader that they are fitting.

READING ASSIGNMENT:
None

Cressida pledges to be true to Troilus, saying, "If I be false or swerve a hair from truth, / . . . yet let memory / From false to false among false maids in love, / Upbraid my falsehood . . . / Yea, let them say, to stick the heart of falsehood, / 'As false as Cressid.'"

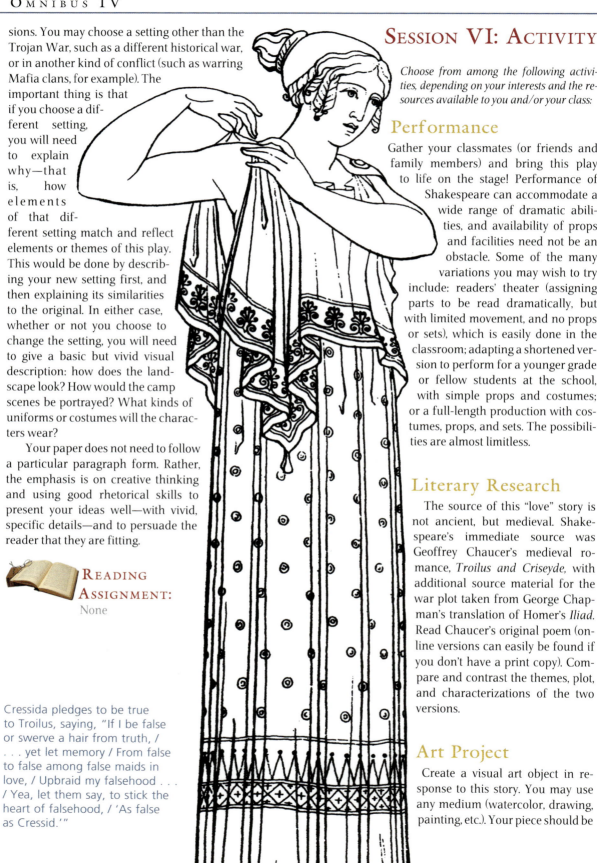

SESSION VI: ACTIVITY

Choose from among the following activities, depending on your interests and the resources available to you and/or your class:

Performance

Gather your classmates (or friends and family members) and bring this play to life on the stage! Performance of Shakespeare can accommodate a wide range of dramatic abilities, and availability of props and facilities need not be an obstacle. Some of the many variations you may wish to try include: readers' theater (assigning parts to be read dramatically, but with limited movement, and no props or sets), which is easily done in the classroom; adapting a shortened version to perform for a younger grade or fellow students at the school, with simple props and costumes; or a full-length production with costumes, props, and sets. The possibilities are almost limitless.

Literary Research

The source of this "love" story is not ancient, but medieval. Shakespeare's immediate source was Geoffrey Chaucer's medieval romance, *Troilus and Criseyde,* with additional source material for the war plot taken from George Chapman's translation of Homer's *Iliad.* Read Chaucer's original poem (online versions can easily be found if you don't have a print copy). Compare and contrast the themes, plot, and characterizations of the two versions.

Art Project

Create a visual art object in response to this story. You may use any medium (watercolor, drawing, painting, etc.). Your piece should be a thoughtful and well-executed response to the themes or characters of this story. For representational art, suggested depictions include: a) a pivotal moment in the play for your chosen character, or a pivotal moment in the play when your chosen theme is most clearly and starkly visible; or b) a moment that is not depicted on stage in this play, but that is crucial to that character's development. You may imagine, for example, Cressida's reunion with her father when she arrives at the Greek camp.

OPTIONAL SESSION: EVALUATION

Grammar

Answer each of the following questions in complete sentences. Some answers may be longer than others. (2 points per answer)

1. This play contains what two parallel plots?
2. Who are Troilus and Cressida?
3. Who is Achilles, and what is the source of the conflict between Achilles and the rest of the army?
4. What happens in the much-anticipated single combat between Hector and Ajax?
5. Identify an example of deception—a failure to tell the truth—in this play.
6. How does Troilus respond to Cressida's unfaithfulness—her failure to be true to him—which he witnesses while spying on her in company with Ulysses?
7. Besides the false lottery, what method does Ulysses use in a personal encounter with Achilles to stir Achilles to act again as a warrior?

Logic

Answer the following question in complete sentences; your answer should be a paragraph or so. Answer two of the four questions. (10 points per answer)

1. Give specific examples of how this play's warriors fail at heroism.
2. How do Troilus and Cressida both wrong each other in this play by failing to fulfill their own roles and responsibilities to be true?
3. How does this play end? Is this ending satisfactory? What is Shakespeare doing here?

4. Both of the parallel plots in this play hinge upon a woman's unfaithfulness: Cressida's betrayal of Troilus, and Helen's of Menelaus. Compare and contrast Shakespeare's portrayal of these two women and their respective roles in the disruption of the social order of their worlds.

Lateral Thinking

Answer one of the following questions. These questions will require more substantial answers. (15 points per answer)

1. Ulysses' great oration on order and "degree" in Act I is the linchpin of the play. Briefly explain Ulysses' conception of order, and how the consequences for being "out of degree" (ignoring this plan for proper order) are borne out and illustrated in the actions of this play. How does this view compare and contrast with the Roman values you might have read about?
2. One of this play's themes is the question of value: is it subjective (resting in others' opinions of the person or object in question—as expressed in the phrase "Beauty is in the eye of the beholder"), or objective (intrinsic to itself, and measured by an external and fixed standard)? What does Scripture teach? What do different characters in this play believe?

ENDNOTES

1 From the Introduction to *Troilus and Cressida* in *William Shakespeare: The Complete Works*, ed. by Stanley Wells, Gary Taylor, et al. (New York: Oxford University Press, 1988), 715.

2 See the section entitled "'Stuff to Make Paradoxes:' Performance History of Troilus and Cressida" in the Introduction to *The Arden Shakespeare: Troilus and Cressida*, ed. by David Bevington (London: Thomson Learning, 2006), 87–117.

3 Bevington, 380–382.

4 See *The Discarded Image* by C.S. Lewis (Cambridge: Cambridge University Press, 1998).

5 *Troilus and Criseyde*, trans. by George Philip Krapp, in *Chaucer*, Vol. 22 in *Great Books of the Western World* (Chicago: Encyclopedia Britannica, Inc., 1952). All Chaucer quotes are from this edition.

First & Second Chronicles

What is your favorite book of the Bible? Anyone who reads the Bible very much usually finds some parts more enjoyable than others. Many would answer Psalms, Proverbs, Romans, or even Revelation. It's unlikely that too many would respond, "I just love the books of 1 and 2 Chronicles!"

Why is that? For one thing, 1 and 2 Chronicles are in the Old Testament, and to some, that fact in itself is a strike against it. Besides that, the Chronicles books come in the *genre* (literary style) of historical narrative, which may also be a deterrent to some Bible readers. Now it is certainly the case that stories from history can be loaded with excitement, bravery, and drama, but somehow, the word "Chronicles" hardly seems to imply high adventure. At best, the word sounds a little dry, and the fact is, a cursory glance through the books of 1 and 2 Chronicles hardly creates a very different impression!

Take a brief look, for example, at the first nine chapters of 1 Chronicles. What do you notice? Lists of names—not exactly the stuff of the latest action movie. If you glance at chapters 23–27, you will also see name after name of people, many of whom are never mentioned again in the Bible. Second Chronicles provides similar apparently unnecessary detail with respect to the building of Solomon's Temple and related matters. It would be natural to wonder whether such archives really have much bearing on the lives of readers removed thousands of years from those moments in history.

Something else you might notice about 1 and 2 Chronicles is its repetition of material from other parts of the Old Testament. Material is borrowed, sometimes with little or no modification, from portions of the books of Samuel or Kings. It is natural to wonder why the author of this book would merely reproduce extended passages from other sources.

So, what are these two volumes about? How should they be read and understood? Why are they even in the Bible, given the repetition from other sources? Hopefully, the following preliminary observations will help in working out some answers to those questions. When the underlying purpose of this remarkable work is understood, it can be seen to be an exciting and encouraging source of help to any reader, even Christians reading it some 2,500 years later.

The author of Chronicles draws together pieces of the history of the chosen people of God to tell a specific story of Yahweh's work.

General Information

Author and Context

Questions related to the authorship and date of 1 and 2 Chronicles continue to intrigue Old Testament scholars. There seems to be a general consensus that the work was produced no earlier than the mid-fifth century B.C. (around 450 B.C.), and no later than the mid-fourth century B.C. The most popular nominee for authorship is Ezra, that great priest and scholar who encouraged the people as they returned to the Holy Land following long years of exile. Arriving in Jerusalem in about the year 458 B.C., he would probably have written or compiled the book over the next twenty years or so.

As you know from your other studies of the Old Testament, the people of Judah had been deported from their land following the fall of Jerusalem to Nebuchadnezzar in 586 B.C. When Babylon itself fell to Cyrus the Great in 539, the Persian king reversed the policies of the Babylonians and authorized the return of any Jewish people who wished to go (cf. 2 Chron. 36:22ff). The Temple in Jerusalem was rebuilt over the next twenty years, and went back into operation under Darius I of Persia in 516 B.C.

A second wave of Jewish immigrants returned with Ezra in about 458 under the Persian king Artaxerxes I. Ezra implemented substantial reforms of worship and practice, as detailed in the book that bears his name, as well as in the book of Nehemiah. Many believe that Ezra's main reason for preparing the books of Chronicles related to his concern over the deteriorating spiritual condition of the people of God and their need to learn important lessons highlighted in that book.

Significance

What were those lessons? What message was he urging his contemporaries to hear and heed? Of equal importance, what lessons can we gather from the pages of this remarkable history?

The answers may not be immediately apparent from simply surveying 1 and 2 Chronicles, especially to the modern reader. It doesn't help much that the author never actually states his purpose. We are, therefore, forced to engage in a bit of detective work as we read, noting what is included or omitted, and paying attention to the themes that are emphasized or repeated, if we are to reach a plausible theory about the purpose and significance of the book. So, as we read the book in this way, what do we notice?

For one thing, even a casual reader cannot help but notice that about five-sixths of Chronicles concerns itself almost exclusively with the history of Judah in general and Jerusalem in particular. The northern kingdom only shows up on those occasions when its story intersects with the southern. Even the lengthy genealogy found at the beginning seems intended mainly to provide a prologue introducing the story of Judah.

Besides the emphasis on Judah, the author narrows his interest even further, paying special attention to the Temple and the rituals of worship as part of his drama. Lengthy descriptions of the courses, routines, and personnel of the Temple show that the author wants his readers to take very seriously the significance of this central venue of worship.

What does all this mean? It seems most likely that the author is addressing specific problems among the people of God in Jerusalem. He believed the people had become less than diligent in restoring a proper view of the Temple and the need to worship God rightly. It seems that Chronicles was written as a book urging reform, renewal, and repentance as the only sure method to avoid a repeat catastrophe.

Main Characters

While many individuals find their way into the story, it doesn't take long to recognize that two personalities dominate the landscape. Fully two-thirds of 1 Chronicles details the career of David, and about one-third of 2 Chronicles highlights the life of Solomon. The lives of these two stand at the center of the work. Preceding material (1 Chron. 1–9) leads up to David, focusing especially on his genealogical record and the dominance of the tribe of Judah. Succeeding material (2 Chron. 10–36) applies the lessons learned from these to the later kings of Judah, evaluating them as to their faithfulness in worship, and reporting the positive or negative consequences of their behavior.

Examining the texts more specifically devoted to David, it may come as a surprise that only two chapters are devoted to David's rise to power, and conspicuously absent from those chapters are his early adventures as giant killer, military leader, and fugitive. The remaining 17 chapters focus almost entirely on his preparations for the building of the Temple. A reader might well wonder what happened to the story of Bathsheba or the revolt of Absalom. Answer: they are simply skipped over. The "David" of Chronicles is idealized and his devotion to the Temple overshadows everything.

In 2 Chronicles, the interest shifts to Solomon, but here again, the Temple lies at the heart of the author's concern. In fact, the first eight of those nine chapters deal with little but the construction and dedication of the Temple. Chapter nine culminates the story with a dramatic account of Solomon's international reputation, highlighted by a visit from the mysterious Queen of Sheba. As with David, Solomon's imperfections are also omitted, notably his dubious family life, his compromises with paganism, and his other breaches of the duties of kings under the Law of Moses (cf. Deut. 17:14ff).

In 1 and 2 Kings we see a more prophetic version of David and Solomon. We see them warts and all. They are shown to be sinners in need of God's grace. In 1 and 2 Chronicles we see a more priestly vision of them that stresses their justification. Thus, we view them through the lens of the sacrifices of the Temple—and the reality (Christ's blood) to which all of the Old Testament sacrifices pointed.

Summary and Setting

Chronicles offers a sweeping and panoramic view of the history of God's people, beginning with Adam and concluding with the remarkable and hopeful decree of Cyrus:

> Thus says Cyrus king of Persia: All the kingdoms of the earth the LORD God of heaven has given me. And He has commanded me to build Him a house at Jerusalem which is in Judah. Who is among you of all His people? May the LORD his God be with him, and let him go up. (2 Chron. 36:23)

The author writes to those who know this history well, but who may have missed its essential lesson—namely, that God has preserved and protected the royal line of Judah and David through the centuries, but God's protection has been moderated substantially depending on whether His people were acting faithfully with respect to their worship.

It is the focus on worship, the place of worship, the ministers of worship, and the heart of worship that occupies center stage in the mind of the author. Certainly God had delivered his people in remarkable and at times miraculous ways over the years, but invariably the author highlights the centrality of heart-felt devotion to God combined with proper outward ritual, rather than great heroic deeds, as the key to understanding the reason for God's favor. He urged this because in the days of Ezra there had been a loss of appreciation for the need for absolute purity in worship—a point also emphasized in the books of Ezra and Nehemiah.

By pointing at true worship and priestly work this book points us again to Christ—the very point of the Old Testament and all of the Scripture.

First Kings 2:10 states that King David was buried in the City of David. His actual tomb has not been discovered by modern archaeologists, but several sites lay claim to being the real one. This statue of the beloved king stands at a traditional burial site on Mount Zion. Wherever David's actual tomb is located, Josephus mentions that King Herod the Great attempted to rob David's tomb but found that other looters had preceded him and left nothing of value.

Worldview

In spite of the impression of some, 1 and 2 Chronicles are actually among the most stimulating books in the Bible, mixing great courage with practical faithfulness. Recognition of those qualities depends, however, on understanding that the book is not exactly what it appears to be at first glance. To read the books as a mere history of Judah would almost certainly lead some to the conclusion that the work is too dull to be of much interest, and others that it is too fantastic to be believed. It is those impressions that have led some to the view 1 and 2 Chronicles as little more than some of the "deadwood" in the Bible. When, however, the real intentions of the author and his methods are grasped, it becomes apparent that 1 and 2 Chronicles have an important and unique place in the Scriptures.

First and Second Chronicles present a view of history on an immense scale, and behind this history is a theology, powerfully and persuasively highlighting three great truths: that humanity dwells under the overruling power of an unchangeable moral order ordained by a sovereign God; that observance of proper forms of worship is of paramount importance for the people of God; and that God's truth applies at all times, both past and present. The author urged these principles, not by abstract argument, but by a method obvious to his contemporaries, although it might seem a little foreign to us. He painted a rich picture of the past, making use of well-known historical episodes to depict greater truths.

The author's method was, at its heart, dramatic. He set forth a vast story beginning with Adam, and climaxing in the destruction of the Judean kingdom. In the first nine chapters, he provides a prelude that encourages us to see that all history, from its earliest roots, led to the crowning moment of David's reign and the astonishing splendor of King Solomon, whose climactic achievement was the construction and dedication of the Temple in Jerusalem, the only place for the true and proper ritual worship of God. From there, the drama descends into a grim recital of the later kings of Judah, men to whom so much had been entrusted, but from whom so little was received.

A consistent feature of the later chapters involves the message of hope for God's people if they will but turn to Him. Again and again, however, that message is rejected. On only two occasions—the reigns of Hezekiah and Josiah—may a flicker of light be seen, but those hopeful moments are transient, and finally spiritual darkness descends on the tragic city, as Jerusalem is captured and destroyed, the Temple burned, the city razed. Kings and people had persisted in wickedness until there was no hope of escaping the inevitable disaster.

Why should such a story be told? In some ways, the answer must be understood first of all in light of *when* it was told. Old Testament scholars generally agree that the 1 and 2 Chronicles were produced many years after the destruction of Jerusalem at a time when it would finally be possible to reflect on both the events and the great themes of Israel's history and learn great lessons from them. The first readers of Chronicles were supposed to recognize that behind the military power that had abolished their political independence was the hand of God. They were also to see that in spite of these disasters, there was still hope, a "shoot out of dry ground," as Isaiah had put it years before.

The first hint of that hope occurred about fifty years after Nebuchadnezzar had destroyed the city, when God permitted their return by the hand of Cyrus the Persian. It is no accident that the entire work of 1 and 2 Chronicles ends on that note. As God's people returned, they were to celebrate a purified religion ennobled by higher thoughts of God and a deeper sense of the heartfelt duty the earlier prophets had demanded.

By the time 1 and 2 Chronicles were written, the Temple had been rebuilt, albeit on a much more modest scale than that associated with Solomon. It was, nevertheless, once again at the center of the life of worship for God's people. At this point, however, something new had been added to the mix. Although a minority of Jewish people lived in the vicinity of Jerusalem, the majority remained dispersed across the vast reaches of the ancient Persian Empire. The author no doubt hoped to stir in them much more than mere emotions of pity and sorrow related to the tragic stories of Judah's history. He was offering living proof of the lessons taught in the pages of that history. He intended that the message of 1 and 2 Chronicles would call them to the vital and solemn life of faith and hope, in which the lessons of trusting in the one God of righteousness and remembering His precepts took on extraordinary importance. They would take to heart the exhortation, "Believe in the Lord your God, and you will be established; believe his prophets, and you will succeed." (2 Chron. 20:20).

So, how does the author set about achieving this purpose? To understand the answer, it is necessary to see past some of the initial impressions a person might have about the book. A casual reader of 1 and 2 Chronicles, for example, while granting that the work includes an inspiring or beautiful verse here and there, might, nevertheless, conclude that at least at a superficial level it often appears unnecessary, uninteresting, defective, and even incredible in comparison with the books of Samuel and Kings.

Why those impressions? Some have thought 1 and 2 Chronicles *unnecessary* given that about half the books appear to be copied verbatim, or with some adaptations, from parts of Genesis, 1 and 2 Samuel, and 1 and 2 Kings. It may seem to others *uninteresting* given the extensive use of the name lists that recur throughout the work, many of which describe the pedigrees of various Levites, and actually seem to have little relevance for later readers. Still others have insisted that 1 and 2 Chronicles are *defective,* giving an exclusive history of Judah that largely ignores the story of the northern kingdom except for a few disparaging references when the actions of certain of its kings affected the history of Judah. Notice, for example, that virtually no mention is made of Elijah and Elisha or other heroic moments important to the history of God's people. On top of that, the stories reported, especially those of David and Solomon, seem to paint them with virtually none of the blemishes that play so prominently in the parallel accounts of the books of Samuel and Kings. Why no men-

SO WHERE IS THE ARK OF THE COVENANT?[1]

In spite of the famous archeological work of Dr. Henry Walton "Indiana" Jones, Jr., a great mystery still surrounds the disappearance of the Ark from history, and even from the biblical record itself. Was it in fact carried off or destroyed by the Babylonian emperor Nebuchadnezzar, either when he first invaded Judea, in 597 B.C., or when he destroyed Jerusalem in 586?

At least three other possibilities have been suggested: the Ark was carried to a hiding place at Mount Nebo (2 Maccabees 2:4–8); pious Israelites buried it safely somewhere within the Temple Mount itself (many have sought for it there); or it was transported to a shrine at Aksum, an ancient capital in northern Ethiopia, by way of Egypt and then up the Blue Nile to its headwaters at Lake Tana. Graham Hancock, an English journalist, made a very extensive investigation about the latter suggestion (*The Sign and the Seal,* 1992) but neither he nor anyone else, outside the designated Ethiopian "inner circle," has ever been allowed inside the Shrine of the Tabot (Ark).

As for the timing of the disappearance of the ancient Ark of Moses, it is suggestive that in the Bible itself the last references to it are those made by the king Josiah and the prophet Jeremiah. Josiah was a godly religious reformer, who reigned following the sinful misdeeds of his antecedents, the kings Manasseh and Amon. He speaks to the loyal Levites, those commissioned to care for the furniture of the Temple, and says to them, "Put the holy Ark in the house which Solomon . . . built. It shall no longer be a burden on your shoulders" (2 Chron. 35:3). There would be no need to say such a thing unless the Ark had been removed from the Temple to avoid desecration by the actions of those evil kings.

Jeremiah, on the other hand, speaks of the time when God's people will return to the holy land from their exile in Babylon. He says, "Then . . . in those days . . . they will say no more, 'The Ark of the covenant of the LORD.' It shall not come to mind, nor shall they remember it, nor shall they visit it, nor shall it be made anymore" (Jer. 3:16). His reason? Jerusalem itself, the entire city, will be called the "Throne of the LORD" (v. 17). There was no Ark in the post-exilic "Second Temple." This in turn points to the ultimate fulfillment of the Ark's purpose, God's presence with His people, by the coming to earth of God Himself, Jesus the Messiah, named Immanuel ("God with us") in the prophecy of Isaiah.

"Now when the queen of Sheba heard of the fame of Solomon, she came to Jerusalem to test Solomon with hard questions. . . ." Historically, Ethiopia was a Christian kingdom, and by the fifteenth century this African nation had developed a tradition of icon painting that rivaled the Orthodox empires of Byzantium and Russia. This illustration of the Queen of Sheba is based on a wall painting that was once in a church in Lalibela, Ethiopia.

tion of David's affair with Bathsheba or of Solomon's drift into paganism during the last years of his reign? Is this not a lopsided and inaccurate picture?

To top it all off, some have concluded that the book is frankly *incredible,* filled with exaggerations that tax the imagination of even the most sympathetic reader. The author appears to exaggerate numbers and amounts beyond all probability. Solomon appears to have amassed a fortune sufficient to meet any modern financial crisis. Jehoshaphat is reported has having 1,160,000 soldiers attending him *in Jerusalem*—this in spite of the emphasis on the fact that the issues of war turned not upon the numbers of soldiers, but upon the power of God! Indeed, whenever a king of Judah, threatened by foes, sought divine aid and obeyed the guidance of a true prophet, victory on a stupendous scale would follow, often without the need for the army to strike a blow (2 Chron. 20; cf. 13:3–20; 14:9–15). On the other hand, if the king relied on any other aid save God's, he suffered cataclysmic defeat, as when Ahaz lost 120,000 soldiers, and had 200,000 men, women, and children taken captive (2 Chron. 28:5-8).

So, what are we to make of all this? At the outset it is worth noting that the purpose and value of 1 and 2 Chronicles lies as much in the lessons they teach as in the history they report. While the lessons are certainly rooted in real history, it may be taken for granted that no decent historian ever attempts to merely recite the facts of the past, cataloging details that fill pages with information but not meaning. Any such work would certainly be a most imperfect survey, dry as dust, useful to only a few who would themselves try to make sense out of the raw data. A good historian consults the best sources, using them as accurately as possible, while at the same time developing themes that make the facts and details meaningful. We ask from a historian both a record of what *happened*, and also a record of what *mattered*, especially with respect to the interests of later readers. We expect the historian to select wisely from available knowledge that which seems to him the most salient and meaningful facts.

In just this way, the author of 1 and 2 Chronicles sets out to depict what mattered in the history of God's people. To accomplish that, he made use of well-known historical accounts but also felt free to emphasize some parts and de-emphasize others in order to produce a narrative that was obviously idealized, but which must have impressed his contemporaries with the things that were really important. He pictures for them how to live and worship rightly, emphasizing the bedrock reality of God and His truth, and the irresistible nature of His designs. The New Testament Gospel writers do the same kind of thing as they report the life of Christ. Each preserves faithfully the underlying events and sayings of Jesus, but also advances its own distinct concerns, and these concerns become noticeable by examining both what is included as well as what is passed over. In just the same way, the author of 1 and 2 Chronicles presents a history that also portrays the principles that enable God's people to faithfully work through life's challenges and choices.

Although these sorts of liberties are taken, at the same time, a set of specific historical events provide the underlying bulwarks against which the story ebbs and flows. These events must be kept in mind. Some of the more important include the following:

1. In 722 B.C., the kingdom of Israel fell to Sargon II of Assyria, who deported some 30,000 Israelites, replacing them with alien settlers.
2. In 586 B.C., the kingdom of Judah similarly fell to Nebuchadnezzar and his Babylonian army, and they sacked Jerusalem, broke down its walls, burned its Temple and palace, and deported its leading citizens and craftsmen to Babylon.
3. Cyrus the Persian conquered Babylon in 539 B.C., releasing the Jewish exiles to return to their homeland if they wished. Some of those who returned were undoubtedly descendents from the official priesthood that traced its lineage back to Aaron—men known at the time as Zadokites in honor of Zadok, the high priest who served under King David.
4. In 516 B.C., construction of a new Temple in Jerusalem was completed. This venue for Jewish worship, commonly known as the Second Temple, seemed humble compared to Solomon's magnificent structure, but it nevertheless inspired high hopes for the future of the Holy City and its people.
5. In about 445 B.C., Nehemiah was appointed governor of Jerusalem and set about the task of rebuilding the ruined walls of the city.
6. During the governorship of Nehemiah, some 1,800 Jews led by Ezra returned to Jerusalem from Babylon, including among them 262 Levites.

The reader of 1 and 2 Chronicles cannot help but notice the extraordinary attention devoted to the Temple and its priests, Levites, musicians, custodians, and other religious staff. Why this emphasis? The answer lies in recalling what had happened in the vicinity of Jerusalem immediately after the Babylonians overthrew it in 586 B.C. While many of the wealthy and noble were deported, many others—the so-called "poor of the land"—remained. Though traumatized at first, these Hebrews eventually recovered some sense of normalcy, albeit greatly modified compared to their prior existence. As these people attempted to understand the calamities that had befallen them, they inevitably must have reflected on the teachings of the prophets who had unambiguously

The Western Wall (also called the Wailing Wall) of the Temple in Jerusalem is a remnant of Herod's Temple after the Romans destroyed the city in A.D. 70. The ornate Dome of the Rock was built in A.D. 691 atop the Temple Mount as a shrine for Islamic pilgrims.

predicted and warned of the very disaster now so richly evident before their eyes. These residents faced up to the fact that the overthrow of their city, kingdom, and way of life was certainly not because the gods of the Babylonians were mightier than the God of Israel, but rather precisely because there really was and is only one God—the Almighty, Yahweh—whose will is just and whose power is irresistible. The disaster had come just as prophets had foreseen, a just retribution for their fathers' and their own iniquities (cf. Lam. 2; 4:13). Now at long last, many of those who had turned a deaf ear to the pleadings of Jeremiah, Zephaniah, Ezekiel, Habakkuk, and others came face to face with a most sobering thought: All this had befallen them for no other reason than that God was perfectly righteous, just, powerful, and true.

Within a few years of Jerusalem's fall, and long before 539 B.C., the worship of God had undoubtedly resumed in the sacred precincts of Jerusalem. Of course the Temple, the Ark of the Covenant, and the other sacred vessels were long gone. Nothing but an eyesore remained—a persistent reminder of lost glory. The people nevertheless offered prayer and praise at the holy site. It is even likely that some limited rituals of worship were re-instituted. While the people gained comfort from the restored routines, their comfort was mixed with a nagging question for which no certain answer could be provided. Who was qualified to lead such worship? Without a priestly caste qualified by ceremony and genealogy, who was truly worthy?

If, as seems probable, such narrowly qualified leaders were in short supply, were there others who could fill in, without once again arousing the anger of the God whose judgments had been so recently poured out? Was

"Solomon gave orders to build a Temple for the Name of the LORD and a royal palace for himself. He conscripted seventy thousand men as carriers and eighty thousand as stonecutters in the hills and thirty-six hundred as foremen over them." (Chron. 2:1–2)

there any precedent for such a thing? As it turned out, there did seem to be an example from Israel's history.

Some years earlier (c. 620 B.C.) the young King Josiah had launched a reform movement more radical than any since the time of David. In his attempts to purify the life of worship, and hopefully avert or postpone God's judgment, he destroyed great numbers of alternative worship venues scattered across Israel and Samaria. He passed laws prohibiting ritual worship anywhere but at the central sanctuary in Jerusalem. His decree may have been devastating to many Levites who had served in various outlying locations without the clear-cut sanction of the inner priestly circle. Josiah's command basically left these "country" Levites unemployed, because they could no longer lead worship in the outlying areas and were not qualified to lead worship at the central sanctuary. Josiah attempted to balance the harsh effects of his reforms with a small dose of leniency, however, granting permission to Levites not strictly within the priestly family to serve in some capacities at the Temple.

When Jerusalem was leveled in 586 B.C., many of its Zadokite clergy were killed or deported, and the tightly knit hierarchy of priests organized under Solomon was essentially dismantled. As worship resumed, a few Zadokites may have returned, but it is likely that the "country" Levites provided a great deal of the priestly service. Even when the Temple was restored in 516 B.C. under Darius I, the need for additional priests was likely supplied by these "country" ministers. The mixture of the Zadokite priests with the less qualified Levites apparently gave rise to some disputes, in which the Zadokites began to assert superiority against the Levites. It may also be the case that the Jewish people of Jerusalem entertained some prejudice against those who had lived in Samaria. Many interpreters of 1 and 2 Chronicles have found considerable evidence that the book was written in part as a criticism of the narrow-minded, vested-interest attitude of some "insiders" against the rest. The author's underlying theme seems to argue powerfully that the faithful Levites of Israel had full right to serve at the Temple, even if they were not in the narrow family of Zadok, and that even those Jewish people who had lived in Samaria should be granted access to the place of worship in spite of earlier years as apostates.

Opposing the narrow and petty jealousy, the author painted a picture of the value of communion and fellowship among God's people. He insisted there should be but one Hebrew people, encouraging them to forget the old prejudices and accept these faithful Levite ministers as their brethren and fellow servants (see e.g., 2 Chron. 29:34ff and 30:25ff). The author exhorted them to think again about the coronation of David, when 400,000 inhabitants of the north had joined 22,000 Judeans in the great celebration (1 Chron. 12:23–38). He reminded them that when two good kings—Hezekiah and Josiah— reigned in Jerusalem, a huge number of Israelites from the north had come to keep Passover, itself a celebration of deliverance and unity (2 Chron. 30; 35).

For us, the message of 1 and 2 Chronicles stands as a constant reminder that God looks on the heart. Without disparaging external form and ceremony, we are consistently reminded that God prefers "mercy" to "sacrifice." Christ, of course, is what all the Old Testament pointed forward to. First and Second Chronicles anticipate the New Testament principle that the true worshippers of God will worship in spirit and truth, the author insisting that God's people must unite behaviors of respect and order with hearts of reverence and humility. We see in 1 and 2 Chronicles history from the perspective of the Temple, from the point of view of the sacrifice, from the viewpoint of the High Priest—from the perspective of justification and sins forgiven by the blood of Christ. In this way, God's kingdom is truly realized and his worship rightly exhibited.

—Bruce W. Gore

For Further Reading

The Interpreters Bible, Vol. 3. New York: Abingdon Press, 1954.

Spence-Jones, H.D.M., ed. and Exell, Joseph. *The Pulpit Commentary*. New York: Funk and Wagnalls, 1950.

Veritas Press Bible Cards: Judges through Kings. Lancaster, Pa: Veritas Press. 59, 65, 71, 77–79.

Veritas Press Bible Cards: Chronicles through Malachi. Lancaster, Pa: Veritas Press. 93.

Session I: Prelude

A Question to Consider

How do hard experiences produce godly character?

From the General Information above and your knowledge of the Old Testament, please answer the following questions:

1. Why were the people of God forced to leave their homeland under the Assyrians (722 B.C.) and again later under the Babylonians (586 B.C.)?
2. The only non-Jewish man in the Old Testament to be called a "messiah" was Cyrus the Persian (Isa. 45:1). Read Isaiah 44:24–45:7. What are the achievements attributed to Cyrus by the prophet?
3. In what way do the actions of Cyrus represent a reversal of the policies imposed by the Assyrians and the Babylonians?
4. Many believe that the author of 1 and 2 hronicles was the Jewish scholar Ezra. Look over Ezra 8:15–36. From your reading of this text, what sort of man would you take Ezra to be?
5. The books of 1 and 2 Chronicles highlight the careers of King David and King Solomon. From your general knowledge of Old Testament history and your reading of the general information above, in what respects were David and Solomon similar? In what respects were they very different?
6. The author of 1 and 2 Chronicles is, among other things, telling a great and sweeping story. Why are stories so powerful as a means of communicating truth?

The next session will be a student-led discussion. Students will be creating their own questions concerning the issue of the session. Students should create three Text Analysis Questions, two Cultural Analysis questions, and two Biblical Analysis questions. For more detailed instructions, please see the chapter on *Death on the Nile*, Session V.

Issue

What does the Ark of the Covenant represent?

Reading Assignment:
1 Chronicles 1–16

Session II: Student-Led Discussion
1 Chronicles 11–16

A Question to Consider

What does the Ark of the Covenant represent?

Students should read and consider the example questions below that are connected to the Question to Consider above. Last session's assignment was to prepare three questions and answers for the Text Analysis section and two additional questions and answers for both the Cultural and Biblical Analysis sections below.

Text Analysis

Example: Why was Uzzah struck dead as he was involved in bringing the Ark of the Covenant to Jerusalem (1 Chron. 13)?

Answer: Uzzah was disobedient to God in several respects. For example, the Ark should have been carried on poles, not an ox cart. As a Kohathite, he was charged never to touch the Ark, lest he die (Num. 4:15). All this was related to the holiness of the sacred objects and the special care to be used in connection with their handling.

Cultural Analysis

Example: Are there "holy objects" in our culture? Are there people, ideas, words, or other things that are off-limits or that will result in "judgment" if violated?

Answer: Every culture has ideas that are off limits—sometimes called "taboos" or "sacred cows." In some cases it is impermissible to question environmentalism, women's rights, naturalistic evolution, multiculturalism, etc., without running grave risk of a social "judgment" for the violation. This law of "politically correct" speech can have a huge effect on public discussion and debate.

Other cultural issues to consider: While the above examples may appear to be a negative aspect of culture, what are some examples of holy objects or people that have a positive effect in culture?

The Ark was a sacred chest made of acacia wood with gold overlay. It resided in the "holy of holies" in the Tent of Meeting (Tabernacle) and then in Solomon's Temple. The Ark's golden cover was named the "Mercy Seat," and it included two cherubim of beaten gold facing each other, their outspread wings touching at the tips. The Mercy Seat symbolized both the throne of Jehovah God, the Great King, and the place of atonement, His forgiving grace. It was the place where the High Priest, and he alone, would once a year—on the Day of Atonement—sprinkle the sacrificial blood for the covering of sins on behalf of all the people.

First and Second Chronicles 517

Biblical Analysis

Example: What is the proper role of sacred things from a biblical perspective?

Answer: Certainly the Bible has much to say about the idea of sacred times, places, and people. The Sabbath was said to be holy, and therefore to be specially respected. The Tabernacle, and later the Temple, were holy places, and indeed the most important of these was called "the holy of holies." A culture may also designate certain things as "holy" in a sense, and worthy of special respect. The National Archives in Washington, D.C., hallow certain pieces of paper as the "holy objects" of the United States, to be cherished and revered. Besides this, traditional American culture has hallowed certain symbols such as the flag, or times such as the Fourth of July.

Other scriptures to consider: Isaiah 6; Revelation 4

SUMMA

Write an essay or discuss this question, integrating what you have learned from the material above.

How should a Christian make the distinction between recognizing holy things as a good and positive aspect of life, as opposed to holy things that actually compete with God's rule and His glory?

Instead of a reading assignment you have a research assignment. Tomorrow's session will be a Current Events session. Your assignment will be to find a story online, in a magazine, or in the newspaper that relates to the issue that you discussed today. Your task is to locate the article, give a copy of the article to your teacher or parent and provide some of your own worldview analysis to the article. Your analysis should demonstrate that you understand the issue, that you can clearly connect the story you found to the issue that you discussed today, and that you can provide a biblical critique of this issue in today's context. Look at the next session to see the three-part format that you should follow.

Issue

Distinguishing true "holiness" from a false "holiness"

READING ASSIGNMENT:
None

Session III: Current Events
1 Chronicles 13

Issue
Holy things

Current events sessions are meant to challenge you to connect what you are learning in Omnibus class to what is happening in the world around you today. After the last session, your assignment was to find a story online or in a magazine or newspaper relating to the issue above. Today you will share your article and your analysis with your teacher and classmates or parents and family. Your analysis should follow the format below:

Brief Introductory Paragraph:
In this paragraph you will tell your classmates about the article that you found. Be sure to include where you found your article, who the author of your article is, and what your article is about. This brief paragraph of your presentation should begin like this:

> Hello, I am Bruce Gore, and my current events article is "200 years on, Lincoln mesmerizes the nation. As Washington marks anniversary, even tiniest relics command reverence" which I found on MSN.com.

Connection Paragraph:
In this paragraph you must demonstrate how your article is connected to the issue that you are studying. This paragraph should be short, and it should focus on clearly showing the connection between the book that you are reading and the current events article that you have found. This paragraph should begin with a sentence like

> I knew that my article was linked to our issue because...

I knew my article was linked to our issue because the subtitle, "...even tiniest relics command reverence" suggests the sense in which Abraham Lincoln has become a national icon of superhuman proportions. Lincoln and his memory have become "holy" objects of American culture. The article details the exaggerated estimate of the man, as illustrated by the following quote:

> The remaining bits of him, locks of hair and pieces of bone among them, are sacred. Things he said or wrote are cherished. But he's still a mystery. "He's approachable and unreachable at the same time," said historian Harold Holzer. Lincoln said he detested slavery but would maintain it to save the Union. He spoke often of religion yet never joined a church. At the peak of his prestige, he was silenced by assassination.

Christian Worldview Analysis:
In this section, you need to tell us how we should respond as believers to this issue today. This response should focus both on our thinking and on practical actions that we should take in light of this issue. As you list these steps, you should also tell us why we should think and act in the ways you recommend. This paragraph should begin with a sentence like

> As believers, we should think and act in the following ways in light of this issue and this article.

The paragraph can continue like this:

> First, we should recognize that there should be sacred objects, places, and people. This is normal and healthy, both in the context of religious devotion, but also in the context of cultural identity. The danger, however, is two-fold. First, a cultural icon may be so elevated that all objectivity is lost, and the ability to consider someone like Lincoln from a detached historical perspective becomes much more difficult. Second, if the cultural icon is actually negative or evil, a matter of calling something good that God calls evil, it becomes extraordinarily difficult to offer a critique without arousing disproportionate hostility from the culture and its media.

Reading Assignment:
1 Chronicles 17–22

Session IV: Recitation
1 Chronicles 17–22

Comprehension Questions
Answer these questions for factual recall.

1. Why is David forbidden to "build a house" for God (1 Chron. 17:4)?
2. What does God mean when he says to David, "I will build a house for you!" (1 Chron. 17:10)?
3. What is the fundamental attitude reflected by King David in his prayer following the announcement given to him by the prophet Nathan (1 Chron. 17:16–27)?

4. In what way does the account of David's victories in chapter 18 confirm the promises made to him in chapter 17?
5. What is the difference between the attitude of David and that of Hanun as reflected in chapter 19? What lesson of character is the author hoping to communicate in this story?
6. In chapter 20, the account of David's relationship with Bathsheba is conspicuously omitted. Why do you suppose the author chose to skip over that rather significant failing on David's part?
7. Why was it wrong for David to take a census of the people of Israel (1 Chron. 21:1)?
8. The author omitted the well-known story of David's relationship with Bathsheba, but he included the story of David's sinful decision to number the people. Why do you suppose one was included and one excluded?
9. How does David stop the spread of the plague following his census?
10. What lesson does the author hope the reader will learn as he describes David's actions to stop the plague?
11. Immediately following the story of the plague, the author details David's preparations for building the Temple. What is the connection between these two stories?
12. What is the principal message that David wishes to communicate to his son Solomon as he instructs him with regard to the building the Temple?

READING ASSIGNMENT:
2 Chronicles 1–9

SESSION V: WRITING
2 Chronicles 1–9

The Queen of Sheba's Diary

This session is a writing assignment. Remember, quality counts more than quantity. You should write no more than 1,000 words, either typing or writing legibly on one side of a sheet of paper. You will lose points for writing more than this. You will be allowed to turn in your writing three times. The first and second times you turn it in, your teacher will grade it by editing your work. This is done by marking problem areas and making suggestions for improvement. You should take these suggestions into consideration as you revise your assignment. Only the grade on your final submission will be recorded. Your grade will be based on the following criteria: 25 points for grammar, 25 points for content accuracy— historical, theological, etc.; 25 points for logic—does this make sense and is it structured well?; 25 points for rhetoric—is it a joy to read?

DESCRIPTION

Your assignment is to write a description following the direction provided below. This may be more difficult than it sounds! Make sure your description guides a reader into an experience of the object. Use language that stirs the senses (what does it look, sound, feel, smell, or taste like?). Make judgments about the object as you describe it. Remember the great rule of description—Show us; don't tell us. Do not tell us that something is good or beautiful or likable. Describe it in a way that shows your reader the object's beauty or ugliness, its goodness, or wickedness.

Give a firsthand (first person) description of the experience of the Queen of Sheba (2 Chron. 9) when she visited Solomon. You should include an account of her initial skepticism, and explain her sense of being overwhelmed at what she saw and heard.

READING ASSIGNMENT:
2 Chronicles 10–19

SESSION VI: AESTHETICS
2 Chronicles 10–19

Art Analysis

In this session, you will get to know a particular piece or type of art related to our reading. It is our job as believers to be able to praise, love, and protect what is beautiful and to condemn, hate, and oppose all that is truly ugly. This task is often harder than one might think at first. We have to first examine and understand the piece objectively. From there it is necessary to try to discern the author's intent, to figure out what the message of the artist might be. Sometimes this is fairly obvious; at other times it might be difficult or impossible. Finally, we need to make our own judgment about the work of art. We might decide that the art piece is untrue, badly done, or wicked. We might on the other hand find we can praise a work as glorious, majestic and true. Often we might find that we can affirm some parts of a work and condemn other parts. It is a mark of immaturity to leap to judgments. It is a mark of maturity to exercise discipline, and it is certainly true that our praise or condemnation means much more after we have first exercised discipline to reflect on the content and meaning of a work.

King Asa of Judah Destroying the Idols

This painting,[2] the most dramatic of de Nomé, is based on the episode in 2 Chronicles 15, in which King Asa destroys a pagan temple in an attempt to restore the people's faith in the one true God. The scene is odd, however, with the right half showing destruction and collapse, while the scene on the left seems unexpectedly serene and peaceful. The source of the destruction is not visible, and apparently not present—as if it were a force off stage. The view is therefore not exactly real and is intended to arouse emotion, rather than portray an event as it actually might have happened.

François de Nomé (c. 1593–c. 1644) was a French painter active during the Baroque era. He also painted under the pseudonym of Monsù Desiderio with several other artists, including his compatriot Didier Barra. His style is almost surrealistic, featuring overcast skies and buildings in ruins.

Technical Analysis

1. Does this work demonstrate the artist's ability and expertise?
2. Describe the scene. What is happening?
3. Does this have balance and symmetry? What is the central or most important element of this work? (To what are your eyes most attracted?)
4. Is this work realistic and proportional or not?
5. How is light used in this work?
6. What colors are used in this work?

Subject Analysis

1. What role is played by the human figures in this painting? Can you tell who they are or what they are doing?
2. What do you suppose is the meaning of the odd contrast between the right side of the painting, filled with destruction, and the left side, which seems undisturbed?
3. What sort of architecture is suggested by the pillars and statuary on the left?
4. How does the lighting in the painting help to communicate its message?

Content Analysis

1. What is the message of this work?
2. What is worthy of praise in this work? What is worthy of condemnation?

OPTIONAL SESSION A: ACTIVITY

The Trial of Josiah

Note to students working alone: This activity will prove meaningful enough to make special efforts to include others. They may be other children near the same age, or it may be worth considering including the entire family.

Today we are going to serve as judge and jury as we consider the case that could be laid out against King Josiah, based on his decision to attack Necho II, Pharaoh of Egypt, as recorded in 2 Chronicles 35:20ff. To do this, follow these steps:

Elect a judge, a prosecutor (to set forth the case against Josiah) and a defense attorney (for Josiah).

The rest of you will be the witnesses and the jury. List charges that could be made against Josiah and the things that might mitigate or lessen his guilt. The judge should write out the charges on the blackboard for all to see. The prosecuting and defense attorney should write the charges on notebook paper.

King Asa of Judah Destroying the Idols is by French painter Francois de Nomé (c. 1593–c. 1644).

The prosecution will then set forth its case, then the defense will have their cases. (Limit the time for presentation by each side.)

The jury should then decide whether Josiah was guilty of unjust warfare (the purposeful, intentional, and unjust declaration of war against the king of Egypt) or negligence (a reckless disregard for the well-being of his nation in meeting Necho in battle). The jury may acquit Josiah on the grounds that he was justified in his actions, based especially on the prophecy of Jeremiah, who had declared repeatedly over the years that God would use Babylon as the instrument of his punishment, and the fact that Necho was attacking Babylon at Carchemish.

OPTIONAL SESSION B: POETRY

Lamentation

In this session you will be challenged to write poetry in a certain form about a particular object, person, event or idea. The challenge for the poet is to lay bare the heart of the truth in language that is beautiful and that inspires its reader to love what is pure and righteous or to hate what is wicked and evil. The best poetry marries true philosophy and beautiful rhetoric.

Writing poetry is a real challenge, so we are providing a sample for you to follow. Remember, poetry is hard, but rewarding work. Consider carefully the following familiar poem of Robert Frost:

Whose woods these are I think I know.
His house is in the village, though;
He will not see me stopping here
To watch his woods fill up with snow.

My little horse must think it queer
To stop without a farmhouse near
Between the woods and frozen lake
The darkest evening of the year.

He gives his harness bells a shake
To ask if there is some mistake.
The only other sounds the sweep
Of easy wind and downy flake.

The woods are lovely, dark, and deep,
But I have promises to keep,
And miles to go before I sleep,
And miles to go before I sleep.

The poem consists of four (almost) identically constructed stanzas. Each line is iambic, with four stressed syllables: Within the four lines of each stanza, the first, second, and fourth lines rhyme. The third line does not, but it sets up the rhymes for the next stanza. For example, in the third stanza, *queer, near,* and *year* all rhyme, but *lake* rhymes with *shake, mistake,* and flake in the following stanza.

The notable exception to this pattern comes in the final stanza, where the third line rhymes with the previous two and is repeated as the fourth line.

Do not be fooled by the simple words and the easiness of the rhymes; this is a very difficult form to achieve in English without debilitating a poem's content with forced rhymes.

Write a lament, in a similar form as the poem by Frost above, as if by Jeremiah, reflecting on the loss of good King Josiah in his battle with Necho. Follow the form of four stanzas of four lines each. If you can get the lines to rhyme without making the language stilted and awkward, do so. If not, be content with good, non-rhyming poetry.

ENDNOTES

1   Adapted from Dr. Milton C. Fisher's forthcoming book, *Through Days of Preparation.* Dr. Fisher worked on portions of the Old Testament for the initial publication the New International Version of the Bible. He has also been involved over the years in lecturing on biblical archaeology as well as participating in digs in Israel related to biblical history.

2   At the time of publication, this art could be viewed online at Link 1 for this chapter at www.VeritasPress.com/OmniLinks.

Ezra, Nehemiah, & Esther

Many athletes have had the disconcerting experience of playing against another team and having to play against the referees as well. A challenging team is difficult enough, but when the other team appears to have recruited the refs as well, it sometimes does not seem worth the effort.

In the books of Ezra, Nehemiah, and Esther, we have a demonstration of how to play faithfully when this kind of thing happens to you. In all three books, the leading characters come into sharp conflict with pagan unbelievers, and so an appeal must be made … to pagan unbelievers. And yet, because God is sovereign over all things, it is possible to be in this position and still not lose.

Nehemiah, the Bible's premiere businessman. He worked in the world at the highest level of civil service then led God's people through a nigh-impossible building project—balancing people's needs, fiscal responsibilites and outside pressures from a "hostile market."

GENERAL INFORMATION

Author and Context

We have before us the books of Ezra and Nehemiah, which were probably one book originally, and the book of Esther, which is closely related. Moreover, it is even possible that Chronicles/Ezra/Nehemiah was originally one book. These books are the last three books in the Hebrew ordering of the Old Testament, and Nehemiah is actually part of Ezra in the Hebrew Bible. As we work through these books together, it would obviously be helpful for you not only to read through these books, but also through the books of Zechariah and Haggai as well. In order to get from books everything that we would like to get, one of our first responsibilities is that of getting oriented.

With Ezra and Nehemiah, the author is probably Ezra—he was a scribe, after all, and he was involved in the action. He was certainly in a position to write this account. But the books themselves do not make this claim, and so we cannot be dogmatic about it. The tone and viewpoint taken in Esther makes it unlikely that Ezra was the author of that story, but we are dealing with the same general outlook shared by the faithful Jews in exile or just coming out of exile.

Significance

The entire Bible gives us the story of a running battle between the seed of the serpent and the seed of the woman. In this longstanding battle, the presence of the great Persian Empire is almost irrelevant—it is the scene for just one of the chapters. The battle began long before the rise of the Persians, and it has continued long after they ceased to be a great power.

As the story of a long war, we have just what you would expect under such circumstances. There are many battles—not just one. Some of them go very well indeed, and others are disasters. We have the protagonists falling into sin and under chastisement, coming to repentance, and being restored. We have a mission assigned to them, which was neglected and therefore failed. But then we have men raised up by God who are eager to return to the mission and equipped by Him to do so—men like Ezra and Nehemiah.

And in the book of Esther, the antagonist Haman was an Agagite, a descendant of Agag. He was the king of the Amalekites, the one whom Samuel killed after Saul had declined to do so. And Mordecai was descended from Kish…Saul's father. When the curtain opens in the book of Esther, the lines are already drawn for a redemptive showdown.

Setting

We are not going to work through these books verse by verse, but it is prudent for us at the beginning to stop at the first verse and ask the questions we need to ask to keep from getting disoriented. "Now in the first year of Cyrus king of Persia, that the word of the Lord by the mouth of Jeremiah might be fulfilled, the Lord stirred up the spirit of Cyrus king of Persia, that he made a proclamation throughout all his kingdom, and put it also in writing, saying . . ." (Ezra 1:1). It is also necessary to explain that on matters of biblical chronology, there is almost always considerable disagreement, so it is necessary for me to explain what chronology we are following here—even if we do not take the time to try to prove it in exhaustive detail. So we begin with Cyrus. Who is he? And what proclamation is this talking about?

The modern Iranians are descended from the Persians, and we will begin by getting straight on their kings from this period. We will start by using the Greek names for them, which are the most common.

Cyrus reigned from 539 to 530 B.C.
Cambyses II reigned from 530 to 522 B.C.
Darius I reigned from 521 to 486 B.C.
Xerxes I reigned from 486 to 465 B.C.
Artaxerxes Longimanus reigned from 465 to 425 B.C.

This period, therefore, stretches from 539 B.C. to 425 B.C. During this time, the Greeks defeated the Persians at Marathon and Salamis, Pericles reigned in Athens, the Greek tragedians flourished, Socrates taught, Cincinnatus was dictator in Rome, and the Buddha and Confucius both lived and died. You might have read about many of these events both in Scripture and in Herodotus's *Histories* covered in *Omnibus I*.

Worldview Essay

As we seek to keep track of all the characters in these important stories, we have a real difficulty. The problem is one of identifying individuals who sat on thrones when we have to take account of the fact that these rulers often used throne names, and not just personal names. We know this readily in other circumstances. If someone today were to refer to "Caesar," a natural question would be, "Which one?" The same is true of "Pharaoh." One of the things we have to deal with is the very real possibility that *Darius* and *Artaxerxes* were throne names. Other throne names in the Bible would be Ben-Hadad (Jer. 49:27; Amos 1:4) or Abimelech (Gen. 20, 26; Ps. 34). So the assumption in the chronology used here is that the shift from Darius to Artaxerxes in Ezra 7 does *not* represent the reign of a different king, but rather a change in the name used for him.

The operating assumption in this approach to the chronology of these books is that the Persian kings named "Darius, Ahasuerus, and Artaxerxes in the books of Ezra, Nehemiah and Esther" are all the same man. In doing this, I am following James Jordan in his important monograph on the subject. I am not following the chronologies of the broader evangelical world here because there seems to be too great a willingness to make biblical statements conform to what we (think we) know about secular history instead of the other way around. And in my mind, this has ramifications for the doctrine of biblical inspiration and infallibility.

Most Bible commentaries assume that the Artaxerxes found in Ezra 7 and following, and in Nehemiah, is Longimanus. This dates the latter part of Ezra between 465–25 B.C. But since the book opens with Cyrus, the beginning of the book is many years before this (in 539 B.C.). If Ezra 1–6 occurs in the early years of Darius, this brings us down to 516 B.C. Then at Ezra 7, we have to skip 57 years, coming down to 459, the seventh year of Artaxerxes. Then Nehemiah takes us even further down the road to the 33rd year of Artaxerxes (433 B.C.). The standard view, therefore, stretches the events of these books over the better part of a century. I am assuming here instead that we need to *telescope* them, and that it all pretty much happened in the reign of Darius. This makes Ezra and Nehemiah contemporaries.

But most Bible chronologists take Artaxerxes (of Ezra) to be Darius. As we study this, remember that Christians of good will differ on these things, and the confusion about these identifications is ancient, even going back to Josephus and the apocryphal books. But if you want to even *attempt* to sort out the history of these books, you have to make certain operating assumptions.

Here are just a few examples from the text as to why I think this telescoped chronology is to be preferred. I said earlier that the matter of biblical infallibility and sufficiency is really at stake, and I want to give just a couple examples of this sort of thing.

Ezra is mentioned in Nehemiah: "And his brethren, Shemaiah, and Azarael, Milalai, Gilalai, Maai, Nethaneel, and Judah, Hanani, with the musical instruments of David the man of God, *and Ezra the scribe before them*. And at the fountain gate, which was over against them, they went up by the stairs of the city of David, at the going up of the wall, above the house of David, even unto the water gate eastward" (Neh. 12:36–37).

Nehemiah is mentioned in Ezra: "Now these are the children of the province that went up out of the captivity, of those which had been carried away, whom Nebuchad-

Although he worked in other media, like stained glass, Marc Chagall once said "My art is an extravagant art, a flaming vermilion, a blue soul flooding over my paintings." This is his lithograph called *Esther*.

nezzar the king of Babylon had carried away unto Babylon, and came again unto Jerusalem and Judah, every one unto his city; Which came with Zerubbabel: Jeshua, *Nehemiah*, Seraiah, Reelaiah, *Mordecai*, Bilshan, Mispar, Bigvai, Rehum, Baanah" (Ezra 2:1–2; *cf.* Neh. 7:7). Unless the writer is trying to confuse us, we should assume that a different Nehemiah would be identified as such (as he in fact was in Neh. 3:16).

Mordecai is mentioned in Ezra also: In the verse quoted above, look at the third name after Nehemiah—Mordecai. Why would this not be the great Mordecai of Esther 10:3? How many Jews would have this Persian name (which, incidentally, meant "man of Marduk")?

All this leads us to a short, telescoped chronology for these books instead of a long chronology. But far more is at stake than simply dates. What matters most is whether we really trust the Word of God in all details.

Another important lesson for us in these books concerns what it teaches us about living with pagan empires. The world is a messy place. Part of the mess for believers is learning to tell the difference between situations that call for martyrdom and those that call for godly acquiescence. One of the more common set-ups where such wisdom is required is when pagan empires are in control. To what extent are we godly members of such a society, and to what extent are we to be radically distinct from it?

> "Now in the first year of Cyrus king of Persia, that the word of the LORD by the mouth of Jeremiah might be fulfilled, the LORD stirred up the spirit of Cyrus king of Persia, that he made a proclamation throughout all his kingdom, and put it also in writing, saying, Thus saith Cyrus king of Persia, The LORD God of heaven hath given me all the kingdoms of the earth; and he hath charged me to build him an house at Jerusalem, which is in Judah…" (Ezra 1:1–11).

Cyrus was a pagan king, and yet it was the Lord who stirred up his spirit to make the proclamation he made (v. 1). In the prophetic word of Isaiah, Cyrus is even called a messiah, an anointed one (Is. 45:1). Cyrus acknowledges that it was the "Lord God of heaven" who granted him his authority and tasked him with the responsibility to build a temple in Jerusalem (v. 2). So the pagan king asks, "Are there any Jews who will go?" (v. 3). Further, the Jews who do not return are charged to help with the task financially (v. 4). In response, three tribes rose up—Judah, Benjamin, and Levi—to return to their ancestral home to build the house of the Lord (v. 5). In addition, from those around there was a willing outpouring of financial support (v. 6). For his part, Cyrus

brought out the vessels from the house of the Lord that Nebuchadnezzar had captured and placed before his pagan gods (v. 7). Midredath the treasurer gave a careful accounting of them to Sheshbazzar, the prince of Judah (v. 8). The details of the transferred treasure were then given (vs. 9–11).

What Cyrus says here in this text sounds pretty good. He wants to build a temple to the true God, he acknowledges that the true God gave him authority over all the nations, and he requires the work be done by the people of God. Moreover, we learn here that the Spirit of God really did motivate him to do this—the heart of the king is in the Lord's hand (Prov. 21:1). So God is at work in Cyrus in Isaiah (Is. 45:1).

But right around the same time, for example, Cyrus gave orders to have the Temple of Sin at Ur of the Chaldees restored. The name Sin was not our "sin," but rather was the name of their moon god. Cyrus went so far as to have the bricks for that temple inscribed with the following: "Sin, the illuminator of heaven and earth, with his favorite sign delivered into my hand the four quarters of the world, and I returned the gods to their shrines. The great gods have delivered all the lands into my hands: the land I have caused to dwell in peaceful habitation."

Cyrus was a religious pragmatist, one who believed in appeasing all the gods. And yet, although he had his own compromised and sinful motives, the Spirit of the Lord on him was not constrained by those motives. And this is why the faithful who are living under pagan emperors must learn to *distinguish* the work of God and the work of man. An artifact called the Cyrus Prism was discovered in 1879, and this excerpt describes very well the policy of Cyrus, along with his reasons for it. But we must not let these reasons trump what the Bible says the real reason was.

> I am Cyrus, King of the World … whose rule Bel and Nebo love, whom they want as king to please their hearts … Marduk, the great lord, induced the magnanimous inhabitants of Babylon to love me, and I was daily endeavoring to worship him … I returned to these sacred cities on the other side of the Tigris the sanctuaries of which have been ruins for a long time, the images which used to live therein and established for them permanent sanctuaries. I also gathered all their former inhabitants and returned them to their habitations. Furthermore, I resettled upon the command of Marduk, the great lord, all the gods of Kiengir and Akkad whom Nabonidus had brought into Babylon to the anger of the lord of the gods, unharmed, in their former temples, the places which make them happy.

Empires come in two kinds. There is the ideological empire, the kind that is fundamentally at war with all who do not conform to its dictates. The attempted reign of Marxism was like this, and the expanding Muslim world is like this—conform or die. We are accustomed to think of this kind of empire as the only kind of tyranny there is. But we have to be careful. The other kind of empire is the syncretistic, pragmatic empire. This empire says you can worship whoever you want, so long as you do nothing to challenge the real god of the system, which is the life of the empire itself, or the circulatory system of that life, which is usually money. Rome was like this, and the rising American empire is like this. The empire of Cyrus was very much like this, and the lives of Ezra and Nehemiah provide us with great wisdom in how to live our lives in a similar situation.

The Spirit of God is not hamstrung by the presence of human sin. We persist in thinking that divine action and human action displace one another, as though they were a couple of billiard balls. If one moves in, the other moves out. But in the sin of Cyrus, the spirit of God stirred him up in order to bless the Jews. The fact that *he* thought he was doing the same thing (for the same reasons) to all the gods of all the other peoples did not alter what was actually happening. God draws straight with crooked lines. God is sovereign. And this glorious dogma is saying much more than just the truth that God is big. God is the uncreated Creator—He is not Zeus; He is not Marduk. Those outside cannot be expected to know this, but we are His people, and so we must know it.

So for us, the central issue is always worship. In a syncretistic empire, what are the lines past which we may not go? The line of division is always worship. While we may cooperate with unbelievers on various projects and tasks, and may even take help from them, we may not do so if the price on the tag spells "compromise in worship." And compromise in worship would be defined as altering or modifying our own worship of the true God to suit them (Dan. 6:11), or of joining with them in the worship of their deities—even if they allow us to continue worshiping our God as well (Dan. 3:12–14). Daniel would not stop praying to his God in order to please them. His faith had nothing to do with them. And his three friends would not bow down to the image of Nebuchadnezzar, because he was not the true God.

The United States is moving into an imperial era. We do not claim to know all the details concerning this, but the broad outlines seem clear. And it is equally clear that our empire is doing what all pragmatic and mercantile empires do—they are trying to get *all* the gods into the same temple, into the same National Cathedral. Let them try. But *we* must not go there with them. So may a faithful Christian serve in the president's cabinet? Of course. For either party? Of course. And may such a man attend the mandatory worship services in the Cathedral? Of course *not*. And if there were such a faithful Christian, he would (in the current climate) find himself in a showdown with all the powers that be, just like Daniel was. And we would all know his name, just like we do Daniel's. But it does not yet appear that we have faithful men with the understanding of Daniel, Ezra, Nehemiah, or Mordecai.

We learn some of the same key lessons in the book of Esther. Esther is a Babylonian name and likely means "Star." Her Hebrew name was the lovely Hadassah, and if we brought it into English, we would call her Myrtle. This is a short book, but the story has just about *everything*. Consider what we have: a sharp conflict between good and evil, a brave and gorgeous heroine, carousing at the royal court, palace and harem intrigues, a Cinderella motif (an orphan girl from an enslaved nation marries the emperor), a really good villain with a waxed mustache and a cloak, helpless victims rescued in the nick of time, a reversal of fortune, a moment of truth in character formation, open battle, and poetic justice. This book has just about everything for a great action movie... except the explosions.

This is not a scriptural case for literary clichés being okay, but it does testify that certain things always make a story work, and that these can be used without falling into cliché.

Here's how the story goes. Vashti is deposed by her husband for refusing to appear at his banquet (1:1–22); Esther, relative of Mordecai, is chosen to replace Vashti (2:1–18); Mordecai tells Esther of a plot on the king's life (2:19–23); Mordecai refuses to bow down before Haman, who consequently plots to kill all the Jews (3:1–15); Mordecai persuades Esther to make an appeal to the king (4:1–17); Esther invites the king and Haman to a banquet (5:1–14); the king makes Haman honor Mordecai publicly (6:1–14); Esther reveals the plot against her and her people at a second banquet, and Haman is hanged (7:1–10); the king sends out a second edict, allowing the Jews to defend themselves (8:1–17); the Jews defeat and kill their enemies (9:1–19); the holiday of Purim is established (9:20–32); and Mordecai is promoted (10:1–3).

Thus we have faithful Jews honored during their life in exile (Nehemiah and Mordecai), and faithful Jews honored for their willingness to return to their ruined city in order to build it again (Nehemiah and Ezra).

—*Douglas Wilson*

Marc Chagall's Ezra (opposite) and Nehemiah from a 1960 publication of the French arts magazine *Verve* in which over one hundred of his biblical drawings were shown in a rare double issue.

For Further Reading

Kidner, Derek. *Ezra and Nehemiah: An Introduction and Commentary.* Downers Grove, Ill.: InterVarsity Press, 1979.

Pilava, Gianluc, Marco Conti, and Thomas C. Oden. *Ancient Christian Commentary on Scripture: 1-2 Kings, 1-2 Chronicles, Ezra, Nehemiah, Esther.* Downers Grove, Ill: IVP Academic, 2008.

Veritas Press Bible Cards: Chronicles through Malachi. Lancaster, Pa.: Veritas Press. 86–94.

Veritas Press History Cards: New Testament, Greece and Rome. Lancaster, Pa: Veritas Press. 16.

Session I: Prelude

A Question to Consider

How can a faithful Christian be a faithful member of an unbelieving empire?

From the General Information above, answer the following questions:

1. What is the main issue in trying to sort out the chronologies of these books?
2. Why are these chronological issues so important?
3. Is it possible for a faithful believer to be a dutiful citizen of an unbelieving nation?
4. Does this mean that believers can fit in just as easily as anyone else?
5. What must a believer in such circumstances not do in order to remain faithful?
6. Why is the book of Esther such a great story?
7. Was Cyrus in sin for the way in which he allowed the Jews to return to Jerusalem?
8. Is Mordecai to be faulted for refusing to bow before Haman?

Reading Assignment:
Ezra 1–6

Session II: Writing
Ezra 1–6

In this session, you will complete a short writing assignment. Please strive for quality rather than quantity. You should write no more than 1,000 words (if typing), or you should write on one side of a piece of paper legibly if you are writing by hand. You will lose points for writing more than this. You will be allowed to turn in your writing three times. The first and second time you turn in your

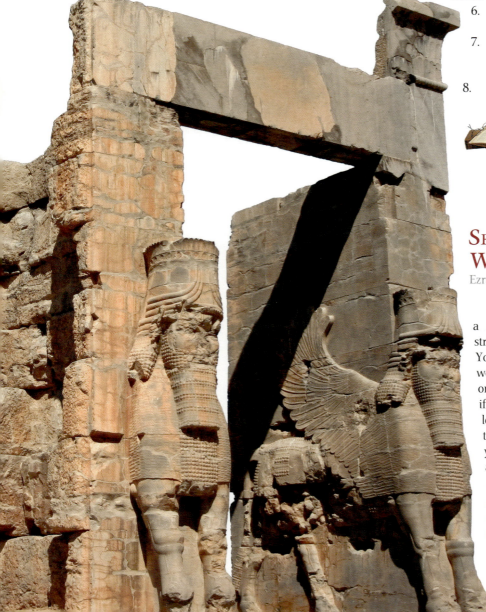

The ruins of the Gateway of Xerxes in Persepolis, the capital city of the Persian Empire, in present-day Iran.

A Reading by Sandra Bowden (1943–), collage mixed media, 2000. Buried beneath the layers of oriental papers and a handwritten passage of the Law are pages from a Hebrew Bible containing the story of Ezra reading the Law to the Israelites after their return to Jerusalem from captivity. Attached to the surface of the collage is a Jewish coin with the Lion of Judah, and a leather cover from an old book with the star of David scratched into its surface, but barely visible.

work, your teacher will grade and edit it. This is done by marking what is wrong and by making suggestions for improving your writing. Your job is to take these suggestions and rewrite your assignment. Your final submission's grade will be recorded. It will be graded in the following manner: 25 points for English grammar; 25 points for content accuracy— historical, theological, etc.; 25 points for logic (does this make sense and is it structured well?); and 25 points for rhetoric (is it a joy to read?).

Your assignment is to write a description according to the instruction below. While this might sound easy, doing it well will be challenging. Make sure your description helps a reader experience the scenario. Use language that stirs the senses (what it looks, sounds, feels, smells, or tastes like). Make judgments about the objects as you describe them. Remember the great rule of description—show, don't tell. Instead of telling us that something is good or beautiful or likable, describe it in a way that shows the object's beauty or ugliness; its goodness or wickedness.

Returning to Jerusalem

The experience of returning to Jerusalem after knowing nothing other than exile in Babylon.

The date: A few years after 538 B.C.

The setting: The Persian king has issued a decree that his Jewish subjects may go back to Palestine to live and to rebuild their temple. When they get there, the place is in shambles and the remnant of poor people is no better off. Yet under the preaching of Haggai and Zechariah, by the godly leadership of Ezra, and through the provision of Persia herself, the people are abuzz with eagerness to rebuild their lives. They are especially stirred to rebuild the Temple so they can draw near to Yahweh properly once again. Imagine you are a teenager who came to Jerusalem with your family. Write a series of journal entries or a letter to a Hebrew friend back in Persia about what you see, hear, smell, feel, and experience as a returnee. Be as creative as you wish, but keep your observations within those important events recorded in Ezra 1–6. For fun, why not identify yourself with a particular name from a particular clan from chapter 2?

Reading Assignment:
Ezra 7–10; Nehemiah 1 and 2

A detail from the coronation of Queen Esther, painted by Jacopo del Sellaio (c. 1441–1493). *"The king loved Esther more than all the other women, and she obtained grace and favor in his sight more than all the virgins; so he set the royal crown upon her head and made her queen instead of Vashti. Then the king made a great feast, the Feast of Esther, for all his officials and servants; and he proclaimed a holiday in the provinces and gave gifts according to the generosity of a king."* —Esther 2:17–18.

Session III: Discussion
Nehemiah 1 and 2

A Question to Consider

Must our prayers be spontaneous and "heartfelt" to be heard by God?

Text Analysis

1. In 1:1–4, what do we learn about Nehemiah himself?
2. Susa was the winter residence of the Persian kings and one of three Persian capitals (Esther 1:2). What was Nehemiah doing in the power center of the Persian king? (See the very end of 1:11.)
3. Why did Nehemiah weep, mourn, and fast at Hanani's news?
4. What was the significance of Jerusalem in redemptive history up to Nehemiah's time? (Read Gen. 12:7–8; Jer. 52:28–30; 2 Sam. 7:4–17; and 2 Chron. 36:15–21 as you answer this question.)
5. Read Nehemiah's prayer in 1:1–5 aloud and then analyze it. He's doing more than simply asking God for something. What different kinds of prayers does he utter? Make a list of all the things that Nehemiah does in this brief prayer.
6. In chapter 2, Nehemiah makes his "prayer" to the king. How is it similar in language to his prayer to the King of Kings?
7. To whom does Nehemiah give credit for his success in 2:8? How is this significant?

Cultural Analysis

1. Is prayer personal or impersonal? How is personhood a critical factor in Nehemiah's prayer (and in any biblical prayer, for that matter)?
2. Sometimes in our popular culture we see advertisements or stories about the "power of prayer." Is prayer itself powerful? Why or why not?

Biblical Analysis

1. Read carefully the disciples' prayer found in Acts 4:23–31 (for context, read 4:13–22 as well). Compare and contrast the various elements of their prayer with Nehemiah's.
2. How is Nehemiah's prayer and intercession before the king a foreshadowing of Jesus Christ's office as High Priest (see John 17; Heb. 7:11–28)?

Summa

Write an essay or discuss this question, integrating what you have learned from the material above.

Must our prayers be spontaneous and "heartfelt" to be heard by God?

Reading Assignment:
Nehemiah 3–9

Session IV: Recitation
Ezra; Nehemiah 1–9

Comprehension Questions

Answer these questions for factual recall:
1. The book of Ezra splits nicely into two parts: chapters 1–6 and chapters 7–10. These parts deal with two distinct issues. What happens in each section?
2. Lists play a significant role in Ezra and Nehemiah because they are historical narratives. Name five of the lists we find in these books.
3. Describe how Nehemiah responds when he hears that the remnant in Jerusalem is downtrodden and that the city walls are in shambles.
4. Who were Nehemiah's opponents in rebuilding the wall?
5. How did Nehemiah keep the wall construction going while their enemies threatened to attack and confuse them (4:8)?
6. What two views exist concerning the chronology of Ezra and Nehemiah?
7. In Nehemiah 8, after the rebuilding of the wall, what did the Levites help Ezra do? How did they do it?
8. Why did the Levites have to tell the Israelites not to fast and weep?
9. Nehemiah chapter 9 records the long and intense prayer of repentance that the Levites prayed on behalf of the people. What particular sin did they confess, and according to Ezra, what did the people do about that sin?
10. What did Nehemiah do in response to the merchants who spent the night outside the city gates on the evening of the Sabbath?

The next session will be a student-led discussion. Students will be creating their own questions concerning the issue of the session. Students should create three Text Analysis Questions, two Cultural Analysis questions, and two Biblical Analysis questions. For more detailed instructions, please see the chapter on *Death on the Nile*, Session V.

Issue

Servant Leadership

Reading Assignment:
Nehemiah 10–13; Esther 1–3

Session V: Student-Led Discussion
Nehemiah 1–13

A Question to Consider

Can a great leader also be a servant? How?

Students should read and consider the example questions below that are connected to the Question to Consider above. Last session's assignment was to prepare three questions and answers for the Text Analysis section and two additional questions and answers for both the Cultural and Biblical Analysis sections below.

Text Analysis

Example: What sort of leadership characteristics do we see in Nehemiah?
1. Love: He had a heart for God's glory, people, and city as a foundation for all he did (Neh. 1:1–4).
2. Faith: His first response to the crisis was prayer. Nehemiah clearly believed that God was active and caring for his people (1:5–11).
3. Giftedness: It is implied that he was a man of outstanding gifts such as integrity, diligence, and loyalty. How else could a Hebrew be cupbearer to a Persian king (1:11)?
4. Position: His employment was critical to the task of rebuilding Jerusalem. Without it, the Jews had no advocate with Artaxerxes I. With it, Nehemiah could ask for nearly anything he wanted (2:1–6).
5. Honesty: Though he was respectful, he spoke boldly with the king, asking for more than just an opportunity to return. His requests were large and specific (2:7–10).
6. Discreetness: Before he attempted to involve his fellow Jewish elders, he took his own private tour of Jerusalem, gathering facts (2:11–20).
7. Administration: He called on and organized all the right labor for the rebuilding (chap. 3). He kept de-

532   OMNIBUS IV

tailed records of all the returnees and their contributions (3:7,10,11–13).

8. Courage: In the face of external opposition, he prayed and spoke succinctly yet firmly for God's glory. He also continued the work undaunted (4:1–9).

9. Brotherhood: In the face of internal turmoil and discouragement, he listened to the people, encouraged them to press on, and provided new strategies for their success (4:10–23). He celebrated with the Israelites over the completion of the wall in providing community feasts (chap. 12).

10. Mercy and Justice: In order to ensure the people were well fed, he put an end to usury and ate only typical provisions, forgoing his governor's allotment (chap. 5).

11. Piety: He led the way for Ezra, the scribes, and the Levites to preach God's Word and bring the Jews back into covenant compliance with Yahweh (chap. 8).

12. Reform: He took a firm stand on morality by purging the Israelites of intermarriage with pagans (chap. 13).

Cultural Analysi

Example: Americans tend to think that romantic inclination trumps religious affiliation when it comes to marriage. Why is it that, so often, young people marry outside their faith community?

Answer: The confluence of hormones with our current culture's obsession with the romantic ideal, along with broken family dynamics, has gotten us where we are today. If children have an enjoyable experience with their family's religion, they tend to stick with that expression of faith. Across the board, healthy experiences in church tend to engender healthy adult attachments. That is borne out by anecdotal reality as well as research. So it stands to reason that some young adults will marry outside their parents' faith just to avoid being like their parents, who either didn't really believe what their church taught or who, worse yet, acted hypocritically. Some also suffer legitimate religious abuse in their churches (and

sometimes, tragically, physical abuses). It makes sense that they would never go back to those churches. Add to this dynamic of rebellion the fact that in America, any religion is deemed "legitimate." Unless a young person is brought up to discern why his family's faith is true or helpful, he will drop it when the urge comes to marry someone he "likes." The presence of a nonbelieving spouse in a marriage does not necessarily spoil the work of God's covenant in families. Also, new converts are told to stay with their unbelieving spouses, yet believers must marry in the Lord.

Other cultural issues to consider: Converting to another faith to marry, deciding which faith to raise children in if father and mother do not agree.

Biblical Analysis

Example: What does Jesus mean in John 13:17 when He says, "I tell you the truth, no servant is greater than his master"? Study the incident of Jesus washing His disciples' feet in John 13:1–17. We see servant leadership in Nehemiah and the impact it had on his fellow Jews. What impact did Jesus' foot washing have on the apostles, who would eventually become the first leaders of Christ's church?

Answer: When Jesus says "no servant," he is referring to each of his friends gathered there in a circle receiving a foot washing. If these men intend to serve Jesus when He is gone, they must get used to the fact that the greatest among them would be the lowliest character of all. Why? Because there's no way any of them could be greater than Jesus, and here He was, acting like a lowly house servant, cleansing dry, dung-encrusted feet. And this cleansing was also a picture of Christ's cleansing of His people by His atoning blood on the cross. The example He set for them must have had a huge impact on each of their egos. We have record in Acts that the apostles did in fact work together in serving Jesus and the early church. None of them tried to exult himself as master. Instead, they wrote,

---

Chart 1: COMPARE AND CONTRAST ESTHER'S "SISTERS"

	PHYSICAL APPEARANCE	INTELLIGENCE, COMPETENCE	RELATIONSHIP WITH GOD	RELATIONSHIP TO MEN
Deborah				
Esther				
Judith				
Susanna				

preached, served, and, for the most part, died in humiliation just like their Master. In the same way, Nehemiah's insistence on refraining from the king's table food and his determination to work shoulder to shoulder with his returnees emboldened them to follow his example and build up Jerusalem.

Other Scriptures to consider: Exodus 18; Isaiah 52:1–53:12; Philippians 2:1–11

Summa

Write an essay or discuss this question, integrating what you have learned from the material above.
Can a great leader also be a servant? How?

Reading Assignment:
Nehemiah 10–13; Esther 4–10

Session VI: Activity
Esther

Esther's Sisters

Compare and contrast some of Esther's "sisters" by completing Chart 1. You will find the information you need on Deborah in Judges 4 and 5. The other two women, Judith and Susanna, lived closer to Esther's time and were considered faithful Jewesses from the inter-testamental period. You should take some time to become familiar with the two Apocryphal books named after these two ladies. Also, be sure to review what you've read about Esther.

Optional Session: Activity

Purim Feast

Jewish families over the centuries have been encouraged to throw a Purim feast in their homes, remembering the victory of Mordecai and Esther that we've just studied. Purim is the action-packed holiday celebrated on the 14th day of the Hebrew month of Adar (early spring).

We will hold our own Purim feast, combining some of the typical home-based and synagogue traditions. Try to set aside two hours for the feast. Also, turn your living room or classroom into a hall suitable for an ancient, Hebrew feast: candles, a special tablecloth, and tapestries (if available) are a good place to start. Part of your classroom time leading up to the feast should be dedicated to preparing the décor. Perhaps a competition for best placemats or wall coverings would motivate your potential Purim partygoers.

Esther by Andrea del Castagno (c.1421–1457)

Purim is a great way to visualize and taste the deliverance of God on behalf of his captive people. We who are Christians also do well to reflect on, and in a way, reenact our deliverance from sin. We do this each time we celebrate the Lord's Supper. Biblical feasts remind us that our salvation is total: body and soul. As surely as we taste the bread and the wine, we can be sure Jesus died and lives for us. By celebrating Purim, we are reminded of the Church's roots in Israel and are given a bridge for communicating the fulfillment of all things in Jesus Christ.

Plan your celebration around five main areas:

1. Liturgy—Reading of the *Megillah*, also known as *The Book of Esther*. In the Jewish tradition, it is often read twice: once on Purim evening (remember, the days begin at sundown) and once on Purim day. The book is 10 chapters long, so have the students take turns reading the *Megillah* once they gather at their tables. You may also choose to read the three traditional blessings before the reading of the *Megillah*.

2. Noise—Purim is a joyous, even silly occasion. As the Jews say, it's supposed to be a *mitzvoh*! So you might want to prepare for this. Traditionally, as the book of Esther is read, people cheer loudly for Esther and Mordecai, and boo or hiss whenever Haman is mentioned. Each student has the privilege of "making a joyful noise" with foot stamping, booing, hissing, and gragger twirling each time Haman's name is read! What is a gragger? It is a noise-making device, similar to a New Year's Eve twirler. For instructions on making typical Jewish graggers for the entire class or family, see the teacher's edition.

3. Feast—The foods of Purim reflects the idea of "hiddenness." Esther's identity as a Jew and a relative of Mordecai, for instance, was hidden from the king. Her purpose of saving the Jews was also hidden. More importantly, God's name is not mentioned in Esther, yet his hand is at work in "hidden" ways.
   a. Prepare food with something hidden inside.
   - Kreplach: pastries filled with meat or mashed potatoes.
   - *Hamantsahen* (meaning "Haman's Pockets") are a traditional Purim treat: a triangular cookie or pastry with filling in the middle.
   - Challah bread with a filling such as raisins.
   b. Décor for the meal should be royal out of respect for Queen Esther. Dress up your table, cups, and napkins. Sprinkle glitter around. You might want to dress up as Middle Eastern royalty.

4. Sharing—Usually, each family gives a charitable gift to someone in need.
   a. Prepare a Purim offering box for your classroom or home where students or family members can discreetly place an offering. Gift ideas may include
   - Non-perishable food items for a local food bank or mission
   - Gently used toys or books for charity
   - Cash gifts in undecorated envelopes
   b. Each person usually prepares a Purim basket for at least two friends or neighbors.
   - These treats can be shared with a grammar school classroom, school administrators, or (given your school's setting) to neighborhood families or businesses.
   - It's always fun to make these deliveries in costume!
   - In a homeschool family, take the gifts to another family in church and talk with them about Purim when you make your delivery.

5. Masquerade—In keeping with the theme of hidden things, all participants in the Purim feast should attend in costume.
   a. Remember that the feast is supposed to be fun, even silly, so an award for the most outrageous costume is certainly a "kosher" idea!
   b. Typically, costumes are derived from the story of Esther and her time frame. However, try a creative twist if you have a larger class and want to go beyond the main characters:
   - Haman as a power-hungry executive or political adviser intent on ruthlessly destroying his enemies
   - Esther as a medieval queen
   - Mordecai as special assistant to the President of the United States
   - The entire story cast as a TV crime drama

Augustus Caesar's World

Have you ever known someone who acted like he was a god? Once I had a student who unwittingly claimed to be one.

One day after school I found myself staring up at the Birthday Bulletin Board in the hallway. On the board there are small pictures of the students whose birthdays fall in that month. Under each picture is a small rectangular white tag bearing the student's name. I did not often look at the board, but today I was waiting for someone and had a few moments to kill, so I stared up at the board.

It is amazing what you can learn about students from singular pictures. Young students, of course, did not pick their own pictures, so most of them had a plain picture that was sent in by their parents. Teenagers, however, were more careful about their photos—particularly the girls. Often they were doing a favorite activity—surfing or riding horses or nibbling watermelon. Their photos were always perfect—especially their hair.

Then I saw it! The photo to end all photos! It was of a young boy enrolled at my school. The picture, at first glance, communicated much more than he, or his parents, ever meant to say. By a series of interesting coincidences this photo made some extraordinary claims. The picture, you see, was from a Christmas photo, and it was one of this young lad in his mom's favorite Christmas sweater. This photo had been turned into the family Christmas card. This card had been sent in to adorn the birthday board. By an act of humorous accidental coincidence, the size of the rectangular name tag exactly matched the size of the Christmas card. The gloss of the paper and the fonts matched. The name tag and the card looked like one item. So don't blame me if I did a double take when I read:

The Savior Is Born
Andrew Smith

The boy was bright, I thought, but having just spent time with him in my office for a disciplinary issue, he was not living up to my messianic expectations. Of course, this photo coincidence was only an accident, and, of course, I already had a Messiah and did not need another. It did cause me to think, however, of what it would be like for people to think that you were a god. The Hebrew word for *glory* means "weight." The most glorious things are the weightiest. God, of course, is all glory and all weightiness—mountains shake when He touches them. What weight would a man have to bear if his friends, acquaintances, and family members thought he was a god? In *Augustus Caesar's World* we will study a man who was called a god. We will see what this weight of glory does to him, his family, and his world because, you see, he owned most of the world. While others were calling Augustus a god, one of the oddest things happened. In Augustus's kingdom, in an out-of-the-way village that meant less than nothing in terms of world politics, in a stable, the true God arrived to begin His rule and reign.

General Information

Author and Context

Genevieve Foster was an inspiring author who lived a quite interesting life. She was born in Oswego, New York, in 1893. Soon after her birth, however, tragedy struck. Her father died, and she and her mother moved to Whitewater, Wisconsin, to live with her grandparents. There she grew up as an only child surrounded by an interesting and artistic group of women. In school her artistic work showed real promise. She attempted her first novel at age ten—it was only one chapter. Later, she earned a degree in classics from the University of Wisconsin. After her undergraduate work she went on to the Chicago Academy of Fine Arts. She ended up working in advertising doing some work in children's literature (which she found to be boring). After marrying Orrington C. Foster, she designed and oversaw the construction of their new home. She continued to do a little work in advertising, but her focus soon was on her home and two children—Orrington Jr. and Joanna. As the children grew, she was involved in their education and became interested in history. Her children's books on history won acclaim and awards beginning with *George Washington's World*. Her approach to her subjects inspired a new sort of thinking about children's history books. She wrote "horizontal history" focusing on what was going on all over the world during a particular person's lifetime. *George Washington's World* not only focuses on the American War for Independence, but also the French Revolution and the rise of the British Empire. Her books make it easy to see the connections between different stories and different histories by blending them into one story. She traveled extensively and wrote with great passion.

Significance

Augustus Caesar's World continued Genevieve Foster's pattern of horizontal history. It covers most of the significant events in all parts of the world during the lifetime of Octavian (who became Caesar Augustus). By doing this, we get to see more clearly many of the external and internal forces driving the young Augustus toward imperial rule. We also witness the rise of many other movements and people—from the movement of Palestinian Jewish Zealots to the rise of rebellious German warlords like Hermann—that affect Rome and Augustus. Chief among these multiple focuses is the Roman province of Judea. Foster provides interesting insight into what scholars call the "Intertestamental Period" between the end of Old Testament prophecy and the coming of Christ. We learn extensively of the rise of Herod the Great, the ruler who tried to kill the infant Jesus to protect that power he had received by serving the Romans. We also learn of Herod Antipas, the son of Herod the Great, who killed John the Baptist. Foster obviously respected Christianity but her perspective on religion in general was more pluralistic, believing that truth can be found in many different religions. Her view can be summed up in her quotation ending the chapter "Questions and Answers" when she says, "No one person or race or nation has ever been or will ever be able to know all Truth or express all the Good to be found in the world." The reader should be wary of her worldview, which subtly seems to affirm Christianity at points while failing to commit to its truth.

Main Characters

Octavian, who later becomes Caesar Augustus, is the main character of this book. His life sets the parameters of the book. We begin by learning of Octavian as a young man. Prophecies are made over him in his youth that he will rule the world. He, however, is an unlikely candidate for world domination. He is often ill and many times on the edge of death. He is not handsome or dashing or known as a great general. He is, however, thoughtful and calculating and disciplined. In this book we witness Octavian's growth as a leader, his conquest of the Roman world, his careful rule and construction of the Roman Empire. We also get a glimpse into Augustus's most trying times. (Of course, Genevieve Foster did not live during his times, but she tries to guess at the feelings and thoughts that would have had to have been running

Augustus Caesar's World   537

through Augustus's mind during his greatest moments of trial.) Foster displays his uncertainty in dealing with the Senate as he jostles with Antony for their favor. We witness his shame as a father as he is forced to exile his wayward daughter, Julia. We see his overarching care for the empire he has founded and his hope that he can pass the care of Rome on to Tiberius.

There is a vast array of other significant characters. Here are just a few:

Julius Caesar: He is, of course, the general and dictator who first consolidates the rule of Rome under his own authority. He adopts Octavian, but is murdered in the Forum by many Senators led by Brutus and Cassius—before he can officially take all power to himself.

Mark Antony: Julius Caesar's friend helps to lead Caesar's army. He seeks control of the empire after Caesar's death and eventually, with Octavian, destroys Brutus and Cassius. He falls in love with Cleopatra and is defeated by Octavian in the Battle of Actium in 31 B.C. He later commits suicide.

Cleopatra: She is the Queen of Egypt whose beauty and wiles attract the attention of both Julius Caesar and Mark Antony. She bears the children of both Julius Caesar and Mark Antony and commits suicide after she and Antony are defeated by Octavian.

Cicero: Cicero is the great orator, protector, and advocate of the Roman Republic. He struggles to maintain the

In Augustus's kingdom, in an out-of-the-way village that meant nothing in terms of world politics, the true God arrived to begin His earthly reign. *The Columba Altarpiece* by Flemish painter Rogier van der Weyden (c. 1399–1464).

republic as it is disintegrating. He famously unmasks the Cataline Conspiracy which thought to overthrow the republic, and he opposes those who would seek to rule Rome personally—like Julius Caesar and Mark Antony. His vocal opposition to Antony causes enmity between them, and when Antony gains control of Rome as part of the Second Triumvirate, he quickly has Cicero killed.

Herod the Great: Herod becomes the king of Judea by carefully and ceaselessly currying the favor of his Roman overlords. He replaces and destroys the Maccabean rulers of Judea. He tries to win the favor of the Jews by rebuilding the Temple and making it more glorious. He is always viewed as an outsider and a Roman servant by faithful Jews. He is consumed by jealousy and tries to kill the Christ child when the Magi bring word of His birth.

Virgil: He is the greatest poet of the Golden Age of Roman poetry. His poem, the *Aeneid*, justifies the rule of Augustus over Rome. Augustus is his patron and loves his poetry. His work becomes something like scripture for the Romans even though he wants it to be burned at his death because he has not fully completed it. Augustus orders that the *Aeneid* be saved.

Jesus: Foster periodically turns her gaze toward Palestine to keep up with Jesus as he is growing up during the reign of Augustus.

Summary and Setting

This book follows the history of the Late Roman Republic and the Early Roman Empire during the lifetime of Augustus Caesar. It also, as horizontal history, tells what is happening all over the world during the time of Augustus's life. We trace out the life of Octavian as he scrambles to avoid being destroyed along with his adoptive father, Julius Caesar, when Caesar is murdered in the Senate on the Ides of March. He allies himself with Antony, but soon finds himself in a struggle to the death with Antony for control of the Roman Empire. As emperor, Augustus works hard to bring peace, stability, and prosperity to Rome. He accomplishes this (it is during his rule that we see the beginning of the *Pax Romana*—or the "Peace of Rome") and sets the pattern of government and rule that is to extend to the end of the empire. He is hailed by Rome as a god and, again, becomes a pattern for future emperor's who will demand that the rest of world view them as gods. Finally, we see Augustus as his years wind down. We see the tragedies in his family—the deaths of his grandsons, Gaius and Lucius, and the exile of his daughter. Finally, he passes on his rule to Tiberius and dies.

Worldview

Growing up in Indiana, I was well acquainted with the gods. Not that any divinity was mentioned in class. No, at the public school I attended the gods came out after school—to be more exact, Friday nights during the winter. Indiana gods put balls through hoops. I was a football and baseball player, so I could have been jealous, but I enjoyed basketball as a cultural event and spectacle. To be a great high school player in Indiana was something like being, if not a full-blown god, a least some sort of lesser deity. The names of these great heroes were recounted from of old and were recited each Saturday morning at the mead hall—or at least at the barbershop. Their nicknames echo in my mind in the voices of the elders of the community as even older men nodded in agreement behind them—the Rocket, the Dynamic Duo, The Big Dog and the Big O. Many simply went by their last name: Bird, Cheaney, Oden, Alford, Graham, Edwards, and Jones. There was one player, however, who stood head and shoulders above all others as I grew up. His name was Damon Bailey.

Damon came from the small town of Heltonville, Indiana. I still remember the first time I heard his name. A friend of mine—a good player in his own right—came back from the summer basketball tournament for seventh grade players. I asked how his team did, and he said, "I played against Damon." The questioning look on my face caused him to add forcefully, "You know. Damon Bailey."

"How did you do?" I inquired.

"I guarded him, and he scored 49 on me," he said. I gasped. He paused. "They took him out at halftime."

Damon's legend continued to grow. It did not shock me then when Damon was featured in Sports Illustrated as an eighth grader.[1] Bob Knight, then the fiery and brilliant basketball coach of Indiana University, was coming to watch his Jr. High games. So my father, brother, and I went to the semi-state games to see Damon the year that both he and I were freshman. He was on his way to the first of his four all state honors in a state that was crazy about basketball. Over 16,000 spectators attended that game at Robert's Stadium in Evansville.[2] Damon led his team, the Bedford North Lawrence Stars, to victory. Bedford's offense was something to watch. He was a sly rabbit running through a forest of moving trees as other players constantly set picks to get Damon open for a short jump shot. He both anticipated and reacted to the movements of the older, usually taller guys who were guarding him. The goal of the offense was to get Damon an open, short

Regardless of what you think about Octavian, you have to admit he must have been something special to have such a yummy salad named after him!

jump shot or a path to drive the ball to the basket. More often than not he got the ball. More often than not he hit the shot. That night, I believe he scored 22 consecutive points for his team. Watching him play was a thing of beauty.

Some of the stories filled my high school years—some must have been apocryphal. He had everything that an emperor would desire. He had a Praetorian Guard that protected him from the media, and crazy fans whisking him away to solitary places after victories. He had legions of fans. He had the hearts of the people, and it was only going to get better. In his high school years, he was All-State four times. He scored over 3,134 points during high school, and in his final game he led his team to the state title in a come-from-behind victory, scoring his team's final 11 points. He scored 30 of his team's 63 points. This all occurred in front of 41,000 cheering fans—the largest crowd to ever watch a high school basketball game. He bore the weight of basketball divinity. His high school built a new gymnasium and named it after him. He was the golden child during the golden age of Indiana high school basketball who was, some thought, to bring balance and restoration to the game—eventually remaking the NBA into something that resembled basketball (as if a 6'3" decently—but not extraordinarily—quick and athletic shooting guard would dominate the game). We all believed he was magic, and watching him play in high school was as close to basketball perfection as I could imagine. His first name served as a one-word summary for the obsession of a state. High school kids wore shirts bearing his name (even some from other schools). Many bowed worshipfully when he scored or was introduced. Wide-eyed old men compared his exploits to Beowulf or Naismith or Bird. The Methodists, Catholics, and Baptists in my home town did not agree on much of anything except they all thought Damon was at least the second coming of Oscar Robertson.[3] I always wondered what it would be like to be Damon with all the pressure, privileges, power, and potential. Still, being a star basketball player in a basketball crazed state like Indiana is a far cry from the power, perks, and privileges that once came with the office of emperor in the city of Rome. Star athletes might get special treatment. Roman Emperor's were once worshipped as if they were gods walking the earth.

The Fall of the Republic

What would it be like to be a god? What would people do for you? How would they react to your words? Few get to experience the feeling of divinity, but Augustus felt the weight of divinity.

At the outset we must admit that there were some things about Augustus that made him a long shot for divinity. He was no Hercules! By all accounts he was, in fact, a rather pale and sickly young man. Often he was near death because of illness. Still, he persisted and gained the favor and attention of Julius Caesar.

He was, however, the right man at the right time for Rome. As Augustus enters history, the great Roman Republic had fallen on hard times. Not that the power of Rome was decreasing—it was in fact at its height—but the forces that made Rome a republic were crumbling. This disintegration was occurring on many levels, but at the deepest level the Roman people had become too slavish and corrupt to maintain a democratic republic.

The power of the Roman Republic (and of all republics for that matter) demands a certain sort of people. The Romans of the republican era were these sorts of men. They were men of austerity, principle, and independence who worked to build their fortunes through industry, thrift, and hard work. Cincinnatus was the pattern of greatness for the Roman Republic. He was a poor farmer called from his field to fend off invasion. He was given absolute power by the state for six months as dictator. In a matter of days he marshaled his troops and beat back the invaders. After the military threat was quelled, he could have used the rest of his six-month term to fill his pockets with the wealth of others or to settle scores with any who were his enemies. Instead, he humbly returned power to the Senate and returned to his farm and relative poverty. The Romans, after the rape of Lucretia (see the chapter on Livy's *Early History of Rome* in Omnibus I), had chased their king out of Rome and decided that Rome could be ruled by a class of aristocrats called Patricians. The men that led Rome served the city, fought in her constant wars as free men, ran their own farms and industries, and struggled mightily to retain their own rights and independence.

These Patricians had to bear great responsibility. While a plurality of political leaders seems normal to us, in the ancient world, Rome was an oddity. Most tribes were ruled by kings who often abused power (as God warns that kings will do in Deuteronomy 17) and abused the people. Year in and year out the Romans fought and overcame the warring tribes surrounding them in Italy. Eventually, Roman armies began to conquer lands outside Italy. Wealth and slaves multiplied. As wealth and slaves multiplied, virtues and principles were forgotten.

Eventually, Roman virtues were in crisis. The sexual immorality of Cleopatra replaced the fidelity of Lucretia. A mad scramble for power and wealth replaced the austere virtue of Cincinnatus as men like Julius Caesar used the wealth of conquest to stake their claims to ultimate power over the republic. At this point the people of Rome had fallen far from the hardy men and women of the republican times who fought in the legion and spun the wool of the republic. They had become addicted to games and welfare represented by the gladiatorial games and free corn meant to keep the mob happy.

The struggle for ultimate power in Rome seemed to be over as Julius Caesar defeated Pompey and entered Rome. He was made dictator for life and was ready to rule the Roman world as his own possession. His murder by the Senate on the Ides of March, however, was the last gasp of republican Rome. Men who harkened back to the virtues of the republic hoped that with the death of Julius Caesar the Senate could be restored to power. This, however, was a baseless hope. Rival forces struggled for absolute power and eventually Octavian took the title of emperor and became the *de facto* ruler of the Roman world.

To this world, he brought peace. With peace came prosperity. With peace and prosperity came the adoration of the Roman people, who eventually hailed him as a god—and the adopted son of another god, Julius Caesar. This peace and prosperity came at a great price. From the Roman people, Augustus took freedom. Shrewdly, he maintained the forms of government that the Romans were accustomed to, but institutions like the Senate existed for show. The will of Augustus was the rule of the empire.

A large portion of the future success of the Roman Empire must be given to Augustus. He, like George Washington, entered into a position that had no history. He carefully lived in a manner that protected the empire. He lived in a manner that portrayed a renewal of Roman virtues. He commissioned poetry—particularly that of Virgil—that bolstered his rule and also sought to inspire Roman virtue. He set a pattern of leadership that—though rejected and abused by future emperors—led to peace and stability. Unlike Washington, however, Augustus did this by diminishing instead of protecting the freedoms of Roman citizens. Gone were the days when Romans needed virtue to govern themselves. Now, the emperor would rule all. There was no balance to his power.

When reminded of his ex-wife and their wayward daughter Julia, Augustus was wont to say, "Would I were wifeless, or had childless died." Julia was described by contemporaries as "tainted by luxury or lust."

The Cost of Divinity

While Augustus was a successful ruler in many ways, he personally paid a great price for his commitment to the Roman state, and his accumulation of power eventually was the undoing of the empire that he sought to protect. All of these shortcomings display that Augustus was, of course, no god, and that the rule of Rome was, like all other rules except that of Christ, to crumble.

Augustus paid a terrible price as a father. His greatest failure was with his daughter, Julia. He, like most fathers, had a soft spot for his intelligent and outspoken girl. In Julia, however, we see Augustus's greatest blind spot. While Augustus was leading a life to inspire virtue (although behind the scenes he was no saint), while he is condemning and punishing vice, his daughter was leading a life of debauchery and sexual immorality. Sadly, everyone around Augustus knew this before him. He eventually was forced to take action, exiling her from Rome. It is said that he avoided saying her name if at all possible. Supposing to be a god, he failed as a father.

Augustus also faced the frustration of being a fallen man rather than a god. He continued to battle illness during his years as emperor. Death surrounded him. The deepest wound he bore on this score was near the end of his life, suffering the deaths of his beloved grandsons Gaius and Lucius within 18 months of each other. So much of Augustus's hopes had been pinned to these boys who were to bear his power after he died. Before death, Augustus is shown to be a man, not a god.

Augustus's claims of divinity eventually bring judgment on the Roman Empire. The Caesars after Augustus continue to claim divinity. The empire sets up its rulers as divine—and eventually seeks to force all its inhabitants to worship the emperor. While Augustus often modeled Stoic virtues, future emperors would, bolstered by the claims of divinity, turn into monstrous beings who devoured everyone and everything around them. History lists them as tyrants and maniacs—

Caligula and Nero (who were in the line of Augustus), but later men like Domitian and Diocletian—men who would send legions to attack the sea and ride in triumph before heaps of sea shells; men who would light their evening parties with the bodies of burning, crucified Christians; men who would slaughter thousands who would not burn incense to the image of an emperor and proclaim that he was a god.

The Battle of the Gods

Augustus's claim of divinity eventually sets up a sort of *theomachy*—or battle of the gods (in this case it is really a battle of God vs. the gods). For in the time of Augustus in a little known village in a corner of the empire that was only a periodic nuisance to the divine Augustus, a male child was born. He was born in Bethlehem because His family was there paying a tax to the emperor. In this young carpenter's son, however, Augustus's empire had met its match. The boy, of course, was Jesus of Nazareth.

The kingdom of Christ and the kingdom of Augustus eventually come to blows. As Christianity spreads throughout the empire, so spreads the worship of the emperor. Eventually, all inhabitants of the Roman Empire are required to burn a pinch of incense before an image of the emperor and recite the words "καισερ κυριος"— or "Caesar is Lord." One did not have to give up one's gods; one did not have to prove that they believed what they said. They simply had to make the sacrifice and say the words. Followers of Jesus, however, refused to make the sacrifice. In 1 Corinthians 12 and Philippians 2 we see the confession that early Christians made as they re-

Augustus's claims of divinity eventually brought judgment on the Roman Empire. Although Augustus often modeled Stoic virtues, later emperors turned into monstrous beings, devouring everyone around them.

fused to recognize the divinity of the emperor—"Ιησους Κυριος" "Jesus is Lord." For this confession and this refusal, multitudes of believers went to their death.

In their deaths, however, these martyrs proved the great difference between the state religion of Rome and the Christian faith. The more the emperors persecuted and killed the Christians, the more believers there were. Augustus would fall in death. Jesus rose from the grave. He disciples and followers did not fear death.

This battle would eventually end with the conversion of Rome's Emperor Constantine, and Christianity became the official religion of the empire. Soon the Roman Empire would be gone, but the Empire of Christ continues and will never fail.

The False Peace of Pluralism

Today, thankfully, we are not pressed to offer sacrifice to the President of the United States and confess that he is a god. We are, however, tempted in more subtle ways to deny the uniqueness of Christ. Roman pluralism let you keep any god you wanted so long as you bowed to the emperor and obeyed Roman law. Modern pluralism demands that we accept all religions as basically valid searches for truth that show us some aspect of the truth. Jesus Christ, however, will have none of this, saying, "I am the way and the truth and the life. No one comes to the Father except by me" (John 14:6). The apostles will have none of this either, saying, "Nor is there salvation in any other, for there is no other name under heaven given among men by which we must be saved" (Acts 4:12). Like the believers of Augustus's day, we must stand firm in the faith, refusing to shave any edge off of the confession that Christ requires of us. "Ιησους Κυριος!"

—G. Tyler Fischer

For Further Reading

Foster, Genevieve. *George Washington's World*. San Luis Obispo, Calif.: Beautiful Feet Books, 1997.

Spielvogel, Jackson J. *Western Civilization*. Seventh Edition. Belmont, Calif.: Thomson Wadsworth, 2009. 134–153.

Suetonius. *The Twelve Caesars*. New York: Penguin, 2007.

Veritas Press History Cards: New Testament, Greece, and Rome. Lancaster, Pa.: Veritas Press. 20–25.

SESSION I: PRELUDE

A Question to Consider

Does power corrupt? Does it always corrupt?

From the General Information above answer the following questions:
1. What is "horizontal history"?
2. Why did the Jewish people hate Herod the Great?
3. What is the *Pax Romana*?
4. What tragedies did Augustus face late in life?
5. How did Augustus set a good pattern for Roman emperors?
6. How did Augustus fail in his own family to uphold family values?
7. How did Augustus's claim of divinity eventually lead to the death of thousands of Christians?

READING ASSIGNMENT:
"Under a Lucky Star" to "Why is July?"

SESSION II: DISCUSSION
"Under a Lucky Star" to "Why is July?"

A Question to Consider
Why do republics fall?

Discuss or list short answers to the following questions:

Text Analysis

1. What does the astrologer do when Augustus tells him his dates?
2. Why does the Senate murder Julius Caesar?
3. Why does Cleopatra return to Egypt after Julius Caesar is murdered?
4. How does Cleopatra portray herself and her son?
5. What does Cicero find when he goes to visit Brutus and Cassius?
6. What does Octavian do to gain favor with the people of Rome? What does this tell you about the Roman populace?

Cultural Analysis

1. Where do you see signs that America is falling into the same sorts of VDD (Virtue Deficit Disorder) as they had in ancient Rome?
2. In *Democracy in America*, Alexis de Tocqueville said that "America is great because she is good. If America ceases to be good, America will cease to be great." Do you believe that this could be happening today? Where do you see it?
3. De Tocqueville also said, "The American Republic will endure until the day Congress discovers that it can bribe the public with the public's money." Is this happening today?
4. Where do you see people being distracted by games rather than paying attention to serious issues in our culture today?

Biblical Analysis

1. What is the danger of having all your needs met (Deut. 8:11–13)?
2. If having a republic is so good, why does God allow His people to have a monarchy (Deut. 17:14ff)?

Summa

Write an essay or discuss this question, integrating what you have learned from the material above.

How can we help save the American republic and keep it from falling into tyranny?

Reading Assignment:
"Gauls, Geese and Black Vultures" to "Horace and the Country Mouse"

Session III: Recitation

"Under a Lucky Star" to "Horace and the Country Mouse"

Comprehension Questions

Answer the following questions for factual recall:

1. What was Octavian's appearance as a youth?
2. In what Triumph did Augustus ride with Julius Caesar?
3. What was Octavian determined to do after the death of Julius Caesar?
4. What was the Cataline conspiracy, and why does Cicero remember it with joy?
5. From what god does Mark Antony claim descent?
6. What does a comet cause the Roman Senate to do with the calendar?
7. How do Cicero and Octavian have a falling out?
8. What does Antony do to Cicero when the Second Triumvirate (Antony, Octavian, and Lepidus) take power?
9. What is Saturnalia?[4]
10. What is Herod the Great's ethnic background, and how does he become the ruler of Galilee?
11. How do Antony and Octavian divide the Empire?
12. Why does the poet Horace lose his farm?

Alexis de Tocqueville

Instead of a reading assignment you have a research assignment. Tomorrow's session will be a Current Events session. Your assignment will be to find a story online, in a magazine, or in the newspaper that relates to the issue that you discussed today. Your task is to locate the article, give a copy of the article to your teacher or parent and provide some of your own worldview analysis to the article. Your analysis should demonstrate that you understand the issue, that you can clearly connect the story you found to the issue that you discussed today, and that you can provide a biblical critique of this issue in today's context. Look at the next session to see the three-part format that you should follow.

Issue

How do the marriage commitments of leaders affect politics and government?

READING ASSIGNMENT:
"Antony and Cleopatra" to "Triumph and Peace"

SESSION IV: CURRENT EVENTS

Issue

How do the marriage commitments of leaders affect politics and government?

Current events sessions are meant to challenge you to connect what you are learning in Omnibus class to what is happening in the world around you today. After the last session, your assignment was to find a story online or in a magazine or newspaper relating to the issue above. Today you will share your article and your analysis with your teacher and classmates or parents and family. Your analysis should follow the format below:

BRIEF INTRODUCTORY PARAGRAPH

In this paragraph you will tell your classmates about the article that you found. Be sure to include where you found your article, who the author of your article is, and what your article is about. This brief paragraph of your presentation should begin like this:

> Hello, I am (name), and my current events article is (name of the article) which I found in (name of the web or published source)...

CONNECTION PARAGRAPH

In this paragraph you must demonstrate how your article is connected to the issue that you are studying. This paragraph should be short, and it should focus on clearly showing the connection between the book that you are reading and the current events article that you have found. This paragraph should begin with a sentence like

> I knew that my article was linked to our issue because...

CHRISTIAN WORLDVIEW ANALYSIS

In this section, you need to tell us how we should respond as believers to this issue today. This response should focus both on our thinking and on practical actions that we should take in light of this issue. As you list these steps, you should also tell us why we should think and act in the ways you recommend. This paragraph should begin with a sentence like

> As believers, we should think and act in the following ways in light of this issue and this article.

The next session will be a student-led discussion. Students will be creating their own questions concerning the issue of the session. Students should create three Text Analysis Questions, two Cultural Analysis questions, and two Biblical Analysis questions. For more detailed instructions, please see the chapter on *Death on the Nile*, Session V.

Issue

What would be needed to create a new civil religion that controlled people and encouraged them to be committed to the state?

READING ASSIGNMENT:
"Augustus Caesar" to "Golden Eagles Come Home"

SESSION V: STUDENT-LED DISCUSSION

A Question to Consider

What would be needed to create a new civil religion that controlled people and encouraged them to be committed to the state?

Students should read and consider the example questions below that are connected to the Question to Consider above. Last session's assignment was to prepare three questions and answers for the Text Analysis section and two additional questions and answers for both the Cultural and Biblical Analysis sections below.

Text Analysis

Example: How does Augustus use poetry to establish a new Roman religion with the Emperor at the center?

Answer: Augustus is the patron of Virgil. Virgil writes the *Aeneid* to inspire and renew Roman virtue by telling the story of Aeneas who escapes Troy and fights his way to rule in Italy. In Book 6 of the *Aeneid,* Aeneas ventures into the underworld and sees a vision of the future of the kingdom that he is founding—Rome. As Roman history passes before the face of Aeneas, it reaches its height when Augustus enters the vision. Thus, Virgil's poetry establishes and supports the rule of Augustus.

Cultural Analysis

Example: Roman religion under Augustus was a civil religion—a religion focused on serving the state. What is the religion of the government of the United States (or what is our civil religion)?

Answer: Our civil religion was once laced with Christian language—although it was never explicitly Christian. Today, however, it is pluralistic. This can be seen by the holidays that our leaders celebrate and the gods that our leaders call on during a time of national tragedy. At the service at the National Cathedral after the 9/11 attacks, our leaders called out to many different gods. Christ was included, but His claims of exclusivity were ignored. Today, the American president celebrates many different holidays of many different religions.

Other cultural issues to consider: pluralism, religious relativism, celebrating Eid at the White House, National Service of Mourning after 9/11.

Biblical Analysis

Example: What was the civil religion of Israel in biblical times? Was it any different than their religion at the family, Temple, or synagogue?

Answer: The civil religion of Israel was focused on adoring and worshipping the one true God. It was not different in its focus than any other religion. The religion of Israel commemorated the great acts of redemption—the Exodus and Passover, the Feast of Booths—celebrating God's salvation of Israel. The king, like the other men of Israel, had duties and responsibilities during these feasts and celebrations, but he did not lead the people. The High Priest did the work in the Temple, making sacrifice to set aside the sins of the people.

Other Scriptures to consider: Leviticus 10, Judges 17–18, Isaiah 40, Romans 13.

Summa

Write an essay or discuss this question, integrating what you have learned from the material above.

Do you see any signs that America might be in the process of creating a new religion—one like the religion of Rome?

Reading Assignment:
"Out of Persia" to "Questions and Answers"

Session VI: Discussion

A Question to Consider

In the chapter "Questions and Answers," Genevieve Foster states the following: "No one person or race or nation has ever been or will ever be able to know all Truth or express all the Good to be found in the world." Is this statement true or false? How do you know?

Discuss or list short answers to the following questions:

Text Analysis

1. What aspects of the Zoroastrian religion are similar to Christianity? Why does the author pick these details?
2. How was the teaching of the great Rabbi Hillel something that should have prepared people for the coming of Christ? Why does the author point this out?
3. Who do the people in the Roman province of Gaul begin to worship as a god?
4. How does Augustus begin to portray himself as divine?
5. What truth is adopted by Pharaoh Akhenaton? (In a world where all religions are true, is this really an insight?)
6. What philosophies were most popular among the Romans?

Cultural Analysis

1. What would happen today if an American president during the State of the Union address announced that Jesus Christ is the way, the truth, and the life and that no one can have a relationship with the true God outside of Christ?
2. In the movie *The Incredibles* little superhero boy Dash and the villain Syndrome keep reminding us that "if everyone is super, then no one really is." In light of this insight what would you say is true if all religions are true?
3. Why does our culture want to avoid having one true religion (at all costs)?

Biblical Analysis

1. In Exodus 32, while Moses was on Mt. Sinai, Aaron led the people in a blended worship service. He created golden calves to represent God and had the people worship them in a manner common to the worship of idols in the ancient world (they had a big party). What did God think of this? Why did Moses throw down the tablets when he saw that the people had run amok?
2. In 1 Kings 12:25ff, Jeroboam the Son of Nebat became the first king of the Northern Kingdom. To

maintain the political unity of the Northern Kingdom, he set up golden calves for the people to worship. What does God think of such religious pluralism (consider 1 Kings 13:34, 14:16, 15:30, 15:34, 16:2, 16:19, 16:26)?

SUMMA

Write an essay or discuss this question, integrating what you have learned from the material above.
How can you be faithful to Christ during periods of intolerant pluralism?

READING ASSIGNMENT:
"Stepson and Stars" to "Buddha and the Kingdom of Truth"

SESSION VII: RECITATION
"Out of Persia" to "Buddha and the Kingdom of Truth"

Comprehension Questions

Answer the following questions for factual recall:
1. Who brings Zoroastrianism to Rome, and what do Zoroastrians worship?
2. When Agrippa and Julia visit Herod in Jerusalem why does Herod complain about the Galileans?
3. What is the Septuagint, and why is it also called the LXX?
4. Why does Pythagoras claim that we can not hear the music of the spheres?
5. Who is Strabo?
6. What do the Mayan's do well?
7. What do the Pharisees do as soon as Herod the Great dies?
8. What sort of philosophy does Confucius teach?
9. What are "castes" in Hinduism, and what do Hindus believe about other religions?
10. What leads Buddha to renounce the world and begin a life of meditation?

The next session will be a student-led discussion. Students will be creating their own questions concerning the issue of the session. Students should create three Text Analysis Questions, two Cultural Analysis questions, and two Biblical Analysis questions. For more detailed instructions, please see the chapter on *Death on the Nile*, Session V.

Issue
What will your legacy be?

READING ASSIGNMENT:
"December 25th, Year 1" to "My Dear Tiberius"

SESSION VIII: STUDENT-LED DISCUSSION

A Question to Consider
What will your legacy be?

Students should read and consider the example questions below that are connected to the Question to Consider above. Last session's assignment was to prepare three questions and answers for the Text Analysis section and

In a Persian version of the emperor cult, the *faravahar* symbolized the winged sun in Zoroastrianism and also the divine authority of the king.

two additional questions and answers for both the Cultural and Biblical Analysis sections below.

Text Analysis

Example: How does Augustus both demonstrate his weakness and his excellence in the banishment of Julia?

Answer: First, Julia's waywardness paints a less than ideal picture of Augustus as a father. He was blind to her indiscretions and only later in life did he recognize the kind of woman that she had become. We see, however, that as the leader, and father, of the Roman Empire he is willing to apply justice to his own family. This example was inspiring to the people of Rome, knowing that the Emperor would not exempt his own family from justice.

Cultural Analysis

Example: How has America profited from the pattern of leadership demonstrated by President George Washington?

Answer: Every time governing power changes hands peacefully in America we should remember and thank God for General Washington. He could have refused to relinquish power. Most people at the time would have applauded his remaining in office. He could have had the titles and privileges of a king, but instead, he served his country, laid his power aside, and returned to his farm. He was called a modern-day Cincinnatus and was, of course, inspired by the example of that great Roman. We benefit from Washington's example in many ways.

Other cultural issues to consider: Term limits (what are the pros and cons); founders of companies, like Bill Gates, John Rockefeller, Steve Jobs, and Andrew Carnegie; for positive examples of leaders who had a great legacy see Elizabeth I, Augustine of Hippo, and Augustine of Canterbury; for negative examples of founding fathers try Robespierre and Vladimir Lenin.

Biblical Analysis

Example: What was David's legacy for Israel?

Answer: While David had some egregiously bad shortcomings (e.g., the census and his sin with Bathsheba), his legacy was overwhelmingly positive. He is the example of a king with his heart in the right place—he was a man after God's own heart. When he failed and sinned, he

Therefore [Jereboam] asked advice, made two calves of gold, and said to the people, "It is too much for you to go up to Jerusalem. Here are your gods, O Israel, which brought you up from the land of Egypt!" —1 Kings 12:28

confessed (without political spin) and repented. He faced trials with courage and faith. He poured out his heart to the Lord in poetry. He faced down a giant who would stand against God's people. He set a standard for kingship and painted a picture of what his descendant, Jesus Christ, would be as a ruler.

Other Scriptures to consider: Consider how Christ's example affected the lives of his disciples in Acts 2:14ff and 4:1–21; consider how the life and example of the father affected the lives of the prodigal son and his older brother in Luke 15:11–32.

SUMMA

Write an essay or discuss this question, integrating what you have learned from the material above.
Where do you or will you have the opportunity to serve as a "father or founder"?

READING ASSIGNMENT:
"Hermann, the German Hero" to "A New Religion for Rome"

SESSION IX: DISCUSSION
"The German Border" to "A New Religion for Rome"

A Question to Consider

What causes are on the horizon that will cause the Roman Empire to fail?

Discuss or list short answers to the following questions:

Text Analysis

1. What do the Romans stop doing at the border of Germany? Why?
2. What does Augustus consider doing to raise more troops to fill the needs of the army during the rebellion in Pannonia?
3. Just as Augustus considers the peace and prosperity of his empire what "gift" arrives from Germany?
4. How does Hermann the German learn to fight so well?
5. Who might have been visiting the Temple in Jerusalem during the census of A.D. 6, and what did he do there?
6. The Empire crucifies Jesus and, eventually, persecutes His followers. What does this cause?

Cultural Analysis

1. The Roman Empire failed both internally and externally. Its virtues turned to vices. Its armies began to falter (as conquests gave way to holding ground). Its people were left without any religion except pleasure seeking. Today, many would say that America has become an empire of sorts. What signs do you see that America is facing the same sorts of internal and external failures that felled Rome?
2. The Roman Empire was pragmatic when it came to philosophy and religion (whatever gets you through the night) so long as people recognized the authority of the empire and did not cause trouble. Theirs was an economic empire built on power and the creation of wealth. Most of the conquered countries did not rebel because of fear but also because Roman rule generally brought prosperity. Do you see any sign that America's position in the world is one that downplays the importance of religion and is built on faith in money instead of any god?

Biblical Analysis

1. Why did the Babylonian Empire fall (Daniel 5)?
2. Why was the wicked empire of the Assyrians spared from God's judgment at least temporarily (Jonah 3)?
3. What did God forecast concerning the empires of this world (Daniel 2)?

SUMMA

Write an essay or discuss this question, integrating what you have learned from the material above.
What can you do to preserve America's strength and place of leadership in the world?

OPTIONAL SESSION A: RECITATION
"Under a Lucky Star" to "A New Religion for Rome"

Comprehension Questions

Answer the following questions for factual recall:

1. What is the Act of Oblivion?
2. Who crossed the Rubicon? Why did he do it?
3. How old is Octavian when he takes office for the first time as Consul?
4. How do Antony and Octavian pay to raise their army to attack Brutus and Cassius?
5. What does Hanukkah, or the Festival of Lights, commemorate?
6. How does Herod the Great become King of Judea?
7. How does Octavian become Tiberius's adopted father?
8. How does Herod's wife Mariamne die?

9. How is Caesar Augustus's trip to Gaul different from Julius Caesar's visit?
10. What happens to Augustus around the time Agrippa takes him to see the Pantheon?

OPTIONAL SESSION B: ACTIVITY

Augustus for a Day

Pick a day for one member of your class or family to serve as Augustus for the day. During their Day as Caesar, they can make any rule that they want. You will need a large bag of M&Ms (or other treat), a stopwatch or clock, and a pair of dice for this activity. Others must follow the rules, but only under the following conditions:

1. The person in your family or class whose birthday is closest to Augustus's, September 23rd, gets to be Augustus for the day.
2. A teacher or parent needs to serve as the judge.
3. Everyone gets 20 M&Ms at the beginning of class. They can do whatever they want with these, but saving them is a good idea. Augustus, however, receives 100 M&Ms. Everyone's M&Ms must be kept in a bag at all times unless they are being eaten.
4. Augustus may not ask anyone to do anything that is *malum in se* (evil in and of itself) or anything that is *malum prohibitum* (evil by prohibition) if the parent or teacher forbids it. He may use his candy to bribe others.
5. Anytime a third- to two-thirds of the empire (i.e., the class or family) rebels against Augustus, he must enter into the Forum to see if it is the Ides of March. To see if it is the Ides, dice must be rolled. If the sum of the two dice is even, then Augustus is removed from office and has to give up three-quarters of his M&Ms. If the sum of the dice is 3, 5, 9, or 11, then

Augustus retains his crown, and he confiscates half of the M&Ms of all who were part of the conspiracy. If the sum of the dice is seven, Augustus retains his crown but no M&Ms change hands.
6. If Augustus is removed from office, then each conspirator chooses a number between two and twelve. The closest wins and becomes the new Augustus. If there is a tie, roll the dice again until one is closer.
7. If more than two-thirds of the class or family rebels, then Augustus retains his crown only if the sum is 6, 7, or 8. On all other sums, Augustus is replaced. (See step #6 for how to choose a new Augustus.)
8. For every 5 minutes that Augustus rules wisely (i.e., is not removed), all players receive 5 additional M&Ms and Augustus receives an additional 15 M&Ms. When a new Augustus is crowned the clock restarts and a new 5 minutes begins.
9. At the end of the time allotted for this activity, you may eat, trade, or share you M&Ms.

ENDNOTES

1   The article is available through Link 1 for this chapter at www.VeritasPress.com/OmniLinks.
2   Back in those days Indiana had classless basketball. All 386 teams played in one tournament to decide a state champion. Theoretically, the smallest school in the state could win the whole thing—thus, the movie *Hoosiers* when the 1954 Milan team basically did run the table.
3   After high school, he continued to do well but was never quite as dominating. He was All-Big Ten Conference at Indiana University. He was chosen in the second round of the NBA draft, but after some injuries never really found a place in the league. He has done well, but I have always wondered what it was like to bear the weight of so many hopes and dreams.
4   Some recent scholarship, however, contradicts Foster's views of Saturnalia. She implies that Christians were trying to use a pagan feast that was already popular. Now there are some who think that it was actually desperate pagans who were trying to "piggy back" onto the increasingly popular Christian holiday of Christmas. More information on this is available through Link 2 for this chapter at www.VeritasPress.com/OmniLinks.

Art and the Bible

Here you are, doing your Omnibus reading. You have been reading great books, thinking big ideas, engaging Western civilization, and getting an education second to none. If you had been born a few decades earlier, you would probably not be doing this.

There was a time not long ago when conservative Protestant Christians largely ignored their cultural heritage and the world outside the walls of their churches. Art, literature, philosophy, politics—all of that was "worldly," they believed. True biblical Christians, many were saying, should separate themselves from such secular concerns and concentrate on their spiritual lives. Many Christian schools concentrated on just teaching the Bible, along with basic reading, writing, and arithmetic—the bare minimum necessary to make a living until the Lord returns.

Those of you who feel run over by the Omnibus may wish that you had lived in those simpler times. You do realize, of course, that this position of Christians having nothing to do with our civilization is another of those modern travesties that, though it sounds pious, it really falls short of biblical truth. You have gone through enough of the Omnibus curriculum to know that Christians have done more than anyone else to build our civilization and that even

The first time God filled someone with His Spirit it was not for preaching, or for battle, but for art. *Then the LORD spoke to Moses, saying: "See, I have called by name Bezalel the son of Uri, the son of Hur, of the tribe of Judah. And I have filled him with the Spirit of God, in wisdom, in understanding, in knowledge, and in all manner of workmanship, to design artistic works, to work in gold, in silver, in bronze, in cutting jewels for setting, in carving wood, and to work in all manner of workmanship."* —Exodus 31:1–5

when it has gone wrong, getting bogged down in false worldviews, Christians have always been battling the bad ideas. Furthermore, you know that even what is seemingly "secular"—art, science, nature, history, and everything else that is real—could not exist apart from God's creation and His sovereignty and that the biblical worldview embraces all of life.

At any rate, one of the men who was most responsible for helping evangelical Christians re-engage the culture again was Francis A. Schaeffer. If you have ever used the term "worldview," if you are an advocate of the pro-life movement, and if your parents allow you to be exposed to anything other than Sunday School art, you probably have Francis Schaeffer to thank.

This is a portrait of Francis Schaeffer mimicking the style of Andy Warhol. And who knows? If Warhol had lived longer, he might have done just such a painting. In *The Religious Art of Andy Warhol* Jane Daggett Dillenberger shows the importance of faith to the pop artist. For example, in the two years before he died, Warhol made seventy paintings based on Leonardo da Vinci's "Last Supper" as well as prints based on Renaissance religious paintings.

General Information

Author and Context

Francis Schaeffer (1912–1984) was a Presbyterian minister, serving congregations in Pennsylvania and St. Louis. Caught up in the various denominational splits and controversies that roiled Reformed churches in the 1930s and 1940s, in which he stood strongly for the inerrancy of Scripture, Schaeffer became burnt out with church politics. In 1948 he left the United States to become a missionary in Europe.

Schaeffer and his wife Edith settled in Switzerland. In 1955 they bought a chalet in the Alps. They called it *L'Abri*, which is French for "the shelter." They opened their home to travelers, and it soon became a study center for whoever wanted to wrestle with the big questions of life.

College students backpacking through Europe trying to find themselves, hippies looking for a new experience, people seeking to fill the God-shaped vacuum in their hearts—they heard about this place in the mountains and made their way to L'Abri. Here Schaeffer and a growing Christian community engaged them with conversation, biblical thinking, and the gospel. Thousands became Christians. Thousands of Christians, many of whom were disillusioned with the shallowness of the Christianity they had known, also passed through L'Abri, eager for the bigger vision of Christianity that Schaeffer opened up for them.

Schaeffer's books, which were based on the lectures he gave at L'Abri, began coming out in the late 1960s and soon brought him a larger audience. In 1976 he came out with a documentary film entitled *How Shall We Then Live?* in which Schaeffer stood among ruins and in front of classic works of art to analyze "the rise and decline of Western culture." This was followed in 1979 with another documentary, *Whatever Happened to the Human Race?*, in which Schaeffer appeared with Surgeon-General C. Everett Koop to attack abortion, euthanasia, and genetic engineering.

Schaeffer developed cancer and in 1978 he and his wife moved to Rochester, Minnesota, so that he could receive treatment at the Mayo Clinic. Another L'Abri site formed around their new home. He died in 1984. L'Abri continues, though, with 11 sites around the world where people can ask questions about Christianity, listen to recordings of Schaeffer's lectures, and think through the implications of the Bible for all of life.

Significance

Schaeffer's little book on art, *Art and the Bible*, based on two of his lectures on the subject, is a good example of how he helped conservative Protestants to re-engage with the larger civilization by means of a rigorous application of the Bible.

He counters the objections that the Bible says little about art—and that what it does say opposes art—by showing that the Bible actually says a great deal about art. At a number of points in Scripture, God commands that art be built. In fact, the Bible mentions favorably nearly every kind of art that there is.

Schaeffer points to Bible passages that are almost never preached on and that are the bane of many well-intentioned Bible-reading projects, the tedious—but no less inspired—directions for constructing the Tabernacle and the Temple, going on and on for chapter after chapter. To adorn His worship, God requires representational art depicting both the spiritual realm (cherubim) and the natural realm (lions, oxen, palm trees, lilies). He demands symbolic art (the Ark of the Covenant) and abstract art (the two freestanding pillars in front of the Temple that support no weight and have no architectural function). He calls for non-realistic art, demanding for the priest's garments not just scarlet and purple pomegranates but blue pomegranates, even though there are no blue pomegranates in God's creation.

The Bible also shows the employment of other kinds of art: drama (in some of the prophets' signs), poetry (the Psalms), songs (of David), instrumental music (in the Levites assigned to play music for the Temple worship). We could also add fiction (the parables), tapestry (the Tabernacle), architecture (the Temple).

The Lamentation of Christ is one of the frescos painted by Giotto di Bondone (c. 1267–1337) for the Scrovegni Chapel in Padua, Italy. His work on this chapel is considered a masterpiece of the Early Renaissance.

Although Scripture warns against the misuse of the arts, as in idolatry, as Schaeffer says, "God is interested in beauty." This is also evident in God's creation, His own art. "Is God's creation totally involved with religious subjects?" Schaeffer asks, in a brilliant question. "What about the universe? The birds? The trees? The mountains? What about the bird's song? And the sound of the wind in the trees? When God created out of nothing by His spoken word, he did not just create 'religious' objects."

In the second chapter, Schaeffer offers, as the title says, "Some Perspectives on Art." He emphasizes that art has value in itself, as art. A painting, a novel, or a piece of music must first be approached, appreciated, and evaluated as an aesthetic object, not just grabbed onto for its message, even if it is a Christian message.

This makes it possible to appreciate a work, even though we may disagree with what it says. Ernest Hemingway, for example, is a really good novelist. His descriptions are vivid, his characters come alive, and his style is gripping. I totally reject, though, his existentialist worldview, in which his characters are always creating some private code of their own so that they can make their way through a meaningless world. I enjoy reading Hemingway, but I do not let that sell me on his sadly deficient worldview.

Conversely, it is possible to agree with an artist while recognizing that their art is utterly incompetent. For example, I won't mention any names, but there are some Christian authors who express a fine biblical message. And yet their descriptions are clichés, their characters are stereotypes, and their style is tedious. The writers who are excellent in both style and content, of course, write the kind of books you read in Omnibus, but these are rare. Schaeffer hopes to inspire evangelical Christians to become that kind of artist.

His other pointers in the second chapter can help to that end. Schaeffer points out that a good artist must possess "validity"; that is, he must not sell out his artistic integrity to the marketplace, producing what will sell, rather than what needs to be expressed. Styles are always changing, he observes, and Christianity can manifest itself in a wide variety of styles. Christian artists of today must not simply follow the styles of the past. "If you are a young Christian artist, you should be working in the art forms of the twentieth [or twenty-first] century, showing the marks of the culture out of which you have

An idol or a beautiful sculpture in tribute to our triumphant Savior? Gian Lorenzo Bernini's *The Risen Christ* was commissioned in 1673 by Pope Clement X to stand atop the tabernacle of the Chapel of the Blessed Sacrament in St. Peter's Basilica. This is the initial, flawed bronze cast. In this sculpture Christ's body is reminiscent of beautiful idols carved of the sun god Apollo. This is in stark contrast to Isaiah's prophecy of Jesus: "He has no form or comeliness . . . There is no beauty that we should desire Him."

come, reflecting your own country and your own con-
temporariness, and embodying something of the nature
of the world as seen from a Christian standpoint."

Schaeffer hoped that this book would inspire and
equip evangelicals to become that "young Christian artist." Maybe that could be you!

Setting

The original debate between the Modernists and the
Fundamentalists in the 1920s and 1930s was a high-
powered intellectual and theological conflict between
those who wanted to liberalize Christianity so that it conformed with the times and those who insisted on holding
to the tenets of historical Christianity. The Fundamentalists, led by intellectual heavy-weights such as J. Gresham
Machen, could be said to have won the argument. But
Machen and the equally formidable Cornelius Van Til
were driven out of Princeton University, whereupon
they founded Westminster Theological Seminary. The
dominant Presbyterian Church of that time embraced
Modernism, as would soon most other mainline Protestant denominations. This, in turn, resulted in a plethora
of smaller, more conservative new church bodies.

With the Scopes trial of 1926, in which a teacher
was prosecuted for teaching Darwin's theory of evolution, "fundamentalists" lost their cultural respectability.
Many Christians in the new church bodies considered
that they had lost the culture wars and that they should
turn their attention away from the world. "Fundamental-
ist" became a synonym for a Christian who believes in
separating from the world. By the 1960s, though, many
conservative Protestants who believed that Christians
should engage the world began calling themselves by
a different name: "evangelical." Francis Schaeffer, who
studied at Westminster under both Machen and Van
Til, became a key figure in this evangelical movement.

Recall too that the 1960s and 1970s, when L'Abri
was at its height, were the age of the counter-culture,
youth rebellion, and non-conformity. Schaeffer—with
his longish hair, goatee, and Alpine garb complete
with lederhosen—came across to the restless young
people of the time as a wise old man of the mountains.
Though Schaeffer acknowledged and agreed with
many of the complaints young people had with "the
establishment"—the rampant materialism, the dehu-
manization of technology, the hypocrisy of previous
generations—he pointed them to Christ and the Bible
as giving the answers they yearned for.

Schaeffer is also credited—or blamed—for promoting Christian political activism. His documentary
Whatever Happened to the Human Race? and his book

A Christian Manifesto spurred evangelical Protestants
to become involved in the pro-life movement. Before
Schaeffer raised the issue, many evangelicals considered abortion to be a "Catholic issue" and were pro-
choice.

When it comes to art, the subject of *Art and the Bible,*
to this very day Protestant Christians—the heirs of great
artists such as Dürer, Cranach, Rembrandt, the Dutch
Masters, the Hudson River school, and many more—are
often indifferent to art and aesthetics. Christians often
insist that art, to be acceptable, has to express an explicit
Christian message. Contemporary churches are often
notoriously ugly. Though Schaeffer's book has inspired
and encouraged legions of evangelical artists, the arts
are arguably the sphere in which Schaeffer's influence
still has a long way to go.

Worldview

That we even are talking about "worldview" is a sign
of Schaeffer's influence. Schaeffer was not so much an
original theologian as a popularizer of the ideas of several
Reformed theologians, specifically, Abraham Kuyper (for
his worldview analysis), Herman Dooyeweerd (for his philosophical approach), and Cornelius Van Til (for his pre-
suppositional apologetics, to which Schaeffer added some
evidentialist elements). This tiny book on art demonstrates
many of the main themes of Schaeffer's thought.

"Despite our constant talk about the Lordship of
Christ," Schaeffer writes at the very beginning of the
book, "we have narrowed its scope to a very small area of
reality. We have misunderstood the concept of the Lordship of Christ over the whole of man and the whole of
the universe and have not taken to us the riches that the
Bible gives us for ourselves, for our lives, and for our culture." In contrast, Schaeffer believes that the Lordship of
Christ extends to all of life, including the arts.

Schaeffer's expansive vision of the Lordship of Christ
has to do with his view of objective truth. "If Christianity
is really true," he writes, "then it involves the whole man,
including his intellect and creativeness. Christianity is
not just 'dogmatically' true or 'doctrinally' true. Rather, it
is true to what is there, true in the whole area of the whole
man in all of life."

Throughout the book, Schaeffer sometimes alludes
to a distinction between the "upper story" and the "lower
story" of human thought and experience. This is a metaphor he developed in some of his other books, particularly *Escape from Reason.* Now that human beings have
largely drifted away from the wholeness of the biblical
worldview, the tendency has been to divide our minds
into an "upper story" of irrationalism and a "lower story"

Madonna and Child by Luca Signorelli (c. 1445–1523) depicts Mary adoring her Son. In Western art the infant Jesus was often shown nude in order to emphasize the humanity of Christ and to refute various Christological heresies.

experience, meaning that it does not have to make any kind of sense. Not only Christianity but also the classical tradition, which sees "beauty" and "truth" as being profoundly related, have a better way of approaching the arts.

Schaeffer, again, was a popularizer. He was not an expert in all of the fields he addressed, so he sometimes made mistakes. Some Christian scholars fault him for under-appreciating our classical heritage with the Greeks and the Romans. He also, arguably, missed much of value in the Middle Ages.

Sometimes he made out-and-out mistakes. For example, in this book he says that the artists Cimabue (c. 1240–1302) and Giotto (1267–1337) are from "the high renaissance." But these men were contemporaries of Thomas Aquinas! The 1200s and the 1300s marked "the high middle ages," not the renaissance, which, properly speaking, reached its "high" mark in the 1500s with Michelangelo and Leonardo da Vinci.

But these are quibbles. We owe Schaeffer a great deal. Especially those of you riding this Omnibus.

—Gene Edward Veith

of logic, common sense, and facts. We live out our everyday lives in the lower story, but we compartmentalize our religion, morals, and whatever gives our life meaning into the upper story. As a result, our religion, morals, and the meaning of our lives tend to be mystical, emotional, and irrational. At the same time, the realm of fact and reason has no meaning.

Thus, some people say they believe God created the universe and they also believe in Darwin's theory of evolution. The contradictions do not bother them because they believe in God's creation "in a religious sense"—in an upper story mystical kind of way that facts can never disprove—while believing in Darwin "in a scientific sense," as a description of what actually happened.

Schaeffer, in contrast, believes that Christianity gives us actual, objective, unified truth. What the Bible says happened did so, in a phrase Schaeffer liked to use, "in space and time."

Modern art has also fallen for this division. Both artists and audiences often take art for an "upper story"

For Further Reading

Bustard, Ned, ed. *It Was Good: Making Art to the Glory of God.* Baltimore, Md.: Square Halo Books, 2006.

Dennis, Lane, ed. *Francis A. Schaeffer: Portraits of the Man and His Work.* Wheaton, Ill.: Crossway Books, 1986.

Hankins, Barry. *Francis Schaeffer and the Shaping of Evangelical America.* Grand Rapids, Mich.: Wm. B. Eerdmans, 2008.

Romaine, James. *Objects of Grace: Conversations on Creativity and Faith.* Baltimore, Md.: Square Halo Books, 2002.

Ryken, Philip Graham. *Art for God's Sake: A Call to Recover the Arts.* Phillipsburg, N.J.: P & R Publishing, 2006.

Schaeffer, Francis A. *The Complete Works.* 5 vols. Wheaton, Ill.: Crossway Books, 1985.

Veith, Gene. *State of the Arts.* Wheaton, Ill.: Crossway Books, 1991.

SESSION I: PRELUDE

A Question to Consider

What place do the arts have in the lives of those who are committed to being followers of Christ?

From the General Information above, answer the following questions:

1. Why did conservative Protestant Christians separate themselves from cultural pursuits like art, literature, philosophy, and politics?
2. What does *L'Abri* mean, and why is it significant in the life of Francis Schaeffer?
3. How did Schaeffer's art essays confront common religious objections to art?
4. What types of art does Schaeffer assert are acceptable according to the Bible?
5. How is it possible to appreciate a work, even though we may disagree with what it says?

READING ASSIGNMENT:
Art and the Bible, Chapter 1

Detail from *Solomon's Dream* by Baroque painter Luca Giordano (c. 1632–1705)

Session II: Recitation
Art and the Bible, Chapter 1

Comprehension Questions

Answer the following questions for factual recall:

1. How is the Christian view of reality directly opposed to the platonic view?
2. Francis Bacon said that man's loss of innocence due to the Fall could be repaired through religion and faith. According to Bacon, how could man's dominion over nature be repaired?
3. Schaeffer says that art can be a doxology in praise of God, but in the Ten Commandments we are told not to make any graven images. How can both be true?
4. The art found in the Tabernacle involves almost every form of representational art in the world. What were some of the styles of art required by God?
5. Schaeffer points out that the Temple was covered with precious stones for beauty: "There was no pragmatic purpose. God simply wanted beauty in the temple. God is interested in beauty." Read 2 Chronicles 3 and list the examples of different art forms.
6. To what did Schaeffer draw our attention to demonstrate secular art in Scripture?
7. How did Jesus use art in His ministry?
8. At the end of the chapter, what other forms of aesthetic expression does Schaeffer show to be scriptural?

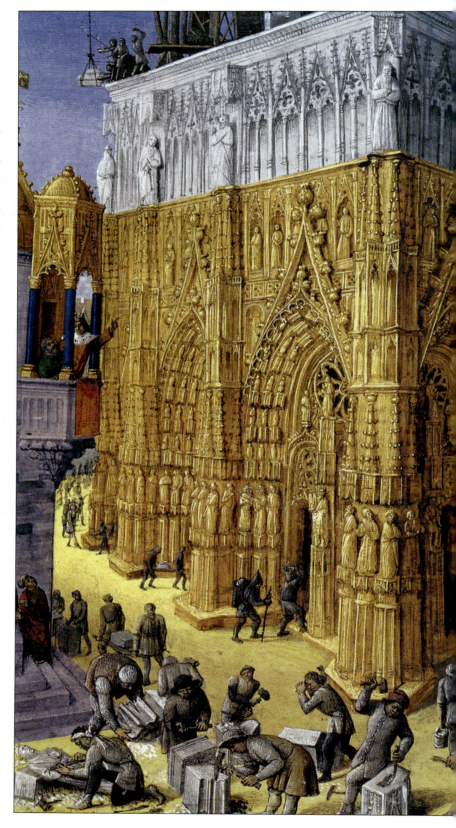

Solomon overseeing the construction of the Temple, as imagined by Jean Fouquet in this fifteenth-century illumination in a French version of Josephus's *Antiquities of the Jews*.

The next session will be a student-led discussion. Students will be creating their own questions concerning the issue of the session. Students should create three Text Analysis Questions, two Cultural Analysis questions, and two Biblical Analysis questions. For more detailed instructions, please see the chapter on *Death on the Nile*, Session V.

Issue

What should a church building look like?

READING ASSIGNMENT:
None

SESSION III:
STUDENT-LED DISCUSSION

A Question to Consider

What should a church building look like?

Students should read and consider the example questions below that are connected to the Question to Consider above. Last session's assignment was to prepare three questions and answers for the Text Analysis section and two additional questions and answers for both the Cultural and Biblical Analysis sections below.

Text Analysis

Example: Schaeffer asserts that God is interested in beauty and that beauty has a place in the worship of God. Then why are so many churches made today that are ugly?

Answer: Schaeffer concludes that the evangelical community fails to understand that beauty should be to the praise of God. This shallowness is reflected in our theology, our worship, our singing, our church architecture, and our lives (chap. 1).

Cultural Analysis

Example: Doesn't good stewardship demand that churches ought to devote their resources to the bare minimum when it comes to facilities and send everything else overseas to missionaries?

Answer: Second Chronicles 3:15–17 says:

Also he made in front of the temple two pillars thirty-five cubits high, and the capital that was on the top of each of them was five cubits. He made wreaths of chainwork, as in the inner sanctuary, and put them on top of the pillars; and he made one hundred pomegranates, and put them on the wreaths of chainwork. Then he set up the pillars before the temple, one on the right hand and the other on the left; he called the name of the one on the right hand Jachin, and the name of the one on the left Boaz.

These two pillars were completely useless for supporting the building or for any other "practical" purpose. They served as huge (literally) reminders that God was interested in beauty in worship that had no pragmatic use. Thus, when building a structure dedicated to worship, believers do have an example that would lead them to consider how to express the beauty and majesty of God even if these expressions are costly and serve no practical purpose.

Biblical Analysis

Example: Jesus said that we are supposed to worship God in spirit and in truth, so therefore isn't it best if we leave all representational art out of worship?

Answer: Worship in spirit and truth should not be contrasted with worship that is beautiful or that is in the material world. God does not expect us to leave our bodies behind when we go to worship. "Spirit and truth" worship is not (has not been and should not be) synonymous with ugly worship—or an ugly worship environment. First Kings 6:29 it says, "Then he carved all the walls of the temple all around, both the inner and outer sanctuaries, with carved figures of cherubim, palm trees, and open flowers."

The Temple was a place of wonder and beauty. It was a place designed by God for His worship. Thus, considerations of beauty should not be set aside but instead should be carefully considered as we build our church buildings.

SUMMA

Write an essay or discuss this question, integrating what you have learned from the material above.
What should a church look like?

READING ASSIGNMENT:
Art and the Bible, Chapter 2

Session IV: Recitation
Art and the Bible, Chapter 2

Comprehension Questions
Answer the following questions for factual recall:
1. Why does a work of art have value in itself?
2. What does art do to a worldview?
3. "Fear No Art" is the slogan of Chicago's Museum of Contemporary Art and can be found plastered on many cars' bumpers. How does that sentiment align with Schaeffer's view of art?
4. What are the four standards of judgment that Schaeffer suggests we apply to any work of art?
5. What three things does Schaeffer assert concerning the style of Christian art?
6. What are the "major" and "minor" themes which should both be present in the art made by Christians?
7. What should be the subject matter of art made by Christians?

 **Reading Assignment:**
None

Chart 1: **TAKING A SECOND LOOK**

MODERN or TRADITIONAL?	CONCEPTUAL or REPRESENTATIONAL?
Is the artist professedly CHRISTIAN or NOT?	Is the subject matter BIBLICAL or NOT?

Optional Activity
Art Walk

Many cities nowadays have a monthly evening set aside where the shops and galleries stay open late to showcase the opening of new art exhibits. Pick one of these evenings and walk downtown with friends to explore and learn. Set a goal for yourself to meet the artist at one of the galleries. Ask him about his work. Be humble. Love your neighbor. Learn what they are trying to show through their work. Remember that Schaeffer says, "the Christian's life is to be an art work. The Christian's life is to be a thing of truth and also a thing of beauty in the midst of a lost and despairing world." Be beautiful, and try to uncover some beauty that you were not expecting to see.

If the artist is not available, pick one piece in the show and devote your time to it. Stare at it. Study it. Read about it. Look for patterns, repeating elements, and other visual clues. Put yourself in the artist's shoes. The artist is your neighbor. Love your neighbor. After you have spent time looking at the piece and "listening" to it. Apply Schaeffer's four standards to it:

TECHNICAL EXCELLENCE

VALIDITY

INTELLECTUAL CONTENT

INTEGRATION OF CONTENT AND VEHICLE

Another way to interact with the piece is to draw a diagram like Chart 1. Thinking through these categories on paper can help you to look at a piece more deeply and see distinctions more clearly, allowing you to better understand how the piece is serving God as it conveys either the "minor" or "major" themes.

It is probable that this activity will require engagement with art that the viewer may not like and might even question if the work can be considered art. But as C.S. Lewis reminds us in *An Experiment in Criticism*:

> We sit down before the picture in order to have something done to us, not that we may do things with it. The first demand any work of art makes upon us is surrender. Look. Listen. Receive. Get yourself out of the way.

Or as Bruce Herman, an art professor at Gordon College has said, "If you want to 'understand' something, you have to be willing to 'stand under' it." Resist jumping to judge the works and try to learn what they are trying to say in the way that they are trying to say it.

Session V: Debate
Nudity in Art

Note to homeschoolers: This activity will prove meaningful enough to make special efforts to include others. Consider other homeschool children near the same age to participate, or include other family members.

Today we are going to debate whether Christian's should depict nudity in their art work. There can be strong feelings over this issue, so make sure that you treat your brothers and sisters in Christ in this debate with care, courtesy and respect. Remember, whichever side of the debate you are on, you might be spending eternity with a number of people that feel differently than you do. Also, it is a wonderful variation on this class to make students argue well for the opposite of the opinion that they themselves hold so that they can see, perhaps, why other believers might feel differently than they do.

Directions

We are going to serve as judge and jury as we consider whether Christian artists should make art depicting nudity. To do this, follow these steps:

Split the participants into two teams. One will defend Christians portraying nudity in art, the other will argue that Christians should not portray nude characters. (If you are working alone, create arguments for both sides and share them with your parents or friends. After you present both sides, ask which side of the arguments was most convincing.)

Edward Knippers' paintings have occasionally been banned and even mutilated by those who viewed his art as heretical. But Knippers is deeply orthodox in his faith and theology, and in *Christ Resisting Temptation* his worldview comes through. We see Jesus, the second person of the Godhead, as fully human. As theologian A.D. Bauer writes, "Jesus' obedience came out of His nature as an unfallen man. Jesus did not easily pass through trials by accessing power from His divinity. Jesus was the second Adam and He was obedient living out His goodness as an unfallen man in a fallen world. Jesus shows the world what Adam and Eve were before the fall and what they would have remained if they had not eaten the fruit."

Spend some time creating your arguments, then choose two people from each group to argue the case.

Ask another class, a group of friends, or your parents to serve as jury members.

Set a time limit for each argument. This format works well:
- 5 minutes per team for opening arguments
- 10 minutes per team for one side to question the other
- 5 minutes per team for closing arguments.
- Any left over time for questions from the audience to either side.

OPTIONAL ACTIVITY

Art Analysis

Edward Knippers is a nationally exhibited artist known as a figurative painter of biblical subjects. He has had over 100 one-man and invitational exhibitions, including a four-person show at the Los Angeles County Museum, and one-man shows at the Virginia Museum, Richmond, the University of Kentucky, Lexington, and the University of Oklahoma, Norman. Knippers's work has been published widely, including by *Life* magazine and *Christianity Today,* and is found in numerous public and private collections including The Vatican Museum, Rome, Armand Hammer Museum, Los Angeles, the University of Oklahoma, Norman, and the Billy Graham Center, Wheaton, Illinois.

Christ Resists Temptation

Knipper's work portrays nudity, but whatever side of the debate you find yourself on concerning nudity in artwork, you might note that many pieces of art produced presently and in the past have employed nudes—as Knippers does. Following are some questions that both praise and question this work.

Technical Analysis

1. Does this work demonstrate the artist's ability and expertise?
2. Describe the piece.
3. Does this work have balance and symmetry? What is the central or most important element (to what are your eyes most attracted)?

Subject Analysis

Read Matthew 4:1–11 and answer the following questions:
1. On what part of the account of Jesus' temptation does this painting appear to be focusing?
2. How does Knippers convey the idea of a spiritual reality in the painting?
3. Why is it significant that Christ is represented in the nude when the account in Scripture does not mention this?

Content Analysis

1. What is the message of this work?
2. Ian Plimer, professor of mining geology at the University of Adelaide, was quoted in the *Washington Times* as saying, "Eco-guilt is a first-world luxury.... It's the new religion for urban populations, which have lost their faith in Christianity." Knippers says that this quote is relevant to the painting. How might that be?

READING ASSIGNMENT:
None

Session VI: Aesthetics

Art Analysis

Rogier van der Weyden (originally Rogier de le Pasture) was one of the finest painters of his day. He was born in Tournai and in 1426 married the daughter of a shoemaker. From 1436 onwards he was the official painter of Brussels and had quite an impact on the art world of his day, although no single work can be attributed to him with certainty based on fifteenth century documentary evidence. He was described by his contemporaries as the most important of all painters, and his works were purchased all over from Belgium to Italy. His paintings feature naturalistic details in expressive compositions that in his day opened up a whole new approach to the great themes of Christian art.

The Deposition

The painting was commissioned by the Greater Guild of Crossbowmen of Louvain, and the tiny crossbows in the side spandrels of the picture allude to the patronage. In the painting the apostle John is helping Mary as she swoons. The women to the left of Mary are her half-sisters Mary Cleophas and Mary Salome. The old man behind Jesus is Nicodemus, and in the gold robes is Joseph of Arimathea. Mary Magdalen is to the far right of the painting, indicated by one of the servants holding the jar that held the costly ointment with which she anointed the feet of Jesus.

Technical Analysis

1. Does this work demonstrate the artist's ability and expertise?
2. Describe the piece.
3. What is the element of the design which most attracts your gaze?

Subject Analysis

1. What moment of the biblical narrative does this depict?
2. What might be the significance of the skull at the bottom of the painting?

The Deposition by Rogier van der Weyden (c. 1400–1464)

Content Analysis

1. What does van der Weyden accomplish by placing all of the action in a shallow space as opposed to a landscape?
2. This image is supposed to be an *Andachtsbild*—a devotional or contemplative image to stir your heart and mind to love for God. What elements does the artist use to move the viewer in such a way?
3. The *Lamentation of Christ* by Giotto reproduced earlier in this chapter, although depicting the same subject as van der Weyden's piece, is very different in composition and feel. Identify some differences.

OPTIONAL SESSION: DISCUSSION

A Question to Consider

Can Christians make images of things, of people and of God without creating idols?

From the General Information above, answer the following questions:

Text Analysis

1. Which of the items in the following list are we forbidden to make an image of by the Second Commandment?

BEAR	LION
FLOWER	STAR
GOD	AUNT SARAH
PEBBLE	JESUS

2. How does Leviticus 26:1 help us to understand and interpret Exodus 20?
3. What then does the Second Commandment actually forbid?
4. Reconsider the list in Question 1. Of which can we make representational artistic images?

Cultural Analysis

1. What does our culture idolize? Does it guard the images of these idols carefully?
2. If you walk into any Christian bookstore (and many churches), you will see hundreds of images of Jesus. Do these images affect your relationship with Christ? Can these images be misleading?
3. Is it possible to worship in churches without using art?

Biblical Analysis

1. Can God use visual objects to represent Himself (Luke 22)?
2. Does Numbers 21 teach us that God can be represented by artwork, or is it, when considered with 2 Kings 18:4, a condemnation of idolatry?

SUMMA

Write an essay or discuss this question, integrating what you have learned from the material above.
Can anyone make an artistic representation of a Divine Being without falling into idolatry?

ENDNOTES

1 *This note appears only in the teacher's edition.*

THE LOST WORLD

Have you ever known something to be true, but nobody would believe you? No matter what you said they would roll their eyes, deride your story and laugh at you when you weren't looking. Sadly, I get this all the time, but I'm a teacher, and it seems to be part and parcel with the job.

However, I remember a particular time when I didn't believe someone else's story and it turned out to be completely true. He was at a homeless shelter and was a Vietnam vet. He happened to be a drunk at the time I met him (and he smelled the part), and we were sitting on a wooden bench in the dining room talking. He told me about a war wound he had received in battle, and for some reason the story sounded implausible . . . so I asked to see it, not because of genuine curiosity, but rather because I was skeptical. He saw right through my young, snot-nosed, little bratty ploy—he knew I doubted him, and right after he showed me, he got up and left. I was particularly embarrassed because I was there to preach the gospel and heal the brokenhearted. Ouch.

As you will see, the same problem—how to prove what you know is true—is afflicting our main character, Professor Challenger, in *The Lost World.* No one will believe his story that he has discovered living dinosaurs, and it seems there is nothing he can do, no matter how fierce his temper tantrums are, to persuade anyone. All he has is his word of honor, and for most that just isn't enough.

GENERAL INFORMATION

Author and Context

In his day, Sir Arthur Conan Doyle (1859–1930) was "one of the most visible literary figures in England."[1] People loved his analytic Sherlock Holmes character and his fast-paced, sci-fi adventure story, *The Lost World* (which are still his most popular works today), but what he believed earned him his knighthood was actually his non-fiction Boer War pamphlets, which were distributed around the world to counteract the overwhelming media bias against Britain. The people loved him for it, and even though he later ran for political office twice and lost, by the end of his life in 1930 he had written 60 Sherlock Holmes mysteries, 60 other short stories and novels, and countless letters and articles expressing his opinions on such diverse topics as literature, religion, science, sports, and international affairs. In his later years he also

became a vocal advocate for spiritualism and considered it his most important endeavor, but more on that in the worldview section below.

Sir Arthur had the added distinction of living through four significant eras. He was born to Irish immigrant parents, Charles and Mary, in 1859 in Edinburgh during the prosperity and optimism of the mid-Victorian Age (1848–1870). Ironically, his birth was also the same year that Darwin published his culture-altering *The Origin of Species.* During the late Victorian Age (1870–1901), he enrolled at the University of Edinburgh in 1876 to become a physician, but he soon discovered his real talent lay in his ability to write. Doyle published his first Sherlock Holmes novel, *A Study in Scarlet*, in 1888.

A copious number of his stories were published throughout the Edwardian Era (1901–1910) and the Georgian Period (1911–1936), including his most popular Holmes novel, *The Hound of the Baskervilles* (1902). *The Lost World* was published in 1912, just two years before the beginning of World War I, but by this time Doyle had established himself as a unique literary figure because, in spite of the shifting attitudes away from the moral certitude and national pride of the Victorian Age, he never abandoned those values himself.

Significance

During Doyle's lifetime, evolution had just begun to package itself as *the* viable alternative to the widely accepted biblical account of creation in the Bible. Today, for some, it has become the *only* accepted probability (just try to dispute it), but in Doyle's time the common man (who today as in Doyle's day often has more common sense than the philosopher) had not yet been convinced. *The Lost World* is significant because it takes Darwin's predictions and clothes them in flesh and blood (not boring fossils), thereby capturing the public's imagination. It is blatantly contrived and yet still fun, humorous (Doyle is said to have laughed often while writing it) and

568 OMNIBUS IV

fast-paced. It is a creative portrayal of how he envisioned skeptics and the public would react if indisputable proof for evolution were presented.

Indeed, for the approximately 50 years between Darwin's publication of *Origin* and Doyle's *World*, evolutionary scientists had

been eagerly searching for the predicted missing link which would ideally sport features of a human-sized cranium and an ape-like jaw. Specimen after specimen contended for the crown of being *the* missing link, but always, upon further review, failed to hold up. All were either too human or too ape-like.

Therefore, what Doyle does in *The Lost World* is to take a tidy snapshot of world history, neatly trapping all of the predicted proofs on a remote South American plateau. Living dinosaurs, ape-men, and primitive natives, are all isolated from external evolutionary influences and

His ferocious cry and the horrible energy of his pursuit both assured me that this was surely one of the great flesh-eating dinosaurs, the most terrible beasts which have ever walked this earth. As the huge brute loped along it dropped forward upon its fore-paws and brought its nose to the ground every twenty yards or so. It was smelling out my trail.

then discovered by our adventurous and intelligent modern men. Doyle knew how influential good storytelling could be on a person's concept of what's real, and he brilliantly constructed a storyline that would be imitated for the next 100 years in such adventures as *King Kong* and *Jurassic Park*. *The Lost World* is one of the earliest novels to use the "thought experiment," effectively fictionalize a scientific theory and imagine what would happen if that theory were undeniably proven true. Basically, "wouldn't it be cool if this happened?"

Main Characters

Doyle's overall success is partly due to the fact that he created authentic characters. He was an astute observer of human behavior, and his characters were modeled after people he knew, the ideals he admired, and the weaknesses he disdained.

For example, the fiery and violent Professor Challenger is modeled after the real Professor Rutherford "with his Assyrian beard, his prodigious voice, his enormous chest and his singular manner." But even though Challenger is extremely hot-tempered, he is also willing to be ridiculed and disbelieved if he is confident he's right.

Lord John Roxton, on the other hand, is the man of action and is modeled after Doyle's friend, Roger Casement, who was a world traveler and outspoken opponent of slavery. Roxton is the practical man who stands up for what is right and likes to be well-armed to do just that. In many ways he embodies the ideals which Doyle admired most. When Edward Malone first enters Roxton's home, he immediately notices that "Everywhere there were mingled the luxury of the wealthy man of taste and the careless untidiness of the bachelor" (chap. VI). He's like Batman without a disguise.

Professor Summerlee, by contrast, is "a tall, thin, bitter man, with the withered aspect of a Theologian" (chap. V). He is a Professor of Comparative Anatomy and is the most vocal opponent of Professor Challenger's claim of having found a pterosaur. Although it is unclear who exactly Doyle had in mind from real life, he fits perfectly the generic, stogy, unadventurous professor. It must have been very fun for Doyle to put such a man in the kind of dangerous situations Summerlee experiences.

Edward Dunn Malone is the narrator of the story, and his calm reflections stand in stark contrast to the fiery brimstone of Challenger. He is a reporter for the *Daily Gazette* (Challenger considers journalists "swine from the devil's herd"), but he earns Challenger's respect for his tenacity (after they get into a brawl) and for his openmindedness in believing his story. Malone also may not be someone specific from Doyle's life, but he is the kind of man he admires: someone who can be convinced of the truth no matter how strange it may sound.

Together, this self-assured foursome makes the most anticipated discovery of Doyle's generation.

Summary and Setting

The Lost World is essentially an exploration of the theory of evolution packaged in a boyish, adventure novel. The four primary characters journey together on a scientific adventure to prove or disprove Professor Challenger's claims to have found an isolated plateau where "creatures survive which would otherwise disappear" (chap. IV). As evidence, he shows the forearm of a pterodactyl to a room full of spectators, but still no one will believe him. After all, bones can be faked. Tired of being ignored, he puts forth his final challenge: "verify my story yourself." Thus begins the adventure of Malone, Lord Roxton, and Professors Summerlee and Challenger.

Doyle himself was a convinced evolutionist, and I believe he based the premise of his story (finding dinosaurs on an isolated plateau) on Darwin's prediction that in just such a scenario life would have "less modification and less extermination."[2] To capture the magical feeling that there were places on this earth left unexplored and ripe for discovery, Doyle put the plateau somewhere in the Amazon River Basin of South America, a remote and mysterious place a hundred years ago.

> Vivid orchids and wonderful colored lichens smoldered upon the swarthy tree-trunks and where a wandering shaft of light fell full upon the golden allamanda, the scarlet star-clusters of the tacsonia, or the rich deep blue of ipomaea, the effect was as a dream of fairyland.[3]

Doyle is at his best with this story, and he himself much preferred the character of Professor Challenger to even his most famous character, Sherlock Holmes. Also, Doyle's favorite stories as a boy were by an Irish American named Mayne Reid, who wrote Old West adventure novels. Doyle successfully melds both of these favorites and then adds in his own unique deductive skills to produce one of the most enduring adventure stories of all time.

Worldview
The Nature of Proof

A question that we all should ask ourselves at some point in our life is: How do I know that what I believe is true? What are the criteria I need to follow? Is it seeing it with my own eyes, getting a photograph, or capturing video footage? I have often wondered that if pictures had been taken of Jesus' death, burial, and resurrection, wouldn't that be far more convincing than just the testimony of the disciples recorded in the Bible? A video tape of the *real* passion of Christ would persuade even the most skeptical unbeliever, right?

Images are powerful, but as all of us know too well, photographs can be faked, and people can be easily fooled. For example, reporters (who sometimes have an agenda to push) have justified altering photographs to "prove" their point because they know that people will more easily believe a photograph. Letters have also been faked, as well as memos, fossils, footprints, alien bodies, and many other so-called pieces of hard evidence. Even lie-detectors can be fooled. Hoaxers abound and, although sometimes it is just an innocent gag to see if they can get away with it, it is often used to perpetrate a lie.

So, to ask the question another way: how do we know when something isn't a hoax?

Proof means "that which confirms or authenticates an assertion." Basically, it means I have hard evidence that what I claim to be true is true. Truth means "the quality of being factual" or that which corresponds with the facts or reality. Put another way, truth "accurately represents what is depicted or described."[4] For example, when we say something is real, we mean that what we are describing has verifiable existence and that it is "true and actual; not imaginary, alleged, or ideal." Anyone who has ever tried to convince their parents of something knows exactly how difficult this can be.

Before we move on, though, we need to recognize a problem which plagues every truth-seeker: denial. If people don't want to believe what the hard evidence proves, they will find all sorts of ways to misrepresent its meaning. Not everyone is an open-minded, honest seeker, and some even actively try to suppress the truth by ignoring or discrediting the evidence. Even though some will believe an obvious fake, it is equally possible that some will refuse to believe an obvious truth. Too often we put blinders on: ignorance is bliss, right?

Our ability to differentiate between truth and error—the authentic and the fraudulent—is becoming more important than ever in our world today. There are a lot of agendas to push and a lot of technology to push it. This is by no means a new problem, though, for even Pilate asked Jesus, "What is truth?" *The Lost World* may give us some helpful insights.

Proof According to Doyle

In the opening chapters of *The Lost World*, the unbelievable story of Professor Challenger is presented to the newspaper man, Mr. Malone. He is a skeptic and asks a series of intelligent questions about each item discovered by Challenger, but then he demonstrates the unusual ability to be persuaded by the evidence. He records: "The cumulative proof was overwhelming. The sketch, the photographs, the narrative, and now the actual specimen—the evidence was complete" (chap. IV). Challenger had previously tried to persuade his colleagues that his story was true, but they couldn't be convinced. It was too absurd. Now, finally, someone was intellectually honest enough to see the truth. Mr. Malone, therefore, represents an important virtue of all truth seekers: the ideal of allowing the facts to guide one's conclusions.

Indeed, Doyle applied this ideal to every aspect of his life. He tried to overturn two unjust court cases where he thought the facts had been misrepresented; he defended the actions of the British Empire in South Africa during the Boer Wars; and he, after years of careful consideration of all the data, believed that fairies were real and that ghosts do exist. He was actually taken in by the famous Cottingley Fairy Photographs.[5] These staged pictures caused quite a sensation in their time. He was kind of like the original Ghost Hunter. Here are some of the typical proofs Doyle would look for in his quest for truth:

- The testimony of reliable witnesses
- Photographs
- Tangible things such as artifacts and fossils
- Personal experiences
- Anecdotes which told a consistent story over time and between social classes.

To his credit, Doyle was never afraid of criticism for any conclusion he came to if he felt he had given it a fair hearing. For example, it takes courage to defend one's belief in fairies scientifically, but as he says in the last line of his book, *The Coming of the Fairies*, "Far from being resented, such criticism [from those who don't believe in fairies], so long as it is earnest and honest, must be most welcome to those whose only aim is the fearless search for truth." He was not afraid of pushing the edge even if the consensus of great scientific minds opposed him:

> . . . when I learned that their [Darwin's, Huxley's, Tyndall's and Herbert Spencer's] derision

The Lost World   571

In 1917 two girls in England took the first of five photographs featuring what they claimed were fairies. Elsie Wright and her cousin Frances Griffiths caused a stir when their photographs came to public attention. Decades later, in 1981, the two women admitted they faked all but one of the photographs. Elsie said they were too embarrassed to admit the truth after duping Arthur Conan Doyle: "Two village kids and a brilliant man like Conan Doyle, well, we could only keep quiet."

had reached such a point that they would not even examine it [life after death] . . . *their action in this respect was most unscientific and dogmatic.* . . .
—*The New Revelation* [emphasis added]

He could not understand how any scientist would refuse to believe what could be empirically proven.

But back to the question regarding *The Lost World* premise: What would it actually mean to find a living dinosaur? It is one thing to believe that Challenger discovered dinosaurs; it is another to believe that it proves evolution. Doyle proposes that if a group of scientists were to bring back indisputable proof that dinosaurs were still alive, that would *prove* the theory of evolution. But my question is: Would it? The difficulty is that, as Ronald Reagan, our fortieth president, once said, "Facts are stupid things." In other words, there is no inherent meaning in the facts; we give meaning to the facts. Truth isn't solely dependent on one's ability to gather facts, but on one's ability to evaluate, sift, and make sense of those facts. And so couldn't finding a living fossil mean something else? Is an evolutionary interpretation the only probable explanation?

One has to wonder whether Doyle's penchant for being duped by fake photographs of fairies and by mediums who were charlatans points to a gullibility that should make us deeply question whether his belief in evolution might not be just another example of his gullibility.

Darwin's Lost World

According to the theory of evolution as Darwin defined it and Doyle defended it,[6] all life forms are "the lineal descendants of some few beings" (*Origin*, chap. 14). If given enough time, adaptations would accumulate which would modify and improve life forms, resulting in the variety of life which we see in the fossil record and all around us today. It is because of the law of Natural Selection that those first few beings evolved into the birds, the sea creatures, the land animals, and every microscopic life form known to us.

Darwin knew very well that his theory of evolution would be controversial because most people in his day believed the Genesis account of creation. Out of consideration for this reality, he sat on his data for twenty years until another naturalist began to publish similar sounding theories, compelling him to finally print his own. It didn't take long for Darwin's ideas to ripple through the universities, but the problem was that his theory still needed some investigation because, admittedly, his data was incomplete. For example, he knew they needed to explore the fossil record for intermediary links and that they needed to study how traits passed from one generation to the next.

We do not know all the possible transitional gradations between the simplest and the most perfect organs; it cannot be pretended that we know all the varied means of Distribution during the long lapse of years, or that we know how imperfect the Geological Record is. Grave as these several difficulties are, in my judgment they do not overthrow the theory of descent with modification (*Origin* chap. 14).

At least Darwin was honest about the lack of evidence, but that is also why other scientists started on their quests to find the missing evidence. In other words, he had published a theory he was confident was true, but which hadn't been fully supported. He had *inferred* trans-speciation evolution from his observations while on his famous voyage around the world; but what is quite amazing is the self-defeating irony of a statement he makes in the introduction and maintains throughout his book: "…much remains obscure …but I can entertain no doubt…" To infer that adaptation leads to trans-speciation stretches his careful observations to a breaking point. Couldn't we just as easily theorize that adaptation is a design feature of the Creator? He completely dismisses that possibility. Notice also the blatant plea to trust his judgment, to take him at his word based upon *his scientific authority*. Darwin's statement clearly demonstrates that he was putting his personal opinion in front of the evidence. What if evidence showed up which disproved his theory? Does his confident statement allow for the possibility that he could be wrong?

In fact, when one reads *The Origin of Species*, it sounds more like a treatise on what Darwin predicted we *should* find if trans-speciation evolution were true (and, of course, he knew it was true), not a book about what he *had* found. But still, as a result of his theoretical model, it initiated a quest to find the proof that Darwin couldn't produce but predicted was there. And it is in the fictional work, *The Lost World*, that Doyle explores that theoretical proof in detail.

Doyle and the Missing Link

Doyle was a true believer in evolution; however, there was still the nagging problem that a true intermediary fossil, the ultimate proof, had not yet been found. There had been some contenders, though. For one, Neandertal man had been found in 1856, but it wasn't until 1864 (five years after the publication of *Origin of Species*, implying that the fossil didn't lead to the conclusion; the conclusion imposed meaning on the fossil), that William King suggested that Neandertals were perhaps the transitional species everyone was looking for. It was exciting at first, and many "scientific" drawings were made, but ultimately Neandertal was just too human. Stephanie Moser in her book *Ancestral Images* makes the case that drawings began to be produced during this time to help sway public opinion about evolution:

> After the evolutionary thinkers made the suggestion that there were missing links which represented an intermediary stage between human and apes, illustrators started to construct images of simian-like ancestors.[7]

As a result some of the first drawings of the original concept of Neandertal Man have indelibly marked our cultural soul as to what a caveman is supposed to look like: a very hairy and very angry hunched over but almost upright ape-man. It doesn't matter that these first images were completely mistaken; *they were drawings of what was predicted*.

The Lost World expands on this image. Once our determined explorers finally find a way up onto the plateau, they not only find dinosaurs, they also find an early species of ape-like men. It is explained in the book how men and dinosaurs could be on the same plateau, so I won't go into that here, but Doyle uses his descriptive powers to flesh out what the scientific community expected to find:

> A face was gazing into mine. . . . It was a human face—or at least it was far more human than any monkey's that I have ever seen. It was long, whitish, and blotched with pimples, the nose flattened, and the lower jaw projecting, with a bristle of coarse whiskers round the chin. The eyes, which were under thick and heavy brows, were bestial and ferocious, and as it opened its mouth to snarl what sounded like a curse at me I observed that it had curved, sharp canine teeth (chap. XI).

Challenger and Summerlee, after they are captured, debate whether they are *dryopithecus* of Java or its earlier cousin, *pithecanthropus*, but the point is Darwin's prediction is living and breathing on this sacred plateau. Wouldn't it be fabulous if it were true!

The Piltdown Hoax

Even though Neanderthals lost their place as *the* missing link, scientists, undaunted, next identified *Cro-Magnon* in 1868 as a viable candidate, and then *Dryopithecus* (Java man) in 1891. Many others were cropping up, but it wasn't until December of 1912, only a month after *The Lost World* had finished running as a serial in *The Strand*, that an amateur archaeologist named Charles Dawson revealed that he had found "the exact combination of features everyone expected to find."[8] Piltdown man had a human-sized cranium and an apelike jaw, and as a result, many skeptics became convinced that evolution had been proven true. Furthermore, it met with Doyle's criteria of physical evidence, and it fit perfectly with Darwin's prediction. What could be wrong with it? Well, for one, it was a complete fraud, and scientists didn't discover or acknowledge this *for over 40 years*. How could this happen to such great men of science?

Some have theorized that Sir Arthur Conan Doyle himself pulled the prank and left clues in *The Lost World*, but this theory did not arise until 1983, and no one in his day

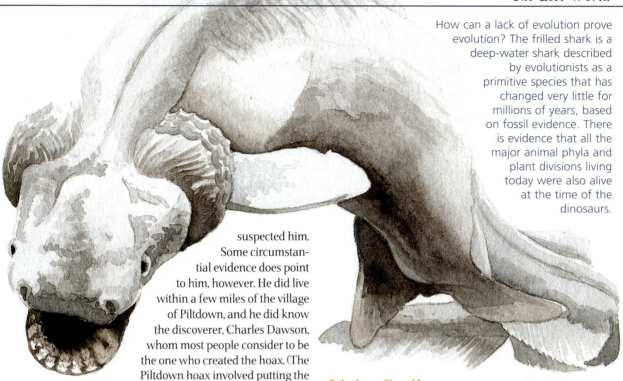

How can a lack of evolution prove evolution? The frilled shark is a deep-water shark described by evolutionists as a primitive species that has changed very little for millions of years, based on fossil evidence. There is evidence that all the major animal phyla and plant divisions living today were also alive at the time of the dinosaurs.

suspected him. Some circumstantial evidence does point to him, however. He did live within a few miles of the village of Piltdown, and he did know the discoverer, Charles Dawson, whom most people consider to be the one who created the hoax. (The Piltdown hoax involved putting the lower jawbone of an orangutan onto the skull of a modern man and claiming that it was the Missing Link. Thus, proof that evolution is true.[9]) Could Doyle have been in on the prank? Could he have given him advice on how to falsify the data?

Personally, I don't think it fits the character of the man who was so devoted to a relentless pursuit of truth. Rather, I think it is more likely that Doyle was simply fooled like everyone else. In a few years he would be completely fooled by supposed photographs of fairies, so why not a forged skull? He believed without question that evolution was true, so when "irrefutable" evidence backed up his belief, how could he deny it? Also, he was immersed in the scientific fervor of his day, and *The Lost World* captures this cultural anticipation of an imminent discovery. Evolution, the theory everyone *knew* to be true, was about to be proven.

Of course, one fraud doesn't disprove the theory, but many skeptics were converted by the Piltdown hoax, and one cannot downplay the effect the *belief* in the Piltdown man had on public opinion for the next 40 years. The fact is that well-trained scientists had been fooled by "evidence" because they *wanted* to believe it. As was pointed out in a PBS episode of NOVA, "…the *desire* to find the earliest Englishman had blinded the scientific establishment" [emphasis added].[10] In other words, in Doyle's day (and ours?) the desire to prove evolution was so strong, some men would do anything—and some would believe anything—if it matched their desired outcome. It is a warning to us all.

Living Fossils

As you read through *The Lost World*, keep in mind that we bring meaning to the facts. Continually ask yourself what the characters' discoveries actually mean. Doyle's willingness to consider any possible conclusion if tangible evidence could be produced is noble, but he was still susceptible to being fooled, as we all are. If an image is convincing enough, we think the source is credible, and we want to believe it, who knows of what things we can be convinced?

Doyle did contain his beliefs within the domain of a Theistic-Christian worldview, but in accordance with the intellectual pressures of the day and his personal choice, he distanced himself from the inspiration of God's Word, and he later grew to despise the Old Testament. He abandoned Scripture as his ultimate authority,[11] and he elevated human reason to that position. In one of his many letters to newspapers, he says: "The Divine Creator has indeed given us one compass, and that is reason, the noblest of all faculties."[12] Note how he makes subtle suggestions of this throughout the story. The problem is that, as we have seen, Doyle's complete faith and reliance in the authority of human reason does not immunize him from being completely fooled by sleights of hand, fraudulent fossils, and faked photographs.

So let's go back to Doyle's premise that discovering living dinosaurs would *prove* evolution. We now need to consider whether this is the only possible explanation.

574 Omnibus IV

The Lost World imagines a long-lost plateau in the dense South American jungle that supports life long extinct in the rest of the world. Creatures from disparate geological ages mingle in a dangerous landscape filled with ancient and modern species. Of particular interest is the idea of the coexistence of modern humans and pre-human ape-men, or hominids. In the story these groups are fierce enemies and fight each other in a constant war for superiority.

According to evolutionary theory, it anticipates finding many extinct species in the fossil record; finding living dinosaurs, therefore, would seem to contradict that prediction. Darwin does suggest that in an isolated situation species may not evolve as quickly, but some of the dinosaurs on Doyle's plateau are from the Jurassic Period, supposedly some 150 million years ago. If they could remain virtually unchanged for 150 million years, how does that "prove" evolution? How can a lack of evolving prove that things evolve? Talk about a sleight of hand!

Doyle's *Lost World*, ironically, makes a better case for special creation than for evolution. Special creation teaches that species were designed to reproduce after their own kind; therefore, even though many extinct species may be found in the fossil record, it is consistent with the special creation theory to find fossilized forms which are still alive *and practically identical* to the fossilized forms.

In fact, this is exactly what we find—and abundantly. Everyone has heard that crocodiles, salamanders, and sharks have remained virtually unchanged for hundreds of millions of years, but the author of *Living Fossils* presents "evidence showing *all* of the major animal phyla and *all* of the major plant divisions living today were also alive at the time of the dinosaurs."[13] Sassafras trees, redwoods, sea cucumbers, lobsters, dragonflies, butterflies, bees, worms, coral, many types of fish, salamanders, frogs, lizards, penguins, owls, ducks, gulls, hedgehogs, possums, flowering plants, etc., are all *living fossils*. The point is that there are many un-evolved life forms living today which are found not only in dinosaur layers, but throughout all the sedimentary layers.

So what would bringing back live dinosaurs actually prove? I believe it would prove that dinosaurs *haven't* adapted (climate conditions are far different today than when they roamed the earth) and that some other explanation for their extinction must be forthcoming. From this abundance of evidence, it would seem a more probable conclusion that life forms don't trans-speciate over time.

We have come back to the question with which we started: How do I know that what I believe is true? After all the questions, after all the debates, after all the inquiries, and after all the doubts, it all comes down to whose testimony do you trust? Like Doyle, do you trust your own judgment, putting your supreme confidence in human reason to figure it all out? Or, as a Christian ought, do you put your trust in God's Word?

Personally, I am saddened by Doyle's unwillingness to dig a little deeper into some of the problems he had with Scripture. He decided to trust mediums over God's prophets, and he chose to trust Darwin's judgment over God's revelation. If someone like him had turned his powers of reason toward a defense of God (who is without flaw) instead of a mere defense of man's reason (which is undoubtedly flawed), who could have contended with him? We don't need to abandon human reason to believe God's Word, but our reason certainly can be enlightened by His Word. We ignore the value of divine revelation to our detriment.

—Corey Piper

For Further Reading

Ape to Men. DVD: A&E Television Networks, 2005.

Behe, Michael. *Darwin's Black Box.* New York: Simon and Schuster, 2006.

Doyle, Sir Arthur Conan. *Memories and Adventures.* Boston: Little, Brown, and Co. 1924.

Johnson, Philip. *Darwin on Trial.* Downers Grove, Ill.: InterVarsity Press, 1993.

Miller, Russell. *The Adventures of Arthur Conan Doyle.* New York: Thomas Dunne Books, 2008.

Symons, Julian. *Conan Doyle: Portrait of an Artist.* New York: The Mysterious Press, 1979.

Session I: Prelude

A Question to Consider

If someone told you a story that seemed too amazing to be true, how would you go about confirming the story?

From the General Information above answer the following questions:

1. What do *proof* and *truth* mean? What is the difference between the two?
2. According to Doyle, what is an ideal any truth-seeker must have? Are there any flaws in this ideal?
3. What does the term "trans-speciation" mean? How is this different from adaptation?
4. What are some of the first candidates for being the missing link?
5. Why was the scientific community fooled by the Piltdown hoax?
6. What did Doyle consider his ultimate authority? Why didn't this immunize him to being fooled?
7. Why does *The Lost World* make a better case for special creation than for evolution?
8. Why is it wiser to trust the authority of God's Word over the authority of man's reason?

Reading Assignment:
The Lost World, chapters I–IV

Session II: Discussion
The Lost World, chapters I–IV

A Question to Consider
What does it mean to be a hero?

Discuss or list short answers to the following questions:

Text Analysis

1. Gladys says that she is in love with an ideal man, although she has never met one. How does she characterize that man?
2. How does Gladys's definition of that ideal man influence Mr. Malone?
3. Why would it take heroic courage for Malone to meet with Professor Challenger?
4. What is Challenger's wife's advice to Mr. Malone?
5. Why did Challenger invite Malone back in after fighting with him for being a fraud?
6. How does Challenger's story in chapter IV illustrate

the heroic virtues of the ideal man?

Cultural Analysis

1. Who are some of the real heroes our culture admires? Why do we admire them?
2. Who are some heroes in the Bible? Why do we admire them?
3. Movies and novels play a huge role in influencing our perception of what a hero should be. Name some famous fictional heroes and the qualities they model.
4. Jesus Christ was not only the perfect man; He defines for us the qualities of a true hero. What qualities does He live out which contrast with our cultural heroes? Which qualities are similar?

Biblical Analysis

1. How do the Beatitudes reflect God's heroic ideal (Matt. 5)?
2. Paul encourages the Philippians to meditate on praiseworthy virtues. Discuss the virtues he lists and their importance to the heroic ideal (Phil. 4:4–9).
3. Isaiah 58:6–12 is one of the most succinct descriptions of the heart of God. Can you identify the heroic virtue to which God wants us to be most devoted?

Summa

 Write an essay or discuss this question, integrating what you have learned from the material above. **What is God's heroic ideal?**

Optional Activity

Identify an injustice that you know about and come up with an action plan to right the wrong. Maybe a friend or a family member has been treated unjustly. Maybe it's a societal injustice. Do you need to write a letter? Do you need to raise awareness? It may require courage to step out and make a difference, but don't forget, with a great adventure comes a great reward.

Reading Assignment:
The Lost World, chapters V–VIII

Session III: Recitation
The Lost World, chapters V–VIII

Comprehension Questions

Answer the following questions for factual recall:

1. About what topic does Mr. Waldron lecture? What does he say that causes Challenger to shout, "Question!" (chap. V)
2. To which great discoverers does Professor Challenger compare himself (chap. V)?
3. What compels Malone to stand up and volunteer to go on the quest (chap. V)?
4. How does Lord John Roxton test the mettle of Malone's character (chap. VI)?

Sir Arthur Conan Doyle

5. Roxton calls himself "the flail of the Lord" in Peru. What did he do (chap. VI)?
6. Whom do they hire at Para to help them on their journey? Describe him (chap. VII)?
7. What is written on the note from Challenger that is to be opened only on July 15 at 12:00 noon sharp (chap. VII)?
8. Even amidst the warning beats of the drums, what do both Summerlee and Challenger do all day (chap. VIII)?
9. What does *Curupuri* mean (chap. VIII)?
10. What does Challenger see, but Summerlee doesn't, when they are only a mile or so from the plateau (chap. VIII)?

READING ASSIGNMENT:
The Lost World, chapters IX–XII

SESSION IV: ACTIVITY
The Lost World, chapters IX–XII

Monster Quest

Our four adventurers experience many strange and alarming creatures, but their quest is not just to know it for themselves; it is to prove it to the rest of humanity. As you may know, there are many eyewitness accounts of strange creatures all over the world. Some of the more famous ones are the Loch Ness monster, Bigfoot, and a South American dinosaur, but people also claim to have seen lake monsters in Turkey, South Africa, and Canada. Indeed, our world is full of strange creatures, such as were purportedly photographed after being washed up by a tsunami. (See Link 6 for this chapter at www.VeritasPress.com/OmniLinks.) Some may be frauds, but are all of them? How can you tell?

In your project seek to follow Doyle's investigative techniques as described in the Worldview essay. Keep in mind the source of your information, and make sure you document it. You may present your information to the class, or to your parents, in the form of a PowerPoint presentation, a video documentary, or a research paper. I suppose one's worldview would have to allow one to believe that such strange creatures could even possibly exist, but since we're theists and believe in a highly creative God, who knows what might actually be out there . . . but don't be fooled. Some things to consider when analyzing photography are: 1) Has the photo been doctored after it was taken? Look for tell-tale signs of repeated, identical patterns that should be random. 2) Were the events shown by the photograph staged? (Doyle and many others were fooled by a supposed fairy photograph because the girls lied. They had cut out pictures of fairies and then taken the photograph. It was an un-doctored photograph, just not of an authentic scene.) A good question to always ask: "Is this photograph too good to be true?" In other words, some people will arrange things that match the prediction perfectly. This is tough to discern, but it should at least raise some skepticism. 3) The trickiest of all is to look out for authentic photographs which are being reinterpreted. The photograph may be of something real, but it is said to be something other than what it is. The only way to discern this is to check sources, study the original artifact or animal yourself, look at other photographs that may provide better context, check dates, and hope the people you are talking to aren't outright lying.

Optional Activity

The Internet is full of pictures of strange creatures supposedly washed ashore during the 2004 Indian Ocean Tsunami. Are they real?

Frances Griffiths and one of the "Cottingley Fairies."

Do a research project on living fossils. Present the information in the same way as described in the activity above. Sassafras trees, redwoods, sea cucumbers, lobsters, dragonflies, butterflies, bees, worms, coral, many types of fish, sharks, salamanders, frogs, lizards, penguins, owls, ducks, gulls, hedgehogs, possums, and flowering plants are all examples of living fossils you might choose.[14] Make sure you consider the implication of finding a living fossil. Would finding a living dinosaur bother you or an evolutionist more?[15] Also, don't forget, one must pay attention to rock layers, not just dates. The dating of rock layers is suspect (a research project in itself).

 **READING ASSIGNMENT:**
The Lost World, chapters XIII–XVI

SESSION V:

WORLDVIEW ANALYSIS
The Lost World, chapters XIII–XVI

Doyle vs. You

Theism in its most basic, structural, form is a belief in a supreme deity who is separate and distinct from creation and yet interacts with and influences humans and events. In its broadest form, then, a theist can be a Muslim, a Jew, or a Christian, and each religion *further defines the characteristics* of the supreme deity in its own way, branching out into its own sub-divisions and nuances. The point is that all of these extensions put their own particular finishing touches on the original, fundamental structure of theism because they are bound within its configuration. Our worldview is refined by our religious and philosophical beliefs, and every person is a complex combination of these various beliefs and cultural influences. Doyle is a great example of how diverse theism can be. In a phrase (which is never fair to anyone) Doyle is a theist, a Christian, and a Spiritualist (which is a blend of science and religion). In Chart 1, fill in specific examples from *The Lost World* or from more research into Doyle's life. Also include what you believe.

SESSION VI: REVIEW

Looking Back at *The Lost World*

The following questions are meant to help you review this book. You should review all of the questions. Some of these questions may be used on a midterm or semester final.

1. Compare and contrast Doyle's vision of the ideal man with that of God's. Use specific examples from *The Lost World* and Scripture.
2. How do we rationally go about figuring out what is true and what is false? Also discuss the impact of a worldview on our investigation.
3. Which of the four main characters best meets Doyle's criteria for being a man of action? Give reasons and

Chart 1: **WORLDVIEW ANALYSIS**

View of:	DOYLE	YOU
God		
Scripture		
Mankind		
Nature		

examples of why you chose the character you did.

4. Describe Doyle's worldview as specifically illustrated in *The Lost World*.

5. What would the discovery of a living dinosaur actually mean? Give the opinion of an evolutionist and a creationist.

OPTIONAL SESSION: ACTIVITY

Watching *The Lost World*

Several movie versions of *The Lost World* have been made, the most recent (and considered one of the better ones) was made for TV by the BBC in 2006. Watch this movie and take special note of how the added characters help focus the evolution/creation debate. There is a specific conversation between Summerlee and a missionary. Write your own scene and include how you might answer Summerlee's criticisms.

After watching the movie, answer the following questions:

1. There is a slight change to how our adventurers become trapped on the plateau. Why is this a significant and very intentional plot change from the book?

2. Another major deviation comes at the end of the movie. Compare the book's version to the movie's ending. Which ending is more realistic? Could you write a better ending from the point of view of a creationist? (Of course, you will have to wait until you finish the book to complete this part of the assignment. Also, be encouraged to read the book's ending before you watch the movie's ending.)

ENDNOTES

1 Miller, Russell. *The Adventures of Arthur Conan Doyle: a Biography*. New York: St. Martin's Press, 2008. 309.

2 *The Origin of Species*, Chapter 4 "Natural Selection." Darwin had observed isolated situations on islands, but he theorized that the same kind of preservation would occur in "a country partly surrounded by barriers, into which new and better adapted forms could not freely enter...." I believe Doyle based his plateau on this prediction.

3 *The Lost World*, chapter VIII.

4 From *Roget's II Thesaurus*, 1995.

5 Information about these famous fairy photos can be found at Links 1 and 2 for this chapter at www.VeritasPress.com/OmniLinks.

6 I am going to primarily document the theory according to Darwin and as Doyle would have understood it. It has "evolved" itself, and in our day many of Darwin's original assumptions have been discarded. One could say the theory had to adapt so it could survive.

7 Moser, Stephanie. *Ancestral Images*. Ithaca, N.Y.: Cornell University Press, 1998.

8 *Ape to Man*. The History Channel DVD, 2005.

9 More information on the Piltdown hoax can be found at Links 3 and 4 for this chapter at www.VeritasPress.com/OmniLinks.

10 "The Boldest Hoax" aired Jan. 11, 2005, on PBS. The transcript from this program may be viewed through Link 5 for this chapter at www.VeritasPress.com/OmniLinks.

11 In an editorial he wrote in response to a man named Mr. Shutte, we get a clear picture of his opinion of the Bible: "He [Mr. Shutte] upholds the absolute and entire inspiration of the Bible. But does he not know that there are in the Bible statements which we know to be untrue? ... Was it He who was author of the statement that the world was created in six days, that the creation was some five thousand years ago, or that Joshua commanded the sun, which was never moving, to stand still? If it was, then alas for our conceptions of the Deity. If it was not, then what becomes of the absolute inspiration of Scripture?" (20 November 1889).

12 From a letter to the *Daily Express* on August, 31, 1906, "Are We Becoming Less Religious? Summing Up." pp. 121–122. He used this argument in the context of devaluing the inspiration of Scripture.

13 *Living Fossils: Evolution: The Grand Experiment, Vol. 2.* Audio Visual Consultants, Inc., 2008. Appendix E.

14 For a video of a swimming, once thought extinct, frilled shark, visit Link 7 for this chapter at www.VeritasPress.com/OmniLinks.

15 An interesting website on this issue can be found by clicking Link 8 for this chapter at www.VeritasPress.com/OmniLinks.

Knowing God

Have you ever gone to a book signing? An author comes to a bookstore to read from his new book, meet fans, and sign autographs. For especially famous authors, people stand in line for a long time to get their books signed. Sometimes there is a chance for readers to ask questions about their favorite characters or plot points. If the readers are fortunate, they get a chance to know the author a little bit and gain a glimpse into why he writes what he does. Our favorite story can come to life by knowing more about who has written it.

The greatest story ever told is playing out before our eyes each day: the story of the world. The central drama in the story was played out on a hill outside Jerusalem two thousand years ago, but the story is far from finished. Because of our distance from the Cross, it can sometimes be hard to see how the story is being told today. Why do terrible things happen in our world, and to us? How can trials, temptations, and sin be for the greater glory of God?

God is the author of this story, of history. By knowing God and His ways, we can start to understand why He has written this story the way He has. We can gain a deeper appreciation for His ways. By learning to love the author, we can learn to love His story.

The Ghent Altarpiece (also called *Adoration of the Mystic Lamb*) was completed by Jan van Eyck in 1432. The central panel shown here depicts Christ seated in triumph and wearing a triple crown, perhaps signifying the Trinity.

General Information

Author and Context

J.I. Packer is a Protestant theologian. He was educated at Oxford University, and it was there that he met C.S. Lewis. In addition to being an executive editor of *Christianity Today*, he served as the general editor of the English Standard Version of the Bible. Currently, Dr. Packer is a professor of theology at Regent College in Vancouver, British Columbia. He was named one of the "25 Most Influential Evangelicals" by TIME Magazine in 2005.

Dr. Packer originally wrote Knowing God as a series of articles for a Christian magazine, but it was compiled in book form in 1973. It has since sold over a million copies and been translated into twelve languages, becoming one of the most significant theological works of the twentieth century.

Significance

The significance of *Knowing God* lies partly in its place in modern Christian writing. Because it has sold so well, it has impacted a vast number of Christians. Dr. Packer gives a straightforward summary of Christian theology without excusing or compromising Scripture.

It is very easy to write theology that attempts to water down the character of God. Many times, God's omnipotence, wrath, or sovereignty are left out in popular theological writings, since those characteristics can make God seem less appealing to the masses. In *Knowing God*, Dr. Packer does not back down from the truths of God and His Word.

Setting

During the 1970s, Dr. Packer felt that Christians were losing sight of who God really was. Humanism had turned man's focus inward rather than outward. Man was focused far more on making God something he could understand simply rather than understanding the God of Scripture.

Dr. Packer also points to skepticism as a motivation for writing his book. Since the Enlightenment in the eighteenth century, Western philosophy has operated from a position of doubt and skepticism. There has been a strong skepticism of anything that cannot be proven using human logic. This has often focused on God Himself.

These twin forces, combined with the cultural degeneration that took place in the decades following World War II, inspired the writing of *Knowing God*.

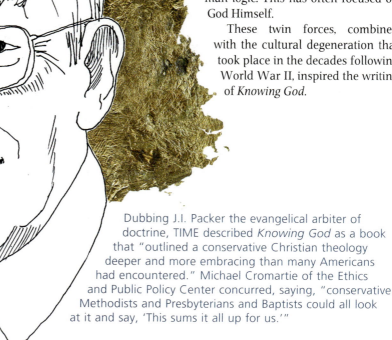

Dubbing J.I. Packer the evangelical arbiter of doctrine, TIME described *Knowing God* as a book that "outlined a conservative Christian theology deeper and more embracing than many Americans had encountered." Michael Cromartie of the Ethics and Public Policy Center concurred, saying, "conservative Methodists and Presbyterians and Baptists could all look at it and say, 'This sums it all up for us.'"

Worldview

What is the first question in the Westminster Confession of Faith? It is, "What is the chief end of man?" The answer to that question is: "Man's chief end is to glorify God and enjoy Him forever." This is our primary duty. We ought to spend our lives glorifying and enjoying God.

As far as the first part goes, we know what it means to glorify God. God is certainly worthy of glory. He is the Creator and King of the universe (Rev. 4:11). Glorifying God means that we obey Him. In the Old Testament, the Israelites glorified God when they kept the covenant, and they shamed God when they chased after other gods. Glorifying God means that we obey Him and worship Him.

But that is only the first half of the answer. Our chief end is also to enjoy God. We are commanded to do this in Scripture (Phil. 4:4). What does it mean to *enjoy* God? We are certainly to enjoy His gifts to us: our families and friends, our shelter from the cold, and chiefly our salvation from sin. We must also enjoy God Himself. To do this properly, we must know who it is with whom we are enjoying fellowship. If we are to enjoy God, we must know who He is.

That is the purpose of *Knowing God*. Dr. Packer wants to explain who God is, how we can know Him, and what knowing Him really means. If we truly know God, it will affect every aspect of our lives.

In the last century, many people developed an unbiblical view of God. The god they thought of was sometimes more akin to the Deist god, the great watchmaker who made the world and then left it to fend for itself. Sometimes this god was a generic, genderless being who cared for people at random. Sometimes this god was another form of "Mother Nature." Many people have also denied God altogether.

Dr. Packer ties these false views of God to two central causes: the rise of humanism and the rise of modern skepticism. This is a two-fold attack on the Person of God. On the one hand, man spends far more time focusing on himself than on His Creator. Our world is obsessed with human accomplishments and human potential. We spend more time dissecting predictions of who we deem mostly likely to win the Oscars than studying God.

At the same time, our culture has been inundated with men claiming that there is no real proof for God. The Enlightenment of the eighteenth century was founded upon the skepticism of Descartes, who trained himself to doubt what he could not prove. One result of the skepticism of the Enlightenment was to give men an excuse to doubt the existence of God. After all, they reasoned, God could not be empirically proven on their own terms. So they attacked the truth of Scripture and ridiculed Christian behavior. We see this still today. When our culture is filled with praise for man and attacks on God, it is little wonder that we ought to reconsider who our God really is.

How can we know God? In the first place, we can look at creation. When we listen to a piece of music, it is possible to identify the artist by his style. We notice that C.S. Lewis wrote differently than William Shakespeare. Just as you can tell an author or musician by their individual styles, we can see the stamp of God's personality on the world. We see God's generosity in the frequent rain that He sends to feed our crops, we see God's love of careful

"Holy, holy, holy! All the saints adore Thee, casting down their golden crowns around the glassy sea; cherubim and seraphim falling down before Thee, who was, and is, and evermore shall be."

detail when we examine the human cell, and we see God's sense of humor when we look at monkeys. Everywhere we look, we see God in His world: we can see what He is like, generally, but not specifically. This is *general revelation.*

Knowledge of God is not only an obligation of Christians. All men are obligated to learn of their Creator, since all things were made by God. If men want to understand the world they live in, they must understand the One who made it. If they deny Him, then "the world becomes a strange, mad, painful place."

But the world is not a perfect picture of God. It is only the creature, and He is the Creator. While a painting shows us something about the artist's personality, it does not show us the artist completely. And this painting is imperfect in another way: it is tainted with sin.

Since we cannot learn everything about God from creation, He has provided special means for us to learn about Himself: His Word. God gave us the Bible in order to show us Himself. We can not only see the basic characteristics of God, but we also learn how God plans to save His people. We learn about God's love. The revelation in God's Word is called special revelation.

Dr. Packer assumes all of this in *Knowing God*. The book is written according to five biblical principles, and the first is that God has spoken unto man, and the Bible is His Word. This is where we must always begin. The Bible is inspired by the Holy Spirit (2 Tim. 3:16; 2 Pet. 1:20–21), and apart from it, there is no true foundation.

The other principles Dr. Packer lists are truths taught clearly in the Bible. The second is that God is Lord and King over the world (Ps. 47:7–8). The Bible teaches us that God has not created the world to leave it to Satan, nor did He lose control of it with the coming of sin. God is, was, and ever will be the King of the world because He has authority and power over *everything* on it (Amos 3:6; Prov. 21:31).

Dr. Packer assumes, thirdly, that God is a Savior, active in sovereign love through Jesus Christ. From the beginning of Scripture to the end, we find that God is seeking out salvation for His people. Only moments after the fall of Adam, God tells our first parents that relief from the rule of the serpent is coming (Gen. 3:15). The end of Revelation is the story of a heavenly city, filled with those whose names are in the Book of Life. The whole Bible is the story of redemption, and God is the Redeemer.

All of God does all that God does. Each person of the Trinity is active in this process of salvation. The Father sends the Son (John 5:36–37), who offers Himself as the perfect sacrifice (Heb. 7:27). The Spirit indwells the people of God as their comforter (John 14:26). *Knowing God* assumes a Triune God.

Finally, Dr. Packer assumes that godliness means responding to God's revelation in trust and obedience. Godli-

ness is not having all the facts right in your head. Godliness is not knowing the right answers on a seminary exam. Godliness is trusting in God and living the way He wants us to. Getting the facts straight is important, but this on its own is dead. Even the demons know there is one God (James 2:19). It is our lives that show whether or not we truly know God.

We can see by examining these principles that Dr. Packer's approach is biblically founded. But this is just a foundation. What does it truly mean to know God? Who is He? What is He like?

We must be very careful to ensure that we are not making God in our own image. God made man in His image, and not the other way around. This is one of the central sins of pagan idolaters: they make gods who are like themselves, only bigger. Their whole perspective is backwards. The results are monstrous, semi-human absurdities like Zeus or Baal.

But we do not have to actually carve an idol to misrepresent God. It is easy to believe that God ignores our sin because we do, or that God is obligated to forgive because we are. It is easy to assume that God likes the things we like, and hates the things we hate. Some people treat God as a supernatural Santa Claus, handing out gifts to those who are good. While God does love to bless His people, He is also a judge, bringing punishment on the wicked. We must make sure that our view of God is biblical, rather than based on ideas from our pop culture.

Many of God's character traits are easy for us to like. God is righteous, God is truthful, God is loving, and God is gracious. God saves His people in miraculous ways throughout Scripture, and He does so joyfully, for He loves to help His people. These are all traits we enjoy, because they benefit us.

Other characteristics, however, are less emphasized in our culture. We are uncomfortable with the idea of God's judgment, and so we downplay the idea of Hell. In recent years, some Christians have felt so uncomfortable with the idea of God's wrath that they have denied it altogether. They argue that God loves all men equally. But this not only presents a false view of God. It also undermines the heart of the gospel: grace. If God is not really angry, or if the penalty for sin is not real, this devalues grace. Why would we need grace if there were no punishment for sin?

Another aspect sometimes ignored is God's sovereignty. Many modern Christians deny God's power over His creation. This happens in areas relating to great evil—how could God have allowed the Holocaust during World War II?—and areas of human choice. But the Bible does not show us a God who is in charge of most things. God is in charge of everything, down to the death of a sparrow (Matt. 10:28–31). This is not limited to the good things, either (Amos 3:6). God is sovereign over every event and every person.

If we do know God, what will our lives look like? Those who truly know God have a relationship with Him. We ask Him to help us when we are in trouble. We praise Him for the easy times *and* the hard times. We call the Son of God our Lord and Savior. When we really know God, we love Him.

When we have a relationship with God, we will also have a relationship with His people. If we really know God, then we will seek to know other Christians and love them as well (John 13:35). John tells us in his first epistle that if we say that we love God, and we hate our brothers, then we are lying (1 John 2:9–11).

If we know God, we will also keep His commands. A few verses earlier, John tells us that "he who says, 'I know him,' and does not keep His commandments, is a liar, and the truth is not in him" (1 John 2:4; 4:20). We cannot claim a personal knowledge of God if we do not obey His Word. How many times in the Bible, or even in history, do we see examples of people who, like Judas, claimed the name of Christ but did not act as if it were true? Our actions speak louder than words, and they speak of our hearts.

But this is all very difficult. How can we know God? How can we really be righteous? After all, we are tainted with the sin of our father, Adam. We cannot hope to please God on our own. Any attempt would not only be full of sin, but it would also be rebellious to think we could succeed on our own.

God knows this. But this is the heart of the gospel. We cannot hope to please God on our own, and so He gives us the strength we need. We cannot hope to save ourselves, so God does so Himself. Apart from God, we can do no good at all, so God shows us Himself so that we might please Him. God is sovereign over this and all other aspects of our salvation. He

We must be careful to ensure that we are not making God in our own image. Our view of God must be biblical rather than based on ideas from our culture. Though it might be easy to emphasize only God's love and mercy, His wrath against sin cannot be ignored. Neither should His sovereign power over all creation be denied. In this detail from the Sistene Chapel, Michelangelo shows a mighty Creator God, full of power. "If there is calamity in a city, will not the LORD have done it?" —Amos 3:6

is sovereign over our lives, and He has told us that He loves us. If we follow God and obey Him—if we know Him—then He will take care of us. He will never leave or forsake us (Heb. 13:5).

This does not mean that our lives will be easy. God promises us trials (John 16:33). Trials are an opportunity for God to grow our faith. When we face trouble, we turn to God for help. God can show us His overflowing grace, while we grow in righteousness and patience. For these reasons, God commands us to count our trials joy (James 1:2). They are an opportunity for blessing.

Too often we doubt that God wants to bless us, especially in the midst of a trial. We think of God as a hostile instructor who is scheming to make us fail. But God has given us His Son. Meditate on that for a moment. If God were scheming to make us fail, would He offer His own Son as a sacrifice in our place? Of course not. The Son of God died and rose again so that God could bless us exceedingly, abundantly, above all we could ask or think (Eph. 3:20).

God wants to save us. God wants to help us through trials. God wants to help us glorify Him. What is left for us to do?

We must have faith. Believe on the Lord Jesus Christ, and we shall know God.

—O. Woelke Leithart

For Further Reading

Packer, J.I. *Evangelism and the Sovereignty of God.* Downer's Grove, Ill.: Intervarsity Press, 1991.

Packer, J.I. *Fundamentalism and the Word of God.* Grand Rapids, Mich.: William B. Eerdmans, 1958.

Warfield, B.B. *The Plan of Salvation.* Avinger, Tex.: Simpson Publishing Group, 1989.

Schaeffer, Francis. *How Should We Then Live?* Wheaton, Ill.: Crossway Books, 1976.

And they told about the things that had happened on the road, and how He was known to them in the breaking of bread. —Luke 24:35

Session I: Prelude

A Question to Consider

Why is it important to know God?

From the General Information above, answer the following questions:
1. What is the purpose of Knowing God?
2. What two problems did Dr. Packer see in the modern church that inspired him to write this book?
3. What are the two ways we can know God?
4. How can we see God in creation? Give an example.
5. How is each Person of the Trinity involved with salvation?
6. What is the result of making God in our own image?
7. What are some characteristics of God that are not emphasized in modern Christian culture?
8. What is the heart of the gospel?
9. How can a trial be a benefit for a Christian?

Reading Assignment:
Preface (1973), Chapters 1–3

Session II: Recitation
Chapters 1–3

Comprehension Questions

Answer the following questions for factual recall:
1. What conviction lies behind the writing of *Knowing God*?
2. On what five basic truths does Dr. Packer plan to base his study of God?
3. Why must we be sure of our reason for studying God?
4. What are evangelicals particularly good at? What are we less good at?
5. What sorts of "great" things do the people who know God show?
6. If we want to know God, what must we realize first?
7. What is the main purpose of man's presence on earth?
8. What are the varying depths of "knowing" something?
9. Who initiates the relationship between God and man? Why?
10. Why is there a great comfort in knowing this?

Reading Assignment:
Chapters 4–7

Session III: Discussion
Chapters 2–7

A Question to Consider

How can you tell if someone knows God or not?

Discuss or list short answers to the following questions:

Text Analysis
1. What is the purpose of man's life?
2. What is the difference between knowing and knowing about?
3. What sorts of evidence do we see in the lives of those who know God?
4. What does it mean to know God?

Cultural Analysis
1. Does our culture believe it is possible to know God? Why or why not?
2. In our culture, do Christians look different? Should they? How could we tell if someone knew God in our culture?

Biblical Analysis
1. How can we know God the Father (John 14:7–11)?
2. How does John say that we can tell if someone knows God (1 John 2:3–4, 9–11)?
3. Did Judas know God? Explain (Matt. 26).
4. What does James mean when he says faith without works is dead (James 2:14–26)? How does this relate to knowing God?

Summa

Write an essay or discuss this question, integrating what you have learned from the material above.
How can we live like people who know God?

Reading Assignment:
Chapters 8–12

Session IV: Writing
Chapters 8–12

Poetry

In this session you will be challenged to write poetry in a certain form about a particular object, person, event, or idea. The challenge for the poet is to lay bare the heart of the truth in language that is beautiful and that inspires

The Trinity, as imagined in Weingarten Abbey's well-known illuminated manuscript, the Berthold Sacramentary.

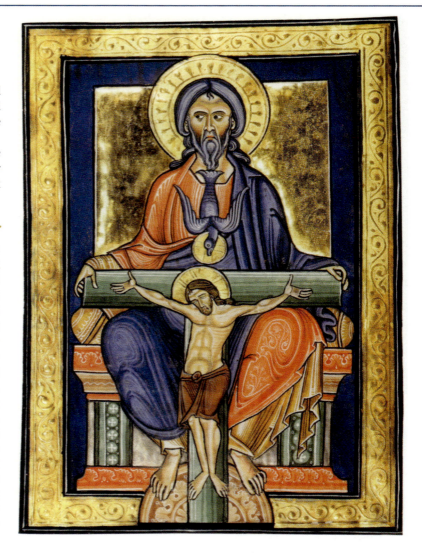

its reader to love what is pure and righteous or to hate what is wicked and evil. The best poetry marries true philosophy and beautiful rhetoric.

Writing poetry is a real challenge so we are going to provide forms for you. Remember, poetry is hard, but rewarding work.

Hymn in Common Meter

Most hymns are written with a set meter and rhyme, with the ending of the second and fourth line in each verse rhyming. In common meter, there are four lines per verse, which alternate between iambic tetrameter (four emphasized syllables) and iambic trimeter (three emphasized syllables). *Amazing Grace* is an example of a hymn written in common meter.

Your assignment is to write a hymn, celebrating the majesty of God. Use things you have learned from the chapter on God's majesty. Feel free to paraphrase biblical passages. Your hymn should be at least five verses long. You can test whether or not it is in common meter by singing your hymn to the tune of *Amazing Grace* or *O, For a Thousand Tongues to Sing*.

O Lord, our Lord, above the earth
You reign in splendor high.
Your majesty fills earth's whole realm,
And all the ages bye.

For in six days you made the world,
It shows your handiwork.
And in each flower, pink or red
Your wondrous secrets lurk.

You made the sun and all its rays
You caused the moon to shine.
And in creation's smallest speck
We see Your touch divine.

You loved your people, sent your Son
To die on Calvary,
And He will come again one day
To bring us all to Thee.

O Lord, our Lord, above the earth
You reign above all things.
While we learn to know you more,
We see creation sings.

READING ASSIGNMENT:
Chapters 17–18

Session V: Writing

Essay

God calls Himself a jealous God in the Ten Commandments when He is warning against idolatry (Ex. 20:5). He tells the Israelites that they are to worship Him alone because He is jealous. As your reading explains, this is not the sort of jealousy where we want what someone else has. God is jealous of His people's time, attention, and worship. He wants their total focus to be on Him, and not on another god. Some other passages that discuss the righteous jealousy of God include Exodus 34:12–14, Psalm 135:4, Psalm 78:58, and 1 Corinthians 10:22.

Husbands should also be jealous to protect their wives from adultery (Prov. 6:34). A husband's duty is not just to love and care for his wife (Eph. 5:25), but also to protect her from other men. She belongs to him only, and he should treat her as such. He should be protective and (in a sense) selfish. Wives are not for sharing. This is what it means for a husband to be jealous of his wife.

How are these two ideas similar? In the Bible, they are closely linked, particularly in the prophets.

This session is a writing assignment. Remember, quality counts more than quantity. You should write no more than 1,000 words, either typing or writing legibly on one side of a sheet

> Packer writes that "statues and pictures of the One whom we worship are not to be used as an aid to worshiping him." An example of such abuse can be seen in the veneration of Veronica's veil, housed in St. Peter's Basilica in Rome and displayed once a year. The legend is that Saint Veronica gave Jesus her veil that he might wipe his forehead during his journey to Calvary. An image of his face was miraculously imprinted on the veil.

of paper. You will lose points for writing more than this. You will be allowed to turn in your writing three times. The first and second times you turn it in, your teacher will grade it by editing your work. This is done by marking problem areas and making suggestions for improvement. You should take these suggestions into consideration as you revise your assignment. Only the grade on your final submission will be recorded. Your grade will be based on the following criteria: 25 points for grammar, 25 points for content accuracy—historical, theological, etc.; 25 points for logic—does this make sense and is it structured well?; 25 points for rhetoric—is it a joy to read?

In this assignment you will be comparing and contrasting adultery and idolatry. First, read the following biblical passages: Jeremiah 3 and Hosea 1–3. Explain how adultery and idolatry are similar and how they are different. Feel free to use other biblical data as well.

READING ASSIGNMENT:
Chapters 21–22

SESSION VI: DISCUSSION
Chapters 21–22

A Question to Consider

Why does God let Christians suffer through so many trials?

Discuss or list short answers to the following questions:

Text Analysis

1. What errors in ministry does the book identify? What results from these errors?
2. Do Christians experience easier lives than other people?
3. How does God use our trials?
4. How should Christians react to God's adoption of us? How does this help us to take comfort in trial?

Cultural Analysis

1. Why does our culture believe that bad things happen?
2. In what does our culture take comfort when things go wrong?
3. How does our culture believe that we can prevent trials in our lives?

Biblical Analysis

1. Why did Job suffer (Job 1–2)? How did he respond when he suffered?
2. What is the proper Christian response to trials (James 1:2; John 16:33)? Why?
3. Why does James tell us that we suffer trials (James 1:2–4, 12)?
4. The ultimate trial is death. How should a Christian view death (Phil. 1:20–26; 1 Cor. 15:54–57)?

SUMMA

Write an essay or discuss this question, integrating what you have learned from the material above.
When we suffer, how should we respond?

OPTIONAL SESSION: DEBATE

A Question to Debate

Is it right to make pictures of Jesus?
The background to this debate can be found in Chapter 4 of *Knowing God*.

Split into two sides of roughly equal size. You should first determine what the rules for the debate will be, such as how long each person will speak, or whether or not you will allow cross examination. If you are going to have a formal debate (with opening statements, closing statements, rebuttals, etc.), then you will need to determine who will speak when, and for how long. After each side is prepared, determine which side goes first. Then proceed!

Antony and Cleopatra

Have you ever fallen *in love*?

I do not mean the sort of common, ordinary, *"thinks she's sort of cute,"* dime-a-dozen attraction that might happen to many eighth grade boys ten times before breakfast. I mean that painful, mind-altering, hurts in the pit of your stomach sensation. The kind of feeling that screams, *"God, you must have made her just for me because (insert 1,000 lame reasons here) and if you make her love me we will serve you as missionaries in India."* The *in love* that makes you ask, "why do my teeth ache?" The kind of *in love* where you alter your schedule to *accidentally* happen to bump into her when she and her family are on vacation in Norway.[1] I mean the see her with your eyes closed, dream of her every night, stop eating and sleeping sort of *in love*.

If you have ever experienced feelings like this, God bless you. It gets better. You should expect that you will find a godly spouse eventually, and you might even marry the person that you are in love with. But if you have felt these odd feelings, I have one further question—or perhaps a list of a few questions:

Did your grades go up or down when you were *in love*?

Did you practice your violin more or less when you were *in love*?

Did you treat other people in your life (parents, siblings—especially nosy younger siblings—and friends) better or worse when you were *in love*?

Did you get better or worse at your favorite hobby or sport while you sat around sighing? If you are like most, being *in love* means lower grades, missed practices, desperate wishes to electrocute younger nosy sisters and lower free-throw percentages (unless you think that any of these will be key to winning the heart of your beloved). When you are *in love* nothing else matters! You would give the world for your beloved, right? Or would you?

In *Antony and Cleopatra* Shakespeare confronts us with one of the greatest and also most destructive love stories in the history of the world. Often lovers feel that they would give the world for their lover. The Bard tells us that once upon a time it actually happened.

Cleopatra stands next to her son Caesarion in this relief from the Temple of Hathor.

His rule lasted less than six years, and he was replaced by the vigorously Catholic Queen Mary (a.k.a. "Bloody Mary" because she persecuted and even killed some Protestants). She left no heir and after five years she left the throne to the Protestant Elizabeth I in 1558. Elizabeth's long rule cemented Protestantism in England, but Shakespeare grew up during a time when the country was still recovering from a serious case of theological and political whiplash. Shakespeare is the greatest English poet and playwright. His poetry continues to feed the souls and imaginations of every generation.

Significance

Antony and Cleopatra is significant because—like the rest of Shakespeare's tragedies—it provides the reader with insight into the human condition, and it does so from an unflinchingly Christian worldview. He demonstrates the destructive powers of sin and how the greatest of human beings are deeply flawed and broken characters.

Antony and Cleopatra is possibly even more important for our day (and particularly for you!) because our culture believes that all things must be thrown overboard in order to achieve or experience or dive after the feeling of being *in love*. Many of the characters in his play have both heroic and wicked characteristics. One might feel at the end, however, like the real villain is simply the feeling of being *in love*. Being *in love* makes people do stupid things. *Antony and Cleopatra* starts off with a haunting line:

> Sir, sometimes, when he is not Antony,
> He comes too short of that great property
> Which still should go with Antony. (*Act 1, scene 1*)

Being *in love* can make people fail to be themselves.[2] Love, of course, is a great blessing and a great joy, but this play can help us, perhaps, put our feelings back into their place.

General Information

Author and Context

William Shakespeare (1564–1616), a.k.a. the Bard, wrote and worked during a tumultuous time in English history. Henry VIII had led the Church of England away from Roman Catholicism a mere thirty years before Shakespeare was born. As we might remember from earlier Omnibus chapters, Henry VIII broke with the Pope not over justification by faith, but because he wanted an heir and needed a divorce. After Henry VIII died Edward VI came to the throne and moved the country toward real Reformation teaching.

Main Characters

The main characters are Mark Antony and Cleopatra (you were expecting someone else?). Mark Antony was Julius Caesar's right-hand man. When Caesar was murdered in the Forum on the Ides of March in 44 B.C., it was Antony who brought revenge against Caesar's murderers (see the chapter in Omnibus I on Shakespeare's *Julius Caesar*). After vanquishing Julius Caesar's enemies, Mark Antony, Lepidus and Octavian Caesar formed the Second Triumvirate (or the Rule of Three Men).[3] These three ruled the Roman Empire, which was the greatest empire in history up to that time. Antony was the greatest soldier of the three and most resembled Julius Caesar in this way.

While Antony had been Caesar's right-hand man, Cleopatra had been Caesar's lover. They had a son together who was called Caesarion (who is mentioned in this play).[4] Before her liaison with Julius Caesar, she had been married twice before, to her brothers Ptolemy the XIII and XIV—a common practice in ancient ruling lines, particularly in Egypt. She was, however, more Hellenistic (influenced by Greek and Roman culture) than Egyptian. She was the queen of Egypt and reportedly extremely beautiful—and equally crafty.

Octavian Caesar is the other main character. He was the adopted son of his great-uncle Julius Caesar. He became Emperor Caesar Augustus in 27 B.C. He was a cautious and calculating ruler who established Roman power throughout the world. He was Antony's competitor and eventual enemy.

There are a number of servants that have important roles throughout this play. Pay attention to them. They are giving commentary on the actions of the main characters. Often Antony can not be trusted to see himself clearly—he is not himself. The servants and advisors, however, offer us unvarnished assessments of what is happening. Roman opinion is represented by these advisors. When Antony is unfaithful to Octavia, a woman renowned for her virtue, the people side with Octavia and her protective brother Octavian against Antony and his barbarian queen.

Summary and Setting

This play swirls around the time leading up to the consolidation of the Roman Empire under one lord—Caesar Augustus. Since the rape of Lucretia (see Livy in Omnibus I), Rome had not had a king, and they were doing all right. The Roman Republic had lasted 450 years before it crumbled at the feet of Julius Caesar The Senate and its legions had survived and won countless battles within Italy, stumbled into major war with a naval superpower, Carthage, and had defeated them, spreading Roman rule across Europe. Rule of this vast empire, which stretched from Spain to Russia, from Belgium to the Sudan, came to Octavian after the Battle of Actium in 31 B.C. Winning this battle made the Mediterranean Sea Octavian's private lake.

The battle was a naval battle off the coast of Egypt and it ended up turning on one major mistake by the forces opposing Octavian. (You will have to read to find out what it is, but it goes without saying that being *in love* has to be involved.)

When Antony was swooning in Egypt, Joseph was likely a boy in Palestine, and Mary had not yet been born.

Worldview

Duty ... Love ...

Balancing these two motives was at the center of Roman life even before there was a Rome. One might remember that in an earlier time, as the story goes, a soon-to-be Roman prince visited an African queen. From the outset things went smashingly. He told her stories. Her heart fluttered. They took walks in the woods and went spelunking. Their hearts were knit together—or so she thought. One morning, however, the soon-to-be prince got a call from his mother. The conversation went something like this:

Mom: What are you doing in Africa?

Prince: Just hanging out. . . . Hey, there's this neat girl I just—

Mom: I know all about this "girl," and she is bad news. Remember, you have a job to do, and it is *not* in Africa.

Prince: But Mom, she is really cool, and she likes my stories, and we both like caves . . .

Mom: Listen young man! You need to get your head out of the sky and get your backside out of the caves and on to a boat and sail north. You have Rome to found.

Prince: But Mom?!?

Mom: But nothing! Now, what are we going to do?

Prince: Found Rome.

Mom: Say it again—this time with more feeling.

Prince: Found Rome!?!?

Mom: Again.

Prince: Found Rome!!!!

Mom: Now, tell your Mommy you love her, and go make her proud.

Prince: Found Ro . . . Oh, I love you Mommy. Thanks for the call. I just wasn't thinking straight.

This conversation occurred between the wandering soldier Aeneas and his mother, the goddess Venus. Aeneas had escaped the fires of falling Troy and was sent, along with his band of men, on a mission to found Rome—the new and greatest Troy. He would be the paradigm for Roman manly virtue. He would leave his love, Queen Dido of Carthage, and do his duty by founding Rome. Aeneas provides a picture of the best case scenario of valuing Duty over Love. (For more on this, see the chapter on the *Aeneid* in Omnibus I.)

Aeneas's departure from Carthage and abandonment of Dido has dire consequences. Dido stabs herself to death on a pile of the gifts that would have reminded her of her Trojan paramour. This pile becomes her pyre. Aeneas sees the smoke rising from Carthage as he sets his sights north. Bad blood continues to boil between Carthage and Rome for centuries. Three Punic wars will ensue as the descendants of Dido's city seek to crush Aeneas's seed. Hannibal marches elephants across the Alps, slaughters Roman armies at Cannae and scares the stuffing out of just about everyone in Italy. Later, P. Cornelius Scipio crosses the Mediterranean, defeats Hannibal, and burns Carthage.

Perhaps Roman princes and African queens are a bad mix!

The story of Mark Antony and Cleopatra takes us back to the love affair between Dido and Aeneas. Rome, however, has not changed. Manly Romans were to value duty above love. But what would happen if the Roman prince, perhaps the most perfect representative of

Aeneas's military prowess, did *not* do his duty and stayed with the African queen? Shakespeare's incredible and historically based play asks us to balance duty and love, honor and passion. This balance is particularly important today because as believers we are bombarded daily with an overriding cultural message: feelings are more important than duty. We have to decide whether we will follow this message—and our hearts; whether we will return to Roman commitment to duty—and our empire; or whether, perhaps, the Bible points us toward a different solution to this dilemma.

Before we consider the Bible's judgment on love and duty, let's take a deeper look at the two main characters involved in this story, Mark Antony and Cleopatra.

Aeneas Perfected and Corrupted

Shakespeare's character of Mark Antony and the actual historical figure are not the same person, but they are very similar. The historical Antony was Julius Caesar's best friend. He served with Caesar's armies during the campaigns in Gaul and Germania. When Caesar defeated Pompey, Mark Antony served as the Master of the Horse, Julius's right-hand man. After Brutus and Cassius murdered Caesar, Antony, surrounded by seasoned veterans from Caesar's army, tracked down, defeated and killed the conspirators. The historical Antony was a wonderful soldier. Shakespeare's Antony is a perfect soldier—a mix and perfection of the virtues of Hercules, Aeneas, Julius Caesar and Achilles all wrapped into a neat package. He is surrounded by the talents of Julius Caesar's legions, which were an unstoppable military force and a wellspring of sound military advice. In this play we see this particularly in the character of Domitius Enobarbus.

Antony is the perfect Roman (that is, when his head is in the game—which, as we enter the play, is not often). His "Achilles heel" is women—or, we should say, one particular woman. (This was true of the historical Antony as well–he was married five times. Antony's willingness to be controlled by romantic love was not typical of the Roman soldier. Romantic love was certainly *not* to pull one away from

Instead of overt melodrama, this sculpture gives us Cleopatra making her decision about suicide. The neoclassical sculptor William Wetmore Story (1819–1895) knew the power of not having a moment reveal everything. As he put it, "What is left undone is as necessary to a true work of art as what is done."

one's duty to the state. Aeneas sets the pattern for this. Julius Caesar had learned this lesson. He, like Antony, had an affair with the alluring Cleopatra, but for Julius Caesar, Cleopatra was kept within her bounds. He loved her. He left her. He had his eyes set on Rome and his destiny. The Antony of the play, it seems, understands this lesson—at least partially—until he meets Cleopatra. He has little attachment to his wife, Fulvia (who is actually Antony's third wife), marries his next wife Octavia for political reasons, and then abandons her. He, however, can not break away from Cleopatra's wiles. From the outset, he is a Roman who has lost the path of Aeneas: Duty . . . Honor . . . Destiny. What is worse, everyone around him sees what is happening. He is making bad decisions because he is following his heart not his head. The empire lies within his grasp, but he is lying on the soft beds of Egypt instead of pursuing his destiny. Aeneas would not have been pleased.

Antony's double-mindedness leads to his destruction. This theme echoes throughout the play. Philo, one of Antony's friends, says this in Act 1, scene 1, speaking of Antony:

Sir, sometimes, when he is not Antony,
He comes too short of that great property
Which still should go with Antony.

Antony, the picture of Roman virtue and manhood is not himself. He has become the "Anti-Aeneas." Aeneas sets aside his feelings and follows his destiny; Antony is trapped by his feelings and kept from his destiny.

Lilith replaces Lucretia

Cleopatra stands Roman feminine virtue on its head. She is the perfect lover for the Anti-Aeneas. Lucretia (see the chapter on Livy's *Early History of Rome* in Omnibus I) was the picture of what a Roman woman should be. She was beautiful, but also functional and hard working. While the other girls were off at the mall or chatting up the latest gossip online, Lucretia was doing the duty of a Roman wife spinning thread for her family. She is a picture of domestic tranquility and happy family life. As the story goes, the evil son of the last Roman king, Sextus Tarquinus, rapes Lucretia. She kills herself because she can not bear the shame, and her death causes such an uproar that the Roman population revolts against and expels their king. Her death causes the founding of the Roman Republic. Not so Cleopatra!

Cleopatra is the Anti-Lucretia. She is sly, moving from man to man for political advantage. She is as unstable as Lucretia was faithful—toying with men, betraying them, lying, cheating and manipulating them. She wins the battle not by her virtue, but by her cunning and her beauty.

You will not find Cleopatra spinning her own thread. She despises any physical labor. She is a picture of feminine glory—but any reality under the veneer is absent. With Cleopatra there is no hope of what Psalm 128 pictures as the blessed domestic life. What then makes up her glory? How does she control and manipulate so many great men? What lies at the root of her power?

Cleopatra is a fantasy that traps men. This fantasy of sexual and romantic fulfillment is pictured throughout history and is alive and well today. We see it in the whore pictured in Proverbs 7:10–18:

And there a woman met him,
With the attire of a harlot, and a crafty heart.
She was loud and rebellious,
Her feet would not stay at home.
At times she was outside,
at times in the open square,
Lurking at every corner.
So she caught him and kissed him;
With an impudent face she said to him:
"I have peace offerings with me;
Today I have paid my vows.
So I came out to meet you,
Diligently to seek your face,
And I have found you.
I have spread my bed with tapestry,
Colored coverings of Egyptian linen.
I have perfumed my bed
With myrrh, aloes, and cinnamon.
Come, let us take our fill of love until morning;
Let us delight ourselves with love.

This lady of the night is the antithesis of godliness. She looks like a fun evening; she ends up being a deep grave. Following her is traipsing ox-like toward destruction. As Proverbs 7:24–27 makes clear:

Now therefore, listen to me, my children;
Pay attention to the words of my mouth:
Do not let your heart turn aside to her ways,
Do not stray into her paths;
For she has cast down many wounded,
And all who were slain by her
were strong men.
Her house is the way to hell,
Descending to the chambers of death.

Cleopatra is just another name for the path of death.

There is a mythological paradigm or model of this sort of woman. She is called Lilith. Although stories of her go in many directions, my favorite is the medieval version of the myth, which says that Lilith was a demon fashioned to look like a woman (technically a *succubus* for those in-

In 1917, still in the infancy of motion pictures, Theda Bara (1885–1955) starred in what was already the third film about Cleopatra. Bara was the celluloid succubus of her time, appearing in revealing, and even transparent, costumes. The studios made up the publicity story that she was Egyptian-born and had spent her early years living under the shadow of the Sphinx. As her fame grew, Hollywood did too and became the center of American film. She moved there to film the Cleopatra epic. No known copies of the film exist today, though various photographs of Bara as Cleopatra have survived.

terested in the classification of imps and lesser demons). The task given to her by Satan was to distract Adam from Eve so that they would not bear children. This would undo God's plan for a Seed to come and eventually crush Satan's head. Satan made Lilith a vision of mankind's carnal lust—short skirt, gaudy lipstick and beds of ease (instead of work in the Garden). As the myth goes she fails in her attempt to turn Adam away from his duty to tend the Garden and his duty to love Eve. There is an important difference between the love of Eve and the *love* of Lilith. Eve's love is productive. It pushes Adam toward fulfillment of his God-given responsibilities. Lilith's *love* instead distracts and destroys God's callings. Eve's love satisfies; Lilith's lust consumes. Lilith pops up all through Omnibus and will continue to pop up in the next few years. She is a paradigm of Duessa in *The Faerie Queen*. We see her in Dante's dream of the witch in Purgatory. She even garners a cameo mention in *The Lion, the Witch and the Wardrobe* (look for her in Mr. Beaver's version of the White Witch's ancestry). Cleopatra, like Lilith, is always feasting, but never working. She also never gets old (*Antony and Cleopatra* 2.2.244-249):

> Age cannot wither her, nor custom stale
> Her infinite variety. Other women cloy
> The appetites they feed, but she makes hungry
> Where most she satisfies. For vilest things
> Become themselves in her, that the holy priests
> Bless her when she is riggish.

Looks like a succubus; talks like a succubus; must be a succubus. Watch out for Lilith/Cleopatra.

What is worse for us is that our culture, to its great peril, has forgotten the difference between Lilith and Eve—between Lucretia and Cleopatra. If you are a young man or woman, you will no doubt be tempted to lust after Lilith or lust after being Lilith rather than following the path of Eve which leads to productive love and fulfillment of God's purposes. Beware of girls that don't work and don't age. Prick them with pins to see if they bleed.

Finding the Biblical Balance

It should not surprise us that the Bible's view of love and duty corrects both extremes by setting both love and duty within their proper context.

Being *in love* is presently one of our culture's most popular idols. People destroy their lives searching for this feeling, thinking that achieving this feeling is their highest and greatest end in life. As believers we must trample this idol underfoot. We must not follow such loves or lusts. We must follow Christ. That said, God is not against emotion or *being in love*. Within marriage love—emotional, romantic love—is to be celebrated, entered into and rejoiced in by both the community and the lovers. Marriages should be big deals and honeymoons should be romantic. In Victorian times newlyweds with means often spent a long time on their honeymoons, touring Italy or the French Riviera. They frequently came back with children.[5] A Christian view of romantic love within its proper covenantal context is glorious. Romantic love outside of its covenantal moorings is a hideous, destructive idol.

Duty—particularly duty to the state—can also be an idol. We should not reject Mark Antony's foolishness so that we can indulge in Aeneas's chase after glory. This idol is not nearly as popular today. It has been a popular idol in the past. As believers, we can not overthrow one idol by replacing it with another.

Commitment and duty to defend the state in a biblical society should be part of defending and loving one's family. Fighting for one's country is simply the men of a country fighting together to defend their wives and children. Thus, when the state calls on men to fight in a just war, the men of that given country should answer with courage and devotion, committing themselves to serving the country's righteous cause against those forces that would unrighteously threaten their families and their future descendants. To fail to fight to protect one's family is cowardice. To fight when the aim is unjust empire-building or undue glory is pride. This service, even death in this service, must not be divorced from affection, passion and even romantic love. In a just war, Christian men leave their families to go off to fight, knowing that some will not return. They do this for love of country, but also for love of their family, their descendants and the families and descendants of their kinsmen. Dying will keep some men from returning to their family and experiencing any sort of love in this life. These men fight, however, so their descendants can have peace and experience the blessings of peace—biblical liberty which is full of hard work, glorious Sabbath and celebration, romantic love, the bearing of children, raising them, loving them, training them and laying down one's life for God, family and community. To fail to follow this path is to embrace slavery and oppression and to reject and deny the faith. This path plays out in the lives of families and community. Believers must be wary when the state calls them to service for the glory of any state that has rejected biblical values and justice.

Of course, defending one's family begins with faithfulness between a husband and a wife. Too often today, people abandon their marriage vows only to find—as Antony does seeing Cleopatra flee at Actium—that faithlessness breeds further faithlessness. Antony loses the empire and his life because he fails in this basic faithfulness.

So the duty of the believer is to love one's family and country. In a perfect world these commitments reinforce each other as they take their rightful place in the life of believers. When, in our world, we see these commitments come into conflict we must prayerfully consider the reasons for this conflict and commit, above all else, to follow Christ—rather than comfort or glory.

—G. Tyler Fischer

For Further Reading

Leithart, Peter. *Brightest Heaven of Invention.* Moscow, Idaho: Canon Press, 1996. (For background on Shakespeare.)

Spielvogel, Jackson. *Western Civilization.* Seventh Edition. Belmont, Calif.: Thomson Wadsworth, 2009. 139–142.

Veritas Press History Cards: Old Testament and Ancient Egypt. Lancaster, Pa: Veritas Press. 32.

Veritas Press History Cards: New Testament, Greece and Rome. Lancaster, Pa: Veritas Press. 12, 17, 19, 20, 22, 26.

Session I: Prelude

A Question to Consider

Can being *in love* make a questionable action righteous?

From the General Information above answer the following questions:

1. Why would it be correct to describe the English spirit as one of religious whiplash at the time of Shakespeare?
2. What was the Second Triumvirate, and who was in it?
3. Who was Octavian, and what does he go on to do?
4. How did Aeneas balance love and duty in the *Aeneid*?
5. What was the connection between Cleopatra and Julius Caesar?
6. In what ways is Antony like Aeneas? In what ways is he different?
7. How does Cleopatra trap, control and manipulate men?
8. How is Cleopatra like Lilith?
9. Is the romantic love of being *in love* against God's will?

Our next session will be a student-led discussion. As you are reading the following assignment, you should write down at least three questions from the text dealing with the issue listed below. These questions will be turned in to the teacher and will be used in classroom discussion. To get full credit for these Text Analysis questions you must create a question that is connected to the reading and to the issue that is the focus of our discussion; you must also answer the question correctly (and include a page or line reference at the end); and your question must be one that invites discussion and debate ("why" questions are excellent; questions that can be answered by "yes" or "no" are to be avoided).

You should also provide two Cultural Analysis and two Biblical Analysis questions. Cultural Analysis questions ask how our culture views the issue that we are discussing. Biblical Analysis questions ask what the Bible says concerning this issue. Again, to get full credit for each question, you must create questions connected to the issue we are studying, answer each question correctly and create questions that encourage and invite discussion and exploration. For an example of each type of question and answer refer to the examples provided in the next session.

If you are working alone, after creating your questions and answers, have your parent or tutor check over them. Also, if possible, share them with your family at the dinner table, helping them to understand why the issue is important, how the issue arises in your reading, how its importance is still evident in our culture, and how understanding this issue might change the way you and your family should think and live.

Issue

Which is more important, love or duty?

Reading Assignment:
Antony and Cleopatra, Acts 1 and 2

Session II: Student-Led Discussion

Antony and Cleopatra, Acts 1 and 2

A Question to Consider

Which is more important, love or duty?

Students should read and consider the example questions below that are connected to the Question to Consider above. Last session's assignment was to prepare three questions and answers for the Text Analysis section and two additional questions and answers for both the Cultural and Biblical Analysis sections below.

Text Analysis

Example: When talking to Cleopatra in Act I, scene 1, how does Antony compare his duty to Rome with his love for Cleopatra?

Answer: Antony says that his love for Cleopatra is much more important to him than his duty to Rome. He says that Rome can melt in the Tiber, and the empire is made of clay. Nothing, he says, can compare to his love for Cleopatra.

Cultural Analysis

Example: Does our culture value duty to country or romantic love more highly? Give an example from current events to support your conclusion.

Answer: Our culture views passionate feeling and sincerity as the most important virtues. Sadly, our culture tends to believe that these forces invalidate all other duties, responsibilities and covenantal commitments. So, if someone has passionate romantic feelings about someone else, they are absolved from all the wrong that they do when they break their covenant commitments to country and family. This is a pernicious evil. God's law defines righteousness—not deeply held passionate feelings. Examples of this abdication occur during almost every divorce involving adultery. Sadly, our county has accepted this false view of covenant commitment.

Other cultural issues to consider: The prominence of pleasure-seeking in our culture or people breaking vows for the sake of romantic love. Also consider the example of Paris from the Iliad (VI.318–324), and no-fault divorce laws.

Biblical Analysis

Example: Should a believing husband be more committed to serving his country or his wife, according to Deuteronomy 20:1–9?

Answer: This passage balances these two covenant commitments in an interesting manner. The issue is complex, because at the deepest level fighting for one's country and being committed to biblical romantic love should be pulling a righteous man in the same direction. In this passage, men who are newlyweds are sent back home to their new wives. Other men (those who have been married for more than a year) should join the army and defend their people. The men who are sent home to their wives are not sent home because romantic love is more important. They are sent home to spend time with their new wives and to raise up the next generation by having children. So, the men who are sent home are sent home to love their wives and to have children who will be the next generation to serve the Lord. The men who are called out to battle go not to defend the abstract concept of a nation-state or an empire, but instead they go to battle to defend their wives and children and all future generations of their descendents who will follow after the Lord.

Other Scriptures to consider: 1 Samuel 3:21–25, 2 Samuel 11 (especially verse 1), 1 Corinthians 7:32–33.

SUMMA

Write an essay or discuss this question, integrating what you have learned from the material above.

How is a righteous man to decide between a call of duty and romantic love?

Instead of a reading assignment you have a research assignment. Tomorrow's session will be a Current Events session. Your assignment will be to find a story online, in a magazine, or in the newspaper that relates to the issue that you discussed today. Your task is to locate the article, give a copy of the article to your teacher or parent and provide some of your own worldview analysis to the article. Your analysis should demonstrate that you understand the issue, that you can clearly connect the story you found to the issue that you discussed today, and that you can provide a biblical critique of this issue in today's context. Look at the next session to see the three-part format that you should follow.

Issue

Sin justified by being *in love*

SESSION III: CURRENT EVENTS

Antony and Cleopatra, Act 2

Issue

Sin justified by being *in love*

Current events sessions are meant to challenge you to connect what you are learning in Omnibus class to what is happening in the world around you today. After the last session, your assignment was to find a story online or in a magazine or newspaper relating to the issue above. Today you will share your article and your analysis with your teacher and classmates or parents and family. Your analysis should follow the format below:

BRIEF INTRODUCTORY PARAGRAPH

In this paragraph you will tell your classmates about the article that you found. Be sure to include where you found your article, who the author of your article is, and what your article is about. This brief paragraph of your presentation should begin like this:

Hello, I am (name), and my current events article is (*name of the article*) which I found in (name of the web site or published source)…

Connection Paragraph:

In this paragraph you must demonstrate how your article is connected to the issue that you are studying. This paragraph should be short, and it should focus on clearly showing the connection between the book that you are reading and the current events article that you have found. This paragraph should begin with a sentence like this one:

I knew that my article was linked to our issue because…

Christian Worldview Analysis:

In this section, you need to tell us how we should respond as believers to this issue today. This response should focus both on our thinking and on practical actions that we should take in light of this issue. As you list these steps, you should also tell us why we should think and act in the ways you recommend. This paragraph should begin with a sentence like this one:

As believers, we should think and act in the following ways in light of this issue and this article.

Reading Assignment:
Antony and Cleopatra, Act 3

Session IV: Recitation
Antony and Cleopatra, Acts 2 and 3

Comprehension Questions

Answer these questions for factual recall.

1. On what does Pompey base his hope of victory (2.1)?
2. What action is taken to bind up the friendship of Antony and Octavian when Antony arrives in Rome (2.2)?
3. After finding out that Antony has married Octavia, what does Cleopatra send messengers to find out (2.5)?
4. When the Triumvirate (Antony, Octavian, and Lepidus) meet with Pompey before the battle, what do they decide (2.6)?
5. What plan does Menas share with Pompey? How does each man react to the plan (2.7)?
6. What does Octavian say that the marriage between Antony and Octavia can be for good or ill (3.2)?
7. What is Cleopatra's reaction to the description of Octavia (3.3)?
8. What does Octavian do to Lepidus after they defeat Pompey (3.5)?
9. What does Octavian report concerning Antony and Cleopatra's behavior and the gift that Antony has given Cleopatra (3.6)?
10. What effect does Enobarbus say that Cleopatra's presence at the battle will have on Mark Antony (3.7)?
11. On what event does the Battle of Actium turn (3.10)?
12. What does Octavian demand of Cleopatra in order that he would pardon her? What is her reaction (3.12 and 3.13)?

Reading Assignment:
Antony and Cleopatra, Acts 4 and 5

Session V: Writing
Antony and Cleopatra, Acts 1 and 5

This session is a writing assignment. Remember, quality counts more than quantity. You should write no more than 1,000 words, either typing or writing legibly on one side of a sheet of paper. You will lose points for writing more than this. You will be allowed to turn in your writing three times. The first and second times you turn it in, your teacher will grade it by editing your work. This is done by marking problem areas and making suggestions for improvement. You should take these suggestions into consideration as you revise your assignment. Only the grade on your final submission will be recorded. Your grade will be based on the following criteria: 25 points for grammar, 25 points for content accuracy—historical, theological, etc.; 25 points for logic—does this make sense and is it structured well?; 25 points for rhetoric—is it a joy to read?

Description

Your assignment is to write a description following the direction provided below. This may be more difficult than it sounds! Make sure your description guides a reader into an experience of the object. Use language that stirs the senses (what does it look, sound, feel, smell, or taste like?). Make judgments about the object as you describe it. Remember the great rule of description—Show us; don't tell us. Do not tell us that something is good or beautiful or likable. Describe it in a way that shows your reader the object's beauty or ugliness, its goodness, or wickedness.

Your Objective:

Describe how Antony and Cleopatra's relationship is an example of the teaching in Proverbs 6:26:

For by means of a harlot
A man is reduced to a crust of bread;
And an adulteress will prey upon his precious life.

Your challenge is to write this assessment from one of two differing perspectives. You can choose to write as Domitius Enobarbus (Antony's right-hand man) or Charmian (one of Cleopatra's servants).

Session VI: Aesthetics

In this session, you will get to know a particular piece or type of art related to our reading. It is our job as believers to be able praise, love and protect what is beautiful and to condemn, hate and oppose all that is truly ugly. This task is often harder than we think. We have to discipline ourselves to, first, examine and understand the piece reflectively. After we understand the content of a piece, we can examine the author's intention concerning the piece and attempt to figure out what the piece of art is communicating. Sometimes this will be easy; other times it will be difficult or impossible. Finally, we need to make judgments about what this work of art communicates. Sometimes we will be able to clearly condemn a work of art as untrue, badly done, or wicked. Sometimes we will be able to praise a work as glorious, majestic, and true. Oftentimes, however, we will find ourselves affirming some parts of a work and condemning others. Remember, maturity is harder than immaturity but also more rewarding. Also remember that our praise or condemnation means more when we have disciplined ourselves to first reflect on the content and meaning of a work.

Art Analysis

The Oath of the Horatii is a famous work created by the artist Jacques-Louis David during the time of the French Revolution. It depicts a famous scene from early Roman history in which the cities of Rome and Alba are at war. This war is to be settled by a battle between three representatives from each city. The Romans send the three Horatian brothers; the Albans send the three Curiatian brothers. The Horatii and the Curiatii had intermarried with each other, but both set aside the ties of family and fight to the death for the sake of their respective states. This work brings one of the main issues of Antony and Cleopatra before us—what should take priority in our lives: our love of the state or our love of family, children, and romantic love?

Jacques-Louis David was an artist and advocate for the French Revolution. He often painted scenes from

Antony held his love for Cleopatra above his love for Rome. We get the opposite in Jacques-Louis David's *The Oath of the Horatii*, painted on the eve of the French Revolution. Patriotism trumps love in this painting as three brothers pledge their loyalty to Rome over family connections, even while the women weep in the background.

Roman history and scenes from the French Revolution. His goal as an artist and as a revolutionary was to inspire people to serve the state and the ends of the revolution.

Discuss or list short answers to the following questions:

Technical Analysis

1. Does this work demonstrate the artist's ability and expertise?
2. Describe the scene. What is happening?
3. Does this work have balance and symmetry? What is the central or most important element (to what are your eyes most attracted)?
4. Is this work realistic and proportional or not?
5. How is light used in this work?
6. What colors are used in this work?

Subject Analysis

1. Who is the man with the swords in his hands, and what is his attitude? How can you tell?
2. Who are the women on the right? How do they feel about what is happening? How can you tell?
3. What are the sons doing? Whose attitude do they agree with? How can you tell?
4. How are light and darkness used by David to help us understand the idea he is trying to convey with this art work?

Film imitated life in the 1963 movie *Cleopatra*, starring Elizabeth Taylor and Richard Burton. The historical Antony and Cleopatra were long mocked by Roman elites for their lack of self-restraint, and the film, too, was notorious for being out of control. It was one of the most expensive films ever made, even by today's standards. No actual shooting script ever existed, and many of the elaborate sets had to be made twice.

5. How are colors used to show unity and agreement or disunity and disagreement between the father, the sons, and the women?

Content Analysis

1. What is the message of this work?
2. What is worthy of praise in this piece of art? What is worthy of condemnation?

OPTIONAL SESSION A: ACTIVITY

Trial of Cleopatra

Note to homeschoolers: This activity will prove meaningful enough to make special efforts to include others. Consider finding other homeschool children near the same age or including the entire family.

DIRECTIONS

Today we are going to serve as judge and jury as we consider the case that could be laid out against Cleopatra. To do this, follow these steps:

Elect a judge, a prosecutor (to set forth the case against Cleopatra) and a defense attorney (for Cleopatra).

All of you will be the witnesses and the jury. List charges that could be made against Cleopatra and the things that might mitigate or lessen her guilt. The judge should write out the charges on the blackboard or somewhere for all to see. The prosecuting and defense attorney should write the charges on notebook paper.

The prosecution will set forth its case. Then the defense will present its case. (Limit the time of each side.)

The jury should then decide whether Cleopatra is guilty of treachery (the purposefully and intentional, unlawfully bringing death to many men and destruction to Antony and his men) or queenly negligence (that she was simply carried away by her passions and made bad decisions). They can also acquit her on the grounds that Antony was to blame rather than Cleopatra for the destruction that came to Rome, Egypt, Antony, and his forces.

Trial of Antony

As an optional activity, have the same kind of trial for Antony. Is he guilty of treason? Is he guilty of negligence (he should have known better but acted with righteous intentions)? Or is he innocent because Cleopatra should bear the guilt for the debacle at Actium?

Antony and Cleopatra 603

OPTIONAL SESSION B: WRITING

Poetry

In this session you will be challenged to write poetry in a certain form about a particular object, person, event, or idea. The challenge for the poet is to lay bare the heart of the truth in language that is beautiful and that inspires its reader to love what is pure and righteous or to hate what is wicked and evil. The best poetry marries true philosophy and beautiful rhetoric.

Writing poetry can be a real challenge, so we are going to provide forms for you. Remember, poetry is hard but rewarding work.

Epigram

Write an epigram from Aeneas to Mark Antony

An epigram is a short poem that is often used as a pithy, brief expression of satirical wit. It is often used in politics to expose flawed thinking or actions on the part of a political opponent. Today we are going to work on writing epigrams that are couplets (a pair of rhymed lines in the same meter). So your epigram should have:

- Two lines
- These two lines should rhyme
- These two lines should have the same meter (meter is the rhythm of your line—so the lines in your epigram should have the same number of syllables, and the emphasis should be on the same syllables in each line).

Imagine what poetry Aeneas would write to Antony. Following is a possible example:

For Roman men example I supplied,
Cleopatra, her eyes fluttered and you cried.

I won glory and my enemies bled,
At Actium the whore turned tail, you fled.

Optional Activity

If time allows, write other epigrams: Mark Antony to Cleopatra, Cleopatra to Octavian, Dido to Cleopatra, or Octavian to Mark Antony.

ENDNOTES

1 I write from the male perspective because it is all that I have. I have some knowledge that females feel like this in some ways. Although I must admit that even though I know women better now than I did when I was 13 (hey, I married one), I must still plead confused ignorance in these matters.

2 Maybe you have experienced this with a friend who fell *in love* and so radically changed that you wanted to slap him or at least make him look in the mirror at the weird clothes that he was wearing, the cologne that he was splashing on (usually way too much) and all the dumb stuff that he was doing. Thankfully, this never happens to *you* when *you* are *in love*, right?

3 The First Triumvirate comprised Julius Caesar, Crassus and Pompey (the father of the Pompey in this play).

4 Yes, Caesar named this son after the mode of his birth. No, just kidding. Remember, it was Julius Caesar himself who lent his name to the Caesarian Section procedure.

5 A short article on the history of the Victorian practice could be found at Link 1 for this chapter at www.VeritasPress.com/ OmniLinks. This and other articles also point out the honeymoon would originally invented in the pre-Christian times when men would capture (kidnap) a bride, run away with her, and hide for a month. A month (a moon) was the traditional time for searching for a lost person, so the kidnapper knew that after this "honey month" he could come out and be safe. This really wrecks the romance.

6 *This note appears only in the teacher's edition.*

7 *This note appears only in the teacher's edition.*

Twenty Thousand Leagues Under the Seas

"Clean your room!"

Has any child ever existed who didn't hear that command at least once in his life? Whether or not he has ever done it properly, or understood the importance of it, is an entirely different matter. When I was growing up, my father would chide me, "Exercise dominion over your room." In other words, I was to show that I was the reigning authority over that space by bending it to my will. I was to put all things in their place according to my use for them. Everything had a place and everything had a name, and it was my job to make it that way.

Often when we hear of dominion we think of grand scale achievements such as God ruling the whole world or a king conquering new lands. Yet real dominion is displayed in even the simplest things, like cleaning your room or washing the dirty dishes. When God placed Adam in the garden, He told him to name the animals and to till the garden. Adam was to have dominion over the individual animals one by one as he named them.

Jules Verne's *Twenty Thousand Leagues Under the Seas* is a story of dominion on many different levels: from despots to sea captains to small individual scientists with their pen and paper. All forms of dominion are necessary and important, but all forms of dominion can also be abused. Just as a king could enslave a nation, so a little boy could steal his brother's toy and claim it as his own. In this story dominion will be abused in several forms.

General Information

Author and Context

Jules Verne lived in a time of great development and growth. He was born in 1828 in the French city of Nantes. This was during the time of European imperialism and scientific inventions that shape our world even today. Verne's fascination with science and inventions was the fuel for much of his work.

Verne's early life did not show promise of a vocation in science or as a writer of fiction. Verne's father was a successful lawyer with his own practice and an intention to have his son follow in his trade. When Verne was old enough he was sent to study law in Paris, but it was there that Verne started writing plays. Verne finished studying law, but convinced his father to let him stay in Paris and write. Most of his early works failed, and he was not able to support himself with his earnings. Because Verne wanted to marry, he attempted to create a more stable income and took up stock trading. Even then he was determined to write. It was at this time that Verne wrote his first large scale success, *Five Weeks in a Balloon*, which enabled him to truly pursue his desire to write.

Throughout his life Verne used science in many of his books, often depicting science as the means through which man would achieve all things. In his later days Verne became skeptical of what man might do with science and the abuses that might occur as a result.

Significance

Imagine life without all of your kitchen appliances. Pop-tarts without a toaster, milk without a refrigerator, cans without openers—life would be much worse, wouldn't it? In our dominion over this world, science is a very useful tool that God has given us. All of those appliances were an invention of applied science at one time or another. Through their use we are better able to fulfill our duty to "fill and subdue the earth." While tools and inventions, used properly, are great things for our good, used wrongly or carelessly they can be harmful to ourselves and to those around us. Even small tools such as car radios can encroach on the liberty of our neighbor if we abuse them.

Jules Verne shows us an imaginary world with great scientific advancement. Humans are able to live under the sea, to walk on the ocean floor, and to see fish in their natural environment. This is a good thing, yet it can also be used for malicious purposes. Verne shows how small tools such as harpoons can be used for good and evil and how large machines like electric submarines can be used for good and for evil. This book is a lesson for all people, whether minimum wage workers or leaders of nations, to not misuse their authority, but to take dominion wisely to the glory of Christ.

Main Characters

"Almighty God! Enough! Enough!" These are the final words of the pivotal character in this book

Captain Nemo. He is at the same time the most intriguing character, the man around whom the book centers, and the villain of this story. Captain Nemo is the commander of the *Nautilus*, the world's only submarine. A lot of mystery revolves around Nemo's origins and motivations. He hates the people who live above the waves and who oppress each other. He has sworn off the land and all who dwell thereon and he seeks to live his life subsisting on what the ocean provides. He is a virtual hermit living under the seas. Yet he is a learned man studying the sea and collecting the wonders thereof. He and his crew have created the world's most advanced seafaring vessel, and they seek to live in it with their own new culture. Aboard the *Nautilus* with Nemo and his crew are three "guests" who would better be understood as prisoners.

Professor Aronnax is a scientist who is fascinated with the work of genius that Nemo has created and with this new access to marine life. Professor Aronnax spends most of his time aboard the *Nautilus* studying both marine life and Captain Nemo. Large portions of the book record Aronnax and his manservant, Conseil, simply classifying fish.

Conseil is a fairly good scientist in his own right. He classifies every creature that he sees and is always trying to learn from his master. He is one of the most loyal servants a man could ask for. In one instance, when the professor falls off a ship in the middle of the night, Conseil jumps in after him, because it is his duty to follow where his master leads.

The last guest is Ned Land, the "simple man." He is a world famous harpooner who is very unhappy about being held on the *Nautilus*. Most of his time is consumed wishing to harpoon something or plotting to escape from Nemo.

The true story in this novel is told between the development and inner workings of these four characters.

Summary and Setting

Jules Verne lived in a time of great scientific advancement. Throughout his life he was a witness to many of the world's great inventions. He was able to predict with surprising accuracy inventions and advancements that would be made much later. Often, though, in the background of his stories is a warning about how horrible the world will be if science is pursued wrongly.

Twenty Thousand Leagues Under the Seas is a fictional story of the world's first submarine, the *Nautilus*. Its creator, Captain Nemo, tries to use it as a retreat from the societies of the world. He makes his own culture and language on board the ship, severing all ties to those who live above the waves. In his rage Nemo also uses his vessel to avenge those who oppressed him earlier in life.

Nemo's life is interrupted when, through a turn of events, he takes in three men who are washed onto the top of his vessel. One of them is the world famous Professor Aronnax, whose book Nemo has read. The professor and his two companions are taken for a journey of 20,000 leagues across the seven seas where they see many strange and amazing sights. (It should be noted to avoid any confusion that the 20,000 leagues is a measurement of the distance traveled not how deep they went. Such a depth is not possible—even for a science fiction writer.) Always looming in the background is the uncertainty of whether they will ever live on land again or what else Nemo has in store for them.

Jules
Verne

Worldview

At the creation of the world God made man and placed him over the animals. Adam was to name the animals and rule over them, taking dominion over the earth. Naming the animals and categorizing them rightly was an important step in taking dominion. Adam and Eve ultimately failed in their task of taking dominion when they misused the creation and broke God's law. They were not to eat of the Tree of the Knowledge of Good and Evil, but they grasped for what was not theirs, and the rule of Adam over creation failed—and creation was horribly marred. The rule of man had failed, but not permanently. A King would come to restore Adam's fallen realm and redeem Adam's fallen race with His own blood, offering Himself

Twenty Thousand Leagues Under the Seas 607

as a sacrifice and atonement for all of men's sins. Dominion, its use and misuse, is the central theme in *Twenty Thousand Leagues Under the Seas.*

Captain Nemo had seen the misuse of dominion. He had even been the victim of the oppression and tyranny of despots and autocrats who sought to impose their own dominion over other men and to oppress them. As a result of this, Captain Nemo secretly crafted a vessel that would carry him under the seas, where no despot could take away his liberty. Here, under the sea, Nemo tries to create a completely separate and self-sustaining culture apart from the rest of mankind who live above the waves. Nemo's ship is self-sustaining, propelled by electricity generated under the sea. Nemo and his crew even speak their own language, and they eat fish and marine vegetation.

Collisions with other vessels, intentional and unintentional, and often resulting in the demise of those vessels unlucky enough to be hit by the *Nautilus*, bring the submarine to the attention of the public. People across the world do not know what the *Nautilus* is or even if it really exists. A large debate begins between those who *believe* that it does exist and that it is a monster and those who are more *scientifically* minded who say it can't exist. After more collisions and sinkings, the debate is renewed, and it becomes general opinion that it is a monster of nature, an enormous sea serpent.

An expedition is formed to destroy the sea monster. Aboard this ship are three men who have an interest in the monster and, as was said earlier, will end up on the submarine. The first man is the story's narrator, the Honorable Pierre Aronnax, professor in the Museum of Paris. He has been invited by the United States government to join the expedition since his expertise on marine life

SO WHAT DID THE *NAUTILUS* LOOK LIKE?

The mysterious craft of Captain Nemo has captured the imagination of readers for years and years. Following are some artists' concepts.

The earliest depictions of the *Nautilus* are Hildebrand's woodcuts from the original publication. It is long, narrow, and cigar-like. Later editions of the book also sported cigar-like designs by artists like Anton Otto Fischer (1932), Kurt Wiese (1946), and Milo Winter (1954).

For Walt Disney's famous *Nautilus* Harper Goff developed an intricate Victorian appearance. Goff threw Verne's stark description overboard and added ornate decoration to the hull, reptilian fins and a bulbulous pilothouse.

Ian Williams's design solves a problem in the text. The hole punched in the *Scotia's* hull was two and a half meters below her waterline while the *Nautilus* was also only two meters below the surface when the collision occurred. So Williams raised the ram. He also gave the salon a larger window than many other renderings, and added two rudders.

Following Groff's lead, Greg deSantis also steered clear of the novel when creating his *Nautilus*. This variation from the Museum of the Improbable includes ornate salon windows, a deck-mounted launch, an elevated cable-braced spar, and a two-sided pilot house with center lantern.

Meinert Hansen developed an interesting design with a spiral screw propeller that had been conceived and patented as a propulsion device for vessels in the late eighteenth century. Verne did not choose this approach, but Nemo might have considered it.

For a fabulous cutaway of the craft, visit Link 1 for this chapter at www.VeritasPress.com/OmniLinks

Suddenly everything became clear! The clearing was a cemetery, the hole a grave, the long object the body of the man who had died during the night! Captain Nemo and his men had come to bury their companion in this shared resting place on the bottom of the inaccessible ocean!

might be invaluable. The second man is Aronnax's servant, Conseil, also a scientist. The third man is Ned Land, a Canadian acclaimed to be the world's best harpooner. They discover that this is not a monster of nature but rather a monster of science. In the power of man's dominion has been elevated, but this dominion is having some terrible results. It has become a monster used to destroy fellow man.

Captain Nemo declares that since their return to land would reveal the secret of his existence, they will never be able to return and must stay forever on board the . Thus, in his attempt to guard his own liberty, Nemo robs them of their liberty.

The Professor and Conseil at first adapt well. They discover a whole new world under the sea, exercising dominion by naming and classifying these new animals, just as Adam named the animals in the beginning. Ned Land, on the other hand, always wants to harpoon the fish that he sees. Eating, of course, is another form of dominion. At points, Ned seems more interested in simply skewering anything that swims. His dominion-taking sometimes is nearer to wanton killing, and he is admonished occasionally by those around him.

Captain Nemo himself exercises dominion over this new world. He sails to the South Pole and claims it as his domain, he studies the ocean so that one day there may be cities under its waves, and he utilizes the sea to provide for all his needs. Captain Nemo, though, brings his dominion to misuse. He uses his vessel for revenge against those who oppressed him when he still lived on the land. He rams their ships in his rage and watches as they sink to the bottom. The only justice he knows is retribution. Throughout the book Nemo regresses into his hatred and rage. In Nemo's world, without the redemption of Christ, all dominion is doomed to fail. Without the blood of Christ, Nemo has no basis for forgiving his enemies. Instead he sinks ships, sacrificing the lives of his enemies (or others that happen to get in his way), and becoming the kind of tyrant he was initially fleeing. Nemo's rage demands that blood be split, but without Christ only the blood of fallen men can be spilt—peace and true dominion are never achieved.

In one incident, after Nemo has destroyed a ship, he boldly declares that he is the law and the judge and that he has made the verdict. He thus positions himself in the place of God as the lawgiver and the judge of mankind. Yet this judge cannot bring lasting peace or salvation. Nemo is clearly overreaching his dominion.

As a consequence, Nemo's world begins to fall down around him. The *Nautilus* is attacked by real sea monsters. The monsters clog the propeller, and the ship is helpless against them. Science and technology cannot save the crew; they must go out and battle with the beast themselves. The monsters must be defeated by man. In their fight against the sea monsters, one of the crew is seized and taken up in the air. In his last breath he calls out in French, his mother tongue, rather than in the language that Nemo has created for his crew. In his last breath this man sees that Nemo's contrived culture is not a savior and can not redeem him. Nemo had made the *Nautilus* to save them from their oppression, but it cannot save them. Nemo's false dominion has fallen. This dying man bears witness to its collapse.

Nemo tries to create a new world for himself free of the men above the waves, yet even he wants to be part of the human community. He has compiled his works of science and his discoveries of marine life into a journal which he has translated into many different languages. He intends that the last survivor of the ship should place it in a water tight sea capsule and cast it upon the waves. This will only help men after Nemo's death.

Nemo finally settles deep into his rage and despair, letting his ship plow into the north seas. In the end, the last words of Captain Nemo are "Almighty God! Enough! Enough!" He has finally come to grips with the Lord, the true Lawgiver and Judge. In his despair he must admit that his own culture and his own creation have failed. Moments later Nemo's creation, the *Nautilus*, is sucked into a whirlpool and destroyed. Dominion, which he used irresponsibly, is taken from him.

—Joshua Shade

For Further Reading

Spielvogel, Jackson J. *Western Civilization*. Seventh Edition. Belmont, Calif.: Thomson Wadsworth, 2009. 605–615, 782, 842.

Unwin, Timothy. *Jules Verne Journeys in Writing*. Liverpool, England: University of Liverpool Press, 2007.

Veritas Press History Cards: 1815 to the Present. Lancaster, Pa.: Veritas Press. 19.

Verne, Jules. *Journey to the Center of the Earth*. New York: Sterling, 2007.

Session I: Prelude

A Question to Consider

How do you take dominion on a day to day basis?

From the General Information above answer the following questions:

1. What is dominion?
2. How is man supposed to exercise dominion?
3. For what purpose does Captain Nemo exercise dominion?
4. In this story how is it shown that man still needs a savior?
5. How does the case of Captain Nemo show that law (at least God's law) is necessary for true liberty?

Reading Assignment:
Twenty Thousand Leagues Under the Seas, Part I, Chapters 1–5

Session II: Discussion

Twenty Thousand Leagues Under the Seas, Part I, Chapters 1–5

A Question to Consider

How conclusive is science? What are the proper limits of science?

Discuss or list short answers to the following questions:

Text Analysis

1. What does the narrator mean in Chapter 1 by his remark that "Wit had proved mightier than science"?
2. What event suddenly dismantles any serious doubts that something is out there?
3. What two options are left and which option is eliminated for the character of the mystery after the impact on the Scotia?
4. What is one of two reasons given that it has to be a monster and not a man-made machine?
5. In the final paragraph of his published article (Part I, Chapter 2), Pierre Aronnax states that what was felt and experienced could have been "nothing at all." Why does Aronnax admit he wrote the paragraph out of cowardice?
6. Why is Ned the harpooner unwilling to believe that such a "narwhal" exists?

Cultural Analysis

1. What part do television and the press play in influencing public perception of science today?
2. What are some scientific issues that the modern press has distorted?
3. In modern societies some people doubt what cannot be satisfactorily proven to be scientifically true. Can you have belief in what you cannot prove?
4. How much is science valued today in terms of determining truth?

Biblical Analysis

1. In light of Paul's challenge to personally walk by faith rather than sight, what is the relationship of science to theology (2 Cor. 5:7)?
2. Is science a worthy profession for the Christian (Gen. 1:26)?
3. What part does God play in science (Prov. 1:7, Rom. 11:36)?

SUMMA

Write an essay or discuss this question, integrating what you have learned from the material above.

What are the proper limits of science?

READING ASSIGNMENT:
Twenty Thousand Leagues Under the Seas, Part I, Chapters 6–11.

SESSION III: RECITATION
Twenty Thousand Leagues Under the Seas, Part I, Chapters 6–11

Comprehension Questions

Answer the following questions for factual recall:

1. How is Ned Land able to face the captain's fear of losing his crew if they use a whaling boat to get to the monster?
2. Why does Ned recommend against launching the whaling boats in the morning?
3. Why was Conseil able to save Aronnax from drowning after the collision?
4. How does Aronnax conclude that "we are saved," despite having seen no sign of life from the iron machine he, Conseil, and Ned are standing upon?
5. What is the "dominant feature" of the second man who walked into the room where Ned, Conseil, and Aronnax were first kept?
6. What argument finally quiets Ned's talk of escape for some moments? What is Ned's new plan?
7. How does Captain Nemo reason that he can trust the story and identities of his captives?
8. Why must Dr. Aronnax cede the argument that he should be treated as an enemy of Captain Nemo?
9. Describe the deal Captain Nemo offers his captives?
10. How does Captain Nemo justify his last remaining connections with the land-bound world, the paintings and music?

READING ASSIGNMENT:
Twenty Thousand Leagues Under the Seas, Part I, Chapters 12–17

SESSION IV: ACTIVITY
Twenty Thousand Leagues Under the Seas, Part I, Chapters 1–17

Learning to Use Coordinates

Study latitude and longitude in an encyclopedia or on the Internet.[1] Points on the earth north or south of the Equator are marked by lines of latitude (also called parallels). The South Pole is 90° S, the Equator is 0°, and the North Pole is 90° N. Each degree is further divided into 60 minutes. Lines of longitude (called meridians) identify points to the east or west of an arbitrary meridian. This arbitrary meridian is called the Prime Meridian. It runs north and south through Greenwich, England and is considered to be 0° longitude. Thus, every point on the earth's surface can be identified by stating its latitude and longitude in degrees and minutes. As an example, Washington, D.C. at 38° 53′N, 77° 02′W is located 38° and 53 minutes north of the Equator and 77° and two minutes west of the Prime Meridian.

Try your own hand at charting points by latitude and longitude. Use a world map with latitude and longitude markings or create your own on poster board or large paper. Chart various events of the voyage of the *Nautilus* based on coordinates given in the story and listed below. If desired, you may draw small depictions of what transpires at each location and pin them to the map.

Scotia's encounter with the "monster":
    45°37′N, 15°12′W
Learning the instruments:
    30° 7′N, 137° 15′W[2]
The forests of Crespo Island:
    32° 40′N, 167° 50′W

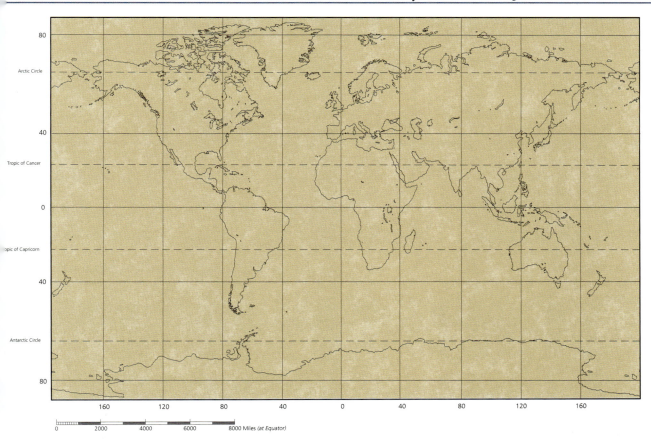

Journey southeast:
    8° 57'S, 139° 32'W
Ocean islands:
    between 13° 30'S and 23° 50'S, and 125° 30'W and 151° 30'W
The Fijian archipelago:
    6° S, 174° W
New Guinea:
    between 0° 19'S and 10° 2'S, and 128° 23'E and 146° 15'E
Cape Wessel:
    10° S, 135°E
Keeling Island:
    12° 5'S, 94° 33'E
13,000 leagues of travel:
    45° 37'S, 37° 53'W
The ice-cap:
    55° S, 50° W
April 1:
    between 53°S and 56° S, and 67° 50'W and 77° 14'W
The wreck of the Vengeur:
    47° 24'N, 17° 28'W

Optional Activity

Dream Cruise

Plan out your own cruise using longitude and latitude. Where would you like to go and what would you like to see? Create your own cruise and then share the itinerary with your family or your classmates.

Reading Assignment:
Twenty Thousand Leagues Under the Seas, Part I, Chapters 18–24

Session V: Discussion
Twenty Thousand Leagues Under the Seas, Chapters 18–24

A Question to Consider
What good came from God's creation of earth?

Discuss or list short answers to the following questions:

Text Analysis

1. Describe the "circulation" that Captain Nemo attributes "the Creator of all things" to have given the ocean?
2. Why does Captain Nemo reason that salt is in the sea for a specific purpose?
3. How will a new, fifth continent extending from New Zealand to Marquesas be formed, according to Dr. Aronnax's observations?
4. What frustrates Ned Land about the under-ocean route through the Torres Strait?
5. What major theme continually recurs in the book when Captain Nemo cannot understand Ned's desire? For what does Ned long?

Culture Analysis

1. How does underwater topography affect international affairs today? Especially, consider how it might affect rights to use land under the sea if the topography pointed to some valuable resource like oil.
2. What cosmic perfections in our world suggest a Creator?
3. What is the nature of machines in man's dominion over nature?

Biblical Analysis

1. Does God want us to have more dominion over some parts of the earth (for instance, is the land more important than the sea?) (Gen. 1:26)?
2. Are there parts of worldliness that are simply so disgusting that one must be Captain Nemo and abandon them completely (John 15:19; Matt. 5:13–16)?
3. There is so much about creation that has not been discovered. Does creation have purpose and value beyond the existence of man (Ps. 19:1)?

SUMMA

Write an essay or discuss this question, integrating what you have learned from the material above.
What good came from God's creation of earth?

Reading Assignment:
Twenty Thousand Leagues Under the Seas, Part II, Chapters 1–6

Why could we not live the life of the fish populating the liquid element, or even that of the amphibians who can move for long hours through the dual realm of land and water as the whim takes them?

Twenty Thousand Leagues Under the Seas 613

Session VI: Recitation
Twenty Thousand Leagues Under the Seas,
Part II, Chapters 1–6

Comprehension Questions
Answer the following questions for factual recall:
1. What is the source of Dr. Aronnax's internal struggle of whether to escape or not?
2. What causes the "sea of milk"?
3. Where are the most fertile land and the most fertile pearl fishing, according to the book?
4. Dr. Aronnax states that "nature's creative power is beyond man's destructive bent." What makes him say this?
5. What does the short poem suggest is the origins of the Red Sea's name?
6. What advice does Conseil give to Ned to ease fears about the Arabian Tunnel?
7. What major body of water does the Arabian Tunnel allow the *Nautilus* to enter?
8. What phenomenon is found near the island of Santorini that causes the water to boil?

 **Reading Assignment:**
Twenty Thousand Leagues Under the Seas,
Part II, Chapters 7–12

Session VII: Worldview
Twenty Thousand Leagues Under the Seas,
Part II, Chapters 7–12

The God of Sci-Fi
What if well before even the telephone was invented you had predicted the fax machine? What if before cars or planes you predicted not only human space flight, but the actual mathematical details of launch location, weight, height, and landing zone of future spacecraft? Jules Verne was one of the most insightful authors in modern history. His predictions of the fax machine, batteries, searchlights, tasers, pollution, and especially electricity as a future source of energy were nearly prophetic. While *Twenty Thousand Leagues Under the Seas* is one of his seminal works, you may also recognize *Around the World in 80 Days, Journey to the Center of the Earth,* and *From the Earth to the Moon.*

In fact, the Apollo 8 mission followed Verne's prediction a full 103 years after he penned it in *From the Earth to the Moon.* One of the astronauts wrote: "Our space vehicle was launched from Florida, like Barbican's; it had the same weight and the same height, and it splashed down in the Pacific a mere two and a half miles from the point mentioned in the novel." It is easy to see why Verne has such a wide fan club of earth shakers, from Antarctic explorers to the father of rocketry to Walt Disney.

Second only to Agatha Christie, his works have been translated more than any other single author of fiction. Yet even Agatha Christie is not considered matriarch of the mystery genre. Jules Verne is widely considered the "father of science fiction" for writing futuristic novels that showed the triumph and progress of technology. Though he did not partake in the twentieth century's technological advances through experience, he led thousands in experiencing in their minds' eyes what we now take for granted. Technology has come a long way since his death in 1905, and we can look back to judge it better.

Clearly Verne was on the cutting edge of technology. What was science for Jules Verne? Did he properly assess it or overvalue its use in the hands of sinners? Could it be, perhaps, that the technology Verne imagined would have best been left in the ideal world of a yarn rather than in actual human hands?

In the twentieth century more humans have died in war than in all of history's previous wars combined. Dynamite, developed to help build passageways through the mountains to assist transport, has been turned into a powerful destructive device. Nuclear energy, which holds potential hope for powerful and long-lasting fuel, was used to wipe out tens of thousands of humans in a single instant. Just like any martial artist, fabulous orator, or rocket scientist can tell you, the extent to which something is good is the extent to which it can be bad. All tools have power, and it is in the hands of a human user to use it for ill or for good. How would God have us view technology?

The fundamental mistake of any human is to think that any success or power he has found comes anywhere but from the Lord. It is almost the story of history that those whom God has raised up eventually praise their own strength for their position. It is a challenge in the workforce to be successful and remind yourself that all success was given by God. Jules Verne, excited by the potential of humans who had marshaled science to their purposes, underestimated the sin nature and the dangers of providing men with raw power. "When Science speaks," wrote Verne, "it behooves one to remain silent."

Humans do have some incredible creative abilities. These are rooted not in man's own doing, but in the divine image of God. Captain Nemo's worldview appears to neglect the source of creativity, and therefore the purpose of it; instead he focuses on what man can achieve. When man focuses on what he can achieve without the proper perspective, wonderful tools will not necessarily be used in wonderful ways. Still, history shows that even when man uses talents for evil, God can turn it to good. Our concern here, however, is with a worldview of false hope in man.

In *Twenty Thousand Leagues Under the Sea* Verne creates a contradiction that in many ways show the pessimism Verne experienced as he aged. The *Nautilus*, an amazing invention that provides heretofore unseen discoveries of the deeps, is a vessel of death. As powerfully as it is good, it is powerfully bad. Eventually, writes Victoria Blake, "he discovered a truth more troubling: Humans might not be saved by science." Technological progress has continued to demonstrate that no material good or skill can save humanity, as the users of such are always fallen men. Instead, the only salvation must come from He who is perfect, the Lord. Verne's end and his religious faith, however, are difficult to discover. He died with a priest by his side, but there is little evidence that he rejected the despair of his later years.

Note: While we must judge Verne by what he wrote, some charity should be granted the man because his publisher, Pierre-Jules Hetzel, deleted many of Verne's references to God in order to make the novels appeal to the widest possible audience.

Prepare for class discussion with a short answer con-

A recent concept drawing of Nemo's diving helmet. The Captain was a classic character in the Steampunk genre—even before there *was* such a style.

taining unbelieving science's answer to each of the following, followed by a Christian answer:

View of Man

Purpose of Man

View of God

Source of Knowledge

Reading Assignment:
Twenty Thousand Leagues Under the Seas,
Part II, Chapters 13–18

Session VIII: Writing
Twenty Thousand Leagues Under the Seas,
Part II, Chapters 13–18

Character Analysis

This session is a writing assignment. Remember, quality counts more than quantity. You should write no more than 1,000 words, either typing or writing legibly on one side of a sheet of paper. You will lose points for writing more than this. You will be allowed to turn in your writing three times. The first and second times you turn it in, your teacher will grade it by editing your work. This is done by marking problem areas and making suggestions for improvement. You should take these suggestions into consideration as you revise your assignment. Only the grade on your final submission will be recorded. Your grade will be based on the following criteria: 25 points for grammar, 25 points for content accuracy— historical, theological, etc.; 25 points for logic—does this make sense and is it structured well?; 25 points for rhetoric—is it a joy to read?

Write a character analysis and biography for one of the main characters (Ned, Nemo, Aronnax, or Conseil). Your task is to creatively extrapolate, based on what you have seen of this character, the history that Jules Verne did not give us. The goal is to understand something more about how an author approaches fictional characters.

Authors of fiction who invent characters often have many pages in their own notes describing each character. Authors say they become "friends" with their imaginary characters. Much like a "method actor" discovers his character by living hours of everyday life "being" that character, understanding a character can require stories and time spent that never appear to anyone who reads the book. In this spirit, get to know your character.

Your "life story" should be two to four pages in length. Here are some suggestions if you struggle coming up with material:

> *Our admiration was still at its peak. Our exclamations continued. Ned named the fish while Conseil classified them. I was in ecstasy at the brilliance of their appearance and the beauty of their forms. I had never before had the chance to observe living animals that could move around freely in their natural element.*

- The essay could be a narrative of some formative fictional events; explain Captain Nemo's nationality and grouchiness; or detail the childhood and family life of your character.
- Describe the character's birth year and formative world events or discoveries during his childhood.
- Detail the character's psychological profile, including traits like the need for affirmation, security, self-confidence, ability to empathize, character, religious conviction, etc.

Optional Activity: Watch the movie version of *Twenty Thousand Leagues Under the Sea* and write a short follow-up essay on how well the director/script-writer developed your particular character. This is an open-ended assignment with a wide range of options available.

Reading Assignment:
Twenty Thousand Leagues Under the Seas, Part II, Chapter 19–23

Session IX: Review

Twenty Thousand Leagues Under the Seas, Part I, Chapter 1–Part II, Chapter 18

Comprehension Questions

Discuss or list short answers to the following questions:
1. Profile each of the following characters in a sentence or two: Captain Nemo, Dr. Aronnax, Ned Land, and Conseil.
2. Read John 15:19 and Matthew 5:13–16. Is Nemo's retreat from society a model for Christians?
3. Jules Verne and his characters place high importance on man and his place in creation. What is man's place in creation?

Optional Session: Evaluation

All tests and quizzes are to be given with an open book and a Bible available.

Grammar
Answer each of the following questions in complete sentences. Some answers may be longer than others. (2 points per answer)
1. Why will Captain Nemo never again touch dry land?
2. What is Dr. Aronnax's role in the book?
3. What are they doing when Ned Land saves Captain Nemo's life?
4. The Suez Canal was not yet completed at the time of the story. What two bodies of water would the canal connect?
5. Recount the story of the iceberg escape.

Logic
Answer the following question in complete sentences; your answer should be a paragraph or so. Answer two of the three questions. (10 points per answer)
1. What were the cycles of doubt and belief in the "monster" that led up to the Abraham Lincoln's voyage to catch it? What does this say about humanity?
2. Is retreat to a "Christian community," similar to Captain Nemo's retreat to his own oceanic world, a godly recourse against the sins of the world?
3. What is the negative side of technological "progress?"

Lateral Thinking
Answer one of the following questions. These questions will require more substantial answers. (15 points per answer)
1. How should Christians guide the advancement of science? Does modern society properly value science? What are science's limitations within a Christian worldview?
2. What responsibilities does dominion require of Christians, as good stewards of the earth?

Endnotes
1 At the time of publication, a very helpful discussion can be found through Link 1 for this chapter at www.veritaspress.com/OmniLinks.
2 Nemo states here (in Part I, Chapter 14) that they are currently about 300 miles from the coast of Japan. In what appears to be a mistake in the original story, these coordinates actually place them closer to California than to Japan.

Phantastes

Not many people have been to Tuvalu, Zanzibar, Maldives, Andorra, or Liechtenstein. Almost as many people have not heard of these countries, even though the latter two are both European nations. Look them up. Knowing these countries just might earn you that obscure geometry quiz bonus or, even better, impress Alex Trebek.

There is a lesson to be learned when we look up these lands out of curiosity to explore the population numbers, topography, climate, and culture of a Tuvalu or Andorra. Even though physically we may not have *seen* them, reading about them does allow us to see them in our minds. When we read about them, we are forming a picture of these lands in us so that we know of Tuvalu or Andorra even though we are not feeling the ground, hearing the wind, smelling the breeze, seeing the landscape, or tasting the fruits of these lands. We *do* see these lands in our minds even though not with our eyes.

This may be a new way of thinking about seeing a country you have never seen. Then again, we are all familiar with the child's debate question: "have you ever seen China with your own eyes?" "Well, no." "Then how do you know China really exists?!"

Any decent logic student will poke holes in that argument. We do not need to see China with our eyes to know that it exits. The faulty assumption at play is that the only things that exist are the things that we see with our physical eyes. If this statement were true, life would be a dull, unimaginative place. Most certainly, if we believe only in the things we can see physically, George MacDonald's *Phantastes* is not a tale we want to pull from the shelf.

The Fairy Fellers' Master-Stroke
by Richard Dadd (1817–1886)

General Information

Author and Context

George MacDonald (1824-1905) was a Scottish clergyman, novelist, poet, and theologian who is most remembered for his Victorian novels and fairy stories, including *Phantastes, Lilith, At the Back of the North Wind, The Princess and the Goblin*, and *The Princess and Curdie*. MacDonald was a great influence on or friend of many great writers including William Morris, C.S. Lewis, Charles Williams, W.H. Auden, G.K. Chesterton, Ruskin, Emerson, Carlyle, Tennyson, L'Engle, and more. Lewis Carroll in particular was a close family friend, and it was through the encouragement of the MacDonald children (six sons and five daughters) that Carroll decided to publish his writings. Of the power of its influence, C.S. Lewis wrote in *Surprised by Joy* that reading *Phantastes* caused the following realization:

> I met there all that already charmed me in Malory, Spenser, Morris and Yeats. . . . But in another sense all was changed. I did not know (and I was long in learning) the name of the new quality, the bright shadow, that rested on the shadows of Anodos. I do now. It was Holiness.

Later Lewis notes that reading *Phantastes* transformed his imagination and began the transformation of his entire life:

> That night my imagination was, in a certain sense, baptized; the rest of me, not unnaturally, took longer. I had not the faintest notion what I had let myself in for by buying *Phantastes*.

MacDonald was born in the western part of Aberdeenshire to George and Helen MacDonald. Unlike many authors, MacDonald did not have a troubled childhood but grew up in a merry family, enjoying especially a fine relationship with his father. MacDonald began attending Aberdeen University in 1840, earning awards in chemistry and natural philosophy. After finishing at Aberdeen in 1845, MacDonald studied for the clergy and was ordained as a Congregationalist pastor in Arundel in 1850. MacDonald preached and wrote theological works throughout his life but never settled for long in one pulpit. In 1860, MacDonald joined the Church of England.

Much is made of MacDonald's revolt from the strong Calvinism that ran through his extended family, but C.S. Lewis is quick to point out that while MacDonald turned from parts of his heritage, he did so without spurning everything in his past:

> All his life he continued to love the rock from which he had been hewn. All that is best in his novels carries us back to that "kaleyard" world of granite and heather, of bleaching greens beside burns that look as if they flowed not with water but with stout, to the thudding of wooden machinery, the oatcakes, the fresh milk, the pride, the poverty, and the passionate love of hard-won learning. His best characters are those which reveal how much real charity and spiritual wisdom can co-exist with the profession of a theology that seems to encourage neither.[1]

Significance

In these modern times, perhaps the first task for anyone reading a fairy story is to clear his mind of so many false assumptions about what fairy stories are, or who they are for. We moderns tend to think that fairy stories are strictly for children, and even then that perhaps they are dangerous since they are not "real." We shall discuss this more below, but it is helpful from the start to remember what J.R.R. Tolkien thought of fairy stories.[2] Tolkien argued that fairy stories are a natural branch of literature that possesses unique abilities to awaken in the reader a sense of "imagined wonder." In other words, we intuitively recognize and greatly yearn for Fairy Land as a beautiful and mysterious place beyond this world. Indeed, *Omnibus* students have read *The Chronicles of Narnia*, and who among you has not yearned to visit Narnia? Or the Shire? At least, we all yearn for such imagined wonder if we have been awakened enough to wonder in the first place. Many of us sadly try to live without wonder or yearning by supposing that this world is serious and mechanical instead of mysterious and joyful. But this is straying from the point on fairy stories. Tolkien, Lewis, Chesterton, and MacDonald all take great umbrage with the notion that fairy stories are just for children. Fairy stories are for all those possessing an imagination, and we can hope this means all men.

Phantastes has delighted countless readers since it was published in 1858, and to be sure it has won its place among the great fairy stories. C.S. Lewis in particular loved this tale and famously claimed that *Phantastes*

George MacDonald

"converted," even "baptized," his imagination.[3] For Lewis the particular value of *Phantastes* lay in the elements of the story itself. Lewis critiques the artistry of MacDonald's words, but praises the pattern of events that makes this story so memorable.[4] In this way, *Phantastes* is like a medieval story that is driven by an episodic narrative, and we should be alert to the plot and symbolism to make the connections between seemingly unconnected episodes. Attentive readers will note similarities between *Phantastes* and Spenser's *Faerie Queene, Sir Gawain and the Green Knight,* and the Arthurian legend, to name a few.

Main Characters

The main character of *Phantastes* is Anodos. In Greek, Anodos means "pathless," and true to his name Anodos wanders from one adventure to the next in Fairy Land, discovering along the way that he possesses the gift of poetry and that he has a touch of fairy blood in him. Anodos's journey in Fairy Land takes him from youth to adulthood. Hence, *Phantastes* is a *bildungsroman,* a literary term coined in the German Victorian era that describes a "coming of age" story in which the hero grows up. This growth is not just—or mainly—physical growth. It is that which occurs as one's mind is shaped into thoughtful maturity. Almost all good fairy stories include a magical landscape where animals and trees can speak, and *Phantastes* is no exception. The forests are living, and two trees in particular are important characters. The Beech tree, long a symbol of knowledge, understanding, and ancient wisdom, is a loving friend to Anodos, saving him from the Ash tree, a grotesque, beastly tree that symbolizes brute power and mastery.

Numerous other characters enter the episodes of *Phantastes,* including two valiant brothers who join Anodos in mortal combat against three giants. Additionally, throughout the story, Anodos visits numerous cottages, each kept by a strong matron. These visits usually signify that a key test for Anodos is on the horizon. One such matron with a sallow, slightly forbidding face is reading a book on darkness when Anodos stumbles by. Ignoring

Am I very like a woman then? . . . I am very glad you think so. I fancy I feel like a woman sometimes. I do so tonight— and always when the rain drips from my hair. For there is an old prophecy in our woods that one day we shall all be men and women like you. Do you know anything about it in your region? Shall I be very happy when I am a woman? I fear not, for it is always in nights like these that I feel like one. But I long to be a woman for all that.

the warnings of this lady of darkness, Anodos is introduced to his own dreadful shadow. While not a real character, this shadow is a real part of Anodos that he must shed in his quest for goodness.

Last, two other characters are important to the tale from beginning to end. Sir Percival is a downcast knight that we should remember from King Arthur's round table brotherhood, and the White Lady is the object of both Sir Percival and Anodos's affections.

Summary and Setting

Phantastes is not a normal story, even by fairy story standards. The quote by Novalis that precedes chapter one of *Phantastes* is telling:

One can imagine stories without rational cohesion and yet filled with associations, like dreams, and poems that are merely lovely sounding, full of beautiful words, but also without rational sense and connections.... This true Poesie can at most have a general allegorical meaning and an indirect effect, as music does.[5]

Phantastes is true to this quote, and readers should beware: as with all of Fairy Land, you must enter this fairy story on its own ground. Reading Anodos's adventures is not like reading most stories but is more like listening to music. Because of this, *Phantastes* is a difficult tale to summarize. After all, how do you summarize a symphony? Nevertheless, there are three parts of the story that help to organize the events. The first section introduces us to the mysteries of Fairy Land that overwhelm Anodos, including a community of singing and feasting fairies who stir up mischief while romping in the playground forest. Soon our hero discovers the wise Beech and violent Ash, visits several cottages, picks up his dreaded shadow, and first meets the beautiful White Lady.

The second section begins when Anodos floats down-river to the Palace of Fairy Land. In this Palace, Anodos wanders for days among the majestic pillars, swimming in a magical

I felt as if I must have seen the knight before; but as he drew near, I could recall no feature of his countenance. Ere he came up to me, however, I remembered the legend of Sir Percival in the rusty armour, which I had left unfinished in the old book in the cottage: it was of Sir Percival that he reminded me. And no wonder; for when he came close up to me, I saw that, from crest to heel, the whole surface of his armour was covered with a light rust.

pool and exploring a library where the books unite with Anodos so that he becomes the object of whatever he reads. Through one such book, Anodos becomes a sword-swinging student in Prague named Cosmo von Wehrstahl, and through Cosmo Anodos learns of mirrored images and ideal verses of sacrificial love.

The last section of *Phantastes* tells of Anodos's adventures after the Palace—fighting giants, finding freedom from his own shadow, and seeing true chivalry and love in Sir Percival and the White Lady. Anodos's final quest calls on all the courage, humility, and sacrificial love he gained in Fairy Land. With these virtues and marks of goodness secured, Anodos returns to his primary world twenty-one days after turning twenty-one.

Worldview

I mentioned above that the world would be a dull place if we believed only in what we can physically see. We should call this view of the world a type of extreme empiricism. Moreover, if this extreme empiricism were true, the world would be dull *and* confusing because language would be nearly impossible. Imagine if you could only talk about the things your eyes were seeing at that moment? If all this were true, mankind would lose much of his freedom to think God's thoughts after Him, all because he would not have the power of imagination.

What then is the imagination? As a simple definition, the imagination is how we make images in our minds. This ability is a wonderful treasure and a distinctly human gift, for while animals have keen instincts and other God-given strengths, only humans can create images. Creating images is a mysterious power that operates on many levels, but for now we should think about the imagination by way of comparison. Namely, the imagination is different from the senses. As an example, when handed a mug of steaming, freshly brewed java, you apprehend the coffee through the warm touch, the taste, the rich aroma, and the appearance of the mug. These ways of knowing the coffee are called *sense-apprehension*. We apprehend the coffee when it is within reach of one of our senses, most importantly in this case, taste and smell. However, what happens when the mug of coffee is beyond the reach of our senses? If we cannot see, smell, touch, or taste the coffee, do we know anything about coffee in general? Do we still know *that* particular mug of coffee? Naturally, yes, we do know about that coffee through the image remaining in our minds once the coffee is gone. However, even more interestingly, at this exact moment that you are reading this, you have an image of a mug of coffee in your mind while having never seen (physically) the hypothetical

mug I have been describing.

This discussion of sense-apprehension versus mental images may seem distant from *Phantastes* until we learn the words for these two concepts. First, the image we have in our minds directly from sense-apprehension is called a *percept*. More importantly for our purposes is the term for mental images: *phantasm*. A phantasm is an image of a thing that is not present to our senses, and this word is the root behind the title of George MacDonald's fairy-story, *Phantastes*.

The Christian Imagination

This excursus into the imagination is helpful because the modern world does not think much of the imagination. At least, most modern people do not seem to take the imagination seriously. We live in an age that exalts factual and scientific knowledge above all other modes of knowing. Yet, as the illustration of the mug of coffee demonstrates, the imagination lies at the root of nearly all thinking and speaking so that it is impossible to ignore the imagination. The Triune God has given us bodies, minds, and souls to know God, God's people and His world, and without the ability to make images, or phantasms, we would lose a distinctive aspect of being made *imago Dei*.

Additionally, for Christians much is at stake with the imagination for we are called to live by faith. The imagination is not the same thing as faith, but the two are related. Hebrews 11:1 tells us: "Now faith is the assurance of things hoped for, the conviction of things not seen." In other words, faith makes real to us the things not visible, things such as the creation of the world by the word of God. Likewise, in John 17 Christ prays that His people will be "in the world" but not "of the world." How are we to live in this world, yet not be of it, if we do not have an idea in us of what Heaven is like? Also, when we pray the Lord's Prayer, we ask for God's will to be done "on Earth as it is in Heaven," and, again, we must have a sense of what Heaven is to pray this. In these ways, faith is related to the imagination, for we are picturing in our hearts and minds what Heaven—as well as what Heaven on Earth—looks like. Christians of all people should be keen to grasp the workings of the imagination, for a practiced Christian imagination will aid our faith.

There is one more point to make on the imagination, or phantasms. Not all phantasms are the same. Just as we can form images in our minds of people, objects, or places on this Earth that may be visible to us presently, so too we can form images of all sorts of things that are not visible at all on this Earth because they are not of this Earth. Consider, for instance, Frodo, the heroic hobbit who has come to us all from the imagination of J.R.R. Tolkien. To the chagrin of many, Frodo does not exist in this world. Frodo is from Middle Earth, yet we should not think less of Frodo because he is not from our time or place. Frodo and Middle Earth really exist in our imaginations. Perhaps we should call this existence an "imaginary reality," a reality true to the God-given imagination. Frodo naturally inhabits the mind of every Tolkien reader, and because of this Tolkien would say Frodo belongs to a secondary reality. Primary reality consists of the things in this world that God created, and secondary reality consists of the creatures, places, and events that we create in our imaginations. In other words, primary reality is God's creation, and, mirroring His creativity, secondary reality is our sub-creation.

What all this means is that we have no need to fear the imagining of things both physically present in this world and of worlds we sub-create. The imagination is a natural faculty and a true mode of knowing that God has given to us. Tolkien, Lewis, MacDonald, and others offer wonderful examples of the Christian imagination in their mythopoeic works. Mythopoeia is a branch of literature that creates myths, or grand stories, about entire worlds apart from ours. When these secondary worlds are founded on biblical principles of beauty, truth, and goodness, these sub-created worlds have much to offer to us in this primary world. For instance, the warm images of simple beauty in the Shire and the noble virtues of Reepicheep, not to mention Anodos's journey to Lady Wisdom, all create in us a longing for the highest things, the best things, and the eternal things. Looking into these sub-created mythopoeic worlds cultivates us in and for this world.

True Heroism in Seeking Goodness

We gain a significant clue about Anodos's fantastic journey in the first chapter of *Phantastes*. Anodos has just celebrated his "one-and-twentieth birthday," a sign that youth should be giving way to the maturity of manhood. *Phantastes* is, after all, a *bildungsroman*, and on his twenty-first birthday Anodos inherits a key to Fairy Land, the place of his quest.

But what is Anodos's quest? As mentioned above, *Phantastes* follows the way of knightly chivalry, and Anodos seeks—at times both knowingly and unknowingly—humility, service, love, and goodness. These virtues define true Christian chivalry, and Sir Percival is a fitting exemplar of such chivalry in *Phantastes*. Sir Percival is known in Grail legend for his chivalry dedicated especially to God. In *Phantastes* Sir Percival appears first in a shell

Cold lady of the lovely stone!
Awake! or I shall perish here;
And thou be never more alone,
My form and I for ages near.
But words are vain; reject them all—
They utter but a feeble part:
Hear thou the depths from
which they call,
The voiceless long-
ing of my
heart.

of rusty armor as a downtrodden, lonely knight, and yet, as a true comedic character, Sir Percival is purged from his failures through sacrificial combat, saving Anodos at a very critical moment. Likewise, Anodos fulfills his quest for goodness when he imitates Sir Percival, and both characters persevere through numerous falls.

This Fairy Land heroism that Anodos learns is quite different from the heroism in ancient Greek literature. Achilles, for example, fights so that the glory of his name will resound long after he has crossed the River Styx, and the code of his glory knows no bounds. Brute strength, cruelty, deception, and favoritism from the gods are all acceptable means to heroism in Homer's world. Hence, Greek heroism is anthropocentric. The heroism Anodos learns, however, follows a code of self-control, humility, and sacrifice, though he rarely learns these lessons the easy way.

Anodos earns his chivalric spurs through many encounters, but perhaps the most telling opponent to achieving heroic goodness is Anodos himself. At times it seems he may never learn to choose the straight and narrow path. Upon a closer look, however, MacDonald is making a specific point in Anodos's repeated failures. Like refining gold, true heroism arises only from persevering through trials and failures, and, for Anodos, most of these failures do not come from some fierce opponent but from subtle temptation. The great symbol for Anodos's sinful inner voice is his shadow that doggedly tracks him. Ironically, avoiding the shadow in the first place required no great deed from Anodos; he needed only to walk away from a door he was tempted to open. However, Anodos fails to resist temptation, and the words of the sallow-faced matron reading the book of darkness haunt him:

> So, then, as darkness had no beginning, neither will it ever have an end. So then, it is eternal. The negation of aught else, is its affirmation. Where the light cannot come, there abideth the darkness. The light doth but hollow a mine out of the infinite extension of the darkness. And ever upon the step of the light treadeth the darkness; yea, springeth in fountains and wells amidst it, from the secret channels of its mighty sea. Truly, man is but a passing flame moving unquietly amid the surrounding rest of night; without which he yet could not be, and whereof he is in part compounded.[6]

As the black-eyed woman (whom Anodos should have recognized as a witch and ogre) reads these words, Anodos should have fled, but he is drawn by the darkness, and throughout the rest of Anodos's ventures, the dark shadow clings to him as a constant reminder of the battle within.

The parallel between the shadow and Anodos's sin nature is not hidden. Most fairy stories are intentionally simple so that we interact directly with such lessons. After all, Fairy Land is not a place of subterfuge but a haven of simple truths that we meet in a special way when we are immersed in imagined wonder. In this state of childlike openness, we can be pierced by truth. Anodos himself is pierced by truth near the end of *Phantastes* when he is forced to confront his shadow at last. Following a prideful encounter with a boasting knight who perfectly mirrors Anodos himself,[7] Anodos is trapped in a tower buried deep within a dark forest. Fittingly, this entrapment is the worst sort for the door is unlocked the whole time. Anodos has only to rise and walk, but he will not. Only through the song of grace and light from a beautiful maid that Anodos had previously harmed is he freed from his dark self-imprisonment to walk in the light. Anodos describes his own lesson learned:

> Then first I knew the delight of being lowly; of saying to myself, "I am what I am, nothing more." "I have failed," I said; "I have lost myself—would it had been my shadow." I looked around: the shadow was nowhere to be seen. Ere long, I learned that it was not myself, by only my shadow that I had lost. I learned that it is better, a thousand-fold, for a proud man to fall and be humbled, than to hold up his head in his pride and fancied innocence. I learned that he that will be a hero, will barely be a man; that he that will be nothing but a doer of his work, is sure of his manhood. In nothing was my ideal lowered, or dimmed, or grown less precious; I only saw it too plainly, to set myself for a moment beside it. Indeed, my ideal soon became my life; whereas, formerly, my life had consisted in a vain attempt to behold, if not my ideal in myself, at least myself in my ideal.[8]

Incarnational Quest for Lady Wisdom

The above lines that describe Anodos's freedom at last from his shadow would seem a fitting end to this fairy story. Indeed, if we thought fairy stories were neat and easy, we would suppose that the proper comedic end to *Phantastes* would leave Anodos free of all troubles. Fairy stories, however, are simple, not simplistic, and Anodos is free of his oppressive shadow, not of all his troubles. Immediately on the heels of his escape from the tower of self-imprisonment, Anodos discovers a "self" that arises within him, taking a "mistaken pleasure in despising and degrading [himself]." Ironically, having just lost his shadow through the intervening grace of a wise maid, Anodos discovers a new pride in his own weakness. This is simply a new form of self-righteousness in which Anodos prides himself for being lowly. However, Anodos's recourse this time is a true turn toward wisdom, and he learns to repent of his own repentance.

> Doubtless, this self must again die and be buried, and again, from its tomb, spring a winged child; but of this my history as yet bears not the record. Self will come to life even in the slaying of self; but there is ever something deeper and stronger than it, which will emerge at last from the unknown abyss of the soul; will it be as a solemn gloom, burning with eyes? Or a clear morning after the rain? Or a smiling child, that finds itself nowhere, and everywhere?[9]

This is an important wisdom lesson for Anodos, and many other similar lessons appear in the pages of *Phantastes*. Biblically, wisdom is personified as a lady, and the harlot is Lady Wisdom's contrary. All the ladies in *Phantastes* fall within these two types, and one way to understand this tale (and your tale, for that matter) is to track Anodos's progression toward Lady Wisdom and away from the harlot. Yet discerning the difference is not always easy. By far the White Lady is Anodos's main love, and the first sight of her stirs the poet in Anodos just as his poetry stirs her to life out of her alabaster tomb, as you shall soon read. However, once he has freed her from this spell, and she is out of sight, Anodos learns the consequences of idealism. Anodos falls in love with love, an idealized romanticism that plays on his emotion and

The whole garden was like a carnival, with tiny, gaily decorated forms, in groups, assemblies, processions, pairs or trios, moving stately on, running about wildly, or sauntering hither or thither. From the cups or bells of tall flowers, as from balconies, some looked down on the masses below, now bursting with laughter, now grave as owls; but even in their deepest solemnity, seeming only to be waiting for the arrival of the next laugh. Some were launched on a little marshy stream at the bottom, in boats chosen from the heaps of last year's leaves that lay about, curled and withered. These soon sank with them; whereupon they swam ashore and got others.

draws him into the snares of the Alder-tree Maid who shreds his belt of wise beech leaves and feeds him to the Ash. Despite his good intentions, Anodos sought after beauty and love in the wrong way, and his reward is the Alder-tree Maid, a type of the harlot.

In Anodos's journey between these two types of women, we can trace a common thread through each fall when he fails to flee the dark harlot: namely, seeking some idealized love or some false mirror of reality smothers Anodos's discernment. What he thinks is a true, pure beauty turns out to be skin-deep tinsel. After his near encounter with the Alder-tree Maid, Anodos turns to a wise woman for advice, asking how he could pursue such beauty that turned out to be evil? She reminds Anodos:

> I am sure she would not look so beautiful if she did not take means to make herself look more beautiful than she is. And then, you know, you began by being in love with her before you saw her beauty, mistaking her for the lady of the marble—another kind altogether, I should think. But the chief thing that makes her beautiful is this: that, although she loves no man, she loves the love of any man; and when she finds one in her power, her desire to bewitch him and gain his love . . . makes her lovely—with a self-destructive beauty . . .[10]

Hence, the first danger Anodos must learn to avoid is the harlot disguised in beauty. Anodos learns a second lesson about idealism, but in this case he seeks a true love in the wrong way so that his love is not love; it is selfishness. The cause of this selfish love comes from pursuing an idealized love that is defined only in Anodos's head, not in something objective. With such an introspective definition of love, Anodos loves another for his own sake. We see this poignantly in the Palace library when Anodos becomes Cosmo von Wehrstahl. Cosmo finds a magic mirror in which he sees a truly beautiful maid, and as the story unwinds, Cosmo is forced to realize that her ideal presence in the mirror leaves her sickly and ill. Only when Cosmo finds the courage to live sacrificially can he free her and actually earn her love.

This theme of ideal versus incarnational love runs throughout *Phantastes*. Be on the watch for mirrors, reflections, sculptures, and other symbols that usually indicate that Anodos is pursuing love on his own fallen terms. In each case, idealized love sours and proves false and/or selfish. Only when the grace of true love from without floods Anodos's soul does he glean the wisdom to love others for their sake like the incarnate One who sacrificed Himself out of love for His own.

—*Matt Vest*

For Further Reading

Lewis, C.S. *On Stories: And Other Essays*. Boston, Mass.: Houghton Mifflin Harcourt, 2002.

MacDonald, George. *A Dish of Orts*. Charleston, S.C.: Biblolife, 2007.

Tolkien, J.R.R. *Leaf and Tree*. London: Harper Collins Publishers, 2001.

SESSION I: PRELUDE

A Question to Consider

Is the imagination an essential aspect of being human? Why or why not?

From the General Information above answer the following questions:
1. What is the imagination?
2. What is the difference between a percept and a phantasm?
3. How does a healthy imagination aid our faith?
4. What is sub-creation?
5. Should Christians be fearful of fantasy literature?
6. Who is Anodos's greatest challenger to completing his chivalric quest?
7. What are the two dangers that stem from Anodos's idealized love?

READING ASSIGNMENT:
Phantastes, Chapters I–VI

SESSION II: DISCUSSION
Phantastes, Chapters I–IV

A Question to Consider

In the first four chapters, Anodos begins his journey into Fairy Land. From the introductory essay, we know that this story is one of a young man "coming of age." How does a young person grow up—what are some things necessary for the journey to maturity?

Discuss or list short answers to the following questions:

Text Analysis

1. What happens when Anodos looks into the eyes of the unusual fairy creature, who says she is his grandmother?

2. What does Anodos learn from the country maid and her mother?
3. What happens to Anodos that confirms at least some of the advice given to him by the country maid and her mother?
4. What happens to Anodos when he consumes the food of Fairy Land?
5. Based on your answers to the above questions, tell what tools Anodos receives for his journey through Fairy Land and into manhood, and whether or not they are similar to the things you listed as important for growing up.

Cultural Analysis

1. What do popular magazine articles, TV programs, and movies you've seen imply that you, as an American youth, are expected to be doing in order to be normal and to have a good time?
2. Imagine that you are giving advice to a 12-year-old about how to grow up to be a really hip, popular American twenty-something; what would you say? Remember, this is not advice about how to be wise, but how to be as much as possible like what is promoted by the media mentioned above.

Biblical Analysis

1. You know that the Bible's teaching on marriage and family is diametrically opposed to the prevalent cultural mindset. Find an example in Scripture of someone who did not grow up according to the ways of God, and paraphrase it. Use a concordance if necessary, and cite your references.
2. In the third chapter of Philippians, Paul speaks of how "those of us who are mature" should think (Phil. 3:15). Read all of Philippians 3. Are there things in this chapter that seem to go along with the things Anodos is learning, or that you listed as important to the journey to adulthood?

SUMMA

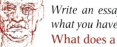

Write an essay or discuss this question, integrating what you have learned from the material above.
What does a young person need for the journey to adulthood?

The next session will be a student-led discussion. Students will be creating their own questions concerning the issue of the session. Students should create three Text Analysis Questions, two Cultural Analysis questions, and two Biblical Analysis questions. For more detailed instructions, please see the chapter on *Death on the Nile*, Session V.

Issue

Is external beauty good, bad, or neutral? What is beauty?

Reading Assignment:
Phantastes, Chapters VII–X

Session III: Student-Led Discussion

A Question to Consider

There is a great emphasis in America on external beauty and youth. Millions are spent each year both in advertising fashion and makeup and in the purchase of these things. Do they contribute to beauty? Is external beauty necessarily a bad thing? What role does the external play in true beauty, and how does one determine true beauty, or become truly beautiful?

Students should read and consider the example questions below that are connected to the Question to Consider above. Last session's assignment was to prepare three questions and answers for the Text Analysis section and two additional questions and answers for both the Cultural and Biblical Analysis sections below.

Text Analysis

Example: In Chapter VII, Anodos discusses the Alder-maid's beauty with the kind old woman. According to her, what makes the Alder-maid beautiful?

Answer: The kind old woman says, first, that Anodos loved the idea of her before he saw her, which made her appear beautiful. Also, that she does things to make herself more beautiful than she is. The main thing, however, is that she "loves the love of any man" because it makes her aware of her own beauty, and that this makes her beautiful. However, she also says that this beauty is self-destructive, "constantly wearing her away within" and that her whole front is just a "lovely mask of nothing."

Cultural Analysis

Example: According to our culture, what is beautiful? Would the Alder-maid fit into cultural standards of beauty?

Answer: The Alder-maid would definitely fit into our cultural standards of beauty. Although Anodos does not describe specific aspects of her beauty, he does say she had a "somewhat girlish figure," and "beautifully moulded features." The kind old woman says she did things "to make herself look more beautiful than she is" (chap. VII). The beauty appreciated in our culture has a certain sameness about it—just take a look at the contestants in any beauty pageant—which almost looks "moulded." The body type seen most often in advertising is more adolescent than womanly, and the flourishing cosmetic industry is testament to the concerted effort among members of the average female population to make themselves look more beautiful than they are.

Biblical Analysis

Example: Read Genesis 12:10–20, Proverbs 7, and Proverbs 31:30, then answer the following question: Should men avoid beautiful women altogether?

Answer: Although it might seem so from reading Proverbs 7, there is no biblical prohibition against beauty itself, or associating with physically attractive people, whether men or women. The emphasis in Proverbs 7 and throughout Scripture is on keeping oneself from evil by being filled with the Word of God and wisdom. The description of events in Proverbs 7 clearly states that the woman was dressed inappropriately (as a prostitute), behaved inappropriately (was loud and wayward, never at home, and was brazenly seductive), and the young man, who is described as "lacking sense," was in the wrong place at the wrong time (on the road to her house when it was getting dark outside). Young men and women who disregard the advice of their elders and the admonition of Scripture either will not recognize these warnings or will ignore them, and may find themselves in similarly dangerous circumstances.

Other Scriptures to consider: Psalm 119:9–16, Romans 1.

SUMMA

Write an essay or discuss this question, integrating what you have learned from the material above.

There are thousands of attractive men and women in ads, on TV, and in movies—these people essentially set the standard of beauty in our culture. Is this a good place to look when judging our own appearance? Why or why not? If not, why not, and where should we look?

READING ASSIGNMENT:
Phantastes, Chapters XI–XIII

Twilight Fantasies by English painter Edward Robert Hughes (1851–1914)

Session IV: Discussion
Phantastes, Chapters VII–X

A Question to Consider
How can beauty and ugliness, faith and unbelief, sorrow and joy, "dwell so near?"

Text Analysis
Discuss or list short answers to the following questions:
1. What distresses Anodos even more than his own folly after his evening with the Alder-maid?
2. Anodos perceives a change in the sad knight, saying that he has "plunged into the torrent of mighty deeds" and that this has washed away the red stains from his armor. What do you think this means?
3. What is the antithesis Anodos experiences between the woman in the cottage and her husband?
4. After he leaves the home of the woman and her husband, Anodos follows a path through the woods to another cottage, where, again, he has a vague misgiving which he ignores. What occurs?
5. What effect does the shadow have on living things and on Anodos himself?
6. Anodos says that the sweetest music always has in it a tinge of sadness, and that the deepest truths and deepest joys cannot come without sorrow. He says this shortly after discussing how reflections in mirrors are lovelier than "what we call the reality." Is there any connection between these statements? Explain.

Cultural Analysis
1. Can you think of any indications in our culture of the belief that difficulties and bad feelings are to be avoided at all costs?
2. Can you think of some areas in which Americans have lost faith in something? What did this loss of faith result in? Are there things which occasionally seem to restore this faith?
3. Are people today so enamored with beauty that they believe external beauty always indicates internal beauty?

Biblical Analysis
1. In Scripture, do sorrow and joy go together?
2. Can you think of any other examples of this sort of antithesis in Scripture?
3. Is it possible for a Christian to wrestle with faith and unbelief? Obedience and disobedience? Give an example from Scripture, and explain why this is the case.

Summa

Write an essay or discuss this question, integrating what you have learned from the material above.
How can beauty and ugliness dwell so near?

Reading Assignment:
Phantastes, Chapters XIV–XIX

Session V: Aesthetics

Peer Gynt Suite
In this assignment you will have the opportunity to listen to some music written in the same era that *Phantastes* was written, evaluate its aesthetic value, and use it as a springboard for your own writing. Evaluating a piece of music can be daunting because, unlike visual art, it occurs in time—you can't stop it to examine it, unless you can read the music. Very often one's reaction to a piece of music is primarily emotional; you either like a piece of music or you don't, but it's sometimes hard to say why. However, since it is our job as believers to be able to praise, love, and protect what is beautiful and to condemn, hate, and oppose all that is truly ugly, we must learn how to do this with music, and practice doing it!

The music you will listen to was written by Norwegian composer Edvard Grieg in 1875. Grieg, Norway's greatest and most beloved composer, is most famous for his Piano Concerto in A minor and the Peer Gynt Suite. This collection of short pieces was written at the request of dramatist and fellow-Norwegian Henrik Ibsen as incidental music for the play, *Peer Gynt*. Ibsen originally wrote *Peer Gynt* as a poetic fantasy to be read, not as a play. It tells the story of the adventures of a young fool, Peer, who is completely self-centered and runs from any sort of commitment. He boasts, is lazy, uses and hurts women, and is disrespectful of his parents. The work was very popular, partly because Ibsen made extensive use of images from Norwegian fairy tales.

Grieg's music was written in two suites of four works each, Suite #1, Opus 46 and Suite #2, Opus 55. If you do not already have access to these works, you may find them at your favorite online music service. You will listen to three pieces from Suite #1 and one from Suite #2. Read the following questions before listening to the music; as you listen, jot down "yes" or "no" in answer to each question for each piece, as well as any descriptive words, emotions, or scenes that come to mind. In addition, tell whether or not each piece "fits" the title it has been given.

Music Analysis

1. Does the music demonstrate the composer's ability and expertise?
2. Is there a clear beginning and ending to each piece?
3. Is there a clear musical theme in each piece—either a melody, or a rhythmic pattern, or both—which occurs throughout the piece and serves to hold it together?
4. Do the pieces seem well-balanced?
5. Is the composer's use of gradual increases and decreases in the volume of the music effective?
6. Does each piece have a clearly discernible climax, perhaps using dissonance, and a resolution to the climax?
7. List the words that come to mind as you listen; calm, exciting, stressful, sad, fast, slow, etc.
8. Whether or not you like this music, is it worthy of praise? Why or why not?

Mythopoeic Description

Select one of the Grieg pieces. If you are in a classroom setting, all students will need to listen to and write about the same one unless they have their own recordings and can do the assignment at home. If you are working at home, you can choose whichever piece you like. Listen to your selection several times, allowing the music to affect your imagination and bring ideas and images to mind. Write a short mythopoeic description of your selection (1,000 words or less if typing—one side of a piece of paper legibly if by hand). You may use any of the characters and images from *Phantastes* if you wish, or you may invent your own.

Optional Activities

Activity 1

Read portions of *Peer Gynt* by Henrik Ibsen; compare his adventures with the experiences of Anodos in *Phantastes*. Discuss them with your family or classmates.

Activity 2

Read a short biography of Edvard Grieg. Compare and contrast his life, experiences, and beliefs with those of George MacDonald.

Activity 3

Listen to more of Grieg's music, and note the distinctive Norwegian flavor of it. Write a short essay describing what the music evokes within you.

Reading Assignment:
Phantastes, Chapters XX–XXV

Session VI: Recitation
Phantastes, Chapters XIV–XVIII

Comprehension Questions

Answer the following questions for factual recall:

1. How does Anodos awaken the White

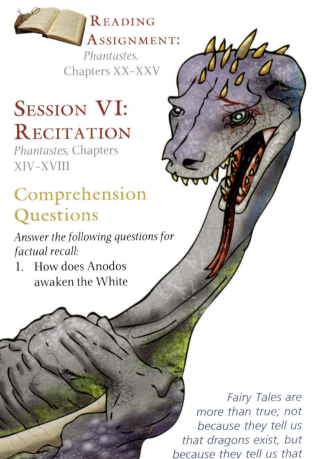

Fairy Tales are more than true; not because they tell us that dragons exist, but because they tell us that dragons can be beaten.
—G.K. Chesterton

630 OMNIBUS IV

Lady the second time?

2. What does the White Lady say when he does this?

3. What does Anodos say is sometimes the saddest of all sounds?

4. The White Lady runs from Anodos, through a large oak door. What is on the other side of the door?

5. The lady descends into a large, dark chasm; Anodos follows, and is harassed by goblins. What does Anodos do that makes the goblins leave him alone?

6. Describe the song that Anodos sings about the White Lady.

7. Why does Anodos have such a tenderness for the White Lady?

8. How does the "goblin Selfishness" reward the "angel Love"?

9. When Anodos emerges from the underground tunnel, he finds himself on a seashore. List the words he uses to describe the place where he finds himself.

10. How does Anodos describe himself in relation to his surroundings?

11. Describe what Anodos experiences after plunging himself into the "heaving abyss" of the sea. What do you think this represents?

12. What happens after he dives in?

13. What makes Anodos feel "almost glad that he had sinned"?

Marble women are pervasive throughout *Phantastes*. This particular lady is on display at the Walters Art Museum in Baltimore, Maryland. But the question is always: Is she Lilith or Lady Wisdom?

OPTIONAL SESSION A: ACTIVITY

Illustrating *Phantastes*

These chapters are complicated, but full of symbolic meaning. For this assignment, you will select one of the readings below and make a drawing to represent it. Present your work to your class and/or your parents and family, using it to explain what happened to Anodos and what he learned through his experience.

READING 1

In Chapter XIX, Anodos enters the cottage of an old woman. Going through each of the four doors of this cottage, Anodos learns some very important lessons. As you read this chapter, pay special attention to the songs that the old woman sings; they will help with understanding the lessons learned beyond each door.

READING 2

Chapters XX and XXI tell of how Anodos meets two young men who call him "brother," and then does "something worth doing."

READING 3

In Chapter XXII, Anodos becomes imprisoned in a tower for a time because of his own weakness and pride.

Select one reading and do one of the following:

a. Draw a diagram of what occurred in your selection, similar to a map with illustrations of the people and events described in each. As you make your drawings, write a list of the sequence of events or a brief description of them.

b. Make a cartoon to tell the story.

c. Rewrite the story as a fairy-tale ("Once upon a time…") and make it a rebus story—the kind where you insert pictures for certain things, feelings, or characters instead of their names.

d. Come up with your own idea— be creative, but check with your teacher for approval before you get started.

Regardless of which selection you choose or the manner of illustration you use, do it with excellence and beauty. Even if all you're doing is an outline drawing of the cottage with a list of events, use a ruler or straight edge, make your lettering neat, finish in ink or colored pencil, etc.

The next session will be a student-led discussion. Students will be creating their own questions concerning the issue of the session. Students should create three Text Analysis Questions, two Cultural Analysis questions, and two Biblical Analysis questions. For more detailed instructions, please see the chapter on *Death on the Nile*, Session V.

Issue

Is there such a place as Fairy Land? Where do we, as Christians, learn our lessons—in the physical realm or in the spiritual?

OPTIONAL SESSION B: STUDENT-LED DISCUSSION
Phantastes, Chapters XXIII–XXV

A Question to Consider

Which is more important for the Christian: the life of the imagination or the physical things and actions we are engaged in?

Students should read and consider the example questions below that are connected to the Question to Consider above. Last session's assignment was to prepare three questions and answers for the Text Analysis section and two additional questions and answers for both the Cultural and Biblical Analysis sections below.

The Artist's Dream by John Anster Fitzgerald (c. 1819–1906), whose nickname was "Fairy Fitzgerald."

Text Analysis

Example: Although many of the stories in *Phantastes* involve beings and happenings that would never occur in real life, there are nevertheless many examples or sayings that we can recognize as applying to our own lives. What example could you provide from Chapter XXIII?

Answer: In Chapter XXIII, the knight, speaking to Anodos, describes Fairy Land as being much like our world, with both "great splendours" and "corresponding horrors." He says "All a man has to do, is to better what he can. And if he will settle it with himself, that even renown and success are in themselves of no great value, and be content to be defeated, if so be that the fault is not his; and so go to his work with a cool brain and a strong will, he will get it done; and fare none the worse in the end . . ." This can easily be applied to our day to day lives.

Cultural Analysis

Example: Describe some examples in our culture of efforts to encourage imagination. How are these different than what occurred to Anodos in Fairy Land?

Answer: Children are encouraged to "be creative," which usually means to do whatever they feel like doing without restrictions of any kind. Adults are encouraged to "find their inner child," which usually means to ignore responsibility and do something crazy. We are often told we should dream big, which usually means to ignore the fact of our genuine limitations and give ourselves to activities removed from our day-to-day responsibilities. Anodos was not asked to do any of these things, and none of the events in the story occurred as if they originated in himself. He was confronted with things he had never imagined and forced to deal with them as best he could. The result of these encounters was the learning of many important lessons.

Other cultural issues to consider: The prevalence of Gnosticism in Western cultural Christianity, which places emphasis on emotional/spiritual "experience" above the plain teaching of Scripture.

Biblical Analysis

Example: Read 1 Peter 4, Romans 8, and James 1 to see if you can find any parallels in these verses to the conclu-sions reached by Anodos in Chapter XXV. Be specific.

Answer: First Peter 4:1 says, "He who has suffered in the flesh is free from sin." This goes along with what Anodos says about setting out to find his Ideal, only to come back "rejoicing that I had lost my Shadow." Romans 8:28 and James 1:2–4 both correspond with the last few sentences of the book, where Anodos says, "Yet I know that good is coming to me—that good is always coming, though few have at all times the simplicity and the courage to believe it. What we call evil is the only and best shape, which, for the person and his condition at the time, could be assumed by the best good."

Other Scriptures to consider: 2 Corinthians 4:10–7:1, John 15:13.

SUMMA

Write an essay or discuss this question, integrating what you have learned from the material above.

How Is there a real "place" which corresponds to Fairy Land, in which we learn about ourselves and life? Or must we learn our lessons in "the other forms that belong to the world of men, whose experience yet runs parallel to that of Fairy Land?" (chap. XXV).

ENDNOTES

1   MacDonald, George. *Phantastes.* Grand Rapids, Mich.: Wm. B. Eerdmans Publishing Company, 2000. vii.
2   Tolkien's essay, *On Fairy-Stories,* is a must-read for teachers and lovers of fairy stories. No detailed analysis of MacDonald's fairy stories or any of the Inklings' literature for that matter would be complete without reading Tolkien's essay or his poem, *Mythopoeia.*
3   MacDonald, xi.
4   Ibid., ix.
5   Ibid., 3.
6   Ibid., 56.
7   Anodos had previously been knighted for a true moment of valor, but an even higher form of chivalry lies in store for our pathless hero.
8   MacDonald, 166.
9   Ibid.
10 Ibid., 49.

Mythology

"Myths are lies," Jack insisted to his friend as they strolled alongside a river. He continued, "I love reading the myths and have done so since I was a boy. Still, they are lies and, therefore, worthless, even though breathed through silver."

John paused for a moment and then responded, "No, they are not lies."

As if to punctuate John's response, at that moment a sudden rush of wind came up on the still warm evening, sending leaves pattering down around them.

John continued his answer, "The myths, though they contain error, also reflect a splintered fragment of true light, the eternal truth that is with God."

The two friends continued the walk, and the conversation, which had begun with dinner, continued on until four o'clock in the morning.

These events took place on September 19, 1931. You are probably quite familiar with the two men, John and Jack. You know John as J.R.R. Tolkien, and Jack was the name that his friend, C.S. Lewis, went by.

Great literature grew out of the friendship, discussions, and even arguments of these two friends. Their literary works grew out of their love of mythology.

What are myths, and what role do they play in our education? Are myths lies? Or do they have some truths to teach us? Do they, in fact, contain some

Athena is a prominent member of the family of twelve Olympians in Greek mythology. This statue of her stands by the main entrance to the Academy of Athens.

"splintered fragment of true light"?

If we had a time machine, maybe we could go back and listen to Tolkien and Lewis discussing mythology. We all know we can't do that, and further, if you stayed up until four in the morning with Jack and John, you would likely fall asleep during math class.

General Information

Author and Context

What do you want to do when you retire? What do you hope for when you are 90? You probably do not think much about these things. Yet Edith Hamilton's greatest accomplishments came after her retirement, and her greatest honor came at age 90.

Hamilton (1868–1963) grew up in a home filled with literature and languages. She and her siblings played games about King Arthur's knights or the Siege of Troy. Edith was a born reader with a phenomenal memory and a gift for telling stories. A cousin remembered her at age thirteen combing her hair while reading a book written in Greek.[1]

Being schooled in the days before classical learning fell from academic graces, Hamilton read Greek and Latin classics for pleasure all her life. After graduating from Bryn Mawr College, she became the first female admitted at the University of Munich.

For twenty-six years she was the Head Mistress at the Bryn Mawr School for Girls, where she won the hearts of her students and raised the school's prestige.

After retiring, Miss Hamilton began sharing her love of classical literature with friends, who soon insisted that she write. At age sixty-three, her first book, *The Greek Way*, came out. Other books followed, including *The Roman Way*, *The Echo of Greece*, and in 1942, *Mythology*, her most popular book.

Her writings earned her numerous awards, but her highest honor came when, at age ninety, she traveled to Athens and received honorary citizenship of the city she had so long loved.

Significance

One of the best-kept secrets in school is how much fun learning literature is. More than just fun, literature enlarges our capacity to understand ourselves and the world. Literature is more fun than riding a roller coaster; however, the fun part of literature requires time and effort.

The enjoyment of literature grows out of reading plenty of literature. The whole shelf of separate books you see in a library is all part of a web or network. To better understand the recent books, you have to go back to the sources. The two main sources for our literature are the Bible and mythology, particularly Greek mythology.

Without an awareness of mythology, you cannot understand ancient, medieval, or modern literature. Without an awareness of mythology, you will not understand numerous literary references or some Bible verses, such as Acts 14:12. Handbooks of mythology are useful, but they usually leave out the poetic and narrative features of mythology. For the myths are stories, some of the greatest

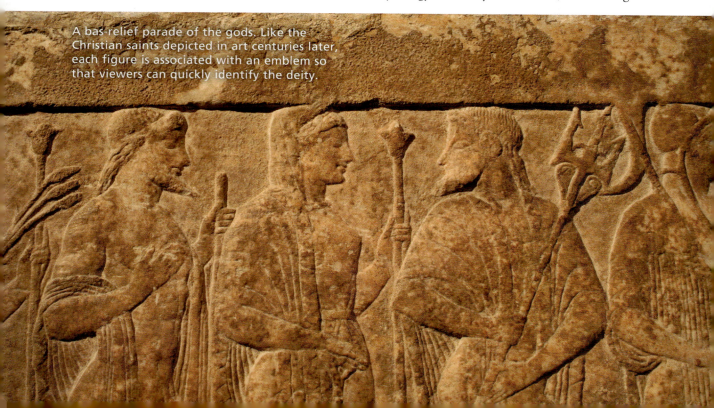

A bas-relief parade of the gods. Like the Christian saints depicted in art centuries later, each figure is associated with an emblem so that viewers can quickly identify the deity.

stories, in fact, ever told.

Mythology can be considered as a short story collection, a reference book, and a guide to understanding ourselves and others. Having a knowledge of mythology at one's fingertips is an intellectual benefit in many ways. Myths are parable-like; myths are philosophical; myths are psychological insights into the mind; myths are pictures of the dangers of pride, ambition, and passion. In reading *Mythology*, you will see the same kinds of stories you learn from the daily newspaper; however, you will remember the myths.

Main Characters

In the northeastern portion of Greece stands Mount Olympus, home to the twelve greatest gods of Greek mythology, who are called the Olympians. The most powerful is Zeus, the Lord of the Sky. His brother, Poseidon, rules the sea, and another brother, Hades, the underworld.

Zeus's wife, Hera, is the protector of marriage. Many myths revolve around Zeus's love affairs and Hera's jealousy. Zeus's children, including Athena, Apollo, Aphrodite, and Ares, each have particular areas of rule.

Other divinities live on earth, such as Dionysus, god of wine, and Demeter, goddess of wheat. There are the Nine Muses, associated with artistic creativity, the three Fates, who determine peoples' destinies, and Furies, Sirens, and other beings, some of whom were neither quite human nor divine.

Some human characters, like Achilles and Aeneas, have both a divine and a mortal parent. Greek mythology is filled with the journeys and battles of heroes. Such were heroes like Jason, Odysseus, and Hercules. Some myths, like Pyramis and Thisbe, focus on love and death among the more ordinary people.

The divinities interact in the world of humans, often resulting in conflicts whenever humans challenge, romantically attract, or somehow please a god.

With so many divine and human characters to remember, begin with the more prominent figures, like Zeus and Hercules. *Mythology* is not only a great book to read, but it is a resource to use over and over again.

Summary and Setting

One of the main sources for classical mythology was the *Metamorphoses* by the Roman writer Ovid. Hamilton says of him, "He told almost all the stories and he told them at great length." Although Hamilton disapproved of Ovid's viewpoint, which she saw as disrespectful toward the myths, she follows his method in her extensive retelling of the stories.

In her introduction, Hamilton describes the key concepts of Greek mythology and discusses the main Greek and Roman sources for the stories. The first major portion of the book describes the pantheon of gods and goddesses, the creation of the world and of mankind, and the earliest heroes. More stories of heroes and their adventures, along with stories of lovers, are then told.

The Trojan War was a major subject for plays, poems, and epics, but the ancient writers assumed the audience knew the whole story of that war. Hamilton provides a complete account of the war and includes summaries of Homer's *Iliad* and *Odyssey* and Virgil's *Aeneid*.

The surviving dramas are summarized in a retelling of the stories of great families, such as the House of Atreus, which includes Agamemnon and Iphigenia, and the Royal House of Thebes, whose descendents include Antigone. In the

This is a fragment of a Roman copy of "Hera Borghese" originally sculpted by Phidias in Athens during the High Classical period. Phidias designed the massive gold and ivory statue of Athena that stood in the Parthenon. His statue of Zeus at Olympia was one of the Seven Wonders of the Ancient World.

latter parts of the book, shorter myths are told.

A brief section near the end of the book covers the key characters and beliefs found in Norse mythology.

Genealogical charts at the end of the book increase its usefulness as a reference work to keep handy while reading the original mythological stories.

Worldview

One of the great by-products of sitting in a classroom listening to a teacher is daydreaming. We know that you always pay attention in class and never daydream, but some of the other students around you daydream quite often.

This is one of the few times you will be encouraged to daydream in class. Imagine being stranded on an island, instead of being in the classroom. The idea of being on a deserted island is popular in books and movies. Remember reading *Robinson Crusoe* and *Swiss Family Robinson*? Or have you watched the movie *Cast Away*? Or did you read the book *Lord of the Flies*? Here's another: *Gilligan's Island*.

We will allow our imaginary island to be in a tropical setting with lots of fruits and berries growing all around and with fish easily caught along the shore. Sorry, but pizza delivery cannot be part of the imagining. We can allow some vital necessities to wash up on the shore after the shipwreck, so you can have tools, clothes, a toothbrush, an iPod, and lots of sunscreen lotion. For the next few years, you have nothing to do but enjoy fun in the sun, sand, and surf. Let's also assume you will be rescued in a few years.

Here's a problem: After your rescue, you will have to complete the high school courses you missed. To prevent that, let's have a box of books wash up on the shore. They would have to be securely sealed and wrapped, since salt water ruins books.

Let's imagine that among the books is one titled *Three Hundred Recipes for Bananas and Fish,* along with another titled *The Dummies Guide to Surviving on a Deserted Island.* The two chief books, however, are the Bible and *Mythology* by Edith Hamilton.

On that small shelf made from a loose board that washed up, you have the foundations for the literature of Western Civilization. With two books, you can understand the two worldviews that have been clashing for thousands of years. With two books, you can gain an understanding of literary references, allusions, phrases, and ideas. With two books, every genre of literature, all of the recurring plot structures, and an inexhaustible supply of character studies are available.

With two books, you have answers to the key questions regarding how the world got here, why we are here, and why things happen as they do. Also, these two books address the great mystery of death and the afterlife. Thank‑

fully, both books are delightfully written and filled with adventure, war, romance, and comedy.

If you look around the room where you are now, it might not resemble our imaginary island. While we likely lack the deep blue ocean waters lapping against the sandy beach, with gulls flying overhead and palm trees swaying in the gentle breeze, we still have the Bible and *Mythology* to read and think about.

Much of the world's oldest and greatest literature dates back to the Greeks. While much has been lost, we still have extensive writings of Plato, Aristotle, Herodotus, and Thucydides, along with shorter collections of Hesiod and Pindar. Some poems and fragments of poems have survived, and out of the hundreds of plays that were performed, quite a few tragedies and comedies have been preserved. Amazingly, we have complete editions of Homer's epics, the *Iliad* and the *Odyssey*. All in all, a rich assortment of Greek literary works has survived.

Long before the surviving manuscripts were first penned, the Greeks had an ever-growing body of mythological stories and characters. Apparently, Greeks already knew these stories. The myths were like a central

Mythology 637

Poor Hermes! He used to be Zeus's messenger, the master thief, guide of the dead, and the god of commerce and the market. He has wings on his helmet and his sandals, but the winged caduceus he once carried has been replaced by modern marketing, his image appropriated to help deliver floral bouquets.

events, but exaggerated and distorted. Or, myths may be totally fictitious, but still illustrate popular beliefs. The power of the myth is not its historic accuracy, but the general truth it portrays. England's cultural myth is King Arthur and his Knights of the Round Table. An actual King Arthur probably once lived, and there could have been a Round Table, but not a Lady of the Lake. If the actual tomb of King Arthur is ever located, it will incite incredible interest, but the myth does not depend upon such a discovery. The Arthurian kingdom provides ideals that have captured the imagination of England's people for centuries. England has endured wars, invasions, and dangers with resolve stemming from the legacy of King Arthur's Camelot. This myth forms a common bond for the English people.

America also has its myths. Have you seen the painting *Washington Crossing the Delaware* by Emmanuel Leutze? Is that painting mythical or historically accurate? The crew shows men, with possibly one woman, representing all the ethnic and social groups that joined the Patriot cause. Central to the picture is General Washington, standing astern in the boat, sternly facing forward. This painting is based on Washington's crossing of the Delaware River on Christmas night in 1776 to launch a surprise attack on the enemy at Trenton. The painting captures Washington's dedication, the soldiers' hardships, and the incredible daring of the American cause in the war. But the painting is mythical.

First, the painting presents this night crossing in bold, bright hues; whereas

casting agency, readily providing characters and plots for poets or playwrights looking for material. Homer's epics grew out of legends from the Trojan War; likewise, playwrights, such as Aeschylus and Sophocles, did not invent new materials, but retold the existing stories, with some occasional variations in the plots.

These myths formed more than just an anthology of favorite stories, for they contained the beliefs and culture of the Greeks. We often use the word *myth* to mean something widely believed, but clearly not true. So, we may say, "It is a myth that all Italians sing opera or that all Scotsmen are tightwads." (By the way, two non-opera-singing Italians have been located, along with a Scotsman who spent money wildly one weekend.)

For our purposes, a more useful meaning is that myths are stories or explanations about the commonly held beliefs of a culture. Myths may be rooted in true

Myths of all nations and cultures take shape around certain central themes. Myths attempt to explain creation, divinity, and religion. They probe the meaning of existence and death and account for natural phenomena. Finally, as in the case of the Washington painting, they chronicle the adventures of national heroes.[2]

All myths are pictures of a culture. If you understand the myths, you understand the culture. Change the myths, and you change the culture. Myths are evidences of the common beliefs and, as such, are evidences of a culture's religious foundations. Mythological beliefs reveal the heart of a culture.

The Greek myths are more than just pre-Christian; they are also anti-Christian. As Tolkien noted, myths contain splintered fragments

an accurate painting of a boat crossing a river by night would be quite dark. Second, if Washington had been standing up in a boat crossing a river, someone would have said, "No disrespect, Sir, but you are rocking the boat. Please sit down." And how likely is it that Washington's boat would have included a New England seaman, an African-American, a Scottish immigrant, a woman, a farmer, a wounded man, a merchant, and Lieutenant James Monroe carrying a half furled flag? But historical inaccuracies aside, the painting still powerfully tells the story of American's War for Independence.

Demeter, goddess of grain and fertility, welcomes her daughter back from the underworld, escorted by Hermes. Each spring Persephone rises from the dead, causing her mother to restore life to the fields and hillsides, but knowing that as winter approaches she will die once again and descend to the land of the dead.

of the true light. As Lewis realized, myths emphasize the theme of the Dying God, which came to historical fulfillment in Jesus Christ.[3] But the myths were man-centered and idolatrous. As Edith Hamilton noted, "The Greeks made their gods in their own image."

Romans 1:18–33 explains why sinful men reject God and worship the wrong things. Men "suppress the truth in unrighteousness" even though the true God may be known through creation (vv. 18–20). Fallen men become "futile in their thoughts, and their foolish hearts are darkened" (v. 21). We can then say of the Greeks, along with other unbelieving cultures, "Professing to be wise, they became fools" (v. 22). The immorality resulting from this suppression of the knowledge of the true God is detailed in verses 24 to 33.

If this Bible passage explains the key thoughts, themes, and practices of the Greeks and of their mythology, why should a Christian study them?

A person wanting to understand the Western world must understand the Greek culture. Paul and his missionary companions knew the Greek language and culture when they began their missionary journeys. At that time, the Greek culture, then referred to as Hellenistic culture, far more than the Roman, Jewish, or Egyptian cultures, permeated the known world.

Without knowledge of things Greek, Paul could not have evangelized Athens, Corinth, and other Greek cities. Since we are not evangelizing the ancient world, can we then dispense with the beliefs common to the Greeks? Knowledge of some ancient cultures can be left to the specialist or confined to the museum, but not the pervasive Greek culture. As often noted, although Rome conquered Greece, Greece conquered Rome in terms of culture.

The Greek cultural presence continued as Christianity spread throughout Europe. During the early Christian era and then into the Medieval era, many aspects of Greek civilization were salvaged from the past. From Aristotle's *Poetics* to Zeno's stoic philosophy, Greek writings and ideas have been taken out of storage, polished up, and used and re-used over and over again.

You cannot understand the Church Fathers without some understanding of Greek ideas. Augustine's *Confessions,* his spiritual autobiography, reveals his experiences with the varieties of Greek thought before his conversion to Christ. Even after his conversion, he never completely removed all Greek ideas from his theology. All studies of philosophy begin with the Greek philosophers, notably Plato and Aristotle. Greek poetic and dramatic literature provides the genres and models for all subsequent literary forms. The four forms listed in Aristotle's *Poetics,* which are lyric, tragedy, comedy, and epic, are still the major classifications of literature. And the canon of

Western literature is drenched with mythological names, references, and re-used plots.

We can benefit from learning from the Greeks without succumbing to the temptation to offer sacrifices to the gods of Mount Olympus. Horrible weapons once used on battlefields become objects for our education and entertainment in a museum. The Greek gods and goddesses may have inspired awe and fear at one time, notwithstanding their foolish and wicked behavior. But to us, their human-like weaknesses and foibles reduce them to pitiful or laughable characters. One can hardly take the womanizing Zeus and the ever-jealous Hera seriously. The gospel has reduced classical myths to objects for our education and entertainment.

Writing to Greeks in Corinth, Paul said that the Christian mission was "bringing every thought into captivity to the obedience of Christ" (2 Cor. 10:5). The Greek culture has now long been a prisoner-of-war held by Christendom. The myths are ours to read and enjoy.

We can learn by comparing and contrasting mythology with Christianity. A recurring theme in classical literature is the interaction of the world of gods and goddesses with mankind. Classical mythology and biblical narratives are similar. Neither the Bible nor the myths are secular. Louise Cowan has noted that one of the defining characteristics of epic literature is "the penetration of the veil separating the human from the divine."[4] Human characters in Greek stories know they must supplicate the gods and that challenging a god usually results in severe judgment. Arachne was turned into a spider because she challenged Minerva (the Latin name for Athena). The Bible narratives are also stories of people who walked faithfully with God or who, in their rebellion, faced the judgment of God.

The great difference between Christianity and Greek mythology is in the object of their worship. The God of the Bible is righteous and holy, and His Word commands righteousness. The Greek gods are notoriously devious, wicked, and capricious. The gods might notice if proper sacrifices are made to them, but humans cannot have trust in the gods' approval. There is nothing like covenantal promises between the gods and mortals among the Greeks.

At the heart of the Greek worldview is their conception of the universe and creation. As Hamilton notes, "The Greeks did not believe that the gods created the universe. It was the other way about: the universe created the gods." With this warped error as the starting point, Greek myths could never proclaim a meaningful and moral universe. All moral and philosophical errors, in fact, grow out of disregarding God's creation of the world.

Mankind, according to the Greeks, is a product of

the same creative processes as the gods. Divine beings are more powerful and beautiful than humans; moreover, they possess immortality, which is the great difference between the divinities and mortals. Mortality is the source of tension and conflict for Achilles in the Iliad. His mother, Thetis, is a divine being, but because he had a human father, Achilles is doomed to mortality. His only hope is for earthly glory, which brings little consolation after you are dead.

In Aeschylus's play *Eumenides*, Apollo says, "Once a man has died, and the dust has soaked up his blood, there is no resurrection." The idea of eternal life was so foreign to Greeks that they thought Paul was preaching two divinities named Jesus and Resurrection respectively in the account given in Acts 17.

Not only is the afterlife without hope, this life is without real freedom of choice or options. For the Greeks, fate is inevitable and the afterlife is not a happy place. Even the Olympians cannot change the Three Fates' power over life. Neither Thetis nor Zeus can change Achilles' fate or the ultimate outcome of the Trojan War. Unlike the biblical doctrine of predestination, there is not a covenantal purpose and goal to a person's fate in Greek mythology. The Greeks cannot say, as Paul did in Romans 8:28, that all things work together for good to those who love God, who are called according to His purpose. Greeks assumed they were hell-bound, and they were right, having not even the concept of grace, salvation, or a joyous everlasting life.

Man's helplessness, mortality, and subjection to fate led the Greeks to emphasize heroic characters. Greek heroes battle against other men, forces of nature, sometimes gods and goddesses, and against fate itself. Such heroes as Theseus and Odysseus are physically strong and crafty in the use of their minds; in contrast, Hercules and Achilles were definitely more brawn than brains.

The hero motif is still ever popular in books and movies. A major change in the character of the hero coming through the Christian tradition is the elevation of the weaker person or unlikely character to hero status. Tolkien chose Hobbits to save the Shire, and Lewis chose children to rule Narnia. Greeks would not have understood the triumph of the underdog. The lowly could often serve the powerful, but the lowly never overcame the powerful.

Throughout the history of literature, many writers, like Dante, Shakespeare, and Milton, blended the Greek and biblical traditions in their works. Christian writers of the future growing up in Asian or African countries may make extensive use of the folk legends and myths of their lands. Even then, they will still be using the Bible and, along with it, mythology to create the literature of their future.

But whatever happened to Jack and John? They continued to talk about myths. Eventually, they discussed

The story of Persephone has provided fertile material for many an artist's imagination. This relief shows Hades forcing her into his chariot, pulled by his coal-black steeds to his dark realm in the underworld.

the gospel. Jack, of course, saw the gospel as one of the many dying-god myths. In the gospel, John told him, "Myth became fact." Maybe Jack wrinkled his brow, but the light would soon dawn. The power of the gospel—*the true myth*—would overwhelm and overpower him and through his words many others as well.

—Ben House

For Further Reading

Grant, Michael. *Myths of the Greeks and Romans.* New York: The World Publishing Company, 1962.

Markos, Louis. *From Achilles to Christ: Why Christians Should Read the Pagan Classics.* Downers Grove, Ill.: Intervarsity Press, 2007.

Reid, Doris Fielding. *Edith Hamilton: An Intimate Portrait.* New York: W.W. Norton & Company, Inc., 1967.

Veritas Press History Cards: New Testament, Greece, and Rome. Lancaster, Pa.: Veritas Press. 6.

Session I: Prelude

A Question to Consider

What are the myths—or basic beliefs and ideals—that we believe about ourselves as a nation? (Remember our national holidays and the Pledge of Allegiance.)

From the General Information above answer the following questions:

1. How did Edith Hamilton's background and schooling prepare her to be a writer?
2. How would a student be hindered if he or she did not have a knowledge of Greek mythology?
3. What are the two primary kinds of characters found in mythology?
4. What is the cultural myth of England, and how did it affect the English people?
5. How can something be historically inaccurate in details and yet tell a greater truth?
6. Why does a Christian need to know about the ancient Greek, or Hellenistic, culture?
7. How do such Christian heroes as those in Tolkien's or Lewis's writings differ from the heroes of Greek mythology?

Reading Assignment:
Mythology, Part One, Chapter I

Session II: Discussion
Mythology, Part One, Chapter I

A Question to Consider

What are some common, yet wrongful, beliefs about God found in our culture?

Hercules, the greatest hero of Greece, displays his overwhelming strength early in life when he kills two snakes that invade his crib. Big of brawn but not of brain, only magic is able to eventually end his life.

Discuss or list short answers to the following questions:

Text Analysis

1. What are the more un-godlike qualities of Zeus?
2. Over what areas of life does Pallas Athena rule?
3. Who is Aphrodite, and how does she come into being?
4. How did the Greeks and Romans differ in their view of Ares (Mars)?

Cultural Analysis

1. If Zeus were a modern-age celebrity, how would his womanizing be viewed?
2. Does our society view war in ways more like the Greek view of Ares (Mars) or the Roman view?
3. Why might Aphrodite make a popular object of worship in our time?

Biblical Analysis

1. How does Mount Olympus as the dwelling place of the gods differ from the biblical view of heaven as the throne of God?
2. In spite of the idolatry of the Greeks and the wickedness of their gods, what truthful views about marriage and family did they still hold?
3. What "splintered fragments of the true light" can be found in Phoebus Apollo, as Edith Hamilton describes him?
4. Why did the people of Lystra think that Barnabas was Zeus and Paul was Hermes (Acts 14:8–13)?

Summa

Write an essay or discuss this question, integrating what you have learned from the material above.
What practical, moral, and social effects occur in a society that believed in the gods and goddesses of Mount Olympus? Consider whether the ancient Greeks really believed in such gods or not.

Optional Activity

Using the book, fill in Chart 1 about the Olympians (all answers are in Part One, chapter I).

READING ASSIGNMENT:
Mythology, Part One, Chapter II

Session III: Discussion

Mythology, Part One, Chapter II

A Question to Consider

As we have become more of an urban and industrial nation, have we lost a sense of the importance of weather, seasons, crops, and harvests? In other words, the things

---

Chart 1: **THE OLYMPIANS**

GREEK NAME	ROMAN NAME	AREA OF RULE	SPECIAL GIFTS OR POWERS	BEST KNOWN FOR
Zeus				
Hera				
Poseidon				
Hades				
Pallas Athena				
Phoebus Apollo				
Artemis				
Aphrodite				
Hermes				
Ares				
Hephaestus				
Hestia				

tied to the soil were very important to our forefathers, but we are not as aware of such things. What is the effect of modern society's distance from the growth of fruits, vegetables, and grains?

Discuss or list short answers to the following questions:

Text Analysis

1. Why was it thought to be natural that the divine power who brought wheat should be a goddess?
2. Why do Dionysus and Demeter both know pain as well as joy?
3. How does the story of Demeter and Persephone account for winter and spring?
4. Who was Semele and what was the cause of her death?
5. What were the two contrary ideas associated with the worship of Dionysus?

Cultural Analysis

1. While women today are not usually employed in harvesting and planting, what areas of life are still largely, although perhaps not completely, viewed as women's work?
2. In the ancient world, the wheat and grape harvests were the key indicators of prosperity. What things, more than agricultural products, are used in our time to indicate prosperity?
3. What are the social uses and abuses of Dionysus's fruit of the vine?

Biblical Analysis

1. What "splintered fragments of true light" can be seen in the stories of Dionysus, the god of wine, and Demeter, the goddess of wheat?
2. What is the Christian answer to the abuses that occur in misusing wine and other alcoholic beverages?

SUMMA

Write an essay or discuss this question, integrating what you have learned from the material above.

As Christians, we should be praying "The Lord's Prayer" (sometimes called "The Model Prayer") either directly or indirectly. In that prayer, we ask that God would "give us this day our daily bread." If your family is not engaged in farming, consider how the season you are in right now and the upcoming season would be different for you if you were to be totally engaged in growing a crop for your daily bread. Consider, for example, the fact that sometimes rainy days ruin our plans for outside activities, but from a farmer's perspective, rainy days are vital for the crop's growth. If your family is engaged in farming, describe how the seasons determine what you do during the year. In either case, write a short description of the seasons and farming.

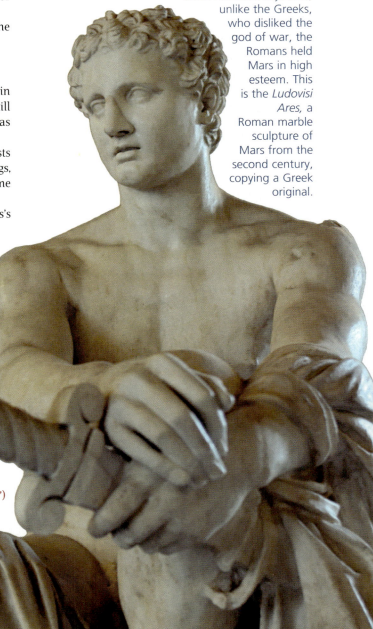

Edith Hamilton says that, unlike the Greeks, who disliked the god of war, the Romans held Mars in high esteem. This is the *Ludovisi Ares,* a Roman marble sculpture of Mars from the second century, copying a Greek original.

Optional Activity

Research one of the following aspects of crops and harvests:
1. The process of growing either wheat or another grain, such as corn, rice, or barley.
2. Maintaining and harvesting a vineyard.
3. The process involved in turning grapes into wine.

Examine an encyclopedia, reference works on farming, or Internet resources for your research. If possible, talk to a farmer about "plowing, planting, and harvesting" a crop.

Reading Assignment:
Mythology, Part One, Chapter IV and Part Two, Chapter II (Pyramis and Thisbe and Orpheus and Eurydice), and Chapter IV (Phaethon and Daedalus)

Session IV: Writing

Modern Greek Myth

This session is a writing assignment. Remember, quality counts more than quantity. You should write no more than 1,000 words, either typing or writing legibly on one side of a sheet of paper. You will lose points for writing more than this. You will be allowed to turn in your writing three times. The first and second times you turn it in, your teacher will grade it by editing your work. This is done by marking problem areas and making suggestions for improvement. You should take these suggestions into consideration as you revise your assignment. Only the grade on your final submission will be recorded. Your grade will be based on the following criteria: 25 points for grammar, 25 points for content accuracy—historical, theological, etc.; 25 points for logic—does this make sense and is it structured well?; 25 points for rhetoric—is it a joy to read?

Objective

Greek stories of heroes, lovers, adventures, and tragedy have been told and retold many times. In plays, novels, poems, and songs, the narrative plots of Greek mythology have been adapted, modified, and put in different settings. You probably recognized that "Pyramus and Thisbe" is a familiar story. William Shakespeare used it in two plays. In *A Midsummer Night's Dream,* some of the characters from the city go to the forest to practice their presentation of the story of Pyramus and Thisbe. In this case, Shakespeare used the myth for comedic purposes (as a play within a play and a comedy within a comedy). In the tragic version, *The Tragedy of Romeo and Juliet,* he borrowed from the plot again to tell a different kind of story.

Stories of a person rescuing the man or woman they love are also popular. Whether it is a cartoon movie like *The Incredibles* or a serious romantic novel like Sir Walter Scott's Ivanhoe, the travails and sacrifices a person is willing to make for the one he or she loves makes for good reading, viewing, or drama. The movie *Cinderella Man,* which tells of the remarkable boxing career of James J. Braddock during America's Great Depression, is the story of a man literally fighting for his family. When it comes to the dangers, uncertainties, and risks a person would take for those he or she loves, literature and history are filled with remarkable accounts. "Orpheus and Eurydice" is just such a story, although it ends in sadness.

This famous sculpture is of the mighty god Zeus. Or is it Poseidon? It all depends on whether he used to be holding a trident or a lightning bolt.

A whole genre of novels are referred to as "coming of age" stories. These stories recount a young person's journey as he or she takes on the challenges and difficulties of adulthood. Several years ago, the movie *Iron Will* told the true story of a young man who raced his sled dogs across the Yukon in Canada in a grueling marathon and won. "Phaethon" tried to step into his father's shoes, but his brashness led to his destruction.

Another popular kind of story is that of the imprisoned and suffering person who survives because of his strength and endurance or who uses his wits to affect an escape. Self-sacrifice, or dying for others, is a recurring theme in these types of stories. Popular movies in this genre include the World War II classic *The Great Escape* and the film versions of *The Count of Monte Cristo*. Prometheus suffered on behalf of others and Daedalus used his wits to escape from prison.

The ultimate love story, which recounts the hero's sacrifices and quest to rescue those he loves, is the story of Jesus Christ. His love for His people was such that He came into a hostile and sinful world, suffered from insults and bodily injuries, and died on the cross. He used His "wits" when confronted in the wilderness by the devil. Like Prometheus, He suffered torments to save mankind. Like Phaethon, Jesus as a young boy boldly took on the task of being about "My Father's business" (Luke 2:49). Like Orpheus, He went to the depths of Hades to rescue His people. Like Daedalus, He escaped from the prison, or in Jesus' case, the grave.

The American author Willa Cather said, "There are only two or three human stories, and they go on repeating themselves as fiercely as if they had never happened before." The future books and movies, which hopefully some of you will be producing, will prove the truth of Cather's statement.

Pick one of the choices below for a writing assignment:

From the readings, pick a story and use the basic ideas or plot to write a new story. Make the short story about 1,000 to 1,500 words in length. Instead of the mythical world of the ancient Greeks, place your story and characters in a different, and preferably more modern, setting. You can, like Shakespeare and many others, change the plot, characters, and even the ending, but keep the story close enough to the Greek myth to be recognized.

READING ASSIGNMENT:
Mythology, Part Three, Chapter III

SESSION V: DISCUSSION
Mythology, Part Three, Chapter III

A Question to Consider

Is it better to be a bold risk taker or to carefully calculate all risks before taking action?

Discuss or list short answers to the following questions:

Text Analysis

1. Why was Hercules not a hero to the Athenians?
2. What event occurred when Hercules was a small child that indicates he is a descendent of Zeus?
3. What was the ultimate tragedy resulting from Hercules' blind rage?
4. Why does Hercules have to undergo what became known as "the Labors of Hercules"?

Cultural Analysis

1. Do people generally admire physical strength more than intellectual abilities?
2. What defenses are used in our time for crimes of passion, like those committed by Hercules?
3. From a human or societal perspective, could a person's great and heroic deeds ever offset or cover his misdeeds? (For example, how should we feel about a murderer or thief who rescues a child from a burning building?)

Biblical Analysis

1. How does Hercules resemble Samson (Judg. 13–16)?
2. How does the Bible deal with the idea of penance for our past actions?
3. How is the story of Hercules rescuing Alcestis from death a "splintered fragment of the true light," or a story resembling the saving work of Jesus Christ?

SUMMA

Write an essay or discuss this question, integrating what you have learned from the material above.

Louise Cowan said, "[T]he immortality of a people is at the expense of a hero." Whether it is our historical, mythical, or spiritual heroes, we live because of the sacrifices of others. What is the role of heroes in our lives, and how is Jesus Christ the fulfillment of the heroic quest?

Optional Activity

Using drawing paper or a poster board, make a series of illustrations of the Twelve Labors of Hercules. Add captions or dialog if you wish. Use humor or satire if you wish.

If drawing is not your cup of tea, then consider this alternative activity: Retell the story of Hercules' Labors by placing him in a modern setting. Come up with twelve seemingly impossible tasks for him to do and then describe how he accomplishes these challenges. For example, you might have Hercules go to Washington, D.C. and root out political corruption.

Reading Assignment:
Mythology, Part Five, Chapter I (The House of Atreus, Agamemnon and His Children and Iphigenia among the Taurians)

Session VI: Recitation

Comprehension Questions

Answer the following questions for factual recall:

1. Identify the following Olympians and other Greek deities. (Part One, chaps. I and II)
   a. Full-grown and in full armor, I sprang from the head of my father fully grown. Like most daughters, I caused my dad to have a headache, but was the best loved of his children.
   b. I am the glorious god of war, but my parents detest me, and that poet Homer called me murderous and bloodstained. Nobody understands me.
   c. I am the twin sister of Apollo. I am the lady of wild things and the huntsman-in-chief to the gods.
   d. I am the god of wine and of having a good time, but like wine, I can be both good and bad.

Zeus is not *always* committing adultery or feuding with his wife Hera, as illustrated in *Jupiter and Juno on Mount Ida,* painted by James Barry (1741–1806).

e. I am the goddess of love and beauty. My mother was Dione; however, I may have arisen from the foam of the sea.
f. I am the supreme god. My thunderbolts back up my claims. I am known for having an eye for the women, and for some reason, that makes my wife really jealous.
g. I am beautiful. I am the god of light and truth, the archer god, and the healer. The laurel is my tree, and no false word ever falls from my lips.
h. I am the goddess of the hearth, the symbol of the home, around which a newborn child must be carried before it can be received into the family. Never, never let the fire go out.
i. I am a brother to the number one god. I rule over the sea and carry a trident. Do you like horses? I gave the first horse to man.
j. I am also a brother to the number one god. I rule over the underworld and the dead. My wife is Persephone.
k. I am Persephone's mother. Every year when she departs from me to go to her husband, I go into mourning, and that causes the earth to grow cold and barren. I am also the goddess of wheat.

2. What mythological story accounts for the beautiful tail feathers of the peacock and what happened in that story?
3. How did the story of Pyramus and Thisbe end tragically?
4. What was the condition imposed upon Orpheus for him to have Eurydice back from the underworld, and did he fulfill that condition?
5. How does the story of "Iphigenia among the Taurians" change the story of Iphigenia's sacrificial death?

OPTIONAL ACTIVITY

Iphigenia in Brooklyn

Classical mythology has been the subject of paintings and poetry, but also music. Concert music, often misleadingly referred to as classical music, has often had themes from Greek classics. Such music is usually quite serious and is performed in concert halls with certain expectations of decorum.

For quite a few years, Peter Schickele, a professor at the University of Southern North Dakota, has been taking a rather unique approach to concert music. He composes, conducts, and presents music supposedly composed by a member of the Bach family, named P.D.Q. Bach. If

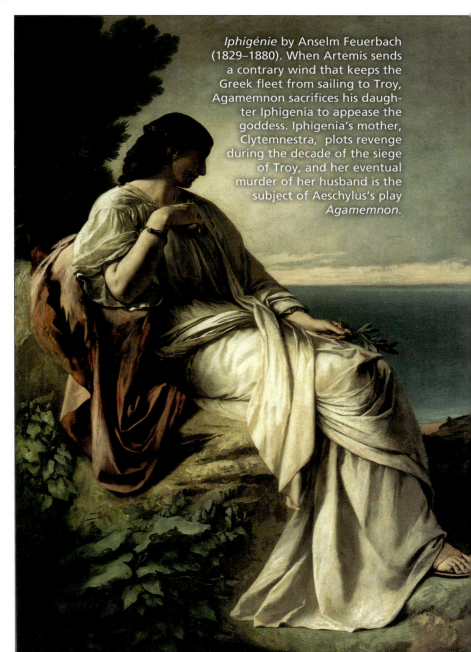

Iphigénie by Anselm Feuerbach (1829–1880). When Artemis sends a contrary wind that keeps the Greek fleet from sailing to Troy, Agamemnon sacrifices his daughter Iphigenia to appease the goddess. Iphigenia's mother, Clytemnestra, plots revenge during the decade of the siege of Troy, and her eventual murder of her husband is the subject of Aeschylus's play *Agamemnon*.

one were to judge the music of P.D.Q. Bach by the higher standards of music, we would have to say that it is quite bad; however, it is quite hilarious. (There is not actually a real composer named P.D.Q. Bach, we hope.)

One of P.D.Q. Bach's/Schickele's "finest" works is "Iphigenia in Brooklyn." As Professor Schickele points out, scholars have debated whether Iphigenia ever was even in Brooklyn. This piece can be found on the DVD titled P.D.Q. *Bach in Houston: We Have a Problem*. It is also available on compact disks and even those old round vinyl devices called record albums.

Find a copy of "Iphigenia in Brooklyn" and listen to it a time or two. Make note of all the actual references to mythology in the music. Be prepared to roll in laughter.

OPTIONAL SESSION: ACTIVITY

John and Jack Discussion

We only have short fragments of the long discussion that J.R.R. Tolkien and C.S. Lewis had on September 19, 1931. But we do have the major premises of both men.

Lewis contended that myths were lies and were therefore ultimately useless, while Tolkien emphasized that myths, though containing error, still reflect "a splintered fragment of true light, the eternal truth that is with God."

Make a list of three to five objections to mythology, including Lewis's objection. (Remember that Lewis was, at that time, being drawn closer and closer to the Christian faith, but that he was not yet a Christian. He later came to agree with his friend, Professor Tolkien, on the issue of myths.)

Using Tolkien's statement and based on your experiences in having read from *Mythology, The Bacchae, Metamorphoses*, and other works containing mythology, make a list of three to five "splintered fragments of true light" gathered from the myths.

If you are in a classroom setting, have one or more students take Lewis's side of the argument. The others will take Tolkien's side. In a homeschool setting discuss the objections with your family or friends or write an imaginary dialogue that fills in the gaps in John and Jack's conversation.

Discuss the topic of the value or dangers of mythology. If your class is small and a river is nearby, hold the discussion while taking a walk. If that is not possible, have tea while holding the discussion. Use your best British accents. Maintain decorum.

If the side presenting Lewis's views trumps the other side in the discussion, re-read and re-think everything in this chapter!

ENDNOTES

1   Reid, Doris Fielding. *Edith Hamilton: An Intimate Portrait*. New York: W.W. Norton & Company, Inc., 1967. 30.

2   Holman, C. Hugh and Harmon, William. *A Handbook to Literature*. New York: Macmillan Publishing Company, 1986. Fifth Edition, 317.

3   Lewis, C.S. "Myth Becomes Fact" from *God in the Dock*. Grand Rapids: William B. Eerdmans Publishing Company, 1970. 66.

4   Cowan, Louise. "Epic as Cosmopoesis," from *The Epic Cosmos*, edited by Larry Allums. Dallas: The Dallas Institute Publications, 2000. 11.

Plutarch's Lives

"Alright, we have time for just one more question for Mr. James." You have one last chance to ask your favorite athlete a question as the Q&A time comes to a close . . . if only he will pick you.

"Yes, sir, in the blue shirt." It's you! What question will you ask as you stand face-to-face with your favorite celebrity?

> *You:* "Ah, um . . . Mr. James, there is one question that I'm dying to ask."
> *Mr. James:* Sure, kid. Ask me whatever you want.
> *You:* Okay, Mr. James, here it is: What did you do when your dog wet the carpet last week?
> *Mr. James:* What!?

Odds are this would not be the question that we would ask—at least I hope not—if we were talking to our favorite athlete or the President of the United States or anyone important.

You might not ask questions like this, but Plutarch would. He wanted the story behind the story. He wanted to see the character of the people he was writing about with crystal clarity. Our reactions in small matters reveal our character. It matters if Mr. James cleaned up after his pooch and perhaps looked-up a dog trainer on the Internet rather than electrocuting his dog or setting him on fire. In the same way, Plutarch was not just interested in all the grand accomplishments of a man's life. In his *Lives*, Plutarch is more concerned to uncover the character of the men he writes about than their public accomplishments, and this leads him to ask different questions and relate different episodes of the *lives* he writes about than a historian might consider most important.

General Information

Author and Context

Although we know few details about Plutarch's life with certainty, we do have a decent outline of his biography. He was born during the reign of Claudius, probably around A.D. 45. His parents were Greeks who lived in a small town in Boetia called Chaeronea. Plutarch grew up in this city and, after a life of study and travel, retired to the same town to write his *Lives*.

Plutarch spent his youth studying philosophy and eventually opened his own school. Unlike many of his Roman contemporaries, he rejected Stoicism and Epicureanism in favor of following the doctrines of Plato. Also unlike many of his contemporaries, his writings are in Greek rather than Latin. Plutarch wrote a number of different essays and dialogues about philosophy, but it is his *Parallel Lives* that have been enjoyed for nearly two thousand years. He traveled widely during his life, visiting Greece, Asia Minor, Egypt, and Italy. His travels furnished him with a wealth of information that found its way into his writings. Plutarch had the privilege of living his entire life under the *pax Romana*, the extended period of peace and prosperity that lasted from the reign of Augustus through much of the second century. His travels, as well as his writings, demonstrate the peace and unity that existed throughout the Mediterranean world during his life.

At home, Plutarch was married to a woman named Timoxena and had at least five children. He also served in a number of public roles, including commissioner of public buildings and city magistrate. Later in life, he was appointed procurator of Greece by the emperor Hadrian and served as a priest of Apollo at Delphi. Plutarch died sometime around A.D. 120 while Hadrian was emperor in Rome.

Significance

Plutarch has been called the first modern biographer, an indication of the novelty of his approach among ancient writers. There were other authors who had been historians, such as Herodotus or Thucydides, and there were certainly other authors who had traced the events of other men's lives. But Plutarch's approach was new. In his efforts to relate the lives of the most important men of Greece and Rome, Plutarch sought to communicate more than just history; he went beyond merely relating events or rehearsing battle details. Plutarch was concerned about understanding the character, motivations, and morality of these men. As Plutarch himself put it, "my purpose is not to write histories, but lives." Plutarch, therefore, stands out because of what he attempted to accomplish with his writing.

Perhaps because Plutarch has been considered the founder of a literary genre, his work has also influenced later authors, particularly in the last few centuries. The fact that the most widely used translation was by John Dryden, a well-known British neoclassical author who opposed the onslaught of French Enlightenment thinking and the deism that often accompanied it. Dryden's interest in Plutarch is one indicator of the importance attached to Plutarch's work in the seventeenth and eighteenth centuries. Plutarch also influenced some of Shakespeare's most famous works, including *Julius Caesar* and *Antony and Cleopatra*. If one compares Shakespeare's play about Julius Caesar with Plutarch's work, he will notice that Shakespeare has taken many of the names and details directly from Plutarch's account. In other words, Plutarch not only introduced a literary genre, but he also provided inspiration and information for important literary works hundreds (and even thousands) of years after him.

Main Characters and Summary

In biographies, the main characters are not just the most important figures in the story or the character with the most lines, the main characters *are* the story. Our selections include the lives of Alexander the Great and Julius Caesar.

Alexander the Great, son of Philip of Macedon, was hungry for glory and great accomplishments from his youth. Plutarch notes that he would shed tears at his father's military success, saying his father had deprived him of a chance for glory. But Alexander had plenty of opportunities to achieve glory, for upon becoming king at age 20, he immediately began his march through Greece, Asia Minor, Persia, and India, establishing the greatest empire up to that point in Western history.

Caesar was also eager for honor, and he was said to cry when reading about Alexander, who had accomplished so much more than he had at a comparable age. Caesar survived the civil war between Marius and Sulla and led Rome as a part of the First Triumvirate with Pompey and Crassus. But after the death of Crassus, Caesar turned on Pompey and defeated him, becoming master of the Roman world.

Alexander and Caesar both transformed the Western world socially, politically, and militarily. The ancient world was overturned in ten years by the young Alexander, who changed the map, introduced a common language, spread Greek learning, and reached the height of military accomplishments by the age of 30. The Roman world may never have become an empire had it not been for the ambition and success of Caesar. He set the stage for the greatest empire the Western world has known. Thus, as Plutarch puts it, it is nearly impossible to summarize the great actions and monumental impact these two men had on ancient history.

Worldview

Bottom of the ninth inning, one out, game four of the American League Division Series. With my favorite team two outs away from ending its season and each member heading to his living room instead of the League Championship Series, two men reached base. The crowd went wild, every single fan standing on his feet and jumping up and down. However, as a small child, all of 32 inches tall, the packed mass of people made it impossible for me to see what was happening. There I was fulfilling my childhood dream of attending a playoff baseball game, and I couldn't even see the action as my team was about to win the game in the last inning! Fortunately, Dad came to the rescue. He hoisted me onto his shoulders so that I could see what was happening and understand the joy of the fans around me. Do you remember sitting on your father's shoulders as a small child in order to see over a large crowd? Perhaps it was at a parade, or a speech by the president, or a baseball game. The crowd around you makes it impossible to see what is going on. Of course, once a father lifts his son or daughter up, the child is able to see even farther than the father.

Those of us who live in the twenty-first century are somewhat like that small child climbing in order to see things more clearly. We are on the shoulders of those who have gone before us in history; their thoughts and writings help us understand who we are and where we are headed, while their lives offer us examples of how we ought (and ought *not*) to live.

But what if every generation ignored the men and women who lived before it and tried to do everything new? Would we have computers—or even electricity—if inventors didn't learn from those who experimented before them? And how much would we understand about medicine, surgery, or the human body if every doctor tried to figure things out himself without considering the research of men who went before him? But we would also lack a tremendous amount of wisdom about life if we ignored those who have lived, thought, and written about their experiences.

Unfortunately, many in our culture have adopted what might be called "massive chronological snobbery syndrome" or MCSS. Chronological snobbery is a logical fallacy that assumes older ideas are less important, less applicable, or untrue just because they are old. While enjoying newer technology is one thing, when our culture begins to reject the wisdom of past generations as well as its technology, then each new generation becomes more and more impoverished intellectually, morally, and spiritually. Our culture seems to believe that previous generations are not worth listening to because they "don't understand," "aren't living in our age," or "are out of touch with the world today." But this attitude ignores the fact that human nature does not change. The experiences of past generations render them very capable of offering wisdom and truth to each new generation.

I once knew a small child who was fascinated with fire. The dancing flames tantalized the young boy, and despite his parents' continued warnings, he did not lis-

Philip II of Macedon had just been victorious in a battle when he received three messages at once: one of his generals had defeated an enemy, his race horse had won in the Olympics, and his son Alexander had just been born. The seers assured him that a son whose birth coincided with these three successes could not help but be invincible.

ten to their advice until he had burned his finger in a candle. Although a teenager might consider himself infinitely wiser than the young boy, his complaint that his "old man" was stuck forty years back in history and didn't understand that now it's okay to do what everyone else in high school was doing, follows the same foolishness as the boy sticking his finger into the fire. When children reject the wisdom and advice of their parents, they are not just rejecting a God-given authority, they are also rejecting a store of wisdom and guidance that God has built into the structure of our lives.

In the Bible, this store of generational wisdom appears in God's covenant with Israel as well. A covenant is something that builds from one generation to another. While each new generation renews or reaffirms the covenant, a proper understanding of the terms of the covenant and the motivation to keep the covenant in obedience come from looking back at those who have lived previously. When God spoke to Israel, He didn't come up with a new contract; He turned back to the covenant of their fathers—Abraham, Isaac, and Jacob. Israel's understanding of who they were, where they were headed, and how they ought to live came from looking back on those who had gone before them. This is also why God commands parents to teach God's commandments to their children and to pass down the stories of His great mercy and salvation. Wisdom is multi-generational. When Israel stopped looking back to the covenant with their forefathers and started to do what was right in their own eyes, the chaos, immorality, and judgment of the period described in Judges resulted. Biblically speaking, only life in covenant with God, which inherently rests on the examples, promises, and wisdom of previous generations, yields obedience and blessing.

In his *Lives*, Plutarch is self-consciously recording the moral examples of men from the past so that future generations might learn from their successes and failures. As he put it, his goal was to "arouse the spirit of emulation" in order to inspire men to imitate the moral exemplars of the past, while at the same time offering clear lessons on the vices, temptations, and mistakes men have made in history.

In his attempt to inspire us with moral examples, Plutarch is doing something profoundly biblical. God's Word repeatedly urges us to pay attention to the lives of those who have gone before us. Paul urges the Corinthians to imitate him (1 Cor. 4:16) and sends Timothy to remind them of how he acts in Christ. While it may sound rather arrogant to instruct others to be more like one's self, Paul clarifies that they should imitate him only because he seeks to imitate Christ (1 Cor. 11:1). The author of Hebrews spends an entire chapter detailing the faith and obedience of the patriarchs, calling them a "great cloud of witnesses," which should encourage us to lay aside sin and temptation and live in obedience, looking to Christ as our chief example (Heb. 11:1–12:2). James uses Abraham as an example of demonstrating the truth of our faith by our actions (James 2:21–23) and Job as an example of perseverance through suffering (James 5:11), while Peter uses Noah and Lot as examples of righteous men staying faithful to God in the midst of pressure from an evil culture and Balaam as an example of a man who could not resist the temptation to do what was wrong (2 Pet. 2:4–16). In other words, God does consider all of life to be a spiritual activity, whether it be someone examining the lives of historical men and women less spiritual or reading the Beatitudes or singing the Psalms. Rather, God repeatedly uses the examples of men and women who have gone before us as inspirations or warnings for our own lives.

Alexander the Great's conquests transformed the Western world in ten short years, changing the map and spreading the Greek language and culture.

Plutarch is keenly aware of the distinction between righteousness and unrighteousness, justice and injustice. Plutarch correctly identifies vices such as greed, anger, bribery, envy, self-centered glory-seeking, and hypocrisy. At the same time, self-sacrifice, justice, integrity, faithfulness, and generosity are virtues that both Plutarch and the Bible commend. But we do have some extra legwork to do, since there are differences between Plutarch's standards of virtue and biblical standards. Reading these biographies can still be a beneficial and even spiritual exercise, but only if we hold these lives up to the standard of Scripture, measuring their virtues and vices by God's standards rather than Plutarch's.

Plutarch does not explain or list his standards of virtue in any one place. His understanding of virtue comes to light only as we read his biographies and observe what he commends and condemns. However, it would be fair to summarize the core of his idea of virtue with what have been called the four classical virtues. These are fortitude, justice, temperance, and prudence.

Fortitude is strength in trial, courage in the face of danger. Plutarch repeatedly praises Alexander and Caesar for their courage and boldness, especially in the face of overwhelming odds. He also mentions that Alexander purposely exposed himself to danger in order to encourage others to follow his example of bravery. On the other hand, one of Plutarch's few condemnations of Demosthenes is his lack of fortitude in battle. Justice was a virtue that applied to everyone, not just lawyers or judges. This virtue meant that a person treated others fairly, honestly, and in accord with what is right. Plutarch praises Alexander for performing his conquest with justice, but condemns his slaughter of the defeated Indians as the one instance of injustice in his campaign. Plutarch praises Cicero for both his justice and his prudence, claiming that Cicero fulfilled Plato's dream of a wise and just man as the ruler of a state. A man who demonstrates temperance is one who shows moderation and acts appropriately, without excess, in all circumstances. Alexander is praised for his temperance when he refused to drink the only water in the camp since no else would have any, and when he rebuked his soldiers for desiring excesses of pleasure over hard work. Finally, prudence refers to a man's wisdom and foresight in making decisions and in his actions. While Cicero ruled with wisdom and Alexander showed foresight in preparing for battle, the sophist Callisthenes comes under condemnation for being a powerful speaker with no judgment. In addition to these four virtues, Plutarch also praises self-sacrifice and generosity while condemning self-praise. In fact, his harshest condemnation falls on Cicero and Alexander for their self-admiration.

Plutarch believed that these virtues could, and should, be found in any man, regardless of his birth or education. While birth and education did benefit a man in life, virtue did not depend on circumstances, but on an ingenuous (or honest) nature and an industrious mind. The latter was the most important, however, for resolution and effort were the most significant factors in developing virtue.

These virtues certainly don't appear contrary to Christian principles. After all, Moses told Joshua to "be strong and of good courage" (Deut. 31:6), Micah urges God's people to "do justice" (Micah 6:8), and temperance is listed as one of the qualifications to be a leader in the church (1 Tim. 3:2). The author of Proverbs repeatedly commends the prudent man. In fact, the medieval church adopted the four classical virtues as part of its summary of godly living. So where does Plutarch go wrong?

Perhaps the better question to ask is not where Plutarch goes wrong, but what happens when we go wrong? Plutarch can acknowledge virtue when he sees it, but he also has condemnations for each of the men he writes about. In the end, every biography is a mixed bag, full of warnings about mistakes and errors in each man's life. The difference between Christianity and paganism does not show up most clearly in defining

654 OMNIBUS IV

The Roman world may never have become an empire had it not been for the ambition and success of Julius Caesar. He set the stage for the greatest empire the Western world has known.

virtuous actions, but in dealing with the problem of every man's lack of virtue. Even fallen men usually recognize virtue when they see it, but only the God of the Bible can provide a solution to the lack of virtue that has confronted all mankind since the Fall.

The biblical model of virtue, then, does not start with fortitude, justice, temperance, and prudence. Those virtues ought to characterize men and women who follow God, but they do so as a result of a fundamental change that occurs in their life as a result of meeting a Person. When Paul offers his life as an example, he does so only while clarifying that his life is based on the example of Jesus Christ, who not only provides a pattern for living, but also provides a way for cleansing and forgiveness when we fail. In the end, it is a Person, not a set of principles, who sets the standard for virtue, and it is only in communion with that Person that we have the strength to act according to that standard and find forgiveness when we contradict that standard.

It is interesting that Hebrews 11 provides a host of examples of the classical virtues. These men and women of God displayed incredible fortitude, justice, temperance, and prudence. Yet they are not praised for the virtues *per se*, but for their faith. Faith becomes the test of virtue, not because the virtues don't matter, but because faith is the means by which we enter into a relationship with the Person who strengthens us in action and forgives us in our failures.

The medieval church did not toss out the classical virtues. Rather, they added three Christian virtues (faith, hope, and love) as the necessary means by which a man could achieve the other four. In the same way, Plutarch and his biographies do not deserve to be set aside. They ought to be read, and they ought to inspire us in our actions, but they ought to be read with the understanding that a Person, Jesus Christ, forges our path to virtue, not our own resolution through an ingenuous nature or an industrious mind.

In addition to the classical standards of virtue and vice, Plutarch also opens a window into a world desperately searching for divine revelation. Darius marched happily to his doom due to a misinterpreted dream. Demosthenes urged Greece to attack the Macedonians against the evidence of every augury and sacrifice. But the problem wasn't stupidity; it was a lack of confidence in the information they received. The ancient mindset was wide open to divine communication, but it was held captive by the false gods of the ancient world, unable to discern what to trust or how to interpret the information they received.

Alexander's last few days of life provide us with the most pitiful picture of this desire for revelation. Battling crows, a tame donkey that attacked a lion, and visions of a crowned king all frightened Alexander and shook his confidence in both the gods and his friends. He seems unable to decide whether he should take heed of the signs or whether sufficient courage would be justification to ignore them as mere superstitions. Plutarch comments that Alexander's mind was filled with fears and follies as he sent around to various oracles for advice. In the ultimate irony, or perhaps the ultimate sign of futility for a man unable to trust his divine sources, Alexander died from a fever just after receiving a favorable answer from one of his oracles.

This picture of random, confusing signs that opened the mind to superstition stands in stark contrast to the God of the Bible, who has clearly revealed Himself to His people throughout the ages. He revealed both His majesty and His mercy to Adam, promising a Savior who would restore the relationship between God and man. He personally spoke with Abraham, Isaac, and Jacob, establishing His covenant with Israel and promising future blessings through their seed. He talked face to face with Moses and wrote down His commandments with His own finger that His people might know how to serve Him. His prophets delivered His messages to the people so that they were not without a witness to His truth or His commands. But finally and most clearly, in fulfillment of all His promises, God Himself came and dwelt with men in the person of Jesus of Christ. Christ then proclaimed God's love for His people and accomplished a way of salvation through His death and resurrection. This restored the broken fellowship between God and man so that through Christ, men might approach God's throne and speak with Him and His Spirit would communicate His will to men. In this way, God has met humanity's desire for divine revelation and restored His communion with them.

The fears, follies, confusion, and misinterpretations that plagued the men of Greece and Rome fade away before the God who has sent His Son and left His Word and Spirit so that we might know Him and His will for our lives. And although Alexander still might not know the future as he desired, his frenzied desire to know the future becomes unnecessary before a God who has repeatedly demonstrated His sovereign faithfulness.

—Christopher Walker

For Further Reading

Cicero, "Against Cataline" in *Selected Political Speeches*. London, England: Penguin Classics, 1989.

Julius Caesar, *The Conquest of Gaul*. London, England: Penguin Classics, 1983.

Spielvogel, Jackson J. *Western Civilization*. Seventh Edition. Belmont, Calif.: Thomson Wadsworth, 2009. 105–110 and 161–166.

Veritas Press History Cards: New Testament, Greece and Rome. Lancaster, Pa.: Veritas Press. 17 and 20.

Session I: Prelude

A Question to Consider

If you could interview any celebrity, who would it be and what would you ask him or her? Why would you ask that question, and what might it reveal about the celebrity's life and character?

From the General Information above, answer the following questions:

1. What are some of the ways in which Plutarch differed from many of his contemporary authors?
2. What was the pax Romana and what opportunities did it provide Plutarch that prepared him for his writing?
3. What is Plutarch's literary significance?
4. According to Plutarch, what caused Caesar to break into tears?
5. What is "chronological snobbery," and how does it apply to our culture?

Reading Assignment:
Plutarch's Lives, vol. II, Alexander, pp. 139–169[1]

Session II: Discussion
Plutarch's Lives, vol. II, Alexander, pp. 139–169

A Question to Consider
Is it appropriate to seek great things in life? Should we have lofty goals?

Text Analysis
1. In what things did Alexander show great temperance and moderation as a young man?
2. What was Alexander eager for in his youth?
3. What did Alexander think about his father's efforts to expand his kingdom?
4. What was Alexander's response when Aristotle published some of his treatises?

Cultural Analysis
1. What goals would our culture consider worth pursuing? Are there any goals or pursuits our culture would look down upon?
2. What does our culture think about seeking glory, honor, and popularity?

Biblical Analysis
1. Read Jeremiah 45. What does this chapter tell us about seeking great things for ourselves? What is God's reason for his admonition?
2. What does James 4:13–15 have to say about our approach to our material goals?
3. What does Philippians 3:12–14 tell us about how we should approach our spiritual goals?

Summa

Write an essay or discuss this question, integrating what you have learned from the material above.

What key principle (or principles) should guide us in determining which goals are worth pursuing? Are some careers or goals better than others?

Reading Assignment:
Plutarch's Lives, vol. II, Alexander, pp. 169–199

These are the ruins of Gordium, the chief city of the Phrygians and the capital of the legendary King Midas. Here is where Alexander is said to have cut the Gordian Knot with his sword after trying unsuccessfully to untie it.

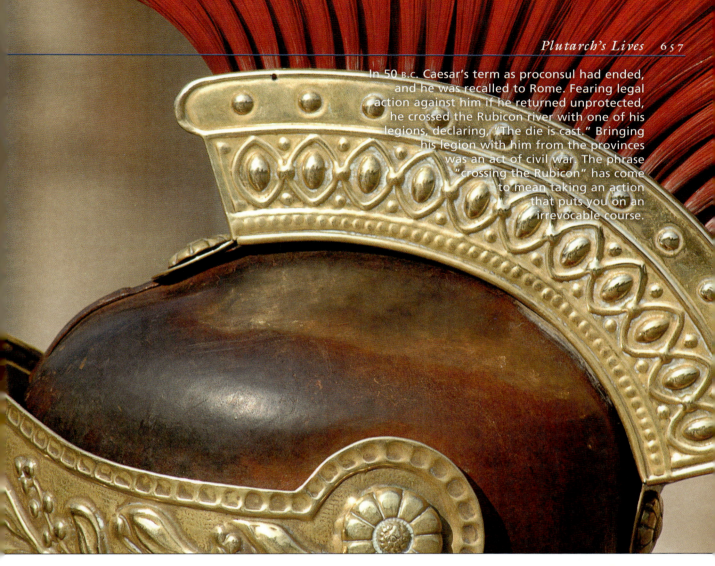

In 50 B.C. Caesar's term as proconsul had ended, and he was recalled to Rome. Fearing legal action against him if he returned unprotected, he crossed the Rubicon river with one of his legions, declaring, "The die is cast." Bringing his legion with him from the provinces was an act of civil war. The phrase "crossing the Rubicon" has come to mean taking an action that puts you on an irrevocable course.

Session III: Discussion
Plutarch's Lives, vol. II, Alexander, pp. 169–199

A Question to Consider
Will the church's influence on the culture be greater if it becomes more like the culture, or if it becomes more distinct from the culture?

Text Analysis
1. What did Alexander change about himself that pleased the Persians but disappointed his fellow Macedonians?
2. Why did the Persians approve of Alexander's marriage to Roxana?
3. What did Alexander do to try to accustom the Persians to Macedonian customs?
4. Why did Alexander wish to see the two cultures intermixed as he continued his campaign?

Cultural Analysis
1. What would our culture think about a church that adopted its habits and customs but kept some thoughts about Jesus?
2. What about the church could be attractive to our culture?

Biblical Analysis
1. What is the significance of Paul's statement in 1 Corinthians 9:19–22? Is Paul becoming just like his culture in order to witness to them?
2. What does 1 Corinthians 1:22–25 tell us about the message of the church in relation to the culture?

Summa
Write an essay or discuss this question, integrating what you have learned from the material above.
What should the church do to strengthen its influence in our culture?

OPTIONAL ACTIVITY: GEOGRAPHY

Mapping Alexander

Using resources from the Internet, make a map of Alexander's conquests. Draw the boundaries of his empire and mark the significant battles he fought in Greece, Asia Minor, Persia, and India. Also, although not mentioned specifically by Plutarch, find out what happened to Alexander's empire after his death, and mark on your map the empires that resulted. If you are so inspired, in the margin of your map you might also make a list of the names and dates of the major battles on his campaign.

READING ASSIGNMENT:
Plutarch's Lives, vol. II, Caesar, pp. 199–219

SESSION IV: WRITING
Plutarch's Lives, vol. II, Caesar, pp. 199–219

Your Own Life

This session is a writing assignment. Remember, quality counts more than quantity. You should write no more than 1,000 words, either typing or writing legibly on one side of a sheet of paper. You will lose points for writing more than this. You will be allowed to turn in your writing three times. The first and second times you turn it in, your teacher will grade it by editing your work. This is done by marking problem areas and making suggestions for improvement. You should take these suggestions into consideration as you revise your assignment. Only the grade on your final submission will be recorded. Your grade will be based on the following criteria: 25 points for grammar, 25 points for content accuracy (historical, theological, etc.), 25 points for logic (does this make sense and is it structured well?), and 25 points for rhetoric (is it a joy to read?).

Your assignment is to write a description following the direction provided below. This may be more difficult than it sounds! Make sure your description guides a reader into an experience of the object. Use language that stirs the senses (what does it look, sound, feel, smell, or taste like?). Make judgments about the object as you describe it. Remember the great rule of description—show us, don't tell us. Do not tell us that something is good or beautiful or likable. Describe it in a way that shows your reader the object's beauty or ugliness, or its goodness or wickedness.

Write your own "Life." You should choose a popular figure such as a politician, sports star, or musician and write a short biography about that figure. You will obviously not have access to every detail of this person's life, or the chance to interview him or her, but feel free to use the Internet or other resources to gather information. Just as Plutarch does, remember to focus not only on the great things this person has accomplished, but also on how the person's actions demonstrate his or her character.

Instead of a reading assignment you have a research assignment. Tomorrow's session will be a Current Events session. Your assignment will be to find a story online, in a magazine, or in the newspaper that relates to the issue that you discussed today. Your task is to locate the article, give a copy of the article to your teacher or parent and provide some of your own worldview analysis to the article. Your analysis should demonstrate that you understand the issue, that you can clearly connect the story you found to the issue that you discussed today, and that you can provide a biblical critique of this issue in today's context. Look at the next session to see the three-part format that you should follow.

Issue

Sacrificing freedom for increased security

SESSION V: CURRENT EVENTS
Plutarch's Lives, vol. II, Caesar, pp. 199–219

Issue

Sacrificing freedom for increased security

Current events sessions are meant to challenge you to connect what you are learning in Omnibus class to what is happening in the world around you today. After the last session, your assignment was to find a story online or in a magazine or newspaper relating to the issue above. Today you will share your article and your analysis with your teacher and classmates or parents and family. Your analysis should follow the format below:

BRIEF INTRODUCTION PARAGRAPH
In this paragraph you will tell your classmates or family about the article you found. Be sure to include where you found your article, who the author is, and what your article is about. This brief paragraph of your presentation should begin like this:

> Hello, I am (name), and my current events article is (name of the article), which I found in (name of the online or published source)…

CONNECTION PARAGRAPH
In this paragraph you must demonstrate how your article is connected to the issue you are studying. This paragraph should be short and should focus on clearly showing the connection between the book you are reading and the current events article you have found. This paragraph should begin with a sentence like:

> I knew that my article was linked to our issue because …

CHRISTIAN WORLDVIEW ANALYSIS
In this section, you need to tell us how we should respond as believers to this issue today. This response should focus both on our thinking and on practical actions we should take in light of this issue. As you list these steps, you should also tell us why we should think and act in the ways you recommend. This paragraph should begin with a sentence like:

As believers, we should think and act in following ways in light of this issue and article.

READING ASSIGNMENT:
Plutarch's Lives, vol. II, Caesar, pp. 219–244

SESSION VI: RECITATION
Plutarch's Lives, vol. II, Alexander and Caesar

Comprehension Questions
Answer the following questions for factual recall:
1. What event happened on the same day as Alexander's birth, signifying his future conquest?
2. How does Alexander demonstrate his courage and wisdom when no one could tame the horse Bucephalus?
3. What was the knot at Gordium, and how did Alexander handle the knot?
4. Why was Darius confident in his attack on Alexander? What was the outcome?
5. What was the one blemish upon Alexander's record of justice and honor in his campaign?
6. Why was Alexander moved by the grave of Cyrus?
7. What was Caesar's response to the pirates who demanded 20 talents for his release? What did he do to the pirates after his release?
8. How and when was Caesar almost killed by Cicero?
9. What was the significance of Caesar's successful attempts to reconcile Crassus and Pompey?
10. What was Caesar's approach to the allies of the enemies he conquered?
11. Why did the citizens of Rome disapprove of the triumph Caesar celebrated after defeating Pompey?

OPTIONAL ACTIVITY
Secret Code
Plutarch mentions that Caesar communicated to his troops in Gaul using secret codes. He is one of the earliest examples of generals using ciphers, or coded messages, to

Julius Caesar is highly regarded for his commentaries on his various military campaigns. His Commentarii de Bello Gallico *describes the wars in Gaul against various tribes. Many modern Latin students have translated this work, as it has been a popular assignment.*

communicate his orders. One way in which Caesar may have written and read his coded messages was by wrapping a thin strip of paper around a standard-size stick so that the random letters on the paper line up, revealing the message. Try making a coded message using this method (use a No. 2 pencil as your stick). What other methods can you come up with to communicate in secret code?

The Optional Session will be a student-led discussion based on additional reading on the life of Demosthenes. Students will be creating their own questions concerning the issue of the session. Students should create three Text Analysis Questions, two Cultural Analysis questions, and two Biblical Analysis questions. For more detailed instructions, please see the chapter on *Death on the Nile*, Session V.

Issue

Does our environment impact who we are? Can we blame our actions on our upbringing?

Reading Assignment:
Plutarch's Lives, vol. II, Demosthenes, pp. 387–408

Optional Session: Student-Led Discussion

Plutarch's Lives, vol. II, Demosthenes, pp. 387–408

A Question to Consider

Does our environment impact who we are? Can we blame our actions on our upbringing?

Students should read and consider the example questions below that are connected to the Question to Consider above. The assignment was to prepare three questions and answers for the Text Analysis section and two additional questions and answers for both the Cultural Analysis and Biblical Analysis sections below.

Text Analysis

Example: What is Plutarch's opinion about the role place of birth plays in a man's happiness?

Answer: He mentions a poet who argues that a man's happiness depends largely on being born in a famous city. However, Plutarch disagrees, contending that happiness is based on a disposition of the mind, and can be achieved by a man born either in a poor, mean city or in one that is wealthy and famous.

Cultural Analysis

Example: What is an example of an issue our culture blames on a person's environment, rather than his personal choice or responsibility?

Answer: Almost any wrong choice can be blamed on a person's environment. Perhaps the most common issues are teen crimes (abuse, theft, murder), which are blamed on the criminal's home environment. The reason they expressed their anger through crime was the abuse they received from their father, or the example of crime they saw in their own family. While this may explain some of the temptations a person faces, it does not excuse that person from responsibility for his actions.

Other cultural issues to consider: What issues might our culture be tempted to blame on a person's environment? What solutions does our culture have to offer for the bad environments that they believe lead to bad choices?

Biblical Analysis

Example: What does Ezekiel 18:1–18 have to say about the responsibility of each individual?

Answer: Ezekiel confronts Israel's complaint that they are being punished because of the sins of their fathers, rather than for their own sin. This is slightly different, but definitely akin to the complaint that a man makes a bad decision because of his father's anger rather than his own. But Ezekiel makes it very clear that a man is responsible only for his own actions, regardless of what his parents or his children do. He will be punished if he disobeys and be rewarded if he serves the Lord faithfully.

Other Scriptures to consider: Gal. 6:7–8; Matt. 7:16–20; 2 Cor. 5:10.

Summa

Write an essay or discuss this question, integrating what you have learned from the material above.

What would be an appropriate way to understand the influence a person's environment has on his behavior?

Endnotes

1 All page citations are from *Plutarch's Lives Volume II*, Arthur Hugh Clough, ed. (New York: Random House, 2001 Modern Library Paperback Edition).

Desiring God

Once there were three goddesses who found themselves at a table on which was set a lovely golden apple addressed to the "fairest of all." Unable to decide among themselves who the rightful owner of the golden apple was, they resolved to ask a gentleman his opinion. One goddess offered the man riches and power if he would choose her, another offered him understanding and wisdom beyond compare, and the third offered him the most beautiful woman in the world as a wife. You may know that Paris ultimately chose door number three, desiring the most beautiful woman in the world, and Aphrodite, the goddess who promised him this reward, was thus named by Paris to be the rightful recipient of the golden apple. Thus began the Trojan War.

Another man once stood on a mountaintop, engulfed in the hazy smoke of burning animal flesh, and God spoke to him from the heavens and promised to grant any request he made. In the end, the man asked for wisdom, for he was a king over many people, and he was most concerned that he rule his nation wisely.

As a young man, Vincent van Gogh wanted to become a pastor. After those hopes were dashed, he left Christian ministry and turned to art. For a time van Gogh abandoned the institutional church, but during his stay at a psychiatric clinic in Saint Remy, where he created some of his greatest art, van Gogh returned to the faith of his youth. He painted pictures with explicitly biblical themes, such as *The Good Samaritan* and *The Raising of Lazarus*. He painted this piece, *At Eternity's Gate* or *On the Threshold of Eternity*, in 1890, a year after he painted *The Starry Night*.

God was very pleased with the king's answer and not only granted Solomon wisdom beyond any other man but also riches and glory for which he *could* have asked.

Consider yet again another man who stood on a mountaintop, gazing out at the nations and kingdoms of the world, and another *god* spoke softly in his ear and said, "All these things I will give to you if you will fall down and worship me." But Jesus refused, quoting words from the ancient Scriptures. The *god* left Him, and the angels came and ministered to Him.

What if you could have anything you wanted? What if you could have whatever you wanted *right now*? Nothing stands in your way. All obstacles will fall before you. The gods or God has spoken and asked you, "What do you want? Ask and it shall be given to you." What would you say?

GENERAL INFORMATION

Author and Context

John Stephen Piper was born on January 11, 1946, in Chattanooga, Tennessee, the son of an itinerant evangelist. He grew up in Greenville, South Carolina, and went to Wheaton College, where he studied literature and philosophy and met his wife, Noel. Piper began theological studies at Fuller Theological Seminary in 1968 and then completed his doctoral work in New Testament studies at the University of Munich in 1974. He taught biblical studies for six years at Bethel College in St. Paul,

Do you feel loved by God because you believe he makes much of you, or because you believe he frees you and empowers you to enjoy making much of him?
—John Piper

Minnesota, before being called to be pastor of Bethlehem Baptist Church in Minneapolis, where at this writing he continues to serve as pastor of preaching. Piper is the author of more than 30 books, and he and his wife have four sons, one daughter, and a number of grandchildren.

John Piper identifies himself as a "Reformed Baptist," embracing the teachings of John Calvin with regard to the sovereignty of God and salvation while holding to baptism upon profession of faith. Piper's teaching and preaching ministry has grown immensely over the years, and his articles and numerous speaking engagements have spread his enthusiastic and clearly articulated explanations of the gospel, the doctrines of grace, and the calling of Christians and the church to discipleship and missions.

Significance

Desiring God is a particularly central theme in Piper's thought and ministry. He describes his entire pastoral philosophy as summarized in the words: "God is most glorified in me when I am most satisfied in him. This is the motor that drives my ministry as a pastor. It affects everything I do."[1] This theology of "Christian Hedonism" has its roots in such great theologians and philosophers as Augustine, Jonathan Edwards, Blaise Pascal, and C.S. Lewis. As Piper explains in the early pages of *Desiring God*, this way of looking at life and the world is not unique to him, and the more he studied and pondered these themes, he saw they were deeply rooted in the very fabric of the Scriptures, wound through nearly every page. This book, then, is immensely significant to Piper and to his pastoral ministry, and it has been significant to many Christians who have benefited from its contents. But insofar as it is an accurate and helpful explanation of some of the greatest themes in Scripture, it is most significant because it is *true*.

Main Characters

As the title suggests, and I imagine John Piper would have us conclude, God is the main character of this book. Piper says, "The ultimate ground of Christian Hedonism is the fact that God is uppermost in His own affections: *The chief end of* God *is to glorify God and enjoy Himself forever.*" Of course, this book isn't a story like many you read in the Omnibus curriculum, but it does have a narrative. In many ways, *Desiring God* is Piper's story of coming to be a Christian Hedonist, coming to see Christian Hedonism throughout the Scriptures, and coming to understand how Christian Hedonism works so fundamentally within many of the central doctrines and teachings of the Christian church. Thus, in this sense, the author, John Piper, is a main character in this book as he unfolds his journey, traveling a lifetime of studies, ministry, and family exploring these themes.

Lastly, I would guess that Piper would be most pleased if you saw yourself in some significant way as a character in this story. As with every Christian doctrine, it must be applied. And therefore you are called upon in many of these chapters to search your own life, to examine your own priorities against the priorities of Christ. What does the call to Christian Hedonism mean for you? How will you respond?

Summary and Setting

Piper writes, "The chief end of man is to glorify God by enjoying Him forever." If you are familiar with the Westminster Shorter Catechism, then you are familiar with these words. Only, one of those little words ought to catch you off guard. Or if you were reading carefully, it may have struck you a little funny. The chief end of man is to glorifyy God *by* enjoying Him forever. In other words, Piper says that the way God is glorified is bound up in the action of man enjoying Him. Man's enjoyment of God is the way he glorifies God. The actual answer to the first question of the Shorter Catechism doesn't say that we glorify God *by* enjoying Him; it says that man's chief end is to glorify God *and* enjoy Him forever. As Piper points out, the "and" does not necessarily imply that these are two completely different actions or pursuits; there is only one "end" after all, but Piper's *by* eliminates all ambiguity. He argues that the Scriptures present us with a direct correlation, a direct kinship—one is a means to the other. And understood rightly, there really is no difference. Our truest, purest pleasure *is* the glory of God. And that's what Piper means by Christian Hedonism. If Hedonism is the belief that life is best lived seeking the greatest pleasure possible, *Christian* Hedonism agrees and goes a step further by identifying the greatest source of pleasure in the world: God Himself.

Worldview

"What is happiness?" Friedrich Nietzsche once asked. He answered, "The feeling that power increases—that resistance is overcome."[2] Nietzsche grounds happiness in the experience of power, the awareness and feelings of overcoming that which hinders us. Later, Sigmund Freud wrote, "Happiness... is a problem of satisfying a person's instinctual wishes.... What we call happiness in the strictest sense comes from the (preferably sudden) satisfaction of needs which have been dammed up to a high degree...." He continues: "...sexual love... affords... the strongest experiences of satisfaction ... the prototype of all happiness."[3] Freud says that sexual gratification and pleasure is the prototype, the foundational image of all happiness. He seems to see his understanding of happiness as being in essential agreement with Nietzsche when he asks, "If one imagines its [civilization's] prohibitions lifted—if, then, one may take any woman one pleases as a sexual object, if one may without hesitation kill one's rival for her love or anyone else who stands in one's way, if, too, one can carry off any of the other man's belongings without asking—how splendid, what a string of satisfactions life would be!"[4]

While Freud seems to relish this sort of moral abandon, he actually realizes that if everyone lived and acted with such unrestraint, cultures would collapse into pure mayhem (can you say "Trojan War"?), and he surmises that the end result would ultimately be one who triumphed over everyone else, and then "only one person could be made 'unrestrictively' happy by such a removal of the restrictions ... and he would be a dictator who has seized all the means to power."[5] For some reason, Freud seems to prefer a sexual democracy to a sexual dictatorship, but ultimately Freud agrees with Nietzsche that power is happiness and takes it a step further by insisting that power finds its greatest pleasure in uninhibited sexual satisfaction. Freud describes this general aim and tendency toward pleasure as a basic principle of human psychology, what he calls the "pleasure principle."[6]

He explains: "We believe, that is to say, that the course of those events is invariably set in motion by an unpleasurable tension, and that it takes a direction such that its final outcome coincides with a lowering of that tension—that is, with an avoidance of unpleasure or a production of pleasure."[7] In other words, Freud says that all human beings exist in a constant tendency toward minimizing what is not pleasurable and ultimately producing that which is pleasurable. Or to put it plainly, people want to be happy, and they act upon that desire.

John Piper's book *Desiring God* carries the subtitle "Meditations of a Christian Hedonist." Of course, *he-*

donism has not enjoyed the most cheery of reviews in Christian circles down through the ages. If hedonism is "a theory according to which a person is motivated to produce a state of affairs in preference to another if, and only if, he thinks it will be more pleasant, or less unpleasant for himself,"[8] then one can easily see that a philosopher like Freud would also be rightly identified at least in broad terms as a hedonist. One might point back to the ancient Greek philosopher Epicurus, who taught his followers to aim at "the absence of pain in the body and of trouble in the soul." And as Richard Mouw notes, Epicurus, though a pagan, was not a particularly crude one, despite the negative connotations of the adjective *epicurean*. Far from endorsing the gluttony and debauchery of drunkenness and orgies and overeating, he encouraged a life of "sober reasoning, searching out the grounds of every choice and avoidance, and banishing those beliefs through which the greatest tumults take possession of the soul."[9] Epicurus taught that the good life was found in pursuing those activities and beliefs that avoided the "greatest tumults." We might substitute "unpleasure" for "greatest tumults," and it looks like we are back at basic hedonism, and Freud is still sitting on the couch talking about sex.

Piper knows that he has chosen a provocative subtitle and has done so on purpose, and the adjective *Christian* is meant to give contours and direction to his case. And yet some may still wonder what Piper is up to. Or to put it more bluntly, how do we know that Piper is not suggesting that we merely "baptize" some kind of Nietzschean or Freudian sex-and-power hedonism? Why should we embrace a theology or philosophy with a name that conjures up pagans and militant atheists? Piper answers these questions in Appendix 5 in the 2003 edition of *Desiring God*. He argues that the meaning of hedonism is general enough to include what he is after, both according to Webster's Dictionary and an encyclopedia of philosophy. He points to "other people, smarter and older" than he who have "felt themselves similarly driven to use the term *hedonism* in reference to the Christian way of life," and he cites C.S. Lewis and Vernard Eller as two instances.

He also says that he prefers to use the term *hedonism* simply because it is shocking. It was shocking to him as he began to see Christian Hedonism in the Scriptures, and he wants it to be equally shocking to the many nominal Christians in the world who need a wakeup call. Finally Piper points to the fact that Jesus did not shy away from provocative language in His ministry, nor is the rest of Scripture embarrassed to use shocking language to call sinners to repentance, and Piper even notes that Paul himself uses the Greek root word for hedonism to describe his own happiness in 2 Corinthians 12:9 and 15.

Christian Hedonism

So what is Christian Hedonism? One of the early steps in Piper's discovery of Christian Hedonism was a printed sermon by C.S. Lewis entitled "The Weight of Glory." Lewis criticizes Kantian and Stoic tendencies in modern Christians who have come to believe that the highest virtues are things like "unselfishness" and "sacrifice" and "self-denial"—all negative terms describing abstinence and denial. But Lewis goes on to point out that while the Scriptures call the disciples of Jesus to denial and sacrifice, those demands always also include "an appeal to desire." He says:

> Indeed if we consider the unblushing promises of reward and the staggering nature of the rewards promised in the Gospels, it would seem that Our Lord finds our desires not too strong, but too weak. We are half-hearted creatures, fooling about with drink and sex and ambition when infinite joy is offered us, like an ignorant child who wants to go on making mud pies in a slum because he cannot imagine what is meant by the offer of a holiday at the sea. We are far too easily pleased.[10]

Lewis says that if Christians are reading their Bibles carefully, they ought to see that the call of the gospel is itself a call to pleasure, a call to true, eternal, and satisfying joy in God through Christ in the Spirit. But that is not all. There is something even prior to that, something of even more importance. Why does God want to call us to pleasure? Piper says that the reason God wants us to be happy is because He is true Happiness Himself. In His presence is fullness of joy; at His right hand are pleasures forevermore (Ps. 16:11). In other words, the foundation of all happiness and joy and pleasure must first be grounded in the reality of God's own pleasure, His own joy, His own perfect happiness. And Piper ties this to God's sovereignty, His rule over all things: "Our God is in the heavens; He does all that He pleases" (Ps. 115:3). Isaiah says, "I am God, and there is no other; I am God, and there is none like Me, declaring the end from the beginning and from ancient times things not yet done, saying, 'My counsel shall stand, and I will accomplish all My purpose'" (Isa. 46:9–10).

The Sovereignty and Happiness of God

But here many people stumble. And they stumble over two things. First is what is commonly referred to as the "problem of evil." If God is all-powerful and all-good and rules over all things, how can He allow evil? Jonathan Edwards described his own experience as eventually coming to see the doctrine of the sovereignty of God as "exceeding pleasant, bright, and sweet," but he says that his "first conviction was not so."[11] At the very least we need to answer this objection with clear statements of Scripture: God "does all that He pleases" (Ps. 115). We have already seen this in Isaiah, and we could just as easily look at the numerous other passages that Piper cites (e.g., Amos 3:6, Acts 2:23, 4:27–28, Prov. 21:1, 16:33, Ezra 6:22, Ps. 135:5–7, Gen. 50:20, Matt. 10:29). Faithfulness to the Scriptures requires us to conclude that Piper is absolutely and wonderfully right: God rules over *everything*.

But there is another possible cause for stumbling, and that is the seeming self-centeredness of such a claim. Insisting that God's sovereignty, His power, is fundamental to His pleasure and glory seems to set us up to describe God in terms that are at the very least somewhat awkward. Piper writes in chapter 1, "The ultimate ground of Christian Hedonism is the fact that God is uppermost in His own affections: *The chief end of God is to glorify God and enjoy Himself forever.*" He explains that since "none of His purposes can be frustrated, then He must be the happiest of all beings." God is the happiest because does whatever He wants.

But this seems strange. Piper anticipates the objection, asking, "How can God be loving and yet utterly devoted to 'seeking His own' glory and praise and joy? How can God be for us if He is so utterly for Himself?" In other words, if we stop here, doesn't it sound like God is Freud's "dictator who has seized all the means to power?" If all we say is that God is all-powerful and therefore God is all Happiness, have we really said anything that is very fundamentally different from Nietzsche or Freud? Piper responds,

> The answer I propose is this: Because God is unique as an all-glorious, totally self-sufficient Being, He must be for Himself if He is to be for us. The rules of humility that belong to a creature cannot apply

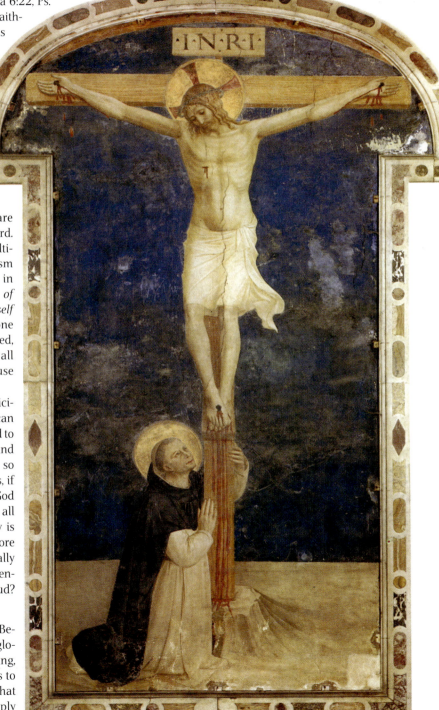

Saint Dominic is depicted desiring God in this fresco (c. 1442) by Fra Angelico from the Museo di San Marco in Florence, Italy. Domingo de Guzmán Garcés was the founder of the Friars Preachers, often called the Dominicans.

in the same way to its Creator. If God should turn away from Himself as the Source of infinite joy, He would cease to be God. He would deny the infinite worth of His own glory. He would imply that there is something more valuable outside Himself. He would commit idolatry.

This is true as far as it goes, but I would suggest that Piper's answer would be greatly strengthened if it were more firmly and *explicitly* grounded in the doctrine of the Trinity. This foundational confession of the Christian church is not of secondary importance. The one, true God of heaven and earth in three persons is not only foundational in terms of our creed, but it is foundational for understand-i n g God's attributes and actions in the world.

For example, when we say that God is love, it simply will not do to merely affirm that God is love as though Allah or the god of the Unitarians could be as well. What does it mean that the Christian God *is* love? Does God radiate "love vibes"? In fact, for the idea of love to have any coherence whatsoever, there must be an "other" to love. If God is a solitary, unitarian being, it is incoherent to say that God is love. One person cannot be or perform the action of love. But the Scriptures are not silent, and they tell us that the phrase "God is love" means that before all worlds the Father loved the Son and the Son loved the Father (1 John 4:7–14; cf. John 17:24). In other words the love of God *is* the love of the persons of the Trinity. And to be sure, Piper knows and even says this in several places explicitly, but it would be wonderful to see it more thoroughly woven into the book.

So in this case, for example,

In the early days of the Church, the triple leaf of the anemone was used to symbolize the Trinity. In Ovid's *Metamorphoses*, Aphrodite transforms the blood of her dead lover, Adonis, into an anemone. This may be the flower Jesus was actually referring to in Luke 12:27 when He said that even Solomon in all his glory was not arrayed as one of these.

where it appears awkward, strange, and even horribly wrong for us to describe God as self-centered and self-serving, we may cheerfully insist that this is nothing like Freud's power-mongering dictator, because the Christian God is the Father, Son, and Spirit who eternally serve and give themselves away for one another. The glory of God is not a static halo; it is not a burning pride that must be protected at all costs. Rather, it is the highly personal action of the Father glorifying the Son and the Spirit, the Son glorifying the Father and the Spirit, and the Spirit giving back all glory to the Father and the Son (e.g., John 16:13–14, 17:5). God is "self-centered" but only as a community of absolutely selfless persons. This mutual glory-giving and honor-giving is the eternal friendship and communion and joy of the one, eternal God. Therefore in this sense, we ought to insist that the rules of humility most certainly do still apply to the Creator and do not require a "unique" status.

In this sense, God sets the rules of humility. God gloriously sets the standard for us to follow. The sovereignty of God is the action of the persons of the Trinity defending, loving, and glorifying one another. The rule and power of God *is* the love that each person of the Trinity has for the others overflowing in creation, in history, and in the gospel. The power of God is His efficacious love found between the persons of the Trinity, shared with His people through the Spirit, which is simultaneously an infinite joy and happiness. As Piper says later, "Love is the overflow of joy in God that gladly meets the needs of others," and he continues, "Love is finding your joy in the joy of another." That sort of love begins in the very being of God and overflows by the working of the Spirit in His people.

Desiring God really is a delight to read. It may raise questions you had not considered before, and Piper carefully works through numerous topics and areas of life, applying the basic thesis that God is busy pursuing His joy in us, and therefore we ought to respond faithfully by pursuing our joy in Him and others. This is Christian Hedonism. And so long as we take that adjective seriously, so long as we understand "Christian" to ultimately mean Trinitarian—grounded in the pleasures of the Father, Son, and Holy Spirit—we are embarking on a pursuit of pleasure that is radically removed from anything Nietzsche or Freud could have imagined.

In their tiny worlds, everything revolved around the self, around the ego, around me. And when all there is in the world is an "I" looking out into the cosmos, the only hope one has is to push, pull, and maneuver into positions of authority, positions of power, hoarding every ounce of pleasure along the way. But they really are like ignorant children clinging to their mud pies in a slum, because they "cannot imagine what is meant by the offer of a holiday at the sea." Nietzsche and Freud and all the other pagan attempts at happiness and joy were failures of imagination. They are "half-hearted creatures, fooling about with drink and sex and ambition" when we have been offered "infinite joy." They were far too easily pleased. They could not imagine the greater pleasures, the deeper treasures, the inexhaustible happiness found in the Father, Son, and Spirit. And there, at the heart of all of reality, the Trinitarian center of the universe, is a community of love, a fellowship of joy, a sharing and giving and sacrificing that turns the world and all the planets with its great pleasure. And we find that this means just the opposite of what Nietzsche and Freud claimed. We find that happiness is found in a power and pleasure that gives itself away, that pours itself out, that becomes the servant of all, and on the other end of that death, that "unpleasure," there is resurrection life and pleasures forevermore.

—*Toby J. Sumpter*

For Further Reading

Mouw, Richard. *The God Who Commands.* Notre Dame, Ind.: University of Notre Dame Press, 1990.

Nicholi, Armand M. *The Question of God: C. S. Lewis and Sigmund Freud Debate God, Love, Sex, and the Meaning of Life.* New York: Free Press, 2002.

Piper, John. *The Dangerous Duty of Delight.* New York: Doubleday, 2001.

Piper, John. *The Pleasures of God.* Sisters, Ore.: Multnomah, 2000.

Session I: Prelude

A Question to Consider
What is happiness?

From the General Information above answer the following questions:
1. What did Nietzsche say happiness was?
2. What did Freud say that happiness was?
3. What does Piper say that happiness is?
4. How does the Trinity make Christian Hedonism radically different from other pagan versions of happiness?
5. What does Jesus' call to discipleship have to do with pleasure?
6. What are some of the reasons Piper gives for using the term *hedonism*?

Reading Assignment:
Desiring God, Introduction and Chapter 1

Session II: Discussion
Desiring God, Introduction and Chapter 1

A Question to Consider
What is glory?

Discuss or list short answers to the following questions:

Text Analysis
1. Why was the area of worship and praise one of the most frustrating areas of Piper's life before he became a Christian Hedonist?
2. What did Blaise Pascal write concerning all men?
3. What did C.S. Lewis suggest actually completes enjoyment? What other theologian agreed with Lewis?
4. What is meant by "a general theory of moral justification"? And how does Piper respond?
5. How is the Heidelberg Catechism just as "hedonistic" as the Westminster Shorter Catechism?
6. Which designs of God are "penultimate," and which design is "ultimate"?

Cultural Analysis
1. What does our culture generally think "glory" is?
2. What does our culture think about seeking your own glory?

Biblical Analysis

1. What is the glory of Joseph in Genesis 45:15?
2. What does it mean that God's glory came down and rested on Mount Sinai (Ex. 24:16)?
3. If the glory of the Lord is going to fill the Tabernacle, what does this suggest about the priests' holy garments that were for "glory and beauty" (Ex. 28:2, 40)?

SUMMA

Write an essay or discuss this question, integrating what you have learned from the material above.

If "glory" has to do with royalty, rule, and presence, what do passages that talk about God's glory "filling the earth" refer to (e.g., Num. 14:21, Ps. 72:19, Isa. 6:3, Hab. 2:14)?

READING ASSIGNMENT:
Desiring God, Chapters 2 and 3

Session III: Recitation
Desiring God, Chapters 2 and 3

Comprehension Questions

Answer the following questions for factual recall:

1. What does Piper say may be "the most straightforward biblical command for conversion" today? Why?
2. Who uses the word *Hell* the most in the New Testament? How many times?
3. What does Piper conclude from the parable of the treasure in the field (Matt. 13:44)?
4. What does Jonathan Edwards call those "feelings" that are not mere physical sensations? What are they?
5. Why is the hedonistic approach to worship the only humble approach?
6. What did Charles Darwin tell his children that he regretted?
7. What does Piper say causes decline in worship?

Saint Lucy was a Christian martyred during the Diocletian persecution in the early fourth century. According to one traditional story, she was born in Syracuse, Sicily, of rich and noble parents. Her desire for God trumped her worldly concerns, and she refused to marry a pagan, instead distributing her dowry to the poor. Her spurned suitor denounced her as a Christian to the governor. She was tortured, and her eyes were put out before being killed. Therefore, art depicting Lucy often shows her holding two eyes on a dish.

The next session will be a student-led discussion. Students will be creating their own questions concerning the issue of the session. Students should create three Text Analysis Questions, two Cultural Analysis questions, and two Biblical Analysis questions. For more detailed instructions, please see the chapter on *Death on the Nile*, Session V.

Issue

Love and Pleasure

READING ASSIGNMENT:
Desiring God, Chapters 4–6

SESSION IV: STUDENT-LED DISCUSSION

Desiring God, Chapters 4–6

A Question to Consider

Does love always make people happy?

Students should read and consider the example questions below that are connected to the Question to Consider above. Last session's assignment was to prepare three questions and answers for the Text Analysis section and two additional questions and answers for both the Cultural and Biblical Analysis sections below.

Text Analysis

Example: How does C.S. Lewis describe the way a bold and silly creature approaches its Creator?

Answer: He says that this bold and silly creature approaches its Creator insisting that it doesn't need anything from its Creator. It says, "I'm no beggar. I love you disinterestedly" (chap. 4).

Cultural Analysis

Example: Sigmund Freud warns people against becoming dependent on a particular love relationship as a primary source of happiness, because by doing so they may face "extreme suffering" if they are "rejected by that object or should lose it through unfaithfulness or death."[12] Does our culture agree with Freud or disagree? Give examples.

Answer: Generally our culture agrees with Freud insofar as it allows for relationships to be broken easily to escape "suffering." Or to turn it around, our culture agrees with Freud enthusiastically insofar as it encourages people to consider their own pleasure first (and avoidance of suffering) and make decisions accordingly. While our culture still has some vague semblance of appreciation for "committed relationships," the definition of "committed" has became more and more diluted, and today frequently only refers to a present-tense pleasure experienced by both parties and not to any sort of formal, long-term constraints. We talk out of both sides of our mouth when we vaguely discourage infidelity in marriage but generally allow for it if it is done in the name of happiness and doing what "feels right."

Other cultural issues to consider: no-fault divorce laws, dating, and courtship habits (especially as our cultural norm becomes pleasure-seeking rather than finding one mate for life), and fear of commitment.

Biblical Analysis

Example: What is the joy that was set before Jesus on the other side of His sufferings and death (Heb. 12:2, Ps. 2:7–8)?

Answer: At the very least, the joy was being seated at the right hand of the throne of God. But being seated there means He has been crowned King of the world, and the entire world has become His inheritance. This means that part of His joy was knowing what His love was going to accomplish in the world, knowing that His acts of sacrificial love would be the means to the salvation and renewal of the world. His joy was in knowing that after His resurrection, He would begin ruling, and all His enemies would be put down.

Other Scriptures to consider: Song of Solomon, 1 Corinthians 13, John 15:9–17.

SUMMA

Write an essay or discuss this question, integrating what you have learned from the material above.

Why should Christians not love "disinterestedly"? Think particularly about the love of God in the Trinity (John 17) and romantic or sexual love (Song of Solomon).

READING ASSIGNMENT:
Desiring God, Chapters 7–9

Session V: Recitation

Desiring God, Chapters 7–9

Comprehension Questions

Answer the following questions for factual recall:

1. How does 1 Timothy 6:9, 18–19 advocate Christian Hedonism?
2. What does 1 Timothy 6:17 teach?
3. Why should Christians work (Eph. 4:28)?
4. What is love in the context of marriage?
5. What does Geoffrey Bromiley say about marriage?
6. What is Frontier Missions?
7. What does Piper mean by saying "missions can be finished"?
8. What do Christian Hedonists love best?
9. Why are missionaries some of the most hedonistic people in the world, according to Piper?

Reading Assignment:
Desiring God, Chapter 10 & Epilogue

So then, after the Lord had spoken to them, He was received up into heaven, and sat down at the right hand of God (Mark 16:19). With great emotion the disciples watch Jesus ascend into Heaven in The Ascension *by Italian Renaissance painter Andrea Mantegna (c. 1431–1506).*

Session VI: Writing
Desiring God, Chapter 10 & Epilogue

Book Review

This session is a writing assignment. Remember, quality counts more than quantity. You should write no more than 1,000 words, either typing or writing legibly on one side of a sheet of paper. You will lose points for writing more than this. You will be allowed to turn in your writing three times. The first and second times you turn it in, your teacher will grade it by editing your work. This is done by marking problem areas and making suggestions for improvement. You should take these suggestions into consideration as you revise your assignment. Only the grade on your final submission will be recorded. Your grade will be based on the following criteria: 25 points for grammar, 25 points for content accuracy—historical, theological, etc.; 25 points for logic—does this make sense and is it structured well?; 25 points for rhetoric—is it a joy to read?

Write a one- to two-page book review of *Desiring God*. This review should be persuasive (fitting, of course, for the rhetoric years). Students should be encouraged to praise the writing style, the content, or the worldview of a book or author. You may also write pieces criticizing a book as well, but look first to find what is praiseworthy—n.b., as a result of today's hyper-cynical culture, we are probably more apt to criticize than praise. In this assignment you should focus on praise, remembering that your admiration must be more than a simple affirmation or denial of "liking" the book.

Use the following outline to fill out your review:

I. Introduction
II. Summarize the book in two or three sentences
III. Describe three specific things you liked in detail (three paragraphs)
IV. Describe one or two things you thought could have been better or you wish had been covered
V. Describe who you think would enjoy reading the book and who it is intended for
VI. Conclusion

Optional Activity

A lengthy portion of chapter 2 of *The God Who Commands* by Richard Mouw is dedicated to critiquing John Piper's Christian Hedonism. Like Piper, Mouw is committed to the Reformed and Calvinistic tradition of theology, and yet his questions and concerns present an interesting counterpoint to Piper. If you can access this chapter, you may add additional paragraphs to your book review engaging Mouw's comments, or with teacher permission, you may write the entire book review as a discussion of these two viewpoints. Note that in the 2003 edition of *Desiring God* Piper has responded to some of Mouw's critique (see the Introduction for the response).

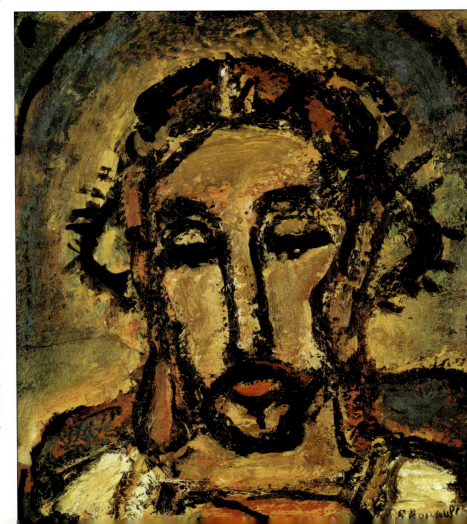

Ecce Homo by Georges Rouault (1871–1958), arguably the most important Christian artist of the twentieth century. Christ and the Cross were central to the art of this French Fauvist and Expressionist painter and printmaker. The heavy black lines his works are known for are probably rooted in his work on stained glass as a youth. Rouault once said, "My life and art make a single whole."

OPTIONAL SESSION: ACTIVITY

Listening to the Teaching

Dr. Piper is a gifted writer. He is also a gifted preacher. The dynamic of reading someone's words and listening to them speak is often quite different. In this activity we are going to explore some of those differences by getting to know Dr. Piper more by listening to him teach.

Locate a video or audio recording of John Piper teaching or preaching. Watch or listen for at least 15 minutes. Take notes and come back to class prepared to share what you learned and what you thought. If you are working as a homeschool student, take your notes and conclusions to the dinner table and discuss these points with the rest of your family.

At the time of publication there was a copious amount (about 25 years worth) of Dr. Piper's preaching online at the Resource Library of Desiring God Ministries (www. desiringgod.org). It is really an incredible body of work, and it is all free.

Use the following questions to guide your note taking:
1. What is Dr. Piper talking about?
2. To what Scriptures is he referring?

3. Does he mention anything that you remember from *Desiring God*? Or is there anything similar?
4. How would you describe Dr. Piper's style of teaching?
5. If you haven't heard or seen Dr. Piper before, does he look or sound like you thought he would?

ENDNOTES

1. This quote may be found at http://www.desiringgod.org/AboutUs/JohnPiper.
2. Cited in Armand M. Nicholi, *The Question of God: C.S. Lewis and Sigmund Freud Debate God, Love, Sex, and the Meaning of Life* (New York: Free Press, 2002), 98.
3. Ibid., 100.
4. Ibid.
5. Ibid.
6. Sigmund Freud. *Beyond the Pleasure Principle, 1.*
7. Ibid.
8. John Piper, *Desiring God*. 2003. (Colorado Springs, Colo.: Multnomah Books, 1986) Reprint. Appendix 5, "Why Call It Christian Hedonism?" in the reprint edition.
9. Cited in Richard Mouw, *The God Who Commands* (Notre Dame, Ind.: University of Notre Dame Press, 1990), 32.
10. C.S. Lewis, *The Weight of Glory and Other Addresses* (Grand Rapids, Mich.: Eerdmans, 1965), 1–2.
11. Jonathan Edwards, "Personal Narrative" in *Jonathan Edwards: Representative Selections*, ed. C.H. Faust and T.H. Johnson (New York: Hill & Wang, 1962), 58–59.
12. *The Question of God*, 101.

APPENDIX I: READING SCHEDULE

Semester 1

	PRIMARY	RATING*	SECONDARY	RATING
	Essay: Philosophy			
Week 1	Proverbs	8.0.2	Aesop's Fables	2.0.8
Week 2	Job	7.1.2	Aesop's Fables	2.0.8
	Essay: Poetry			
Week 3	The Iliad	2.2.6	Death on the Nile	0.2.8
Week 4	The Iliad	2.2.6	Death on the Nile	0.2.8
Week 5	The Iliad	2.2.6	Joshua, Judges, Ruth	5.4.1
Week 6	The Iliad	2.2.6	Joshua, Judges, Ruth	5.4.1
Week 7	Psalms	7.1.2	Joshua, Judges, Ruth	5.4.1
Week 8	Peloponnesian War	1.8.1	Troilus and Cressida	1.2.7
Week 9	Peloponnesian War	1.8.1	Troilus and Cressida	1.2.7
Week 10	The Bacchae	1.2.7	1 and 2 Chronicles	5.5.0
Week 11	The Clouds	1.2.7	1 and 2 Chronicles	5.5.0
Week 12	Hippocratic Oath	3.5.2	Ezra, Nehemiah, Esther	5.4.1
	Essay: Politics			
Week 13	The Republic	5.2.3	Ezra, Nehemiah, Esther	5.4.1
Week 14	The Republic	5.2.3	Augustus Caesar's World	1.8.1
Week 15	The Republic	5.2.3	Augustus Caesar's World	1.8.1
Week 16	Nicomachean Ethics	6.1.3	Augustus Caesar's World	1.8.1
Week 17	Nicomachean Ethics	6.1.3	Art and the Bible	9.1.0
Week 18	Poetics	2.2.6	Art and the Bible	9.1.0
Week 19	Finals			

Semester 2

	PRIMARY	RATING	SECONDARY	RATING
	Essay: Aesthetics			
Week 1	Apocrypha	3.5.2	The Lost World	0.1.9
Week 2	Euclid's Elements	1.7.2	The Lost World	0.1.9
Week 3	The War with Hannibal	0.9.1	Knowing God	10.0.0
Week 4	The War with Hannibal	0.9.1	Knowing God	10.0.0
Week 5	On the Nature of Things	6.1.3	Anthony and Cleopatra	1.2.7
Week 6	Cicero	1.7.2	Anthony and Cleopatra	1.2.7
	Essay: Cultural Anthropology			
Week 7	Annals of Imperial Rome	1.8.1	20,000 Leagues	0.1.9
Week 8	Annals of Imperial Rome	1.8.1	20,000 Leagues	0.1.9
Week 9	Eclogues and Georgics	1.2.7	20,000 Leagues	0.1.9
Week 10	Metamorphoses	2.1.7	Phantastes	1.0.9
Week 11	Metamorphoses	2.1.7	Phantastes	1.0.9
Week 12	Gospel of Mark	7.2.1	Mythology	2.7.1
Week 13	Philippians and Colossians	9.0.1	Mythology	2.7.1
	Essay: Law			
Week 14	The Jewish War	3.7.0	Plutarch's Lives	1.8.1
Week 15	The Jewish War	3.7.0	Plutarch's Lives	1.8.1
Week 16	Meditations	6.2.2	Desiring God	10.0.0
Week 17	Apostolic Fathers	7.2.1	Desiring God	10.0.0
Week 18	Finals			

The books are weighted in the following order: Theology, History and Literature

APPENDIX II: *Timeline* 675

		1600 B.C.	1500 B.C.

EGYPTIAN

c. 1570–1300 B.C.
Early New Kingdom in Egypt

GREEK

c. 1450–1200 B.C.
Mycenaen Culture

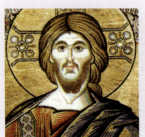

BIBLICAL

c. 1446 B.C.
The Exodus

c. 1445 B.C. Ten Commandments

c. 1444–1435 B.C.
The Tabernacle and Ark of the Covenant

ROMAN

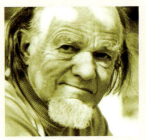

OTHER

676 OMNIBUS IV

EGYPTIAN

GREEK

BIBLICAL

1400 B.C.

c. 1406 B.C.
Moses Dies, Joshua Assumes Command

c. 1400–1350 B.C.
Israel Given the Promised Land

c. 1389–1050 B.C.
The Judges of Israel

c. 1377–1337 B.C.
Othniel and Ehud

c. 1350 B.C.
Deborah the Prophetess

c. 1350 B.C.
Gideon Delivers Israel

c. 1350 B.C.
Jephthah's Foolish Vow

ROMAN

OTHER

APPENDIX II: *Timeline* 677

1300 B.C.   1200 B.C.   1100 B.C.

c. 1300–1090 B.C.
Later New
Kingdom in Egypt

c. 1200 B.C.
Trojan War

c. 1200 B.C.
Iliad Homer

c. 1200 B.C.
Troilus and Cressida
Shakespeare

c. 1100 B.C.
Naomi and Ruth

c. 1200–1000 B.C.
Phoenician Civilization
and the Alphabet

678 OMNIBUS IV

1000 B.C.

EGYPTIAN

GREEK

BIBLICAL

c. 1080 B.C.
Samson and
Delilah

c. 1011–971 B.C.
The Davidic
Kingdom

c. 1000 B.C.
David Writes
Many Psalms

c. 971–931 B.C.
Solomon's Reign

c. 970 B.C.
Solomon Given
Wisdom

c. 970 B.C.
Writings of
Solomon

c. 967–960 B.C.
The Temple
is Built

ROMAN

OTHER

APPENDIX II: *Timeline* 679

900 B.C. 800 B.C. 700 B.C.

c. 900 B.C.
Life of Homer

c. 776 B.C.
The Olympics

c. 750–508 B.C.
Greece Colonized,
Democracy Begins

c. 750–500 B.C.
City-States in
Greece

c. 950 B.C. The
Queen of Sheba
Visits Solomon

c. 931 B.C. Israel
Divides into Two
Kingdoms

c. 760 B.C.
Hezekiah Trusts
the Lord

722 B.C. Israel
Falls to Assyria

c. 753 B.C.
Founding of Rome

680 Omnibus IV

600 B.C.

EGYPTIAN

c. 530–522 B.C.
Cambyses II and
Conquest of Egypt

GREEK

c. 620–560 B.C.
Aesop's Fables
Aesop

c. 570–500 B.C.
Life of
Pythagoras

BIBLICAL

c. 635 B.C.
Josiah Repairs
the Temple

c. 586 B.C.
Fall of Jerusalem
to Babylon

ROMAN

OTHER

c. 563–483 B.C.
Life of Buddha

c. 559–530 B.C.
Conquests
of Cyrus

c. 551–479 B.C.
Life of Confucius

c. 530–522 B.C.
Cambyses II and
Conquest of Egypt

APPENDIX II: *Timeline* 681

500 B.C.

c. 500–480 B.C.
Persian Wars

500–338 B.C.
Golden Age
of Greece

c. 485–406 B.C.
Euripides, author
of *The Bacchae*

520 B.C. Jews Return Under
Zerubbabel, Temple
Restoration Begins

c. 516 B.C.
Esther Becomes
Queen

c. 510 B.C.
Esther Saves the
Jews

c. 509–366 B.C.
Roman Republic
Developed

c. 521–486 B.C.
Reign of Darius

c. 486–465 B.C.
Reign of Xerxes

682 OMNIBUS IV

EGYPTIAN

GREEK

  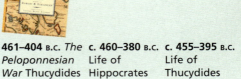

490 B.C. Battle of Marathon

480 B.C. Battles of Thermopylae and Salamis

c. 469–399 B.C. Life of Socrates

461–404 B.C. *The Peloponnesian War* Thucydides

c. 460–380 B.C. Life of Hippocrates

c. 455–395 B.C. Life of Thucydides

c. 450–322 B.C. Greek Philosophers

BIBLICAL

c. 458 B.C. Ezra Forbids Intermarriage

ROMAN

OTHER

465–425 B.C. Reign of Artaxerxes Longimanus

APPENDIX II: *Timeline* 683

400 B.C.

c. 449–380 B.C. Aristophanes, author of *The Clouds*

427–347 B.C. Life of Plato

384–44 B.C. *Lives* Plutarch

c. 384–322 B.C. Life of Aristotle

c. 384–322 B.C. Life of Demosthenes

c. 360 B.C. *Republic* Plato

356–323 B.C. Alexander the Great

c. 444 B.C. Nehemiah Rebuilds Walls of Jerusalem

684 Omnibus IV

300 B.C.

EGYPTIAN

332 B.C. Alexander the Great conquers Egypt

GREEK

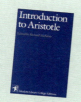

c. 350 B.C.
Nicomachean Ethics and *Poetics* Aristotle

c. 325–265 B.C.
Life of Euclid

c. 300 B.C. *The Elements* Euclid

c. 300–200 B.C.
Translation of the Septuagint

c. 287–212 B.C.
Life of Archimedes

BIBLICAL

ROMAN

c. 250 B.C.
Architectural Advances in Rome

OTHER

APPENDIX II: *Timeline* 685

200 B.C.

c. 215–164 B.C.
Reign of
Antiochus IV
Epiphanes

235–183 B.C.
Life of Scipio
the Elder

222–201 B.C.
*The War with
Hannibal* Livy

c. 167–165 B.C.
Maccabean
Revolt

146 B.C. Rome
Rises to World
Power

133–31 B.C.
Decline
and Fall of
the Roman
Republic

106–43 B.C.
Life of Cicero

248–c. 183 B.C.
Life of Hannibal

c. 200 B.C.–A.D. 100
The Apocrypha

686 Omnibus IV

100 B.C.

EGYPTIAN

69–30 B.C.
Life of Cleopatra

GREEK

BIBLICAL

ROMAN

c. 99–55 B.C.
Life of Lucretius

83–30 B.C.
Life of
Mark Antony

75 B.C.–A.D. 14
Golden Age of
Latin Literature

c. 74–4 B.C.
Life of Herod
the Great

70–19 B.C.
Life of Virgil

c. 63 B.C.–A.D. 24
Life of Strabo

59 B.C.–A.D. 17
Life of Livy

OTHER

APPENDIX II: *Timeline* 687

50 B.C.

41–30 B.C. *Antony and Cleopatra* Shakespeare

31 B.C. Battle of Actium

30 B.C. Egypt Falls to Rome

 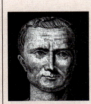 

c. 55 B.C. *On the Nature of Things* Lucretius

47–44 B.C. Reign of Julius Caesar

43 B.C.–c. A.D. 17 Life of Ovid

41–30 B.C. *Antony and Cleopatra* Shakespeare

c. 37–29 B.C. *Eclogues and Georgics* Virgil

31 B.C. Battle of Actium

688   Omnibus IV

1 B.C.

EGYPTIAN

GREEK

BIBLICAL

C. 4 B.C.–A.D. 67
Life of Paul the Apostle

C. 3 B.C.
Birth of Christ

ROMAN

27 B.C.–A.D. 14
Reign of Caesar Augustus

3 B.C.–A.D. 65
Life of Seneca

A.D. 8
Metamorphoses
Ovid

A.D. 14–66 *Annals of Imperial Rome*
Tacitus

A.D. 14–37
Reign of Tiberius

OTHER

A.D. 30

C. A.D. 27 Twelve Apostles Appointed

C. A.D. 27–30 Ministry of Christ

C. A.D. 29 Death of John the Baptist

C. A.D. 30 Crucifixion, Resurrection and Ascension of Christ

C. A.D. 30 Pentecost

A.D. 37–54 Reign of Caligula

A.D. 37–c. 100 Life of Josephus

A.D. 50

EGYPTIAN

GREEK

BIBLICAL

C. A.D. **45–47** Paul's First Missionary Journey

C. A.D. **50–51** Paul's Second Missionary Journey

C. A.D. **53–57** Paul's Third Missionary Journey

C. A.D. **58–60** Paul in Rome

C. A.D. **60** Gospel of Mark

ROMAN

A.D. **41–54** Reign of Claudius

A.D. **45–125** Plutarch, author of *Lives*

A.D. **54–68** Reign of Nero

C. A.D. **55–117** Life of Tacitus

OTHER

APPENDIX II: *Timeline* 691

C. A.D. **61**
Letter to the Colossians Paul

C. A.D. **61**
Letter to the Philippians Paul

A.D. **64** Rome Burns, Nero Persecutes Christians

A.D. **68–69**
Reign of Galba

A.D. **69**
Reign of Otho

A.D. **69**
Reign of Vitellius

A.D. **69–79**
Reign of Vespasian

692 Omnibus IV

A.D. 70

EGYPTIAN

GREEK

BIBLICAL

ROMAN

OTHER

A.D. 70
Destruction of Jerusalem

A.D. 70–c. 150
Apostolic Fathers

C. A.D. 70–155
Life of Polycarp

A.D. 73
Masada Falls to the Romans

A.D. 79
Pompeii Burns

A.D. 79–81
Reign of Titus

A.D. 81–96
Reign of Domitian

APPENDIX II: *Timeline* 693

A.D. 100

A.D. 96–98
Reign of
Nerva

A.D. 98–117
Reign of
Trajan

DIED C. A.D. 99
Life of
Clement of
Rome

DIED C. A.D. 115
Life of Ignatius

A.D. 117–138
Reign of
Hadrian

A.D. 138–161
Reign of
Antoninus
Pius

A.D. 161–180
Reign of
Marcus Aurelius

A.D. 161–169
Reign of
Lucius Verus

694   Omnibus IV

A.D. 200

EGYPTIAN

GREEK

BIBLICAL

ROMAN

c. A.D. 170–180 *Meditations* Aurelius

A.D. 177–192 Reign of Commodus

A.D. 286 Split of the Roman Empire

A.D. 313 Constantine and the Edict of Milan

A.D. 367 Closing of the Canon

OTHER

c. 250–900 Classic Period of Mayan Culture

APPENDIX II: *Timeline* 695

1500   1800

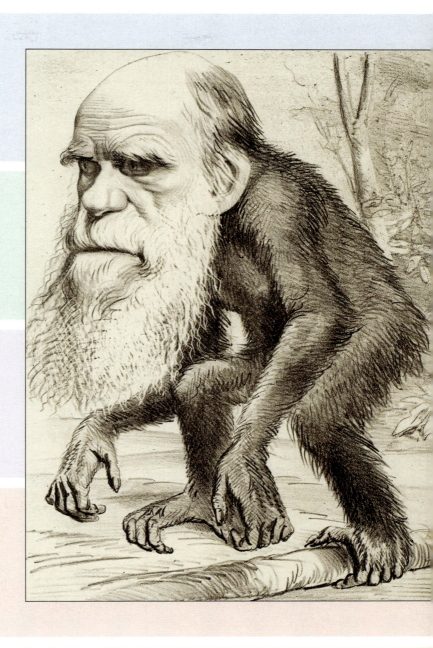

1564–1603
Life of
Shakespeare

1596–1650
Life of Rene
Descartes

1824–1905
Life of George
MacDonald

1828–1905
Life of Jules
Verne

1858 *Phantastes*
MacDonald

1859–1930
Life of Sir
Arthur Conan
Doyle

1859 *The Origin
of Species*
Darwin

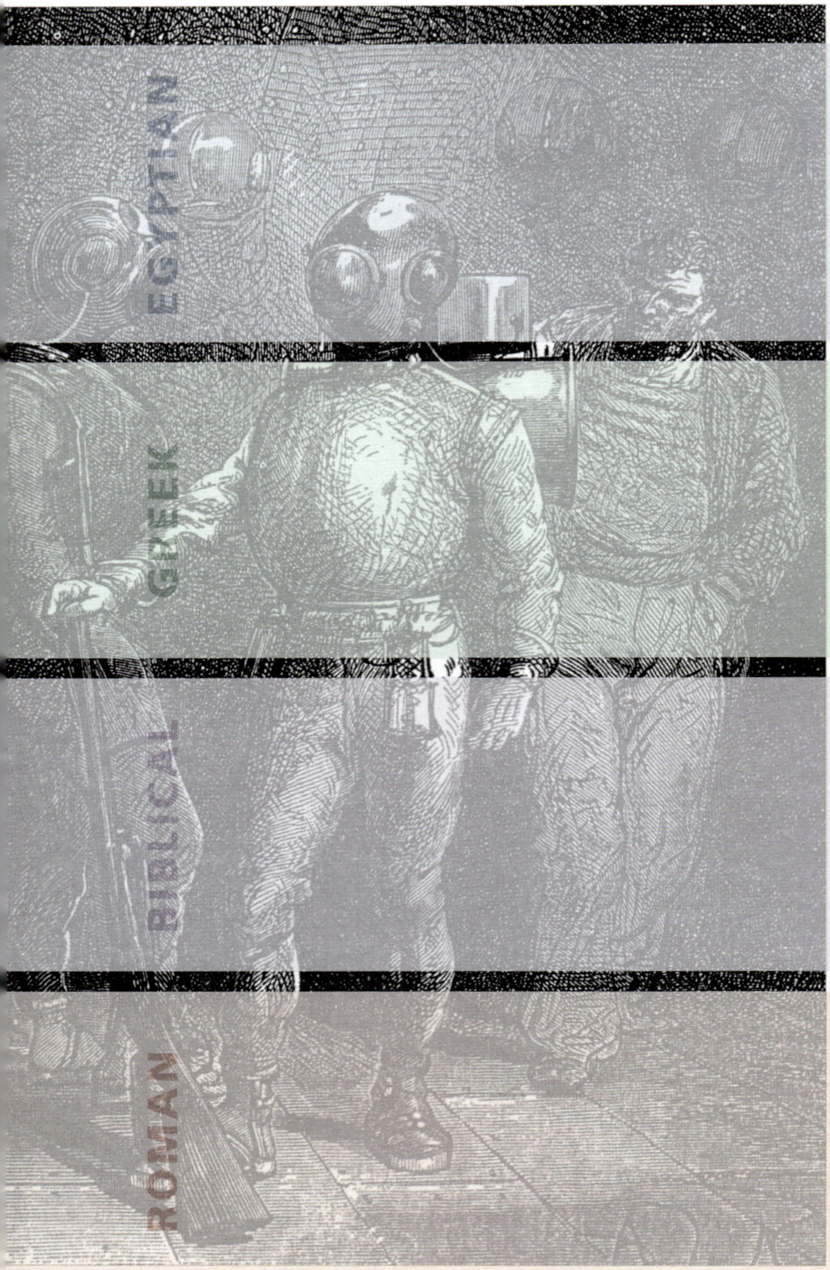

EGYPTIAN

GREEK

BIBLICAL

ROMAN

OTHER

1900

1868–1963 Life of Edith Hamilton

1869–1870 *Twenty Thousand Leagues Under the Seas* Verne

1890–1976 Life of Agatha Christie

1893–1979 Life of Genevieve Foster

1912–1984 Life of Francis Schaeffer

1912 *The Lost World* Conan Doyle

1914–1918 World War I

J.I. Packer, author of *Knowing God*

APPENDIX II: *Timeline* 697

1950

1934–1996 Life of Carl Sagan

1937 *Death on the Nile* Christie

1939–1945 World War II

1942 *Mythology* Hamilton

John Piper, author of *Desiring God*

1947 *Augustus Caesar's World* Foster

1973 *Knowing God* Packer

1973 *Art and the Bible* Schaeffer

1986 *Desiring God* Piper

INDEX

A

Aaron 513, 546
Abednego 162
Abel 108, 382, 385, 459
Abimelech 477, 524
Abraam 42. *See also* Abraham
Abraham 16, 28, 31, 34, 140, 317, 378, 390, 453, 474, 476, 479, 652, 655. *See also* Abraam; Abram
Abram 13, 382, 383, 387. *See also* Abraham
Absalom 140, 508
Accuser, The 28–31, 33, 34, 36. *See also* Satan
Achan 76, 471, 483
Achilleus (Achilles) 59, 60, 62–66, 68, 69, 71, 72, 74, 76–78, 81, 104, 186, 203, 219, 493, 494–501, 503, 505, 594, 623, 635, 640
Achish 251
Actaeon 359, 360
Acte, Claudia 338
Adad 42
Adam 13, 15, 16, 19, 21, 28, 30, 31, 34, 36, 76, 111, 201, 294, 355, 377, 382–384, 424, 459, 479, 481, 490, 501, 509, 510, 561, 584, 585, 596, 606, 608, 655
Adams, James E. 92
Adams, Jay E. 97, 98
Adams, John 165
Adeimantus 174
Adelard of Bath 257
Adler, Mortimer J. 200, 207, 224
Adonis 363
Aeneas 78, 79, 353, 494, 593–595, 597, 598, 603, 635
Aersten, Pieter 344
Aeschylus 100, 101, 118, 122, 218, 637, 640, 647
Aesculapius 146. *See also* Asclepius
Aesop 24, 215, 445–447, 450–452, 455, 456, 458, 502
Agag 524
Agamemnon 60, 62, 63, 66, 68, 69, 71, 72, 76, 77–79, 81, 104, 186, 187, 494, 496, 635, 647

Agaue 119, 128
Agrippa, Marcus Vipsanius 547, 550
Agrippina, Julia Augusta (Agrippina the Younger) 323, 324, 332, 338
Agur 15
Ahab 318, 383, 464
Ahasuerus 525. *See also* Darius I (the Great)
Ahaz 512
Aias 62, 71. *See also* Ajax (son of Telamon)
Ajax (son of Telamon) 47, 494, 496–498, 500, 503, 505. *See also* Aias
Akhenaton (Amenhotep IV) 546
Alcestis 645
Alcibiades 101, 104, 105, 112, 114
Alder-tree Maid 625, 626, 628
Alexander, Leo 145, 147, 148
Alexander the Great 3, 197, 200, 212, 216, 218, 223, 244, 256, 402, 499, 650–653, 655–659
Alexandros 72, 73
Alexis 341
Alford, Steve 539
Alfred the Great 16
Alice 200
Allah 384, 666
Allen, R.E. 12
Allerton, Mrs. 461
Allerton, Tim 461, 469
Allums, Larry 648
Almond, Gabriel A. 170
Alphesiboeus 341
Alter, Robert 35
Ambrose, Saint 174, 299
Amin, Idi 142
Amon 511
Amos 26, 418
Ananias 404, 475
Anaxagoras 100
Andersen, Hans Christian 15
Anderson, Norman 399
Andromache 65, 494–496
Andromeda 360, 361
Angelico, Fra (Guido di Pietro) 377
Anodos 618–626, 628–630, 632
Anscombe, Elizabeth 12

Anselm of Canterbury, Saint 255, 261
Antenor 503
Antigone 635
Antiochus III 281
Antiochus IV Epiphanes 248, 402
Antiochus V Eupator 254
Antoninus Pius (Titus Aurelius Fulvus Boionius Arrius Antoninus) 331
Antony, Mark 268, 298–301, 305, 306, 308, 344, 345, 378, 537, 538, 544, 545, 549, 592–595, 597, 598, 600–603
Anubis 464
Aphrodite 60, 62, 67, 72, 73, 635, 642, 661, 666. *See also* Venus
Apollo 66, 68, 69, 79, 110, 123, 125–127, 142, 144, 146, 178, 179, 190, 198, 203, 218, 352, 356, 362, 635, 640, 642, 646, 650
Aquinas, Thomas 4, 106, 201, 223, 232, 556
Arachne 356, 357, 361, 639
Aragorn 363
Arcas 359
Archidamus 102, 109
Archimedes 260, 265, 266, 395
Arendt, Hannah 167
Ares 60, 62, 635, 642, 643. *See also* Mars
Aristophanes 131–138, 171, 218
Aristotle 3, 7, 12, 16, 46, 99, 107, 116, 164, 169, 174, 175, 181, 196–226, 228, 256, 257, 259, 283, 299, 636, 639
Arius 16, 389
Arnold, Matthew 285
Aronnax, Professor Pierre 606–610, 612, 613, 615, 616
Artaxerxes I (Longimanus) 508, 524, 525, 531
Artemis 110, 642, 647. *See also* Diana
Artorius 416
Asaph 84
Asclepius 142–145, 149. *See also* Aesculapius
Ash tree 619, 620, 625
Aslan 117, 118, 301, 345

Asom 42
Athanasius 16
Athene (Athena) 60, 62, 71, 219,
    360, 633, 635, 639, 642
Atreus 73
Auden, W.H. (Wystan Hugh) 46, 49,
    55, 58, 462, 618
Augustine of Canterbury 548
Augustine, Saint 4, 11, 55, 90, 92,
    98, 106, 148, 164, 171, 173–175,
    181, 182, 184, 215, 292, 341, 345,
    432, 437, 482, 548, 639, 662
Augustus (Gaius Julius Caesar
    Octavianus) 268, 269, 322, 324,
    331, 340, 345, 352–354, 368, 380,
    420, 536–538, 540–546, 548–550,
    593, 650
Aurelius Antoninus 420. See
    also Antoninus Pius (Titus
    Aurelius Fulvus Boionius Arrius
    Antoninus)
Austen, Jane 12
Azarael 525
Azarias 246

B
Baal 270, 384, 584
Baanah 526
Baburen, Dirck van 348
Bacchus 117, 118, 124. See
    also Dionysus
Bach, Johann Sebastian 233, 238–
    241
Bach, P.D.Q. 647, 648
Bacon, Francis 558
Baggins, Frodo 621, 622
Bailey, Damon 539
Bainton, Roland 97
Balaam 652
Balac 42
Baldad 42
Baldung, Hans 32
Bambi's mother 220, 221
Barach, John 390
Barad 42
Barak 485, 487, 488
Bara, Theda 596
Barnabas 366, 642
Barnhart, Bruno 57
Barra, Didier 520
Barry, James 38, 646
Basho, Matsuo 58

Basil 85, 86
Bathsheba 464, 466, 491, 508, 512,
    519
Batman (Bruce Wayne) 569
Baucis 358, 361, 362
Baudelaire, Charles 58
Bauer, A.D. 561
Bavinck, Herman 290
Beardsley, M.C. 242
Beaver, Mr. 596
Beech tree 619, 620
Beethoven, Ludwig von 44
Behe, Michael 575
Bel 249
Bellefort, Jacqueline de 461, 463–
    467, 469
Benedict, Ruth 311, 320
Ben-Hadad 524
Benjamin (Ben-Jamin) 142
Bennett, Mary 23
Ben-Oni 142. See also Benjamin
    (Ben-Jamin)
Beowulf 540
Beren 363
Berge, Edward 178
Berlioz, Hektor 79, 80
Bernini, Gian Lorenzo 8, 352, 362
Bessner, Dr. 461, 467
Bevington, David 505
Bezalel 551
Big Dog, The (Glenn Robinson) 539
Big O, The 539. See also Oscar
    Robertson
Bigvai 526
Bildad (the Shuhite) 28, 32, 34, 36,
    37
Bilshan 526
Bird, Larry 539, 540
Bismarck, Otto von 100
Blackstone, William 394
Blake, Victoria 614
Blake, William 29, 30, 32, 37, 39, 40,
    42, 55, 57, 58
Blood, Sweat & Tears 120
Bloom, Allen 182
Boas, Franz 311–313, 320
Boaz 318, 471, 473, 474, 479–482,
    488–491
Boccaccio, Giovanni 352
Boethius, Anicius Manlius Severinus
    4, 198
Bondone, Giotto di 553

Bonfigli, Benedetto 47
Bonhoeffer, Dietrich 91, 397
Bono (Paul David Hewson) 93, 95
Bosch, Hieronymus 273
Bosorrha 42
Botticelli, Sandro 293
Bottom, Nick 352
Bourget, Louise 461, 469
Bowden, Sandra 529
Bowers, Miss 461
Braddock, James J. 644
Brasidas 101
Briseis 63, 203, 496
Bromiley, Geoffrey 670
Brother Lawrence 57
Browning, Robert 55, 58
Bruce, F.F. 250, 400
Bruegel, Pieter, the Elder 362
Brutus, Marcus Junius 378, 537, 543,
    549, 594
Bucephalus 659
Buddha 524, 547
Burgess, John 166
Burke, Edmund 234, 276
Burne-Jones, Edward 64
Burton, Richard 602
Bush, George H.W. 100
Bush, George W. 100, 163
Bustard, Ned 242, 556
Butler, Tanja 487
Byblis 357
Byron, Lord (George Gordon) 58

C
Cadmus 119, 123, 128, 353, 360
Caesarion 592, 593
Cage, John 195
Cahn, Steven M. 242
Cain 108, 382, 385, 459, 464, 465
Cairns, Scott 53, 58
Calchas 494, 495, 503
Caleb 484
Caligula 322, 324, 331, 368, 542. See
    also Gaius (Gaius Julius Caesar
    Augustus Germanicus)
Callisthenes 653
Callisto 357, 358, 359
Calvin, John 11, 84–86, 89, 90, 97,
    320, 662
Cambyses II 524
Cameron, Nigel M. 149
Camilla 47

INDEX 701

Campbell, Roderick 97
Carlyle, Thomas 618
Carnegie, Andrew 548
Carolsfeld, Julius Schnorr von 252
Carr, Edward 100
Carr, John Dickson 460
Carroll, Lewis 618
Carson, D.A. 250, 373, 375
Carus, Paul 12
Carville, James 308
Casement, Roger 569
Cash, Johnny 240
Cassandra 494, 498, 499, 503
Cassius (Gaius Cassius Longinus) 378,
    537, 543, 549, 594
Castagno, Andrea del 533
Cataline (Lucius Sergius Catilina)
    284, 298
Cather, Willa 645
Caunus 357
Caxton, William 446
Cephalus 174, 180, 183, 186, 194
Ceres 345, 351, 361 *See also* Demeter
Cestius Gallus 404, 408
Chagall, Marc 489, 525, 527
Challenger, Professor Edward 567,
    569–572, 575–577
Chapman, George 504
Charybdis 347
Chaucer, Geoffrey 45, 58, 352, 363,
    494–499, 504, 505
Cheaney, Calbert 539
Cheney, Dick 170
Cheshire Cat 200
Chesterton, G.K. 11, 423, 445, 446,
    450, 462, 618, 629
Chiron 143
Chodkiewicz, Jean-Luc 320
Christie, Agatha 460, 461, 463, 465,
    466, 469, 614
Christie, Archibald 460
Chryses 203
Chrysostom, John 215
Cicero, Marcus Tullius 106, 175, 269,
    284, 297–308, 537, 538, 543, 544,
    653, 655, 659
Cimabue, Cenni di Pepo (Giovanni)
    556
Cinderella 527
Clapton, Eric 240
Clark, Desmond M. 12
Claudius (Tiberias Claudius Drusus

Nero) 321–325, 331, 336, 368,
    369, 650
Clement of Alexandria 85, 90, 97
Clement of Rome 433–435, 438, 439
Cleon 101, 105, 110, 112, 131
Cleopatra 344, 537, 540, 543, 545,
    592–598, 600–603
Cline, Patsy 240, 241
Clinton, Bill 100
Clio 231
Clodius 284
Clough, Arthur Hugh 266, 660
Clytemnestra 647
Coleman, Robert 349
Coleridge, Samuel Taylor 43, 51,
    55, 58
Cole, Thomas 232–235
Collini, Stefan 170
Collins, Billy 12, 54
Colonel Nathanson 159
Colson, Charles 149
Commodus (Lucius Aurelius
    Commodus Antoninus) 331, 420
Conan Doyle, Sir Arthur, *see* Doyle
Confucius 524, 547
Connor, W. Robert 107
Conseil 606, 608, 610, 613, 615, 616
Constantine (Caesar Flavius Valerius
    Aurelius Constantinus Augustus)
    345, 380, 387, 432, 543
Conti, Marco 528
Copleston, Frederick 182, 207, 216
Correggio, Antonio Allegri da 134
Corydon 341
Coulter, Ann 308
Cowan, Louise 639, 645, 648
Cranach, Lucas, the Elder 64, 555
Crane, Gregory 107
Crassus, Marcus Licinius 298, 603,
    650, 659
Creon 186
Cressida 493–500, 503–505
Crick, Bernard 170
Crito 188
Crotty, William 170
Crystal, Billy 217
Cummings, E.E. 50
Cupid (Eros) 73, 356, 360
Cyclops 286, 287
Cyrus 15, 508–510, 513, 516, 524,
    526–528, 659

D
Dadd, Richard 617
Daedalus 362, 645
Dali, Salvadore 64
Dame Folly 15, 21, 23
Damoetas 341, 348
Damon 341, 342
Daniel 28, 162, 249, 527
Dante Alighieri 55, 58, 175, 179,
    198, 223, 269, 345, 352, 441, 596,
    640
Daphne 352, 356, 362
Daphnis 341
Darius I (the Great) 508, 515, 524,
    525, 655, 659
Darwin, Charles 5, 285, 294, 555–
    572, 574, 575, 579, 668
David 13, 26, 55, 60, 69, 76, 84, 85,
    87–89, 91, 94, 95, 98, 251, 277,
    324, 343, 375, 383, 435, 453, 464,
    466, 473, 474, 479, 488, 490,
    508–513, 515, 516, 518, 519, 525,
    548
David, Jacques-Louis 73, 187, 188,
    601, 602
Da Vinci, Leonardo 134, 556
Davis, Dale Ralph 481
Davis-Henry, Denise 358
Dawkins, Richard 471, 481, 486, 487
Dawson, Charles 572, 573
Day, John N. 98
Deadalus 362
Deborah 36, 484, 485, 487, 491, 532,
    533
DeCamp, Ira W. 146
Demeter 635, 638, 643. *See also* Ceres
Demetrias 85
Demetrius I Soter 254
Demosthenes 113, 300, 653, 655,
    660
Dennis, Lane 556
deSantis, Greg 607
Descartes, René 4, 5, 12, 257–261,
    583
Desiderio, Monsù, *see* Nomé,
    François de
Desmoulins, Camille 298
Devil, The 89. *See also* Satan
DeVito, Danny 217
Devlin, Lord Patrick 392
De Vos, Cornelis 129
Dewald, Carolyn 107

Diamond, Jared 320
Diana 358–360. *See also* Artemis
Dickens, Charles 242
Dickinson, Emily 43, 44, 58
Dido 594, 603
Dillenberger, Jane Daggett 552
Dillon, John 12
Diocletian (Gaius Aurelius Valerius Diocletianus) 542, 668
Diodore 84
Diodotus 101, 110, 112
Diogenes 482
Diomedes 60, 71, 78, 79, 494–499
Dione 647
Dionysus 117, 119, 120, 122–128, 131, 136, 140, 178, 635, 643. *See also* Bacchus
Dis 351. *See also* Hades; Pluto
Disney, Walt 607, 614
Dolon 78
Domitian (Titus Flavius Domitianus Augustus) 322, 331, 542
Donne, John 12, 52, 55, 58, 238, 500
Dooyeweerd, Herman 320, 555
Dorsey, David 97
Douglas, Lisa 339
Douglas, Mary 320
Douglas, Oliver Wendell 339, 342
Doyle, Sir Arthur Conan 567–579
Doyle, Charles 567
Doyle, Linnet 461, 463, 464, 469. *See also* Ridgeway, Linnet
Doyle, Mary 567
Doyle, Simon 461, 464, 466, 467, 469
Drew, Charles 92, 98
Dr. Seuss (Theodor Geisel) 43, 450
Dryden, John 58, 494, 650
Duchess of Death 460. *See also* Christie, Agatha
Duessa 596
Du Fu 58
Duke Frederick 340
Duncan 40
Dürer, Albrecht 32, 555
Dyke, Anthony van 480

E

Ebimelech 489
Echo 360
Edge, The (David Howell Evans) 95
Edison, Thomas 240
Edwards, Jay 539

Edwards, Jonathan 232, 662, 664, 668, 672
Edward VI 592
Eglon 473
Ehud 36, 473, 475
Einstein, Albert 260
Eleazar ben Simon 404, 412
Elihu 29, 37, 42
Elijah 270, 511
Elimelech 479–481, 488, 491
Eliot, T.S. 54, 55, 58, 238
Eliphaz (the Temanite) 28, 30, 32, 34, 36, 37, 42
Elisha 511
Elizabeth I 548, 592
Elizabeth of Austria 77
Eller, Vernard 664
Ellington, Duke 241
Elwell, Walter A. 373
Emerson, Ralph Waldo 43, 56, 618
Ennius 285
Ennon 42
Enobarbus, Domitius 594, 600, 601
Epaphroditus 381
Ephraim 491
Epicurus 283, 284, 287, 289, 291, 295, 664
Eris 198
Esau 42
Esolen, Anthony 285, 287–289, 291, 295
Esther 527, 530, 532–534
Euclid 255, 256, 258–266
Euodia 378
Euripides 70, 118, 119, 122, 123, 125, 126, 218
Europa 360
Eurydice 358, 647
Eusebius of Caesarea 366, 380, 426, 432
Eve 30, 459, 479, 561, 596, 606
Everitt, Anthony 305
Ezekiel 14, 366, 514, 660
Ezra 118, 131, 508, 509, 513, 516, 524, 525, 527, 529, 531, 532

F

Fabius (Quintus Fabius Maximus Verrucosus) 270, 280
Fanthorp, James (Jim) 461, 463, 466, 467, 469
Farr, James 170

Father Christmas 117
Faust, C.H. 672
Felix, Marcus Antonius 402
Ferguson, Mr. 461, 463, 467, 469
Ferry, David 340, 346, 349
Feuerbach, Anselm 64, 647
Finifter, Ada 170
Fischer, Anton Otto 607
Fisher, Milton C. 521
Fitzgerald, John Anster 631
Flaminius 277
Florus, Gessius 404
Forde, Steven 107
Foster, Genevieve 536–538, 543, 546, 550
Foster, Joanna 536
Foster, Orrington C. 536
Foster, Orrington C., Jr. 536
Fouquet, Jean 558
Fowler, F.G. 116
Fowler, H.W. 116
Fränkel, Hermann 364
Franklin, Aretha 240
Franklin, Benjamin 16, 419, 454
Freccero, Yvonee 125
Freeman, Derek 320
Freud, Sigmund 663, 664–667, 669, 672
Friedrich, Carl Joachim 400
Frost, Robert Lee 44, 46, 51, 52, 54, 58, 340, 349, 521
Frye, Northrop 450

G

Gaius (Gaius Julius Caesar Augustus Germanicus) 322, 323. *See also* Caligula
Gaius Julius Caesar, *see* Julius Caesar
Galba (Servius Sulpicius Galba Caesar Augustus) 331, 404
Galen 143
Galileo Galilei 258
Gallus 341, 342
Garfield 243
Gates, Bill 240, 548
Gauguin, Paul 316
Geertz, Clifford 313, 320
Geisel, Theodor, *see* Dr. Seuss
Genghis Khan 394, 395. *See also* Taizu
Genius 363
Gentileschi, Artemisia 243, 245
George III 188

Gewirth, Alan 393, 394
Ghandi, Mohandas Karamchand 161
Gibbon, Edward 102
Gideon 36, 477, 487, 488
Gilalai 525
Ginsberg, Irwin Allen 50
Giordano, Luca 557
Giotto di Bondone 556, 564
Girard, Rene 35, 125, 499
Glaucon 174, 186, 194, 195, 198
Goethe, Johann Wolfgang von 58, 285
Goff, Harper 607
Goizueta, Roberto 456
Goliath 62, 69, 85
Gonzalez, Justo 426, 437
Goodman, Martin 411, 418
Gorgias 133
Gower, John 363
Graham, Greg 539
Grant, Michael 308, 641
Grateful Dead 120
Gratian (Flavius Gratianus) 106
Greene, Nathaniel 432
Greenleaf, Simon 399
Green, Peter 282
Gregory the Great
    (Pope St. Gregory I) 299
Grieg, Edvard 628, 629
Griffiths, Frances 571, 578
Groton, Anne H. 346
Guinan, Patrick 149
Guliuzza, Frank 170
Gummeson, Janet 45, 46
Gylippus 113
Gynt, Peer 628

H
Habakkuk 514
Haberman, David 320
Habermas, Jürgen 167
Hadas, Moses 338
Hadassah. See Esther
Hades 635, 640, 642, 645.
    See also Dis; Pluto
Hadot, Pierre 283
Hadrian (Publius Aelius Hadrianus)
    331, 419, 650
Haggai 402, 529
Haggard, Merle 240
Haik-Ventoura, Susan 97
Hall, Christopher 97

Hals, Frans 5
Haman 524, 527, 528, 534
Hamilcar 267, 268, 269, 275
Hamilton, Alexander 165, 166
Hamilton, Edith 68, 305, 634–636,
    639, 641, 642, 643, 648
Hamlet 52
Hanani 525
Hancock, Graham 511
Handel, George Frideric 333
Hankins, Barry 556
Hannah 473
Hannibal 267–270, 272, 274–282,
    594
Hannity, Sean 308
Hanno 269
Hansen, Meinert 607
Hanun 519
Hardie, Peter 358
Hardy, Thomas 58
Harmer, J.R. 441
Harmonia 198
Harmon, William 648
Harris, Marvin 313, 320
Harstad, Adolph 481
Hart, H.L.A. 392
Hasdrubal 269
Hatch, Orrin 159, 170
Heaney, Seamus 58
Hegel, Georg Wilhelm Friedrich 5,
    165
Hegeman, David 320
Heidegger, Martin 10
Hekademos 172
Hektor (Hector) 59–66, 71, 72, 78,
    79, 219, 494–498, 500, 503, 505
Helen of Troy 60, 65, 68, 70, 80, 134,
    210, 308, 494, 496–500, 503, 505
Heliodorus 253
Hell's Angel 121
Hemingway, Ernest 554
Hendrix, Jimi 120
Henry, Matthew 320
Henry VI 340
Henry VIII 592
Hensley, Joanna 217, 218
Hephaestus 642. See also Vulcan
Hera 60, 65, 70, 74, 79, 119, 635,
    639, 642, 646. See also Juno
Heraclitus 180
Herbert, George 16, 50–52, 55–58,
    238

Hercules 353, 361, 447, 461, 540,
    594, 635, 640, 641, 645, 646
Herman, Bruce 560
Hermann 536, 549
Hermaphroditus 354
Hermas 433, 434, 436, 441
Hermes 70, 637, 638, 642. See
    also Mercury
Herod Antipas 536
Herodotus 60, 70, 99, 102, 197, 231,
    310, 320, 446, 524, 636, 650
Herod the Great 141, 142, 403, 407,
    509, 536, 538, 543, 544, 547, 549
Herter, Ernst 77
Hesiod 198, 340, 636
Hestia 642
Hetzel, Pierre-Jules 614
Heyen, William 58
Hezekiah 15, 113, 383, 510
Hildebrand 607
Hillel 546
Hinds, Stephen E. 364
Hippocrates 100, 142, 143, 145, 149,
    150, 155
Hitchcock, Alfred 217
Hitchens, Christopher 287
Hitler, Adolf 142
Hobbes, Thomas 100, 165, 258, 285
Holford, George 411
Holman, C. Hugh 648
Holmes, Sherlock 567, 569
Holofernes 243
Holzer, Harold 518
Homer 58–60, 62, 65, 66, 68, 70, 72,
    73, 79, 104, 197, 198, 203, 220,
    223, 285–287, 340, 494–497, 499,
    504, 623, 635, 636, 637, 646
Hopkins, Gerard Manley 48, 55, 57,
    58, 238
Horace 544
Hornblower, Simon 107, 364
Hosea 299
Housman, A. E. 43
Hubbard, Robert L., Jr. 481
Hughes, Edward Robert 627
Hulme, T.E. 46
Hume, David 5, 6, 12
Hungerton, Gladys 575
Hur 551
Huss, John 26
Hutchinson, D.S. 207
Huxley, Aldous 195, 198, 570

Hygieia 144

I

Ibsen, Henrik 628, 629
Icarus 361, 362
Ignatius of Antioch (Theophorus) 432–436, 440
Io 354
Iphigenia 635, 647
Iphis 357
Iris 72
Isaac 140, 453, 652, 655
Isaiah 345, 526, 664, 665
Isis 357

J

Jabin 485, 487
Jachin 559
Jackson, Mahalia 241
Jacob 28, 30, 31, 33, 36, 317, 318, 476, 652, 655
James the Apostle 28, 38, 56, 390, 447, 587, 590, 652
James, Henry 460
Jason 253, 353, 360, 635
Jay, John 166
Jefferson, Thomas 165, 188
Jehoshaphat 90, 512
Jemimah 29
Jephthah 477, 487, 488
Jeremiah 142, 253, 511, 514, 521, 524
Jeroboam 546, 548
Jerome 85, 245
Jeshua 526
Jesus Christ 7, 8, 10, 11, 13–16, 19–21, 23, 26, 28, 34–36, 38, 40, 53, 57, 62, 65, 84, 85, 88, 90–92, 98, 117, 124, 125, 127–129, 134, 137, 138, 140–142, 148, 154, 155, 158–160, 162, 171, 178, 179, 181, 182, 184, 189, 193, 194, 200, 201, 205, 207, 209, 210, 220, 222, 223, 238, 246, 247, 269, 271–275, 281, 283, 300, 305, 306, 315, 318, 322, 324, 326–328, 342–345, 348, 355, 358, 365–390, 392–400, 403–408, 410–413, 415, 420, 421, 424, 425, 427, 428, 432–437, 440, 446, 448–451, 453, 459, 460, 465, 473, 475, 476, 478, 479, 481, 482, 484, 485, 487–491, 509, 511, 512,

515, 530, 532, 534, 536, 538, 542, 543, 546, 549, 551, 553–557, 559, 561–564, 570, 576, 584–586, 589, 590, 597, 605, 608, 614, 639, 640, 645, 652, 654, 655, 662–664, 666, 667, 669–671
Jiminy Cricket 394
Job 28–40, 42, 179, 377, 453, 590, 652
Jobab 28, 42. *See also* Job
Jobs, Steve 548
Job's wife 28, 30, 31
John of Gischala 404, 408–411, 413, 414
John of the Cross 55, 58
Johnson, James Weldon 58
Johnson, Lydon B. 158
Johnson, Philip 575
Johnson, T.H. 672
John the Apostle 4, 34, 182, 380, 563, 585, 587
John the Baptist 365, 366, 371, 374, 402, 536
Jonathan 277
Jones, Indiana (Henry Walton Jones, Jr.) 511
Jones, Paul S. 92, 97
Jones, Rick 539
Jonson, Ben 58, 219
Joplin, Janis 120
Jordaens, Jacob 405
Jordan, James 15, 23, 31, 481, 525
Joseph 15, 490, 491, 593, 668
Joseph of Arimathea 563
Josephus (Yosef bar Mattathyahu) 401–404, 407–416, 509, 525, 558
Joshua 375, 471–476, 482–486, 491, 579, 653
Josiah 375, 383, 510, 511, 515, 520, 521
Jove 353, 354, 356, 358–360. *See also* Jupiter
Juanes, Juan de 181
Judah 479, 491, 509
Judas Iscariot 377, 587
Judas the Galilean 403
Judith 243, 249–251, 532, 533
Julia the Elder 537, 541, 547, 548
Juliet 46, 52, 55, 503
Julius Caesar (Gaius Julius Caesar) 268, 284, 298, 310, 320, 340, 353, 354, 537, 538, 540, 541, 543, 544,

550, 593–595, 598, 603, 650, 651, 653–655, 659, 660
Juno 272, 354, 357, 360, 372. *See also* Hera
Jupiter 271, 272, 351, 356, 357, 360, 361, 372, 384, 447. *See also* Zeus
Juvenal 281, 282

K

Kagan, Donald 107
Kalypso 68
Kant, Immanuel 5, 11, 12, 260, 393, 394
Kaplan, Justin D. 224
Kauffmann, Angelica 495
Kaufmann, Walter 12
Keats, John 44–46, 58, 340, 349, 363
Kemos, Alexander 116
Kennan, George F. 100
Keren-Happuch 29
Kerr, Hugh 437
Kevorkian, Jack 149
Key, Francis Scott 485
Keziah 29
Kidner, Derek 528
Kierkegaard, Søren 5
King Arthur 620, 634, 637
King, Martin Luther, Jr. 161, 307
King, William 572
Kipling, Rudyard 460
Kish 524
Kissinger, Henry 100
Kitto, H.D.F. 125
Knight, Bob 539
Knippers, Edward 561, 562
Koop, C. Everett 552
Korah 87
Krapp, George Philip 505
Kraut, Richard 182
Kroeber, Alfred 311
Kuyper, Abraham 320, 555

L

Lady Geometry 257
Lady Justice 391
Lady Macbeth 40
Lady Mallowan 460. *See also* Christie, Agatha
Lady Wisdom 622, 624, 630
Lady Wisdom (of Proverbs) 15, 16, 18–21, 24
Lamech 383

Land, Ned 606, 608–610, 612, 613, 615, 616
Lane, William L. 373
Lasagna, Louis 147
Leda 134
Lee, A. 358
Lee, Charles 431, 434, 435
LeGeis, Trevor 51
Leibniz, Gottfried Wilhelm 258
Leithart, Peter J. 23, 24, 66, 125, 137, 358, 476, 491, 597
Lemuel 15
L'Engle, Madeleine 618
Lenin, Vladimir 548
Leonard, William Ellery 284, 295
Leutze, Emanuel Gottlieb 210, 211, 637
Levi 373
Lewis, C.S. 11, 58, 65, 72, 90, 97, 117, 118, 301, 302, 314, 320, 345, 499, 505, 560, 582, 583, 618, 619, 622, 625, 633, 634, 639–641, 648, 662, 664, 667, 669, 672
Lieber, Francis 166
Lightfoot, J.B. 441
Lilith 595, 596, 598, 630
Limbaugh, Rush 308
Lincoln, Abraham 135, 264, 265, 518, 616
Linnet's father 469
Linton, Irwin H. 400
Li Po 58
Livy (Titus Livius) 267–278, 280–282, 368, 540, 593, 595
Locke, John 5, 12, 165
Longimanus 525. See also Artaxerxes I (Longimanus)
Lorca, Federico García 58
Lot 390, 652
Lotto, Lorenzo 50
Louis IX (Saint Louis) 484
Lowell, Robert 58
Lowie, Robert 311
Lucian 100, 116
Lucilla 284
Lucius Domitius Ahenobarbus 368. See also Nero (Nero Claudius Caesar Drusus Germanicus)
Lucius Julius Caesar 538, 541
Lucius Verus (Lucius Aurelius Verus) 331, 420

Lucretia 368, 540, 593, 595
Lucretius (Titus Lucretius Carius) 283–295
Lucy, Saint 668
Luke 365, 366, 432, 475
Luther, Martin 64, 84, 88, 97, 223, 299, 320, 397, 400
Luthien 363
Lycaon 356
Lycidas 340–342, 349

M
Maai 525
Macaulay, Thomas Babington 285, 286
Macbeth 40
Maccabeus, Judas 254, 402
MacDonald, George 617–619, 621–623, 625, 629, 632
MacDonald, Helen 618
Machen, J. Gresham 251, 555
Machiavelli, Niccolò 100, 164, 198
MacIntyre, Alasdair 202, 207
MacLeish, Archibald 44
Madison, James 105, 165, 166
Maher, Bill 308
Maier, Paul 426
Malachi 402
Malinowski, Bronislaw 312, 320
Mallowan, Max 460
Malone, Edward Dunn 569, 570, 575, 576
Malory, Thomas 618
Manasseh 383, 491, 511
Mantegna, Andrea 670
Mao Zedong 471
Marcellus, Marcus Claudius 265, 266
Marcovaldo, Coppo di 388
Marcus Annius Verus. See Marcus Aurelius (Marcus Aurelius Antoninus Augustus)
Marcus Aurelius (Marcus Aurelius Antoninus Augustus) 331, 419–430, 433
Marcuse, Herbert 167
Marduk 526, 527
Mariamne 549
Marion, Francis 432
Marius, Gaius 297, 650
Markos, Louis 641
Mark the Evangelist (John Mark) 365–367, 369–376

Marlowe, Christopher 58, 340, 349
Marple, Miss Jane 460
Mars 356, 642, 643. See also Ares
Marshall, George C. 100
Martin, Charles 353, 364
Marvell, Andrew 58
Marx, Karl 165
Mary 435, 490, 556, 563, 593
Mary Cleophas 563
Mary I (Bloody Mary) 592
Mary Magdalen 355, 563
Mary (Mother of Mark the Evangelist) 366
Mary of Bethezuba 416
Mary Salome 563
Masinissa 272, 275
Mason, Steve 411
Mattathias 253
Matthew 141, 142
Matthew, Victor 318
Mays, James Luther 92
Mazzola, Girolamo Francesco Maria (Parmigianino) 379
McClatchey, J.D. 58
McCleary, Mary 177
McKeon, Richard 12
McLean, Don 121
Mead, Margaret 311, 320
Medea 360, 361
Medusa 358
Melancthon, Philipp 299
Meliboeus 340, 341
Mellon, James 266
Menalcas 340, 341, 348
Menas 600
Menelaos (Menelaus) 60, 65, 69, 70, 72, 494, 496, 497, 505
Mercury 361, 447. See also Hermes
Meshach 162
Meskin, Aaron 242
Metzger, Bruce 250
Meyers, Jeffrey 34, 35
Meyers, Ken 97
Micah 653
Michelangelo Buonarroti 290, 556, 585
Midas 656
Midredath 526
Milalai 525
Miller, Agatha Mary Clarissa 460. See also Christie, Agatha
Miller, Dennis 308

Miller, Russell 575, 579
Milosz, Czeslav 58
Milton, John 55, 58, 233, 238, 242, 340, 349, 352, 640
Minadeo, Richard 291
Minerva 356, 372, 639.
    See also Athene (Athena)
Minos 104
Mispar 526
Moeris 341, 342
Moliere, Jean-Baptiste 219
Monroe, James 638
Montesquieu, Baron 310
Montgomery, John Warwick 400
Moo, Douglas 373, 375
Moon 138
Moore, Marianne 58
Mopsus 341
Moran, Thomas 233
Mordecai 524, 526–528, 533, 534
Moreau, Gustave 122
Morgan, Lewis Henry 310, 312, 320
Morgenthau, Hans 100
Morgoth 363, 364
Morison, Frank 400
Morris, Leon 373, 375
Morris, William 618
Moser, Barry 493
Moser, Stephanie 572, 579
Moses 15, 65, 84, 87, 116, 141, 399, 411, 435, 472, 474, 475, 546, 551, 653, 655
Most, Glen W. 465
Mouw, Richard 664, 667, 671, 672
Mozart, Wolfgang Amadeus 239, 241
Murch, A.E. 465, 469
Myers, Kenneth 240
Myrrha 357

N
Nabonidus 526
Naboth 318, 464
Nahash 111
Naismith, James 540
Naomi 473, 479, 480, 488–491
Narcissus 360
Nathan 464, 466, 490, 518
Nebuchadnezzar 141, 142, 250, 508, 510, 511, 513, 525–527
Nebuzaradan 142
Necho II 520, 521

Needham, N.R. 426
Nehemiah 118, 131, 513, 523, 525–527, 530–533
Nemo, Captain 606–610, 612, 614–616
Neptune 372. *See also* Poseidon
Nero (Nero Claudius Caesar Drusus Germanicus) 269, 321–328, 331, 332, 334–338, 368–373, 380, 386, 401, 404, 542
Neruda, Pablo (Neftalí Ricardo Reyes Basoalto) 45, 58
Nerva (Marcus Cocceius Nerva) 322, 330, 331
Nestor 71, 79, 81, 494, 500
Nethaneel 525
Newton, Isaac 258, 260
Nicanor 401
Nicholi, Armand M. 667, 672
Nichols, James Hastings 86, 97
Nichomachus 199
Nicias 101, 105, 113
Nicodemus 563
Nietzsche, Friedrich 6, 12, 663, 665, 667
Niobe 357, 361
Noah 28, 652
Noll, Mark 320
Nomé, François de 520
Noonan, Peggy 157, 159
North, Gary 320
Novalis 620
Nozick, Robert 167
Nysa 341, 342

O
Obama, Barack 100
Obed 480
Octavia, Claudia 336
Octavia Minor 593, 600
Octavian 268, 284, 331, 368, 378, 536–539, 541, 543, 544, 549, 593, 598, 600, 603. *See also* Augustus (Gaius Julius Caesar Octavianus)
Oden, Greg 539
Oden, Thomas C. 528
Odysseus 59, 60, 65, 71, 78, 81, 223, 494, 635, 640. *See also* Ulysses
Oecolampadius, John 247
Oedipus 34, 96, 222, 497
Old Yeller 220
Olorus 100

Onan 320
Origen 91
Orpheus 176–179, 198, 358, 645, 647
Orwin, Clifford 107
Osborne, Charles 465, 469
Otho (Marcus Salvius Otho Caesar Augustus) 331, 404
Otterbourne, Rosalie 461
Otterbourne, Salome 461, 469
Ovid (Publius Ovidius Naso) 351–354, 356–360, 362–635, 666
Owen, Wilfred 48

P
Pacino, Al 110
Packer, J.I. 582–584, 586–589
Pan 97
Panacea 144
Pandarus 494, 495, 498, 499, 503
Papias 366
Paris 60, 65, 68–70, 72, 80, 494, 496–498, 500, 503, 599, 661
Parker, Charlie 241
Parr, Dash 546
Parsons, Theophilus 399
Pascal, Blaise 662, 667
Pasture, Rogier de le, *see* Weyden, Rogier van der
Patroklos (Patroclus) 60, 63, 74, 76, 78, 79, 494–497, 500, 501
Paul the Apostle 7–9, 16, 22, 61, 62, 72, 89, 92, 98, 158, 167, 179, 182, 189, 202, 206, 218, 247, 249, 250, 300–302, 314, 322, 324, 325, 356, 366, 367, 372, 374, 378–388, 390, 394, 398, 403, 412, 423, 424, 428–430, 432, 434–436, 439, 440, 447, 449, 469, 474–476, 576, 610, 626, 639, 640, 642, 652, 654, 657, 664
Pavarati, Luciano 241
Peneus 362
Pennington, Andrew 461, 463, 466, 467
Pentheus 119–121, 123–126, 128, 129
Percival, Sir 620–623
Pericles 100, 101, 104, 105, 107, 109, 110, 112, 524
Perkins, Caroline 358
Perkins, David 58
Persephone 638, 640, 647. *See also* Proserpina
Perseus 353, 358, 360, 361

INDEX 707

Peterson, Eugene H. 20, 92, 93, 98
Peter the Apostle 303, 314, 322, 366, 367, 372, 376, 399, 476, 652
Petrarch (Francesco Petrarca) 352
Pevensie, Lucy 117
Pevensie, Susan 117
Phaedrus 446
Phaethon 359, 645
Pheidippides 131–133, 135–140
Phidias 635
Philemon 358, 361, 362
Philip II of Macedon 216, 218, 244, 300, 378, 650, 651
Philo 595
Philomela 357
Phoebus 359
Phoinix 63, 71
Picasso, Pablo 64
Pilate, Pontius 322, 328, 370, 403, 435
Pilava, Gianluc 528
Pindar 636
Piper, John Stephen 662–668, 670–672
Piso, Gaius Calpurnius 338
Placidus 413
Plantinga, Alvin 7
Plath, Sylvia 48, 51, 58
Plato 3, 5, 7, 12, 90, 131, 133, 164, 169, 171–183, 188–191, 194–201, 203–206, 212, 218, 219, 224, 256, 283, 287, 383, 421, 446, 636, 639, 650, 653
Plimer, Ian 562
Plotinus 4, 12
Plutarch 116, 265, 269, 298, 322, 649–655, 657–660
Pluto 360. See also Dis; Hades
Pocock, J.G.A. 167
Poirot, Hercule 460, 461, 463–466, 469
Pole, Jill 345
Polemarchus 174, 183, 186
Pollack, Jackson 233
Pollio, Gaius Asinius 344, 345
Polo, Marco 320
Pol Pot (Saloth Sar) 142
Polycarp 432, 433, 436, 440
Pompey (Gnaeus Pompeius Magnus) 298, 403, 600, 603, 650, 659
Pope, Alexander 46, 58
Poppaea Sabina 336, 338

Popper, Karl 393
Poseidon 74, 635, 642, 644. See also Neptune
Postman, Neil 241
Prescott, Catherine 53
Priam 60, 63, 64, 494
Prince (husband of Lady Wisdom) 15
Procne 357
Prometheus 191, 341, 348, 645
Proserpina 351, 360, 361. See also Persephone
Protagoras 118
Ptolemy I Soter I 256
Ptolemy XIII 593
Ptolemy XIV 593
Puddleglum 345, 347
Pye, Lucian W. 170
Pyramus (Pyramis) 352, 360, 635, 644, 647
Pythagoras 354–356, 359, 364, 547

Q
Queen of Sheba 512, 519

R
Rabshakeh 113
Race, Colonel 461, 463
Rachel 141, 142
Racine, Jean 219
Rackham, Arthur 445
Radamistus 333
Radcliffe-Brown, Alfred Reginald (A.R.) 312
Rahab 251, 474, 482, 483, 491
Raimondi, Marcantonio 64
Ramses II 462, 466, 468
Ramsey, Anne 217
Rand, Edward 364
Raphael (from the Book of Tobit) 251
Raphael (Raffaello Sanzio) 204, 205, 382
Rawls, John 167, 393, 394
Reagan, Ronald 157, 571
Reelaiah 526
Reepicheep 622
Rehoboam 23, 71, 115, 116
Rehum 526
Reid, Doris Fielding 641, 648
Reid, Mayne 569
Rembrandt Harmenszoon van Rijn 197, 233, 234, 238, 245, 555

Remus 303
Rhoades, James 349
Rhoda 441
Ribera, Jusepe de 124
Richetti, Signor 461, 467
Rich Young Ruler 376
Ridgeway, Linnet 461, 463, 466, 468. See also Doyle, Linnet
Rimbaud, Arthur 58
Robertson, Oscar 540. See also Big O, The
Robespierre, Maximilien 548
Rockefeller, John 548
Roddenberry, Gene 303
Roethke, Theodore 58
Romaine, James 556
Romeo 45, 46, 52, 55, 503
Romulus 303
Rood, Timothy 107
Roosevelt, Theodore 107, 116
Rorty, A.O. 224
Roscius, Sextus 297
Ross, Dennis 100, 116
Rossetti, Dante Gabriel 351
Rouault, Georges 239, 671
Rousseau, Jean-Jacques 198, 395
Roxton, Lord John 569, 576, 577
Rubens, Peter Paul 64, 67, 68
Ruskin, John 232, 233, 238, 242, 618
Ruth 318, 375, 473, 474, 479–481, 488–491
Rutherford, William 569
Ryken, Philip Graham 556

S
Sagan, Carl 5, 292
Sallust (Gaius Sallustius Crispus) 284
Salome 371
Samaritan, The Good 220
Samson 16, 36, 62, 473, 477, 487, 488
Samuel 60, 375, 473, 474, 487, 524
Sandburg, Carl 264
Santa Claus 397, 584
Santayana, George 285
Sapir, Edward 311
Sapphira 475
Sarah 251
Sargon II 513
Sarpedon 72
Satan 21, 28–30, 34, 121, 122, 365, 596. See also Accuser, The; Devil, The

Satie, Erik 195
Saul 13, 62, 111, 473, 474, 524
Schaeffer, Edith 552
Schaeffer, Francis 11, 164, 320,
    552–560, 586
Schickele, Peter 647, 648
Schlossberg, Herbert 320
Scipio, Publius Cornelius 269, 270,
    272, 276, 279, 282, 594
Scott, Walter 644
Scotus, Duns 5
Scrubb, Eustace 345
Scylla 341, 347, 357
Seerveld, Calvin 242
Seidelman, Raymond 170
Sejanus, Lucius Aelius 323, 325,
    328–330, 332
Seleucid 253
Sellaio, Jacopo del 530
Semele 119, 122, 128, 643
Seneca, Lucius Annaeus (Seneca the
    Younger) 323, 326, 328, 336, 338
Seraiah 526
Seward, Desmond 411, 418
Shadrach 162
Shakespeare, William 12, 40, 45, 46,
    52, 55, 58, 218, 219, 233, 238,
    239, 242, 255, 340, 352, 460,
    493–500, 502–505, 583, 591–594,
    598, 640, 644, 650
Shaw, George Bernard 352
Shaw, Luci 47, 58
Sheesley, Joel 241
Shelley, Percy Bysshe 43, 58, 363, 462
Shemaiah 525
Sherlock, Thomas 400
Sheshbazzar 526
Shutte, Mr. 579
Sigmund, Paul E. 12
Signorelli, Luca 556
Silas 366, 378
Silenus 341, 347
Simon bar Giora 404, 414
Singer, Peter 146, 147, 155
Sisera 487
Smith, Andrew 535
Smith, Standley Barney 295
Socrates 3, 7, 12, 118, 131–135,
    137–139, 142, 164, 171, 173–183,
    185–195, 197, 198, 200, 214, 218,
    219, 273, 446, 524
Solomon 13–19, 21–26, 28, 31, 76,

82, 84, 116, 248, 356, 405, 453,
    465, 490, 507–516, 519, 558, 662,
    666, 669
Somit, Albert 170
Sommerstein, Alan H. 135, 137, 140
Sophar 42
Sophocles 97, 118, 122, 218, 637
Southwood, Joanna 461, 466, 467,
    469
Spawforth, Anthony 364
Spence-Jones, H.D.M. 515
Spencer, Herbert 175, 352, 570
Spenser, Edmund 52, 55, 58, 340,
    349, 618, 619
Spielvogel, Jackson J. 66, 107, 125,
    137, 182, 207, 224, 275, 305, 328,
    346, 411, 426, 437, 543, 597, 609,
    655
Spinoza, Baruch 258
Spitz, Vivien 155
Spock, Mr. 303
Stalin, Joseph 142
Stapert, Calvin R. 97, 98
Stephen 390
Stevenson, Leslie 320
Stevens, Wallace 45, 58
Steward, Julian 313, 320
Storkey, Alan 320
Story, William Wetmore 594
Strabo 547
Strauss, Leo 167
Strepsiades 131–135, 137–140
Stryk, Lucien 58
Suetonius (Gaius Suetonius
    Tranquillus) 368, 370, 373, 543
Sulla (Lucius Cornelius Sulla Felix)
    297, 650
Summerlee, Professor 569, 572, 577,
    579
Superman (Clark Kent) 6
Susanna 245, 249, 532, 533
Sydney, Philip 44
Symons, Julian 575
Syndrome 546
Syntyche 378
Syphax 275

T
Tacitus, Publius (or Gaius) Cornelius
    310, 321–330, 332, 335–338, 370,
    373
Taizu 395. See also Genghis Khan

Tarquinus, Sextus 595
Tarrant, Harold 12
Taylor, A.B. 358
Taylor, Elizabeth 602
Taylor, Gary 505
Teen Angel 220, 221
Teiresias 119, 123, 128
Tenny, Merrill C. 373
Tennyson, Alfred 48, 49, 52, 58, 284,
    285, 618
Tereus 357
Tertullian (Quintus Septimius Florens
    Terullianus) 179, 198
Themistocles 109
Theocritus 340
Thersites 494, 495, 503
Theseus 353, 640
Thetis 78, 79
Thielman, Frank 387
Thisbe 352, 360, 635, 644, 647
Thomas, Dylan 44, 58
Thompson, Francis 55
Thoreau, Henry David 57
Thrasymachus 174, 176, 177, 183,
    185, 186, 192, 194, 195
Thucydides 99–112, 114, 116, 131,
    172, 173, 231, 636, 650
Thyrsis 341
Tiberius (Tiberius Claudius Nero
    Caesar) 322–325, 328–332, 338,
    368, 370, 537, 538, 547, 549
Tiepol, Giovanni Battista 439
Timothy 381, 432, 434, 439, 652
Timoxena 650
Tintoretto, Jacopo 288
Tinuviel 363. See also Luthien
Titian (Tiziano Vecelli) 355
Titus (Titus Flavius Sabinus
    Vespasianus) 322, 331, 401–405,
    413, 414, 416, 417, 439
Tityrus 341
Tobias 251
Tobit 251
Tocqueville, Alexis de 544
Tolkien, J.R.R. 12, 97, 238, 242, 363,
    618, 621, 622, 625, 632–634, 638,
    640, 641, 648
Traherne, Thomas 58
Trajan (Marcus Ulpius Nerva
    Traianus) 322, 331, 424
Trebek, Alex 617
Troilus 493–500, 503, 505

INDEX 709

Turner, Frank M. 295
Turner, Joseph Mallord William 274, 276
Turnus 287
Twain, Mark 60
Tylor, Edward Burnett 310–312
Tyndall, John 570

U

Ulysses 494–496, 498, 500, 502, 503, 505. *See also* Odysseus
Unwin, Timothy 609
Uri 551
Uriah 466
Uzzah 516

V

Valens 436
van Dyck, Anthony 245
van Eyck, Jan 581
van Gogh, Vincent 661
Van Schuyler, Marie 461
Van Til, Cornelius 10, 11, 320, 555
Van Til, Henry 60
Varro 272, 280
Vashti 527, 530
Vaughan, Henry 58
Veith, Gene Edward 242, 556
Veith, Joanna. *See* Hensley, Joanna
Veith, Mary 217
Veith, Paul 217
Velázquez, Diego 56
Venus 284–287, 289, 293, 356, 363, 447, 593. *See also* Aphrodite
Vermeer, Johannes 231
Vermigli, Peter Martyr 201
Verne, Jules 605–607, 609, 613–616
Vernon Jones, V.S. 445, 450
Veronica 589
Verres 284
Vespasian (Titus Flavius Sabinus Vespasianus) 269, 322, 325, 331, 401–404, 409, 411, 413, 418
Vetus, Lucius Antistius 336
Virgil (Publius Vergilius Maro) 58, 79, 81, 179, 284, 285, 287, 339–349, 352, 353, 368, 538, 545, 546, 635
Vitellius (Aulus Vitellius Germanicus) 331, 404
Vulcan 356. *See also* Hephaestus

W

Wagoner, Mary 463, 469
Waldron, Mr. 576
Walker, Jeanne Murray 58
Walker, Williston 437
Wallace, Robert 58
Walther, C.F.W. 400
Waltke, Bruce 14, 23
Warfield, B.B. 586
Warhol, Andy 552
Washington, George 210, 211, 240, 431, 432, 434, 541, 548, 637, 638
Waterhouse, John William 334, 335, 363
Watts, Alan 45
Wehrstahl, Cosmo von 621, 625
Weil, Simone 57
Wells, H.G. 195, 198
Wells, Stanley 505
Wenner, Jann 83, 97
Westmacott, Mary 460. *See also* Christie, Agatha
Weyden, Rogier van der 371, 537, 563, 564
Whitehead, Alfred North 3, 173
White Lady 620, 621, 624, 629, 630
White, Leslie 313
White Witch 596
Whitman, Walt 46, 50, 58
Wiese, Kurt 607
William of Ockham 4
Williams, Charles 618
Williams, Hank 240
Williams, Ian 607
Williamson, G.I. 250
Williams, William Carlos 45, 48, 49, 54, 55, 58
Winter, Milo 607
Wittgenstein, Ludwig 6, 12, 393, 395
Wodehouse, P.G. 12
Wolterstorff, Nicholas 242
Wood, Peter 68
Wordsworth, William 43, 55, 58
Wormwood 72
Wright, Christopher 476, 491
Wright, Elsie 571
Wright, Franz 58
Wright, James 49
Wright, N.T. 380, 384–387, 390

X

Xenophon 102, 116
Xerxes I 524, 528

Y

Yarbrough, Robert W. 373
Yeats, William Butler 45, 58, 618

Z

Zadok 513, 515
Zare 42
Zechariah 402, 529
Zenobia 333
Zephaniah 514
Zerah 471
Zeus 60–62, 69, 71, 72, 74, 75, 118, 119, 122, 134, 135, 219, 384, 402, 428, 496, 527, 584, 635, 637, 639, 640, 642, 644–646. *See also* Jupiter
Ziffel, Arnold 339
Zipes, Jack 450
Zophar (the Naamathite) 28, 34, 36, 37
Zuck, Roy B. 35
Zwingli, Ulrich 90

SELECT ILLUSTRATION CREDITS

Charles Beyl 159, 292, 576. *More of his work can be seen at www.CharlesBeyl.com.*

Jennifer Brown 93, 512, 517, 552, 624. *More of her work can be seen at www.NyeDesignStudio.com.*

Ned Bustard 89, 161, 202, 301, 450, 475, 541, 551, 582, 591. *More of his work can be seen at www.WorldsEndImages.com.*

Matthew Clark 6, 61, 86, 95, 136, 149, 223, 303, 306, 328, 356, 364, 385, 406, 416, 417, 433, 452, 490, 567–569, 572–574, 577, 607, 614, 620, 629, 662. *More of his work can be seen at www.DrawingMatthewClark.com.*

Keith Criss 478. *More of his work can be seen at www.TraditionalWorks.com.*

Glenn Howell 319. *More of his work can be seen at www.GOHowell.com.*

Judith Hunt 267, 454, 459, 523, 619. *More of her work can be seen at www.HuntJudith.com.*

Lydia Midwood 410, 412, 513.

Barry Moser 493. *More of his work can be seen at www.Moser-Pennyroyal.com.*